1e

American Government

Your Voice, Your Future

Matthew R. Kerbel
Villanova University

ATOMICdogPUBLISHING

Cincinnati, Ohio
www.atomicdog.com

Book Team

Vice President, Publisher Laura Pearson
Managing Editor Kendra Leonard
Director of Interactive Media and Design Joe Devine
Director of Quality Assurance Tim Bair
Senior Production Coordinator Mary Monner
Digital Designer Zach Hicks
Web Production Editor Joyce Powers
Quality Assurance Editor Dan Horton
Marketing Manager Mikka Baker

**When ordering this title, use ISBN 1-59260-134-0.
To order only the Online Edition of this title,
use ISBN 1-59260-135-9.**

Cover photos: Photofest and PhotoEdit.

ISBN 1-59260-133-2

Library of Congress Control Number: 2004114038

Printed in the United States of America by Atomic Dog Publishing,
1148 Main Street, 3rd Floor, Cincinnati, OH 45202

10 9 8 7 6 5 4 3 2 1

**To Gabrielle and her generation,
so they may never lose the love of learning**

Brief Contents

Contents

Preface
Understanding and Using This Book

Unifying Themes: Accessibility, Relevance, and Choice

For many of us, government seems distant and irrelevant—in part because it's so big, in part because it's hard to draw the connection between what political figures do and the things that have meaning in our lives. I constantly talk to students who don't care about the political world, don't see how it affects them, or don't wish to find out. Maybe you feel that way, too. If you do, it certainly doesn't help to have an American government text that portrays government as a far-away abstraction. Too often, I've heard my students complain about government texts being too plodding and inaccessible. I've heard similar complaints from professors.

Here, you'll be presented with an entirely different version of American government. Think of it as an up-close version, where abstractions give way to gritty fundamentals, revealing a government composed of all-too-ordinary people who share our daily concerns and priorities. Members of Congress struggle to fit in and find ways to get their homework done. Lobbyists struggle to beat out other lobbyists and make the case that will win over members of Congress. Supreme Court justices play high-stakes poker with their colleagues in an effort to shape their decisions on a case without realizing they've been influenced. The political system is filled with situations like these and with people trying to do their jobs under conditions of uncertainty and in the face of great time pressures.

If this sounds familiar, that's the point. Government cannot be relevant to our lives until we're able to see it in terms that make sense to us. This book will encourage you to experience American government in a way to which you can relate, because the truth is that when you strip away the generalizations and remove the distance, the people and situations you encounter in Washington or in your state capital are remarkably like those you encounter in any institution or social situation—including college.

Making government less mysterious and more real should make it easier for you to wrestle with the central question of the book: What do you want your relationship to government and politics to be? We all have a choice to participate in the political system or to opt out, and if we choose to participate, we also can decide how much and in what form we want to get involved. There are a lot of options, starting with voting and branching out to include reading about politics, getting involved with a political weblog online, giving money to a political cause or candidate, sending email to an elected representative, engaging in protest demonstrations, and much more.

Because the choice of whether and how to participate is deeply personal, only you can make it, and by the time you've finished with this book, I sincerely hope you are interested in doing just that: deciding what you want your political role to be. I could spend sixteen chapters telling you why I believe it's important for you to participate—and I do believe it's important, or I wouldn't have bothered writing this book—but what's the point of that? It's far more important for you to decide for yourself what, if anything, you're going to do, to have ownership of your decision, and to feel comfortable with it. You may conclude that you don't want to have a role in politics or that it doesn't matter whether or not you get involved. With this book, I'll help you make an informed decision, whatever that decision may be.

How This Book Is Organized

Think of this book as a round-trip journey on which you are the navigator. It's a round-trip journey because if you were to read the book straight through, you'd find that in the last four chapters of the book, we're back to talking about some of the same issues we discuss in the first two, reconsidering them in light of everything we've learned along the way. In five parts encompassing sixteen chapters, *American Government: Your Voice, Your Future* maps out a route designed to take you from understanding your place in the political system to how people connect with government, how the political system works and what it does, and finally—to come full circle—how responsive it is to your demands and desires.

Part 1 Why Should We Care about American Democracy?

We'll start with background on the fundamental concepts you'll need to understand if you're going to be able to make an intelligent decision about what you want your political role, if any, to be. Although this is the most abstract portion of the book, the concepts are illustrated with concrete examples. Think of this part as a presentation of the building blocks you'll need for the rest of the book and the place where you'll encounter foundational questions about the role and purpose of government that will set the tone for the discussions that follow.

- *Chapter 1 Should We Care about Politics?* The question posed by the chapter title is one you will be able to answer for yourself by the time you've finished reading this book. It's a personal question with no correct answer, but an informed response necessitates understanding how government fits into everyday life—whether we care about politics or not. Chapter 1 addresses how societies come together to make choices about governing themselves, discussing the fundamentals of such things as authority, legitimacy, power, equality, and liberty.

- *Chapter 2 The Constitution and Federalism: Setting the Ground Rules for Politics* The Constitution establishes the broad outlines for how American government operates, and federalism is one of the most important and distinctive features of the American system. Together, the Constitution and federalism shape the rules for American politics. We'll look at the origin, makeup, and evolution of both, keeping an eye on how the ground rules influence who is favored and who is disadvantaged in the political process.

Part 2 Citizenship and Democracy

Moving from a discussion of concepts to a discussion of their application, this section explores the parallel issues of how the United States developed as a nation and how individual Americans develop—or don't develop—into political creatures. We'll examine public opinion about politics and politicians, the elements of political culture that lead people to identify as Americans, aspects of political socialization that acquaint us with that culture while teaching the basics of civic involvement, and the kinds of political participation in which, once socialized, we may choose to engage.

- *Chapter 3 What Is Public Opinion, and What Does It Have to Do with Me?* To answer the question posed in the chapter title, we'll look at three important components of public opinion: political knowledge, attitudes, and beliefs. Political knowledge is our factual understanding of politics, and we'll find that it tends to be not particularly extensive. Political attitudes encompass how we feel about politics, such as whether we feel distant from political figures and what they do. Political beliefs involve what we think is true about politics. Together, these elements of public opinion influence the way we relate to what politicians do.

- *Chapter 4 Who Are We, and What Do We Do?* By broadening the discussion of public opinion to include issues of national and individual identity, we consider ways that Americans unite as a nation, come of age as political individuals, and engage in political action. National self-identification is rooted in something we call political culture. The process of political socialization explores how important people in our lives shape our adult perspectives on politics and government. The political activities we might consider doing encompass a variety of forms of political participation—from voting to attending protest rallies.

Part 3 Connections between Citizens and Government

Once we have explored the nature of public opinion and the origins of political involvement, we'll look at three institutions that link us to the people who represent us in government: the mass media, political parties, and interest groups. When working properly, each of these institutions functions like the connective tissue of government by channeling citizen demands and concerns to political figures and information about political figures to citizens. As we'll see, sometimes, these connections aren't as clear or as simple as you might expect.

- *Chapter 5 Mass Media: Influencing What We Think About* The media comprise the first of the three linking institutions that we'll examine. Most everyone is familiar with media like television, radio, newspapers, and the Internet, but we may have thought of these media only as sources of entertainment. They also play a central role in politics by providing us directly and indirectly with information that can shape the way we think about our government and the people in it. We'll look at how they do it and evaluate how effectively the media keep us informed about politics and government.

- *Chapter 6   Political Parties: Connecting Us to the Electoral Process* Political parties may be less familiar to us than the media, even though they help to organize a lot of political activity, particularly in terms of how candidates for office are recruited, funded, and ultimately elected. This is the case despite the fact that the Constitution does not provide for parties. We'll look at why the United States has only two major parties (most nations have more), explore how political parties have evolved through American history, and examine how parties are organized and what they do.

- *Chapter 7 Campaigns and Elections: Vehicles for Democratic Expression* One of the most important functions of political parties is structuring the way we choose elected officials. We'll devote a chapter to examining this essential role of parties in connecting candidates and voters. We'll spend some time in the cutthroat world of political campaigns, where the stakes are high and the winner takes all, examining the process for selecting candidates, the strategies candidates use to try to win elections, and the vital role of money in the campaign process.

- *Chapter 8 Interest Groups: Accessing Government through Common Membership* Probably the least familiar of our three linking organizations, interest groups are nonetheless vital to determining important national policies, as people who organize around common interests are the ones who are best positioned to be heard by elected leaders. We will consider what interest groups are, where they come from, why people belong to them, the resources they have to get the ear of government officials, and the way they use those resources to advance their agendas.

Part 4 Institutions of Democracy

The discussion of institutions that connect us with government will lead directly to Part 4, where we address the operation of the institutions that constitute government: Congress, the presidency, the federal bureaucracy, and the judiciary. Rather than regarding them as abstractions, we will treat these institutions as organizations run by people just like us, who (also just like us) have goals and objectives and a lot of work to do, and who try to advance their objectives as best they can with limited resources. We'll look at the world of Washington as a place where lots of people press to get all sorts of things done, looking for allies to help them, while trying to dodge the equally determined efforts of those who oppose them.

- *Chapter 9   Congress*   We will begin Part 4 by looking at Congress. Like any institution, including your college or university, Congress operates under a set of unspoken rules that attempt to promote civility and encourage compromise. We'll look at these rules and how Congress is organized to facilitate legislative work—a rather messy process in which it's far easier to frustrate someone else's initiative than it is to get something accomplished.

- *Chapter 10   The Presidency*   The presidency is probably the most visible office in the world, yet it can be surprisingly mysterious—and complex. There is a highly institutionalized side to the presidency composed of a web of offices and presidential advisors operating within the White House. At the same time, the presidency is the most personal of government institutions, responding more to the character of its chief occupant than any other political office. We'll look at how strong presidents have shaped the office and at the many—often contradictory—roles we ask the president to assume.

- *Chapter 11   The Federal Bureaucracy*   The president is the chief executive, and the branch of government he ostensibly heads is the executive branch, or the federal bureaucracy. Even though it may be less well known than the president himself, the federal bureaucracy has an important place in the functioning of Washington. Hierarchical and specialized, it is a sometimes explosive mix of lifelong civil servants and political appointees who serve at the president's pleasure. With the president as the head of the executive branch, you might think that bureaucrats would be responsive to him, but the reality is far more complicated. We'll explore why as we examine the functions bureaucrats perform.

- *Chapter 12   The Judiciary*   Perhaps the most mysterious branch of government, the judiciary can be just as political as any other institution—despite its dark-robed justices and secretive deliberations. From state courts to the federal courts, up to and including the United States Supreme Court, the judiciary faces a dilemma: It is charged with making judgments it has no power to enforce. As we look at how the court system is constituted, we will explore the informal mechanisms available to judges and justices that give them standing to confront others in the political system.

Part 5   What Government Does and How Well It Works

We ask our government officials to do two important things: (1) to protect the rights and liberties discussed in Part 1 and (2) to make policy on behalf of the country. We'll see how some policies are more controversial than others and how even the least controversial policies can have their detractors. Does discord mean government isn't responding well to our needs—or is it just a characteristic of being human that we're going to have disagreements about the policies government produces? We'll consider these issues by looking at policy from the standpoint of government responsiveness. We'll examine how effectively the officials we discussed in Part 4 listen to the voices expressed through the institutions we discussed in Part 3—voices reflecting opinions and participation styles of people like us, as we discussed in Part 2.

- *Chapter 13   Establishing Civil Rights*   Civil rights policies ensure that the law treats everyone equally and protects individuals from discrimination. We will explore the history and development of civil rights law as it pertains to the struggle for equal treatment fought for by groups that have historically experienced discrimination in America: African Americans, Native Americans, Latinos, women, Asian Americans, disabled individuals, gays and lesbians, and senior citizens.

- *Chapter 14   Protecting Civil Liberties*   Civil liberties are constitutional and legal protections against government infringement on personal freedoms. This encompasses a wide range of freedoms, almost all of which are universally accepted in principle but may be controversial in practice. For instance, the Constitution prohibits the government from restricting religious freedom, but does this right extend to permitting prayer in public places? The Constitution establishes the right of Americans to bear arms, but is this a relatively unrestricted personal right to own firearms or a collective right to form militias? We will explore questions like these, which illustrate the complexity of civil liberties.

- *Chapter 15 Domestic Policy and Policy Making* Domestic policies include budgetary decisions, regulations, and legislation pertaining to how Americans resolve domestic problems. Regulatory policies give government a role in adjusting the marketplace in ways that would not otherwise occur, in order to minimize hazards created by a free market or to maximize its benefits. Domestic legislation comes in several forms, most notably distributive policies, which claim tax dollars for projects or programs that could potentially benefit anyone, and redistributive policies, which transfer resources from one group to another. Because domestic policy decisions have "losers" who bear the cost and "winners" who benefit, they can be controversial. We'll explore this controversy in detail.

- *Chapter 16 Foreign and Defense Policies* Foreign policy is about how the United States conducts itself as a nation among other nations. It encompasses a host of economic, diplomatic, and military concerns, ranging from questions about global trade to relationships with other nations and how much to invest in maintaining a military. An extensive network of political advisors, diplomats, military personnel, and international leaders shape the direction of foreign policy and influence foreign policy decisions, which because of their life-and-death implications are among the most crucial decisions a nation has to make.

A Word on Critical Thinking

You'll find that the more you learn about how American government operates and affects your life, the more important it will be to have the skills to assess the many claims that politicians and elected officials make. Critical thinking skills make navigating the political process possible. With them, you can evaluate the content of news stories, determine if a policy proposal is in your best interest, assess whether claims made by your senator about her performance in office accurately represent her record—all things you'll need to do to have a meaningful political voice.

That's why this book approaches the American political system as a forum for developing critical thinking skills. From the outset, when we talk about the origins and foundation of the political system, through the closing chapters that connect those foundations with policies that affect our daily lives, we'll never stop asking questions about how theory is connected to practice, or why citizens, politicians, reporters, lobbyists, and judges act the way they do, or whether an observation about government is rooted in opinion or fact. Questions like these will develop and sharpen the analytical tools that will make us better citizens—and students—and help us make intelligent decisions about whether and how to participate in politics.

Before You Start: How to Use This Book

Six things set *American Government: Your Voice, Your Future* apart from conventional textbooks. They are:

- Print and Online Editions
- Natural and relaxed writing style
- Modular presentation
- Interactive examples
- Ease of navigation and repetition
- Customization

Here's a quick overview of each one.

Print and Online Editions

American Government: Your Voice, Your Future is available in two parallel forms: as a traditional Print Edition and as an Online Edition with a host of interactive features. If your professor gave you the option to use both, you will find that the two versions are designed to work together.

The content of the two books is identical, and the Print Edition contains all the features of the Online Edition in static form, including static screen captures of items that are animated or interactive in the Online Edition. The Print Edition also offers freedom from being tied to your computer. The people at Atomic Dog Publishing recognize that it's difficult to read from a screen all day and that most of us read much faster from a piece of paper. The Print Edition is particularly useful when you have extended print passages like this one to read. Then, if you have the option, you can turn to the Online Edition to take full advantage of the interactive features.

Think of the Online Edition as an interactive version of what you will find in the Print Edition. It gives you access to the navigation, updating, and customization features we'll be addressing shortly, taking advantage of the nonlinear characteristics of the Internet, so you won't be constrained by sequences of pages. Use the Search feature to locate and jump to discussions anywhere in the book. You can move out of the book to follow web links. You can navigate within and between chapters using a clickable Table of Contents and Table of Figures. These features allow you to work at your own pace and in your own style, as you read and surf your way through the material. The Online Edition gives you the flexibility to customize the process of learning so that it feels right for you.

Whether you're working in print or online, each chapter concludes with a set of features designed to reinforce and expand what you've learned, including a concise chapter review, a list of key terms, ten multiple-choice review questions, an annotated bibliography (called "In Their Own Words") that lists readings you could consult for research projects, and a list of notes with follow-up information.

Natural and Relaxed Writing Style

Conventional textbooks supply you with information. *American Government: Your Voice, Your Future* is a book that can teach. It's not a substitute for the learning you do in class—no book can be—but it is a core learning tool in a way that traditional books cannot be. The difference lies in the way the material is presented to you. Some of this comes from the interactive capability of working online, but an important component of teaching is how information is presented. That's where the style of the book comes into play.

I'm sure you've already noticed that this book has an informal, open quality. That's by design. The intent is to have a conversation between author and reader, much like you would find in a first-person novel or an in-class lecture. The philosophy that guided the writing of this book is that learning is a dynamic process and that we learn best when we interact with the material—when we feel engaged in the story a book tells. In this regard, both the Print and Online Editions are designed to be interactive learning devices. Both present a detailed and thoughtful account of the people, processes, systems, and institutions that comprise American government in an engaging, challenging, personalized, true-to-life manner that talks to you rather than down to you or past you.

Modular Presentation

Most of us are used to learning one chunk of information at a time. So *American Government: Your Voice, Your Future* reduces information to its component parts for easier digestion. You may have noticed how this preface is broken into small, modular sections; in the online version, it's on several brief screens that you can move through quickly and easily. The entire book follows this format.

Moreover, the construction of this book permits some deviation from the traditional linear textbook model, where material is presented through a running text narrative offset with secondary material in boxes. In this book, the set-aside information is not secondary at all, but core text that appears in boxes in the Print Edition or pops up when you click on "LearnMore" icons in the Online Edition. Boxes in the Print Edition are identical to online "LearnMore" items, so you get the same complete text in both versions of the book. These features may illuminate or elaborate on a point in the text, or they may use something in the text as a point of departure for a related discussion. Either way, they should be regarded as core material, not peripheral content you can ignore.

This is important to remember because it defies convention. You may have seen textbooks that are dotted with little bordered "boxes" that scream, "This is secondary material—don't read me!" Such is *not* the case with the boxes and LearnMore features in this text. Far from it. You'll find glossary terms and footnotes in this material, just like you'll find in the body of a chapter. The only difference is in the way you navigate through them. Having material set aside like this permits you to read ahead and come back if you so choose. It's another way this book presents you with a nonlinear approach to the material. You just have to remember not to ignore it.

Interactive Examples

Throughout the Online Edition, you'll find interactive devices, which are another way that *American Government: Your Voice, Your Future* can teach rather than simply convey material. With interactive examples, static figures come alive to demonstrate how political phenomena change over time. Tables become vehicles for you to click through for easy comparison of data. Complex concepts are illustrated with animated images. You can listen to snippets of a "fireside chat" by President Roosevelt or to the Oval Office tapes that brought down President Nixon, rather than simply having them described to you.

Some interactive examples allow you to register your opinions about political matters and then see how your responses compare with the class as a whole. Others invite you to participate in games and exercises built around important course themes. The particulars vary by chapter; the guiding philosophy is that we can learn best from experiences with self-explanatory and self-motivating learning tools that are instructive and enjoyable.

Icons like those shown in the margin on the right appear next to a number of figures, tables, and boxes in the Print Edition. The icons indicate that the corresponding figure, table, or box in the Online Edition is interactive in a way that applies, illustrates, or reinforces the concept under discussion.

Ease of Navigation and Repetition

Whether you're working in the Print Edition or the Online Edition, you'll find that the design of the book allows you to move quickly and easily within and between chapters, jumping ahead to explore an essay or game that applies to what you're reading, bouncing back to a place you've already been to review something you haven't seen in awhile. Because repetition is an important part of learning, key terms introduced early in the book are emphasized again when they appear in later chapters, and because we often forget some of what we learned weeks and months ago, key segments of early chapters are repeated for quick review when they are relevant to understanding material in later chapters. It's all part of the philosophy of having a book that teaches rather than simply presents information.

In the Online Edition, navigation features make it easy to surf through the book the way you're used to surfing the web. You can read about these in the section titled "Working Online."

Customization

You can customize *American Government: Your Voice, Your Future* to fit your study habits. The Online Edition offers you the capability to take notes and highlight material for future reference. The points you highlight automatically appear in the study guide at the end of the chapter. Your professor can also highlight important points in the text and even supplement the text with lecture notes or other material he or she considers important for you to know (see "Supplementing and Customizing the Book").

Working Online

American Government: Your Voice, Your Future contains the following online features to facilitate learning and to make using the book an easy, enjoyable experience:

- *Clickable Table of Contents* You can surf through the book quickly by clicking on chapter headings, or first- or second-level section headings, or you can move forward or backward between sections by clicking on "Next" or "Back" icons. The Table of Contents can be accessed from anywhere in the book.

   To assist those who use the Online and Print Editions together, the primary heads and subheads in each chapter are numbered the same. For example, the first primary head in Chapter 1 is labeled 1-1, the second primary head in this chapter is labeled 1-2, and so on. The subheads build from the designation of their corresponding primary head: 1-1a, 1-1b, etc. This numbering system is designed to make moving between the Online and Print Editions as seamless as possible.

- *Clickable Table of Figures* Simply click on the title of an illustration to navigate directly to it. The Table of Figures can be accessed from anywhere in the book.

- *Key concepts search* Type in a term, and a search engine will return every instance of that term in the book; then jump directly to the selection of your choice with a click of your mouse.

- *Clickable glossary* Glossary terms appear as highlighted "hot spots" within the narrative. Click on the term, and a definition instantly pops up in a separate window. The study guide at the end of each chapter contains a key term matching quiz.

- *Clickable footnotes* Footnotes are called out by a superscript letter *f*; click on it and the footnote will pop up, complete with a hot link to a related website when one is available, for easy access to more information.

- *Hyperlinks* Get instant access to supplementary resources like newspaper or magazine articles and websites supported by government institutions or political groups, so that you can immediately get more information on topics that interest you.

- *LearnMores* Items of importance to the book's central narratives are noted in the margins by a "LearnMore" icon like that in the margin to the left.

Supplementing and Customizing the Book

In addition to containing unique online features, *American Government: Your Voice, Your Future* comes with the following supplements on an instructor's CD:

- *Test Item File* A customized test bank available in ExamView Pro containing 100 short-answer questions per chapter for creating original quizzes and exams

- *Instructor's Manual* An enhanced version of the book offering assistance in preparing lectures, identifying learning objectives, developing essay exams and assignments, and constructing course syllabi

- *PowerPoint® Presentations* Concise outlines of the book's main points in PowerPoint® format that can be used to visually illustrate key material

- *Animations* from the Online Edition included as *Lecture Animations* with the PowerPoint® Presentations

All material on the instructor's CD are Blackboard and WebCT compatible.

Instructors also have the capability to customize the following features in the Online Edition:

- *Editable LearnMore boxes* Professors can customize book content by adding text boxes and hyperlinks anywhere in the Online Edition.
- *Editable QuickChecks* Professors can insert original follow-up questions at the end of all major sections of the Online Edition.
- *Editable review questions* Professors can substitute their questions for the review questions at the end of each chapter of the Online Edition.

Reviewers

The scholars listed here have read and commented on this text, contributing valuable insights and suggestions, both large and small, that collectively shaped the book's content and presentation. I am indebted to them for permitting me to incorporate their ideas, and I am particularly grateful to the many specialists who contributed their insights into material that I appreciate only as a generalist. Their labors were critical to the completion of this project.

Evelyn Ballard
Houston Community College

Ken Baxter
San Joaquin Delta College

Melanie Blumberg
California University of Pennsylvania

Robert Bradley
Illinois State University

Barry Burden
Harvard University

Craig Curtis
Bradley University

Michael Good
California State University

Catherine Grott
Montana State University

Randy Hagerty
Truman State University

William Hall
Bradley University

James Hanley
Adrian College

James Harrigan
LeMoyne College

Marjorie Hershey
Indiana University

Donna Hoffman
University of Northern Iowa

Mark Joslyn
University of Kansas

William Kelly
Auburn University

Jeffery Kraus
Wagner College

Paul Lermack
Bradley University

Norm Luttbeg
Texas A&M University

Tim Nokken
University of Houston

Mark Peterson
Washburn University

Rob Preuhs
The University of Denver

Beth Rosenson
University of Florida

Scot Schraufnagel
University of Central Florida

Mark Tiller
Houston Community College

David VanHeemst
Olivet Nazarene University

Joe Wert
Indiana University Southeast

Garry Young
George Washington University

Acknowledgments

I was sitting in the restaurant of a generic conference hotel in Chicago—or maybe it was San Francisco—complaining to Ed Laube about the slow pace of negotiations with a Very Large Publisher over the rights to a concept book I was developing, which I described as a "book that can teach." I had known Ed for some time—long before he was editor-in-chief of Atomic Dog—and I knew he was an original thinker who embraced unconventional approaches to conventional problems. We commiserated about the state of textbook publishing—the Very Large Publisher was holding up my concept project while it gobbled up a Not-So-Large Publisher and shuffled its editorial staff—and agreed that the conventional publishing model that produced carbon copies of bulky, oversized, uninteresting texts was in need of an overhaul.

It took two more conversations before we both realized that what Ed wanted to accomplish at Atomic Dog Publishing meshed beautifully with what I wanted to do with my concept book. This sparked a collaboration in which Ed helped fashion a book that would become the first large-scale title written from scratch to Atomic Dog guidelines. In part, those guidelines evolved in tandem with this book because of Ed's openness to feedback about Atomic Dog's production, development, and marketing strategies as problems and questions arose during the time this book was being written. Authors simply don't have the kind of input to the publication process that I was permitted because few editors are as secure as Ed or as committed to true collaboration between writer and publisher. For everything he contributed—for his support, insight, and steadiness—Ed from the start made certain that this huge project would get done, and he did this without sacrificing creativity or compromising objectives.

If Ed is the reason why this book exists, Kendra Leonard's hard work is the reason why it looks and feels the way it does. While Ed handled large issues, Kendra addressed the details, where the murkiest problems always reside. If there was a technical problem or stylistic concern, Kendra was there to point it out and offer ways to address it. If there was a substantive point that called out for improvement, Kendra offered suggestions, countless numbers of which found their way into the final manuscript. Any author would be lucky to have a developmental editor of Kendra's talent and devotion, a claim that I'm sure she would reject owing to her tremendous modesty, but it must be said that this book would have been impoverished without her influence.

Countless others have made their mark on this book as it went through development and production, including copy editor Jean Privitt and senior production coordinator Mary Monner. The collaborative effort that produced this book had such a strong hold on me that several months into the process I found myself starting to speak and act as if I worked for Atomic Dog. I have never experienced anything quite like the spirit and energy displayed by the people who contributed to this book. Atomic Dog is a company that understands that everyone is enriched when everyone is empowered.

If not for my wife Adrienne, I may never have begun this odyssey with Atomic Dog. When I raised doubts about the wisdom of working with a publisher that had such an unconventional imprint, she looked at me the way someone who knows you better than you know yourself can look at you and said, essentially, if *you* don't write for them, who on earth will? I never looked back after that, and Adrienne never stopped supporting my efforts. This project is a labor of love on her part as much as mine, for the way she appreciated and nurtured my writing is a selfless expression of her love and a product of her unending support, without which I could not have taken on a manuscript of such massive scope.

If Adrienne was my sustenance for this project, my daughter Gabrielle was my inspiration. Every time I picked her up at kindergarten and watched her bubble over with excitement about what she had done in school that day, I redoubled my efforts to write a textbook that could tap into that innate love of learning that all too often dissipates with time. My wish is that she and all young people can find a way to cherish or, if lost, rekindle the joy of exploration and knowledge that so easily gets buried in the daily grind of work and the pressure to get good grades. In this spirit, I dedicate this book to her.

Matthew R. Kerbel

About the Author

Matthew R. Kerbel is professor of political science at Villanova University outside Philadelphia, where he teaches and writes about the way the mass media influence American politics, especially national political campaigns and presidential governance. He is the author of four books on the subject, including *Remote and Controlled: Media Politics in a Cynical Age* and *If It Bleeds, It Leads: An Anatomy of Television News*. His interest in political communication was sharpened by stints working in television news as a writer for the Public Broadcasting Service in New York City and in radio as an on-air news anchor in exceedingly small markets. He lives in Wayne, Pennsylvania, with his wife Adrienne and daughter Gabrielle.

Part

1

Why Should We Care about American Democracy?

Should We Care about Politics?

1

1-1 Introduction

During your teenage years, when you may or may not have been paying attention to politics, the United States experienced in rapid succession a string of unprecedented shocks to its political system.

Conservatives, led by Republican Newt Gingrich, swept away forty years of Democratic control of the House of Representatives in a massive upset that installed a new order in Congress that ruled at will—for a little less than a year. The Gingrich group soon overplayed its hand and was repudiated by a crafty Bill Clinton, who used his platform as president to turn public opinion against his political adversaries.

Yet, just as Clinton appeared to ascend politically, events surrounding his extracurricular activities with a White House intern named Monica Lewinsky snowballed into impeachment proceedings against him. It was only the second time in history that a president was brought to the brink of political extinction by a Senate impeachment trial. Clinton survived, only to see his handpicked successor, Vice President Al Gore, lose the next presidential election, despite winning more votes than his opponent—only the fourth time in history that happened—and only after the election went into a seven-week overtime period of ballot challenges that culminated in an unprecedented 5–4 Supreme Court decision that effectively installed George W. Bush in the White House. No one had ever witnessed anything quite like it.

The Republican Bush took office with razor-thin Republican majorities in the House and Senate, only to see the Senate flip to Democratic control within months of his inauguration when one moderate Republican, feeling ignored by the conservative White House, left his party to become an independent. Nothing like this had ever happened before.

If afternoon soap operas had a political theme, this one would have had enough intrigue, sex, and ego to run a long, long time.

But if you didn't notice much of this, or didn't get too worried by it— join the club. For all of its great story elements, during times of peace and prosperity, many of us pay little attention to politics, and even if we do pay attention, we often have vague impressions of what's going on rather than fully formed opinions. That's just the way politics works in our lives.

Then came the horrific events of September 11, 2001: the terrorist attacks on the World Trade Center and the Pentagon, and a virtual declaration of war by Washington on terrorism. For many of us, politics was instantly thrust into the center of our daily lives. As anthrax-coated letters began appearing in the mail, Americans of all gener-

During a long period of peace and prosperity, American politics took on characteristics often indistinguishable from daytime talk shows. *(Left)* Bill Clinton and Monica Lewinsky. *(Right)* An audience at *The Jerry Springer Show*.

Source: (Left) AP/Wide World Photos. *(Right)* Photofest.

ations began turning to our elected leaders for reassurance and to government agencies for help. Such is the way of life in a crisis, when public decisions supersede private actions. This, too, is the way politics works in our lives.

Whether we pay a lot of attention to politics or ignore it completely, whether in times of comfort or times of anxiety, we live in a country where you can draw a straight line between your choice of whether or not to get involved and the kind of government we get. No one will make you vote if you don't want to, and no one will make you watch the news (well, your professor might, but you'll be back to having free choice over your viewing habits in a few months). You can make your own choices about what you know and whether or how much to get involved. Some combination of these individual decisions—and the choice to be apolitical is a decision—determines what happens in Washington, in your state capital, in your community, and to you.

So, should we care about what happens in politics? Does it really matter? Does it only matter in times of crisis? Wait—don't answer yet. Let's talk first about where you fit in—about the big and small ways your American citizenship invites you to interact with democracy—before deciding whether it's worth your time and energy to give politics and government a second thought once you're done with this course. Take the quiz in Table 1-1 to find out.

1-2 Democracy and Everyday Life

Ever since grade school, we've had a pretty basic sense of what it means to live in a democracy. At the same time, we don't always know what democracy means in everyday life, except maybe for some of the obvious things like voting and making contributions to political candidates. These are the most direct and visible ways we interact with government. Think, though, about some of the choices in the "Is it relevant?" game. We can also interact indirectly, passively, or without direct knowledge that we're in a political situation at all. We may even interact against our will, like if the dues we pay the American Automobile Association (AAA) for that convenient towing service end up being spent on efforts to get elected officials to support policies we don't agree with.

That's because a democracy as big and complex as ours has great reach in our lives—greater than we probably realize.

In any form, **democracy** entails a few basic things: participation by the people, the willing consent of the people to accept and live by the actions of government, and the recognition that we all have basic rights that government can't take away from us. These

▶**democracy** A government created by the people over whom it rules.

TABLE 1-1	
Is It Relevant? 	Here's a list of activities that may or may not constitute ways we can interact with democracy. Select the ones you believe have something to do with your relationship with government or politics.

1. Voting in a congressional election
2. Watching *The Daily Show* on Comedy Central
3. Joining AAA to get towing services when your car breaks down
4. Trying to drive only 10 miles over the speed limit to avoid getting a ticket
5. Making a $10 contribution to a candidate for mayor
6. Attending a private college or university
7. Camping out at Yosemite
8. Buying a Diet Coke
9. Buying a lottery ticket
10. Flushing the toilet

They're all "Yes" answers. Surprised? Here are the reasons why:

1. Yes. Easy question—voting is the most obvious way we interact with democracy.
2. Yes. Political and social satire get us to think about what government is doing and teach us a little about what's in the news.
3. Yes. You may be really surprised by this one. Even though it may not be why we join, organizations like the American Automobile Association (AAA) use our dues to lobby elected officials for legislation.
4. Yes. Government officials write a lot of the rules we live under, like speed limit laws, and enforce them with agents like police officers who determine whether 10 miles over the limit is bending the law too much.
5. Yes. Another easy one—money plays a big role in politics.
6. Yes. Whether it's adhering to national antidiscrimination policy on admission or hiring decisions or administering federally subsidized student loans, even private schools find it hard to escape the influence of government.
7. Yes. National parks like Yosemite are preserved through government actions.
8. Yes. Almost every state imposes a sales tax on food items. If you live in Delaware or New Hampshire and you answered "no," go ahead and give yourself credit because there's no sales tax there.
9. Yes. Lotteries are established and supported by state governments, and the proceeds are often used to pay for government programs.
10. Yes. You can't even find privacy from government actions here. Most places have a sewer system that wouldn't be there if not for the government. Give yourself credit for a "no" answer if you have a septic tank at home.

Score Yourself

If you got 8–10 correct, you pay more attention than most people to politics and government. Odds are you know what C-SPAN is.* If you got 5–7 correct, you have a pretty good feel for the role government plays in our lives. If you got fewer than 5 correct, you're in for a lot of interesting surprises!

*You may not know where to find the C-SPAN website, however. It's at http://www.cspan.org.

are the things Abraham Lincoln was talking about in the passage from the Gettysburg Address that mentions "government of the people, by the people, and for the people."

It's easy to imagine how these prerequisites for democracy might not always hold. We often choose not to participate—or may end up unknowingly participating without giving consent. At various times in our history, those who did not own property, people of color, women, and young people were denied the most basic political freedoms. Even today there are indications that poor individuals and minorities are more likely to have their voices dismissed through such inequities as living in communities that use cheaper and less reliable methods of counting votes (see Box 1-1). We saw evidence of this as recently as the 2000 election.

Box 1-1 Ballots That Disenfranchise

Months after the conclusion of the disputed 2000 election, the question of ballot inequity was still a big topic of discussion. George W. Bush had won the presidency following a pitched battle over the official vote count in the state of Florida—a battle that included questions about confusing and irregular ballots, and machines that made a significant number of mistakes reading ballots.

On the surface, counting votes seems straightforward. We've all voted in class elections—you write your choice on a piece of paper, someone reads the votes and adds them up to get a winner. Easy. But when you start to count votes in large numbers, more sources of error are introduced to what seems like such a simple process. In 2000, one of the problems was with punch-card ballots that worked by using a stylus pen to push little perforated squares called chads out of a piece of cardboard. A machine designed to scan the holes created by the vacated chads counted the votes automatically. The only problem was that it didn't always work well. Chads that didn't fully detach or that weren't punched through could confuse the scanner, a mechanical device that couldn't discern the intent of the voter. Votes that confused the scanner would be set aside without being counted. The voter, in essence, would be **disenfranchised**—denied the right to cast a vote—by virtue of his or her ballot not being included in the final tally.

Any mechanical method of vote counting is going to have its problems, and if these problems were spread evenly throughout the country, we might be able to write it off as an unfortunate but necessary side effect of trying to count a lot of votes quickly and efficiently. Even though some individual votes would be lost, the outcome of the election wouldn't change. But what if there is reason to believe that some groups of people are disproportionately affected by counting errors?

That's the charge leveled by a congressional report released several months after the 2000 election. It found that voting systems like the punch-card method, which tend to make more errors than expensive systems using more advanced technology, were more likely to be used in districts containing low income and minority voters. Consequently, it found a higher rate of uncounted ballots in those districts. If these results are substantiated, they suggest that the inevitable problems caused by vote counting methods fall more heavily on low income and minority voters. In relation to affluent voters, individuals in these groups are disenfranchised at a higher rate.

The seriousness of this charge should be understood in the political environment in which the investigation was undertaken. Congressional Democrats conducted the study, and the groups they allege are being disenfranchised are groups that tend to vote for Democrats. That adds a partisan slant to the issue of disenfranchised voters. At the same time, it's an issue that goes to the core of what it means to have rights in a democracy. So, as we consider the possibility that a balloting method systematically disenfranchises groups of voters with shared characteristics, we might ask another question about finding truth in the political process: Can a group with a partisan stake in the outcome nonetheless conduct a fair investigation? On the other hand, if a group with a stake in the outcome didn't take the initiative to investigate possible wrongdoing, how would potential problems with the political system ever emerge?

▶ **disenfranchised** Losing or being denied the legal right to vote by intentional or unintentional means.

1-3 Making Democracy Practical

Does this mean that the democratic ideals that our politicians like to praise at Memorial Day parades don't really work in America? Does it mean that they work, but unevenly? How much does government act poorly or inappropriately, simply because the principles it's based on don't fully translate to real world conditions? No system is perfect, but which imperfections are you willing to live with, and which ones, if any, are intolerable? These are hard questions that don't invite a single answer. And they go to the heart of how we function as a people.

Democracy is both an imperfect system and a complex idea. In fact, the broad principles we're talking about can take on different forms depending on the circumstances—with different results. In the small towns of colonial New England, a form of **direct democracy** took hold that enabled everyone to have a personal say in what government did. On this small scale, it was possible for every citizen of a town to gather in a meeting place and directly influence the way the community governed itself. When you stop to consider the wait for the bathroom if a nation of 284,796,887 people[1] tried to do something like this, you realize why even when we were a much smaller country we decided to take a different course. Instead of direct democracy, we opted to choose people to represent our wishes in government decision making through the indirect mechanisms of **representative democracy.** This system—also called a republican system (you may have heard the United States

▶ **direct democracy** Democracy without representation, where each eligible individual participates in decision making.

▶ **representative democracy** A form of democracy in which eligible individuals choose others to make decisions on their behalf.

> **republic** Any nation with provisions for the selection of representatives who make decisions on behalf of those who select them. James Madison said a republic was "a government in which the scheme of representation takes place," as compared to direct democracy.

referred to as a **republic** for this reason)—depends heavily on some familiar things, like holding free elections and keeping elected officials accountable to the voters. It's far more practical than direct democracy, but the trade-off is that it's also more complex.

1-4 Buying in to Authority

For a democracy—or any political system—to function effectively, we have to buy in to the basic principles it's based on. That's not always so automatic, especially in a large and diverse country like ours where we often disagree on what government should do and even on what society should look like. Some people want government to tax less, while others want it to spend more on social services; some people oppose the death penalty or abortion rights, while others feel differently. Some of these differences take on a moral dimension, where people hold views that they feel reflect the correct way to live, or the way a just society should act. When feelings about these things become intense, people often don't want to give in. At the same time, governing ourselves in a democracy is all about finding room for compromise.

Against this backdrop of different values and objectives, there has to be some agreement on the rules of the game—on the way we're going to set up our democracy—or else the entire system could topple under the weight of our vast disagreements.

Let's say your candidate for president loses the election. What are you going to do about it? You may stage protests against the winner, speak out against his actions, or work against him in the next election. But even if you think the winner is an incompetent swine, you're probably going to accept what he does as representing the official actions of the president of the United States.

> **authority** The right to act in an official capacity by virtue of holding an office like president or member of Congress.

That's because Americans generally respect the **authority** of a victorious candidate—his or her right to assume office and to carry out the responsibilities pertaining to that office. It's one of the rules of the game the vast majority of us accept, even if we sometimes don't like it, and it makes democracy possible. There is nothing automatic about this response; many nations—even democratic ones—struggle to resolve contested claims to authority, sometimes to the point where a military coup results in the overthrow of a legitimately elected government.

Americans have a long history of avoiding violent conflicts over authority disputes. As a society, we've shown a preference for investing authority in officials we may not like on the understanding that there will be other elections that may produce outcomes more to our liking. Even the most outspoken opponents of President Bush and his policies worked within the system for his political defeat in 2004, rather than advocating the violent overthrow of the government. Similarly, maybe you don't like the way one of your professors exercises authority—maybe you feel he or she is arbitrary in grading—but you try to deal with it by remembering it's only for a semester or a quarter, and there'll be other classes.

So, even a candidate elected by the slimmest margin assumes the jurisdiction to act with the authority of the office to which he was elected. In 1998, Jesse "The Body" Ventura narrowly won a three-way race for Minnesota governor. Almost two-thirds of those voting had chosen someone else. But Ventura became governor and assumed the authority of the office—the jurisdiction to propose legislation, negotiate the state's budget, grant clemency to prisoners, and a host of other serious functions. Some cringed when he continued to do color commentary on XFL football broadcasts and referee World Wrestling Federation matches, but these actions didn't interfere with the authority he had from having been duly elected governor of a state.

1-5 Inheriting Legitimacy

Now, some people would say that Jesse Ventura was making a mockery of his office when as governor he dressed in the flamboyant outfits of his wrestling days. (Of course, you might just think it was a pretty cool thing to do—but like we said before, people hold all kinds of opinions about things.) If you're the type of person who thinks governors should wear suits (or at least shirts), then seeing Ventura in feathers might make you respect him less as governor. Although that does nothing to undermine his formal authority to act as

He may not dress the way we expect a public official to dress, but former governor Jesse Ventura still had the authority to veto acts of the Minnesota legislature.

Source: AP/Wide World Photos.

governor, it could diminish his **legitimacy,** the widespread acceptance of his actions. Diminished legitimacy, in turn, could make it harder for him to maneuver politically because of the resistance he would face from people who doubted him.[2]

> ▶**legitimacy** Widespread public acceptance of the official standing of a political figure or institution.

Legitimacy is a funny thing because, unlike authority, which is granted by virtue of holding an office, legitimacy is partly inherited and partly earned. One source of legitimacy evolves over time and is rooted in the way we come to accept an office and by extension its occupant as being rightful and appropriate. The German sociologist Max Weber suggested this kind of legitimacy is rooted in tradition and law—that after hundreds of years, for instance, we have come to accept the presidential winner as the legitimate occupant of that office for a period of four years, under a plan set up long ago in the Constitution. This is why most Americans who voted for someone else accept a new president who attains office through normal, legal, time-tested channels. Even his strongest opponents do not call for tanks in the streets.

The legitimacy an official inherits is usually at its peak at the start of a term of office and is often the reason for the "honeymoon" or grace period we tend to give new officials. That even applies to the nontraditional 2000 election, where—as you'll see in Box 1-2—tensions ran high as the election was decided by the most unconventional legal maneuvering.

1-6 Earning Legitimacy

In order for our elected officials to act effectively—whether it be in addressing terrorist threats or trying to get Congress to approve a budget—we have to accept their actions as appropriate, even if we don't always approve of them. An official can squander or enhance his well of legitimacy through his behavior in office. That's why those of you who think a public official shouldn't be involved in professional wrestling activities might see Governor Ventura as a less legitimate public servant because of his continued wrestling connections (not to mention the fact that some people even say those wrestling events are *fixed*). Those of you who think it's a pretty cool thing to do might see Ventura as charismatic and honest, and that could elevate his legitimacy in your eyes. Similarly, Ronald Reagan used his communication skills as president to project an image of strength that enhanced his legitimacy. Bill Clinton's involvement with Monica Lewinsky and his subsequent impeachment diminished his legitimacy in the eyes of some.

Authority and legitimacy may seem like distant abstractions, but we deal with them almost every day. You're dealing with them in your classroom right now, as you navigate your response to the way your professor has decided to structure this class. Before you enrolled, your professor chose to assign this text, and made decisions about the work you would be required to do, the way grades would be calculated, how course material would

Box 1-2 Legitimacy in Doubt?

D id the way he came to power keep President Bush from inheriting some of the goodwill he might have otherwise enjoyed?

The postelection period that resulted in President Bush taking office was highly unorthodox and infused with partisanship on both sides. There was the unsavory spectacle of lawyers for the Bush and Gore teams working to count every ballot in areas where large numbers of their likely supporters lived while trying to disqualify as many ballots as they could in the other guy's strongholds. The governor of the disputed state of Florida was the brother of the Republican candidate. The question of whether to continue recounting ballots was ultimately decided by the United States Supreme Court in a split decision that broke along ideological lines, with the most conservative justices voting successfully to stop the recount in an action that essentially handed the election to President Bush.

Aspects of legitimacy based in tradition and law were tested and, to a degree, undermined by what happened in November and December 2000. In fact, the circumstances surrounding this postelection period were so unconventional and irregular that some people were led to the unusual position of questioning the legitimacy of the outcome. With lawyers and Supreme Court justices having had a decisive say in Bush's election, some partisan Democrats and even some reporters talked about whether George W. Bush should be regarded as the legitimate presidential winner. This sentiment was particularly pronounced in the African American commu-

nity because of the sense that African Americans had been disproportionately disenfranchised by the balloting irregularities we discussed earlier.

There is another side to the story, and it speaks to the strength of American political traditions even in the face of actions that question those traditions. Even under the irregular circumstances of Election 2000, a majority of Americans *accepted* the legitimacy of the Bush administration—even some who did not approve of the way he won the office. This speaks to the depth of the American tradition of accepting the declared winner and moving on. It suggests just how strong American traditions are, and how important Americans feel it is as a nation to legitimize elected officials.

In one important respect, the question of President Bush's legitimacy was put to rest for many Americans on September 11, 2001, when the terrorist attacks on the World Trade Center and the Pentagon created an emergency atmosphere in which Americans sorely needed leadership. Bush used his authority as president to speak out against the attacks and lead the American response against al-Qaeda, earning him a level of acceptance originally denied him by virtue of how the election was decided. Even Al Gore publicly stated that George W. Bush was his commander-in-chief.

This was a highly unusual way to develop legitimacy, following an election that ended in the equally unusual circumstance of withheld legitimacy.

be presented, whether you would have the opportunity to earn extra credit, how much emphasis to place on attendance and class participation, and a host of related items.

Other professors who teach this course probably would have made different choices because each professor has the authority to define the parameters of instruction—and you're left to contend with those choices. You may find you like that style of instruction, appreciate the course, and end up recommending it to your friends. Or you may take issue with anything from the reading load to how you're evaluated to the way lectures are delivered. In turn, you may find yourself acquiescing to things you dislike, or you may react by daydreaming during lectures, cutting classes, not reading the material fully, or engaging in any number of time-tested ways to rebel against academic authority figures. Regardless of your reaction, though, chances are you never question your professor's *right* to teach the course as he or she chooses. In other words, you accept your professor's authority to determine the contours of the course.

That is, unless your professor does something that you feel defies the boundaries of his or her authority. Let's look at a hypothetical example of this. Imagine that your professor randomly assigned everyone in your class to one of two groups and permitted everyone in the *other* group to skip this week's lectures, declaring that they would not be held accountable for the work they missed. You'd probably agree that your professor has the authority to determine if someone is entitled to an excused absence from class. To do so in an arbitrary manner, though, without explanation, feels wrong.

This capricious quality could well undermine your professor's legitimacy by making it seem as if he or she is acting unfairly. Randomly dismissing some classmates but not others is a heavy-handed thing to do, even if it's technically within your professor's authority to do it, which brings the legitimacy of the act into question. To be legitimate, you might expect everyone to be offered the option to miss the lectures, or at least to be provided with a rationale for why some people will be exempt from attending.

▶ Box 1-3 Information and Power in the New Millennium

It's been widely said that knowledge is power. It's been just as widely said that we're living in the information age and that what we know defines our place in society. These may be overworked sayings, but they're overworked for a reason. The fact is that our world is so technical and so specialized that what we know really does go a long way to determining how powerful we are. That's just another way of saying that information is one of the most important resources we'll encounter in our exploration of politics and government.

It shouldn't take too much thought to find places where information matters. Computers are obviously about information, and as we'll find out in a few weeks, the signature media of the twenty-first century like the Internet and twenty-four-hour cable television play a huge role in how we understand political issues, how candidates get elected, and a host of other situations where power is at stake.

We'll also find information popping up (literally and figuratively) in less expected places. Members of Congress can't survive without it. Neither can bureaucrats. Next to money, it's the lifeblood of many interest groups. The president relies on all sorts of information about public preferences before making decisions that could affect his political career. So, when you think about power, think about information as one of the foremost tools of power.

When the legitimacy of authority figures is brought into question, it's natural to raise doubts about their right to act as they did, and your choice of how to respond may take on greater urgency than if you simply took issue with their methods of evaluation or one of the many things a professor plainly has the authority to do. Do you accept it and move on, with their legitimacy permanently diminished in your eyes? Do you take action by confronting your professor, or by lodging a complaint with the dean? When you make your decision, how much do you take into account that you're dealing with someone who for the next few months has some leverage over your future—someone who will grade you at the end of the semester?

1-7 Power Surge

If you find yourself thinking you would probably not want to risk your grade in a confrontation with your professor, you would be giving up doing something you wanted to do in order to protect your GPA. In this case, you would be reacting to the **power** your professor has over you in your class. Someone has power when they can prevent you from doing something you want to do or make you do something you might not want to do. They can do it by coercing you through implied or overt threats or by influencing you with the promise of something you want or need. In the case of our fictional random dismissal from class, your behavior would be in response to a calculation about the likely cost of a confrontation with the professor. No words have to be spoken because the threat of a lower grade would be implied by the situation.

In a raw, basic sense, power is about might rather than right. You could even say that, initially, the people who get to decide the right way of doing things—who determine how authority is constituted—are the ones who wield power most successfully. Power isn't simply the use of force, though. It's subtler than that. It's about convincing other people of mutually shared interests, or threatening them with the loss of something they want, or actually denying them something they want, or providing them with a favor, or any number of other things that might move someone to act the way the person with power wants them to. In this regard, the person with power has tools in his or her arsenal—**resources** that may be used to change another person's behavior.

When the president says he'll veto an act of Congress in an effort to prevent its passage, he is exercising power over Congress, and the resource he's using is the threat of the veto. But the president can also exercise power by using personal charm or sharing the glow of his popularity—if he happens to have these resources at his disposal because he's charming or popular. Computer firms that make contributions to congressional candidates in an effort to influence their positions on high-tech matters exercise power with the use of money. Lawyers with expertise, lobbyists with information (see Box 1-3), you with your ability to vote in elections—all have resources that are desired by others in the political process. Power is exercised when resources are used to achieve a desired outcome.

▶ **power** The ability to make others act in a way that they otherwise might not have done.

▶ **resources** Anything of value to others that can be used to sway another individual.

Box 1-4 Do I Have Resources That Matter?

Everyone has resources, but you can argue—to borrow from George Orwell—that some resources are more equal than others. Some people believe that the resources that most influence political officials are concentrated in the hands of a few, giving this small group disproportionate power to determine political outcomes. Others point to the way Americans like to join groups and feel that the resources held by groups with broad memberships greatly influence the decisions that come out of the political process. Whether you believe the resources that move the political system are held by a few people or many people determines whether you believe political power is wielded by the few or the many.

You probably know people who say there's no reason to vote because your vote really doesn't matter, since voting doesn't overrule the actions of powerful, unelected people with wealth, prestige, or access to sophisticated information who make decisions that affect our lives. People who think like this have a lot in common with people who say the political system is characterized by **elitism,** or the belief that government is in practice controlled by a small, centralized hierarchy of people with a wealth of resources at their disposal. Advocates of elitism believe that a stable, resource-rich, permanent elite drives political decisions in the United States, rendering the vast majority of Americans effectively powerless.

On the other hand, many Americans join groups like service organizations; mosques, churches, or synagogues; and other community groups—all sorts of organizations where we expend time (a resource) pursuing matters of interest to us. These groups operate in public, allowing us to voice our interests and concerns in a manner in which they'll be heard. As these groups compete with each other for public attention, it's possible that they shape the way government officials listen and respond. If you agree with this assessment, you're in line with those who say the political system is characterized

by **pluralism,** or the belief that government in practice responds to the many (plural) voices expressed through group membership. One advocate of this position is political theorist Robert Dahl, who once wrote of the central role of "all the active and legitimate groups in the population," who "can make themselves heard at the same crucial state in the process of decision.*

Obviously, pluralism and elitism present divergent and mutually exclusive ways of understanding who holds power, and sorting through the two approaches is not that simple because it's easy to see where each has merit. It may even be tempting to say that they both describe our political system, but you shouldn't lose sight of the fact that pluralism and elitism assume the system is structured in entirely different ways. Figure 1 illustrates the different ways elitists and pluralists describe the structure of the political system.

▶ **elitism** The theory that government responds to a small, stable, centralized hierarchy of corporate and academic leaders, military chiefs, people who own big media outlets, and members of a permanent government bureaucracy. People who subscribe to this position believe the actions of regular citizens, like voting and joining groups, simply mask the real power exercised by elites.

▶ **pluralism** The theory that government responds to individuals through their memberships in groups, assuring that government is responsive to a wide range of voices. People who subscribe to this position believe that the wide distribution of resources in society drives the decisions government officials make.

*Robert Dahl, *Preface to Democratic Theory* (Chicago: University of Chicago Press, 1956), 137.

When you stop to think about it, we're involved in power relationships with other people all the time. Sometimes we are in the powerful position of being able to offer or withhold resources others want. Sometimes people have power over us because they control resources—like grades—that matter to us. Any individual or group with resources can engage in a power relationship, and power relationships are among the most fundamental at every level of politics from the White House to school boards. Quite often, maybe surprisingly, a mutually beneficial exchange of resources gets others to act in a way they might not have intended. In the American political system, the exercise of power is about mutual benefit a lot more than we might suspect.

When we start to think of power in terms of relationships, we're getting to the heart of what **politics** means. We all have things we want to accomplish and things we want to avoid. And we're always involved in relationships with other people. When you bring human desire and human relationships together, you have the essentials of a process that ultimately determines who gets what. When this process happens in a public sphere so that everyone in the country is potentially affected by what happens, we have politics of the sort that matters in government. Almost seventy years ago, a student of the process, Harold Lasswell, called politics "the study of who gets what, when and how."[3]

▶ **politics** The process of determining who gets what, when, and how.

Some of us may be more powerful by virtue of having more resources (see Box 1-4); some of us may get heavily involved by virtue of our interest in what government does. But

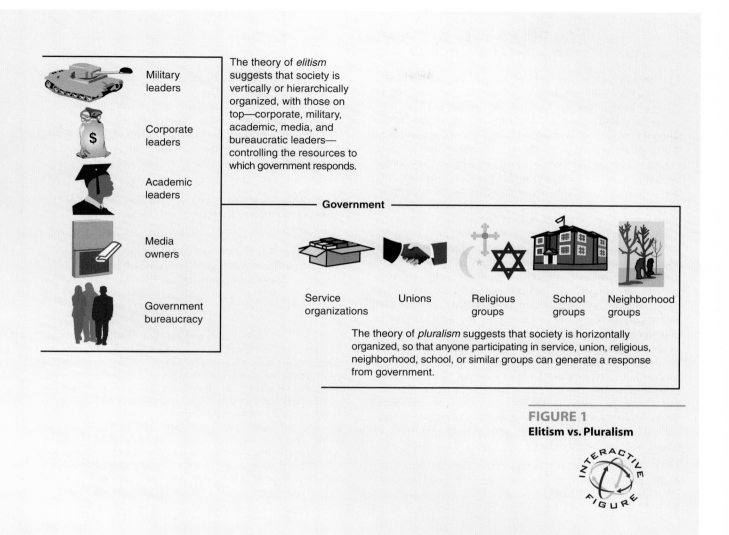

The theory of *elitism* suggests that society is vertically or hierarchically organized, with those on top—corporate, military, academic, media, and bureaucratic leaders—controlling the resources to which government responds.

Military leaders

Corporate leaders

Academic leaders

Media owners

Government bureaucracy

Government

Service organizations

Unions

Religious groups

School groups

Neighborhood groups

The theory of *pluralism* suggests that society is horizontally organized, so that anyone participating in service, union, religious, neighborhood, school, or similar groups can generate a response from government.

FIGURE 1
Elitism vs. Pluralism

INTERACTIVE FIGURE

regardless of our level of power or interest in this process, we are all affected by it—even if you never had a single thought about politics before you registered for this course. That's because politics produces winners and losers on everything from whether we'll be sent to war to how much we'll have to pay in taxes to who gets to operate your favorite TV station to whether embryonic stem cells can be used for scientific research to whether you may legally drink beer. Think of something you encounter in your daily life, and the chances are that in some way it's influenced by politics.

1-8 It's Not Fair!

Let's return one more time to the hypothetical example of your professor randomly dismissing part of your class. Whether you thought it was ridiculous that a professor would dismiss some of the class at random, or whether you thought it was wrong that someone else would get to be excused from work for what appeared to be no good reason, your reaction to the example was based on an assumption about how people should be treated. It must seem fairly obvious that if you're going to make an exception for someone, there had better be a good reason for it.

What may seem less obvious is that sentiment like this doesn't have to be automatic or universal. It's a value judgment, and we're going to find that people make all kinds of

Box 1-5 Facts and Judgments

Throughout this course, we're going to be making observations based on analysis of information and observations based on our judgments or evaluations of circumstances. These are different kinds of observations. When we evaluate data or information, we make **empirical** or factual observations about the world around us. No value judgments are involved when we do this. When we say something like, "Americans tend to prefer equality of opportunity over all other possible kinds of equality," we're making an empirical observation based on our analysis of what we understand to be the preferences of Americans.

But when we say something like, "It's a good thing for American society that Americans tend to prefer equality of opportunity over all other possible kinds of equality," we're making a **normative** observation or value judgment that involves assessing a standard or making an evaluation. We could easily apply different norms or standards and argue that it's *not* a good thing for American society that Americans tend to prefer equality of opportunity.

Let's do a quick check. See if you can figure out which of the following statements are normative and which ones are empirical. If some of the statements appear to fit into both categories, it's because the line between a factual evaluation and a value judgment is not always as clean as you might think—which can be a source of misunderstanding in a political discussion if someone makes a value judgment that you take to be a statement of fact!

1. The painting contains three shades of blue oil paint.
2. The painting would be more dramatic if it contained nine shades of blue oil paint.

3. The painting would be more effective if it were displayed in a brighter light.
4. The United States can be classified as a republic rather than as a direct democracy because elected representatives make decisions on behalf of the public.
5. The United States is better suited to being a republic than a direct democracy because of the vast size of the country.

▶ **empirical**   Any statement based on the assessment of data or the analysis of information, without regard to value judgments.

▶ **normative**   Any statement that invokes a judgment or evaluation. Think of the word "norm," which implies a standard for evaluating something.

Answers: 1. Empirical. The color of the paint and the number of shades of the color are all assessments of data. 2. Normative. What makes something dramatic? It's a value judgment. You could also apply a different norm and contend that fewer shades of blue would make the painting more dramatic. 3. Normative again. There's no fixed standard for what makes a painting effective, so you're utilizing a norm to make a judgment. 4. Empirical. "Republic" and "democracy" can be defined (in fact, they already were), and the rationale for making the claim that the United States is better classified as a republic comes directly from the facts of the definition. 5. Normative. Any time you talk about why something is better or worse, you're applying a norm. The fact that the statement expresses why the United States is better suited to being a republic simply helps make the case for the norm.

▶ **equality of opportunity**
One of several ways of understanding equality, this way values giving people comparable advantages for succeeding in life, regardless of the unequal outcomes that may result.

judgments about what seems right and fair—judgments that, in their scope and range, contribute to the complexity of political debate. Before moving on, take a few minutes to look at Box 1-5, where you'll learn an important distinction about normative judgments like this, which are based on values, and empirical observations based on fact.

Once you're clear about what constitutes a normative judgment, we can return to the matter at hand—fairness. Would it have been different if you and everyone else had been given the *choice* to stay or go? Perhaps that would seem less arbitrary and, accordingly, more acceptable. If it feels this way, you're tuned into a prominent way many Americans understand the notion of equality. It's called **equality of opportunity,** and it's about everyone having the same chance for advancement, free from obstacles that might limit some people from realizing their potential. This is essentially what Thomas Jefferson had in mind when he wrote in the Declaration of Independence that "all men are created equal," although his eighteenth-century perspective excluded women, African American slaves, and Native Americans from consideration. Over time, efforts have been made to incorporate groups Jefferson left out, but the basic idea that people are "created equal" still applies to where we start out in life, not where we end up—to the chances life affords us rather than to the results we achieve.

Valuing equality of opportunity is consistent with supporting government efforts to make the "starting line" more equal. That's why Americans usually support government programs to help underprivileged kids have access to higher education, because education is considered the gateway to opportunity. It's also why Americans generally value **political equality** and believe that everyone should have the same political and legal rights as everyone else. If all votes count the same and if everyone has the same rights in a court of law, the theory goes, then the playing field isn't tilted toward some groups and away from others. Everyone has the same opportunity to make the most of themselves without the political or legal system getting in the way. When you think about it this way, you can apply the language of equal opportunity to the question we were discussing earlier about whether some individuals or groups were disenfranchised during the 2000 election.

To value opportunity is a choice, and it's a different choice than some other countries make. In places like Norway and Sweden, for instance, people place more emphasis than Americans do on **equality of outcome,** on diminishing economic and social disparities among people through government actions that try to level off differences between rich and poor by redistributing resources from top to bottom. If Americans as a group were as interested as Scandinavians in equality of outcome, then our government might provide cradle-to-grave health care, long stretches of paid maternity leave, and generous retirement benefits like they do in Norway and Sweden. Of course, we'd have to pay a lot more in taxes to support programs like these, and that would result in a lot of resources shifting around so that rich and poor alike would benefit equally. A country makes choices like that when it primarily values **economic equality** and **social equality**—both forms of equal outcomes—in which economic and social distinctions are minimized as a matter of policy and choice.

Just take a quick look at social and economic patterns in the United States, and you'll probably begin to realize how much equality of outcome takes a back seat to equality of opportunity. We're aware of the existence of social classes, of the great distance there is between the wealth of someone like software magnate Bill Gates and people who have to work for a living, to say nothing of people who can't find work at all or who live in poverty. But the size of the disparity might be even greater than you imagine. In 1998, the wealthiest 1 percent of American households had more than 190 times the net worth of the bottom 40 percent *combined*. The disparity is even greater than it was fifteen years earlier, when the top 1 percent had "only" thirty-seven times more. Figure 1-1 illustrates recent trends in wealth ownership. Although we'll find that some efforts are made to address these inequalities, as a matter of policy—and as a matter of choice—Americans tend to make the normative judgment that providing opportunity is generally preferred over equalizing outcomes.

Because we tend not to value equality of outcome, groups that have historically met with discrimination lag behind in their share of economic resources. The earning power of African Americans, Hispanics, and other minority groups falls below the earning power of whites—sometimes well below. For instance, according to the U.S. Census Bureau, in 1999 one in ten whites lived in poverty, compared with better than one in four African Americans and Hispanics. Figure 1-2 will show you more details.

Similarly, the earning power of women is less than the earning power of men who do comparable work. In 1999, women were paid only 72 percent of what men in comparable jobs were paid—a difference that amounts to over a half-million dollars for the average twenty-five-year-old woman over the course of her working life.[4] The federal government is quite aware of these disparities—there's even a Women's Bureau at the U.S. Department of Labor that in past administrations provided a checklist you could use if you were a working woman and you thought you were being unfairly compensated for what you do.[5] Still the inequalities remain, as the statistics show, in violation of a primary assumption about how equality of opportunity should work. Box 1-6 explains.

1-9 Equal *and* Free?

How much of your income would you be willing to pay in taxes if you received government benefits in return? Twenty percent? Thirty? Fifty? Eighty? At some point, it'll feel like a drag on your earning power and you'll resist. In America, we tend to reach that point pretty quickly. We see taxes—along with some of the government programs the taxes pay for—as an imposition on our ability to make choices for ourselves about what to do with our money. Many Americans prefer voluntary action to government mandates.

▶ **political equality**
Establishing political and legal rights on the basis of the individual, so that everyone has the same right to vote and is equal under the law. An alternative would be to grant political rights to elite individuals based on wealth or social standing.

▶ **equality of outcome** One of several ways of understanding equality, this way values leveling the social and economic inequities among people, rather than attempting to give people comparable advantages for succeeding in life.

▶ **economic equality** A form of equality of outcome that values using government policy to minimize the economic disparities found in society.

▶ **social equality** A form of equality of outcome that values using government policy to minimize social class distinctions found in society.

FIGURE 1-1
**Recent Trends in Wealth
Ownership, 1983–1998**

Source: Edward N. Wolff, "Recent Trends in
Wealth Ownership, 1983–1998," Working
Paper #300, Jerome Levy Economics
Institute, Table 2; http://www.levy.org/docs/
wrkpap/papers/300.html.

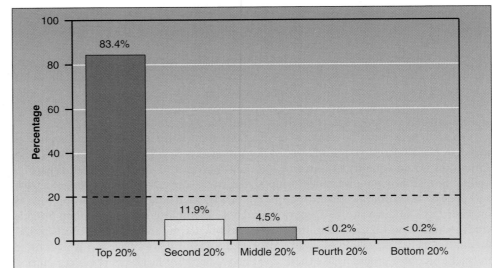

If wealth were distributed evenly across the population (see dashed line above), then there would be no economic classes. Everyone would have the same net worth—that is, each one-fifth of the population would have one-fifth of the wealth.

In reality, we're very far from equal outcomes in the United States. The upper one-fifth of the population controls over four-fifths of the wealth, and almost half of that is in the hands of the top 1 percent. In contrast, the bottom 40 percent combined accounts for only 0.2 percent of the wealth, meaning that the top group has more than 400 times the worth of the bottom two groups combined.

FIGURE 1-2
Minority Income Levels

Source: U.S. Census Bureau, *Statistical
Abstract of the U.S. 2000: The National Data
Book,* 43, 46.

This resistance to being told what to do has deep roots in our country, which was born in a rebellion against a strong central government. It's about **liberty,** about having the freedom to act without others interfering with what we do, and it's at the center of so many of the choices we make when we govern ourselves. Americans place a premium on preserving liberty. It was the rationale for fighting two world wars and the cold war with the former Soviet Union, and it's the thing Americans most fear losing to terrorists. Hours after the World Trade Center was destroyed, President Bush told the nation, "Our way of life, our very freedom came under attack."[6]

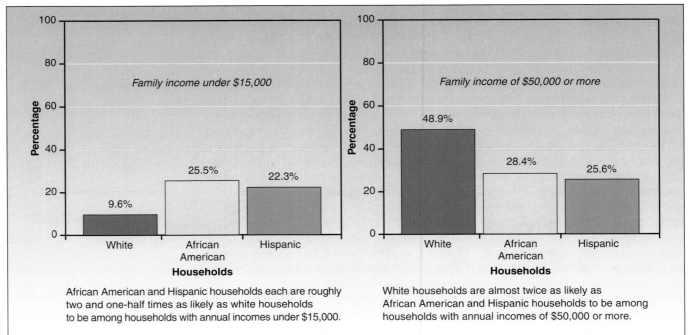

African American and Hispanic households each are roughly two and one-half times as likely as white households to be among households with annual incomes under $15,000.

White households are almost twice as likely as African American and Hispanic households to be among households with annual incomes of $50,000 or more.

Box 1-6 Unequal and Different

The tendency in the United States to emphasize opportunity over outcomes raises important questions about the relationship between the condition of being unequal and simply being different.

Think of someone you know—perhaps a friend, significant other, or classmate. Start thinking of some of the outward differences between you. Maybe there are gender differences, or differences in eye, skin, or hair color. You could be different heights or weigh different amounts. The more you think about it, the longer the list of differences should become because so many factors contribute to the unique way we look.

You would no sooner want these physical differences to determine how others treat you than you would for your professor to randomly determine who gets to be excused from your next class. Neither, in a normative sense, is fair. Both undermine the central idea of equality of opportunity, which is that all people should be in a roughly comparable situation that permits them to express their talents and abilities.

In theory, we should have the same chance to succeed despite these many differences. Rather, our capabilities and interests should determine what we achieve. Some of us will become shopkeepers, while others become bookkeepers; there will be lawyers and landscapers and teachers and day-care providers and salespeople and waiters and chief operating officers. If we have an even shot at all these outcomes and reach the one we choose because of where we decide to direct our energy, you could say equality of opportunity is working well. There should be no relationship between the outcomes we choose and our surface differences, which have no bearing on our talents and interests.

The fact that we see disparities in outcome based on gender, racial, and ethnic characteristics is a sign that equality of opportunity does not work in practice the way it does in theory. Remember, the dilemma isn't that people end up in different places—that's to be expected—it's that people end up in different places for surface reasons that have no bearing on their talents or ability. It suggests that some groups face obstacles to achievement simply because they are different.

If an inner-city Hispanic teen scores lower on the SAT than does a white suburban kid, she will likely be denied admission to the best state and private schools and will face a more limited set of college options. Is her score lower because she isn't as bright as her suburban counterpart, or is it because she attended an overcrowded high school and didn't have access to good academic counselors or SAT prep classes? Is it possible that if she had had the advantages of a wealthier school system, her SAT scores would have been higher, and she would have had the same educational opportunities as someone from an affluent suburb?

Like the inner-city teen, other groups—like African Americans facing hiring discrimination and women who are paid less money to do the same work as men—find the playing field tilted against them because of surface differences. At times in our history, these obstacles have become political issues, in that they became the focus of public debate. But the fact that the debate over advancing equality of opportunity needs to consider group differences says a lot about the tricky nature of how our society handles diversity and how diversity poses a challenge to the fundamental American idea that individuals should be provided opportunity free from arbitrary obstacles.

In an absolute sense, if we had total liberty, there would be chaos because everyone would do whatever he or she wanted. So, we make choices. One of the biggest trade-offs we make is between liberty and equality. We've already seen how there are several ways to understand what it means for people to be equal. Certain types of equality are more compatible with having liberty, while others may only be attained by placing restrictions on liberty.

Let's see if you can identify the trade-offs between liberty and the five types of equality we've talked about: equality of opportunity, equality of outcome, political equality, social equality, and economic equality. Take a look at Figure 1-3 to gain a sense of the balancing act that has to be maintained in order to preserve both liberty and equality.

> **liberty** (see p. 14) The ability to pursue your ends and objectives, tempered by socially defined boundaries and limited government impediments.

1-10 Whose Choice?

We've been saying that society makes choices between liberty and equality, normative choices that involve judgments about what we value and what we're willing to trade off to achieve those values. And while this is the case, it's also very abstract. Who is society, after all, but you and me? We didn't write the rules of the game—other people for a complicated set of reasons made the choice to value liberty over equality of outcome long ago—but on an everyday basis, we're faced with lots of choices that we can affect.

We're constantly faced with situations where we are asked voluntarily by others or involuntarily by government to give up some of our liberty to act in order to benefit others. Sometimes, we do this with no problem; other times, it's inconvenient, and

FIGURE 1-3
Balancing Liberty and Equality
It's a difficult task to balance
liberty and equality.

we gripe about it or perhaps take things into our own hands and resist the restrictions placed on us.

Take, for instance, the simple act of listening to music. Maybe you live in a dorm or apartment and have a roommate or two. If your roommate isn't around and it's the middle of the afternoon, you can probably feel pretty good about blasting a CD if you want to without having to think about how it affects anyone else. Your liberty to act is absolute. But if your roommate is there and you have different musical tastes, you've got a choice to make between doing what you want—exercising your liberty to listen to music—and imposing a restriction on your wishes in order to take your roommate's feelings into account. Some of us might factor our roommate's wishes heavily into our decision, whereas some of us might not consider them at all.

If our decision caused conflict, we may or may not be able to manage it privately and peacefully without an RA (a resident advisor in a dorm) or the campus police intervening. If our decision entailed curtailing what we would have done if we were left alone, like listening to a different CD or turning down the volume, we might grumble at our loss of liberty but accept it as a condition of having a roommate.

On a larger scale, conflicts like this between personal liberty and the rights of others are the very things government tries to resolve every day. These conflicts involve trade-offs between liberty and **social responsibility,** or the concern for the rights of others in society. Because our actions constantly affect other people, and because it's human nature to want to pursue our desires and objectives despite this, we are continually asking government to resolve disputes between personal liberty and social responsibility. Essentially, we turn to government to draw the boundaries that determine where individual liberty stops and the needs of society start.

Obviously, not everyone will draw that line in the same place. Not everyone believes that government is always the appropriate arbiter, either, believing instead that individuals should work out their conflicts without government getting involved. A lot of political debate turns on these two facts.

Drinking laws are among those that you may have strong feelings about. As a society, as you're no doubt quite aware, we've decided that it is illegal to purchase or consume alcohol until you turn twenty-one. You probably know the rationale for this, which has to do with the desire to cut down on alcohol-related driving accidents. Essentially, if you are under twenty-one, your liberty (some would call it a right) to drink has been curtailed by government action in favor of the socially responsible position that it is more important to protect the lives of everyone on the roads. That's a choice that stems from a value judgment. You may agree with it or not. But it's the law.

So, what do you do about it? One option is to do nothing—to plan a big celebration on your twenty-first birthday and to do nothing before then. You might take this course of action if you agree with the law or even if you disagree with it but recognize its legitimacy. Another option is to violate the law and try not to get caught. You might do this if you dis-

▶**social responsibility**
Concern for the protection of the rights of individuals in a community or society, at the expense of some degree of personal liberty.

agree with the trade-offs behind the law, or if you feel drinking alcohol should be a matter of personal choice and not a matter for government to consider. There would be sanctions if you were caught because you would be breaking the law, not changing it. But that would be a consequence you would have to face.

The dual questions of when to give up liberty to protect the rights of others and whether government or private individuals should make the decision have a long history in our country's political debates. As you can probably see, when *your* liberty is at issue, feelings can get pretty intense. Also, as with all interesting political questions, there are winners and losers, which can make the result of what government does hard for some to swallow.

Compounding the issue is the great range of reactions we have to the tension between liberty and responsibility as well as other questions regularly placed before our political system. The great diversity of America that we were talking about before is both a strength and a complicating factor for our politics. It's a strength inasmuch as the expression of a wide range of viewpoints tends to enhance the decisions we make for ourselves, because a variety of voices coming from different vantage points can make for intelligent and gratifying solutions to problems, much like the blending of many ingredients can make food tastier and more satisfying.

At the same time, diverse perspectives can make it harder to reach a conclusion, complicating the process by which decisions are made. A system designed over two centuries ago to hear primarily the voices of white land-owning males has been required to expand to accommodate the views and desires of people with a wide range of backgrounds, perspectives, and beliefs. How it has managed to do this, and what it means in real terms for you and me, is part of the story you'll read in the next chapter.

1-11 So—Should I Care about Politics?

Whether you should personally care about politics is a normative judgment. It's also a personal matter that you'll probably approach differently from your friends. You'll make a judgment that depends in part on how much you think politics matters in your life. No one else can make that judgment for you.

We started out by asking whether it makes sense to care about the political system enough to engage in it because the question goes right to the heart of why you're in this course. If there's absolutely no reason to care about politics, then it's going to be a long semester or quarter! There are certainly reasons to get involved, but you may feel they don't apply to you. In the end, you may decide like many people that you're just not a political person. At that point, you'll be able to draw your conclusions with your eyes open to the evidence.

But before we can make an informed decision about whether and how much we should care about the public side of life, we should grow to understand it much better. There may already be things you know now that you didn't realize before you started reading this chapter, like how you're involved in power relationships at times when you're totally unaware of them—whether it's in the classroom with your professor or with a membership you may have in the American Automobile Association.

We've already seen that we can be involved in politics even if we don't care about it and even if we're not paying attention. We've talked about how the republican form of democracy we practice in this country reaches into things we may take for granted in our daily life, like having other people elected by us (or by our neighbors if we don't take part) make decisions on our behalf. We've talked about how we tend to act around authority figures, whether they're our professor or our president, and how their ability to wield resources can influence our lives—especially if we see their actions as legitimate.

We identified ways we're involved in power relationships with people every day—directly with people we work and live with, indirectly through the actions of political figures that make decisions on our behalf. We even looked at equity issues—matters of fairness—and how they balance the freedoms that a lot of us feel are extremely important in our lives. We talked about how liberty and equality are much more than abstractions. They're values, and as such, the extent to which we enjoy them, as well as the form they take, are the product of choices and trade-offs made by our society and shaped by government action. Whether we feel it's important to try to contribute to the political dialogue that shapes those trade-offs may be one part of the answer to our question about whether interacting with government matters to us.

We've hinted at the idea that in order to make choices about who gets what, when, and how, we set up rules and then play by them (to a greater or lesser extent). In fact, a specific set of rules is in place that determines how politics works in this country. Some of the rules are legal in nature; a lot of them are set out in the Constitution. But even the Constitution has its roots in a struggle between different ways to define the political ground rules. As we understand those rules, we'll probably come to recognize a little more about where we come from as a nation, and how the resolution of some of our earliest political struggles shaped the political options before us today, some two centuries later. How can the struggles of people long gone be relevant to how we live our lives in the twenty-first century? Chapter 2 has some answers to that question.

Chapter Review

Even though people often speak of America as a democracy, it is best understood as a republic because we elect representatives to make decisions on our behalf. In that respect, our country is a representative democracy rather than a direct democracy, where people would make decisions on their own behalf. A representative democracy is far more practical for a nation as large as the United States, but it is also more complex and can be controversial inasmuch as there can be strong differences of opinion about what representatives should do in our name.

For a republic to function effectively, there has to be agreement on the principles on which it's based. Americans typically respect the authority of elected representatives to act in an official capacity by virtue of holding an office, and for the most part, grant legitimacy to elected officials even when they disagree with them. However, political figures can undermine their legitimacy through their actions because, unlike authority, legitimacy is partly earned.

Elected officials can use their authority and legitimacy to exercise power, although their ability to do so is hardly automatic. Power is about getting others to act the way you want them to, even if they prefer to act otherwise, in order to determine who gets what, when, and how. The tools of power are resources, which can encompass a wide range of things, such as a politician's personal charm, the information supplied to members of Congress by a lobbyist, or the promise of campaign money.

Who gets to exercise power is an important—and open—question. Those who subscribe to the theory of elitism believe that a permanent, unelected elite of corporate and academic leaders, military chiefs, media operators, and bureaucrats holds the resources that matter in government decision making. Those who subscribe to the theory of pluralism believe that ordinary individuals can exercise

power in a republic because the resources that matter to people in government are widely distributed in society.

Many Americans value equality of opportunity, or trying to give people a fair start in life, knowing that people of different interests and abilities will end up in different places. Equality of opportunity comes at the expense of equality of outcome and produces economic and social disparities in the name of protecting individual initiative. Many value political equality on the assumption that ensuring everyone the same right to vote and equal rights under the law promotes equal opportunity.

In truth, we have neither equality of opportunity nor equality of outcome in America, although we are much more likely to support government actions that promote the former. One place where equal opportunity breaks down is in the unequal economic and social outcomes of women and historically disadvantaged racial and ethnic groups because unequal outcomes are supposed to be a product of our different talents, interests, and abilities, not our physical differences.

There are also important trade-offs to be made between equality of opportunity and liberty, which is the ability to pursue our objectives, tempered by socially defined boundaries and limited government impediments. Liberty is consistent with equal opportunity because it supplies the freedom to make individual choices. Absolute liberty would generate chaos, so liberty is bounded by social responsibility, or the concern for the rights of others in society. We turn to government to draw the boundaries that determine where individual liberty stops and the needs of society start. But we won't all draw that boundary in the same place, which can lead to political disputes over whether government should create boundaries or leave matters of social responsibility to individuals.

Key Terms

authority (p. 6)
democracy (p. 3)
direct democracy (p. 5)
disenfranchised (p. 5)
economic equality (p. 13)
elitism (p. 10)
empirical (p. 12)

equality of opportunity (p. 12)
equality of outcome (p. 13)
legitimacy (p. 7)
liberty (p. 14)
normative (p. 12)
pluralism (p. 10)
political equality (p. 13)

politics (p. 10)
power (p. 9)
representative democracy (p. 5)
republic (p. 6)
resources (p. 9)
social equality (p. 13)
social responsibility (p. 16)

Review Questions

Note: You can find the correct answers to these questions by taking the quiz and then submitting your answers in the Online Edition. The program will automatically score your submission. If you miss a question, the program will provide the correct answer, a rationale for the answer, and the section number in the chapter where the topic is discussed.

1. "A government created by the people over whom it rules" is a way to define
   a. democracy.
   b. direct democracy.
   c. representative democracy.
   d. republic.

2. Which of the following is partly inherited and partly earned?
   a. authority
   b. legitimacy
   c. custom
   d. power

3. Information is one of many resources that can be used in the exercise of what?
   a. authority
   b. legitimacy
   c. custom
   d. power

4. Someone who subscribes to the theory of pluralism would believe that power can be exercised by
   a. voters.
   b. corporate leaders.
   c. military leaders.
   d. bureaucrats.

5. Americans tend to resolve the trade-offs between the various forms of equality by favoring
   a. equality of opportunity.
   b. equality of outcome.
   c. economic equality.
   d. social equality.

6. Americans tend to believe that ensuring everyone the same right to vote is an excellent way of advancing
   a. equality of opportunity.
   b. equality of outcome.
   c. economic equality.
   d. social equality.

7. Because women receive less pay than men for comparable work, one may argue that
   a. unequal opportunities undermine equality of outcome.
   b. unequal outcomes undermine equality of opportunity.
   c. pay inequities are normative rather than empirical.
   d. women are being denied political equality.

8. Liberty is consistent with equal opportunity because it
   a. tempts us to violate drinking laws.
   b. always comes with socially defined boundaries.
   c. provides us with the freedom to make choices that allow us to realize our potential.
   d. requires us to make trade-offs.

9. When we permit government to place restrictions on our actions out of concern for the rights of others, we trade off liberty in the name of
   a. pluralism.
   b. chaos.
   c. social responsibility.
   d. power.

10. One source of political disputes originates in differences in where to draw the line between
   a. individual action and social responsibility.
   b. authority and legitimacy.
   c. pluralism and elitism.
   d. normative and empirical judgments.

In Their Own Words

You might be interested in examining some of what the following authors have said about the topics we've been discussing:

Dahl, Robert. *Preface to Democratic Theory.* Chicago: University of Chicago Press, 1956. Different approaches to American democratic theory, with special attention paid to majority and minority rule—things we're going to talk more about in Chapter 2.

Lasswell, Harold D. *Politics: Who Gets What, When, How.* New York: Meridian Books, 1958. A classic discussion of the meaning of power.

Machiavelli, Niccolò. *The Prince.* New York: Penguin Books, 1999. Written 500 years ago, it contains observations about power that still ring true.

Notes

1. 2001 U.S. Census Bureau estimate. See http://quickfacts.census.gov/qfd/states/00000.html.
2. In fact, toward the end of his single term as governor, Ventura found that a large number of Minnesotans had soured on his persona or were unhappy with his official performance. This made it difficult for him to maneuver politically.
3. Harold D. Lasswell, *Who Gets What, When, How* (New York: Meridian Books, 1958), 3.
4. See the AFL-CIO website at http://www.aflcio.org/issuespolitics/women/equalpay/.
5. You may access the Women's Bureau at the U.S. Department of Labor website, at http://www.dol.gov/wb/.
6. "Day of Infamy," *Time,* September 12, 2001.

The Constitution and Federalism:
Setting the Ground Rules for Politics

2

2-1 Introduction

Think back for a second to grade school. Try to remember what your classroom and playground felt like. For many, these places provided our first encounter with rules and structures in social situations. The restrictions generated by those rules may have been unpleasant. At the same time, it's not hard to imagine how chaotic things would have been without them.

This essentially describes the trade-off we face when we consider how to establish the ground rules for politics. Rules place limits on our liberty. But the total lack of rules is a recipe for chaos. A functional government rests somewhere between the extremes of no liberty and chaos—but precisely where is an open question that can cause some intense political disputes.

In the early days of the republic, political disputes over how to write the rules of the game were commonplace because there were different points of view about how deeply government should reach into everyday life. The differences were rooted in the experiences people had with government prior to and during the American Revolution. Some people were influenced by what felt to them like government repression under the British and were determined to avoid establishing a strong central government here. Others feared that if the central government were too weak, it would be impossible for the new nation to function. Out of this debate came America's first halting attempts at self-government.

The results weren't very pretty, at least initially. Many early decisions did not withstand the test of time, and there were ongoing, heated political debates as people on both sides of the strong government question jockeyed for political advantage. Because setting the rules is never a neutral exercise—some groups are inevitably favored at the expense of others—the question of how government should operate was a central issue that consumed American politics for years after the Revolution ended. It's a lively story with implications for how Americans live today because the rules that were settled on still favor some at the expense of others, some 215 years after they were written. So, as we go back in time to revisit these events, we're really looking at the roots of how we make choices for ourselves in the twenty-first century.

2-2 Ground Rules for Revolution

The multiethnic, industrial America of the twenty-first century still operates under rules created by European male settlers in response to circumstances long forgotten by most of us. To understand what America is now we should understand what it was then—

who settled this country, what they were looking for, how they were different from some of the people they left behind, and what they experienced in colonial America.

Primarily, European settlers were risk takers, people willing to leave their homes and everything familiar in search of religious freedom or economic opportunity. If you imagine for a second what it would take for someone to cross a dangerous ocean in a small, precarious vessel on a journey of great uncertainty, you can probably get a sense of how those who came to America differed from those who decided not to make the trip. Notwithstanding the sense of community found in some of the religious groups that came here, there was certainly enough individualism to go around.

Risk-taking and self-reliance are consistent with the desire for government to do less so individuals can maintain more liberty and seek opportunities. From the start, America's white settlers were inclined to favor placing restrictions on government so they could preserve the freedom to go it alone—a freedom they found wanting in the old world.

Their perspective mattered most to America's political development. In the eighteenth century, America's nonwhite settlers and natives were composed primarily of African American slaves and Native Americans, both of whom—to expand on a term from Chapter 1—were **disenfranchised** by Europeans by being kept out of the decision making that produced our constitutional and legal system.[1]

▶**disenfranchised** Losing or being denied the legal right to vote by intentional or unintentional means.

The inclination toward individualism exhibited by white settlers—which goes a long way toward explaining how the rules were written in America—was compounded by events in the decade leading up to the American Revolution, a time when many colonial settlers experienced British policy as heavy-handed and burdensome. Not surprisingly, a string of British legislative acts passed during this time were widely regarded as impositions on liberty. Table 2-1 illustrates some of the more salient actions.

The series of events depicted in the timeline, starting with the imposition of the Stamp Act and concluding with the First Continental Congress, represented a British crackdown on colonial life. True, the colonies had never been autonomous, but the vast ocean separating London and Boston effectively afforded the colonies a certain amount of self-rule. The King and Parliament were simply too far away and too preoccupied with other matters to maintain tight control on colonial life. So, for the better part of 150 years prior to the Boston Massacre, colonial settlers drafted constitutions to govern the colonies, created representative assemblies with the authority to draft laws, and held free elections. They had to share this authority with royal governors, but they had a taste of self-government, and they liked it. Against this backdrop, and considering their personal inclination toward preserving liberty, it's no wonder why so many of them found the Coercive Acts to be intolerable.

Within months of the First Continental Congress, the tense, cold standoff turned violent. Clashes between colonists and British soldiers at Lexington and Concord, Massachusetts on April 19, 1775, marked the start of the American Revolution. One month later, the **Second Continental Congress** convened in Philadelphia to coordinate the war effort. One year later, it would declare American independence from Great Britain.

▶**Second Continental Congress** A gathering of representatives from the colonies in Philadelphia in 1775, necessitated by the need to coordinate planning during the Revolutionary War, that functioned as the first central government in colonial America.

From the outset, the American Revolution differed from other revolutions in the sense that the objective was not to overthrow the existing order and replace it with something new. There was no talk of overthrowing the British monarchy, and the government of Great Britain continued to exist outside the former colonies after conceding defeat to the Americans. Instead, the American Revolution was more of a separation—perhaps the way some of us as teenagers move away from our parents and establish autonomy when we begin to see ourselves as adults and question parental authority. To Americans supporting the war, the purpose was to rebel against the existing order. The British crackdown in America had led some to begin to question British authority, and even though the idea of going it alone was far from universally popular in the colonies (many opposed revolution and hoped to reconcile their differences with the British), by 1775, it had become a viable option.[2]

2-3 Ground Rules for Independence

What gave Americans the right to separate from Great Britain? Law and tradition bound them to the British, who saw the Revolution as a profound act of treason. Supporters of

TABLE 2-1   British Policy Prior to the American Revolution

Year	Events and Consequences
Early 1760s	In the early 1760s, American colonists fought alongside the British in the French and Indian War. It was a long and expensive war, and the British turned to the colonies to help pay for the war through a series of Parliamentary acts.
1764	The American Revenue Act was passed in 1764. It was widely called the **Sugar Act** because of the tariff it placed on sugar, along with other goods. The Sugar Act was followed the next year by the **Quartering Act,** which forced colonists to shelter British troops, and the **Stamp Act,** which taxed everyday legal documents like marriage licenses and newspapers.
1765	The Stamp Act of 1765 created uproar in the colonies, leading some colonies to refuse to import British goods and to the outcry "no taxation without representation." The protest led to the repeal of the Stamp Act, but in 1767, Parliament imposed a new round of taxes on goods imported from Great Britain, which led to a new boycott and growing tensions.
1770	The British sent troops to Boston to maintain order, but their presence inflamed tensions. On March 5, 1770, tensions erupted into a skirmish. Shots were fired, and five colonists were killed in what history remembers as the **Boston Massacre.**
1773	When Great Britain imposed the Tea Act of 1773, giving the East India Tea Company a monopoly over the tea trade in North America, tensions rose again. In the protest known as the **Boston Tea Party,** a group of colonists masquerading as Native Americans boarded ships loaded with tea and dumped the contents into Boston Harbor.
1774	Parliament moved swiftly and severely in response to the Boston Tea Party, initiating what became known as the **Coercive Acts** (in the colonies, the Intolerable Acts). Loading and unloading ships in Boston Harbor was prohibited, and the Quartering Act was revitalized.
1774	In response, representatives from most of the colonies gathered in 1774 at the **First Continental Congress** to protest the action, voting to boycott British goods. The Continental Congress lacked **authority,** but it represented a major step forward in forging among the colonists a sense of collective purpose and the ability for collective action.

Stamp Act protest in the Pennsylvania Journal

The Boston Massacre

Source: National Archives and Records Administration.

▶**social contract**
The arrangement in which people agree to give up some of their liberty to establish a government that will protect basic rights that are threatened in the state of nature.

▶**Thomas Hobbes (1588–1679)**
The seventeenth-century British social thinker and author of *Leviathan* who believed that people need to trade off liberty for a strong government that can protect their fundamental right to live.

the Revolution, though, believed the British had forfeited their right to govern the colonies when they began to deny colonists their liberty. In this idea, they had support from theorists who had written in the abstract about why governments form and under what circumstances they may be overturned.

The founders read widely and were influenced by theorists dating back to antiquity. You could turn to the theoretical influences of two Enlightenment thinkers in particular to find the origins of one of the key philosophical justifications for the Revolutionary War. The seventeenth-century British philosophers Thomas Hobbes and John Locke differed in their view of human nature and their prescriptions for how government should operate, but they both spoke of government as being the product of a **social contract** among individuals.

Thomas Hobbes wrote that without governments, people existed in what he called the **state of nature**—a ruthless place with absolute liberty where people can easily deny others their liberty and their lives by simple force. Hobbes had a negative view of human nature and painted a brutal picture of what life would be like if we permitted ourselves to exist in the state of nature. In a passage from his book *Leviathan*, Hobbes claims that life in the state of nature is "solitary, poor, nasty, brutish, and short."[3]

The Boston Tea Party

Source: National Archives and Records Administration.

The Continental Congress

Source: National Archives and Records Administration.

▶ **Sugar Act** The first in a string of taxes levied by Great Britain on the American colonies. Formally called the American Revenue Act of 1764, it taxed a number of colonial imports, including sugar.

▶ **Quartering Act** An act of the British Parliament requiring colonists to house British troops; first imposed in 1765 and then again in 1774 as part of the Coercive Acts.

▶ **Stamp Act** A particularly vexing tax levied by the British on scores of legal documents, which led to a colonial boycott of British goods.

▶ **Boston Massacre** A precursor to the war that was still five years away, it was the first mortal conflict between colonists and British troops in Boston and resulted in the deaths of five colonists in 1770.

▶ **Boston Tea Party** A protest against the Tea Act of 1773 in which fifty colonists dressed as Native Americans boarded British trade ships loaded with tea and threw the contents into the water.

▶ **Coercive Acts** Called the Intolerable Acts in the colonies, the Coercive Acts represented the British attempt to clamp down on the colonies following the Boston Tea Party.

▶ **First Continental Congress** A gathering of representatives from twelve of the thirteen colonies in Philadelphia in 1774 to protest the Coercive Acts and chart a unified colonial response.

▶ **authority** The right to act in an official capacity by virtue of holding an office like president or member of Congress.

The only way to protect people from this ugly situation is for them to give up liberty in exchange for the security of a strong government (a "leviathan," representing government to Hobbes, is a big, powerful monster), essentially to form a social contract with others in which liberty is the price of protection. Hobbes believed that people had to give up most of their liberty—far more than colonial settlers would have been happy with—in exchange for the right to live, which is why he was a supporter of a strong and forceful monarchy.

Although he had a somewhat more upbeat view of mankind, **John Locke** also advocated for a social contract as the basis of civil society. Locke believed that in the state of nature people possess **natural rights**—to life, liberty, and property—which they enter into a social contract to protect. Since the purpose of government in this contract is to do more than provide physical safety, the reins of government shouldn't be as tight as in Hobbes' vision. To Locke, liberty is something for government to protect as much as it is what you give up to have government protect you. In other words, government needs to be strong enough to protect individual rights but not so strong that it becomes a threat to liberty, so there have to be limits on government that monarchy cannot provide.

▶ **state of nature** (see p. 22) The condition of total liberty in which people are free to act on their impulses, but where individual rights are afforded no protection.

▶ **John Locke (1632–1704)** A seventeenth-century British social contract theorist whose ideas about government getting its authority from the consent of the governed in order to protect fundamental human rights greatly influenced the leaders of the American Revolution.

▶**natural rights** (see p. 23)
Inalienable rights inherent to every individual that cannot be taken away by individuals or government, and that government should be designed to protect.

▶**Declaration of Independence**
The document drafted by Thomas Jefferson and approved by the Continental Congress in July 1776, stating the reasons for the Revolutionary War and declaring a formal break with Great Britain.

Locke went much further than Hobbes, asserting that people form governments and people can dissolve them, through revolution if necessary, should they become too strong and violate individual rights. This was fairly radical thinking in an era of monarchy, when you consider that monarchs claimed their authority came from God. Locke rejected this "divine right of kings," arguing that governments receive their authority from the consent of the governed.

Locke's fingerprints are all over the **Declaration of Independence,** whose author, Thomas Jefferson, was heavily influenced by Locke. The idea that everyone is equal in the state of nature; that people are born with natural rights; that governments are formed to protect these rights; that individuals and not deities form governments; that governments must derive their authority from the people they govern; that people have the right to overthrow a government that fails to protect individual liberty—it's all there, and it all has its roots in Locke's writing.

Perhaps because of what was at stake in the Declaration of Independence, Jefferson can be forgiven for not footnoting Locke. And educated people in 1776 understood where Jefferson's ideas came from. The full text of the Declaration of Independence can be found in Appendix A.

For much of this country's history, Americans have subscribed to Locke's generally positive view of humanity. Having two great oceans to shelter us from the conflicts of the rest of the world surely contributed to American optimism. But, at times of great stress, it may be easier to subscribe to Hobbes' view of the state of nature than to Locke's, and to ask government to step in and provide greater fundamental protection. There are indications that some people reacted this way in the aftermath of the September 11, 2001, terror attacks on the United States, turning to government for protection against a world that appeared to become dramatically more dangerous overnight. See Box 2-1.

Americans wait in long lines and tolerate an unprecedented military presence at domestic airports, giving up the liberty to travel freely and without intrusion for the promise of government protection from Hobbes' state of nature.

Source: Courtesy of Mark Ide.

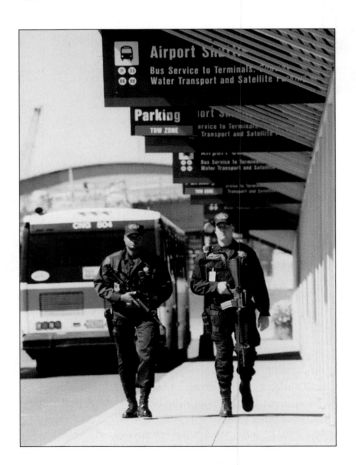

> **Box 2-1   Hobbes, Locke, and Terror**

For two decades, political debate in the United States revolved around the question of whether government had grown so large as to be intrusive. After a period in the 1950s, 1960s, and 1970s in which the national government addressed problems of segregation, poverty, crime, women's rights, and a host of other social and economic dilemmas, debate turned to whether in the course of addressing these issues government had grown so strong as to infringe on personal liberties. Through the 1980s, the Reagan and George H.W. Bush (senior) administrations advocated the position that government is a problem more than a solution to problems. In the 1990s, Congress picked up this line of reasoning. You could draw a straight line from Jefferson and Locke to the contemporary argument that big government is a threat to personal liberty.

Then terrorists destroyed the World Trade Center and heavily damaged the Pentagon. Anthrax began showing up in the mail. American troops were dispatched to Afghanistan, and America shifted to a war footing. People stopped talking about government as an intrusion. The state of nature suddenly resembled Hobbes' dark views more than Locke's hopeful ones. People looked to government for aid and assistance in numbers not seen for decades. In keeping with Hobbes' prescription that a strong government is needed to keep us safe and alive, many Americans even began saying they would be willing to give up liberty in return for protection.

An article that ran in *The Philadelphia Inquirer* toward the end of 2001 discussed how "a new view of freedom" had settled into the national psyche, a view far more restrictive than what had been the norm for generations.[*] It told of how trust in government shot up after the attacks because Americans had become "newly appreciative of safety" and therefore "willing to give [government] unusually broad powers to fight terrorists." Americans expressed willingness to "put up with more government" and give the president "a little more latitude to do what he thinks is right."

Immediately after the attacks, three in four Americans had reservations about immigration and wanted to make it harder for people of other nations to enter the United States, essentially limiting the free passage to America that has been one of the hallmarks of American liberty. Unease about foreigners settled into this nation of immigrants, with the call going out to government to do what was necessary to keep America safe.

Large numbers of people supported a Bush administration directive to try alleged terrorists in secret military tribunals, out of view of the public and apart from the normal judicial system—essentially denying these suspects the ordinary rights allowed others charged with crimes. One individual quoted in the article acknowledged, "That is kind of scary, taking away one of the freedoms Americans believe in." But, he added, "We are at war. I'm more tolerant of that at the moment."

The question is, how long will the moment last? This may be a temporary shift in attitudes, or it may have long-lasting consequences. How well can a nation that declared its independence on Locke's principles fare under Hobbes' perspective of human nature? In the long run, how much liberty will Americans really be willing to give up in order to feel safe?

[*]*The Philadelphia Inquirer,* December 26, 2001, sec. A.

2-4 Ground Rules for Self-Governance— First Attempt

Almost immediately after declaring independence from Great Britain, the Continental Congress went to work to create a framework for collective government. It was a difficult job because the practical need for the new United States to act in concert was balanced by strong concerns about the individual states giving up too much authority to a distant national government that might not be responsive to local concerns. Fears were widespread that a strong national government would be an obstacle to liberty, especially in light of colonial experiences with British rule over the past generation. Furthermore, even though the Declaration of Independence announced a new United States of America, most citizens of this new country identified with their respective state rather than with the collection of states. People would refer to themselves as New Yorkers, Virginians, or Rhode Islanders—not as Americans. Why, then, would they accept a strong government of the United States?

At the same time, members of the Continental Congress knew that without a central government, they would not be able to maintain an army, negotiate treaties with other nations, or coordinate commerce among the states. The rules of the game would have to be written carefully.

When a framework did materialize in the form of the **Articles of Confederation,** which were adopted by Congress in 1777 and ratified by all thirteen states in 1781, the results were problematic. The Articles addressed the fear of a strong centralized government by creating a loose federation or "league of friendship" among the states in which

> **Articles of Confederation**
> The first constitution of the United States, which created a loosely functioning national government to which the individual states were supreme. It addressed concerns about a strong national government undermining individual liberty, but it created a national government that was unable to regulate commerce or conduct foreign policy and was abandoned in favor of the United States Constitution just eight years after it was ratified.

▶**Shays' Rebellion**   A rebellion by debtor farmers in western Massachusetts, led by Revolutionary War Captain Daniel Shays, against Boston creditors. It began in 1786 and lasted half a year, threatening the economic interests of the business elite and contributing to the demise of the Articles of Confederation.

▶**confederal system** An arrangement for establishing a government out of a set of component states, in which the national government is the creation of the states and subservient to them. The Articles of Confederation established a system like this in the United States. In today's world, the United Nations may be the most prominent example of a confederation.

▶**unitary system**   The inverse of a confederal system, in which a centralized national government creates subnational units like states, provinces, and counties, which derive their authority from the national government. Most nations are unitary systems. In the United States, the relationship between each individual state and its counties, townships, and cities is a unitary relationship, with the states creating and empowering the local governments.

▶**federal system** The arrangement created by the United States Constitution, in which the national government and the states share authority over citizens. States may act autonomously to do such things as create school districts, levy taxes, or assemble a police force; at the same time, powers are reserved for the national government, which is supreme to state laws. In addition to the United States, only Canada, Germany, India, and a small group of other nations have federal systems.

"each state retains its sovereignty, freedom, and independence, and every power, jurisdiction, and right, which is not by this Confederation expressly delegated to the United States." In other words, the laws and actions of the individual states were supreme to the actions of the United States. The national government took its cues from the thirteen state governments.[4]

The Articles further protected the states by requiring that national action of any kind would have to win the approval of nine states. The national government was composed of a Congress in which each state had one vote, but any five states could keep the national government from acting. Because of concerns about centralized authority, there was no independent chief executive like the modern-day president. There was no national court system for resolving disputes. The Articles were inflexible: All thirteen states had to agree to amend the Articles; one lone dissenter could put an end to change.

These features conspired to create a national government that was weak and ineffective. The Articles of Confederation created a national government that would not undermine individual liberty, but it also created a national government that could barely act. It couldn't keep states from putting up barriers to trade with other states or resolve trade wars between them. It couldn't raise taxes. It could pass laws, but it couldn't make the states follow them. It was severely limited in its ability to conduct foreign affairs. Because changes had to be approved unanimously, it couldn't do much to fix these weaknesses, especially when groups in some states benefited from the rules as they were written in the Articles.

Small farmers and debtors, of whom there were many in the years following the Revolutionary War, appreciated the fact that the Articles kept politics close to home and receptive to local needs and were among the Articles' strongest supporters. But the industrial revolution was about to hit the new country with the force of a tidal wave, and anyone involved in banking or the trade or manufacture of merchandise was frustrated by the inability of the Articles to regulate commerce among the states and maintain stable international ties. From the standpoint of conducting normal relations with other countries, the Articles of Confederation was a disaster.

If that wasn't enough, hard economic times fell upon the new country following the Revolutionary War. Things were particularly bad in Massachusetts, where heavy taxes and an economic depression placed a disproportionate burden on small farmers, many of whom lost their land and landed in debtor's prison. Suffering farmers in western Massachusetts blamed their plight on Boston merchants, who pressed for taxes so the state could repay the money it had borrowed from them during the war. In a case of borrowers rising up against unfair conditions they attributed to lenders, a group of debtor farmers took up arms to prevent Massachusetts courts from convening and sentencing debtors.

The insurrection was led by Revolutionary War officer Daniel Shays, and **Shays' Rebellion** started in August 1786 and lasted half a year until the Massachusetts militia put an end to it. It was typical of the type of rebellion that characterized this unsettled time. The national Congress had been powerless to deal with either the complaints or the actions of the debtors, and business groups who had previously been frustrated with the Articles of Confederation now worried that their fundamental interests were threatened.

It was 1787, and the ruling elite had seen enough. It was time to change the ground rules.

2-5 Ground Rules for Self-Governance— Second Attempt

The rules of the game under the Articles of Confederation turned out to be bulky and unworkable. They were also unusual rules. Most nations do not establish a **confederal system.** They are not a confederation of essentially independent states that band together to create a weak central union. Of course, there were special circumstances involved in trying to bring together thirteen largely autonomous colonies into a single nation, so the type of structure most common in the world—the **unitary system**—was never really an option. And when the framers of the government tried a second time, they again opted for an atypical structure in a **federal system,** still trying to find a way to balance the needs of the states with the need to function as a nation. This time, after a tough political debate, they

A *unitary system* is like a jigsaw puzzle made out of only one piece. Unitary contains the word *unit*, meaning one or singular. In the United States, each state is a unitary system with respect to its counties, cities, and townships. There are county governments, city governments, and township governments, but they're all chartered by the state and completely dependent on the state for their existence. Only the state can create a county or change county lines. Most nations of the world operate as unitary systems, where the national government creates all the local governments.

A *confederal system* is like a jigsaw puzzle made up of many noninterlocking parts. The whole picture is the sum total of the pieces, but it isn't strong and can easily fall apart. In a confederation, the national government has only those powers granted to it by the states, like in the Articles of Confederation. If a small number of states disagree with what the national government wants to do, the national government is restricted from acting.

A *federal system* is like a jigsaw puzzle with interlocking parts. Each state can still act on its own, but it is bound to the others through a national government. Each piece is still important in its own right, and in a federal system, a lot of power is reserved to the states. But the federal government has a lot of power too and functions as its own entity, not simply as a creation of the states. There are powers denied to the states that only the federal government has, like negotiating treaties with other countries. But at the same time, the federal government cannot interfere with the internal actions of any state, eliminate a state, or redraw state boundaries like in a unitary system.

Figure 2-1
Unitary, Confederal, and Federal Systems

▶ **Constitutional Convention**
A meeting of representatives from twelve of the thirteen states held in Philadelphia in 1787, which produced the federal system of government outlined in the United States Constitution.

fared much better. Figure 2-1 explores the differences among unitary, confederal, and federal systems.

Although by the spring of 1787 there was widespread sentiment that the Articles of Confederation had to be revised, there were different opinions about what that meant. Those benefiting from the rules of the game would fight hard to maintain their advantages. Others wanted a stronger and more functional central government that would dramatically change the rules. Most everyone was fearful of creating a system that could suppress liberty in the effort to make government more effective. Even if life under the Articles was chaotic, memory of British rule tempered the temptation to overreach in the other direction.

So, a delicate political challenge confronted the fifty-five men who gathered in Philadelphia in May 1787, ostensibly to revise the Articles. In what became known as the **Constitutional Convention,** delegates from every state but Rhode Island[5] assembled for the stated purpose of strengthening the confederation. (See Box 2-2.) It was clear from the start, though, that the convention was going to abandon the confederal system and replace it with something that might protect against chaos without burying individual liberties.

Box 2-2   Delegates to the Constitutional Convention

George Washington

The fifty-five delegates to the Constitutional Convention were an elite group of educated and privileged men. About half had had the rare opportunity to attend college. More than half were lawyers or had legal training, and almost one-quarter were businessmen or merchants. Several, like George Washington, were among the wealthiest people in the new nation, and many of the nation's most prominent families were represented. In keeping with their wealth and status, the delegate list read like a "who's who" of colonial and American politics. Although only eight delegates had signed the Declaration of Independence and only six had signed the Articles of Confederation, 80 percent had been members of the Continental Congress. Not surprisingly, the delegates would be a strong presence in the government they created. The convention boasted two future presidents (Washington and Madison), one future vice president, four cabinet secretaries, five Supreme Court justices, nineteen senators, and thirteen House members.

A few delegates had an important influence on the proceedings. By presiding over the meeting, Virginia's George Washington supplied the gathering with an important element of **legitimacy.** As leader of the Continental Army during the Revolutionary War, Washington was easily the most heroic figure in America.

Scene at the signing of the Constitution
Source: Painting by Howard Chandler Christy.

Benjamin Franklin
Source: National Archives and Records Administration.

Old and frail, the eighty-one-year-old inventor, writer, publisher, and diplomat Benjamin Franklin said little at the convention, but his presence made an important public statement about the significance of the proceedings. His democratic sentiments were well known, but the elder statesman from Pennsylvania could work behind the scenes to facilitate compromise among the divergent perspectives held by the delegates.

▶Virginia Plan A proposal for the new Constitution, supported by large states, that would have based representation on population and provided for a centralized national government that could overrule the states.

▶New Jersey Plan A proposal for the new Constitution, supported by small states, that would have provided for equal representation of large and small states in the national legislature, while limiting the power of the national government over the states.

The recognition of that goal was the easy part. Getting there—and getting political support for something new—would pose immense hurdles.

Despite widespread support for a federal system to replace the confederation, the convention nearly fell apart over two central issues: large versus small state representation in the new federal government and the legality of slavery.

Large, populous states like Virginia and Pennsylvania, mindful of their ability to dominate the new national government, advocated a method of representation based on population. Early in the convention, Edmund Randolph introduced what would be known as the **Virginia Plan,** which called for representation in the legislature based on population and a strong national government that would reign supreme over the states. Small states strenuously objected, and in turn, offered an alternative, the **New Jersey Plan.** Far less ambitious, it was essentially a stronger version of the Articles of Confederation, with representation based on states where each state would have one vote in the legislature.

In politics, it helps tremendously to set the agenda, and the Virginia group, by virtue of the fact that they were prepared with a plan, had the advantage of going first and structuring the course of the debate. The New Jersey Plan was offered in reaction to it, but it was voted down by the convention, as was a proposal by Alexander Hamilton that would have provided for an extremely strong central government with a powerful executive who served for life. With the rejection of the New Jersey Plan for a state-centered government

George Mason
Source: Gunston Hall Plantation,
http://www.gunstonhall.org.

Alexander Hamilton

One of the more critical voices was Virginia's George Mason, who, despite being a vocal and influential delegate, refused to sign the Constitution. His reservations centered on the concern that the government created by the Constitution would be too strong and might trample on the freedoms of those who created it. He feared the lack of a bill of rights (which was subsequently added by constitutional amendment) and the potential for abuses of power by Congress and the judiciary to hurt those without many resources and take power from the states (see Appendix E).

Delegates who feared the new government would not be strong enough represented the other end of the spectrum. New York's Alexander Hamilton, who had married into an aristocratic family, was more concerned about creating a strong central government that could pay its debts and function on the world stage than he was with establishing democratic mechanisms or protecting individual rights. He unsuccessfully proposed to the convention something resembling the British monarchy.

James Madison
Source: Library of Congress.

Virginia's James Madison occupied the middle ground between these two perspectives, which helped to make him the most influential member of the convention. Although not an imposing figure or speaker, and despite being one of the younger delegates at age thirty-six, Madison had the greatest influence on the Constitution. An advocate of a stronger central government than what the Articles of Confederation provided, Madison was a tireless campaigner and natural politician who was able to fashion compromise while successfully advocating his ideas.

You can read more about the delegates to the Constitutional Convention by visiting the National Archives at http://www.archives.gov/national_archives_experience/charters/constitution_founding_fathers_overview.html.

▶ **legitimacy** Widespread public acceptance of the official standing of a political figure or institution.

and the Hamilton plan for what looked to many like a monarchy, it became clear that the Virginia Plan—soundly positioned between the two—would be the foundation for the new Constitution.

It was equally clear, however, that nothing was going to happen unless the small states were on board, and as structured, the Virginia Plan would never come close to winning broad-based support. The convention deadlocked over the issue, and as May turned into June, tension was as thick as the Philadelphia humidity. Delegates from states large and small didn't want to sacrifice their essential interests, although most everyone wanted to return home with something better than the Articles. In the long run, this created an environment where compromise was possible.

The logjam was broken by the **Connecticut Compromise,** which provided a bicameral or two-house legislature. Representation in the lower house—the House of Representatives—would be determined by population, and states would be equally represented in the upper house, or Senate. Voters would directly elect members of the House of Representatives, while state legislators would appoint senators. In this arrangement, the configuration of the House of Representatives would address the concerns of the large states, and the configuration of the Senate would address the concerns of the small states. Apart from the fact that senators are now also directly elected, the Connecticut Compromise established the structure for Congress that exists to this day.

▶ **Connecticut Compromise**
A compromise between the Virginia and New Jersey Plans that broke the deadlock over representation at the Constitutional Convention by providing for a bicameral legislature. Large states would get their demand for representation based on population in the House of Representatives, while every state, regardless of size, would have two senators, which pleased small states.

▶ Three-Fifths Compromise
A compromise between northern and southern states that broke the deadlock over how slaves should be counted for purposes of representation. Three-fifths of slaves would be included in population totals, benefiting southern states that had the largest concentration of slaves by inflating their representation in the House of Representatives.

▶ Baron de Montesquieu (1689–1755) An eighteenth-century French political theorist whose ideas about decentralizing power to ensure personal liberty greatly influenced the government created by the Constitution.

▶ separation of powers
The division of political power among several equal and independent branches of government to prevent power from being consolidated in any one branch.

▶ checks and balances
The ability of any one of several equal and independent branches of government to keep the others from acting, designed to prevent power from being consolidated in any one branch. Because any branch can put a check on the others, government can only act when there is cooperation between the branches, a situation that necessitates compromise.

▶ republic Any nation with provisions for the selection of representatives who make decisions on behalf of those who select them. James Madison said a republic was "a government in which the scheme of representation takes place," as compared to direct democracy.

▶ representative democracy
A form of democracy in which eligible individuals choose others to make decisions on their behalf.

With the Connecticut Compromise came the hope that the convention would bear fruit, but one serious problem remained. If representation in the House of Representatives was to be based on population, should slaves be among those counted? Delegates from southern states, where slavery was concentrated, argued they should be, even though slaves were denied all rights granted to free persons. Of course, counting slaves for purposes of representation would have enhanced the power of southern states in the new Congress.

Some delegates from outside the South would have been happy to outlaw slavery entirely in the Constitution. It wasn't difficult to see the ironic contrast between the language of the Declaration of Independence, justifying separation from Great Britain, and the practice of slavery. As a pragmatic matter, though, slavery was essential to the southern economy, and there would be no union of the states if the convention insisted on pursuing the matter. So, slavery would be left to fester like a raw wound in the body politic for generations as the price of establishing a federal system.

Northern delegates did strenuously object to the southern proposal to count slaves for representation purposes, but this matter was addressed in the **Three-fifths Compromise**— a purely pragmatic attempt to split the difference between the two camps by counting each slave as three-fifths of a person for the purpose of determining representation in the House. As a reflection of the odious nature of the compromise, the final draft of the Constitution never mentions slaves, distinguishing instead between "free persons" (who would be counted fully) and "all other persons."

The summer of 1787 was coming to a close, and compromise was making possible a blueprint for a new federal government.

2-6 Ground Rules in Theory and Practice

If the Virginia Plan set the agenda for the Constitutional Convention, Virginia's James Madison developed the blueprint for some of the new government's most important features. Madison was an advocate of a strong central government, but he recognized that if it were to survive, it couldn't be so strong as to threaten individual liberties. Returning to the rationale for independence, Madison reasoned that the new government could be no more threatening to natural rights than American colonists believed the British government had been. That was a tall order to fill. It was one thing to declare independence on the basis of Locke's theoretical principles about the nature of government. It was quite another to design a functioning government that would uphold those principles.

For guidance, Madison turned to the writings of John Locke and eighteenth-century French political theorist **Baron de Montesquieu.** A supporter of democracy, Montesquieu believed that the best way to protect individual liberty was to make sure that power wasn't concentrated in any one place. He advocated separating powers into three distinct branches of government—an executive, a legislature, and a judiciary—each dependent on the others and therefore able to limit the powers of the others.

These ideas were incorporated into the design of the federal government. The Constitution provides for a system of **separation of powers,** whereby the executive (president), legislature (Congress), and judiciary (Supreme Court) are independent of one another. They represent different constituencies, are chosen by different means, perform distinct functions, and serve for terms varying from two years to life. Because nothing can get done unless they agree to work together, any one can frustrate the initiatives of the other two, a process known as **checks and balances** (see Box 2-3). You can find a quick overview of the workings of separation of powers in Table 2-2 and checks and balances in Figure 2-2 on page 32.

Along with separation of powers and checks and balances, the Constitution contained other safeguards designed to protect citizens from the new government it created. As we saw in Chapter 1, the Constitution called for a **republic** or **representative democracy** in which the House of Representatives would consist of people selected by and accountable to voters. Representatives have to face the voters again after a fixed term of two years, and can be tossed out of office if their actions defy the wishes of the people they represent. Originally selected by state legislators, senators are now chosen in the same manner and serve a fixed term of six years.

> ## Box 2-3 Inefficiency and Liberty
>
> I t's human nature to want to get things done, but, as we've seen, separation of powers and checks and balances purposely make it difficult for the federal government to accomplish things. One way to think about this frustrating situation is that it's actually a feature of the Constitution designed to protect individual liberty. Here's how it works: Because Congress, the president, and the Supreme Court each can check the initiatives of the other two branches, things can only get done when they work together. Often, their interests won't line up, and one branch will put a check on everyone else—such as when the Supreme Court declares an act of Congress unconstitutional, the president vetoes a bill, or the Senate refuses to confirm a presidential appointee.
>
> It's an inefficient way of trying to do business. Things happen much more slowly than they would if everyone worked together. When the branches continue to disagree, nothing gets done at all. In these situations, the whole process stalls. Everything grinds to a halt. No bill is passed, or the law is struck down, or the appointment doesn't happen.
>
> At the same time, the process makes it hard for any one group or interest to achieve its goals at the expense of everyone else. It forces deliberation and compromise. That helps protect the wishes of those who otherwise might be overwhelmed by the quick actions of like-minded government officials. So, while it may be frustrating, the inefficiency of a decentralized system is also a safeguard. The Constitution's framers chose to create frustration as part of the price of protecting personal liberty.

Other safeguards followed from the ideas of John Locke. Representative democracy implies a government based on **popular sovereignty,** where the government is run by the people it is designed to serve based on the free expression of their will to be governed. Recall that Locke argued against the divine right of kings to rule, asserting that government gets its authority from individuals and must protect the natural rights of those it serves. By implication, if the new government had failed in this endeavor, it would have been appropriate for Americans to reject it and try again.

The Constitution also established a **limited government** by placing specific restrictions on what government can do. This, too, is consistent with Locke's thinking because it is based on the principle that the people rightly decide the appropriate role for government, and that Americans can restrict the government from acting in ways that they feel might jeopardize their liberty. So, for instance, Congress is prohibited—by constitutional amendment—from restricting religious freedom. Contrast this way of thinking with the traditional rationale for monarchy, in which a king's broad authority doesn't take into account restrictions on individual liberty.

A final safeguard—**federalism**—was more a product of necessity than design, but it serves the purpose of placing a check on the actions of government that can be just as strong as separation of powers, checks and balances, representative democracy, popular sovereignty, or limited government. We've already seen how a federal government contrasts with a confederal government, like the one created by the Articles of Confederation, and a unitary government, which is the model for most governments in the world. Federalism regards the bulky architecture of shared authority between the national (federal)

▶**popular sovereignty**
Rule by the people based on the consent of the governed.

▶**limited government** The idea that power can be denied to government and the people who serve in it, in order to restrict those in positions of authority from infringing upon individual liberty.

▶**federalism** The division of power between a sovereign federal government and sovereign state governments, which provides that some functions will be performed by the national government, some by the state governments, and some by both the national and state governments. As a feature designed to limit the strength of government, federalism works to decentralize power by creating dual levels of authority.

| | Executive/ President | Legislative/Congress | | Judicial/Courts |
		House	Senate	
Represents	Entire nation	Small districts	States	The Constitution
Chosen by	Electoral College	The people	The people (originally state legislatures)	The president, confirmed by the Senate
Term	4 years, renewable once	2 years	6 years	Life
Function	Carrying out laws	Writing the laws	Writing the laws	Judging the laws

TABLE 2-2

The Three Branches

Congress
Legislative Branch

Supreme Court
Judicial Branch

President
Executive Branch

1. If the Constitution designed a government that was strong enough to get things done, you might think the institutions created by the Constitution—the executive, legislature, and judiciary—would have a common purpose, like hockey players on the same team. But we know that separation of powers gives the president, Congress, and the Supreme Court different constituencies, different terms of office, and different functions to perform. This can put them at cross-purposes. And the Constitution gives each one the ability to frustrate the others through checks and balances. It's as if players on the same hockey team started to block each other, putting personal interests above the combined interests of the team.

2. If the House and Senate can agree on legislation, they have to pass it to the president for his signature. But the president can block it with a veto and send it back to Congress, where Congress has the power to override the president and make a bill law without his approval. At the same time, the Supreme Court can nullify the law by declaring it unconstitutional, just as it can nullify an action taken by the president by declaring it unconstitutional.

3. The three branches can block each other on nominations as well. The president nominates people to positions in the executive branch and on the courts. But the nominations will die if the Senate doesn't confirm them. So Supreme Court justices can only take their seats if approved by the Senate after nomination by the president.

4. The three branches also have a say in each others' job security. If the House impeaches the president and the Senate convicts him, the president is removed from office. If the House impeaches a Supreme Court justice and the Senate follows with a conviction, that justice is removed from office.

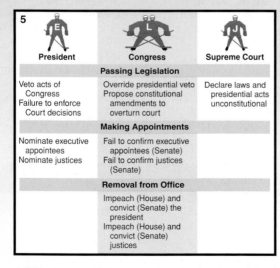

President	Congress	Supreme Court
Passing Legislation		
Veto acts of Congress Failure to enforce Court decisions	Override presidential veto Propose constitutional amendments to overturn court	Declare laws and presidential acts unconstitutional
Making Appointments		
Nominate executive appointees Nominate justices	Fail to confirm executive appointees (Senate) Fail to confirm justices (Senate)	
Removal from Office		
	Impeach (House) and convict (Senate) the president Impeach (House) and convict (Senate) justices	

5. To review, the three branches of government can check each other in three important ways. One, when making legislation, the president may veto acts of Congress and resist enforcing Court directives; Congress may override presidential vetos and propose constitutional amendments to overturn Court decisions; and the Court may overrule Congress or the president by declaring a law or presidential act unconstitutional. Two, the president nominates people to serve in the executive branch of government and on the courts, but if the Senate fails to confirm them, the appointments die. Three, the House may impeach and the Senate may convict the president or Supreme Court justices, thereby removing them from office.

6. With checks and balances, each branch has the opportunity to assert its interests and put a stop to the work of the other two. Only when their interests align will they work together as a team instead of blocking one another.

Figure 2-2
Checks and Balances

Article I	Establishes the legislative branch of government, with instructions for electing representatives and senators, and gives basic guidelines for how Congress should run and what it should do.
Article II	Establishes the executive branch or the presidency. It says that the president shall be commander-in-chief of the armed forces, grants the president the power to make treaties, mandates that the president report to Congress from time to time on the state of the union, and devotes a lot of attention to presidential selection.
Article III	Establishes the judiciary. It mandates the establishment of a Supreme Court, stipulating the matters over which it should have jurisdiction, and gives Congress the authority to set up lower courts.
Article IV	Addresses the relationship between the federal government and the states, including procedures for admitting new states to the union, and defines the relationship of each state to the others.
Article V	Sets up the mechanism for amending the Constitution.
Article VI	Transfers to the new government all outstanding debts acquired by the United States under the Articles of Confederation and establishes the Constitution as the supreme law of the land.
Article VII	Sets the procedures for ratifying the Constitution.

government and the states as a feature of the republic. By assigning some functions to the federal government, others to the states, and still others to both, the framers of the Constitution ensured that there would be multiple centers of power.

Throughout our history, federalism has been the source of intense political disputes the likes of which you won't find in too many countries. We'll take a closer look at these disputes in Section 2-10, "Federalism: Only in America."

For something so important, the Constitution is a simple document. It consists of seven articles and twenty-seven amendments, the first ten of which constitute the Bill of Rights (see Appendix B). Take a look at Table 2-3 to see what was in the original, unamended document.

2-7 "If Men Were Angels"

The clearest rationale for why the new nation might benefit from all these institutional safeguards appeared in a series of essays written after the Constitutional Convention by Alexander Hamilton, James Madison, and John Jay. First published anonymously between October 1787 and May 1788 in several New York newspapers under the name "Publius," which is Latin for "public man," the eighty-five essays that came to be known as *The Federalist* (to many today, *The Federalist Papers*) were meant to persuade a reluctant New York State of the advantages of the Constitution. Notwithstanding their political purpose, *The Federalist* remains one of the clearest expressions of how the Constitution was designed to work, not to mention the best surviving glimpse into the thinking of the Constitution's authors.

As a body of work, *The Federalist* addressed the "defects" in the Articles of Confederation (in a series of essays believed to have been written by Alexander Hamilton) and detailed how the new Constitution would correct them without costing citizens their liberty (in an argument made by Madison). Additionally, John Jay, who had experience in foreign affairs, authored a few essays dealing with constitutional structure and foreign relations.

Madison made the argument that the new government had to have numerous power centers in order to protect people from the worst motives of their neighbors, both in and out of government. "If men were angels, no government would be necessary," he wrote. "If angels were to govern men, neither external nor internal controls on government would be necessary." But common sense and knowledge of human nature tells us that we need to be cautious in social endeavors, especially when power is involved.

▶ *The Federalist* A collection of essays written by Alexander Hamilton, James Madison, and John Jay in an effort to persuade a reluctant public to support the Constitution.

faction A group of individuals who are united by a desire that, if realized, would threaten the liberty of the larger community—in James Madison's words, individuals who are "united and actuated by some common impulse of passion, or of interest, adverse to the rights of other citizens, or to the permanent and aggregate interests of the community." A faction may be defined by size, such as when a majority of citizens threatens the liberty of the minority, or by intensity, such as when a minority of citizens with intensely held preferences threatens the liberty of a disinterested majority.

tyranny The denial of liberty to individuals through the actions of a faction or through the actions of government itself.

We've all at times questioned the motivation of people we've met. Maybe they were trying to sell us something, or trying to befriend us, and for whatever reason, the way they acted didn't feel right to us. Madison acknowledged these types of experiences happen all the time, and when you're trying to govern yourself as a nation, you run the risk that a group of people with malevolent motives will band together as a **faction** and work to impose their will on everyone. Even if they are small in number, a faction of highly motivated people can threaten the rest. Madison's fear was that if they were not controlled, factions could impose their will on others and produce **tyranny,** denying liberty to those who did not share the wishes of the faction.

Madison lays out the problem in detail and assesses the possible solutions to it in Federalist #10, ultimately explaining why the new Constitution provided the surest and safest way to address the dangers of faction. In Federalist #51, he goes on to detail how separation of powers and checks and balances work to protect against the danger of tyranny from the government.

In Federalist #10, Madison addresses alternative ways to deal with the dangers posed by factions. Here's a simple way of thinking about what he said. Let's say you wanted the liberty to dress in whatever style appealed to you. Further assume that there is a group of people—a faction—that wanted to impose a national dress code that would forbid the wearing of baggy pants and nose rings. They could be small in number but highly motivated, plotting to find ways to get you to dress like they do while you're busy going about your life, not giving a second thought to what you wear. Or, they could be large enough in number to overwhelm you. Either way, they could pose a threat to your free expression.

Madison looks at ways to prevent that from happening and considers two options: removing the causes of faction—the things that motivate others to gang up on you—or controlling their effects. Removing the causes of faction would require either removing liberty or giving everyone the same preferences and desires. Neither is a particularly attractive option. In the first case, what's the point of removing liberty if the objective is to *preserve* liberty? Madison says this remedy would be "worse than the disease" of faction itself. He likens liberty to air: We need it to breathe, and fire needs it to burn, but if you eliminated air just to put out fires, you'd be extinguishing life in the process. So, this solution is effective, but way too expensive.

What about giving everyone the same preferences and desires? That would result in a society where everyone would look, act, feel, and believe the same things—a place where, say, everyone wore baggy pants and nose rings. If you're having trouble imagining how this might come about, it's because this is not a practical solution. As long as people have liberty, different opinions will form, and with them, the risk that factions will form. "The latent causes of faction," Madison says, "are thus sown in the nature of man." It's a condition we simply have to deal with.

Madison concludes that if we can't regulate the causes of faction, we need to control their effects so that liberty can be protected. This is where the safety features of the Constitution come into play, starting with the establishment of a republican form of government. As we know, unlike direct democracy, a republic is characterized by elected representatives who are accountable to the people through popular sovereignty. In this depiction of events, our dress-code advocates can vote along with everyone else for representatives to Congress. Their intensely expressed wish for everyone to dress in a particular manner may result in the election of some representatives who share their views, which, in turn, will be expressed in Congress to other representatives who speak for different people who do not share their views. Because they are a faction, it will be hard for them to attain enough support in Congress to impose their wishes on others, although Congress will give them a forum for having their views heard. In a country as large as the United States, Madison speculated that there would be many factions concerned with a host of issues, none of which would be able to dominate the government.

To make things more secure, the Constitution makes it difficult for any one group to dominate the workings of government by separating powers into different branches and through checks and balances. Add staggered terms for elected representatives, different constituencies for elected representatives, and federalism—all the safeguards we talked about earlier—and it becomes difficult for a single faction to manipulate the machinery of government.

At the same time, Madison was sensitive to the need to protect the public *from* the government. In Federalist #51, he describes the benefits derived from separation of powers and checks and balances, which make it difficult for government to overwhelm individual liberty. By creating different institutions with separate and distinct roles, representing different groups in society, the three branches are likely to adhere to distinct agendas, which they cannot advance alone. As a consequence, each branch will have to moderate its wishes through compromise with the others or submit to the reality that nothing will get done. Either outcome protects the public from the threat of centralized power. "Ambition must be made to counteract ambition," Madison writes. "The interest of the man must be connected with the constitutional rights of the place."

Essays in *The Federalist* are not long, but they were written in the language of eighteenth-century America and should be read slowly. You can access the original text of Federalist #10 and Federalist #51 in Appendixes C and D, respectively.

2-8 Selling the Constitution

It may be strange to think of politicians writing essays in an effort to win a political battle, but that's essentially what *The Federalist* was about. Today, Hamilton and Madison would set up an organization to collect contributions from wealthy like-minded donors and use that money to buy thirty-second television ads in states where ratification of the Constitution seemed shaky. At the same time, even if their methods seem quaint by comparison, the bitter struggle over ratification was as partisan and nasty as anything in politics today.

Those who favored ratification cleverly called themselves "Federalists," leaving their opponents with the negative tag "Anti-Federalists." Since the way you characterize your political opponent goes a long way to structuring the debate (see Box 2-4), this choice of label gave the Federalists the upper hand in the discussion because it's always better to be for something than to want to obstruct something. And if the Anti-Federalists were opposed to the Constitution, and people at large were widely opposed to the Articles of Confederation, then it was reasonable to wonder exactly what the Anti-Federalists were for.

In fact, the Federalists did have the advantage of being more organized than the Anti-Federalists, and of having a cohesive argument for ratification. They had the stature of national figures like Washington and Franklin behind them. They had frustration over the Articles to help their cause. What they didn't have was enough votes.

It was clear to the Federalists that ratification was in serious jeopardy in a number of states. Because state legislatures (rightly) feared losing power under the new constitutional arrangement, they were among the Constitution's strongest critics, and the Constitutional Convention shrewdly maneuvered to have ratification considered in state conventions rather than in the legislatures. But ratification still had to take place at the state level, where officials stood to lose a lot of power and could be counted on to lead the charge against change.

To confront this difficulty, the Constitution's supporters opted to require ratification from only nine of thirteen states before the new constitutional arrangement would take effect—even though unanimity had been required to revise the Articles. They recognized that unanimity was an unrealistic objective, and were savvy enough to realize that if faced with the reality of the new government taking effect elsewhere on the continent, reluctant states would find themselves with no alternative but to go along.

There were other huge obstacles as well. Anti-Federalists made much of the apparent class bias at the Constitutional Convention, claiming that a group of lawyers and merchants had created a new government that would undermine the interests of farmers and debtors. Considering the conflicts between debtors and creditors that helped fuel the Constitutional Convention, it's not at all surprising that this argument carried a lot of weight. Add this to the sentiment that the country had just finished fighting a war to get away from a strong central government and the Anti-Federalists had a strong case.

Box 2-4   The Politics of Language

Couching the ratification debate in the language of "Federalists" and "Anti-Federalists" is akin to how language is used in present-day debates over contentious policy issues. Think about the way each side in the abortion debate implicitly characterizes the other through the selection of the labels they claim for themselves. Abortion rights supporters call themselves "pro-choice," suggesting that their opponents—implicitly "antichoice"—stand in opposition to liberty. Those on the other side of the question label themselves "pro-life," with clear implications for what that makes the other side. Would anyone willingly claim to be "pro-death"?

In what would become typical of politics in America, the battle was spirited, impassioned—and dirty. Rumors flew in the newspapers. Pagans would control the government. Federal crimes would be punished by torture. The Pope would be elected president.[6]

The claims about punishment and torture stuck, and the Federalists found that they had to respond to charges that the Constitution did not protect people from fundamental abuses of liberty by the federal government. Their answer was a promise to amend the Constitution immediately in a way that would protect individuals from abuses by government. The result of this promise was the first ten amendments to the Constitution—the Bill of Rights—passed as promised by the First Congress and ratified by the states within two years.

The First Congress quickly took up the matter of a Bill of Rights as promised by the Federalists in their campaign to win ratification of the Constitution. On September 25, 1789, Congress passed and sent to the states twelve amendments designed to protect people from abuses of their liberty by the new government. The first amendment, which addressed the number of constituents each House member would represent, was not ratified. The second amendment, which set restrictions on congressional compensation, took 203 years to ratify and became the Twenty-seventh Amendment to the Constitution on May 7, 1992. The remaining ten were ratified December 15, 1791 and became known as the Bill of Rights. Table 2-4 describes each amendment included in the Bill of Rights.

The promise of a Bill of Rights turned out to be a particularly important maneuver by the Federalists. By January 1788, Delaware, Pennsylvania, New Jersey, Georgia, and Connecticut had ratified the Constitution, but the remaining states were either strongly opposed or too close to call. The outcome in Massachusetts was in question when its convention met in February, and the Bill of Rights concession is credited with making the difference in a narrow vote to approve. It would help make the difference in other narrow votes to come.

Things remained tenuous, though. New Hampshire was leaning against ratification, and in March, Rhode Island held a referendum that rejected the Constitution by a large margin. It was up to Maryland to regain the momentum for the Federalists, which it did in April with a vote to ratify. South Carolina soon fell in line, and when New Hampshire became the ninth state to ratify on June 21, 1788, the Constitution had been officially adopted.

Nonetheless, the battle continued. As a practical matter, the constitutional plan could not have been implemented without the blessing of two of the largest states, New York and Virginia. This was hardly forthcoming. Owing in part to the hard work and political skills of James Madison in Virginia and Alexander Hamilton in New York—of which the publication of *The Federalist* was a part—and in part to the relative disarray of the Anti-Federalists, these two populous states eventually ratified the Constitution, even though the vote in each case was harrowingly close (the margin in the New York convention was three votes of fifty-seven cast). It's quite likely that a majority of New Yorkers and Virginians opposed the Constitution at the time their states ratified it. Hamilton assumed a majority of Americans opposed it, but the Federalists had outmaneuvered their opponents. North Carolina would ratify the Constitution following Washington's inauguration as president.

		TABLE **2-4**
First Amendment	The First Amendment prevents government from interfering with several key personal freedoms, including the freedom to worship, speak, and assemble peacefully. It also prevents the government from restricting freedom of the press and the freedom to petition government.	**The Bill of Rights**
Second Amendment	The Second Amendment protects the right to bear arms.	
Third and Fourth Amendments	The Third and Fourth Amendments provide a right to privacy from government interference. The Third Amendment prevents government from forcing citizens to house soldiers during peacetime—addressing one of the complaints the colonists had against the British. The Fourth Amendment protects against unreasonable searches and seizures of property or personal effects.	
Fifth through Eighth Amendments	The Fifth through Eighth Amendments establish a host of protections for individuals accused of a crime. These include the right not to be tried twice for the same crime, the right to be indicted by a grand jury before being tried for a capital crime, the right not to be forced to testify against yourself, the right to due process of law, and the right not to have property confiscated by government without compensation (all in the Fifth Amendment); and the right to a speedy and impartial trial, the right to be informed of charges against you, the right to call and confront witnesses, and the right to a lawyer (all in the Sixth Amendment); and the right to a jury in civil trials (Seventh Amendment); the right to be free from excessive bail and from the infliction of cruel and unusual punishments (Eighth Amendment).	
Ninth and Tenth Amendments	The Ninth Amendment is a safety net establishing that any rights not specifically mentioned in the first eight amendments are not necessarily denied. The Tenth Amendment establishes that any powers not granted to the federal government or prohibited to the states are reserved for the states.	

Rhode Island, the final holdout, would sign on almost two years after the document had become official, and there would be a federal republic in the United States. Table 2-5 details how the new government unfolded.

2-9 Changing the Constitution

The rules of the game set out in the Constitution have evolved over time, and much of that change has been gradual and evolutionary, rather than sudden and dramatic. Although there are formal mechanisms for amending the Constitution, the greatest change has come through differences in the way the Constitution is interpreted. This has afforded the Constitution the flexibility to respond to two centuries of dramatic social, economic, and political change.

The Constitution's authors were determined not to repeat the mistakes of the Articles of Confederation, which were impossible to amend. At the same time, they wanted it to be difficult to change the supreme law of the land. They decided on two methods for proposing and ratifying amendments to the Constitution, which are described in Box 2-5.

Formally changing the Constitution has proved difficult. Since 1789, only twenty-seven amendments have been ratified—ten of which were the Bill of Rights. Many of the ratified amendments broadened the grant of constitutional rights or strengthened the power of the federal government. Table 2-6 provides an overview.

Box 2-5   Amendment Ratification

Amendments need to be proposed, then ratified. The Constitution allows the process to begin at either the federal or the state level. At the federal level, an amendment is proposed if it is approved by a two-thirds vote of both the House of Representatives and the Senate. Every amendment to the Constitution has originated this way. It then follows one of two paths. The most typical path is for the amendment to be considered by the legislatures of the fifty states. The amendment is ratified if it is approved by three-fourths of the state legislatures. All but one amendment was ratified this way.

The lone exception was the Twenty-first Amendment, which repealed the Eighteenth Amendment outlawing the sale or manufacture of alcohol. The Twenty-first Amendment followed the other ratification path permitted by the Constitution: It was approved by special ratifying conventions in three-fourths of the states. These were like the state ratifying conventions that approved the original Constitution.

For an amendment to be proposed at the state level, two-thirds of the state legislatures would have to ask Congress to call a national convention, similar to the Constitutional Convention that produced the Constitution. Whatever amendment or amendments the national convention approved would then require the approval of three-fourths of either the state legislatures or state conventions for ratification. This method has never been used.

To review, amendments need to be proposed, then ratified. The Constitution provides two ways to propose amendments and two ways to ratify them. Every amendment in our history has been proposed by a two-thirds vote of both houses of Congress, and all but one has been ratified by a vote of three-fourths of the state legislatures. The one exception was approved by ratifying conventions in three-fourths of the states. Amendments may also be proposed if two-thirds of the state legislatures request a national constitutional convention. This method has never been used.

TABLE 2-5

Constitutional Timeline

It took a while before the machinery created by the Constitution came on line. Some of it was being put into place while the ratification process was still playing out. Here's how the new government unfolded, from the ratification of the Constitution to the establishment of all three branches of the new federal government.

June 21, 1788	The Constitution is adopted when New Hampshire becomes the ninth state to ratify.
September 1788	Congress sets dates for voting for president.
January 1789	Presidential electors are chosen in states that ratified the Constitution.
February 1789	Presidential electors meet and select George Washington as the first president.
March 3, 1789	The government established by the Articles of Confederation ceases to exist.
April 6, 1789	The first Congress of the United States meets to begin organizing.
April 8, 1789	Members of the House of Representatives take the oath of office.
April 30, 1789	George Washington is sworn in as the first president of the United States. The executive branch becomes operational.
June 1, 1789	The first act of Congress provides for senators to take an oath of office and recognizes the oath that House members took on April 8th as official.
June 3, 1789	Senators take the oath of office, and John Adams is sworn in as vice president. Congress becomes fully operational.
February 2, 1790	The Supreme Court meets in first full session. All three branches of the new government are now operational.

Source: National Archives at http://www.archives.gov/national_archives_experience/constitution_q_and_a.html.

TABLE **2-6**

Amendments to the Constitution

Apart from the Bill of Rights, the amendments to the Constitution—in order of appearance—did the following:

Eleventh (1795)	Limited federal court jurisdiction in suits against states
Twelfth (1804)	Modified the method of selecting the president
Thirteenth (1865)	Abolished slavery
Fourteenth (1868)	Expanded the federal guarantees of equal protection of the law and due process of law to the states
Fifteenth (1870)	Extended voting rights to African Americans
Sixteenth (1913)	Authorized a federal income tax
Seventeenth (1913)	Changed the method of choosing senators from selection by state legislatures to direct popular vote
Eighteenth (1919)	Abolished the sale and production of alcohol; repealed by the Twenty-first Amendment (1933)
Nineteenth (1920)	Extended voting rights to women
Twentieth (1933)	Established that presidential terms expire on January 20th and that congressional terms expire on January 3rd
Twenty-first (1933)	Repealed the Eighteenth Amendment (1919)
Twenty-second (1951)	Established presidential term limits
Twenty-third (1961)	Extended the right to vote in presidential elections to residents of the District of Columbia
Twenty-fourth (1964)	Abolished the poll tax in federal elections
Twenty-fifth (1967)	Provided procedures for handling presidential disability and for filling a vacancy in the vice presidency
Twenty-sixth (1971)	Extended voting rights to eighteen-year-olds
Twenty-seventh (1992)	Prohibited midterm congressional pay increases

The Thirteenth, Fourteenth, and Twenty-fourth Amendments expanded civil rights.

The Fifteenth, Seventeenth, Nineteenth, Twenty-third, and Twenty-sixth Amendments expanded the right to vote.

Because so many parties have to agree to amend the Constitution, a large number of efforts have failed. Some of the more significant proposals that never made it include:

- *A proposed Equal Rights Amendment that would have made sex discrimination unconstitutional*—It was proposed in 1972 with a time limit for ratification. Three-fourths of the state legislatures failed to ratify it by 1982, and it expired.

- *Full congressional representation for the District of Columbia*—This amendment was proposed in 1978 and expired, unratified, seven years later. To this day, residents of the nation's capital have no representation in the Senate and are represented in the House by a delegate who cannot vote.[7]

- *A proposal to allow Congress to limit child labor*—Proposed in 1926, it remains ten states short of ratification and has no time limit. But no state has acted on the amendment since 1937.

Many more proposals of lesser note have been unsuccessful, typically unable to muster the congressional support necessary to send them to the states for ratification. Some of the failed attempts over the past few years would have established:

- A constitutional right to health care
- A constitutional restriction against the early release of convicted criminals
- A constitutional right to own a home

It's pretty easy to see how difficult it would be to get all the necessary parties to come together to modify the Constitution around these relatively specific issues. It may be less obvious to see how profound changes have occurred through judicial interpretation and political circumstance. Rather than alter the physical document, changes of this nature alter the way we understand the physical document.

The courts have had to deal with countless disputes over constitutional interpretation, and in the process, they have shaped the way the Constitution is applied and understood, sometimes in ways its authors never could have imagined. The Supreme Court is the arbiter of constitutional disputes, but in a good example of how judicial interpretation has modified the Constitution, nothing in the Constitution itself actually grants this authority to the Supreme Court. As we will see in Chapter 12, early in its history, the Supreme Court interpreted the Constitution to say that the Court's power to review the Constitution was intended by the document's framers.

Changes in political circumstances have similarly shaped the Constitution in unintended ways. For instance, political parties are never mentioned in the Constitution, and with good reason—the Federalists equated parties with factions and saw them as a threat to liberty. Yet, the years immediately following the ratification of the Constitution saw the emergence of political parties, and they have been a central part of our political process ever since. The Constitution has been flexible enough to adapt to this change.

Soon we'll learn about the complex constitutional mechanism for presidential selection, called the Electoral College. It originally provided for an elite group of individuals, called electors, to debate the merits of the candidates and vote for the one they felt most qualified. Through natural evolution, political parties acquired that function. But the electors still exist, even though they only go through the motions of voting for president. The Constitution was flexible enough to adjust to a situation its authors simply couldn't anticipate.

2-10 Federalism: Only in America

Well—almost only in America. Apart from a handful of countries like Canada, Germany, and Switzerland, federal systems are unusual in the world. In this country, federalism has a lot to do with how political debates play out.

Having states and a federal government as independent power centers is an effective feature of the Constitution designed to keep power from being concentrated in a single set of hands. It is also an awkward design that has caused conflict throughout American history.

The dilemma centers around which power center—the states or Washington, D.C.— gets to have the final word in American politics. There's no doubt that Madison intended the national government to be supreme to the state governments. But this was a point of contention at the Constitutional Convention that wasn't put to rest until the Civil War settled the matter some seventy years later by establishing that the South did not have a right to depart from the Union to form a new confederation.

The Constitution does contain wording that appears to support Madison's position. Article VI states, "This Constitution, and the laws of the United States which shall be made in Pursuance thereof . . . shall be the supreme Law of the Land." This seems to suggest that actions of the federal government should override actions of the states, but not everyone saw it this way at first. Only over time, through precedent and judicial interpretation, did this **supremacy clause** cement the position of the federal government as superior to the states.

> **supremacy clause**
> A constitutional provision (Article VI) establishing the relationship between the federal and state governments. The supremacy clause asserts that any conflict between the federal government and the states will be decided in favor of the federal government.

There are other hints that the Constitution's framers intended for the states to be subservient to the federal government. In Article I, Section 8, Congress is given the authority "To make all laws which shall be necessary and proper for carrying into Execution . . . all other Powers vested by this Constitution in the Government of the United States." Implicit in this statement is a large grant of power to the national government that, when broadly interpreted, gives Congress the ability to make laws that states would be obligated to follow.

The key word here is *interpreted*—and there are several different ways of understanding the intent of the Constitution's framers with respect to federalism that could be conveniently applied by people on both sides of the strong federal government question. Beyond giving the federal government the upper hand in its relationship with the states, the Constitution provides little guidance on how federalism is to operate in practice. Consequently, the specific relationship between the federal and state governments has varied at different points in our national history and has evolved over time.

Madison's vision was what might best be termed **nation-centered federalism,** whereby the Constitution was the supreme law of the land, the federal government was a creation of the Constitution, and the states—despite their broad grant of authority—were subservient to both. But those favoring greater state and local control of politics advocated a form of **state-centered federalism,** which turned Madison's perspective on its head with the claim that the Constitutional Convention itself was a meeting of the states intended to revise the Articles of Confederation. Therefore, the Constitution it produced and the federal government it established were essentially a creation of the states, which should have the final say in disagreements over which level of government had the ultimate authority to act.

This might seem like an academic argument, but the implications were tremendous. When southern states seceded from the union during the period leading up to the Civil War, they justified their actions on the basis of state-centered federalism—that the federal union was created by the states, who maintained the right to opt out. In turn, northern states opposed secession—and justified military action—on the basis of nation-centered federalism, that the union of the states was greater than the sum of its parts.

During the decades following the drafting of the Constitution, many took a middle perspective that worked as long as the states and the federal government didn't have to confront irreconcilable differences—the perspective of **dual federalism,** which contended the Constitution had given both the states and the federal government distinct authority over a broad range of matters. In other words, the grant of authority to the federal government could coexist with a different but equally broad grant of authority to the states, sidestepping the matter of which would win a battle of wills.

Dual federalism provided a reasonable way to manage the natural tension arising between the federal government and the states because, during the period stretching from the Constitutional Convention to the Civil War, the federal government and the states for the most part did operate in distinct spheres. Government at both levels was small by today's standards and didn't participate in a wide range of activities, so disputes could be minimized.

When the two clashed, though, they made a loud noise. The most notable conflict during this period came to a head in 1819, when the U.S. Supreme Court had to determine whether the federal government had the right to charter a federal bank and locate it, free of taxes, in one of the states. The decision, in the case *McCulloch v. Maryland,* was the first to clearly enumerate **national supremacy,** or the dominance of the federal government over the states. See Box 2-6.

If the Civil War put an end to the claim that the federal government was a creation of the states, it also ushered in a period of rapid growth in the United States, which posed new challenges for federal/state relations. As waves of immigrants flocked to American cities during a period of rapid industrialization, government at both the federal and state levels had to address a host of new social and economic concerns. By the start of the twentieth century, a new intergovernmental relationship was forged that lasted for the better part of

▶**nation-centered federalism**
One of several perspectives on federalism, which argues for the supremacy of the Constitution and federal law over state actions.

▶**state-centered federalism**
One of several perspectives on federalism, which argues that the Constitution and the federal government are creations of the states and therefore can be overruled by the states.

▶**dual federalism**   One of several perspectives on federalism, popular during the early years of the republic, which stated that the federal and state governments operated concurrently in separate arenas, and that each had the final say in those areas where it had a clear grant of authority.

▶*McCulloch v. Maryland*
The 1819 Supreme Court case that established federal supremacy over the state governments.

▶**national supremacy**
The doctrine that the federal government has the final word in disputes with the states. National supremacy was established through court rulings, precedent, and the victory of the North in the Civil War, eventually resolving the conflict between nation-centered federalism and state-centered federalism in favor of the former.

Box 2-6   *McCulloch v. Maryland* (1819)

The dispute before the U.S. Supreme Court in *McCulloch v. Maryland* centered on two questions about the scope and reach of the federal government: Could the federal government engage in activities that were not expressly delegated to it in the Constitution, and does the federal government supersede the states when a conflict arises between them? In both cases, the verdict was a resounding yes, setting the stage for the future growth of national power and the eventual repudiation of state-centered federalism.

The particulars center on the establishment by the federal government of a Bank of the United States. First chartered by Congress in 1791 as a means for coining currency, making loans, and centralizing the financial affairs of the United States, the first Bank of the United States was controversial. Not surprisingly, supporters of nation-centered federalism, like Treasury Secretary Alexander Hamilton—always an advocate of a strong central government—were behind the idea. Hamilton justified the creation of the bank on the grounds that the Constitution gave Congress a broad grant of power that extended to just about anything not expressly denied to it. Just as predictable were the Bank's opponents: debtor farmers (who still didn't trust the actions of lenders) and advocates of state-centered federalism, who felt Congress had grossly overreached its authority because the Constitution did not specifically give Congress the power to charter a national bank.

The charter on the bank expired in 1811, but the financial demands of the War of 1812 were justification for President Madison—the same James Madison who guided the development of the Constitution—to recommend that Congress revisit the charter. A second Bank of the United States was subsequently established, and it met with a heightened level of opposition. The state of Maryland imposed a tax on the Baltimore branch of the Bank in 1818, which the Bank's cashier, James McCulloch, refused to pay on the grounds that a state did not have the power to tax a federal entity. Shortly afterwards, the dispute landed in the U.S. Supreme Court.

The decision, written by Chief Justice John Marshall, backed both the power of Congress to establish the bank and the right of the federal government to do so without having to submit to taxes levied by a state. In so doing, Marshall invoked both the "necessary and proper" clause and the supremacy clause of the Constitution.

In ruling to support the right of the federal government to charter a bank, Marshall took a broad interpretation of the **"necessary and proper" clause,** arguing that the language of Article I, Section 8, gave Congress powers that were not specifically delegated to it in the Constitution—powers that were implied but not stated. This interpretation allowed Congress to act with great flexibility in future years, permitting the federal government to grow in authority in relation to the states.

In ruling against Maryland on the tax issue, Marshall invoked the reasoning of nation-centered federalism and a broad reading of the supremacy clause. He argued that as long as the federal government acted constitutionally, its actions were binding on the states. Since Marshall had already established that the bank charter was a "necessary and proper" move for Congress in its constitutionally enumerated capacity to regulate commerce, it followed that the states had no choice but to permit Congress to establish branches of the Bank, tax free, wherever it wished.[*]

▶ **"necessary and proper" clause** A constitutional provision (Article I, Section 8) giving Congress a broad grant of authority to make laws that are binding on the states.

[*]You can find the text of Marshall's ruling at http://usinfo.state.gov/usa/infousa/facts/democrac/10.htm or by looking up the case, *4 Wheaton 316 (1819).*

▶**cooperative federalism**
One of several perspectives on federalism, popular during the first two-thirds of the twentieth century, which was defined by joint endeavors between the federal and state governments. Typically, state governments would carry out federal initiatives, using federal money and federal guidelines.

seventy years. Dubbed **cooperative federalism,** it was characterized by federal-state partnerships, where federal funds were used to help states administer federal priorities at the state level.

The story of American government in the twentieth century is a tale of increasing demands on government through the first two-thirds of the century, followed by a reaction against central government activity in the latter one-third. It's a story with all kinds of implications for how government developed and how it works today, so we'll be coming back to it a lot. Table 2-7 on pages 44–45 demonstrates how federal-state relations evolved over the course of the twentieth century and continue to evolve today. Box 2-7 describes the continuing debate over big government.

2-11 Who Would Create a System Like This?

If you had set out to design a constitutional system, you probably never would have come close to creating the complicated mechanism in place in the United States. The combination of factors leading to the adoption of the Constitution was unparalleled, contributing to the development of a political system the likes of which had never been attempted.

> ## Box 2-7   Big Government: Fighting Words

It's said that the more things change, the more they stay the same. So it is with the debate over the size and role of the federal government. If you listen to some of the arguments for a smaller federal government that have been made over the past twenty-five years, you might think you were back at the Constitutional Convention. When President Reagan said in his inaugural address, "the federal government did not create the states, the states created the federal government," he was echoing the philosophy of state-centered federalism that had been advocated by those who feared strong federal control some two hundred years earlier—a philosophy that had been rebuffed by Chief Justice Marshall in *McCulloch v. Maryland,* discredited by the outcome of the Civil War, and forgotten in the activism of the New Deal and the Great Society.

When no less a spokesman than the president of the United States makes the case for a smaller, state-centered government, an argument long dead can come roaring back. By the time President Reagan made his pronouncement in 1980, the United States had already taken a few steps back from the activism that was the hallmark of the previous half-century. Subsequently, Reagan took the case much farther than most people imagined he could. Ever since the Reagan years, where you stand on the question of federal versus state power has been a defining question in political debate.

The issue has both practical and philosophical significance. As a practical matter, the more the federal government does, the more it costs—a price that must ultimately be paid in taxes. And, as a practical matter, how effectively government spends those tax dollars can have a bearing on how much people want government to do. A large, strong federal government was popular when it put people to work during the Great Depression, but less popular when it failed to cure social ills as Great Society programs promised it would.

As a philosophical matter, the big government debate raises the normative question of what government *should* do. Ronald Reagan was philosophically opposed to the federal government trying to cure social problems, and felt that government is most effective at the local level, where it is closer to the people. He saw a large federal government as the problem, not as the solution to other problems.

When George W. Bush took office in 2001, the large government/small government debate continued to define American politics. Bush cast himself in the Reagan mold, and advanced policies designed to limit what government could do. In his first months in office, during a time of federal surpluses, he successfully advocated the largest tax cut in twenty years, which he argued was a matter of returning excess federal money to the public. Two years later, during a period of mushrooming deficits, he followed up with another substantial tax cut, arguing that it was necessary to get the economy moving again. Opponents argued that the Bush tax cuts would hamstring the ability of government to provide a wide range of programs and services. Supporters did not disagree—and did not complain.

Ironically, just weeks after signing his first tax cut into law, President Bush found himself in the unexpected position of presiding over a large *increase* in government spending to enhance security in the wake of the September 11, 2001, terrorist attacks. Circumstances had changed, and with them, public attitudes on what government should do. A consensus quickly formed around the desire for the federal government to spend more money in order to ensure our security and well-being.

In one noteworthy debate, congressional supporters of a smaller federal government had to give in to public demand that airport security personnel be federal officials rather than private citizens. The thought of federal employees rather than minimum-wage workers staffing security checkpoints simply comforted a lot of people. It was the first significant setback to advocates of smaller federal government in a generation.

At the same time, President Bush continued to act aggressively to shift federal programs to the states and to advocate full or partial privatization of federal responsibilities. It remains to be seen whether the penchant for smaller government in nondefense areas will result in a more limited federal operation, or whether national security needs will move things in the other direction. Either way, debate about the appropriate role of the federal government shows no signs of letting up. Far from a dull academic exercise, the debate over federalism in American politics structures a host of questions about what government will and should do, with real implications for who gets what, when, and how.

Look at what the authors of the Constitution had to contend with. Any central government they created had to enter into a relationship with the states. For their creation to be viable, they had to produce a government that was strong enough to deal with the social unrest that the Articles of Confederation couldn't handle. If there was going to be any hope for constitutional ratification, they had to address the fears of small states that they would be dominated in the federal government by the commercial interests of the larger states. They had to face the fact that slavery ran the southern economy. They couldn't create a strong, centralized government or detractors would fear they were reproducing the type of system they had just fought to leave. And they had to do this knowing they were going to ask the states to ratify a document that diminished their power. Above all, they set about creating a system that would produce a new set of winners and losers from the power structure that was in place, and people are often reluctant to buy into new rules when they're not sure how or if they'll benefit.

TABLE 2-7

Federalism in the Twentieth and Twenty-First Centuries

Franklin Delano Roosevelt
Source: Library of Congress.

Lyndon Baines Johnson
Source: LBJ Library photo by Yoichi R. Okamoto.

1932–1964: Unprecedented Federal Authority

With the start of the Great Depression at the dawn of the 1930s, state governments were unable to handle the demands created by massive unemployment. With the election of President Franklin D. Roosevelt in 1932, the relationship between the federal and state governments changed dramatically. The programs of Roosevelt's **New Deal** produced an unprecedented expansion in the size and role of the federal government. For the first time, the federal government was involved in such things as unemployment compensation and Social Security. The federal government also took a bigger role in regulating the economy, and spent money on construction projects to get people back to work. With the New Deal, the federal government became a presence in the lives of American citizens like it never had before.

1965–1968: Federal Authority Peaks

This active federal role reached its peak in the 1960s during the administration of President Lyndon B. Johnson. The **Great Society** initiatives of the Johnson administration took the philosophy of the New Deal one step further, seeking to use the federal government to solve broad social problems, like eliminating poverty and hunger in America. State governments became agents of a federal agenda, carrying out a large number of new social programs that were funded and regulated by Washington. The Great Society created a complex web of programs and regulations, some of which fell short of their goals. As a consequence, the latter one-third of the twentieth century witnessed a gradual reaction against the strong role of the federal government characterized by the New Deal and the Great Society.

1969–1980: Things Begin to Change

In the late 1960s, President Richard M. Nixon launched an initiative he called **New Federalism,** an attempt to simplify the federal government while shifting the balance of power in running government programs toward the states. One characteristic of Nixon's New Federalism was less federal regulation of federal money so that states could have more freedom to decide how to address social problems.

Soup line during the Great Depression
Source: Hulton Archive/Getty Images.

Poverty in Appalachia
Source: Photo by D. Lange.

Richard Nixon
Source: National Archives and Records Administration.

CHAPTER 2 The Constitution and Federalism: Setting the Ground Rules for Politics

1981–1992: The Reagan Revolution

With the election of Ronald Reagan in 1980, the movement toward less federal involvement in everyday life begun in the Nixon administration took a dramatic turn with an effort to shift responsibility for social programs from Washington to the states. Though largely unsuccessful, it represented a bold departure from the New Deal and Great Society. The rhetoric and actions of the Reagan administration reflected the philosophy of those who advocated a limited role for the federal government some 200 years earlier, as Reagan sought to vastly limit the size and scope of the federal government.

1993–2000: The Shadow of Reagan

President Bill Clinton took office in the wake of the smaller government debate of the Reagan years. Despite a natural inclination for a large, active federal government along the lines of Roosevelt and Johnson, Clinton found himself swimming against the strong Reagan tide. His response to New Federalism was to make the federal government smaller by making it more efficient. Clinton's **Reinventing Government** initiative met with modest success.

2001–Present: An Unexpected Turn

The small government argument remained popular through the start of the millennium, with George W. Bush as its most visible advocate. In the wake of the September 11, 2001 terrorist attacks on the United States, though, President Bush found himself in the position of advancing a larger role for the federal government in military matters and homeland security, as public sentiment took a turn toward renewed acceptance of a stronger role for Washington in security matters. At the same time, President Bush's successful tax-cutting policies raised speculation among critics that he seeks to starve the federal government of its funding in an attempt to return federal-state relations to what they were before the growth of the federal government with the New Deal.

Ronald Reagan
Source: National Archives and Records Administration.

Bill Clinton
Source: Clinton Presidential Library.

▶ **New Deal** The name given to the programs of President Franklin D. Roosevelt, which vastly expanded the role of the federal government in an effort to deal with the debilitating effects of the Great Depression on American society.

▶ **Great Society** The name given to the programs of President Lyndon B. Johnson, which elevated the federal government to the most prominent role it would play in the twentieth century. The philosophy of the Great Society was that government should try to solve large social problems like hunger and poverty.

▶ **New Federalism** The name given to the programs of Presidents Richard M. Nixon and Ronald Reagan, which started as an effort to streamline the federal government produced by the Great Society and ended up as a movement to reverse fifty years of federal growth by returning authority to the states.

▶ **Reinventing Government** The name given to President Bill Clinton's initiative to make the federal government smaller by making it more efficient.

To this effort, the Constitution's framers brought a keen understanding of key political writers and a willingness to put political theory into practice. The fact that *The Federalist* could articulate a constitutional *philosophy* is a good benchmark of how much abstract thought guided the writing of the Constitution. The safeguards to liberty built into the Constitution were a consequence of the belief that abstractions could be brought to life. You could call it a crazy belief because, throughout history, violence and not reason had been the hallmark of great changes in governments, where new rules meant new winners and losers. As experimental as the Constitution was in its day, the United States is still using the bulky, complex mechanism designed around the ideas of Locke and Montesquieu.

If the Constitution's authors created the playing field on which to go about the business of politics and government, it remains up to us how and how much we want to get into the game, if at all. We didn't create the rules of American democracy, but these rules shape the decisions we face about everything political, from the options available for political participation, to how we express our views about our leaders, to how we can have a role in deciding what government does or does not get done.

The political world may be all around us, and it may affect our everyday world in ways we may not readily recognize, but that doesn't mean our everyday world has a lot of room for the political world. The process of becoming politically aware and knowledgeable takes time and effort; having opinions about elected officials takes a certain level of interest that not everybody has. Let's take a look at public opinion—what we know, think, and believe about politics, and how it influences the way we relate to what politicians do. We'll have that discussion in Chapter 3, which opens Part 2 of the book, called "Citizenship and Democracy."

Chapter Review

Years before the American Revolution, conditions were building in the colonies for an eventual separation from Great Britain. The British imposed a series of acts that the colonists found restrictive, including taxes on tea and other goods through the Sugar Act and the Stamp Act, and a requirement that colonists house British soldiers through the Quartering Act. These actions clashed with a long colonial tradition of limited self-rule, including the free election of representative assemblies, and contributed to a growing feeling that something needed to be done—even though separation from Great Britain was far from universally popular.

The colonists were reluctant to give up too much liberty in exchange for security, so when they won their independence they established a weak confederal system of government under the Articles of Confederation, in which the national government was a creation of the states. The Articles turned out to be ineffective, and the new United States had difficulty conducting foreign policy, regulating commerce, and even settling disputes among the states.

The Articles were far from easy to revise, however, because concerns remained about the harmful effects of a strong central government, and because changing the structure of government would create a new—sometimes uncertain—set of winners and losers. Disputes centered on the competing interests of large and small states, and of free and slave states. Eventually, these differences were ironed out through compromise. The Constitution's framers also built a series of institutional safeguards into the new government, including separation of powers, checks and balances, popular sover-

eignty, limited government, and federalism. These addressed concerns that a strong central government would overwhelm personal liberty.

Because of the political controversy caused by changing the rules of the game, the Constitution was not easily ratified. Those who supported ratification called themselves Federalists. They engaged in a long and sometimes nasty debate with Anti-Federalists in an attempt to get the requisite nine states to endorse the Constitution. Federalists Alexander Hamilton, James Madison, and John Jay authored eighty-five essays known as *The Federalist* (today, some people call it *The Federalist Papers*), which detailed how the Constitution would address the weaknesses of the Articles while protecting the public from tyranny at the expense of factions. One of the strongest arguments against ratification was that the new Constitution did not contain a Bill of Rights. A Federalist promise to add one as soon as the new government was established tipped the balance in favor of ratification.

Although federalism is an institutional safeguard designed to disperse authority, it has also been a source of great controversy. Prior to the Civil War, the relationship between the federal and state governments was a matter of great controversy. In 1819, the Supreme Court supported national supremacy in *McCulloch v. Maryland,* ruling that the interests of the federal government are supreme when they conflict with the interests of the states. Many still subscribed to the concept of state-centered federalism—the belief that the Constitution and the federal government it established are creations of the states, which maintain ultimate authority. Because the two levels of government typically addressed different matters, regular conflict could be avoided through the principle of dual federalism, which contended that the federal government and the states had their own distinct grants of authority. Dual federalism, however, was insufficient to avoid large conflicts like the one created by slavery.

The nature of federalism changed as government at both levels became more involved in everyday life in response to the growing complexity of America in the twentieth century. Joint endeavors between the federal government and the states, called cooperative federalism, characterized the relationship during the first two-thirds of the last century. In the 1960s, President Nixon introduced an initiative called New Federalism, the first step in an effort to limit the federal role in daily life that was accelerated in the Reagan administration and embraced by the Bush administration. Even though federalism was established over two centuries ago, dramatic changes since then in the relationship between the federal government and the states show how the rules of the political game are always evolving—with consequences for who gets what, when, and how.

Key Terms

Articles of Confederation (p. 25)
authority (p. 22)
Baron de Montesquieu (1689–1755) (p. 30)
Boston Massacre (p. 22)
Boston Tea Party (p. 22)
checks and balances (p. 30)
Coercive Acts (p. 22)
confederal system (p. 26)
Connecticut Compromise (p. 29)
Constitutional Convention (p. 27)
cooperative federalism (p. 42)
Declaration of Independence (p. 24)
disenfranchised (p. 21)
dual federalism (p. 41)
faction (p. 34)
federalism (p. 31)
The Federalist (p. 33)

federal system (p. 26)
First Continental Congress (p. 22)
Great Society (p. 44)
Hobbes, Thomas (1588–1679) (p. 22)
legitimacy (p. 28)
limited government (p. 31)
Locke, John (1632–1704) (p. 23)
McCulloch v. Maryland (p. 41)
nation-centered federalism (p. 41)
national supremacy (p. 41)
natural rights (p. 24)
"necessary and proper" clause (p. 42)
New Deal (p. 44)
New Federalism (p. 44)
New Jersey Plan (p. 28)
popular sovereignty (p. 31)
Quartering Act (p. 22)

Reinventing Government (p. 45)
representative democracy (p. 30)
republic (p. 30)
Second Continental Congress (p. 21)
separation of powers (p. 30)
Shays' Rebellion (p. 26)
social contract (p. 22)
Stamp Act (p. 22)
state-centered federalism (p. 41)
state of nature (p. 23)
Sugar Act (p. 22)
supremacy clause (p. 40)
Three-Fifths Compromise (p. 30)
tyranny (p. 34)
unitary system (p. 26)
Virginia Plan (p. 28)

Review Questions

Note: You can find the correct answers to these questions by taking the quiz and then submitting your answers in the Online Edition. The program will automatically score your submission. If you miss a question, the program will provide the correct answer, a rationale for the answer, and the section number in the chapter where the topic is discussed.

1. Each of the following contributed to the American Revolution except
   a. the British forcing colonists to house British soldiers.
   b. a colonial tradition of free elections.
   c. overwhelming support in the colonies for a split with England.
   d. a series of taxes levied by the British on the colonies.
2. What's the best way to contrast the writing of Thomas Hobbes and John Locke?
   a. Only Hobbes believed in a social contract.
   b. Only Locke wrote about the state of nature.
   c. Only Hobbes believed in monarchy.
   d. Only Locke believed in the divine right of kings.
3. A national government created by the states would be termed
   a. federal.
   b. confederal.
   c. continental.
   d. unitary.

4. Shays' Rebellion was
   a. brought about by a failing of the Three-fifths Compromise on slavery.
   b. bought about by a tax burden not unlike what the colonists experienced under British rule.
   c. an uprising of merchants against farmers.
   d. one of the first crises facing the new constitutional system.
5. Delegates from small states agreed to support the Constitution when the Constitutional Convention agreed to
   a. the Three-Fifths Compromise.
   b. a bicameral legislature.
   c. the Electoral College.
   d. representation based on population.
6. The constitutional safeguard that keeps one branch of government from amassing unlimited power is called
   a. checks and balances.
   b. representative democracy.
   c. popular sovereignty.
   d. limited government.
7. Which of the following does *not* apply to *The Federalist*?
   a. It addressed the dangers of tyranny.
   b. It made a strong case for the Articles of Confederation.
   c. It explained the value of separation of powers.
   d. It was originally a series of political documents.

8. Constitutional change can come about as a result of each of the following *except*
   a. formal amendments.
   b. congressional action.
   c. judicial interpretation.
   d. changes in political circumstances.
9. In *McCulloch v. Maryland,* the Supreme Court endorsed the concept of
   a. cooperative federalism.
   b. dual federalism.
   c. New Federalism.
   d. national supremacy.

10. The relationship between the national government and the states during the first two-thirds of the twentieth century is best characterized as
    a. cooperative federalism.
    b. dual federalism.
    c. New Federalism.
    d. national supremacy.

In Their Own Words

You might be interested in examining some of what the following authors have said about the topics we've been discussing:

Hobbes, Thomas. *Leviathan.* New York: Oxford University Press, 1996. This version contains the original text and notes explaining Hobbes' reasoning.

Locke, John. *Two Treatises of Government.* New York: Cambridge University Press, 1994. This is a student version of the text of one of Locke's most influential works, including background on the author and his times.

McWilliams, Wilson C., ed. *Federalists, the Antifederalists, and the American Political Tradition.* New York: Greenwood Press, 1992. Seven essays explore the thinking and motivation of the people who fought on both sides of the constitutional ratification question, and examine the relevance of their observations to today's politics.

Millican, Edward. *One United People: The Federalist Papers and the National Idea.* Lexington, KY: University Press of Kentucky, 1990. If you're interested in *The Federalist,* this book explores the arguments of Hamilton, Madison, and Jay, and the many ways they have been interpreted over the years.

Rossiter, Clinton L. *1787: The Grand Convention.* New York: W.W. Norton, 1987. A richly detailed, illuminating account of the people, politics, and events that shaped the Constitution.

The Debate on the Constitution: Federalist and Antifederalist Speeches, Articles and Letters during the Struggle over Ratification. New York: Viking Press, 1993. For those who like original source material, this two-volume set offers a wealth of original speeches from advocates on both sides of the federalist question.

Notes

1. See John W. Kingdon, *America the Unusual* (New York: Worth Publishers, 1999).
2. For an overview of the events of the Revolutionary War, courtesy of the History Channel, go to http://www.historychannel.com and type "American Revolution" at the search bar.
3. Thomas Hobbes, *Leviathan* (New York: Oxford University Press, 1996), 84. This edition contains the original text and notes explaining Hobbes' reasoning.
4. You may access the text of the Articles of Confederation at http://www.usconstitution.net/articles.html#Preamble.
5. Rhode Island refused to send delegates because small farmers with large debts who feared the actions of a convention filled with wealthy creditors controlled the state politically.
6. You can read about these false allegations and the whole story of constitutional development in the article, "A More Perfect Union: The Creation of the New Constitution," at the National Archives website at http://www.archives.gov/national_archives_experience/charters/constitution_history.html
7. The politics of full representation for the District of Columbia makes it unlikely that this situation will change any time soon, even though it may seem strange that people living in the nation's capital do not have the same rights to representation as everyone else. Because the District of Columbia is a heavily Democratic city, it would certainly send Democrats to the House and Senate—ensuring that Republicans will work to prevent this from happening.

What Is Public Opinion, and What Does It Have to Do with Me?

3-1 Introduction

Did you know that more than two in three Americans have a favorable impression of Britain's Queen Elizabeth?[1] That 16 percent of the U.S. population is actively disengaged at work?[2] That 32 percent of Americans say figure skating is their favorite Olympic sport while only 3 percent prefer luge?[3] How do we know this? *Why* do we know this? Why do we *want* to know this?

We know these and many other details about our society because we have at our disposal the means to gather information about **public opinion**—information that tells us what people think in matters relating to politics and society. We gather information about public opinion because it's of interest to lots of different groups—corporations looking for the best way to market a product, elected officials concerned with how their actions are being perceived by voters, and even political scientists who want to learn more about how government works.

We're not likely to be interested in everything there is to know about public opinion, but there's a highly attentive audience for every bit of information that's gathered. Maybe you find the high level of disengagement in the American workplace to be little more than an interesting factoid, but it could be valuable information to a corporation looking to boost its productivity. Perhaps you could live a contented life never knowing that Americans prefer figure skating to luge, but if you're an NBC television executive looking to maximize the size of the audience for the Olympics, this small kernel of public opinion is a golden nugget.

Public opinion about politics encompasses a range of things—from what people know and understand about what's going on in Washington, D.C. or in their state capitals, to what people think government should and should not do, to how people evaluate the job elected officials are doing, and more. Public opinion in a representative democracy is a two-way street: It's the basis for officials to understand public concerns and for the public to gauge official actions.

Collecting public opinion is an **empirical** enterprise, in that it's based on systematic, scientific measurement of opinions. But the substance of public opinion has an important **normative** component. Public opinion measures the values people place on such things as the characteristics people desire in politicians or the policies people say government should pursue.

Websites *You Can Use*

To get a quick sense of some of the issues that make up public opinion today, take a minute to check out a brief public opinion quiz offered by the Gallup Organization, one of the leading collectors of public opinion data. It's also a fun way to test your knowledge of public opinion. You can access the quiz at http://www.gallup.com/poll/quiz.

Before we look at the particulars of public opinion, there are a few things we could consider about its structure. At its most basic, public opinion often has a "thumbs up" or "thumbs down" quality. We tend to think that Congress is either doing a good job or a bad job. In other words, public opinion is **directional**—it can be positive or negative. We can think of this as an expression of people's preferences—good or bad, hot or cold—about a candidate for office, the performance of the president, or a policy idea that's being batted around in Congress. When we said that 68 percent of Americans have a favorable impression of Queen Elizabeth, we were making a statement about the direction of public opinion. The simplicity of positive and negative expressions allows us to get a quick sense of where the nation stands collectively on important political matters.

Public opinion is also characterized by **intensity,** by how deeply or strongly an opinion is held. If you're capable of living a happy and satisfied existence without thinking about which Olympic sport is your favorite, we'd say you have a low intensity of feeling about the issue. You may have an opinion, of course, but it wouldn't be a deeply held one. Many issues that surface in American politics are low-intensity issues.

A good example is campaign finance reform, or whether changes should be made to the way candidates for office raise money. For many years, Americans have generally supported the idea of campaign finance reform, meaning the direction of opinion on the issue was positive. At the same time, Americans ranked it as a low-level concern, meaning that they didn't feel strongly about it. Not coincidently, without intense public support for change, it took Congress years to seriously consider meaningful campaign reform legislation.

High-intensity issues tend to be ones that hit home for people. They can be bread-and-butter economic issues, like whether President Bush should have pursued tax cuts during the slow economic times of 2003; fundamental foreign policy issues, like whether the United States should have gone to war with Iraq; or social issues with personal or moral ramifications, like abortion rights and whether gay couples should be allowed to marry. Beyond issues like these, Americans typically have lots of opinions, but few strong opinions.

Finally, public opinion is fluid. People change their minds about things. Circumstances change, causing people to assess situations differently, which is why it is common for public opinion on the president's job performance to fluctuate widely over the course of an administration. This speaks to the **stability** of public opinion, or changes in the direction of public support for an official, candidate, institution, or policy. When opinions are less intensely held, they are susceptible to large swings.

Let's look at two figures that contrast stable public opinion with unstable public opinion. Figure 3-1 is an example of stable public opinion. Notice that most Americans consider religion to be an important part of life at a level that's virtually unchanged between 1980 and 2000.

Now look at Figure 3-2, which measures public opinion about whether the United States should concern itself with world problems. The percentage of people seeking involvement in world affairs generally tends to be on the low side, but look at how it jumps around. In 1960 and 1998, the United States was outward reaching as a nation; in the

▶ **public opinion** (see p. 50)
A collection of opinions people hold on matters relating to government, politics, and society.

▶ **empirical** (see p. 50)
Any statement based on the assessment of data or the analysis of information, without regard to value judgments.

▶ **normative** (see p. 50)
Any statement that invokes a judgment or evaluation. Think of the word *norm*, which implies a standard for evaluating something.

▶ **directional** An aspect of public opinion that measures whether people feel favorably or unfavorably toward a political figure, institution, or policy.

▶ **intensity** An aspect of public opinion that measures how strongly people feel toward a political figure, institution, or policy.

▶ **stability** An aspect of public opinion that measures how much change or variability there is in the way people feel toward a political figure, institution, or policy.

Figure 3-1

Percentage of Americans Saying Religion Is an Important Part of Life, 1980–2000

Source: Data from National Election Studies, at http://www.umich.edu/~nes/nesguide/toptable/tab1b_3.htm. The National Election Studies, Center for Political Studies, University of Michigan. Electronic resources from the NES World Wide Website (www.umich.edu/~nes). Ann Arbor, MI: University of Michigan, Center for Political Studies [producer and distributor], 1995–2000. These materials are based on work supported by the National Science Foundation under Grant Nos.: SBR-9707741, SBR-9317631, SES-9209410, SES-9009379, SES-8808361, SES-8341310, SES-8207580, and SOC77-08885. Any opinions, findings, and conclusions or recommendations expressed in these materials are those of the author(s) and do not necessarily reflect those of the National Science Foundation.

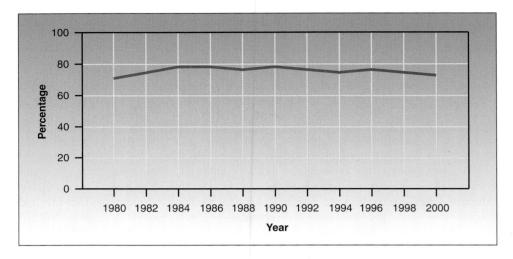

middle 1970s and late 1980s, Americans were less likely to want to get involved in foreign entanglements.

The direction, intensity, and stability of public opinion combine to create a barometer of where Americans stand on political issues as time passes. An example of how these factors interact—one with real implications for politics—may be found in patterns of public approval of the job performance of the president. Changes in opinions of President Bush (senior) provide a good example of how variable, shallow, and unstable opinions can be. Figure 3-3 shows the dramatic variations in public opinion that occurred over the course of the first Bush presidency.

3-2 How Much Do We Know about Politics?

One component of public opinion is political knowledge—what we know about how government is structured, the policies it considers or carries out, and who serves in or is running for elected office. Let's try a variation on the Gallup Poll quiz, customized to political knowledge, and see how your knowledge of a few political items compares to what Americans as a whole know.

Figure 3-2

Percentage of Americans Saying the United States Should Not Concern Itself in World Problems, 1956–2000

Source: Data from National Election Studies, at http://www.umich.edu/~nes/nesguide/graphs/g4d_1_1.htm. The National Election Studies, Center for Political Studies, University of Michigan. Electronic resources from the NES World Wide Website (www.umich.edu/~nes). Ann Arbor, MI: University of Michigan, Center for Political Studies [producer and distributor], 1995–2000. These materials are based on work supported by the National Science Foundation under Grant Nos.: SBR-9707741, SBR-9317631, SES-9209410, SES-9009379, SES-8808361, SES-8341310, SES-8207580, and SOC77-08885. Any opinions, findings, and conclusions or recommendations expressed in these materials are those of the author(s) and do not necessarily reflect those of the National Science Foundation.

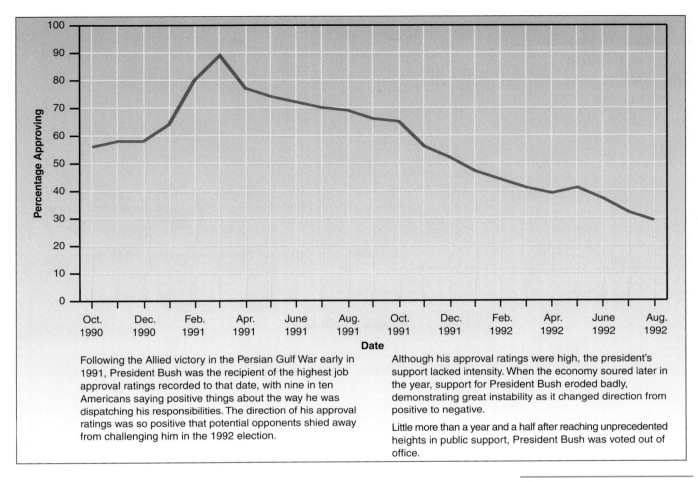

Following the Allied victory in the Persian Gulf War early in 1991, President Bush was the recipient of the highest job approval ratings recorded to that date, with nine in ten Americans saying positive things about the way he was dispatching his responsibilities. The direction of his approval ratings was so positive that potential opponents shied away from challenging him in the 1992 election.

Although his approval ratings were high, the president's support lacked intensity. When the economy soured later in the year, support for President Bush eroded badly, demonstrating great instability as it changed direction from positive to negative.

Little more than a year and a half after reaching unprecedented heights in public support, President Bush was voted out of office.

Figure 3-3
The Rise and Fall of President George Bush (Senior)
Source: The Gallup Organization.

A few years ago, researchers Michael X. Delli Carpini and Scott Keeter took a comprehensive look at levels of political knowledge in America over the past fifty years. Table 3-1 shows a few of the questions they included in their study. Try to answer them to the best of your ability.

If you missed some of these questions, don't feel bad. You're in good company. As you can see, some of these questions were answered correctly by large numbers of people, whereas others were correctly answered by only a few. As Delli Carpini and Keeter found, most people retain some political knowledge and some people have large reserves of political information, but many people are quite limited in what they know about politics. Some of us are totally lacking in knowledge of our political institutions and political policies.[4]

People who are capable of rattling off the names of the starting pitchers on their hometown baseball team may be at a loss to recall the names of their U.S. senators. People who can readily identify Regis Philbin or Elton John may go blank trying to place Condoleezza Rice.[5] For many of us it's a matter of priorities. Americans simply do not make politics a main concern.

This is not a new story. Low levels of political knowledge have characterized American public opinion for as long as anyone can remember. Delli Carpini and Keeter found that levels of political knowledge are essentially unchanged from what they were a half century ago. Their findings reinforce a study of political knowledge that was conducted fifty years ago, when three researchers named Bernard Berelson, Paul Lazarsfeld, and William McPhee set out to understand how people made up their minds when they voted in the 1948 presidential election. Their study included a look at how much voters knew about the issue positions of the candidates. The answer: like today, not very much. Only about one in three voters had an accurate perception of the candidates' positions on major issues.

T A B L E 3-1	**Political Institutions and Processes**

A Quick Political Knowledge Quiz	1. Do you happen to know how many times an individual can be elected president?
	  a. once
	  b. twice
	  c. four times
	  d. indefinitely
	
	2. What percentage vote of Congress is needed to override a veto by the president?
	  a. a bare majority
	  b. two-thirds
	  c. three-fourths
	  d. 90 percent
	
	3. A district attorney's job is to defend an accused criminal who cannot afford a lawyer.
	  a. true
	  b. false
	
	4. Every decision made by a state court can be reviewed and reversed by the U.S. Supreme Court.
	  a. true
	  b. false

Foreign and Domestic Politics

5. The Social Security tax money collected from an individual is set aside specifically for that person's retirement benefits.
   a. true
   b. false

6. Is the United States a member of NATO, the North Atlantic Treaty Organization?
   a. yes
   b. no

7. Do you think the United States has to import oil to meet our needs, or do we produce as much oil as we need?
   a. has to import oil to meet our needs
   b. produce as much oil as we need

8. According to the U.S. Census, approximately what percentage of the U.S. population is African American?
   a. 6 percent
   b. 8 percent
   c. 13 percent
   d. 16 percent

Answers
1. b (Those answering correctly in 1990: 73 percent)
2. b (Those answering correctly in 1985: 63 percent)
3. b (Those answering correctly in 1983: 47 percent)
4. b (Those answering correctly in 1983: 11 percent)
5. b (Those answering correctly in 1981: 75 percent)
6. a (Those answering correctly in 1989: 60 percent)
7. a (Those answering correctly in 1991: 51 percent)
8. c (Those answering correctly in 1990: 17 percent)

Source: Michael X. Delli Carpini and Scott Keeter, *What Americans Know about Politics and Why It Matters* (New Haven: Yale University Press, 1996).

If you think for a second about the sources of political information we have today that didn't exist in 1948—or 1968 or 1988—the stability in our lack of political knowledge is noteworthy. We've lived through an information explosion since you were born, featuring twenty-four-hour cable news services, live television coverage of Congress, newspapers with websites, weblogs—all sorts of facts and opinions conveniently available like never before. Yet, our low levels of political knowledge remain unshaken.

Box 3-1 More Information, Less Knowledge?

Berelson, Lazarsfeld, and McPhee's study of how people decide to vote found that knowledge of election issues and correct understanding of candidate positions on major issues was higher among those who paid close attention to media reports. This suggests that people who watch or read the news more often are likely to acquire more political information.

But how do we know that the information we're getting is entirely accurate?

News reports seem very authoritative when they're delivered by well-groomed anchors on television or when they appear in sharp print in the newspaper. So, when something comes along that's misleading, it can be hard to spot, even if we know not to believe everything we see or read.

Here's an example. The Bush administration engaged in an ongoing struggle with Congress over its plan to drill for oil in the Alaskan wilderness. Since being ecologically sensitive is popular and therefore good politics, the administration had an interest in downplaying the extent of environmental disruption its plan might produce. At one point during a series of exchanges between the two branches of government, Interior Secretary Gale Norton* claimed the impact of the Bush proposal would be "limited to just 2,000 out of 1.9 million acres" of the Arctic National Wildlife Refuge (ANWR).

Is this true? In a narrow, technical sense, yes. But it is also misleading, to the point where *New York Times* columnist Paul Krugman labeled this statement "a fraud." Krugman wrote,

> Development won't be limited to a small enclave: According to the U.S. Geological Survey, oil in ANWR is scattered in many separate pools, so drilling rigs would be spread all across the coastal plain. The roads linking those rigs aren't part of the two thousand acres: They're not "production and support facilities."

And "surface acreage covered" is very narrowly defined: If a pipeline snakes across the terrain on a series of posts, only the ground on which those posts rest counts; bare ground under the pipeline isn't considered "covered."[†]

In other words, when you count up all the land potentially affected by the Bush plan, it's difficult to support the conclusion that drilling in ANWR will be a limited venture. Krugman calls it a case of "deceptive advertising" by the administration. If he's correct, it certainly wouldn't be the first time a presidential administration has attempted to use words to make their initiatives politically palatable.

What do we do with this information? It's difficult to say. Even if we had the high levels of political knowledge that might help us make informed and intelligent decisions about politics, it would be impossible to place Norton's statement about the Bush plan in context because no context was provided. We would have to find our way to Krugman's opinion piece about what Norton said, and then we'd have to have a basis for believing or challenging Krugman's interpretation. All in all, that's asking a lot of us.

We can be surrounded by information and still be uninformed. If we wanted to protect the environment, we might conclude that the Bush plan does just that when in fact there is reason to believe it does the opposite. We might find ourselves supporting the plan against our real interests. Even if we took the time to learn about the administration's position on drilling for oil in ANWR, we could find ourselves with more information, but less knowledge.

*The interior secretary is the member of the president's cabinet responsible for overseeing America's natural resources.

[†]Paul Krugman, "Two Thousand Acres," *New York Times,* March 1, 2002, sec. A.

One explanation is that it's simply difficult to learn new information or to be motivated to learn new information. Another explanation is that it's possible to be exposed to *too much* information—to find the noise and chatter of twenty-four-hour news overwhelming and to tune it out. A variation on this explanation is that it can be hard to make sense of the information we get, to put it together in a meaningful way, even to decipher what's truthful and what is not. See Box 3-1.

On the face of it, having a nation of people who don't know much about politics seems at odds with the underlying assumptions of a representative democracy that the Federalists advocated during the battle over ratification of the Constitution. After all, to have an effective democratic republic, it follows that those who elect representatives should have some knowledge of what they stand for, so there can be a meaningful connection between representative and represented. It makes sense that information is an important resource for connecting our interests to the actions of our representatives, to make sure they're acting according to our wishes. As Berelson and his colleagues put it:

> The democratic citizen is supposed to be well informed about political affairs. He is supposed to know what the issues are, what their history is, what the relevant facts are, what alternatives are proposed, what the party stands for, what the likely consequences are. By such standards, the voter falls short. Even when he has the motivation, he finds it difficult to make decisions on the basis of full information when the subject is relatively simple and proximate; how can he do so when it is complex and remote?[6]

Is democracy compromised if our political knowledge is far less than what democratic theorists suggest is necessary for us to be able to make complex political decisions? Berelson and company do not believe so. No place is political knowledge more important than in the decisions Americans make in the voting booth, but people are able to make those decisions all the time without detailed knowledge of the candidates or issues. As we'll see in Chapter 4, people use all kinds of shorthand methods to figure out how to vote. While levels of political knowledge in America may fall short of what John Locke would have found desirable, the argument can be made that the political process survives just fine without highly informed citizens.

Or does it? Here's another view: Delli Carpini and Keeter say that whites, males, older people, and financially well-off individuals tend to know more about politics than blacks, women, young people, and people with low incomes. Since informed people are better able to identify what they want from the political system, people who already have economic and social advantages may be better positioned to get the political system to respond to them. From this perspective, there is an "information elite" whose control of an important resource—information—gives it political power, while the lack of political knowledge serves as a detriment to those who need it the most.

3-3 Political Attitudes: From the Heart

▶**attitudes** A component of public opinion that measures people's orientations toward politics.

If political knowledge is scarce in the population, political attitudes—another component of public opinion—are commonplace. People have attitudes about all sorts of things. **Attitudes** tap how people feel about politics or how people are oriented to political figures, institutions, issues, or events. Like any feeling, attitudes are something people experience; they cannot be right or wrong in a normative sense. Maybe you have an attitude about New Age music: You hate it, love it, or just don't get it. Or maybe you couldn't care less. That's an attitude too. There's nothing inherently wrong or right about any of these positions—they're just how you feel. Political attitudes work the same way.

We have attitudes about a wide range of things. Let's look at a few and see how our attitudes compare with others in our class, and with the nation as a whole. We'll consider our attitudes toward big government, levels of trust we place in government, political efficacy, and tolerance of diversity.

3-3a Big Government

As we said in Chapter 2, the debate over how large and strong the federal government should be continues to divide people as much now as it did two hundred years ago. Table 3-2 contains a question pertaining to the matter of government power that has appeared for many years in the National Election Studies (NES), a major survey of American public opinion. Take a minute to think about the question and decide what option best reflects your attitude.

Many people responding to the NES survey had no opinion on this matter. But among those who did, age-old concerns about a strong federal government are apparent in contemporary attitudes. More than twice as many people who had an opinion on the matter expressed concern that government was becoming excessively powerful.

Although the percentage of Americans voicing this sentiment has bounced between 30 and 50 percent over the past forty years, you have to go back to 1970 to find the last time a greater percentage of people had the attitude that government was not too strong. In recent times, concerns about the power of government reached their peak in the mid to late 1970s, in the aftermath of the abuses of power that characterized the Watergate scandal. This trend is displayed in Figure 3-4.

Even when unease about abuses of power began to abate in the 1980s, a large percentage of Americans continued to feel that government was too strong. This is a reflection of how concerns about government creeping too far into daily life are both deeply rooted in American history and a prominent part of how Americans experience government. Perhaps the opinions of your classmates reflect this attitude as well.

It is also the case that not all groups of Americans share the same degree of concern about the power of the federal government. Take a close look at how men and women

TABLE 3-2

Big Government

Some people are afraid the government in Washington is getting too powerful for the good of the country and the individual person. Others feel that the government in Washington is not getting too strong. What is your feeling? Do you think the government is getting too powerful, or do you think the government is not getting too strong?

- Government is getting too powerful.
- Government is not too strong.
- Don't know/have no opinion.

National Results

Thirty-nine percent of respondents felt that government is getting too powerful, while 17 percent answered that government is not too strong. The majority, 44 percent, did not know or had no opinion.

Source: Data from 2000 National Election Study. The National Election Studies, Center for Political Studies, University of Michigan. Electronic resources from the NES World Wide Website (www.umich.edu/~nes). Ann Arbor, MI: University of Michigan, Center for Political Studies [producer and distributor], 1995–2000. These materials are based on work supported by the National Science Foundation under Grant Nos.: SBR-9707741, SBR-9317631, SES-9209410, SES-9009379, SES-8808361, SES-8341310, SES-8207580, and SOC77-08885. Any opinions, findings, and conclusions or recommendations expressed in these materials are those of the author(s) and do not necessarily reflect those of the National Science Foundation.

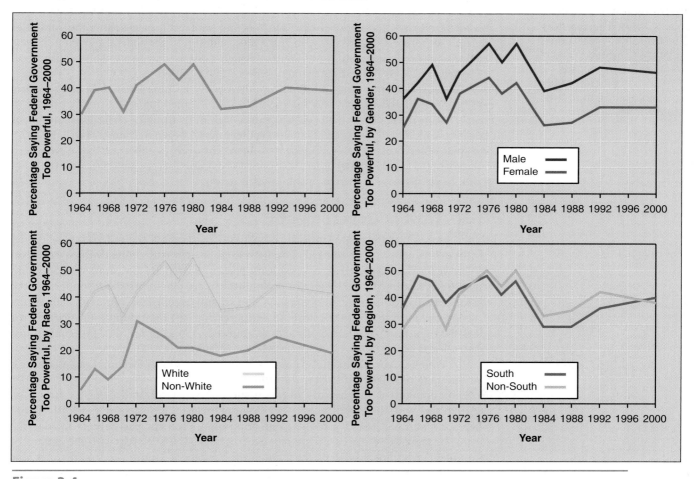

Figure 3-4

Percentage of Americans Who Feel Government Is Too Powerful, 1964–2000

Source: Data from 2000 National Election Study. The National Election Studies, Center for Political Studies, University of Michigan. Electronic resources from the NES World Wide Website (www.umich.edu/~nes). Ann Arbor, MI: University of Michigan, Center for Political Studies [producer and distributor], 1995–2000. These materials are based on work supported by the National Science Foundation under Grant Nos.: SBR-9707741, SBR-9317631, SES-9209410, SES-9009379, SES-8808361, SES-8341310, SES-8207580, and SOC77-08885. Any opinions, findings, and conclusions or recommendations expressed in these materials are those of the author(s) and do not necessarily reflect those of the National Science Foundation.

differ in their attitudes toward government by revisiting the gender statistics in Figure 3-4. The top line tracks the percentage of men who since 1964 have expressed the opinion that government is too strong; the bottom line does the same for women. Notice how for both women and men the level of concern about government moves up and down with the overall pattern, but at every point women express less concern than men about government encroachment on their personal lives.

One way of understanding this difference is to think of it in terms of the policies government produces and the way they're received by men and women. Women as a group tend to be receptive to policies that assist the poor, minorities, and the poorly educated, while men are more likely to question whether these are appropriate things for government to be doing—or whether the fact that government involvement in policies such as these is a sign that government is doing too much.

We see an even more striking version of this when we look at racial differences. Look at the racial statistics in Figure 3-4, and notice how nonwhites are far less likely to be concerned about the power of government than whites. Again, this difference may be explained by the tendency for nonwhites as a group to be more receptive than whites to the idea of a strong central government.

When we look at regional differences, a less stable pattern of public opinion emerges. Review the regional statistics shown in Figure 3-4. You'll see two lines—one tracking opinion among southerners, the other tracking opinion among people living elsewhere in the country. Traditionally, the South has been highly sensitive to federal power. As we saw in Chapter 2, southern states were the strongest early advocates of **state-centered federalism,** seceded from the Union prior to the Civil War, and were reconstructed after the war under federal authority. More recently, in the 1950s and 1960s, the federal government was responsible for desegregating the South through policies that some white southerners regarded as excessive use of government power.

Not surprisingly, during the 1960s, southerners were more likely than others to feel that the federal government was too powerful. Then something interesting happened in the 1970s. As the era of dramatic policy changes stemming from the civil rights movement began to wind down, attitudes about government power began to change as well. By 1972, regional differences virtually disappeared. In recent years, southerners have even been incrementally *less* likely than others to express the opinion that the government is too powerful. As circumstances change, attitudes often follow.

> **state-centered federalism**
> One of several perspectives on federalism, which argues that the Constitution and the federal government are creations of the states and therefore can be overruled by the states.

3-3b Trust in Government

When your political history is infused with strong doubts about centralized authority, you might expect people to be somewhat hesitant to place their trust willingly in government. When we look at how much trust Americans place in the federal government to do what's right, we in fact find an undercurrent of doubt—not enough to bring our support for the institutions of government into question, but doubt nonetheless. Although only a tiny fraction of Americans feel their government never does the right thing, a majority feels it does the right thing only some of the time. And only 4 percent feel that government just about always gets it right.

In Table 3-3, you'll find another question from the National Election Studies, this one pertaining to the matter of trust in government.

Like opinions about government power, there has been a great deal of change over the years in this attitude as well, suggesting that Americans are not entirely predisposed to skepticism and that events can affect our disposition. Over the past several decades, the degree of trust we've placed in government has tracked very closely with the actions of prominent government officials, most notably the president. Figure 3-5 demonstrates how the amount of trust we've placed in government has taken a roller-coaster ride since 1958.

Back in the late 1950s and early 1960s, trusting government was almost a unanimous sentiment. That was a lifetime ago, before the Vietnam War and Watergate drained the well of universal trust. As the United States became deeply entrenched in Vietnam, the administration of President Lyndon Johnson purposely misrepresented the extent and likely duration of the war. His successor, Richard Nixon, assumed Johnson's misleading

TABLE 3-3

Trust in Government

How much of the time do you think you can trust the government in Washington to do what is right—just about always, most of the time, only some of the time, or none of the time?

- Just about always
- Most of the time
- Only some of the time
- None of the time
- Don't know/have no opinion

National Results

Fifty-five percent of respondents felt that government could be trusted to do what was right only some of the time, while 40 percent agreed that government could be trusted to do what was right most of the time. Four percent answered that this was true just about always, while 1 percent felt it was true none of the time, and 1 percent did not know or express an opinion. (*Note:* The option "None of the time" was not asked in the original question; respondents volunteered it.)

Source: Data from 2000 National Election Study. The National Election Studies, Center for Political Studies, University of Michigan. Electronic resources from the NES World Wide Website (www.umich.edu/~nes). Ann Arbor, MI: University of Michigan, Center for Political Studies [producer and distributor], 1995–2000. These materials are based on work supported by the National Science Foundation under Grant Nos.: SBR-9707741, SBR-9317631, SES-9209410, SES-9009379, SES-8808361, SES-8341310, SES-8207580, and SOC77-08885. Any opinions, findings, and conclusions or recommendations expressed in these materials are those of the author(s) and do not necessarily reflect those of the National Science Foundation.

approach to Vietnam, then fell from office as a result of the Watergate scandal, during which he obstructed justice and concealed illegal activities. Gradually, Americans began to feel that their leaders were deceiving them as a matter of policy, and trust in government dropped accordingly—from a high of 76 percent in 1964 to only 36 percent by 1974.

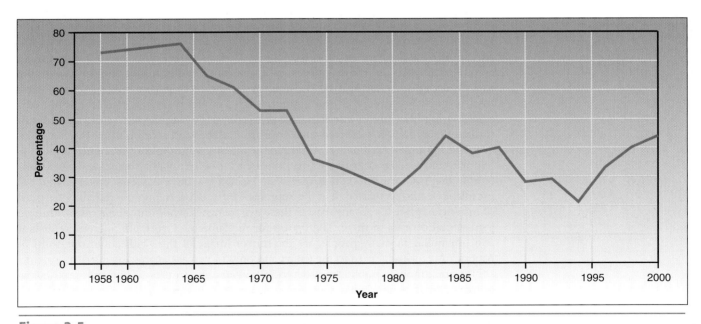

Figure 3-5
Percentage of Americans Who Always or Usually Trust Government to Do What Is Right, 1958–2000

Source: Data from 2000 National Election Study. The National Election Studies, Center for Political Studies, University of Michigan. Electronic resources from the NES World Wide Website (www.umich.edu/~nes). Ann Arbor, MI: University of Michigan, Center for Political Studies [producer and distributor], 1995–2000. These materials are based on work supported by the National Science Foundation under Grant Nos.: SBR-9707741, SBR-9317631, SES-9209410, SES-9009379, SES-8808361, SES-8341310, SES-8207580, and SOC77-08885. Any opinions, findings, and conclusions or recommendations expressed in these materials are those of the author(s) and do not necessarily reflect those of the National Science Foundation.

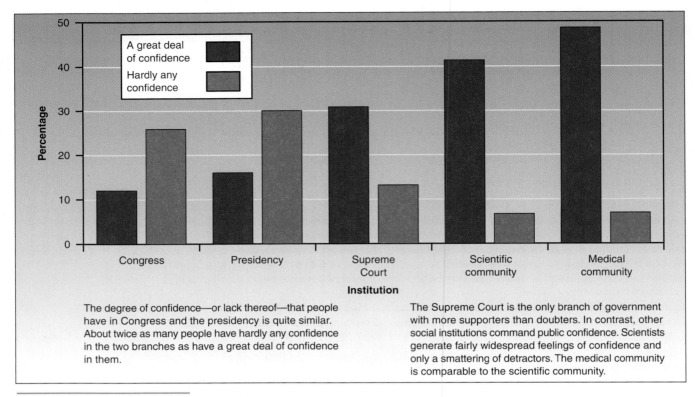

The degree of confidence—or lack thereof—that people have in Congress and the presidency is quite similar. About twice as many people have hardly any confidence in the two branches as have a great deal of confidence in them.

The Supreme Court is the only branch of government with more supporters than doubters. In contrast, other social institutions command public confidence. Scientists generate fairly widespread feelings of confidence and only a smattering of detractors. The medical community is comparable to the scientific community.

Figure 3-6
Percentage of Americans Expressing High and Low Levels of Confidence in Key Institutions, 2000

Source: Data from 2000 General Social Survey, http://www.icpsr.umich.edu/GSS/.

cynicism A pervasive attitude of mistrust about politics that may lead people to withdraw from political participation.

And trust continued to fall. President Gerald Ford pardoned Nixon for his role in Watergate, which at the time was widely regarded as a move that sheltered Nixon from accountability. President Jimmy Carter presided over what many considered a hapless administration characterized by a sour economy and frustration overseas. By the end of Carter's term in 1980, only one-quarter of Americans felt they could trust government to generally do what is right.

Feelings of trust recovered during the Reagan administration, but hardly to the optimistic levels reached in the early 1960s, then dropped again in the wake of widespread disappointment with President Bush (senior). In 1994, President Bill Clinton unsuccessfully attempted to make government more responsible for providing health care—after running as a moderate who downplayed the desire to create more government programs—and trust in government crashed to its modern-day low. Trust in government was buffeted again during the Clinton impeachment proceedings. During the fast economic times of the late 1990s, though, trust recovered once again to the modest levels of the Reagan years.

The amount of confidence we have in the major institutions of government is consistent with our feelings of trust. In what may be a case of familiarity breeding a bit of contempt, the two branches of government elected by the people—Congress and the presidency—are less trusted than the Supreme Court. Between one-quarter and one-third of Americans place hardly any trust in these two branches, while only about one in six have a great deal of trust in them. The figures for the Supreme Court, although more distant and unfamiliar to many people, are the mirror image of this, with about one-third of Americans expressing trust in the Court and only 15 percent expressing distrust.

Overall, though, public trust—even in the Supreme Court—is low and ranks below nongovernmental figures like scientists and doctors (see Figure 3-6).

Another interpretation of what's happened since the early 1960s is that Americans have become more cynical about government. **Cynicism** is a pervasive feeling of mistrust or suspicion, and can be distinguished from skepticism, which is having doubts or wanting proof before believing something. Skepticism offers the possibility of acceptance when one's doubts are satisfied, but cynicism holds no such promise. Skepticism is captured in Missouri's nickname—the "Show-Me" state: Prove it to me before you ask me to believe you. Cynicism is expressed when someone rolls their eyes, looks at the sky, and says, "whatever."

The distinction is important because cynicism and skepticism can generate entirely different reactions to politics. We can be skeptical but still be engaged in the political process. It's probably fair to say that many of the framers of the Constitution were skeptical about creating a strong central government, but their reaction was to attempt to create a system that kept government under control. If they had been cynics, it's doubtful that they would even have tried.

When we're suspicious of something, we tend to withdraw from it or at least search for evidence to validate our suspicions. If we're cynical about government, we may find ourselves pointing out things we don't like about politicians or what they do, and using this as justification for feeling cynical. Or we might just withdraw from politics entirely. Of course, if we do that, we're leaving the system to others who will engage it to advance their interests.

3-3c Efficacy

The flip side of cynicism is **efficacy,** or the sense that you can get results from the political system if you engage in political action. One way to measure the extent of cynicism is to assess the degree of efficacy people feel. The more efficacy people feel, the less cynical they're likely to be.

Efficacy can be hard to measure because it can be difficult for survey questions to distinguish someone who feels the system isn't responding to them from someone who feels totally alienated from government. For this reason, we'll approach efficacy from several directions by using three National Election Study questions (see Table 3-4) to determine how efficacious you feel.

> **efficacy** The attitude that you can be effectual and effective in your dealings with government.

TABLE 3-4
Efficacy

1. "Sometimes politics and government seem so complicated that a person like me can't really understand what's going on."
   - Agree
   - Disagree
   - Neither
   - Don't know/have no opinion

2. "Public officials don't care much about what people like me think."
   - Agree
   - Disagree
   - Neither
   - Don't know/have no opinion

3. "People like me don't have any say about what the government does."
   - Agree
   - Disagree
   - Neither
   - Don't know/have no opinion

National Results

1. Sixty percent of respondents agreed with this statement, 32 percent disagreed with it, 7 percent neither agreed nor disagreed, and 0 percent felt they didn't know or had no opinion.
2. Fifty-six percent agreed with this statement, 33 percent disagreed, 10 percent neither agreed nor disagreed, and 1 percent felt they didn't know or had no opinion.
3. Forty-one percent agreed with this statement, 50 percent disagreed, 9 percent neither agreed nor disagreed, and 0 percent felt they didn't know or had no opinion.

Source: Data from 2000 National Election Study. The National Election Studies, Center for Political Studies, University of Michigan. Electronic resources from the NES World Wide Website (www.umich.edu/~nes). Ann Arbor, MI: University of Michigan, Center for Political Studies [producer and distributor], 1995–2000. These materials are based on work supported by the National Science Foundation under Grant Nos.: SBR-9707741, SBR-9317631, SES-9209410, SES-9009379, SES-8808361, SES-8341310, SES-8207580, and SOC77-08885. Any opinions, findings, and conclusions or recommendations expressed in these materials are those of the author(s) and do not necessarily reflect those of the National Science Foundation.

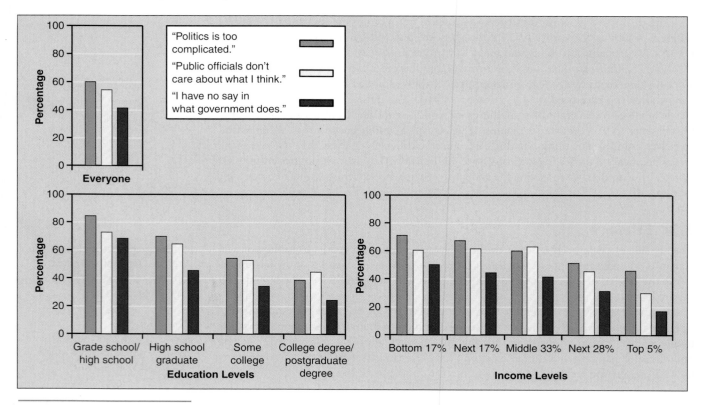

Figure 3-7
Different Perspectives on Efficacy

Source: Data from 2000 National Election Study. The National Election Studies, Center for Political Studies, University of Michigan. Electronic resources from the NES World Wide Website (www.umich.edu/~nes). Ann Arbor, MI: University of Michigan, Center for Political Studies [producer and distributor], 1995–2000. These materials are based on work supported by the National Science Foundation under Grant Nos.: SBR-9707741, SBR-9317631, SES-9209410, SES-9009379, SES-8808361, SES-8341310, SES-8207580, and SOC77-08885. Any opinions, findings, and conclusions or recommendations expressed in these materials are those of the author(s) and do not necessarily reflect those of the National Science Foundation.

As you can tell, there are limits to the degree of efficacy many people feel. Six in ten find politics to be too complicated to really understand, and only slightly fewer feel that public officials don't care much about what ordinary people think. However, these sentiments do not fully extend to attitudes about having a say over what government does, as one in two people still feel they have some determination over the political results they get from government. In other words, many are confounded by the complexity of government and have doubts about the motives of elected officials, but not as many feel powerless to control what government does.

When we take a little closer look at this situation, something interesting pops out of the data. The degree of efficacy people feel turns out to have a lot to do with their social and economic situation, as captured by their level of education and income. You can see this by looking at how people with different levels of education and income responded to the three NES questions you just answered. See Figure 3-7.

Figure 3-7 makes it pretty clear that the less education and income people have, the less efficacy they feel. There are striking attitude differences between the wealthiest or most educated people and the poorest or least educated people. For instance, 83 percent of people whose education falls short of a high school diploma find politics too complicated. That figure falls to 56 percent in your group—people with some college education—and drops even further to 39 percent among college graduates and people with postgraduate education. Accordingly, almost three of four high school dropouts feel they have no say in what government does, compared to less than one in four college graduates.

This suggests a relationship between having command of the kind of information and skills that come with formal education and the feelings we develop about our place in the political system. It makes sense that if something like government feels complicated because we don't understand it, we're probably not going to give it a big place in our lives. It also follows that people would feel disconnected from government if they don't understand it, and feel that elected officials don't care about them and that what they say doesn't matter. Even if formal education doesn't entail formal education *about* government— think of your friends who avoid taking courses in political science!—the skills that come with higher education can produce a sense of confidence that's associated with feeling efficacious about government.

> ## Box 3-2   Building Political Efficacy on the Internet

When people feel cynical about politics, it's partly a consequence of feeling disconnected from a political community. It's easy to be disbelieving of political figures who seem distant and detached, and even though the United States is connected electronically through television, overall levels of cynicism have grown over the years since television became a central feature in our lives. Television has not proven to build efficacy, and may, in fact, undermine it by creating a false connection to others that does not provide the nourishment of the real thing.[*]

Although still in its infancy compared to other media, there is some reason to believe that the Internet may work in the opposite direction, building efficacy by building community. During the 2004 election cycle, Democratic presidential candidate Howard Dean became the first political figure to test the potential of the Internet to bring people into the political process. Defying conventional wisdom that campaigns should be run on a top-down basis, the once-anonymous former Vermont governor built a viable political following by bringing people together online and listening to their suggestions for how to run his campaign.

Tapping into a nation that has become increasingly comfortable with the Internet, the Dean campaign created a space where supporters could interact virtually through weblogs (or "blogs") to discuss how to promote their candidate. His web page also directed supporters to a website called meetup.com, where people could sign up to attend campaign meetings in person on the first Wednesday of every month. Over the course of the year leading up to the election, tens of thousands of people joined these virtual and real communities, with the number involved in the Dean campaign growing steadily as word about what Dean was doing spread online.

Comments posted by users of Dean's official campaign blog suggested that people were reacting emotionally to the experience, expressing feelings of political efficacy that had eluded them for decades—or, for younger participants, for their entire lives. People reacted to being part of a community working together for a common goal, and they were getting out of their houses to get involved in the political process—many of them for the first time. Their comments suggested they were experiencing the full range of what politics can be—fun, exciting, purposeful and meaningful.

It is still too early to determine how widely the Internet can bolster political efficacy by building community, although the Dean experiment suggests the possibilities are promising.

[*]For an interesting account of this phenomenon, see Roderick P. Hart, *Seducing America: How Television Charms the Modern Voter* (Thousand Oaks, CA: Sage Publications, 1999).

The income figures tell a similar story, possibly with an important wrinkle for who gets what, when, and how. Look at the responses people give to the question about having a say about what government does. Slightly more than half the people in the bottom one-sixth of the income scale feel they have no say politically. Only 18 percent of the wealthiest Americans feel this way. It can make you wonder whether wealthy people feel more efficacy toward government because government really *is* responding to their interests with greater regularity.

Of course, if having information fuels empowerment, the Internet—which promises access to information and easy ways to link to other people—may offer a new way of building efficacy (see Box 3-2).

3-3d Tolerance

Following the terrorist acts of September 2001, public officials, religious leaders, and educators, among others, spoke poignantly about the need for tolerance of those who may look or act differently, particularly people of Middle East origin and of the Muslim faith. Were those messages going out to an already tolerant and accepting public?

There are as many ways to determine tolerance as there are different groups with which people identify. Here's one that's been discussed in the United States for a long time: Would you vote for a woman or an African American presidential candidate? The questions in Table 3-5 were asked in the 2000 General Social Survey (GSS), a large biennial study of trends, changes, and constants in how Americans feel, think, and act, conducted by social scientists based at the University of Chicago. You can register your response to these questions now.

There was a time when a large percentage of Americans would have opposed the idea of a woman or minority president. Accordingly, every president has been a white male and all but one has been Protestant.[7] In 1984, When Democratic presidential nominee Walter Mondale chose Representative Geraldine Ferraro as his vice presidential running mate, it was considered an historic and risky choice. But as you can see, in 2000, overwhelming majorities of people claim to be open to the possibility of a woman or an African American serving at the highest levels of government.

For most of our history, presidential politics was the exclusive province of white male Protestants. As more Americans have become accepting of diversity at the highest levels of government, real and would-be nominees from different backgrounds have begun to emerge. *(Top)* Geraldine Ferraro (with Walter Mondale). *(Bottom, left to right)* Elizabeth Dole, Colin Powell, and Joseph Lieberman (with Al Gore).

Source: (Top) AP/Wide World Photos. *(Bottom, left to right)* AP/Wide World Photos; U.S. Department of State; AP/Wide World Photos.

T A B L E **3-5**	
Tolerance	1. "If your party nominated a woman for president, would you vote for her if she were qualified for the job?" • Yes • No • Don't know/have no opinion 2. "If your party nominated a black (African American) for president, would you vote for him if he were qualified for the job?" • Yes • No • Don't know/have no opinion **National Results** 1. A resounding 83 percent of respondents answered yes, with 14 percent disagreeing and 3 percent expressing no opinion. 2. Similarly, a striking 82 percent of respondents answered yes, with 14 percent disagreeing and 4 percent expressing no opinion.

Source: Data from 2000 General Social Survey, http://www.icpsr.umich.edu/GSS/.

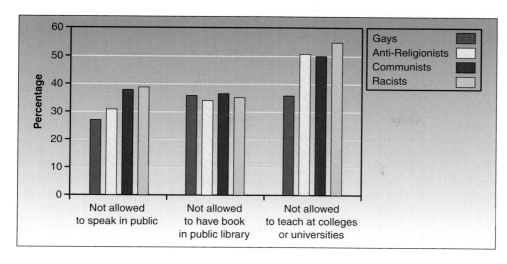

Figure 3-8
Putting Tolerance to the Test
Source: Data from 2000 General Social
Survey, http://www.icpsr.umich.edu/GSS/.

There may be something to this professed tolerance.[8] The last decade has seen the emergence of diversity among real and potential national candidates. In 2000, former transportation secretary and American Red Cross president Elizabeth Dole ran an unsuccessful but credible campaign for the Republican presidential nomination (she later won election to the Senate from North Carolina). Former secretary of state Colin Powell, an African American, has been prominently discussed as a presidential candidate since his emergence as a public figure during the first Persian Gulf War (he repeatedly asserts his disinterest). Al Gore was almost elected president in 2000, running on a ticket with Connecticut senator Joseph Lieberman, the first national candidate in American history to be Jewish.

When we look beyond diversity in national candidates, though, our capacity for tolerance is more dubious. From the Boston Tea Party to Shays' Rebellion to the Revolutionary War itself, America is a nation built on protest and dissent. Nonetheless, a solid minority of the population is reluctant to accept either. We don't know their opinions of Revolutionary-War activists, but one-third of Americans responding to questions in the 1990 GSS said they are intolerant of youthful protest. They disagreed—6 percent strongly disagreed—with the statement that it was good for young people (like yourself) "to have greater freedom to protest against things they don't like and to 'do their own thing.'" Likewise, 21 percent disagreed with the statement that "it is good to treat dissenters with leniency and an open mind, since new ideas are the lifeblood of progressive change."

When people are asked to be lenient in less abstract settings, their tolerance is strained even more. Respondents to the 2000 GSS were asked if they were comfortable allowing people whose ideas or values were not mainstream to speak publicly, to have books advocating their views on the shelves of public libraries, or to teach at a college or university.

Take a look at what they said. Figure 3-8 displays the responses people gave regarding four groups whose views could be considered outside the mainstream of American public opinion: gays, anti-religionists (people who oppose all churches and religions), Communists, and racists. The figure shows that most Americans would be willing to permit each of them to speak. But a sizable minority would not, ranging from 27 percent who would object to a gay speaker publicly advocating homosexuality to 39 percent who would have a problem with a racist speaker publicly proclaiming personal views on the inferiority of African Americans.

Roughly one-third of Americans have a problem with library books proclaiming positions outside the mainstream, regardless of the position at issue. When it comes to permitting members of these groups to teach in colleges or universities, Americans are at their most intolerant. Although we think of universities as being places where dissenting opinions are welcomed, accepting diverse and perhaps distasteful discourse in the classroom requires a high level of tolerance, considering the authority claimed by professors— tolerance to a degree not exhibited by many Americans.

Box 3-3   Saying the "Right" Thing

Some attitudes are simply easier than others to admit to, and as a result, we need to be a little careful about the face value of data on controversial attitudes like intolerance. What if you feel that gay people shouldn't be allowed to teach in universities, but you also feel that if you express this, you're going to look narrow-minded? Situations like this can give people strong motivation to cover up their antisocial attitudes and behaviors, and report positions that don't reflect what they really feel. If enough people do this, pollsters won't get an accurate reading on the extent of social intolerance. Something called a **social desirability bias** results when public opinion polls reflect what people want others to believe instead of what they really believe.

Questions about voting can produce this kind of bias. Everyone knows they're *supposed* to vote, but many people do not. It's easy to imagine some nonvoters claming they voted to avoid the social embarrassment of publicly admitting they didn't do something they felt they should have done.

Surveys of public opinion can anticipate this problem and try to mitigate it with questions worded to offset social desirability bias. For instance, questions about voting can start out with a disclaimer that many people don't vote because they lack the time or interest, suggesting that not voting is an acceptable behavior with no social consequences. In the end, of course, it's up to the individual to decide whether to admit to something that may cause them some discomfort.

▶ **social desirability bias**   A form of error in public opinion polls, whereby opinions or behaviors that could be considered undesirable are not fully reported in the data.

So, are we a tolerant people? Answering this question may be like asking if the glass is half empty or half full. From one perspective, the answer would seem to be yes. Most measures of tolerance won the support of majorities of Americans, even large majorities. Some circumstances, like objecting to racist teachings, actually could be interpreted as being intolerant of an intolerant message, even though this position disregards the constitutionally protected freedom of the speaker in the effort to discard the message.

On the other hand, the numbers of people professing intolerant positions is significant. And there's always the possibility that data like these may not fully reflect the depth of intolerant attitudes. After all, it's not always easy to admit to having a position that many people would find unpopular. See Box 3-3.

3-4 Political Beliefs: From the Head

▶ **beliefs**   A component of public opinion that measures what people think is true about politics.

If political attitudes are plentiful and come from your heart, political beliefs are just as plentiful, but they're of an entirely different nature. Whereas attitudes stem from what people feel, political **beliefs** are things people think to be true about politicians, politics, and policy. You might say they come from our head or mind.

We said that attitudes could never really be wrong because they're simply a reflection of how we're oriented toward political people, institutions, and events. Beliefs are more complex. People can believe things that are not true, such as that Social Security isn't a government program (it is) or that 15 percent of the federal budget goes to foreign aid (the real figure is much less). Months after Saddam Hussein was overthrown, a majority of Americans incorrectly believed that the Bush administration had found a link between Iraq and al-Qaeda.[9] Though false, people hold to beliefs like these as if they *are* true, muddying the political decision-making process.

Beliefs can even influence attitudes. Some people believe there was a conspiracy to assassinate President Kennedy that included members of the government. It's not hard to imagine how having a belief like this could negatively influence attitudes like efficacy and trust in government.

Similarly, people may fiercely believe that something is right or wrong when in truth their belief cannot be supported by objective facts. Some people equate legalized abortion with murder because they believe that life begins at conception. Others endorse abortion rights with as much fervor because they believe that before a fetus is viable outside the womb it is part of the mother's body, and the mother has the right to make decisions affecting her body. As a matter of scientific principle, the question of when life begins eludes clear definition. An argument can be made for both positions but neither can be proved. Of course, if you fervently hold to a belief it might be impossible to convince you that it's a belief and not a fact. It will certainly seem factual to you.

Intensely held beliefs can motivate people to political action. Recall that one dimension of public opinion is intensity, which is perhaps most clearly visible when it comes to the public expression of beliefs. Sometimes political activity stems from the actions of an intense minority of citizens whose strong beliefs lead them to make demands on government, even if most of the population feels less strongly about the matter than they do. In cases like this, which might remind you a little of Madison's argument about the dangers of minority **factions,** the political system is supposed to diffuse the intensity of the feelings these groups express by providing them with an outlet for articulating their beliefs as part of a broader dialogue on the subject that concerns them.

Again, the abortion issue is an excellent example of this. It is prominently placed in the news, and a subject of widespread discussion, in part because of the efforts of activists on both sides of the issue. Over the years, there have been a series of legislative and judicial debates about the legal parameters of abortion. Many people view abortion as an emotional issue with complex moral dimensions.

This would suggest that abortion is a matter about which most Americans hold strong and intense beliefs. But it is not. Data from the 2000 GSS indicate that the abortion issue is one of the most important issues of the day to only 14 percent of the public. Another 14 percent say it is not at all important to them. And the rest fall somewhere in between, concerned about it perhaps but not in a deeply committed way. One-third of Americans claim to be "personally concerned" about the abortion issue, and another 44 percent claim to be somewhat concerned. They are aware of the matter and likely have beliefs about it, but the issue is not pressing enough to spur them to act. Instead, the political action we see on the issue most likely originates with the 14 percent who experience abortion as the most important issue to them.

The abortion issue also provides an excellent illustration of the complexity of beliefs. Sometimes during the course of trying to be persuasive in political debate, advocates can overly simplify an argument, even though public opinion may well be quite complicated. If pollsters were to ask people the deceptively simple question "should abortion be legal?" they might get answers, but it's unlikely that these answers would reflect the complex array of beliefs people hold on the matter.

The question "should abortion be legal?" supposes that abortion should be legal under any circumstances, a position held by four in ten Americans. Figure 3-9 demonstrates how these figures can change dramatically when people are asked to consider different circumstances under which abortion could be permitted.

The unqualified condition that abortion should be legal under any circumstances is really a baseline for public opinion on the issue. Adding conditions to it alters what some people believe about legalizing abortion. Conditions that appear to be in the mother's control increase support for legalized abortion, but only incrementally. If a married woman doesn't want more children, if a woman is unmarried and becomes pregnant, or if a low-income family faces the prospect of an additional child, support for legalized abortion grows slightly. Conditions that are more clearly out of the mother's control alter public opinion more dramatically. Better than eight in ten Americans support legalized abortion in the event that the child likely will have serious birth defects, or if a woman becomes pregnant as a consequence of being raped. Nine in ten support legalized abortion if the woman's health is seriously threatened by the pregnancy.

So it is with many issues: Beliefs can be more complex than any single measure indicates. This can make definitive statements about public opinion hard to come by. If you were affiliated with the Right to Life movement and wanted to make the case to legislators that there is strong antiabortion sentiment in America, you could point out that 60 percent believe that abortion should not be freely available under all circumstances. If you represented the abortion rights movement and wanted to make the case to legislators that most Americans are supportive of the principle of abortion, you could point to the figures on birth defects, rape, and the health of the woman. Both arguments would be accurate, at least to the degree that both arguments capture an element of public opinion on the issue.

> **faction** A group of individuals who are united by a desire that, if realized, would threaten the liberty of the larger community—in James Madison's words, individuals who are "united and actuated by some common impulse of passion, or of interest, adverse to the rights of other citizens, or to the permanent and aggregate interests of the community." A faction may be defined by size, such as when a majority of citizens threatens the liberty of the minority, or by intensity, such as when a minority of citizens with intensely held preferences threatens the liberty of a disinterested majority.

Figure 3-9
Abortion Should Be Permitted If . . .

Source: Data from 2000 General Social Survey, http://www.icpsr.umich.edu/GSS/.

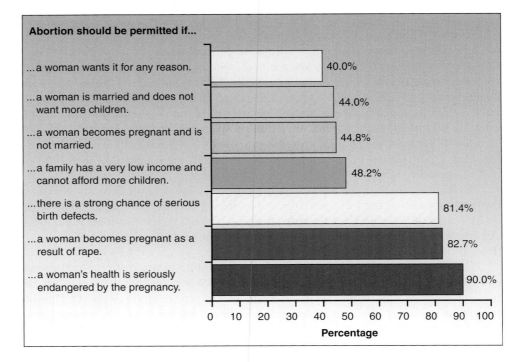

Abortion should be permitted if...

...a woman wants it for any reason. — 40.0%

...a woman is married and does not want more children. — 44.0%

...a woman becomes pregnant and is not married. — 44.8%

...a family has a very low income and cannot afford more children. — 48.2%

...there is a strong chance of serious birth defects. — 81.4%

...a woman becomes pregnant as a result of rape. — 82.7%

...a woman's health is seriously endangered by the pregnancy. — 90.0%

Percentage (0 10 20 30 40 50 60 70 80 90 100)

Several other prominent issues are listed in Figure 3-10. See if your sense of what Americans believe is in line with what Americans say they believe.

3-5 Political Ideology: Beliefs That Make Sense

Just like opinions are neither right nor wrong, nothing says people have to hold beliefs that make collective sense. It's pretty commonplace for people to be perfectly happy holding contradictory beliefs—even without realizing it.

For instance, when people are asked if they believe government is spending too much or too little on a host of domestic social programs, large majorities repeatedly say too little. Look at Figure 3-11 to see some of the things that majorities of Americans say are underfunded.

Spending more on any of these priorities means either taking money away from other things, going into debt, or raising taxes. While it's possible to imagine a spirited debate about which priorities might be cut to make money available for the initiatives listed in Figure 3-11 or about the feasibility of borrowing to live beyond our means, it's practical to assume that in order to follow through on the funding increases that so many people say they want, the government would have to raise more money.

So, does a comparable percentage of Americans want to raise taxes? Not at all. A comparable percentage—64.4 percent—wants to *lower* taxes. Less than 1 percent advocates raising taxes. How exactly do those large majorities of people expect government to find the additional money they want spent on education, health care, and crime prevention?

The answer is they're probably not thinking about it that way. They're not connecting the matter of tax increases with their sincere desire to have government spend more money. They simply hold contradictory beliefs: that government doesn't spend enough, and that taxes are too high.[10]

When people's beliefs fit together in a coherent way, they're considered to be ideological thinkers. We would say they have an **ideology,** or an intricately woven, complex set of beliefs that fit together in a logical manner. Many people assume their beliefs fit together in a logical manner—perhaps you do—but that alone does not make you an ideological thinker. A dispassionate observer would be able to identify an ideological individual through the lack of contradictions among the ideas he or she holds. For instance, someone

▶**ideology** A wide-ranging set of beliefs that logically fit together.

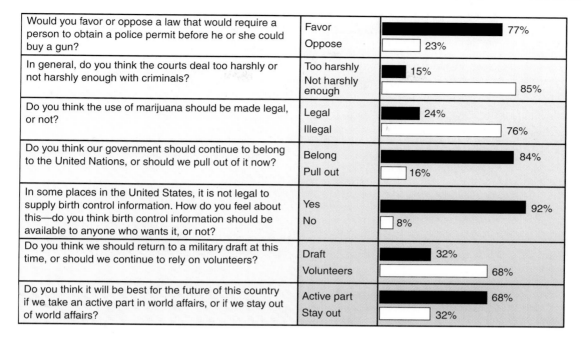

Would you favor or oppose a law that would require a person to obtain a police permit before he or she could buy a gun?	Favor	77%
	Oppose	23%
In general, do you think the courts deal too harshly or not harshly enough with criminals?	Too harshly	15%
	Not harshly enough	85%
Do you think the use of marijuana should be made legal, or not?	Legal	24%
	Illegal	76%
Do you think our government should continue to belong to the United Nations, or should we pull out of it now?	Belong	84%
	Pull out	16%
In some places in the United States, it is not legal to supply birth control information. How do you feel about this—do you think birth control information should be available to anyone who wants it, or not?	Yes	92%
	No	8%
Do you think we should return to a military draft at this time, or should we continue to rely on volunteers?	Draft	32%
	Volunteers	68%
Do you think it will be best for the future of this country if we take an active part in world affairs, or if we stay out of world affairs?	Active part	68%
	Stay out	32%

Figure 3-10
What Americans Believe
Source: Data from 2000 General Social Survey, http://www.icpsr.umich.edu/GSS/.

might be considered an ideological thinker if he or she supported a balanced budget *and* higher taxes or spending cuts to make it possible.

It's difficult to pinpoint the exact percentage of Americans who think this way, but the best evidence is that it's not very high. If you go back three generations, you'll find an influential study of how Americans reason about politics in a book called *The American Voter*. Angus Campbell and his colleagues set out to understand how Americans make sense of political parties and candidates for office, and as part of their inquiry they isolated and identified ideological thinkers.[11] They found that back in 1956, less than 3 percent of the people they studied could be classified as "ideologues," in the sense that their beliefs were "functionally related" to each other. Another 13 percent could be termed "near-ideologues" for their tendencies to use ideological labels like "conservative" and "liberal" without demonstrating that they fully grasped the meaning of the terms. That meant that the remaining 85 percent of the public did not think about things ideologically.

The government is spending too little on...

...solving the problems of the big cities.	53.4%
...Social Security.	54.9%
...protecting the environment.	60.4%
...improving education.	61.3%
...dealing with drug addiction.	63.3%
...health care.	64.7%
...assistance for childcare.	65.1%
...fighting crime.	69.9%
Income taxes are too low.	0.7%

0 10 20 30 40 50 60 70 80 90 100
Percentage

Figure 3-11
Consistent Beliefs?
Source: Data from 2000 General Social Survey, http://www.icpsr.umich.edu/GSS/.

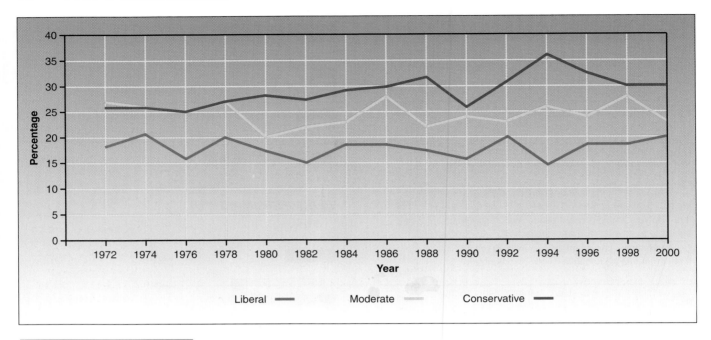

Figure 3-12
Liberal-Conservative Self-Identification, 1972–2000

Source: Data from 2000 National Election Study. The National Election Studies, Center for Political Studies, University of Michigan. Electronic resources from the NES World Wide Website (www.umich.edu/~nes). Ann Arbor, MI: University of Michigan, Center for Political Studies [producer and distributor], 1995–2000. These materials are based on work supported by the National Science Foundation under Grant Nos.: SBR-9707741, SBR-9317631, SES-9209410, SES-9009379, SES-8808361, SES-8341310, SES-8207580, and SOC77-08885. Any opinions, findings, and conclusions or recommendations expressed in these materials are those of the author(s) and do not necessarily reflect those of the National Science Foundation.

liberalism An ideology that advocates the use of government power to address economic and social problems, like unemployment and environmental protection, while limiting government involvement in moral matters like abortion rights and prayer in public schools.

One generation later, a different team of researchers working in a different era found that ideological thinking had increased dramatically since the late 1950s, perhaps as a consequence of the traumatic political and social events of the civil rights era and the Vietnam War. Writing in *The Changing American Voter,* Norman Nie, Sidney Verba and John Petrocik claimed that by 1972, one-third of the public could be classified as "ideologues" and about half were either "ideologues" or "near-ideologues."[12] That's a huge shift upward from what *The American Voter* authors found in the 1950s, and it is possible that the relative political stability of the Eisenhower era at that time had a depressing influence on the number of ideological thinkers.[13] Given a stringent definition of ideology, though, it's probably safe to say that ideological thinking is not particularly widespread in America.

Even if by the most generous standards more than half the population falls short of ideological thinking, many people use ideological labels like "conservative" and "liberal" in everyday conversation. National Election Studies data show that over the past three decades anywhere from 40–50 percent of Americans used these labels to describe themselves, with about another one-quarter claiming to be less ideological "moderates." There's been some movement between liberals and conservatives over the years, although self-professed conservatives have outnumbered liberals throughout the period. Figure 3-12 tells the story.

Do you think of yourself as being conservative or liberal? If you do, can you come up with a clear explanation for why? Many Americans will say "yes" to the first question, then struggle with the second. If most people aren't ideological thinkers, what do these labels really mean? In Table 3-6 on pages 72–73, you'll find a list of questions relating to some of the issues we've been discussing—issues people have beliefs about—along with a question about whether you consider yourself a conservative or a liberal. Answer the questions and then evaluate how reliably you take liberal or conservative positions.

Liberalism in its broadest sense endorses an active role for government in addressing social and economic problems, and a more limited role for government in refereeing matters involving personal or moral values.

Liberals advocate government activism (which in a practical sense translates into spending money on government programs) for such social issues as environmental protection, health and child care, urban decay, education and drug addiction, and for such economic issues as welfare and Social Security. In this regard, liberals seek to use the power of government to assist those in need (for instance, through welfare and drug programs) and to compensate for the inequities (like unequal access to health care) or consequences (like air and water pollution) of the economic marketplace.

At the same time, liberals typically believe government should stay out of matters that they consider to be of a moral nature. Consequently, liberals may oppose using government power to limit abortion rights, impose the death penalty, or require prayer in public schools (however, they may be quite comfortable engaging the government to protect abortion rights and defend against school prayer). Liberals may also favor gun control laws, limits on military spending, and tax laws that benefit lower-income people.

Conservatism applies different principles to arrive at mirror-image positions. In its broadest sense, **conservatism** values the power of the marketplace to address economic concerns and individual initiative to confront social problems, therefore advocating a limited role for government power in economic and social matters. Contemporary conservatism for many years has accepted the reality of America's social welfare programs (although some of today's conservatives have spoken about the need to privatize or eliminate social programs), but conservatives tend to be suspicious of government programs that are not subjected to what they regard as the beneficial self-correcting forces of the marketplace, and that therefore take money out of taxpayer's pockets that could be put toward free enterprise.

Consequently, conservatives advocate less involvement in (and less money for) government programs on environmental protection, health and childcare, urban issues, education, and drug addiction. They regard welfare as a program that can undermine individual initiative, and have been successful in recent years in restructuring government welfare benefits to orient the program toward getting people to find jobs. Conservatives, like liberals, embrace Social Security, but are more likely to be interested in making it a market-oriented program.

Where conservatives seek to keep government out of economic and social matters, a hallmark of American conservatism since the Reagan administration has been an attempt to use government power to advance positions with a clear moral dimension. This, too, is a mirror image of liberalism, and it leads conservatives to seek government intervention to restrict or eliminate legal abortion, legalize the death penalty, permit prayer in public schools and forbid gay marriage. Conservatives may also oppose gun control laws, value military spending, and favor tax laws that benefit those at the top of the income scale out of the belief that it helps them produce wealth for society.

Chances are, if you call yourself a liberal or conservative, your positions on all of these issues do not align perfectly with the prescribed ideological positions advocated by the "left" (the traditional designation for "liberals") or the "right" (the designation for "conservatives"). If that's the case, you're not alone. Just like the authors of *The American Voter* discovered, most people don't hold internally consistent beliefs. That may not stop us from using the conservative or liberal labels to describe ourselves. It just means that using the labels doesn't make us ideologues.

For instance, while liberals in general favor more spending than conservatives on social and economic concerns, majorities of conservatives support the liberal position on such issues as protecting the environment, providing health care and child care, improving education and combating drug addiction. In turn, many liberals are aligned with conservatives in opposition to welfare and in support of the death penalty. See Figure 3-13 on page 74. Box 3-4 on page 75 explores whether President Bush would have been considered liberal at an earlier point in American history.

Although most Americans are not ideological thinkers, and most ideological dialogue in the United States takes place between conservatives and liberals, there are other ideological positions as well. If you think of ideologies as being points on a line, with liberals on the left and conservatives on the right (remember, we said that liberals are commonly referred to as being "left" or "left-wing" and conservatives as "right" or "right-wing"), and you extend the line in both directions, you'll arrive at these other positions.

To the left of liberalism you'll find **socialism,** which subscribes to some of the same principles as liberalism but carries them to a different conclusion. American liberals place a premium on **equality of outcome,** but they strive to enhance outcomes at the margins while accepting the American preference for **equality of opportunity.** Socialists, on the other hand, strive for equality of outcome in place of equality of opportunity, and view the government rather than the free market as the vehicle for getting there. Socialists would

▶**conservatism** An ideology that advocates limits on government power to address economic and social problems, relying instead on economic markets and individual initiative to address problems like health care and education, while promoting government involvement in moral matters to, for instance, minimize or eliminate abortions or permit prayer in public schools.

▶**socialism** A left-leaning ideology centered on the use of government power to advance equal outcomes.

▶**equality of outcome** One of several ways of understanding equality, this way values leveling the social and economic inequities among people rather than attempting to give people comparable advantages for succeeding in life.

▶**equality of opportunity** One of several ways of understanding equality, this way values giving people comparable advantages for succeeding in life, regardless of the unequal outcomes that may result.

TABLE 3-6	**Questions**
Are You Ideological?	1. We hear a lot these days about liberals and conservatives. Where would you place yourself? Would you say you are liberal, conservative, moderate, or you don't know? a. liberal b. conservative c. moderate d. don't know/have no opinion 2. Please tell me if you think it should be possible for a pregnant woman to obtain a legal abortion if the woman wants it for any reason. a. yes b. no c. don't know/have no opinion 3. Are we spending too much, too little, or about the right amount on the environment? a. too much b. too little c. about right d. don't know/have no opinion 4. Are we spending too much, too little, or about the right amount on health care? a. too much b. too little c. about right d. don't know/have no opinion 5. Are we spending too much, too little, or about the right amount on childcare? a. too much b. too little c. about right d. don't know/have no opinion 6. Do you favor or oppose the death penalty for persons convicted of murder? a. favor b. oppose c. don't know/have no opinion 7. Are we spending too much, too little, or about the right amount on solving the problems of the big cities? a. too much b. too little c. about right d. don't know/have no opinion

fascism A militant, ultra-nationalistic ideology of the extreme right that rejects liberal ideas about personal rights.

libertarianism An ideology centered on the reduction of government power to advance personal liberty.

advance what they consider a common, collective interest, and believe the creation of wealth should serve the common good instead of going to make a small number of people rich.

To the right of conservatism you'll find **fascism,** the ultra-nationalistic ideology of the far right that favors developing a strong military and police apparatus to defend the interests of the state. A militant ideology, fascism endorses the concentration of power by any and all means, and rejects liberal notions of individual rights. Following the defeat of fascism in World War II, the term became so widely discredited that it is unusual for anyone but small, militant fringe groups to use it in the United States.

Libertarianism is typically placed far to the right as well, but it can be harder to place on a left-right continuum. It covers a range of political and economic theories, but the basic intent of libertarians is to advance individual liberty free from government interference. In this regard, libertarians take the ideas of classical liberalism beyond where conservatives would go. Mainstream contemporary conservatives have accepted the social policies and programs of twenty-first century America—even as they may work to limit them in scope and size. Libertarians would work to roll back all but the most basic func-

8. Are we spending too much, too little, or about the right amount on welfare?
   a. too much
   b. too little
   c. about right
   d. don't know/have no opinion

9. Are we spending too much, too little, or about the right amount on improving the nation's education system?
   a. too much
   b. too little
   c. about right
   d. don't know/have no opinion

10. Would you favor or oppose a law that would require a person to obtain a police permit before he or she could buy a gun?
    a. favor
    b. oppose
    c. don't know/have no opinion

11. Are we spending too much, too little, or about the right amount on Social Security?
    a. too much
    b. too little
    c. about right
    d. don't know/have no opinion

12. Are we spending too much, too little, or about the right amount on dealing with drug addiction?
    a. too much
    b. too little
    c. about right
    d. don't know/have no opinion

Evaluate Your Answers

Compare your answers with the liberal, conservative, and moderate responses listed here. In which category do your answers most often fall?

- Liberal: The "liberal" answer to each question is *b*, except for Questions 2 and 10, where the liberal answer is *a*.
- Conservative: The "conservative" answer to each question is *a*, except for Questions 2 and 10, where the conservative answer is *b*.
- Moderate: The moderate answer to each question is *c*.

tions of government, like defense and some elements of criminal justice. At the same time, many libertarians advocate social positions that are typically rejected by conservatives, like legalizing abortion, drugs, and prostitution.

3-6 Measuring Public Opinion

It puzzles a lot of people exactly how we can know what a nation of 285 million citizens believes about gun control or feels about political efficacy. You may be wondering this yourself: Where do these precise-looking figures in opinion polls come from, and how much faith should we place in their accuracy? When the Gallup Organization tried to find out about people's confidence in the work of pollsters—essentially by conducting a poll about polls—it found that despite widespread sentiment that polling produced accurate results, most people said it simply was not possible to get reliable data about a whole nation by talking to only one thousand or so people. In other words, people believe polls work even as they doubt the science that makes them work.

That's not so hard to understand, when you consider that it's not intuitive how a poll of a tiny number of people can accurately capture the beliefs and opinions of many

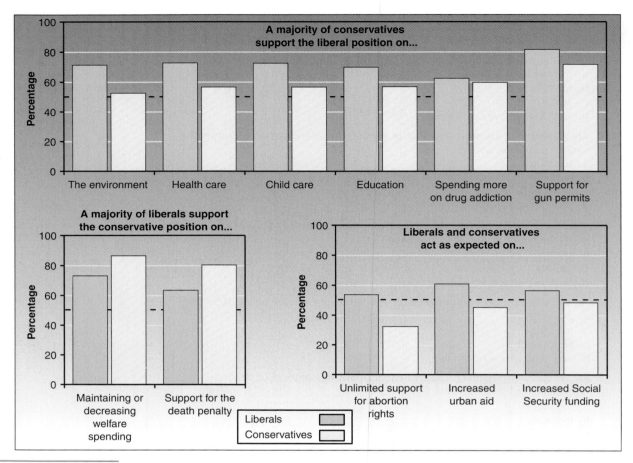

Figure 3-13
Nonideological Liberals and Conservatives

Source: Data from 2000 General Social Survey, http://www.icpsr.umich.edu/GSS/.

millions. It's not an easy thing to explain either. Maybe the best way to think about it is to imagine a bowl of hot soup. If you put a spoon in the bowl, mix it around, take a spoonful to your mouth, and spit it out because it's too hot and making your tongue blister, you don't need to finish the whole bowl to know that it's boiling hot. That little sample told you everything you had to know, and you got an accurate measure as long as you mixed up the soup so you weren't taking it from a part of the bowl that might have been cooler, like the edge or the top.

Polls work pretty much the same way. The key to conducting a good poll is making sure that the "soup" is all mixed up or, to put it another way, that everyone in America has the same chance of being selected for the poll. If you only taste from the edge of the bowl where perhaps the soup is always cooler—or if you only talk to a select group of people with the same set of characteristics—you can end up misjudging the broader group. The soup you eat has to be representative of the soup in the bowl, just like the people you talk to in your survey have to be representative of the people in the country.

Early political polls ran into this problem. A magazine called the *Literary Digest* had been conducting opinion polls on how Americans were going to vote for president, and between 1916 and 1932, it had called every presidential election correctly using a method whereby millions of people were contacted and asked to fill out sample ballots. The *Literary Digest* got the names of these people from phone books and automobile registration lists, and they operated on the (flawed) assumption that the more people you contact, the more accurate the results. To continue our analogy, they wanted to finish off about one-third of the soup before deciding they had enough information to conclude that the soup was hot.

Their approach worked for many years. Then, in 1936, with Franklin Roosevelt facing reelection, the *Literary Digest* got it badly wrong, predicting a lopsided win for challenger Alf Landon, when in fact Roosevelt won in a landslide. It seems the phone books and auto-

> ## Box 3-4   George W. Bush: A Liberal?
>
> A limited role for government. Suspicion of centralized power. Abiding faith in individual initiative. We've said these are all contemporary conservative beliefs. In fact, President Bush, a self-described conservative, regularly articulates all these ideas.
>
> But if you think back for a second to Chapter 2, you may remember that we've encountered these characteristics before, when we were talking about John Locke and the ideas that influenced the early Federalists.
>
> We said that in Locke's time, the idea of **limited government** was pretty radical stuff. In its day, Locke's writing was considered quite liberal since it advocated protecting the rights of the individual from encroachment by either government or the cruelty of the state of nature.
>
> Today, Locke is regarded as a classical liberal, as someone who was a liberal in the context of the time in which he lived, and his writing is viewed as an expression of **classical liberalism.** He regarded monarchy, the strong central government of his day, as an obstacle to the advancement of individual rights and liberties.
>
> As American government has grown in size, scope, and function, particularly in the twentieth century, liberals and conservatives have switched some of their philosophical clothes. Liberals have emerged as those who advocate using government power because they regard contemporary government social programs as a means to the traditional goals of protecting individual rights. Conservatives disagree, and have emerged as those who seek to maintain the once radical ideas of limited government advocated by classical liberals two centuries ago.
>
> In this respect, had George W. Bush lived two centuries ago and expressed the positions he does today, there is little doubt he would have been considered a liberal.
>
> ▶ **limited government** The idea that power can be denied to government and the people who serve in it, in order to restrict those in positions of authority from infringing upon individual liberty.
>
> ▶ **classical liberalism** A term given to the philosophy of John Locke and other seventeenth- and eighteenth-century advocates of the protection of individual rights and liberties by limiting government power.

mobile registration lists came back to haunt them. With Roosevelt's New Deal policies assisting people hurt by the Depression, the votes of those who couldn't afford phones and cars differed wildly from the votes of the wealthy and middle class that were not as affected by the Depression and were more likely to pay for than to benefit from Roosevelt's programs. This group was much less likely to support Roosevelt, and their opinions were given disproportionate weight. Without realizing it, the *Literary Digest* was sampling from only one part of the soup bowl.

That same year, the Gallup Organization predicted the election outcome correctly by talking to only a few thousand people. It was as big a win for scientific polling methods as it was for Roosevelt because it demonstrated the inherent accuracy of taking small, careful samples and discredited methods that reached out to large numbers of people. It also made a name for George Gallup, who put his reputation and a lot of money on the line by betting that his results would be more accurate than the *Literary Digest* results.[14]

What the *Literary Digest* did was comparable to what happens when we ask our friends their opinions (or compare opinions with our classmates like we've been doing in this chapter). We'll get a response but it will only tell us about the opinions of the people we talked to—we won't be able to apply their opinions to what a larger group might say because our friends are self-selected. They just aren't representative of a larger group. Box 3-5 discusses random sampling in polls.

> ## Websites *You Can Use*
>
> If you're interested in knowing more about how surveys are taken, the Gallup Organization has a clear and intuitive explanation of how it conducts its opinion polls. You can access Gallup Organization Frequently Asked Questions online at http://www.gallup.com/help/FAQs/poll1.asp.

76   P A R T **2** Citizenship and Democracy

Box 3-5 Speak to a Few, Speak for Many

Randomization is the key to being able to discern the opinions of many people by contacting only a few. Scientific surveys are based on **random samples** of individuals, meaning that everyone contacted for an opinion poll had the exact same chance of being contacted as everyone else. The *Literary Digest* poll didn't do this because people without cars and phones had no chance of being part of their survey. You also don't do this when you ask opinions of your friends.

Professional pollsters, though, collect random samples all the time. The most cost-effective way to create a random sample is to program a computer to generate and call a random list of telephone numbers. Commonly called random-digit dialing, this method works because you can program a computer to select telephone numbers on the condition that every number has the same chance of being selected. Unlike 1936, today virtually everyone has a telephone, so you can use phone numbers as the basis for conducting a scientifically valid poll.* Furthermore, selecting telephone numbers this way avoids the problem of missing unlisted numbers not published in phone directories.

If everyone has an equal chance of being selected for a poll, it turns out you don't have to talk to many people before you generate an accurate view of public opinion. This can be confusing because it seems counterintuitive, but it's what makes scientific polling possible. After only several hundred interviews with randomly selected individuals, pollsters can begin to speak with some degree of accuracy about how well the opinions they collected reflect national public opinion. Statistical models can tell them how likely it is that a survey of, say, one thousand people represents the opinions of the larger group they were sampled from.

The key word here is *likely*. Opinion polls never *definitely* say what the larger group feels or believes, but they do tell pollsters the *odds* that the figures in the poll represent national public opinion within a specified range, called a margin of error (which can be determined by statistical models). If the odds are good that the poll is accurate and the margin of error is narrow enough to be useful, they're in business.

Of course, people who use the poll still have to know how to interpret the results. Reputable surveys will claim an accuracy rate of at least 95 percent, meaning if you repeated the survey one hundred times (interviewing the same number of different, randomly selected people each time), in 95 percent of the surveys you should expect to find results that are within the margin of error of the survey you conducted.

For instance, let's say a recent Gallup Poll found that the president had a job approval rating of 55 percent (meaning 55 percent of those surveyed thought he was doing a good job as president), and the survey had a margin of error of 3 percent. We'd conclude that the president's national job approval rating was within three percentage points of 55 percent, or between 52 percent and 58 percent. We'd further conclude that we're 95 percent certain of this result because we'd expect to find a result in this range in 95 percent of the surveys we could conduct.

Of course, we could be wrong, and some surveys are indeed off base. On average, five in one hundred surveys are out of the real range of public opinion, and we can never know which ones these are. Still, the odds are with you each time you do a survey, and the overwhelming majority of them get it right, which is why random sampling is a far more accurate way of conducting opinion polls than grazing through phone books.

▶ **random sample** The basis for a scientifically accurate public opinion poll, in which everyone in the community being polled has an equal chance of being selected to give their opinions to pollsters. In a poll of national opinion, everyone in the country would have to have an equal chance of being selected to participate in it.

*Gallup estimates that about 5 percent of Americans still do not have a telephone, meaning the opinions of these people never have a chance of being included in polling. They would still have a fair chance of being included if pollsters collected information face-to-face, as they did twenty years ago, but telephone surveys are faster and more economical, so overlooking this group is a trade-off contemporary pollsters have decided to make.

For all the mathematical sophistication that goes into designing and conducting public opinion polls, the degree of accuracy they return depends at least as much on the human element as scientific acumen. Both science and art go into the process of writing questions, ordering questions in a survey, and asking questions in an impartial manner. It's not always easy to anticipate how seemingly simple changes in the wording of a question can dramatically alter the answers people give, or how small voice modulations can unconsciously direct someone toward a particular response.

For instance, take a look at this question from the 2000 General Social Survey: "Are you in favor of the death penalty for persons convicted of murder?" Straightforward and simple, it generated a "yes" response of 60.3 percent. Now look at this equally straightforward variation on the question from the same survey: "Do you favor or oppose the death penalty for persons convicted of murder?" It sounds like exactly the same question, but in this form, 73.8 percent said they "favor" the death penalty, a nontrivial increase of 13.5 percentage points.

Why such a noticeable difference? One possibility lies in a subtle variation in how the two questions are constructed. The first question asks people to consider the death penalty in the affirmative, simply asking them if they favor it for persons convicted of murder. The second question asks people to make a thumbs up/thumbs down choice on the same matter, inviting them to consider whether they favor the death penalty in the context of whether they may also oppose it. It's possible that when people are invited to think about support for the death penalty in the context of opposition to the death penalty, more of them voice their support than when they're not encouraged to think about the possibility of opposing it.

At this point, you could be forgiven for wondering how pollsters can figure out how to word questions *at all,* if something as seemingly simple as the addition of couple of benign words can significantly alter the response to a question. In fact, a lot of attention is paid to precision in question wording because the effects can be so strong. Pollsters with a long history of conducting surveys can rely on the results they have gathered over time to fashion questions in a way that they are confident will generate accurate results. New questions are routinely tested in several forms in order to identify and weed out leading or misleading wording.

Likewise, reputable polling firms are attentive to the sequence of questions in a survey, to the fact that asking questions about one topic could unintentionally prompt people to think about subsequent topics in the context of the earlier questions. For instance, a battery of questions about the war in Iraq placed immediately before a question about President Bush's job performance might unintentionally lead some people to think about Bush's job performance *in terms of* the Iraq War, yielding lower performance scores during times when the war was unpopular than if the job performance question had been asked first.

Similarly, people who administer surveys over the telephone are trained in techniques for asking questions in a balanced and neutral fashion. Without careful attention to how questions are asked, the beliefs or biases of those reading the questions could influence how a respondent answers, and neither questioner nor respondent might be aware of what's going on.

For all these reasons—question wording, sequencing, and delivery—opinion polls should be regarded as imperfect mechanisms that, even in the best of cases, are susceptible to some human error. Good surveys minimize the problems, but when you add human error to the statistical error present in surveys (addressed in Box 3-5), it should be easy to see why survey results need to be approached with some caution. Good surveys are a powerful tool and they can sketch a remarkably accurate picture of public opinion. Still, they're best approached as a snapshot of opinion that's accurate within a narrow range, rather than as unarguable numbers printed for eternity in indelible ink.

3-7 Measuring Public Opinion in Politics

Early in his campaign for reelection, Bill Clinton consulted with one of his political advisors about a weighty and critical issue: where he should take his vacation. It seems the president and those who helped him make political decisions felt it was important to use the vacation as a vehicle for sending the right image of the commander-in-chief to undecided voters. So, Clinton's advisors commissioned a public opinion poll. It turned out that taking the First Family to a wealthy friend's compound in the exclusive Massachusetts retreat Martha's Vineyard, as Clinton had done in the past, smacked of elitism to those swing voters who might determine the outcome of the next election. Polls showed these voters preferred camping trips.

So, the president took his family to Wyoming.

Polling has become so prevalent in politics that it's hard to find a part of the political system that polling hasn't touched. Public officials at all levels of government have come to depend on polls for a host of purposes, from figuring out what legislation to promote to crafting a public image. President Clinton relied heavily on opinion polls to decide which policies to promote, steering away from issues that were controversial with important voting groups while embracing issues, like welfare reform, that polls said voters wanted addressed. President Bush was careful to characterize his policy initiatives with language that opinion polls suggested would appeal to large groups of voters, for instance, by speaking of his 2003 tax cut initiative as a "growth" and "jobs" program.

Candidates use polls for every facet of their work, from determining what issues to talk about to figuring out what slogans to use. Interest groups—which we'll discuss in Chapter 8—use polls showing public support for their positions to win the votes of legislators. The media build stories around polls, especially during election campaigns when reporters turn to them as a source of hard data for assessing likely winners and losers.

3-7a Candidates and Opinion Polls

The 1996 election, in which Bill Clinton sought a second term against Republican Senator Robert Dole, provides an excellent example of how thoroughly polling has permeated the political world. During that election, it seemed as if no item was too small to avoid being subjected to opinion polls that would guide the two national campaigns in what they said and how they said it. For instance:

- The Clinton campaign polled four different versions of a slogan before arriving at "Building a Bridge to the Twenty-First Century," which was preferred by far more people than the self-serving alternative, "Building a Bridge to a Second Term."

- The Dole campaign, looking for a way to talk about values without scaring away moderate voters, conducted an opinion poll and found that an anti-Hollywood theme would do the trick with conservative voters who worried about the movies and music their kids were exposed to.

- When polling showed that 80 percent of Americans favored a balanced budget, Clinton's pollsters urged him to endorse the idea, to the chagrin of some of his more principled liberal advisors who simply thought it was bad policy. (Clinton eventually sided with the pollsters.)

- Both the Dole and Clinton campaigns used polls to shape their television commercials. Ideas for ads were frequently "mall tested" by pollsters, meaning that prototype ads were shown to people in shopping malls who were then polled for their reactions.

- The Clinton campaign conducted a poll to end all polls—a "neuropersonality poll" that asked questions about every facet of people's lives in order to put together a blueprint of the electorate. From this poll, Clinton's aides were able to discern precisely which messages would appeal to the voters they needed. It played a major role in shaping the strategy that carried Clinton to a second term.[15]

There are two schools of thought about the polling phenomenon. You could argue that polling at this level is consistent with the way democracies are meant to function, with candidates finding out exactly what the public wants to know so they can closely align themselves with public opinion in the best model of representative democracy. You could also contend that there's something a little spineless about candidates relying on opinion polls to decide how to act and what to say. Think about whether the heavy reliance by candidates on polls seems like the ultimate expression of representatives responding to what people say they want, or whether it suggests a craven willingness for candidates to twist themselves like claymation figures into whatever shape pollsters say people want to see.

3-7b The Political Value of Misleading Polls

You may not have much familiarity with interest groups at this point (that will change soon), but the important thing to know is that they are organizations that try to get government officials to promote their views on issues they care about. Since elected officials tend to perk up when they hear that large numbers of people (read: potential voters) hold a particular viewpoint, an interest group can be persuasive if it can demonstrate widespread public support for a position it's promoting. Public opinion polls are one way for interest groups to make their case.

Remember what we said about the artistic component of polling? Scientific polls like the ones conducted by the Gallup Organization regard the nuances of question wording and question order as potential obstacles to producing accurate and reliable results. Polls commissioned by interest groups may be less inclined toward objectivity and more oriented toward demonstrating public support for the group's position—whether or not it really exists. In other words, pollsters working for interest groups may be intentionally "creative," wording questions in such a way as to generate the response that the group desires.

For instance, a group promoting widespread tax cuts might conduct a poll with questions like, "Would you support tax relief in the form of a government effort to return hard-earned money to people through a capital-gains tax cut?" It's hard to be against "tax relief" or "returning hard-earned money" to people, so questions like these could easily produce results that exaggerate the level of support for the tax cut. Where pollsters looking to accurately capture public opinion would avoid loaded phrases like these, interest groups might deliberately include them because it serves their political purposes.

Push polls are the most unethical example of using surveys to produce an outcome rather than measure opinion. With push polling, someone who sounds like they work for a professional polling firm but who really works for a political candidate calls people to ask questions that are highly biased against the candidate's opponent. The purpose is to trash the opposition by leaving people with a negative impression of them. In the 2000 election, the campaigns of George W. Bush and one of his Republican opponents, Senator John McCain, accused each other of using push polls. Not surprisingly, both campaigns denied the charge.[16]

> **push polls** Surveys that appear legitimate but in fact are a dirty campaign trick designed to generate negative opinion about an opponent in a political contest.

The moral of the story is: When you're looking at poll numbers, remember the motivation of the people who commissioned the poll.

3-7c Media and Opinion Polls

Whereas candidates, elected officials, and interest groups use public opinion to try to gain political advantage, the media use public opinion as an easy and convenient way to tell political stories. Media outlets conduct polls about all sorts of social and political issues, and use results they find interesting to fashion stories for newspapers or television news programs.[17]

Media polls are most prevalent during presidential election years, when campaign news is saturated with poll results about how the race is shaping up. On television, tracking polls—which show a daily running average of support for major candidates—are a fixture in the weeks leading up to the election.

On election nights, the major television networks rely on exit polls for early predictions of the outcome. Exit polls are based on interviews with randomly selected voters as they leave the polling place. These voters are asked a small number of questions, including questions about how they voted in the day's most prominent contests. Since most respondents can accurately recollect how they voted just moments earlier, exit polls are often a highly reliable source of information. Consequently, networks are often able to use them to predict the outcome of races before all the votes are counted.

Survey methods have become so reliable, in fact, that in races that are not close, network television personnel sometimes know the results of an election hours or even days *before* anyone has voted. This has generated intense discussion among network television officials and political observers about the appropriate use of opinion polls to predict election outcomes. See Box 3-6.

When we don't have an election going on, media organizations rely on the information in opinion polls to write stories about whether people feel the country is going in the right direction, the degree of their support for highly visible policies or policy proposals being debated by Congress, and how much they approve of the job the president is doing.

Box 3-6 Knowing Too Much?

One of the bizarre twists of polling technology is that in some instances it's possible to know the outcome of an election before anyone votes. In 1980, Jimmy Carter's chief pollster informed the president that he was not going to be reelected several *days* before the polls opened. In 1992, George Bush (senior) experienced the same surreal fate. Not a vote had been cast, but the outcome was assured.

From what we know about polling, it's not too hard to understand how this can happen. The 1980 and 1992 elections produced lopsided defeats for the incumbents, well beyond the margin of error of good opinion surveys. As people put the finishing touches on their voting intentions several days before the election, pollsters captured the one-sided nature of their decisions and had a high degree of confidence in the findings.

Media outlets had access to the same information, but unlike the losing candidates (whose only use of the poll numbers was to brace themselves for what was about to happen to them), news executives confronted a serious dilemma about what to do with the information. As we'll see in Chapter 5, journalists see themselves as purveyors of information, and there are a lot of pressures on newspeople to report valuable information as quickly as possible. Knowing the winner of the next presidential election counts as having some of the juiciest and most coveted information a reporter can get.

Releasing that information before Election Day, though, poses a serious threat to the democratic tradition of one person–one vote because it would appear that news organizations were selecting the president on the basis of polling data. It would be reasonable for people to ask why they should go to the polls at all, especially if they intended to vote for the eventual loser. Because news organizations want to avoid the appearance of undermining democratic processes, they studiously avoid calling the outcome of elections before people get a chance to cast their vote, despite strong pressures to quickly release important information.

But what about on Election Night itself? Television networks try to hold back on making predictions about an election until all the polls have closed, but competitive pressures to make a fast call have led to some unfortunate consequences. In 1980, the major networks announced that Ronald Reagan had defeated Jimmy Carter before all the polls had closed in the West, leaving some residents of California, Oregon, Washington, Alaska, and Hawaii to wonder why they should vote at all. Considering the many other races on the ballot in those states, it's reasonable to ask if the effects of the early call could have worked their way down the ballot if some Carter voters stayed home after finding out the probable results of the presidential contest.

In 2000, the major television networks used exit polls to declare that Al Gore had won the presidential vote in the state of Florida, even though the polls were still open in a small portion of the Florida panhandle that's in the Central Time Zone. Then, in an embarrassment of unprecedented proportion, the networks one by one retracted the call as the actual votes began to indicate the exit polls might be incorrect. Late on Election Night, the networks awarded the Florida presidential vote to George W. Bush—only to retract *that* call when the final vote tally turned out to be too close to call. It was an ugly case of competitive pressures producing hasty judgments about what to report. We'll examine it in more detail in Chapter 7.

Still, since newspeople regard their job as disseminating information (and are rewarded for being first with what they know), it's difficult for them to sit still when they know something important is about to happen. In the case of exit polls, restraint is often the best policy for democracy, but it flies against all the competitive, commercial, and professional interests of journalists. It's a rare case where polling technology can create the burden of knowing too much.

3-8 What Should We Make of Public Opinion?

Like any tools, opinion polls can be of value if you know how to use them. That means remembering both what they can and cannot tell us. Experienced political advisors know a great deal about the science and art of polling and can discern the currents of public opinion quite effectively.

On the other hand, journalists, who are not schooled in the ways of opinion polls, sometimes do a sloppy job of interpreting them. We know that polls present us with a good bet that public opinion reflects the numbers in the poll, but there is always a margin of error. When journalists forget to include the margin of error (see Box 2-5) in their interpretation of polls—which happens frequently—they run the risk of misinterpreting what's going on. For instance, a poll with a margin of error of three points that shows one candidate three points ahead of the other is telling us that the contest is a dead heat. But it's not uncommon for journalists to inaccurately report that one candidate holds a three-point lead.

Even when polls are accurately interpreted, they still need to be handled with care. We know that Americans often do not hold strong or stable opinions about things. It's a mistake to accept poll data as a measure of deeply held or carefully considered attitudes and beliefs when in fact polls may be measuring opinion that's weak or fleeting. Polls are of limited value if the opinion they're measuring is soft or poorly developed, or if people are poorly informed about the matter in question. People will give all sorts of answers to pollsters' questions, but that doesn't automatically make their answers thoughtful or meaningful.

Even for public officials who are advised by the most sophisticated professionals, there is a difference between being responsive to public opinion and making responsible public decisions. Sometimes, simply doing what the public wants can produce policy with undesirable outcomes. Something like this happened in the 1980s. Polls showed that people wanted lower taxes. They also showed that people wanted the government to continue spending on a host of popular programs. As we saw earlier, it's not uncommon for people to hold contradictory opinions like these.

This isn't necessarily a problem unless officials follow public opinion to the letter. During the Reagan administration, the president wanted to cut taxes and spending on domestic policies; majorities in Congress wanted to maintain or increase spending on domestic programs, although a majority was also willing to go along with cutting taxes. So, the president got his way on tax cuts while Congress got its way on maintaining domestic spending. This split reflected public opinion fairly well, but it was problematic as the government soon began spending more money than it was taking in. Many years of large budget deficits followed, and while each side blamed the other for this outcome, a case can be made that the president and Congress were being more responsive than responsible.

An important component of effective leadership involves following public opinion. Another important component can be making unpopular decisions if, in the view of elected officials, public opinion is ill conceived. Governing through polls doesn't typically encourage this type of leadership.

Making decisions for a large, diverse population is a difficult proposition anyway, with or without opinion polls. From a largely homogeneous population at the turn of the eighteenth century, today's America is a multiethnic place where a rich variety of traditions support a range of sometimes incompatible approaches to how Americans should live and be governed.

We're going to explore this cultural terrain next. We'll look at how people become political creatures—to the extent that we know or appreciate politics at all—by examining some of the influences that shape political development. We'll also explore the possibilities available to us for participating in politics, if we are so inclined. All this lies ahead in Chapter 4.

Chapter Review

Public opinion is information that tells us what people think about matters relating to government, politics, and society. Because public opinion is gathered through careful scientific measurement, it is derived from empirical means. But public opinion also has an important normative component because it tells us what people value about government and politics.

There are several elements to the structure of public opinion. The direction of public opinion gives us a "thumbs up/thumbs down" reading on the degree of support people feel for a political individual, institution, or action. The intensity of public opinion tells us how strongly people hold to an opinion. The stability of public opinion tells us whether an opinion is fleeting or endures over time.

One component of public opinion is knowledge. Americans have never exhibited high levels of political knowledge, probably because politics is not a high priority for many Americans. Some argue this lack of knowledge does not prevent people from making intelligent political decisions. Others decry what they call an "information elite" of resource-rich individuals whose relatively high levels of political knowledge permit them to effectively identify what they want from government—and get it—while the poor have relatively less knowledge and therefore achieve less from government.

Another component of public opinion is attitudes, or how people feel about political figures, institutions, issues, or events. People hold attitudes on a wide range of things. For instance, many Americans say that the government is too strong, a view predominantly held by men, whites and, until the 1970s, southerners. Over the years, trust in government has declined from its pre-Vietnam highs. Cynicism has increased and efficacy has declined. However, efficacy remains generally higher among people with higher levels of education and income, suggesting the possibility that wealthy people feel greater efficacy because government is more likely to respond to their wishes.

Beliefs address what people think is true about politics. While attitudes can never be incorrect because they reveal how people feel, it is possible to hold incorrect beliefs. Strongly held beliefs can motivate people to political action. Beliefs may also be quite complex and hard to capture with single survey questions.

When beliefs fit together in a logical order, we call it an ideology. Most people in America are not ideological thinkers. The most frequently used labels are liberal and conservative. In its broadest sense, liberalism endorses an active role for government in addressing social and economic problems, and a more limited role for government in refereeing matters involving personal or moral values.

In its broadest sense, conservatism values the power of the marketplace to address economic concerns and individual initiative to confront social problems, therefore advocating a limited role for government power in economic and social matters.

There are other ideological positions as well. For instance, socialism subscribes to some of the same principles as liberalism but carries the desire for equal outcomes much further. Libertarianism subscribes to the conservative desire for freedom from government action, but also endorses moral positions conservatives would likely reject.

The most efficient way to measure the opinion of a large group like a nation is to take a random sample of the opinions of a small subset of that group, making sure that everyone in the nation had an equal chance of being selected for questioning. Opinion polls can provide an account of public opinion, if they are conducted and interpreted properly. Officials, candidates, interest groups, and the media utilize opinion polls to determine or demonstrate how Americans react to public events, although there is a difference between being responsive to public opinion and making responsible public decisions. Sometimes simply doing what the public wants can produce policy with undesirable outcomes.

Key Terms

attitudes (p. 56)
beliefs (p. 66)
classical liberalism (p. 75)
conservatism (p. 71)
cynicism (p. 60)
directional (p. 51)
efficacy (p. 61)
empirical (p. 50)
equality of opportunity(p. 71)

equality of outcome (p. 71)
faction (p. 67)
fascism (p. 72)
ideology (p. 68)
intensity (p. 51)
liberalism (p. 70)
libertarianism (p. 72)
limited government (p. 75)
normative (p. 50)

public opinion (p. 50)
push polls (p. 79)
random sample (p. 76)
social desirability bias (p. 66)
socialism (p. 71)
stability (p. 51)
state-centered federalism (p. 58)

Review Questions

Note: You can find the correct answers to these questions by taking the quiz and then submitting your answers in the Online Edition. The program will automatically score your submission. If you miss a question, the program will provide the correct answer, a rationale for the answer, and the section number in the chapter where the topic is discussed.

1. When we say that the president has a job approval rating of 54 percent, we are making a statement about what element of public opinion?
  a. direction
  b. intensity
  c. stability
  d. accountability

2. How do levels of political knowledge among Americans today compare with levels of political knowledge among Americans fifty years ago?
  a. They are higher today but relatively low overall.
  b. They are lower today but relatively high overall.
  c. They are lower today and relatively low overall.
  d. They are fundamentally unchanged.

3. Delli Carpini and Keeter argue that there is an "information elite" in America, whereby financially advantaged white males
  a. use shorthand measures when making political decisions.
  b. are better positioned to get what they want from the political system.
  c. lack the knowledge necessary to get the political system to respond to them.
  d. are no more capable of deciding how to vote than everyone else.

4. The component of public opinion that addresses how people feel about politics is called
  a. knowledge.
  b. attitudes.
  c. beliefs.
  d. ideology.

5. Which of the following best describes the attitude "cynicism"?
  a. seeking proof before believing something
  b. a pervasive feeling of mistrust or suspicion
  c. the sense that you can get results from the political system
  d. the feeling that the government will generally do what is right

6. Social desirability bias can occur because
   a. people often lie to pollsters.
   b. attitudes are frequently unstable.
   c. people don't like to admit to attitudes they think are not publicly acceptable.
   d. attitudes are often fleeting.
7. Beliefs
   a. can never be right or wrong.
   b. rarely motivate political action.
   c. are simple to measure.
   d. deal with what people think is true about politics.
8. Liberals
   a. generally favor a smaller role for government than Libertarians.
   b. generally favor equality of outcome more than Socialists.
   c. sometimes take conservative positions on political issues.
   d. are always ideological thinkers.

9. Public opinion polls
   a. should be regarded as literal representations of public opinion.
   b. are more science than art.
   c. can generate incorrect results because of the sequence of the questions.
   d. will be exactly right 95 percent of the time.
10. Opinion polls are commonly used for all of the following purposes *except*
   a. officials crafting a public image.
   b. media organizations attempting to influence the outcome of elections.
   c. candidates deciding what issues to talk about during a campaign.
   d. interest groups persuading public officials.

In Their Own Words

You might be interested in examining some of what the following authors have said about the topics we've been discussing:

Berelson, Bernard R., Paul F. Lazarsfeld, and William N. McPhee. *Voting: A Study of Opinion Formation in a Presidential Campaign.* Chicago: University of Chicago Press, 1954. A classic study of how people in the upstate New York city of Elmira decided how to vote in the 1948 elections, with important observations about political knowledge and the subject of our next chapter, political participation.

Campbell, Angus, Philip E. Converse, Warren E. Miller, and Donald E. Stokes. *The American Voter.* New York: John Wiley and Sons, 1960. A seminal study on how Americans vote, with

an interesting section on ideological thinking in 1950s America.

Delli Carpini, Michael X., and Scott Keeter. *What Americans Know about Politics and Why It Matters.* New Haven: Yale University Press, 1996. A recent and thorough account of political knowledge in America.

Nie, Norman H., Sidney Verba, and John R. Petrocik. *The Changing American Voter.* Cambridge, MA: Harvard University Press, 1979. One generation after *The American Voter*, this book challenges some of the assumptions about how people understood politics during the relatively sleepy 1950s.

Notes

1. The exact figure is 68 percent, from a December 1998 Gallup Poll cited in Darren K. Carlson, "Queen Elizabeth: 50 Years of Public Opinion," Gallup Poll News Service, February 6, 2002.
2. Add to this an additional 55 percent of the population that's simply not engaged, and you have a picture of a turned-off workforce. Kenneth A. Tucker, "A Passion for Work," *Gallup Management Journal,* February 18, 2002.
3. Not too many Americans enjoy ski jumping either. The figures are from a February 2002 Gallup Poll cited in Jeffrey M. Jones, "Figure Skating Tops List of Americans' Favorite Winter Olympic Events," Gallup Poll News Service, February 8, 2002.
4. Michael X. Delli Carpini and Scott Keeter, *What Americans Know about Politics and Why It Matters* (New Haven: Yale University Press, 1996).
5. She is secretary of state and was the assistant to President Bush for National Security Affairs in his first term.
6. Bernard R Berelson, Paul F. Lazarsfeld, and William N. McPhee, *Voting: A Study of Opinion Formation in a Presidential Campaign* (Chicago: University of Chicago Press, 1954), 308.
7. John F. Kennedy was the only Catholic president.
8. Up to a point, at least. The GSS also finds that one-third of Americans feel that most men are better suited emotionally for politics than most women.

9. Steven Kull, *Americans on Iraq: WMD, Links to al-Qaeda, Reconstruction.* The PIPA/Knowledge Networks Poll, July 1, 2003, 4. You can access the poll results at http://www.pipa.org/OnlineReports/Iraq/july1_iraqreport.pdf.
10. This is not a new story, either. In 1935, after two years of Franklin D. Roosevelt's New Deal policies, the Gallup Organization reported that six in ten Americans thought the federal government was spending too much money on programs designed to bring relief from the Great Depression. At the same time, nine in ten supported the Social Security program.
11. Angus Campbell, Philip E. Converse, Warren E. Miller, and Donald E. Stokes, *The American Voter* (New York: John Wiley and Sons, 1960), 216–255.
12. Norman H. Nie, Sidney Verba, and John R. Petrocik, *The Changing American Voter* (Cambridge, MA: Harvard University Press, 1979).
13. It is also possible that the authors of *The Changing American Voter* were more lenient in the standards they used to classify ideologues, inadvertently inflating the number of ideological thinkers in their study.
14. The story of early scientific polling is an interesting one that you can read about in transcripts from the PBS program, "The First Measured Century," which you can access online at http://www.pbs.org/fmc/segments/progseg7.htm.

15. Richard Stengel and Eric Pooley, "Masters of the Message: Inside the High-Tech Machine That Set Clinton and Dole Polls Apart," *Time*, November 6, 1996. You may access the full article at http://cgi.cnn.com/ALLPOLITICS/1996/elections/time.special/pollster/. It's colorful and fast moving, filled with accounts of power, personal jealousies, infighting, backstabbing, an ill-timed rendezvous with a prostitute—and enough opinion polls to make your head spin.

16. See "Push Polling," BBC News, February 22, 2000, at http://news.bbc.co.uk/2/hi/in_depth/americas/2000/us_elections/glossary/n-p/652168.stm.

17. One way to get a sense of the wide range of topics in media polls is to check out the ABC News "poll vault," which you may access online at http://abcnews.go.com/sections/politics/PollVault/PollVault.html.

Who Are We, and What Do We Do?

4-1 Introduction

Are you an American?

Easy question, right? If you were born in or live legally in this country, your answer is probably "sure" (otherwise, it's probably "no"). Still, if you are an American, when you think about your identity, is "American" qualified with something else?

Irish American?
African American?
Italian American?
Chinese American?
Cuban American?
German American?
Native American?
Vietnamese American?
Mexican American?

Those qualifiers tell us about where we came from. Many people think of themselves as Americans while simultaneously seeing themselves in terms of their heritage. This says a lot about the richness of the American identity, and helps explain why American politics can be so complex.

On one hand, Americans are many different people with deep roots in a variety of diverse, sometimes conflicting traditions. On the other, Americans share a common set of values, attitudes and beliefs, which together form an American **political culture.** Those values tend to be about "buying in" to the idea of America and how it operates, which is essential in order for the United States to function as a nation.

We saw in Chapter 3 just how much disagreement there is in America on specific issues of policy. At the same time, there's a lot of agreement on how to set up the political rules of the game. A basic accord supplies the framework for American political culture. It encompasses things like:

- Acceptance of representative democracy and capitalism as superior political and economic arrangements
- Acceptance of the rule of law for resolving disputes and determining political winners and losers
- Belief in compromise with others as a way of achieving objectives

Box 4-1   Political Culture in Comparative Perspective

The American political culture is so universally accepted that when we talk about it, you may just think we're stating the obvious. That's not uncommon for something that's part of a core identity—it seems obvious because it's so deeply ingrained. This tends to make it difficult to imagine that the political cultures of other nations may look quite different because of the human tendency to believe that others fundamentally think like we do and want what we want. Because of this, American political culture may be best understood in a comparative perspective, in which we're open to the possibility that people in other nations have a different relationship to their government and to what constitutes acceptable political action.

Have you ever heard someone say that something is "un-American," like "it's un-American not to reward someone for hard work"? Now try to imagine someone saying something is "un-Canadian" or "un-Vietnamese." Most likely, you'll never hear anything like that because thinking about one's nation in terms apart from others is not a part of all political cultures. That's not to say that people of other nations do not notice cultural differences, but they don't necessarily define and describe themselves in terms of those differences. In the

United States, though, it's probably not necessary to explain what it means for something to be un-American because, as vague as that phrase is, for many Americans, it encompasses a set of ideas associated with what it means to be an American. In that respect, it is both a part of the political culture and a way of reflecting that culture to others.

In the early 1960s, researchers Gabriel Almond and Sidney Verba wrote a pioneering study comparing political cultures of different nations. In *The Civic Culture,* they attempt to explain differences in the levels of political attachment by people in different nations, and identify the characteristics that motivate people to political action.[*] You can find the full reference for *The Civic Culture* in the "In Their Own Words" section at the end of the chapter, where you'll also find a reference for a book called *The New Political Culture,* which offers an updated discussion of political culture in different nations.[†]

---

[*]Gabriel A. Almond and Sidney Verba, *The Civic Culture: Political Attributes and Democracy in Five Nations* (Newbury Park, CA: Sage Publications, 1989).

[†]Terry Nichols Clark and Vincent Hoffmann-Martinot (eds.), *The New Political Culture* (Boulder: Westview Press, 1998).

- Agreement on the rules for electing representatives
- Approval of the fundamental choice of liberty and opportunity over equal outcomes (which we talked about in Chapter 1)

These bedrock qualities of the American political culture help to maintain the legitimacy of the system. If they seem obvious to you, to the point where you find yourself thinking, "Who wouldn't agree with these things?", then you are deeply enmeshed in American political culture. In practice, there is no reason to believe people will automatically accept these positions, and individuals in many other cultures do not. That most Americans would accept these points without thinking about it addresses how political culture works: It is composed of principles that are so fundamental as to be almost invisible.

Accepting this broad framework doesn't imply that everyone agrees with the specific choices made in America on matters of policy—far from it, as we saw in Chapter 3. But it does mean that there's a sense of acceptance and even pride in the American system that is a basic part of the identity of many Americans, regardless of their origin. You might even say that without that acceptance, Americans wouldn't have the means for working through the many political differences that arise. It's the same way in other countries, too, even if the particulars of other political cultures are different (see Box 4-1).

In this chapter, we're going to explore American political culture in order to get a sense of who Americans are and how American political culture affects politics. Then, we'll move from the collective portrait of a diverse nation to political socialization, the processes that shape our individual awareness of and relationship to politics. Finally, we'll put these general observations together with the individual ones when we look at how political culture and political socialization relate to participation in the political arena in ways large and small.

> ▶ **political culture** (see p. 86)
> The common set of attitudes, beliefs, and values that provide the foundation of support for a political system.

4-2 Political Culture: Who Are We?

A few years ago, the Institute for Advanced Studies in Culture at the University of Virginia attempted to identify some of the constants in American political culture. They discovered nearly unanimous buy-in among Americans for what they call the "American creed"— ideals about the public life of America. Take a second to see how much you subscribe to the "American creed" by answering the five brief questions in Figure 4-1.

Pretty clearly, Americans overwhelmingly are proud of their country, believe in its goodness and the goodness of its citizens, and even feel that America has a mission to serve as an example for the rest of the world. These elements of political culture may seem abstract, and in one important sense, they are: The nearly universal acceptance of others in *theory* does not translate into universal tolerance for the *practice* of people expressing unpopular ideas, as we saw in Section 3-3d, "Tolerance," in Chapter 3. Political culture is manifested through abstract perceptions about self and nation, rather than through specific attitudes, beliefs, and actions that may be at odds with how many Americans view themselves. This infuses political culture with a generous portion of mythology (see Box 4-2).

4-2a Group Membership and Tolerance

The tendency for Americans to join organizations is one characteristic of American political culture that separates it from the political cultures of other nations. Observers of American culture have noted this characteristic for centuries. In 1831, the French nobleman Alexis de Tocqueville spent the better part of a year touring the United States, an experience that culminated in publishing his observations in the two-volume work, *Democracy in America,* in 1835 and 1840. In it, he made the observation that America is a nation of joiners, and that through participating in groups with fellow citizens, Americans learned the fundamentals of compromise necessary to a functioning democracy.[1] Tocqueville noted how, "Americans of all ages, all stations in life, and all types of disposition are forever forming associations. There are not only commercial and industrial associations in which all take part, but others of a thousand different types—religious, moral, serious, futile, very general and very limited, immensely large and very minute."[2] Today, we would call these voluntary groups: civic and religious organizations, political clubs, sports leagues, neighborhood associations, charitable and service organizations, and educational and cultural groups. They need not be expressly political in order to teach how to tolerate and work with others; in fact, most of these groups are not political, and may be devoted to pursuits as recreational and ordinary as intramural sports or playing trumpet in the band or working on the school newspaper.

Recent research confirms what Tocqueville saw over 170 years ago: Americans tend to join groups more frequently and more widely than people in other nations.[3] The more

Figure 4-1
Shared American Ideals?

Source: 1996 Survey of American Political Culture, University of Virginia Institute for Advanced Studies in Culture (IASC).

Questions	National Percentage That Agree
1. America from its beginning has had a destiny to set an example for other nations.	87%
2. America's contribution is one of expanding freedom for more and more people.	94%
3. America is the world's great melting pot, in which people from different countries are united into one nation.	95%
4. With hard work and perseverance, anyone can succeed in America.	96%
5. Democracy is only as strong as the virtue of its citizens.	95%

Box 4-2 Political Culture during Times of Stress

We saw the connection many Americans have to their political culture at work in the public reaction to the terror attacks of September 2001. American flags and American flag stickers blossomed overnight on homes, office buildings, and cars. The near-universal sentiment that *we* had been attacked was an expression of an attitude about identifying as an American. At that moment, being conservative or liberal didn't matter, nor did the national origin of one's ancestors. (One unfortunate and important exception to this involved Americans of the Muslim faith and of Middle Eastern origin, who experienced increased discrimination that reflected the worst elements of the hybrid American culture.)

We saw the contours of our political culture during the cold war as well, even during times of great unrest as a result of strong differences of opinion about such things as the civil rights movement and the Vietnam War. For a while in the 1960s, the American flag became a symbol adopted by those who supported American policy in Vietnam. Some on the other side of this issue burned the American flag as a way of expressing their views, a manifestation of our cultural acceptance of dissent. We know from Chapter 3 that dissent is something people don't embrace quite as strongly as the "American creed." In this regard, everyone may not always accept all cultural values.

Still, even at a moment of great divisions over policy, Americans expressed attitudes and beliefs rooted deep in the political culture. Although at times vocal minorities have advocated the overthrow of the American system, an overwhelming number of Americans—including many who opposed the Vietnam War—continued to feel a patriotic attachment to the American system and rejected the Communist system of the Soviet Union as an inferior alternative.

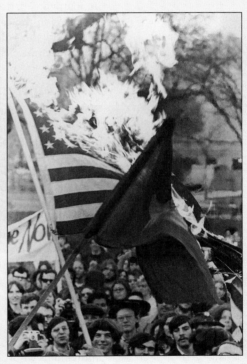

Images of American political culture: The flag is a powerful symbol of national unity in the aftermath of the September 2001 terrorist attack on America *(left)*, as well as a symbol of free expression during the Vietnam War *(right)*.

Source: (Left) AP/Wide World Photos. *(Right)* Getty Images.

groups we join, the more experience we get in the give-and-take with other people that teaches us how to be tolerant. Therefore, people who join more groups tend to be more tolerant of the rights of others. It is the isolated individual who is likely to be the least tolerant of all.[4]

However, there are indications that over the course of your lifetime, civic engagement has diminished. Historically, there have been peaks and valleys in the degree to which Americans engage in group activities, and evidence suggests that for the past several decades we have been living through one of the valleys. Political scientist Robert D. Putnam writes that over that period, Americans have become increasingly isolated from one another by joining fewer organizations and spending less time with neighbors and friends. As a consequence, Putnam argues that Americans have become detached from the relationships that reinforce basic democratic and civic values. The title of his book, *Bowling Alone*, refers to the disappearance of bowling leagues that once provided a social connection for many people, while providing a visual metaphor for the isolation that characterizes the leisure and work lives of so many people who spend their days living in places where they don't know their neighbors, working alone in cubicles, commuting alone in cars, and recreating alone in front of the television.[5]

Putnam sees in these trends the loss of social capital—the connections we make with each other when we spend our time in association with others. The value of social capital is in its ability to nurture trusting relationships, through which we learn how to compromise and reciprocate with others. These values are associated with having a rich civic life and stand in sharp contrast to the isolation from one another that, according to Putnam, characterizes our time and makes us feel detached and alienated from each other, our communities, and our government.[6]

To reverse these trends, Putnam advocates the daunting task of creating social capital through renewed civic engagement in all facets of life: promoting family-friendly workplaces; designing communities with common areas that promote socializing with neighbors; encouraging clergy to spark a spiritual awakening that will promote religious tolerance; developing Internet activities that engage people in communities; and participating in social and political activities.[7] For many, this would require changing some of the fundamental patterns of our lives—from turning off the TV to joining groups to spending less time in the car. The benefit to individuals could be greater personal fulfillment. The benefit to the political culture would be a deeper investment in the bonds that help a republic endure. See Box 4-3.

4-2b Immigration

Because one component of political culture is the belief that America is an open place accepting of others in need—the idea symbolized by the welcoming torch of the Statue of Liberty—America has been able to incorporate numerous subcultures that immigrant groups have brought with them to this country. This simultaneously makes American government more interesting—and more complicated. It brings texture to the American tapestry while assembling a much wider set of values than those subscribed to by the Anglican males who wrote the Constitution, making governing the country a challenge.

Changes in political culture—and politics—may be anticipated through the changing face of diversity in America. Cultural changes have also been driven in recent years by shifting migration patterns and the growing number of senior citizens in America. Let's look a little closer at these factors. We'll examine America's long history of immigration and the nature of American cultural diversity, recent patterns of geographic mobility, and the aging of America.

It's probably not overstating things to say that America is a place where just about everybody comes from someplace else. Even the Native American civilizations that European settlers encountered when they came to North America were likely populated by individuals whose origins may be traced to Asia, and to a long walk over what thousands of years ago was a land bridge across the Bering Straits between Alaska and Russia.

Between 1820 and 2000, a total of 66 million immigrants came to the United States, changing the tenor of American life. Of these, better than half (58 percent or 38,460,000) came from Europe. (See Figure 4-2.)

European immigration tells only part of the story, though. More recently, America has become home to large numbers of new immigrants from different parts of the globe. Specifically:

- Almost three-quarters (72 percent) of the total immigration to the United States from Mexico and the Caribbean has happened since 1970.

- Almost two-thirds (62 percent) of the total immigration to the United States from Asia has happened since 1980.

Box 4-3 Virtual Civic Engagement

There is intriguing evidence that one impetus for renewed civic engagement may be found on the Internet, as people turn to websites that actually encourage them to turn off the computer and meet in person.

The premier example of this is meetup.com, a free Internet service designed to allow people to find others online who share their interests and arrange in-person get-togethers. People looking to reach out to others can go to meetup.com and search the database of topics until they find what they're looking for. Topics cover the range of civic and personal interests that Putnam identified as central to community life: books, films, games, health, music, pets, hobbies, work and politics—everything from Audi owners to ferret lovers. You can scan today's list of groups by going to http://www.meetup.com/browse/.

Site users can join an existing group or suggest a topic for the purpose of attracting others with the same interest. When a topic attracts enough people in the same geographic area, members vote on a time and a place for a meeting and get together in person, typically in an informal location like a bar, café—or bowling alley. Meetup.com brings together people with the same interests who otherwise might not find each other, but the interaction takes place off line, in the community.

Meetup.com was created with social activities in mind, but it unexpectedly developed an important political function in 2003, as supporters of Democratic presidential hopeful Governor Howard Dean began using the website to organize on behalf of their candidate. The official campaign rapidly recognized the value of meetup.com for national grass roots organizing, and in early 2003, placed a direct link to meetup.com on the candidate's website. Shortly thereafter, Dean's meetup numbers started to soar, growing from several hundred in January to over 65,000 in July, to better than 180,000 before Dean ended his presidential bid the following February. John Kerry's presidential campaign, taking a cue from Dean's success, began promoting meetup.com in the summer of 2003, building its own network of grassroots volunteers.

The first Wednesday of every month became the designated day for Dean meetups, at which thousands of volunteers at hundreds of locations across America would gather in small groups to plan strategy for the Dean campaign. The Dean website trumpeted this activity as the first true grassroots presidential campaign of the Internet era, and attributed the sharp rise in Dean's profile during 2003 to the high degree of interest the candidate generated through meetup.com. As a civic matter, meetup.com became the vehicle by which people who were previously detached from or passive about politics could get involved in a presidential campaign—many for the first time in their lives. It offered a tantalizing glimpse of how the Internet could bring people together in the real world to work for a political cause—a far cry from the couch-potato politics of passive observation and detachment offered by television.

- Slightly more than three-quarters (77 percent) of the total immigration to the United States from Africa has happened since 1980.

- Slightly more than one-third (34 percent) of the total immigration to the United States from Central and South America has happened since 1990.

Figure 4-3 will give you a sense of how immigration to America has come in waves from different parts of the world over the course of two centuries.

After each great wave of immigration, Americans' tolerance has been tested, starting with the first influx of Irish immigrants in the 1840s. Nativist Protestants opposed to the foreign, "contaminating" influences of Roman Catholics formed secret societies with names like "The Order of the Star-Spangled Banner" in an effort to combat citizenship for Irish immigrants. Because these organizations operated in secrecy, with their members never claiming to know anything about its leadership, the anti-Catholic crusade was dubbed the **"Know-Nothing" movement.** It survived as a national movement for almost 20 years, until it dissolved over differences about slavery just prior to the Civil War.

The "Know-Nothing" movement showed how tolerance can be sorely tested when some people feel threatened by large-scale changes to their way of life. This regrettable chapter in American history has been repeated several times, as people with different religious practices, skin colors, and native languages came to America and, by virtue of their numbers, modified the cultural and political landscape. Jews arrived in large numbers in the early twentieth century to widespread anti-Semitism. The wave of German immigrants was subsiding around World War I, but American involvement in the war generated public hostility to immigrants of German dissent. During the 1990s, the most recent wave of

▶**"Know-Nothing" movement**
An anti-Catholic movement that formed in the 1840s as a reaction to the first large wave of Irish immigration.

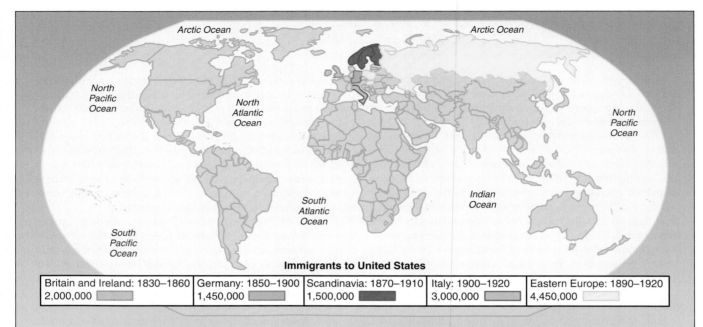

Immigrants to United States

Britain and Ireland: 1830–1860	Germany: 1850–1900	Scandinavia: 1870–1910	Italy: 1900–1920	Eastern Europe: 1890–1920
2,000,000	1,450,000	1,500,000	3,000,000	4,450,000

Much of the immigration from Europe came in waves, starting with British and Irish immigrants in the early to mid-nineteenth century, German immigrants following the Civil War, and immigrants from Eastern Europe in the first decades of the twentieth century.

One of the first waves of immigration came from the British Isles, especially Ireland. Between 1830 and 1860, almost 2 million Irish immigrants came to America, representing 40 percent of all immigrants to the United States during that period. Almost another 1.5 million arrived between 1860 and 1890. Many Irish immigrants were Catholic, adding a religious mix to what had been an overwhelmingly Protestant nation.

Germany was the next big departure point. Between 1850 and 1900, following the initial wave of Irish immigrants, a large group of German immigrants came to the United States. The peak was in the 1880s, when 1,450,000 German immigrants represented more than 25 percent of all immigrants during that time.

A large influx of immigrants from the Scandinavian countries overlapped the wave of German immigrants. Over 1.5 million Scandinavians, many of them Norwegians and Swedes, came to America between 1870 and 1910.

The turn of the twentieth century witnessed a large influx of Italian immigrants—over 3 million between 1900 and 1920—representing 20 percent of all immigrants during that time.

The same period was a peak time for Eastern European immigrants. Three million Russians arrived between 1890 and 1920, 1.2 million Hungarians arrived between 1900 and 1920, and 250,000 Poles arrived during the 1920s. This wave of immigration included a large number of Jews, Russian Orthodox, and other non-Protestants. Notice how as time passed, European immigration moved clockwise, from western to central to eastern Europe.

Figure 4-2

Native Countries of Immigrants to the United States, 1830–1920

Source: Data from Immigration and Naturalization Service Fiscal Year 2000 Statistical Yearbook.

American immigrants produced a "close-the-borders" backlash aimed at Latinos. Box 4-4 (see page 94) discusses anti-immigrant sentiment at different points in our history.

Apart from the psychological component of adjusting to people who may look different or speak and act in an unfamiliar way, periods of widespread immigration invariably put a strain on the resources that government must provide to its swelling population. This poses a material problem for the government and a political problem for elected officials. It's why anti-immigration dictates found a sympathetic audience among those Californians who felt their pocketbooks were being stretched to provide for the needs of a flood of immigrants, many of whom had snuck into California through the Mexican border (see Box 4-4 for more details).

Turn over this picture, however, and you'll find the beneficial side of immigration. People from different cultures bring variety to everything from the arts to politics, adding richness to the things people consider uniquely American. Individuals willingly coming to the United States tend to embrace the "American creed," which provides a common sense of self-identification. Many immigrants—even from vastly different political cultures—instinctively subscribe to key elements of the American approach to government and society. For instance, Irish immigrants who came to America to escape poverty accepted the idea of opportunity as an avenue toward self-betterment. Contemporary immigrants from

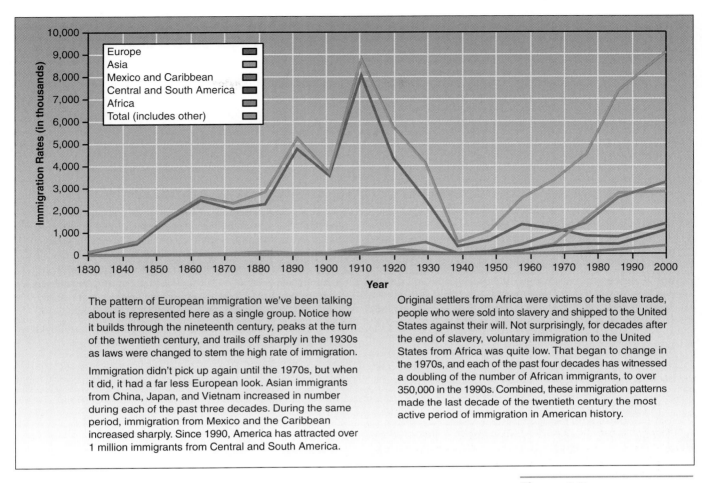

The pattern of European immigration we've been talking about is represented here as a single group. Notice how it builds through the nineteenth century, peaks at the turn of the twentieth century, and trails off sharply in the 1930s as laws were changed to stem the high rate of immigration.

Immigration didn't pick up again until the 1970s, but when it did, it had a far less European look. Asian immigrants from China, Japan, and Vietnam increased in number during each of the past three decades. During the same period, immigration from Mexico and the Caribbean increased sharply. Since 1990, America has attracted over 1 million immigrants from Central and South America.

Original settlers from Africa were victims of the slave trade, people who were sold into slavery and shipped to the United States against their will. Not surprisingly, for decades after the end of slavery, voluntary immigration to the United States from Africa was quite low. That began to change in the 1970s, and each of the past four decades has witnessed a doubling of the number of African immigrants, to over 350,000 in the 1990s. Combined, these immigration patterns made the last decade of the twentieth century the most active period of immigration in American history.

Cuba who came to America to escape the repression of the Castro regime fiercely embrace the American values of liberty and limited government.

Every generation of immigrants brought with them the myth of the American dream, that their children would find a better life despite the hardships and discrimination that might await them. However glorified this myth may be, to a certain extent, Americans have eventually accepted groups that in their day were derided as dangerously threatening to the established social order. History suggests this may eventually be the fate of the groups contemporary Americans find threatening.

4-2c Diversity

With immigration comes variety. Just look at the 2000 Census. The Constitution requires that a **census** be taken every ten years, in which everyone in the country is supposed to be counted. The census says a lot about the composition of the United States, and tells us how it has changed since the last census was taken a decade ago. Box 4-5 tells why an accurate census is so important.

Figures from the 2000 Census confirm the story of America's immigrant past and present. Although about seven in ten Americans is a non-Hispanic white, roughly one in eight is African American, slightly less than one in eight is of Hispanic origin, and one in 25 is Asian American. Also, just as immigrant groups have traditionally settled in specific states or regions, the Census reveals that the South, Southwest, and portions of the Northeast are the most diverse regions of the country. The Latino population is largest in California, Texas, Florida, New York, and New Jersey. The Asian American population is concentrated in California. African Americans are most numerous in the states of the deep South and in the large industrial states of the East and Midwest. In contrast, northern New

Figure 4-3
Patterns of Immigration to the United States, 1820–2000

Source: Immigration and Naturalization Service Fiscal Year 2000 Statistical Yearbook.

▶**census** An accounting or, as Article I Section 2 of the Constitution puts it, an "actual Enumeration" of the residents of the United States, taken every ten years by constitutional decree to assess population growth and population shifts. Census figures are used to determine representation in Congress, as states that lose population between censuses stand to lose House seats to states that gain population.

Box 4-4   Immigration as a Perceived Threat to Social Order

The immigrants of the late twentieth and early twenty-first century, most notably Latino and Asian immigrants, have been subjected to angry reactions from some quarters. In the 1990s, as a large number of Latino and Asian immigrants were descending—legally and illegally—on California, Governor Pete Wilson advocated tightening immigration laws by denying government health and education benefits to illegal immigrants and denying citizenship to their children. His positions set off a fiery debate over what it means to be an American and how the United States should treat people living within its borders.

When Pat Buchanan, a speechwriter and columnist, unsuccessfully contested the 1992 Republican presidential nomination, he turned heads by speaking about a "culture war" in America, in which, as he told the Republican Convention, "we must take back our cities, take back our culture, take back our country," presumably from anyone who didn't look and think like middle-aged white males of European origin like Pat Buchanan. Ironically, as a Roman Catholic, Buchanan himself would have been viewed by the "Know Nothings" as representing the group from whom others wished to "take back our country" 150 years earlier.

The fact that the Buchanan candidacy emerged when it did is not surprising, considering the social stress fissures always caused by large immigrant waves. Immigration poses psychological challenges to a society (this is not unique to the United States). It requires accepting people who may look, speak, or act differently, which some people can do more easily than others. Inevitably, immigration booms produce friction and hostility, as tends to be the case when any group appears threatening to established interests.

That's why anti-immigrant sentiment mirrors the treatment of other groups whose presence threatened the existing order. Following emancipation, African American slaves—brought to this country against their will—faced generations of institutionalized discrimination in the South and social and economic discrimination throughout the country, as we'll see later in the chapter. Native Americans faced decades of discrimination at the hands of an often hostile American government which itself could be seen as composed of late-arriving immigrants.

Box 4-5   Slipping through the Cracks

As you can probably imagine, it's impossible to count everybody in a nation as vast as the United States. Some people live in remote areas; others are homeless; many others simply elude the reach of census takers. In fact, the Census Bureau estimates that in 1990, about four million people were missed—amounting to 1.6 percent of the population.

This probably doesn't sound like a big deal unless you're really compulsive about record keeping, but from a political perspective, it's huge. Real resources ride on the outcome of the census—big dollars and real power. Some policies provide for federal money to be allocated to states based on population, so states where a disproportionate percentage of the population was undercounted will lose funds they would otherwise be eligible for, while still having to provide for the undercounted people. When we talk about Congress in Chapter 9, we'll see that the census is used to determine which states will gain or lose seats in the House of Representatives, so states where a disproportionate percentage of the population was undercounted will lose representation to which they're entitled.

Compounding the political tension is the fact that all population groups are not undercounted equally, with minority group members far more likely to be overlooked. The Census Bureau estimates that in 1990, 0.9 percent of the white population eluded census takers, compared with 4.4 percent of African Americans and 5 percent of Hispanics. So, members of

these groups—not just states—lost out on federal funds and representation in Congress because they were not fully counted.

It turns out that there's a remedy for this disparity, but it's highly controversial. The Census Bureau can estimate the true population using statistical methods, correcting the errors produced by the actual head count.

This possibility generated a huge political battle in the days leading up to the 2000 Census. Because the underrepresented minority groups tend to disproportionately support candidates of the Democratic Party, any statistical adjustment to the census would favor Democrats, probably resulting in the creation of more congressional districts favorable to Democratic candidates. Not surprisingly, Republicans ferociously opposed the statistical estimate, claiming it would amount to a mere guess at the true population—a far cry from the hard numbers required by the Constitution. They argued that even a flawed head count was better than an estimated count, and closer to what the nation's founders had in mind. In 1999, the Supreme Court put its stamp on this reasoning, claiming that using estimated figures for determining congressional representation was unconstitutional.[*]

---

[*]The case was *Department of Commerce et al. v. United States House of Representatives et al.*, 98–404 (1999).

Box 4-6 Review: Liberalism and Conservatism

Liberalism in its broadest sense endorses an active role for government in addressing social and economic problems, and a more limited role for government in refereeing matters involving personal or moral values.

Liberals advocate government activism (which in a practical sense translates into spending money on government programs) for such social issues as environmental protection, health and child care, urban decay, education, and drug addiction, and for such economic issues as welfare and Social Security. In this regard, liberals seek to use the power of government to assist those in need (for instance, through welfare and drug programs) and to compensate for the inequities (like unequal access to health care) or consequences (like air and water pollution) of the economic marketplace.

At the same time, liberals typically believe government should stay out of matters that they consider to be of a moral nature. Consequently, liberals may oppose using government power to limit abortion rights, impose the death penalty, or require prayer in public schools (however, they may be quite comfortable engaging the government to protect abortion rights and defend against school prayer). Liberals may also favor gun control laws, limits on military spending, and tax laws that benefit lower-income people.

Conservatism applies different principles to arrive at mirror-image positions. In its broadest sense, **conservatism** values the power of the marketplace to address economic concerns and individual initiative to confront social problems, therefore advocating a limited role for government power in economic and social matters. Contemporary conservatism for many years has accepted the reality of America's social welfare programs (although some of today's conservatives have spoken about the need to privatize or eliminate social programs), but conservatives tend to be suspicious of government programs that are not subjected to what they regard as the beneficial self-correcting forces of the marketplace and that therefore take money out of taxpayer's pockets that could be put towards free enterprise.

Consequently, conservatives advocate less involvement in (and less money for) government programs on environmental protection, health and childcare, urban issues, education, and drug addiction. They regard welfare as a program that can undermine individual initiative, and have been successful in recent years in restructuring government welfare benefits to orient the program toward getting people to find jobs. Conservatives, like liberals, embrace Social Security, but are more likely to be interested in making it a market-oriented program.

▶ **liberalism** An ideology that advocates the use of government power to address economic and social problems, like unemployment and environmental protection, while limiting government involvement in moral matters like abortion rights and prayer in public schools.

▶ **conservatism** An ideology that advocates limits on government power to address economic and social problems, relying instead on economic markets and individual initiative to address problems like health care and education, while promoting government involvement in moral matters to, for instance, minimize or eliminate abortions or permit prayer in public schools.

England and the Great Plains and Rocky Mountain states tend to have the highest percentage of white residents.

If diversity influences politics, then it should be pretty easy to imagine that national politics is far from a singular phenomenon. Although political activity is about much more than racial or ethnic identification, it still stands to reason that states and regions with greater diversity are likely to voice different concerns and interests than states and regions with less diversity. The politics of New York is different than the politics of Idaho in part because of the different groups that settled there.

Some of these differences go back to the distinctions between liberals and conservatives that we talked about in Chapter 3, although this too can be oversimplified. (Box 4-6 reviews the concepts of liberalism and conservatism.)

For instance, we mentioned that African Americans are more likely to express the liberal position supporting government activity in economic and social matters—adding a liberal bent to politics in regions with large African American communities. Not every minority group has liberal inclinations, though. Cuban Americans, for instance, can be quite conservative politically, lending a conservative quality to regions with large Cuban American communities, like southern Florida.

Probably the biggest story in the 2000 Census is the emerging majority of minority groups, so to speak. Those figures we were just talking about from the year 2000 are simply a snapshot of America at a given time. It's also possible to look at trends in immigration patterns and birth rates, and try to estimate what America will look like in the years

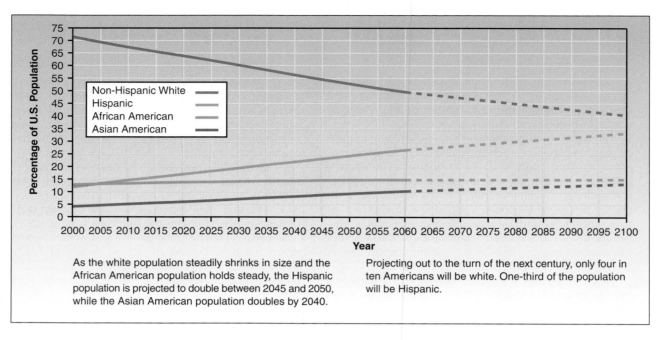

Figure 4-4
Projected Ethnic Group Demographics for the Twenty-First Century
Source: U.S. Census Bureau.

As the white population steadily shrinks in size and the African American population holds steady, the Hispanic population is projected to double between 2045 and 2050, while the Asian American population doubles by 2040.

Projecting out to the turn of the next century, only four in ten Americans will be white. One-third of the population will be Hispanic.

ahead. The Census Bureau has developed a projection like this, and you can see the results in Figure 4-4.

Keep in mind that this is an estimate based on current trends, and that if immigration or birth rates should change, the estimates could be off. Nonetheless, the most notable thing about the projection is that during your lifetime, the white majority that has always characterized this country will become a numerical minority. By the year 2060, non-Hispanic whites are projected to dip below the 50 percent mark in total population, remaining the largest group in America but shrinking from a majority to a plurality of the population, as Hispanics, African Americans, and Asian Americans will together constitute a numerical majority of Americans.

For a nation that's always seen itself as primarily Anglican, these changes promise to create an entirely different identity—one with potentially profound political implications. The questions are speculative, but interesting, even if the answers are unknowable. What would it mean for whites to be just another minority under these new circumstances? Would whites see themselves as a minority? As the largest minority? Or still as a majority? Would they continue to control a disproportionate amount of economic resources by virtue of having been a majority group for so long? Would greater diversity in the population translate into greater diversity among elected representatives, and if so, what might that mean for the direction of our politics?

4-2d Migration

In addition to being an immigrant nation, America has always been a mobile nation. As large numbers of people move around within the United States, politics is inevitably affected. Once an agrarian country centered on rural concerns, America was redefined by industrialization, which brought about massive movement toward urban centers in the late nineteenth and early twentieth centuries. With urban development, political attention turned to urban issues like transportation, sanitation, labor laws, and a host of matters that were irrelevant in an earlier time.

In recent decades, there have been two politically meaningful population shifts: regionally from the old industrial cities of the Midwest and Northeast to the South and Southwest, and nationally from cities to suburbs.

The regional shift is evident when you compare where people lived in 1920 with where they lived in 1960 and 2000. Eighty-odd years ago, the most populous states were in the industrial centers of the Midwest and Northeast that in recent years have been dubbed the

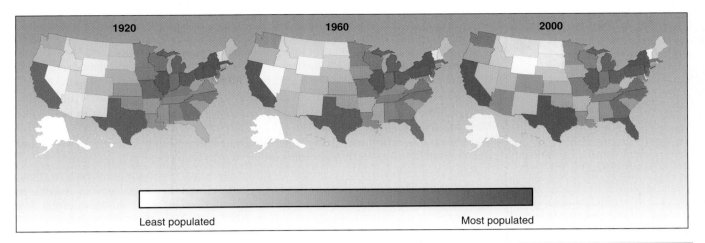

1920   1960   2000

Least populated   Most populated

"Rust Belt" region, after the aging industries of twentieth-century America that were once their crowning jewels. By 1960, the move to warmer "Sun Belt" states had already begun, and by 2000, America's center of gravity had shifted to the South and West. Figure 4-5 illustrates these population shifts.

The ascendancy of conservative national politics coincided with this migration. Through the 1960s, heavily populated industrial centers were the engine of liberal politics, a key base of political support for presidents like Franklin Roosevelt and Lyndon Johnson who, as we noted in Chapter 2, presided over a large expansion in the role of the federal government. These regions lost political clout as they lost population to the Sun Belt states, which traditionally have been more socially and economically conservative.

Now it's easy to overstate the relationship between population shifts and changes in political currents—there's a lot more to it than where people live, as we'll see as we go along. For instance, liberal presidents like Roosevelt and Johnson drew support from outside the Rust Belt. It's also the case that the greatest population binge happened in California, now the nation's most populous state and in recent years a center of liberal politics. Still, as people move, congressional districts move with them, and national officials take notice of where the votes are.

The other meaningful migration in recent years has been the steady nationwide exodus of city dwellers to ever-expanding rings of suburbs. The urban exodus began after World War II, and by 2000, a country that originated as a rural nation and experienced urban migration in the twentieth century had become suburbanized. A glimpse of the nation at night, with lights radiating out from core cities, communicates a sense of how America's population spreads out for miles from downtown.

When we think of suburbs, we tend to think of affluence, and it is true that part of the motivation for the post-war migration from inner cities by people with resources was to escape growing urban decay. Today's suburbs are more complex than this; some older suburbs have predominantly working class neighborhoods, and in some places, suburbs are starting to become ethnically diverse.

Figure 4-5
Population Shifts, 1920–2000
Source: Data from U.S. Census Bureau.

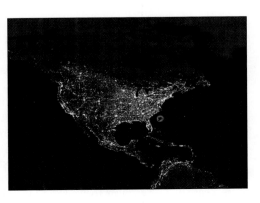

America at night: A portrait of urban sprawl

Source: Data courtesy Marc Imhoff of NASA GSFC and Christopher Elvidge of NOAA NGDC. Image by Craig Mayhew and Robert Simmon, NASA GSFC.

Traditionally more conservative than residents of urban areas, suburbanites today are a politically complex lot. In the 1996 election, for instance, political analysts made a lot out of the phenomenon of "soccer moms"—suburban women with young kids (whom they shuttled to soccer games, hence the name). These voters tended to be social moderates who were attracted in large numbers to the policies of President Clinton, permitting the Democratic president to make inroads through conservative suburban areas. In 2004, those same analysts labeled these voters "security moms" concerned with terrorism, who were more likely to support President Bush.

The politics of affluence does play a role in some urban-suburban issues, however, like education. Public schools in many states are supported with property taxes, meaning affluent suburban communities of private dwellings are able to collect more money to spend on education. This can create wide disparities in the educational opportunities available to urban and suburban schoolchildren, an arrangement that challenges the American notion of equality of opportunity but that, nonetheless, will be defended by suburbanites who benefit from it. As we will see in Section 4-6, "Black and White, Rich and Poor," with more resources at their disposal than residents of poorer urban neighborhoods, affluent suburbanites have an advantage should they wish to defend the status quo against efforts to fund public schools more equitably.

4-2e Age

If you had been born 50 years earlier, the sight of someone over 100 years old would have been highly unusual. Today, it isn't surprising if you know or are related to someone who reached the century mark, and U.S. Census Bureau projections indicate the longevity trend should continue. Add to this the huge number of people in the aging baby boom generation—all those people who were born in the twenty years following the end of World War II—and you have the makings for age to be a key political divide in the years ahead.

In 2000, the U.S. Census Bureau reported that people 65 years or older composed 12.4 percent of the population. Among these, 1.5 percent or 4.2 million were 85 years or older. As these figures increase, the swelling ranks of seniors is bound to put pressure on a Social Security system that is not prepared to handle the burden it will face when you're approaching middle age and will have to support it.[8]

As Baby Boomers age, we're also likely to see increased political attention paid to health care matters, both routine and extraordinary. As more Americans require medical assistance in their advanced years, it's easy to imagine a heated political debate over the question of how much government will be asked to do to defray the cost, especially for those who cannot afford medical services or prescription drugs. We're already witnessing an intense ethical debate over emerging medical technologies like cloning and performing research using stem cells from human embryos—research that has the potential to advance treatments for diseases like Alzheimer's that affect people later in life but that, by its very nature, raises controversial questions about what constitutes life itself.

4-3 Political Socialization: How We Become Political Creatures

How do we become political creatures? That may be a strange question to ask after spending so much energy in Chapter 3 talking about how many of us simply *aren't* political creatures. The fact is, though, that while we are often not very political by choice, we're still exposed to a multitude of political influences, starting from the time we're very young, through the process of **political socialization.**

▶**political socialization**
The process by which we acquire political knowledge, attitudes, and beliefs.

Take a minute and think back. Try to identify your earliest political memory—the first time in your life that you can remember being aware of a politician or a political event. It can be about an election, a national event—anything where a political figure was involved.

Chances are, the event you remembered took place when you were between six and ten years old, around the time kids begin to open up to the larger world. And chances are also that it involved the president. For most kids, the president is the first political figure we're aware of, our gateway to appreciating politics. Of course, when kids become aware of the president, it's in the simple way you would expect kids to process information. They really don't understand what the president does, even as they recognize that he is someone important. In other words, young kids will have a limited **cognitive** or factual understanding of the president. Instead, their relationship to the president will be highly **affective** or emotional.[9]

Initial impressions of the president are that he is powerful and good. This was the case in 1958, when presidential scholar Fred Greenstein examined the impressions of President Eisenhower held by fourth through eighth graders,[10] and it was the case in 2000 when Greenstein's study was replicated on the same age groups with respect to impressions of President Clinton.[11] With the exception of eighth graders in the 2000 study, kids in 1958 and 2000 ranked the president as more important than a host of authority figures they knew firsthand, including teachers, principals, doctors, police officers, and religious leaders.[12] In both years, kids were inclined to view the president in positive terms as well, although the 2000 study reveals a tendency for today's generation to hold less positive views overall than kids did in the late 1950s.

This could be the result of greater negative media coverage of the president, or of kids having access to the Internet at a young age, where they are exposed to a wider variety of political messages. The 2000 study revealed that 81 percent of fourth through eighth graders use the Internet, changing patterns of socialization by accelerating exposure to adult political messages.[13] It has long been the case that as kids age, they abandon the generally positive affect toward political leaders that characterizes early socialization, precisely because age exposes us to a more adult appreciation of the political world and, with it, a less childlike view of politicians. Attitudes like **cynicism** that we discussed in Chapter 3 traditionally develop during adolescence when a more complex understanding of politics sets in.

Political socialization doesn't just happen passively as we age, though. There are forces that act on us, shaping the way we become political as we venture beyond our childhood homes. These **agents of socialization** are many and varied, and they work on us from birth through early adulthood because political socialization is a process that plays out over a long period of time. There are several important agents of socialization, starting with our parents and siblings in our home as we grow up, continuing with our friends as we get older, our teachers in school, our coworkers when we get a job, and the media throughout our lives.

4-3a Family and Friends

Maybe you heard your parents talking about Bill Clinton's involvement with Monica Lewinsky, or about whether they thought the president should be impeached for his actions. Perhaps you have older sisters or brothers who were involved in a cause and liked to talk about it. If your parents voted, maybe they took you to the polls when you were very young. Or you may remember them talking about the price of gas or food or how high taxes are, and blaming it on one politician or another.

It doesn't take much for kids to learn about politics from parents and siblings. The home can be a laboratory for young kids, who absorb an awful lot of information just from the tone of their parents' voices and from what their parents say about political figures and issues. Kids don't even have to be involved in the conversation; they're pretty good at putting together what they hear to figure out how the world works—or, at least, how the world works based on the way it looks at home. Because kids interact heavily with their families, and because families are where kids figure out who they are by the way others relate to them, parents and siblings are considered a **primary agent of socialization.**[14]

One's childhood home is the place where people experience early life socialization. It's where we internalize a set of values about how the world works that will structure our relationship to politics as we age. From their parents and families, young children learn messages about authority, order, trust, tolerance, cooperation, and obedience. If you grew up in a home with strict parents, you likely internalized different values than if you grew up in a permissive home.

Such early learning is very important as it sets the stage for the continuing socialization of our later years, when we develop a mature sense of our political selves. By no means does this suggest that we become a carbon copy of our parents—far from it. In fact, for all

cognitive A factual awareness or appreciation of someone or something. Cognition implies knowledge and the ability to exercise judgment. This is why we would say that a young child's understanding of the president is not cognitive because kids' awareness of the president as an important figure lacks appreciation of what the president does and why he is important.

affective Existing in the realm of emotion or feeling.

cynicism A pervasive attitude of mistrust about politics that may lead people to withdraw from political participation.

agents of socialization External influences that shape the way we are socialized to politics, including parents and siblings in the home, friends and coworkers outside the home, and institutions like schools and the media.

primary agent of socialization Parents and siblings exert disproportional influence on the political development of children by virtue of the initial influence they have on kids, giving the family a primary role in the process of political socialization.

the power of the family to socialize us to politics, you can probably think of many ways you're different from your parents politically. At the very least, you probably hold different positions on many political issues.

Instead, the strongest relationship between parents and kids tends to be on the general level of **party identification,** or the political party you identify yourself with. You could think of party identification as being socialized much like religious identification. In other words, chances are you identify with the same religious group as your parents. At the same time, you may hold different attitudes about the nature or importance of religious worship, or about some of the specific positions of your religious group. This is analogous to holding the same party identification as your parents but disagreeing on particular political issues.

One major study on how effectively party identification is socialized showed that six in ten children had the same partisanship as their parents when both parents had the same partisanship—both were Republicans or both were Democrats.[15] While this is a large percentage—much larger than anything else that's socialized from parent to child—consider that it also means that four in ten children whose parents share a partisan attachment end up identifying with a different party or not identifying with any party. Furthermore, not every child comes from a home where the parents share partisanship. You can pretty much flip a coin to determine the partisanship of kids who come from homes where their parents do not have the same party identification because they are equally likely to be Democrats or Republicans.[16]

From childhood through college and beyond, friendship groups rival the family as an important socializing agent, taking on a central role in political socialization during adolescence. Because peer groups are interpersonal, they are a primary agent of political socialization. But, unlike our families, we get to choose our friends. As teens and even now, we may look for friends who help us fit in at school. If we do, we look for friends who are a lot like us. This means that for many people, peers reinforce rather than challenge existing political beliefs—to the extent that politics enters into friendships at all.

As we get older and the initial influence of family socialization fades, we may be more open to a broader spectrum of opinion in our friendships. If this happens, peers can actually challenge our earlier political learning and serve as an agent for change.[17] This typically does not happen while we're still young, though.

> ▶ **party identification**
> An individual's association with a political party. The most common parties Americans identify with are the two major parties, Republican and Democrat. Party identification—also called party I.D.—varies in intensity such that it may be strong or weak. Those who do not identify with any party are typically called independents.

4-3b Schools and the Media

It's pretty obvious that a lot of formal learning about politics happens in school. After all, it's happening right now. And it starts in preschool, where we begin to learn about the president and about holidays commemorating political figures. In this regard, schools are an excellent source of political information and a fairly direct agent of political socialization.

Perhaps the strongest contribution of schools to political socialization is a bit less obvious. If you grew up in the United States, do you remember what your kindergarten classroom looked like? Was there a flag over the chalkboard? Did you pledge allegiance every morning, to "one nation, invisible?" Was the room decorated in paper cutouts of turkeys and Pilgrims in November, Lincoln and Washington in February, or were there paper ballots with the names of real candidates on Election Day? Exposure to political symbols and engaging in patriotic rituals works to develop a national identity, making the classroom a subtle but important source of political socialization.

How thoroughly do the schools act as an agent of socialization? Not as thoroughly as family and friends, with whom we are engaged in close interpersonal relationships. Although schooling can give us a basic civic education, for many kids the amount of political learning that occurs in secondary school is limited—you probably remember from Chapter 3 that levels of political knowledge tend to be low among adults. Also, while kindergartners may be taken by stories of how George Washington could not tell a lie, we saw in Chapter 3 that adults are more cynical about politicians, meaning that attitudes learned in school eventually change, beginning in adolescence when we start to see the political world as a complex place.

Much of the political socialization that occurs in school may be found in the trappings of the classroom rather than in the curriculum.

Source: PhotoEdit.

For these reasons, we may think of school as a **secondary agent of socialization.** Schools matter to our political development, but not as much as parents, siblings, and peers, with whom we have strong and regular interpersonal relationships.

The same may be said of the media, even though common sense may tell us that the media exert a strong influence on our development by virtue of how pervasive television, radio, newspapers, and the Internet are in our daily life. Like schools, the media can be a source of political learning. As we'll see in Chapter 5, we live in an information environment so cluttered with noise that it's often hard to make good judgments about what's factual and what's simply opinion. This limits the ability of the mass media to serve as a reliable source of political information.

The media are also surprisingly limited in their ability to shape our political attitudes. The primary reason for this is media messages are impersonal, and have trouble competing with family and friends. We're more likely to pay attention to or believe media messages that reinforce our existing attitudes, while ignoring others—a phenomenon called **selective exposure.** We may even unconsciously filter out messages that don't conform to our prevailing attitudes, through a process called **selective perception.** Between consciously being uninterested in messages that conflict with our attitudes and unconsciously filtering messages that conflict with our attitudes, the way we use the media puts the brakes on its effectiveness as a socializing agent.

The media are not without effect, however. They may have a socializing influence through their ability to set the boundaries of what we're aware of politically, determining the issues and people we think about. This process is called **agenda setting.** It can be a powerful effect in the sense that things that are *not* on our agenda will have no place in public political discussion, making them less likely to be considered for political action. The power of agenda setting is limited, though, to influencing what's on our mind. Remember, agenda setting is different from generating opinions—we're not saying that the media have the kind of reach into our lives necessary to formulate opinions on our behalf.

Agenda setting influences what we think about, rather than the attitudes and opinions we hold about the things on our mind.[18] If you find yourself talking to your friends about terrorism or global warming or other topics you know about because they're in the news, you could say that the media helped place those topics on your personal agenda. Your attitudes and opinions about these topics are less likely to be shaped by the media—although we will see that when television commentators consistently portray a politician or an issue in a particular light, our thinking tends to follow from what they say. That, too, is covered in Chapter 5—so stay tuned.

4-3c Other Influences on Political Socialization

Not everyone is socialized under the same circumstances, which means there may be sharp differences among us in the way we come to understand the political world, even though we will all be exposed to the same agents of socialization. African Americans and women, for instance, have for a long time been socialized differently than whites and men.

Generations of African Americans have had to contend with a political system that produced obstacles to participation, and have had to face the dilemma of how to become socialized to a system that was in some important respects unwelcoming.[19]

Studies indicate that as early as grade school young girls begin to react to messages that suggest they should be less interested in political life than young boys, despite demonstrating greater proficiency with language and greater maturity than boys of the same age.[20]

These varying experiences with political socialization help explain why some African Americans may feel conflicted about embracing the shared experiences of American political culture that we talked about earlier, or why, despite recent gains, women remain disproportionately underrepresented in elected offices with respect to their numbers in the population. They may also help explain why it is possible for us to talk about patterns of public opinion that are distinct to African Americans and women. In the aggregate, African Americans are much more likely to support government solutions to social problems and Democratic candidates for public office than the population as a whole. The

secondary agent of socialization Schools and the media have an effect on political socialization, but the effect is less than from primary agents like the family because we do not form close interpersonal bonds with either institution.

selective exposure The tendency to pay attention to messages that are consistent with existing attitudes or beliefs, while overlooking messages that conflict with them.

selective perception An unconscious process by which we filter information that we deem irrelevant, uninteresting, or inconsistent with our attitudes and beliefs, while absorbing information that conforms to our self-perception.

agenda setting The tendency for topics given great weight by the media to be given equally great weight by those who use the media, such that the people and events considered important by those who determine media coverage will become the people and events that the public considers important.

tendency for women to hold more liberal positions on social issues than men may also have its origins in the different ways men and women are socialized.

The things that happen when you're young and as you reach adulthood can also shape the way you're socialized to politics. Imagine that you were born into a home that was hit hard by the Great Depression, where food and money were scarce and you had to live from day to day with what little you could find. Perhaps your grandparents or your great-grandparents came of age in an environment like this. It's not too difficult to imagine that the development of their political attitudes could have been driven by issues of scarcity, and perhaps an attachment to government assistance to help mitigate the painful effects of poverty.

Maybe your parents had to contend with the Vietnam War when they were younger. Perhaps they had to confront a decision about whether to go to Vietnam or to resist the draft—a common experience for young people in the middle and late 1960s and early 1970s. Perhaps they were influenced by counterculture demonstrations against the war, which were politically and socially anti-establishment in nature. Intense social experiences like these can have as great an impact as the Depression on shaping the relationship an entire generation develops toward politics. Such **generational effects** on political socialization help explain why large groups of people, like the "Baby Boomers" born in the twenty years after World War II, move through life with a commonly held set of political and social attitudes developed from their formative experiences.[21]

At the same time, where you are in life can interact with how you respond to the formative political events of your generation and alter the way you relate to politics as you age. Baby Boomers like Bill Clinton, who protested the system when in their twenties, were hardly radical in their approach to government when their turn came to run things twenty years later. Maybe you have strong ideals right now about what you hope to do with your life, or how you can contribute to society. That wouldn't be unusual because many people have strong ideals when they're in college, and are really open to the idea of social change.

That's not to suggest you won't have strong ideals twenty years from now—the last thing you need is someone twenty years older than you telling you that you're going to outgrow idealism—far from it! You may instead find your idealism living side by side with a growing sense of pragmatism. **Life cycle effects** studied in older people point to the emergence of a kind of practical outlook on things when people acquire jobs, families, and the other trappings of middle age. As you might expect, the older we get, the less open we become to political and social changes. Still, it will be interesting to see how life cycle effects compete with generational effects as the Baby Boom generation ages, to see if generational influences remain strong into old age. How hard is it to imagine grandparent Boomers taking their kids and grandkids to see an octogenarian Mick Jagger in concert?

4-4 Political Participation: Getting Involved

Fresh from the process of childhood political socialization, armed with a sense of our political selves, we can go forward into the adult world of politics and participate in a variety of political activities.

Or not.

Truth is, while some people are heavily engaged in politics, it's not all that unusual to find people whose participation is limited to voting—or less. Just like the civic activities we discussed in Section 4-2a, "Group Membership and Tolerance," involvement in political activities is less than it was a generation ago, with particularly sharp declines in the percentage of people who engage in the most widespread political activity, voting.

To many people, **political participation** only means voting. However, it can be a lot more than going to the polls. If you take a look at Figure 4-6, you'll find a list of eight different ways we can participate in politics. Take a second and think about which of these activities you've done in the last year. This should begin to give you a sense of just how much—or how little—Americans get involved politically beyond the voting booth.

▶**generational effects**
Historical influences felt by an entire generation during their formative years, which shape the way they are socialized to politics.

▶**life cycle effects** Changes to the way we relate to politics and society that naturally occur during the course of aging, which typically leave us less open to political and social change as we get older.

▶**political participation**
The range of activities people can engage in to influence the political process. While voting is the most commonly performed political act, participation encompasses a host of things—from writing letters to public officials to contributing time or money to a campaign or protesting the actions of government.

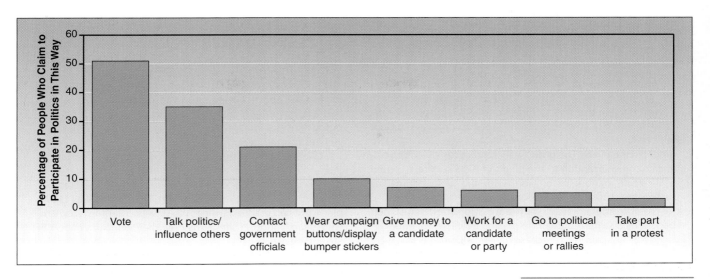

4-4a Conventional Participation

Roughly half the eligible voters participated in the 2000 election, in which both major political parties offered a fresh alternative for president, and in which one-third of the Senate and the entire House of Representatives was up for grabs. During "midterm" elections—the elections that fall during the middle of a presidential term in which congressional and gubernatorial seats are the biggest draw—turnout typically falls to about one-third of eligible voters.

That's roughly comparable to the percentage of Americans who claim they talk about politics from time to time, perhaps with the intent of influencing others. Talk may not be cheap, but it is relatively inexpensive compared to other forms of participation, and as the amount of effort involved in an activity increases, the number of people engaged in that activity predictably declines. So it is that only about one in five of Americans will call or send a letter or email to an elected official on an issue they feel strongly about.

Only one in ten will wear a campaign button, put a bumper sticker on their car, or display a sign in front of their house in support of a political candidate. Fewer will contribute money to a political candidate or volunteer time to work for a candidate or a political party. Only one in twenty will attend political meetings or campaign rallies.

4-4b Unconventional Participation

Even fewer will get involved in less conventional forms of political participation, like engaging in a protest or demonstration, even though American history is replete with examples of protest activity. From the Boston Tea Party prior to the Revolution to Shays's Rebellion during the period of the Articles of Confederation, small but intensely committed groups of dissenters have sought to bring about political change through acts of defiance.

Sometimes, these activities are peaceful but dramatic acts of **civil disobedience,** like those led by the Reverend Dr. Martin Luther King Jr. against segregationist policies in the South in the 1950s and 1960s. Simple but defiant and courageous acts, like Rosa Parks' refusal to give up her seat on a bus to a white man in Montgomery, Alabama, in 1955, drew attention to and helped to change unjust laws.

Sometimes, protest activity is violent. In stark contrast to Dr. King's peaceful demonstrations, African American neighborhoods in cities across the United States were the site of violent rioting in the 1960s. In the highly charged atmosphere of the Vietnam War, college campuses across the country became centers of sometimes violent protests. At Kent State University in 1970, police killed four students and wounded nine others during a protest against President Nixon's decision to escalate the war. The 1960s also witnessed political assassination as a tool of protest, including the murders of President John F.

Figure 4-6

How Politically Active Are We as a Nation?

Sources: Data from 2000 National Election Study. The National Election Studies, Center for Political Studies, University of Michigan. Electronic resources from the NES World Wide Website (www.umich.edu/~nes). Ann Arbor, MI: University of Michigan, Center for Political Studies [producer and distributor], 1995–2000. These materials are based on work supported by the National Science Foundation under Grant Nos.: SBR-9707741, SBR-9317631, SES-9209410, SES-9009379, SES-8808361, SES-8341310, SES-8207580, and SOC77-08885. Any opinions, findings, and conclusions or recommendations expressed in these materials are those of the author(s) and do not necessarily reflect those of the National Science Foundation. Data for percentage who voted from official turnout figures from the 2000 election.

▶ **civil disobedience**
A peaceful means of protest whereby individuals draw attention to laws they consider unjust by disobeying them and being arrested for their actions.

Box 4-7   Vaccine? Animal Rights? You Decide

In June 1999, hundreds of gay and lesbian demonstrators belonging to the group ACT UP (AIDS Coalition to Unleash Power) disrupted a Philadelphia fund-raiser by presidential candidate Al Gore. Some in attendance had protested a Gore rally in New Hampshire days earlier and were on hand to organize the event. The group, which practices civil disobedience to draw attention to the plight of AIDS sufferers, carried a life-sized marionette of Gore with big drug companies pulling the strings.

Their complaint was that Gore supported legislation backed by pharmaceutical firms making it difficult for impoverished African nations to purchase generic AIDS drugs that were far less expensive than the brand-name drugs produced by American drug companies. This policy, said the protesters, sealed the fate of countless numbers of people with AIDS in order for large sums of money to flow to the drug companies—and from the drug companies to the Gore campaign war chest.

The protesters were not supporting Gore's opponent. In fact, they were clear about their position that they did not want George W. Bush to become president. But they did want to bring attention to their plight and felt that without dramatic action, the entire issue, to say nothing of the large matter of finding a cure for AIDS, would go unnoticed. In its manual on civil disobedience, ACT UP instructs would-be participants in nonviolence training, how to stage a demonstration, and how to act when you're arrested and sent to jail.[*]

It's hard to know how many ACT UP members are also sympathetic to the rights of animals. But another organization, People for the Ethical Treatment of Animals (PETA), has a problem with AIDS activists. PETA objects to the use of animals in AIDS research and stages protests in the attempt to put an end to research that harms or kills animals. In their manual for activists, they make the point that animals, like humans, have rights, and that human use of animals for the purpose of experimentation (or for consumption or clothing) violates those rights.[†]

Like many protest groups, their activities can be passionate and extreme. The *Wall Street Journal* reported that PETA had engaged in attacks on laboratory facilities at Stanford University where AIDS research with live animals was taking place and had used legal means to slow and at times stop similar research at other sites.[‡] They see their work as a matter of life and death.

So do the AIDS activists.

So, the two groups are in conflict. PETA activists would probably be happy to leave AIDS research alone if researchers would stop using animals in their experiments. But an AIDS cure is not possible without animal research. For their part, AIDS activists might be sympathetic to PETA objectives if they didn't feel that people would die in the name of protecting animal rights.

And what of people who voice support for animal rights *and* an AIDS cure? On the surface, it seems possible to be sympathetic to both, and it's not uncommon for celebrities and public figures to endorse both causes. The work of protest groups makes it plain that beneath such verbal proclamations of support lies a disagreement that is deadly in its intensity.

[*]You can access the ACT UP Civil Disobedience Manual at http://www.actupny.org/documents/CDdocuments/CDindex.html.

[†]You can access the PETA website at http://www.peta-online.org/.

[‡]The *Wall Street Journal*, June 13, 1996.

Kennedy, his brother Senator Robert F. Kennedy, and Dr. King. Box 4-7 discusses current examples of civil disobedience.

4-5 Young and Old, Men and Women

OK, so maybe you looked at the list of activities in Figure 4-6 and thought, "I don't wear campaign buttons. I don't give money to political candidates. I'm not into meetings and rallies, and I don't know anyone who is." That wouldn't be very surprising. Not only are these types of political activities not widespread, they're especially uncommon among young adults. All forms of political participation are—and with good reason.

Think of the things that are on your mind right now or that have been on your mind at one time or another since you started school. Maybe you're worried about your grades, or how you're going to pay for your education. Friendships and relationships might take up a lot of your time. You could be preoccupied with where you're going to live next semester, or maybe you've got an issue with a roommate that's taking a lot of your energy. Perhaps you have some unresolved matters with your family. You could just be thinking about the plans you have for this weekend or for after you stop reading about political participation.

Grades, money, friends, dating, housing, roommates, family, social plans—some or all of these things are typical of what we spend our time thinking about as young adults. That

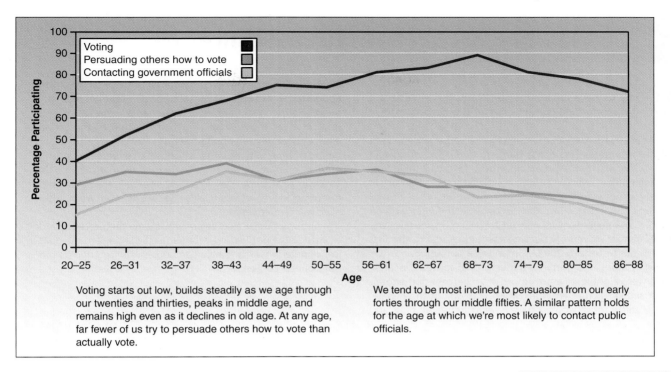

Voting starts out low, builds steadily as we age through our twenties and thirties, peaks in middle age, and remains high even as it declines in old age. At any age, far fewer of us try to persuade others how to vote than actually vote.

We tend to be most inclined to persuasion from our early forties through our middle fifties. A similar pattern holds for the age at which we're most likely to contact public officials.

doesn't leave a lot of time for joining political campaigns, especially if politics feels so much more remote than these other immediate things.

After a while, this starts to change for some of us. We graduate from college and find work. Many people find a long-term partner and settle down in an apartment or house that they rent or own. Life takes on a new rhythm, a more settled rhythm conducive to greater political involvement. For some, this newfound appreciation of political engagement is interrupted briefly as the responsibilities of having young children encroach on time available for civic activity. Otherwise, the tendency to participate in politics builds through middle age, as having the time to get involved coincides with having interests to protect—like a family, a job, or a house—and growing responsibilities like loans and an ever-increasing tax bill. We still have a lot going on like when we were younger, but the things we're doing are more likely to be the sorts of things that lend themselves to political action.

Political participation begins to tail off as we get older and begin to slow down, although senior citizens are among the most politically active of any group when it comes to voting. Even though there is a drop-off in voting after people reach retirement age, the decline is gradual. People in their eighties are still far more likely to vote than people in their twenties!

Figure 4-7 gives you a sense of how age influences three of the more commonplace types of political participation: voting, persuading others to take a particular political position, and contacting public figures. It's based on self-reports from people of different ages that appeared in the 2000 General Social Survey. As you look at the figure, notice how political participation throughout the life cycle takes on a kind of upside-down U-shape that reflects the things we've been discussing, with participation starting out low in young adulthood, growing in fits and starts into middle age, and declining gradually thereafter.

It has also been the case historically that women have tended to participate less than men. Some of this is no doubt because women were denied the right to vote until 1920. In recent years, women have demonstrated greater political involvement, particularly in the areas of voting and running for elective office. The women's vote has been especially important in recent years—in fact, if only men voted, Bill Clinton would have lost the 1992 and 1996 elections. Additionally, women are starting to serve in elected office at a higher rate than ever before. See Box 4-8.

Figure 4-7
The Influence of Age on Political Participation

Source: Data from 2000 General Social Survey, http://www.icpsr.umich.edu/GSS/.

> ## Box 4-8 The Rise of Women in Elected Office

A good way to gauge the rise in the level of political activity by women is to look at how many women in recent years have run for and won election to the nation's highest offices.

As of 2004, twenty-five women had served as governors of twenty-two states (Texas has had two and Arizona has had three). The first two women governors followed their husbands in office—Miriam Ferguson in Texas and Nellie Ross in Wyoming, both elected in 1925. After them, fifty years passed before Connecticut's Ella Grasso became the first woman elected to a governorship without following a spouse. In the 1980s, female governors became commonplace for the first time in our history. By 2002, women were serious contenders in half of that year's thirty-six gubernatorial contests. In 2004, there were eight female governors, or 16 percent of the total.

A similar picture emerges when you look at the Senate, where thirty-three women have served between 1922 and 2004. As with governorships, a number of these women were appointed to fill seats left vacant upon the death of their husbands. Hattie Wyatt Caraway of Arkansas was the rare exception: She was the first woman to be elected to the Senate without benefit of an appointment, in 1931. Then, after a long period of time in which only a handful of women served, the number of female senators increased dramatically in the 1990s. In 2004, there were fourteen women in the Senate representing eleven states (California, Maine, and Washington have two female senators).

Although these figures are well below the percentage of women in the population, they suggest a change in the political climate in which female candidates are regarded as serious political contenders.

Even in places where women appear to participate less than men, some of the disparity can be understood in terms of differences in education. In fact, how much education you have has a lot to do with how likely it is for you to get involved politically.

If you look at Figure 4-8, you'll find the percentage of men and women who told the General Social Survey that they engaged in several types of political participation—attending political events, contributing to candidates, and contacting government officials. Overall, men are slightly more likely to get involved than women.

But watch what happens to the differences between men and women when you look at their levels of participation in terms of how much education they have. Participation rates rise steadily for men and women as they amass more years of schooling, really shooting up for college grads. As participation rates go up, gender differences shrink or disappear. College-educated women are just as likely as college-educated men to contribute to political campaigns, almost as likely to contact government officials, and more likely to attend political rallies.

4-6 Black and White, Rich and Poor

Just as differences in political participation rates between men and women can be explained by education rather than gender differences, participation differences between African Americans and whites defy simple racial explanations. There are multiple reasons why whites participate in some—but not all—political activities at a higher rate than blacks, including a legacy of institutional restrictions against African American voting, and a complex relationship among participation, social and economic resources, and psychological factors that adversely affects African Americans.

In 1972, political scientists Sidney Verba and Norman Nie published a groundbreaking study of American political participation, in which they found that a greater share of African Americans are entirely uninvolved politically than their numbers in the population would suggest. At the same time, Verba and Nie found that African Americans vote at about the same rate as whites and are about even with the rest of the population among the small group of people who are highly active politically. In other words, blacks opt out of the political process at a higher rate than whites, but those that are highly involved are about as active and engaged politically as whites.[22]

The fact that we don't find significant racial differences in voting patterns is noteworthy when you consider the obstacles to voting that African Americans faced in the South until very late in the twentieth century. Although granted the legal right to vote following

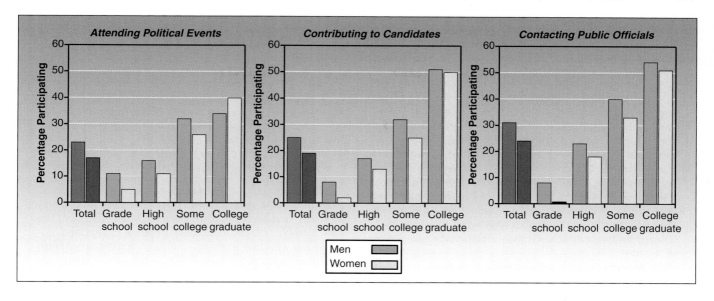

Figure 4-8

Gender, Education, and Participation

Source: Data from 2000 General Social Survey, http://www.icpsr.umich.edu/GSS/.

the Civil War, it took a century before those rights were more than words on a piece of paper.

The years immediately following the Civil War gave few hints that it would take a century before one-time slaves would be free to embrace the political rights promised to them during Reconstruction.[23] A string of federal acts promised to immediately enfranchise African Americans. In rapid succession:

- The Military Reconstruction Act of 1867 required all southern states to give former slaves the right to vote as a condition of being readmitted to the Union.

- The Fourteenth Amendment, ratified in 1868, extended citizenship to former slaves.

- The Fifteenth Amendment, ratified in 1870, specifically forbade states to deny the vote to someone on the basis of race, color, or the fact that they were once a slave.

- The Enforcement Act of 1870 imposed criminal penalties on anyone who would try to deny blacks the right to vote.

- The Force Act of 1871 shifted the right to oversee elections from the states (some of which vehemently resisted black voting rights) to the federal government.

Initially, hundreds of thousands of former slaves flocked to the political process. African Americans voted in large numbers and were elected to offices at all levels of government. However, as Reconstruction ended and federal troops withdrew from the South in the late 1870s, whites who vehemently opposed black involvement in politics did everything they could to lock them out of the process. Using a combination of violence and political tactics, white southerners ruthlessly put an end to black participation. As northern troops departed the region, southern whites employed violent attacks against African Americans as an intimidation tactic designed to keep them from voting. By the 1890s, with whites back in control of state legislatures, many southern states passed a series of laws designed to make it impossible for blacks to vote. These included:

- Literacy tests, which required voters to demonstrate knowledge of the Constitution that might be advanced for you, even if you've already read Chapter 2 of this book. Because many African Americans lacked formal education, literacy tests were an effective way to disenfranchise them.

- Poll taxes, which required voters to pay a tax in order to exercise their right to vote. Although the tax was generally nominal, it had the practical effect of disenfranchising countless black voters who were too poor to pay it.

Box 4-9　How Well Would You Do on a Literacy Test?

For decades, African Americans had to endure hardship and humiliation in order to register to vote. It was not uncommon for voter registration offices to be open only a few days a month, during work hours. White employers who permitted black workers to take time off to register were subjected to organized economic retaliation designed to threaten the jobs of African Americans who registered. At the Registrars Office, it was common for local deputies to harass, threaten, and intimidate blacks who tried to register. Information on African American applicants would likely find its way from the registrar to the Ku Klux Klan, which would use violence or the threat of violence against blacks who dared to try to register.*

If would-be voters actually made it to the literacy test, they faced an exam designed for them to fail. A case in point is the Alabama Literacy Test, which consisted of three parts: a reading of a portion of the Constitution, which the applicant had to interpret orally to the registrar, and two written sections on constitutional, federal, and state law that were evaluated in secrecy by a Board of Registrars. Here are some questions from that test. See if you can answer them:

- If a person charged with treason denies his guilt, how many persons must testify against him before he can be convicted?
- At what time of day on January 20 each four years does the term of the president of the United States end?
- If the United States wishes to purchase land for an arsenal and have exclusive legislative authority over it, consent is required from _____.

- Name one area of authority over state militia reserved exclusively to the states.
- The power of granting patents, that is, of securing to investors the exclusive right to their discoveries, is given to the Congress for the purpose of _____.
- In what year did Congress gain the right to prohibit the migration of persons to the states?†

As you can see, these questions are challenging (or trivial) even for people with a formal education. They would only humiliate and discourage someone with no education. The combination of legal roadblocks, physical threats, and violence was effective; in many southern counties, the African American registration rate was zero, and it remained this way for decades.

By the way, the answers are: Two persons must testify against someone charged with treason; the president's term ends at noon on January 20; consent for purchasing land for an arsenal has to come from the legislature; the states have exclusive authority over the appointment of officers to militia; Congress grants patents for the purpose of promoting progress; Congress gained the right to prohibit the migration of persons to the states in 1808. Be honest—how many of these did you get right?

*See "Voting Rights," from the Civil Rights Movement Veterans, at http://www.crmvet.org/info/lithome.htm.

†To see the complete literacy test, go to http://www.crmvet.org/info/litques.pdf.

- Grandfather clauses, which exempted whites—many of whom were as uneducated as African Americans—from having to take literacy tests or pay poll taxes because they were eligible to vote or were descended from someone who was eligible to vote in 1867—before passage of the Fourteenth Amendment.
- "White primaries," which circumvented the Fifteenth Amendment by keeping African Americans from voting in Democratic Party primaries by declaring the Democratic Party to be a private organization exempt from laws requiring equal participation. In southern states dominated by the Democratic Party, primary winners invariably won elections, and exclusion from primary voting was an effective way to disenfranchise blacks.

▶**socioeconomic status (SES)**
A measure of an individual's social position based primarily on education, income, and occupation. High socioeconomic status individuals are more likely to have advanced education, high incomes, and occupations that award high status and demand great responsibility, like professional or managerial work. The abbreviation for socioeconomic status is SES.

These discriminatory laws remained on the books for decades. Although the Supreme Court ruled grandfather clauses unconstitutional in 1915[24] and "white primaries" unconstitutional in 1944,[25] southern states continued to disenfranchise African Americans (see Box 4-9) until the Supreme Court and Congress actively intervened in the 1960s. By then, African Americans had to overcome the effects of having been locked out of the political process in the South for four generations.

For African Americans who choose not to participate in politics, the underlying causes start with the relationship between race and class. Verba and Nie found that people with higher **socioeconomic status (SES)**—well-educated people with high incomes and high-status jobs—are more likely to have resources that facilitate political participation, and that African Americans are less likely to be represented in the high-SES group. These resources include time, money, and information about politics.

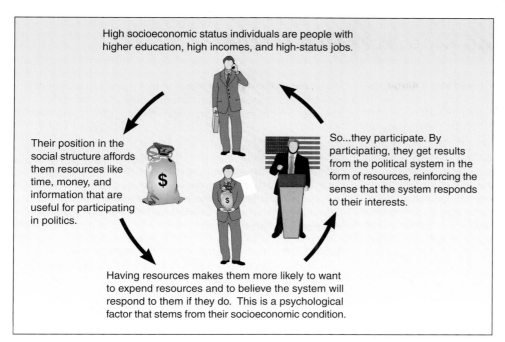

Figure 4-9
Resources, Psychological Factors, and Participation

Verba and Nie speculate that there is an intricate relationship between having resources, having the motivation to use them, and getting results. They contend that this relationship explains who is likely to participate and why African Americans are less likely to be represented among political participants.[26] The economic disparity that distinguishes high-SES individuals from low-SES individuals is associated with a psychological divide. People with more resources to use in the political process, a group in which African Americans are less well represented than whites, are more likely to be oriented toward the political process. They're more likely to be aware of and concerned about the political process, and have a high sense of political **efficacy,** which you may recall from Chapter 3 is the feeling that you can get results if you enter the political arena. This should make sense: If you start out with the necessary tools, you're more likely to feel you can get the job done. You feel motivated. You participate.

We've already talked about how participation is linked to getting results when we said in Chapter 1 that not participating is always a choice but that people who participate are more likely to get results from government. This works to reinforce the psychological drive to participate because when you actually accomplish something by participating, it's natural to feel like you can get the system to respond to your wishes. You've already done it! To the degree that what people get through participating is tangible, which it often is, participating also works to bolster their supply of political resources that were the catalyst for participating in the first place.

The process works something like that shown in Figure 4-9.

You can probably see how the tangible and psychological rewards that come from participating work to reinforce the tangible and psychological advantages that high-SES individuals start with. So, if African Americans are underrepresented in the high-SES group, they will ultimately be less likely to participate and less likely to believe that participating will make a difference. That's because the process can work in reverse to keep low-SES individuals from wanting to engage in political activity. Low SES means having fewer resources that are useful for participating in politics, which can reinforce the psychological orientation that political participation is a waste of time because the system will not be responsive. This low sense of efficacy discourages participation—and is self-fulfilling.

You can probably also see how participation can reinforce social status, independent of race. With people from higher socioeconomic groups participating more, the political system is going to be more responsive to their interests, which you can probably imagine are different from the interests of people with lower socioeconomic status. For instance, the political interests of unemployed people for job training or unemployment insurance

efficacy The attitude that you can be effectual and effective in your dealings with government.

Box 4-10 Revisiting Resources That Matter

Remember in Chapter 1 when we talked about **pluralism** and **elitism** as different ways to understand who gets what, when, and how? (If not, take a quick trip back to Section 1-7, "Power Surge," in Chapter 1.) In a way, when we talk about the connection between having resources and having the motivation to participate in politics, we're revisiting the question of whether political power is held by many or few.

Let's look a little more closely at the case of the long-term unemployed population, typically low-SES individuals who lack the resources and therefore the motivation to participate politically. If political officials are more sensitive to the needs of people who participate, and unemployed individuals tend not to participate, you could make the case that the political system will not be responsive to their interests, choosing instead to respond to the interests of a smaller group of resource-rich, high-SES individuals. You'd be making an argument in support of an elitist perspective of American government, in which few people with a lot of resources exercise power. This conclusion seems to be supported by the claim that people without many resources and who lack efficacy are unlikely to be able to get political figures to respond to their needs.

On the other hand, we might also observe that government does not ignore the needs of the unemployed. There are unemployment insurance policies, job-training programs, and economic plans during periods of high unemployment designed to lower the unemployment rate. Presidents like to boast about how many new jobs were created under their administration. Why does any of this happen when unemployed people are not likely to participate in the political process in large numbers?

Political scientists who have studied this question[*] claim that other groups will speak for the unemployed in the politi-cal system. For instance, unions and civil rights groups, out of self-interest or social justice concerns, may advocate policies that benefit unemployed people. Is this consistent with the pluralist perspective that resources are distributed widely enough for many to wield political power? Is it simply a modification of an elitist argument because unemployed people inadvertently benefit from the convergence of their interests and the interests of a powerful elite? Is it possible that government would respond more quickly or lavish more attention on the needs of the unemployed if they participated in the political process?

▶ **pluralism** The theory that government responds to individuals through their memberships in groups, assuring that government is responsive to a wide range of voices. People who subscribe to this position believe the wide distribution of resources in society drives the decisions government officials make.

▶ **elitism** The theory that government responds to a small, stable, centralized hierarchy of corporate and academic leaders, military chiefs, people who own big media outlets, and members of a permanent government bureaucracy. People who subscribe to this position believe the actions of regular citizens, like voting and joining groups, simply mask the real power exercised by elites.

[*]Kay Lehman Scholzman and Sidney Verba, *Injury to Insult: Unemployment, Class, and Political Response* (Cambridge, MA: Harvard University Press, 1979), 333–356.

are worlds apart from the concerns of high SES individuals, but the unemployed are not oriented to participate in large numbers in the political process, so they are in a weakened position to make demands on the system.[27] Political officials will be more sensitive to the needs of high-SES individuals, who will be well positioned to reap the rewards of government. See Box 4-10.

4-7 I Couldn't Care Less!

▶ **apathy** A sense of indifference to or lack of interest in politics.

Maybe you couldn't care less about who participates and what happens to them. There's a word for that. It's called **apathy.** It's a word that is widely used in the media and in conversation to describe the way many people relate—or fail to relate—to politics. Americans are widely perceived to be apathetic as a result of having low levels of political knowledge and involvement. People who are apathetic avoid political participation because they genuinely don't care about it. (They might want to avoid reading about it, too.)

Or do they? Some research on the topic points to a different conclusion, based on observations of people in social settings who avoided talking about politics. This line of thought suggests that people seem apathetic not so much because they don't care about what's going on but because they feel powerless to do anything about it. Big political problems, even those that could affect us directly, are just that—big—and they can leave us feeling overwhelmed.[28]

In the face of this, and to avoid the social embarrassment that could come from making it appear that we actually believe our opinion might matter or that we could exercise some control over the situation, a lot of people resort to saying "I'm not interested" or "I'm just not paying attention." They strike an apathetic pose, and they resist political involvement, even on issues that hit home, like rapidly increasing tuition costs, where they're quite aware that what happens does matter to them.

Doing this takes work. We have to try hard to be apathetic because it's so natural to care about what happens to us and to those around us. Maybe your parents grew up during a time when it was cool to be "involved." Under different social circumstances, you might also find that it can be cool to talk about political problems with friends and neighbors.

You may have noticed that this section on apathy is a lot shorter than others in the book. Do you care?

4-8 Why Vote?

Bad jokes about apathy aside, when you look at the most commonly engaged form of participation—voting—it's reasonable to ask why anyone would take the time to do it at all. When you look at what you have to do in order to vote in an election in this country, you might reasonably ask how our turnout can be as *high* as 50 percent in presidential election years.

Some countries, like Australia, have close to perfect turnout. In these countries, voting is compulsory because it is regarded as an obligation rather than a right. There's actually a fine for not voting. Under those circumstances, plenty of people manage to find their way to the polls. It doesn't happen that way in the United States, though, where the process is much more complex and there is no monetary cost to not participating.

First, you have to register to vote. This typically involves satisfying age and residency requirements, although the specifics vary by state. Alabama, for instance, makes you affirm your allegiance to the Constitution and swear that you have no plans to overthrow the legally elected government of the state.

If you live in North Dakota, you have it easy because there's no registration requirement there—you can just skip to the part where you show up at the polls on Election Day. If you live in any other state, you have to be aware of the need to register, know the registration deadline in order to register in time to vote in the next election (it's typically a couple of weeks or so before Election Day), and know how to register.[29]

Until recently, registering to vote in most states involved locating and visiting a state office, like your County Board of Elections. Things got easier with the passage of the **National Voter Registration Act** of 1993. It's commonly called the "Motor Voter Act," because of a provision that makes it possible for you to register to vote when you apply for or renew your driver's license.

The Motor Voter Act has other provisions, also designed to make registration more convenient. All states except for Minnesota, Wyoming, Wisconsin (and, of course, North Dakota) must accept mail-in registration forms, including a national mail-in voter registration form made available by the Federal Election Commission. Agencies that provide public assistance, like Medicaid and food stamps, or services to people with disabilities, are also required to provide voter registration services. Some states, like California, let you register online, while others let you download application forms off the Internet.

▶**National Voter Registration Act** Passed in 1993 to simplify and standardize voter registration requirements, the "Motor Voter Act" allows residents of most states to register to vote at the same time as they apply for or renew their driver's license. It also provides for a standardized, national registration form that can be downloaded from the Internet.

 You Can Use

If you would like a copy of the national mail-in voter registration form, you can find it at http://www.fec.gov/votregis/pdf/nvra.pdf

Box 4-11   Why People Vote

Why do you vote? Some people say:

- Because it's my obligation to vote
- Because it makes me feel good
- Because I feel that I can influence what's happening

If you say, "I vote because I feel it's my obligation to vote," then you're expressing a sentiment about **civic responsibility,** the sense that there are certain things we're obligated to do as citizens of a democracy. Some people feel that the inconvenience of voting is part of the price we pay to maintain privileges like the freedom to speak our mind or to complain when we don't like something.

If you say, "I vote because it makes me feel good," then you know that you don't have to make *the* difference in an election to feel like you've made *a* difference. It's efficacy again, in a specific form that relates to voting. Some people get a sense of efficacy from voting because they feel like their voice will be included in the mix of voices expressed on Election Day. Also, it can be gratifying to speak up.

If you say, "I vote because it gives me the feeling that I can influence what's happening," then you are trying to shape your world. Influence is a different type of feeling than efficacy. Some people feel that voting equals influence, regardless of the outcome of an election. They see voting as a way to shape the future course of politics, either by contributing to a candidate's winning margin or by making a show of support for the loser.

▶ **civic responsibility** A sense of duty or obligation to society that some people believe comes along with citizenship.

The Motor Voter Act makes registration easier than it used to be—if you know about it. If you're like many people, though, you didn't know about it until about a minute ago, unless you stumbled across it when you got your driver's license. It still requires the expenditure of a valuable resource—time—to complete the registration form, and turnout figures suggest it has not significantly boosted voter turnout.

Also, don't forget that registering to vote is only the first step in the process. You then need to find and get directions to your polling place—information that will take time to get—and arrange to take time out of your day to vote. Polls open early in the morning in most states, and typically remain open until seven, eight, or nine in the evening, giving people who work the opportunity to vote without taking time away from their jobs. However, this can mean the added inconvenience of having to get up a little earlier or delay an evening activity, and possibly wait in line during these "prime time" hours.

In other words, voting can be a pain. It requires work and time, and the sacrifice of something else you might want to be doing, like sleeping or going out or being with your family. It may seem particularly burdensome if you're one of those low-efficacy Americans who feel the political system is not going to respond to your wishes and interests anyhow. If you believe your vote does not matter, or politicians are all just a bunch of hypocrites, you're not likely to invest your resources in registering and voting.

So, if voting is such a hassle, why does anyone want to do it? You'll find a few explanations in Box 4-11.

Because the mathematics of voting makes the likelihood of casting the deciding vote in an election remote, many people vote because of the attitudes they have about living in a democracy. People vote because they feel they should, or because it makes them feel good, or because it gives them the sense that they have a voice in public affairs.

4-9 How Can I Decide?

Chances are some people in your class have voted in a real election, others are eligible but have never voted, and still others may be ineligible to vote in the United States because they're not 18 years old or American citizens. So, to make sure everyone has had a voting experience (or something close to it) before we move on, let's take a minute and cast a vote in a hypothetical congressional election. You'll find your ballot in Figure 4-10, marked with the names and party identification of the candidates—the same information you would have in a real voting booth. Imagine there are other people in line behind you, so try not to linger too long over your decision.

Figure 4-10
Let's Vote

So, what was your decision? Did you make a choice? Or did you go for the "no vote" option? Maybe you were thinking, "I don't know any of these people. How can I vote?" And, of course, you don't know anything about them—which precisely mirrors the situation of many people who cast ballots in real elections. They still manage to vote. Perhaps you did too. Let's look at how they do it.

4-9a Party I.D. Voting

One of the few clues you had to guide you was party affiliation, so if you identify as a Republican, you may have voted for Leonard Fitzsimmons, or if you identify as a Democrat, you may have voted for Marjorie Carp. Even without knowing anything else about these candidates, this is a reasonable thing to do because a simple party label can convey a lot of information. Perhaps you assumed that the Republican candidate is the more conservative of the two. Often, you would be correct. Perhaps you reasoned that you don't know what Carp's positions are on issues that matter to you, but if you're a Democrat, the chances are that she's closer to your beliefs than Fitzsimmons. That seems like a pretty reasonable assumption as well.

You may even have voted for the candidate who shares your partisanship without even wondering what the candidate stands for, simply because you're a strong partisan. Remember, party identification is socialized more strongly than political attitudes and beliefs, and if we're predisposed to thinking of ourselves as Republicans or Democrats, it's natural to gravitate to a candidate who shares our identification.

So, party identification can help strip away the confusion of an unfamiliar ballot and provide a reasonable guideline for how to vote. It wouldn't be surprising if many of your classmates voted this way, just as it wouldn't be surprising to find many Americans voting this way in real elections. In recent years, party identification has been a good way to predict how people will vote.

At the same time, party identification may not be quite as strong as it was many years ago. In 1952, 47 percent of Americans claimed to be Democrats and 28 percent identified themselves as Republicans, according to the American National Election Studies. Half of these called themselves strong partisans. That left one-quarter of the electorate as either independent or apolitical.

Compare that to 2000, when only 34 percent identified themselves as Democrats and 24 percent as Republicans, leaving 41 percent of us as independents or apolitical. Although about one-third of the independents said they "lean" toward the Democratic Party and an equal number "lean" toward the Republican Party, we find that people who identify loosely with a political party are a bit more likely than strong supporters to shop around when they vote.[30]

More independents and fewer strong partisans in the electorate can produce **ticket splitting** among voters, where people vote for, say, a Republican candidate for president and a Democratic candidate for Congress. This type of voting pattern can generate divided

▶ **ticket splitting** Voting for candidates of different parties for different offices, rather than voting a "party line" for all Republicans or all Democrats. Ticket splitting, which has increased in recent years, is a sign of how Americans have been growing independent from political parties.

Box 4-12 The Surprising Success of Victor Morales

It's not every day that someone with no political experience, hardly any money, and no backing from the political establishment can make a credible run for a Senate seat from a major state. However, that's exactly what high school geography teacher Victor Morales did in Texas—twice—as the nominee of the Democratic Party for the Senate in 1996 and as the runner-up in a three-way race for the same nomination in 2000.

To the political establishment, Morales came out of nowhere in 1996, riding around Texas on a shoestring budget in an old pickup truck, to defeat two members of the U.S. Congress for the Senate nomination in a race he lost to incumbent Republican Senator Phil Gramm. Four years later, using the same low-budget strategy, he came in second in a field of three candidates, only to lose a head-to-head runoff with Ron Kirk, the well-funded, party-endorsed former mayor of Dallas.

Part of Morales' success no doubt stemmed from the fact that he was a maverick outsider in a state that likes anti-

politicians, and an underdog who achieved a kind of celebrity status through news coverage of his seemingly impossible quest. But Texas Democratic Party leaders promoting Kirk were sensitive to the fact that Morales could count on a large turnout among Latino Democrats, a force in Texas politics, because of his roots in the Latino community. They feared Latino support would not be enough for Morales to be elected to the Senate, but it might just be enough to defeat Kirk for the Democratic nomination.

Eager to avoid a second Morales nomination, Democrats supporting Kirk's candidacy arranged for high-profile endorsements from gubernatorial nominee Tony Sanchez and former San Antonio mayor and U.S. Secretary of Housing and Urban Development Henry Cisneros. The extent to which these endorsements from high-profile Latino figures helped Kirk win the Democratic nomination may never be known, but it illustrates how much political leaders believe voters will support candidates with backgrounds similar to their own.

government, where one party controls the White House and the other controls at least one house of Congress, like we saw during eighteen of the twenty years between 1980 and 2000.

4-9b Candidate Characteristics

Did you think about voting for Leonard Fitzsimmons because he has an Irish-sounding name? Maybe you cast your vote for Marjorie Carp because she is the only woman on the ballot.[31] Ethnic and gender identification can be other useful voting shortcuts. In fact, candidates with ethnic sounding names may count on votes from people who will identify with their background. See Box 4-12.

Candidate character, as well as characteristics, may also play a role in voting. Sometimes the character of the candidate—their integrity, or the way they handle their personal or public life—can factor into whether people will vote for them. Bill Clinton is an excellent example of a political figure who conducted his personal life in a way that lost him the respect—and in some cases, the votes—of people who otherwise approved of his performance in office. Another example is California Congressman Gary Condit, initially well respected in his conservative district as a family man. In 2001 he became embroiled in scandal when he denied, then admitted, a romantic involvement with Chandra Levy, a twenty-four-year-old congressional intern who was found dead in a Washington, D.C. park (Representative Condit was not involved in Levy's death, but her disappearance put their relationship in the headlines.) Condit's unwillingness to cooperate with authorities investigating Levy's disappearance and his less than truthful demeanor in a nationally televised interview cost him the support of voters in his district, who in 2002 decided not to send him back to Congress.

Of course, these are high-profile cases of politicians in the news. Voting for or against a candidate because of their personal characteristics requires having more information about them than their last name or their party identification, and information can be costly to acquire. This limits the circumstances under which people will find themselves in a position to vote on a candidate's character.

issue voting Choosing a candidate in an election on the basis of his or her proximity to your position on an issue or issues you consider important.

4-9c Issue Voting

More limited still may be the opportunity to vote on the positions a candidate takes on issues. **Issue voting** requires satisfying several conditions, which involve having fairly spe-

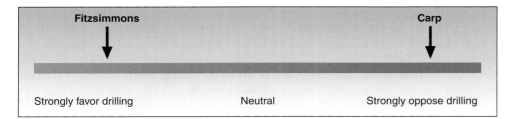

Figure 4-11
Issue Voting: Positions of Two Hypothetical Congressional Candidates on Drilling for Oil in Alaska's Arctic National Wildlife Refuge

cific information about the candidates running for an office and the motivation to use it to determine how you'll vote. To cast a vote on an issue, you must:

- Have enough awareness of an issue to have a position on it
- Be aware of where the candidates stand on the issue
- Differentiate the candidates' positions on the issues
- Vote for the candidate whose position is closest to yours

Take a second and try it. Imagine that our two congressional candidates have announced their position on President Bush's initiative to drill for oil in Alaska's Arctic National Wildlife Refuge. The plan would permit oil drilling in a remote portion of the Alaska wilderness presently preserved for wildlife. Supporters argue we need to become less dependent on foreign oil by tapping domestic reserves. Opponents claim that the habitat is fragile and that drilling will do irreparable harm to the animals living there (there's more information on this issue in Section 15-2e, "How Much Regulation?" in Chapter 15, in case you want to learn more about it now).

Leonard Fitzsimmons favors the initiative, calling it a matter of "responsible development." Marjorie Carp opposes it, calling the plan "environmentally risky." You can find their positions in Figure 4-11.

To cast an issue vote, you would vote for a candidate based on this issue, regardless of where he or she stands on all other issues, and regardless of his or her party identification.

Clearly, you'd have to feel pretty strongly about the issue to do this, and some people do feel that strongly about some issues. Perhaps caring deeply would then motivate you to be informed about the issue, but information can be difficult to come by or complicated to wade through for even the most dedicated voter. Case in point: You could have educated yourself on the issue in our issue voting exercise by going to Section 15-2e, "How Much Regulation?" in Chapter 15—but did you?

When a team of political scientists investigated voters' decision-making processes in 1956, they found that no more than one-fifth to one-third of voters could satisfy the informational requirements for issue voting.[32] A more recent study of this question found that, in 1992 and 1984, more people—on average, better than half—were able to navigate the informational requirements necessary for issue voting on a host of issues including government spending, crime, job policies, the environment, aid to minorities, and women's rights.[33]

However, the figure was lower in 1988, 1980, and 1976, jumping around a bit from election to election. This could reflect how the information environment isn't always the same from issue to issue or from year to year. Some issues are more complex than others and sometimes it's just harder to differentiate where the candidates stand. In fact, political candidates eager to reach as many voters as possible may intentionally take broad or vague positions, complicating our ability to place ourselves clearly in one camp.

4-9d Retrospective Voting

Issue voting is prospective in nature because we're looking ahead and making judgments about what candidates are likely to do after they're elected. Some people make decisions about candidates by looking at the past. When an incumbent is running for reelection, it's fairly typical for voters to view the election as a referendum on his job performance. **Retrospective voting** provides an opportunity for people to look back and evaluate how the official has performed in office to determine whether the incumbent should be retained or replaced.[34]

▶**retrospective voting**
Evaluating the past performance of an incumbent to make a judgment about the future—whether the incumbent should be retained or replaced.

We might take any number of things into account when making a retrospective evaluation about an official. The candidate's actions on a particular issue or set of issues could be prominent in our thinking, particularly if it's an issue that affects us personally like the economy, or something the candidate made a big deal about when running for office the last time. We might take character into account when making a retrospective evaluation and ask if the official is worthy of our continued support.

It's hard to know exactly what people will look for, but incumbents assume that voters will be judging their actions and record and try to be prepared as best they can. They can never control the timing of events, though. In Chapter 3, we saw how in 1991, following the swift and decisive American victory in the Persian Gulf War, President Bush (senior) probably believed he would be judged—and rewarded—for his efforts at putting together an effective war coalition. When a recession hit a year later, he found himself vulnerable to assessments that he wasn't sympathetic enough to people who were hurt by the downturn or proactive enough to do something to combat it. This type of reaction is not surprising: Historically, presidents are punished if they have the misfortune to preside over bad economic times during an election year.

George W. Bush faced reelection during a time of economic and international uncertainty, when a majority of Americans said they felt the country was going in the wrong direction. Normally, this spells difficulty for an incumbent, and throughout 2004, President Bush ran even with his challenger, Massachusetts senator John Kerry. Although President Bush was reelected, the country remained divided on his performance to the end, handing the president a narrow three-point victory with a slim majority in the Electoral College.

When Al Gore sought the presidency in 2000, he ran as a *de facto* incumbent. As Bill Clinton's vice president, Gore was in a position to take credit for the prosperity of the Clinton years. Of course, he was also in line to take the blame for the scandals of the Clinton years. Fearful of being seen as too close to Clinton's shortcomings, Gore ran away from his administration's record, never asking voters to give him credit for good economic times. Whether or not this was an error in political judgment will never be known, but it did neutralize a powerful tool that fortunate incumbents have at their disposal when inviting voters to make a retrospective evaluation of their term of office.

4-10 A Look Ahead: Apathy, Efficacy, and the Media

Remember a little while back, in Section 4-7, "I Couldn't Care Less!", when we were saying that apathy might be about powerlessness? That people may come across as uncaring because problems seem so overwhelming that we might actually feel uneasy suggesting that we believe we can do something about them? It's possible that the media contribute to this situation.

That's because the choice to participate in politics is made in a prevailing climate of public opinion, which is influenced by the media. In the 1960s, when getting involved was cool, the prevailing climate of public opinion supported political participation, even activism and protest—some of the less conventional forms of participation we talked about earlier.

The climate has been quite different in recent years, and this is reflected in the way society is mirrored back to us on television and in newspapers. If those messages preach conformity, it's possible that we'll feel reluctance to express ourselves, especially if our opinions differ from the norm. We may be discouraged from talking about politics, from participating in political campaigns, possibly even from voting. We'll seem and act apathetic, not just because we may feel overwhelmed by the magnitude of the problems we face, but because we're reacting to a social climate perpetuated by media messages that are unsympathetic to political participation.[35] We're apathetic because we want to fit in.

Media coverage of political events may have an impact on feelings of efficacy as well. From news shows to tabloid talk shows to MTV to Internet websites, we're bombarded with lots of information about politics and government, but we don't have a clear way to make sense of it all. It's easy to get lost or confused in the free market of messages, where everyone seems to have a point of view and it can be hard to figure out whom to believe. As we'll see in Chapter 5, even "credible" media sources like network and local news programs play on our fears and doubts, inviting us to anticipate the worst possible outcomes from events or to accept that our political leaders are motivated by the basest instincts. There's evidence that as television replaced newspapers as our primary source of information, feelings of efficacy began to decline—a pattern that began taking shape more than a generation ago.[36]

The tone of our political discussion just makes things worse. To call it "discourse" or "debate" risks putting a refined label on political coverage that's often harsh and shrill. In an environment where there are so many channels that everyone has to yell to get our attention, how can we know what's truthful, what's partially truthful, what's rumor, and what's totally fabricated? The answer is, very often we don't have a reliable way of navigating through the noise.

Sometimes, we end up believing things about our public officials that aren't entirely true. Sometimes, we just turn the noise off altogether. These are both reasonable responses to our twenty-first-century media environment. Neither does much to facilitate feelings of efficacy.

Of course, it's easy to blame the media for everything from political apathy and inefficacy to why there was no hot water in the shower this morning. The media are so pervasive that they make an easy target, and even though there are places where the media play a critical role in the way the political system operates, it is possible to exaggerate the extent of that role. We'll be sure to aim carefully as we begin to explore the role the media play in connecting us to—or distancing us from—the political world. That's the matter we'll take up next, in Chapter 5.

Chapter Review

American political culture comprises a widely held set of values, attitudes, and beliefs that people have about the United States. It unifies America as a nation despite its great diversity by giving people a sense of an "American creed" that most Americans subscribe to, despite differences about how America should be governed.

Holding these shared values can ease the strain caused by diversity. Throughout history, periods of heavy immigration have typically produced an intolerant reaction, like the anti-Catholic "Know-Nothing" movement of the mid-1800s and, more recently, anti-Latino and anti-Asian sentiments of the 1990s. New groups put a strain on resources and bring different customs and traditions that may seem alien and threatening to those who were here before them, although immigrant groups typically embrace American political culture, and over time contribute to the diversity that is one hallmark of that culture.

Changes in our political culture—and our politics—may be anticipated through the changing face of diversity, migration patterns, and the growing number of senior citizens in America. As Asians and Hispanics replace Europeans as the largest immigrant groups, whites are steadily becoming a smaller percentage of the population, and census projections estimate that whites will be a minority by the middle of the twenty-first century.

Political socialization is the process by which we acquire knowledge about politics, along with the attitudes and beliefs that we carry into adulthood. Socialization is a lifelong process facilitated by a series of agents, primary among them our parents, siblings, and friends. Although parents are the most important single agent of political socialization, many parental attitudes and beliefs are not socialized between generations, with party identification the most widely acquired parental characteristic. Secondary agents of socialization include schools and the mass media, which influence political discourse through agenda setting. Political socialization is also affected by the circumstances of our upbringing, with African Americans and women confronting a political environment that has not always embraced their participation; by large-scale events that shape our generation; and by where we are in the life cycle.

There are many ways beyond voting that people participate in politics, like working for a candidate, contacting public officials, contributing money to a campaign, talking about politics, or participating in a protest or an act of civil disobedience. Of these, voting is the most common political activity, although only about half the eligible voters participate in presidential elections. The likelihood of participating in politics is influenced by age, education, socioeconomic status, and efficacy.

Participation takes effort, and given time and information costs, you can make the case that it's sensible not to vote. Still, people find the motivation to vote because they feel it is their civic responsibility, they get a sense of efficacy from voting, or they believe that voting gives them some influence over politics. Voting decisions may be based on party identification, attributes of the candidate, issues, or retrospective evaluations of candidate performance.

Key Terms

affective (p. 99)
agenda setting (p. 101)
agents of socialization (p. 99)
apathy (p. 110)
census (p. 93)
civic responsibility (p. 112)
civil disobedience (p. 103)
cognitive (p. 99)
conservatism (p. 95)
cynicism (p. 99)

efficacy (p. 109)
elitism (p. 110)
generational effects (p. 102)
issue voting (p. 114)
"Know-Nothing" movement (p. 91)
liberalism (p. 95)
life cycle effects (p. 109)
National Voter Registration Act (p. 111)
party identification (p. 100)
pluralism (p. 110)

political culture (p. 86)
political participation (p. 102)
political socialization (p. 98)
primary agent of socialization (p. 99)
retrospective voting (p. 115)
secondary agent of socialization (p. 101)
selective exposure (p. 101)
selective perception (p. 101)
socioeconomic status (SES) (p. 108)
ticket splitting (p. 113)

Review Questions

Note: You can find the correct answers to these questions by taking the quiz and then submitting your answers in the Online Edition. The program will automatically score your submission. If you miss a question, the program will provide the correct answer, a rationale for the answer, and the section number in the chapter where the topic is discussed.

1. Political culture
   a. explains political socialization.
   b. exists largely in myth.
   c. is a unifying force that transcends differences people may have about policy issues.
   d. is learned through the elementary school curriculum.

2. Periods of heavy immigration can put a strain on
   a. resources.
   b. political culture.
   c. political socialization.
   d. both *a* and *c*.

3. Estimated census figures for the twenty-first century suggest that we may have to rethink what it means to be
   a. an immigrant.
   b. a minority group.
   c. Hispanic.
   d. included in a census count.

4. Parents are considered a primary agent of political socialization because
   a. we are socialized to take on our parents' party identification.
   b. we have close interpersonal relationships with our parents.
   c. parents reinforce preexisting political attitudes and beliefs.
   d. the attitudes we learn at home stay with us our entire lives.

5. Which of the following is an example of an unconventional form of participation?
   a. participating in a protest in front of the White House
   b. attending a rally for a Senate candidate
   c. sending an email to a member of Congress
   d. convincing a friend to vote for a particular candidate

6. Gender differences in political participation disappear when you factor in
   a. age.
   b. apathy.
   c. education.
   d. socioeconomic status (SES).

7. All of the following were efforts by the federal government to extend voting rights to African Americans after the Civil War *except*
   a. the Military Reconstruction Act.
   b. the Enforcement Act.
   c. the National Voter Registration Act.
   d. the Force Act.

8. People with high socioeconomic status
   a. are more likely to be white than African American.
   b. are too busy at high status jobs to participate in politics.
   c. share psychological characteristics with people of low socioeconomic status.
   d. typically lack political efficacy.

9. All of the following are reasons why someone might vote *except*
   a. civic responsibility.
   b. influence.
   c. efficacy.
   d. apathy.

10. Which of the following methods of deciding how to vote requires that you anticipate the future actions of candidates?
   a. party I.D. voting
   b. issue voting
   c. retrospective voting
   d. name recognition

In Their Own Words

You might be interested in examining some of what the following authors have said about the topics we've been discussing:

Almond, Gabriel A., and Sidney Verba. *The Civic Culture: Political Attitudes and Democracy in Five Nations.* Newbury Park, CA: Sage Publications, 1989. This study of several countries lends a comparative perspective to political culture.

Clark, Terry Nichols, and Vincent Hoffmann-Martinot, eds. *The New Political Culture.* Boulder, CO: Westview Press, 1998. This edited volume of essays on comparative political culture reflects contemporary thinking on the subject.

Dawson, Richard E., and Kenneth Prewitt. *Political Socialization: An Analytic Study.* Boston: Little, Brown, 1969. As the name suggests, this volume is a good overview of political socialization, containing a particularly good discussion of the agents of socialization.

Eliasoph, Nina. *Avoiding Politics: How Americans Produce Apathy in Everyday Life.* New York: Cambridge University Press, 1998. An interesting and surprising take on the widely held belief that Americans do not participate in politics because they are apathetic.

Fiorina, Morris P. *Retrospective Voting in American National Elections.* New Haven, CT: Yale University Press, 1988. For those who want to learn more about the evaluations people make about incumbents running for reelection and how those evaluations factor into how people vote.

Putnam, Robert D. *Bowling Alone: The Collapse and Revival of American Community.* New York: Simon and Schuster, 2000. This influential book presents an impressive array of data to support the argument that Americans have become increasingly detached from each other, weakening the civic bonds on which a vital democracy depends.

Tocqueville, Alexis de. *Democracy in America.* New York: Vintage Books, 1945. One of the first and most perceptive observers of American civic life, Tocqueville comments on the American tendency to join groups—a characteristic of American political culture that still holds true.

Notes

1. Alexis de Tocqueville, *Democracy in America* (New York: Vintage Books, 1945).
2. Cited in Robert D. Putnam, *Bowling Alone: The Collapse and Revival of American Community* (New York: Simon and Schuster, 2000), 48.
3. Gabriel A. Almond and Sidney Verba, *The Civic Culture* (Newbury Park, CA: Sage Publications, 1989).
4. Allan Cigler and Mark R. Joslyn, "The Extensiveness of Group Membership and Social Capital: The Impact on Political Tolerance Attitudes," *Political Research Quarterly* 55:1 (March 2002), 7–25.
5. Putnam, *Bowling Alone*, 15–28.
6. Ibid., 18–24.
7. Ibid., 402–414.
8. If you work or have worked, you've already started to support the Social Security system. As you age, there will simply be fewer workers contributing to the system and more retirees claiming benefits, so your share of the burden will increase.
9. Fred I. Greenstein, "Children and Politics," in Greenberg, Edward S. (ed.), *Political Socialization* (New York: Atherton Press, 1970), 56–63.
10. Fred I. Greenstein, "The Benevolent Leader: Children's Images of Political Authority," *American Political Science Review* 54 (1960): 934–943.
11. Amy Carter and Ryan L. Teten, "Assessing Changing Views of the President: Revisiting Greenstein's Children and Politics," *Presidential Studies Quarterly* 32: 3 (September 2002): 453–462.
12. Eighth-graders in the 2000 group ranked doctors ahead of the president as the most important authority figures.
13. Carter and Teten, op. cit.
14. Richard E. Dawson and Kenneth Prewitt, *Political Socialization: An Analytic Study* (Boston: Little, Brown, 1969), 105–126.
15. Frank Sorauf, *Party Politics in America,* 2nd ed. (Boston: Little, Brown, 1972), 144.
16. Ibid.
17. Dawson and Prewitt, *Political Socialization,* 127–142.
18. Maxwell McCombs and Donald Shaw, "The Agenda-Setting Function of the Mass Media," *Public Opinion Quarterly* 36 (Summer 1972): 176–187.
19. Dwaine Marvick, "The Political Socialization of the American Negro," in Dawson and Prewitt, *Political Socialization,* 151–177.
20. Greenstein (1970), ibid., 59.
21. The term "baby boomers" applies to the generation born during the years 1945–1965, the older members of which came of age during the Vietnam War. See M. Kent Jennings and Richard G. Neimi, *Generational Politics* (Princeton, NJ: Princeton University Press, 1982).
22. Sidney Verba and Norman Nye, *Participation in America: Political Democracy and Social Equality* (New York: Harper and Row Publishers, 1972), 125–137.
23. Material discussed here may be found in greater detail in "Introduction to Federal Voting Rights Laws," United States Department of Justice, Civil Rights Division, Voting section website. To learn more, go to http://www.usdoj.gov/crt/voting/intro/intro_a.htm.
24. *Guinn v. United States,* 238 US 347 (1915).
25. *Smith v. Allwright,* 321 US 649 (1944).
26. Verba and Nye, op. cit., 125–173 and 334–343.
27. Kay Lehman Scholzman and Sidney Verba, *Injury to Insult: Unemployment, Class, and Political Response* (Cambridge, MA: Harvard University Press, 1979).
28. Nina Eliasoph, *Avoiding Politics: How Americans Produce Apathy in Everyday Life* (New York: Cambridge University Press, 1998).
29. You can find registration deadlines for your state from the electionline.org website, at http://www.electionline.org/site/docs/html/voter_registration_deadlines.htm.
30. The NES Guide to Public Opinion and Election Behavior, which may be accessed at http://www.umich.edu/~nes/nesguide/toptable/tab2a_1.htm. Figures do not sum to 100 percent because of rounding error.
31. Or maybe because you like fish?

32. Angus Campbell, Philip E. Converse, Warren E. Miller, and Donald E. Stokes, *The American Voter* (New York: John Wiley and Sons, 1960), 168–187.

33. Paul R. Abramson, John H. Aldrich, and David W. Rhode, *Change and Continuity in the 1996 and 1998 Elections* (Washington, D.C.: Congressional Quarterly Press, 1999).

34. Morris P. Fiorina, *Retrospective Voting in American National Elections* (New Haven: Yale University Press, 1988).

35. Elisabeth Noelle-Neumann, *The Spiral of Silence* (Chicago: University of Chicago Press, 1984).

36. Michael J. Robinson, "Public Affairs Television and the Growth of Public Malaise: The Case of the Selling of the Pentagon," *American Political Science Review* 70 (June 1976): 409–432.

Mass Media:
Influencing What We Think About

5-1 Gatekeeping

"World Exclusive!"

"Sunday December 17, 2000. Bill Clinton TV Show Pitched; Post-Presidency Plans Take Shape."[1]

One month before leaving the White House, it was widely reported in the press that one of Bill Clinton's postpresidency options would be to host a television talk show on NBC. The story with the previous headline stated that producer friends of the soon-to-be ex-president had approached NBC to pitch the idea of a *Bill Clinton Show.*

There was only one problem with the story.

It wasn't exactly accurate.

Yes, there had been a discussion about a possible Clinton talk show at NBC, except the president hadn't gone hat in hand, knocking on the network's door, like the story implied. It turns out it was the network's idea, the brainchild of an NBC executive from Clinton's native Arkansas. Although a discussion had taken place, it was far from the formal "pitch" that producers make when they're trying to get a network interested in a show. The real facts of the story make Bill Clinton appear something of a bystander to the whole thing, rather than a publicity hog unwilling to give up the television spotlight after his turn as president came to an end.

Before the story could be publicly challenged, it had been picked up by newswire services that are used by many local newspapers and television stations, and had run in one large daily paper, *New York Newsday.* Their source: an Internet site known for its mix of news and gossip, "The Drudge Report," operated by a man named Matt Drudge—someone with no formal training as a reporter whose journalistic credentials stem from the fact that he has a web address.[2] Because anybody—including you and me—can post information on the web without having to apply standards of accuracy, it can be difficult to know how much of what we're reading is true. The problem is compounded when information on the web becomes the basis for information in mainstream newspapers, where accuracy is supposed to be beyond question.

How could this happen? How could information from cyberspace end up supporting a story at organizations where they're supposed to check their facts? Welcome to the twenty-first century world of news and information.

> ### Box 5-1 Just Passing Through

The word *media* is the plural form of the word *medium,* which is defined as an element through which something passes. In the spiritual world, a medium is the person at a séance who claims to be able to receive and relay messages from the dead to the living. In the world of communication, a medium is a tangible element like a newspaper, television, radio, computer, book, movie, CD, or DVD—anything that can transmit information, which is the thing that passes through the medium.

The media in the previous list would all be considered mass media because they're capable of passing information to large numbers of people. In contrast, hand-printed newspapers or books of which only a few copies were produced would still be media, but not in a mass sense. It's easy to associate mass media with technology because technological innovations from mass production of newspapers, to radio and television, cable, and the Internet have profoundly enhanced the reach of contemporary media. For this reason, our "information age," as it is sometimes called, could accurately be termed an age of mass media.

We tend to use the words *media* and *press* interchangeably—you'll even see a little of that in this chapter—but they're really different. *Press* evokes journalism, or the process by which information is gathered, whereas *media* evokes the methods of communicating the information journalists gather. There can also be a normative difference between the terms, with *press* suggesting the careful gathering of factual information, and *media* implying something faster, flashier, and perhaps more slipshod. "I'm a journalist" can have a more substantive ring than "I'm with the media."

In an ideal world, if you were inclined to participate in the political process, you'd be able to get all the information you need to make intelligent political decisions from the wide variety of **mass media** at your disposal: newspapers, television, radio, magazines, and the Internet (see Box 5-1). What you'd learn from these information sources would be clear and valid, believable, and easy to understand. Facts would be neatly distinguished from opinion, they would be accurate, and there would be no rumors or half-truths. You'd wade your way through this information until you learned what you needed or wanted to know. Your information environment would offer you both clarity of content and diversity of ideas.

The mass media of your parent's generation offered more clarity than the mass media of our time, but in its own way, it was also far from ideal. In that world, only a small number of people—newspaper editors, television news producers, select prestigious journalists, and evening news anchors—were the decision makers or **"gatekeepers"** of news content, making the choices about what to cover and what not to cover. Even today, the same small number of highly influential editors and producers make decisions about news content for the traditional media, like newspapers and television news programs.

The choices they made in that earlier time tended to be stable and consistent, which has its advantages and disadvantages. On the plus side, the stable choices of traditional gatekeepers offered a clear view of key political officials and candidates, which could be pretty helpful in evaluating their performance, deciding how to vote (retrospectively or on issues), and figuring out exactly what Congress, the president, the courts, and state and local officials were up to. You might even say that this kind of linkage between people and their political leaders could be a valuable political resource because the media are a major source of political information, which we know can be critical to informed political involvement.

But there is a price to be paid for this stability. Because gatekeepers traditionally made predictable story choices, typically favoring recurring news themes and relying on the same set of official sources, there were limits on the range of ideas available to think about.[3] The information may have been clear, but it was limited in scope. What was gained in clarity was lost in diversity.

Today, the media environment is hardly limited, but it is murky. It's like a noisy bazaar, where literally hundreds of media outlets are clamoring for a few seconds of your attention. Anyone with a web address can be a gatekeeper. Nonstop cable news demands interesting around-the-clock content. How can you be sure that they're giving you reliable

> **mass media** Vehicles, such as television, radio, newspapers, magazines, and the Internet, capable of rapidly communicating information to large numbers of people over large distances. Note that *media* is the plural form of *medium:* Television *is* a *medium,* whereas television and the Internet *are media.*

> **gatekeepers** Television producers, newspaper editors, and prestigious reporters and anchors who make the decisions about what stories will be published or aired. Think of the imagery of a guard who decides who will be allowed to pass through a gate. In this case, news gatekeepers determine which information will be allowed to pass through the medium.

information? Which media outlets are exaggerating the truth, or trading in rumor and innuendo? How can we be intelligent news consumers and reasonably informed citizens when we can't easily answer these questions? This is what we'll be talking about as we go through Chapter 5.

Political theorist Robert Dahl points to two criteria for effective democratic processes that can guide us as we attempt to figure out how well we're served by the media. They are "effective participation" and "enlightened understanding." The first of these entails assuring that we have an equal and effective opportunity to participate in political decision-making (which is already complicated, as we saw in Chapter 4, by unequal patterns of participation resulting from the unequal distribution of resources). Enlightened understanding makes effective participation possible in that, unless we have a way to understand the terms of political debate, we won't be able to arrive at sensible decisions. In other words, in order to have a flourishing democracy, we have to have access to good information. Suppress critical information, and people may well make different—and inferior—decisions.[4]

As we examine the role of the media in the political process, we'll keep returning to the question of how well they promote—or how much they discourage—effective participation and enlightened understanding. First, we'll look back on the media through history to see how they have evolved from being a limited factor in early politics to a major player today. Then, we'll try to figure out exactly what counts as news at the turn of the millennium and talk a little about how *privately* owned newspapers and television stations and the like came to play such an important role in *public* life.

We'll try to figure out how we can differentiate information from entertainment, both in coverage of elections and news coverage of people in office, while exploring the paradox that an ever-expanding menu of media choices has developed alongside an ever-diminishing pool of media owners. Finally, we'll examine the effect the mass media can have on the public beyond setting the political agenda and raise the question of whether there is bias in coverage. When we're done, we may or may not be better positioned to draw on the mass media for useful information about politics and government, but we should have a better idea of how to approach news coverage.

5-2 Political History of the Media—From Colonial Press to Global Media

The United States is a media-saturated nation where sources of information too numerous to count are available through the click of a mouse or television remote control. It certainly didn't start out that way. In colonial America, there wasn't much of a press, and what there was didn't concentrate much on political issues until just before the Revolutionary War. The colonial press needed government approval to operate, and under British law, any publisher who circulated material that criticized the government was subject to prosecution for seditious libel. So, newspaper publishers tended to avoid hot-button political issues, and the British authorities more or less left them alone.[5]

▶ **Stamp Act** A particularly vexing tax levied by the British on scores of legal documents, which led to a colonial boycott of British goods.

Then came the **Stamp Act,** which you may recall from Chapter 2 placed a tax on newspapers. With their interests at stake, publishers used their newspapers to defy the Stamp Act, in the process transforming newspapers into vehicles for arousing public opinion. Newspapers sympathetic to the revolutionary cause played an important role in setting the agenda for the war by recounting stories of British corruption and war atrocities, and of the colonists' military resistance.[6]

▶ **party press** Newspapers functioning as an arm of a political party, communicating information about partisan politics from party leaders to their supporters. Newspapers functioned in this capacity from the inception of political parties in America around 1790 through the 1830s.

The emergence of political parties following the Revolutionary War ushered in the era of the **party press.** From about 1790 through the 1830s, newspapers became an important vehicle for reaching and "educating" the party faithful in order to advance the political objectives of party leaders. No longer apolitical, the press had become a mouthpiece for the views of party leaders, which meant that newspapers also weren't objective. However, press objectivity wasn't highly valued in the early nineteenth century, and it wasn't important to the survival of newspapers, which had a built-in readership from party faithful, who loved partisan rhetoric.[7]

Newspapers of this time were expensive, costing upwards of six cents. Most people couldn't afford the price, but most people couldn't vote—or read. So, party newspapers were limited in circulation and purchased by a small, loyal following. As the 1830s approached and voting rights were extended to men who didn't own property, political parties became larger, mass political activity emerged, and newspapers became an important link between party leaders and their growing legions of loyalists.

Major technological changes were taking place at this time as well, lowering printing costs and creating new markets for manufactured goods that had to be advertised. The **penny press** emerged in response to these conditions. Starting in the early 1830s, publishers found they could sell newspapers to readers for a penny if they also sold advertising to manufacturers interested in alerting emerging mass markets about their products.[8] The marriage of publisher and advertiser had begun.

Not coincidently, so had the marriage of media and entertainment. In order to bolster advertising revenues, penny newspapers required large circulation figures, just like today's newspapers. The best way to sell papers to a large number of readers was to emphasize sensational stories and tell them in lurid detail—just like today. In 1835, the *New York Herald* ran a series of stories telling in graphic detail of the ax murder of a prostitute, and circulation figures soared. If this sounds like something from today's local television news programs, it's because stories about sex and violence have always commanded an audience.

The penny press did not put the party press out of business, and partisan publications continued to survive even as they were pushed aside by mass publications. But the necessity of reaching a large audience argued against outright partisanship in coverage. Publishers who wished to have their political views represented began relegating them to the editorial page. Also, while many penny publications focused on fires and murders, the penny press provided a forum for the emergence of the journalism of ideas. Horace Greeley, a well-known political activist and writer in the mid-nineteenth century, published the *New York Tribune* as an intelligent alternative to sensational journalism. A number of reputable journalists of that era found their start under his tutelage; he even hired Karl Marx as a foreign correspondent.

The period that followed witnessed the emergence of newspapers as big businesses. The immigrant influx at the turn of the twentieth century created new markets for newspapers, which began to increase in value. Trends in newspaper ownership anticipated the corporate mergers which, as we will shortly learn, are characteristic of our era, with declining competition, owners buying newspapers in multiple cities to form chains, and businessmen buying existing papers to get into the newspaper business. Publishers like William Randolph Hearst and Joseph Pulitzer engaged in ferocious competition with each other, while amassing enormous fortunes and great power. In this competitive climate, much like today, newspapers began to figuratively scream for attention, offering sensational human-interest stories about crime and sex, large headlines, photographs, and comic strips set off with yellow ink—hence the term **"yellow journalism."**[9]

The age of yellow journalism also ushered in a period of reporting on corporate abuses and political corruption, subjects with great appeal to members of the lower classes. Dubbed **"muckraking,"** this investigative reporting was the engine behind an era of progressive reforms, which included child labor laws, food inspection, and land conservation.

As newspapers became big business, journalism became a profession. Schools of journalism began to appear on college campuses, and journalists enjoyed a high level of prestige. As yellow journalism diminished after World War I, professional journalists ushered in a period of objectivity, which placed a premium on detached, balanced reporting. The ideal story presented a compilation of facts without a theme, as reporters saw themselves as purveyors of details rather than as storytellers. This continued until competition from television pushed the pendulum back to thematic story telling in the 1970s.

Of course, the twentieth century was also the time when mass communication emerged in its numerous forms, including telephones, movies, radios, and eventually television. The rise of radio as a national medium in the 1930s began a transformational period in which emerging media networks integrated the nation. The NBC radio network premiered in 1926, CBS in 1927, and by the 1940s, better than 60 percent of radio stations

▶ **penny press** High-circulation newspapers, emerging after 1830, that kept costs down by selling advertising. These newspapers brought in large numbers of readers with lurid and sensational reporting.

In the competition between Hearst's *New York Journal* and Pulitzer's *New York World,* the publishers tried to arouse public opinion to ignite a war with Spain. Pictured is the sensational way the *World* covered Admiral Dewey's victory at the Battle of Manila during the Spanish-American War.

▶ **yellow journalism** The term given to the sensational newspaper coverage prevalent during the turn of the twentieth century, noteworthy for its emphasis on violence, sex, human-interest stories, and exposés of official corruption.

▶ **muckraking** Investigative reporting prevalent during the turn of the twentieth century, which centered on uncovering corruption in government and industry for the purpose of promoting progressive reforms.

Figure 5-1
The Power of the Mass Media: Uniting—at Times Scaring—a Nation
Source: War of the Worlds broadcast clips courtesy of Earthstation1.com.

"Ladies and gentlemen, this is the most terrifying thing I have ever witnessed. Wait a minute. Someone or something I can see is turning out of that black hole through luminous disks—the eyes, it might be a face. Good heavens, something's wriggling out of the shadow like a gray snake. Now it's another one, and another one and another one. They look like tentacles to me. There, I can see the thing's body now. It's large as a bear and it glistens like wet leather. But that face. It—it's, ladies and gentlemen, it's indescribable. I can hardly force myself to keep looking at it, it's so awful. The eyes are black and they gleam like a serpent. The mouth is kind of V-shaped with saliva dripping from its rimless lips that seem to quiver and pulsate. The monster or whatever it is can hardly move. It seems weighed down by possibly gravity or something. The thing is rising up now and the crowd falls back. They've seen plenty. This is the most extraordinary experience, ladies and gentlemen. I can't find words. I'll pull this microphone with me as I talk. I'll have to stop the description so I can take a new position. Hold on, will you please, I'll be back in a minute."

were network affiliates.[10] With them came the first evidence of what we now take for granted: When electronic media become a routine part of life, they have the power to connect and move an entire society.

Even though newspapers had long reached large audiences, before radio there was nothing close to what we now call mass media. On October 30, 1938, Americans learned how profoundly and how immediately people could be touched by mass media. The forum was a radio adaptation of H.G. Wells' science-fiction story "The War of the Worlds," about a Martian invasion of earth. It was presented as a Halloween show by the gifted young director Orson Welles (no relation), who decided to tell the story as a real-time "newscast," with announcers appearing to break into regular programming with bulletins describing a supposed Martian invasion transpiring in New Jersey (that's right, New Jersey). There was a disclaimer at the start of the show that everything you were about to hear was a dramatization, but not everyone heard it. Imagine how you would react if you turned on your radio that night and heard the urgent report in Figure 5-1, believing it was real.

People panicked. They ran, hid in basements, or covered their noses to protect themselves from Martian poison gas. Believing the realistic reports of a Martian invasion were in fact *real* reports of a Martian invasion, they moved quickly to defend themselves from what they believed was a dangerous and imminent threat. It wasn't until later that people learned—through *real* radio news reports about the panic—that the invasion was just part of a radio play. And it wasn't until much later that people realized they had lived through an accidental demonstration of something we now experience every day: the power of the mass media to dramatically influence massive numbers of people.

Although television entered the scene in the late 1940s, its potential wasn't felt until the 1950s, when news reporters and political figures began to recognize how profoundly the visual medium could stir public opinion. For the next three decades, television news dominated the media landscape, filling our homes with images of political events like civil rights violence, urban riots, political assassination, war, and scandal, while changing the way candidates run for and act in office. Television remains a potent but altered force today, thanks to the emergence of satellite and cable technology, which gave birth to multiple channels and around-the-clock programming. Of course, television now shares the media spotlight with the Internet, whose full potency as a political tool remains to be discovered.

Both the Vietnam War and the Watergate scandal initially aroused interest in investigative reporting. Then, after many years of official government sources lying to journalists as a matter of policy, investigative reporting gave way to a kind of aggressive journalism that redefined the relationship between reporters and officials and lent a negative cast to political coverage that's still with us today. Add to this the swirl of new technology and an increasingly competitive media marketplace, and you have an information environment that resembles the yellow journalism period of one hundred years ago, only faster-paced and all-encompassing.

We'll examine how to make sense of news reporting in this environment, sort out the way reporters and officials interact, and clarify what coverage of politics and government looks like, and why. Before we do, let's take a few minutes to check out the timeline in Table 5-1 that illustrates the evolution of the press by detailing key moments in American media.

5-3 How Do We Know If It's News?

The printed word makes things seem so—authentic. So does the smooth, baritone voice of a news anchor. Of course, we know that we should never believe everything we read or hear, but how can we know *which* media reports to accept, reject, or question?

Take a look at the four news stories in Table 5-2 on page 129, which come from a variety of mass media. Read them, and for each one, try to determine if it is truthful, deceptive, irrelevant—or flat-out false.

It should be easy to see how even a careful reader can be misled. The first story addresses a major problem with the Internet—that anyone can be a journalist, editor, and publisher. If you missed this one, don't feel bad, because you're in good company. Former presidential press secretary and ABC News foreign correspondent Pierre Salinger made international headlines when he claimed to have a government document stating that the 1996 crash of TWA Flight 800 was caused by a missile fired by the U.S. military. In fact, Salinger was the victim of an Internet hoax; his document turned out to be identical to a fake one that had been floating around the web.[11]

The third and fourth stories raise questions about how mainstream journalism approaches news events. News Story 3 poses disquieting questions about air travel based on the *possibility* that something *could* happen. News Story 4 uses facts deceptively, to get us to fear car theft at a time when car thefts are declining. Both confuse more than they illuminate, raising concerns in order to get our attention.

A big part of the problem of navigating the information environment is that the traditional rules for what constitutes news have changed. A journalist working for a newspaper in the mid-twentieth century would have approached news coverage from a factual standpoint, ferreting out a series of answers to questions about what happened, when it happened, where it happened, and who was involved. He or she then would have attempted to evaluate the significance of these facts and report them in **inverted pyramid** fashion, so named because the most salient facts would be reported at the top of a story, with smaller, less critical facts noted in subsequent paragraphs. You could read the first few paragraphs and be fairly well informed, and if you were interested, you could read more and fill in smaller details. After you read the first paragraph, though, you could stop at any time and be fairly certain that you had covered the most critical factual material.

> **inverted pyramid** A style of reporting typical of twentieth-century newspaper coverage, in which stories were constructed with the most important factual material in the first paragraph, followed by successively less important facts.

Many (though far from all) newspaper stories are still written in the inverted pyramid style. Figure 5-2 on page 130 shows an example from the *Washington Post*.[12] Notice how the journalist puts the most important "who," "what," "where," and "when" facts in the first paragraph. Subsequent paragraphs fill in the story with secondary facts.

Television news and some print journalism do it differently. Television news reports tell a *story* in the classic sense of the word. They have a beginning, middle, and end, and a theme to tie them together. Because television news is thematic, it has to be about something more than the basic who, what, when, and where facts of the inverted pyramid story. Typically, "why" questions cement television news stories together. That's because why questions are analytical in nature; they permit the reporter to probe the subject, offering a hypothesis or a theory about what's happening in the news. When this happens, the reporter's perspective becomes inseparable from the facts of the story.

This makes things tricky for us because we're probably not aware of the fact that we're being shown information that's being filtered through a prism of the reporter's choosing. When you watch the ABC News version of the terror story that's transcribed in Box 5-2 on page 131, it's natural to wonder whether the president or the FBI acted irresponsibly because the reporter leads you to that question. If you find yourself asking the same question after reading the *Washington Post* version of the story in Figure 5-2, it would be because you had formulated it yourself.

T A B L E 5-1	Three Hundred Years of Media Development

Colonial Press (1700–1790)

1704	The weekly *Boston Newsletter* debuts as the first continuously published newspaper in the American colonies. It depended on foreign newspapers for much of its news content, even though those papers were months out of date.
1784	The *Pennsylvania Packet and Daily Advertiser* becomes the young nation's first daily newspaper.

Party Press (1790–1830)

1789	John Fenno publishes the *Gazette of the United States,* which becomes the first Federalist party newspaper, frequently featuring the writing of Alexander Hamilton.
1791	James Madison and Thomas Jefferson persuade writer Philip Freneau to establish the first Republican (anti-Federalist) party newspaper, the *National Gazette.*

Penny Press (1830–1880)

1833	Benjamin Day publishes the *New York Sun* for the remarkably low sum of one cent, using advertising revenue to make up the balance of his costs.
1841	Horace Greeley establishes the *New York Tribune* as an intelligent alternative among penny newspapers.

Yellow Journalism (1880–1920)

1883	Joseph Pulitzer acquires the *New York World,* dramatically increasing its circulation with sensational coverage and crusading journalism that appealed to immigrant readers.
1895	William Randolph Hearst purchases the *New York Journal* and enters into fierce competition with Pulitzer as the period of "yellow journalism" reaches its peak.

Emerging Mass Media (1920–1950)

1920	KDKA/Pittsburgh becomes America's first commercial radio station and the first radio station to report the results of a presidential election. (In case you missed the broadcast, Harding defeated Cox.)
1926	NBC radio begins operation as two networks: the Red Network and the Blue Network (which eventually became ABC). CBS radio followed one year later.
1947	The first regularly scheduled television newscast appears on NBC. The *Camel News Caravan,* sponsored by Camel cigarettes, featured an announcer at a desk and a cigarette constantly burning in an ashtray.

Age of Television (1950–1980)

1954	Broadcaster Edward R. Murrow uses his television program *See It Now* as a platform for exposing the anticommunist crusade of Senator Joseph McCarthy as a hollow smear campaign.
1960	John F. Kennedy and Richard Nixon hold the first televised presidential debate.
1968	CBS anchorman Walter Cronkite goes to Vietnam and reports that the best outcome the United States could expect in the Vietnam War is "stalemate." President Lyndon Johnson interprets Cronkite's commentary as a sign that he has lost the support of mainstream America.
1974	Richard Nixon becomes the first American president to resign from office after his involvement in the Watergate scandal and cover-up is revealed by investigative reporters Bob Woodward and Carl Bernstein and in widely viewed televised congressional hearings.

Age of New Media (1980–present)

1982	Satellite technology makes possible the national publication of *USA Today.*
1991	CNN provides real-time worldwide coverage of the Persian Gulf War.
1996	Internet users top sixty million worldwide, as major daily newspapers begin to maintain websites.
2003	Obscure former Vermont Governor Howard Dean momentarily becomes the front-runner for the Democratic Party's presidential nomination behind an unprecedented Internet fund-raising and organizing effort.

Source: Library of Congress and Richard Davis, *The Press and American Politics: The New Mediator,* 3d ed. (Upper Saddle River, NJ: Prentice Hall, 2001).

News Story 1	TABLE **5-2**

"Top GOP operatives who feel there is a double standard of only reporting Republican shame believe they are holding an ace card: New [Clinton]White House recruit Sidney Blumenthal has a spousal abuse past that has been effectively covered up. 'There are court records of Blumenthal's violence against his wife,' [said] one influential Republican, who demanded anonymity."*

Truthful, Deceptive, Irrelevant—or False?

- Truthful
- Irrelevant
- Deceptive
- False

News Story 2

"Pakistan was preparing to possibly fire nuclear weapons during a 1999 border conflict with India, moving the countries closer to nuclear war than was commonly known at the time, according to a new article by President Bill Clinton's chief White House advisor on South Asia. U.S. intelligence had developed 'disturbing evidence that the Pakistanis were preparing their nuclear arsenals for possible deployment.'"†

- Truthful
- Irrelevant
- Deceptive
- False

News Story 3

"It's been compared to potholes in the sky. Turbulence is often nothing more than a minor bump in flight, but there are some times when it can take you on a roller-coaster ride at thirty thousand feet. Veteran flyers insist that it's nothing to be afraid of because planes are designed to take that kind of punishment. But that's little comfort when you're being tossed around in the cabin in a pocket of terrifying turbulence."‡

- Truthful
- Irrelevant
- Deceptive
- False

News Story 4

"Car theft remains America's most expensive property crime, one every twenty-three seconds, adding up to almost one-and-a-half million stolen cars a year. And while that number is down over the past decade, police actually recover fewer cars now. One-third of them are never found."§

- Truthful
- Irrelevant
- Deceptive
- False

Answers

News Story 1, from the aforementioned Drudge Report, was based on an anonymous source. It was false. Drudge retracted it the next day, but it was the basis of a lawsuit by Blumenthal against Drudge.**

News Story 2 is factual, even though it may seem incredible. The conflict in question was over the disputed Kashmir territory.

News Story 3 is a real story—about nothing. It's about something that may happen but didn't actually happen. And if something may happen, it also may not.

News Story 4 is a deceptive story about a nonevent. Car theft was and is still America's number one property crime—there's nothing new there. And car theft has declined over a ten-year period, even though this story makes it *seem* as if it's gone up by creating the sense that there's an urgent problem. Wrap the same statistics in different words, and you'll see that two-thirds of a smaller number of stolen vehicles are returned to their owners.

*The Drudge Report, August 11, 1997. See http://drudgereport.com/.

†*Washington Post,* May 15, 2002.

‡WXYZ-TV Detroit, February 26, 1997, cited in Matthew R. Kerbel, *If It Bleeds, It Leads: An Anatomy of Television News* (Boulder, CO: Westview Press, 2000), 36–37.

§*NBC Nightly News,* June 15, 1999, cited in Kerbel, *If It Bleeds,* 108.

**A summary of the lawsuit may be found at http://www.techlawjournal.com/courts/drudge/Default.htm.

Figure 5-2
Just the Facts

Source: © 2002, The Washington Post, reprinted with permission.

Paragraph 1
President Bush and his top advisers **were informed** by the CIA **early last August** that terrorists associated with Osama bin Laden had discussed **the possibility of hijacking airplanes,** according to reliable sources.

Paragraph 2
The information, given to Bush as part of **his daily intelligence report,** lacked **specific details about how the terrorist plans would be carried out,** the sources said. The White House said last night that law enforcement agencies were **quietly placed on alert as a result of the intelligence.**

Paragraph 9
The information provided to Bush was included as part of the president's **daily briefing, a highly restricted classified document** prepared by the CIA. **The document** is seen by only a handful of people, White House officials said: **Bush, Vice President Cheney, CIA Director George J. Tenet, National Security Adviser Condoleezza Rice and, less frequently, Chief of Staff Andrew H. Card Jr.**

What ■   When ■   Who ■

▶**newsworthy** The conditions under which a story warrants publication or dissemination, based on a set of values applied by newspaper editors and television producers. Newsworthy stories typically have conflict, proximity and relevance to the audience, timeliness, and familiarity.

Television reporters don't have to reach far from traditional ways of doing business to find the themes for their reports. Journalists have long used a set of standards to determine if a story is **newsworthy**—that is, if it has enough news value to be published or broadcast. Media scholar Doris A. Graber says newsworthy stories typically exhibit a mix of the following five characteristics:

1. *Conflict:* Natural or man-made disasters, scandals, or accidents hold the interest of news audiences.
2. *Proximity:* People are more likely to be interested in things that happen close to home or that can affect their lives.
3. *Timeliness and originality:* News should have happened recently, and it should involve something that doesn't happen every day.
4. *Relevance:* We like stories that have some relationship to our lives, that have an impact on our lives, or that we can identify with. This is why a small earthquake in the United States would receive more news coverage than a devastating earthquake in China.
5. *Familiarity:* We are drawn to familiar situations and people, which can extend to celebrities and public figures that we "know" through the media.[13]

If you think about it, these characteristics are likely to make news stories appeal to readers and viewers more than they are likely to reflect a story's political, social, or educational value.[14] What makes a story newsworthy, then, does not always stem from normative judgments by journalists and their editors and producers about what information the audience should have. It is not uncommon for news stories to be selected for their audience appeal rather than for their ability to keep us informed about important political and social events. Although it is possible to capture our attention and inform us at the same time, not every informative story contains conflict or feels like it's close to home. So, a story about, say, congressional deliberation over farm subsidy legislation probably wouldn't have the staying power to compete for airtime with a good scandal or a shooting spree.

The stories that do make it on television use conflict to support reporter analyses of political figures and events that are often negative and cynical. After all, that's what's going to draw our interest. It's a far more interesting story if President Bush had advance warning that a terrorist attack was brewing than if he did not. Public figures acting irresponsibly are always more fun to read about than those that behave. So, if the facts can be used to suggest that a politician behaved poorly, television news will naturally gravitate to this perspective.

5-4 Infotainment and Its Implications

If this sounds to you like the news media are in the business of entertaining us, you're right on target. At the same time, the news media are charged with the vital civic responsibility

Box 5-2　The Facts—and a Lot More

Here are key paragraphs from the ABC News version of the story you just read in Figure 5-2 about how President Bush had some early knowledge of a pending terrorist attack.* Although this version also tells you a bit about who was involved and what they did, it has an overarching theme that was absent in the print version, namely, *why* did September 11 happen if there was any official suspicion that terrorists might strike the United States? The reporter explores the hypothesis that the president or the FBI could or should have done more.

Paragraph 1

U.S. intelligence told President Bush before the attacks on September 11 that Osama bin Laden's terrorist network might try to hijack American airplanes. But White House officials say the president and his advisors had no way of knowing the precise details of how the planes would be used.

Paragraph 4

The report about the president's knowledge comes on the heels of fresh criticism of the FBI, for failing to piece together various bits of information that might have suggested terrorists were planning an attack using commercial airlines.

Paragraph 6

FBI Director Robert Mueller admits that when it comes to intelligence gathering, his agency needs an overhaul.

*ABC World News Tonight, May 15, 2002, Bill Ritter reporting.

---

of keeping us informed so that we can make intelligent decisions about what government does. These responsibilities can easily conflict, often to the detriment of our ability to have the information we need to understand political events.

Because newspapers, television and cable stations, and many Internet sites are privately owned, they strive to maximize their profits. If they don't make money, they don't last long. They make money by attracting advertisers, who in turn seek large or targeted audiences for their products. Large audiences, in turn, are drawn to interesting, entertaining, and dramatic stories.

When public events naturally generate drama—such as following the 2000 presidential election standoff or the September 11 terror attacks—the media's need to attract us coincides with their responsibility to inform us. Often, the two do not overlap, though, leading to a problematic outcome: The ever-present pressure to make a profit encourages the media to emphasize dramatic stories that arguably are not central to our civic lives, while downplaying or ignoring dull but important political and policy issues. Whether basketball star Kobe Bryant is guilty of rape is an important matter *for the parties involved,* whereas Federal Reserve Board decisions on interest rates directly affect the size of your credit card payments and the possibility that you will be able to afford to buy a home. When the media give us a lot of news about the former and precious little about the latter, we risk becoming entertained spectators without the information we need to make intelligent public choices.

5-4a　Distinguishing News from Entertainment

Often, it's hard to draw the line between information and entertainment. Many people in their late teens and early twenties get their news from MTV, which you probably know is an entertainment network that mixes political and social issues with a heavy dose of music, celebrity news, and reality programming.

On other networks, news programs can be so sensational—or sensational programs can look so much like news programs—that it's hard to tell where information stops and entertainment begins. Some media critics use the term **infotainment** to describe this phenomenon, which captures the entertainment value of information and the blending of news and entertainment programs. Take a program like *Entertainment Tonight*, with its reporters and stories that resemble the evening news. At times, like during the Monica Lewinsky scandal in the Clinton administration, it even covered some of the same stories as the evening news. Does that make *Entertainment Tonight* a news program? Not in the traditional sense, but it is infotainment.

> **infotainment** News reports and information-based programs that use information to entertain by playing on sensational topics, such as celebrities, violence, and the like.

Box 5-3 How Circulation Figures and Ratings Work

It's fairly easy to determine how many people read a daily newspaper because publishers adjust the number of copies they print to meet the demand for their product. This is captured in circulation figures, which will vary by the popularity of the paper and by the size of the metropolitan area (commonly called a market) served by the newspaper.

For instance, for the six months ending in September 1998, the circulation of the Denver *Rocky Mountain News* for a weekday edition averaged 332,000. The *Knoxville News-Sentinel* (Tennessee), serving a smaller community, had an average daily circulation of 122,000 over the same period.[*] The circulation of the Denver paper is slightly less than three times the circulation of the Knoxville daily. But that's consistent with the population difference between the two cities. In 1998, Denver had 1.9 million people, or slightly less than three times Knoxville's 666,000.[†]

Television ratings are a bit more complicated to determine. An organization called Nielson Media Research estimates how many people are watching television and what they are watching at any given time, using statistical techniques similar to those we discussed in Chapter 3 when we looked at how pollsters could assess public opinion by only talking to a small but carefully selected random sample of people.[‡]

The two most important figures for advertisers—and, therefore, for everyone associated with a television production—are the ratings and share figures. Ratings measure the percentage of households with a television that have the television turned on to a program. The share is the percentage of that group with the television on that is tuned in to a particular program. A program with a large share of a large audience can command higher advertising rates, just like a paper with healthy circulation figures. Of course, programs that cannot maintain a large enough audience to cover their production costs and turn a profit come under careful scrutiny by media ownership. This includes news and information programs.

[*]The E.W. Scripps Company 1998 annual report, which may be accessed at http://www.scripps.com/annrpt/98/scripps/newspaper_info.shtml. The Scripps Company owns both newspapers.

[†]U.S. Census Bureau Metropolitan Area Population Estimates, July 1998.

[‡]If you'd like to learn more about how television ratings are calculated and what they mean, you can go to the Nielson Media Research website at http://www.nielsenmedia.com. Click on "Nielson Top 10 TV Ratings" in the upper right corner, and then select "Ratings 101" from the "See Also" box at the right.

---

soft news Feature stories, stories about celebrities, and other news items that do not derive their news value from proximity, timeliness, or relevance to the reader or viewer.

hard news Traditional news items that derive their value from recent, relevant events that have some bearing on the lives of readers or viewers.

Traditional journalists would probably explain infotainment by saying that it resides in the realm of **soft news,** which shares some of the values of newsworthiness with **hard news,** but without the requirements of proximity, timeliness, or even relevance. Soft news stories are sometimes called feature stories because they're about things that could have happened at any time, without specific connections to the recent events that serve as the basis for hard news, like the type of story you'd find on *Entertainment Tonight.* You could classify the airplane turbulence and car theft stories we read about earlier as soft news (and these ran on evening newscasts). So, it really is hard to make the distinction between news programs that entertain and entertainment programs built around information.

5-4b The Profit Motive

Because entertaining stories provide the media with the most expedient way to build the audience they need to attract advertisers, they can be an irresistible source of news content. Newspapers and television networks make money from advertising in a manner that links advertising dollars to audience size. You may have heard about television ratings, which measure the size of the audience for television programs. Circulation figures do the same for newspapers and are the key to profitability. Box 5-3 explains ratings and circulation figures.

Ratings and circulation figures are a central part of our discussion of the media because the vast majority of news outlets in the United States are privately owned, for-profit ventures. The United States is unusual in this respect. Newspapers in many Western democracies are run by or maintain strong links to political parties (the way the American press operated in its early days) and receive government subsidies or tax breaks to offset their costs. Governments of all other industrialized democracies, such as Great Britain, Japan, Canada, Italy, France, and Germany, exercise some form of ownership over broadcast media. This translates into all or a portion of operating revenue coming from public money rather than advertising dollars and coincides with government regulations that

> ### Box 5-4   Libel: One Win, One Loss

I f you've never read the *National Enquirer,* you've probably seen it at a grocery store checkout stand, and you may well know it by reputation. Even though its feature stories include such journalistic gems as "Bad-Girl Britney Goes Dirty Dancing" and "Cher Bushwhacked by Oprah,"* it publishes under the same laws and restrictions as mainstream newspapers.

In the mid-1970s, the *National Enquirer* ran a story about a loud, public fight that comedienne Carol Burnett allegedly had at a Washington restaurant with former Secretary of State Henry Kissinger. The fight never happened, and Burnett sued for libel, claiming the *National Enquirer* was selling papers and making money at the expense of her good name. A jury agreed, awarding Burnett $1.2 million, an amount later reduced to $200,000 by an appeals court.

Not every jury is as sympathetic, and not every libel case as straightforward as Burnett's. In 1982, CBS News ran a pro-

gram that accused General William Westmoreland of misleading public officials about American progress during the Vietnam War. Westmoreland sued the network for $120 million, but settled out of court when he was unable to prove that CBS had acted out of malice.†

The high standards for proving libel in court deter public figures from filing suit every time their name is mentioned in an outrageous story and give publications like the *National Enquirer* the license they need to operate on (or beyond) the boundaries of truth.

---

*The National Enquirer, May 19, 2002.

†Steven Pressman, "Libel Law in the United States," in *An Unfettered Press,* ed. Hedley Burrell (United States Information Agency, 1994).

---

range from requiring mandatory coverage of Parliament sessions, to free air time for candidates, to requirements that political programming demonstrate balance and facilitate democratic debate.[15]

The closest the United States comes to taxpayer-supported media is a public television and radio network, neither of which is entirely public. Both are supported in part by public money and in part by corporate and private contributions. The Corporation for Public Broadcasting (CPB) is a private nonprofit corporation created by Congress in 1967 to serve the public interest through educational, news, public affairs, and cultural programming that might not be found on commercial broadcasts. It supports National Public Radio (NPR) and the Public Broadcasting Service (PBS), which you may recognize if you spent any time as a kid watching Big Bird on *Sesame Street.*

5-4c Media Regulation and Deregulation

Beyond that, the United States is not entirely without regulation of the media, although what regulation exists pertains mostly to electronic media, pales in comparison to what we find in other democracies, and is less than it was a generation ago.

There are **libel** laws that prohibit all media from printing or broadcasting baseless material that could damage someone's reputation or defame their character. But libel is difficult to prove in court, especially because the Supreme Court has said the standard for proving libel requires demonstrating malice by the press.[16] In other words, to demonstrate libel, you have to prove malevolence on the part of the press, not simply incompetence. Box 5-4 discusses libel in more detail.

There is also an independent government agency called the **Federal Communications Commission (FCC),** established by Congress as part of the **Federal Communications Act of 1934,** to make sure the public interest was represented in the emerging radio (and later, television and cable) industry. The point of regulating the airwaves was to use government authority to counterbalance the profit motive and to make sure that private broadcast companies serve the public interest in the way they operate. The FCC has the authority to license radio and television stations, giving it leverage over broadcast outlets to enforce its public interest requirements.

The most important of these regulations is Section 315 of the Federal Communications Act, known as the **equal time provision.** In order to make sure a full range of political views receive just treatment, the equal time provision directs broadcast outlets to make an equal amount of commercial time available to all candidates running for elected office.

> **libel** The legal restriction against the malicious publication of material that knowingly damages an individual's reputation.

> **Federal Communications Commission (FCC)** The federal agency responsible for regulating broadcast communications, including radio, television, wire, satellite, and cable transmissions. The FCC is directed by five commissioners who are appointed by the president and confirmed by the Senate for five-year terms.

> **Federal Communications Act of 1934** The act of Congress that established the Federal Communications Commission (FCC) and the equal time provision.

> **equal time provision** The federal requirement that broadcast outlets selling commercial time to a political candidate must make equal time available to other candidates running for office.

▶**fairness doctrine** The FCC requirement, no longer in force, that electronic media provide a balanced forum for controversial public discourse.

In 1949, the FCC established the **fairness doctrine** to make sure that broadcasters devoted airtime to the discussion of controversial public issues, obligating them to present opposing views. Because anyone can start a magazine or newspaper without government approval, the government posed no obstacles to those who wanted to establish a print forum for their ideas (the fact that not everyone has the resources to publish a magazine or newspaper is another matter). However, since you need government licensing to run a radio or television station, the fairness doctrine was designed to ensure a balanced and vigorous public debate among the relatively few electronic media outlets. Regardless of this rationale, broadcasters opposed the fairness doctrine as a burdensome obligation not required of their print brethren, and in 1987, a sympathetic FCC agreed and revoked the measure.

By 1987, a trend toward media deregulation that had started in the late 1970s was in full swing. In addition to the fairness doctrine, a number of other FCC provisions were eliminated or relaxed, permitting broadcasters greater leeway to operate without government input. These include:

- Eliminating guidelines limiting broadcasters to eighteen minutes of commercials per hour
- Eliminating a rule requiring broadcasters to devote a fixed percentage of time for local, public affairs, and nonentertainment programming
- Lengthening of the term of broadcast licenses to five years for television and seven years for radio, reducing the frequency of government review
- Increasing the number of television and radio stations that could be owned by a single broadcast organization[17]

▶**Telecommunications Act of 1996** Legislation that overhauled the Federal Communications Act of 1934 by deregulating a range of communications technologies in an effort to promote competition in the development and provision of telecommunications services. If your local telephone company now offers long-distance service, or if your cable television provider also offers high-speed Internet access, it's because the opportunity for them to do so was made possible by this law.

In addition, the deregulation trend led to passage of the **Telecommunications Act of 1996,** the first major revision of telecommunication law since the FCC was founded. The purpose of the legislation was to foster competition in the emerging electronic marketplace of cable, satellite, and Internet communications by removing government barriers to ownership.

Overall, deregulation provides owners of electronic media with greater flexibility to serve the public interest as they see fit, without input or restrictions from government—and that returns us to the dilemma posed by privately operated media in a democracy. On one hand, media organizations seeking profitability behave just like corporations that manufacture cars and refrigerators. If entertainment is what brings in the audience, gets high ratings, and enables media corporations to charge top dollar for advertising, self-interest and an obligation to stockholders mandates that media owners bring on the infotainment. On the other hand, because the news media carry a civic responsibility, they are qualitatively different from manufacturers of cars and refrigerators.

After all, newspapers (and, over time, all news media) are the only private institutions afforded constitutional protection. It's there in the First Amendment, where it says "Congress shall make no law . . . abridging the freedom of speech, or of the press."

This protection is warranted because it's expected that privately owned media would serve the public good by providing a platform for the advancement of public discussion. The Code of Ethics of the U.S. Society of Professional Journalists puts it this way: "The primary purpose of gathering and distributing news and opinion is to serve the general welfare by informing the people and enabling them to make judgments on the issues of the time."[18] To do that responsibly at times means presenting exactly the kind of metered, sober (read: boring) material that can turn away audiences. This is the reason broadcasters resisted the fairness doctrine for so many years. In the wake of government deregulation of the industry, though, media organizations have less incentive to supply the type of news that provides the information we need to make intelligent political judgments.

5-5 More Choices, Fewer Options?

Some say the solution to this dilemma rests with competition. They point to the proliferation of media options that the marketplace has given us just in the time since you left

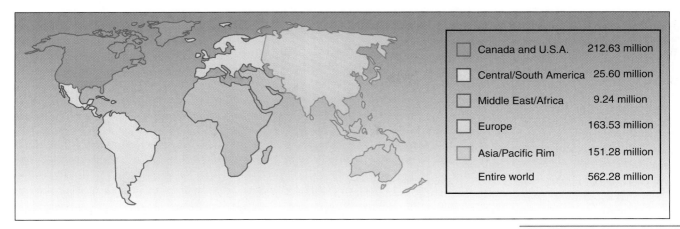

Canada and U.S.A.	212.63 million
Central/South America	25.60 million
Middle East/Africa	9.24 million
Europe	163.53 million
Asia/Pacific Rim	151.28 million
Entire world	562.28 million

Figure 5-3
Worldwide Internet Users, 2002

Source: Data from "Internet Users by Continent, 2002 to 2006," June 2, 2002, available at http://www.computer economics.com/article.cfm?id=592.

grade school. If a wide array of ideas is available to us through cable television or the Internet, perhaps it matters less if any single outlet provides a detailed or balanced treatment of political and social issues. We can find pretty much anything if we just look for it. In part, this approach guided the deregulation movement that crystallized with the Telecommunications Act of 1996.

5-5a Lots of Channels

There's no question the media are more diversified than they were a generation ago, with the Internet being the obvious but not the only example. When you were born, the system that would grow into the Internet we use today was an obscure network used mainly by scientists doing research. By 2002, however, it was estimated that there were 562 million Internet users worldwide, with almost 40 percent of them in North America alone.[19] Take a minute to check out the map showing worldwide levels of Internet use in Figure 5-3.

Maybe you've heard your parents tell stories about how they had to actually walk over to the television and turn a dial to move from channel to channel, the sum total of which probably numbered anywhere from three to possibly eight, if they were lucky. Today, there are that many programming choices from HBO alone. One count of television channels lists 217 distinct offerings available on cable services throughout the country.[20] Depending on where you live and whether you have a cable or satellite service, it's possible to receive so many channels that you need a search engine to tell you what's available to you.

These include a lot of channels like CNN, MTV, and ESPN that are available through most services, as well as more obscure offerings like The California Channel, the Military Channel, and the Idea Channel.[21] The proliferation of television channels permits specialized programming, or **"narrowcasting,"** that appeals to small but interested audiences.

The media explosion is not limited to television or the Internet, either. Radio experienced something of a rebirth in the 1990s with the growth of talk radio programs. Once the exclusive province of music, radio has been redefined as a platform for talk programs that feature celebrity hosts and listener call-ins. In 2004, there were 9,370 FM stations and 5,026 AM stations,[22] and about 10 percent included talk programs on their schedules.[23] Although Rush Limbaugh may be the most recognized talk radio host, the airwaves are filled with talkers who incite their listeners to call in and share their political perspectives—sometimes by making outrageous and incendiary political claims that stir the passions of sympathetic listeners. Talk radio programs offering a conservative perspective, like Limbaugh's, have been the most durable. Well-known liberal figures like Mario Cuomo and Jesse Jackson have tried their hand as talk radio hosts, but they failed to produce high ratings. Still, in 2004, a liberal group began operating a national radio network called "Air America" with liberal hosts like comedian Al Franken in an attempt to catch up to the popularity of conservative talk radio.

Even newspapers, which died off in large numbers due to their inability to compete with network evening news broadcasts in the 1970s and 1980s, have had something of a resurgence (see Figure 5-4). Over the last fifty years, the number of evening daily

▶**narrowcasting** Programming oriented to a small segment of viewers, like that found on cable television stations. It contrasts with broadcasting, like that found on traditional television networks, which seeks to reach a larger audience with programming that has wide appeal.

Figure 5-4

Newspapers Respond to Television

Evening newspapers began losing readers to television news programs in the 1970s and 1980s. However, starting in the 1980s, an increase in morning and Sunday newspapers began to compensate for some of the lost evening readership.

Source: Data from *Editor and Publisher.*

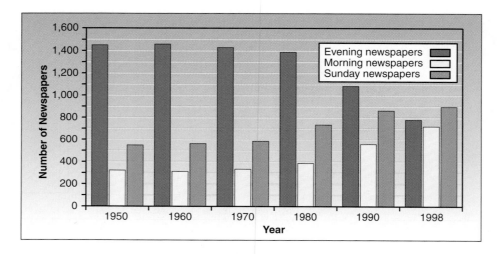

newspapers has been cut in half as people preferred to come home to news from Walter Cronkite and David Brinkley, the forerunners of Dan Rather and Brian Williams. However, a countertrend has emerged in the past twenty years, with the growth of morning newspapers and Sunday editions. When you take everything into account, the total number of newspapers in the United States is essentially what it was fifty years ago.

As newspapers have held their own and adjusted to changing patterns of news usage, they also have dramatically changed their look and approach to reporting. Soft news, once the domain of feature sections in the "back" of the paper, now appears more prominently, and in a trend that emulates television news reporting, thematic coverage is creeping into stories that once would have been presented in the inverted pyramid fashion. Technology that enables the printing of color pictures has brightened up the look of newspapers. Even the staid *New York Times* and the stogy *Wall Street Journal* now feature color images, as newspapers emulate the up-tempo appearance of television news.

USA Today is perhaps the most successful example of using television news techniques to market a newspaper. Colorful and fast-paced like a television news program, it features headline-length stories; pages of "factoids" from every state, designed to attract local readers; prominently placed pictures of celebrities; a statistics-laden sports section; feature-rich health, living, and technology sections; and a bright, detailed weather map. Even the curbside box that it's sold from has something in common with television. Take a look next time you pass one.

5-5b Very Few Owners

Nonetheless, there is an ironic flip side to this proliferation of media resources. At a time when more information outlets are available than ever before, the free market fostered by

Unlike those traditional, boxy newspaper vending machines, *USA Today*—the newspaper that tries to be TV news on the printed page—is sold from a slick receptacle that evokes a television set.

Source: AP/Wide World Photos.

deregulation has concentrated media ownership in very few hands. Passage of the Telecommunications Act of 1996 accelerated a process of media mergers and acquisitions that had begun in the 1980s during the Reagan administration, some of the highlights of which are:

- Capital Cities Corporation purchases the ABC television network.

- Loews Corporation purchases the CBS television network.

- General Electric purchases the NBC television network and its parent company, RCA.

- Australian media magnate Rupert Murdoch's News Corporation purchases Metromedia Television and forms the Fox Television Network.

- Time, Inc. buys Warner Communications in a $14.1 billion deal to create Time Warner

- Viacom purchases Paramount Communications and Blockbuster Video.

- Gannett, America's largest newspaper chain, purchases Multimedia, Inc., to increase its newspaper, television, and radio holdings.

- Disney buys Capital Cities, which had previously bought ABC, for $19 billion.

- CBS television gets a new corporate parent as Westinghouse Corporation buys it for $5.4 billion.

- Time Warner buys Turner Communications[24] (and is itself later bought by America Online and for a brief time is known as AOL Time Warner).

Remember, this was all *before* the Telecommunications Act was signed into law and deregulated the industry.

The consequence of this is what political scientist Dean Alger calls the emergence of "megamedia," a few giant corporations who dominate media ownership. Alger refers to a "dominant dozen" who together control the means of mass communication: conglomerates like Disney, Time Warner, General Electric, News Corporation, and Microsoft. Let's take a look at one of those conglomerates—Disney, circa 1998—in Figure 5-5 to get a sense of Disney's size, scope, and reach.

What of this centralized ownership? Even though we have an enormous number of media options, the fact that very few corporations control so many of those choices may work to undermine our enlightened understanding of politics if, instead of presenting many perspectives, the media are presenting one perspective through many outlets. Alger writes:

> If a few megamedia corporations control most of the major print, broadcast, cable, and other media that most of the public relies on as their *main sources* of information, opinion, and creative expression, then this fundamental pillar of democracy is likely to be seriously threatened. Indeed, the Florida Supreme Court concluded:
>
>> The right of the people to know all sides of a controversy and from such information to make an enlightened choice is being jeopardized by the growing concentration of ownership of the mass media into fewer and fewer hands, resulting in a form of private censorship. *(Miami Herald v. Tornillo)*[25]

Notwithstanding Alger's warning, media deregulation efforts continued into the Bush administration, with a controversial ruling in 2003 by the Federal Communications Commission that permitted even greater concentration of media ownership by further relaxing restrictions on the number of media outlets that a single corporation could own in any media market (see Box 5-5 on page 139). The ruling met with stiff public opposition, leading Congress to weaken but not entirely roll back the FCC ruling.

5-6 The Politics of Entertainment I: Elections

Have you ever had a love-hate relationship with someone? You know, a situation where you always seem to be arguing with them, but you can't bear the thought of life without them? That may be the best way to think about how reporters and political figures relate to each

Disney-Capitial Cities-ABC*		
Broadcasting		ABC television network (223 affiliated stations), including ABC News, ABC Sports, and ABC Entertainment; ABC Radio; 10 local television stations; 21 local radio stations; 14% share of Young Broadcasting (8 local television stations)
Cable		Disney Channel; ESPN and ESPN2 (80% ownership); Lifetime Entertainment Services (50% ownership); Arts & Entertainment (A&E) television network (37.5% ownership); Disney Interactive software
Internet		ABC Online
Movies, Video, Music		Disney Television Productions; Walt Disney Studios; Buena Vista Television; Buena Vista Home Video; Miramax Pictures; Touchstone Pictures; Buena Vista Pictures Distribution and Buena Vista International (distributors of Disney and Touchstone films); Walt Disney Records; Hollywood Records
Publishing		Six daily (local) newspapers; 40 weekly newspapers; *Discover* magazine; *Women's Wear Daily* magazine; *Los Angeles* magazine; *Institutional Investor* magazine; *ESPN* magazine; Disney Publishing; Chilton Publications (trade publishers); Guildford Publishing Company; Hitchcock Publishing Company
Resorts/ Travel		Disneyland; Walt Disney World Resort; Disneyland Resort Paris (part owner); Tokyo Disney Resort (part owner); 12 resort hotels; Disney Vacation Club; the Disney Cruise Line
International Holdings		Tele-Munchen Fernseh GmbH and Company (German television and film production, 50% owner); RTL Disney Fernseh GmbH and Company (German broadcasting company, 50% owner); RTL2 Fernseh GmbH and Company (German broadcasting company, 23% owner); TM3 Fernseh GmbH and Company (German broadcasting company, 37.5% owner); Eurosport network, Spanish Tesauro SA TV, and Scandinavian Broadcasting System SA (20–33% owner); TVA (Brazilian pay TV, 20% owner)
Other		Over 500 Disney Stores; Disney product licensing; Anaheim Mighty Ducks professional hockey team; Anaheim Angels professional baseball team (25% owner)

* Circa 1998.

Figure 5-5

The Mouse That Roars

Source: Dean Alger, *MEGAMEDIA: How Giant Corporations Dominate Mass Media, Distort Competition, and Endanger Democracy* (Boulder, CO: Rowman & Littlefield, Inc., 1998), 36–38.

▶**free media** The news coverage that major candidates for high office can expect to receive on a regular basis. Although free, candidates cannot control the content of this coverage or guarantee that it will be favorable.

▶**paid media** Radio and television ads paid for and produced by political campaigns.

other. Their relationship is adversarial, inasmuch as it is defined by conflict. However, it is also symbiotic, in that it is a relationship of mutual benefit and dependence. The consequence of this relationship is fierce competition for command of the news agenda, where candidates and reporters vie to control each other in a dance that shapes the news in a way that—like deregulation and centralized media ownership—may leave the viewer and reader without the most useful information for making an informed political choice.

Reporters and politicians are professionally joined at the hip. Reporters depend on politicians, especially important ones, to be sources for their stories. Politicians need coverage to keep their names in front of the public. This is what's typically called **free media** because all major candidates know they can count on the publicity that comes from being newsworthy without having to use any campaign money to get it.

Of course, candidates don't just want free coverage—they want *favorable* free coverage that will advance their political interests. This conflicts with reporters' professional autonomy in determining what the content of stories should be. That's the source of the struggle.

The other portion of a candidate's media exposure comes from, not surprisingly, **paid media.** These are the advertisements that candidates purchase on television and radio to promote their campaign—or to disparage their opponent. Paid media gives campaigns far more control over their message, as they can craft their own ads, but it doesn't give them the legitimacy that comes with messages communicated by journalists, so candidates need to engage journalists for coverage no matter how much money they have available to spend on buying commercials. Instead of struggling for message control, the major strategic challenges facing candidates when it comes to paid media are finding an effective message and raising the money to pay for ads. Television ads are expensive—they can be extremely expensive in large media markets—and are the biggest reason why the cost of running for office has become so high.

> *Box 5-5* **Do They Want to Discuss *All* the Things They Bring to Life?**

Earlier, we said that any organization that deals in news reporting is not simply manufacturing refrigerators. But it is possible that a corporation that manufactures refrigerators could own an organization that deals in news reporting, and in fact, one does—General Electric, which owns NBC News. What may be less well known is that GE makes more than household appliances. It also produces nuclear weapons. If you see the potential for controversy and conflict of interest, you're thinking clearly about the situation.

Nuclear weapons production is a contentious topic of great importance, making it a newsworthy subject, particularly when it is the target of a major boycott. In the early 1990s, a corporate watchdog group called Infact was leading a boycott against GE for its role in the production of nuclear weapons. Would NBC cover the boycott?

The network had to address this question when, in 1990, a member of the *Today* show production staff contacted Todd Putnam, an expert on consumer boycotts, to appear as a guest to talk about "the biggest boycott going on right now."* The Infact boycott of GE was the one that stood out to Putnam, so he suggested it to the *Today* employee. "We can't do that one," was her response. "Well, we could do it, but we won't."

And they didn't. When Putnam raised the topic with a *Today* show producer, his reaction was, "You guys … I'll be looking for a new job on Tuesday."

Putnam was interviewed on the *Today* show, but about other boycotts he considered less paramount. The only time anyone at NBC asked him about the Infact boycott of GE was after the interview, in a hallway—by an NBC janitor.

When we talked about the media's role in **agenda setting** in Chapter 4, we said that we tend to think about things that are covered prominently in the news. If an issue is not covered, then unless we or a friend are directly involved in the issue, there is no easy way to form an opinion on it, much less an informed opinion. Is the case of the GE boycott an instance where Alger's concern for enlightened choice is undermined? Or are you confident you could find news of the boycott in other media, as the NBC janitor possibly did? Is our ability to make enlightened decisions undermined if the centralization of media ownership in the hands of large corporations makes it less likely that their other corporate actions will receive scrutiny?

▶ **agenda setting** The tendency for topics given great weight by the media to be given equally great weight by those who use the media, such that the people and events considered important by those who determine media coverage will become the people and events that the public considers important.

*Todd Putnam, "The GE Boycott: A Story NBC Wouldn't Buy," *Extra!*, January/February 1991. *Extra!* is published by an organization called FAIR (Fairness and Accuracy in Reporting), a media watchdog group with a liberal tilt, which works to expose news organizations when it believes they are suppressing important information. The author is the expert who was contacted to appear on *Today*. All quotations in this section come from this article. You can read the whole article on the FAIR website at http://www.fair.org/extra/best-of-extra/ge-boycott.html.

5-6a The Candidate's Perspective

Candidates and reporters each have resources at their disposal to try to get the upper hand in coverage. Good campaigns are disciplined. They develop a message they want to communicate to the public and repeat that message constantly so that people learn it. Candidates who stay "on message" are generally able to set the agenda for the election because they make it difficult for reporters to deviate from what they are being told by campaign officials. By doing so, however, candidates communicate information about themselves that is more rhetorical than substantive—empty messages that serve the candidate's interests but leave voters without a sound basis for making an electoral choice.

In 2000, then-governor George W. Bush wanted voters to change the widespread perception that had developed over the previous few years of the Republican Party as callous and unsympathetic to the concerns of ordinary voters. At every campaign stop, Bush referred to himself as a "compassionate conservative," a rhetorical label that was more about image-building than promoting a specific agenda. Bush's advisors calculated that if he repeated that phrase without deviation, reporters would begin to use it. The strategy worked, owing in large part to the candidate's discipline with the message. Repeated stories that called Bush a "compassionate conservative" helped to make the label stick, enabling Bush to define the contest on his terms.

Candidates have a few tools at their disposal to assist them with "message control." They can get the attention of reporters by staging **media events**—activities that appear to be news but that in fact are produced by the campaign to get reporters to give them free

▶ **media events** Activities staged by campaigns or political officials that have enough news value to draw press attention to a message the politician wants to communicate.

Ronald Reagan was a master of the photo opportunity. By posing in front of the Statue of Liberty, as he did in this 1980 picture, he associated himself with a set of patriotic values designed to convince voters to see him in a positive light. Michael Dukakis, the 1988 Democratic presidential nominee, wasn't as skillful. The picture you see here is the result of a photo opportunity designed to communicate the message that the candidate would be a strong leader of the armed forces. You can judge the photo's effectiveness for yourself.

Source: (Left) Ronald Reagan Library. *(Right)* AP/Wide World Photos.

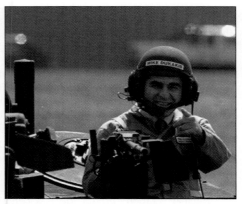

▶**photo opportunities** Staged appearances by politicians in visually appealing settings designed to produce images that will be widely disseminated in the press.

▶**spin** A technique used by political figures to characterize events in a favorable way in order to get the media to report them in a favorable way—regardless of what the facts of a story may indicate.

coverage of their message. Media events work if they are convenient for journalists to cover, if they offer good pictures for television, and—in the era of infotainment—if they are interesting or fun to watch. In 1988, when George Bush (senior) wanted to send the message that he was more patriotic than his opponent, he staged a media event at a factory that produced flags. It looked like news (the candidate visits with factory workers), but it was a well-executed ploy to use free media to communicate his message.

The Bush campaign also knew that every newspaper and television news program would run a picture of him surrounded by American flags. Candidates know that if they give the media a chance to get a picture of them in an appealing setting, editors and producers will find the images irresistible. So, campaigns look for **photo opportunities,** where they can project an image of the candidate consistent with the message they want to communicate. In 1980, Ronald Reagan wanted to associate himself with the American values we discussed in Chapter 4, so he staged a photo opportunity in front of the Statue of Liberty. Vice President Al Gore gave his wife a long, lingering kiss before making his acceptance speech at the 2000 Democratic National Convention—a photo opportunity designed to communicate the message that Gore was more of a family man than Bill Clinton and more passionate than his wooden image might suggest. In both cases, the resulting pictures played widely in the press and favorably for the candidate.

Of course, not all campaign experiences go the candidate's way, and when campaigns find themselves facing negative coverage, they often try to **spin** events to their liking, characterizing things in the best possible fashion in the hope that the press will report events the way the campaign wants them reported. (The term *spin doctor* is generally applied to political aides who work on reporters to accept their version of events.) In Chapter 7, we'll learn about primary elections, where decisions are made about which candidate will be nominated by a party to run for office. When you run for president, you enter quite a few primary elections. In 1992, Bill Clinton finished in second place in the important New Hampshire primary, but he didn't want reporters saying that he had lost. Since opinion polls taken before the vote indicated that it was possible for him to have finished as low as third place, he told supporters at a rally after the votes were counted that he was the "comeback kid"—a characterization that implied he had won. The press picked it up, and Clinton was on his way to the Democratic Party nomination. He was able to successfully spin a loss into a victory.

Campaigns need to be vigilant about the way they employ these techniques. With so many media outlets competing for information and with some operating around the

Box 5-6   Technology and the News Cycle

Competition among media is part of what accelerates the news cycle. There are so many news outlets that the demand for original information is ferocious; the presence of twenty-four-hour news services means the demand for information never ends. This demand could not be satisfied without the appropriate technology. Satellites that make it possible to beam information around the world in real time; videotape that can be easily recorded and viewed immediately; cell phones that permit instantaneous communication from remote locations—these are at the technological heart of today's mass media. Consider that during the Vietnam War, battlefield footage was recorded on film, which had to be shipped by airplane to New York for development before it could be edited and aired—a process that took days. Twenty-five years later, when allied forces began their attack on Iraq in the Persian Gulf War, people around the world could watch the events on CNN as they were happening.

clock, the shelf life for information is very short. The time between when a candidate does something and when it ends up in the news, or the **news cycle,** is so short as to be in some cases instantaneous (for example, you can turn CNN on any time). The continuous, never-ending news cycle means campaigns have to be on guard all the time, always staying on message, always thinking about ways to get their message in the news. It can easily strain their relationship with reporters, especially because reporters have resources of their own to battle the campaign's "message control," including technological advantages that fuel the news cycle. See Box 5-6.

While it's probably true that television reporters can't resist a great photo opportunity, that doesn't mean that they will spin the story the way the campaign wants it. No one likes to feel controlled, but that's exactly the way reporters feel in the wake of campaign news management techniques. Their defense is that they get to decide what goes into the story.

> **news cycle** The time between when an event happens and when it gets press coverage. With twenty-four-hour news services setting the pace, the demand for new information is enormous and immediate, greatly accelerating the news cycle.

5-6b The Reporter's Perspective

To most journalists, simply relating a candidate's message makes them feel like a mouthpiece for the campaign. Giving in to that feels like an abandonment of their responsibilities. To battle back, reporters can choose a **frame** or context for their stories that sidesteps the message the campaign is trying to present. Frames give meaning to factual information by putting it in a perspective that the reporter chooses. Three popular reporter frames are the strategy a campaign is using, the campaign's prospects for winning and losing, and the candidate's character flaws. Each of these permits the reporter to cover the campaign on his or her own terms.

One way some reporters avoid feeling controlled is by reporting on how the campaign is trying to control the media message, rather than discussing what that message is. In other words, reporters will focus on the candidate's strategy for controlling the message rather than on the message itself, talking about how the campaign engages in spin or crafts media events in order to manipulate reporters and, by extension, everyone. Arguably, this information is not very useful to a voter trying to decide among the candidates.

For example, on March 6, 1992, President Bush (senior) was giving a campaign speech to a crowd of enthusiastic supporters, but his press secretary was convinced that reporters in the pressroom were not paying attention to either Bush's words or the crowd's reaction to them. So, he had the audio feed of the speech turned off in the pressroom in an effort to force reporters to attend the speech and cover Bush's message. CNN reacted with the following story, which makes no mention of the president's message but goes into great detail on how the Bush campaign was trying to manipulate the press:

> **frame** The frame of reference for a news story, or the context around which the facts of a story are organized. If a news story is thematic, like most television news stories, the frame determines what the specific theme of the story will be.

> As President Bush steamrolled through the South, his press secretary was rolling over the national press following Mr. Bush, calling them—quote—lazy bastards, telling them to get out of the press work space and go to a Bush rally to report on it for real. [Press Secretary] Marlin Fitzwater then cut off the public address system that routinely provides an audio feed of the president's remarks to reporters who must file their stories under tight deadlines.[26]

horserace That element of a political campaign that deals with winning and losing, whether a candidate is leading or trailing an opponent, and what the candidate may be doing to improve or solidify his or her electoral prospects.

Another favorite approach of election reporters is to cover the contest for president—who's up and who's down—rather than the substance of what the candidates are saying. This emphasis on the **horserace** aspect of the campaign protects reporters from the candidate's agenda-control efforts by explaining what the candidate is saying and doing in terms of the candidate's electoral prospects. Although voters learn about likely winners and losers, horserace coverage (like stories about how candidates manipulate reporters) offers little information on how best to vote (unless you simply want to vote with the likely winner).

The logic of horserace coverage says that any action of a candidate who is trailing in public opinion polls should be reported as an effort to climb back into the race, and any action of a candidate who is leading in opinion polls should be reported as an effort to extend that lead or protect against backsliding (regardless of whatever nonstrategic explanations there may be for the candidate's behavior). In either case, the actual content of what the candidate does or says is of secondary importance, permitting the journalist control of the message, but on terms that might not benefit the public.

Sometimes, events occurring outside the campaign become the subject of horserace scrutiny. For instance, in the closing hours of the 2004 presidential race, a tape of Osama bin Laden—in which the al Qaeda leader addressed the upcoming American election—was released to the American media, which wasted no time assessing the effect it might have on the contest between President Bush and Senator Kerry. The *Washington Post* framed the horserace implications of the bin Laden tape this way:

> As Bush and Kerry responded with dignified statements of unity against Osama bin Laden, the two campaigns struggled to game out their reactions, and to figure out how such a surreal event—the feared, ghostly image returning to Americans' TV screens after a long absence—would alter Tuesday's outcome.[27]

Finally, reporters can latch on to the character of the candidate and make that the centerpiece of their coverage. Before the investigative reporting of the Watergate period turned into aggressive reporting, the private lives and actions of public figures were off limits to reporters. Not so today. When a story broke several days before the 2000 presidential election that George W. Bush had many years earlier been arrested for driving while impaired, it ran on every media outlet nationwide. During the 1992 campaign, Bill Clinton faced a barrage of stories about his character, including whether he had avoided the draft, smoked pot, and engaged in extramarital affairs. The 2004 campaign was filled with allegations about whether John Kerry could be trusted not to change his mind or "flip flop" on decisions.

attack journalism A form of aggressive coverage in which reporters latch onto an allegation of misdoing by a candidate or public official and engage in a "feeding frenzy" in which they cover it intensely and to the exclusion of other news.

Sometimes, when a character story hits the airwaves, reporters pile on it and cover it at the expense of everything else. When this happens, it's as if the candidate is under attack by the press for something he or she allegedly did, and aggressive reporting becomes **attack journalism,** where reporters latch on to the hint of a candidate indiscretion and, in the words of political scientist Larry Sabato, "go after a wounded politician like sharks in a feeding frenzy."[28] Sometimes, media critics refer to this as "gotcha!" journalism because the point of coverage appears to be catching a politician in a compromising situation, and reporters can seem to be playing a vengeful role.

Apart from providing reporters with a way to maintain control of the news agenda, strategy, horserace, and character stories have the advantage of being entertaining. Strategy stories bring us inside the campaign and can make us feel like we're privileged to information we wouldn't normally have. Horserace stories have the appeal of a high-stakes race or playoff game, complete with the dramatic tension that winning and losing provides. Character stories are of innate interest in much the same way that many people enjoy reading gossip about the personal lives of celebrities. Even feeding frenzies can have an appeal not unlike looking at an accident on the side of the road. So, reporters are certainly not doing a disservice to media owners by framing campaigns in a way that's inherently interesting.

They may be doing a disservice to the audience, though. Once again, we're faced with the trade-off between using information to entertain and using it to inform. Even in some of their coverage, reporters acknowledge that in their attempt to wrestle control of the news agenda from the candidate, they may be getting in the way of what the audience needs. Consider these quotes from television news coverage of the 1992 presidential election:

Journalists' Questions	Public's Questions
"[Independent candidate] Ross Perot claims you're hiding from him. Will you debate him?"	"Would you give money to Russia?"
"Is it proper for Perot, with his vast wealth and no spending limits, to use that to attain the presidency?"	"What is your view on trade between the United States and Mexico?"
"You say you haven't been good at getting your message across, but don't the polls indicate a rejection of the message in and of itself?"	"What would you look for in a Supreme Court nominee?"
"Do you share the view of Ross Perot as a man who, if he doesn't get his way, stomps off and goes home?"	"Would you release loans to Israel?"

T A B L E 5-3

Public vs. Journalists

Source: Thomas E. Patterson, *Out of Order* (New York: Alfred A. Knopf, 1993), 55–56.

The trouble for Clinton [is] the press hounds him about his character; *voters seem more worried about other things.*

[There is] a feeling among many voters [in New Hampshire] that some of *the press and the public are not necessarily interested in the same things,* and a feeling that much of the press . . . is actually cutting the candidates off from the voters.

[Clinton tries to] get past the press in order to talk to the voters.[29]

How far does the press deviate from what we say we want them to talk about? In Table 5-3, you'll find questions that were asked of George Bush and Bill Clinton during the 1992 presidential campaign. Some come from a viewer call-in program, in which people like you and me were able to ask questions of the candidate. Some come from a press interview.

Political scientist Tom Patterson says the difference between the two lists in Table 5-3, in which the public primarily asked issue-oriented questions while journalists asked strategy, horserace, and character questions, is a difference in perspectives on what the election is about. Reporters simply have a different framework for processing information about the election than the public does, built around the attitude that the election is a game. Their perspective is reflected in the stories they report.[30]

Patterson claims this difference leaves us lacking in information that we need to make intelligent political choices. In particular, the emphasis journalists place on strategy, horserace, and character frames means:

- *More negative news.* If you think about the tone of the reporter questions in Table 5-3, it's overwhelmingly negative. Reporters imply that President Bush is running from an opponent and failing to get his message to the public. Negative news, which by Patterson's count more than doubled between 1960 and 1992,[31] can weaken the bonds between public and politicians by undermining our confidence in those who run for office.

- *More cynical perspectives on politics.* In the course of their struggle with candidates for control of the news agenda, reporters communicate the message that candidates will do anything to win and that everything they do is designed to help them win. This is a cynical view that can leave us feeling like candidates are empty shells who make hollow, self-serving promises.[32]

- *Less issue coverage.* As reporters emphasize the horserace, stories about issues and policies are squeezed out. This leaves us with less information about where the candidates stand on issues, should we want to use this information to decide how to vote. By one count, issue stories on network evening news programs fell 26 percent between 1996 and 2000, while horserace stories increased by an almost identical percentage.[33] By another, as the number of horserace stories on the front page of the *New York Times* doubled between 1960 and 1992, the number of policy stories fell from over 50 percent to only 20 percent.[34]

5-7 The Politics of Entertainment II: Governing

The dynamics of election coverage also apply to coverage of elected officials, with the important exception that once in office, politicians have more resources at their disposal to try to manage the news message. They still engage in media events, hold photo opportunities, and spin the news to their advantage whenever possible. Once in office, though, they are even more newsworthy than when they were running for office. This is particularly true for the president. It means the struggle with the press can be heightened as well.

5-7a The President

Reporters approach stories about the president as if they were covering a campaign, placing presidential actions in the context of strategy, horserace, and character. In a political reporter's characterization of governing, presidents look to score political points by racking up victories over Congress as they work for approval of their legislative program. Discussion of the merits of the president's proposals is often supplanted by discussion of the political necessity of getting a legislative "win." Strategy stories address the tactics used by the White House to engineer legislative victories. As in a campaign, a feeding frenzy can happen at any time.[35]All in all, this type of news can be quite entertaining, while sending the message that the political values of a campaign (that is, winning at all costs) are what serving in public office is all about. See Box 5-7.

Presidential efforts at image and message control date back over a century. Teddy Roosevelt, serving at the turn of the twentieth century, predates the mass media by a generation, but he could be viewed as a prototype for his media-savvy successors. Roosevelt actively cultivated reporters to advance his political purposes. As photography was central to selling newspapers during the period of yellow journalism that coincided with his administration, Roosevelt shrewdly cast an image of a strong and engaged president in order to sell an activist agenda to an American public that would never meet him personally or hear his voice.

Thirty years later, Franklin D. Roosevelt would have radio at his disposal for crafting a media image and engaging in a message control campaign that knew no equal in its time. He was not the first president to have radio as a tool, but FDR was the first to realize its political potential. In a world where most Americans had never heard a president's voice, Roosevelt realized that he could use radio to achieve a level of familiarity his predecessors never had, deliberately crafting an image of himself that to millions would be inseparable from the office he held (and, not coincidentally, that he would be elected to four times). He mastered the medium the way today's presidents try to conquer television, through strong, reassuring performances during times of peril—the Great Depression and World War II. A CBS radio bureau chief dubbed these talks **"fireside chats"** for their intimate, personal nature, and the name stuck.[36]

▶**fireside chats** The term given to Franklin Roosevelt's radio addresses to the American public, which demonstrated Roosevelt's ability to master the medium and build a sense of rapport with ordinary Americans.

Before Franklin D. Roosevelt, presidential speeches were long, impersonal orations. Roosevelt's Fireside Chats were brief, and delivered directly to the American people as though the president was talking personally to everyone in the radio audience. He addressed listeners as "my friends," and spoke in a familiar manner that inspired listeners to feel as if they personally knew this distant figure. Careful not to undermine the power of his message through overexposure, FDR resisted public calls for more Fireside Chats, giving only four during his first year as president and only twenty-six in the next eleven years. He chose his topics carefully, speaking primarily about the Depression, his New Deal economic recovery program, World War II, and national security issues.[37]

It's probably hard to imagine what it was like to have faced the extreme hardship of the Great Depression or the tremendous sacrifice and uncertainty of World War II, no less imagine a time when most adults had never heard a president's voice. If you can use your

Box 5-7   The Health Care Horserace

Early in his first term, President Clinton unsuccessfully attempted a dramatic overhaul of the American health care establishment. To follow press coverage of the initiative, you might think he was running for president all over again.

Winning and losing was a prominent theme running through mainstream coverage of the health care events of late 1993. The terms for success were clear: Congressional approval of anything resembling the president's package would constitute a "win" for the White House; compromise resulting in something less than the president wanted would register as a loss. Complete failure to win legislative approval for health care reform—the actual result of the president's efforts—would go down as a major setback, a sign of the president's weakness akin to losing an election.

Notwithstanding the fact that separation of powers and checks and balances necessitate compromise if anything is going to get done in Washington, framing the development of health care policy as a political horserace sidesteps questions about the merits of the policy under consideration. It's a misleading frame, and not a particularly relevant one. With its big-stakes winners and losers and its glimpses into the workings of power, though, it can be a captivating human drama.

Every step of the way, news audiences were treated to glimpses into the strategic logic of the Clinton health care team's effort to "sell" its health care plan, as CNN put it.* For instance, an administration critique of the insurance industry was reported on NBC as a strategic attempt to find a scapegoat that the public could blame for high health care costs. Media events like televised viewer call-in programs featuring the president were covered as strategic attempts to put pressure on congressional representatives by building support for the Clinton plan with the public. The *New York Times* wrote in detail about the administration's "double-barreled strategy" of appealing to voters and pressuring members of Congress.

Then, in spring 1994, a feeding frenzy erupted around questionable real estate dealings involving the president and first lady Hillary Rodham Clinton. True to campaign form, the "Whitewater" frenzy (named for the real estate development in question) was covered as a scandal that could dramatically undermine Clinton's health care initiative. Because Hillary Rodham Clinton was a central figure in both the development of the administration's health care proposals—where she had been receiving positive press coverage—and in the Whitewater affair, the frenzy assumed the personal attributes of attack journalism by focusing on her character. "She's got to be either Tonya or Nancy," said one cable television report of the first lady, in a reference to a widely covered attack on figure skater Nancy Kerrigan that was arranged by rival Tonya Harding. "Her once dazzling image is now tarnished," agreed CBS News.

And what of the health care proposals that the Clintons were trying to advance through the political system? Would it have been good for the country had the president succeeded in winning approval for his plan and basked in press coverage of a major victory? Did his political failure spare the country a bad policy? Coverage that treats making policy like winning an election doesn't give us the information we need to reach a judgment.

*This and all other references in this section may be found in Kerbel, *Remote and Controlled: Media Politics in a Cynical Age* (Boulder, CO: Westview Press, 1998), 112–119.

imagination, try to envision how comforting it could have been to hear the strong voice of the president say, "I pledge myself to a New Deal for the American people," or to reassure you that "The only thing we have to fear is fear itself" (see Figure 5-6).

It certainly would have been inconceivable to many Americans hearing those words from their radios that they were delivered by a man confined to a wheelchair, the result of adult polio. Ever aware that Americans in the 1930s and 1940s could perceive his wheelchair-bound presence as a sign of weakness, FDR worked assiduously to keep this

New Deal
I pledge myself to a New Deal for the American people.

Rendezvous with Destiny
There is a mysterious cycle in human events. To some generations, much is given; of other generations, much is expected. This generation of Americans has a rendezvous with destiny.

Fear Itself
So, first of all, let me assert my firm belief that the only thing we have to fear is fear itself.

Figure 5-6
How FDR Sounded to a Worried Nation
Source: Courtesy of the Franklin D. Roosevelt Library and Digital Archives, http://www.fdrlibrary.marist.edu/audio.html.

basic fact about himself hidden from view. He carefully cultivated reporters, maintaining an open relationship with the White House press corps and permitting them access to power.[38] The relationship was symbiotic without being adversarial, and it paid off in the form of largely sympathetic coverage of FDR and his agenda. It was an era when reporters didn't consider it a sign of weakness on *their* part to acquiesce to White House requests not to write about or photograph the president in his wheelchair.

As media politics began to change in the generation that followed FDR, presidents began to employ different tactics to achieve the same objectives of news management and message control that the two Roosevelts accomplished so effectively in their time. John F. Kennedy won the loyalty of reporters by granting them access to his administration in much the same way as FDR, but he also implemented a strategy built around television to communicate an image of leadership directly to American homes that circumvented the traditional press. As Kennedy once remarked to a reporter, "When we don't have to go through you bastards, we can really get our story out to the American people."[39]

Both FDR and JFK held regular **press conferences,** meetings with journalists that allowed them to ask direct questions of the president on matters of policy. Kennedy permitted television cameras to broadcast these events live to the public in prime time, transforming press conferences from events designed to brief journalists to TV shows designed to showcase the president's quick wit and command of detail. A knowledgeable man with a good sense of humor, Kennedy commanded the stage at televised press conferences and used the conferences to construct an image of a substantive leader in charge of his administration and world events.[40]

A generation after Kennedy, presidential message control efforts increased in intensity, to the point where they came to resemble the love-hate struggle characteristic of election campaigns. Ronald Reagan used his acting skills coupled with strict control of information to create a likeable, strong persona who could dominate the news agenda. Unlike FDR or JFK, Reagan limited access to the reporters covering him. His media operations were tightly controlled by advisors, who would begin each day by deciding what they wanted coverage to look like on the evening news, and then would spend the rest of the day creating media events, producing sound bites, and spinning the statements necessary to realize their vision.[41]

The Reagan team was so successful in crafting and selling its message that Reagan became known in press circles as the "Teflon president," because even bad news seemed to slide right off of him. For the better part of his eight years in office, President Reagan was viewed positively by large numbers of Americans.[42] His success made his operation the model for those who followed him in office, and even if none of his successors has matched his level of effectiveness, they have all employed the tools of message control that have long since institutionalized the skeptical stance presidents and journalists have toward one another.

press conferences Scheduled meetings between reporters and political figures like the president, which give the press access to the official and an opportunity to ask him or her questions firsthand.

5-7b Congress

If the single occupant of the presidency is a natural focus for television's personalizing qualities, Congress poses something of a dilemma for a medium that thrives on telling individual stories. With a combined 535 senators and representatives, Congress is an unwieldy branch of government that doesn't offer its occupants easy entrée to television news. To compound matters, much of what happens in Congress occurs in committees and private meetings, which are largely out of the reach of cameras, and Congress is a deliberative branch of government where progress happens slowly; television, as we know, demands action and drama.

What is often visible to cameras is the infighting that's inevitable even among members of the same political party when political interests collide. This is sometimes sufficient to supply the drama otherwise missing from staid hearings and floor speeches, and it plays naturally on the strategy and horserace frames typical of presidential coverage.

So, members of Congress are not immune to the kind of "sky is falling" coverage that presidents experience when their proposals are not sailing along through the legislative process. At the same time that reporters were covering President Clinton's health care initiative as a political horserace, they were painting the legislative branch in similar tones, as in this story from NBC News:

> Behind the scenes, the infighting among Senate Democrats is fierce. Democratic senators told NBC News that the president's key allies are undermining [Senate Finance Committee Chairman Daniel Patrick Moynihan], saying he's too eager to compromise with Republicans. Both [Senators] Mitchell and Rockefeller deny the charge. Another Clinton ally said the president is also exasperated because Moynihan "won't shut up." . . . Key [Democrats] warn that undercutting Moynihan could destroy chances for health reform this year.[43]

You'll note that principled ideological differences are not the source of the conflict in this story, which emphasizes petty partisanship and great clashes of egos.

When politics interferes with action and Congress fails to act, reporters are quick to cover the **gridlock** that ensues. Gridlock is typically reported as a problem, rather than as a natural institutional response to complicated problems. The expectation among reporters is that Congress *should* be able to report out legislation rather than fall victim to inaction, despite the fact that, by constitutional design, it is a place where passions and interests that might be adverse to the wishes of much of the country are frustrated or subjected to compromise (as we saw in Chapter 2 and as we'll see again when we get to Chapter 9). Coverage of Congress in gridlock is the legislative equivalent to coverage of a president's failure to win a policy horserace, taking the inability to achieve an outcome as a sign of weakness independent of the merits of the policy under discussion.

> **gridlock** The term given to legislative inaction, when members of Congress are unable to reach agreement and legislation stalls.

For many years, Congress was reluctant to open its proceedings to public view. The Senate, especially, with its long tradition as an exclusive club, was determined to maintain its privacy from the cameras that today seem to define public life. But as television naturally gravitated to the president, and presidents learned how to manipulate television coverage, some members of Congress grew concerned that their relative obscurity in the mass media was facilitating a flow of power toward the far more visible presidency.[44] By the late 1970s, the House of Representatives permitted cameras to broadcast its floor proceedings. The Senate followed suit in the 1980s. Today, you can view major House floor debates and key committee meetings on C-SPAN, and Senate proceedings on C-SPAN2.[45]

5-7c The Court System

Maybe Congress has become less private in the face of television cameras. Not the federal court system. The Supreme Court may be equal by design with Congress and the president, but its refusal to permit cameras in its proceedings and deliberations places it a clear third in the media's picture of the federal government.

Lack of press access to court activities has forced coverage of the Supreme Court to emphasize places where the Court's actions rub against the other, more observable federal institutions. Court rulings on matters of great visibility, like affirmative action or abortion rights, receive media scrutiny that typically explores how groups on different sides of the issue will be affected by the Court's actions. This can include analysis of how these groups might petition the president or members of Congress, or what their next move might be in light of how the court ruled. This perspective fits nicely with the policy-as-strategy approach the press takes in its coverage of the president and Congress.

In a similar fashion, a recurring story involves how the ideological balance of the court shifts in response to presidential judicial appointments. This, too, is fundamentally a political horserace story, in which the president seeks to alter (in the case of Clinton) or preserve (in the case of Bush) the Supreme Court's conservative tendencies. The side that's "winning" the horserace is determined in part by the alignment of justices who "swing" between the court's conservative and liberal factions—whether they're consistently siding with one group or the other. Unlike private deliberations, the votes of justices are a matter of public record, available to reporters who wish to speculate on how tightly conservatives maintain their grip on the institution.

5-8 Beyond Agenda Setting

So, what difference does it make if the media insist on framing politics and policy-making in terms of winners and losers, strategies and tactics, and personalities and scandals? If the struggle between reporters and candidates or officials results in news coverage that does not enhance informed decision-making, how much of this coverage gets through to the public and how do people process it?

In Chapter 4, we saw how the media can have an important influence over what we think about through their agenda-setting ability, tempered though it may be through **selective exposure** and **selective perception.** Now, perhaps, we have a better sense of what those things are that we're invited to think about. Even if many of us are like the callers to the television program that chose to ask policy questions of Bill Clinton, the basis that many of us have for understanding our complex government is information that skirts substantive issues. When a feeding frenzy breaks, it's pretty easy to imagine what will be on the agenda of many Americans the next day.

Beyond agenda setting, there's evidence to suggest that the media can turn up the volume on a particular issue by covering it more intensively and affect the way we think about political figures by the context in which they're presented. Political scientists Shanto Iyengar and Donald Kinder performed a creative experiment in which they showed people television news reports that had been manipulated to emphasize stories about specific policy concerns. In most cases, people were more sensitized to the manipulated issue following exposure to the news reports than they were beforehand, attaching greater importance to it after being exposed to it in the news.[46]

Furthermore, exposure to stories featuring political figures in favorable contexts had the effect of bolstering people's impressions of them. News reports were found to unintentionally produce this **priming** effect, whereby the manner in which a politician was discussed in the news cued viewers to think about the politician in terms defined by that context.

Months after the September 11 attacks, President Bush continued to ride a wave of unparalleled popularity that can be explained in part by how the media covered him in the context of his efforts to fight terrorism, for which he received vast public support. When questions began to surface in May 2002 about whether the president had done everything possible to prevent the attacks, the White House acted swiftly to change the subject to terrorist threats that still remained, seeking to get the press to portray the president in a context where he was widely regarded as competent and to avoid reminders about some of the doubts people had about Bush's capability to serve as president prior to September 11.

The same thing happened in July 2003, following the first stages of the war with Iraq, when questions surfaced about whether the administration had misrepresented the dangers posed by Iraq in order to win public support for the war. In this instance, top White House officials attempted to reframe coverage around the benefits of having toppled the Iraqi government. In each case, the administration's concern was that if people were primed to think about President Bush's competence or integrity, they would begin to evaluate him in a critical light.

5-9 Media Bias?

Were stories like the ones questioning whether President Bush had misrepresented intelligence data to promote the Iraqi war a product of media bias? Some Bush operatives thought so, believing that the media were biased against the president and his conservative philosophy. Is there evidence to support this claim?

There's a widely held belief that mainstream media are biased toward liberal positions. During the 1990s, some conservatives derided CNN as the "Clinton News Network," and Fox News deliberately presents a conservative perspective on the news in a self-described effort to counter what it perceives as a liberal bias elsewhere. Critics point to the personal beliefs of journalists, many of whom admit to being liberal, and argue that it is impossible for journalists to keep their worldview out of coverage, claims of objectivity notwithstanding.

---

selective exposure
The tendency to pay attention to messages that are consistent with existing attitudes or beliefs, while overlooking messages that conflict with them.

selective perception
An unconscious process by which we filter information that we deem irrelevant, uninteresting, or inconsistent with our attitudes and beliefs, while absorbing information that conforms to our self-perception.

priming A media effect whereby the context in which a political figure is presented in the news can create a positive or negative cue for how viewers think about and evaluate that figure.

Conservative organizations like the Media Research Center seek to publicize instances of liberal bias in mainstream reporting, like those shown in Table 5-4 regarding the defection of Vermont Senator Jim Jeffords from the Republican Party, a move in the spring of 2001 that gave working control of the Senate to the Democratic Party. Take a minute to look at each claim and decide whether you agree that it amounts to slanted coverage.

So, what do you think? If you found bias in three or more of the claims in Table 5-4, would you also say you consider yourself conservative? It's not always the case, but people tend to find bias against the positions they hold, be they conservative or liberal. Those who have attempted to take an objective look at the issue are typically hard pressed to find systematic ideological bias in the news. Remember, when we try to quantify bias in the news, we're drawing a line between our view of the world and the news message. Coming up with an objective understanding of bias can be difficult because what's perceived as bias may depend partly on where we stand ideologically.

In fact, there's a left-wing critique of the media that claims there's a bias *toward* conservative institutions and ideas. From this point of view, the media support the interests of those who own the media, not those who report the news. This perspective includes an uncritical acceptance, for instance, of free enterprise, American military might, and American foreign policy interests. In specific terms, such critics might argue that patriotic coverage of the Iraq war, in which reporters presented American interests as "our" interests, ignored the perspective that the conflict served the needs of large oil companies and put business considerations ahead of regard for human life.[47] Consistent with this critique, it became an article of faith among many liberal critics that George W. Bush did not get the same level of press scrutiny as Bill Clinton.

There's a third perspective on bias that sidesteps ideological positioning to find a **structural bias** in the news—that is, a tendency for the media to cover the same limited set of individuals and institutions. When gatekeepers decide what's newsworthy, they're not starting out by looking at an infinite set of events to cover. Most events that could potentially be reported never even make it into the discussion.[48] However, events involving high-level elected officials, entertainment and business leaders, and other well-known individuals are never far from their radar screen. Consequently, these individuals and the institutions they represent are disproportionately featured in media coverage.[49]

▶ **structural bias** The possibility that news stories are skewed toward the limited set of sources and topics selected by gatekeepers for publication and broadcast.

Although news organizations appear to be ready to cover news anywhere it's happening at a moment's notice, in fact the process of making news is cumbersome and requires a lot of planning. High-ranking government officials, political party leaders, the heads of a few prominent interest groups, and academic experts offer gatekeepers a ready supply of reliable sources, giving their perspectives disproportionate media play. From this point of view, bias is not introduced because the media report on George W. Bush more than John Kerry or John Kerry more than George W. Bush, but because they cover both Bush and Kerry far more reliably than they cover sources without official positions or high standing.

5-10 Making Sense of Media Coverage

What happens, then, when the media's desire to entertain us clashes with their obligation to inform us; when the proliferation of media give us more news options than our parents could have dreamed of but less clarity about who's doing the gatekeeping; when news cycles turn over at the speed of light? Under these circumstances, it's understandable if we're a bit confused, or feel like tuning out.

Look at Table 5-5 to see how easily facts seeped into innuendo and mainstream media blended with marginal media in the rush to report the news about Bill Clinton's alleged affair with Gennifer Flowers. The year was 1992, and Flowers had decided to go public with what at the time was a bombshell announcement: that the front-runner for the Democratic presidential nomination had had an extramarital affair with her. Her vehicle for making this announcement: the supermarket tabloid *Star*, which had paid her for her story.

As shown in Table 5-5, in one quick turn of the news cycle, unsubstantiated claims about the source of the Flowers story were being reported with confidence on NBC's *Today* program, while rumor of the alleged Flowers-Clinton liaison was headline news everywhere.

TABLE 5-4	**Bias Claim 1**
Is This Coverage Biased? INTERACTIVE TABLE	The media labeled Jeffords a disgruntled "moderate" or "maverick" when in fact he was a liberal who had no place in the Republican Party, making Jeffords appear sympathetic and mainstream rather than out of step with national Republicans. Example: "He is a maverick, he is an independent. This was really about having his own moderate views heard within what he thinks is an increasingly conservative Republican Party." (ABC News) Is this coverage biased? ____Yes ____No

Bias Claim 2

The media blamed conservatives for making the Republican Party too conservative, not Jeffords for being too liberal. Example: "Jeffords' frustration with his increasingly conservative party has been building for a long time.... Jeffords felt his views on taxes, the poor, the environment were dismissed by Republican leaders." (ABC News)

Is this coverage biased?   ____Yes   ____No

Bias Claim 3

The media blamed the Bush White House for Jeffords' defection, saying they punished him for voting against them and did not respect his views. This perspective disregards Jeffords' own disrespect for the policy views of his own party. Example: "So, why is Jeffords on the brink of bolting? Mostly, friends say, because he is deeply offended by lack of respect from the White House and from key Senate Republicans.... The last straw: After Jeffords votes against Bush's tax cut, the White House retaliates by not inviting him when a Vermont educator is honored as teacher of the year." (NBC News)

Is this coverage biased?   ____Yes   ____No

Bias Claim 4

The media reported Jeffords' actions as noble, virtually ignoring the perspective of his constituents in Vermont, who might have felt betrayed by his party switch. Examples: CBS News said "He was treated like a rock star when he went home to explain his reasons for quitting the Republican Party." NBC News said Jeffords "embraced a flinty kind of New England independence."

Is this coverage biased?   ____Yes   ____No

Bias Claim 5

The media adopted the preferred liberal conclusion that Jeffords' departure should force President Bush to moderate his views and abandon some of his conservative positions, rather than the preferred conservative conclusion that the president should stand by his conservative ideas and take the case for his agenda directly to the people. Example: Without Jeffords, Bush faces congressional obstacles to "new legislation and confirmation for judicial nominees. The president's options? Political analysts say bipartisan compromise." (NBC News)

Is this coverage biased?   ____Yes   ____No

Source: Media Research Center website: http://www.mrc.org/cyberalerts/2002/cyb20020524.asp#3.

How much of what was reported could be believed? Flowers, the source of the allegation, had sold her story to the *Star*, a newspaper reputable journalists would never touch. But everyone was willing to report on how the *New York Post* had reported on the *Star* press conference, laundering the story through a somewhat more respectable source but not changing a thing about its questionable origins.

10 A.M., Day 1	Gennifer Flowers holds a press conference, sponsored by the tabloid *Star,* alleging an affair with presidential candidate Bill Clinton.
2 P.M., Day 1	Press conference is mentioned in the quasi-tabloid, but more mainstream, *New York Post.*
4 P.M., Day 1	Newspapers and television news programs nationwide that would never go near a story in the *Star* report on the *Post's* coverage of the press conference.
5 P.M., Day 1	Flowers repeats her allegations on the evening tabloid television program *A Current Affair.*
7 P.M., Day 1	Clinton campaign consultant James Carville alleges that Flowers' story was the handiwork of the rival Bush campaign, saying Roger Ailes, a Bush advisor, had links to *A Current Affair.*
9 P.M., Day 1	That evening on CNN's *Larry King Live,* talk show host Larry King asks his guest, Bush Labor Secretary Lynn Martin, what she knows about the Roger Ailes/*A Current Affair* connection.
9:30 P.M., Day 1	King's question prompts an on-air telephone call from Hollywood producer and Clinton supporter Linda Bloodworth-Thomason, who insists that she knows "one-hundred percent that Mr. Roger Ailes is a consultant for . . . *A Current Affair.*"
6 A.M., Day 2	The next morning, Roger Ailes appears on NBC's *Today* show, where host Bryant Gumbel asserts with certainty: "The word is out that the Gennifer Flowers story was leaked by one Roger Ailes."

TABLE 5-5

Rumor at the Speed of Light: The Spread of the Gennifer Flowers Story

Source: Matthew Kerbel, *Remote and Controlled: Media Politics in a Cynical Age* (Boulder, CO: Westview Press, 1998), 138.

The claim that the Bush campaign was behind the whole thing was equally dubious, starting with an allegation by a Clinton operative and bolstered by a nationally televised phone call from a Clinton friend, both of whom had a political interest in redirecting coverage away from Flowers' allegation. However, once the *Today* show reported that the Bush campaign was behind Flowers' charge as though it were a fact, it took on the legitimacy of an undeniable claim, even though it remained unsubstantiated.

If you're not sure what to make of this, you're not alone. Even professional media critics have a hard time coming up with suggestions for how to make good sense of the world as it appears in the media. Political communication specialist Roderick Hart makes the point that the pervasiveness of mass media, particularly television, has changed the way we feel about politics. Remember the cynicism and disillusionment we said so many Americans feel about government? Hart lays a lot of it at television's doorstep, claiming that while watching television can make us *seem* closer to our world, in reality it creates a false sense of intimacy that can leave us feeling empty. He would have us get more involved in the political world we can touch, relying less on the mass media for our information and more on the immediate attachments we can find in our communities, from which real satisfaction can flow.[50]

That's one solution—one that requires effort and desire on our part, and the ability to look past the messages in mainstream media that confound clear and informed understanding of political events. To this end, there is tentative but powerful evidence that as the Internet matures, new media may provide us with a vehicle for combating the often cynical and unhelpful messages of the old media.

In early 2003, Howard Dean was a largely unknown former governor of Vermont who had been running for president on a shoestring budget for about a year. The quintessential long shot, Dean received virtually no notice from television and newspaper reporters, who considered him a footnote to the emerging field of Democratic presidential hopefuls.

Then, a confluence of forces propelled him to national attention in a short span of time. One was his outspoken condemnation of the Iraq war, which set him apart from his rivals and resonated with a group of attentive Democratic primary voters. The second was a penchant for unvarnished plain talk, which differentiated him from politicians who carefully choose their words for reporters. The third was the Internet.

Supporters attracted to Dean's substance and style began self-organizing through meetup.com, the website designed to bring together people with similar interests, as we mentioned in Chapter 4. Dean's campaign took advantage of this phenomenon by putting a link to meetup.com on its website and encouraging people to get involved. As hundreds, then thousands and tens of thousands flocked to Dean meetups over the following months, the campaign further utilized the Internet by hosting an official weblog or "blog" where citizens could interface with campaign strategists, suggesting ideas (which the campaign at times adopted), offering moral support to fellow Dean enthusiasts, and commenting on the campaign's progress. The candidate began using the language of empowerment, calling his campaign the first great grassroots effort of the electronic era. The claim was validated as the number of people who subscribed to Dean's email list rose through the thousands to the hundreds of thousands by mid-summer, fully one and one-half years before the presidential election, during a period when observers of political campaigns assume most people are not focused on politics.

Then the Dean campaign did something that caused the mainstream press to take notice. In the days prior to June 2003, when candidates close their books on fund-raising for the second quarter of the year, Dean appealed to his online followers to donate small amounts to his campaign in order to boost his fund-raising totals. They responded in numbers rarely seen before, raising at one point $800,000 in online contributions in one day (just short of the one-day Internet record of $1,000,000 set by John McCain following his success in the New Hampshire Republican primary in 2000). Because of his successful Internet effort, the once obscure Dean bested his eight Democratic rivals in fund-raising in 2003. The Internet had made the dark horse into a viable presidential contender.

Dean's fund-raising success was all the more noteworthy because it came on the heels of what Washington media insiders considered a damaging performance on the political talk show *Meet the Press*. Unable to specify the number of American troops in Iraq and unsteady in his responses to questions about the death penalty and a constitutional Balanced Budget Amendment, media commentators universally declared the Dean candidacy dead or gravely wounded.

Supporters would have nothing of it. Dean's blog—and dozens of "unofficial" blogs that had been started by private citizens—abounded with postings about how the *Meet the Press* interview was a classic case of cynical Washington reporters playing "gotcha" with politicians, trying to deflate politicians in an effort to gain the upper hand in setting the agenda. Dean's Internet supporters refused to be sucked into the negativity of mainstream coverage, and responded by recruiting new backers and giving money to the Dean campaign in large amounts. As representatives of the old media declared the Dean campaign to be not ready for prime time, representatives of the new media declared that "prime time" is itself a construct belonging to the old media—and not relevant to their approach to politics.

Ultimately, the rules of the old media prevailed. Despite his online fund-raising and organizational success, Dean's Internet effort failed to win him the Democratic Party's presidential nomination, in large part because his heated, outspoken, off-the-cuff demeanor played poorly on television, where most voters still get their political news and where coolness and control win the day. Nonetheless, it did cause reporters and other candidates to take notice. The Dean phenomenon raises the prospect that a candidate who resonates with the electorate can motivate people to engage in political action through the new media, even at a time when television still rules as the primary medium of political communication. As the Internet matures, it offers the tantalizing possibility that a new generation of wired citizens may be able to engage politicians in a two-way dialogue that enables us to be informed and active rather than amused and detached, in a manner consistent with Robert Dahl's call for enlightened understanding and effective democratic participation.

Chapter Review

The mass media—encompassing newspapers, television, radio, magazines, and the Internet—are an important link between the public and government, although the variety of media messages and their sometimes uncertain origins can make it challenging to distinguish truth from half-truth, rumor, and gossip. This can confound our ability to make enlightened political choices by presenting us with inadequate or irrelevant information about politics and government.

For many years, we didn't have anything resembling mass media. During the Revolutionary War, newspapers found they could move public opinion, and with the establishment of political parties after 1790, newspapers became vehicles for rallying the party faithful. In the 1830s, the penny press emerged as an alternative to the party press. By the end of the nineteenth century, newspapers had become big businesses, drawing audiences with sensational "yellow journalism" and widely popular "muckraking" investigations of political and corporate corruption. The era of mass media followed in the twentieth century, first with radio, then television, cable, satellite, and Internet communication.

Traditional media like major newspapers and television news programs employ editors and producers to act as gatekeepers of news content and determine the stories that appear in print or on the air. On the Internet, things can be more confusing; anyone with a web address is a potential gatekeeper, and it can be hard to know if the material being reported is factual. Historically, gatekeepers have applied a set of standards to determine if a story is newsworthy, centering on characteristics like conflict, proximity to the news audience, timeliness and a sense of the unusual, relevance and familiarity.

The blending of information with entertainment, or "infotainment" complicates the media environment. Feature-laden "soft news" has become a large part of mainstream coverage, and gossip programs share news subjects with newspapers and television news shows because they draw widespread attention, which serves the commercial needs of media operators. This is happening at a time when the government is actively deregulating the media industry, which is facilitating the concentration of media ownership in the hands of a few "megamedia" organizations. The risk of such concentration of power is that stories threatening to these corporate interests will not be exposed in the news, undermining the level of information we need to make intelligent political decisions.

As mass media became a central part of our lives, it became a key resource for candidates and elected officials, and the source of a struggle between politicians and journalists over control of the news message. Candidates try to get their version of events in the news by staging media events for the press, holding photo opportunities, and spinning news items in a favorable direction. Reporters have the last say in how a story is framed, or the context in which it is presented. In recent years the techniques of campaign coverage have filtered into coverage of how officials govern, turning the process of governing into a kind of horserace with political winners and losers.

In addition to agenda setting, in which media coverage influences what we think about, news stories can prime us to think about and evaluate political figures in specific ways. Some people believe the news media are ideologically biased, although bias is a difficult thing to prove. A structural critique of news coverage argues that bias is not ideological so much as it is about the disproportionate attention centered on a small set of well-known individuals.

Making your way through the freewheeling, decentralized news environment can be difficult, and even professional media critics have a hard time coming up with suggestions for how to make sense of the world as it appears in the media. News messages may encourage cynicism and create a false sense of intimacy about the political world that ultimately leaves us feeling empty. At the same time, the Internet offers the intriguing promise that the new media may facilitate informed participation.

Key Terms

agenda setting (p. 139)
attack journalism (p. 142)
equal time provision (p. 133)
fairness doctrine (p. 134)
Federal Communications Act
   of 1934 (p. 133)
Federal Communications Commission
   (FCC) (p. 133)
fireside chats (p. 144)
frame (p. 141)
free media (p. 138)
gatekeepers (p. 123)
gridlock (p. 147)

hard news (p. 132)
horserace (p. 142)
infotainment (p. 131)
inverted pyramid (p. 127)
libel (p. 133)
mass media (p. 123)
media events (p. 139)
muckraking (p. 125)
narrowcasting (p. 135)
news cycle (p. 141)
newsworthy (p. 130)
paid media (p. 138)
party press (p. 124)

penny press (p. 125)
photo opportunities (p. 140)
press conferences (p. 146)
priming (p. 148)
selective exposure (p. 148)
selective perception (p. 148)
soft news (p. 132)
spin (p. 140)
Stamp Act (p. 124)
structural bias (p. 149)
Telecommunications Act of 1996 (p. 134)
yellow journalism (p. 125)

Review Questions

Note: You can find the correct answers to these questions by taking the quiz and then submitting your answers in the Online Edition. The program will automatically score your submission. If you miss a question, the program will provide the correct answer, a rationale for the answer, and the section number in the chapter where the topic is discussed.

1. Gatekeepers
   a. are the small number of influential people who own media organizations.
   b. decide what is newsworthy.
   c. could be almost anyone in traditional news organizations.
   d. would include people who regularly watch television news.

2. "Muckraking" was popular during the period of
   a. the colonial press.
   b. the party press.
   c. yellow journalism.
   d. television.

3. Traditional print news stories are typically structured
   a. around the newsworthy criterion of conflict rather than relevance.
   b. thematically.
   c. around "why" questions.
   d. in inverted pyramid style.

4. "Infotainment" is incompatible with
   a. programs like *Entertainment Tonight*.
   b. stories about sex scandals.
   c. hard news.
   d. soft news.

5. Which of the following is most closely associated with the deregulation of mass media?
   a. the Federal Communications Act of 1934
   b. the Telecommunications Act of 1996
   c. the equal time provision
   d. the fairness doctrine

6. "Megamedia"
   a. may hinder our "enlightened understanding" of politics.
   b. is the reason for the large variety of media choices we have today.
   c. began to emerge after passage of the Telecommunications Act of 1996.
   d. includes Internet weblogs.

7. In the competition between reporters and political candidates, which of the following is a powerful tool at the disposal of reporters?
   a. spin
   b. media events
   c. framing
   d. photo opportunities

8. Presidential efforts to control news messages
   a. require that reporters be kept at a distance.
   b. may include holding televised press conferences.
   c. were largely invented by Franklin D. Roosevelt.
   d. are applied with great effect by all presidents.

9. When we're cued to think of a political figure in a specific context, we call the effect
   a. agenda setting.
   b. selective exposure.
   c. framing.
   d. priming.

10. The fact that most small party presidential candidates did not get mainstream media exposure during the 2000 election is an example of
    a. "megamedia" bias.
    b. liberal bias.
    c. conservative bias.
    d. structural bias.

In Their Own Words

You might be interested in examining some of what the following authors have said about the topics we've been discussing:

Alger, Dean. *Megamedia: How Giant Corporations Dominate Mass Media, Distort Competition, and Endanger Democracy.* Boulder, CO: Rowman & Littlefield, 1998. Alger presents a clearly constructed analysis of how very few organizations own most of our favorite media outlets, and what that means for the quality of information we get.

Graber, Doris A. *Mass Media and American Politics,* 6th ed. Washington, DC: Congressional Quarterly Press, 2002. A thorough overview of media politics.

Hart, Roderick P. *Seducing America: How Television Charms the Modern Voter.* New York: Oxford University Press, 1994. Hart offers an original and thoughtful analysis of how television misleads us into feeling clever and involved when in fact it has the effect of making us cynical and detached.

Patterson, Thomas E. *Out of Order.* New York: Alfred A. Knopf, 1993. It's the political system that Patterson claims is out of order, owing to the misplaced role of the media as the primary link between candidates and voters.

Sabato, Larry J. *Feeding Frenzy: How Attack Journalism Has Transformed American Politics.* New York: The Free Press, 1991. An account of the rise of attack journalism, including many examples of feeding frenzies from the recent past.

Iyengar, Shanto, and Donald R. Kinder. *News That Matters.* Chicago: University of Chicago Press, 1987. A creative approach to capturing media effects beyond agenda setting.

Tuchman, Gaye. *Making News: A Study in the Construction of Reality.* New York: Free Press, 1978. For readers interested in the question of what is included in and omitted from the news and why, Tuchman offers an interesting account of how gatekeepers determine the content of news reports.

Notes

1. The Drudge Report, Sunday, December 17, 2000. See http://drudgereport.com/.
2. A story about the error appeared in the *Washington Post* (December 19, 2000), and an excerpt from the story also appeared in the Drudge Report.
3. Doris A. Graber, *Mass Media and American Politics,* 6th ed. (Washington, DC: Congressional Quarterly Press, 2002), 110–112.
4. For a full discussion of these points, see Dean Alger, *Megamedia: How Giant Corporations Dominate Mass Media, Distort Competition, and Endanger Democracy* (Boulder, CO: Rowman & Littlefield, 1998), 4–20.
5. Richard Davis, *The Press and American Politics: The New Mediator* (White Plains, NY: Longman Publishing, 1992), 43–45.
6. Ibid., 47–49.
7. Richard L. Rubin, *Press, Party, and Presidency* (New York: W. W. Norton, 1981).
8. Ibid.
9. Davis, *Press and American Politics,* 70–79.
10. Ibid., 92.
11. For an interesting account of the Salinger incident that blames traditional media for the rapid spread of Internet misinformation, take a look at this piece from Salon.com, at http://www.salon.com/media/media961112.html.
12. Dan Eggen and Bill Miller, *Washington Post,* May 16, 2002, sec. A.
13. Graber, *Mass Media,* 116–120.
14. Ibid., 120.
15. Davis, *Press and American Politics,* 128–134.
16. The case is *New York Times Co. v. Sullivan,* 376 US 354 (1964).
17. Davis, *Press and American Politics,* 122.
18. Alger, *Megamedia,* 4–20.
19. If you're interested, you can find a brief and interesting Internet timeline at http://www.pbs.org/opb/nerds2.0.1/timeline/.
20. You can find a full list of cable selections from Zap2it.com, a supplier of television and movie information and a division of Tribune Media Services, at http://tv.zap2it.com/resources/stations/us/cable/.
21. Ibid.
22. U.S. Radio and TV Directory, at http://www.100000watts.com.
23. Carla Gesell-Streeter, "Talk Radio History," at http://www.radiotalk.org/history.html.
24. Alger, *Megamedia,* 5–10.
25. Ibid., 20, emphasis in original.
26. CNN, March 6, 1992, Jill Dougherty reporting. Cited in Matthew R. Kerbel, *Edited for Television: CNN, ABC, and American Presidential Elections,* 2nd ed. (Boulder, CO: Westview Press, 1998), 35.
27. Dana Milbank, "Impact of Tape on Race Is Uncertain," *Washington Post,* October 30, 2004, p. A1.
28. Larry J. Sabato, *Feeding Frenzy: How Attack Journalism Has Transformed American Politics* (New York: Free Press, 1991), 1.
29. Kerbel, *Edited for Television,* 38, emphasis in original.
30. Thomas E. Patterson, *Out of Order* (New York: Alfred A. Knopf, 1993), 53–93.
31. Ibid., 20.
32. Ibid., 78–81.
33. "Campaign 2000: More News, Less Filling," Center for Media and Public Affairs, September 21, 2000.
34. Patterson, *Out of Order,* 73–74.
35. Kerbel, *Remote and Controlled,* 102–129.
36. Betty Houchin Winfield, *FDR and the News Media* (Urbana: University of Illinois Press, 1990).
37. You can skim though the text of Roosevelt's fireside chats, archived at the Franklin D. Roosevelt Presidential Library, at http://www.mhrcc.org/fdr/fdr.html.
38. Graham J. White, *FDR and the Press* (Chicago: University of Chicago Press, 1979).
39. Mary Ann Watson, *The Expanding Vista: American Television in the Kennedy Years* (New York: Oxford University Press, 1990), 76.
40. You can read transcripts of some of Kennedy's press conferences through the John F. Kennedy library at http://www.jfklibrary.org/jfk_pressconf_menu.html.
41. Mark Hertsgaard, *On Bended Knee: The Press and the Reagan Presidency* (New York: Farrar, Straus and Giroux, 1988). Hertsgaard says the objective of the Reagan media team was "not simply to tame the press but to transform it into an unwitting mouthpiece of the government," and quotes NBC anchorman Tom Brokaw as calling the Reagan staff "killers" for their ability to get the coverage they wanted on a regular basis (p. 5).
42. Kerbel, *Remote and Controlled,* 51–52.
43. *NBC Nightly News,* May 18, 1994. Cited in Kerbel, *Remote and Controlled,* 122.
44. Norman J. Ornstein, "The Open Congress Meets the President," in Anthony King (ed.), *Both Ends of the Avenue: The Presidency, Congress, and the Executive Branch in the 1980s* (Washington, DC: American Enterprise Institute, 1983).
45. Curious about what's on now? Check out the C-SPAN schedule at http://inside.c-spanarchives.org:8080/cspan/schedule.csp.
46. Shanto Iyengar and Donald R. Kinder, *News That Matters* (Chicago: University of Chicago Press, 1987).
47. Calvin Exoo, *Politics of the Mass Media* (West Publishing Company, 1994). Exoo makes this point about the Persian Gulf War.
48. See, for instance, Gay Tuchman, *Making News: A Study in the Construction of Reality* (New York: Free Press, 1978).
49. Herbert J. Gans, *Deciding What's News: A Study of CBS Evening News, NBC Nightly News, Newsweek, and Time* (New York: Vintage Books, 1980).
50. Roderick P. Hart, *Seducing America: How Television Charms the Modern Voter* (New York: Oxford University Press, 1994).

Political Parties:
Connecting Us to the Electoral Process

6

6-1 Introduction

What exactly is going on in the photo at the top of the next page? It's the serious business of formally ratifying the selection of a candidate who will seek to become the most powerful person in the world and crafting the positions on which he will campaign. So, why are these people dressed like . . . Uncle Sam? Because politics in America is and always has been a blend of fun and responsibility, spectacle and power, sideshow and serious deal making.

These people are delegates to the 2004 Democratic National Convention in Boston. Their outfits may not exactly seem presidential, but they allow the delegates to get involved in the fun of politics. If the essence of democracy is self-expression, then political party conventions like this one are bastions of democracy. It may not always be dignified, but you can probably see how political parties can provide an important link between ordinary people and the political process.

A **political party,** in the words of political scientist Leon Epstein, is "any group, however loosely organized, seeking to elect government officeholders under a given label."[1] There are other definitions as well, but they hold in common the idea that parties are organized groups that share the desire to win power by contesting elections. If you take away the requirement about trying to elect officeholders, and instead talk about organized groups that try to influence the political process, you'll end up with something closer to the interest groups we'll be talking about in Chapter 8. Parties are about political competition, about winning and losing, and through our involvement in that competition, they can connect us to the electoral process.

Even though political parties are organized groups, that doesn't mean that they're tightly integrated. Parties exist at all levels of our federal system, and state and local parties can exercise a fair amount of autonomy from national parties. There are also different venues for parties, where they perform unrelated functions: in government, where Republicans and Democrats want to fulfill different legislative agendas, and among ordinary people in the **electorate,** where Republicans, Democrats, and a host of smaller parties run campaigns to compete in elections. So, it's fair to say that parties are organizations, but not hierarchical ones.

In the United States, two parties dominate the political landscape. That's not the case in other countries, though, and we're going to take a look at why. In fact, two parties have competed in elections in this country since its founding, and we're going to take a look back at that history to lend some perspective to where today's parties come from. Once we do that, we'll talk about the government and campaign venues

Delegates to the 2004 Democratic National Convention in Boston
Source: AFP/Getty Images.

where parties do most of their work, to get a sense of how they're set up and how they operate.

Since a big part of party activity is running political campaigns and competing in elections, we'll also take some time to look at how that works. Campaigns are complex, multistage enterprises that engage political parties and the mass media, and therefore require a lot of attention and explanation. So, we'll devote Chapter 7 to examining them.

6-2 Why Two Parties?

There's something that seems natural about the idea of two parties in competition, like two baseball or basketball teams facing off against each other. But, in truth, two political parties competing against each other is something that doesn't happen in most nations. Great Britain has three parties: two major ones and an active minor one. Nine parties had some hope of success in the last French elections. Italy boasts more than one dozen parties. So does Israel. Figure 6-1 provides an overview of the wide range of viable political parties competing for power in governments around the world.

So, what is it about the United States that supports just two parties in regular competition? There are several explanations.

6-2a Winner-Take-All Elections

What would happen in a basketball game if we decided to award a partial victory to the team that scored the second largest number of points? Suddenly, you wouldn't have to win in order to be competitive. If we extended the rule to award a partial victory, say, to any number of teams that could score at least fifty points, we might end up with a lot of basketball teams on the same court trying to score their points before the clock ran out.

Sound silly? Perhaps—but that's pretty much the way election rules work in nations with **proportional representation,** where voters select the party of their choice, and representation in the legislature is awarded in rough equivalency to each party's percentage of the total. Proportional representation systems feature **multimember districts,** meaning several people, typically of different parties, represent one district. Any party receiving more than a minimum percentage of the vote—which may be as low as 10 percent—is eligible for representation in the legislature, so it makes sense that many parties will take a

political party (see p. 156) An organized group of individuals with common interests seeking to gain power in government by electing officials to public office.

electorate (see p. 156) The portion of the public eligible to vote in elections.

proportional representation Electoral systems that encourage the participation of many parties by awarding representation on the basis of the share of the vote won by each party in an electoral district.

multimember district The structure of electoral districts in proportional representation systems, in which each electoral district sends several representatives to the legislature.

Bahrain: Bahrain does not allow political parties.

China: China's political party is the Communist Party of China. This party allows so-called democratic subparties, but all of their functions are handled by the primary party.

Colombia: Colombia's parties include the Colombian Liberal Party, the Colombian Conservative Party, Radical Change, Team Colombia, and the Movement of National Salvation, among others.

Denmark: Denmark's parties include the Liberal Party of Denmark, Social Democrats, the Danish People's Party, the Conservative People's Party, and the Socialist People's Party, among others.

France: France's parties include Rally for the Republic; the Liberal Democrats; the Socialist Party; the National Front; the Greens; the Left Radicals; the Communist Party; Republican Pole; and Hunting, Fishing, Nature, Traditions; among others.

Germany: Germany's parties include the Social Democrats, the Christian Democrats, the Greens, and the Free Democrats, among others.

Haiti: Haiti's parties include the Water Fall Family, the Christian Movement, and Open the Gate, among others.

Iceland: Iceland's parties include the Independence Party, the Alliance of the Women's List, and the Progressive Party, among others.

Italy: Italy's parties include Forwards Italy, the National Alliance, the New Italian Socialists, Olive Tree, Communist Refoundation, League North, the Christian-Democratic Centre, and Democrats of the Left, among others.

Israel: Israel's parties include Avoda (Labour), Likud (Consolidation), Geshur (Bridge), and Meretz (Energy), among others.

Philippines: The Philippines' parties include the National Union of Christian Democrats, the United Muslim Democratic Party, and the Struggle for Democratic Filipinos, among others.

Russia: Russia's parties include the Communist Party, Apple, Fatherland All-Russia, Women of Russia, Interregional Movement Unity, Union of Right Forces, the Stalinist Bloc for the Soviet Union, and the Zhirinovsky Bloc, among others.

Saudi Arabia: Saudi Arabia does not allow political parties.

Singapore: Singapore's parties include the People's Action Party, the Worker's Party, and the Singapore Democratic Alliance, among others.

South Korea: South Korea's parties include the Grand National Party, the Democratic Party, and the United Liberal Democrats, among others.

Spain: Spain's parties include the People's Party, Spanish Socialist Workers, the United Left, Convergence and Union, and the Basque Nationalist Party, among others.

United Arab Emirates: The United Arab Emirates does not allow political parties.

Figure 6-1
Other Political Systems

shot at electoral competition. Proportional representation systems are popular in Europe, which helps explain why so many European nations have **multiparty systems,** with a large number of active parties successfully competing for a role in government.

The United States does things differently. The American **two-party system** discourages many parties from forming because the standard for being represented in government is nothing short of complete electoral victory. Unlike proportional representation systems, the American **winner-take-all system** awards all the representation to the candidate of the

PROPORTIONAL REPRESENTATION SYSTEM				
Party	Number of Votes	Percentage of Votes	Number of Legislative Seats Won	Percentage of Representation
Centrist Party	3,450	34.5%	2	33.3%
Conservative Party	3,375	33.8%	2	33.3%
Labor Party	1,275	12.8%	1	16.7%
Green Party	1,200	12.0%	1	16.7%
Socialist Party	700	7.0%	0	0.0%
Totals	**10,000**	**100.1%***	**6**	**100.0%**

*Rounding

WINNER-TAKE-ALL SYSTEM				
Party	Number of Votes	Percentage of Votes	Number of Legislative Seats Won	Percentage of Representation
Centrist Party	3,450	34.5%	1	100.0%
Conservative Party	3,375	33.8%	0	0.0%
Labor Party	1,275	12.8%	0	0.0%
Green Party	1,200	12.0%	0	0.0%
Socialist Party	700	7.0%	0	0.0%
Totals	**10,000**	**100.1%***	**1**	**100.0%**

*Rounding

TABLE 6-1

Change the Rules, Change the Outcome

▶**multiparty systems** (see p. 158) Political systems in which more than two parties have a realistic chance to win representation in government.

▶**two-party system** (see p. 158) A political system, like ours in the United States, in which only two parties have a realistic chance to win most elections.

▶**winner-take-all system** (see p. 158) The electoral system in use in the United States, whereby the candidate of the party receiving the most votes in an electoral district gets to represent that district.

▶**plurality** Winning the most votes in an election, or at least one more vote than the next closest candidate or party.

▶**majority** Winning more than half the votes in an election, or 50 percent plus one.

▶**single-member district** The structure of electoral districts in winner-take-all electoral systems, in which each electoral district sends only one representative to the legislature.

party that wins a **plurality** of votes, which simply means that the candidate has to win the most votes. He or she doesn't even need to win a **majority** of votes or more than half. In a winner-take-all system, just win one more vote than the next candidate, and you get to be the lone representative from your **single-member district,** which is represented only by the candidate of that winning party.

There's a pronounced difference between winner-take-all rules and proportional representation rules. Take a look at Table 6-1, where five fictional parties are competing in a hypothetical legislative district. The voting between the top two parties was close, with only a handful of votes separating the first-place Centrist Party from the second-place Conservative Party. The remaining three parties lagged behind.

If a proportional representation system with multiple-member districts were in place, several people would have the opportunity to represent the district. For the sake of example, let's say the district would have six representatives. Assume also that any party with at least 10 percent of the vote would be eligible for representation. Based on the proportion of the vote won by each party, the first-place Centrist Party and the second-place Conservative Party would each be awarded two seats and would be able to send two of their members to serve in the legislature. The third-place Labor Party and fourth-place Green Party would each get to send one of their members to the legislature because each party received close to one-sixth of the vote and cleared the 10 percent threshold for representation. Only the last-place Socialist Party, with 7 percent of the vote, would be shut out entirely.

If the American winner-take-all system were in place, the same results would produce a radically different outcome. With only 34.5 percent of the vote, the candidate of the Centrist Party would win the right to be the sole representative for the district, taking 100 percent of the representation, despite the fact that almost two-thirds of the voters preferred someone else. Furthermore, because the winner takes everything, small shifts in support can produce dramatically different results. Had the Conservative Party managed to poll just seventy-six more votes, it would have won all the representation and the Centrist Party would have won nothing.

6-2b Election Laws

If the electoral system discourages competition from minor parties, election laws compound this inequity by stacking the deck in favor of Republicans and Democrats. Candidates running under a major party label are guaranteed a spot on the ballot. Candidates of smaller parties often have to earn their way on by collecting signatures from a sufficient number of voters to demonstrate their viability. The effort and expense required to do this discourages poorly organized and poorly financed third parties from trying.[2] In order to qualify for his third-party presidential run in 1992, businessman Ross Perot needed to file petitions in all fifty states, an enormous undertaking that required money, coordination, legwork, and legal assistance in interpreting the fifty individual state election laws in place across the country.

In 1980, Republican Representative John Anderson lost out to Ronald Reagan for the nomination of his party but decided to run as an independent candidate against Reagan and incumbent Democrat Jimmy Carter. Like Perot, Anderson had to overcome election laws designed to discourage this kind of insurgent candidacy. Unlike Perot, Anderson could not self-finance the effort to qualify on fifty state ballots, and the money it took simply to get into the game left him with limited resources to run a general election campaign.

The problems Anderson faced weren't restricted to money, either. By the time he had made the decision to run as an independent in late April 1980, the deadline for filing to get on the ballot had already passed in five states: Kentucky, Maine, Maryland, New Mexico, and Ohio. Anderson had to set up a separate petition drive in every state and in the District of Columbia. To qualify for the ballot in California, he needed 100,000 signatures, but he needed more than half that number in the much smaller state of Georgia. Qualifying for all fifty-one ballots in 1980 required a total of 1.2 million signatures gathered under fifty-one different sets of rules.[3]

6-2c Public Opinion and Party Flexibility

Back in Chapter 3, we said that, by and large, Americans agree on the rules of the political game. It's been a characteristic of American politics that, for all our disagreements on particular issues, most of us tend to prefer democracy, capitalism, liberty, and equality of opportunity to their alternatives. We also tend to support moderate positions, such as those balancing individual liberty with social responsibility, over extreme positions. As a consequence, parties advocating socialism, communism, fascism, or libertarianism simply don't find a big audience in America.

Since public opinion tends toward the political center rather than the political extremes, the Republican and Democratic Parties find themselves crafting positions that reflect this relative moderation. After all, parties and their candidates have to go where the votes are. The centrist nature of public opinion dovetails with the winner-take-all electoral system, as both forces move political parties to embrace broad and moderate political messages in the effort to capture the most votes.

You might look at this situation and conclude that there's no real difference between Democrats and Republicans. Or you could say that both major parties are like big umbrellas containing several factions, which would probably go their own way in other nations where the electoral system rewarded multiple small parties.[4] The Republican Party is composed of several conservative factions that have different interests and agendas, including:

- *Religious conservatives* concerned about moral issues, but not economic issues
- *Business conservatives* favoring free enterprise, who are not particularly concerned about moral questions

- *Small government conservatives* whose laissez-faire views on social issues may conflict with the direction religious conservatives want government to take

Similarly, the Democratic Party is composed of several relatively liberal factions that also have different and at times competing agendas:

- *Economic liberals,* centered around unions, who are concerned with wages, benefits, job creation, and the interests of workers
- *Social liberals,* such as African Americans and many Jews, with a liberal social agenda, including concern for minority rights
- *Social and economic moderates* ("New Democrats" as Bill Clinton called them), especially suburbanites and women concerned with crime, education, and the environment, whose support of globalization and free trade may conflict with the interests of union workers

Even within these groups, there can be flexibility and overlap. Union workers with conservative social values were dubbed "Reagan Democrats" when they were persuaded to vote Republican in the 1980s. Business leaders in the entertainment field who have liberal social agendas often support Democratic candidates.

Because of the fluid and diverse nature of the groups that identify with the two major parties, Republicans and Democrats need to engage in the process of **interest aggregation** to bring together a wide variety of sometimes-conflicting demands, in order to enter into successful electoral competition. What makes U.S. parties interesting in this respect is that interest aggregation takes place *within* the party *before* it contests an election. In multiparty systems, where many narrow parties are represented in government, the process of negotiating among interests takes place when multiple victorious parties bargain with each other after the election for a place in the new government. The result of this negotiating is a **coalition** government made up of multiple parties.[5]

Since the groups that make up the two large parties are always negotiating with each other (or fighting among themselves) to get the party to represent their agendas, the parties are pretty adept at moving to where the votes are as public opinion shifts. In the 1980s, as public opinion took a conservative turn, the Republican Party shifted rightward and began a successful electoral run. Eventually, following a protracted battle among its more liberal constituencies (which tend to participate disproportionately in the process of selecting presidential candidates), the Democratic Party shifted rightward as well in the 1990s, only to revisit its earlier struggles following Bill Clinton's departure from the White House. See Box 6-1.

This flexibility also permits the major parties to move into space occupied by smaller parties, should they begin to make electoral inroads. Ross Perot's economic pragmatism appealed to enough voters to make him a force (if not a factor) in the 1992 presidential contest. Over the next four years, both major parties deliberately made appeals to Perot supporters, and by 1996, they were able to cut the maverick Texan's vote-getting ability in half.

Figure 6-2 should give you a picture of what public opinion looks like in the United States and how the two major parties respond to it. The curved line captures the distribution of opinions people hold, from very liberal to very conservative. It bulges in the middle, meaning that most people hold moderate views. If you think of this line in terms of votes, there are more votes where the line peaks. Public opinion may shift over the years to the (conservative) right or the (liberal) left, but it tends to avoid extremes. As it shifts, the parties follow, like two big, wobbly Jello molds, capturing as many votes as they can while squeezing out smaller parties that could try to capitalize on changing public attitudes.

6-2d Third and Minor Parties

With the rules stacked against them, you might think that third parties and minor parties simply wouldn't form at all. However, throughout our history, parties that have been unsuccessful at winning elections have repeatedly formed, and some of them have flourished. What's with that?

▶**interest aggregation** The process by which groups with different and potentially conflicting agendas are brought together under the umbrella of a political party.

▶**coalition** A government formed as a partnership among several victorious parties in a multiparty system, following negotiations about the agenda that each party will be allowed to pursue in exchange for its participation in the new government.

Box 6-1 Bush Lite?

In order for us to be presented with real alternatives on Election Day, the major political parties need to offer us a discernable choice. However, political writers and casual observers regularly criticize the parties for being carbon copies of each other. This critique can be overdrawn, but because Republicans and Democrats hunt for votes in the center of the political spectrum, there is a tendency for each party to downplay its differences with the other on issues where there is broad public agreement. When this happens with respect to important national concerns—the things on which issue voters might want to base a decision—the parties can leave themselves open to questions about what they stand for.

Events surrounding the buildup to the Iraq war and President Bush's 2003 request for a large tax cut produced exactly this type of debate within and about the Democratic Party. In late 2002, President Bush asked Congress for support in the event that he decided to invade Iraq. The war was unpopular with many liberal Democrats, and privately, numerous congressional Democrats expressed reservations about whether Iraq was the right target at the right time and whether it was wise to invade preemptively without broad international support.

However, the politics of the war made it difficult to oppose. Many Americans trusted the president to do the right thing and were willing to support the conflict, even if they had reservations about its outcome. Democrats feared that opposing the war would make them look "soft" on the larger issue of combating terrorism and therefore out of step with public desire for a tough approach to terrorists. With congressional elections only weeks away, many congressional Democrats

joined with Republicans to give the president the authorization he wanted. This included four Democrats with presidential aspirations: Senator John Kerry of Massachusetts, Senator Joseph Lieberman of Connecticut, Senator John Edwards of North Carolina, and Representative Richard Gephardt of Missouri.

A similar calculation entered into the picture when Democrats agreed to a scaled-back version of a tax package requested by the Bush administration shortly after the major fighting in Iraq ended. Privately, most Democrats believed that the package would help the very rich at the expense of the poor and middle class, that it would not create jobs as the president predicted, and that it would cause budget deficits to balloon to record levels. However, they also knew that people like tax cuts, and they feared being cast as obstructionists to a popular effort. They feared that to be characterized as soft on security issues *and* opposed to lower taxes is to appear so far from the center of public opinion as to be unelectable. So, they compromised with the administration.

These actions produced a firestorm among activist Democrats and many regular partisans. Moderate Democrats defended the Iraq and tax positions on pragmatic grounds, saying that the Democratic Party has to go where popular opinion lies if it wants to be competitive. Liberals responded with outrage, calling Democrats who supported the president on these matters "Bush Lite," while arguing that saying "me too" to the Republican Party on these important matters would undermine the Democrats' competitive position. From their perspective, the two major parties appeared to blend together, offering no alternatives on the key issues of the day.

Figure 6-2
The Two Large Parties Maintain Their Dominance

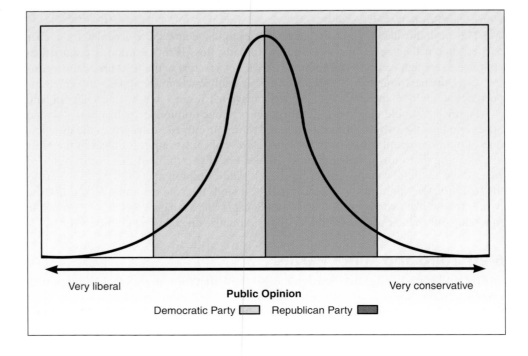

There are a couple of answers to this question. In some cases, winning is less important than giving party identifiers a place to go. Communists may not win too many elections in the United States, but if you're a Communist, then neither of the two major parties is going to represent your beliefs. That's why **ideological parties** like the Communist Party, Socialist Party, and Libertarian Party have a long history in the United States, complete with fielding candidates for office. Even though almost all ideological party candidates go down to defeat, having the opportunity to publicize their views can be a goal in its own right, apart from electoral victory.[6]

In a similar vein, some parties that endure from election to election formulate around a concern for a particular issue rather than a broad ideology. Such **single-issue parties** operate like ideological parties in that they compete in elections largely to draw attention to the issue they espouse. For instance, a Right-to-Life Party appears on the ballot in New York State elections. Nationally, the Green Party is a single-issue party devoted to the cause of environmentalism.

In 2000, the Green Party nominated noted consumer advocate Ralph Nader as its presidential candidate. Given the media's natural affinity for personality and celebrity, Nader's candidacy generated more media attention for the Green Party than a single-issue party normally would attract (although much of this centered around the horse race elements of Nader's candidacy—whether Nader would claim liberal votes that might otherwise go to Democrat Al Gore—rather than on environmental concerns espoused by the Green Party). Nader won 2.7 percent of the national presidential vote, which is quite sizable for a single-issue candidate (and quite a bit more than the margin that separated George W. Bush from Al Gore).

Other minor parties develop in reaction to the temporary failure of the major parties to satisfy a sizable constituency. Unlike ideological or single-issue parties, these **splinter parties**—named because of their propensity to splinter away from the broad Democratic or Republican Party coalitions—tend to be pragmatic. They typically form around a charismatic figure and compete for one or two election cycles until the major parties successfully address the concerns of the group that split away, move into the space occupied by the splinter party, and effectively put it out of business.

There were several notable splinter parties in the last century. In 1912, former Republican president Theodore Roosevelt attempted a comeback after a falling-out with incumbent Republican President William Howard Taft. Unable to wrest the nomination of the Republican Party from the conservative Taft, Roosevelt ran as the nominee of the Progressive or "Bull Moose" Party (a nickname that captured Roosevelt's hearty physical characteristics). On the strength of his personal popularity, Roosevelt secured more than one-quarter of the vote, better than any third-party or independent candidate of the twentieth century. However, his presence on the ballot drained Republican votes from Taft and enabled the election of Democrat Woodrow Wilson.

After the election, the Republican Party absorbed the disaffected progressives, and the Progressive Party faded away. It reemerged briefly in 1924 under the leadership of one of its original founders, Sen. Robert M. LaFollette of Wisconsin, whose showing was less impressive than Roosevelt's. LaFollette died shortly after the election, and although the Progressive Party continued to function for a while, it never again competed effectively in national elections.

In the mid-twentieth century, it was the Democratic Party's turn to see a faction walk out and compete against it. The issue of civil rights split southern Democrats from the rest of their party, as first Harry S Truman and then John F. Kennedy and Lyndon B. Johnson took increasingly progressive positions on race relations. In 1948, President Truman beat back a challenge by disaffected "Dixiecrats," who unsuccessfully ran Democratic South Carolina Governor Strom Thurmond as a regional alternative to Truman. Thurmond won only 2.4 percent of the vote, although he polled ahead of Truman in four southern states.[7]

A more serious split occurred in 1968, when fiery Alabama Governor George C. Wallace, a Democrat, received 13.5 percent of the vote as the candidate of the American Independent Party, on a platform of racial segregation. With the national Democratic Party

ideological parties Third parties that form around a broad ideology not represented by the two major American parties. They endure from election to election despite the fact that they rarely achieve electoral success.

single-issue parties Third parties that form to advance a specific issue agenda, like environmentalism, which members feel is not being adequately addressed by the two major American parties. They endure from election to election despite the fact that they rarely achieve electoral success.

splinter parties Third parties that split away from one of the major parties in protest against the direction taken by the Republicans or Democrats. They often form around a charismatic leader and last a short time, after which the major parties address their concerns and they lose their reason to continue.

John Anderson's uphill presidential bid got an early boost from popular comic strip character Michael Doonesbury, whose support gave the independent's campaign an image of youthful energy and a place in the popular culture. But even Michael Doonesbury recognized how hard it can be to run for president without a lot of resources, and in the long run, Anderson lost some credibility by being pigeonholed as the candidate who was endorsed by a cartoon character.

Source: DOONESBURY © 1980 G. B. Trudeau. Reprinted with permission of UNIVERSAL PRESS SYNDICATE. All rights reserved.

▶**Reform Party** The organization built by businessman Ross Perot in a mostly unsuccessful attempt to create a competitive third party.

supporting policies promoting civil rights for African Americans, Wallace's defection heralded the departure of white southerners as a Democratic Party constituency. Socially conservative white southerners eventually found a new home in the Republican Party, and the American Independent Party faded from the scene.

John Anderson's 1980 independent run for president and Ross Perot's 1992 independent bid were born more from widespread doubts about the major party nominees than from disagreements over the direction of a major party. In 1980, Republicans nominated former California Governor Ronald Reagan to face incumbent Democrat Jimmy Carter. At the time, Reagan was widely regarded as being more conservative than mainstream America and highly belligerent toward the Soviet Union, while Carter was saddled with a sour economy and a lingering crisis in which Americans were being held hostage in Iran.

In this environment, where one candidate did not inspire trust and the other was perceived to lack competence, undecided voters were looking for an alternative. Anderson, a previously obscure Republican congressman from Illinois who had lost his party's nomination to Reagan, presented himself as someone trustworthy and competent. Although his campaign received a fair amount of press interest because of its potential to complicate the horserace, Anderson's independent bid fell way short and, as many Americans warmed to Reagan during his first term, there was no rationale for Anderson to try again four years later.

In a similar fashion, Perot offered himself as an alternative to unpopular incumbent Republican George Bush (senior) and scandal-plagued Democrat Bill Clinton. Unlike Anderson, Perot could bankroll his campaign with the considerable fortune he had acquired as the founder of Electronic Data Systems, a multibillion-dollar corporation. In a year when many voters were disillusioned with the major nominees, Perot's candidacy polled almost 19 percent of the vote. He tried to organize his independent bid into a permanent third-party organization, but as disaffected voters returned to the major parties, Perot's **Reform Party** candidacy did less well in 1996, and by 2000, the third-party movement had effectively run out of steam. Box 6-2 discusses the creation of third parties in more detail.

Even though a number of third-party and independent presidential candidates performed admirably at the polls, they rarely had any traction in the Electoral College, which ultimately decides who becomes president (no third-party or independent candidate has won any electoral votes since George Wallace in 1968). In Chapter 7, we'll explore how the Electoral College works, but for now, the important thing to know is that in contemporary elections it takes 270 electoral votes to be elected president, which are awarded state by state on a winner-take-all basis. When you look at how even the more successful third-party and independent candidates did over the last hundred years, it's clear that none of them came close (see Table 6-2). Even in Perot's case, because his support was evenly spread throughout the country, he was unable to dent the Electoral College.

> *Box 6-2* ## Building a Viable Third Party—for a Few Months

I f splinter parties gain momentum from charismatic figures, certainly Ross Perot fits the mold. The feisty self-made Texas billionaire surprised political observers when, during an appearance on CNN's *Larry King Live* in February 1992, he announced that he would put his considerable fortune behind an independent presidential run if people would circulate petitions sufficient to get his name on the ballot in all fifty states. People responded in large numbers. Perot coordinated and financed the effort—and advertised it by appearing on other television talk shows.

Perot was an unconventional candidate. He understood television and used the media to maximum effect. By late June, he was running neck-and-neck with his major party opponents—only to suddenly drop out of the race at a time when questions about his character threatened to foment into a feeding frenzy. Then, just as suddenly, Perot reentered the contest with just weeks to go before the election. His personal fortune permitted him to pick up where he had left off, albeit with a smaller base of supporters. Perot spent heavily to purchase thirty-minute long "Infomercials" focusing primarily on economic issues that interested his supporters. Ultimately, a combination of money, media, and misgivings about the major candidates contributed to Perot's strong showing.*

After the election, Perot remained a visible figure, energizing his followers and encouraging them to begin a third-party movement. As disaffection with the major parties continued into the first years of the Clinton administration, the Perot-backed organization "United We Stand America" became the basis for the Reform Party, which was organized with Perot's support in 1995. Leaders of the new party hoped to run candidates for numerous offices and to build on Perot's impressive showing in the 1992 presidential election.

However, the Reform Party faltered as the political climate changed. After a halting start, President Clinton began to connect with a large segment of the population. By 1996, a lot of the anger from four years earlier had dissipated, and with it, more than half of Perot's vote. Because the Reform Party had been built from the top down—around Perot's dynamic television persona—rather than from the bottom up, there was little to sustain it once Perot's television "act" grew stale. In 1998, the Reform Party captured a major office when Jesse Ventura was elected governor of Minnesota in a tight, three-way race, but Perot's legions were learning how hard it is to build a viable third party in the United States.

By 2000, the national Reform Party had split into two camps: one loyal to its founder and one supportive of conservative television commentator Patrick Buchanan, who had been denied the nomination of the Republican Party and who was looking for a ready-made platform from which to launch a presidential campaign. Perot supporters cried foul and accused Buchanan of hijacking their organization. In a raucous and testy convention, the two camps nominated different candidates (the Perot group supported physicist Dr. John Hagelin), and it was left to the courts to decide who would be the official nominee. In September 2000, a federal judge declared Buchanan to be the Reform nominee. Buchanan turned out to be a candidate who did not resonate with the times, and his campaign went nowhere. In 2002, Ventura decided not to seek a second term as Minnesota governor, and the once high-flying Reform Party was left battered and irrelevant.†

*Steven J. Rosenstone, Roy L. Behr, and Edward H. Lazarus, *Third Parties in America: Citizen Response to Major Party Failure* (Princeton, NJ: Princeton University Press, 1996), 231–268.

†To read the story of the movement that gave rise to the Reform Party (from the perspective of a supporter of that movement), go to the Reform Party website at http://www.reformparty.org/PrinciplesIssues/history.html.

TABLE 6-2

Significant Third-Party and Independent Candidates of the Twentieth Century

Year	Candidate	Party	Type of Third Party	Percentage of Votes	Electoral Votes
1912	Theodore Roosevelt	Progressive/Bull Moose	Splinter	27.4%	88
1992	Ross Perot	Independent	Splinter	18.9%	0
1924	Robert M. LaFollette	Progressive	Splinter	16.6%	13
1996	Ross Perot	Reform	Splinter	8.4%	0
1980	John B. Anderson	Independent	Splinter	6.6%	0
1912	Eugene V. Debs	Socialist	Ideological	6.0%	0
1968	George C. Wallace	American Independent	Splinter	3.5%	46

Source: William J. Keefe, *Parties, Politics, and Public Policy in America* (Washington, DC: CQ Press, 1998), 60.

6-3 Party Systems

So, America has a two-party system and always has. From the time the Constitution went into effect, with the formation of rudimentary political parties, there have been two parties in regular competition with each other. In a **party system,** the *same* parties enter into regular competition with each other year after year, and although the number of parties has been stable over the past two centuries, party labels and the groups identifying with the parties have changed several times.

We can divide our history into five distinct periods, each characterized by a party system with a uniquely constituted pair of major parties competing against each other. Within each of these five party systems, the groups identifying with the two parties remained stable. But between each period, there was a **realignment,** or a significant, lasting, long-term shift in the groups that identified with the parties in the previous system, precipitating the change to the new system. Typically, realignments have followed a major social upheaval, like war or depression, which created new social cleavages that the existing parties were simply unable to address. Political scientist V. O. Key noted that each realignment followed what he called a **critical election,** in which large numbers of voters shift their allegiances in what turns out to be lasting fashion.[8]

The story of these five party systems and the realignments that fashioned them is in one respect the story of the major events that shaped American political history. Let's look briefly at that story and get a sense of the foundation beneath the parties we know today as Republican and Democrat.

6-3a Formation of a Party System, 1796–1824

The framers of the Constitution did not look kindly on political parties and did not anticipate their existence. If you look at the Constitution, you'll find that parties aren't mentioned anywhere. That's because parties were perceived to be synonymous with **factions,** and you probably remember how poorly factions were regarded. Regardless, the fact that parties were feared as organizations that could produce **tyranny** didn't stop some of the same people who wrote negatively of them from organizing what would become the first party system.

George Washington, in his farewell address of 1796, spoke directly of "the baneful effects of the spirit of party:"

> It serves always to distract the public councils and enfeeble the public administration. It agitates the community with ill-founded jealousies and false alarms; kindles the animosity of one part against another; foments occasionally riot and insurrection. It opens the door to foreign influence and corruption, which finds a facilitated access to the government itself through the channels of party passion.[9]

All well and good, but at the same time Washington was urging his countrymen to put aside partisan differences, others—notably others who served in Washington's administration, like Alexander Hamilton and Thomas Jefferson—were at work forming what would soon become America's first political parties. By 1800, two factions in Congress had developed around the major issue of the day: the strength of the federal government relative to the states. Supporters of Hamilton's position in favor of a strong federal government with a strong national bank formed the camp that would eventually be known as the Federalists. Followers of Jefferson's position on states' rights would become known as the Democratic-Republicans (they were also called Anti-Federalists, Republicans, Jeffersonian Democrats, and even sometimes simply Jeffersonians).

In 1800, the two groups, or caucuses, began acting and looking like political parties. The Democratic-Republican congressional caucus nominated Thomas Jefferson for president, while congressional Federalists lent their support to the incumbent (and eventual loser) John Adams. Congressional partisans also began building connections with supporters in the states.[10] Despite widespread apprehension about political parties, the first party system was in full swing.

party system The regular, over-time competition of the same major political parties, composed of the same groups of identifiers.

realignment A shift from one party system to another, the result of a lasting, long-term adjustment in the groups that identify with the major political parties.

critical election An election that heralds a realignment, during which large numbers of voters deviate from their traditional party allegiances in what turns out to be a lasting change.

faction A group of individuals who are united by a desire that, if realized, would threaten the liberty of the larger community—in James Madison's words, individuals who are "united and actuated by some common impulse of passion, or of interest, adverse to the rights of other citizens, or to the permanent and aggregate interests of the community." A faction may be defined by size, such as when a majority of citizens threatens the liberty of the minority, or by intensity, such as when a minority of citizens with intensely held preferences threatens the liberty of a disinterested majority.

tyranny The denial of liberty to individuals through the actions of a faction or through the actions of government itself.

The Federalists never organized as effectively as the Democratic-Republicans, and John Adams was the only president who would wear their label. The Democratic-Republicans, with strength in the rural South, elected a succession of Virginians to the presidency between 1800 and 1824: Jefferson, James Madison, and James Monroe. In fact, the Federalists had such a hard time of it that by 1816 they stopped nominating presidential candidates altogether. From the time the Federalists called it quits until 1824, the country went through a brief period when there was little party activity at the national level.[11] This so-called "Era of Good Feelings" masked conflicts that were rumbling below the surface, however. It was only a short period of time before party competition would be back.

6-3b The Second Party System: Jackson Democrats versus the Whigs, 1828–1856

The electorate was changing in the 1820s as states began removing property ownership as a requirement for political participation. This led to conditions that supported the emergence of the mass political parties that we know today. More than anyone else, Andrew Jackson—backwoodsman, lawyer, congressman, senator, and charismatic general in the War of 1812—would surface as the architect of the new political party.

"Old Hickory" was a popular, strong, and divisive figure, determined to democratize government and bring ordinary people into the political process. Elected to the presidency in 1828 as a Democratic-Republican, Jackson was a polarizing force who expanded Jefferson's party to include newly enfranchised voters while sending disaffected Jeffersonians into the opposition as National Republicans, or Whigs. Leaders of the new Whig Party—people like Henry Clay and Daniel Webster—feared Jackson's form of democracy meant trampling individual liberties. For its part, Jackson's party began competition under the abbreviated name "Democrats"—a label meant to capture the broad-based nature of the party and the same label it uses today.[12] In fact, the modern-day Democratic Party is the nation's oldest continually operating political party, tracing its roots back to Jefferson and Jackson.

Under Jackson's leadership, the Democrats held their first national nominating convention in 1832—the forerunner of the conventions we talked about at the start of the chapter—replacing the congressional caucuses that had selected previous presidential candidates. It was more democratic, and it drew more people into the political process. Presidential campaigns, once dominated by a congressional elite, became mass exercises. Something resembling modern political parties had been born.[13]

The Democrats drew their strength from the rural southern and western elements of Jefferson's party, but they were a national party with a base in New York led by the pragmatic Martin Van Buren, who would follow Jackson in the White House. The Whigs were also national in scope, and more of an elite party, supported by southern plantation owners and northern commercial interests. For three decades, they entered into regular competition with each other, with the Democrats winning most of the presidential contests (the two Whig victories were with military figures William Henry Harrison in 1840 and Zachary Taylor in 1848, both of whom promptly died in office not long after their inaugurations).

However, as the 1850s approached, the national coalitions in both parties came under enormous strain. Abolitionist sentiment grew in the northern and frontier states, while public debate over extending slavery to new western states intensified divisions over the issue of slavery. Northern Whigs aligned with strong antislavery forces and split from southern Whigs, who had been promoting compromise positions designed to preserve the union while maintaining the institution of slavery. Northern Democrats, who long differed with their pro-slavery southern counterparts, found themselves in alliance with northern Whigs, and in the middle 1850s, they joined forces to create the Republican Party as an antislavery party.

The Whigs and the Democrats had originally organized around common economic perspectives. But their internal similarities were irrelevant to the issue of slavery, and as slavery became the overriding political concern, regional differences within each party pulled them apart. The realignment that ensued left the Democrats as a southern, pro-slavery party. It destroyed the Whigs entirely. And it enabled the emergence of the Republicans, the only "third" party ever to attain major party status.[14]

Based in Wisconsin, Michigan, Ohio, and Illinois, the Republican Party began competing successfully in statewide elections, as it spread through the Midwest eastward to antislavery regions of the North. By 1856, state Republican parties had unified, and the first Republican national convention was held. In 1860, the Republican Party elected its first president, Abraham Lincoln, ushering in secession, Civil War, and the third party system.[15]

6-3c The Third Party System: Ascendancy of a New Party, 1860–1892

From 1860 on, Republicans and Democrats engaged in regular competition with each other. Even though the labels haven't changed in over 145 years, the issues the parties have confronted and the groups aligning themselves with each party have shifted dramatically over the years.

The Republican Party dominated national politics during this era of the third party system, when the parties were organized over divisions stemming from the Civil War and Reconstruction of the Union. The Democratic Party had become a southern conservative party, while the Republican Party was essentially a northern party devoted to extending rights to freed slaves.

Still, just like the second-party system had been organized around economic groups and fell apart when the parties weren't able to address the issue of slavery, the third party system, organized around the issue of slavery, was unprepared to address emerging economic concerns as the nation headed into the industrial era.

In the West, farmers became politicized in opposition to an eastern financial class that they felt had a tight grip over the economy. In cities, workers in the new industrial economy were concerned with issues of trade, wages, and as the century progressed, monopoly ownership of business. Neither party responded adequately to their complaints, which rose in volume over the latter third of the nineteenth century until they came to dominate national politics. The coming division in American politics would pit East against West, bankers and lenders against farmers and laborers, much as the previous conflict had divided North and South.[16]

6-3d The Fourth Party System: Republicans Again, 1896–1928

In 1893, the country plunged into economic depression. The Democratic Party was split down the middle between eastern forces of commercialism that favored the stability of a gold standard for currency, and western forces of populism—rural advocates of currency backed by silver, which by virtue of its greater availability would have a devaluing effect that would assist rural debtors.

By 1896, the agrarian forces had emerged victorious within the Democratic Party, which nominated Nebraskan William Jennings Bryan for president on a platform of "free silver." The Republicans, with the strong support of commercial interests, cast Bryan as a radical and stoked fears of a populist takeover of the government that resonated in the industrial Northeast and Midwest. Banks and corporations heavily funded the Republican nominee, William McKinley. The nation was polarized. For the first time in over a generation, a presidential election offered a stark choice over economic issues long ignored by the major parties.

McKinley's victory in the critical election of 1896 cemented Republican control of national politics through the first one-third of the twentieth century. Even though the Republicans had been the majority party before, the 1896 vote revealed an entirely new set of allegiances for the two parties that would hold for decades. McKinley's victory was concentrated in the commercial centers of the Northeast and the industrial Midwest. Bryan swept the South and the West.[17]

The Republican Party established itself as the party of bankers, industrialists, urban laborers, and African Americans (who remained loyal to the party of Lincoln). The Democrats emerged as the party of rural interests and southerners (whose attachment to the Democratic Party was as strong as it had been since the Civil War). These two groups would compete against each other for more than thirty years, with the Republicans maintaining a clear advantage. Between 1896 and 1928, in a time marked by rapid immigration and industrialization, Republicans would lose the White House only in the wake of Teddy Roosevelt's third-party challenge in 1912 and again in 1916.

That is, until the next great economic depression.

6-3e The Fifth Party System: Democrats Emerge as Liberals, 1932–1964

Herbert Hoover, the last in the line of Republican presidents who served during the fourth party system, no doubt had little sense of what was coming. The Great Depression hit suddenly and ferociously in 1929, ending a decade of prosperity. Hoover spent the rest of his term unsuccessfully grappling with an economic downturn that proved deeper and more enduring than he had initially anticipated.

With the unemployment rate soaring above 20 percent, voters were ready for a change. In what emerged as a campaign of the powerful versus what Democratic nominee Franklin D. Roosevelt called the "forgotten man at the bottom of the economic pyramid," the Democratic Party won a landslide victory in 1932 that would establish it as the majority party for over three decades. Roosevelt himself would claim the presidency four times—breaking with the two-term tradition established by Washington—and between 1932 and 1964, popular General Dwight D. Eisenhower would be the only Republican to crack the Democrat's lock on the White House.[18]

After the election, Democrats embraced government activism to ease the burden felt by an increasingly angry and despondent America. In office, Roosevelt moved swiftly to enact an agenda that was far more activist than the one on which he had campaigned. Working in tandem with Democratic majorities in the House and Senate, Roosevelt implemented the **New Deal** policies that would cement the electoral changes evident in the critical election of 1932. Key members of what would be termed the **New Deal coalition** included:

- *Urbanites,* particularly in the North, many of whom were first-time voters
- *Jews,* many of whom were urbanites, and who were among the Democrats' strongest supporters
- *Catholics,* many of whom were first drawn to the Democratic Party in 1928, when its nominee was New York Governor Al Smith, the first Catholic presidential nominee of a major party
- *African Americans,* who abandoned the party of Lincoln after seventy years of affiliation
- *Organized labor,* who benefited greatly from Roosevelt's New Deal reforms
- *Liberals,* whose ideas were well received in FDR's reformist administration
- *Southerners,* who remained true to the party of the Civil War, despite conservative voting patterns that were out of sync with the progressive reforms of the New Deal[19]

Following Roosevelt, Harry S Truman maintained the New Deal coalition with his **Fair Deal** policies that built on popular New Deal programs by, for instance, raising the minimum wage and increasing Social Security benefits. In the 1960s, Lyndon B. Johnson presided over a second wave of government activism ushered in by his **Great Society** programs aimed at conquering poverty and extending civil rights protection to African Americans.

However, Johnson's emphasis on civil rights alienated white southerners, and his prosecution of the Vietnam War deeply divided elements of the New Deal coalition. Although Democrats would continue to compete successfully in southern statewide elections, they

▶**New Deal** The name given to the programs of President Franklin D. Roosevelt, which vastly expanded the role of the federal government in an effort to deal with the debilitating effects of the Great Depression on American society.

▶**New Deal coalition** The political coalition composed of urbanites, ethnic and racial minorities, unions, liberals, and southerners that made the Democratic Party the majority party during the fifth party system.

▶**Fair Deal** The name given to the domestic policies of President Harry S Truman, which built on the popularity of the New Deal.

▶**Great Society** The name given to the programs of President Lyndon B. Johnson, which elevated the federal government to the most prominent role it would play in the twentieth century. The philosophy of the Great Society was that government should try to solve large social problems like hunger and poverty.

no longer dominated. Republicans were emerging as a competitive force on the statewide level and, gradually, as a dominant force in presidential elections. Richard Nixon exploited cracks in the Democrats' southern base during his presidential campaign of 1968, and by 1972, Nixon swept the South against antiwar Democrat George McGovern, who was perceived as too liberal to be in touch with southern political sentiment.

Nonetheless, Democrats maintained control of the House of Representatives until 1994, and of the Senate until 1980 (they would regain control for six years in 1986 and for less than two years following Senator Jeffords' defection from the Republican Party in 2001). During this period, more Americans still claimed to be Democrats than Republicans. There had been no political earthquakes on the scale of depression or civil war, and no obvious critical elections to usher in the start of a new political system. Yet, clearly, something had changed. What was it?

6-3f Divided Government in a Conservative Era, 1968–Today

In the wake of the social turmoil of the turbulent 1960s, large numbers of people who previously identified with one of the political parties had been shaken from their partisan moorings. As the majority party in the fifth party system, the Democrats felt this shift more strongly than the Republicans. The percentage of people claiming to be independent of party identification has increased since the 1960s, and the percentage of Democrats has declined. This suggests a **dealignment** in American politics: not the establishment of a new party system so much as a weakening of the existing system.

Scholars who study political parties do not universally agree that the United States has gone through a dealignment, especially because the percentage of independents in the electorate stabilized in the late 1980s. If you want to make the case that dealigning forces have influenced party affiliation over the past two generations, though, it's easy to see where you would claim the trend started. It coincides with the fraying of the New Deal coalition during the Johnson administration in the mid-1960s. In Figure 6-3, check out the way the percentage of independents, which had hovered around 20 percent in the 1950s and early 1960s, shot up to 30 percent in 1968 and to 40 percent in 2000.

One source of this possible dealignment is the weakening attachments of some of the original members of the New Deal coalition. Southerners, for sure, as well as Catholics—both groups that were never ideologically liberal—over time relinquished their support for the Democratic Party. Part of the movement away from the Democratic Party came in reaction to the political dialogue of the twentieth century's last two decades, which was markedly different from the New Deal and Great Society periods. With the election of Ronald Reagan in 1980 on a platform of social conservatism, issues like abortion rights and gun ownership came to the forefront of debate.

> **dealignment** The weakening of party affiliation, signified by an increase in the number of people who call themselves independents.

Figure 6-3
Weakening Party Ties
The percentage of independents increased dramatically in the mid-1960s, while Democrats declined in strength and Republicans held their own. *(Note:* Independents include people who claim to lean slightly toward one of the two major parties.)

Source: Data from National Election Studies, at http://www.umich.edu/~nes/nesguide/toptable/tab1b_3.htm. The National Election Studies, Center for Political Studies, University of Michigan. Electronic resources from the NES World Wide Web site (www.umich.edu/~nes). Ann Arbor, MI: University of Michigan, Center for Political Studies [producer and distributor], 1995–2000. These materials are based on work supported by the National Science Foundation under Grant Nos.: SBR-9707741, SBR-9317631, SES-9209410, SES-9009379, SES-8808361, SES-8341310, SES-8207580, and SOC77-08885. Any opinions, findings and conclusions or recommendations expressed in these materials are those of the author(s) and do not necessarily reflect those of the National Science Foundation.

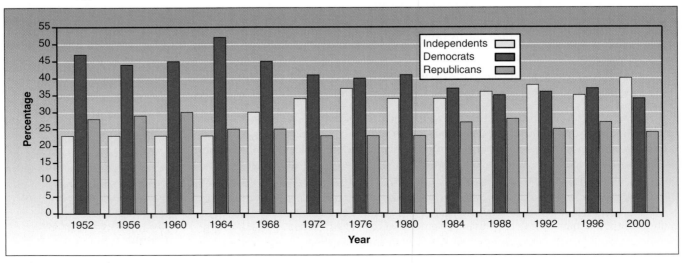

> ## Box 6-3   Are Republicans "from Mars," While Democrats Are "from Venus"?
>
> Since 1980, at the national level, it would only be exaggerating things a little to say that Republicans have been the "Male Party" and Democrats have been the "Female Party." When Ronald Reagan defeated Jimmy Carter that year, 54 percent of men supported Reagan, while only 46 percent of women did—a gap of eight points. There has been a gap of at least this magnitude in almost every subsequent presidential election. In fact, in 1996, when Bill Clinton was reelected with close to a seven-point cushion, his opponent Bob Dole was actually favored by men. Clinton's reelection could be attributed to the gender gap, as women voted for him by a huge 54–38 margin.
>
> This is not to suggest that women vote as a unit or that there aren't important differences among women voters. Socially conservative and security-oriented women tend to support Republicans, for instance, while so-called "Soccer Moms"—suburban women with young kids—helped Democratic candidates during the 1990s. But it does point to the tendency for women more than men to be supportive of the activist agenda promoted by the Democratic Party and to the importance of women as an electoral force.[*]
>
> [*]Anna Greenberg, "Deconstructing the Gender Gap," John F. Kennedy School of Government Working Paper, Harvard University, 1998.

However, while divisive, these issues have not proved to be of enough importance to voters to serve as the basis for realignment. The history of realignments since the Civil War has been that deeply felt economic issues have been the engine of political change, and the history of the late twentieth century has been that during times of economic difficulty, discussion of social issues tends to disappear.[20]

Additionally, while some groups moved away from the Democratic Party since Reagan, the "New Democrats" we mentioned earlier have shifted in the opposite direction. Middle-class suburbanites have become less strongly affiliated with the Republican Party over this period, as have women, whose lukewarm response to cultural conservatism is apparent in a **gender gap,** whereby women have supported Republican presidential candidates by a much lower margin than men. Box 6-3 talks more about gender and the political parties.

Loosening political ties mean people are less likely to vote for the candidate of the same party for every office on the ballot, something that was quite commonplace during earlier periods of strong party allegiance. As we noted in Chapter 4, since 1968, we've been much more willing to engage in **ticket splitting,** disaggregating or dividing our vote between the parties. This can result in **divided government,** in which one party controls the White House while the other party controls at least one house of Congress. Perhaps more than anything, divided government characterizes the politics of our recent past. In the thirty-six years from 1968 to 2004, the same party has controlled the White House and both houses of Congress only four brief times: during the four years of the Carter administration, during the first two years of the Clinton administration, during the first few months of the George W. Bush administration (prior to the defection of Republican Senator James Jeffords of Vermont), and following the congressional elections of 2002. During President Bush's first term, the margin of Republican control in the House and the Senate was slim, although Republican strength in the Senate did increase with the president's reelection.

To put this in perspective, when Republican Dwight D. Eisenhower was reelected president in 1956, Democrats won control of both houses of Congress, marking the first time in over a century (since Zachary Taylor's election in 1848) that an election had produced a president of one party and a Congress of another. Since 1968, it's happened six times in ten elections.[21] As we identify less with political parties, we feel more freedom to pick and choose among individual candidates, regardless of party label. Presidents no longer have **coattails,** carrying senators and representatives into office on the strength of their victory. If anything, representatives and senators commonly have *reverse* coattails—outpolling the presidential nominee of their party. As a consequence, governing becomes more ad hoc, and more difficult.

That's one reason why this period of divided government has often been characterized by the **gridlock** we talked about in Chapter 5. When voters place majorities of different

gender gap A difference in the voting pattern of men and women, evident since 1980, whereby men are more likely than women to support Republican presidential candidates.

ticket splitting Voting for candidates of different parties for different offices, rather than voting a "party line" for all Republicans or all Democrats. Ticket splitting, which has increased in recent years, is a sign of how Americans have been growing independent from political parties.

divided government Partisan division of the national government, in which each of the two major parties can claim control of one branch (or one legislative house) of the federal government.

coattails The ability of a victorious presidential candidate to sweep congressional candidates of the same party into office on the strength of people voting for one political party.

gridlock The term given to legislative inaction, when members of Congress are unable to reach agreement and legislation stalls.

Party System Number	Dates	Main Issue	Parties			Major Figure
1	1796–1824	Federalism	Federalists	vs.	Anti-Federalists (Democratic-Republicans)	Jefferson
2	1828–1856	Expansion	Whigs	vs.	Democrats	Jackson
3	1860–1892	Slavery/reconstruction	Republicans	vs.	Democrats	Lincoln
4	1896–1928	Industrialization	Republicans	vs.	Democrats	McKinley
5	1932–1964	New Deal	Republicans	vs.	Democrats	F. D. Roosevelt
?	1968–present	(Dealignment?)	Republicans	vs.	Democrats	Reagan

Figure 6-4
Party Systems

ideological persuasions in the White House and Congress, officials will naturally disagree, and those checks and balances designed to slow progress kick into high gear. Without strong party ties, this has happened with great frequency over the past thirty-five years. To be sure, one-party control is not a recipe for moving legislation through the system: Democrats Jimmy Carter and Bill Clinton (in his first two years) had comfortable House and Senate majorities but had limited success winning legislative approval for their major agenda items. However, divided government can accentuate partisan differences.

We've covered a lot of ground talking about over 210 years of party history. Let's stop for a second and take a look at Figure 6-4, which summarizes the main points about partisan realignment and party systems. The majority party in each system is the one in blue type.

6-4 The Party in Government

"Do something!"

That's the cry heard for years from Americans frustrated with the inability of the federal government to make quick progress on important issues. When Democrat Bill Clinton first became president, he was in the enviable and unusual situation of having a Congress dominated by his party. But his attempt in 1993 to pass a controversial budget that raised taxes squeaked by in the House of Representatives only after intense White House pressure on wavering Democrats. Clinton's proposal to reform the health care system went nowhere. President Bush, despite high job approval ratings in 2002, was unable to move large portions of his domestic agenda through a House of Representatives controlled by his party.

Both presidents had to deal with the limitations of partisanship in our institutions of government. When we talk about the **party in government,** we're talking about an elite group: the members of the Republican and Democratic Parties who serve in our governing institutions. We can contrast this with what we call the **party in the electorate,** which involves all of us who through our party identification make up rank-and-file party membership.

party in government That component of political parties composed of elected officials that organizes and runs our governing institutions like Congress, the presidency, state governorships and assemblies, and the like.

party in the electorate
Party identifiers who make up the rank-and-file membership of the political parties.

Box 6-4 Responsible Parties Abroad

I n some countries, political parties act cohesively in the legislature. Great Britain is a good example. Candidates run for office on a party platform, and when in office, leaders of the majority party advance that platform with the unified support of its members. Leaders of the minority parties will also vote as a unit, forming a reliable opposition group.

The British system offers incentives for responsible party behavior that don't apply to the American system. The British prime minister is selected by the majority party in the House of Commons and remains in office only with the continuing support of a legislative majority. If the prime minister loses the support of the majority, the government falls. So, it's in the interest of members of the majority party to act in concert in order to maintain their majority status. Separation of powers and fixed terms of office in the American system do not give legislative parties in the United States the same incentive to unify, as legislative majority status is conferred by the voters every two years, whether or not members of a party vote together.[*]

[*]Paul Allen Beck, *Party Politics in America,* 8th ed. (New York: Longman, 1997), 303.

The party in government is an interesting and sometimes confounding entity. Remember, the Constitution established Congress and the presidency as institutions that would be filled by people who did not carry party labels. Nonetheless, both institutions are infused with partisanship. In Congress, party strength determines who runs the institution and who controls the agenda. Individual members, though, still have the freedom to go their own way, regardless of party membership. That's how Senator Jeffords' defection from the Republican party could upend President Bush's agenda and why Presidents Clinton and Carter were frustrated by members of Congress who shared a common party affiliation but not always common political interests.

6-4a How Parties in Government Function

Even when we don't have divided government, it can be difficult for members of the same party in Congress and the White House to work as one because of the way political parties function in government. They're flexible. They're not ideological. They're not **responsible parties,** which is simply to say that party leaders cannot impose an agenda on their members in the House or Senate, and legislators will not automatically heed the wishes of a president of their party. To say we do not have responsible parties in the United States is not to suggest that parties act irresponsibly; rather, it is to say that members of a party do not act as one unit. See Box 6-4.

In theory, there are advantages to having responsible parties. Parties could run campaigns around clearly articulated programs, accentuating the choices between the parties and providing voters with the information they need to base their vote on the kind of policy they want government to make. There would be no fudging or fuzziness to the candidate's positions of the sort that can complicate **issue voting** like we talked about in Chapter 4— what you see would be what you get. All candidates of a party would run on the same program and in office would be accountable to that program (see Box 6-5). The party winning the most seats in the legislature would therefore be expected to move ahead and implement its program, while the minority party would play the role of loyal opposition.[22]

Because our political parties are those large, catchall groups we were talking about earlier, it shouldn't be surprising to find members of the same party disagreeing with each other and coming down on different sides of an issue. Perhaps the most pronounced example of this is southern Democrats, who are typically more conservative than the rest of their party and often vote their own way. In fact, you could say that when you take into account how broad-based the parties are and how hard it is for party leaders to impose discipline, it's remarkable how much party cohesion there is in Congress.

In recent years, Democrats and Republicans have been able to muster large majorities of their members to stick together on votes where the parties take a position. As you can

responsible parties Political parties whose legislative members act in concert, taking clear positions on issues and voting as a unit in accordance with their stated positions.

issue voting Choosing a candidate in an election on the basis of his or her proximity to your position on an issue or issues you consider important.

Box 6-5 The Contract with America

In 1994, the Republican Party organized its congressional campaigns around a platform it called "The Contract with America." Republican candidates signed a document pledging that, if elected as a legislative majority, they would work collectively to implement a carefully articulated set of policies, what they called "a detailed agenda for national renewal." It included provisions for how the House would operate and listed ten bills that would be considered during the first one hundred days of the congressional session on such things as a constitutional amendment requiring a balanced budget, a crime bill, a welfare reform proposal, and congressional term limits.*

The idea of coordinating congressional campaigns around a national party theme was novel: Congressional campaigns are typically waged independent of each other, revolving around local rather than national concerns. Nonetheless, Republican congressional candidates endorsed the "Contract with America" with the discipline you'd expect to find in a system that has responsible parties. It's not clear how much their efforts contributed to the sweeping victory they realized in the 1994 elections—postelection polls suggest very few vot-

ers knew about the Contract—but after reclaiming the majority in the House of Representatives for the first time in four decades, the new Republican majority went forward with the promises they made during the campaign.

Republicans kept their promises in line with the realities of the American system by agreeing only to bring the items in the Contract to a vote. They recognized that a president of the other party with an entirely different agenda was likely to be an obstacle to turning proposals into laws, and they understood that they might not be able to exercise the discipline necessary to get the votes to approve all their ideas. In fact, four of the Contract items failed because the president did not support them, and one item—term limits—failed to carry the votes of forty Republicans who had signed the Contract. But to be able to organize a party around a specific governing agenda, bring it to the public, and then follow through after the election is perhaps as close as a party can come in the American system to governing in a cohesive, disciplined way.

*You can read the full text of the Republican proposals at http://www.house.gov/house/Contract/CONTRACT.html.

tell from the party unity scores in Table 6-3, in the 1960s and 1970s, Republicans were somewhat more unified than Democrats as conservative southern Democrats crossed over to vote with Republicans. In the 1980s, during the Clinton administration, there was growing polarization in the priorities of the parties, leading to greater internal cohesiveness in voting.[23]

6-4b How Parties in Government Are Organized

Although party members may not always come together to vote on policy issues, they invariably speak with one voice when it comes to organizing the legislature. Parties organize the U.S. Congress and forty-nine of the fifty state legislatures, with the party holding the most seats commanding the power to set the rules (only Nebraska, which has a unicameral or one-house legislature, elects its representatives on a nonpartisan basis). We'll see in Chapter 9 how this gives majority party members many advantages, if they can stay together and control the organizational process. So, when it comes to organizational matters, it's in everyone's interest to get with the program and vote along party lines.

Let's use the U.S. Congress as an example of how parties organize legislatures. Before the start of each two-year session of Congress, party members meet in groups closed to members of the other party (Democrats call their group a "caucus" and Republicans call their group a "conference"), to select their candidates for leadership positions in the coming session. It's understood that the candidates selected in caucus will receive the backing of all party members later on, when leadership votes are held in the full House or Senate. At that point, with everyone falling in line behind their party's choices, the party with the most seats will elect their candidates to positions in the majority, while the candidates of the other party will take their place as part of the minority leadership.

We'll also see in Chapter 9 that the leadership of the House of Representatives is vested in a Speaker of the House, who is selected on a party-line vote—essentially, as the top leadership choice of the majority party. In both the House and Senate, each party has a leader (majority leader or minority leader, depending on whether they are the majority or minority party), who plays an important role in assigning party members to committees, shap-

TABLE 6-3

**Party Unity in
Congress, 1961–1995**

Party unity among congressional Democrats increased greatly in the 1980s and 1990s, while Republicans became a very cohesive party when they took over Congress in 1995 following the "Contract with America" election. (*Note:* Figures combine votes in the House and the Senate where a majority of one party voted against a majority of the other party.)

Year	Democrats	Republicans	Year	Democrats	Republicans
1961	71%	72%	1979	69%	72%
1962	69	68	1980	68	70
1963	71	72	1981	69	76
1964	67	69	1982	72	71
1965	69	70	1983	76	74
1966	61	67	1984	74	72
1967	66	71	1985	79	75
1968	57	63	1986	78	71
1969	62	62	1987	81	74
1970	57	59	1988	79	73
1971	62	66	1989	81	73
1972	57	64	1990	81	74
1973	68	68	1991	81	78
1974	63	62	1992	79	79
1975	69	70	1993	85	84
1976	65	66	1994	83	83
1977	67	70	1995	80	91
1978	64	67			

Source: Marjorie Randon Hershey and Paul Allen Beck, *Party Politics in America* (New York: Longman, 1997), p. 322 (Table 13.2). Reprinted by permission of Pearson Education, Inc.

ing and moving the legislative agenda, and campaigning and raising money for party members. There are also several "whips," who work to maintain as much party discipline as possible on legislative votes.[24]

Some leaders exercise power more strongly than others—for instance, Newt Gingrich went to great lengths to hold his fellow Republicans accountable for their actions when he was Speaker of the House—but in any event, the majority party exercises a lot more control over the legislature than the minority. This is particularly true in the House of Representatives, where the rules give the speaker a lot of formal authority. Not surprisingly, this manner of organization produces a lot of competitive pressure within both parties to attain (or remain in) the majority.[25] The pressure was particularly intense through 2004 as the parties were so close in number that majority status remained within the reach of both. See Box 6-6.

6-5 The Party in the Electorate

Are you a Democrat? A Republican? If so, do you have your party membership card stored carefully in your pocketbook or wallet?

Can't find it? Don't spend too much time looking. There are no membership cards for American political parties, just like there are no meetings to attend and no dues to pay. You can be a Republican simply by virtue of identifying with Republicans, a Democrat with no more effort than it takes to think, "I guess I'm a Democrat." In some states, when you

Box 6-6 Message Teams

The one thing every member of a congressional party agrees on is the importance of getting all party members reelected to obtain or maintain majority status, from which every party member would enjoy the fruits of power. In recent years, it's been commonplace for parties in government to coordinate their legislative strategy with an eye toward the next election, even as party members are going their separate ways on individual votes.

An example of one such effort is illustrated in a June 2002 article from *The Hill*, a newspaper that covers Congress, which discusses the way minority House Democrats established "message teams" in a coordinated effort to set the agenda for the upcoming 2002 election. The idea was to try to fashion the news agenda around issues where people tend to side with the Democratic Party, which in 2002 included things like Social Security reform, the environment, and education policy. Teams of representatives were selected to arrange **media events** around the Democrats' issues in order to keep their party's message in the news. A similar effort was underway in the Senate.

For all their planning, the Democrats' message teams found themselves outmaneuvered by a Republican president who, by virtue of his position, had a much louder megaphone. While the Democrats were trying to run on domestic issues, President Bush was preparing the country for a war in Iraq. To the Democrats' dismay, the weeks preceding the 2002 election were dominated by discussion of whether to support the president's war plans—an issue that played to Republican electoral strengths.

▶ **media events** Activities staged by campaigns or political officials that have enough news value to draw press attention to a message the politician wants to communicate.

▶ **political socialization**
The process by which we acquire political knowledge, attitudes, and beliefs.

▶ **party identification**
An individual's association with a political party. The most common parties Americans identify with are the two major parties, Republican and Democrat. Party identification—also called Party I.D.—varies in intensity such that it may be strong or weak. Those who do not identify with any party are typically called independents.

register to vote, you may be asked if you want to register with a party so you can participate in that party's primary election contests (we'll go into more detail on this in Chapter 7). But you can change your registration any time you want, and you can consider yourself a party member without ever registering.

When we talked about **political socialization** in Chapter 4, we said that **party identification** was the most well-socialized political phenomenon and that many of us hold to our party affiliation in a manner similar to the way many people are attached to a religious affiliation. This gives party identification a psychological component unrelated to whatever policy agreements we may have with the party we call our own. Through these associations, be they emotional or policy-based, we align ourselves with a party and become a small portion of that party's base of support. In effect, *we are* the party in the electorate— any of us who wish to claim allegiance to a political party, for whatever reason.

Now, there's a connection between us—the party in the electorate—and the party in government, inasmuch as party supporters typically want their candidates to succeed politically, or to have an effect on public policy making, or both. The extent to which the electorate acts on these wishes often depends on how much the electorate is motivated or mobilized. The composition of the party in government depends on how much we indulge our partisan instincts through the kinds of political participation we talked about in Chapter 4—contributing funds, campaigning, or voting for members of our party.

6-5a Who Makes Up the Party in the Electorate?

Because we don't have to declare our partisan allegiances, the composition of the Democratic and Republican Parties in the electorate will shift and change. Nonetheless, there are differences in the relative attachments of various groups of Americans to the two parties, which are best understood by looking at the remnants of the New Deal coalition. Democrats are more likely to attract people who are older, less well educated, less well off, nonwhite, ethnically diverse, and female (see Figure 6-5).

6-5b How Are Political Parties Organized to Reach the Electorate?

As much as party organizations inside the legislature are structured and hierarchical, party organizations that don't perform a legislative function are more decentralized. Instead of

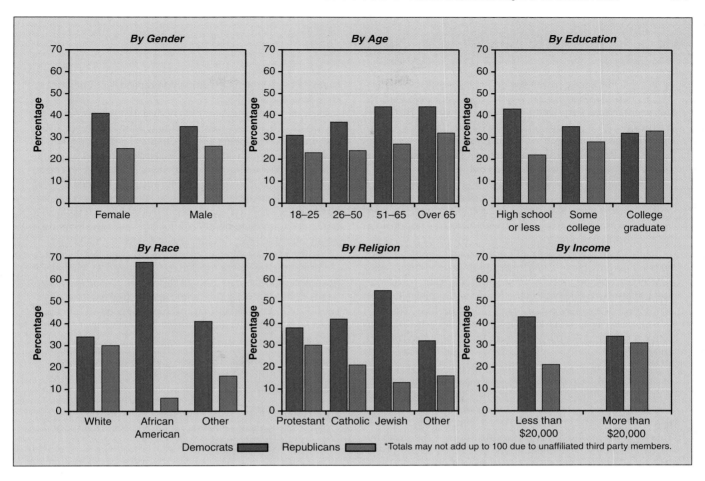

Figure 6-5
Democrats and Republicans in the Electorate
Source: Data from 2000 General Social Survey, http://www.icpsr.umich.edu/GSS/.

imagining a singular, cohesive, national Republican or Democratic Party, try to picture each party with several national organizations, fifty statewide organizations, and lots of local organizations, connected to each other but not organized from top to bottom. Each has a slightly different perspective on the same goal: electing Republicans or Democrats to office. From the standpoint of what they're about, party organizations outside the legislature are concerned with contesting elections—getting us to the polls to vote for their candidates—not with governing or advancing legislation. They share political interests with the party in government, but they operate separately.

Nationally, each party has three organizations: a national committee (the Democratic National Committee, or DNC, and the Republican National Committee, or RNC), run by a national committee chair, and House and Senate campaign committees.

The national committees govern the national parties, and include among their members representatives from the state parties. The party that controls the White House typically finds that the president exercises a great deal of control over the actions of the committee, from selecting the chair to setting the goals and objectives for the national party. The party that is not in the White House typically finds that the national chair is an important force in establishing the direction of the party and laying the groundwork to contest the next national election.[26]

As the main national organization for their respective parties, the DNC and RNC are responsible for arranging their party's national convention. However, the parties only meet in convention once every four years, for the purpose of nominating a presidential and vice-presidential candidate. On a more regular basis, the national committees are responsible for raising money for campaigns, establishing the guidelines for nominating presidential candidates, and helping state parties recruit candidates, develop campaign strategies, and build their organizations (you can probably imagine how the state parties perform

Box 6-7 "Only Vote 'Em Once"

While national parties have grown in strength, local parties have become far weaker than they were early in the twentieth century, when some were so strong that they overpowered free democratic competition. In many cities, party organizations were **political machines** run by party bosses who controlled electoral competition by controlling **patronage,** or favors that were doled out to political supporters.[*] The image of a machine might bring to mind a smoothly running vehicle with many component parts, and that's pretty much the way party machines operated. Cities were divided into small districts or wards, each with its leader responsible for dispensing patronage.

Here's how it worked: At a time when cities were flooded with immigrants, party leaders through their connections and control of public services could provide jobs, make sure tenement apartments had heat in the winter, and supply a host of other necessary services to poor constituents who had nowhere else to turn for help. In exchange, they were asked to support the party—a fairly easy price to pay when you're cold and hungry.

So, in one respect, political machines used the resources of government to supply social services. In another respect, they were thoroughly corrupt, ensuring through patronage that there would be no competition against them. If, to maintain control, the names of deceased people happened to appear in the voting logs prepared to support the machine candidates in the next election, who was going to complain? There's an old (and not particularly funny) joke about two machine politicians who, while looking at names on headstones in a cemetery, came across some particularly long names that they planned to copy down and have "vote" for machine candidates in the next election. One politician blurted out that the names were so long, they could vote them twice, to which his companion replied, "Let's be honest. Only vote 'em once."

Of course, there was nothing honest about it, even though the political machines were providing people with resources they needed. If you think back to Chapter 2, when we said that in order to maintain liberty, the Federalists created an inefficient system where factions would keep each other in check, you might recognize that just the opposite happened with the highly efficient political machines that denied people the liberty of free political competition. Madison argued that, in a big country, it would be difficult for one faction to dominate politics, but such was not the case in relatively small cities.

Party machines began to decline as they lost exclusive control of the resources needed for patronage. As the federal government began to turn its attention to social welfare needs during the New Deal and Great Society eras, it claimed control of the resources that machines needed to function.[†] Patronage still exists at all levels of politics, but political machines are largely a thing of the past.

▶ **political machines** The name given to urban political parties that used patronage to overrun their competition and maintain power.

▶ **patronage** Jobs, favors, and other resources that party officials provide in exchange for people's political support.

[*]Martin and Susan Tolchin, *To the Victor: Political Patronage from the Clubhouse to the White House* (New York: Random House, 1971), 5.

[†]John F. Bibby, "State Party Organizations: Coping and Adapting to Candidate-Centered Politics and Nationalization," in L. Sandy Maisel, ed., *The Parties Respond*, 3rd ed., 23–49.

parallel functions to the national committees). On the fund-raising front, the national committees are joined by the four congressional committees—the National Republican Congressional Committee (NRCC) and Democratic Congressional Campaign Committee (DCCC), which raise money for House candidates, and the Democratic Senatorial Campaign Committee (DSCC) and National Republican Senatorial Committee (NRSC), which do the same for Senate candidates.[27]

For a long time, national party organizations were weak, victims of campaigns that had become candidate-centered. With the growth of television as a central campaign tool, the locus of campaigning shifted from the national committees to the candidates and their personal campaign organizations. As we'll see in Chapter 7, political consultants, hired by the candidates to run campaigns and direct fund-raising techniques, made the national party organizations less important to candidates.

In recent years, the national party organizations have rebounded, owing in large part to the ability of the national parties to provide expertise to candidates who face an increasingly complex campaign environment. As national parties began providing candidates with resources like political information and technical knowledge, and as they became more proficient in raising money, they became stronger and more relevant.[28] Box 6-7 discusses the concurrent declining role of local parties.

We'll get a deeper sense of how parties operate as we take a closer look at political campaigns and elections, the subject we'll discuss in Chapter 7.

Chapter Review

Political parties are organized groups that link us to government through the role they play in recruiting and running candidates for elected office. We have two major parties in the United States; many nations have more than that. But a two-party system is consistent with our electoral mechanisms that award representation on a winner-take-all basis to the plurality vote winner of an election. Election laws and the moderate tendencies of American public opinion also encourage two parties, although they are broad parties made up of groups that sometimes disagree. When these disagreements become pronounced, a faction might temporarily leave and form a splinter party that competes as a third party against the Democrats and Republicans. Typically, one of the major parties is able to capture the allegiance of the disaffected faction in a future election, and the third party disappears. Third parties built around an ideology or single issue endure from election to election but rarely win public office.

Since parties emerged in the late eighteenth century, we have had five party systems in which two parties have faced each other in regular competition. Each party system gave way to a new one when a major issue arose which shattered the prevailing party coalitions, causing a realignment to a new party system following a critical election. The most recent realignment coincided with the emergence of the fifth party system under the leadership of the Democratic Party during the Great Depression, but since the 1960s, some observers say we've witnessed a period of dealignment characterized by weak party ties, more independent voters, and divided government.

We can understand political parties by distinguishing between the party in government and the party in the electorate. The party in government is composed of elected officials who serve in government, and our legislative branch is organized around parties, with the majority party controlling leadership positions and exercising great influence over the legislative agenda. Even though party leaders often have an agenda, party members do not always follow it because we do not have responsible parties that would obligate members to vote the party line. The party in the electorate is composed of those of us who identify as Democrats or Republicans, although American parties do not require formal membership.

Key Terms

coalition (p. 161)
coattails (p. 171)
critical election (p. 166)
dealignment (p. 170)
divided government (p. 171)
electorate (p. 156)
faction (p. 166)
Fair Deal (p. 169)
gender gap (p. 171)
Great Society (p. 169)
gridlock (p. 171)
ideological parties (p. 163)
interest aggregation (p. 161)
issue voting (p. 173)

majority (p. 159)
media events (p. 176)
multimember district (p. 157)
multiparty systems (p. 158)
New Deal (p. 169)
New Deal coalition (p. 169)
party identification (p. 176)
party in government (p. 172)
party in the electorate (p. 172)
party system (p. 166)
patronage (p. 178)
plurality (p. 159)
political machines (p. 178)
political party (p. 156)

political socialization (p. 176)
proportional representation (p. 157)
realignment (p. 166)
Reform Party (p. 164)
responsible parties (p. 173)
single-issue parties (p. 163)
single-member district (p. 159)
splinter parties (p. 163)
ticket splitting (p. 171)
two-party system (p. 158)
tyranny (p. 166)
winner-take-all system (p. 158)

Review Questions

Note: You can find the correct answers to these questions by taking the quiz and then submitting your answers in the Online Edition. The program will automatically score your submission. If you miss a question, the program will provide the correct answer, a rationale for the answer, and the section number in the chapter where the topic is discussed.

1. Political parties are
  a. tightly organized and hierarchical.
  b. loosely organized and decentralized.
  c. organized only on the state level.
  d. disorganized.

2. An electoral system featuring proportional representation is likely to support
  a. single-member districts.
  b. winner-take-all elections.
  c. plurality winners receiving 100 percent of the representation.
  d. multiple competitive parties.

3. In multiparty systems, coalitions form between parties in the government. In the American two-party system,
  a. a set of factions identifies exclusively with each party.
  b. each party studiously avoids moving into the other's territory.
  c. interest aggregation occurs within the parties.
  d. there is no way for groups to express their interests.

4. The Reform Party was unable to survive for more than two election cycles because, like so many third-party movements,
  a. it lacked a charismatic figure.
  b. it was an ideological party.
  c. its agenda was absorbed by the major parties.
  d. it had depended too heavily on ticket-splitting.

5. The movement between party systems is characterized by
  a. the loss of dominance by one of the two major parties.
  b. the disappearance of one of the major parties.
  c. a lasting shift in the party identification of large groups of people.
  d. a lasting decline in the strength of party identification of large groups of people.

6. The framers of the Constitution opposed political parties because they feared
   a. critical elections.
   b. plurality elections.
   c. tyranny.
   d. realignments.
7. Which party system was characterized by a reaction to economic depression and the forces of industrialization that resulted in the maintenance of majority party status for the majority party from the previous system?
   a. second
   b. third
   c. fourth
   d. fifth
8. "Responsible parties"
   a. refers to parties in the electorate.
   b. facilitate legislative cohesion.
   c. complicate issue voting.
   d. work best in a system with separation of powers.

9. Outside of government, parties are organized as
   a. a decentralized organization of national, state, and local parties.
   b. a hierarchical organization of national, state, and local parties.
   c. a strong, single national organization.
   d. a weak national organization unaffiliated with state and local parties.
10. Patronage arrangements
   a. stifled political competition and had no apparent benefits.
   b. denied political freedom of choice to people in exchange for the provision of social services.
   c. died out entirely when political machines disappeared.
   d. provided government jobs and services to dead people.

In Their Own Words

You might be interested in examining some of what the following authors have said about the topics we've been discussing:

Beck, Paul Allen. *Party Politics in America,* 8th ed. New York: Longman, 1997. This is a good source if you're looking for a comprehensive overview of American parties and party systems.

Keefe, William J. *Parties, Politics, and Public Policy in America,* 8th ed. Washington, DC: CQ Press, 1998. Like *Party Politics in America* by Paul Allen Beck, a good, comprehensive overview of political parties.

Maisel, L. Sandy, ed. *The Parties Respond: Changes in American Parties and Campaigns,* 3rd ed. Boulder, CO: Westview Press, 1998. A recommended assortment of essays assessing the role and status of contemporary political parties.

Rosenstone, Steven J., Roy L. Behr, and Edward H. Lazarus. *Third Parties in America: Citizen Response to Major Party Failure,* 2nd ed. Princeton, NJ: Princeton University Press, 1996. A thorough review of third parties and third-party voting from the nineteenth century through Ross Perot.

Sabato, Larry J. *The Party's Just Begun: Shaping Political Parties for America's Future.* Glenview, IL: Scott, Foresman, 1988. Along with an overview of party systems, Sabato provides ideas for party reform.

Sundquist, James L. *Dynamics of the Party System: Alignment and Realignment of Political Parties in the United States.* Washington, DC: Brookings Institution, 1983. A good place to turn for a descriptive and theoretical discussion of party realignments in American history.

Tolchin, Martin, and Susan. *To the Victor: Political Patronage from the Clubhouse to the White House.* New York: Random House, 1971. An interesting and well-written look at political machines and patronage at all levels of government.

Wattenberg, Martin P. *The Decline of American Political Parties, 1952–1996.* Cambridge, MA: Harvard University Press, 1994. An interesting source to turn to on the phenomenon of dealignment.

Notes

1. Leon D. Epstein, *Political Parties in Western Democracies* (New Brunswick, NJ: Transaction Books, 1980), 9.

2. William J. Keefe, *Parties, Politics, and Public Policy in America,* 8th ed. (Washington, DC: Congressional Quarterly Press, 1998), 60.

3. Steven J. Rosenstone, Roy L. Behr, and Edward H. Lazarus, *Third Parties in America: Citizen Response to Major Party Failure* (Princeton, NJ: Princeton University Press, 1996), 21.

4. See Theodore J. Lowi, *The End of the Republican Era* (Norman, OK: University of Oklahoma Press, 1995); Richard S. Katz and Peter Mair, eds., *Party Organizations* (London: Sage Publications, 1992), 871–876; Steven B. Wolinetz, ed., *Parties and Party Systems in Liberal Democracies* (New York: Routledge, 1988), 272–279.

5. Epstein, *Political Parties,* 283.

6. Rosenstone and others, *Third Parties in America,* 88–92. If you're interested in the positions of a few ideological parties, and want to know more about the issues that concern them, check out the websites for the U.S. Communist Party at http://www.cpusa.org/; the U.S. Socialist Party at http://sp-usa.org/; the U.S. Green Party at http://www.gp.org/; and the U.S. Libertarian Party at http://www.lp.org/.

7. For the political junkies among us, if the name Strom Thurmond sounds familiar, it's because the "Dixiecrat" who ran for president in 1948 is the same Strom Thurmond who retired from the Senate in 2003 at the age of 100. First elected to the Senate in 1954, he switched parties and became a Republican in 1964.

8. James L. Sundquist, *Dynamics of the Party System* (Washington, DC: Brookings Institution, 1983), 1–18.

9. You can read the full text of Washington's farewell address at the U.S. Department of State website, http://usinfo.state.gov/usa/infousa/facts/democrac/49.htm.

10. Larry J. Sabato, *The Party's Just Begun: Shaping Political Parties for America's Future* (Glenview, IL: Scott, Foresman, 1988), 32–33.

11. Ibid.

12. If you'd like to read a brief but interesting biography of Andrew Jackson, you can find one at the White House website, http://www.whitehouse.gov/history/presidents/aj7.html.

13. Paul Allen Beck, *Party Politics in America,* 8th ed. (New York: Longman, 1997), 23.

14. Sundquist, *Dynamics,* 50–105.

15. The modern-day Republican Party rightfully claims to be the party of Lincoln, tracing its roots to the election of 1860.

16. Sundquist, *Dynamics,* 106–146.

17. Ibid., 146–169.

18. Ibid., 198–214.

19. Sabato, *The Party's Just Begun,* 34.

20. Sundquist, *Dynamics,* 412–449.

21. Martin P. Wattenberg, *The Decline of American Political Parties: 1952–1992* (Cambridge, MA: Harvard University Press, 1994), 162–167.

22. Responsible parties have had their advocates in the United States. Over a half-century ago, the American Political Science Association issued a report in which it advocated responsible parties for the United States. The report is called "Toward a More Responsible Two-Party System," and it can be found in the *American Political Science Review* 44: 3 (1950). Or, if you like, you can look at the proceedings of a conference commemorating the fiftieth anniversary of the report, at http://www.apsanet.org/~pop/APSA_Report.htm.

23. Beck, *Party Politics in America,* 321–322.

24. For a more detailed account of the leadership positions in each house, by party, as well as the names and backgrounds of the current occupants of these positions, go to The Congressional Institute website at http://www.conginst.org/congressleaders/, and click on any of the four boxes on the right-hand part of the screen (House Republican Leadership Positions; House Democratic Leadership Positions; Senate Democratic Leadership Positions; Senate Republican Leadership Positions).

25. Keefe, *Parties, Politics, and Public Policy,* 218–236; and Beck, *Party Politics in America,* 305–311.

26. Beck, *Party Politics in America,* 85–91.

27. Paul S. Herrnson, "National Party Organizations at the Century's End," in L. Sandy Maisel, ed., *The Parties Respond,* 3rd ed. (Boulder, CO: Westview Press, 1998), 50–82.

28. Ibid.

Campaigns and Elections:
Vehicles for Democratic Expression

7

7-1 Introduction

Imagine that you got up at 5:30 this morning, and you won't get to bed until after 1:00 tonight. You eat bad food whenever you have a second to grab some, which is rarely, because from the time you wake up until the time you go to sleep, you're constantly on the move, flying in and out of places so fast you lose track of where you are. In between, you go to meeting halls and auditoriums, where you're either talking to ten yawning people at a time or, if you're lucky, you're swamped by crowds and overwhelmed by reporters, leaving you no time to think for yourself. Either way, you find yourself repeating the same speech over and over until it feels like a stale, meaningless mantra. And when you're done speaking, you ask everyone you can find for money—people you know, people you don't know, it doesn't matter. You just keep asking for money—and lots of it.

Now imagine doing this every day for two years—more if you're not particularly well known. Think you can handle it?

Good. You're ready to run for president.

The process of running for president doesn't ensure that we'll send the brightest or most experienced candidates to the White House, but it does guarantee that they'll be durable. Running for president means making the sacrifice of personal time and family life for several *years* in the long-shot gamble that you'll be the last one standing on Election Day. "Running" for president is an appropriate term because the system in place for attaining the office is a marathon that can devour the weak.

We'll see that it incorporates some things we're already familiar with, like the media strategies that we talked about in Chapter 5. We'll also find that the Electoral College, an arcane and often misunderstood structure that usually has the last word on who is elected president, invariably drives general election strategies. Later in the chapter, we'll try to make sense of it.

As we proceed, we'll try to assess whether the process by which we select people for high office adequately provides us with a real and significant opportunity to have input to policy decisions, as we would expect if political parties are to function as effective linkages between citizens and officials. The point is not so much to determine if you would want to try your hand at running for president as it is to see if campaigns can engage you in politics in a meaningful way.

Our discussion of campaigns will focus on presidential races because they're by far the most complex, encompassing a two-step process of winning a party nomination and engaging a candidate of the other major party in the general election. This two-phase process is typical of campaigns for other offices as well, but only the presidential campaign lasts years and is always hotly contested. Many congressional seats, in contrast, are uncontested because the incumbent has successfully scared off possible challengers by raising large sums of money (something that congressional incumbents have an easier time doing than challengers who do not hold power), or because congressional district lines have been drawn to protect incumbents by including a disproportionate number of Democratic or Republican partisans within their boundaries. Both parties attempt to draw district lines in this fashion, creating as many "safe seats" as possible.

7-2 Decisions, Part I: The Selection Process

There are two stages in the marathon process of choosing a president: the selection stage, which takes place within the political party, and the election stage, in which party candidates are pitted against each other. We'll look at them in that order, illustrating how the process unfolds, the strategies candidates use to advance their campaigns, and the importance of money and media to winning the race.

7-2a The Ground Rules

The end point of the selection process occurs when one candidate receives the **nomination** of a political party, formally making that candidate the official choice of the party. The race for the presidential nomination is really fifty-one individual contests (counting the District of Columbia). To win the presidential nomination of a major political party, a candidate needs to compete in these contests, called primaries or caucuses, which are held in every state to select delegates to the party's national convention, held the summer before the presidential election. The candidate who receives a majority of the votes of the delegates at the convention wins the nomination of the party.

Because of the influence of federalism, election laws are state laws, leaving each state to determine its own rules for how its delegates will be chosen. Most states select their convention delegates in a **primary,** which is an election open to party identifiers for the purpose of selecting among candidates for an office. In states that hold primaries, Republicans and Democrats hold separate contests. In presidential primaries, voters select delegates pledged to support a candidate at the national convention. For lower offices, voters select the candidate directly; in most instances, the plurality winner receives the party's nomination.

A **caucus** works quite differently from a primary. It's a series of open meetings, starting at the local level and progressing over a period of time to meetings covering larger jurisdictions, like counties or congressional districts. At each stage of the process, party members select representatives pledged to a variety of candidates to attend the next caucus stage. At the last stage of the process, representatives are selected to attend a state convention, where delegates are chosen to attend the national convention. Unlike a primary, which is a secret ballot, caucus participants make their preferences public.[1] Picture the first stage of a caucus as being small groups of people meeting simultaneously in school buildings, lodges, and social halls across a state, discussing or even debating their presidential preferences with one another. It's a lot different than going to a voting booth and making your choice in private.

The number of states holding primaries has grown steadily in your lifetime, to the point where primaries are now by far the preferred method of delegate selection. In 2000, forty-four states held Democratic primaries and forty-three held Republican primaries. In 1968, only fifteen states held primaries, and the Democratic nominee, Vice President Hubert Humphrey, didn't enter any of them.[2]

In 2004, more than in recent years, states scheduled their primaries and caucuses early. A brief look at the Democratic Party primary calendar shows how many states pressed to get into the action early (see Table 7-1).

A cluster of states held their contests following the first events—the Iowa caucuses, held in late January, and the traditional first primary in New Hampshire, held the following week. In a brief, six-week stretch beginning January 19 and culminating in ten contests

nomination The official endorsement of a candidate by a political party, making that candidate the one whose name will appear on the ballot next to the party label in the next general election.

primary A method of candidate selection in which party identifiers vote for the candidate who will run on the party label in the general election. In presidential primaries, voters select delegates to the national convention.

caucus A method of candidate selection in which party identifiers gather in a series of meetings to select delegates to the national convention.

TABLE 7-1	Date	Primary/Caucus
The Early 2004 Primary and Caucus Calendar	**January 19**	Iowa caucuses
	January 27	New Hampshire primary
	February 3	Arizona primary
		Delaware primary
		Missouri primary
		New Mexico caucuses
		Oklahoma primary
		South Carolina primary
		North Dakota caucuses
	February 7	Michigan caucuses
		Washington (state) caucuses
	February 8	Maine caucuses
	February 10	Tennessee primary
		Virginia primary
	February 17	Wisconsin primary
	February 24	Hawaii caucuses
		Idaho caucuses
		Utah primary
	March 2	California primary
		Connecticut primary
		Georgia primary
		Maryland primary
		Massachusetts primary
		Minnesota caucuses
		New York primary
		Ohio primary
		Rhode Island primary
		Vermont primary

Source: The Federal Election Commission, at http://www.fec.gov/pages/2004pdates.htm.

on "Super Tuesday" (March 2), enough primaries were held to assure that John Kerry would be the Democratic nominee (on the Republican side, President Bush ran unopposed). We'll come back to this point in a little while.

If you think it's silly to select a presidential nominee by compressing the primary schedule into a few hectic weeks, you're not alone. Politicians and pundits regularly second-guess the primary system, and party leaders have been tinkering with the rules for over thirty-five years. During this period, dramatic changes have occurred in the way we select presidential nominees, many of them occurring in the name of reform.

7-2b Reforming the Ground Rules

In Chapter 6, we said that presidential candidates in the first party system were selected by a caucus of the members of their party in government. This system allowed a small, tightly controlled congressional elite to determine presidential nominees. As Jacksonian democracy came into vogue with the second party system, the congressional caucus fell out of favor and was replaced by the more open system of selecting nominees at national party conventions. So, ever since the 1830s, parties have been holding nominating conventions, but the way convention delegates are selected has changed over the years.

For much of the nineteenth century, state conventions, state party committees, or even state governors chose delegates. Initially, this reform permitted states to have a hand in the selection process, but the system remained elite-based, permitting state party bosses

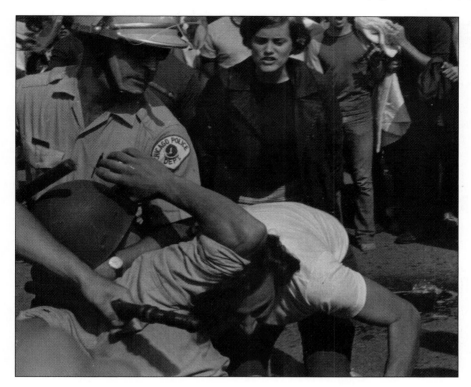

Chicago police battled antiwar protestors during the 1968 Democratic Convention. Media-savvy and conscious of the impression they were making on the television audience, the protestors chanted "The whole world is watching" as a way of bringing attention to what they saw as police brutality that mirrored administration policy in Vietnam.

Source: Copyright Jo Freeman.

to exercise a heavy hand over which delegates were chosen. By the turn of the twentieth century, reformers complained that rank-and-file voters should have more say over the nomination process.

Enter the presidential primary. By 1916, more than half the states held them, but in the ensuing years, their popularity waned as party leaders objected to them, candidates ignored them, voters didn't turn out for them, and states didn't want to pay for them.[3] This permitted party bosses to continue to exercise leverage over the process and explains how Hubert Humphrey could enter the 1968 convention with the support of the Democratic Party elite and win the nomination without having contested any primaries.

The 1968 Democratic Convention was no ordinary gathering, though. Fighting in Vietnam was at a crescendo—the result of the policies of President Lyndon Johnson, a Democrat. An antiwar faction composed mostly of young activists planned to protest what was expected to be Johnson's renomination in Chicago that August. Even though Johnson dropped out of the race months before the convention, the antiwar faction of the Democratic Party marched in protest through the streets of Chicago, putting them at odds with the law-and-order Democratic Party boss, Chicago Mayor Richard Daley.

While the convention nominated Vice President Humphrey, the choice of party insiders, over the vocal protests of antiwar delegates, demonstrators clashed with police outside the hall. Scenes of mayhem and violence—of tear gas, arrests, and police beatings—appeared on television screens nationwide, portraying a deeply divided and torn Democratic Party. Humphrey's candidacy failed, and the cry went out to change the nomination system in a way that would shift control to rank-and-file Democrats from the party elites that had supported Humphrey.[4]

The reforms that changed the way party nominees are selected came between 1969 and 1971 from the Democratic Party Commission on Party Structure and Delegate Selection, commonly called the **McGovern-Fraser Commission** after its chairs, Senator George McGovern of South Dakota and, later, Representative Donald Fraser of Minnesota. The commission made the delegate selection process more open, egalitarian, and mass-based, making it harder for party elites to control the nomination. Major reforms of the McGovern-Fraser Commission are shown in Figure 7-1.

▶**McGovern-Fraser Commission** The commission organized by the Democratic Party following its 1968 convention to democratize the process of delegate selection to party conventions.

Figure 7-1
Major Reforms of the McGovern-Fraser Commission

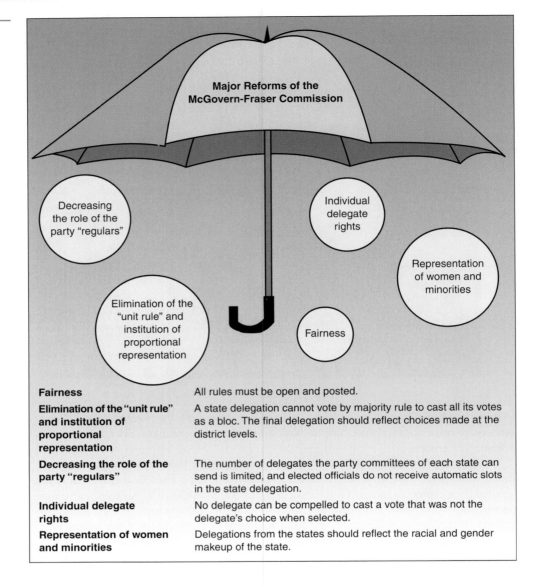

Fairness	All rules must be open and posted.
Elimination of the "unit rule" and institution of proportional representation	A state delegation cannot vote by majority rule to cast all its votes as a bloc. The final delegation should reflect choices made at the district levels.
Decreasing the role of the party "regulars"	The number of delegates the party committees of each state can send is limited, and elected officials do not receive automatic slots in the state delegation.
Individual delegate rights	No delegate can be compelled to cast a vote that was not the delegate's choice when selected.
Representation of women and minorities	Delegations from the states should reflect the racial and gender makeup of the state.

> **media events** Activities staged by campaigns or political officials that have enough news value to draw press attention to a message the politician wants to communicate.

Like so many well-intentioned efforts, there were unexpected consequences to the McGovern-Fraser reforms. Although the Commission didn't expressly advocate the expansion of primaries, many states found that moving to a primary system was the easiest way to implement the letter if not the spirit of the reforms. Because these changes were being made on a state-by-state basis, the Republican Party soon followed suit. This shifted the arena for candidate selection in both parties to the primaries and away from the national conventions, which became vehicles for ratifying the victorious primary candidate, rather than deliberative forums for selecting the candidate.[5] Since 1968, there has not been a national convention that convened with the identity of the party's presidential nominee in doubt, and conventions have become staged **media events** showcasing the victorious nominee to the nation.

This not only resulted in control over the selection process passing from party elites to rank-and-file voters, it changed the entire nominating process from one centered in the party to one centered in the individual campaigns, with unprecedented emphasis on the personality and communication skills of the candidate. Successful candidates no longer had to be champions of party insiders if they could compete successfully in primary races by appealing directly to voters. After 1968, the nominating process became a long string of individual statewide campaigns, in which candidates appealed through television to primary voters in order to pile up enough delegates to win the nomination outright at the con-

Year	Commission	Objective	Major Change	Result
1972	Mikulski	No McGoverns	Delegates better represent voter preferences	Carter elected
1978	Winograd	Reelect Carter	Bind delegates on first ballot	Carter defeated
1982	Hunt	No Carters	Elite "super delegates"	Mondale defeated
1986	"Fairness"	No Mondales	No "winner-take-all" primaries	Dukakis defeated

TABLE 7-2

Tinkering with the Rules

vention. Perhaps no one understood this better than the man who wrote the rules—George McGovern—a liberal who lacked the backing of the party's deal makers but who parlayed his appreciation of the new system into the 1972 Democratic presidential nomination.

The McGovern candidacy was a general election disaster, though, carrying only one state and the District of Columbia in the most lopsided Electoral College defeat to date. The new rules had opened up the system as intended, but they had produced a candidate without the elite backing that in past years had been helpful in winning a general election. So, the Democrats continued to tinker. For four straight presidential elections following McGovern's defeat, Democrats convened commissions to revise the rules. Each commission reacted to the perceived flaws of the one that came before, as all but one led to electoral failure.

The outcome of these commissions, and the political results they produced, are summarized in Table 7-2. The Mikulski Commission attempted to avoid a repeat of the McGovern debacle by ensuring that delegates more accurately represented the preferences of primary voters. This opened the process to a little-known, one-term ex-governor of Georgia, Jimmy Carter, who never would have had a chance at the presidential nomination under the old rules and who might have been locked out under the McGovern procedures.

When Carter took hold of the Democratic Party apparatus as president, he attempted through the Winograd Commission to solidify his position through changes making it harder to challenge his renomination, such as by binding delegates to support the candidate they were selected to represent. Carter survived a nomination challenge by Massachusetts Senator Edward Kennedy but was denied a second term. Party insiders blamed Carter's defeat and the shortcomings of his administration on the fact that he had been an inexperienced outsider, and a movement began to return elite control to the selection process. The Hunt Commission introduced "super delegates"—state and local party leaders, members of Congress, and other elected officials—who would represent 14 percent of convention delegates and serve to throw the nomination to an experienced candidate acceptable to the party elite if needed. And in 1984, the Democrats nominated a candidate with a long resume—former Vice President Walter Mondale—who promptly took his party to its second forty-nine-state loss in twelve years.

Candidates who had lost to Mondale in the 1984 primaries, like the less established Colorado Senator Gary Hart, argued for reforms that would make it easier for challengers to compete in the primaries. Democrats responded with the "Fairness" Commission, which instituted proportional representation methods designed to make this happen. The result was as planned: In 1988, Democrats nominated Massachusetts Governor Michael Dukakis, who was not one of his party's better known national figures. He had marginally more success than Mondale, but his inexperience showed in the national campaign he waged, and the Democrats once again lost the general election.[6]

The experiment with formal commissions ended in 1986, but changes in the selection process continued to evolve. During the past few years, one of the most notable changes has been the compression of the primary schedule that we mentioned earlier. In 1976, Carter didn't secure the nomination until primaries were held in California, Ohio, and New Jersey on June 8, four months after the Iowa caucuses. In 2004, a hotly contested

Democratic nomination battle ended within a matter of weeks after the Iowa caucuses because so many states—particularly delegate-rich large states—had moved their primaries up to the early stage of the selection process.

The reason for this movement has to do with the political advantages of going early. Not all primaries and caucuses carry the same importance, and a state's position on the calendar is more important in the scheme of things than its population or diversity. By custom, Iowa holds the nation's first caucus, typically in late January, and New Hampshire follows with the nation's first primary roughly one week later. Throughout all the years of reform, this custom remains untouched. Both are small, sparsely populated states without urban centers, demographically atypical of the rest of the country. But they receive a disproportionate share of media attention over all other primaries and caucuses because they're first. Horserace-centered reporters, hungry for real voters to make real decisions, magnify the results of these first contests disproportionately.

In the primary-centered selection process that the McGovern-Fraser Commission set into motion, candidates get a critical boost coming out of Iowa and New Hampshire, and larger states began to realize that the closer they could schedule their primaries to the early contests, the more influence they would have over the outcome. Conversely, the closer they were to the end of the primary calendar, the greater the risk of being cut out entirely, as challengers dropped out and the eventual nominee became clear.

California, the largest state, traditionally held its primary in June, but in every election since 1976, the nominee was essentially decided by then. So, in 2004, California moved its primary date to March. So did New York.[7] The effect: an earlier, accelerated, and more expensive primary race, as candidates now have little time to catch their breath while expending resources to compete in populous states where buying television time is very expensive.

As for those of us who would wish to influence the presidential selection process, geography is destiny. If you live in a state that held its 2004 Democratic Party primary or caucuses after March 2, the choice was already made before you had a chance to vote. Even if you live in a state that voted in middle or late February, you faced a more limited choice than the residents of Iowa and New Hampshire, as unsuccessful candidates like Representative Dick Gephardt, Senator Joseph Lieberman, General Wesley Clark, and Governor Howard Dean fell by the wayside quickly after losing a handful of early contests. Even though it is the product of reforms designed to democratize the selection process, the system in place through 2004 offers disproportionate influence to voters in the states that go first.

7-2c Money

As campaigns became primary-centered, they also became incredibly expensive to wage. One of the greatest costs in a primary campaign is television advertising, and as political parties have lost control of the nominating process to individual candidates, it is arguably the most critical resource for a campaign to have. To win primary votes, candidates have to reach those rank-and-file voters that reformers wanted to bring into the process. That means advertising and lots of it—which of course means raising a lot of money.

The rules that govern how money can be collected in a presidential campaign have gone through two significant changes during the period since the McGovern-Fraser reforms and have had as much influence on how campaigns operate as changes in the delegate selection rules. Both were campaign finance reform laws. The first was instituted in 1974, the second in 2002.

As a consequence of illegal contributions to President Nixon's reelection campaign brought to light during the Watergate scandal, Congress turned its attention to reforming the way candidates solicit money. The result was the 1974 **Federal Election Campaign Act,** which set limits on campaign contributions, set practices for public disclosure of campaign contributions, established a method of partial public funding of presidential campaigns, and created the **Federal Election Commission (FEC)** to oversee the process. In an attempt to keep the FEC nonpartisan, its six commissioners are equally divided between

▶**Federal Election Campaign Act** The 1974 act aimed at limiting the influence of big-money contributions on political campaigns.

▶**Federal Election Commission (FEC)** The federal regulatory agency that administers and enforces campaign finance laws.

> ### Box 7-1   **Political Action Committees**

PACs are organizations formed by special interest groups of the sort we will be discussing in Chapter 8 for the purpose of contributing money to political candidates. Most PACs represent labor unions, business groups, or organizations with an ideological agenda—all of which have an interest in affecting the public agenda. Because PACs get their money directly from group members rather than from the organization's funds, they were technically legal before the implementation of the 1974 Federal Election Campaign Act because the language of the law prohibited contributions *directly* from unions and businesses.

After 1974, PACs became officially sanctioned, and limits were placed on how much they could contribute. From that point, the number of PACs (and PAC dollars) grew astronomi-

cally. According to the nonpartisan Center for Responsive Politics, in 1974, 608 PACs were registered with the Federal Election Commission, and they had contributed a combined $15 million to presidential and congressional candidates. In 1998, 3,798 registered PACs had contributed $220 million.[*]

In Chapter 8, we'll take a closer look at who organizes PACs, how much they contribute to politics, and how much they influence the decisions of victorious politicians.[†]

[*]The Center for Responsive Politics, at http://www.opensecrets.org/pubs/bigpicture2000/pac/index.ihtml.

[†]In the meantime, if you want to take a closer look at the role of PACs, go to http://www.opensecrets.org/pubs/bigpicture2000/pac/index.ihtml.

Republicans and Democrats. Under the law, limits were placed on how much individuals and **political action committees** or **PACs** could contribute to candidates and party organizations. Box 7-1 discusses PACs in more detail.

Individuals could contribute no more than $1,000 to a candidate, and PACs could contribute no more than $5,000. The limits were applied to each election, with primaries and general election campaigns regarded as separate contests. Also, there were restrictions on contributions that could be made to party organizations and annual limits on individual giving. These limits were modified in 2002, resulting in the funding limits shown in Table 7-3.

In presidential campaigns, a system of matching public funds was established to place limits on spending, while tightening the bonds to the political system for those of us interested in participating through contributing money. The idea was to give ordinary voters who might not think to make political contributions a convenient way to participate in the political process, while democratizing fund-raising at the margins by limiting the amount of big-dollar contributions in the system.

Here's how it works: The government retains a Presidential Election Campaign Fund financed by those of us who check a box on our tax return authorizing $3 of our tax payment to go to the fund (checking the box simply allocates the money—it doesn't increase the tax payment). Money from the fund can go to candidates who demonstrate broad-based support by raising $5,000 in small contributions in each of twenty states. Once a candidate qualifies, the government matches up to $250 in contributions made by individuals; PAC contributions are not matched. In turn, the candidate agrees to a spending limit, which in 2004 was $37.3 million for the primaries and $74.6 million for the general election. During the primaries, there are also spending limits candidates must adhere to within individual states.[8]

> **political action committees (PACs)** Organizations formed by interest groups such as labor unions, businesses, and ideological groups for the purpose of contributing money to political candidates.

T A B L E 7-3	**Annual Campaign Contribution Limits**			
	To a Candidate (Per Election)	**To a National Party Organization**	**To Any Other Party Organization**	**Total**
Individuals	$2,000	$25,000 per party committee	$10,000 to each state or local party committee	$95,000 every two-year election cycle
PACs	$5,000	$15,000	$5,000	None

Source: The Center for Responsive Politics, at http://www.opensecrets.org.

Figure 7-2

Campaign Spending before and after Campaign Finance Reform

Source: Data from Nelson W. Polsby and Aaron Wildavsky, *Presidential Elections,* 10th ed. (New York: Chatham House Publishers, 2000), 55.

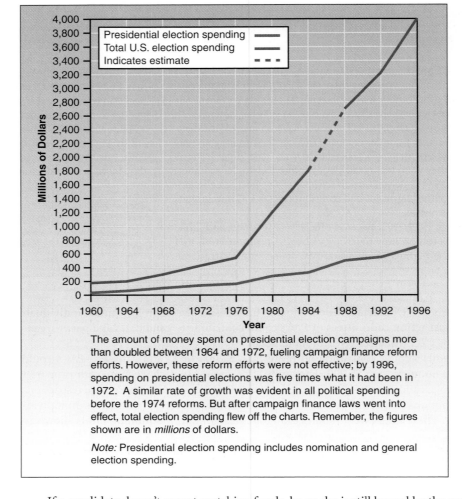

The amount of money spent on presidential election campaigns more than doubled between 1964 and 1972, fueling campaign finance reform efforts. However, these reform efforts were not effective; by 1996, spending on presidential elections was five times what it had been in 1972. A similar rate of growth was evident in all political spending before the 1974 reforms. But after campaign finance laws went into effect, total election spending flew off the charts. Remember, the figures shown are in *millions* of dollars.

Note: Presidential election spending includes nomination and general election spending.

If a candidate doesn't accept matching funds, he or she is still bound by the campaign contribution limits in Table 7-3, but not by the spending limits. Because matching funds can stretch a candidate's coffers, they're hard to pass up, and since the law went into effect, only five candidates have declined public money, but—notably—all but one of them competed in the last two elections. Former Texas governor John Connelly in 1980 and businessman Steve Forbes in 1996 and 2000 tapped personal fortunes in unsuccessful efforts to win the Republican Party nomination. George W. Bush in 2000 and 2004 assembled a remarkably proficient fund-raising organization that shattered all fund-raising records to fuel two successful Republican nomination bids. Former Vermont Governor Howard Dean in 2003 set fund-raising records for a Democrat by relying on a previously untapped source—the Internet—before his campaign deteriorated in early 2004. To keep pace with Dean, eventual nominee John Kerry declined matching funds, although before his campaign took off, he borrowed against one of his homes to finance his campaign.[9]

Despite the best intentions of the reformers, there were loopholes in the system that could be exploited even by candidates who accepted matching funds, and given the pressure candidates felt to spend money on media (and travel and consultants), it wasn't long before spending dramatically increased. Campaigns were becoming expensive prior to the establishment of the FEC, but take a look in Figure 7-2 at how spending shot up *after* public financing went into effect in 1974.

What went wrong? Campaign finance limits restricted what's often called **hard money**—contributions made directly to candidates. They did not cover **soft-money** contributions, or money donated to state and local party committees or to the national parties' nonfederal accounts. The Federal Election Campaign Act left soft-money contributions unregulated, on the assumption that funds from these accounts would be used for state elections, voter registration, get-out-the-vote drives, and other "grassroots" activities.

hard money Funds contributed directly to candidates or national parties by individuals or PACs for the purpose of electing candidates to federal office. Federal law regulates hard-money contributions.

soft money Funds contributed to state and local parties or to national parties for the purpose of running state elections or conducting local "grassroots" political activity.

This, in turn, provided parties and contributors with a loophole for circumventing campaign finance limits. With a little creativity, it's easy to see how the parties could spend soft money on, say, campaign overhead, permitting candidates to spend more of their hard money on campaign commercials and other political functions. One of the more popular uses of soft money is for what are euphemistically called "issue ads" by political professionals. These are commercials produced on behalf of a candidate, which appear to advocate the candidate's election (or the defeat of his or her opponent) by spotlighting an aspect of the candidate's record (typically by putting an opponent's record in a negative context). As long as these ads do not *expressly* advocate the election or defeat of a candidate, they are considered educational and can be paid for with unlimited soft money.[10]

In recent years, Congress has wrestled with changing the campaign finance structure to make contributing to presidential campaigns more democratic, but it's been a hard sell. Incumbent members of Congress of both parties have been reluctant to change a system that brought them to power, and although finance reform is a widely popular issue, it's not the sort of thing that gets most people out of their homes on Election Day. Finally, in 2002, the political climate worked in favor of reform. By a narrow margin, both houses of Congress passed a version of campaign finance reform advocated by Republican Senator John McCain and Democratic Senator Russell Feingold, and a reluctant President Bush signed it into law.

The major feature of the Bipartisan Campaign Reform Act of 2002, commonly called the **McCain-Feingold Act,** is a prohibition of the use of soft money in federal elections, including a ban on "issue ads" funded with soft money. In exchange, after the 2002 elections, the annual limit that individuals can contribute in hard-money contributions to candidates and party organizations doubled—to $2,000 and $10,000, respectively.

Even after passage, McCain-Feingold met with resistance. Although ardent reform activists felt it was little more than a Band-Aid over a gaping wound, just about everyone directly influenced by the changes resisted them. Both major parties immediately searched for ways to circumvent the soft-money restrictions, while some PACs argued it went too far, challenging soft-money limitations as restrictions on free expression.

Detractors included four of the six FEC commissioners who were in office at the time the law went into effect. Because they were responsible for interpreting and enforcing the law, they were able to weaken some of the law's reforms, restoring large portions of the soft-money loophole that McCain-Feingold was designed to fill and providing exceptions under which federal candidates could still collect soft-money contributions. That led to a fight with Senator McCain, who vowed to undo the FEC action. The law got a boost in December 2002, when a divided Supreme Court upheld the soft-money ban, but McCain-Feingold was unable to prevent massive soft-money expenditures in the 2004 contest.[11]

7-2d Off to the Races: Money, Media, and Momentum

Perhaps the most accurate way to characterize the presidential selection season is to say it's a marathon leading up to the primaries, then a fast sprint to the nomination (followed by another marathon to the fall election for the primary winners). The strategy followed by candidates is dictated partly by the realities of the calendar and partly by the resources at their disposal.

Every potential president starts out with advantages and disadvantages, but not in equal amounts. As the 2004 Democratic presidential contest began to take shape, potential candidates like Al Gore and Joseph Lieberman, the 2000 Democratic nominees for president and vice president, held one obvious advantage over, say, Carol Moseley Braun.

Who's Carol Moseley Braun? That's the point. If you live in Illinois, you may know that she once represented your state in the Senate (she was later U.S. ambassador to New Zealand). But for the millions of Americans who do not live in Illinois (and who do not pay close attention to American ambassadors), she had a lot of catching up to do when it came to **name recognition** because, as a one-term senator who had been out of office for several years, she was not exactly a household name.

Name recognition gives candidates credibility; no one is going to question whether Gore or Lieberman could mount a viable presidential campaign the way one might raise that question about, say, Gary Bauer.[12] (Look at the endnote if you don't know who Gary

▶ McCain-Feingold Act
The name commonly used to describe the Bipartisan Campaign Reform Act of 2002, which prohibits the use of soft money in federal elections in an attempt to close a loophole in the 1974 Federal Election Campaign Act.

▶ name recognition
An informal measure of how much the public is aware of a candidate or elected official, based on how widely people are able to identify who the candidate or official is.

Box 7-2 As the Rich Get Richer, the Poor Drop Out

Running for president has become so expensive that, in 1999, a few fairly well-known contenders dropped out *before* the primaries began because they were unable to raise enough money. By June 30, 1999, more than half a year before the first primary and caucus votes were cast, George W. Bush had raised a staggering $37.2 million for his campaign. In stark contrast, former Vice President Dan Quayle and former Labor Secretary Elizabeth Dole had "only" been able to raise $3.5 million each, while former Tennessee Governor Lamar Alexander, who had essentially never stopped running after his unsuccessful presidential bid four years earlier, had raised one million less than that.* All three would call it quits by October 1999, recognizing that they simply did not have a realistic chance of attracting the kind of dollars they would need to compete.

Despite all the dollars that flow to politics, there is still a finite source of contributors. In 1999, Bush was aided by his connections to the oil industry, which is a key source of Republican money. Democrats, for their part, traditionally tap big Hollywood contributors. For Democratic primary hopefuls, 90210 isn't just an old TV show—it's the zip code identifying one of the most lucrative sources of Democratic money (Beverly Hills, California)—a zip code that Bill Clinton frequently visited in 1992 and 1996.

The fact remains that once money is committed to a candidate, it's out of play, and with the frontloading of expensive contests, money raised early counts the most. In the days following the McGovern-Fraser reforms, candidates could expect to be able to raise money during the long primary season if they experienced early success. Today's compressed primary calendar makes that impossible. If big money doesn't flow early, a campaign is doomed.

As with a primary schedule that awards political influence unevenly, depending on where you live, there's a big irony in the way campaign finance reforms have restricted political competition. The reforms that produced today's primary system were intended to democratize the selection process, giving voice to the wishes of the party's rank-and-file voters. As candidates drop out before the voting starts because of inability to raise the huge sums necessary to run a primary campaign, candidate selection shifts from people willing to go to the ballot box to people willing—and able—to open their checkbooks.

*Nelson W. Polsby and Aaron Wildavsky, *Presidential Elections,* 10th ed. (New York: Chatham House, 2000), 100.

Bauer is.) With credibility comes the ability to raise resources. It's easier to raise money if you look like you can mount a serious campaign. You'll attract seasoned campaign advisors. The media will pay more attention to you.[13]

By far, the greatest benefit of name recognition is the advantage it gives a candidate in attracting donors. Long before a single primary vote is counted in New Hampshire, well in advance of the snowy Iowa caucuses, the primary race takes shape as prospective candidates travel the country looking for financial support. (See Box 7-2.) This preprimary phase, which could legitimately be called the "money primary," can stretch out for a year or two for candidates with name recognition, even more for candidates who are less well known. Considering the cost of buying television commercials in large states that now hold their primaries early in the process, raising large amounts of money is essential to any candidate who hopes to have a serious chance of making the race.

Similarly, viable campaigns will strengthen their position by attracting a team of advisors with proven track records. Any successful campaign needs organization, and potential staff members will want to place their professional futures in the hands of candidates who seem to be going somewhere. That's why candidates with name recognition are in a better position to attract the people who make a campaign run: fund-raisers, pollsters, speechwriters, and political consultants who can organize a national strategy, an advance staff to organize events, and grassroots political teams in key primary and caucus states who can get out the vote.[14] See Box 7-3.

The more a candidate demonstrates the ability to amass resources in the year or so before the primaries begin, the more seriously political reporters and pundits will regard the candidate. Achieving a high level of notice from the press is as critical as raising money because a campaign that depends on reaching voters on a state-by-state basis cannot survive without media attention. Press coverage then begets press coverage in a kind of self-fulfilling cycle: A candidate who gets press coverage is taken seriously by reporters, who react by bestowing even more press coverage on the candidate. Of course, this attention

Box 7-3   Doing It Differently

At the end of Chapter 5, we noted how long-shot presidential candidate Howard Dean became a serious contender in the summer of 2003 by drawing supporters to his Internet site and raising money—much of it online—in small amounts. Because campaign finance law matches the first $250 contributed, the Dean campaign had the opportunity to stretch its resources further by qualifying for matching funds for a large proportion of the contributions that flooded his coffers via his website, before he raised so much money that he opted to reject matching funds and spending limits entirely. This method of fund-raising will not work for everyone; some of Dean's rivals tried to leverage support from the Internet but were unable to do so. It is, however, another indication of how emerging technology may make it possible to counter some of the undemocratic forces in the electoral process. Without an active Internet presence, the Dean fund-raising effort could not have kept pace with rival campaigns, and it is likely that his campaign would not have survived, no less become competitive.

Even though Dean raised enough money to hire professional consultants, he continued to rely on his web-based supporters to plan and organize events, and to turn out crowds—something they proved surprisingly adept at doing. During the summer of 2003, Dean addressed crowds that numbered in the hundreds and, at times, thousands—far greater than any of his opponents and unprecedented for a nonincumbent so early in the process. Professional campaign workers dream of being able to generate that type of response. In Dean's case, much of it was the product of individual initiatives on the part of ordinary citizens who found, through the Internet, a niche they could fill in the campaign process.

---

just works to help the candidate raise more money and build a better organization. It can work in reverse as well, with struggling candidates facing longer odds as the press ignores them.

But with the benefits of an effective early-stage campaign come the pressures of high **expectations.** Horserace coverage comes early to a campaign marked by a long march to raise money and establish credibility, and reporters will handicap the odds against each contender well before primary voters have their say.[15] When reporters see that candidates with name recognition like George W. Bush in 1999 are succeeding at fund-raising and attracting a professional staff, they will treat them as serious contenders who are expected to perform well once the voters actually have their say. Likewise, reporters will express doubts about a candidate like Connecticut Senator Joseph Lieberman, who entered the 2004 Democratic presidential primary with higher name recognition than his opponents but failed to best them at fund-raising in the year before the primaries.

Bush's fund-raising efforts so outclassed his Republican opponents that he went into the 2000 primaries as the perceived **front-runner**—the candidate reporters said everyone had to beat. In contrast, reporters handicapped former labor secretary (and current North Carolina senator) Elizabeth Dole as a main challenger to Bush, by virtue of her high level of name recognition and position in the Republican establishment (she is the wife of 1996 Republican presidential nominee Bob Dole). As a serious challenger, reporters expected less of her than of Bush; she would have to run close enough to the front-runner to take the lead in the event he stumbled. A candidate like Arizona Senator John McCain (the same McCain who has his name on the 2002 campaign finance law), whose limited fund-raising and organizational success put him in a **long-shot** position, could afford to run behind the leaders in the early going without suffering negative press coverage.

The press reliably assigns these labels every four years. In the 2004 Democratic race, the early leader of the "money primary" was John Kerry, who was stripped by reporters of his front-runner status and replaced by Howard Dean following the latter's Internet fund-raising success, only to reclaim the front-runner designation after winning the Iowa caucuses and New Hampshire primary. When Dean faltered, Senator John Edwards of North Carolina emerged as the main challenger to Kerry in the February and March contests, before Kerry secured the nomination.

Whether you're a front-runner, main challenger, or long shot, your strategy is largely dictated by your position in the race and the media-generated expectations that follow from it. When the primaries begin, a campaign generates **momentum** by meeting or exceeding expectations. This puts the greatest pressure on the front-runner to win early

expectations The benchmark for how well a campaign needs to perform in presidential primaries in order to receive positive horserace coverage, based on reporter assessments of the campaign's viability.

front-runner The presidential candidate who leads the primary horserace, based on media assessments of the campaign.

long shot A presidential candidate who is not expected to fare well in the primary horserace, based on media assessments of the campaign.

momentum The ability of a presidential campaign to maintain viability by meeting or exceeding press-generated expectations during the long primary period.

and often, while long shots simply need to do better than expected. In fact, a long shot who surprises reporters by finishing close to the top of the pack in the Iowa caucuses or New Hampshire primary can receive a goldmine of media coverage—even if he or she doesn't finish first. In that case, a candidate can win in the media without winning with the voters.

However, when long shots beat their expectations, they're no longer long shots, and reporters will require that they begin to win, and win soon. Failure to meet newly elevated expectations can stall momentum just as surely as a front-runner that underperforms runs the risk of being tossed from the race. Momentum has tangible rewards because resources follow winners, and if you're presented as a winner in the press, the money and organization you'll attract might just be enough to validate what reporters are saying about your campaign. See Figure 7-3 on pages 195–197.

After a long buildup to the first caucus and primary decisions, selection contests run under contemporary rules always sort themselves out fast. The logic of horserace coverage places so much weight on Iowa and New Hampshire that candidates must exceed expectations in these early contests if they hope to survive. As Bush demonstrated in 2000, winning Iowa does not sew up the nomination. As McCain demonstrated, neither does winning New Hampshire. But doing better than expected gives a campaign momentum at a critical time, creating an opportunity for the campaign to demonstrate to the press that it's worthy of the higher expectations that come with success. When Forbes could not win New Hampshire or Delaware, the momentum he had generated in Iowa vanished. When McCain lost nationally on Super Tuesday, his campaign could not recover. Of course, candidates who actually *do* win contests they're "expected" to lose find themselves in a strong position. John Kerry came out of nowhere to beat Howard Dean in Iowa; when he finished first the following week in New Hampshire, his campaign got such a media boost that Kerry was able to ride the momentum it generated to the 2004 Democratic Party nomination.

The strategic importance of the early races means that all candidates need to invest a disproportionate amount of money, time, and organizational resources into Iowa and New Hampshire, while trying to save sufficient resources to carry them through the next steps. If you're trying to get a sense of whether a prospective candidate is serious about running, just pay attention to how much time he spends in Iowa and New Hampshire during the year before the election. Between March 15 and August 2, 1999, Lamar Alexander spent a combined thirty-nine days in Iowa and New Hampshire, compared to twenty-six days in his home state and twenty-three days in all other states combined. Elizabeth Dole spent a combined twenty-nine days in Iowa and New Hampshire, thirty-nine days everywhere else. Howard Dean spent the better part of *two years* in Iowa and New Hampshire, visiting each of Iowa's ninety-nine counties during 2002 and 2003. No other state comes close to commanding that kind of attention. But since 1972, no candidate has won a nomination after finishing below third place in either state.[16]

While campaigning in these and other primary and caucus states, candidates fashion a message that can define their campaigns. Along with investing resources in the early contests, developing an effective message is a key part of attaining viability because it's not enough to tell people you're running for president simply because you want to be president. Candidates need to give people a reason to vote for them.

Typically, candidates need to do two things. They need to distinguish themselves from their rivals, which is sometimes difficult to do in a selection contest where your rivals come from within your party and probably agree with you more than they disagree. They also need to appeal to the people who are likely to turn out to vote.

One way candidates can draw distinctions with their opponents is by positioning themselves to the "right" or "left" of the opposition. For instance, Howard Dean took a stand against the Iraq War, positioning himself as a more liberal candidate than John Kerry, even though Kerry had a more liberal record. George W. Bush used the term "compassionate conservatism" to portray a conservative philosophy with a moderate temperament that suggested unity and inclusiveness, as we noted in Chapter 5.

Even as Bush sought the middle ground, it was the middle ground *within* his party. Primary voters are more likely than general election voters to be closer to the poles of public opinion. Republicans are likely to be more conservative than the general population; Democrats are likely to be more liberal. Candidates need to reach these voters in order to

January 1999

These are the candidates for the 2000 Republican presidential nomination in early 1999. In the lead is Texas Governor George W. Bush, the popular governor of a big state, which gives him name recognition and the ability to raise money fast. Behind him is Elizabeth Dole, well-known former labor secretary and Red Cross president; former Vice President Dan Quayle; and former Tennessee Governor Lamar Alexander, who established himself as a contender during an unsuccessful run for the 1996 nomination.

Further back, we have wealthy businessman Steve Forbes, who also ran unsuccessfully in 1996 and who has the money to finance a long campaign, and maverick Arizona Senator John McCain.

Bringing up the rear are three candidates who have never held elected office: television commentator Pat Buchanan, columnist and talk-show host Alan Keyes, and conservative activist Gary Bauer.

Figure 7-3
Money, Media, and Momentum in 2000

Starting Order
#1- G. W. Bush
#2- E. Dole
#3- D. Quayle
#4- L. Alexander
#5- S. Forbes
#6- J. McCain
#7- P. Buchanan
#8- A. Keyes
#9- G. Bauer

July 1999

In the contest to see who can raise the most money, the early front-runner clearly excels. Dole, Quayle, and Alexander are having unexpected problems raising money and seem to be falling back.

Running Order
#1- G. W. Bush
#2- E. Dole
#3- D. Quayle
#4- L. Alexander
#5- S. Forbes
#6- J. McCain
#7- P. Buchanan
#8- A. Keyes
#9- G. Bauer

October 1999

Uh, oh—Quayle and Alexander are having serious difficulties, and they're out of the race. Meanwhile, Bush is padding his appreciable lead. And now it appears that Elizabeth Dole is also out of the race because of her inability to attract enough campaign contributions. So, we're left with Bush, the biggest fund-raiser, in the lead, followed by the vastly wealthy Steve Forbes, with McCain and the other long shots in the distance.

Running Order
#1- G. W. Bush
#5- S. Forbes
#6- J. McCain
#7- P. Buchanan
#8- A. Keyes
#9- G. Bauer
#2- E. Dole - out
#3- D. Quayle - out
#4- L. Alexander - out

Figure 7-3 continued on next page

November 1999

What's this? The Buchanan car is leaving the racetrack for a different one. Looking like a sure loser in this race, Buchanan is leaving to join the contest for the Reform Party nomination.

Running Order
#1- G. W. Bush
#5- S. Forbes
#6- J. McCain
#8- A. Keyes
#9- G. Bauer
#2- E. Dole - out
#3- D. Quayle - out
#4- L. Alexander - out
#7- P. Buchanan - out

January 2000

Three viable competitors and one long shot are out of the race, all before the first hurdle involving real voters. The Iowa caucus results are coming in now, and it's a big win for the front-runner, plus a surprisingly strong second-place showing for Forbes, with Keyes and Bauer finishing three and four ahead of a disappointing showing for McCain. Are the media going to take Forbes seriously enough to make him a strong main challenger to Bush?

Running Order
#1- G. W. Bush
#5- S. Forbes
#8- A. Keyes
#9- G. Bauer
#6- J. McCain
#2- E. Dole - out
#3- D. Quayle - out
#4- L. Alexander - out
#7- P. Buchanan - out

February 2000

What's happening now? The New Hampshire results are coming in, and it's a stunning upset for long-shot challenger John McCain. Bush finishes second in New Hampshire as the long-shot McCain pulls into a tie for the lead. Campaign money is flowing McCain's way. Last week's impressive showing by Forbes in Iowa doesn't help him in New Hampshire, where he finishes a disappointing third, way below his expectations, and he seems to be sputtering.

Running Order
#1- G. W. Bush
#6- J. McCain
#5- S. Forbes
#8- A. Keyes
#9- G. Bauer
#2- E. Dole - out
#3- D. Quayle - out
#4- L. Alexander - out
#7- P. Buchanan - out

February 2000

Bush easily beats Forbes in the Delaware primary. Delaware is a tiny state, but it borders on Forbes' home state of New Jersey, so reporters expected him to win big. Instead, Forbes is out of the race just days after his strong second-place finish in Iowa. New Hampshire is also the end for Bauer's long-shot candidacy. That leaves Bush and the surprising long shot McCain neck and neck, with Keyes well in the rear. Next comes the South Carolina primary. Bush is well organized there. Can he stop McCain?

Running Order
#1- G. W. Bush
#6- J. McCain
#8- A. Keyes
#2- E. Dole - out
#3- D. Quayle - out
#4- L. Alexander - out
#7- P. Buchanan - out
#5- S. Forbes - out
#9- G. Bauer - out

February 2000

Perhaps he can. It's a big win for Bush in South Carolina.

Running Order
#1- G. W. Bush
#6- J. McCain
#8- A. Keyes
#2- E. Dole - out
#3- D. Quayle - out
#4- L. Alexander - out
#7- P. Buchanan - out
#5- S. Forbes - out
#9- G. Bauer - out

February 2000

But wait, it's not over yet. McCain scores a big win over Bush in Michigan, and he's looking to Super Tuesday to take the lead for good. Bush is starting to falter a little. The big battle is ahead.

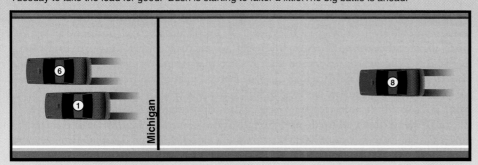

Running Order
#1- G. W. Bush
#6- J. McCain
#8- A. Keyes
#2- E. Dole - out
#3- D. Quayle - out
#4- L. Alexander - out
#7- P. Buchanan - out
#5- S. Forbes - out
#9- G. Bauer - out

March 2000

It's a battle in which the original front-runner, with his money and organization, has all the advantages. McCain does well in New England, but Bush prevails nationally, with primary victories from California to New York. It's all over for the long shot. Six weeks after the Iowa caucus, the original front-runner pulls ahead to stay. George W. Bush will be the Republican Party's presidential nominee in 2000.

Finishing Order
#1- G. W. Bush
#6- J. McCain
#8- A. Keyes
#2- E. Dole - out
#3- D. Quayle - out
#4- L. Alexander - out
#7- P. Buchanan - out
#5- S. Forbes - out
#9- G. Bauer - out

> ### Box 7-4 Koppel Walks Out

It was all too much for ABC News reporter Ted Koppel, who left the Republican Convention early and refused to go to the Democratic Convention at all. Insisting that there was no longer any news made at the conventions, Koppel refused to give his blessing to the media events they had become. Traditionally, conventions had been big news, and the major television networks had interrupted prime time programming to broadcast them. In 2000, in a reflection of the love-hate relationship between reporters and politicians that we were talking about in Chapter 5, Koppel felt the convention event had become too manipulative. His reaction was to regain some control by walking away, essentially removing the convention from the news agenda.*

Of course, with coverage on cable networks, it was still possible to watch the whole convention if you wanted to. It's also likely that Koppel would have been right back there if something unexpected happened that deviated from the candidate's script.

*Paul S. Herrnson, "National Party Organizations at the Dawn of the Twenty-First Century," in L. Sandy Maisel, ed., *The Parties Respond*, 4th ed. (Boulder, CO: Westview Press, 2002), 19–46.

be selected as the nominee of the party, so it's not uncommon for Republican hopefuls to sound more conservative during the primary race and for Democrats to sound more liberal.

Once the nomination is secure and the nominees start running against each other, they typically shift their campaign rhetoric toward the center of public opinion where most voters lie, and where general elections are won and lost.

7-3 Decisions, Part II: The Election Process

When a roll call of the delegates at the national convention ratifies the primary victor, the candidate becomes the official party nominee, and the general election campaign begins. Typically held in late summer before the November election, conventions are a four-day gathering that in recent years has been a protracted "infomercial" for the party nominee.

Stage-managed by the victorious campaign, conventions produce the sort of balloon-and-streamer-filled pictures that television can't resist. Celebrities join political figures to speak at the convention podium in order to maximize press interest. Everything is designed to play well on television and to maximize positive exposure for the candidate, who may have been in politics for years but who is "introducing" himself to the American public as a future president. It's typical for each newly minted nominee to get a "bounce" in the polls from favorable reaction to four days of positive press exposure.

In 1996, Elizabeth Dole (then in the role of the nominee's spouse) walked through the convention floor with a handheld microphone, talking about her husband in a made-for-television act that evoked a talk show. In 2000, the Republican Convention studiously featured minority supporters, like General Colin Powell and former Oklahoma Representative J. C. Watts, in an effort to portray the party as diverse and inclusive. Democrats countered with celebrities like Christopher Reeve, who spoke of the Democratic Party's compassion for people like himself who had suffered severe spinal cord injuries.[17] In 2004, John Kerry surrounded himself with veterans who had served with him in Vietnam to communicate the message that he would be a strong commander-in-chief. See Box 7-4.

platform The official document produced at the major party conventions that serves as a philosophical and policy blueprint for the party's presidential nominee.

Behind the scenes, delegates perform serious work in the form of writing the **platform** on which the nominee will run. The platform is a long document listing the principles that the party stands for under the leadership of its presidential nominee. Since the early resolution of the primary battle guarantees that the winning candidate will be able to stock the convention with his or her delegates, recent platforms have been written by supporters of the victorious candidate to reflect that candidate's views. So, if you were to read the party platforms, you'd get a pretty good sense of the philosophical differences among the candidates and probably have a good sense of how they would govern. Of course, few of us even

2000 PLATFORM PLANKS		TABLE 7-4
Democrat	**Republican**	**Party Differences**

Democrat	Republican
"Millions of Americans already have benefited from the Family and Medical Leave law. Now we need to expand it so that it covers parent-teacher visits and children's routine medical appointments."	"We support the traditional definition of 'marriage' as the legal union of one man and one woman, and we believe that federal judges and bureaucrats should not force states to recognize other living arrangements as marriages."
"We need mandatory child-safety locks on guns to protect our children. We should require a photo license I.D., a full background check, and a gun safety test to buy a new handgun in America."	"To guard against future tax hikes, we support legislation requiring a super-majority vote in both houses of Congress to raise taxes."
"By the end of the next presidential term, high-quality, affordable preschool should be fully available to every family, for every child, in every community in America."	"We affirm traditional military culture. We affirm that homosexuality is incompatible with military service."
"We stand behind the right of every woman to choose [whether to have an abortion], consistent with *Roe v. Wade* and regardless of ability to pay. We support contraceptive research, family planning, and policies that support healthy childbearing."	"In the final analysis, education remains a parental right and responsibility. We advocate choice in education—not as an abstract theory but as the surest way for families, especially low-income families, to free their youngsters from failing or dangerous schools."

think to do this, but that doesn't diminish the value of the platform as a blueprint for the next administration's priorities.

Because the party activists who become convention delegates and help shape the platform are generally more ideological than rank-and-file party adherents, it shouldn't be surprising that the Democratic and Republican platforms reveal differences in priorities and in approaches to problems. Perhaps no place is the difference between the two parties more clearly defined than in these documents.

In Table 7-4, take a look at a few "planks" from the 2000 Democratic and Republican platforms and see if you can spot some of these differences.

Platform writing generally happens out of view of television cameras, and with the victorious candidate in control of the process, it typically generates little suspense. In 1996, a minority of pro-choice Republicans talked about challenging the language of the platform's antiabortion plank, threatening to create a newsworthy spectacle. Nothing came of it, though: A revolt was avoided, and the platform was constructed in private and with no excitement.

In fact, because conventions are no longer the scene of suspenseful balloting or factional jockeying, the only real surprise to emerge from most conventions is the identity of the nominee's vice presidential running mate (who is selected by the nominee and ratified by the convention delegates). Some nominees have even drained the convention of this small element of suspense by revealing the running mates' identity before the convention starts in order to generate excitement among the delegates and extra press coverage. John Kerry did this in 2004, announcing his selection of Senator John Edwards several weeks before the Democratic Convention assembled.

Nominees typically select as running mates people who promise to balance them on such factors as experience, ideology, or geography. In 1988, Michael Dukakis, a liberal Massachusetts governor, covered all three bases by selecting as his running mate Texas Senator Lloyd Bentsen, a southern centrist with Washington experience. Nominees who survived a bruising primary fight might invite their vanquished rival to run with them in a play for party unity, as Ronald Reagan did in 1980 with his selection of primary opponent George Bush (senior). Strategically, selecting running mates from large, electoral-rich states is an attractive proposition for nominees, although in 2000 this did not figure into the calculations of either George W. Bush (whose running mate, Dick Cheney, was from Wyoming) or Al Gore (who selected Connecticut Senator Joseph Lieberman).

Nominees facing an uphill fall battle may go against conventional wisdom to generate excitement with their pick. Bill Clinton defied expectations by running with a political twin: Al Gore, a fellow southern Baby Boomer from a neighboring state. In 2000, Al Gore's selection of Senator Lieberman produced the first Jewish nominee on a major party ticket. Sixteen years earlier, Walter Mondale generated a buzz with his selection of New York Representative Geraldine Ferraro to be the first national female nominee of a major party.

Still, as far as excitement goes at party conventions, that's about it. The primary victor's name is placed in nomination. The delegates vote. They vote for the nominee's vice presidential selection. The nominee makes a big speech and tries to stir excitement among the party faithful. Balloons and streamers drop from the rafters.

Then the other major party does the same thing.

And the general election campaign begins.

7-3a Organization, Media, Information—and Endurance

It's tempting to begin this section with a disclaimer because here we are talking about how political parties form a link between us and our elected officials—we've already witnessed places where that link is problematic, from the primary calendar to campaign fundraising—and what you are about to read may at times seem coldly calculated to manipulate our voting patterns more than to engage us in spirited political discourse. What you're going to read about is, frankly, an example of why many people are turned off by politics. So, if you can, try to keep an open mind, and remember that running for president is an intense ordeal, where the biggest political prize on earth hangs in the balance.

From the convention to Election Day, party nominees have roughly seventy-five days to bring their case for election to the American people. It's hard work—and it's big business, requiring a more extensive campaign structure than the candidate had during the primary season, careful attention to paid and free media, an effective information-gathering apparatus, and, as always, the ability to remain sharp with little sleep.

Today's campaigns are an amalgam of professionals brought in to manage different components of the effort, meaning the candidate becomes a client to a series of political "hired guns" responsible for plotting and executing campaign strategy.

In addition to a campaign manager to handle the daily responsibilities of the effort, the campaigns hire media consultants, pollsters, fund-raisers, press officials, and staff members in much larger numbers than they had during the primary campaign. Their work entails designing, planning, and executing campaign events; testing themes for and developing television ads (media consultants); gauging and responding to public reaction to the candidate (pollsters); raising money (fund-raisers); and working to get reporters to cover the candidate's message (press secretary).

Much of this effort revolves around maximizing results from the **paid media** and **free media** we discussed in Chapter 5. In successful campaigns, the messages communicated in ads and in the press work together, are simple, and target groups of voters that the campaign needs to be victorious. As they did during the primaries, successful presidential candidates will go around the country giving essentially the same speech several times a day, hitting the same themes and staying "on message" in the hope that news stories that evening will reflect the theme crafted by the campaign. Only now, they will come under even greater press scrutiny.

In a savvy campaign, the same themes will appear in the candidate's paid advertising, allowing for a potentially powerful reinforcement tool because political professionals believe that if people hear a consistent message they're more likely to absorb it. We know from Chapter 5 that reporters often rebel against this kind of message control by retaining the last word in framing news stories. Nonetheless, when a campaign can sustain a coordinated message in paid and free media, it can typically wage the election on its terms.

paid media Radio and television ads paid for and produced by political campaigns.

free media The news coverage that major candidates for high office can expect to receive on a regular basis. Although free, candidates cannot control the content of this coverage or guarantee that it will be favorable.

In order to determine which groups of voters the candidate needs to win over and what messages will reach them, professional pollsters conduct public opinion surveys throughout the campaign. Initial polls reveal a wealth of information that can be used to plot strategy, especially information about how voters view the candidates' strengths and weaknesses. By looking closely at survey results, pollsters can identify groups that strongly support the candidate, strongly support his opponent, and all-important "swing" groups that are within the candidate's reach and that could determine the outcome of the election.

Typically, campaigns will gather more information on how targeted groups of voters are reacting to the candidate by conducting **focus groups,** which bring together a small number of people sharing a targeted demographic, like suburban women or southern white men, to "talk" about the candidate. Unlike opinion polls, which you may recall consist of random samples in which theoretically anyone can be contacted, focus groups are nonrandom and nonscientific. They can quickly and inexpensively produce a wealth of useful details for the campaign about how the selected group feels about the candidate that can help them fine-tune their strategy.

> **focus groups** A small group of voters chosen by a political campaign for their demographic similarities who are brought together to gauge how the group they represent feels about the candidate.

For instance, in his 1988 acceptance speech, George Bush (senior) referred to Americans as being "like a thousand points of light in a broad and peaceful sky." During the general election campaign, Bush kept using the phrase "a thousand points of light," often to refer to American volunteerism—until a focus group revealed that most people had no idea what he was talking about.[18]

Getting out the message requires travel—and lots of it. In the early days of the republic, it was customary for presidential candidates to stay home and say nothing; anything more was considered undignified. Nothing could be farther from the description of today's general election campaigns, which feature nonstop travel by the candidate and his entourage, who crisscross the country at jet speeds in a test of endurance that taxes all but the strongest constitutions. Candidates watch the country go by in a blur as they are chauffeured about in what some describe as a "bubble" of advisors, advance people (who arrange the events), reporters, and the electronic gear of twenty-first-century politics: television cameras, microphones, wires, and the like.

Although no day can be considered "typical," Table 7-5 shows a page from the first President Bush's 1992 campaign agenda. It captures the hectic nature of what a presidential nominee goes through every day before the election.

In all, Bush attended five public events and a private function in four cities during a thirteen-and-a-half-hour day that began after a night away from home. If something was delayed at any point in the day, everything else would be pushed off, and the day would run longer. During the entire period, the schedule provided him with a grand total of forty minutes of personal time. Of course, while he was doing all this he still had to perform his presidential responsibilities.

7-3b Strategy Again

With an infinite number of possible events to attend and a finite amount of time, campaign strategists need to set the candidate's agenda for maximum political benefit. This is accomplished by identifying where the candidate needs to shore up strength among voters.

As we'll soon see when we talk about the Electoral College, presidential elections are decided on a state-by-state basis. Each state is accorded electoral votes, awarded as a bloc to the candidate who carries the state, and a candidate must win a majority of electoral votes (270) to be elected. This fact drives fundamental strategic decisions. Where the candidate visits and where he or she purchases commercial airtime is determined by the states that campaign operatives believe they need to carry to win the election.

Each campaign's fundamental strategic decisions are based on dividing the map into three groups: states the campaign feels it will lose no matter what it does (where there's no realistic chance to win electoral votes); states the campaign feels it will win no matter what it does (where it feels assured of winning electoral votes); and competitive states, which get the most attention. Many of these can be determined by recent voting patterns. For instance, in 2004, the Bush campaign knew that most states on the Great Plains and in the

T A B L E 7-5	October 3, 1992
The Schedule of George H. W. Bush	8:25 A.M.: Depart Holiday Inn, Clearwater, Fla.
	8:42 A.M.: Arrive at Top of the World Retirement Community
	9:05 A.M.: Begin remarks at retirement community
	9:55 A.M.: Depart retirement community en route to St. Petersburg Airport
	10:15 A.M.: Arrive St. Petersburg Airport and board Air Force One
	10:20 A.M.: Depart St. Petersburg for Homestead, Fla.
	11:15 A.M.: Arrive Homestead to view hurricane relief efforts
	1:45 P.M.: Depart Homestead en route to Fort Lauderdale, Fla.
	2:10 P.M.: Arrive Fort Lauderdale to welcoming ceremony
	2:15 P.M.: Give remarks
	2:20 P.M.: Depart for Naval Warfare Center
	2:55 P.M.: Arrive Naval Warfare Center for Historical Association ceremony
	3:25 P.M.: Depart Naval Warfare Center for AMR COMBS Hangar
	3:30 P.M.: Private time at AMR COMBS Hangar
	4:10 P.M.: Depart Ft. Lauderdale en route to Orlando, Fla.
	5:15 P.M.: Arrive Orlando International Airport
	5:20 P.M.: Depart Orlando International Airport en route to Church St. Market
	6:00 P.M.: Remarks at rally
	6:35 P.M.: Private reception
	7:35 P.M.: Depart Church St. Market en route to Orlando International Airport
	7:40 P.M.: Depart Orlando, Fla. for Andrews Air Force Base
	9:25 P.M.: Arrive Andrews Air Force Base
	9:30 P.M.: Board Marine One en route to White House
	9:45 P.M.: Arrive White House

Source: Paul S. Herrnson, "National Party Organizations at the Dawn of the Twenty-First Century," in L. Sandy Maisel, ed., *The Parties Respond,* 4th ed. (Boulder, CO: Westview Press, 2002), 19–46.

Rocky Mountain West reliably support Republican candidates. Likewise, the Kerry campaign knew it could count on California, New York, and the lower New England states. So, there was no point for *either* campaign to devote resources to Utah, North Dakota, Rhode Island, or Massachusetts.

The remaining states make up the campaign battleground. These are "swing" states that have a history of supporting either Democrats or Republicans in recent elections, and which both candidates feel could break in either direction. The more populous of these become key to the strategies of both campaigns. In reality, the national campaign for president isn't a national campaign at all; it plays out mostly in these swing states. If you live in places like Ohio, Missouri, Michigan, Pennsylvania, and Florida, you are showered with candidate visits and campaign promises and commercials, as both campaigns advance a strategy that will move them toward Electoral College victory. If you live in a state that's reliably in one column or the other, you're more of a bystander to a contest being played out elsewhere (see Box 7-5).

Once target states have been identified, the campaign's pollsters go into action to assess the strength of the candidate and his or her opponent. The result of this assessment determines how resources are allocated. Campaigns will start with the electoral votes of their "base"—the states they can count on—and subtract that number from 270 to arrive at the number of electoral votes they need to win the election. They can identify where

> **Box 7-5** **Vote Swapping**
>
> Candidates aren't the only ones who can engage in election-year strategy. In 2000, when consumer advocate Ralph Nader was the presidential candidate of the Green Party, some Nader voters living in battleground states faced a dilemma: They were concerned that if they voted for Nader (their first choice) instead of Gore (their second choice), the loss of a vote for Gore would boost the prospects of Bush (their third choice). In a close race, they were concerned that a vote for Nader would be a vote for Bush.
>
> The solution: Trade votes with Gore voters in states where the outcome wasn't in doubt. In an example of spontaneous, grassroots political involvement, Internet sites emerged that allowed Nader voters in battleground states to find Gore vot-
>
> ers in states where one candidate or the other was sure to win so they could agree to "swap votes." The Nader voter in the battleground state would agree to cast a vote for Gore, believing that a Gore voter in a state where the race wasn't close would cast a vote on their behalf for Nader. Of course, these "agreements" were unenforceable, and neither voter would ever know if the other carried out the agreement. Still, it demonstrates that it's not just the professionals who can be sophisticated strategists in a presidential election and that, given the opportunity to reach others via the Internet, it's possible for ordinary people to play with the electoral rules in order to maximize their political expression in presidential campaigns.

these votes might come from by looking at the number of electoral votes in the states that are up for grabs. From the survey data, they can determine which of the battleground states are likely to be the most competitive and devote the most resources to them.

Pollsters constantly take the temperature of the race in battleground states, and campaigns use the data to modify where they allocate resources. If the campaign's polls indicate that a state is starting to tip one way or another, resources can be pulled from that state and reallocated to a more competitive state.

In the closing weeks of the 2000 contest, when Gore's polling indicated that Bush was pulling ahead in Ohio, the campaign made the decision to shift advertising funds from Ohio to other battleground states whose polls showed the race was still close (a questionable decision in hindsight, as Bush narrowly won the state). Around the same time, the Bush campaign's polling showed the race tightening in California—a state both campaigns believed would go to Gore. Bush made the strategic decision to campaign in California, assuming that even if he eventually lost the state (he did), his presence there might force the Gore campaign to expend scarce resources in the final days that could have helped him more in other close states. Such is the gamesmanship of presidential campaigns.

As Election Day nears, pollsters can generally predict with great accuracy how the election will turn out, making it possible to fine-tune the campaign in its final hours if it's going to be close. Sometimes, that's not necessary. In 1992, Bill Clinton's pollsters told him several days before any votes were cast that he was going to be the next president of the United States.

Other times, it can be very helpful. In 2004, after months of strategic calculations based on the electoral map, the Bush and Kerry campaigns both knew that their tight contest would be determined in Ohio, Pennsylvania, and Florida. All three states were close, and based on the electoral vote totals both campaigns believed they could count on elsewhere in the country, the only way they could reach 270 electoral votes was by carrying two of the three. Whichever candidate carried two of the three would be president. (Bush, in fact, won by carrying Florida and Ohio.) Both campaigns had reached the same conclusion from their polling, so both campaigns focused intently on these three states in the campaign's final hours.

7-3c Going Negative

It's always tempting for campaigns to use television commercials to define their opponent's character or record in negative terms through the use of negative ads (euphemistically called "comparative ads" by campaign professionals because they aim to highlight the positive qualities of the candidate by dragging down the candidate's opponent). The reason is

Figure 7-4
The Daisy Ad
Source: LBJ Library Video by DNC.

simple: Advertising specialists believe they work. They permit the candidate to focus attention on the weaknesses of the opponent that the candidate's polling indicates will matter to undecided voters. If an opponent is relatively unknown, negative advertising can define the opponent in the most critical light to viewers who have no basis for challenging the assessment. In 2004, negative ads about John Kerry portrayed him as an unprincipled "flip-flopper" and questioned his heroism in Vietnam.

The environment produced by pervasive negative advertising can drive people away from politics, depressing turnout and increasing cynicism. However, political consultants bent on winning an election for their client will not be concerned with these serious systemic effects, and the fact is negative advertising exists because it's effective. People tend to remember negative messages, especially if they are repeated enough or left unchallenged. Even if they are challenged, the response from the opposing candidate can make him look defensive. Some campaigns actually anticipate negative ads and answer the charges *before* they're made in order to avoid looking defensive and "inoculate" the public against a charge they believe is coming.

Because people are repelled by negative messages even as they internalize negative allegations, negative ads can be risky to use. They can backfire by making the candidate who runs them appear mean-spirited. For this reason, negative ads will typically be shown first to focus groups to get a sense of how people from targeted demographic categories react to them. When they run, pollsters monitor public reaction closely, and campaigns will quickly pull negative ads at the slightest hint that they are hurting the campaign.[19]

Negative ads are not new to American politics, although in recent years the threshold for what we seem to be willing to accept has gone up. For a good sense of how we've become more open to negative campaigning, consider the ad in Figure 7-4, which you can access online. It's still one of the most controversial in our history, even though it ran back in 1964 on behalf of President Johnson.

President Johnson's opponent, Republican Senator Barry Goldwater, generated concerns among many people who felt he might be trigger-happy and who worried that he might be too willing to use nuclear weapons. So, the Johnson campaign ran this commercial to reinforce these concerns. It juxtaposes images of a little girl pulling petals from a daisy with pictures suggesting nuclear Armageddon. Although that sounds heavy-handed, consider that Goldwater is never mentioned by name, and his policies are never discussed. The voice you hear at the end of the ad is Johnson's.

Forty years later, it's still powerful. When the "Daisy Ad" ran, the Goldwater campaign cried foul, saying it unfairly implied that its candidate was a threat to world peace. Johnson agreed, and the ad never ran a second time. In today's charged political environment, unless the ad began to backfire politically, it's hard to imagine a campaign responding the same way.

> ## Box 7-6   The First Debates

The first televised debates between Kennedy and Nixon occurred in part because both candidates stood to benefit from them. The race was close when Kennedy issued his debate challenge to Nixon, so neither candidate had the luxury of avoiding a direct confrontation by sitting on a large lead. Kennedy was knowledgeable and quick on his feet, and believed he could use the debate forum to dispel the idea that his youth was a liability in a contest against an incumbent vice president. Nixon knew that he wasn't the most trusted politician and believed that a strong performance could give him an opportunity to erase that impression. Besides, he had a record as a good debater, and to refuse Kennedy's invitation would make it appear that he was running scared.

Nixon's debating skills turned out to be of limited value, though. He failed to grasp what Kennedy's media consultants understood: that the debates would be about television. Kennedy's advisors knew that people are more likely to look at the pictures than listen to the words. They were savvy about

the use of makeup to present a healthy image, and the inviting impression made by a blue shirt on a black-and-white television screen. They could coach their candidate to look into the camera and talk to the voters, not to his opponent on stage. In short, they knew how to make Kennedy appear "telegenic," and in so doing, to invite a positive emotional reaction to the candidate.

That Nixon was recovering from an illness, looked pale, needed to shave, and perspired too much simply served to underscore the different impressions made by the two candidates. Perhaps the most valuable lesson of the Kennedy-Nixon debates was what the debates taught about the power of pictures more than words to communicate a message on television.[*]

[*]Mary Ann Watson, *The Expanding Vista: American Television in the Kennedy Years* (New York: Oxford University Press, 1990).

A tense and shadowy Richard Nixon looks away from the audience as his youthful opponent, engulfed in light, prepares to talk directly to the camera.

7-3d Televised Debates

Since 1976, televised presidential debates have been a part of every fall campaign. Box 7-6 talks about the first debates. Nonetheless, debates do not have a long history in our presidential campaigns, and they regularly form a point of contention between the candidates, who struggle over the strategic advantages and disadvantages of debating. Before 1960's showdown between John F. Kennedy and Richard M. Nixon, there were no presidential debates at all.

It's rare that the strategic interests of both candidates will bring them into a high-stakes showdown with each other on the same stage in front of a huge national audience. Typically, one candidate will have more to gain by participating, leading an opponent to believe it is in his or her best interest to opt out.

That's why, after 1960, it took sixteen years before presidential debates resumed. In 1964, President Johnson was so far ahead in opinion polls that he could simply refuse to debate Barry Goldwater. With Nixon on the ballot again in 1968 and 1972, there was probably no way that debates were going to happen, considering his bad experience in 1960.

It wasn't until 1976, when imperiled incumbent Gerald Ford was locked in a tight race with Jimmy Carter, that both sides felt it was in their interest to debate. Ford, whom Nixon appointed to the vice presidency after Spiro Agnew resigned in scandal, was elevated to the Oval Office following Nixon's resignation, making him the only president ever to serve without winning a national election. Two years into his brief term, Ford was still trying to convince Americans that he was up to the job, and his campaign operatives felt a televised debate would give him that opportunity. For his part, Carter was relatively unknown, and his campaign handlers felt a debate would give him positive exposure and a chance to show off his command of details.

Four years later, the political dynamics again favored a debate. This time, Carter was the imperiled incumbent, and Ronald Reagan was the challenger who needed a way to reassure cold war voters that he would not act like a cowboy with America's nuclear arsenal.

Both debates worked to the advantage of the challenger, who received a boost by appearing on stage with the president. In 1984, with Reagan far ahead in opinion polls, his campaign calculated that it would make the president look magnanimous if he debated his opponent. This established the expectation that after three consecutive presidential elections with candidate debates, future campaigns would be expected to engage in debates as well. By 1988, debates had become the norm, and reluctant candidates found that the cost of looking like they were ducking their opponent had become too high for them to resist debating.

If you're on the debate team at school or if you know someone who is, you may be surprised at how little actual debating takes place at presidential debates. They tend to be more like joint press conferences, where both candidates repeat the same messages they've been talking about at campaign events. This can create a disconnected feeling, where candidates talk past each other or avoid questions in order to jump to their campaign talking points. In 2004, the Bush campaign went so far as to insist on guidelines that precluded the candidates from addressing each other directly. The name of the media game is to control the message by staying "on message," and that's how political advisors instruct candidates to approach televised debates.

They also instruct candidates to speak to the camera and try to relax. Because we react to what we see more than to what we hear, candidates who are unable to come across naturally in televised debates can find themselves at a disadvantage. In the 2000 debates, Al Gore was eager to show off his detailed policy knowledge, believing that it would show him to be more presidential than his less worldly opponent, George W. Bush. This turned out to be an incorrect assumption. Opinion polls conducted by both campaigns revealed that Gore turned off many undecided voters by coming across as somewhere between a bully and the smartest kid in the class. Gore may have won most of the debating points, but Bush appeared at ease and more likeable. Impressions like these can linger and factor into how people vote.

7-4 The Electoral College: Is This Any Way to Elect a President?

It's probably safe to say that no institution like the Electoral College has ever been created anywhere. It's been with us since the Constitutional Convention of 1787, modified once to account for political party competition, and has been the object of numerous reform proposals over the centuries, all of which have failed to materialize. It's complex, often misunderstood, and difficult to explain. Yet, it is almost always the final arbiter of who will enter the White House.

First, let's make sure we understand how it works—see Box 7-7.

7-4a Why Would Anyone Create a System Like This?

Although it may seem like the Constitution's framers created the Electoral College to make life miserable for government students, in truth, it was a compromise that solved a couple of key dilemmas. The framers wanted an elite to identify the most qualified presidential

Box 7-7 The Electoral College

The president and vice president are chosen by an Electoral College consisting of electors allocated to each state and (by virtue of the Twenty-third Amendment) the District of Columbia, which gets three electors. Electors are allocated by adding the number of senators (two) to the number of representatives in each state. Since the least populous states have one representative, the smallest number of electors a state can have is three.

In total, there are 538 electors in the Electoral College. Each gets one vote. Figure 1 shows how many electors are allocated to each state. When you vote for president and vice president, you're really selecting the electors pledged to vote for the presidential and vice presidential candidates of your choice.

Electors are real people, chosen by state party leaders in numbers equal to the electoral vote of each state. So, since Illinois has twenty-one electoral votes, the Illinois Republican Party selects twenty-one loyal Republicans to act as electors, and the Illinois Democratic Party selects twenty-one loyal Democrats to act as electors.

Independents and third parties that qualify to be on the ballot also get to field a slate of electors. We determine which slate of electors represents our state when we go to the polls to vote for president. Our votes for president are called the **popular vote.** The party of the candidate receiving a **plurality** of popular votes for its slate of electors wins all the electors in that state.

In 2000, Al Gore won 366 more popular votes than George W. Bush in New Mexico, out of 598,605 cast. It was less than a majority, but Gore's slim plurality was enough to give him all five of the state's electoral votes. Maine and Nebraska have the only exceptions to the winner-take-all rule. In those states, two electors are awarded to the candidate receiving a plurality of the statewide popular vote, and the rest are awarded to the plurality winner of the popular vote within each of the state's congressional districts. So, it's possible for these states to send a combined slate of Republican and Democratic electors to the Electoral College.

On the Monday following the second Wednesday in December, the winning slate of electors gathers in the state capital to cast their votes for president and vice president. In some states, election law requires the electors to vote for the state's popular-vote winner. Other states do not have this restriction, making it possible for a **faithless elector** to vote for a different candidate. Because electors are strong partisans and have devoted a lot of time and energy to their party, few ever deviate from supporting their party's candidate.

The electoral votes are sent from the states to Washington, D.C., where on January 6, the vice president, acting in his constitutional capacity as president of the Senate, records the votes. The presidential and vice presidential candidates receiving an outright majority of electoral votes—270—are elected. If no candidate receives 270 electoral votes, which could happen if there were a third-party candidate in the mix, the House of Representatives selects the president from the top three electoral-vote recipients. The Senate selects the vice president from the top two electoral-vote recipients.

The House votes for president by state delegation, with representatives from each state together getting one vote. The candidate who receives a majority of the fifty state delegations is elected. In the Senate, each senator casts one vote for vice president. The candidate who wins a majority of votes is elected.

▶ **popular vote** The votes individuals cast in a presidential election. Technically, these are votes for a slate of electors representing the candidate. A candidate who wins a plurality of the popular vote in a state gets all the electoral votes allocated to that state.

▶ **plurality** Winning the most votes in an election, or at least one more vote than the next closest candidate or party.

▶ **faithless elector** A member of the Electoral College who does not cast a vote for the plurality winner of the popular vote in his or her state.

	State	Electors	State	Electors	State	Electors	State	Electors
	Alabama	9	Illinois	21	Montana	3	Rhode Island	4
	Alaska	3	Indiana	11	Nebraska	5	South Carolina	8
	Arizona	10	Iowa	7	Nevada	5	South Dakota	3
	Arkansas	6	Kansas	6	New Hampshire	4	Tennessee	11
	California	55	Kentucky	8	New Jersey	15	Texas	34
	Colorado	9	Louisiana	9	New Mexico	5	Utah	5
	Connecticut	7	Maine	4	New York	31	Vermont	3
	Delaware	3	Maryland	10	North Carolina	15	Virginia	13
	District of Columbia	3	Massachusetts	12	North Dakota	3	Washington	11
	Florida	27	Michigan	17	Ohio	20	West Virginia	5
	Georgia	15	Minnesota	10	Oklahoma	7	Wisconsin	10
	Hawaii	4	Mississippi	6	Oregon	7	Wyoming	3
	Idaho	4	Missouri	11	Pennsylvania	21		

Figure 1
Number of Electors Allocated to Each State

candidates, but they didn't want presidents to be beholden to the elite that selected them. Also, they didn't want to undermine separation of powers by simply having Congress select the president. In the Electoral College, the framers created a mechanism for assembling an elite that would go out of business as soon as its work was done, meaning it wouldn't be in a position to ask anything of the new president. As complex as it is, the Electoral College is consistent with federalism by giving the states a key role in presidential selection, and separation of powers, by putting the choice of the president in the hands of Congress as a matter of last resort.

In its original incarnation, the Electoral College was really established as a mechanism that would perform the selection function that soon became the province of political parties. Electors were to identify the worthiest candidates in their respective states, and if a majority could not agree on a single best choice, the House of Representatives would settle the matter. By 1800, the selection process was already being performed through party nominations, and the mechanics of the Electoral College had to be changed.

In its original form, electors cast two votes, one for a candidate from another state in an effort to avoid parochial choices. The runner-up in electoral votes would become vice president. With the advent of two-party competition, it quickly became apparent that this meant the vice president could be the losing presidential candidate of the opposition party. As parties started nominating separate candidates for president and vice president, the possible outcomes became even more bizarre. In 1800, the Democratic-Republicans nominated Jefferson for president and Aaron Burr for vice president, resulting in an Electoral College tie as Democratic-Republican electors cast one vote each for Jefferson and Burr. The resulting complications led to passage of the Twelfth Amendment, providing for separate electoral tallies for president and vice president.[20]

In its time, the Electoral College was intended as a deliberative body, but as candidate selection shifted to the congressional caucus, then party conventions, then primaries, the functions of the Electoral College became much more automatic. Today, network anchors talk about electoral votes as if they were coupons you clipped from a newspaper. On election night, they sit in front of big maps, rapidly assigning electoral votes to one candidate or another as soon as the popular vote from a state is determined. As the map fills in—red states for the Republican nominee, blue states for the Democrat—it becomes a race to 270, no more than a mathematical exercise.

7-4b Changing or Eliminating the Electoral College

The automatic quality that the Electoral College has assumed encourages reformers to question the wisdom of retaining a system that could produce a president who finished second in the popular vote. After all, every office but the highest one is determined by simple plurality vote. It's unlikely, but mathematically possible, for the electoral vote winner to be different from the popular vote winner. This has happened three times in our history; a fourth disputed election involved the House bypassing the Electoral Vote winner:

1824: In a disputed election that wound up in the House of Representatives, John Quincy Adams was chosen president, despite the fact that Andrew Jackson had won more electoral votes.

1876: In another disputed election involving questions about the accuracy of the vote in three southern states, Rutherford B. Hayes was elected president, despite having lost the popular vote to Samuel Tilden by three percentage points.

1888: In an undisputed election, Grover Cleveland won a majority of popular votes but lost the electoral count to Benjamin Harrison.

2000: In the closest election of our time, George W. Bush narrowly prevailed in the Electoral College on the basis of a contested victory in Florida, despite finishing second in the national popular vote count.

Not surprisingly, every time the popular vote and the electoral vote go in different directions, there's renewed call for Electoral College reform. However, if history is a guide, the odds aren't very good. Electoral College reform is a highly charged, big-stakes partisan issue; changing the rules will inevitably favor one side or the other and, quite possibly, could introduce unintended effects that everyone would be reluctant to face. The Twelfth Amendment is the only successful alteration to the process in over two hundred years and more than one thousand attempts.[21]

Also, consider that even if these aberrant outcomes produced challenges to the legitimacy of the eventual winner, they didn't create a legitimacy crisis for the system. There was even something of a self-correction involving the first three disputed winners: Each served only one term, in two cases (1824 and 1888) to be followed in office by the candidate they had "defeated" four years earlier. Box 7-8 discusses the 2000 election.

7-5 Leading or Following?

As a linkage to the candidates who will become our public officials, political parties should be a vehicle for channeling our preferences to those who wish to lead us. The most important function they perform in this capacity is contesting elections. Whether parties carry out this function effectively in the electoral arena is a matter of some discussion. On one hand, through careful attention to public opinion polls and focus groups, candidates are acutely sensitive to political currents. But to what end? Is it leadership to listen to what people want and give it to them? Or does this amount to campaigning without principle?

Harry S Truman, who was president in an age before professional political consultants dominated campaigning, mused that he "wondered how far Moses would have gone if he had taken a poll in Egypt." The former president saw polls as interfering with the judgments politicians are hired to make, distinguishing *popular* decisions from *good* decisions. The natural remedy for officials who make decisions that their constituents dislike is to vote them out of office. Yet, politicians may use public opinion polls to guide their actions so as to maximize their chances of staying in office, making it harder for elections to perform a corrective function. Perhaps this is as it should be, or perhaps it comes at the cost of establishing principled links between voters and officials.

Add to this the explosion in campaign spending, and you have another potential strain on the connections parties can supply voters. Campaign finance reforms designed to strengthen the bonds between individuals and candidates by maximizing the role of small individual contributions have been undermined by the soft-money loophole. As large contributions from wealthy individuals and organizations flood the political process, it's reasonable to ask how much political influence is returned in the bargain, and to what effect. A disproportionate share of campaign money goes to incumbents who can use it to create a lopsided advantage in reelection contests. Like polls that can be used by candidates to stake out safe and popular ground, big money flowing to incumbents can drain the competition from elections.

As we noted earlier, political money is channeled through PACs that operate on behalf of organized interests. In turn, organized interests are established to represent constituencies, functioning like parties as a linkage to government. How strong and effective is this connection, and how closely do interest groups represent the wishes of people like us? Is all that PAC money advancing the agendas of people who identify with and support interest groups, or is it largely serving an elite? We'll turn to these questions next, in Chapter 8.

> Box 7-8
The 2000 Election: What Happened?

During the weeks leading up to the 2000 election, public opinion polls consistently showed a narrow preference for George W. Bush over Al Gore, with a fair number of undecided voters. A lot of people simply couldn't make up their mind. On election night, it turned out that the "undecideds" got it right.

We saw in Chapter 3 how, as the television anchors at ABC, CBS, NBC, CNN, and Fox sat in front of their wall-sized maps assigning blue states to Gore and red states to Bush, something unprecedented happened. On the basis of survey results conducted as people were leaving their polling places, the major television networks predicted that Gore was the winner in Florida. The state of Florida turned blue on every major network map and stayed that way—for about an hour. Then, inexplicably, every network took it back, saying that as the actual votes were being counted, it appeared that Florida was in fact too close to call. As the evening progressed, the vote tally in Florida remained breathtakingly close. It soon became clear that Florida mattered because electoral votes in the rest of the states were breaking in such a way that the entire election would hinge on the Florida outcome.

In the early morning hours, the networks finally called Florida for Bush, and the state that hours before had been posted on the map in "Gore" blue was now "Bush" red. Gore called Bush to congratulate him. The election was over, and Bush had won.

For about forty-five minutes. As he was about to leave his motorcade to address his supporters, Gore received word that the final Florida tally showed him within a few hundred votes of Bush out of almost six million cast. Gore called Bush again to retract his concession. The networks reversed themselves—again. Americans woke up to the news that the 2000 election was too close to call. There would be a recount in Florida.

What followed can best be described as high-stakes political hardball by two campaigns that had been thrown into overtime by the Electoral College. Each assembled legal teams to contest voting irregularities and public relations teams to win a heated media war that would determine how long the public would tolerate political wrangling over the outcome. The Gore team tried to build sympathy by saying that time was needed to count every vote, while the Bush team—ahead in the original balloting—created pressure to limit the scope and length of the recount with the line that the votes had been counted and counted and counted again.

The legal battle played out on several fronts. There were questions about the clarity of the ballot in Palm Beach County, a booklet with a "butterfly" design bearing candidate names on both sides of a central column. Arrows from both sides of the booklet pointed to holes in the column that the voter was supposed to punch to register his or her choice. When it was revealed that conservative Reform Party candidate Pat Buchanan—whose name appeared opposite Gore on the ballot—received a disproportionate vote in this liberal county, the Gore team tried unsuccessfully to have those Buchanan votes reconsidered.

There were questions about voting rights, as civil liberties groups charged that thousands of African Americans had been prohibited from voting as the result of having been erroneously purged from the voter registration lists in a statewide effort to delete the names of felons. Because the "purge" was supervised by Katherine Harris, the Republican secretary of state with close ties to the Bush campaign, and because 93 percent of African Americans in Florida voted for Gore, the issue immediately assumed political overtones.

In the end, the outcome came down to which votes would be recounted and under what guidelines. The Gore campaign jumped on the fact that there had been a disproportionately high percentage of "undervotes," or ballots indicating no presidential choice, in southern Florida counties that used punch-card voting. This makes sense, considering the stylus used for removing indented squares or chads in the ballot card sometimes doesn't make it all the way through.

Because these counties also went disproportionately for Gore, a struggle ensued over the terms of the recount. What if a chad is perforated but still hanging from the card? What if it is bulging but attached on all sides? What if it is simply dimpled? The Gore camp argued for the most liberal standards for recounting, in an effort to claim the most votes, while the Bush camp argued for consistent standards—a move that helped them win public support as the nation witnessed different counties performing manual ballot recounts using different rules for what constituted a vote.

Legal and public relations wrangling dragged on into December. Gore continued to trail in the recount, and political pressure mounted for him to concede. Ultimately, the matter was decided in court. The Florida Supreme Court agreed with Gore's argument that ballots that did not indicate a clear presidential choice should be recounted, noting that Florida law gives each county the responsibility of determining as best it can the intent of the voter. But a bitterly divided U.S. Supreme Court ruled differently. In a 5–4 decision in *Bush v. Gore,* the Court upheld the legality of the recount but determined that it should be conducted under clear and consistent guidelines, an impossible task given the limited time before members of the Electoral College were constitutionally obligated to cast their votes. In effect, their ruling halted the recount in its tracks. Gore was out of legal options; Bush would become president.*

It's possible to draw all sorts of conclusions from the 2000 postelection spectacle. As with the disputed elections of 1824 and 1876, the political saga was bitter, but the system continued to function. The public relations methods used by both sides illustrated the importance of a strong media campaign to set the public agenda in order to create political momentum. The often-confusing actions of well-meaning election officials who tried to decipher the "intent of the voter" demonstrated how the apparently simple act of counting ballots is not as straightforward as we might think. Americans were exposed to a range of voting irregularities that are probably

very common but usually go unnoticed because few elections of this magnitude have required looking at the balloting so closely.

Finally, the Florida recount experience said something about our political divisions at the turn of the millennium. It's striking to look at the final electoral vote map (see Figure 1) and see the stark regional divisions between the "blue" Gore states of the coasts and upper Midwest and the "red" Bush states of the South, plains and mountain West. New Hampshire was the only northern state won by Bush; New Mexico, the only western interior state won by Gore—and both were decided by razor-thin margins. Essentially, the country divided along regional lines between Gore's message of activist government and social liberalism, and Bush's fiscal and social conservatism. The Electoral College results told us that we had essentially produced a tie, the result of divisions that continue to define our politics.

Bush v. Gore 531 US 98 (2000).

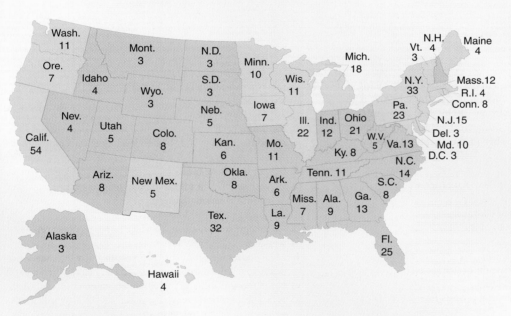

Figure 1
**The Red States
and the Blue States, 2000**

Chapter Review

One of the most important functions of political parties is competing in elections. Party nominees for all elected positions are selected in primaries or caucuses, depending on the state; presidential candidates enter a series of primaries and caucuses to win delegate support at the party's nominating convention. For many years, party elites selected presidential nominees at party conventions, but following 1968, a series of reforms instituted by the Democratic Party led to the proliferation of primaries and a shift away from elite control of the nominating process. Today, would-be nominees can secure enough delegates to win the nomination by competing in primaries, provided they can acquire enough resources—money, staff, and media attention—to remain viable.

Money is particularly critical for waging successful campaigns, and candidates typically spend years raising it. The 1974 Federal Election Campaign Act attempted to regulate campaign contributions, but a loophole permitted unlimited soft-money contributions. The McCain-Feingold Act is designed to close that loophole, but parties can still find ways to raise and spend large sums.

A candidate emerges as the nominee by raising sufficient money and maintaining momentum through the primaries by meeting or beating performance expectations generated by reporters. Nominees are introduced to the country at a national convention that has largely become a media event, and organize a professional staff of campaign aides who, with the use of opinion polls and focus groups, develop a strategy for allocating the candidate's time and money. Strategies may include running negative commercials in order to undermine support for the candidate's opponent; in recent years, nominees have faced off in televised debates. Strategy is largely shaped by the demands of the Electoral College, which makes the presidential race a state-by-state endeavor. The candidate who wins a plurality of the popular vote in enough states to win a majority of the electoral vote becomes president.

Key Terms

caucus (p. 183)
expectations (p. 193)
faithless elector (p. 207)
Federal Election Campaign Act (p. 188)
Federal Election Commission (FEC)
   (p. 188)
focus groups (p. 201)
free media (p. 200)

front-runner (p. 193)
hard money (p. 190)
long shot (p. 193)
McCain-Feingold Act (p. 191)
McGovern-Fraser Commission (p. 185)
media events (p. 186)
momentum (p. 193)
name recognition (p. 191)

nomination (p. 183)
paid media (p. 200)
platform (p. 198)
plurality (p. 207)
political action committees (PACs) (p. 189)
popular vote (p. 207)
primary (p. 183)
soft money (p. 190)

Review Questions

Note: You can find the correct answers to these questions by taking the quiz and then submitting your answers in the Online Edition. The program will automatically score your submission. If you miss a question, the program will provide the correct answer, a rationale for the answer, and the section number in the chapter where the topic is discussed.

1. Primaries differ from caucuses in that primaries are
   a. secret ballots.
   b. attended mostly by active party loyalists.
   c. only used to select presidential nominees.
   d. held in fewer states.
2. The McGovern-Fraser Commission
   a. expressly advocated the expansion of primaries.
   b. created convention "super delegates."
   c. shifted control of the nominating process from party elites.
   d. boosted the importance of national party conventions.
3. Political action committees (PACs)
   a. did not exist before the 1974 Federal Election Campaign Act.
   b. are regulated by the Federal Election Commission (FEC).
   c. were banned by the McCain-Feingold Act.
   d. get their money from the Presidential Election Campaign Fund.

4. The increase in campaign fund-raising since 1974 could be attributed to
   a. hard money.
   b. soft money.
   c. spending limits in the 1974 Federal Election Campaign Act.
   d. federal matching funds.
5. In the year leading up to presidential primary contests, what's the relationship among name recognition, media coverage, and money?
   a. Campaign contributions produce name recognition, which produces media coverage.
   b. Media coverage produces momentum for candidates who beat expectations in primaries and caucuses, which creates name recognition and increases campaign contributions.
   c. Name recognition gives a candidate credibility, which makes it easier to attract media coverage and raise money.
   d. Name recognition increases a candidate's expectations, and higher expectations increase campaign contributions and intensify media coverage.
6. Reporters would likely consider a candidate going into the Iowa caucus with low name recognition, little media coverage, and limited campaign funds to be
   a. the front-runner.
   b. a main challenger to the front-runner.
   c. a long shot.
   d. crazy.

7. How is a candidate's primary campaign message likely to be different from his general election campaign message?
  a. In the primary campaign, a candidate's message is likely to be more conservative in an effort to distinguish himself from his rivals.
  b. In the primary campaign, a candidate's message is likely to be more liberal in an effort to distinguish himself from his rivals.
  c. In the primary campaign, a candidate's message is likely to be more ideologically extreme to appeal to party supporters who vote in primaries.
  d. In the general election campaign, a candidate's message is likely to be more ideologically extreme to appeal to general election voters.

8. Today's political conventions are
  a. media events.
  b. sources of factional jockeying.
  c. where party elites choose the nominee.
  d. exciting.

9. In the general election campaign, candidates decide how to allocate their resources based on
  a. the requirements of the Electoral College and the advice of consultants.
  b. the effectiveness of negative advertising.
  c. whether they plan to debate their opponent.
  d. focus groups more than opinion polls.

10. What's the relationship between popular votes and electoral votes?
  a. In each state except Maine and Nebraska, electoral votes are allocated proportionately based on the candidate's share of the popular vote.
  b. In each state, the plurality popular-vote winner gets to field a slate of electors equal in number to that state's electoral vote.
  c. In each state except Maine and Nebraska, the plurality popular-vote winner takes all the electoral votes.
  d. The plurality electoral-vote winner becomes president, regardless of the combined popular vote total.

In Their Own Words

You might be interested in examining some of what the following authors have said about the topics we've been discussing:

Abramson, Paul R., John H. Aldrich, and David W. Rohde. *Change and Continuity in the 1996 and 1998 Elections.* Washington, DC: CQ Press, 1999. A good overview of the selection and election stages of the campaign, with an emphasis on recent congressional and presidential elections.

Cramer, Richard Ben. *What It Takes: The Way to the White House.* New York: Random House, 1992. A firsthand account of the 1988 presidential contenders, written like a novel, that explores the character and motivation of those who roll the dice to enter the high-risk, marathon presidential sweepstakes.

DeClerico, Robert E., and James W. Davis. *Choosing Our Choices: Debating the Presidential Nominating Process.* Lanham, MD: Rowman & Littlefield, 2000. The pros and cons of the way we select our presidential nominees, with suggestions for how we might do it differently.

Michael Nelson, ed. *The Elections of 2000.* Washington, DC: CQ Press, 2001. The 2000 election was one for the history books, and this book examines it from a variety of perspectives.

Polsby, Nelson W., and Aaron Wildavsky. *Presidential Elections: Strategies and Structures of American Politics,* 10th ed. New York: Chatham House, 2000. A comprehensive overview of campaigns and elections.

Schumaker, Paul D., and Burdett A. Loomis, eds. *Choosing a President: The Electoral College and Beyond.* New York: Chatham House Publishers, 2002. Everything you would ever want to know about the Electoral College is contained in this thoughtful volume that emphasizes proposals for reform.

Notes

1. Paul R. Abramson, John H. Aldrich, and David W. Rohde, *Continuity and Change in the 1996 and 1998 Elections* (Washington, DC: CQ Press, 1999), 16.
2. Robert E. DiClerico and James W. Davis, *Choosing Our Choices: Debating the Presidential Nominating Process* (Lanham, MD: Rowman & Littlefield, 2000), 22.
3. Ibid., 3–6.
4. If you'd like to read more about what happened that August week in Chicago, CNN/Time offers a summary at http://www-cgi.cnn.com/ALLPOLITICS/1996/conventions/chicago/facts/chicago68/index.shtml.
5. DiClerico and Davis, *Choosing Our Choices,* 28–29.
6. Ibid., 14–23.
7. Nelson W. Polsby and Aaron Wildavsky, *Presidential Elections,* 10th ed. (New York: Chatham House, 2000), 110–126.
8. Federal Election Commission website: http://www.fec.gov/pages/brochures/pubfund_limits_2004.html.
9. DiClerico and Davis, *Choosing Our Choices,* 16–17.
10. For a sense of who has been giving the most soft money to candidates in recent years—and how much they give—return to the Center for Responsive Politics website, at http://www.opensecrets.org/bigpicture/softtop.asp?cycle=2002.
11. Center for Responsive Politics Statement on McCain-Feingold Decision, December 10, 2003, at http://www.opensecrets.org/pressreleases/2003/SCtDecision.asp.
12. He's a conservative political activist who ran unsuccessfully for the Republican presidential nomination in 2000.
13. Polsby and Wildavsky, *Presidential Elections,* 10th ed., 99–101.
14. Ibid., 101.
15. Matthew R. Kerbel, "The Media: Old Frames in a Time of Transition," in Michael Nelson, ed., *The Elections of 2000* (Washington, DC: CQ Press, 2001), 109–132.
16. Polsby and Wildavsky, *Presidential Elections,* 10th ed., 109–110.
17. Paul S. Herrnson, "National Party Organizations at the Dawn of the Twenty-First Century," in L. Sandy Maisel, ed., *The Parties Respond,* 4th ed. (Boulder, CO: Westview Press, 2002), 19–46.
18. Ibid., 178.
19. Ibid., 190–193.
20. Donald Lutz, "The Electoral College in Historical and Philosophical Perspective," in Paul D. Schumaker and Burdett A. Loomis, eds., *Choosing a President* (New York: Chatham House Publishers, 2002), 31–51.
21. Ibid., 35.

Interest Groups:
Accessing Government through Common Membership

8

8-1 Introduction

In July 2002, an economic crisis was building in America. The stock market was in a free fall as investors lost confidence in corporate leadership following a string of revelations about wrongdoing at corporations like Enron, WorldCom, and the accounting firm Arthur Anderson. The sting of scandal reached the Bush White House, as questions emerged about whether President Bush and Vice President Cheney engaged in illegal or unethical practices when they were businessmen. Older Americans who were depending on investments to cushion them in retirement began to worry that market losses would undermine their living standards or make it impossible to retire. Members of the House and Senate, most of whom would face the voters in a few short months, leaped into action and legislated different versions of corporate reform, then tried to hammer out language that would be acceptable to both chambers.

As representatives of the House and Senate met to address their differences, representatives of the American Institute of Certified Public Accountants (AICPA) went into overdrive to make sure the final product was as soft as possible on CPAs. They were facing the possibility of legislation that would impose greater government regulation and tighter accounting standards, changing the way accountants operate and, they feared, adversely affecting their bottom line.

So, the AICPA sprang into action to defeat what it saw as the most restrictive provisions of the emerging legislation, pressing senators and House members to water it down while simultaneously urging their own members to pressure Washington to guard their interests. In an email to its members, AIPCA wrote, "We cannot allow . . . the fierce search for blame [in the corporate scandals] to taint the 350,000 CPAs in this country who stand for integrity, competence and objectivity."[1] Translation: Your future is in danger—protect your turf.

You probably didn't know there was an American Institute of Certified Public Accountants, did you? Don't feel badly—not many people do. AICPA is not a high-profile organization. It seldom makes news. However, with one-third of a million members, it can speak with a pretty loud voice to defend its interests.

So, a group you might not have heard of is trying to influence legislation that will reverberate through the economy, potentially affecting your personal finances and your job prospects after graduation. Do you share their concerns? If you want to make your living one day as an accountant, you probably do. If not, or if you happen to be one of the people calling out for Congress to tighten accounting procedures to shore up confidence in business and help the economy, you probably don't. In that case, who is developing strategies to represent your interests to those who make laws?

Welcome to the world of interest groups, which, like the mass media and political parties, provide us with a way to access and influence our government. Unlike the media, which are all around us, and parties, which are pretty visible, interest groups are the least discernible link between government and us. There is probably a lot we don't know about interest groups because we'd have to pay close attention to government to be aware of how they operate, and we know that most people don't. Interest groups complement political parties by giving people another way to make demands on government. Where parties permit access to the system by fielding candidates for us to choose among, interest groups provide access through membership in a group that presses its agenda on government officials.

The thing for us to figure out is whether the system of interest groups in place in America provides a strong and direct link to government that serves individual interests. We'll do that by looking at whose interests are being represented as we explore what interest groups do.

8-2 Factions Again?

Will we ever stop bringing up the subject of factions? Eventually, but it makes sense to think back for a minute to what we said about factions in Chapter 2 because it should make the whole concept of interest groups easier to understand. See if you remember whether the following statements are true or false:

1. A faction is always a majority of people whose interests conflict with the minority.
2. James Madison, writing in *The Federalist*, expressed the belief that people naturally group into factions.
3. Madison felt the best way to handle factions was to allow them to compete with each other in a system where the clash of interests would require compromise.

The first statement is false because a faction can be either a majority or an intense minority (see Section 2-7). The second statement is true. Madison wrote that the causes of faction "are sewn into the nature of man" (see Section 2-7). The third statement is also true. This is the basis for all the safeguards in our political system. It's also an important thing to remember when we talk about how interest groups work (see Section 2-7).

Remember in Chapter 6 when we said that there are no mentions of political parties in the Constitution because the framers equated them with factions and felt they were to be avoided? Interest groups can be regarded as factions as well—as the groups people naturally form to promote interests that are potentially detrimental to others. **Interest groups** are organizations of individuals with common objectives who seek to advance those objectives through the political process. Unlike parties, interest groups operate outside the formal political system, even as they work closely with elected representatives inside the system to advance their agenda. Unlike parties, which are broad organizations, interest groups form around narrowly defined issues. And, unlike parties, which were not anticipated by the framers, groups like these were expected to form naturally. The key thing is that they're supposed to compete with each other, and out of that competition should come compromises that serve the general interest. The question is—does it work that way?

Interest groups are sometimes called **pressure groups** because of the perception that they achieve their objectives by putting pressure on politicians. In fact, one of the main purposes of an interest group is **lobbying** government officials, trying to exert influence on the way they develop public policy. Interest groups are also called **special interest groups** because of the narrowly defined nature of their objectives. These terms capture key characteristics of interest groups, which act on the political system from the outside to advance agendas that serve specialized needs rather than broad, common interests.

▶**interest groups** Organized associations that seek to promote common objectives through government action.

▶**pressure groups** Another term for interest groups that emphasizes the demands interest groups make on the political system.

▶**lobbying** Attempting to influence the content of policy by exerting influence on government officials.

▶**special interest groups** Another term for interest groups that emphasizes the narrow scope of their concerns.

How specialized? How about:

- The Beer Institute
- American Society of Home Care Inspectors
- Beauty and Barber Supply Institute
- American Ceramic Society
- Hosiery Association[2]

Beer? Ceramics? Hosiery? That's pretty narrow. They're all interest groups whose industries can benefit from favorable government action on things like taxes and trade policy. Other groups may not be affiliated with business but can have interests that are just as narrow.

Now, if the system is working the way Madison imagined it would, all these narrow groups will engage in competition with each other for government action, and out of that competition will come compromise, which in the long run will serve collective interests because no one will be positioned to get everything they wanted. This perspective is consistent with **pluralism,** where a wide distribution of resources in society is reflected in the large number of individual special interest groups competing for the attention of government officials. It's a pretty clear example of how interest groups can link us to government through political action.

However, you may also remember the competing perspective, called **elitism,** that says ordinary people do not have a say in making important political decisions. Take the competition among interest groups out of the political process, and you have something that looks more like an elitist perspective on government than what Madison envisioned. If interest groups can find a way to hook into the political system, the argument goes, they can cozy up to officials and get what they want without having to compete with other groups. Small groups like the Beauty and Barber Supply Institute can win small victories this way. Large interests like huge corporations, foundations, and professional associations with disproportionately more resources, though, stand to win large victories that can dictate the way public policy is made—like what the CPAs were after when they tried to block changes in accounting procedures.

So, as we become familiar with what interest groups are and how they work, we'll keep in mind this question about whether they fit in the pluralist or elitist camp. We'll revisit the question later on, after we get a better feel for the different types of interest groups that are out there, and whose interests are served and whose are not.

8-3　Types of Interest Groups

Just like clothing, interest groups are not one-size-fits-all. Consistent with the pluralist perspective, there are a wide variety of interests that cover a host of agendas that operate in Washington and in state capitals to promote their objectives to officials who can help group members get what they want. Most are organized to enhance their self-interest, although some work for the collective good or to promote a particular vision of society.

Some of these groups seek to advance economic objectives, such as business, professional, agricultural, and labor interest groups. Others advance noneconomic interests, such as ideological, civil rights, public interest, and single-issue interest groups.[3]

8-3a　Economic Groups

If you're just looking at it in terms of raw numbers, economic groups compose by far the largest number of organized interests. Of these, business groups make up the largest share, followed by professional associations, unions, and agricultural interests.[4] You can take a look at some examples of economic groups in Table 8-1 on pages 218–219, along with how much money they put into the political system.

Business groups are among the most prevalent of interest groups; by one count, they constitute 71 percent of all registered lobbying organizations,[5] spending over one billion

---

▶**pluralism** The theory that government responds to individuals through their memberships in groups, assuring that government is responsive to a wide range of voices. People who subscribe to this position believe the wide distribution of resources in society drives the decisions government officials make.

▶**elitism** The theory that government responds to a small, stable, centralized hierarchy of corporate and academic leaders, military chiefs, people who own big media outlets, and members of a permanent government bureaucracy. People who subscribe to this position believe the actions of regular citizens, like voting and joining groups, simply mask the real power exercised by elites.

Box 8-1   Money, But Not Power

With $21,480,000 on hand in 2000, the Business Round-table would appear to be a formidable organization. At one time it was. Organized as an association of 200 CEOs in the 1970s, the Business Roundtable was instrumental in beating back a number of labor-friendly proposals under consideration by Congress.

You can't always draw a straight line between money and clout, though, and today the Business Roundtable has lost the reputation it once had in Washington. There are a couple of reasons why. The rise of PACs, as we saw in Chapter 6, has created a marketplace of options for politicians seeking campaign funds, leaving the Business Roundtable in a competitive position with respect to other interest groups. Differences among CEOs worked to undermine that position, and made it harder for the organization to speak with one voice.

Even its considerable cash contributions cannot be leveraged for maximum effectiveness, as a large percentage of spending goes to Democrats, making it unlike most business groups, which tend to overwhelmingly support Republican officials. That's the choice of some of the CEO members, but it has weakened the Business Roundtable's influence among Republicans, who choose to listen to other groups considered to be more loyal. Said one Republican official of the Business Roundtable, "They're a wasted resource and just plain irrelevant.*

So, it's possible to put tens of millions of dollars into lobbying and be considered an empty shell by the people you're trying to influence.

---

*H.R. Mahood, *Interest Groups in American National Politics: An Overview* (Upper Saddle River, NJ: Prentice Hall, 2000), 33–34.

---

dollars in 2000 to promote their interests to government officials. Much of this money comes from businesses themselves, who hire professional **lobbyists** in an effort to achieve or—more often—protect favorable regulatory and tax rules.

Additionally, there are groups that speak for broad business concerns. The first such organization was the United States Chamber of Commerce—a name you may be familiar with but perhaps never thought of as an interest group. The Chamber of Commerce was founded in 1912 as a federation of state and local organizations committed to the advancement of free enterprise. Accordingly, it lobbies for business tax relief, against federally mandated wage and benefit requirements for workers, and against the expansion of social welfare programs.[6] More recently, the Business Roundtable was established in the 1970s to advance the interests of large businesses. Box 8-1 discusses why the Business Roundtable has little clout politically, despite having money to spend.

In a more specialized vein, **trade associations** lobby on behalf of businesses that are widely regarded as trades, like bankers, manufacturers, and retailers. The American Bankers Association is the voice of the banking industry, the National Association of Manufacturers speaks for the manufacturing industry, and the National Association of Convenience Stores works on behalf of retail outlets. You may not have heard of these groups unless you know someone involved in the trade in question, but trade associations are often well-funded and important players in Washington, protecting and advancing the interests of their members.

Professional groups are powerful organizations representing the interests of professionals like doctors, lawyers, and educators. With large memberships and deep pockets, groups like the American Medical Association, the American Bar Association, the Association of Trial Lawyers of America, and the National Education Association are as influential as large business and trade groups.

It's not exaggerating to say that the road to creating or changing health care policy runs through the American Medical Association (AMA) offices. President Clinton found that out the hard way in the 1990s, when the AMA led the charge against his ambitious attempt to change the way health care is provided. Previous presidents also found their efforts frustrated when they attempted to change the health care system in ways opposed by the AMA.

When it comes to the matter of placing limits on the liability of health care providers, however, other powerful voices take a position at odds with the AMA. The American Bar

lobbyists Professionals hired by interest groups to influence the political process on behalf of the group.

trade associations Groups that advance the concerns of specific business interests, such as banks, energy companies, real estate firms, and car manufacturers.

TABLE 8-1	Business and Trade Groups: $1,048,475,000	
Economic Lobbies, 2000	*General*	Business Roundtable: $21,480,000 National Federation of Independent Business: $2,300,000
	Banks	American Bankers Association: $3,770,000 Chase: $4,680,000
	Communications	American Electronics Association: $4,000,000 AT&T: $7,400,000 Microsoft: $6,360,000
	Construction	American Council of Engineering Companies: $1,570,000 Portland Cement Association: $1,200,000
	Defense	Lockheed Martin Corporation: $9,740,000 Northrop Grumman Corporation: $6,880,000
	Energy	American Public Power Association: $1,920,000 Edison Electric Institute: $12,000,000 ExxonMobil: $7,077,000
	Manufacturing	National Association of Manufacturers: $3,980,000 General Electric: $16,000,000 P&G: $3,540,000
	Real Estate	National Association of REALTORS®: $8,920,000 Consumer Mortgage Coalition: $1,540,000
	Retail Sales	National Association of Convenience Stores: $1,500,000 Wal-Mart Stores: $1,020,000
	Transportation	Alliance of Automobile Manufacturers: $3,100,000 Ford Motor Company: $8,000,000 The Boeing Company: $7,820,000

Association (ABA) has lobbied for the expanded right of individuals to sue their health care plans for damages resulting from being turned down for medical treatment, claiming it would result in few lawsuits and marginal increases in health care costs. Not surprisingly, the AMA warns against frivolous lawsuits that would result in much higher medical premiums. It would also like to limit lawsuits against doctors, claiming too many physicians are losing their liability insurance as costs are driven up by expensive legal judgments.[7]

This debate tends to divide the political parties as well, with Democrats generally favoring expanded legal protections and Republicans favoring limits on medical malpractice awards. Consistent with this is the tendency for money from the legal community to find its way into the hands of Democrats and for health care money to flow to Republicans. In 2000, two-thirds of the political contributions from lawyers went to Democrats, and 60 percent of the political contributions from the medical field went to Republicans.[8]

Unions are the political counterparts to large business interests. Born of the discontentment workers felt with conditions in the industrial plants of late nineteenth century America, the labor movement remains a powerful political force, although the declining number of union workers has diminished its standing since the 1940s and 1950s. The AFL-CIO is the premier voice of organized labor, representing thirteen million workers in sixty-six different unions, ranging from electricians to plumbers to teachers to sanitation workers.[9] The AFL-CIO mission emphasizes establishing economic and social justice in the workplace, focusing on traditional bread-and-butter issues like wages, benefits, and working conditions, as well as such things as equal pay for women, trade policy, job retraining in emerging industries, and giving workers a greater say over production.

Professional Groups: $314,830,000

Education	National Education Association: $1,364,000
Law	Association of Trial Lawyers of America: $3,000,000
	American Bar Association: $1,080,000
Medicine	American Medical Association: $16,580,000
	American Hospital Association: $10,440,000

Agriculture: $77,700,000

Crops	American Farm Bureau Federation: $4,700,000
Dairy	Dairy Farmers of America: $280,000
Livestock	National Cattlemen's Beef Association: $400,000
	National Chicken Council: $120,000
Tobacco	Philip Morris USA: $11,220,000
	Brown and Williamson Tobacco USA: $2,460,000

Unions: $27,200,000

Industrial Unions	AFL-CIO: $3,342,000
	United Auto Workers: $1,850,000
	United Mine Workers of America: $1,810,000
Municipal Workers	American Federation of State, County, and Municipal Employees (AFSCME): $1,440,000
Trade Unions	United Association (formerly Plumbers/Pipefitters Union): $256,000
	Sheet Metal Workers International Association: $120,000
Transportation Unions	Teamsters: $1,320,000
	United Transportation Union: $1,248,000

Source: Data from http://www.opensecrets.org.

Other large, influential unions include the Teamsters (which represent truckers, airline employees, and others in the transportation field), the United Auto Workers, the United Mine Workers of America, and the American Federation of State, County and Municipal Employees (AFSCME).

If business interests generally show a preference for supporting Republican candidates, unions have traditionally been an important source of support for Democrats. During the 2000 election, labor PACs channeled $48 million or 91 percent of their contributions to Democrats, including $12 million each from industrial unions, transportation unions, and public sector unions, and $10 million from building trade unions.[10]

Agricultural groups have been organized for almost a century and a half, dating back to the establishment of the national Grange some 130 years ago. Today, with small family farms dwindling, agricultural interests largely represent "agribusiness:" large corporations involved in farming as well as the processing and trade of food products. Umbrella organizations like the American Farm Bureau Federation lobby on behalf of broad agricultural interests, such as farm price supports (a government subsidy to farmers forced to sell crops at a market price that's below their targeted price), federal worker safety laws, and government pesticide controls.[11] Organizations like the Dairy Farmers of America and the National Chicken Council represent specialized agricultural industries.

One of the biggest spenders in the agricultural sector is the tobacco industry, whose status as producers of a hazardous product puts it in an unusual lobbying position. For years, the tobacco lobby spent considerable sums to prevent restrictions on cigarette advertising, particularly to teenagers, and federal health and safety regulations of firsthand and

TABLE 8-2	Type of Group	Specific Groups
Noneconomic Lobbies, 2000	**Single-Issue Groups: $75,100,000**	
	Religious	Evangelical Church Alliance: $240,000
	Abortion/Reproductive Issues	National Right to Life: $635,000 Planned Parenthood Federation of America: $580,000
	Guns	Gun Owners of America: $4,150,000 National Rifle Association: $1,150,000 Handgun Control, Inc.: $340,000
	Seniors	AARP: $4,000,000
	Environment	National Wildlife Federation: $420,000 Americans for Affordable Electricity: $246,000
	Women's Issues	Women First National Legislative Committee: $100,000 National Women's Law Center: $60,000
	Veterans' Issues	Disabled American Veterans: $400,000 Veterans of Foreign Wars: $240,000
	Government Groups: $38,800,000	
	States and Territories	Commonwealth of Puerto Rico: $4,380,000
	Cities	National League of Cities: $0
	Counties	National Association of Counties: $100,000
	Civil Rights and Public Interest Groups: $11,980,000	
	Civil Rights	American Civil Liberties Union: $1,420,000
	Public Interest	Common Cause: $1,420,000 Public Citizen: $120,000 Consumer Federation of America: $80,000
	Ideological Groups: $6,024,000	
	Conservative	Christian Coalition of America: $1,760,000 Traditional Values Coalition: $300,000
	Liberal	People for the American Way: $140,000

Source: Data from http://www.opensecrets.org.

secondhand smoke. It fought having to put health warnings on cigarettes, and when warnings were mandated, it fought to keep the wording mild and innocuous. In recent years, the industry has been engaged in a battle against government lawsuits alleging the tobacco industry willfully misled Americans about the addictive nature of nicotine. Despite its funding and clout, the tobacco lobby has found itself on the defensive, in part because of changing public attitudes about smoking. As the industry's situation evolved, its lobbying approaches and objectives changed accordingly.

8-3b Noneconomic Groups

Interest groups organized around noneconomic matters generally do not command the big dollars that economic interests channel into the political system. However, you'll still find a strong political influence exerted by single-issue groups, government groups, civil rights and public interest groups, and ideological groups. Table 8-2 gives you a sample of some of the interests promoted by noneconomic groups, along with a sense of how much money they're spending on their cause.

Most *single-issue groups* are fairly small, but there are a lot of them, and they can be surprisingly effective. In part, this is because of the dedication of group members to their cause, whether it be heartfelt support for or opposition to abortion laws, gun ownership, environmental protection, or a host of other specific issues. Single-issue group representatives may not mobilize politically around any other issue, but the issue that compels them

Box 8-2 Lobbying the Abortion Issue

Public opinion polls suggest that while many of us have opinions about abortion policy, most of us do not hold opinions intense enough to drive us to political action. However, for the few who feel passionately about the matter, it's a single issue that's strong enough to motivate intense political activity—and conflict. For many engaged in the abortion debate, the outcome has a moral as well as a policy dimension, with some feeling that it is simply wrong to terminate a pregnancy and others believing that it is wrong to deny women the right to determine what to do with their bodies.

Complicating matters is the fact that the legal status of abortion procedures is debated as a **zero-sum policy,** in that any gains for one side come at the expense of the wishes of the other side. This adds to the ferocious quality of lobbying by groups on opposite sides of the issue. Policy debates that don't have a zero-sum quality—which is to say most policy debates—leave open the possibility for compromise. The abortion debate pits two dramatically different perspectives on the issue against one another in an all-or-nothing battle.

Look at how two powerful interest groups on opposing sides of the abortion issue frame the debate. The National Right to Life Committee believes that abortion ends life and takes the position that "a new individual human being begins at fertilization, when the sperm and ovum meet to form a single cell. If the baby's life is not interrupted, he or she will someday become an adult man or woman. Worldwide, millions of unborn babies are killed each year. In the United States, over 40 million unborn babies have been killed in the twenty-nine years since abortion was legalized, and more than 1.3 million are killed each year."*

To Planned Parenthood, a fetus is part of the mother's body, and maintaining a legal right to abortion is a matter of human dignity and personal choice. Their policy statement asserts that "it is the policy of Planned Parenthood Federation of America to ensure that women have the right to seek and obtain medically safe, legal abortions under dignified conditions and at reasonable cost. . . . Abortion must always be a matter of personal choice. Planned Parenthood recognizes its responsibility to guard equally against coercion or denial of services in connection with a patient's decision about continuing a pregnancy. No one should be denied abortion services solely because of age, or economic or social circumstances."†

▶**zero-sum policy** A policy debate in which any victory by one side comes at the expense of the opposing side, negating the possibility of compromise.

*You can read more about their position at http://www.nrlc.org/.

†You can read more about their position at http://www.plannedparenthood.org/.

to action does so totally, and the intensity of the beliefs of single-issue group members makes them a powerful force. Box 8-2 discusses abortion as a lobbying issue.

In some quarters, lobbying even takes place among different levels of government. As a consequence of **federalism,** the national government maintains a relationship with the states and localities, which, as we'll see in Chapter 15, includes the transfer of federal dollars to the states. This doesn't involve for-profit lobbying like we see with business or professional groups, but the competition among jurisdictions can be significant, so *government groups* lobby Washington for their share of this funding. The National League of Cities, the National Association of Counties, and a host of individual states, counties, and cities hire lobbyists to advance the transfer of federal money to their locale.[12]

So far, we've addressed groups organized around the promotion of economic or social self-interest. But *civil rights* and *public interest groups* promote objectives whose benefits extend far beyond group members to the broader society. If the American Medical Association is able to scuttle changes to health care policy that would end up costing doctors money, the primary beneficiaries of their action are AMA-member doctors. However, if a public interest group like Public Citizen is able to get the federal government to impose tighter standards for child seatbelt restraints on automobile manufacturers, then all car owners with kids are the potential beneficiaries.[13] Similarly, if a civil rights group like the American Civil Liberties Union successfully petitions government to protect the anonymity of Internet users,[14] many who are not directly involved with the interest group stand to gain—including you, if you ever send personal data over the web.

Why the selflessness? Contemporary civil rights and public interest groups trace their origins to the social and political turmoil of the 1960s, to the antiwar, civil rights, and women's movements, when the social and political *status quo* was being challenged and questioned. That's why groups of this nature focus on issues of equal opportunity, minority and women's rights, environmental protection, racial equality, religious liberty, the rights of people with disabilities, and consumer safety.

▶**federalism** The division of power between a sovereign federal government and sovereign state governments, which provides that some functions will be performed by the national government, some by the state governments, and some by both the national and state governments. As a feature designed to limit the strength of government, federalism works to decentralize power by creating dual levels of authority.

Box 8-3   Ralph Nader and the Politics of Public Lobbying

More than anyone else, Ralph Nader has been the face of the public interest movement over the past thirty-five years. You may be familiar with his name—he most recently ran for president on the Green Party ticket in 2000 and as an independent candidate in 2004, and he has been a celebrity figure since long before you were born. Nader emerged on the national scene in 1965 with the publication of the book *Unsafe at Any Speed*, which challenged General Motors' commitment to automobile safety. When it became public that GM had hired a private investigator to tail Nader and dig up dirt from his background, congressional hearings ensued, and the serious lawyer became a media star. Cast in the role of the defender of the little person, Nader became something of a folk hero and bankrolled his fame into the interest group Public Citizen, which engages in public action on behalf of such

things as health and safety measures and environmental protection.*

In the 1970s, when there was a lot of campus activism, Nader used colleges as sort of a farm system for public advocates. He sponsored Public Interest Research Groups—or PIRGs—on campuses all over the country (you may have one at your school) and encouraged young lawyers, dubbed "Nader's Raiders," to join him in the pursuit of government action they felt opposed the greater public good.†

*For a look at the full range of issues on the Public Citizen agenda, go to: http://www.publiccitizen.org/.

†Jeffrey M. Berry, *The New Liberalism: The Rising Power of Citizen Groups* (Washington, DC: Brookings Institution Press, 1999), 25–28.

▶**McGovern-Fraser Commission** The commission organized by the Democratic Party following its 1968 convention to democratize the process of delegate selection to party conventions.

The popularity of reforming the system and giving voice to the concerns of those lacking representation gained expression in the late 1960s through the political party reforms of the **McGovern-Fraser Commission** we talked about in Chapter 7. The interest group counterpart to this movement was a program by the Ford Foundation that offered start-up money to law firms willing "to advance necessary social change constructively."[15] Just as McGovern-Fraser engaged the Democratic Party on a path that diminished the authority of party elites, the Ford grants produced sixteen public interest law firms with a parallel objective: to open the political system to a broad range of public interests that were not being advocated by the powerful elite groups that had the ear of elected officials. These firms used the judicial system to press for change in the way government did business that would serve the broad public interest. As they achieved success, they were able to attract more contributors to the idea of challenging the system from within.[16] Box 8-3 discusses public interest lobbying.

Civil rights and public interest groups are unique in a couple of important ways. They are pluralistic in character, expending resources on behalf of others who may not hold a lot of resources, even if those others are not group members. In contrast, the economic interest groups and some of the noneconomic interest groups we discussed are elitist in nature, channeling resources collected from a closed group of members into government action designed to aid those members. Also, where much of the lobbying that's done by business, trade, and professional groups, agribusiness, and unions is aimed at preserving benefits already in place, civil rights and public interest groups engage in the (far more difficult) process of changing the law. From their inception as organizations designed to reform the political process, civil rights and public interest groups have positioned themselves in opposition to powerful elites, fighting battles that most likely would not be waged without an organized voice to speak out against entrenched interests.

If civil rights and public interest groups want to protect the general public from inequality and hazardous conditions, *ideological interest groups* seek to restructure society around a set of ideas about how they believe it should work. Like civil rights and public interest groups, their ends are nonmaterial and derived from an idea about the proper relationship between government and its citizens. Unlike civil rights and public interest groups, ideological interests are rooted more in a philosophy than in a cause. Their perspectives may be conservative, liberal, or otherwise, but in any case, they draw their energy from supporters who believe strongly in the organization's agenda.

▶**libertarianism** An ideology centered on the reduction of government power to advance personal liberty.

Think back to when we were talking about **libertarianism** in Chapter 3. We said libertarians subscribed to an ideological perspective whose basic intent is to advance individual liberty free from government interference. The Cato Institute is an ideological interest group that reflects a libertarian agenda. Its mission statement says: "The Cato

Institute seeks to broaden the parameters of public policy debate to allow consideration of the traditional American principles of limited government, individual liberty, free markets, and peace."[17]

Off to the left of the political spectrum, you'll find groups like People for the American Way Foundation. Their goals are quite a bit different than those of the Cato Institute's. Note how Cato emphasizes individualism through liberty and limited government, while People for the American Way focuses on community through equality and diversity: "People for the American Way Foundation (PFAWF) is committed to defending democracy and bringing the ideals of community, opportunity, diversity, equality, and fairness together to form a strong, united voice. To achieve this, PFAWF . . . monitors and researches the Religious Right movement and its political allies."[18]

By **"Religious Right,"** People for the American Way is referring to groups like the Christian Coalition, a powerful, religious-based organization with a sweeping conservative agenda at odds with the goals of PFAWF. Founder Pat Robertson (whom you may recognize from his CBN cable station), describes the Christian Coalition as "a pro-family citizen action organization" established "to promote Christian values in government."[19]

> **Religious Right** Ideological interest groups promoting a conservative political agenda consistent with an evangelical religious perspective.

The different worldviews described by PFAWF and the Christian Coalition should give you a pretty good idea of just how strongly these two ideological groups clash. Calling itself "America's leading grassroots organization defending our Godly heritage," the Christian Coalition is on a self-described moral mission. It supports legislation that advances traditional views of heterosexual marriage, opposes legalized abortion, and favors the use of tax money for private schools. People for the American Way, in contrast, is on a mission to limit the reach of the Christian Coalition. It supports gay rights, legalized abortion, improved public education, and religious freedom not defined in terms of Christian values or teachings.

The Christian Coalition has been a key political force since its establishment in 1989. Drawing support from a large base of Evangelical Christians, it effectively mobilized supporters to take its vision of America into the political arena. By getting evangelicals to the polls and helping to elect conservatives to public office, the Christian Coalition became an important political player in the 1990s, with a say over the public agenda. It's a record that liberal groups have not been able to match, although for its part, the Christian right has had limited success in expanding its base beyond the Evangelical community.[20]

One way ideological groups flex their muscle is by monitoring key legislative votes and issuing ratings of legislators, based on how closely their voting record supports the groups' cause. The ratings are a way of motivating the faithful to work against legislators who have low ratings and to support those who are perceived to be friends. Not surprisingly, many legislators score ideological ratings that are either very high or very low, and a high rating from a conservative group invariably predicts a low rating from a liberal group, and vice versa. Take a second and see how your senators were rated for key votes they cast in 2002 by the conservative group American Conservative Union (ACU) and the liberal group Americans for Democratic Action (ADA). Find your home state in Table 8-3 to reveal the name of your senators from 2002 and their (conservative) ACU ratings and their (liberal) ADA ratings. Ratings are on a 100-point scale, where 100 represents perfect ideological alignment with the interest group, and 0 represents total opposition.

8-4 Would You Join an Interest Group?

In Chapter 6, we said that you don't have to join a political party to consider yourself a Republican or Democrat. Not so with interest groups, which rely on membership fees for their lobbying efforts. So, what might lead you to join?

For the sake of argument, let's say you're concerned about the environment. Many of us are, so the chances are it's not too much of a stretch for you to imagine being at least a little concerned about fresh air, clean water, or open forests (if you couldn't care less about the environment, try to use your imagination and play along for a few minutes).

You're probably not going to consider joining a lot of groups; for many people, one would be enough (possibly too much). You look around, and the first thing that surprises you is how many environmental interest groups are out there. Maybe you know about

TABLE 8-3

How Your Senators Rate—Ideologically, 2002

Name of Senator	State	Party	ACU (conservative)	ADA (liberal)
Sessions	Alabama	Republican	98	10
Shelby		Republican	74	10
Murkowski	Alaska	Republican	83	0
Stevens		Republican	63	10
Kyl	Arizona	Republican	97	0
McCain		Republican	84	20
Hutchinson	Arkansas	Republican	97	5
Lincoln		Democrat	23	70
Boxer	California	Democrat	2	90
Feinstein		Democrat	12	80
Allard	Colorado	Republican	97	5
Campbell		Republican	54	30
Dodd	Connecticut	Democrat	8	80
Lieberman		Democrat	20	85
Biden	Delaware	Democrat	14	80
Carper		Democrat	22	80
Graham	Florida	Democrat	18	75
Nelson		Democrat	20	70
Cleland	Georgia	Democrat	16	65
Miller		Democrat	54	30
Akaka	Hawaii	Democrat	7	80
Inouye		Democrat	7	80
Craig	Idaho	Republican	94	5
Crapo		Republican	93	10
Durbin	Illinois	Democrat	7	95
Fitzgerald		Republican	87	20
Bayh	Indiana	Democrat	21	70
Lugar		Republican	79	5
Grassley	Iowa	Republican	83	10
Harkin		Democrat	9	80
Brownback	Kansas	Republican	97	5
Roberts		Republican	88	0
Bunning	Kentucky	Republican	96	0
McConnell		Republican	90	0
Breaux	Louisana	Democrat	46	65
Landrieu		Democrat	17	70
Collins	Maine	Republican	57	35
Snowe		Republican	52	30
Mikulski	Maryland	Democrat	6	100
Sarbanes		Democrat	5	100
Kennedy	Massachusetts	Democrat	3	100
Kerry		Democrat	6	85
Levin	Michigan	Democrat	6	95
Stabenow		Democrat	4	95
Dayton	Minnesota	Democrat	4	95
Wellstone		Democrat	3	100
Cochran	Mississippi	Republican	80	25
Lott		Republican	93	0
Bond	Missouri	Republican	82	10
Carnahan		Democrat	19	90

Name of Senator	State	Party	ACU (conservative)	ADA (liberal)
Baucus	Montana	Democrat	14	75
Burns		Republican	91	10
Hagel	Nebraska	Republican	84	10
Nelson		Democrat	53	50
Ensign	Nevada	Republican	92	15
Reid		Democrat	20	85
Gregg	New Hampshire	Republican	79	10
Smith		Republican	93	10
Corzine	New Jersey	Democrat	3	100
Toricelli		Democrat	12	80
Bingaman	New Mexico	Democrat	13	90
Domenici		Republican	73	15
Clinton	New York	Democrat	11	95
Schumer		Democrat	6	85
Edwards	North Carolina	Democrat	15	70
Helms		Republican	99	0
Conrad	North Dakota	Democrat	20	95
Dorgan		Democrat	18	90
DeWine	Ohio	Republican	83	15
Voinovich		Republican	81	5
Inhofe	Oklahoma	Republican	98	10
Nickles		Republican	96	0
Smith	Oregon	Republican	76	35
Wyden		Democrat	10	85
Santorum	Pennsylvania	Republican	87	5
Specter		Republican	42	35
Chafee	Rhode Island	Republican	47	45
Reed		Democrat	7	100
Hollings	South Carolina	Democrat	37	85
Thurmond		Republican	91	10
Daschle	South Dakota	Democrat	14	85
Johnson		Democrat	21	90
Frist	Tennessee	Republican	90	0
Thompson		Republican	86	10
Gramm	Texas	Republican	95	0
Hutchison		Republican	94	5
Bennett	Utah	Republican	88	5
Hatch		Republican	90	5
Jeffords	Vermont	Independent	26	95
Leahy		Democrat	6	95
Allen	Virginia	Republican	90	10
Warner		Republican	82	15
Cantwell	Washington	Democrat	16	80
Murray		Democrat	3	90
Byrd	West Virginia	Democrat	31	75
Rockefeller		Democrat	9	90
Feingold	Wisconsin	Democrat	10	90
Kohl		Democrat	15	85
Enzi	Wyoming	Republican	93	10
Thomas		Republican	89	10

Source: American Conservative Union and Americans for Democratic Action, 2003.

T A B L E 8-4	

**Do I Join the
Sierra Club?**

Answer yes or no to each of the following questions and keep track of your answers. When you're done, read on to see if you'd join up.

1.   I'll get a one-year subscription to *Sierra Magazine,* complete with great nature photography and articles on hot environmental issues. Do I want this enough to pay $25 to join? (Y/N)

2.   I'll get discounts on books and nature calendars. Do I want this enough to pay $25 to join? (Y/N)

3.   I'll be eligible to go on Sierra Club outings and service trips, like ski tours and visits to archeological sites. Do I want this enough to pay $25 to join? (Y/N)

4.   I'll have the satisfaction of knowing I'm doing something good for the planet. Do I want this enough to pay $25 to join? (Y/N)

If you responded "No" to all four questions, you've decided not to join the Sierra Club. None of the incentives was strong enough to get you to pay $25 for membership.

If you responded "No" to the first three questions and "Yes" to question 4, then you've decided to join the Sierra Club because of the satisfaction you feel from contributing to a cause you believe in, rather than because of any tangible incentives the club offers to members.

If you responded "Yes" to at least one of the first three questions (regardless of how many "Yes" responses you gave and regardless of your response to question 4), you've decided to join the Sierra Club because you want benefits that you can only get by being a member.

some of the big ones, like the National Wildlife Federation, the Sierra Club, the Audubon Society, or Greenpeace. Maybe you're surprised to learn that your options include smaller, more targeted groups like Pheasants Forever, the American Loon Fund, and the National Wild Turkey Federation.[21] How can you decide?

One easy way is to indulge your particular concern for the fate of pheasants, loons, or turkeys, and join the group that's tailored to your interests. Now, assuming you don't have a strong passion for fowl that leads you to one of these options, you'll probably choose among the groups you know about and decide whether it's worth your while to become a member.

You look at the Sierra Club, where an introductory membership is $25. It turns out the Sierra Club offers a few incentives to ease you into membership, which are listed in Table 8-4. Take a look at the options, figure out which (if any) appeals to you, and decide whether you're going to join.[22]

If you decided to join the Sierra Club because the trips or the calendars seem pretty cool, you gave in to the lure of **selective benefits**—tangible goods that flow only to members after they pay their dues. Many interest groups offer selective benefits to members because group leaders realize that not everyone will join a group simply because they share the group's objectives. Some selective benefits are just material goods with widespread appeal that have nothing to do with the group's lobbying objectives, like car rental discounts and inexpensive life insurance. Box 8-4 discusses a lobbying group for professors who teach political science courses.

Here's the thing: Without the appeal of selective benefits, it makes perfect sense for people not to pay dues to an interest group, even if they share the group's objectives. Think about it: If the Sierra Club is successful in reducing pollutants in water, it can't restrict access to clean water to Sierra Club members. The clean water is a **collective good**—something everyone is free to enjoy, whether or not they join the interest group that worked to bring it about.

This poses a problem to interest groups that wish to expand their membership because sympathetic, would-be members can enjoy the benefit of the collective good without paying a penny. Economist Mancur Olson calls this a **"free rider"** problem because the

selective benefits Incentives offered exclusively to interest group members as a means of getting people to join.

collective goods Benefits stemming from the work of an interest group that are available to everyone, whether or not they join the group.

free rider Someone who is sympathetic to the objectives of an interest group and enjoys the benefits produced by that group without making a contribution. Accordingly, he or she "rides free" on the backs of dues-paying members.

> **Box 8-4   Interest Groups for People Who Teach about Interest Groups**
>
> Even professors have special interests.
> Find out if your professor is a member of the American Political Science Association, a professional association that lobbies on behalf of the interests of academic political scientists (you may not have thought of political scientists as a professional group, but they are). If he or she is a member, find out why. Chances are it's because membership includes a subscription to the *American Political Science Review*, a leading
>
> source of current academic research, and *P.S.*, a journal that offers lots of professional information about what's happening in the field of political science. This information can be really helpful to political scientists engaged in research and teaching. If that's not enough, membership also includes a break on admission to the Association's annual professional meeting—and a car rental discount.

would-be member gets to benefit from the work of the group without making a contribution and argues that groups need to rely on selective benefits to get people to sign up.[23] In large groups, which are going to survive with or without your membership dollars, the free rider problem can be a real dilemma—hence, the need for particularly attractive membership incentives if they're going to maximize their membership size.

However, it is also the case that quite a few groups manage to thrive without offering selective benefits to members.[24] How do they make it? One possibility is that Olson's attention to tangible goods as a means of attracting members overlooks other, less tangible rewards. Remember **efficacy**—that sense that you can get government to respond to your interests? Plenty of people get satisfaction from being part of a cause they believe in or from feeling they've expressed their ideas—something called a **purposive benefit.** It's what would lead someone—maybe you—to join the Sierra Club because of the satisfaction created by pitching in to help a worthwhile cause (if you, in fact, feel the Sierra Club does worthwhile things). This could explain the appeal of membership in a civil rights or public interest group: The collective good produced by the group may be enough to compel people to belong.

There's one other reason why people join interest groups. Have you ever worked at a plant or company that was unionized? Perhaps a relative of yours does. If so, you might have encountered a twist on the incentive structure we've been talking about in order to entice people to join groups. Many unions operate as "closed shops," strengthening their numbers by compelling workers to pay union dues.[25] Because unions derive their benefits from collective bargaining, and because benefits flow to all workers, it's in the interest of unions to represent everyone at a work site and often in the interest of workers to join. However, the use of coercion to compel membership takes away the choice, making unions unique among interest groups in the manner in which they go about getting members.

efficacy The attitude that you can be effectual and effective in your dealings with government.

purposive benefit The gratification an interest group member gets by contributing to a cause.

8-5 Lobbyists and Lobbying

One obvious reason why interest groups want to encourage membership is that lobbying costs money. A less obvious reason is because there's power in numbers. Any interest group that can claim to speak for a lot of people simply has more clout. For instance, there's a group called the American Association of Retired Persons, which now goes by its initials, AARP. If you go to the membership page on their website, you'll find that it says, "Anyone over fifty can get all the great benefits of membership in AARP."

Anyone over fifty? In an organization dedicated to retired people?

That's not a misprint. By opening group membership to people fifty and over instead of moving the cutoff closer to the standard retirement age of sixty-five, AARP can expand its membership base and claim to speak for far more people—thirty-five million in all—making it second only to the Roman Catholic Church as the nation's largest organization.[26] When a group representing that many people speaks, official Washington tends to listen, as it did in 2003 when AARP came out in support of a measure subsequently approved by Congress to add a prescription drug benefit to the Medicare program.

access The ability to maintain
personal contact with public
officials. Many lobbying
strategies depend on
maintaining an open door
to contacts in the legislative
and executive branches.

inside strategies Lobbying
approaches that rely on direct
relationships between
lobbyists and officials.

outside strategies Lobbying
approaches that rely on
mobilizing group members
to influence the actions of
officials.

Money and membership numbers are key resources used in lobbying. So is information because, as we'll see, one reason officials listen to lobbyists is because they can supply them with information they need in order to do their jobs intelligently. Interest groups have other important resources, too. Larger groups can depend on the media as a resource for publicizing their aims and objectives, and lobbyists rely on **access** to public officials—the ability to contact them on a regular, ongoing basis and know they'll be welcome.

With these resources—money, membership, information, media, and access—interest groups engage in a host of strategies to achieve their ends. We can group them into **inside strategies,** where direct personal contacts with officials or their staffs are the source of lobbying efforts, and **outside strategies,** where groups appeal to their membership in an indirect effort to get officials to respond to their wishes.

8-5a Inside Strategies

A lot of lobbying involves face-to-face interaction between lobbyists and officials. In fact, the term *lobbying* derives from the way interest group representatives would gather in the lobby of the legislative chamber—they aren't allowed inside—waiting to corner representatives as they emerged from the legislature.

Lobbying can take a lot of specific forms, but it tends to involve the same collection of activities. By one count, some of the most widely utilized inside strategies are:

- Making direct personal contacts with officials
- Presenting technical information to officials
- Helping to draft legislation
- Testifying at legislative hearings
- Making campaign contributions[27]

Inside strategies involve the use of access, information, and money to advance group goals. That sounds pretty abstract, but in reality, inside lobbying is about building relationships.

Just take a look at some of the inside strategies in the previous list to get a feel for how it works. Direct personal contacts, targeted at members of Congress, their staff, and people who serve in the many agencies that constitute the executive branch of government, happen regularly and frequently. They can be made formally or at social gatherings. Official Washington loves to socialize, and it can be impossible to distinguish business from pleasure because when lobbyists are at a restaurant or social function with members of

Lobbyists wait for their contacts outside the legislative chamber, ready to resume their ongoing dialogues.

Source: AP/Wide World Photos.

Congress, they are maintaining the personal contacts that make their job possible (yes, there's actually a career where part of the job description involves going to parties). In an important respect, lobbying is forever: It's an endless, ongoing process of cultivating relationships because interest groups are constantly engaged in the process of seeking what they want and protecting what they have.[28]

Because interest groups are also called pressure groups, it would make sense that personal contacts are used to twist the arms of legislators who stand in the way of the group's goal. That's the picture of lobbyists that a lot of people have in their heads—people who are always working whatever angle they can find to change the minds of opponents—and to a point this happens. However, maybe the more interesting contacts take place between lobbyists and officials who are *sympathetic* to the group's goals. You might think that interest groups don't have to lobby their friends, but in fact, sympathetic officials form an important base of support that groups constantly nurture, and interest groups commonly target friendly or undecided officials before they invest their time into trying to change people's minds.[29]

In this vein, lobbyists provide a service to sympathetic officials when they supply them with technical information and assist representatives and senators in drafting legislation. It's the business of interest groups to be familiar with the policy details of the interests they represent, and that expertise is incredibly valuable to busy officials who simply don't have the time to immerse themselves in the particulars of a legislative area. Of course, lobbyists who help draft legislation will do so with their interests liberally represented, but this doesn't cause a problem to allied legislators who will introduce the bill (and it in no way guarantees that the legislation they draft will pass through Congress in the form in which it is written, if it passes through Congress at all).

Information also comes into play when lobbyists testify at legislative hearings, where they get to display their expertise as members of Congress deliberate the merits of legislation. Hearings provide lobbyists with a forum for making the case for their position while showing off what they know, and because the substance of hearings is often covered by the press (even if it's an industry newsletter or trade publication), the lobbyist can use a hearing as a source of free publicity, playing the role of expert to set the press agenda in a manner that's favorable to the group's cause.[30]

8-5b Outside Strategies

While inside strategies are about networking, outside strategies are about mobilizing group supporters to demonstrate political demand for the group's position. Some of the most widely used outside strategies are:

- Contacting the press
- Mobilizing grassroots members
- Publicizing legislative voting
- Advertising and public relations efforts
- Endorsing candidates
- Engaging in protests or demonstrations[31]

Outside strategies entail the use of media and membership to advance group goals, expanding the arena in which interest groups can gain momentum for their cause beyond official Washington. The purpose is to get officials to take notice of an issue, either by demonstrating that group members are energized by it (meaning it might influence how they vote in November) or by publicizing it through the media.[32]

Outside strategies can be as routine as organized interest group efforts to get members to write to their representatives about an issue, but on occasion, outside strategies can be dramatic. There's a terrific story about a group of seniors in Chicago who were mobilized to protest a tax on catastrophic health care insurance, endorsed by AARP and guided through the House by powerful congressman Dan Rostenkowski. With big interests lined up behind it, Congress approved the tax. However, smaller senior citizen interests opposed it, such as the National Committee to Preserve Social Security and Medicare. For more than a year, the smaller lobby ran television ads framing the tax as unfair to seniors, helping to make seniors aware of the tax and raise the visibility of their antitax position to legislators.

When Rostenkowski agreed to meet with a group of seniors in his district about the measure, the Committee to Preserve Social Security and Medicare went into action. Playing on the ire of their members, they recruited angry seniors to attend the meeting with signs protesting Rostenkowski's support of the measure. They were energized, and—prompted by interest group leaders—they wanted the congressman to talk to them personally. Rostenkowski left the meeting without doing so. Indignant, a group of about twenty seniors surrounded the congressman's car, in full view of television cameras and reporters—who had been tipped off to the potential for good pictures by interest group leaders. They were led by sixty-nine-year-old Leona Kozien, who to that point had never been involved in political action of any kind and certainly never dreamed that her name would end up in an American government textbook.

> The seniors stood in front of the car and waved placards. The congressman's driver honked the horn and moved the car a few inches. The front bumper brushed against Kozien's thigh, and she staggered a bit. Some man shouted, "You knocked her down! You hurt her!" This same man then turned to Kozien and said quietly, "Lay down under the car."
>
> "Are you crazy? No way, he'd run me over!" retorted Kozien, who was barely over five feet tall. The car moved again, and this time Kozien fell on the hood of the car. Her face was inches from Rostenkowski's, with glass separating them. She was still carrying her placard, and from inside the car, Rostenkowski saw her placard, her face, and her body sprawled across the windshield.
>
> "Killer! Killer!" the crowd shouted.
>
> Rostenkowski then got out of the car and ran through a parking lot, while angry seniors chased after him. The driver maneuvered through the crowd, drove around the block, and caught up with Rostenkowski down the street.[33]

Considering what we know about the media, it's not hard to imagine that pictures of a senior citizen hanging in protest from a congressman's car got national play—which is exactly what the group organizers had hoped for. The results were remarkable. It thrust the catastrophic health care tax on the national agenda. Interest group leaders used it as a rallying point to motivate seniors across the country to write letters to their representatives urging Congress to repeal the tax. The effort culminated in an about-face by Congress, which voted overwhelmingly to ax the tax just one year after it had instituted it (even AARP changed its position). Working from the outside, strategically using media and membership, a small but determined interest group succeeded in getting Congress to reverse itself.

Although the outside strategies we listed previously are often employed independently, the case of the angry seniors combined most of them into a coordinated campaign. An organized public relations effort incorporating television advertising paved the way for the protest by making the issue of the catastrophic health care insurance tax visible to seniors and officials.

Grassroots members were mobilized to attend the meeting with Rostenkowski, something they might not have done without encouragement when you consider that these were seniors who did not have a record of social activism or even tremendous political participation.

The press had been contacted about the event and informed by group leaders about the potential for great pictures to support a good story line (little old ladies with placards confront powerful House member). The media showed up because the promise of seniors picketing a congressman was too hard to resist.

Then, of course, there was the protest itself, which took place with more than a little coaching from organizers, who were out to get the pictures they knew could catapult their cause into national headlines. When they succeeded, more grassroots mobilizing took place in the form of an organized letter-writing campaign from seniors to representatives from districts across the country.

> **Box 8-5   How *Not* to Write a Letter to Your Representative**
>
> How can members of Congress or their staff tell if an interest group orchestrates a seemingly spontaneous outpouring of sentiment? One way is by looking at what's in the letters arriving at the representative's office. When groups contact their members, they often coach them about what to write, typically including a "sample" letter for the group member's reference. Lots of people will copy the sample letter verbatim and send it to their member of Congress. So, if duplicate of copies of the same letter start showing up in the halls of Congress, members know that they're dealing with an organized effort. Some people have been known to make it easy for members of Congress to figure out what's going on by dutifully copying the "sample" letter, then enclosing the sample along with their rewritten copy in the envelope they mail to Washington, D.C. It can do a number on the element of surprise when a representative gets a "spontaneous" letter from a constituent that includes an interest group mailing urging the constituent to write a letter that looks spontaneous.

The two outside strategies on our list that didn't come into play in the catastrophic health care tax example—publicizing legislative voting and endorsing candidates—serve a similar purpose to the strategies that did. Earlier, we talked about how ideological interest groups rate members of Congress based on how they vote on key issues in order to direct the support of members toward sympathetic representatives or to get them to work against representatives deemed hostile to the cause. Interest groups with large memberships may publicize legislative voting records as a way of putting pressure on members of Congress by publicly stating that the group is watching what they're doing. The implication, of course, is that members of Congress who don't act in accordance with group goals will face the wrath of interest group members at the polls.

Endorsing candidates works much the same way. Powerful interest groups with lots of members like the National Rifle Association (NRA) or the AFL-CIO will target candidates for defeat, while showering supportive candidates with PAC money and working to get rank-and-file members out to the polls to vote for them. The NRA alone spent $14.6 million between 1977 and 1994 just to support or oppose congressional and presidential candidates based on their positions on gun laws. In 1994, it spent over $3 million and claimed an 84 percent success rate—a figure that makes candidates look over their shoulder if they're on the wrong side of the spending spree.[34]

That said, there are limits to outside strategies. Not every group is like the NRA, with large numbers of motivated members that cast their votes with the group's agenda in mind. The senior citizen protest, although highly effective, is an unusual tactic to employ: Interest groups tend to shy away from protests and demonstrations. For that matter, if the great pictures of Leona Kozien dangling from the hood of Congressman Rostenkowski's car had not materialized, it's unlikely that there would have been national media coverage of the issue.

Even the letter-writing campaign that followed has its boundaries. Members of Congress can often tell if the cards and email they're getting are the product of an orchestrated effort (see Box 8-5), and if so, they're easier to discount than a more spontaneous outpouring of discontent. Interest groups can go to a lot of effort to get members to write to their representatives, but, ironically, they'll be more effective if they can generate a big response with little prodding.[35] Of course, that only happens when group members are already upset about an issue, something group leaders cannot easily manufacture.

On the whole, lobbying is an insider's game. In a survey of interest groups, almost *all of them* claimed to engage in key inside strategies: contacting government officials, testifying at hearings, and presenting officials with technical information. By comparison, they relied less heavily on outside strategies, as Figure 8-1 demonstrates.

8-5c More Money

Looking at interest group strategies permits us to revisit the matter of PACs from the perspective of where all that money is coming from. For starters, not every PAC is formed by an interest group and not every interest group has a PAC. Some PACs are organized and

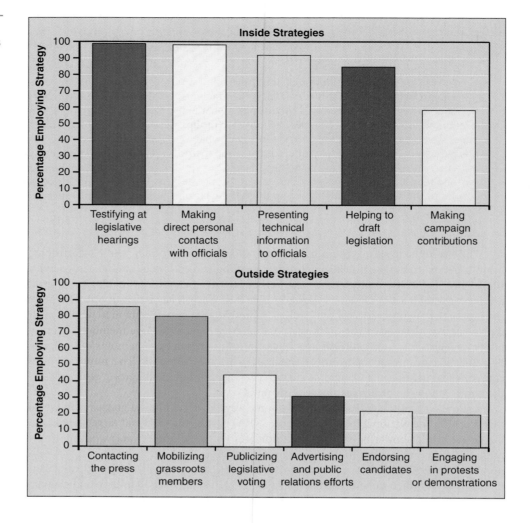

Figure 8-1

Inside versus Outside Strategies
Interest groups widely employ almost every inside strategy available to them, whereas outside strategies are used more selectively—or rarely, as in the case of advertising, endorsing candidates, and protesting.

Source: Data from Kay Lehman Schlozman and John T. Tierney, *Organized Interests and American Democracy* (New York: Harper & Row, 1986), 150 (Table 7.1).

run by single individuals or small groups (as an example, see if you can find Al Gore's Leadership 98 PAC, which promoted Gore's presidential ambitions by raising money for Democratic congressional candidates, in Table 8-5). Still, many are the money-giving arms of organized interests. They tend to be formed by interest groups that are heavily engaged in advancing policy goals in a competitive political environment, where lobbying can get expensive and contributions to political officials are thought to be productive.[36]

Business interests are most likely to have PACs—by one recent count, better than 40 percent of PACs are affiliated with corporations, like Coca Cola PAC and the Ford Motor Company Civic Action Fund. Ideological groups compose the next largest group of PACs, with organizations like the American Conservative Union and People for the American Way raising large sums of money in an attempt to influence a broad political agenda. Labor Unions and Trade Associations are also big players in the use of PAC money to advance their interests.[37]

A list of the top fifty PAC contributors from 1998 (see Table 8-5 on pages 234–235) gives you a pretty good idea of who the biggest players are. Here's how the top of the top shakes down: Coming in at number one overall is the Association of Trial Lawyers of America, with total contributions of nearly $2,700,000. Barely below in total dollars is the American Federation of State, City, and Municipal Employees (AFSCME). In fact, five of the top ten and almost half the top fifty PACs represent unions, in part because of their ability to pool large numbers of small contributions from members. The biggest spending corporate PAC is the United Parcel Service PAC ($1,687,000), and honors for the top single-issue/ideological PAC go to the National Rifle Association ($1,700,000).[38] It is also a stable group; seventeen of the top twenty PAC contributors in 2004 appear on this list.[39]

You can see how, as we noted earlier, unions have a preference for Democrats, and business interests are more likely to support Republicans, although not to the same overwhelming degree. With the large number of unions at the top of the list, this would appear to give the Democrats an advantage in the quest for PAC money. Remember, though, campaign funds also come in the form of **soft money,** with Republican-tilting businesses topping the list. So, tobacco giant Philip Morris is forty-ninth on the PAC contribution list at just slightly under one million dollars donated but jumps to number two on the list of overall contributors when you factor in the $2,447,000 the company forked over in soft money—83 percent of which went to the Republican Party.

Table 8-6 on pages 236–237 lists the top fifty soft-money contributors in 1998. In this group, businesses constitute seven of the top ten contributors and 80 percent of the list (including WorldCom and Enron, two of the largest culprits in the 2002 corporate scandals). The list takes in a wide range of business concerns: tobacco, banking, shipping, mass media, phone companies, pharmaceuticals, agribusiness, beer manufacturers, oil and gas production, and airlines, to name a few. Take a minute to compare it to the PAC contribution table (Table 8-5), and see if you can tell the difference in terms of who's giving soft money and who's getting it.

In 2004, Democrats bridged the soft-money gap with Republicans through the active fund-raising of advocacy groups or "527 Committees"—named for the section of the tax code under which they are authorized. These groups are chartered to advocate issues and mobilize voters, for which they can raise unlimited amounts of soft money. The top 527 group—the Joint Victory Campaign—alone raised over $65 million to assist John Kerry's presidential campaign.[40]

8-5d Lobbying the Executive Branch

The inside and outside strategies we've discussed can, for the most part, be applied to lobbying the legislative and executive branches. Although some approaches, like advertising voting records and endorsing candidates, apply specifically to Congress, lobbyists find themselves heavily engaged in trying to influence the executive branch.

That's because the game isn't over once a group has successfully gotten Congress to act in its interest. Any new legislation that Congress creates is interpreted and put into effect by the **executive branch,** or the **bureaucracy.** As we'll see in Chapter 11, bureaucrats in the executive branch have a lot of freedom over how to implement acts of Congress, which means lobbying efforts extend to getting them to interpret the law in ways that are sympathetic to the group's wishes. As it turns out, bureaucrats can be influenced by the organizational clout of interest groups or benefit from the expertise interests groups can offer.

We hinted at the importance of the executive branch in Chapter 7, when we mentioned that the Federal Election Commission (FEC) had weakened key provisions of the McCain-Feingold campaign finance reform law, making it possible for political parties to collect soft money in apparent contravention of the spirit of the law. If you don't remember the discussion, here it is, repeated from Chapter 7 (Section 7-2c, "Money"):

> Even after passage, McCain-Feingold met with resistance. Although ardent reform activists felt it was little more than a Band-Aid over a gaping wound, just about everyone directly influenced by the changes resisted them. Both major parties immediately searched for ways to circumvent the soft-money restrictions, while some PACs argued it went too far, challenging soft-money limitations as restrictions on free expression. Detractors included four of the six FEC commissioners who were in office at the time the law went into effect. Because they were responsible for interpreting and enforcing the law, they were able to weaken some of the law's reforms, restoring large portions of the soft-money loophole that McCain-Feingold was designed to fill, and providing exceptions under which federal candidates could still collect soft-money contributions.

In this instance, the FEC is the arm of the executive branch charged with putting into effect the campaign finance law passed by Congress. Interest groups concerned with closing the soft-money loophole, like public interest groups that work for campaign reform, found it necessary to lobby the FEC to press for a strict interpretation of the law, despite having already spent years trying to get Congress to pass the law in the first place.

▶**soft money** Funds contributed to state and local parties or to national parties for the purpose of running state elections or conducting local "grassroots" political activity.

▶**executive branch** The institutional component of the branch of government we think of as the presidency, charged with carrying out laws passed by Congress. Sometimes, the executive branch is referred to as the bureaucracy.

▶**bureaucracy** Another name for the executive branch of government, the institutional component of the presidency, which is charged with carrying out laws passed by Congress.

| T A B L E 8-5 | Top PAC Contributors, 1998 |

Rank	Sponsor	Amount Spent	Percent Contributed to Democrats	Percent Contributed to Republicans	Type of Group
1	Association of Trial Lawyers of America	$2,698,000	85%	14%	Professional
2	American Federation of State, County, and Municipal Employees (AFSCME)	$2,632,000	96%	4%	Union
3	American Medical Association	$2,609,000	30%	69%	Professional
4	National Association of REALTORS®	$2,594,000	40%	60%	Trade group
5	International Brotherhood of Electrical Workers	$2,325,000	96%	4%	Union
6	Teamsters	$2,305,000	93%	7%	Union
7	National Automobile Dealers Association	$2,237,000	30%	70%	Trade group
8	National Education Association	$2,210,000	93%	7%	Union
9	United Auto Workers (UAW)	$2,079,000	99%	1%	Union
10	National Association of Home Builders	$1,991,000	31%	69%	Trade group
11	National Association of Letter Carriers	$1,944,000	83%	17%	Union
12	International Association of Machinists and Aerospace Workers	$1,874,000	99%	1%	Union
13	Laborers' International Union	$1,844,000	90%	10%	Union
14	National Rifle Association	$1,709,000	17%	83%	Single issue
15	United Parcel Service	$1,687,000	23%	77%	Business
16	United Food and Commercial Workers	$1,672,000	97%	2%	Union
17	American Federation of Teachers	$1,600,000	98%	1%	Union
18	American Marine Offiers	$1,563,000	52%	48%	Union
19	United Brotherhood of Carpenters and Joiners of America	$1,535,000	93%	6%	Union
20	AFL-CIO	$1,527,000	96%	4%	Union
21	Communications Workers of America	$1,507,000	99%	1%	Union
22	American Bankers Association	$1,491,000	41%	59%	Trade group
23	Service Employees International Union	$1,476,000	97%	3%	Union
24	National Association of Health Underwriters	$1,441,000	37%	63%	Trade group

In the case of McCain-Feingold, key public interest groups employed an outside strategy in order to pressure the FEC into a strict interpretation of the law. The effort was not lost on FEC commissioners, who, according to the *Washington Post,* "bristled" at the tactics, complaining that "the leaders of such groups as Common Cause and Democracy 21 were trying to influence commission decisions by lobbying through the news media."[41]

The executive-branch parallel to the interest group strategy of trying to influence congressional elections is trying to influence bureaucratic appointments. Because it's always easiest to lobby someone sympathetic to your cause, groups may support or oppose presidential appointees based on how closely an appointee's philosophy matches the group's objectives. In the case of the FEC, you would expect Common Cause and Democracy 21

Rank	Sponsor	Amount Spent	Percent Contributed to Democrats	Percent Contributed to Republicans	Type of Group
25	National Beer Wholesalers Association	$1,422,000	21%	79%	Trade group
26	United Transportation Union	$1,408,000	85%	15%	Union
27	Credit Union National Association	$1,367,000	46%	54%	Business
28	Bank of America	$1,316,000	44%	56%	Business
29	Leadership 98 (Al Gore)	$1,313,000	100%	0%	Political
30	American Institute of Certified Public Accountants	$1,244,000	35%	65%	Professional
31	Ironworkers International	$1,243,000	92%	8%	Union
32	Sheet Metal Workers International Association	$1,242,000	96%	4%	Union
33	FedEx	$1,242,000	28%	72%	Business
34	Citigroup	$1,213,000	42%	58%	Business
35	National Federation of Independent Business	$1,210,000	7%	93%	Business
36	Lockheed Martin Corporation	$1,186,000	36%	64%	Business
37	American Hospital Association	$1,174,000	48%	52%	Professional
38	American Dental Association	$1,170,000	47%	53%	Professional
39	PricewaterhouseCoopers	$1,160,000	35%	65%	Business
40	United Steelworkers of America	$1,149,000	100%	0%	Union
41	United Association (formerly Plumbers and Pipefitters Union)	$1,103,000	93%	7%	Union
42	Ernst & Young	$1,045,000	41%	59%	Business
43	Americans for Free International Trade	$1,030,000	18%	82%	Trade group
44	Bank One Corporation	$1,021,000	39%	61%	Business
45	Air Line Pilots Association	$1,006,000	80%	19%	Union
46	Associated Builders and Contractors	$996,000	2%	98%	Trade group
47	Bell Atlantic	$990,000	38%	62%	Business
48	National Rural Electric Cooperative Association	$989,000	50%	50%	Single issue
49	Philip Morris USA	$989,000	32%	68%	Business
50	AT&T	$988,000	46%	54%	Business

Source: Data from http://www.opensecrets.org.

to push for commissioners who are sympathetic to campaign finance reform as vacancies emerge on the commission.

8-6 Who Are These Guys?

If you pick up a copy of *Washington Representatives*, a comprehensive source of information on lobbyists, you'll find listings for around seventeen thousand individual lobbyists and eleven thousand lobbying firms.[42] That's enough lobbyists to fill a small city. Who are these guys?

For starters, lobbyists are guys. They are mostly white males, although women are becoming more visible as lobbyists, especially for health care issues. It's a profession that

TABLE 8-6	Top Soft-Money Contributors, 1998

Rank	Sponsor	Amount Spent	Percent Contributed to Democrats	Percent Contributed to Republicans	Type of Group
1	Philip Morris USA	$2,447,000	17%	83%	Business
2	Communications Workers of America	$1,464,000	100%	0%	Union
3	American Federation of State, County, and Municipal Employees (AFSCME)	$1,341,000	100%	0%	Union
4	Amway	$1,313,000	0%	100%	Business
5	American Financial Group, Inc.	$1,210,000	21%	79%	Business
6	WorldCom	$1,143,000	37%	63%	Business
7	RJR Nabisco	$1,138,000	12%	88%	Business
8	National Education Association	$1,126,000	97%	3%	Union
9	Loral Space & Communications	$1,027,000	100%	0%	Business
10	AT&T	$1,024,000	33%	67%	Business
11	Buttenwieser & Associates	$934,000	100%	0%	Single issue
12	FedEx	$928,000	28%	72%	Business
13	Bell Atlantic	$912,000	28%	72%	Business
14	Freddie Mac	$876,000	26%	74%	Business
15	The Walt Disney Company	$855,000	56%	44%	Business
16	American Federation of Teachers	$854,000	100%	0%	Union
17	Citigroup	$841,000	23%	77%	Business
18	Goldman Sachs	$790,000	79%	21%	Business
19	Microsoft	$775,000	19%	81%	Business
20	Joseph E. Seagram & Sons	$754,000	52%	48%	Business
21	Pfizer, Inc.	$747,000	13%	87%	Business
22	BellSouth Corp.	$737,000	46%	54%	Business
23	AFL-CIO	$722,000	100%	0%	Union
24	US West, Inc.	$722,000	20%	80%	Business
25	Enron Corp.	$692,000	16%	84%	Business

disproportionately draws well-off middle-aged Protestants, with Catholic and Jewish lobbyists more likely to represent unions and professional associations. Politically, Democrats are more likely to represent such areas as energy and labor, whereas Republicans are more likely to be drawn to business and agricultural issues.

Lawyers are also heavily represented among lobbyists, as are people with deep roots in Washington, D.C. This makes sense, if you consider that lawyers are well situated to understand the ramifications of making changes to legislation. Being well connected in Washington helps open the doors that lobbyists need to walk through in order to implement inside strategies. In fact, it's not at all uncommon to find among the ranks of lobbyists former members of Congress and the executive branch, who can offer interest groups easy access to the corridors of powers and familiarity with how official Washington works.[43]

If lobbying is about implementing a variety of strategies designed to win the support or neutralize the opposition of officials toward an issue, then lobbyists are first and foremost strategists. Good lobbyists recognize the resources they have to work with and can design and implement an approach to convert those resources into the outcome they seek.

Rank	Sponsor	Amount Spent	Percent Contributed to Democrats	Percent Contributed to Republicans	Type of Group
26	BlueCross BlueShield Association	$688,000	24%	76%	Business
27	Service Employees International Union	$662,000	95%	5%	Union
28	Slim-Fast Foods Company	$650,000	94%	6%	Business
29	CSX Corporation	$642,000	12%	88%	Business
30	United Food and Commercial Workers	$639,000	100%	0%	Union
31	MA Berman Company	$600,000	100%	0%	Business
32	Bristol-Myers Squibb Company	$560,000	25%	75%	Business
33	Northwest Airlines	$560,000	42%	58%	Business
34	Brown and Williamson Tobacco USA	$559,000	4%	96%	Business
35	Atlantic Richfield	$551,000	38%	62%	Business
36	Tele-Communications, Inc.	$536,000	41%	59%	Business
37	Alfa Insurance	$532,000	20%	80%	Business
38	JW Childs Associates, L.P.	$530,000	0%	100%	Business
39	The Boeing Company	$530,000	43%	57%	Business
40	Bank of America	$524,000	26%	74%	Business
41	News Corporation	$523,000	11%	89%	Business
42	AMR Corp.	$522,000	33%	67%	Business
43	Archer Daniels Midland Company	$518,000	51%	49%	Business
44	Ernst & Young	$515,000	54%	46%	Business
45	Anheuser-Busch Companies	$502,000	40%	60%	Business
46	Fannie Mae	$501,000	38%	62%	Business
47	Sprint	$497,000	55%	45%	Business
48	Novartis	$496,000	30%	70%	Business
49	New Republican Majority Fund	$475,000	0%	100%	Political
50	Time Warner	$471,000	45%	55%	Business

Source: Data from http://www.opensecrets.org.

To do this effectively, lobbyists need to know which officials can help them, then be thorough and follow through. Just like success in college, effective lobbying involves doing a lot of homework.[44] Box 8-6 gives tips for effective lobbying.

8-7 Competition . . . or Cooperation?

You're probably starting to get the idea that for all the competition between groups and for all the arm-twisting and threats to endorse political opponents, interest groups benefit from having a lot in common with the people they lobby. While it's true that some groups engage in zero-sum competition with other groups, a lot of the positions that groups advance are encouraged by like-minded officials who benefit magnificently from their relationships with lobbyists.

The term **"iron triangle"** describes the exchange of mutual self-interest among interest groups, legislators, and bureaucrats in the executive branch. Also called **"subgovernments"** for their highly specialized nature, iron triangles are enduring relationships based

▶ **iron triangle** The ongoing, mutually beneficial relationship among an interest group, members of Congress sharing the interest group's objectives, and bureaucrats in federal agencies responsible for carrying out legislation pertaining to the interest group's field. Iron triangles can develop in any policy area, and many distinct iron-triangle relationships form because the federal government is responsible for a large number of policies.

Box 8-6   The "Five Commandments" of Lobbying

Bruce C. Wolpe and Bertram J. Levine, two students of the process, offer five "commandments" for effective lobbying.

- *Tell the truth.* A lobbyist's reputation lasts forever, and failing to provide lawmakers with a full appreciation of the obstacles they face could lead to political embarrassment for the legislator, and professional oblivion for the lobbyist.
- *Never promise more than you can deliver.* As tempting as it is to make grandiose claims, if you promise a legislator that you're going to enact a grassroots letter-writing campaign to other members of Congress, you better deliver. This is why it's important for lobbyists to know their resources.
- *Listen and understand.* Words from an official that sound like a commitment could turn out to be much less, and a good lobbyist can tell the difference. So, if legislators say,

"I want to help you," or "I believe you have a good case," they're expressing their support—but not their commitment to your cause.

- *Work with staff.* In Chapter 9, we'll see just how busy members of Congress are. Their schedules make them dependent on their staff for decision making and processing a heavy workload. Personal relationships with members of Congress are important and may be an ego boost, but working with their staffs can clear the way to get things done.
- *Spring no surprises.* Politicians hate surprises. Their staff members hate surprises. And lobbyists who do their homework can avoid unpleasant surprises.[*]

[*] Bruce C. Wolpe and Bertram J. Levine, *Lobbying Congress: How the System Works,* 2nd ed. (Washington, DC: CQ Press, 1996), 13–19.

▶ **subgovernments** (see p. 237)
Another term for iron triangles, which captures the specialized (and often hidden) relationship among lobbyists, members of Congress, and bureaucrats, who share mutual professional and policy interests and objectives.

on the mutual gratification of the needs of the three participants, and they can spring up around any policy area, no matter how tiny. Iron triangles capture the way interest groups can inject themselves into the heart of policy making, and they define the way interest groups held sway over government for the latter portion of the twentieth century (as we'll see in a little while, the iron lock started getting rusty as the twenty-first century approached). They're "iron" because, with each participant getting something they need from the others, there's no incentive for anyone to leave, either voluntarily or through persuasion. Figure 8-2 should give you a good idea of how they work.

As you look at the image in Figure 8-2, try to imagine lots of these iron triangles, encompassing all sorts of policy areas, and you can perhaps get a feel for how subgovernments could easily become their own little mutually beneficial worlds, operating autonomously from all other subgovernments.

Where's the competition in a system like this, the clash of interests that Madison said was supposed to produce policy to serve the greater good? Critics say it isn't there. For instance, it's easy to imagine that there are common interests among, say, Lockheed Martin Corporation (one of our top fifty PAC contributors and a major manufacturer of missile systems), the Pentagon, and members of the House and Senate Armed Services Committees. Lockheed Martin has a commercial interest in selling its systems to the military, and the Pentagon has a professional interest in expanding and upgrading its stockpile of weaponry. Members of Congress serving on the Armed Services subcommittee that handles acquisitions of military hardware have a political interest in having expensive weapons systems constructed in their districts because it means jobs for their constituents.[45]

▶ **revolving door**
A consequence of the close relationships between interest groups and government officials that makes it possible for lobbyists to become government officials charged with regulating the organizations they once worked for, or for government officials to become lobbyists who influence friends in their former agency.

Mutual interest keeps this small community together. Mutual expertise stemming from a shared knowledge base, combined with the natural, human enterprise of networking, can perpetuate the community through a **"revolving door"** in which it would not be uncommon for officers of Lockheed Martin to be prime candidates for service as ranking Pentagon officials (where human nature says they would look favorably on projects developed by their former employer), or for former Pentagon officials to use their expertise and connections to become lobbyists for Lockheed Martin, working closely with their one-time associates in government to promote corporate interests. This is why iron triangles are sometimes called "cozy triangles." See Box 8-7 on page 240.

Through cooperation, mutual interests are protected and everyone in a small, closed, iron-triangle community can get something they want. Nonetheless, it's reasonable to have

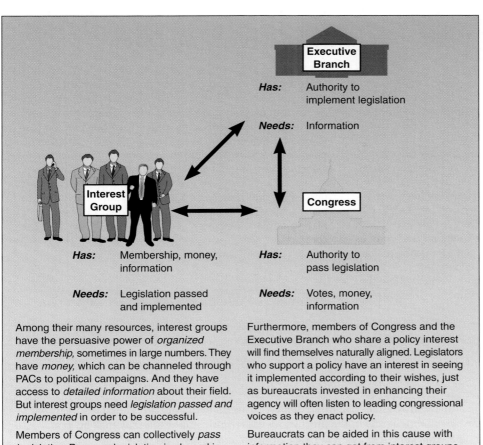

Figure 8-2
Here's Why They Call Them "Iron"

Among their many resources, interest groups have the persuasive power of *organized membership,* sometimes in large numbers. They have *money,* which can be channeled through PACs to political campaigns. And they have access to *detailed information* about their field. But interest groups need *legislation passed and implemented* in order to be successful.

Members of Congress can collectively *pass legislation.* Because legislation is shaped in committees, iron triangles are typically said to operate through the congressional committee structure. But, individually, members of Congress need the *votes* of large numbers of people, *money* to run for reelection, and *information* to do their committee work intelligently and effectively.

Similarly, bureaucrats in the Executive Branch have the authority to *implement legislation.* Implementing legislation can be detailed, technical work, and like members of Congress, bureaucrats in the Executive Branch need *information* to do their jobs intelligently and effectively.

Furthermore, members of Congress and the Executive Branch who share a policy interest will find themselves naturally aligned. Legislators who support a policy have an interest in seeing it implemented according to their wishes, just as bureaucrats invested in enhancing their agency will often listen to leading congressional voices as they enact policy.

Bureaucrats can be aided in this cause with information they can get from interest groups, in exchange for favorable implementation of policy.

Members of Congress can look to interest groups for votes from their membership, PAC money for reelection, and information to assist them in the details of legislating, in exchange for their determined effort to pass legislation supported by the interest groups.

Iron triangles hold tightly together because each participant has resources that benefit the other two, while benefiting, in turn, from the resources the other two participants can offer.

doubts about whether the common good is best served by decisions made in this manner. Political scientist Theodore J. Lowi calls the system of subgovernments "interest group liberalism," a contorted version of pluralism in which public policy becomes the sum total of the combined self-interested actions of interest groups that can lock in to the political system. To Lowi, self-serving interests replace—but do not speak for—collective interests, which ultimately silences our voices in favor of the voices of the organized and connected.

If you look at some of the following characteristics of "interest group liberalism," you can get a sense of the consequences of the iron-triangle system, as interest groups have worked their way to the heart of the political system, where their demands can be translated into official policy.

- Because interest groups are organized, representation is based on organization. That means large interests with a lot of the resources we were talking about before will

Box 8-7   The Vice President and the Revolving Door

Y ou can look to the Bush White House for a good illustration of the "revolving door." Long before he was vice president, Dick Cheney was a young chief of staff to President Ford, a member of Congress from Wyoming, and defense secretary to President Bush (senior).

While serving as defense secretary, Cheney oversaw the easing of a restriction on outside contractors providing maintenance and construction services to military bases. The first of those contracts went to a company called Kellogg, Brown & Root—a subsidiary of Halliburton, a Texas oil company.

When Cheney left Washington after his time in the Bush (senior) administration, he spent time in the private sector as CEO of Halliburton. He brought with him a Pentagon military assistant who became a senior vice president with jurisdiction over Pentagon contracts.[*] Other high-ranking Defense and State Department personnel were brought in as lobbyists and consultants. Kellogg, Brown & Root secured billions in government contracts over the next few years.

Cheney brought his Halliburton connection with him when he returned to Washington in 2001. As the Defense Department developed plans for global antiterrorism bases, billions of dollars in contract work were awarded to Kellogg, Brown & Root. Critics charge that the contracts are a gravy train for a politically connected firm. They argue that the cost will be far higher than if the Pentagon's own construction operation handled the job; the contractor is permitted to make a 9 percent profit and is not subject to public oversight.

Because criticism like this suggests the revolving door is unseemly, politicians like to keep it from public view. They're often successful. For his part, Vice President Cheney denies playing a role in helping Kellogg, Brown, and Root land the contracts.[†]

[*]Robert Scheer, "Dick Cheney's Slimy Business Trail," *Salon,* July 17, 2002. You can find the article at http://www.salon.com/news/col/scheer/2002/07/17/cheney/.

[†]Pratap Chatterjee, "The War on Terrorism's Gravy Train," *CorpWatch,* May 2, 2002. You can find the article at http://www.corpwatch.org/article.php?id=2471.

thrive in a system like this. Issue concerns that are not represented by organized groups are losers in the process, no matter how important they may be in a normative sense: They can have no voice if they have no body.

- Because organized interests typically want to protect what they have, government policy becomes inflexible. With well-positioned friends in government, groups can exercise their power by protecting their turf, even if this is not the best result for the country or the result that would come out of true pluralist competition.

- Because organized interests typically want more of what they have, they will make demands on government that can result in the need for more or bigger agencies to handle growing implementation needs. As the size of government is the sum total of its agencies, bureaus, and the like, it means that interest groups become the driving force behind the growth of the bureaucracy, assuring new programs, agencies, and regulations.

- Because organized interests operate independently of each other, each in their own subgovernment, the sum total of their separate actions becomes government policy. There's no overall plan, no sense of how government officials might make overarching decisions that address collective interests rather than a laundry list of individual interests.[46]

As an example of how interest groups can frustrate broad national interests, take the matter of "big government," which we know is an idea that's not part of American political culture. Many Americans complain about large government bureaucracies, and opinion polls invariably demonstrate wide support for cutting back the bureaucracy. Every president for the past thirty years has pledged to make government more efficient (Carter) or smaller (both Bushes), or saw it as the enemy (Reagan), or promised to reinvent it (Clinton). These positions generated popular support.

However, the bureaucracy has not gotten smaller—in large part because no president can seriously undermine subgovernments without running the risk of alienating the members of Congress who derive important political resources from the interest groups that would lose out if the president's popular plan were enacted. As we'll see in Chapter 9, no president can afford to do this on a wide enough scale to make a meaningful difference

> ### Box 8-8 The Expanded Community of Abortion Lobbying

The abortion issue provides a good example of how new groups have been pulled into an issue area that was once exclusively the province of a few single-issue interest groups primarily concerned with abortion law.

Traditionally, single-issue groups, like the ones we discussed earlier when we talked about abortion as a zero-sum issue, were the only players in the abortion lobby. "Pro-life" groups like the National Right to Life Committee lobbied against "pro-choice" groups like Planned Parenthood. The ramifications of abortion policy have since seeped into other areas of policy, particularly as medical technology has advanced, bringing new groups into the mix.

Interest groups concerned with health care policy became engaged in abortion lobbying as it arose as a topic in discussions about reforming the health care system. The Committee for the Separation of Church and State became involved in the issue—despite not having a position on abortion rights, women's rights, or health care issues—when it became concerned that a religious dimension to some abortion lobbying jeopardized the church/state boundary.

Doctors and researchers engaged in addressing infertility became intertwined with the abortion issue when their medical approaches became entangled with abortion legislation. Abortion procedures can be involved in infertility approaches that include implanting or using drugs to produce, then selectively terminate, multiple embryos. As a consequence, interest groups representing doctors, nurses, hospitals, and medical schools have engaged in lobbying in the abortion arena in an effort to represent the interests of those involved in reproductive medicine. More recently, questions over medical research using fetal tissue have thrust a new community of scientists into the abortion debate.[*] The result is a wide-ranging policy community involving a wealth of organized interests whose primary concerns are matters other than abortion rights.

[*]Laura R. Woliver, "Abortion Interests: From the Usual Suspects to Expanded Coalitions," in Allan J. Cigler and Burdett A. Loomis, eds., *Interest Group Politics,* 5th ed. (Washington, DC: CQ Press, 1998), 327–342.

to the size and scope of government. So, a broadly held collective interest falls victim to the logic of "interest group liberalism."

8-8 Triangles or Networks?

If you were reading carefully earlier, you might have picked up the reference to the iron lock getting rusty as the twenty-first century approached. This doesn't mean that subgovernments have disappeared, or that revolving doors have stopped rotating. Nonetheless, the interest group community has become more diverse, broad issues have drawn interest groups into policy areas they once ignored, new public interest groups have emerged, and many iron triangles have given way to more broadly defined **issue networks.** In an issue network, there are more players, and more light comes in from the outside. Interest groups with competing agendas have access to the system, opening the range of possibilities for how government will respond to an issue.

What changed to bring this about? For one thing, as the problems that government addresses became more complex, the needs of interest groups became more complicated, causing them to expand their relationships with officials. Many smaller triangles by necessity became larger webs.

Add to this the emergence in your lifetime of greater diversity among interest groups—most notably the rise of public interest groups, which now have a say in the direction of policy making—and you have the makings of a more complex system. At one time, environmental policy would not have been made with input from groups like the Environmental Defense Fund and Population Zero because they simply did not exist. Today, agendas of groups like these are included in broader policy networks that in a previous generation would have been restricted to the agendas of groups lobbying to avoid the cost of environmental regulation.[47] See Box 8-8.

Does this mean that the interest group system has become more pluralistic? At the very least, it means it has grown more fluid. Does this mean it has become more open and representative?

Writing in 1960, political scientist E. E. Schattschneider said that interest groups simply do not represent most people because the number of groups is exceedingly small, especially when you compare it with the range of interests and concerns that people have.

> **issue network** A fluid policy community permeable to a wide range of interest groups, permitting a broad array of policy outcomes.

Because, as we know, those with more resources are more likely to participate, he says the interest group system is both narrow and tilted toward the interests of well-to-do individuals. This is especially so when you compare the interest group system to broad-based political parties, which appeal to a more general range of concerns.[48]

We've seen how political parties have been declining in strength, and it seems that interest groups walked into the void created when party reform unintentionally undermined the controlling grip of party elites.[49] Interest groups now work closely with political parties and often coordinate their efforts, with business groups and religious conservatives aligning with the Republican Party and unions aligning with the Democrats. Reliance on campaign contributions and voter mobilization efforts, commonplace among such groups as the Christian Coalition for Republicans and the AFL-CIO for Democrats, blends interest group tactics with party politics.

Does this lead to more broad-based representation? It doesn't change the fact that interest groups remain narrowly focused and speak for defined segments of the population. It does return an element of competition to the system that was missing when subgovernments were more prominent. It's up to you to decide whether the system is broad-based enough to be considered pluralistic.

8-9 Does Access Equal Influence?

One way to approach the pluralism question is to determine whether the access interest groups have to the political system translates into influence over politicians—or more specifically, how much influence it permits over politicians. We already know that access is a group's ability to open doors to political officials, and there should be no doubt that between PAC contributions and the exercise of mutual interests, officials grant access to interest groups. Influence is another matter, though. To have **influence** is to have the ability to shape the decisions of political officials. Influence when successfully applied means getting things you want, and it's what all those PAC contributions are *intended* to produce.

There's evidence that this happens, at least some of the time. Journalist Jeffrey H. Birnbaum has covered money and politics for over twenty years, and he tells of the role interest groups played in the Republican takeover of the House of Representatives following the 1994 "Contract with America" election:

> When Republicans took control of the House of Representatives in January 1995 after forty years in the minority, they reached out to their most loyal backers—in large measure their *financial* backers—and rewarded them with seats at the table. And they, in turn, used that position to help House Republicans pass Newt Gingrich's Contract with America, which was, in effect, their wish list, ranging from limits on corporate lawsuits (a favorite of the U.S. Chamber of Commerce) to an increase in tax breaks for stay-at-home moms (beloved by the Christian Coalition). The point is that moneymen are *players*. They aren't figures lurking in the background, plotting political intrigue. They are central to the drama. They make a difference in the way laws are made and implemented.[50]

Birnbaum says interest groups may have the greatest sway over those few but important policy decisions that are not determined by local concerns (a senator from Kansas could never vote against wheat interests) or by clear partisan divisions. When a representative does not have an unambiguous direction on how to vote, Birnbaum says interest group influence provides them with the crucial road map.[51] That, by definition, is influence.

While you're questioning how well the pluralist model applies to the interest group system, you might want to go back to the lists of top PAC contributors in Table 8-5 and soft-money contributors in Table 8-6, and think about who's likely to be influential in Washington. Does the influence trail seem long and varied or, as Schattschneider suggests, is influence concentrated in the hands of the few? Think also about public interest groups and whether they fill in enough gaps to compensate for the possibility that issues of widespread concern do not otherwise have an organized voice. Ask yourself if they provide sufficient balance to special interest influences.

Also, think about whether having influence always means getting results. In some instances, like the way Halliburton apparently benefited from its relationship with Vice

influence The ability to shape political outcomes to your liking.

> Box 8-9   **Big Business in Retreat**

Tighter government regulation of corporate finances. A new, independent board with subpoena power to oversee the accounting industry. New and longer prison terms for corporate fraud, coupled with new rules that make executive officers personally liable for the truthfulness of their corporate reports. You can probably imagine that none of this was at the top of the business agenda, but these provisions were put into effect as part of what the media called the biggest crackdown on fraudulent business practices since the 1930s. In fact, it was signed into law by a pro-business Republican president.

How could something like this happen?

An exceptional confluence of political forces produced the corporate reform legislation that passed Congress and was signed into law by President Bush in July 2002 in response to the stock market free fall we mentioned in the opening section of the chapter. It started with revelations about how several prominent companies, including Enron and WorldCom, had employed a variety of accounting tactics to overstate their value. The revelations shook investor confidence and rattled the stock market, which began to collapse. Among those hurt by the falling market were millions of middle-class investors (read: voters) who sat by helplessly as the gains they had realized during the 1990s stock market boom simply vanished into the ether. It didn't help matters that the top executives of fallen companies walked away with multi-million-dollar gains by selling out before the collapse.

Political pressure came fast and furious from a number of directions. The president and vice president's political fortunes were taking a hit as their own past business practices were being scrutinized for some of the same irregularities that were at the heart of the business scandal. Congressional elections were just months away, and Democrats saw an issue they felt would work in their favor, so they began criticizing

the administration while moving their version of reform legislation through the Senate, where they were the majority party.

Congressional Republicans were worried too. In the Senate, because they didn't have a choice and had to move quickly, they got behind the Democrats' legislation even though it was far tougher than what most Republicans would ever want, and the legislation passed on a unanimous vote. In the House, the Republican majority passed a weaker version of corporate reform, but Democrats knew they had the upper hand in the effort to reconcile the different bills because Republicans couldn't face the voters without having passed something on a matter of grave concern to a lot of people. If Republicans objected to provisions of the Senate version, Democrats were ready to walk away and cast Republicans as obstacles to reform, aligned with the business interests that at the moment were a target of voter anger. So, Republicans agreed to the tougher Senate bill without changes, and the president—feeling the same pressure to do something—signed it (and took credit). This is clearly not the outcome that business lobbyists wanted, but the political momentum for action was more than they could stop.

In most cases, that is.

With Democrats running the show, computer firms who support Democratic candidates successfully lobbied to exclude a potentially expensive provision that would have changed the way they account for executive stock options. They were able to exercise leverage because they were able to convince Senate Democratic leaders that excluding this provision wouldn't undermine their claim that they were moving swiftly to write strong legislation. They had access to and influence with the right people in this battle, so they were able to turn it into results in a way that business interests with access to and influence with congressional Republicans could not.

President Cheney, it's easy to draw a clear line from access to influence to results. In other cases, the connections are not as strong. Combined annual soft-money contributions approaching $2 million could not prevent Enron and WorldCom from becoming victims of their shady business practices (see Box 8-9). All the business PAC money in the world—which, as you know, is a big number—could not keep Congress from passing a package of corporate reforms that business opposed. Sometimes, access equals influence, but it does not always equal effective influence.

Even if influential interest groups do not always get what they want, you might ask if the sum total of what interest groups do accomplish equals some version of the national interest. Supporters of the system might say that when we add everything up, we get policy that approximates what most people want. With self-interest, special interests, single interests, and public interests all having their say, the process may not be pretty to watch, but the outcome represents a mix of salient items on the public agenda. They could point to the rivalry within issue networks as evidence of ambition counteracting ambition in a competition among groups that doesn't explain all interest group interactions with government, but that characterizes how things work in large and important policy areas. From this perspective, interest groups manage to channel our concerns effectively to government and to turn some of those concerns into policies.

Detractors would argue that we get policy that approximates what a select group of people want, most notably that group with a lot of resources, who may not get everything they're after but who get an awful lot. The effectiveness of public interest groups notwithstanding, they might point to the strong track record of moneyed groups in preserving a status quo that's beneficial to them. In the process of defending what they already have, the argument goes, these groups are responsible for preempting an open debate on our national direction—a debate that could well lead to changes that entrenched groups would find expensive. Critics could point to the powerful role money plays in keeping officials from seeking this debate, noting how incumbents are reluctant to act boldly out of the (reasonable) fear that it will cost them precious dollars they need to underwrite outsized election expenses. From this perspective, interest groups not only fail to represent the greater good, they're responsible for making the political process stall out.

▶ **dealignment** The weakening of party affiliation, signified by an increase in the number of people who call themselves independents.

We could also look at the trend toward partisan **dealignment** that we talked about in Chapter 6 in the context of the entrenchment of special interests in the political system. As party allegiance weakens, we know there are more nonaligned voters who will not automatically vote for one party or another. As parties and interest groups become more intertwined, it's possible that candidates become more responsive to the concerns of the interest groups that help them with the resources they need to get elected rather then to the concerns of nonaligned voters. This helps cast our politics adrift, leaving voters feeling alienated. An article in the *Washington Post* about the strength of independent candidates in Minnesota makes this claim:

> Neither Republicans nor Democrats have a clear majority in Minnesota because neither party is successfully appealing to the majority—a diagnosis that could apply to other states. Instead, strategists try to build winning coalitions from relatively narrow interest groups—a few percent here and there. The parties draw their energy from the extreme wings, left and right. . . . The result, so far, is an ever-growing middle, untethered, restlessly seeking candidates with whom it can connect.[52]

As we understand more about how the major branches of government operate, we'll be better positioned to decide what results when interest groups interact with government officials and what the ramifications are for how those officials act. We've suggested that members of Congress, for instance, are overburdened with work and that a lot of what lobbyists do can greatly simplify their lives. This is surely a good thing for representatives. But is it a good thing for us? We're ready to turn now to Part 4, where we'll find the background we need to consider a question like this, as we put a human face on the institutions of the federal government, starting in Chapter 9 with Congress.

Chapter Review

Interest groups are specialized organizations of individuals with common purposes who seek to advance their objectives in the political process. Unlike political parties, their objectives are narrowly defined, and they operate outside the political system. Interest groups engage in lobbying legislators and bureaucrats, attempting to exert influence over the shape of public policy.

Groups promoting economic self-interest constitute the largest number of interest groups, with business, trade, and professional groups leading the way. Business groups generally support Republicans, while unions provide a vital source of support for Democrats. Noneconomic groups promote a variety of single issues and ideological concerns, and include civil rights and public interest groups that advocate agendas designed to advance the pubic good.

Some people will elect to join interest groups for the purposive benefit of being part of something they believe in, but many will not. Because the benefits of interest group membership are often collective goods that are not limited to members, many groups offer incentives in the form of selective benefits to get people to join. Unions operating closed shops can get members to join through coercion.

Professional lobbyists do the work of interest groups, employing a range of inside and outside strategies. Inside strategies revolve around face-to-face interactions with officials and can include such things as testifying at congressional hearings, helping to draft legislation, presenting technical information to legislators and bureaucrats, or generally remaining in touch through direct personal contact. Outside strategies involve mobilizing members to pressure officials and can include a range of activities from engaging in public relations efforts to publicizing legislative voting records to endorsing candidates to, in unusual cases, engaging in protests or demonstrations. Financial contributions of hard and soft money made through PACs comprise an important part of lobbying as well. Unions top the list of PAC contributors, while businesses top the list of soft-money contributors.

Lobbying often brings to mind the application of pressure by interest groups on members of Congress (interest groups are sometimes called pressure groups for this reason), but a lot of lobbying is cooperative. Iron triangles, or subgovernments, describe mutually beneficial relationships among lobbyists, legislators, and bureaucrats who share legislative interests. Each has resources needed by the others, leading them to form lasting bonds of mutual self-interest. The emergence of public interest groups and the growing complexity of policy questions have picked the lock on some iron triangles, opening some policy areas to broader issue networks. Nonetheless, interest groups continue to use access to the political process to wield influence over political decision making.

Those who feel interest groups do not exercise undo influence over the process point to the fact that even the most powerful and wealthy groups do not get everything they want, and that enough interests have a place in the system to provide a rough approximation of the pubic interest. Critics say interest groups exercise too much influence and, through the lack of direct competition between groups, undermine the pluralist ideal of policy development stemming from competition over ideas.

Key Terms

access (p. 228)
bureaucracy (p. 233)
collective goods (p. 226)
dealignment (p. 244)
efficacy (p. 227)
elitism (p. 216)
executive branch (p. 233)
federalism (p. 221)
free rider (p. 226)
influence (p. 242)

inside strategies (p. 228)
interest groups (p. 215)
iron triangle (p. 237)
issue network (p. 241)
libertarianism (p. 222)
lobbying (p. 215)
lobbyists (p. 217)
McGovern-Fraser Commission (p. 222)
outside strategies (p. 228)
pluralism (p. 216)

pressure groups (p. 215)
purposive benefit (p. 227)
Religious Right (p. 223)
revolving door (p. 238)
selective benefits (p. 226)
soft money (p. 233)
special interest groups (p. 215)
subgovernments (p. 237)
trade associations (p. 217)
zero-sum policy (p. 221)

Review Questions

Note: You can find the correct answers to these questions by taking the quiz and then submitting your answers in the Online Edition. The program will automatically score your submission. If you miss a question, the program will provide the correct answer, a rationale for the answer, and the section number in the chapter where the topic is discussed.

1. James Madison made all of the following claims about factions *except*
    a. a faction is a majority of people whose interests conflict with the minority.
    b. people naturally group into factions.
    c. the causes of faction "are sewn into the nature of man."
    d. the best way to handle factions is to allow them to compete with each other in a system where the clash of interests would require compromise.
2. Most interest groups lobby on behalf of
    a. business.
    b. unions.
    c. single issues.
    d. the public interest.
3. One way to distinguish noneconomic interest groups from economic interest groups is
    a. there are more noneconomic interest groups.
    b. there are fewer noneconomic interest groups but they raise and spend more money than economic groups.
    c. noneconomic groups are not exclusively devoted to the promotion of self-interest.
    d. noneconomic groups include unions and government groups.

4. A zero-sum issue precludes
    a. lobbying.
    b. influence.
    c. compromise.
    d. access.
5. If you join the Sierra Club because you're concerned about the condition of the environment, you're motivated by
    a. selective benefits.
    b. purposive benefits.
    c. collective goods.
    d. coercion.
6. The American Association of Retired Persons (AARP) extends membership to people many years away from retirement because it allows them to increase all of the following resources *except*
    a. organization size.
    b. access to public officials.
    c. media attention.
    d. information.
7. Which of the following is an example of a lobbyist using an "outside" strategy?
    a. testifying at a legislative hearing
    b. attending Washington social events
    c. drafting legislation
    d. publicizing a legislator's voting record
8. Subgovernments are characterized by all of the following *except*
    a. flexible government policies.
    b. a revolving door between agencies and interest groups.
    c. a bias toward organized interests.
    d. the mutually supportive sharing of resources among interest groups, Congress, and the bureaucracy.

9. Subgovernments have diminished in prominence because
   a. business groups have come to prefer issue networks.
   b. public interest groups have emerged as an important legislative force.
   c. interest groups lack the resources to maintain iron-triangle relationships.
   d. the zero-sum nature of most policy making necessitates a more complex relationship between legislators and lobbyists.

10. Access is related to influence in that
   a. access is always necessary for influence.
   b. few groups have access to policy makers, but many have influence.
   c. influence is always necessary for access.
   d. access permits influence, which always produces results.

In Their Own Words

You might be interested in examining some of what the following authors have said about the topics we've been discussing:

Birnbaum, Jeffrey. *The Money Men: The Real Story of Fund-Raising's Influence on Political Power in America.* New York: Crown Publishers, 2000. An easy-to-read journalist's account of money in politics, which bridges our discussions of interest groups and political parties.

Cigler, Allan J., and Burdett A. Loomis, eds. *Interest Group Politics,* 5th ed. Washington, DC: CQ Press, 1998. A good overview of topics related to interest groups from a wide range of perspectives.

Kollman, Ken. *Outside Lobbying: Public Opinion and Interest Group Strategies.* Princeton, NJ: Princeton University Press, 1998. If you're interested in knowing more about the outside strategies interest groups employ, this is a good choice.

Lowi, Theodore. *The End of Liberalism: The Second Republic of the United States,* 2nd ed. New York: Norton, 1979. An interesting and influential argument about how interest groups have emerged as central to the political system and the consequences this poses for democracy.

Mahood, H. R. *Interest Groups in American National Politics.* Upper Saddle River, NJ: Prentice Hall, 2000. This well-written overview of interest group activity includes, among other topics, a discussion of PAC influences, an analysis of the strategies interest groups employ, and a review of elitist and pluralist perspectives on interest groups.

Olson, Mancur. *The Logic of Collective Action: Public Goods and the Theory of Groups.* Cambridge, MA: Harvard University Press, 1965. This seminal work on interest group formation considers the question of why people join interest groups if they can be a "free rider" and benefit without joining.

Schattschneider, E. E. *The Semisovereign People: A Realist's View of Democracy in America.* New York: Holt, Rinehart and Winston, 1960. Another seminal work addressing how the nature of organizations limits political involvement and input.

Schlozman, Kay Lehman, and John T. Tierney. *Organized Interests and American Democracy.* New York: Harper & Row, 1986. A widely cited overview of organized interest groups featuring an original survey of the attitudes of Washington lobbyists.

Wolpe, Bruce C., and Bertram J. Levine. *Lobbying Congress: How the System Works,* 2nd ed. Washington, DC: CQ Press, 1996. If you ever thought you'd want to be a lobbyist (and even if you never did), this book offers a practical guide to the basics.

Notes

1. "Accountants Attack Senate Reform Bill," *Los Angeles Times,* July 19, 2002.
2. All are registered as interest groups. For a complete list, go to http://www.opensecrets.org/lobbyists/indus.asp?Ind=N and click on the industries in the table for the names of specific groups and how much they spent on lobbying activities in 2000.
3. H. R. Mahood, *Interest Groups in American National Politics: An Overview* (Upper Saddle River, NJ: Prentice Hall, 2000), 26–28.
4. Kay Lehman Schlozman and John T. Tierney, *Organized Interests and American Democracy* (New York: Harper & Row, 1986), 70.
5. Ibid., 70–71.
6. Mahood, *Interest Groups,* 32–34.
7. You can track the issue by going to the American Bar Association website at http://www.abanet.org/poladv/priorities/health.html. The AMA's side of the story may be found at http://www.ama-assn.org/ama/pub/category/6087.html.
8. Opensecrets.com, at http://www.opensecrets.org/industries/indus.asp?Ind=K (legal community) and http://www.opensecrets.org/industries/indus.asp?Ind=H (health care).
9. See the AFL-CIO website at http://www.aflcio.org/aboutaflcio/about/.
10. Opensecrets.com, at http://www.opensecrets.org/pacs/sector.asp?txt=P01&cycle=2000.
11. Mahood, *Interest Groups,* 29–30.

12. Is a city or county close to your heart on the lobbyist list? Find out at http://www.opensecrets.org/lobbyists/indusclient.asp?code=W03&year=2000.

13. Public Citizen has recently been involved in such an action, as you can see by going to its website at http://www.publiccitizen.org/publications/release.cfm?ID=7172.

14. Such an action is ongoing, as you can see at http://www.aclu.org/Privacy/Privacy.cfm?ID=10160&c=131, the American Civil Liberties Union website.

15. Jeffrey M. Berry, *The New Liberalism: The Rising Power of Citizen Groups* (Washington, DC: Brookings Institution Press, 1999), 25–28.

16. Ibid.

17. You can access the Cato Institute home page at http://www.cato.org/about/about.html.

18. You can access the People for the American Way Foundation website at http://www.pfaw.org/pfaw/general/default.aspx?oid=163.

19. You can access the Christian Coalition website at http://www.cc.org/about.cfm.

20. James L Guth and others, "Thunder on the Right? Religious Interest Group Mobilization in the 1996 Election," in Allan J. Cigler and Burdett A. Loomis, eds., *Interest Group Politics*, 5th ed. (Washington, DC: CQ Press, 1998), 169–192.

21. No, I'm not making this up. See Paul E. Johnson, "Interest Group Recruiting: Finding Members and Keeping Them," in Cigler and Loomis, *Interest Group Politics*, 36.

22. By the way, if you want to seriously consider joining the Sierra Club, you can get more information online at https://ww2.sierraclub.org/membership/.

23. Mancur Olson Jr., *The Logic of Collective Action: Public Goods and the Theory of Groups* (Cambridge, MA: Harvard University Press, 1965).

24. Jack Walker, *Mobilizing Interest Groups in America: Patrons, Professions, and Social Movements* (Ann Arbor, MI: University of Michigan Press, 1991).

25. Olson, *Logic of Collective Action*, 75–76.

26. Burdett A. Loomis and Allan J. Cigler, "The Changing Nature of Interest Group Politics," in Cigler and Loomis, eds., *Interest Group Politics*, 5th ed., 12.

27. Schlozman and Tierney, *Organized Interests*, 150.

28. Bruce C. Wolpe and Bertram J. Levine, *Lobbying Congress: How the System Works*, 2nd ed. (Washington, DC: CQ Press, 1996), 63–64.

29. Beth L. Leech and Frank R. Baumgartner, "Lobbying Friends and Foes in Washington," in Cigler and Loomis (eds.), *Interest Group Politics*, 5th ed., 217–233.

30. Ernest Wittenberg and Elisabeth Wittenberg, *How to Win in Washington: Very Practical Advice about Lobbying, the Grassroots, and the Media* (Cambridge, MA: B. Blackwell, 1990), 109–110.

31. Schlozman and Tierney, *Organized Interests*, 150.

32. Ken Kollman, *Outside Lobbying: Public Opinion and Interest Group Strategies* (Princeton, NJ: Princeton University Press, 1998), 109–110.

33. Ibid., 29.

34. Kelly Patterson, "The Political Firepower of the National Rifle Association," in Cigler and Loomis, eds., *Interest Group Politics*, 5th ed., 136.

35. Kollman, *Outside Lobbying*, 75.

36. Mahood, *Interest Groups*, 71–77.

37. Ibid., 74–75.

38. Opensecrets.org, at http://www.opensecrets.org/pubs/bigpicture2000/top_contrib/pac.ihtml.

39. Opensecrets.org at http://www.opensecrets.org/pacs/topacs.asp?txt=A&Cycle=2004.

40. The Joint Victory Campaign raised funds for two liberal advocacy groups, America Coming Together and the Media Fund. See opensecrets.org at http://www.opensecrets.org/527s/527cmtes.asp?level=C&cycle=2004.

41. Thomas B. Edsall, "FEC to Allow 'Soft-Money' Exceptions," *Washington Post*, June 21, 2002, sec. A.

42. *Washington Representatives*, 26th ed. (Washington, DC: Columbia Books, 2002).

43. Mahood, *Interest Groups*, 48–49.

44. Wolpe and Levine, *Lobbying Congress*, 10–11.

45. Mahood, *Interest Groups*, 16–17.

46. Mahood, *Interest Groups*, 16–17; and Theodore J. Lowi, *The End of Liberalism: The Second Republic of the United States*, 2nd ed. (New York: Norton, 1979), 57–61 and 310–313.

47. Mahood, *Interest Groups*, 20–21.

48. E. E. Schattschneider, *The Semisovereign People: A Realist's View of Democracy in America* (New York: Holt, Rinehart and Winston, 1960).

49. Burdett A. Loomis and Allan J. Cigler, "The Changing Nature of Interest Group Politics," *Interest Group Politics*, 1–32.

50. Jeffrey H. Birnbaum, *The Money Men: The Real Story of Fund-Raising's Influence on Political Power in America* (New York: Crown Publishers, 2000), xiii, emphasis in original.

51. Ibid., 11.

52. David Von Drehle and Dan Balz, "GOP, Democrats Locked in Race toward Decline," *Washington Post*, August 4, 2002, sec. A.

Congress

9

9-1 Introduction

You don't spend a lot of time thinking about Congress, do you? You're not alone. Many people are capable of having a great day without giving any thought to the workings of Congress, the presidency, the bureaucracy, or the court system. You may well be one of them. However, because we tend not to pay too much attention to our political institutions, it's easy to misinterpret what they do and how they do it.

A place like Congress can seem totally unrelated to our everyday experiences, when, in fact, in many important ways, it's a lot like places that are very familiar to us—your university, for instance—filled with people doing their best to find a way to fit in, manage their time amidst great pressure to do way too much, and avoid making mistakes that could hurt their future careers. If this sounds a little bit like some of what you face in school, it's because you have a lot more in common with members of Congress than you probably think.

In the pages ahead, we'll explore some of those similarities. We'll look at who gets to serve in Congress—the people who choose to run in elections and the characteristics of those who win. We'll examine how new members (called freshmen, just like in school) adjust to unfamiliar surroundings. We'll take some time to figure out what members of Congress do: what it means to serve in Congress, to be part of the congressional leadership, and to handle an unbelievable amount of work—way more than anyone can do at any one time (this may sound familiar to you, too). For some members, the work is just too much, and they decide to drop out, despite the thrill and privilege of serving in Washington. We'll figure out why.

When people do take the time to think about Congress—or when pollsters ask them to think about it—responses are typically negative, at least when they think about Congress as a large, disorganized group of 435 representatives and 100 senators. In a 1992 survey, only 24 percent of those responding had a positive opinion of all members of Congress. However, two out of three people evaluated their *own* representative *positively*.[1] In another study taken in 1998, the comparable figure was even higher—82 percent.[2] So, when we put a single human face on the institution, we're much more likely to react positively. As we'll see, Congress is a complex and chaotic institution, but it can be appreciated as the scene of hundreds of individual human dramas.

9-2 Getting to Congress—Who Wins and Why?

Many things determine the composition of that relatively small group of people who represent us in Congress. Candidates have to be motivated to run. They need to be willing to put everything in their lives on hold for up to a year so they can knock on doors, make phone calls, plead for money, give speeches, eat large quantities of mediocre chicken, and engage in all the campaigning activities we talked about in Chapter 7. Even if potential candidates have the passion to serve, they still may not run if they're not a good match to their district—say, if the candidate is a Democrat in a heavily Republican area.

9-2a Drawing the Lines

The first step in determining who gets to Congress happens before a single candidate decides to run, when lines are drawn on a map that determine the partisan composition of each district that will send someone to Congress. Congressional districts are drawn every ten years following the release of the decennial census. The Constitution requires that each state have at least one House district, with each district represented by a single member (each state, of course, also has two senators). In states with more than one House district, each district has to include roughly the same number of people.

This sounds pretty uninteresting and straightforward, but in fact, the way district lines are drawn can go a long way to determining who gets elected, so the process of **redistricting** is the basis of some pretty intense political battles. For starters, states that gain or lose large numbers of residents in the ten years since the previous census may gain or lose congressional seats.[3] Other states may see significant shifts in their populations, like from cities to suburbs. New lines need to be drawn to reflect these changes, a process that can lead to redrawing the boundaries of many or all previous districts.

> **redistricting** The process by which congressional districts are redrawn every ten years following the release of new census data.

If computers did redistricting, it would be pretty dull, but people do it—elected officials with an interest in stacking the deck in favor of their party. District lines can be drawn in lots of ways to satisfy the population requirement, and the governors and legislators in each state who are responsible for redistricting will look for the best ways to divide the opposition while putting majorities of their supporters in as many districts as possible. See Box 9-1.

Redistricting is a complex process that takes place in several rounds and draws a lot of attention from interested parties. Because of federalism, each state has its own procedures for redistricting. A few rely on nonpartisan boards to draw the lines, but most commonly, the governor and state legislators draw district boundaries. Because of the stakes, it's not uncommon for interest groups to get into the act and lobby for boundaries that will help sympathetic candidates. Often, the courts have the final say, either because the governor and legislators couldn't arrive at a plan or because there's a question about the legality of the new districts. It's not uncommon for the courts to completely overturn the work of the legislature. It's also not impossible for a group challenging a redistricting plan to seek relief in a court that's historically supportive of their position.[4]

In 2002—the first congressional election year following the 2000 census—Republicans were well positioned to take advantage of the opportunity to draw new district lines. By controlling the governorships of twenty-seven states and holding majorities in at least one legislative house in thirty-four states, Republicans believed they could strongly influence many redistricted maps. Their political superiority turned out to be balanced by demographic factors, though, like increases in the numbers of Hispanic and African American voters, who tend to favor Democrats.[5] In the end, Republicans were able to turn the playing field to their advantage in some states, like Pennsylvania and Michigan, but nationally, the 2002 redistricting battles ended up largely as a partisan wash.

When states lose House seats, unless an incumbent retires, it's inevitable that two incumbents are going to be thrown together in a newly redrawn district, forced to fight against each other for their political lives. Depending on which party has the political advantage in drawing the new districts, incumbents of the same party could be forced to battle it out in a primary, or incumbents of different parties could be pitted against each other in the general election. In 2002, we saw both types of spectacles, and it got ugly. Because (as we'll see) incumbents can generally depend on an easy ride back to Congress, redistricting can cause a sudden and unexpected end to a House career.

In Michigan, the longest-serving House member, seventy-six-year-old Democrat John Dingell, was forced into a primary against a more liberal four-term incumbent, Lynn

► *Box 9-1* Texas Republicans versus the "Killer D's"

With the nation deeply divided along partisan lines, and with a handful of closely divided congressional districts determining which party gets to run Congress, any plan to tinker with congressional boundaries can lead to open political warfare. Nowhere was this more evident than in Texas, where Republicans sought to redraw congressional district lines in the summer of 2003—two years *after* the issue had been revisited at the scheduled time following the decennial national census.

Republicans were in control of the Texas governorship and legislature for the first time in generations, leaving them in a strong position to have their way with the boundaries for their thirty-two congressional districts that favored Democrats by a narrow 17–15 margin. With direction and encouragement from national Republican leaders, Texas Republicans flexed their muscles. They proposed legislation to redraw district lines in such a way as to secure as many as five additional Republican seats in the U.S. Congress.

Democrats saw this as a power play and cried foul, saying it was unprecedented for a political party to alter district lines except in response to a new census. Republicans countered that they weren't doing anything that Democrats wouldn't have done when they ran the state—they were simply exercising their right as the majority party to draw the congressional map. The Republicans were in a perfect position to play hardball politics because with the governorship, state Senate, and state House under their control, they held all the cards. Except one.

Texas Democrats couldn't block passage of the redistricting plan, but if enough of them failed to report for work, they would deny the legislature the quorum (or minimum number of members) it needs to conduct business. So, in May 2003, fifty-one Democratic members of the Texas House fled to Oklahoma, where they stayed until the end of the regular session of the legislature. Now it was the Republicans' turn to cry foul, but there was nothing they could do, as Oklahoma's Democratic governor welcomed and protected the Texas Democrats. The fifty-one refugees became partisan folk heroes to opponents of the redistricting plan, who dubbed them the "Killer D's" (for Democrats).

The battle wasn't over, though. That summer, Texas Governor Rick Perry called a special session of the legislature for the purpose of considering the redistricting bill. This time, eleven Democrats in the Texas Senate exiled themselves to New Mexico, again preventing a quorum and bringing the special session to a halt. Said one state senator, speaking from a hotel in Albuquerque, "We're availing ourselves of a tool given to us by our Texas constitution to break a quorum. It's not about Democrats, it's about democracy."[*]

Perhaps, but in the end, the Democrats' tool turned out to be a delaying tactic that only worked as long as everyone stayed together. Texas Republicans knew that the opposition couldn't remain in New Mexico forever, and they eventually won the redistricting war when the Democrats' unity cracked. In the 2004 election, their efforts bore fruit, as five additional Republicans were elected to Congress from Texas, sending four incumbent Democrats to early retirement.

[*]"Texas Senate Democrats Flee Session," *Washington Post*, July 29, 2003, sec. A.

Rivers. The two ran neck and neck, as unions, environmentalists, and women's groups that normally unite behind Democrats took sides and battled it out in an intense race that Dingell narrowly won. In Connecticut, Nancy Johnson, a powerful Republican incumbent, was forced by redistricting into a general election battle with James Maloney, a popular Democratic incumbent. In a normal year, both would be expected to win reelection easily. In the redistricting year of 2002, Johnson defeated Maloney after a bitterly fought race.[6]

9-2b It Looks Like Some Kind of Serpent

What do you see in Figure 9-1?

Sometimes partisan state legislators go out of their way to construct districts like this in order to give one party a distinct edge, pulling voters from small enclaves of partisan supporters and allowing district lines to meander over a wide range of territory in the most unlikely fashion. It's called **gerrymandering,** and it's an age-old political practice whose origins predate the actions of nineteenth-century Massachusetts Governor Elbridge Gerry, who in 1811 signed off on a salamander-shaped district (hence the name gerrymander) designed to be a safe haven for Jeffersonian Democrats. Does it work? The evidence is mixed, although a case can be made that strong candidates from the disadvantaged party are discouraged from running in gerrymandered districts.[7] Certainly, partisans from both sides of the aisle continue the practice because they *believe* it gives them an edge.

Since 1990, some states have engaged in the controversial practice of **racial gerrymandering,** drawing district lines that group together far-flung populations of African

► **gerrymandering** Drawing district lines in a way that favors the electoral prospects of the party in power.

► **racial gerrymandering** Drawing district lines in a way that combines disparate populations of minority groups in order to guarantee representation by those groups in Congress.

American or Hispanic voters for the purpose of assuring representation for these groups. The effort began in response to language added to the Voting Rights Act in 1982 prohibiting states from diluting the voting power of racial minorities, which was interpreted broadly in some states as a green light to gerrymander in order to bolster the influence of minorities.

The effects of racial gerrymandering cut two ways. Although the districts it created sent generally liberal African American and Hispanic representatives to Congress, *neighboring* districts that lost these voters became more conservative. In 1992, seven districts represented by Democrats lost at least 10 percent of their African American constituents to racial gerrymandering. By 1996, all seven were represented by Republicans—enough to help Republicans hold the majority in Congress.[8] Ironically, a procedure designed to enhance minority representation in Congress had the effect of diluting minority influence because, as we will see, influence in Congress flows to those in the majority.

Because it's so controversial, racial gerrymandering has been the subject of court challenges. A sharply divided Supreme Court has voted to curtail the process on multiple occasions, overturning some of the more far-reaching districts on the grounds that they represented an effort to segregate voters.[9] By the end of the 1990s, a number of states reacted to the Court's position by redrawing the boundaries of racially gerrymandered districts to reduce the concentration of minority voters.

9-2c Who Runs for Congress—And Who Makes It?

Against this backdrop of partisan maneuvering over district boundaries, a potential candidate needs to take a good, long look in the mirror before embarking on an expensive and time-consuming public campaign that could easily come to nothing. If you were thinking of running, you'd want to take a look at who lives in the district and assess how closely your background and political views match your would-be **constituents.** You would also need to make sure the timing is right for a run, especially if you have to abandon a lower office where you could probably win reelection.

A big part of this calculation involves whether or not you will have to face an **incumbent.** Challengers don't like to face incumbents, and for a good reason. With the contacts they have and with their ability to raise large sums of money, incumbents are hard to topple. Since World War II, better than nine in ten incumbent representatives and almost eight in ten incumbent senators seeking reelection have been victorious—a figure that (as we'll see later on) has only been increasing in recent years. Incumbents may play to their strength by raising large sums of money in an effort to scare off strong competition,[10] and the strategy is likely to work, unless the nation is going through an economic downturn or experiencing a moment when voters are unhappy with the status quo.

Some candidates are self-starters who make the judgment to run on their own, although to have a chance at success it helps if they have a high level of **name recognition** from a previous job. This favors amateurs who've previously worked as television commentators, actors, athletes, or at other high-visibility jobs. Many candidates are encouraged to run by political party operatives, who (as we mentioned in Chapter 6) engage in candidate recruitment as one of the formal functions of political parties. Candidates with strong personal qualities that attract voters are always in demand. Lately, given the high cost of campaigning and the central role of money in winning elections, Democrats and Republicans are looking more frequently toward wealthy candidates who can self-finance campaigns. Fame and fortune do not guarantee electoral success, of course, but as Box 9-2 indicates, candidates with these qualities are in great demand because of the prospect of what they could deliver on Election Day.

As a constitutional requirement, you have to be at least twenty-five to serve in the House of Representatives, a resident of the state from which you're seeking election, and an American citizen for seven years. You don't have to live in the district you represent as long as you live in the same state, although as a practical matter, it's bad politics to ask people to vote for you when you live somewhere else. To be a senator, you have to be at least thirty and an American citizen for nine years.

Figure 9-1
Is It a Serpent?
Actually, it's a congressional district. Specifically, it's Florida's Third Congressional District, stretching through parts of nine counties, in some cases not much wider than a highway. But it sure looks like a serpent.

constituents Individuals living in a district represented by an elected official.

incumbent An official presently serving in office.

name recognition An informal measure of how much the public is aware of a candidate or elected official, based on how widely people are able to identify who the candidate or official is.

Box 9-2   Today's Candidates: Fame and Fortune

When you're the one-time chairman of the investment firm Goldman Sachs, you can afford to pump $60 million of your personal fortune into your quest for a U.S. Senate seat. That's exactly what Jon Corzine did in his successful 2000 attempt to become Senator Jon Corzine of New Jersey. Though a political novice, Corzine's personal fortune made him an attractive candidate to the Democratic Party as it attempted to hold the Senate seat being vacated by Senator Frank Lautenberg. For his part, Corzine said the money was necessary to level a political playing field that included opposition from a former governor and a well-known member of Congress, each of whom had far greater name recognition.*

In 2002, Republican Party officials helped pave the way for former Red Cross President Elizabeth Dole to run for the North Carolina Senate seat left vacant by the retirement of Republican Senator Jesse Helms. In Dole's case, name recognition rather than personal wealth was the reason for Republican enthusiasm. The former transportation secretary, presidential candidate, and spouse to 1996 Republican presidential nominee Bob Dole is a highly visible and widely well-regarded public figure (despite her unsuccessful attempt to win the 2000 Republican presidential nomination), and something of a celebrity in her own right. Having a candidate of that stature and visibility helped Republicans hold on to Helms' seat.

*You can read about what Senator Corzine says about his self-funded campaign online at http://www.opensecrets.org/newsletter/ce74/interview.asp.

---

pluralism The theory that government responds to individuals through their memberships in groups, assuring that government is responsive to a wide range of voices. People who subscribe to this position believe the wide distribution of resources in society drives the decisions government officials make.

elitism The theory that government responds to a small, stable, centralized hierarchy of corporate and academic leaders, military chiefs, people who own big media outlets, and members of a permanent government bureaucracy. People who subscribe to this position believe the actions of regular citizens, like voting and joining groups, simply mask the real power exercised by elites.

substantive representation The ability of a legislator to represent the agenda or interests of a group to which he or she does not personally belong.

On paper, this appears to open membership in Congress to most of us (at least in a few years). However, with the emphasis on wealth and popularity in candidate recruitment, it shouldn't be too surprising that Congress is far from a mirror of American society. (See Box 9-3.) What may be surprising is how different it is from the country as a whole on such things as occupation, education, religion, race, and gender. Remember our earlier discussion about **pluralism** and **elitism**? When it comes to the characteristics of congressional members, background similarities favor some groups over others, even though Congress is a less homogeneous place than it was when you were born. Check out Figure 9-2 for some demographics on the 106th Congress that convened in 1999.

So, what of these apparent inequities between congressional members and the populations they represent? If Congress is largely an educated, professional, white, male and Protestant bastion, can it function as a representative institution? The answer depends on how we look at the idea of representation. As a descriptive matter, the answer would have to be no because the congressional class picture doesn't look very much like the portrait of America. As a substantive matter, the answer could still be yes. To engage in **substantive representation,** a member of Congress has to be able to act in the interests of groups to which he or she does not belong. If you believe that a white representative can promote the interests of African Americans or Hispanics, that a male representative can advance the agenda of women's groups, or that a college-educated lawyer can advocate the concerns of blue-collar workers, then you may be able to make the case for Congress as a representative institution, despite the fact that it draws its members from a nonrepresentative elite group of Americans.[11]

9-3 Adjusting to Congress

Think back for a minute to freshman orientation, to what it felt like to be in a new place surrounded by new people. Maybe you traveled far from home, and everything looked new. Maybe you're a commuter, or going to a local school, and you had to confront new ways of doing things and new people as you made the transition from high school to college. Remember how you felt? Many people experience moments of frustration or confusion, even sadness or homesickness, during those first crazy days of college. You want to fit in, but everything is new, and you're not always sure how to do it.

As distant and remote as Congress may seem, new members are human and experience many of the same feelings. No place can compare with Congress (just like nothing exactly compares with college), so arriving there several months after experiencing the thrill of being elected (much like arriving at school several months after the excitement of getting that acceptance letter) can leave a person bewildered.

> ### Box 9-3   Changes to the All-Male Club

I n 1992, an unprecedented number of women were elected to Congress in what the press dubbed the "Year of the Woman." Ever since, although the vast majority of members are male, there has been a notable female presence in an institution that previously functioned as something of an all-boys club.

The presence of female lawmakers has made some differences in the ways of Congress. Legislative matters considered to be "women's issues," like family leave during pregnancy and illness, funding for breast cancer research, and workplace discrimination, have found their way onto the agenda.* Some have made it into law.

It takes time to accumulate power in Congress, and more than a decade later, some women are beginning to do just that. In 2001, Representative Nancy Pelosi became the first woman elected to a leadership position in Congress when she was chosen to be the House Democratic Whip; one year later, she became House Democratic leader.

As in any institution, though, change can be slow and those who are there at the start can find it frustrating. Marjorie Margolies-Mezvinsky, a member of the Class of 1992, has stated that she and her female colleagues suffered indignities

from congressional workers and some male members who treated them as second-class citizens. She recalls an experience she had during a presidential State of the Union Address to a joint session of Congress, which she felt provided a good measure of how far women in Congress had come—and how far they still had to go:

> I remember sitting with my colleagues, looking around at all 435 of us. The women stood out in a truly dramatic fashion, and I thought, my gosh, people are going to turn on the tube tonight and see us and they're going to realize that the rest of the nation has begun to inch itself into this body. I was sitting next to North Carolina Democrat Martin Lancaster, who was trying to point out somebody on the other side of the aisle, and he said, "He's the guy with the receding hairline, gray hair." And I said, laughing, "You've eliminated nobody!" My point is that the people who have always been outside of the system are now beginning to infiltrate it. There aren't enough of us, but we're working on it—all the time.†

*Roger H. Davidson and Walter J. Oleszek, *Congress and Its Members*, 7th ed. (Washington, DC: CQ Press, 1999), 130–131.

†Marjorie Margolies-Mezvinsky, *A Woman's Place: The Freshmen Women Who Changed the Face of Congress* (New York: Crown Publishers, 1994), 38–39.

One member relates the story of getting to her new office to find it unfurnished. She was advised by a senior member to roam through the office building corridors looking for discarded furniture. So, she did, furnishing her office with stuff other people had cast off, not unlike the way some people furnish an off-campus apartment.[12]

One way we try to fit into a new place, be it college or Congress, is by learning the ways of the institution, the **norms** people live by as they try to get along with each other. Norms are unspoken and unwritten rules of behavior. No one has to teach us about them—we observe norms and internalize them, and if we violate them, we'll probably hear about it from a friend or from someone in a position of authority. For instance, it may be okay for you to get a visit from a friend at midnight while you're living at school. The norm for late-night visits when you're back at home with your parents over the summer could be something quite different. No one has to tell you this—you know what's going on—although your parents probably will say something if you violate the norm.

Norms help people ease into a new institution, but they also serve the institution by helping it run more smoothly. Many people don't get to choose their freshman roommate, and sometimes, things don't work out too smoothly, but by observing the norms for good roommate behavior, you can make the best of a bad situation. In much the same way, members of Congress do not get to choose their colleagues—voters in other districts do—but they have to find a way to work together. Norms help smooth the way for members who might not choose each other as colleagues if they had the option.

The five norms in Table 9-1 have existed in Congress for decades. Take a look at the table for a definition of each norm and an explanation of how it benefits members of Congress.

The last norm you looked at—reciprocity—can assume a couple of specific forms. The example in the table, where members trade support for each other's pet projects, is called **logrolling,** evoking the kind of cooperation people exhibit when they stand on a log and try to roll it down a river.[13] Logrolling helps members get the kind of projects for their home districts that constituents love—and that can only help their reelection prospects—

norms Unspoken rules of behavior that people adhere to in an institution like Congress that allow people to fit in and help the institution run smoothly.

logrolling A form of reciprocity in which members of Congress exhibit mutual cooperation for each other's pet projects.

Figure 9-2
Who Gets to Serve?

Source: Data regarding the 106th Congress are from Roger H. Davidson and Walter J. Oleszek, *Congress and Its Members,* 8th ed. (Washington, DC: CQ Press, 2002).

Occupation

Not too many organizations can claim that better than 40 percent of its members are lawyers (apart from law firms, of course), but that's the case in Congress, where lawyers far outnumber all other professionals. Business people come in second, followed by educators.

Remember we said that celebrities make good candidates? Recent congresses have included several astronauts, including former Senator John Glenn; former football players like Representative Steve Largent; and former baseball players like Senator Jim Bunning, who once pitched a perfect game in the major leagues.

On the other side of the coin, farmers, laborers, and blue-collar workers are severely underrepresented in Congress.

Education

Unlike the population at large, almost everyone in Congress is college educated. Two-thirds have graduate or professional degrees.

Religion

Almost everyone in Congress has a religious affiliation, compared with about 70 percent of Americans. Most are Protestant, although more than one-quarter of the membership is Catholic (slightly more than the nation as a whole) and about 7 percent are Jewish (almost three times the national figure).

Race

Even with advances by minority groups in recent years, Congress is still overwhelmingly white. Only 7 percent of members are African American and 5 percent are Hispanic, roughly half the percentage of their numbers in the population. Out of 535 representatives and senators, there are six Asian Americans and two Native Americans.

Gender

Once a nearly exclusive male club, Congress has seen an influx of women in recent years. Still, at about one-eighth the membership of Congress, women are well under-represented with respect to the population.

▶ **compromise** A form of reciprocity in which members of Congress exhibit flexibility over their legislative objectives in exchange for future flexibility from their colleagues.

▶ **integrity** A key component of reciprocity in which members of Congress are expected to keep their word with each other and honor their commitments.

although as Box 9-4 points out, it's often the case that one member's beneficial project is a case of wasteful spending to those in other districts who do not benefit.

Reciprocity can also be expressed through **compromise,** or flexibility, over an issue that a member may feel strongly about—like the wording of legislation. Since what goes around comes around, members have an investment in compromising with each other, with the expectation that at some later time, others will offer the same courtesy to them. The same is true with **integrity,** which is a critical component of reciprocity. You probably know from personal experience how you feel about a friend who promises something and doesn't deliver. As one member put it, "you don't have to make these commitments [to other members], . . . but if you *do* make them, you had better live up to them."[14]

TABLE **9-1**

Congressional Norms

Norm	Example	Benefit
Specialization	Becoming an expert on global warming	Congress addresses a wide range of complex issues and needs members' expertise to handle them intelligently.
Legislative work	A subcommittee chairman being prepared for a hearing	If some members are not prepared, the burden of their negligence is passed to other members.
Courtesy	Referring to a member you may personally dislike as "honorable" or "distinguished"	Kind words cool the heat of conflict and keep debate moving forward.
Institutional patriotism	Avoiding getting entangled in a bribery scheme	Discredit brought upon the institution undermines every member's base of power.
Reciprocity	An urban representative voting for agricultural price supports with the expectation that rural representatives will support aid for mass transit	When everyone reciprocates, everyone benefits; if no one reciprocated, no one would benefit.

▶ **specialization** The legislative norm that members of Congress should become experts in a legislative field.

▶ **legislative work** The legislative norm that members of Congress should stay on top of the work required by the committee that deals with their area of specialization.

▶ **courtesy** The legislative norm that members of Congress should treat each other with respect and avoid personal attacks, regardless of how much they may disagree.

▶ **institutional patriotism** The legislative norm that precludes members of Congress from acting or speaking in ways that would discredit the institution.

▶ **reciprocity** The legislative norm that encourages members of Congress to support each other's initiatives, even if there is no direct political benefit in doing so.

Remember, norms are enforced by the people in the institution, and stay in effect because the institution benefits along with its members. So, specialization is held in place by virtue of the tremendous amount of detailed work that Congress has to handle and the fact that it's in everybody's interest for the work to get done, which can best be accomplished if every member contributes. Likewise, the norm of doing legislative work is held in place by the fact that everyone benefits if everyone does a small share of the heavy lifting. If you've ever been in a group project where not everyone contributed equally (but everyone was in the same boat when it came to getting graded), you can probably appreciate how easily resentment could be generated toward those who did less work. Since congressional legislative work is like a big group project, specialization keeps the institution moving forward while minimizing those resentful feelings.

Of course, if norms no longer benefit those involved, they can evolve out of existence. One norm that's not in Table 9-1 is **apprenticeship,** even though it was a hallmark of how Congress did business for the better part of the twentieth century. Freshmen members were expected to refrain from voicing their opinions in committees, introducing legislation, or drawing attention to themselves as they learned the ropes from senior members and acclimated to the ways of Congress. Apprenticeship maintained institutional stability and was a great way for new members to learn other norms.

If you happen to be a freshman, you probably don't think much of a norm that has you speaking only when you're spoken to and holding back on what you came to Congress

▶ **apprenticeship** The legislative norm that says freshmen members of Congress should limit their activity and defer to senior members as they learn the ways of the institution. Apprenticeship is no longer enforced in Congress.

> ### Box 9-4   The Golden Fleece
>
> One commonly expressed knock against Congress is its tendency to waste money. You can probably see how logrolling could encourage spending on dubious projects because to win the support of colleagues for a pet venture, members only have to signal that they want support for a particular item (and show their willingness to support the pet projects of others). They don't have to justify the importance of the undertaking, and other members who want their projects supported aren't in a position to raise questions.
>
> Although you can always find someone ready to defend the merits of any congressional action, some things seem on the surface to be just a bit more dubious than others—projects that are criticized as being **pork-barrel** items because of their apparent wastefulness. In 1975, former Wisconsin Senator William Proxmire began issuing a monthly "Golden Fleece" award to those projects funded by Congress that in his view seemed particularly wasteful. His purpose was to bring logrolling out of the shadows of congressional deal making and to shine light on pork-barrel spending in order to curtail it.
>
> What kinds of things did Proxmire single out over the years? How about $1.2 million to preserve a Trenton, New Jersey, sewer as an historical site; $20,000 to build a limestone replica of the Great Wall of China in Bedford, Indiana; and $6,000 for a report instructing the Army on how to buy a bottle of Worcestershire sauce!*
>
> ▶ **pork barrel** Wasteful or unnecessary spending that can result from logrolling. Whether something is a pork-barrel project or a valuable use of taxpayer dollars may depend on whether you stand to benefit from it.
>
> *An interest group called Taxpayers for Common Sense has a more complete list online at http://www.taxpayer.net/awards/goldenfleece/history.htm.

to accomplish. If you had a large enough group of like-minded peers, you might want to do something about it.

That's essentially what happened to apprenticeship in Congress. In 1974, in the wake of the Watergate scandal that rocked the Nixon administration, a huge freshman class of 103 young, reform-minded newcomers was elected to Congress. They felt they had a mandate to change things in Washington, and they weren't about to be quiet or wait their turn. Backed by the strength of their large numbers, they fashioned themselves as a new type of member, more entrepreneurial and outspoken, as they brushed aside apprenticeship as an antiquated norm.[15]

Today, the effects of their independent spirit continue to change the ways of Congress and strain some of the other norms. Members have become more media-savvy and self-promotional; many (especially in the Senate) devote great energy to positioning themselves to run for president. In the process, they may be absent from Congress more than in the past, and fail to keep up with their legislative work the way you may at times let extracurricular activities cut into the time you devote to your homework.[16] Likewise, when Republicans took control of the House of Representatives in 1994, testy moments followed between the two parties as Democrats, not used to being in the minority, chafed at what they considered heavy-handed tactics employed by the new Republican majority who were rewriting the informal rules of the institution. Courtesy was severely tested in the process, but perhaps because in the end everyone benefits more from cooperation than conflict, the norms that had developed over the decades were bent but not broken. Even as partisanship produces tension in Congress, members continue to rely on existing norms to find their place in a complex institution.

9-4 Serving in Congress: How Congress Works

New members of Congress arrive at an institution that's been shaped by centuries of history, but the broad contours of what Congress does—and what members are expected to do in Congress—can be traced to the parameters established in the Constitution.

Article I of the Constitution establishes a **bicameral** legislature with a House of Representatives (created in Section 2) and a Senate (created in Section 3) as the two branches. As constitutional articles go, it's pretty long because it takes great pains to spell out exactly what the Congress would do. The powers specifically granted to the House and Senate are called **enumerated powers,** and they go well beyond what the national legislature could do under the Articles of Confederation.

▶ **bicameral** A legislature composed of two houses.

▶ **enumerated powers** Powers directly granted to Congress by the Constitution.

> **Box 9-5   How Congresses Get Their Numbers**

Maybe the phrase "the first Congresses" in the first paragraph of Section 9-5 sounded a little funny to you. If it did, it's because you're probably used to thinking of Congress as a singular (albeit bicameral) entity. It is, of course, but when we talk historically about Congress, we classify each group that serves together as "a Congress," and we give it a number.

So, the First Congress served from 1789–1791, with the first year constituting the first "session" of the First Congress and the second year constituting the second session. Why two years? That's the stretch between congressional elections. The entire House of Representatives is up for election every two years (a short period designed to keep representatives responsive to public opinion). One-third of the Senate is also up for election every two years (a full Senate term is six years). When they reconvene in January following the election, the new collection of members—the "new Congress"—gets a new number.

The 109th Congress was elected in November 2004 and sworn in January 2005, to serve until January 2007.

Enumerated powers include the power to tax, with all revenue bills required to originate in the House of Representatives, the body designed to be closer to the people. Other important enumerated powers include the ability to regulate commerce among the states and with other nations, coin money, raise a military, declare war, establish post offices and roads, and create a court system below the Supreme Court (which is itself established by the Constitution).

Then Article I gives Congress the ability "To make all Laws which shall be necessary and proper for carrying into Execution the foregoing Powers, and all other Powers vested by this Constitution in the Government of the United States, or in any Department or Officer thereof." This "necessary and proper" clause has been interpreted over the years as a broad grant of **implied powers,** which has allowed Congress to consider matters that could not have been anticipated by the Constitution's authors.

Despite going into detail on a range of congressional responsibilities, the Constitution leaves it up to each house to determine how it's going to put into place the procedures to do its job. The Constitution dictates that a majority of members of a house is required to form a quorum (which, as we noted in Box 9-1, is the number of members required for a legislative body to meet and do business) and that each house has to keep a record of its public votes and proceedings, but it leaves to each house the ability to determine how to do business. As a consequence, the two houses operate under a different set of rules.

9-4a How the House Works

In a simpler time, the first Congresses (see Box 9-5) debated important matters as a group, and if legislation was deemed appropriate, a committee was established to discuss the nuts and bolts. However, it didn't take long before the need to process a growing workload led to the establishment of permanent or **standing committees,** which were organized to deal with ongoing matters like budgetary or military concerns. By the 1820s, standing committees would debate legislation before it was brought before the full House.

Today, the House has nineteen standing committees (the Senate has sixteen), but even with that large number, many of the thousands of proposals introduced each session for consideration never make it to committee. Because most legislation needs to go through the committee process to make it to the floor for a vote, all those measures that never get a hearing simply die on the vine. The relatively few proposals that make it to committee are typically sent to one or more **subcommittees** of the standing committee. The detail work of legislating takes place in subcommittees, which are specialized units suited to ongoing relationships with sympathetic interest groups of the sort we talked about in Chapter 8 when we discussed **iron triangles.** Together, the nineteen standing House committees support eighty-four subcommittees, each with its own chairperson and agenda (the Senate's sixteen standing committees support sixty-nine subcommittees).[17] Table 9-2 lists the names of the standing committees of the House, along with the number of House members serving on the committee and the number of subcommittees each

implied powers The broad constitutional grant of power to Congress that allows it to make all laws that are "necessary and proper" to carry out its enumerated functions.

standing committees Permanent congressional committees that handle matters related to a specific legislative topic.

subcommittees Subunits of standing committees that do the detail work involved in writing legislation.

iron triangle The ongoing, mutually beneficial relationship among an interest group, members of Congress sharing the interest group's objectives, and bureaucrats in federal agencies responsible for carrying out legislation pertaining to the interest group's field. Iron triangles can develop in any policy area, and many distinct iron-triangle relationships form because the federal government is responsible for a large number of policies.

TABLE 9-2

House Committees and Subcommittees

Agriculture [51 members; 4 subcommittees]

Appropriations [61 members; 13 subcommittees]

Armed Services [60 members; 5 subcommittees]

Banking and Financial Services [59 members; 5 subcommittees]

Budget [43 members; 0 subcommittees]

Commerce [53 members; 5 subcommittees]

Education and the Workforce [49 members; 5 subcommittees]

Government Reform [43 members; 7 subcommittees]

House Administration [9 members; 0 subcommittees]

International Relations [49 members; 5 subcommittees]

Judiciary [37 members; 5 subcommittees]

Resources [52 members; 5 subcommittees]

Rules [13 members; 2 subcommittees]

Science [47 members; 4 subcommittees]

Small Business [36 members; 5 subcommittees]

Standards of Official Conduct [10 members; 0 subcommittees]

Transportation and Infrastructure [75 members; 6 subcommittees]

Veterans' Affairs [31 members; 3 subcommittees]

Ways and Means [39 members; 5 subcommittees]

Source: Roger H. Davidson and Walter J. Oleszek, *Congress and Its Members,* 8th ed. (Washington, DC: Congressional Quarterly Press, 2002), 202.

committee had in 2002 (the names and sizes of committees and subcommittees may vary slightly from Congress to Congress). Notice how some of these committees have more people in them than an upper-division political science class!

If a bill fails to clear a subcommittee, it dies; otherwise, it's sent back to the full committee where it can again die if it fails to win passage. Even if it wins full committee approval, it's not out of the woods yet. That's because the House places restrictions on the terms of debate and on what bills get to move to the floor for final consideration. As with the development of standing committees, House rules on debate evolved over the years. Initially, House debate was fluid and unlimited. As the House grew in size and legislation grew in complexity, the House began placing limits on how long members could speak, and procedures were instituted to control the flow of legislation.

In the late nineteenth century, the House established a process by which legislation would be channeled from standing committees through a **Rules Committee** before it could come to the floor for debate and a vote. Despite the fact that a standing committee may have worked for months or longer on legislation, if it failed to be assigned a "rule" from the Rules Committee, it would simply disappear from legislative consideration. If the Rules Committee decides to assign a rule and bring a measure to the floor, it can set the terms of the debate, including whether amendments can be offered that would change the bill. If a bill is brought to the floor with a rule that prohibits amendments, then members have only the choice to vote the bill up or down as it's written. This gives the Rules Committee—and the political party controlling it—enormous power to set the terms of the House agenda.[18]

If an issue lends itself to short-term review, the House may establish a **select committee** (also called a special committee) to investigate. Senate rules permit the establishment of select committees as well. Select committees are established for one congressional session and then expire. Instead of reporting bills like a standing committee, they usually review a matter and make recommendations for action. For instance, prior to the start of

▶**Rules Committee** The committee of the House that channels legislation to the floor for debate and a vote on passage.

▶**select committee** A House or Senate committee established on a temporary basis to review a specific matter. Typically, select committees make recommendations but do not move legislation.

the millennium, the Senate established a select committee to investigate the much-talked-about Y2K computer problem, which threatened to shut down computer systems on January 1, 2000 if software mistakenly read the date as January 1, 1900.[19]

A member introduces legislation in the House by literally dropping it in a wooden box at the front of the chamber. Any member can do it for any reason—to advance a personal priority or the priorities of constituents or interest groups. At that point, the bill is referred to a committee or, in some cases, multiple committees that have jurisdiction over the content of the proposal. For most bills, that's the end of the line. A select few undergo the generally slow process of moving through subcommittee, where hearings are held that shape the content of the emerging bill or determine whether it will ever come to a committee vote.

These are the textbook procedures for moving legislation through Congress and, well, this is a textbook, so what better place than here to describe it? Not every bill travels that route, however. There are House procedures that allow the leadership to circumvent the committee process entirely, which they may do in politically sensitive situations. It happened in 1996, when House Republican leaders moved a last-minute budget resolution directly to a floor vote following an unsuccessful confrontation with President Clinton over spending priorities. There's also a procedure called a **discharge petition,** which, if signed by half the membership (218 representatives), plucks a bill from committee and brings it to the House floor for a vote. It's usually very difficult to get half the House to go along with a discharge petition, although it can happen—like it did in 2001, when supporters of campaign finance reform forced a vote on the campaign reform bill that would eventually become the McCain-Feingold Act.[20]

9-4b How the Senate Works

The early Senate operated like the early House, first as a deliberative body then through the work of standing committees. Owing to its smaller size, it never faced quite the same pressures as the House to limit debate or control the flow of legislation. So, the Senate doesn't channel legislation through a Rules Committee, and senators maintain the privilege of unlimited debate time. This gives senators a legislative weapon not available to their colleagues in the House: the **filibuster,** or the ability to talk a bill to death on the Senate floor. If one or more senators simply refuse to stop talking about a matter under discussion, they can bring the Senate to a halt. A filibuster can only be ended by a vote of **cloture,** which requires a supermajority of three-fifths, or 60 percent of the Senate to enact. This means a minority of 41 senators can block a bill if they stick together and refuse to support cloture. Before the cloture provision was enacted in 1917, it was even harder to silence a senator because a unanimous vote was required to make a determined senator sit down. As Box 9-6 indicates, the filibuster can be a powerful procedure in the hands of a determined Senate minority—and a tool of last resort for outnumbered senators.

The standing committee, subcommittee, and select committee structure is much the same as it is in the House, although with fewer members, there are more committee and subcommittee leadership opportunities. Virtually every senator has a leadership role somewhere, even newly elected senators. Table 9-3 lists the names of the standing committees of the Senate, the number of senators serving on each committee, and the number of subcommittees associated with each committee, circa 2002. Notice how much overlap there is between House and Senate committees, even though each house organizes its standing committees independently.

In some cases, the House and Senate establish **joint committees** to commonly investigate or study a matter that concerns both houses. Much of what joint committees do is routine and detailed. For instance, the Joint Taxation Committee pools House and Senate staff to help with the technical details of writing tax legislation.[21]

In an entirely different context, the two houses of Congress will form **conference committees** when they pass different versions of the same legislation. The Constitution requires that the House and Senate pass identical legislation before it's sent to the president for consideration, but it's probably easy to see how that's not likely to happen when legislation has to pass separately through the network of rules and committees in each house. So, when both houses pass their own version of a bill, they form a conference

discharge petition A House procedure that forces a floor vote on legislation stalled in committee. To succeed, a discharge petition must be signed by half the House membership.

filibuster The strategy available to senators to delay or derail legislation by refusing to relinquish their time on the Senate floor. The filibuster is possible only in the Senate, where rules permit unlimited time for debate.

cloture The procedure for ending a filibuster. A cloture vote requires a 60 percent majority of the Senate.

joint committees Committees composed of members of the House and Senate that consider matters of interest to both houses.

conference committee A committee made up of members of both houses of Congress, assembled when the House and Senate pass different versions of the same legislation. If the conference committee can iron out the differences, a compromise version of the legislation is sent back to both houses for final passage. If it cannot arrive at a compromise, the legislation dies.

Box 9-6   No One Can Tell Them to Sit Down and Shut Up

When a senator has the floor during debate, he or she can talk about anything for as long as he or she wants. Although the picture of a senator reading listings from the phone book or talking about his or her grandchildren may seem funny (and, yes, it's really happened), a filibuster is serious business because it gives a minority of the Senate the opportunity to delay or prevent legislation they oppose despite the presence of majority support.

For years, the filibuster was a favorite tool of conservative senators opposed to civil rights legislation. A filibuster that lasted seventy-four days delayed the landmark Civil Rights Act of 1964 from coming to a vote. South Carolina Senator Strom Thurmond personally held the Senate floor for over twenty-four hours (a Senate record) in an unsuccessful effort to block the earlier Civil Rights Act of 1957.* In recent years, controversial legislation has routinely faced blocking tactics in a closely divided Senate, with such items as campaign finance reform, crime legislation, abortion restrictions, and agriculture funding all at some point facing filibusters from senators across the political spectrum.

Filibusters have also come into play during the judicial confirmation process. When Democrats controlled the Senate for the majority of the first two years of the Bush administra-tion, they could keep President Bush's judicial nominations bottled up in committee if they were so inclined, as we'll see in Section 9-5c, "Confirming Presidential Appointments." When Republicans regained Senate control after the 2002 election, Democrats turned to the filibuster as the only tool available to them to block court appointments. However, it was a tool they used selectively. Recognizing the danger of being painted as obstructionists by the majority, Democrats filibustered only a few Bush appointees. As a counterstrategy, Republicans repeatedly called for cloture votes, forcing Democrats to go on record numerous times against the president's appointees while attempting to chisel away at the opposition. Perhaps because only a few judges were targeted, Senate Democrats repeatedly held together to sustain their filibusters.

After padding its majority after the 2004 session, there was even talk among the Republican leadership about implementing a so-called "nuclear option" of prohibiting filibusters of judicial nominees. Such a change would represent a jarring departure from traditional methods of doing business in the normally staid Senate.

*See http://www.senate.gov/artandhistory/history/common/briefing/Filibuster_Cloture.htm.

committee made of up of representatives and senators that tries to hammer out differences between the two versions of the legislation, writing compromise language that committee members believe will be acceptable to majorities in both chambers. If they fail to do so, the legislation dies. If they succeed, the bill they produce still has to be approved by both houses.

TABLE 9-3

Senate Committees and Subcommittees

Agriculture, Nutrition and Forestry [18 members; 4 subcommittees]

Appropriations [28 members; 13 subcommittees]

Armed Services [20 members; 6 subcommittees]

Banking, Housing, and Urban Affairs [20 members; 5 subcommittees]

Budget [22 members; 0 subcommittees]

Commerce, Science, and Transportation [20 members; 7 subcommittees]

Energy and Natural Resources [20 members; 4 subcommittees]

Environment and Public Works [18 members; 4 subcommittees]

Finance [20 members; 5 subcommittees]

Foreign Relations [18 members; 7 subcommittees]

Governmental Affairs [16 members; 3 subcommittees]

Health, Education, Labor and Pensions [18 members; 4 subcommittees]

Judiciary [18 members; 7 subcommittees]

Rules and Administration [16 members; 0 subcommittees]

Small Business [18 members; 0 subcommittees]

Veterans' Affairs [12 members; 0 subcommittees]

Source: Roger H. Davidson and Walter J. Oleszek, *Congress and Its Members,* 8th ed. (Washington, DC: CQ Press, 2002), 202.

Introducing a bill in the Senate works pretty much the way it does in the House. However, because the Senate is less formal and "clubbier" than the House, individual senators have more range to influence the path of legislation. In contrast to the formal discharge petition required by the House to bypass the committee process and bring a bill to a floor vote, any senator can request that a bill go directly to the floor (in reality, though, a senator would need the support of the Senate leadership to be successful). Because the Senate doesn't use a Rules Committee to prohibit a bill from being modified during floor debate, any senator can introduce an amendment to a bill being debated on the floor—forcing the Senate to act on the amendment even if it has nothing to do with the legislation being discussed. This privilege effectively circumvents the committee process. If a senator wishes to introduce a civil rights amendment to a bill on veteran's benefits, the rules allow it.[22]

Figure 9-3 provides an overview of the whole process of how a bill becomes law. Despite procedural differences between the two houses, notice the parallel structures in place between the House and the Senate for considering legislation. Notice, also, how each step in the process provides opponents with an opportunity to derail legislation. When you think for a second about all the places where proposals can die, it's not surprising that thousands of proposals flood into Congress but only a handful become law.

9-5 Serving in Congress: What Congress Does

As the legislative branch of government, Congress has its hands in the development of both domestic and foreign policy. Of course, because power is separated among the branches of the federal government, Congress is continually engaged in a push-pull relationship with the president, sometimes spearheading the national agenda and sometimes following the president's lead.

Generally speaking, Congress is more assertive in domestic issues and follows presidential leadership in foreign affairs. Every president comes to office with a domestic policy agenda—President Bush, for instance, wanted to cut taxes and partially privatize Social Security—but members of Congress can be fairly vocal about putting their imprint on the president's ideas, rejecting the president's agenda, or advancing an agenda that's entirely different than the president's.

The two branches may act together, particularly if the president's party also runs Congress, as was the case when President Bush won approval for his tax cut proposal in 2001. As we noted in Chapter 6, though, even shared party affiliation is not a guarantee of mutual objectives. President Clinton failed to marshal support for the largest initiative of his first term—an overhaul of the health care system—even though his party controlled both houses of Congress. When Congress and the president are of different parties, congressional leaders can be in a position to steer the national agenda. When Democrats regained control of the Senate in 2001 after Vermont Senator Jim Jeffords bolted the Republican Party, the Senate immediately discarded President Bush's agenda to consider items that the president had no interest in pursuing, like campaign finance reform.

Foreign affairs are another matter. Although the Constitution gives Congress important tools for the conduct of foreign policy, it also gives a broad grant of authority to the president, and over time, the president has emerged as the premier voice in international matters. Congress has the power to declare war (something it has not done since World War II), and the Senate has the power to confirm ambassadors and ratify treaties. In turn, the president is commander-in-chief of the armed forces, and, as we'll see in Chapter 10, best positioned to move public opinion in times of international tension. As a consequence, Congress typically defers to presidential leadership on foreign and defense issues. As Box 9-7 on pages 266–267 illustrates, Congress often has very little choice but to go along with the president.

On the other hand, Congress plays a central role in several important government activities: making budgets, overseeing the actions of the bureaucracy, confirming a wide range of presidential appointments, and removing other officials from office. Let's look at each one in turn.

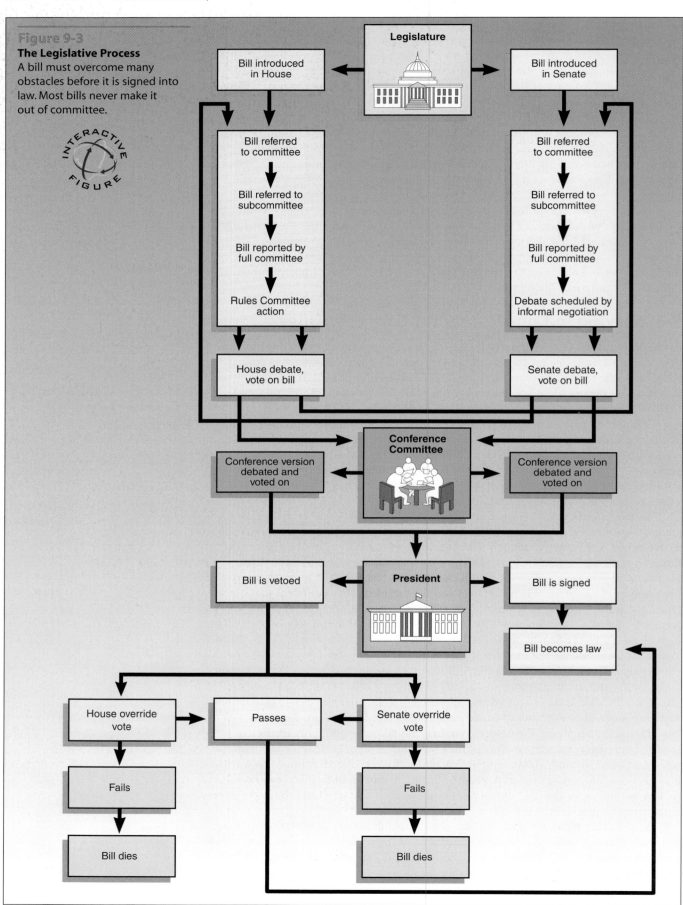

Figure 9-3

The Legislative Process
A bill must overcome many obstacles before it is signed into law. Most bills never make it out of committee.

9-5a Making Budgets

If you've ever tried to save for something or figure out how you're going to spend limited funds on a bunch of needs, then you know how tricky it can be to write a budget. Add the individual wishes of hundreds of members of Congress and the president into the mix, and it shouldn't be hard to see how writing a budget is one of the most complex, sensitive, and important things Congress has to do. Members who sit on committees with a hand in budget writing find that they are rarely lonely.

Budget writing is an annual affair that typically takes an entire year to complete. A number of committees get into the act, in keeping with the decentralized way the House and Senate function. The process has been more coordinated, though, ever since the passage of the **Congressional Budget and Impoundment Control Act of 1974.**[23] A lot of the action happens in the House and Senate Appropriations Committees, which are charged with reporting bills that determine how much money government agencies and programs will have to spend (**appropriations** refer to legislation authorizing the government to spend money).

The procedure is complex, but it follows this outline: First, the House and Senate budget committees set guidelines and budgetary priorities. Then the appropriations committees are supposed to allocate money in line with those priorities. They approve spending bills to cover the variety of items in the federal budget. If the sum of these expenditures exceeds the budgetary guidelines, the expenditures are brought into line with the budget targets through a process called **reconciliation.** For both houses to end up with the same budget, differences between them are resolved in a conference committee, after which final approval on a budget can be sought in both houses.[24]

If budget guidelines necessitate changes in tax law, the House Ways and Means Committee and the Senate Finance Committee get into the act. As the tax-writing committees of Congress, they draft legislation specifying which taxes will be raised and by how much.

Because so much money is at stake, and because real policy changes can be made by the act of budgeting, there are always a lot of congressional fingerprints on the final act. We'll take a closer look at budgeting when we talk about domestic policy in Chapter 15.

9-5b Oversight of the Bureaucracy

Congress may pass laws, but as we discussed in Chapter 8 and as we'll see in greater detail in Chapter 11, the bureaucracy is responsible for implementing laws, or carrying them out. This gives the bureaucracy a lot of freedom to interpret the intent of Congress, although Congress does have a function that can allow it to retain some control over how the bureaucracy implements legislation. It's called **oversight,** the process by which Congress reviews the actions of the bureaucracy to see that laws are being enacted as Congress intended. Most congressional oversight is carried out through the committees and subcommittees that share jurisdiction over a policy area with agencies and departments in the bureaucracy.

This sounds fairly neutral, but in fact, congressional oversight can be politically charged. The bureaucracy is part of the executive branch, and the president's political opponents in Congress can try to interfere with agencies they feel are implementing the law in accordance with the president's wishes instead of their own. Oversight can be a weapon for members of Congress who seek to diminish what they regard as excessive or unnecessary government programs. During the budgeting process, oversight can have dramatic consequences for government programs, as Congress can reduce (or threaten to reduce) funds to agencies, or put restrictions on how money is spent, all set against the backdrop of competing political and ideological agendas about what government should and should not do. In recent years, for instance, congressional Republicans have cut the budgets of programs they feel do not warrant government spending, such as Amtrak and public broadcasting.

At the other end of the spectrum, oversight can be anything but acrimonious. The cooperative nature of iron-triangle relationships can turn oversight into something of a lovefest between bureaucratic agencies and the congressional committees supposedly

> **Congressional Budget and Impoundment Control Act of 1974** An act designed to centralize the congressional budgeting process, which established current procedures and timetables for writing a budget.

> **appropriations** Legislation permitting the government to spend money that determines how much will be spent and how it will be spent.

> **reconciliation** A procedure in the budget-writing process, whereby appropriations made in a number of congressional committees and subcommittees need to be brought in line with spending targets established early in the process.

> **oversight** The process of congressional review of the bureaucracy.

Box 9-7 Input? Approval? Consent?

In late summer 2002, rumors percolated through Washington that the Bush administration had made up its mind to conduct a military strike against Iraq in the not-too-distant future. The president himself fueled these rumors, as he spoke in increasingly belligerent tones about the dangers posed by Iraqi President Saddam Hussein's efforts to stockpile biological, chemical, and nuclear weapons.

The idea of a military campaign against Hussein was controversial. Among America's allies, only Great Britain expressed public support (a position not shared by a large portion of the British public), and some members of Congress expressed concern about the United States moving ahead without the United Nations' involvement. Others in Congress felt an unprovoked attack on Iraq would constitute a serious and potentially dangerous departure from the American position to use military options in self-defense, possibly giving cover to other nations to use force against their adversaries. Still others raised questions about the risks and costs of an all-out assault, whether the administration had a workable vision for a post-Hussein Iraq, and if war with Iraq would deflect resources and attention away from the campaign against terrorism.

Against this background, the Bush administration began sending signals that it might consider taking action without congressional backing. This possibility generated a firestorm of congressional criticism, and in September, President Bush relented: He would not take action against Iraq without first consulting Congress.

What exactly did that mean? Would he ask Congress for its input and then take action against Iraq regardless of what Congress said? Would he seek a vote of approval from Congress, with the understanding that he would move against Iraq even if congressional approval were not forthcoming? Would he ask Congress for its consent to take action, and change course if it wasn't granted?

As commander-in-chief, Bush was in a strong constitutional position to order an attack on Iraq even without congressional backing. He would be doing it without a formal declaration of war, but there are many precedents for doing that, from the Korean War to Vietnam to the Persian Gulf, as Figure 1 demonstrates. He was in a strong political position as well. Many members, regardless of their views on the wisdom of an invasion, would regard a congressional vote as a demonstration of American resolve, which is why history shows that Congress is reluctant to position itself against a president who is about to commit American troops to fight overseas. This situation was no different. In fall 2002, Congress voted to support the war against Iraq that the United States would wage early the following year.

overseeing them, fueled by mutual friendships with like-minded interest groups. When this happens, congressional committees work to protect agencies from scrutiny, investigations, and loss of funding.[25]

9-5c Confirming Presidential Appointments

The Constitution simply gives the Senate the responsibility to offer "advice and consent" when the president nominates people to fill vacancies in the bureaucracy and the court system. In reality, the function of confirming presidential appointees can be an institutional and ideological tug-of-war between the legislative and executive branches, as we saw when we were discussing the filibuster—especially when senators and the president have dramatically different ideas about how conservative or liberal appointees should be.

When a presidential nomination is made, it is referred to the appropriate Senate committee for deliberation, and if approved, to the floor for a final vote. The committee holds hearings on the nominee, which are often smooth and uneventful, although they can be contentious if there is a philosophical rift between the nominee and committee members. Presidents are most likely to win approval for major cabinet-level appointments made as they come into office, on the grounds that a president has the right to appoint people of his choosing to key positions. However, even this is not guaranteed if an appointment is controversial. For instance, President Bush's appointment of conservative former Senator John Ashcroft as Attorney General angered liberal interest groups, who vocally opposed the nomination. Ashcroft was approved, but the vote was close.

Traditionally, Senate hearings center on the nominee's qualifications for office, but in recent years, almost anything goes: moral issues, personal or family background, financial dealings, medical history—any or all of these could be open for discussion. Senators looking for justification to turn down a nominee can turn almost anywhere for a rationale to vote no.[26] This is particularly true for judicial nominations, which tend to be more contentious than other presidential nominations. Box 9-8 on page 268 looks at why.

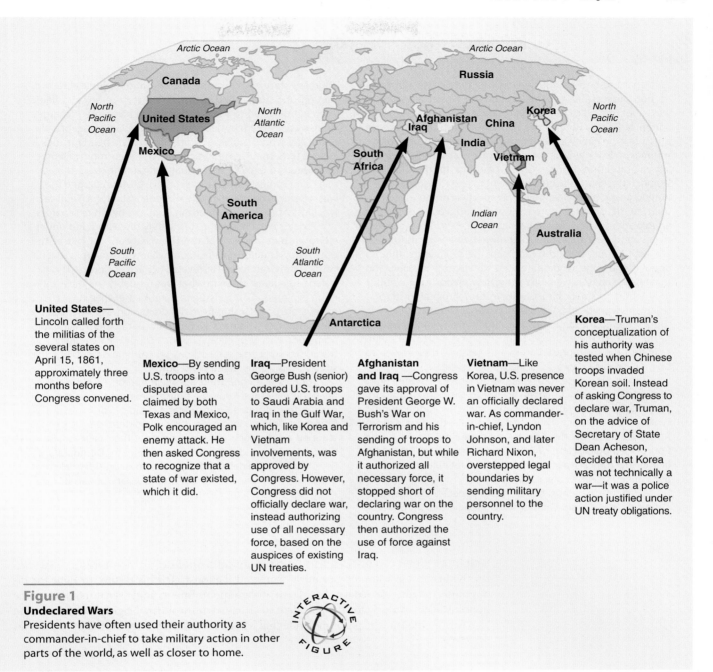

United States—
Lincoln called forth
the militias of the
several states on
April 15, 1861,
approximately three
months before
Congress convened.

Mexico—By sending
U.S. troops into a
disputed area
claimed by both
Texas and Mexico,
Polk encouraged an
enemy attack. He
then asked Congress
to recognize that a
state of war existed,
which it did.

Iraq—President
George Bush (senior)
ordered U.S. troops
to Saudi Arabia and
Iraq in the Gulf War,
which, like Korea and
Vietnam
involvements, was
approved by
Congress. However,
Congress did not
officially declare war,
instead authorizing
use of all necessary
force, based on the
auspices of existing
UN treaties.

Afghanistan
and Iraq —Congress
gave its approval of
President George W.
Bush's War on
Terrorism and his
sending of troops to
Afghanistan, but while
it authorized all
necessary force, it
stopped short of
declaring war on the
country. Congress
then authorized the
use of force against
Iraq.

Vietnam—Like
Korea, U.S. presence
in Vietnam was never
an officially declared
war. As commander-
in-chief, Lyndon
Johnson, and later
Richard Nixon,
overstepped legal
boundaries by
sending military
personnel to the
country.

Korea—Truman's
conceptualization of
his authority was
tested when Chinese
troops invaded
Korean soil. Instead
of asking Congress to
declare war, Truman,
on the advice of
Secretary of State
Dean Acheson,
decided that Korea
was not technically a
war—it was a police
action justified under
UN treaty obligations.

Figure 1
Undeclared Wars
Presidents have often used their authority as
commander-in-chief to take military action in other
parts of the world, as well as closer to home.

Senators can also drag their feet on holding hearings for nominees. Senate Democrats accused Senate Republicans of using this tactic during the Clinton administration to block liberal judicial appointees; then, Senate Republicans accused their Democratic counterparts of dragging their heels on a host of President Bush's bureaucratic and judicial nominees when they controlled the process. When the Senate fails to act on a nomination, the position simply remains vacant.

The president can attempt to fill a vacancy created by Senate inaction by appointing someone on an "acting" basis, or by making "recess appointments" when the Senate is out of session. Recess appointments don't require approval, and those appointed can serve until the end of the congressional session—but they're highly controversial. In 2004, President Bush appointed Charles Pickering and William Pryor to the U.S. Court of Appeals after both had been blocked by a prolonged filibuster staged by Senate Democrats. The

Box 9-8   "Bork" Becomes a Verb

It's hard to find a single reason why the Senate confirmation process has become so ugly—it wasn't always that way—but one place to look is President Reagan's 1987 nomination of Robert Bork to the Supreme Court. Under intense pressure from liberal interest groups who feared Bork's constitutional philosophy was too conservative, and with the ideological direction of the Court hanging in the balance, Democratic senators subjected the nominee to rigorous questioning about his philosophical perspective, pronounced him unfit to sit on the Supreme Court, and voted down his appointment. Many conservatives were livid. They claimed that a nominee's philosophy had never been grounds for Senate action, that the president had the legitimate right to appoint someone who shared his ideological outlook, and that liberal senators were distorting Bork's record and writings in an effort to smear him. Civility in the nomination process fell by the wayside as an ideological war of sorts was declared; "Bork" entered the language as a verb. To many conservatives, to be "Borked" meant to be ambushed and destroyed politically through misrepresentation and lies, and they vowed to be more media savvy and proactive next time.

Things got worse four years later, when President Bush (senior) nominated Clarence Thomas to the Supreme Court. Thomas, a conservative African American judge, would replace liberal justice Thurgood Marshall—the first African American to sit on the Court—guaranteeing a shift in the Court's ideological center. Again, interest groups on both sides of the ideological spectrum geared up for full-scale battle, determined to win at any cost.

When the hearings began, little appeared to stand in Thomas's way. A southerner who began life in poverty, Thomas's story was a compelling one, and his judicial record, though undistinguished to critics, didn't raise any red flags. Then word leaked to the press of sexual harassment charges leveled against him by a former employee, University of Oklahoma law school professor Anita Hill, and the hearings took a bizarre turn. The Senate Judiciary Committee, run by Democrats, opted to explore the sexual harassment charges as the television cameras rolled. Conservative groups charged that it was a setup; Thomas himself pointedly called it a "high-tech lynching" of an African American nominee by white senators.

Today, sexual harassment is widely discussed and understood (in part, because of the Thomas hearings), but at the time, many Americans were not familiar with the topic, so it hit with tremendous force. Hill leveled her accusations as Thomas defended against them in what was arguably the most thorough exploration of the issue to date. All the while, it was hard to separate partisanship from the discussion, as evidenced by the pattern of Thomas's Democratic detractors grilling the nominee as his Republican supporters put Hill's credibility on trial. Ostensibly, the subject was sexual harassment, but the subtext was clearly politics and power.

Thomas was confirmed, 52–48, in one of the closest Senate votes ever for a Supreme Court nominee, and he took his seat on the Supreme Court under a cloud of controversy. The bitterness of the battle never fully dissipated, even as people stopped asking each other whose story they believed. Such bitterness is on display whenever Senate Democrats or Republicans try to delay, defeat, or destroy a presidential nomination that threatens to move the judiciary or the bureaucracy in a direction they don't like.

---

action permitted two of President Bush's more contentious court nominees to take seats on the bench for a limited period of time and demonstrated his resolve to fight for his appointees. It also carried a political cost. Recess appointments anger senators, who see the appointments as a way for the president to circumvent the normal legislative process, and also further inflame the partisan divide that has characterized the appointment process for a generation.

9-5d Impeachment

impeachment The power granted to Congress to remove from office the president, vice president, judges, and other federal officials.

No political power is greater than the power to throw someone out of office, and the Constitution grants that power exclusively to Congress. **Impeachment** is a two-step process involving both houses. The House of Representatives can impeach any federal official, including the president, vice president, Supreme Court justices, and federal court judges. Impeachment requires a majority vote of the House and is similar to an indictment in court in that it charges the official with one or more counts of misconduct. Once articles of impeachment are approved, a trial is held in the Senate, where evidence is presented to support each accusation. With the chief justice of the Supreme Court presiding, the impeached official is permitted to offer a defense against the charges. At the conclusion of the trial, each senator casts one vote on each article of impeachment, with a two-thirds majority required to remove the official from office.

The Constitution is especially vague on what constitutes an impeachable offense, stipulating only "Treason, Bribery, or other high Crimes and misdemeanors." Through the years, it has fallen to others to determine what this means. Invariably, the interpretation is political because, although the impeachment process looks like a trial, the jurors are elected officials responsive to public opinion. Regardless of the merits of the case, it's politically difficult to impeach and convict an official who has a lot of popular support.

It's also the case that impeachment doesn't happen very often. It's a complicated process with a low likelihood of conviction, designed that way so that political adversaries wouldn't routinely employ it. Only seventeen officials have been impeached since the Constitution was ratified, and only seven were convicted—all federal judges.[27]

There have been only two presidential impeachment trials—Andrew Johnson in 1868 and Bill Clinton in 1998—and both took place against the backdrop of partisan politics. Johnson, a southerner who took office upon the assassination of Abraham Lincoln, was strongly at odds with a Congress unsympathetic to the South in the period following the Civil War. When Congress passed the Tenure of Office Act, requiring congressional approval before a presidential appointee could be removed from office, Johnson ignored it, believing it to be unconstitutional. The House rushed to impeach him, eager to see Johnson removed for political reasons. He prevailed in the Senate by one vote.

President Clinton's impeachment grew out of charges that he perjured himself when he lied under oath about his sexual relationship with White House intern Monica Lewinsky. Since the charges did not stem from an issue related to the president's official conduct of his office, reporters, political analysts, and constitutional scholars questioned whether President Clinton's alleged offenses were impeachable. These questions were reinforced by the political nature of the proceedings, as the House voted almost along party lines to impeach. A dramatic Senate trial concluded in Clinton's acquittal on one count of perjury and one count of obstruction of justice. Both counts failed to produce even a simple majority of senators supporting conviction.

Richard Nixon is the one president who likely would have been convicted, on charges related to his conduct during the Watergate scandal, but he circumvented the impeachment process by becoming the first president to resign from office. Nixon faced removal in the wake of evidence pointing to a broad pattern of abuse of power stemming from his participation in and cover-up of events surrounding the break-in at Democratic Party headquarters. When a bipartisan majority of the House Judiciary Committee voted to recommend that the full House impeach the president, it became apparent that Nixon lacked the votes to avoid impeachment in the House or conviction in the Senate. Had the proceedings continued, it would have been the only time in history that the gravity of the charges against a president would have compelled significant numbers of his own partisans to vote to remove him from office.

President Clinton's political fate rested with the legislative branch as the Senate met to consider the removal of a president from office for only the second time in its history.

Source: AP/Wide World Photos.

TABLE 9-4		House	Senate
Comparing the House and Senate	Number of Members	435	100
	Districts	Congressional districts	States
	Member Terms	2 years	6 years
	Elections Held	Every 2 years for everyone	One-third of Senate seats every 2 years
	Distinctive Functions	Originate revenue bills; write articles of impeachment	Ratify presidential appointments; ratify treaties; hold impeachment hearings
	Most Powerful Committees	Appropriations, Budget, Commerce, Rules, Ways and Means	Appropriations, Armed Services, Commerce, Finance

This is probably a good time to stop for a second and review the broad outlines of what we've been discussing. Let's do it by briefly comparing a few key elements of the House and Senate—see Table 9-4.

9-6 Leading Congress

When the authors of the Constitution left it up to each house to figure out how it was going to function, they didn't imagine a role for political parties because, as we know, they viewed parties as factions and assumed (or hoped) that they would never develop. As it turns out, parties mean everything in Congress. They determine who gets to lead Congress, control congressional committees, set the agenda, and set the rules. Power flows to the majority party; frustration visits the minority. For this reason, congressional leaders are highly motivated to attain and keep majority status.

In both houses, the majority is simply the party with the most seats. However, just like in congressional elections where all the representation goes to the winner, all of the leadership benefits go to the majority party. Even a one-seat advantage (like Senate Democrats had in 2001 and 2002) permits the majority party to have a majority of its members on all committees, to have its members chair all committees and subcommittees, and to have its leader set the legislative agenda. That's why when Senator Jeffords defected from the Republican Party during the 2001 legislative session and decided to become an independent who votes with Democrats on leadership issues, the entire chamber was turned on its head. Overnight, (mostly liberal) Democrats replaced (generally conservative) Republicans as leaders and committee chairs, bringing with them an entirely different set of legislative priorities and the power to have them heard.

9-6a Leadership Structure

The different traditions and procedures in the House and Senate translate into differences in the degree to which the majority party can clamp down on the minority. The Senate offers more opportunities to members of the minority party to express their will through the filibuster and through courtesies extended individual members. It operates on the principle of **minority rights,** whereby deference is granted to the concerns of those whose party does not control the chamber.

The House, in contrast, functions on a **majoritarian principle** that frustrates dissent. After more than a century of dealing with rules that permitted legislative minorities to derail legislation, the House, around the turn of the twentieth century, instituted rules that give the leadership of the majority party tight control over all proceedings.

The **Speaker of the House** is the foremost leader in the chamber. Chosen by a caucus of the majority party, then ratified by a party-line vote of the full House, "Mr. Speaker" (as

minority rights Procedures, such as those in place in the Senate, that permit members of the minority party the opportunity to resist legislative actions they oppose.

majoritarian principle Procedures, such as those in place in the House of Representatives, that limit the ability of the minority party to influence the shape of legislation or the direction of the legislative agenda.

Speaker of the House The leader of the majority party in the House of Representatives who exercises control over the operation of that branch through formal and informal means.

he is addressed) is one of the premier leaders in Washington (not to mention second in line for the presidency after the vice president). He has both formal and informal powers, which allow him to advance his priorities and the priorities of his party, regardless of the wishes of the minority. Formally, the Speaker presides over the House, resolves disputes as they arise, decides which committees will consider legislation, and determines who will serve on conference and select committees. Informally, the Speaker can influence the Rules Committee (affecting the scheduling of debate and votes on legislation), reward members for their loyalty (or punish members for their independence), influence assignments to standing committees, and function as the spokesperson for the House of Representatives in the press.[28]

Unlike other congressional leadership offices, the position of Speaker of the House is mandated by the Constitution. Article 1, Section 2 says that "The House of Representatives shall choose their Speaker and other Officers," leaving the rest of the leadership structure to evolve through custom and practice. What the Constitution does *not* say is that the Speaker has to be a member of a majority party (remember, no parties are mentioned in the Constitution) or even a member of the House. However, every Speaker has been a House member, and every contemporary Speaker has been a majority party member with many years of service in the House.

The Speaker is assisted by the rest of the majority party leadership, which, like the Speaker, is selected by a caucus of the majority party at the start of each congressional session. The key positions are the **majority leader** and the **majority whip.** The majority leader is the floor leader for the majority party, responsible for doing the everyday work of moving the party's legislative agenda through the House: lining up the support of committee chairs, gauging levels of support among House members, and persuading members to vote the party position. Because, as we mentioned in Section 6-4a, "How Parties in Government Function," we do not have **responsible parties** in government, members—even powerful committee chairs—cannot be assumed to support the positions of leadership. See Box 9-9.

The majority leader is assisted in this effort by the majority whip. The name suggests whipping up or rounding up votes, which is a good description of what the whip does. The whip reminds party members of key votes, counts heads to determine if the party position is likely to prevail, and when necessary, leans on members to vote with the leadership.

The minority party counterparts to these leadership positions are the **minority leader** and **minority whip.** As leaders of the party out of power, their roles parallel their counterparts in the majority but without the ability to shape the legislative agenda. So, the minority leadership advocates the policy alternatives of the minority as they look for opportunities to develop alliances with wayward members of the majority in an effort to frustrate the majority party's agenda.

Leadership in the Senate operates a little differently. There is no counterpart to the Speaker of the House. Instead, the Constitution makes the vice president of the United States the presiding officer of the Senate, where his formal title is president of the Senate, and his one formal power is the ability to cast tie-breaking votes. However, unless it looks like the Senate is heading for a tie vote, you probably won't find the vice president anywhere near the Senate. In his absence, the chore of presiding over the Senate falls to the **president pro tempore,** a mostly honorary position that typically goes to the longest serving member of the majority party. Apart from being third in line for presidential succession behind the vice president and the Speaker of the House, the president pro tempore has no formal powers and typically finds the job of presiding over the Senate to be as dull as the vice president does. That's why, on any given afternoon, it's not unusual to find junior senators presiding over the proceedings, not as an honor but as an obligation assumed by those with the least standing in the chamber.

In the absence of a powerful figure like the House Speaker, the Senate is led by the majority leader and majority whip. They determine the items on the legislative agenda and work to keep their majority in line. It can be a harder job than what befalls their House counterparts because of the Senate's less hierarchical traditions that permit individual senators to go their own way. The minority leader and minority whip function much like their

▶ **majority leader** The number-two leadership position in the House of Representatives and the number-one leadership position in the Senate. In the House, the majority leader is the chief assistant to the Speaker; in the Senate, the majority leader is the chief leader on a par with the House Speaker.

▶ **majority whip** The number-three leadership position in the House of Representatives and the number-two leadership position in the Senate. In both instances, the whip is responsible for mobilizing party members to support the leadership on key issues.

▶ **responsible parties** Political parties whose legislative members act in concert, taking clear positions on issues and voting as a unit in accordance with their stated positions.

▶ **minority leader** The number-one leadership position for the opposition party in the House of Representatives and Senate, whose responsibilities mirror those of the majority leader but without the ability to set or advance the legislative agenda.

▶ **minority whip** The number-two leadership position for the opposition party in the House of Representatives and Senate, whose responsibilities mirror those of the majority whip.

▶ **president pro tempore** The senator charged with the honorary duty of presiding over the Senate in the absence of the vice president of the United States.

Box 9-9　Going Their Own Way

Remember, even when we don't have a divided government, it can be difficult for members of the same party in Congress and the White House to work as one because of the way political parties function in government. They're flexible. They're not ideological. They're not responsible parties, which is simply to say that party leaders cannot impose an agenda on their members in the House or Senate, and legislators will not automatically heed the wishes of a president of their party. This fact has been the cause of a lot of anguish over the years as party leaders have tried—some more successfully than others—to keep their members in line.

For example, in 2003, President Bush and Republican congressional leaders faced a revolt by a few congressional representatives of their own party over the Medicare prescription drug benefit discussed in Chapter 8. Republican leaders kept the final vote on the measure going all night in a frantic effort to convince enough recalcitrant conservatives to give their president a victory. One reporter recalled feverish efforts by House Speaker Dennis Hastert and his lieutenants:

> The House's reigning Caesars were running around in circles, going back once, twice, and three times to conservatives who were clearly hard "no's" and had been that way for days. Tom Feeney, R-Fla.? No thanks. Steve Chabot, R-Ohio? Didn't like the means-testing provision. Todd Akin, R-Mo.? The [Republican] whip, fellow Missourian Roy Blunt, had him out in the Speaker's lobby all alone and was getting nowhere.[*]

It took close to three hours and a few personal phone calls by the president to round up enough votes to secure passage of the measure. In time, however, the victory raised serious questions about the tactics used by the House leadership and the administration—including the prospect that Republican leaders had employed bribes and threats to change the votes of reluctant members, and that the White House knowingly withheld the true cost of the measure to keep conservatives on board—in an extreme example of what can happen because congressional representatives are free to go their own way.

[*]Mike Viqueira, "Medicare Vote Got Surreal in House," MSNBC News, November 24, 2003, at http://msnbc.msn.com/id/3606311/.

House counterparts. Figure 9-4 on pages 274–275 shows the House and Senate leaders after the 2004 presidential election.

Maybe you're getting the sense that political parties have emerged as the organizations that hold Congress together, structure its operations, and help to centralize an institution staffed by hundreds of ambitious people from different regions of the country with varying personal agendas and objectives. Without parties to provide structure, it's quite possible that the legislative branch would be a much harder place to run—particularly in the Senate, where customs and procedures give voice to individual and minority opinions.

The other side of this coin is that during times of close partisan division like we've experienced over the past few years, the efforts of party leaders can serve to heighten philosophical differences between the two camps, leading to intensely fought battles over legislation and, more broadly, the general direction of the country. When only a handful of seats separates the majority from the minority in the House—and when only a single seat creates the same distinction in the Senate—leaders have no margin for error in carrying out their legislative plans. A defection or two can hand victory to the other side, so there is intense pressure on leadership to keep members in line. Under the circumstances, things can get nasty.

There are a number of things the leadership can do to appeal for party cohesion. Leaders can shower members with rewards for adhering to the party line on key votes. They can listen to members and incorporate their interests as legislation is formulated. They can help them get committee assignments that will promote their career goals—by putting them on committees that afford them power in Congress or that address their personal legislative interests or the interests of their constituents. Leaders can go to member districts and campaign for them, and use their clout to raise money for member reelection efforts.

Any or all of these things can just as easily be withheld from members who cause trouble for the leadership, but only to a limited extent. Remember, it's in the leaders' self-interest to help party members win reelection because holding the majority fulfills the promise of power in Congress, and every reelected member brings an incumbent or would-be majority leader closer to that goal.

9-6b Party Structure

For the congressional member who is not part of the leadership, party business is conducted primarily through participation in the **party caucus.** Each party in each house has a caucus, which conducts leadership elections and finalizes committee assignments at the start of each new Congress, and provides a forum for discussion of policy issues and party legislative strategies. The caucus is the place where House Republicans, House Democrats, Senate Republicans, or Senate Democrats can articulate their interests or concerns about the positions the party might take, in an effort to build general agreement for the positions that the leadership will move forward. (Although it's the same term, this use of *caucus* should not be confused with a caucus that meets to elect delegates to a political party convention, like the Iowa caucuses we talked about in Chapter 7.)

> **party caucus** The group of all members of a political party in the House or Senate that meets to discuss and formulate legislative priorities.

Caucus can also be used as a verb: When Senator Jeffords left the Republican Party in an evenly divided Senate to become an independent, he altered majority control because of his willingness "to caucus" with Democrats. By attending the Senate Democratic caucus and supporting Democratic leadership candidates, he gave Democrats enough votes to elect their leaders and become the majority party.

Complementing the relatively informal caucus are party committees (see Table 9-5 on page 276) that help coordinate the political and policy interests of the parties. Because these committees serve partisan purposes rather than institutional purposes, they're different and apart from the standing committees and subcommittees we talked about earlier. These committees give partisan advice on developing legislative strategy, recommend committee assignments by matching members with committees that can help them politically, and help party members with reelection needs.

A quick glance at a couple of these committee websites could give you a richer sense of how they operate and what they do. For instance, the Senate Republican Policy Committee (RPC) bills itself as "helping shape the GOP game plan:"

> Every Tuesday that the Senate is in session, Republican senators gather in the Capitol for a policy lunch meeting. This is the one scheduled time each week for all Republican senators to gather and discuss issues before the Senate, review the anticipated agenda, and discuss policy options.

> Republican staff directors of the Senate committees meet weekly in the Policy Committee office to review pending issues. The RPC also hosts weekly briefings for Republican legislative directors and press secretaries, as well as meetings with outside speakers and policy experts to facilitate discussion on key issues and explore new ideas for legislative action.[29]

The Senate Democratic Steering and Coordination Committee, in addition to its committee assignment function, works to coordinate the Senate Democratic legislative strategy with Democratic allies outside Congress:

> The Steering Committee works with Senate Democrats to develop and maintain relationships with leaders and organizations off of Capitol Hill. In its capacity as liaison between the Democratic Caucus and elected officials, constituency groups, and community organizations across the country, the Steering Committee keeps individuals and groups apprised of the positions, proposals, and activities of Senate Democrats, while reaching out to build relationships with communities and groups across the United States.[30]

Beyond these committees, members can find numerous opportunities to gather in less formal or smaller partisan group settings to discuss goals, map strategies, and mediate disputes. Congressional parties in both houses occasionally hold retreats (typically in a pleasant setting outside Washington) for the purpose of boosting party unity. Like on a college

Figure 9-4
House and Senate Leaders

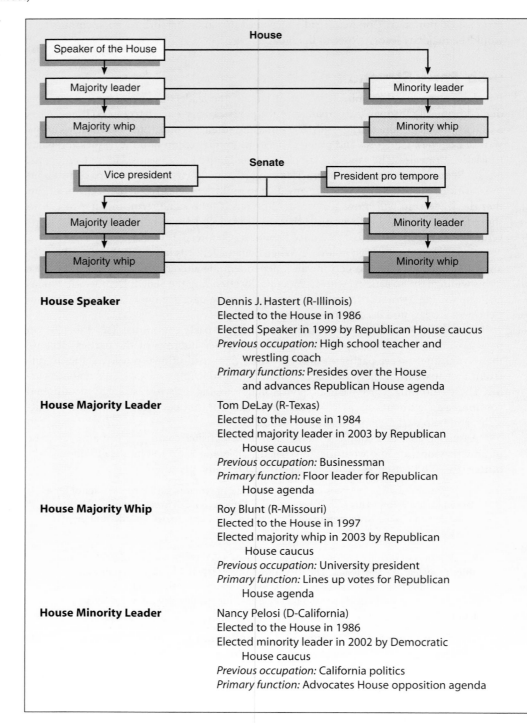

House Speaker	Dennis J. Hastert (R-Illinois) Elected to the House in 1986 Elected Speaker in 1999 by Republican House caucus *Previous occupation:* High school teacher and wrestling coach *Primary functions:* Presides over the House and advances Republican House agenda
House Majority Leader	Tom DeLay (R-Texas) Elected to the House in 1984 Elected majority leader in 2003 by Republican House caucus *Previous occupation:* Businessman *Primary function:* Floor leader for Republican House agenda
House Majority Whip	Roy Blunt (R-Missouri) Elected to the House in 1997 Elected majority whip in 2003 by Republican House caucus *Previous occupation:* University president *Primary function:* Lines up votes for Republican House agenda
House Minority Leader	Nancy Pelosi (D-California) Elected to the House in 1986 Elected minority leader in 2002 by Democratic House caucus *Previous occupation:* California politics *Primary function:* Advocates House opposition agenda

campus, there are plenty of extracurricular groups you can join in Congress, where you'll find other people with similar partisan or ideological interests. For instance, the Congressional Black Caucus and the Congressional Hispanic Caucus are organized around identity politics. The Blue Dogs are a group of moderate-to-conservative House Democrats that tries to build bridges between liberal Democrats and Conservative Republicans. The Blue Dogs would never be confused with the CATS (Conservative Action Team), a House Republican group dedicated to advancing a small-government agenda.

House Minority Whip	Steny Hoyer (D-Maryland) Elected to the House in 1981 Elected minority whip in 2002 by Democratic House caucus *Previous occupation:* Maryland politics *Primary function:* Maintains support for House opposition agenda
U.S. Vice President	Dick Cheney (president of the Senate; R-Wyoming) Became Senate president upon taking office as U.S. vice president in 2001 *Previous occupation:* Government service and businessman *Primary function:* Ceremonial; presides over Senate; casts tie-breaking vote
Senate President Pro Tempore	Ted Stevens (R-Alaska) Elected to the Senate in 1968 Elected president pro tempore in 2003 when Republicans became majority party *Previous occupation:* Law *Primary function:* Ceremonial; presides over Senate
Senate Majority Leader	Bill Frist (R-Tennessee) Elected to the Senate in 1994 Elected majority leader in 2003 *Previous occupation:* Surgeon *Primary function:* Advances Republican Senate agenda
Senate Majority Whip	Mitch McConnell (R-Kentucky) Elected to the Senate in 1984 Elected majority whip in 2003 *Previous occupation:* Government service *Primary function:* Lines up votes for Republican Senate agenda
Senate Minority Leader	Harry Reid (D-Nevada) Elected to the Senate in 1986 Elected minority whip in 1999; elected minority leader in 2005 *Previous occupation:* Law *Primary function:* Advocates Senate opposition agenda
Senate Minority Whip	Richard J. Durbin (D-Illinois) Elected to the Senate in 1996 Elected minority whip in 2005 *Previous occupation:* Law *Primary function:* Maintains support for Senate opposition agenda

9-6c Committee Structure

Congressional leadership and party structures play big roles in the organization of the committee system. There are so many committees—the structure is so decentralized—that parties step in to hold things together. We've already talked about how committees are organized around parties and how leadership plays a critical role in making committee assignments, attempting to match members with committees that will advance their careers.

TABLE 9-5

Party Committees and Their Purposes

	Committee	Approximate Number of Members	Purpose
House	Republican Policy Committee	39	Build consensus for party policy positions
	Democratic Policy Committee	36	Establish and communicate party priorities
Senate	Republican Policy Committee	26	Research and draft party policy positions
	Democratic Policy Committee	24	Develop party positions and priorities
House	Republican Steering Committee	27	Assign Republicans to committees
	Democratic Steering Committee	44	Assign Democrats to committees
Senate	Republican Committee on Committees	9	Assign Republicans to committees
	Democratic Steering and Coordination Committee	20	Assign Democrats to committees and coordinate Democratic policy agenda
House	National Republican Congressional Committee	33	Elect Republicans to the House
	Democratic Congressional Campaign Committee	40	Elect Democrats to the House
Senate	National Republican Senatorial Committee	11	Elect Republicans to the Senate
	Democratic Senatorial Campaign Committee	15	Elect Democrats to the Senate

Source: Roger H. Davidson and Walter J. Oleszek, *Congress and Its Members,* 7th ed. (Washington, DC: CQ Press, 2000), 189.

However, there are a few things we haven't addressed about the committee structure that are important to the way they operate. One is how the ratio of Republicans to Democrats is determined. Another is how member preferences are matched to committees. Then, there's the all-important matter of seniority.

We've said that the majority party receives a majority of seats on all committees, but the magnitude of that advantage will vary, depending on how many seats the majority party occupies. In a closely divided legislature of the sort we've seen in recent years, the majority party will command only a small advantage on most committees, but there can be exceptions. For instance, the majority party may demand disproportionate representation on the House Rules Committee, allowing majority leadership to control the flow of legislation to the floor.

At the start of every Congress, new members will seek committees on which they want to serve and will typically lobby their leadership to get them. Members are goal-directed, and see committee service as an opportunity to advance career objectives. Those interested primarily in making laws will gravitate to policy-oriented committees, like the House International Relations Committee or the Senate Health, Education, Labor and Pensions Committee. Those seeking to climb the leadership ladder in Congress will be drawn to committees where they can exert influence on the congressional agenda, like the Ways and Means Committee or the Rules Committee in the House. Members from competitive districts with reelection on their minds will want to join committees where they can benefit from the perks of pork, like the House Resources Committee.[31]

Although leaders try to accommodate assignment requests, not everyone gets what they want. Just like in many universities, where seniors have priority over freshmen when enrolling for courses, **seniority** gives long-serving members an edge in having their committee requests fulfilled. Seniority also plays an important role in committee leadership. As a long-standing matter of custom, each **committee chair** is the member of the majority party with the longest continuous service on the committee. The longest-serving member of the minority party is the **ranking minority member.** Although there have been a few cases over the past several decades of a party caucus granting a committee chair to someone other than the longest-serving member, the seniority custom is rarely violated.

Because most legislation first goes to committee for a hearing, a committee chair can have enormous power over the legislative process. A committee chair is no longer the iron-fisted dictator of an earlier time, although he can still influence the committee's agenda, budget and staff, and may have influence over determining subcommittee memberships. He can decide how—or whether—to route legislative proposals to subcommittees. He can decide when—or whether—to schedule a vote to send legislation on for consideration by the full chamber. By delaying action on a bill he doesn't like, a chair can keep the rest of Congress from considering it, even if the bill has widespread support. As a result, chairs are well positioned to fashion committees to suit their interests.[32]

9-7 Working in Congress: Washington

Okay, see if this sounds familiar to you. It's final exam week. You have four tests in the next three days, and while you've done your best to keep up with most of the reading, you realize you're facing a few long days and nights.

Now imagine that finals week goes on forever, and you'll have a sense of what the workload is like for members of Congress. There's always more to do than can get done, and just like you're always aware that you'll be getting graded at the end of each term, every member keeps an eye on when their term ends and they have to face the voters again.

Members have to fulfill a number of obligations, all with implications for how well they'll do on Election Day. When they cast a vote on legislation, when they do work on committees, when they address the concerns and complaints of constituents, they realize they're doing things with the potential to assist—or undermine—their reelection prospects. It's a lot to cover, and it's probably not exaggerating things too much to say that a big misstep, or a lot of small missed steps, could put their future in jeopardy.

9-7a On the Job

Representatives can be easily overwhelmed. They need to make judgments about a wide range of issues, many of them detailed and technical. With the exception of perhaps one or two issues, members are limited in their level of expertise. It would be like taking a series of liberal arts courses in everything from biology to art history to sociology to psychology, and feeling a sense of command only in your major subject—except, where you probably take no more than five courses per term, representatives are inundated with many more than five complex issues they need to address.

Members of Congress typically spend more time in committee rooms than you spend in classrooms; just like the job of learning takes place in class, the detail work of Congress takes place in committee. Between committee and subcommittee assignments, members are regularly overbooked and have to make choices about which hearings to attend. It would be as if you registered for seven three-credit courses and some of them met at the same time.

More than committee work pulls members in competing directions. They need to meet with lobbyists and constituents, they're expected to spend time on the floor of Congress debating and voting on legislation, they have to pay attention to their public image by devoting time to the media and by making public speaking engagements, and they are presented with a steady supply of social functions that offer opportunities to "network" and conduct business. It's not unusual for a representative's day to begin early and end late in the evening.

Then there's the commute. Members must return to their districts regularly or they risk losing touch with their constituents at the grass roots. Some members who live close

seniority The custom of awarding committee chairs on the basis of length of service.

committee chair The member of Congress responsible for running a committee, who can have great influence over the committee agenda and, by extension, the legislative process.

ranking minority member The minority party counterpart to the committee chair, but without the power to influence the direction of the committee.

Box 9-10 ## A Typical Day on the Hill

Conflicts in congressional schedules are the rule, rather than the exception. Every decision disappoints some group. Which options would you choose?

Option 1

7:50 A.M. Breakfast with Chamber of Commerce officials from home district to discuss business interests and the Chamber's political support for your reelection campaign

8:00 A.M. Breakfast meeting with fellow Blue Dog Democrats to discuss centrist legislative strategies

Meeting with lobbyists connected to your district instead of going to a regularly scheduled meeting with other conservative Democrats is the less risky choice. Maintaining good relationships with sympathetic groups will help you earn their money and support for your next reelection effort. It would be nice to contribute to the Blue Dogs' strategic plans, but you can always meet with them next week.

Option 2

8:55 A.M. A long, impromptu meeting with a Republican colleague who wants your vote for a bridge construction project in her district; she is willing to support construction of a military helicopter in your district in return

9:00 A.M. Meeting with computer company lobbyists about adding funding to combat cyberterrorism in the homeland security bill

This is a tough call with no obviously good choice. The trade-off you're arranging with your colleague will help you bring an important pork-barrel project back to your constituents, and your willingness to talk shows you are a good colleague. However, the computer lobbyist you're neglecting is a potential political supporter who wants to talk about an important legislative matter.

Option 3

10:15 A.M. Meeting with a postal worker from your district who is retiring after 50 years of service without ever calling in sick

10:20 A.M. Floor vote on designating an official "National Asparagus Day"

The meeting will matter to the postal worker (who may turn out to vote in the next election), it will likely get you favorable coverage in the local papers back home, and you'll build up good will with postal workers in your district. The vote, on the other hand, is symbolic; missing it would only be a problem for a member from a district that produces asparagus.

to Washington are able to divide their time between the Capital and their district, spending long weekends at home or even driving or taking the train if they're very close. Others have a much longer way to go: Imagine if you represented California—or Hawaii. Once home, members keep working, often on weekends, taking care to meet with constituents, locally based interest groups, and financial supporters.

9-7b Staff to the Rescue

Of course, they don't have to do it alone. The typical House member has a full-time staff of fourteen and nine college interns. The typical senator has a paid staff of thirty-four and nine unpaid interns. Typically well educated, young, and willing to trade off higher pay elsewhere for the thrill of working with powerful people and the ability to make important professional contacts, staffers help manage the workload by performing a number of important roles:

- *Administrative assistants (AAs)* help manage the Washington office, provide political advice to the representative or senator, and function as an intermediary in dealings with constituents, lobbyists, and other members.

- *Legislative assistants (LAs)* help manage the member's committee work by writing speeches and bills, analyzing legislative proposals, and following up on committee and subcommittee meetings the member misses.

- *Caseworkers* devote their time to helping constituents with problems and work either out of Washington, D.C., or out of one of the member's home offices. Representatives on average have two or three "branch offices" in their districts; senators average four offices in their state.

- *Press aides* are responsible for the member's media relations, including communicating the member's message to the press and managing communications

Option 4

10:45 A.M. Hearing on acid rain (Committee on Energy and Commerce Subcommittee on Energy and Air Quality)

11:00 A.M. Hearing on possible NASA expedition to Mars (Committee on Science Subcommittee on Space and Aeronautics)

You can't go to every hearing. Of the two, the hearing on acid rain is probably the more important one to you because your constituents will have a direct interest in the effects of acid rain. Your legislative assistant can keep tabs on the meeting you missed.

Option 5

1:15 P.M. Floor debate. Prepared remarks (two minutes) on proposed homeland security bill

1:20 P.M. Unscheduled visit by elementary school group from home district looking for personalized tour of Congress

1:20 P.M. Hearing on affordable housing: Committee on Financial Services Subcommittee on Housing and Community Opportunity, on which you are ranking minority member

It makes sense that you'd want to deliver your remarks on an important measure like homeland security. However, it's difficult to miss a meeting of a subcommittee where you're the ranking member without violating the norm of doing your legislative work. An alternative would be to arrange to have your remarks made part of the permanent record without actually presenting them. As hard as it is to overlook school kids from home—remember, their parents may be voters—

the visit was unannounced and could probably be handled by your staff caseworkers.

Option 6

3:00 P.M. Taped interview with CNN on affordable housing issue

3:00 P.M. Floor vote on raising the minimum wage by 40 cents an hour

This is another tough call. You want the publicity that CNN can give you, but by not voting on an important measure like the minimum wage, your opponent in the next election could raise questions about why you're not doing your job.

Option 7

8:00 P.M. Evening reception in Georgetown with lobbyists from Greenpeace

8:00 P.M. Evening function at the White House honoring the Canadian prime minister, an opportunity to discuss the topic of acid rain

8:00 P.M. Quiet time with family

The Greenpeace reception would allow you to mix with sympathetic lobbyists from a group that supports your environmental concerns. However, the presidential function has the added benefit of allowing you to talk to the Canadian prime minister about one of your pet issues—and it's at the White House. All this weighs against personal time with your family, which is always a tough choice to make.

with constituents through newsletters and, in some cases, surveys of constituent opinion.[33]

Take a look at some of the things a member of Congress might face on a typical day. You'll find them in Box 9-10. This is a fictional composite, but it's based on the real thing. Imagine you're the representative with the scheduling conflicts in Box 9-10 (in some cases, this will require a lot of imagination): a conservative, pro-business Democrat from a competitive district in the Northeast with an interest in affordable housing, air pollution (particularly the problem of acid rain), and homeland security—all of which are important to the constituents who support you. During much of the day, scheduling conflicts make it impossible for you to be everywhere and do everything you would like. You'll have the chance to decide how you will resolve these conflicts by selecting the events you're going to attend and those you're going to miss from a set of available options. Remember, some of what you miss can be taken care of by your staff—but not everything.

Also, remember that there's a potential cost every time members of Congress fail to show up for an event that a staff member can't cover, either in the form of a lost opportunity, an angry constituent, a violated congressional norm—or the appearance that they are just not doing their job.

9-7c Voting on Legislation

If you felt it was an intrusion on your busy schedule to have to vote on legislation creating a "National Asparagus Day," you can probably get a sense of the range of things—big and small—that representatives are called upon to decide. Maybe which way to vote on something like an honorary holiday is a no-brainer (you support it!), but there are a lot of more substantive votes a member has to cast and—let's face it—with so many technical issues to decide, members have to cast plenty of votes on things they know nothing about.

cue taking Looking to other members of Congress for guidelines on how to cast a vote on a technical or unfamiliar matter.

So, they need voting strategies. To simplify what could be confusing decisions on unfamiliar matters, members of Congress engage in **cue taking,** looking to other members for reliable signals on how to vote. There are several commonsense shortcuts that members might take. They could turn to a colleague who shares their philosophical outlook and vote the way the colleague is voting. They could seek advice from a member with expertise on the legislation being considered, such as a member of the committee that held hearings on it. If they are junior members, they might look for someone with seniority who has been around long enough to be familiar with the matter at hand. If they are in the House, they could turn to a member of their state delegation, someone from their area who is known and trusted. This sort of cue makes particular sense if the legislation could have an impact back home, like a measure that could affect an industry in the member's state.[34]

If a member's vote on the issue is important to other members but does not concern the member or his or her constituents, it would probably be an appropriate time to engage in logrolling, where the member would exchange his or her vote for future support on something that does matter to the member. Logrolling can be accomplished informally before a final vote on legislation, and it can involve a number of members. One former senator, sounding a whole lot like anyone who has ever called in favors from a friend, explained how he put together majority support for a bill: "Maggie said she talked to Russell, and Tom promised this if I would help him on Ed's amendment, and Mike owes me one for last year's help on Pete's bill."[35]

Cue taking is necessary when a lawmaker doesn't know much about the legislation on the table, and logrolling is effective when the outcome of a vote doesn't matter to the representative. Every so often, though, members have to cast votes that matter to their constituents on things their constituents are aware of and feel intensely about. These are the votes that get noticed, the votes that could influence how constituents react the next time they see the member's name on a ballot. Perhaps it's a vote involving an industry that employs a lot of people back home, like the automobile industry in the Midwest or the tobacco industry in the South. Maybe it's a vote about something that touches people's lives in a direct way, like tax increases, health care costs, Social Security benefits, or education. These votes require extra care.[36]

Likewise, members will take notice when an issue mobilizes elite groups in their districts. Issues of this nature tend to be narrow and don't involve large numbers of constituents, but they can matter strongly to the group with a stake in the outcome—like, for instance, cigarette manufacturers facing a new surcharge on their product. Because elites are politically active, resource-rich groups that can use their clout to help or hinder a member's reelection prospects, they can command a lot of notice despite their size.

On occasion, these votes can be tricky, depending in part on how strongly representatives feel about the matter at hand, whether their position is at odds with the position of their constituents, and if they believe they should vote their mind rather than the preferences of the people who elected them. Box 9-11 explains.

It's unusual for a single vote to mean the difference between political life and death. Often, members will consider their overall voting record as they look toward the next campaign, rather than worry about any particular vote. They'll try to avoid casting what political scientist John Kingdon calls a "string of votes" against a series of constituent interests that could form the basis for a future campaign against them. They'll also try to be conscious of ways to explain the more controversial parts of their voting record to their constituents, perhaps by pointing to other actions more in line with constituent wishes, or by finding shelter for their vote in the supportive words of the president or other authorities their constituents might respect.[37]

They do these things because they recognize that while most votes will be inconsequential, there will always be a handful of votes on salient issues that can generate political risk. The riskiest type of vote is on a highly visible and unpredictable matter that the member cannot avoid, like the decision members of Congress had to face in 2002 over whether to support military action against Iraq. Some representatives who were in Congress in 1991 remembered agonizing over whether to support President Bush (senior) on the Persian Gulf War. Some who voted against it were attacked by opponents for being weak on defense issues—a charge that can have devastating political consequences. However, at

Box 9-11   Burke's Dilemma

Before you get the sense that legislators try to make everyone happy all the time, you should consider a couple of things. Legislators have values, and sometimes, they want to cast votes on principles that could contradict constituent wishes. Some legislators believe that they were hired to vote their conscience and experience, to do what they felt was best for the nation even if it contradicts the views of their constituents. These considerations can factor into their voting decisions, depending in part on how they view the notion of representation.

Edmund Burke, eighteenth-century political philosopher and member of the British Parliament, espoused the view of representatives as **trustees** who are elected to exercise their best judgment of the national interest. His perspective conflicts with the more widely held contemporary American view that representatives are **delegates** of the people who put them in office and are thereby obligated to vote their constituents' wishes. Both are legitimate ways to understand representation.

Most of the time, the difference between the trustee and delegate approaches to representation isn't relevant. Because most votes are not controversial, and because the personal philosophy of candidates recruited to run for office typically matches the prevailing views of the district, sharp differences between representative and constituent do not emerge often or can get lost in the shuffle of legislation.

However, should members face a rare, highly visible vote on a matter where their best judgment puts them at odds with their constituent's wishes, they face a dilemma. In fact, they face "Burke's Dilemma," as Burke himself found his view of the national interest in conflict with the wishes of his constituents.

It's probably easy to see how the trustee view of representation can have its political costs. On matters of principle, it's also easy to see how representatives might wish to risk these costs and vote against their constituents' wishes in order to do what they feel is best for the nation.

trustee A philosophy of representation that says officials are elected for their wisdom and to exercise their judgment of the national interest, even when it is at odds with their constituents' wishes.

delegate A philosophy of representation that says officials are elected to carry out constituent interests, even when these interests conflict with what the representative believes is the right thing to do.

the time they were asked to vote, members had no way of knowing that the war would produce a swift military success with little cost to the United States. Had the war gone differently, their vote against would have appeared cautious and wise. Members faced the same type of uncertainty in the vote on the second Iraq campaign. See Box 9-12.

9-8   Working in Congress: Back Home

Whether members regard themselves as delegates or as trustees, the folks back home are the ones who will decide whether they get to return to Washington for another term. Legislative voting is, of course, one of the determining factors that constituents might use when they decide whether to reelect an incumbent. There's another side to the job that's more personal and often more mundane than what a member does in Washington. It's about constituent service, and it's a key part of what members of Congress do to keep their voters satisfied with their performance.

Constituent service can help the entire district at once or serve one constituent at a time. Members are always looking out for things to bring back to their districts—tangible items like public projects or federal jobs. These are the fruits of logrolling, and since every member needs them, every other member is sympathetic to the need to trade off favors for favors. Even the most vocal opponents of government spending will be happy to allow the government to write a check for something that benefits their district, and their colleagues—understanding how the game is played—will say nothing about it.

Remember the $1.2 million historical sewer in Trenton, New Jersey, that we mentioned in Box 9-4? That represents a $1.2 million federal outlay to a congressional district. The replica of the Great Wall of China in Bedford, Indiana? That's a $20,000 outlay to a congressional district. Members can point to them at reelection time as concrete evidence of their effectiveness in serving community interests and needs.

On a more individual level, members (with an important assist from their staff) regularly perform **casework** for constituents who have problems they would like to see handled by the federal government. Casework is homework in the literal sense of the word because it requires members to use their legislative positions to address requests from

casework Service performed by members of Congress for constituents with individual problems or complaints that they would like the government to address.

Box 9-12   Iraq: Weighing the Pros and Cons

From a purely political perspective, the vote on whether to support the Iraqi invasion had a couple of important wrinkles. Typically, members of Congress like to support the president on military matters, in deference to his role as commander-in-chief. This is particularly true for a popular president, which President Bush was in late 2002. Members also try to avoid being labeled as "soft" on something as important as national security. On the other hand, representatives know that it can be even more devastating to an official's career to support a war that bogs down in heavy fighting, produces a lot of American casualties, emboldens anti-American terrorists, damages the economy, or unleashes unexpected and unwanted side effects—such as the use by Iraq of chemical or biological weapons against American troops.

In 2002, there was no way to predict that the capture of Baghdad would be quick, American casualties would be light, and Saddam Hussein would not use weapons of mass destruction against American troops. Of course, there was also no way to predict that the American occupation of Iraq after the war would be difficult and costly in lives and dollars, and

that some of the justifications offered by the administration for supporting the war—like the existence of Iraqi weapons of mass destruction—would be brought into question. In the immediate aftermath of the overthrow of the Hussein government, the war was wildly popular with Americans. In the months following that high point, opinion was more divided.

How do you vote when you can't anticipate events or public reaction to events? You can listen to your constituents, but if they tell you to support the war, you know it won't mean anything if later on they've turned against it. You can take a calculated risk and make the decision that you feel will be the least likely to come back and haunt you later. Or you can listen to your inner voice and vote according to what you feel is best for the country. This would allow you a clear conscience, knowing you voted responsibly on a matter of grave importance, but it could also leave you politically exposed if events turn against your position.

So, think about it—if you were in Congress in 2002, how would you have voted, and why?

people back home that can be serious and important—as well as mundane or tedious. Just like the relationship that so many of us have to doing homework, it's fair to say that most legislators do not find this to be the most fulfilling part of their job. However (just like our homework assignments), it's important to do (your grade—and their reelection prospects—hinge on doing it), and the work never stops pouring in.

Some casework involves problems constituents have with government agencies. For instance, a constituent having trouble getting his Social Security check or veteran's benefits might contact a member of Congress for help. Someone having trouble getting a passport also could turn to his or her member for assistance. So might somebody whose child wants a congressional nomination to attend West Point.

Not all casework is about navigating the bureaucracy. Lots of people contact their member of Congress because they want to receive a flag that was flown over the Capitol (flags are raised and lowered over the dome with great frequency in order to provide this service).[38] Many are interested in arranging a tour of the House, Senate, or White House during their family trip to Washington.

Other requests are just downright odd. Members have been asked for recipes, transportation on military aircraft, help changing a grade in a college course (don't bother trying—it can't be done), and all sorts of unusual, personal items. These requests are granted if possible, or turned down gently, but they're always taken seriously because there's no point in antagonizing a potential voter, even though responding to these requests takes time.

All constituent requests may get a hearing, but members of Congress do not regard all constituents the same way, especially as they think about the next election. Members try to be alert to the groups of constituents they can count on to vote for them, those they can count on to support them intensely, and those whose support they probably can never win. The strong supporters can be pretty easy to identify, but at the margins, many representatives will confess to some fuzziness in their picture of whom they can rely on politically.

home style The way legislators approach constituents, determined partly by how they size up their support in the district.

Political scientist Richard E. Fenno uses the term **home style** to describe the way members approach these different constituency groups. The way representatives size up the political inclinations of people in their district can affect the way they allocate staff resources in the district, how they fashion their trips home, and how they explain to their constituents what they do in Washington.[39]

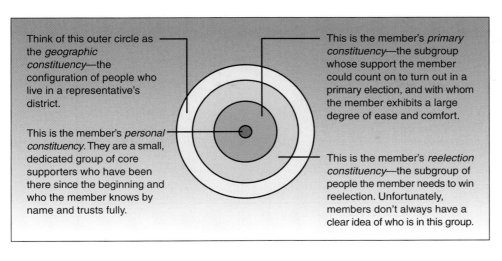

Think of this outer circle as the *geographic constituency*—the configuration of people who live in a representative's district.

This is the member's *personal constituency.* They are a small, dedicated group of core supporters who have been there since the beginning and who the member knows by name and trusts fully.

This is the member's *primary constituency*—the subgroup whose support the member could count on to turn out in a primary election, and with whom the member exhibits a large degree of ease and comfort.

This is the member's *reelection constituency*—the subgroup of people the member needs to win reelection. Unfortunately, members don't always have a clear idea of who is in this group.

Figure 9-5
Constituencies inside Constituencies

Fenno says members—without being fully conscious of it—divide their districts into a set of overlapping constituencies based on perceptions of political support. From this perspective, a relatively small number of people can have a disproportionate influence on the member's approach to the whole district. Figure 9-5 illustrates the different layers of constituents that make up a member's district. Imagine that the circles in the figure represent different constituent groups in a district. Consider that constituents who are closer to the "bull's-eye" have more influence with their representative.

9-9 Staying in Congress

It shouldn't be too hard to figure out that when you add up the cost of all those staff members and the price of travel back to the district, members of Congress have a number of perks that ease the burden of their jobs and help grease the way towards reelection. The truth is, we haven't even scratched the surface of the rewards members of Congress get when they serve.

9-9a Perks

You can start with the prestige of office (which is greater for senators but not so shabby for representatives). Tack on an annual salary of $145,100.[40] Then, there are the perks, such as:

- Administrative and clerical staff allowance: $632,000 (House); $1.2–2.2 million (Senate)
- Legislative staff allowance (Senate): $396,000
- Office expenses: $195,000 average (House); $175,000–$470,000 (Senate), including:
  - Travel allowance
  - Franking (postage) allowance
  - Long-distance telephone allowance
  - Recording studio allowance
  - Automobile leasing allowance
  - Computer supplies
- Pension plan (typical lifetime benefit with retirement at age 60 after 20 years: $1,000,000)
- Free office and airport parking
- Richly furnished offices for senior members and secret Senate "hideaway" offices
- Subsidized health and life insurance
- House and Senate gymnasium, staffed by physical therapists

Figure 9-6
Congressional Pay Increases, 1975–2001

Source: Data from *Congressional Quarterly.*

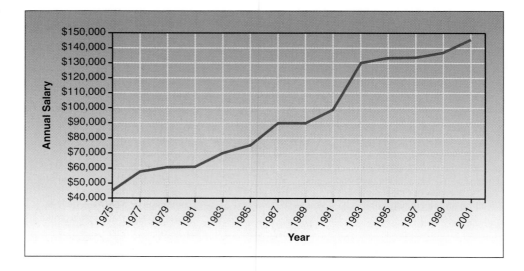

- Subsidized haircuts (Senate only)
- Subsidized House and Senate restaurant privileges[41]

It's hard to put an exact figure on the salary and benefits a member receives because a lot depends on sliding scales adjusted by the distance a member has to travel from home or by the population of a senator's state. But it should be pretty easy to see that service in Congress can easily return annual salary and benefits at least in the $2 million range, along with perks that you wouldn't be able to find in most other jobs.

These numbers have been growing steadily over the last quarter century. Take the salary figures as an example. Since 1975, members of Congress have voted to increase their salaries no less than 14 times, creating the steady increase displayed in Figure 9-6 (notice how most of these increases happened in odd-numbered years without elections). It's a steep increase in a relatively short time—and quite a change from the $6 per day members earned in the First Congress!

More importantly, much of what members get in the form of taxpayer-subsidized benefits helps them stay in office. Travel allowances enable members to return to their districts to bolster support among their primary and reelection constituencies. The "franking" privilege, which allows members to substitute their signature for postage, enables them to send newsletters to constituents at no charge—newsletters that keep constituents familiar with their members' name and accomplishments (as told from the perspective of the member, of course). Access to video and audio recording equipment enables media-savvy members to take their positions to constituents in a more visible way.

9-9b Media Access

In fact, the media-saturated environment in which all political figures operate gives members of Congress a number of opportunities to keep their images and messages in front of constituents in a way that most political challengers would find hard to match. Your representative and senators almost certainly have websites where you can go to find the latest "news" about what they've been up to, packaged to present your member in the most favorable light. Websites also facilitate casework by giving constituents an easy way to make frequently asked requests.

It's worth taking a second to check out one of your representative's websites; they're listed at http://www.senate.gov. The next chance you get to work online, just click on your home state from the list and the names of your senators will appear in the screen on the right (if you're not from the United States, you could select the state your school is in, or any state you like). Click on either name and you'll be directed right to their website. Take a minute to look around, especially at the way they present themselves. The website is a great opportunity for members to portray themselves the way they want you to see them. What's your reaction?

Members of Congress can implement media strategies that go beyond maintaining a website. By virtue of their position in Congress, members are **newsworthy** and can command the attention of local media in their districts with little effort. Depending on the news agenda and their seniority, members can have easy access to national media as well, although the national press often gravitates to members based on their seniority and expertise. Committee chairs presiding over an issue in the news will find themselves in demand, as will members of the leadership of both parties and practically any senator regardless of the story. Chairs or leaders who call press conferences to discuss an issue will certainly get coverage.

Everyone in Congress can take advantage of C-SPAN, the cable service that provides coverage of floor debate and key hearings on three channels operating 24/7. If a member wants to make points with the folks back home, a two-minute appearance from the floor of the House or Senate broadcast on C-SPAN offers an opportunity that wasn't available a generation ago.[42]

The value of all this media attention rests with the ability it gives members to publicize themselves and their actions. Members naturally want to claim credit for doing things they know their constituents will support, and the media (supplemented by member websites and newsletters) provide a natural way to do this. Leaders want to do the same thing for their party and will use the media to communicate whatever messages they feel give them an advantage over their adversaries, even to the point of staging media events to draw attention to their message.

> **newsworthy** The conditions under which a story warrants publication or dissemination, based on a set of values applied by newspaper editors and television producers. Newsworthy stories typically have conflict, proximity and relevance to the audience, timeliness, and familiarity.

9-9c The Incumbency Advantage

Although it's difficult to pin the reelection advantage incumbents have on the fact that they have perks that tilt the electoral playing field strongly in their direction, it's not difficult to see how an incumbent's resources can be used to get the better of potential competition. Members use perks to personalize their office in an attempt to make reelection contests a judgment on them as someone constituents have come to recognize, feel comfortable with, and relate to as their representative in Washington. With people feeling weaker partisan attachments than in the past, it's a strategy that makes sense.

The one thing that is clear is that competitive elections—especially in the House—are going the way of the *Tyrannosaurus Rex.* Incumbents are being reelected in higher numbers than ever and, in many cases, by higher margins. The number of uncontested seats has swollen, due in no small part to redistricting. During the last two decades of the twentieth century, incumbent House members were reelected on average 90 percent of the time, a figure that's notably higher than it was during the previous two decades.[43] In 2000, two-thirds of Senate incumbents and 82 percent of House incumbents won with 60 percent or more of the vote.[44] In 2002, Democrats needed only to claim seven seats in the 435-seat House to win the majority. It should have been easy to do with every seat in contention. They were unsuccessful, though, in part because close to four hundred of those contests were over before they began, with the incumbent party virtually assured of remaining in power.

In addition to incumbents strategically using the perks of office to personalize elections in a time of decreasing partisanship, other possible explanations for this strong incumbency advantage are the decline of strong challengers and the redrawing of more district lines to keep them safe for the party in power. Looming over everything is money. PAC money flows more freely to those who hold the reigns of power than to those who wish to replace them, and Chapter 8 showed us just how much money now floods the political system.

Incumbents overall are able to far out-raise their challengers—in some cases, acting preemptively to raise so much money well in advance of the election that strong challengers never make the race. Challengers looking at an incumbent with name recognition, access to the perks of office, *and* a huge wallet are acting rationally if they think they'll never be able to catch up, and in the process, never be able to communicate their message and structure the agenda of the race. (This also explains the reason why both parties have recently looked to wealthy candidates who can self-finance campaigns against incumbents.)

The ability to raise large sums of money has a darker side. Members know they *have to* raise money to maintain their advantage, and they have to raise it in large quantities as campaign costs are high and continue to soar higher. The average cost of a successful House campaign increased 17 percent just between 1998 and 2000.[45] Imagine serving in the House and having to run for reelection every two years. You'd never be done with your fund-raising. Senators have six years between contests but have to run statewide—a more expensive proposition, except in small states. In 2000, the average Senate seat cost $7.2 million to win.[46]

Money may be easy to come by, but members still have to ask for it. Some find the process distasteful. If you think about it for a second, no matter how big your ego or how much you feel you're worth it, many people cannot glide easily into a room filled with strangers, give a five- or ten-minute presentation about how important their reelection is to everyone in attendance, and then ask for large sums of cash.

Herein lies a key dilemma of twenty-first century legislative politics. Members of Congress are showered with perks. They have power and visibility. Once elected, the likelihood of keeping their job is greater than at any time in memory.

But the job has become more distasteful than ever before.

Between constant fund-raising, intense partisan bickering, endless casework, and long hours away from home and family, members can be forgiven for wondering whether the demands of such a seemingly glamorous occupation are worth it. In an era when it is more possible than ever to make a long career out of serving in the national legislature, it's not unusual for members to ask themselves whether it pays to serve.

Would you stay? It's a difficult question to answer if you've never put in the effort to run for office, just like it's hard for you to say if you'd go to college again until you've been through it once. It might seem easy to say no to staying in Congress, but if you were elected to one term in the House, you have already spent two years campaigning and raising money before you were sworn in, and another two years in office doing more campaigning and raising more money for your anticipated reelection campaign. That's four years of campaign work in order to serve two years in office. It's hard to walk away from an investment like that.

So, while some walk away, many stay despite the complaints—and some of them strive for higher office. For those who see elected office as a career, an eye is often turned to the next level of the political food chain. House members with long-term ambitions will wait for a Senate seat to become vacant. Many senators look in the mirror at some point in their careers and see a future president.

And why not? Even though the Constitution makes Congress the centerpiece of the political establishment, in the contemporary world no one is more visible than the American president. As an office, the presidency is quite different from Congress—less deliberative, less collaborative, and far more dependent on the actions and even the personality of one individual. It's also hard to make a successful bid for the presidency from Congress, even though so many members have tried (John Kerry was the most recent senator to try and fail). Given the huge differences between the two offices, maybe it's not surprising that during the twentieth century, only John F. Kennedy and Warren Harding successfully made the move down Pennsylvania Avenue to the White House. Let's turn to Chapter 10 and see what they found waiting for them when they got there.

Chapter Review

People tend to hold negative opinions of Congress but positive opinions about their representative, which in some ways, is fitting for an institution that in recent years has become much more personalized. Before you can get to Congress, you have to run for election, and the way House district lines are drawn is a political matter that can dramatically influence who wins elections (senators, elected statewide, don't face this issue). Gerrymandering is the process of drawing district lines for political purposes, to bolster the prospects of one party at the expense of the other.

With the high cost of campaigning, wealthy candidates who can finance their own race have become popular in recent years. Although women have been elected to Congress in larger numbers than ever before, members are still overwhelmingly male. Most members of Congress are white, college-educated professionals.

Like any institution, Congress has informal norms of behavior that members learn as they become familiar with the institution. Congressional norms emphasize flexibility, compromise, and civility—qualities that might not arise spontaneously in the often-contentious legislative environment.

The House and the Senate are organized differently, with the House less likely to tolerate minority dissent. Where the House places strict limits on debate, the Senate is respectful of the individual wishes of its members to the point that a single senator can filibuster legislation unless sixty colleagues vote to terminate debate. Both houses are organized around standing committees and subcommittees that hold hearings on legislative matters. Among the important functions Congress performs are writing an annual federal budget and overseeing the actions of the bureaucracy. The Senate confirms presidential appointments, and both houses play a role in the impeachment of federal officials.

A parallel leadership structure is in place in both chambers, with the majority party responsible for determining the legislative agenda and chairing committees. The leader of the majority party in the House is the Speaker, who presides over the chamber. The vice president of the United States presides over the Senate, but this is largely a ceremonial role with the important exception of being able to cast tie-breaking votes. Both parties have leaders and whips. With few exceptions, committee leadership is determined by seniority.

Members of Congress face an intense legislative workload and the responsibility for handling constituent problems. Staff members help manage the work, but members still rely on shortcuts like cue taking from other members to figure out how to vote on a wide range of issues they know nothing about. Voting is a particularly important concern for members, who need to avoid casting a string of votes against different constituent groups, who might oppose them in the next election.

Members tend not to see their district as a uniform entity, instead focusing their energy on maintaining good relationships with voters they believe are most likely to renominate and reelect them. It can be a demanding job. For all the perks of office that give incumbents an electoral advantage over challengers—including access to media resources that help them boost their name recognition and communicate messages to voters—the demands of casework and fund-raising can make the job a taxing one. This leads some members to walk away from public service, although many make a career out of running for and serving in Congress.

Key Terms

apprenticeship (p. 257)
appropriations (p. 265)
bicameral (p. 258)
casework (p. 281)
cloture (p. 261)
committee chair (p. 277)
compromise (p. 256)
conference committee (p. 261)
Congressional Budget and Impoundment Control Act of 1974 (p. 265)
constituents (p. 253)
courtesy (p. 257)
cue taking (p. 280)
delegate (p. 281)
discharge petition (p. 261)
elitism (p. 254)
enumerated powers (p. 258)
filibuster (p. 261)
gerrymandering (p. 252)
home style (p. 282)

impeachment (p. 268)
implied powers (p. 259)
incumbent (p. 253)
institutional patriotism (p. 257)
integrity (p. 256)
iron triangle (p. 259)
joint committees (p. 261)
legislative work (p. 257)
logrolling (p. 255)
majoritarian principle (p. 270)
majority leader (p. 271)
majority whip (p. 271)
minority leader (p. 271)
minority rights (p. 270)
minority whip (p. 271)
name recognition (p. 253)
newsworthy (p. 285)
norms (p. 255)
oversight (p. 265)
party caucus (p. 273)

pluralism (p. 254)
pork barrel (p. 258)
president pro tempore (p. 271)
racial gerrymandering (p. 252)
ranking minority member (p. 277)
reciprocity (p. 257)
reconciliation (p. 265)
redistricting (p. 251)
responsible parties (p. 271)
Rules Committee (p. 260)
select committee (p. 260)
seniority (p. 277)
Speaker of the House (p. 270)
specialization (p. 257)
standing committees (p. 259)
subcommittees (p. 259)
substantive representation (p. 254)
trustee (p. 281)

Review Questions

Note: You can find the correct answers to these questions by taking the quiz and then submitting your answers in the Online Edition. The program will automatically score your submission. If you miss a question, the program will provide the correct answer, a rationale for the answer, and the section number in the chapter where the topic is discussed.

1. Racial gerrymandering
   a. has been upheld by the Supreme Court.
   b. cleared the way for substantive representation of African Americans.
   c. diluted the voice of minorities in Congress.
   d. helped produce Democratic majorities in Congress.

2. Logrolling is an example of the norm of
   a. reciprocity.
   b. courtesy.
   c. institutional patriotism.
   d. pork barreling.

3. Powers granted to Congress under the "necessary and proper" clause of the constitution are
   a. enumerated.
   b. normative.
   c. implied.
   d. substantive.

4. Which of the following will you find in the House of Representatives but not in the Senate?
   a. select committees
   b. cloture votes
   c. discharge petitions
   d. majority leaders

5. Which of the following will you find in the Senate but not in the House of Representatives?
   a. select committees
   b. cloture votes
   c. discharge petitions
   d. majority leaders

6. Congressional review of the actions of the bureaucracy is called
   a. impeachment.
   b. reconciliation.
   c. appropriation.
   d. oversight.

7. The vice president of the United States
   a. casts a vote in the event of a Senate tie.
   b. presides over the House of Representatives.
   c. is president pro tempore of the Senate.
   d. owes his position as president of the Senate to the majoritarian principle of representation.

8. Caseworkers are staff members who
   a. help manage the Washington office.
   b. help manage the member's committee work.
   c. help solve constituent problems.
   d. communicate the member's message to the press.

9. Cue taking
   a. makes it likely that a member of Congress will cast a string of votes against key constituency groups if it is done repeatedly.
   b. permits members of Congress to vote intelligently even when they don't have all the facts about a bill.
   c. provides members of Congress with an opportunity to exhibit the norm of institutional patriotism.
   d. is a relatively ineffective time management technique.

10. One explanation for the incumbency advantage in Congress is
    a. competitive congressional races are disappearing.
    b. incumbents can raise more money than challengers.
    c. members are paying more attention to casework.
    d. term limits.

In Their Own Words

You might be interested in examining some of what the following authors have said about the topics we've been discussing:

Davidson, Roger H., and Walter J. Oleszek. *Congress and Its Members,* 7th ed. Washington, DC: CQ Press, 1999. A comprehensive overview of topics relating to the operation of Congress, including congressional structure, leadership, and decision making.

Dodd, Lawrence C., and Bruce I. Oppenheimer, eds. *Congress Reconsidered,* 7th ed. Washington, DC: CQ Press, 2001. A selection of essays covering a variety of topics related to the operation of Congress.

Fenno, Richard F. *Home Style: House Members in Their Districts.* Boston: Little, Brown, 1978. The author traveled with members of Congress to see how they approach their constituents as they work for reelection.

Kingdon, John W. *Congressmen's Voting Decisions,* 3rd ed. Ann Arbor, MI: University of Michigan Press, 1989. A pioneering study of how members of Congress decide to vote.

Margolies-Mezvinsky, Marjorie. *A Woman's Place: The Freshmen Women Who Changed the Face of Congress.* New York: Crown Publishers, 1994. A former member of Congress discusses how the institution was changed by the largest influx of female representatives in its history.

Ornstein, Norman J., Thomas E. Mann, and Michael J. Malbin. *Vital Statistics on Congress, 2001–2002.* Washington, DC: American Enterprise Institute, 2002. A thorough source of data on Congress, available online at http://www.cfinst.org.

Sinclair, Barbara. *Unorthodox Lawmaking: New Legislative Processes in the U.S. Congress.* Washington, DC: CQ Press, 1997. A realistic look at how things get done in Congress.

Notes

1. John R. Hibbing and James T. Smith, "What the American Public Wants Congress to Be," in Lawrence C. Dodd and Bruce I. Oppenheimer (eds.), *Congress Reconsidered*, 7th ed. (Washington, DC: CQ Press, 2001), 52–53. Hibbing and Smith also note that when people were asked to think about Congress as an important national institution rather than as a large group of people, approval shoots up to 88 percent.

2. Ibid.

3. States can even gain population and lose seats if their growth was slower than population growth in other states.

4. Roger H. Davidson and Walter J. Oleszek, *Congress and Its Members*, 7th ed. (Washington, DC: CQ Press, 2000), 48–49.

5. Davidson and Olezek, *Congress and Its Members.*

6. You can read more about the repercussions of members facing members in the *Washington Post* at http://www.washingtonpost.com/ac2/wpdyn?pagename=article&node=politics/elections/redistricting&contentId=A9881-2002May25&notFound=true.

7. Linda L. Fowler, *Candidates, Congress, and the American Democracy* (Ann Arbor, MI: University of Michigan Press, 1993), 84–87.

8. Davidson and Oleszek, *Congress and Its Members,* 53–56.

9. Ibid., 56–59. The central cases were *Shaw v. Reno* 509 US 630 (1993), which you can read about online at http://www.votinglaw.com/racialfaq.html, and *Miller v. Johnson* 515 US 900 (1995).

10. Davidson and Oleszek, *Congress and Its Members,* 64–69.

11. Hannah Pitkin, *The Concept of Representation* (Berkeley, CA: University of California Press, 1967).

12. Marjorie Margolies-Mezvinsky, *A Woman's Place: The Freshmen Women Who Changed the Face of Congress* (New York: Crown Publishers, 1994), 35. The member this happened to is Representative Jennifer Dunn, a Washington State Republican.

13. Sure, people roll logs down rivers. Check out http://www.tamarackcamp.com/LogRoll/logroll.html. The origin of the term, though, is believed to be in the nineteenth century custom of neighbors cooperatively rolling logs to build a fire.

14. David W. Rhode, Norman J. Ornstein, and Robert L. Peabody, "Political Change and Legislative Norms in the U.S. Senate, 1957–1974," in Glenn R. Parker (ed.), *Studies of Congress* (Washington, DC: CQ Press, 1985), 151; emphasis in original.

15. Burdett Loomis, *The New American Politician* (New York: Basic Books, 1988), 6–19.

16. David W. Rhode, Norman J. Ornstein, and Robert L. Peabody, "Political Change and Legislative Norms in the U.S. Senate, 1957–1974," in Glenn R. Parker (ed.), *Studies of Congress* (Washington, DC: CQ Press, 1985), 181–184.

17. Davidson and Oleszek, *Congress and Its Members,* 201–205.

18. Barbara Sinclair, *Unorthodox Lawmaking: New Legislative Processes in the U.S. Congress* (Washington, DC: CQ Press, 1997), 5–6.

19. Davidson and Oleszek, *Congress and Its Members,* 205.

20. Sinclair, *Unorthodox Lawmaking,* 9–31

21. Davidson and Oleszek, *Congress and Its Members,* 205–206.

22. Sinclair, *Unorthodox Lawmaking,* 32–50.

23. You can read about the Congressional Budget and Impoundment Control Act of 1974 online at http://www.house.gov/rules/jcoc2y.htm.

24. Sinclair, *Unorthodox Lawmaking,* 63–69.

25. Davidson and Oleszek, *Congress and Its Members,* 324–330.

26. Ibid., 314–317.

27. Ibid., 328.

28. Ibid., 165.

29. Senate Republican Committee website, at http://www.senate.gov/~rpc/aboutrpc.html.

30. Senate Democratic Steering and Coordination Committee website, at http://democrats.senate.gov/steering/.

31. Richard Fenno, *Congressmen in Committees* (Boston: Little, Brown, 1973).

32. Christopher J. Deering and Steven S. Smith, *Committees in Congress,* 3rd ed. (Washington, DC: CQ Press, 1997), 124–182.

33. Davidson and Oleszek, *Congress and Its Members,* 153–155.

34. John W. Kingdon, *Congressmen's Voting Decisions,* 3rd ed. (Ann Arbor: University of Michigan Press, 1989), 75–96.

35. Davidson and Oleszek, *Congress and Its Members,* 279.

36. Kingdon, *Congressmen's Voting Decisions,* 29–45.

37. Ibid., 43–54.

38. If you're interested in obtaining one, keep in mind that there's a charge and you should allow six weeks for delivery.

39. Fenno, *Congressmen in Committees,* 1–53.

40. Figures are as of 2001.

41. Figures are as of 1999 and are compiled from Davidson and Oleszek, *Congress and Its Members,* 153–155 and the National Taxpayer's Union at http://www.ntu.org/main/press.php?PressID=343

42. If you're curious about who's on C-SPAN right now, just go to their website at http://www.c-span.org/.

43. Fowler, *Candidates, Congress, and the American Democracy,* 74–81.

44. The Campaign Finance Institute, at http://www.cfinst.org/studies/vital/commentary.html.

45. Ibid., at http://www.cfinst.org/studies/vital/commentary.html.

46. Ibid., at http://www.cfinst.org/studies/vital/commentary.html.

The Presidency

10-1 Introduction

When we approach the presidency, we enter a place that is fundamentally different from the world of Congress. Five hundred and thirty-five people give way to a single individual with a large supporting cast. The decentralized, institutional feel of the legislative arena disappears in favor of the personal mystique of a powerful man who lives and works in the shadows of the few others who have served before him.

Many of us have emotional reactions to the president that we don't have toward Congress. He can generate strong feelings in us—both positive and negative. We can be quick to comment about the job he's doing. His personal life is on display for us to judge. His quirks and foibles are magnified by television. Comedians make fun of him. We compare him to others who held the job, even presidents long ago that we don't personally remember, and have opinions about how he stacks up. We measure him for greatness, even as we are critical of his actions.

Many of us also have specific ideas about the qualities we want in our presidents (something we probably never think about in relation to members of Congress), personal characteristics we expect them to have. Take a second to think about this. Table 10-1 contains qualities that some people look for in the president.

If you're so inclined (or if you're asked by your professor), compare notes with your classmates about what they want in a president. Chances are, many of them have a long wish list. Are they looking for honesty? Integrity? Intelligence? Curiosity? Strength? Determination? Flexibility? The ability to bring people together? Legislative skills? Communication skills? Good looks? These are just a few things people commonly say they expect their presidents to have. Does George W. Bush have all these qualities? Of course not—it's such a demanding set of characteristics that we're much more likely to find them in a comic-book superhero than a person. But demand we will—and we feel disappointed when our presidents let us down.

Political scientist George Edwards sums up the dilemma by noting that "all" we want from our presidents is "leadership yet responsiveness, flexibility yet firmness, statesmanship yet political skill, openness yet control, and empathy for ordinary people yet uniqueness. In other words, the president is expected to be all things to all people."[1]

If in reality presidents don't have all of the personal characteristics we want them to, you might wonder why we maintain such high expectations of them. Maybe it's that past presidents set our expectations, and we want our recent ones to measure up. As part of our socialization to politics in elementary school, we internalize legends about the giants who held the office long ago, people like Washington, Jefferson, and Lincoln.

Which of the following characteristics do you want in a president?		TABLE **10-1**

Brave	Has integrity
Can bring people together	Has practical life experience
Curious	Honest
Decisive	In control
Determined	Intelligent
Empathetic	Leadership skills
Faithful	Open to different ideas
Firmly held convictions	Politically savvy
Flexible	Responsive to public opinion
Good communication skills	Sensitive
Good legislative skills	Strong
Good-looking	Thoughtful
Good politician	Understands people like me

Things I Want in a President

In contrast, we hear so much criticism of recent presidents. Table 10-2 lists criticisms widely leveled against three recent presidents in the press and in public opinion.

Maybe you've heard comedians make fun of George W. Bush's intelligence. Lots of people—even his friends—felt Bill Clinton flip-flopped on important things and was deceptive, even dishonest. And Richard Nixon—during the Watergate scandal—was widely criticized by members of both political parties for disregarding personal liberties and trampling on the Constitution. Maybe you made these connections, maybe not.

What you may not have realized is that these are *exactly* the things that critics said about some of our more respected presidents, long before their faces were depicted on currency. It may surprise you to know that the things some people say about George W. Bush were also said about George Washington. Thomas Jefferson thought the first George wasn't particularly bright. Alexander Hamilton thought Washington craved power and control. His critics thought Washington paid way too much attention to his image and not enough to substance.

The things people said about Clinton echo what critics said of Thomas Jefferson, who was widely mistrusted, even by his allies, and believed to be someone who would say one thing and then turn around and say something contradictory if it suited his purposes.

Trampling on the Constitution? It was said about Lincoln as well as Nixon, by critics who watched Lincoln shut down opposition newspapers, arbitrarily arrest political dissenters, and deny prisoners who felt they were unlawfully incarcerated the right to petition for their release.

President	Popular Criticism	Criticism Also Leveled Against	TABLE **10-2**
George W. Bush	Secretive; not substantive; some say he is not very bright	George Washington	
Bill Clinton	Duplicitous; deceptive; inconsistent; dishonest	Thomas Jefferson	
Richard Nixon	Shows total disregard for the Constitution and personal liberties; not trustworthy	Abraham Lincoln	

Criticism of Recent Presidents

TABLE 10-3

Ranking the Presidents

1. Lincoln	22. Carter
2. F. Roosevelt	23. Ford
3. Washington	24. Taft
4. T. Roosevelt	25. Nixon
5. Truman	26. Hayes
6. Wilson	27. Coolidge
7. Jefferson	28. Taylor
8. Kennedy	29. Garfield
9. Eisenhower	30. Van Buren
10 L. Johnson	31. B. Harrison
11. Reagan	32. Arthur
12. Polk	33. Grant
13. Jackson	34. Hoover
14. Monroe	35. Fillmore
15. McKinley	36. Tyler
16. J. Adams	37. W. H. Harrison
17. Cleveland	38. Harding
18. Madison	39. Pierce
19. J. Q. Adams	40. Johnson
20. G. H. W. Bush	41. Buchanan
21. Clinton	

Sources: Reuters; Tim H. Murray and Robert K. Blessing, *Greatness in the White House: Rating the Presidents from George Washington through Ronald Reagan* (University Park: Pennsylvania State University Press, 1994); and Harold W. Stanley and Richard G. Niemi, *Vital Statistics on American Politics 1999–2000* (Washington, DC: CQ Press, 2000).

So, how did Washington, Jefferson, and Lincoln end up on Mount Rushmore if in their day they were criticized like our current presidents? The answer partly lies in the difference between myth and reality. Time has a way of making mortals heroic, of glossing over the flaws that make people human, especially if those mortals served at a critical time in our history like during the establishment of the constitutional system or the Civil War (our recent presidents did not have the opportunity to lead the United States to victory in the Revolutionary War, draft the Declaration of Independence, or emancipate the slaves). As a nation, we crave our heroes, and because of the psychological attachments people have to the presidency, our past presidents naturally fill the role. We *know* Washington didn't chop down that cherry tree, but deep down, many of us want to believe in leaders who could not tell a lie.

Besides, the presidency is the one office where greatness is the yardstick of performance. For many years, historians led by Arthur M. Schlesinger Jr. have been classifying past presidents as great, near great, average, below average, and failures.[2] Table 10-3 shows an updated ranking of the presidents. Some names remain affixed at the top—Lincoln, Washington, Franklin D. Roosevelt. Others are hopelessly in the cellar—Grant, Buchanan, Harding. What's interesting is that some presidents move around the rankings over time. Dwight D. Eisenhower was ranked twenty-first in Schlesinger's 1962 survey (low average) but rose to tenth (high average) in his 1996 results. Every president who served in the twenty-five years leading up to the most recent survey was bunched right in the middle. Will they look that way twenty-five years from now? Like most everything else, presidential performance looks different when viewed through the prism of time.

Presidents and presidential candidates, of course, are well aware that greatness is the standard by which they will be measured, and they play to it. You never hear presidential candidates promising to be the next Herbert Hoover. If there is a reason for caution in all this, it's that the Mt. Rushmore myth can influence the expectations we have of our presidents, elevating them to a place that's out of proportion to the realistic expectations of a complex and complicated office.

President Ford recognized this and played against the myth when he was elevated to the presidency upon Richard Nixon's resignation. "I'm a Ford, not a Lincoln," he told the nation, explicitly lowering expectations about his performance. It's only when we're offered the promise of a Lincoln that we can be set up for disappointment, because even Lincoln wasn't the Lincoln of myth when he walked the earth.

The wide-ranging and wildly unrealistic characteristics we look for in our presidents coincide with equally unrealistic and contradictory performance expectations. Just look at some of the things we expect the president to deliver:

- *Policy leadership:* On fundamental issues, we look to the president rather than Congress for leadership and direction. More than anyone else in the political system, we expect the president to keep us prosperous and safe, and we tend to punish presidents who fail to deliver. We hold these expectations despite the fact that the president is subject to forces beyond his control in the conduct of economic and foreign policy.[3]

- *Global leadership:* We expect the president to be the embodiment of America in the world, projecting a strong and compassionate image in line with how many of us like to view our global presence. In relations with other countries, the president is expected to act both wisely, as a statesman, and shrewdly, as a politician, despite the fact that this would require playing a unifying and divisive role simultaneously.

- *Crisis management:* The president is the person we turn to in a crisis, and we expect him to be in command. We expect the president to use his expertise and political skills to end a crisis successfully and in short order, with minimum harm to Americans, even though confusion may reign in the White House, information about what's happening may be incomplete, situations may change swiftly and unexpectedly, and good options may not be available.

- *Symbolic leadership:* We expect the president to be someone we can look up to and identify with, almost like a parent is to a young child. We want to be moved when he speaks. We want him to embody the best of us, and through his words and actions, project those positive characteristics back to us. Symbolically, we want him to be the image on Mount Rushmore, and many of us are sorely disappointed when he projects his human flaws rather than his idealized strengths.

- *Legitimacy for the system:* The president is as close as we get to a monarch, and like a king, we want the president to confer legitimacy on our collective sense of ourselves. We want him to act honorably so that his actions reflect well on American democracy and so that we may regard him as a unifying force. We want this despite the fact that the presidency is a political job, and politics is inherently divisive.

So, the myth of presidential greatness encourages a series of performance expectations that are at best contradictory and at worst impossible to fulfill. Presidents attempt to deal with this by compartmentalizing what they do, acting out different roles at different times, making a rousing speech for public consumption at a summit meeting with other world leaders while working outside the spotlight on the divisive politics of policy making. The compartmental approach can work up to a point, but presidents inevitably run up against their limitations and the many roadblocks built in to the federal system. Some presidents simply play one or two of these roles better than others. President Bush has received high marks for providing crisis management. President Clinton was considered a strong policy leader. President Reagan provided a lot of people with symbolic leadership. It's a lot to expect them to perform all these roles at the same high level. But we do.

Box 10-1   You Want to Be President?

You'd better be thirty-five years old. And you must be a natural-born citizen of the United States who's lived here fourteen years. So says the Constitution.

Here are a few other procedural matters pertaining to the presidency that are set down in Article II:

- The presidential term is four years.
- Congress establishes the president's salary but can't change it while he's in office.
- If the president dies or resigns, the powers and duties of the office "devolve on the Vice President." The Twenty-fifth Amendment, ratified in 1967, allows the president to temporarily assign his powers to the vice president if he is going to be incapacitated, such as if he's going under general anesthesia during an operation. It also provides for the vice president and a majority of Congress or the president's cabinet to make the vice president "Acting President" if they judge the president to be unable to function; and it permits the president to fill a vacancy in the vice presidency, subject to

confirmation by a majority vote of both Houses of Congress.

- The president has to "from time to time" give Congress "Information of the State of the Union," but it doesn't have to be in a formal speech, and there's no provision for it to be televised.
- The president and vice president may be removed from office if impeached for and convicted of "Treason, Bribery, or other high Crimes and Misdemeanors." We discussed impeachment in Chapter 9 (Section 9-5d, "Impeachment").
- At his inauguration, the president is required to take the following oath: "I do solemnly swear (or affirm) that I will faithfully execute the Office of President of the United States, and will to the best of my Ability, preserve, protect and defend the constitution of the United States." George Washington added: "So help me God." So has everyone who came after him.

10-2 Growth of the Presidency

What's more, we have high expectations for performance in a presidential office that, on paper, doesn't have very much substance. The presidency started out as a poorly defined second cousin to Congress. Only time, precedent, and the actions of some of its more aggressive occupants have shaped the presidency into the powerful branch we know today.

Take a look at Article II of the Constitution, which establishes the presidency (you can find the full text in Appendix B and a discussion of the highlights in Box 10-1). Notice how short it is compared to Article I, which establishes Congress. It's only four sections (compared to the ten sections composing Article I)—and if you take away the material on the president's term of office, presidential elections, eligibility requirements, compensation, the oath of office, the requirement that the president make a State of the Union address to Congress, and **impeachment,** you're left with a grand total of two paragraphs dealing with what the president is supposed to do.

Article II opens with the declaration: "The executive Power shall be vested in a President of the United States," but it doesn't elaborate. The executive power? What's that supposed to be?

The authors of the Constitution were purposely vague about this central point. In colonial America, they had been pretty familiar with strong executives, both in the form of the King of England and the royal governors he appointed to oversee the colonies—who were widely regarded as corrupt officials who abused their power. In contrast, as we saw in Chapter 2, freely elected colonial legislatures served as a democratic check on these executives. The experience led them to conclude that strong legislatures were the best way to protect personal liberties.[4] So, they created a strong legislature in Article I, paying detailed attention to how it would function. Secondarily, they created the office of the president, whose grant of executive power was meant to be more vague than broad.

From these beginnings, the office of the presidency grew erratically, strengthened by precedent and by a few opportunistic presidents inclined to use ambiguous constitutional language to enhance their power. George Washington established expectations for the office by instituting standards for everything from how the president should be addressed (he preferred the constitutional designation of, simply, "the President of the United States" to Vice President John Adams' more regal, "His Highness the President of the United States

impeachment The power granted to Congress to remove from office the president, vice president, judges, and other federal officials.

and protector of their Liberties"), to procedures for how the executive branch would conduct business, to how long the president should serve (two terms, long before it was mandated by constitutional amendment).[5]

Andrew Jackson, who took office in 1829, was the first to assert a direct presidential connection to the people, strengthening the office with respect to Congress, which had previously played that role. Abraham Lincoln claimed unilateral power for the presidency as he led the Union through the Civil War. Following a period of congressional reemergence in the second half of the nineteenth century, a succession of presidents from Grover Cleveland to William McKinley to, most notably, Theodore Roosevelt, contributed to the expansion of presidential power.[6] Echoing Jackson, Roosevelt articulated his philosophy of a presidency limited only by what the Constitution *prohibited* him from doing (which, admittedly, is not much), calling himself "a steward of the people bound actively and affirmatively to do all he could for the people."[7]

The twentieth century witnessed a line of presidents who exercised aggressive leadership. Woodrow Wilson sought to be a strong party leader who could move public opinion and, with it, command congressional support. Franklin D. Roosevelt, governing during the Great Depression and World War II, was a proactive leader who presided over unprecedented expansion in the size and scope of the executive branch. Lyndon Johnson dominated Congress, establishing the center of policy making in the White House. Richard Nixon went to war with Congress over his attempts to expand presidential prerogatives, impounding funds for congressional initiatives he disliked and acting unilaterally in his prosecution of the Vietnam War. Ronald Reagan used the force of his personality and strong communication skills to move public opinion and congressional opponents.[8]

10-3 Formal and Informal Sources of Presidential Power

Over the last century, success in the presidency came to hinge on the ability to articulate a message and establish a bond with voters. The advent of mass media made direct communication with the public more possible—and more necessary. Today, it's unthinkable for a day to go by without the president appearing in, or even dominating, the news agenda. The ubiquitous president is a late twentieth-century phenomenon that's worked to supplement the president's limited formal powers with a wealth of informal powers—for those presidents who know how to use them.

10-3a Formal Presidential Powers

Apart from giving the president that vague grant of "executive Power" and the equally vague (or broad) mandate to see to it that "the Laws be faithfully executed," the Constitution gives the president very few formal powers. The only specific powers expressly granted to the president are:

- *Appointments:* The Constitution gives the president the power to appoint ambassadors, Supreme Court justices, and other federal officers, like federal court judges, cabinet secretaries, and agency heads. The Senate has to confirm the president's nominees.
- *Treaties:* The president can negotiate treaties with other nations, subject to ratification by two-thirds of the Senate.
- *Commander-in-chief of the army and navy:* The Constitution makes the president the civilian commander of the military.
- **Veto power:** The president can veto an act of Congress, though Congress can override the veto with a two-thirds vote of both houses.
- **Recess appointments:** Presidential appointments made while the Senate is out of session do not require ratification, and stand until the end of the congressional session. We discussed them in Section 9-5c, "Confirming Presidential Appointments" in Chapter 9.

veto power
The constitutional power granted to the president to block an act of Congress. It takes a two-thirds vote of both houses of Congress to override a presidential veto.

recess appointments
The constitutional power granted to the president to make nominations while Congress is out of session that do not require Senate approval. The appointments stand until the end of the congressional term.

Box 10-2 Pardon Me?

The presidential pardon power has its origins in the traditional right of kings to be the final arbiter of disputes, which is why it is an absolute power. In fact, it's something of an anomaly: Nowhere else in the federal system can an elected official unilaterally grant clemency. This can cause controversy if a president is viewed as issuing pardons for political purposes.

On his last day in office, President Clinton ignited a scandal by issuing 140 pardons, some of them controversial pardons of political supporters, including a pardon of fugitive international financier Marc Rich, who was wanted by the Justice Department on fraud charges, and a pardon of his half-brother Roger, who faced trouble over alleged illegal lobbying efforts. The Justice Department lists the pardons and itemizes the (often sleazy) allegations against the pardon recipients on its website at http://www.usdoj.gov/opa/pardonchartlst.htm.

Perhaps the most famous use of the pardon power was President Ford's full pardon of his predecessor Richard Nixon

for all actions taken by Nixon while he was in office. The pardon eliminated the possibility that the former president would be tried as a private citizen for illegal activities stemming from the Watergate scandal. Ford defended the pardon as a necessary action to get the country past the scandal, arguing that the specter of a former president on trial for criminal activity would prevent the nation from healing. Critics derided the pardon by saying it placed Nixon above the law, shielding him from facing responsibility for his actions. There was even speculation at the time that Ford had agreed to pardon Nixon in exchange for the latter's resignation, but if this was so, it exacted a great political cost from Ford, who narrowly lost election to the presidency two years later. Also, it should be remembered that a president has the power to pardon anyone: Before he resigned, Nixon easily could have pardoned himself.

• *Convene Congress:* The president may call a session of Congress at any time.

• *Receive ambassadors:* The president officially greets representatives of other nations on behalf of the United States.

• *Pardon power:* The president may pardon anyone suspected, accused, or convicted of any crime for any reason without explanation (see Box 10-2). Presidential pardons are final and cannot be overturned.

pardon power The unilateral power of the president to grant unconditional clemency to anyone for any reason.

executive privilege The power of the president, established by custom, to keep Congress, the courts, and the public from having access to presidential documents and communications.

Time and tradition have supplemented the president's constitutional powers. For instance, the Constitution never mentions **executive privilege,** and Congress has never fully accepted it, but presidents have been known to use it freely. It's the power to keep material originating in the executive branch confidential. Although presidents find it helpful—and convenient—to be able to designate material as "privileged," executive privilege is far from an absolute power and can best serve as a defensive maneuver against Congress.

Typically, presidents have claimed executive privilege on matters surrounding national security, on the grounds that public exposure would undermine sensitive government operations—a position that's been upheld by the courts. Presidents have relied on executive privilege to keep members of the executive branch from testifying at congressional hearings and to prevent the release of sensitive documents.

They have also claimed executive privilege in political circumstances to avoid the release of politically damaging information. President Nixon tried unsuccessfully to use executive privilege as a rationale to prevent the release of tapes of Oval Office conversations that implicated him in the Watergate affair.

The Bush administration, arguing an important principle and not politics is involved, claimed executive privilege to prevent the release of information related to meetings between the vice president and energy company officials regarding the development of the administration's national energy policy—even though the vice president isn't the chief executive.

When you add up the president's formal powers, there's not a whole lot a president can use on an everyday basis that will help him politically. Most of the powers are situation-specific and only come into play when the president is faced with treaties he can negotiate, ambassadors he can receive, legislation he can veto, or individuals he can pardon. Recess appointments can only be made during those few weeks when Congress is out of session, and as we said in Chapter 9, the Senate regards them as hostile acts, so many presidents have been reluctant to make them. The appointment power can be formidable and can enable the president to put his mark on the executive branch and the judiciary—but it's only one aspect of the president's job. Likewise, commanding the military is an awesome power, but much of the president's involvement in domestic and foreign affairs doesn't involve military matters. The constitutional powers granted the president simply do not have a lot of day-in, day-out value.

10-3b Informal Presidential Powers

Unlike formal powers, the prerogatives of the presidency can be enormously helpful to a president who wants to put his imprint on politics and policy. Political scientist Richard Neustadt distinguished formal, constitutional powers from informal means of exercising political power, saying the president may not occupy the strongest constitutional position with respect to Congress (which has the final word in overriding vetoes, confirming appointments, and even impeaching the president), but a skillful president can dominate Washington politically through careful use of the informal advantages his office provides. In fact, we will see that most of the president's power comes from informal sources. Neustadt recognized that the doctrine of separation of powers created three branches of government that need to find common ground in order to get anything accomplished. In this environment, a skilled and determined president can emerge a political leader.[9]

He does it by using **persuasion,** by convincing others in Washington whom the president needs to get things done that his interests are their interests. There is no strict formula for doing this, but Neustadt claims the president can have maximum leverage if he enjoys a strong professional reputation in Washington and a high level of public prestige. Maintaining these requires creating favorable impressions of his ability and support.

A president's **professional reputation** is the judgment of him made by others in Washington, based on what he says and what he does. A president who rises above what is expected of him, acts consistently, and stands behind his beliefs is in a solid position to bargain for what he wants.[10] Immediately following the terrorist attack of September 2001, many in Washington who previously doubted whether he was up to the job perceived President Bush as steady, firm, and reassuring. His political stock soared as Bush erased impressions that he was a political lightweight.

A president's **public prestige** is the impression formed by others in Washington of his standing with the public, and like the president's reputation, high levels of prestige can enhance his persuasiveness by making him a political force to be dealt with. In this regard, the president's public prestige and professional reputation can reinforce each other.[11] When President Bush asked Congress for approval to use military force against Iraq in September 2002, his strong public standing on matters of security and defense made it difficult for some members of Congress to oppose the request, despite their doubts about the advisability of the Iraq mission. If President Bush had been an unpopular president at the time, congressional opponents of the Iraq War might have found it easier to voice their disapproval without worrying that their constituents would blame them for defying the president.

10-3c Malleable Public Opinion

Writing over forty years ago, Neustadt saw the president's personality and popularity as secondary factors in determining the president's prestige. Today, anyone who works as a political advisor to the president would pay a great deal of attention to these things. Earlier presidents could take their **mandate** to lead from the election results, but contemporary presidents have to contend with a never-ending barrage of public opinion polls commissioned by independent research firms, major newspapers and television networks, political parties—even the White House—that measure presidential approval on an ongoing basis.

This gives the president a sliding mandate—a pliable environment for governing that can make him more or less persuasive as his term progresses.[12] Bill Clinton came to office having failed to secure a majority of the popular vote in a three-way race, and his early months were scarred by missteps that caused his public support to plunge so low that

▶**persuasion** An informal source of presidential power that gives skilled presidents the opportunity to influence the decisions of members of Congress and others in Washington whose support the president needs to accomplish his political objectives.

▶**professional reputation** The sense among Washington officials of the president's political skills and abilities. It is one of the keys to effective persuasion, as it enhances the president's ability to bargain.

▶**public prestige** The sense among Washington officials about whether the president is well regarded by the public. It is one of the keys to effective persuasion, as it enhances the president's ability to bargain.

▶**mandate** A directive by voters to the president to move ahead with the program he promised when he was a candidate. A large mandate produced by a lopsided vote gives the president a strong bargaining position with respect to Congress to set and advance the agenda in Washington.

political commentators were speculating that the new president would never be able to win a second term. Clinton made adjustments, and by the time he returned to face the voters, opinion polls showed his standing with the public had vastly improved; he was reelected easily.

Because public support is neither steady nor reliable, presidents can have a difficult time mobilizing the public. Even a president with a high standing in public opinion polls can find that it is an effort to rally Congress and the public behind his policies. Much depends on the substance and style of his approach, and on events beyond his control that might independently move public opinion away from him. Starting in late 2003, President Bush tried to unite the public beyond the postwar effort in Iraq, but ongoing casualties to American troops complicated his efforts. Sometimes, the best the president can hope to do is move public opinion at the margins, getting some people who were opposed to become indifferent, or some who were indifferent to be supportive. Sometimes, small movements in public opinion are enough to secure the results the president wants—for instance, getting a wavering senator or two to support the president—while at other times, they fall short.[13]

The summary figure that president-watchers (and presidents) look at to gauge presidential effectiveness is support for the president's performance in office: the percentage of Americans who approve and the percentage who disapprove. However, the polling environment is complex because pollsters ask so many questions—about individual policies, hypothetical approaches to problems, approval of the president as an individual, and much more.[14] We talked about this in Section 3-6, "Measuring Public Opinion," in Chapter 3. Box 10-3 demonstrates how data on presidential performance are used.

With all the variables involved in opinion polls, there is one constant to the shape of presidential job approval that applies to almost all contemporary presidents: It goes down with time (see Figure 10-1). Flush with the excitement and great expectations produced by a winning campaign, new presidents often come to office with a reservoir of goodwill that translates into a **honeymoon** period with the press and the public.[15] Trading on the unrealistic expectations of the presidential myth, new presidents offer the promise of great things; even people who supported the losing candidate are typically willing to give the new president a chance.

It doesn't take long for reality to set in. After a few weeks or months, unrealistically high expectations give way to the reality of governing, where hard choices by necessity begin to alienate groups of constituents. This is particularly the case during difficult economic times, which are generally blamed on the person in the White House. Presidential approval falls. The honeymoon becomes a distant memory.[16]

Even though the general trend in presidential approval is downward, events can conspire to bolster a president's public standing. Typically, if a president is reelected, there is a brief "second honeymoon" characterized by an uptick in public approval. It is also quite commonplace for traumatic national events to produce a **rally effect,** whereby people turn to the president for leadership, temporarily bolstering his support scores in the process.

The interesting thing about a rally effect is that it tends to happen regardless of what the president does, how well he performs, or whether he does anything at all. After President Reagan was shot in a failed assassination attempt in 1981, his job approval went up seven points. Early in his administration, President Kennedy ordered a failed assault on Cuba known as the Bay of Pigs invasion. It was a fiasco, the president admitted it was a mistake—and his job approval ratings went up. Americans were taken hostage in Iran during the Carter administration, the president did nothing, and his approval scores went up, too.[17] But gravity inevitably takes its toll on rallies. In Carter's case, as the Iranian hostage crisis dragged on for 444 days, people soured on the president's inability to work out a resolution, and public support for his ability to handle foreign policy took a nosedive. Box 10-4 on page 300 talks about the unusual pattern of George W. Bush's job approval scores.

Rally effects aside, presidents labor—often unsuccessfully—to keep their performance ratings up in an effort to marshal their power. Political scientist Theodore Lowi, writing during the Reagan administration, saw a democratic dilemma in what he calls the personal presidency, where presidential power is built on popular support for things the president realistically can't deliver because the constitutional system is designed to frustrate his

▶**honeymoon** The initial weeks of a new presidential administration when enthusiasm and good press typically translate into high public-approval ratings.

▶**rally effect** The tendency for Americans to unite around the president during a crisis, temporarily bolstering his job-approval ratings.

Box 10-3   When Do Polls Get in the Way of Governing?

In film and on television, hypothetical presidents make decisions from the heart or the gut without obsessing over the details of polling data. Real presidents are far more likely to keep trusted pollsters as close advisors and rely on their counsel when deciding what positions they should take and how they should act.

There are a couple of ways to view this reliance on survey data, which mirror the different legislative roles we discussed in Chapter 9—the delegate and the trustee.

When the president keeps his finger on the pulse of public opinion, it could be argued that he's acting like a delegate to govern as the public wishes. However, more than members of Congress, presidents are valued for their wisdom and leadership abilities, characteristics of the trustee role, which include the ability to set a national direction and build support when it's lacking. This is a daunting task for presidents who rely heavily on the safety of public approval.

It's also possible to put polling data ahead of principle. Polls might direct the president to do what's expedient or politically convenient, rather than what he would like to do or what in his judgment is best to do. For instance, it may be responsible but politically unpopular to propose changes to the Social Security program in order to address a projected shortfall in Social Security funding. President Bush campaigned on a controversial change that would have permitted limited private investment of Social Security funds—a plan that looked politically appealing when the stock market was booming. Two years later, as stock values fell sharply, pollsters advised Bush to stop talking about the proposal and to stop using the term "privatization" because voters now viewed it negatively. This was good political advice, but the policy problems posed by a potential Social Security shortfall remained.

At another level, when we see the president changing or shading positions in response to polls, it can work against the desire some people have to view the president as an independent leader. True, part of this desire is rooted in those sometimes unrealistic expectations of the president that we talked about earlier. Unrealistic or not, though, expectations can translate into attitudes. In theory, we might like to see the president move boldly on principle against the tide of public opinion. In practice, the president's political advisors would most likely say it's not worth the risk of alienating the electorate.

Not every president will listen to this advice. Despite the primacy of polling data in White House decision making, presidents have been known to buck the suggestions of their pollsters when facing problems that demanded risky, unpopular solutions. President Bush (senior) violated his most prominent campaign pledge—"read my lips: no new taxes"—and supported a tax increase in order to win congressional support for an economic package he felt on the whole was best for the economy (thus triggering a political backlash that undermined his reelection prospects). Back in the 1950s, when the science of modern polling was emerging, President Truman (who was often beset with weak job approval ratings) was fond of saying, "I wonder how far Moses would have gone if he had taken a poll in Egypt? What would Jesus Christ have preached if he'd taken a poll in Israel? . . . It isn't polls or public opinion of the moment that counts. It is right and wrong and leadership."[*]

---

[*]Paul Brace and Barbara Hinckley, *Follow the Leader: Opinion Polls and the Modern Presidents* (New York: Basic Books, 1992), 19.

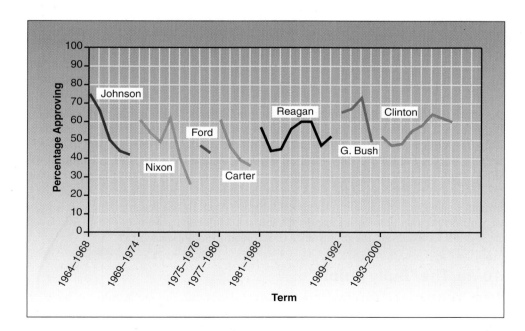

Figure 10-1
Down They Go
The general direction of presidential job performance scores is down. Of the seven presidents to hold office before George W. Bush, only Ronald Reagan left office on the upswing.

Sources: Lyn Ragsdale, *Vital Statistics on the Presidency,* revised edition (Washington, DC: Congressional Quarterly, 1998) and http://www.gallup.com/.

Box 10-4   George W. Bush: Presidential Approval during Extraordinary Times

Presidential approval scores typically start out high, fall when the "honeymoon" ends, rally briefly during crises, and decline during difficult economic times. The unconventional way President Bush came to power and the dramatic impact of the 2001 terror attacks altered this pattern somewhat—at least for the first year of the president's term. Instead of coming to Washington awash in good feelings, Bush had a stunted honeymoon following his contested election. Then the tragic events of September 11, 2001, united the public around the president, who saw his job approval top 90 percent—an unprecedented level commensurate with events. Although a year later, better than 25 percentage points had been shaved off this mark, Bush's job approval scores remained high, even as large numbers of Americans expressed concern about the direction of the economy. It seems that many people were willing to forgive the president for falling stock prices and a poor job market, either because

they blamed the terror attacks for bad economic times or because their support for Bush's work in foreign affairs weighed more heavily in their overall assessment of his job performance.

In his second and third years, President Bush experienced a more customary pattern of public support. The president continued to realize a decline in popular support into his second year as unemployment mounted. This decline was halted by another rally event—the Iraq War—which briefly produced a surge in presidential approval that dissipated over the summer of Bush's third year, when American troops faced violence in postwar Iraq and the job market remained weak. The capture of Saddam Hussein in late 2003 produced another temporary bump in support for President Bush, but he faced strong political opposition throughout the 2004 presidential campaign as his approval rating sagged into the high 40 percent range.

initiatives, not advance them. Only rarely can a president prevail over institutional checks and balances—like during a national crisis when he can rally Congress to his side. These are the exceptions—but we expect them to be the rule, an expectation that's inflated by our mythical notion of what the president can do and by presidents who play to that myth for political reasons, making promises that are hard to deliver.

Lacking the institutional powers necessary to play to public expectations, Lowi claims presidents engage in sales efforts to convince the public that they've met those expectations. He says that following a sincere effort to keep their promises, presidents spend their terms trying to create the illusion of success. Appearance replaces performance, sending performance expectations further out of whack with reality.[18]

With the personal side of the presidency playing such a large role in how the president governs, the makeup of the president's character can be more important to understand than, say, the character of individual senators or Supreme Court justices. Admittedly, character takes into account a lot of factors—it can be hard to pin down exactly what it is, much less figure out how it relates to presidential performance. One provocative approach to understanding presidential character is considered in Box 10-5.

10-4 The Media as a Presidential Resource

It's easier for presidents to sell the idea that they're performing than it is to actually perform because they have greater access to tools that allow them to speak effectively than to act effectively. Belying the chronic drop-off in public support that awaits most presidents is the fact that they have considerable resources at their disposal in their ongoing efforts to keep the public behind them. Most noteworthy is the megaphone the president can use to amplify his voice above the din of official Washington and command the attention of the press: There are 535 members of Congress, and the nine Supreme Court justices operate largely out of public view; the president is the only officer who alone can speak for a branch of government, an administration, or the nation. In this regard, the president can depend on the media to be an important source of informal power that enables him—if he is skillful—to elevate the importance of a constitutionally weak office.

10-4a The "Bully Pulpit"

Teddy Roosevelt called the president's elevated vantage point the "bully pulpit" ("bully" in Roosevelt's day meant wonderful), and presidents who have been skillful communicators (or who have had shrewd and skillful communications aides) have been able to command

Box 10-5 Presidential Character

Political scientist James David Barber suggests that one way to think about presidential character is to assess whether a president has an energetic, active approach to his job or a removed, passive style, and then to determine if the president takes pleasure in his activity or feels burdened by it. By crossing these two characteristics (activity and self-esteem), Barber arrives at four presidential character "types" or patterns with a long history in psychological research and into which every president can be classified.

The four types are displayed in Figure 1: "active-positive;" "active-negative;" "passive-positive;" and "passive-negative." [*]

Barber was heavily influenced by the behavior of Presidents Johnson and Nixon, whom he considered dangerous because of what he saw as "an energy distorted from within."[†] Both active-negative types, Johnson deceived the press and public while pulling the nation irrevocably into the Vietnam tragedy, while Nixon deceived the press and public while pulling the nation irrevocably into the Watergate scandal.

Barber claims that presidents with different character profiles would have behaved less compulsively and self-destructively, and he says we need to be aware of character issues before "hiring" a new president in order to avoid future troubles. However, his work is not without controversy. He admits to a preference for active-positive presidents (a categorization that even *sounds* more appealing than "passive" or "negative"), who display the energy of a Johnson or a Nixon but who are flexible and adaptive. However, this choice could be said to favor a governing model in which the president is an activist, rather than one where the president delegates the particulars of a limited agenda. Furthermore, because Barber's categories are broad, classifying presidents using his framework leaves room for a fair amount of interpretation (should Reagan, for instance, be classified as "active" rather than "passive?").

What do you think of the value of Barber's approach to presidential character? Do you think it would be helpful to have information like this before voting for president? Do you think it would make a difference in how people voted if it were widely available?

[*]James David Barber, *The Presidential Character: Predicting Performance in the White House,* 4th ed. (Englewood Cliffs, NJ: Prentice Hall, 1992), 1–11.

[†]Ibid., 9.

Active-Positive	Active-Negative
Examples: Franklin D. Roosevelt John F. Kennedy • Flexible and adaptive • Develops and grows over time • Feels capable of meeting job challenges • Well-grounded • Results-oriented	*Examples:* Lyndon B. Johnson Richard M. Nixon • Compulsive and insecure • Distorted ambition, which compensates for low self-esteem • Trouble managing aggressive feelings • Unable to correct misguided actions • Dangerous power-seeker
Passive-Positive	Passive-Negative
Example: Ronald Reagan • Compliant • Reacts to events instead of being assertive • Nice guy searching for affection • Low self-esteem • Often disappointing in public office	*Example:* Dwight D. Eisenhower • Does little and enjoys little of what he does • Motivated by duty and service • Inflexible • Withdraws from conflict • Could lead the nation adrift

Figure 1

Barber's Presidential Character Types

Source: James David Barber, *The Presidential Character: Predicting Performance in the White House,* 4th ed. (Englewood Cliffs, NJ: Prentice Hall, 1992).

it with some success. Roosevelt served at a time when mass-circulation newspapers were becoming popular, and he shrewdly recognized the president's ability to use the mass media to reach out to the public and advance his agenda.[19] Contemporary presidents who routinely engage in intricate media strategies can trace their efforts to what Roosevelt started one hundred years ago.

One of the more typical ways that presidents use the "bully pulpit" is by appealing directly to Americans through the media to support their agenda. Political scientist Samuel Kernell calls this strategy **"going public,"** and although it can be traced back in some fashion to Teddy Roosevelt, it has become the centerpiece of modern presidential governing styles.[20] President Bush "goes public" every time he makes a televised speech, appears at

▶ **going public** The presidential strategy of using the media to appeal directly to the public to support presidential initiatives.

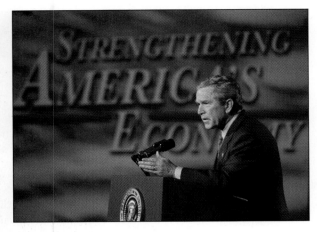

Presidents have been "going public" for years, and in media-savvy ways that have changed as communication technology grew up. Franklin D. Roosevelt *(left)* used his command of radio to give "fireside chats" that made people feel like he was a visitor in their living rooms. George W. Bush *(right)* uses clear, simple slogans to underscore the point he wants to convey in his televised message.

Source: (Left) Picture History. *(Right)* White House photo by Paul Morse.

events around the country or the world, or employs **media events** to draw attention to and build support for an initiative. Today, presidents will go so far as to talk about policy initiatives in front of a backdrop bearing a slogan that tersely reinforces his main point—something like "Protecting Worker's Rights" or "Preserving Precious Natural Resources." It may seem cheesy and more suited to a salesperson than a national leader, but when the president goes public, he in effect becomes salesperson-in-chief.

Even casual attention to television or the Internet would reveal that presidents frequently engage in public sales efforts. The point is to put pressure on members of Congress, while circumventing them at the same time. In Neustadt's terms, "going public" involves the president leveraging public prestige by moving voters to his position, rather than bargaining with members of Congress directly. Because these are the same voters who pass judgment on members of Congress, the strategy can be effective.

10-4b Media Operations

As objectionable as it may be to some people, public relations and advertising campaigns have become an integral part of White House operations and an essential part of being president. A large number of high-level White House staff members devote their time to developing, managing, and communicating the president's message on a daily basis. In the Bush White House, the key players reside in the **Communications Office,** contributing to the strategic planning of the president's policy agenda by formulating daily messages and planning media events designed to get the press to discuss the president's agenda and to do so in the way the president desires. In effect, the Communications Office tries to set the agenda for the agenda-setters in the press.

As part of this effort, the Communications Office coordinates the following communications functions:

media events Activities staged by campaigns or political officials that have enough news value to draw press attention to a message the politician wants to communicate.

Communications Office The White House office responsible for coordinating the president's media operations, including speechwriting and liaison with national and local reporters.

press secretary The liaison between the White House and the national press covering the president.

- *Contact with national reporters.* The **press secretary** is the conduit between the president and the press. He or she manages requests for interviews with White House officials and holds regular **press briefings** with national newspaper, television, radio, magazine, and wire-service reporters who cover the White House, answering their questions—or avoiding them if doing so is in the president's interest. In recent administrations, the press secretary has worked to keep tight control over the flow of information.

- *Contact with local reporters and special interest media.* The Media Affairs Office is responsible for handling requests by local television and radio stations, newspapers, and specialized media, such as business, religious, and sports publications, for

Box 10-6   Is Presidential News Management a Problem?

It may be a normatively good thing for democratic processes when the White House is unable to control the message it wants to communicate on a daily basis. After all, it's critical for information to flow freely if we're going to have the chance to be well informed, and at its core, presidential news management is about *restricting* information to the press and, by extension, to us. The argument against coordinated presidential news management strategies is that controlling the flow of information to the press will always serve the president's political purposes—presenting him and his policies in the best possible light. It may not simultaneously serve the public interest if, in the process, information is withheld or manipulated.

News management in the George W. Bush White House fell under intense scrutiny in 2003 when it came to light that the president may have intentionally or unintentionally misstated the level of the threat posed by Saddam Hussein prior to the American invasion of Iraq. As part of his effort to win public support for the Iraq War, President Bush made the claim that Hussein possessed weapons of mass destruction and was engaged in developing nuclear weapons. After the war, Iraqi weapons of mass destruction were not immediately found, and reports surfaced that claims about Hussein's nuclear capability were based on faulty intelligence that high-level administration officials may have known to be false.

Critics who wanted to know how the White House could successfully exaggerate and misrepresent the Iraqi threat when war hung in the balance blasted a highly efficient White House news management operation that prevented careful press scrutiny of the facts. With the president, vice president, and key advisors speaking in concert about information they tightly controlled, critics charged the administration could not be effectively challenged as it led the nation to war under what they said were false pretenses. The president himself only met with the press once during the prewar period—see the discussion of press conferences that follows—and that was in a controlled setting in which the reporters who would get to ask questions were preselected to minimize the likelihood that they might raise issues the president did not want to address.

To those who felt it was in the national interest for the administration to convince the public to support the Iraq War by any means, careful news management advanced their desired outcome. To those who argued that the best way for citizens of a republic to make informed life or death decisions is for them to be provided with an honest rendering of pertinent information, the White House news management strategy was seen as undermining intelligent public decision-making. What do you think?

---

interviews with White House personnel and official information. The Media Affairs Office also maintains the White House website at http://www.whitehouse.gov.

- *Speechwriting.* The president employs a number of people who put words in his mouth, scripting everything from formal addresses to talking points for presidential appearances.[21]

The point of the effort is to get the White House to speak with one carefully crafted voice, which is often difficult to accomplish. The job of coordinating a single message can be daunting because so many people work with and around the president, all of whom have personal agendas that are not always the same as the president's. Administration officials routinely circumvent the official communications operation by giving **news leaks** to the press when it serves their purposes, even if it undermines the president's official message. Some White Houses are "leakier" than others. The Clinton White House was known for its lack of discipline. The Bush White House is highly intolerant of news leaks, unless they are put out on purpose with the blessing of the Communications Office to test public reaction to a policy move the White House is planning.[22] Box 10-6 discusses presidential news management in more detail.

Presidents also have a couple of other tools to get their message to the public through the press. Presidents skilled in structured question-and-answer formats have relied on **press conferences** with reporters who cover the White House to disseminate the official line on topics of importance to the administration. Press conferences can either be conducted privately or staged as television events. President Kennedy, for instance, was fond of televised press conferences because he could use them to speak directly to the public, in effect turning them into media events where reporters were props.[23]

Presidents cannot control what happens at a press conference, of course (apart from the press conference discussed in Box 10-6, where reporters agreed to let the White House determine who would get to ask questions of President Bush), but press conferences don't

press briefings (see p. 302) Formal exchanges of information between the press secretary and the national press covering the president.

news leaks The tactic used widely by White House officials of releasing information to the press on an anonymous basis when it serves their interests to have the information publicized. Some leaks are unauthorized and unwanted by the White House.

press conferences Scheduled meetings between reporters and political figures like the president, which give the press access to the official and an opportunity to ask him or her questions firsthand.

have to be risky ventures for them. They can take questions from reporters known to be friendly to the administration. Presidential advisors can usually anticipate the major questions reporters will ask, and speechwriters can craft responses in advance. Even if a question isn't about something he wants to address, the president can give a quick and general response and move rapidly to something he wants to talk about. Because reporters customarily are limited in their ability to follow up, it can be hard for them to get the president to address something he doesn't want to talk about. All this restricts how informative press conferences can be.[24]

President Clinton held press conferences less frequently than some of his recent predecessors; President Bush rarely holds them, opting instead to let his press secretary interact with reporters. However, every president since Franklin D. Roosevelt has held background briefings or **"backgrounders,"** where reporters are given information "off the record"—meaning they can use it as long as they don't attribute it to its source. Any administration official may hold a backgrounder, and unlike press conferences, they can be a good source of information for reporters. The administration can use backgrounders to float a policy idea without having the president's fingerprints on it in case it flops with the public (much like the way news leaks can be used), or even to send messages to other nations about possible foreign policy initiatives without yet having to defend them as official policy.[25]

10-4c Tensions with Reporters

As presidents have come to view the press as a tool in a public relations campaign, reporters have pushed back by looking critically, even cynically, at the president's motives and by reporting his actions accordingly. Today, presidential news is more likely to be about the motivation underlying what the president said or did than simply about his words or actions. By reporting on the presidential public relations machine, reporters try to dilute its effects by drawing attention to it.

It may be hard to believe that for a period before the Vietnam War, the president was widely regarded by the press as a public servant who spoke for the nation, and reporters would pass his words on uncritically. That was before the Johnson administration lied to reporters about American progress in Vietnam and the Nixon administration lied about the president's involvement in Watergate. Media advisors to Presidents Reagan, Clinton, and George W. Bush relentlessly stage-managed the president's image, leading reporters who felt they had been lied to by Johnson and Nixon to experience the additional burden of feeling controlled by the White House. The cumulative product of these experiences has been the creation of an adversarial relationship between reporters and the president, in keeping with the relationship between reporters and political figures that we discussed in Chapter 5.

It is, however, a complex relationship. Presidents want to control the timing and content of news stories. So do reporters. Because the president's ability to persuade the public and official Washington depends so heavily on the media, he can't do without the reporters who cover his actions. At the same time, because the prestige and career advancement of those who cover his actions depend on having access to the White House, reporters can't do without the president.[26]

Because it's an ongoing relationship, both parties typically find a way to cooperate, although reporters will find some administrations to be more forthcoming than others, and levels of cooperation change over the course of time. Political scientists Michael Grossman and Martha Kumar identify three distinct phases in the relationship between the president and the press, starting with a period of *alliance* when an administration is new and reporters are engaged in developing relationships with new people in the president's press operation. It's a time when reporter and administration self-interest calls for cooperation, as both groups benefit from covering the administration in a favorable light.

It usually doesn't last long. Once the administration gets down to the business of governing, conflicts and controversies are inevitable. Reporters, seeing these items as **newsworthy,** diverge from the White House view of how (or whether) the story should be covered. A phase of *competition* sets in, leading reporters and White House officials to

▶ **backgrounders**
Off-the-record exchanges between the president or administration officials and reporters. Whatever a reporter learns at a backgrounder can be used in a story, but the source of the information cannot be revealed.

▶ **newsworthy** The conditions under which a story warrants publication or dissemination, based on a set of values applied by newspaper editors and television producers. Newsworthy stories typically have conflict, proximity and relevance to the audience, timeliness, and familiarity.

engage in manipulative actions for control of the agenda. The competition phase can endure for a long time before giving way to *detachment,* when the administration gives up on trying to build support for its agenda, abandoning its most intensive efforts to control the press. During the detachment phase, the president more or less avoids the press, and his schedule is tightly controlled.[27] Detachment is likely to set in during the final years of a president's second term, when reporters find greater newsworthiness in the race to replace the incumbent. In the Bush administration, the phase of competition has left reporters griping that the Communications Office controls information so tightly that, in the words of one reporter, "If the National Hurricane Center were as stingy with its information, there would be thousands dead."[28]

10-5 Chief Executive

For an officer with a brief constitutional job description, the president performs a wide range of policy and political roles: chief executive, chief legislator, chief of state, commander-in-chief, and chief of party. We'll look at each one in turn. Although we will find in these roles the occasional constitutional power like the ability to make appointments, the veto power, and the power to negotiate treaties, almost every tool the president wields has developed through custom and practice, placing them in the realm of informal powers—like the president's use of the media—that have expanded the capacity of a constitutionally limited branch.

When we talk about the president as the **chief executive,** we mean he's the chief executive officer of the United States, as well as the chief of the executive branch of government, or the bureaucracy (which we'll be talking about in Chapter 11). In this capacity, he exercises "the executive Power" in a number of specific ways.

> **chief executive** The role the president plays as head of the executive branch, in which he carries out the constitutional directive to "take Care that the Laws be faithfully executed."

10-5a Making Appointments

We said in Section 10-3a ("Formal Presidential Powers") that presidents have the formal power to make appointments to key federal positions, which are subject to Senate confirmation. A big part of his role as chief executive rests with the appointments the president can make to upper-level positions in the bureaucracy. These include top appointments to the departments, agencies, and commissions that comprise the federal bureaucracy—and there are a lot of them, from large departments like Defense, Justice, and Treasury, to more narrowly focused agencies like the Federal Election Commission, the Federal Trade Commission, and the Nuclear Regulatory Commission. The Library of Congress has a complete list, which you may find online at http://www.loc.gov/global/executive/fed.html. If you go there, be sure to scroll down to the bottom of the screen to get a sense of the scope of the executive branch.

There are serious limits to the president's appointment power. All in all, over 1.75 million people (not including postal workers) were employed in the executive branch in 2000.[29] Of these, the president appointed only a few thousand. The rest are civil servants, who get and hold their jobs independent of political considerations and, as we'll see in Chapter 11, are not indebted to the president. Furthermore, there are limits to the president's ability to remove people he appoints. The president cannot remove appointees who have fixed terms of office, like members of the Federal Communications Commission or the Federal Reserve Board, just as he can't remove judicial appointees. He has a lot more latitude over political assistants and cabinet members, whom he can remove at will.

The President's Cabinet The Constitution does not give the president the power to appoint a **cabinet.** It doesn't even mention one. However, every president has had one. George Washington had four cabinet secretaries: State, War, Treasury, and Justice. Today, there are fifteen (see Table 10-4).

In the Bush administration, six other people also have cabinet "rank." At the end of the president's first term, they were: the vice president, the president's chief of staff (Andrew Card), the United States trade representative (Robert Zoellick), and the directors of the Environmental Protection Agency (Michael Leavitt), the Office of Management and

> **cabinet** The name given to the collection of secretaries of the executive departments. Despite commonly held beliefs to the contrary, the cabinet rarely serves as an advisory body to the president.

TABLE 10-4	Department	Date Created	2004 Bush Cabinet
The President's Cabinet	State	1789	Secretary of State Colin Powell
	Defense*	1789	Secretary of Defense Donald Rumsfeld
	Treasury	1789	Secretary of the Treasury John Snow
	Justice	1789	Attorney General John Ashcroft
	Interior	1849	Secretary of the Interior Gale Norton
	Agriculture	1862	Secretary of Agriculture Ann Veneman
	Commerce	1903	Secretary of Commerce Don Evans
	Labor	1913	Secretary of Labor Elaine Chao
	Health and Human Services†	1953	Secretary of Health and Human Services Tommy Thompson
	Housing and Urban Development	1965	Secretary of Housing and Urban Development Alphonso Jackson
	Transportation	1966	Secretary of Transportation Norman Mineta
	Energy	1977	Secretary of Energy Spencer Abraham
	Education	1979	Secretary of Education Rod Paige
	Veterans' Affairs	1988	Secretary of Veterans Affairs Anthony Principi
	Homeland Security	2002	Secretary of Homeland Security Tom Ridge

*Established as the Department of War; combined with the Departments of the Navy and Air Force and renamed in 1947.

†Established as the Department of Health, Education and Welfare; renamed in 1979 with the creation of a separate Department of Education.

Budget (Joshua Bolton), and the Office of National Drug Control Policy (John Walters).[30] Cabinet rank is assigned at the president's discretion, so these other individuals will vary from administration to administration. Apart from the director of the Environmental Protection Agency, these other cabinet-level officials in the Bush administration are all part of the White House staff, or what is more formally called the **Executive Office of the President (EOP)**—the large, sprawling staff that assists the president in making political and policy decisions on a wide range of matters. We'll look more closely at the EOP in Section 10-10, "The Institutional Presidency."

Contrary to widely held popular belief, presidents rarely convene their cabinets to get advice and make decisions because cabinet members function first as the head of their respective departments and only second as presidential advisors.[31] More often, communication in cabinet meetings flows in one direction: from the president to the cabinet secretaries, on whom the president relies to advance administration policies. It would be frustrating for the president to try to do otherwise because cabinet secretaries, as specialists in their own areas of expertise, have little in common with each other. As the heads of large departments, they may also have conflicting interests and agendas—something that doesn't lend itself to a frank and open exchange of ideas and advice.

Executive Office of the President (EOP) The large staff of advisors to the president that comprises the president's political and policy operation.

10-5b Preparing Budgets

Congress has the power of the purse, but as chief executive, the president has a hand in formulating the budget. Like the cabinet, this role is not mentioned in the Constitution, but as the federal government took on more responsibilities in the twentieth century, the executive branch grew in size (revisit Table 10-4 to see how many cabinet departments were created after 1900). The president as chief executive naturally assumed a larger role in creating the budgets for these departments.

This role was formalized in the **Budget and Accounting Act of 1921,** which detailed the president's responsibility in the budget process. Among its key provisions are:

- The requirement that the president submit an annual budget proposal to Congress, reflecting his spending priorities and estimating how much money it's going to take to keep the executive branch operational for another year.

- The establishment of the **Office of Management and Budget (OMB),** formally the Bureau of the Budget, which assists the president in formulating his budget.

- The establishment of a congressional investigative office, the General Accounting Office (GAO), designed to ensure the accountability of the executive branch.

The president's budget proposal is just a recommendation, and in a Congress controlled by the opposition party, it's likely to be "dead on arrival." However, because the president gets to draft a formal proposal, he gets to be a player in the budget debate that takes place in Congress. At a minimum, he has a forum for presenting his priorities. If he's dealing with a sympathetic Congress, he'll find that his recommendations are given serious consideration.

10-5c Issuing Executive Orders

The Constitution instructs the president to "take Care that the Laws be faithfully executed," but without a road map showing how to do this, presidents since Washington have used **executive orders** to make directives to the bureaucracy that do not require congressional approval and that carry the force of law. Executive orders are another informal presidential power because they are based on a broad interpretation of the Constitution. They permit the president to act unilaterally on matters that are not itemized in the Constitution, and the courts have generally upheld the president's right to issue them.

Most executive orders are procedural or of little interest, but on occasion, presidents have used executive orders to do an end run around Congress and create policy. President Truman used an executive order to desegregate the armed forces (which are part of the executive branch). President Johnson used an executive order to require that private businesses receiving federal contracts (through executive branch departments) implement affirmative action policies. President Reagan used an executive order to ban abortion counseling in federally supported clinics. President Clinton used an executive order to overturn it.[32]

10-6 Chief Legislator

In addition to being chief executive officer and presiding over the executive branch, the president plays a central role in the legislative process by shepherding an agenda through Congress. Or, more accurately, every president *tries* to get Congress to approve his initiatives. In making the president **chief legislator,** the Constitution gives the president the vantage point from which to lead Congress but offers no guarantee of success. Much of the capital a president accumulates by developing a strong professional reputation and enhancing his public prestige goes to convincing Congress to support his legislative initiatives. Win or lose, presidents know their leadership skills will be evaluated in the next election on the basis of how well they moved their program through Congress.

10-6a Proposing an Agenda

The origins of a president's agenda may be found in the election campaign—in the platform drafted at the party convention where the president was nominated and the rhetoric of his campaign speeches—and in the issues the president makes a priority upon taking office. Advancing that agenda can be difficult, as presidents meet with mixed degrees of success in converting their priorities into congressional priorities. Sometimes, this is because what the president wants to accomplish is simply not what the congressional

Budget and Accounting Act of 1921 The act providing the legal basis for presidential participation in the budget process, by requiring the president to submit an annual budget to Congress for its consideration.

Office of Management and Budget (OMB) The executive office responsible for developing the president's annual budget proposals by evaluating requests for funding among departments and setting the president's spending priorities.

executive orders Presidential directives to the bureaucracy that are legally binding and do not require congressional approval.

chief legislator The role the president plays when he offers a legislative agenda and attempts to win congressional approval for it.

leadership wants to do. President Nixon had to deal with this when he came to office. Sometimes, it's because presidents set out too many priorities for Congress to handle and find that their effort to accomplish a lot of things results in little or nothing getting done. President Clinton met with this fate when he tried to make four huge issues—health care, trade, spending, and taxation—his top priorities in his first term.

It's often hard to predict how effectively a president is going to manage his role as chief legislator. President Nixon faced resistance from an opposition Congress, but so did President Reagan, and Reagan was able to get Congress to accept his agenda, whereas Nixon was not. President Clinton tried unsuccessfully to get a Congress controlled by his own party to do a lot; President Johnson faced the same situation and was largely successful.

The differences? They can be explained in part by the situation surrounding the president's rise to power. President Johnson took office upon John F. Kennedy's assassination, and a year later won a lopsided election victory over a weak opponent. President Reagan won only slightly more than half the popular vote but carried better than 90 percent of electoral votes. Even though Reagan's election was in part a repudiation of incumbent Jimmy Carter, the press interpreted the election as a mandate for Reagan's legislative agenda, and that helped shape the public's response. The same interpretation followed Johnson's election, with similar results. Whether or not either interpretation was warranted, it had the effect of creating a climate in which the new president could place his agenda at center stage. Neither Nixon nor Clinton had this advantage.[33]

10-6b Lobbying Congress

Still, a mandate—or the appearance of a mandate—is simply a tool. Presidents need to maximize their resources of persuasion if they're going to put this tool to good use. They and their aides need to quickly identify their top legislative priorities. They need to organize staff members who will be responsible for **legislative liaison**—maintaining ongoing contact with Congress and lobbying for the president's proposals at every step of the legislative process. They need to develop a strategy about how they're going to do this. They need to access and absorb volumes of technical information on their policy priorities so they're ready for the inevitable questions or problems that will arise with Congress. They need to have insight into the ways of the federal government, or be clever enough to surround themselves with others who do. They need to persevere through the long and often frustrating legislative process, despite the emotional or physical toll it may take.[34]

> **legislative liaison** White House lobbyists who maintain regular contacts with members of Congress and congressional committees, in order to help guide the president's legislative agenda.

If the administration has its priorities straight, is organized, efficient, strategic, informed, familiar with Washington, and tireless, it can approach Congress from a position of strength. Then, if the president has capital by virtue of his electoral mandate, professional reputation, and public prestige, he has a chance of seeing his legislative priorities move through Congress. At least, that's the way it would work in an ideal world.

Everything could be in place for the president, and circumstances might still work against his best efforts. If an international crisis arises, it's likely that the president's domestic agenda will get sidetracked. If members of Congress are gearing up for reelection, it's possible that little legislating will get done because members will be more interested in drawing partisan distinctions than in making the compromises necessary to advance legislation.

That's why the timing of a president's actions is so important. There's a good reason we've been talking about legislative efforts during the early days of a presidential administration—during the honeymoon—when official Washington is typically most open to listening to what the president has to say. Time is the president's enemy if he wishes to lead Congress.

One presidential aide put it this way: "You've got to give it all you can that first year. Doesn't matter what kind of majority you come in with. You've got just one year when [members of Congress] treat you right and before they start worrying about themselves."[35] Another presidential assistant picks apart the typical four-year presidential administration like this: "You should subtract one year for the reelection campaign, another six months for the midterm [elections], six months for the start-up, six months for the closing, and

> **Box 10-7   Some Constitutional Tricks**

The Constitution lets the president pull a nifty maneuver if Congress passes legislation he doesn't want to sign and then adjourns within ten days of acting. It's called a **pocket veto,** and it lets the president veto a bill by doing absolutely nothing. Because Congress is out of town, a presidential veto could not be delivered to Congress for its consideration. So, the Constitution under these circumstances gives the president two options: Sign the bill, or put it in your pocket and forget about it. After the ten-day window is over, if the bill doesn't have the president's signature, it dies. This makes a pocket veto absolute—it cannot be overridden.

On the other hand, if Congress is in session and the president receives legislation he doesn't particularly like but has

decided not to veto, he has the option of leaving it on his desk for ten days, at which point, it becomes law without his signature. A president might do this as a way of signaling that he recognizes he doesn't have the support to sustain a veto, but because he dislikes the legislation, he's going to let the bill become law without his name on it.

▶ **pocket veto**   The presidential prerogative to veto a bill without taking action. Presidents may issue pocket vetoes only if Congress has passed legislation within ten days of adjournment. A pocket veto cannot be overridden.

another month or two for an occasional vacation. That leaves you with a two-year presidential term."[36]

10-6c Vetoing Legislation

Perhaps the president's strongest legislative weapon is negative. The Constitution gives the president the formal power to veto legislation sent to him by Congress, which has to muster a two-thirds vote in both houses to **override** the veto and make the legislation into law without the president's approval. The veto can be a strategic tool that a president can use to try to shape legislation to his liking and can be particularly useful to presidents who face a Congress controlled by the opposing party. If the president threatens to veto legislation while it's being considered by Congress, and the threat is credible—meaning members of Congress believe the president will go through with it—they could decide to reshape elements of the legislation to the president's liking. Considering how hard it is to muster two-thirds majorities in both houses to override a veto, such shifting might make sense to legislators who would at least come out with some of what they want. It also means that a president doesn't always have to use the veto for it to be a potent weapon; the mere threat of action sometimes will suffice. Box 10-7 discusses other options the president has when considering how to act on legislation.

▶ **override**   The congressional power to overturn a presidential veto by a two-thirds vote of both houses of Congress.

If a president does veto a bill, the odds are great that the veto will hold up. Of 1,484 regular vetoes[37] cast between 1789 and 2002, only 106 have been overridden—about 7 percent. Presidents only have to worry about an override if they veto a bill that has widespread public support or if they're up against a Congress dominated by the other party. The latter situation is rare, although it has happened. President Ford, a Republican, faced overwhelming Democratic House and Senate majorities, which kept passing legislation he did not support. Ford's response was to use the veto pen forty-eight times in two and a half years, only to see twelve of them, or 25 percent, overridden—a rate of override about three and a half times the presidential average.[38] Under the circumstances, the strategy of using the veto as a way to get Congress to bend to the president's wishes was unavailable to President Ford. His only viable strategic option was to use the veto to send a message of disapproval to the legislature. Figure 10-2 shows how many vetoes the presidents since John F. Kennedy have cast.

10-7 Chief of State and Foreign Policy Leader

If the president's chief executive and chief legislator roles are marked by the strategic allocation of resources in an ongoing, often frustrating tug-of-war with Congress, the president as **chief of state** lives a much more charmed existence. A chief of state is a nation's

▶ **chief of state**   The role the president plays as ceremonial head of the United States.

Figure 10-2
Presidents and Their Vetoes
(*Note:* Does not include pocket vetoes.)

Source: Office of the Clerk, U.S. House of Representatives.

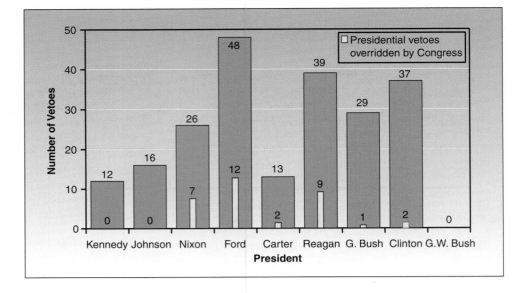

The president's role as chief of state can range from the ceremonial fun of a T-ball game on the White House lawn *(left)* to the serious business of representing the United States abroad. President Bush and South Korean President Kim Dae-Jung may have been smiling about their World Cup jackets *(right)*, but the reception they were attending was an important diplomatic function.

Source: (Left) White House photo by David Bohrer. *(Right)* White House photo by Eric Draper.

official envoy to the world, a nation's symbolic and ceremonial head. The chief of state greets foreign dignitaries and has formal state dinners in their honor. The chief of state gets to light the official White House Christmas tree, and grants honorary recognition to celebrities. He speaks for the nation and is the nation's representative to the world.

If you think about it, this is an odd combination of roles, with the chief executive and chief legislator engaging in gritty political maneuvering while the chief of state rises above the political fray. Although there can be diplomatic substance to the president's responsibilities as chief of state (see Box 10-8), for the most part, the functions he performs in this capacity are symbolic. That's why so many nations separate the roles, leaving the political stuff to a head of government and permitting a nonpartisan figure to assume the ceremonial role. In Great Britain, for example, a partisan prime minister, selected from the majority party in Parliament, performs the functions that are comparable to our chief executive and chief legislator. But the queen is the chief of state, the ceremonial leader who can rise above politics and represent Great Britain to the world.

Because we roll all these roles into one job, we ask the president to unify us as our symbolic representative and move us forward as our government leader—even though politics is, by definition, a divisive business. This can lead to some interesting wrinkles in the way presidents act and in the way we relate to our presidents. For instance, while opinion polls

Box 10-8   Chief Diplomat

The pageantry, pomp, and really good food that serve as the trappings of the chief of state can mask a substantive role accorded the president. Think of him as the **chief diplomat**—as the person the Constitution makes responsible for receiving "Ambassadors and other public Ministers." Officially, this means that before ambassadors of other countries can set up shop in the United States, they must present their credentials to the president. This apparently ceremonial function gives the president the right to extend American **diplomatic recognition** to other nations—to decide whether the representative of a nation has legitimacy in the eyes of the United States.

Recognition by a major power like the United States can build instant global credibility for a new nation or a regime

that takes power following a revolution or uprising. Situations like this don't come around often, but when they do, decisions about whether or when to extend diplomatic recognition can reverberate globally. For instance, in the confusion surrounding the demise of the Soviet Union, the United States faced the prospect of recognizing a host of self-declared independent states that previously had been part of one nation.

▶ **chief diplomat** A constitutional role of the president, in which he has the power to recognize ambassadors from other nations.

▶ **diplomatic recognition** Formal acceptance of the legitimacy of another nation or its representatives.

repeatedly showed large percentages of Americans approved of Bill Clinton's policy agenda, the litany of finance and sex scandals that pockmarked his administration undermined his ability to function as chief of state. Some who saw Clinton as unprincipled or shady objected to him being the official voice of the United States, preferring instead someone they could relate to or be proud of.

George W. Bush tapped this desire when he campaigned for office as someone who people would be proud to have as their symbolic leader. Following the 2001 terror attack, President Bush continually emphasized his role as chief of state, both to unify the nation and, subsequently, to leverage the support he was receiving for his partisan political battles with Congress. For Bush, being a successful chief of state became a resource in his role as chief legislator.

In addition to the pomp and ceremony of the chief-of-state role, the president performs key foreign policy functions, making him the paramount voice in American foreign affairs. He is responsible for formulating the nation's foreign policy, overseeing the nation's intelligence activities, and functioning as commander-in-chief of the armed forces.

10-7a Formulating Foreign Policy

In keeping with the general tendency for the chief-of-state role to be less contentious than the president's domestic policy roles, the president typically finds himself with more leeway in foreign affairs than he does when he engages in the inevitable domestic clashes with Congress. This distinction led political scientist Aaron Wildavsky to contend that there are "two presidencies" with distinct patterns of political support—a domestic policy presidency, where presidential initiatives often get bogged down in the thistle of congressional opposition, and a foreign and defense policy presidency, where a determined president can almost always have his way.[39]

The key place Wildavsky looks for evidence of the two presidencies is in the record of success presidents have had in the formulation of policy. Where presidents have had mixed results moving domestic proposals through Congress, succeeding most thoroughly in the rare instances when they are propelled by a major crisis (like Franklin Roosevelt during the Great Depression) or when their party comprises an overwhelming congressional majority (like Lyndon Johnson in the 1960s), Wildavsky finds that presidents who wanted to pursue a foreign or military course typically succeeded.

Wildavsky finds several reasons for this. Unlike domestic policy, foreign policy is dangerous; events can move quickly and the consequences can be monumental. This tends to focus the public on the president's foreign policy actions and motivate presidents to devote a lot of resources to foreign policy formulation. No one else in Washington can rival the administration's investment in foreign policy expertise or its ability to speak with one voice.[40]

Wildavsky wrote during the heightened tensions of the cold war, leading some to reevaluate his argument with the passage of time.[41] Today, in a world where protection from terrorist threats dominates the foreign policy agenda, we can find some anecdotal evidence that the president again may have a relatively free hand in formulating foreign policy. It took only a few weeks in 2002 for President Bush to convince a reluctant Congress to endorse his plans to invade Iraq if that nation refused to permit open inspection of its weapons programs. Yet, at about the same time, the president remained unable to advance key elements of his domestic agenda, including legislative proposals on tax and Social Security reform.

10-7b Negotiating Treaties and Making Executive Agreements

The president's formal constitutional prerogative to negotiate treaties with other nations seems on the surface to contradict that idea that it's smooth sailing for presidents in foreign affairs. Because treaties have to be ratified by a two-thirds vote of the Senate, presidents may find that the negotiating they have to do with the legislative branch is much more difficult than the negotiating they had to do with the other nation or nations involved in the treaty. Historically, the Senate has not been shy about defeating even high-profile treaties with strong presidential backing; probably the most notable twentieth-century example is the defeat of the Versailles Treaty by the Senate following World War I, which kept the United States out of the League of Nations.

executive agreements
Legally binding presidential agreements with other nations that do not require congressional approval.

However, as is often the case with the president, there is an informal mechanism available to him that circumvents the constitutional complexity of navigating treaties through the Senate. Presidents can avoid a resistant legislature by issuing **executive agreements,** which do not require congressional action. The president can negotiate executive agreements with leaders of other nations, a practice with a long history even though it is not provided for in the Constitution. Once signed, executive agreements have the force of law. This gives the president great latitude in foreign policy negotiations, provided those nations are willing to forego the stature of a treaty. When President Bush and Russian President Vladimir Putin were negotiating nuclear arms reduction in 2002, one point of discussion was whether any agreement produced by the talks would be subject to congressional approval—a move that would offer Russia the type of respect afforded the Soviet Union during the cold war days of joint superpower arms talks.

10-7c Supervising Intelligence Activities

Since September 11, 2001, many of us have become more aware than before of our intelligence operations and the complex business of gathering information about groups or individuals who might pose a threat to national security. The secretive world of intelligence gathering falls under the auspices of the president through the director of central intelligence, whom the president appoints with Senate approval. It's been that way since the National Security Act of 1947 established the Central Intelligence Agency (CIA), the organization responsible for providing the president with information on security threats, under the supervision of the director of central intelligence.[42]

National Security Council (NSC) The group of senior policy advisors responsible for helping the president shape national security policy.

The CIA also reports to the **National Security Council (NSC),** the primary body for assisting the president with security-related decisions. In addition to the president's national security advisor, the NSC includes select cabinet officials (including the secretaries of state, defense, and treasury) and receives military briefings from the chairman of the **Joint Chiefs of Staff,** the president's primary military advisor.[43]

Joint Chiefs of Staff
The group of military advisors comprised of the heads of the army, navy, air force, and marines.

In response to the attacks on the World Trade Center and the Pentagon, President Bush proposed and established a cabinet-level Department of Homeland Security, which entailed conducting the largest reorganization of the federal government since Franklin D. Roosevelt was president. The new department combined a host of security-related and information-gathering organizations under one administrative umbrella in an effort to create a coordinated agency charged with border security, emergency preparedness, and antiterrorist intelligence gathering.

10-8 Commander-in-Chief

The Constitution gives Congress the power to declare war, but it gives the president the power to wage war. In the eighteenth-century world of the Constitution's framers, where troops were committed to battle following a formal declaration, the president's military powers were expected to be secondary to Congress. In a twenty-first century world, where the military response to crisis is often swift and troops are sent into battle without formal declarations, the president's power as **commander-in-chief** of the armed forces looms large.

> **commander-in-chief**
> The president's constitutional role as civilian leader of the armed forces.

The president has several advantages over Congress in the conduct of military affairs. He has the formal power to move American forces overseas and commit them to battle. As we just noted, he has an intelligence and advisory structure that can keep him abreast of international developments, providing him with information that Congress does not have. He can act unilaterally and swiftly. Informally, he can move public opinion behind him once he acts.

The swelling of the president's military resources follows the growth of the United States as a world power. Until about seventy years ago, presidents had access to very limited advice and data for making military judgments, as there was little in the way of a defense establishment like we have today.[44] That was before the commander-in-chief was responsible for a nuclear arsenal, and before America's permanent military establishment ballooned in size and reach in response to the country's central place in world affairs. Although presidents have claimed the power to commit troops without congressional authorization since John Adams sent the navy to do battle with France, the scope, magnitude, and extent of American involvement overseas has made presidents serving since the middle of the twentieth century the central figures in military affairs.

In the 1970s, Congress tried to fight back. In the wake of the divisiveness of the Vietnam War, many members of Congress felt Presidents Johnson and Nixon had overstepped the boundaries of their role as commander-in-chief, and they were determined to reassert their constitutional prerogative over military matters. The result was the **War Powers Act of 1973** (which passed over President Nixon's veto), the intent of which was to limit the president's ability to initiate military action without congressional approval. It does this by requiring in the absence of a declaration of war that the president consult with Congress before taking action and periodically while troops are in the field. If Congress does not ratify the president's action within sixty days, the president has to bring the troops home (this may be extended to ninety days if the president claims immediate withdrawal poses a risk to the troops).

> **War Powers Act of 1973**
> A congressional attempt to reassert the role of the legislature with respect to the president in military affairs by restricting the president's ability to wage war.

The promise of the War Powers Act was that balance in military affairs would be reestablished between Congress and the president, but it hasn't quite worked out that way. Presidents have ignored the War Powers Act, choosing instead to continue to commit troops as they always did—and Congress hasn't tried to reign in the president. There are good political reasons why. As Vietnam faded into memory, passions subsided, and subsequent congresses weren't eager to confront the president. If Congress pressed the point and the president decided to challenge the constitutionality of the War Powers Act, it's not at all clear that the act would hold up to scrutiny if the Supreme Court decided that it provides Congress with a veto over the president's actions (this would be considered a "legislative veto," and the Constitution only grants veto power to the president). Also, because the president can typically rely on the public rallying behind him at least briefly when he sends troops abroad, it's difficult for Congress to stand up to the president when he's engaged in the role of commander-in-chief.

10-9 Chief of Party

It's nowhere to be found in the Constitution, but by custom, the president is the head of his political party. We found out in Chapter 6 that political parties are decentralized organizations built from the ground up. Despite this structure, as the highest elected national official, the president is well positioned to give a face and a voice to his party and, if he enjoys popular support, contribute heavily to party campaigning and fund-raising functions. It's an advantage the party out of power simply can't match.

Particularly when it comes to raising money, the president can be a party's biggest weapon. When President Clinton was in office, he routinely barnstormed the country, headlining fund-raisers that brought in record sums of money for the Democratic Party. President Bush exceeded Clinton's fund-raising records to the benefit of the Republican Party, raising over $260 million for his reelection campaign.

Being party chief is not without its complications. An unpopular president can leave a party effectively leaderless, and because no one else commands the national stage like the president, no one else can step in as party leader if a president lacks popular support. Candidates for other offices will not want to be seen on the same stage with him for fear that their association will cost them votes. President Clinton was so unpopular during the congressional elections held in the middle of his first term that he became a powerful political weapon for the *opposition* party. More than one Democrat running for Congress conveniently found himself with something else on his schedule when word came that the president wanted to campaign for them.

> **coattails** The ability of a victorious presidential candidate to sweep congressional candidates of the same party into office on the strength of people voting for one political party.

Even popular presidents may find that there are limits to their political reach. Two generations ago, when more people voted strictly by party, presidential candidates routinely carried members of Congress into office on their **coattails.** Today, as we saw in Chapter 6, people are more likely to split their ticket, voting for Republicans for some offices and Democrats for others. It's not uncommon for congressional candidates to get more votes than their party's presidential candidate receives in their district. This leaves the president—even a popular one—with limited political leverage, as the congressional candidates they campaign for often do not win their office on the strength of the president's campaign. In 2001, President Bush put his prestige and support behind the Republican nominees for the two governorships up for election that year, in Virginia and New Jersey. Despite his efforts, both candidates lost.

The president may also face problems reconciling the blatant partisanship of the party-leader role with the president's other responsibilities. President Bush wrestled with this dilemma right before the 2002 congressional elections as he tried to remain above politics as chief of state while campaigning for Republican candidates as chief of party.[45] The balancing act was particularly delicate: The president tried to look serious and statesman-like as he moved the nation closer to a conflict with Iraq, while also hopping around the country unleashing partisan rhetoric at political rallies. In his chief-of-state role, he was trying to unify the nation and prepare the world for military action, but the chief-of-party role required the president to get down into dirty, divisive partisan muck in order to rally the faithful and win votes for Republicans. The strategy carried risks for Bush's professional reputation, which would have been undermined had he appeared too partisan or divisive at such a somber moment.

You could say that Bush's problem reflects the crosscutting expectations we place on our presidents. It illustrates the dilemma that presidents face as they juggle contradictory roles.

10-10 The Institutional Presidency

It seems as though the more we ask the president to do, the more help he requires—and the more assistance he gets in the form of a large, bureaucratic staff centered around the Oval Office. In Section 10-5a ("Making Appointments"), we briefly made note of this staff in our passing reference to the Executive Office of the President (EOP). When the presidency was a fairly small office prior to the major expansion in federal functions that occurred during Franklin D. Roosevelt's administration, the White House staff was equally small. By way of comparison, Roosevelt left behind a personal staff of fifty-three people, which had swollen to over 350 by the time Bill Clinton took office. During the same period, the president's budget advisors almost doubled in number, and his national security staff more than tripled.[46]

10-10a Inside the Executive Office of the President

Every administration organizes the EOP a little differently, but there are a number of constants that have endured from administration to administration. Every recent president has organized the **White House Office** around a **chief of staff,** who coordinates the workings of the White House Office and serves as a key advisor with intimate access to the president. The White House Office typically includes the president's personal secretary, legal advisors, political advisors, and in recent administrations has grown to include the Communications Office and offices that handle contacts between the White House and Congress, interest groups, and the president's political party.[47]

The inner circle of the White House Office contains the president's most trusted and influential confidants. Typically, these people are the president's longtime associates or personal friends, including people who worked with the president when he held lower offices and people who had high-level positions in the president's election campaign.

The rest of the EOP is just as compartmentalized, containing offices that assist the president on things ranging from budgetary to security matters.

> ▶**White House Office**
> That portion of the Executive Office of the President organized to serve the president's immediate needs.

> ▶**chief of staff** One of the president's top political advisors and the formal head of the White House staff.

10-10b The Office of the First Lady

The Executive Office of the President is housed in the West Wing of the White House. Across the way, in the East Wing, you'll find the offices of the first lady. There's no official role for the first lady, but the wife of the president is an important symbolic figure in American life, especially in an era when television cameras make her a public figure (whether or not that's her wish). Jacqueline Kennedy was the first to play the role of national hostess on television, projecting an air of youth and glamour akin to her husband's televised persona.

Traditionally, the first lady has played a social role, hosting guests at the White House. A few presidential spouses have seen themselves as more than official greeters. Eleanor Roosevelt, wife of Franklin, played an active role in her husband's administration. Ahead of her time, anticipating the revolution in women's roles that would begin twenty years after she left the White House, Eleanor Roosevelt lobbied her husband on behalf of the social issues she advocated. She wrote a newspaper column and was a media presence, promoting causes like rights for women and minorities.

Nancy Reagan maintained a far more traditional public image, but behind the scenes, she was influential in her husband's administration. People who worked in the Reagan White House understood the importance of being on good terms with the president's wife, and her close relationship with the president made her an important, though informal, advisor. Once, when reporters were shouting questions at President Reagan that he was unable to hear against the din of background noise, television cameras picked up Nancy Reagan whispering an answer in her husband's ear, which promptly came out of his mouth. It was a rare glimpse of how involved she was in the workings of the administration.

Hillary Rodham Clinton took the role of first lady to a place none of her predecessors had been—directly into the West Wing, where she set up shop with a personal staff. An attorney with experience as a congressional aide, she came to the White House with the resume of someone who might have applied for work in the Executive Office of the President. As a candidate, Bill Clinton joked about his wife's ability and influence by saying that they offered voters a "buy one, get one free" option.

In office, it came to pass. Bill Clinton put his wife in charge of a task force exploring proposals for restructuring the way Americans receive health care, a role so out of sync with the traditional work of a first lady that it sparked a national debate. When the Clinton health care proposal tanked, Hillary Clinton shared the blame with her husband and never again took a visible policy role in her husband's administration. Nonetheless, she continued to be an influential advocate in the White House, and in the last year of the

Websites You Can Use

Here is some information about the various members of the EOP and the URLs of their websites.

White House Office
The "inner circle" of the White House, where you'll find the president's closest political advisors.

National Security Council
Senior advisors responsible for making national security policy recommendations to the president, helping the president manage foreign policy crises, and coordinating national security related actions of other agencies, like the CIA. See Section 10-7c and http://www.whitehouse.gov/nsc/.

Office of Management and Budget
The president's policy and political arm for budget making. OMB assists the president in preparing the annual budget proposal he sends to Congress and reports to the president on the efficiency of a range of federal programs that the budget funds. See Section 10-5c and http://www.whitehouse.gov/omb/.

Council on Environmental Quality
The president's key environmental policy advisory group. Its purpose is to assess environmental conditions and recommend environmental policies for the president's consideration. The CEQ tends to be staffed and funded more fully by administrations that emphasize environmental concerns. See http://www.whitehouse.gov/ceq/.

Office of Homeland Security
Established by President Bush in response to the attacks of September 11, 2001, this office coordinates other agencies involved in providing protection against domestic attacks. See Section 10-7c and http://www.whitehouse.gov/homeland/.

Office of the Vice President
Before the Kennedy administration, the vice president had to operate with a small staff out of an office on Capitol Hill. Then the Office of the Vice President was established, and gradually, his staff, funding, proximity to the president—and clout—began to increase. See Section 10-11.

Clinton administration, she became the only first lady to be elected to public office when she won a Senate race in her adopted state of New York. In 2001, as President Clinton was moving out of the Oval Office, Senator Clinton was settling into her new workspace on the other end of Pennsylvania Avenue.

She was replaced in the East Wing by Laura Bush, a more traditional first lady who keeps a much lower and less controversial profile. Like many contemporary first ladies, she has become a public advocate for a cause—in this case, literacy and childhood education—which she has promoted since her days as a teacher and librarian in Texas.[48]

10-11 Second In Command

Here's a job description for you to consider: You get to attend the occasional funeral for a head of state, preside over the Senate (where no one will complain that you hardly ever show), and otherwise make yourself available just in case something happens to your

Office of Administration
The office that coordinates the other offices in the Executive Office of the President (EOP). It provides support services for facilities, information technology, research assistance, human resources, security, and mail operations. It also oversees development of the annual EOP budget.

Office of National Drug Control Policy
Establishes objectives for the administration's antidrug strategy and coordinates the work of drug-related federal agencies. See http://www.whitehousedrugpolicy.gov/about/ index.html.

Office of Science and Technology Policy
A formal grouping of technical advisors who can assist the president in developing a range of scientific and technological policies in conjunction with the states and private industry. For instance, the OSTP provides technical advice on homeland security matters. See http://www.ostp.gov/html/_aboutostp.html.

Office of the U.S. Trade Representative
The office responsible for developing U.S. trade policy, advising the president on trade policy, and conducting international trade negotiations. See http://www.ustr.gov/Who_We_Are/Section_Index.html.

Council of Economic Advisors
Economists who serve the president with economic analysis used for developing national and international economic policies. See http://www.whitehouse.gov/cea/.

Office of Policy Development
The domestic policy counterpart to the National Security Council, the OPD provides the president with advice on domestic issues. It includes the National Economic Council (http://www.whitehouse.gov/nec/) for coordinating and developing economic policy, and the Domestic Policy Council (http://www.whitehouse.gov/dpc/) for policy development in such areas as health, education, welfare, transportation, labor, and veterans' affairs. The DPC also oversees the Office of National AIDS Policy, the Office of National Drug Control Policy, and the Office of Faith-Based and Community Initiatives.

boss. For this, you will be well compensated with a good salary and a nice house in a great location.

Perhaps, you find the prospect of a job like this appealing, but many of the people who have served as vice president have commented on the remarkable emptiness of a position that is, after all, the only *other* nationally elected office in the United States. The first vice president, John Adams, bemoaned, "My country has in its infinite wisdom contrived for me the most insignificant office that ever the invention of man contrived or his imagination conceived." Thomas Marshall, vice president under Woodrow Wilson, compared his situation to "a man in a cataleptic fit: He cannot speak; he cannot move; he suffers no pain; he is perfectly conscious of all that goes on, but has no part in it." John Nance Garner, Franklin D. Roosevelt's first vice president, put it more succinctly: "The vice presidency isn't worth a pitcher of warm spit."[49]

It's probably not surprising that ambitious men could feel hamstrung in the vice presidency, or that the office itself was a late addition to the Constitution, where it was never more than a pencil sketch of an institution. The vice presidency gave the Constitution's authors a method of presidential succession that didn't violate separation of powers by relying on a congressional officer, and it resolved the issue of who would preside over the Senate and cast tie-breaking votes when necessary. It also created a dilemma for its occupants, who are given little authority and no power, and who until recent administrations have been reduced to waiting around in case something happened to the president.

Throughout the nineteenth century and well into the twentieth, vice presidents were frequently the object of ridicule or neglect. Selected by party leaders to provide geographic or ideological balance to the presidential nominee, qualifications for the number two office rarely advanced beyond the ability to carry a state or a voting group that the presidential candidate could not. As political circumstances evolved from year to year, necessitating a different balance in the next election, vice presidents found themselves highly expendable commodities: No nineteenth-century vice president was renominated for a second term by a major political party. After Martin Van Buren in 1836, none was nominated for president.[50]

Since seeking the office wasn't much of a career move, it didn't draw the interest of big political names. Daniel Webster rejected overtures from Whig Party leaders to be their vice-presidential nominee in 1848, saying facetiously, "I do not wish to be buried until I am dead."[51] The nomination went instead to Millard Fillmore, who apparently didn't mind. So, most vice presidents were second-tier political figures who spent their time looking for something useful to do. Some didn't even bother to stay in Washington. Van Buren's vice president, Richard M. Johnson, left town in 1837 to operate a tavern.[52]

Circumstances changed dramatically in the middle of the twentieth century, making the modern vice presidency a much more desirable office both substantively and politically. When Harry Truman became president upon the sudden death of Franklin D. Roosevelt in 1945, World War II was ending. America and its allies were drawing plans for the shape of the postwar world, and the United States had been secretly developing an atomic bomb, but Truman was uninvolved in and largely unaware of these efforts. When he became president, he had to come up to speed quickly and was left to make life and death decisions that affected the future shape of the world. From that point on, it became clear that the vice president had to be someone who could step into a role that now had global implications.

That didn't mean that vice-presidential candidates didn't still have to give political balance to a ticket. But after 1945, presidential candidates needed to assure the country that they were running with someone who had the capability and experience to become president at a moment's notice. Their choice would come to be seen as an example of their judgment and leadership ability.

This applied in 1976 when Jimmy Carter selected Senator Walter Mondale to be his running mate. The liberal Mondale, a midwesterner and Washington insider, provided natural political balance to Carter's more conservative southern base. Mondale's four years as vice president turned out to be historic, as Carter offered him more policy responsibility than any vice president in history. He had a West Wing office, access to presidential information, and met regularly with the president, serving as a key advisor. Al Gore played an even larger role in the Clinton administration, as the president made him primarily responsible for making decisions in a range of policy areas, including the environment, technology, and telecommunications.[53] Dick Cheney followed Gore as vice president and played a highly influential role, serving as one of President Bush's most trusted advisors. But can a vice president capitalize on this experience? Box 10-9 looks at the success of vice presidents with presidential aspirations.

10-12 The Ebb and Flow of Presidential Influence

As an institutional matter, the president and Congress have long been in a tug-of-war befitting two institutions dependent on each other to get things done. The early presidents who stretched the reach of the presidency through a broad interpretation of the presidential role—presidents like Thomas Jefferson, Andrew Jackson and Abraham Lincoln—did so at the expense of Congress. This is why we've seen strong presidencies followed by peri-

> ### Box 10-9   Moving from Number Two to One

The revamped, contemporary vice presidency is viewed as a stepping-stone to the presidency, but how successful have recent vice presidents been in achieving that ambition? When George Bush (senior) was elected president immediately after serving eight years as vice president to Ronald Reagan, he became the first vice president to take that step on his own since Martin Van Buren succeeded Andrew Jackson in 1836.

Al Gore tried to replicate the feat in 2000 but fell short. His troubles illustrate how the vice presidency can cut both ways when its occupant seeks the top prize. As a visible national fig-ure, Gore had no trouble raising money and winning the nomination of his party. At the same time, he was saddled with the scandals of the Clinton years, and as a member of the administration, he had trouble distancing himself from them. Journalists wrote of Gore's dilemma trying to emerge from President Clinton's shadow, but the reality of the vice presidency is that it's hard for its occupant to run for president as his own person.

Still, the vice presidency has been fertile ground for presidential candidates in recent years. Table 1 offers a quick look at the political trajectories of its last ten occupants:

TABLE 1   Political Trajectories of the Last Ten Vice Presidents

Vice President	President Served	Became President through Presidential Death or Resignation	Ran for President, Won	Ran for President, Lost
Nixon	Eisenhower		Yes	Yes*
Johnson	Kennedy	Yes		
Humphrey	Johnson			Yes
Agnew†	Nixon			
Ford	Nixon	Yes		
Rockefeller‡	Ford			
Mondale	Carter			Yes
G. Bush	Reagan		Yes	
Quayle	G. Bush			Yes§
Gore	Clinton			Yes

*Nixon ran and lost when he was an incumbent vice president in 1960; he ran again and won eight years later.

†Agnew resigned the vice presidency under a cloud of scandal and was replaced by Ford.

‡Rockefeller had been an unsuccessful presidential candidate before Ford selected him to serve as vice president; he did not run for president afterward.

§Quayle ran in the Republican presidential primary in 2000, eight years after leaving office. He did not win the nomination.

ods where Congress grabbed back some of the authority that it felt rightfully belonged to the legislature.

The War Powers Act was passed during such a time, following a string of presidential administrations considered "imperial" for their regal tone and extensive claims of authority. If Franklin D. Roosevelt forever enhanced the role of the president when his administration dramatically increased the sweep of federal authority, the advent of America as a global power and the nuclear tension of the cold war gave late twentieth-century presidents godlike power over life and death. We looked to them to protect civilization and keep us safe from nuclear annihilation, giving them unprecedented opportunities to use their informal powers to strengthen the office. People started calling them the "leader of the free world." That's why the "imperial presidency" reached its height under Presidents Kennedy, Johnson, and Nixon, in the frostiest days of the cold war.[54]

It's not too hard to see how presidents serving under these conditions might take on imperial characteristics. The president has always had personal privileges, but the benefits of the presidency assumed regal characteristics under cold war circumstances. Imagine how you'd feel if you never had to wait in line for anything. You never had to drive a car, and you never got stuck in traffic because roads were closed off when you were coming. Every time you walked into a room, people would stand. Military bands would play "Hail to the Chief" when they spotted you. Airplanes would take off within thirty seconds after you boarded. It would be hard for most people not to let this go to their heads. Now consider what happens when they're also calling you the "leader of the free world." The effect would be to create a sense of privilege befitting an emperor.

As the president took on the characteristics of a monarch, the Executive Office of the President took on the air of a court. George Reedy, who served as press secretary to President Johnson, compared the situation in the White House to one you'd find in a palace, where courtiers cater to the king's ego, fight among themselves for the leader's attention, and engage in petty acts to undermine each other in the larger pursuit of winning the king's favor.

What does *not* happen in this atmosphere is an honest, hard-hitting exchange of ideas. Aides feel pressed to say yes to the president, regardless of how much they may privately disagree with what he's doing. To disagree was to risk the wrath of the chief executive and to be displaced from power. No one felt they could do what Reedy believed was necessary to reestablish a healthy atmosphere in the White House: Occasionally tell the president to "go soak his head."[55]

Bad ideas can be hatched in such an insular environment, without dissent to sharpen the president's thinking—and they were. The prosecution of the Vietnam War proceeded as President Johnson listened to advisors who assured him that escalating the conflict was the best policy, partly because they feared punishment if they dissented. This effectively trapped Johnson inside a gilded echo chamber, where the failure to hear dissenting voices kept him from recognizing that he was losing the support of the public. President Nixon's administration was secretive to a fault—the chief of staff tightly controlled all contact with Nixon—and in his imperial seclusion, Nixon believed he could get away with illegally thwarting his political opposition. He was, after all, the "leader of the free world."

That was when Congress fought back—with the War Powers Act and with impeachment proceedings against Richard Nixon, stemming from illegal activities conducted in a climate of White House secrecy. A period of congressional dominance followed, coinciding with the weak presidencies of Gerald Ford and Jimmy Carter. Box 10-10 goes into more detail on these presidencies.

Events continued to shape the office after Carter's term, facilitating the conditions for a return to the imperial presidency, punctuated by an interlude defined by more down-to-earth politics. With the cold war still raging, many Americans found security in the regal trappings of the Reagan years. At the same time, the Reagan administration advocated policies that, for the first time since Franklin Roosevelt, assumed government was the source of our problems, not the solution to our problems. There was a profound transformation in the political debate, which for the first time in generations made it acceptable to consider shifting power away from Washington. In the process, President Reagan undermined one of the two pillars on which the imperial presidency had been built: the sense that the president, as the chief executive of the national government, was ultimately responsible for providing a huge range of services that could not be had elsewhere. As power began to flow out of Washington and to the states, the president's royal position was inevitably diminished.

Then the Berlin Wall came down, the Soviet Union crumbled, the cold war ended, and the other pillar supporting the imperial presidents—the fact that each was the "leader of the free world"—lost its currency. Without having to assume the posture of someone faced with decisions of global life and death, Bill Clinton could reach out to voters as a pop-culture figure rather than as a regal figure. He could appear on a late-night television variety show wearing shades and playing the saxophone, as he did during his presidential campaign. He could turn up on MTV and answer a question about the kind of underwear he prefers. In their day, no one could have imagined Presidents Johnson or Nixon answering a question about whether they liked boxers or briefs. For that matter, no one could have imagined either man being in a situation where the question would have been asked.

Box 10-10 The Weak, Accessible Presidencies of Jerry and Jimmy

Recognizing that presidential grandeur had taken the presidency too far away from its political roots, President Gerald Ford followed Richard Nixon in office with a deliberate effort to make the president ordinary. Naturally unaffected and down to earth, Ford fit the role perfectly. In his first days in the White House, he held a media event designed to communicate the message that this president would not be an emperor: There in the kitchen was the new president in a bathrobe, making his breakfast toast. We had entered a period of the anti-imperialist president, the president of the people. Ford did away with the pomp that surrounded his predecessors, even to the point of requesting at times that "Hail to the Chief" be replaced by the fight song of his alma mater, the University of Michigan.

His successor also used populist symbols to communicate the message that his presidency was the antithesis of Johnson's and Nixon's. President Carter broke with tradition by leaving the limousine that carried him to the White House after his inauguration, choosing to walk the parade route, hand-in-hand with his wife. He wore cardigan sweaters instead of suits and ties. He invited people to call him "Jimmy."

Interestingly, the public eventually tired of this folksy presidential style, in no small part because of how it became intertwined with downsized presidential performance. It's impossible to know if Ford would have become a folk hero—the ordinary man in the White House—had he not generated so much ill will by pardoning President Nixon for his Watergate-related crimes or presided over an ailing economy. Likewise, the image of a plainspoken peanut farmer might have become Jimmy Carter's presidential legacy had he been able to tackle the rampant inflation that undermined the nation's standard of living, and crises abroad that left many feeling that America had become a weak nation.

Ironically, despite the wrenching experiences of Vietnam and Watergate, the events of the Ford and Carter administrations left many people yearning for a return to the imperial presidency. Ronald Reagan promised to restore pomp and glitter to the office as part of a broader message of regaining a sense of national strength and pride. For many, it was the right message at the right time, playing to the enduring wish that the president provide a king-like legitimacy to the American system.

During the ten years or so while you were going through adolescence, the presidency was experiencing a kind of adolescence as well. The office had returned to pre-imperial dimensions. Congress reasserted itself to the point where in the first months following the 1994 Republican takeover of the House and Senate, the president briefly became secondary to Congress in political importance. Several years later, an energized Congress impeached but failed to convict President Clinton for his actions stemming from the Monica Lewinsky scandal.

Perhaps, things would have continued on this path had America not been the object of a major terrorist attack. Having elected in George W. Bush a president with admittedly no foreign policy experience, foreign affairs ironically became the focal point of his administration. With this came a return to the serious business of being global leader, and not coincidentally, a return to some of the trappings of the cold war administrations: increased secrecy and the reassertion of presidential authority over Congress. In time, we'll see if this signals a lasting return to the imperial presidency.

One of the ironies of the modern presidency is that even at its most imperial, the one branch that the president seemed to have the least influence over was his own. There are interesting reasons why the "leader of the free world" often comes across as the head of the bureaucracy in name only. In reality, things are often different than what you'd expect from an organizational chart of the executive branch that has the president's name at the top. We'll look at the peculiar relationship between the chief executive and the executive branch as we turn to Chapter 11.

Chapter Review

Because the presidency is the only federal office that's personified by an individual, it's the only office where performance expectations are elevated to unrealistic heights. It's not uncommon for people to evaluate the president against a mythical ideal derived from the presidency's vast folklore, nor is it unusual for people to feel disillusioned when presidents do not live up to this standard.

The Constitution gives the presidency few formal powers, initially designing it to be secondary in importance to Congress. Over time, through the efforts of strong presidents who mostly served during crises, the office has greatly expanded in size and influence. This permits savvy and skillful presidents to exercise the informal prerogatives of their office and wield power by effectively persuading others in the Washington community to support their interests. Cultivating a strong professional reputation and high levels of public prestige can bolster presidential persuasion.

Contemporary presidents rely heavily on public relations to boost public approval—they have a Communications Office to do the work—though despite their best efforts most presidents lose support over time. Their office gives them a big megaphone for influencing the news agenda, and presidents like to stage media events in order to take their message to the public on their own terms. However, journalists typically struggle against the president's desire to set the agenda, causing friction that's part of the competitive relationship between the White House and reporters.

The multiple and mutually exclusive roles the president must play contribute to the complexity of the office. As chief executive, the president is in charge of the government's executive branch or bureaucracy, and is responsible for executing the laws passed by Congress. As chief legislator, the president can propose a legislative agenda and attempt to persuade Congress to accept it, relying on his legislative liaison staff to lobby Congress. The president also plays the largely symbolic chief-of-state role, whereby he attends official functions and hosts foreign dignitaries. As chief diplomat, the president has the ability to extend diplomatic recognition to leaders of other nations, lending credibility to their regimes.

As commander-in-chief, the president is the civilian head of the armed forces. This gives him the power to commit troops and to wage war. Congress retains the power to declare war, but because contemporary wars are often waged without being declared, the military balance between the two branches has shifted heavily toward the president. In 1973, Congress tried to regain some of its military authority by passing the War Powers Act, requiring the president to get congressional approval to commit troops for more than sixty days, but presidents have largely ignored the measure.

The president's most divisive role is chief of party. Being the most prominent and powerful member of his party gives the president a platform for raising campaign money and stumping for his party's candidates for lower office. Contemporary presidents have rarely had coattails, though, limiting their influence over other races.

Over the past seventy years, the presidency has grown into a multifaceted institution centered in the Executive Office of the President. The White House Office contains the president's closest aides and coordinates the daily workings of the White House. Other offices handle national security issues, domestic policy, trade and budget issues, and environmental matters.

The president and Congress historically duel with each other for dominance in the federal system. The executive branch became ascendant with the New Deal programs of Franklin Roosevelt's presidency and the importance of the president as global leader during the cold war. The end of the cold war and a shift in public support toward a philosophy of less government growth permitted Congress to reassert itself in the 1990s. The shift in national priorities following the 2001 terror attacks may again revitalize the presidency.

Key Terms

backgrounders (p. 304)
Budget and Accounting Act of 1921 (p. 307)
cabinet (p. 305)
chief diplomat (p. 311)
chief executive (p. 305)
chief legislator (p. 307)
chief of staff (p. 315)
chief of state (p. 309)
coattails (p. 314)
commander-in-chief (p. 313)
Communications Office (p. 302)
diplomatic recognition (p. 311)
executive agreements (p. 312)
Executive Office of the President (EOP)
* (p. 306)*

executive orders (p. 307)
executive privilege (p. 296)
going public (p. 301)
honeymoon (p. 298)
impeachment (p. 294)
Joint Chiefs of Staff (p. 312)
legislative liaison (p. 308)
mandate (p. 297)
media events (p. 302)
National Security Council (NSC) (p. 312)
news leaks (p. 303)
newsworthy (p. 304)
Office of Management and Budget (OMB)
* (p. 307)*
override (p. 309)

pardon power (p. 296)
persuasion (p. 297)
pocket veto (p. 309)
press briefings (p. 303)
press conferences (p. 303)
press secretary (p. 302)
professional reputation (p. 297)
public prestige (p. 297)
rally effect (p. 298)
recess appointments (p. 295)
veto power (p. 295)
War Powers Act of 1973 (p. 313)
White House Office (p. 315)

Review Questions

Note: You can find the correct answers to these questions by taking the quiz and then submitting your answers in the Online Edition. The program will automatically score your submission. If you miss a question, the program will provide the correct answer, a rationale for the answer, and the section number in the chapter where the topic is discussed.

1. The degree to which the president is someone we can identify with will most directly determine our judgments of his
  a. policy leadership.
  b. global leadership.
  c. crisis management.
  d. symbolic leadership.

2. Which of the following is *not* a formal presidential power?
  a. pardon power
  b. power to convene Congress
  c. power to persuade Congress
  d. appointment power

3. Which of the following does *not* apply to executive privilege?
  a. It is never mentioned in the constitution.
  b. It permits the president to withhold sensitive information from Congress.
  c. It permits the president to negotiate binding agreements with other nations.
  d. It is typically justified in the name of national security.

4. A rally effect
   a. is typically produced by a traumatic national event.
   b. is typically produced by an effective presidential response to a traumatic national event.
   c. results in a lasting increase in presidential job approval.
   d. is an artifact of the way public opinion polls are conducted.

5. According to James David Barber, the most dangerous type of presidential character is the
   a. active-negative.
   b. active-positive.
   c. passive-negative.
   d. passive-positive.

6. The White House is always in control of each of the following press contacts *except*
   a. press briefings.
   b. press conferences.
   c. backgrounders.
   d. news leaks.

7. The veto can be a powerful presidential weapon
   a. if Congress intends to adjourn within ten days.
   b. if the president uses it often.
   c. if the president waits more than ten days before acting on a bill.
   d. if Congress is not composed of supermajorities of the other party.

8. Having coattails can assist the president in performing which of the following roles?
   a. chief diplomat
   b. chief of party
   c. commander-in-chief
   d. chief of state

9. Which office in the Executive Office of the President houses the president's "inner circle" of close advisors?
   a. National Security Council
   b. White House Office
   c. Council of Economic Advisors
   d. Office of Administration

10. Historically, the vice president
   a. has been a second-tier political figure.
   b. has had an excellent chance of becoming a future presidential nominee.
   c. has been a close presidential confidant.
   d. exercised tremendous authority presiding over the Senate.

In Their Own Words

You might be interested in examining some of what the following authors have said about the topics we've been discussing:

Barber, James David. *The Presidential Character: Predicting Performance in the White House,* 4th ed. Englewood Cliffs, NJ: Prentice Hall, 1992. Barber's effort to understand presidential performance by systematically classifying presidential character is as interesting as it is controversial.

Brace, Paul, and Barbara Hinckley. *Follow the Leader: Opinion Polls and the Modern Presidents.* New York: Basic Books, 1992. Domestic matters may be one thing, but when there's a foreign crisis, the public rallies around the president—whomever he may be.

Burke, John P. *The Institutional Presidency: Organizing and Managing the White House from FDR to Clinton,* 2nd ed. Baltimore: Johns Hopkins University Press, 2000. A look at the way the institutional White House is structured.

Edwards, George C. *Presidential Approval: A Sourcebook.* Baltimore: Johns Hopkins University Press, 1990. Edwards examines how popular support influences what the president is able to do.

Grossman, Michael Baruch, and Martha Joynt Kumar. *Portraying the President: The White House and the News Media.* Baltimore: Johns Hopkins University Press, 1981. Grossman and Kumar look at the push-pull relationship between the president and the press, and how the relationship goes through phases.

Jones, Charles O. *The Presidency in a Separated System.* Washington, DC: Brookings Institution, 1994. Do we expect too much from our presidents, considering the limits the Constitution places on the office?

Lowi, Theodore J. *The Personal President: Power Invested, Promise Unfulfilled.* Ithaca, NY: Cornell University Press, 1985. Lowi explores the president as symbolic figure who fills a complex emotional role with the public.

Milkis, Sidney, and Michael Nelson. *The American Presidency: Origins and Development, 1776–1998,* 3rd ed. Washington, DC: CQ Press, 1999. An historical account of growth and change in the presidency.

Neustadt, Richard E. *Presidential Power: The Politics of Leadership.* New York: Wiley, 1960. In a seminal work on presidential power, Neustadt makes the case that personal persuasion, not formal authority, is the key to presidential effectiveness.

Notes

1. George C. Edwards III, *The Public Presidency: The Pursuit of Popular Support* (New York: St. Martin's Press, 1983), 188.

2. Arthur M. Schlesinger, Sr., who published a list of great presidents in 1948, initiated presidential rankings. Lincoln came in first, followed by Washington and FDR. Grant and Harding pulled up the rear.

3. Edwards, *The Public Presidency,* 187–191.

4. Sidney M. Milkis and Michael Nelson, *The American Presidency: Origins and Development: 1776–1998,* 3d ed. (Washington, DC: CQ Press, 1999), 2–3.

5. Ibid., 66–84. Washington might have served a third term if he hadn't wanted to retire so badly. After his successor, John Adams, became the first president to be voted out of office, Thomas Jefferson honored the two-term tradition, and it stood until Franklin D. Roosevelt sought and won four terms in office starting in 1932. The Twenty-second Amendment (ratified in 1951) makes the two-term limit a constitutional requirement.

6. Ibid., 85–221.

7. Ibid., 196. This was most evident in international affairs, where Roosevelt exercised strong leadership independent of Congress—a model for American presidents of the twentieth century who served during America's emergence as a global power. See also 206–212.

8. Ibid., 222–241, 262–276, 307–327, and 340–353.

9. Richard E. Neustadt, *Presidential Power: The Politics of Leadership* (New York: Mentor Books, 1964), 42–63.

10. Ibid., 64–87.

11. Ibid., 88–106.

12. Paul Brace and Barbara Hinckley, *Follow the Leader: Opinion Polls and the Modern Presidents* (New York: Basic Books, 1992), 18–19.

13. George C. Edwards III, *At the Margins: Presidential Leadership of Congress* (New Haven: Yale University Press, 1989), 142–143.

14. If you want to get a sense of the variety of matters that pollsters get into, take a look at the home page of one polling firm, Zogby International, at http://www.zogby.com/.

15. Not every president gets the benefit of a honeymoon period. President George W. Bush did not have much of a honeymoon because of the raw feelings left by the unprecedented events surrounding how he came to office. President Clinton's early difficulties securing approval for key Cabinet appointees and his controversial early steps supporting gays in the military energized Republicans to oppose him immediately.

16. Brace and Hinckley, *Follow the Leader,* 22–27.

17. Ibid., 27–30.

18. Theodore Lowi, *The Personal President: Power Invested, Promise Unfulfilled* (Ithaca, NY: Cornell University Press, 1985), 1–21.

19. Milkis and Nelson, *The American Presidency,* 200–202.

20. Samuel Kernell, *Going Public: New Strategies of Presidential Leadership* (Washington, DC: CQ Press, 1986), 1–4.

21. You can read more about the Communications Office at http://www.whitehouse.gov/government/off-descrp.html.

22. Edwards, *At the Margins,* 141–146. If an administration is considering a policy and wants to see how the press would react to it, they can leak the information anonymously and see if reporters shoot down their "trial balloon" before the president officially announces it.

23. Ibid., 112–115.

24. Ibid., 115–119.

25. Ibid., 119–121.

26. Michael Baruch Grossman and Martha Joynt Kumar, *Portraying the President: The White House and the News Media* (Baltimore: Johns Hopkins University Press, 1981), 3–13.

27. Ibid., 273–298.

28. Jim Rutenberg, "White House Keeps a Grip on Its News," *New York Times,* October 14, 2002. The *New York Times* discussed the conflict as it played out in the Bush White House, which included press complaints about the lack of presidential press conferences and news leaks.

29. United States Office of Personnel Management, Demographic Profile of the Federal Workforce, at http://www.opm.gov/feddata/demograp/table1-1.pdf.

30. If you're interested in what these folks look like, you can find their pictures at http://www.whitehouse.gov/government/cabinet.html.

31. George Washington tried to rely on his cabinet for advice, but found it to be ineffective because of sharp differences among its members. Subsequent presidents didn't fare much better.

32. You can find a list of recent presidential executive orders at http://www.whitehouse.gov/news/orders/.

33. Charles O. Jones, *The Presidency in a Separated System* (Washington, DC: Brookings Institution, 1994), 147–181.

34. Paul Charles Light, *The President's Agenda: Domestic Policy Choice from Kennedy to Carter* (Baltimore: Johns Hopkins University Press, 1982), 13–25.

35. Ibid., 13. Attributed to Harry McPherson, aide to President Johnson.

36. Ibid., 17.

37. The figure does not include pocket vetoes. If you include all vetoes, the total for the period is 2,551.

38. Ford issued a total of sixty-six vetoes. This total includes eighteen pocket vetoes. See Office of the Clerk, U.S. House of Representatives, at http://clerk.house.gov/histHigh/Congressional_History/vetoes.html.

39. Aaron Wildavsky, "The Two Presidencies," *Trans-Action 4* (December 1966), 7–14.

40. Ibid.

41. See Donald A. Peppers, "The 'Two Presidencies' Thesis: Eight Years Later," in Steven A. Shull, ed., *The Two Presidencies: A Quarter Century Assessment* (Chicago: Nelson-Hall Publishers, 1991), 26–35; and Richard Fleisher and John Bond, "Are There Two Presidencies? Yes, But Only for Republicans," in Shull, *The Two Presidencies,* 119–142.

42. You can read more about the Central Intelligence Agency online at http://www.cia.gov/cia/information/info.html.

43. To read more about the National Security Council, go to http://www.whitehouse.gov/nsc/.

44. Wildavsky, "The Two Presidencies," 7–14.

45. See "Bush Feels Heat of U.N. Debate, U.S. Elections," *Washington Post,* October 27, 2002, sec. A.

46. John P. Burke, *The Institutional Presidency: Organizing and Managing the White House from FDR to Clinton,* 2d ed. (Baltimore: Johns Hopkins University Press, 2000), 13–18.

47. Ibid., 14–15.

48. You can read more about Laura Bush at http://www.whitehouse.gov/firstlady/flbio.html.

49. Milkis and Nelson, *The American Presidency,* 401–407. That last quote is commonly circulated but not exactly accurate. Garner, salty Texan that he was, actually compared the office to a different bodily fluid.

50. Ibid., 404.

51. Ibid.

52. Ibid., 405.

53. Ibid., 410–416.

54. Arthur M. Schlesinger Jr., *The Imperial Presidency* (Boston: Houghton Mifflin, 1973).

55. George E. Reedy, *The Twilight of the Presidency: From Johnson to Reagan* (New York: New American Library, 1987).

The Federal Bureaucracy

11-1 Introduction

Chances are, at some point, you've had a close encounter with some sort of bureaucracy. Maybe it was in a government office, like the Department of Motor Vehicles if you've gone for a driver's license. Perhaps you've had to fill out forms or wait in line to process a college loan application. Most of us can't get through college without dealing with some type of bureaucracy, either surrounding financial aid or course registration or at the bursar's office.

So, what comes to mind when you think about bureaucracy? Long lines? Paperwork? Inefficiency? Workers who could stand to be a little more, say, pleasant or concerned?

Impressions like these influence the way a lot of us think about bureaucracies. When we specifically think about the *federal* bureaucracy, seemingly so distant and far away, some people would add cold, heartless, and unfeeling to the description.

These impressions may be compounded by the way bureaucracy is treated as an object of ridicule in the popular culture. The media, always looking for sensational stories to hold our attention, periodically find maddening or ridiculous bureaucratic breakdowns that they know will capture our attention, like these unearthed by public administration scholar Charles T. Goodsell:

- A Chicago woman undergoing chemotherapy for cancer of the breast applied for Medicare. She received a computer-produced letter indicating she was ineligible since she had died the previous April.

- A chronic alcoholic was arrested and mistaken for another man. When he protested, his claims of misidentification were diagnosed as paranoia and schizophrenia, and he was committed to a mental hospital.

- The Department of Energy set out to declassify millions of documents inherited from the Atomic Energy Commission. Eight of the released documents contained the basic design for the hydrogen bomb.

- A unit of what is now the Department of Health and Human Services sent fifteen chimpanzees to a Texas laboratory for the purpose of launching a chimp-breeding program. All were males.[1]

Of course, since we understand what makes something **newsworthy,** we know that the press was drawn to these incidents precisely *because* they were exceptional. Ordinary

When we imagine the bureaucracy, many of us picture something like this: waiting in long lines to speak with a bureaucrat working on the other side of a desk. It's an unpleasant and familiar image for many of us, which can lend a negative cast to our impressions of bureaucracy.

stories of bureaucratic functioning wouldn't be very interesting because they would be about what happens when things go smoothly.

You say you're still not convinced because your encounters with bureaucracy tell you otherwise? Fair enough. But read on. There are a number of widely held beliefs about the bureaucracy that simply aren't true because there's more to the federal bureaucracy than meets the eye. In truth, the bureaucracy is staffed by people—millions of them—who are multidimensional and far more dedicated than we may give them credit for: people much like us, many of them knowledgeable about their field and passionate about what they do.

See if you can accept the possibility that:

- Bureaucracies don't always cause more problems than they solve. Much of the time the bureaucracy functions without incident, exactly as it's intended to operate. If you don't want to take my word for it, look at public opinion surveys. Large majorities of people who've had bureaucratic encounters came through them feeling positive. Even the postal service gets good reviews from three-quarters of the public.[2]

- Bureaucracies aren't always inefficient. The key word here is *always*. Sure, there's waste, although as we'll see, some waste is in the eye of the beholder and some of it is the result of political forces operating outside the bureaucracy. Many departments and agencies are actually efficient and effective. Of course, these aren't the ones we hear about in the news.

- Bureaucrats care about ordinary people. In fact, they *are* ordinary people. And they're not forced to do what they do. They choose to do it for the same reason that so many of us choose our jobs: because they're interested in their field and they enjoy their work.[3]

If our myths about our presidents are unrealistic because we expect too much, perhaps our myths about the bureaucracy are unrealistic because we expect too little. It just may be that the bureaucracy is more beneficial than we imagine.

11-2 What's the Bureaucracy Really Like?

The executive branch or the federal **bureaucracy** is a large web of departments, agencies, and bureaus charged with carrying out the laws and regulations passed by Congress and signed by the president. To handle the complexity of this task, the bureaucracy is organized in a way that would look recognizable to any of us familiar with a university, the military, or the workings of a large corporation. The German sociologist Max Weber noted these characteristics of bureaucratic structures:

- *Hierarchy*—Authority is clearly structured in bureaucracies, and is designed to operate on a top-down basis.

▶**newsworthy** (see p. 326) The conditions under which a story warrants publication or dissemination, based on a set of values applied by newspaper editors and television producers. Newsworthy stories typically have conflict, proximity and relevance to the audience, timeliness, and familiarity.

▶**bureaucracy** Another name for the executive branch of government, the institutional component of the presidency, which is charged with carrying out laws passed by Congress.

- *Specialization*—Bureaucrats function in specific capacities, dictated by their place in the organization.

- *Formalization*—Rules and procedures are made clear, and everyone doing business with the bureaucracy is subject to the same set of rules.

- *Permanent staff*—Bureaucrats make a career of service to their organization, making them accountable to the institution rather then to prevailing political tides.[4]

Taken collectively, these characteristics lend a sense of the impersonal to bureaucracies, and in fact, that's the point of Weber's model. Organization is supposed to ensure efficiency and protect against favoritism. If you don't put faces and personalities to the people in the bureaucracy, it's easy to confuse impersonal structures with impersonal individuals. In truth, bureaucrats do a lot more than go to meetings and write memos.

The bureaucracy is highly *specialized,* and many bureaucrats are skilled policy experts. "Bureaucrats," says Goodsell, "operate bridges, investigate crimes, manage forests, program computers, arbitrate labor disputes, counsel teenagers, calculate cost-benefit ratios, operate sea-rescue cutters, run libraries, examine patent applications, inspect meat, negotiate contracts, and so on and so forth."[5]

It's also misleading to think of the bureaucracy as a single, massive entity. Departments and agencies dealing with diverse, unrelated concerns in practice have nothing to do with one another. This lends a *fragmented* and *decentralized* quality to the federal bureaucracy. Someone in the Department of Energy has interests and expertise in entirely different issues than someone in the Department of Justice. There would be no reason for their paths to cross, and there would be no common area of overlap if they did.

Furthermore, each department has its own way of doing things. Over time, departments develop distinct *organizational cultures,* which distinguish them from other departments, even to the point of making them incompatible with one another.

It's hard to define organizational culture. The scholar James Q. Wilson calls it "a persistent way of thinking about the central tasks of and human relationships within an organization."[6] He compares organizational culture to individual personality traits, as something passed along through generations, resistant to change.

You've probably had experiences with different organizational cultures if you've visited friends at other universities. Maybe you noticed that their approaches to work and play were a little different from what you're used to—seemingly little things, like how at some schools no one would think of studying on a Thursday night and at other schools no one would think of partying on Thursdays. Things like this reflect the way people at different schools experience college, and they tend to be passed along as each freshman class acclimates to the college or university.

In the bureaucracy, the comparable effect could be like what Wilson found in the Department of State among bureaucrats trained mostly as diplomats, who by virtue of what they do value openness and communication over secrecy and security. As a consequence of these tendencies, Wilson found the culture of the State Department to be a culture of openness, where people in charge of the secretive business of maintaining security lose out in the battle for money, staff, and status, and where security in general is regarded as an annoyance.[7] It shouldn't be too hard to imagine other agencies made up of people with different approaches to the world—those doing intelligence work, for instance— making different choices in a different environment.

It also shouldn't be too difficult to imagine what could happen if something threatened to uproot an organization's culture—like the changes that occurred to agencies that were folded into the Department of Homeland Security, which was created by restructuring and reorganizing a host of existing bureaucratic entities. Bureaucrats brought to the new department an established understanding of how to approach their work that put them in conflict with bureaucrats from other agencies who wanted to apply to the new department different approaches developed in *their* organization's culture. The urge to do so is embedded in human nature, but it can pose a serious obstacle to merging bureaucratic operations.

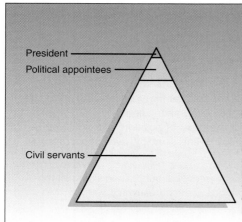

Political appointees are the top-level department and agency heads. At the highest level, they are people who are close to the president and may have assisted in the president's election. At every level, they can be expected to share the president's philosophy of government. With few exceptions, political appointees stay no longer than the president, making their maximum service eight years. In practice, many serve far less than the maximum.

Civil servants make up the vast majority of bureaucratic positions. They get their jobs on the basis of their qualifications and by law are not permitted political connections to the presidential administration. After a period of time, they are eligible for tenure, making them difficult to fire. This insulates civil servants from shifting political winds and promises them longevity in office.

Figure 11-1
Staffing the Federal Bureaucracy

11-3 Who's in the Bureaucracy?

If you were to visualize the bureaucracy as a big pyramid with the president at the top (it is, after all, the executive branch), as you worked your way down you'd find layers of top-level executives, followed by a large assortment of specialists holding just about every white-collar and blue-collar job imaginable. The top executives are **political appointees,** consisting of roughly 3,000 people including the department secretaries who serve in the president's cabinet, their undersecretaries and assistant secretaries, and bureau chiefs. The remaining employees, several million in number, are **civil servants**—the workers who permanently staff the bureaucracy. See Figure 11-1.

11-3a Political Appointees

One of the first tasks facing a new president is the responsibility—or opportunity—to fill top bureaucratic posts with people of his choice. Senior appointments are invariably the subject of great speculation in Washington, and the choices a president makes can send a clear message about the type of administration he intends to conduct. President Bush, for instance, filled key domestic policy positions with people who had backgrounds as business leaders, signaling his intention to bring a private-sector approach to governing and the affection his administration would have for business. President Clinton said he wanted the top levels of the bureaucracy to "look like America," underscoring the importance he placed on diversity.

Appointments below the top two or three positions in a department are generally subject to a national search of candidates, although cabinet secretaries may bring in associates to fill some of these jobs, and large political contributors have been known to land appealing spots in government. Bush and Clinton, like many of their predecessors, liberally placed financial supporters in attractive ambassadorships.

Vacant bureaucratic posts that need to be filled by presidential appointment are publicly listed in something called the Plum Book. Take a look at Box 11-1 for details.

Historically, presidential appointees have been overwhelmingly white, male, affluent, middle-aged, educated individuals from high-status occupations. Perhaps the most important characteristic they share is their tendency to come to government with limited public-sector experience, and to leave after a relatively brief period of time, often never returning to serve another administration. During the short time they are in government service, political appointees spend time in their department or agency, but not with each other. This makes political appointees a detached, disconnected group and a fairly transient elite.[8]

▶ **political appointees**
Top-level bureaucratic officials whom the president appoints, typically pending Senate confirmation, and who serve at the pleasure of the president.

▶ **civil servants** Career employees who staff the bureaucracy in a wide range of positions and who get their jobs independent of political considerations.

> ## Box 11-1 The Plum Book
>
> I nterested in putting your hat in the ring for an upper-level political position one day? There's an easy resource you can use to find out what's available. Every four years, following a presidential election, would-be public executives turn their attention to the **Plum Book,** a congressional publication listing the bureaucratic positions available through presidential appointments. (The document's official name is the "United States Government Policy and Supporting Positions," but since the top positions it lists could be considered "plums," it's acquired a name that's much easier to remember.) The Plum Book lists positions by department and rank, and includes salary information and the name of the present officeholder. It attracts intense interest when the White House passes to a president of a different political party, since every job in the book is eventually filled by someone new.
>
> To get a feel for the types of positions available, you can access the Plum Book online at http://www.gpoaccess.gov/plumbook/2004/.
>
> ▶ **Plum Book** The congressional publication listing all top-level political positions in the bureaucracy.

11-3b Career Civil Servants

Their transience also sharply distinguishes political appointees from career civil servants, where the term "career" should be a strong clue as to their length of service in the bureaucracy. While political appointees come and go, typically more quickly than the presidents who appoint them, civil servants stay much longer, often serving in a department or agency until retirement. Although between one-quarter and one-third of political appointees can expect to be working elsewhere within a year of assuming their job,[9] the average civil servant in 2000 had started working in the bureaucracy in 1983.[10]

As a group, civil servants are middle aged and male, better educated than the population as a whole and more Anglo, although during the 1990s the ranks of women and minorities increased somewhat. Figure 11-2 tells the story, comparing civil servant demographics from 1990 and 2000.

What do career civil servants do? Anything and everything—more than you can probably imagine. The range of civil-service work is unbelievably far-reaching: You could literally run a city with the variety of skills and specialties represented by civil servants. Between civil servants who work in Washington and those who work for the federal government across the country and around the world, you can find a full palette of white-collar and blue-collar specialties. Of course, there are letter carriers and park rangers and the folks who answer questions at the Social Security Administration, but as of September 1999, the government also employed:

- 363,953 clerical workers
- 139,132 health care workers
- 123,183 engineers
- 115,369 accountants and budget specialists
- 93,897 investigators
- 86,377 lawyers and legal workers
- 18,197 artists and information specialists
- 13,624 mathematicians and statisticians
- 8,045 librarians and archivists
- 5,667 plumbers and pipe fitters
- 5,414 machinists
- 3,869 cooks
- 597 chaplains
- 205 nuclear materials couriers
- 39 sociologists

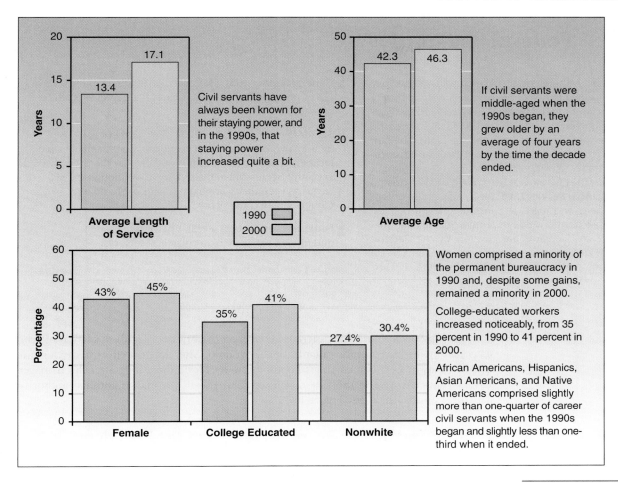

Civil servants have always been known for their staying power, and in the 1990s, that staying power increased quite a bit.

If civil servants were middle-aged when the 1990s began, they grew older by an average of four years by the time the decade ended.

Women comprised a minority of the permanent bureaucracy in 1990 and, despite some gains, remained a minority in 2000.

College-educated workers increased noticeably, from 35 percent in 1990 to 41 percent in 2000.

African Americans, Hispanics, Asian Americans, and Native Americans comprised slightly more than one-quarter of career civil servants when the 1990s began and slightly less than one-third when it ended.

Figure 11-2
Who Are the Civil Servants?

Source: United States Office of Personnel Management, *The Fact Book* (1990–2000 editions), Trend of Employment.

- 27 clothing designers
- 24 funeral directors
- 2 beauticians
- 1 bartender[11]

The main reason why civil servants stick around for so long is that after a probationary period many of them are eligible for **tenure.** Much like tenure in a university that protects your professors from losing their jobs if they publish controversial research, tenure in the civil service protects employees from being penalized by changing political currents. It also makes it difficult to let them go.[12]

The same logic of protection from political influences explains how white-collar civil servants get their jobs. Employment is merit based, keeping it outside the political process. Typically, applicants take an objective civil service exam, which forms the basis for their eligibility. Jobs are publicly posted, along with a description of responsibilities and a clearly defined pay grade. Federal pay grades are very specific, in fact—as Box 11-2 indicates.

Things weren't always like this. In Section 11-6b ("From the Spoils System to the Merit System"), we'll see that standardized hiring, pay and promotion procedures were a reform designed to protect the bureaucracy from undue political influence.

▶ **tenure** Job security afforded civil servants following a probationary period, to protect them against losing their jobs for political reasons.

11-3c Appointees vs. Careerists: Going Native

So, civil servants serve for years, are protected by tenure, and are experts in their respective field, while political appointees come and go, serve at the president's pleasure, and share no common political bonds. This can make things challenging for political appointees. In private bureaucracies, like the ones you find in large corporations, lines of authority work

Box 11-2 Federal Pay Grades

White-collar civil servants are covered by a detailed pay scale designed to reflect the complexity and difficulty of the jobs they perform. The **General Service (GS)** classification contains eighteen grades (GS1 to GS18); the higher the grade, the more specialized the work and the higher the pay. Within the first fifteen grades, there are ten steps for advancement in each grade, allowing employees pay raises without changing grades. The Civil Service Reform Act of 1978 created the **Senior Executive Service (SES)** for a small group of top-level policy experts and managers, including some political appointees whose positions do not require Senate confirmation. Blue-collar civil servants are covered by the **Federal Wage System (FWS),** which typically pays the customary rate for services in the region of the country where the civil servants are employed.*

▶ **General Service (GS)** The system of eighteen grade levels (GS1 through GS18) that determines the pay level of white-collar civil servants.

▶ **Senior Executive Service (SES)** The payment scale used for a small group of upper-level government managers and technical experts. Most positions covered by the Senior Executive Service are in the civil service, although the SES covers select political appointees whose jobs do not require Senate confirmation.

▶ **Federal Wage System (FWS)** The system used to determine salaries for blue-collar civil servants.

*Ronald N. Johnson and Gary D. Libecap, *The Federal Civil Service System and the Problem of Bureaucracy* (Chicago: University of Chicago Press, 1994), 98–99.

from the top down. Things are different in the executive branch, regardless of what may be suggested by the bureaucratic organizational pyramid. After all, how effective can a manager be if his or her tenured subordinates know they'll be there long after the manager leaves? That's the case in the federal bureaucracy, and it can turn traditional authority structures upside down. See Figure 11-3.

11-3d Bureaucratic Responsiveness to the President

Given this environment, the president may choose to approach the bureaucracy strategically, to maximize his influence and the influence of his appointees. One place where the president can attempt to assert his will is through the approach he takes to making appointments. This is, after all, one area where he has a fair amount of leeway. Some presidents make loyalty a key criterion when selecting high-level appointees, hoping to find people who will resist the temptation to **"go native"** and become advocates for the department they run at the expense of the president's agenda.

▶ **"go native"** The tendency for political appointees to adhere to the organizational culture of the department they are sent to run, making them advocates of the department rather than advocates of the president.

However, presidents have to make their selections carefully because beyond the upper echelon of appointees, there are limitations to how broadly the law permits the president to remove the people he has appointed. Presidents often find it easier to lean on sympathetic appointees by reminding them of past loyalties than by threatening dismissal for noncompliant behavior. See Figure 11-4 on page 334.

A more extreme version of the presidential appointment strategy entails naming deeply ideological individuals committed to the president's goals to as many bureaucratic levels as the president can appoint people. This strategy assumes that the philosophical commitments of "true believers" will outweigh the temptation for them to "go native," and that strategic appointments reaching below the highest echelon of agencies and departments give the president more leverage with career civil servants.

This approach was used by President Nixon and replicated by President Reagan, both of whom faced a bureaucracy that housed a large number of liberals philosophically opposed to the president's objectives. It was part of a broader strategy of implementing an **administrative presidency** designed to maximize the president's ability to achieve policy objectives through tight administrative control of the bureaucracy, counteracting the strong tendencies of political appointees to become advocates for their agencies by:

▶ **administrative presidency** A strategic approach to the bureaucracy relying on ideological political appointees and tight presidential management to combat the tendency for political appointees to "go native."

- Requiring all agencies and departments to submit funding requests through the president's Office of Management and Budget (OMB), to try to short-circuit the close relationships civil servants have with the congressional allies who fund them.

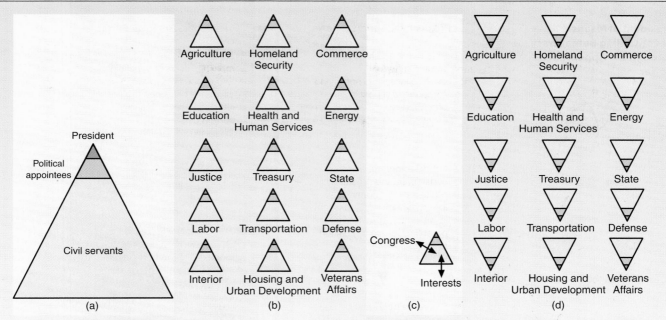

(a) This is the pyramid representing the structure of the federal bureaucracy that we saw a little earlier, with the president and political appointees ostensibly on top.

(b) However, we now know that the bureaucracy isn't one integrated mass, but a group of unrelated departments and agencies. These fifteen represent only the major departments and don't include independent agencies, independent regulatory commissions, and government corporations.

(c) Since each department has its own organizational culture, each one is a little like a "native village" where civil servants, who have longevity, define the culture. They're engaged in long-term relationships with members of Congress and interest groups with whom they share concerns and interests—the ones we talked about when we discussed the iron triangle. These enduring relationships define their everyday experiences. Political appointees have no such relationships: They are essentially outsiders in the village.

(d) With no ties to bind them to each other, political appointees find that their best option is to join the village—to "go native"—and identify with the culture of the department they were selected to run. As they do, they leave behind whatever mandate they got from the president to lead the department, becoming instead a spokesperson for the agency's interests. They become followers, in a sense, as traditional lines of command are upended. Real bureaucratic power rests with the careerists who would appear to be at the bottom of the organizational chart.*

*Hugh M. Heclo, *A Government of Strangers: Executive Politics in Washington* (Washington, DC: Brookings Institution, 1977), pp. 111–112.

- Requiring all agencies and departments to submit proposed rules changes to OMB to make sure they're in line with the president's program.

- Exploiting loopholes in the law to transfer or demote career civil servants who stand in the way of political appointees.

- Having lower-level appointees loyal to the president's program carry out functions typically reserved for high-level career civil servants.[13]

How well did it work? In the Reagan administration, the results were mixed, but in many respects positive. Career civil servants were largely responsive to Reagan's administrative presidency in the sense that there were few observable attempts to undermine the president's policies. However, the level of responsiveness varied by department, partly in reaction to how each department treated dissent. For instance, in the Food and Nutrition Service and the National Highway Traffic Safety Administration, the prevailing attitude among civil servants was that they were there to serve the president, and even if they didn't agree with what he was trying to do, they kept quiet and did their work. In the Civil Rights Division, there was vocal disagreement between appointees and careerists, and a number of resignations and threats of resignation.[14]

Figure 11-3
The Structure of the Federal Bureaucracy: A Second Look

Figure 11-4
Presidential Means of Controlling Bureaucracy through the Appointment Power

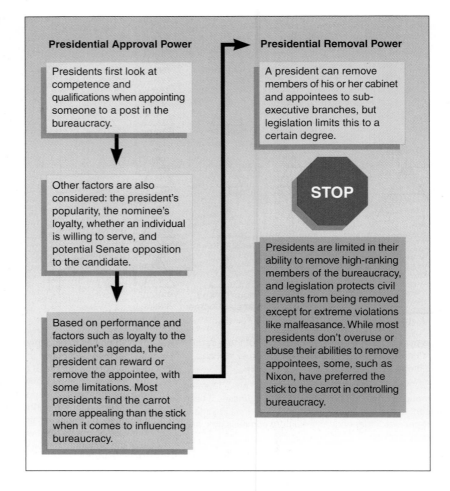

Presidential Approval Power

Presidents first look at competence and qualifications when appointing someone to a post in the bureaucracy.

Other factors are also considered: the president's popularity, the nominee's loyalty, whether an individual is willing to serve, and potential Senate opposition to the candidate.

Based on performance and factors such as loyalty to the president's agenda, the president can reward or remove the appointee, with some limitations. Most presidents find the carrot more appealing than the stick when it comes to influencing bureaucracy.

Presidential Removal Power

A president can remove members of his or her cabinet and appointees to sub-executive branches, but legislation limits this to a certain degree.

STOP

Presidents are limited in their ability to remove high-ranking members of the bureaucracy, and legislation protects civil servants from being removed except for extreme violations like malfeasance. While most presidents don't overuse or abuse their abilities to remove appointees, some, such as Nixon, have preferred the stick to the carrot in controlling bureaucracy.

There was variation in the responsiveness of bureaucrats within individual bureaucratic units as well. In the Environmental Protection Agency, many civil servants complied with the president's policies while others strenuously resisted them. Often, the ones that went along did so out of the sense that it was better to acquiesce to the administration's wishes than to risk limiting career prospects, at least for the immediate future.[15] A determined president, then, can expect to have some success counteracting the forces that, if left to their own devices, put control of bureaucratic units in the hands of career civil servants.

11-4 Departments, Agencies, Commissions, and Corporations

Let's take a minute and figure out the maze of departments, agencies, commissions, and corporations that make up the bureaucracy.

11-4a Departments

In Chapter 10, when we talked about the president's cabinet, we said that the cabinet secretaries each head a department in the executive branch. The largest portion of the bureaucracy is composed of the fifteen departments headed by those cabinet secretaries (see Table 10-4).

Although departments and agencies have offices that are scattered around the country, the nerve center of the federal bureaucracy is located in a remarkably small section of Washington, D.C., where cabinet department headquarters are clustered in a narrow power corridor centered on the White House and Congress. Notice in Figure 11-5 how three of the oldest departments—Treasury, Justice, and State—are fairly close to the cen-

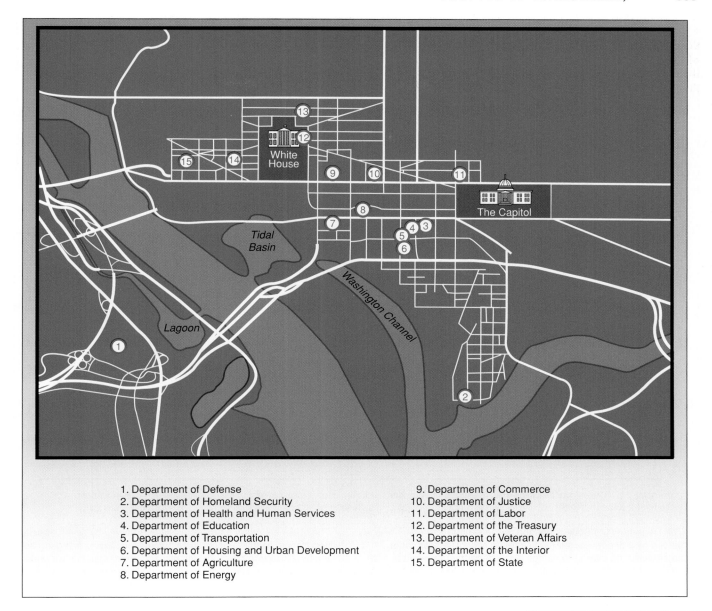

1. Department of Defense
2. Department of Homeland Security
3. Department of Health and Human Services
4. Department of Education
5. Department of Transportation
6. Department of Housing and Urban Development
7. Department of Agriculture
8. Department of Energy
9. Department of Commerce
10. Department of Justice
11. Department of Labor
12. Department of the Treasury
13. Department of Veteran Affairs
14. Department of the Interior
15. Department of State

ter of executive power, the White House. Some of the departments that serve specific political constituencies, like Labor, Education, and Health and Human Services, are closer to the Capitol.

On paper, each of these departments is organized in a top-down fashion that seems to defy the upside-down power dynamics we were just talking about. Remember, though, organizational charts simply detail how the component parts of an institution fit together, not how it actually operates. It's worth looking at an organizational chart or two in order to get a sense of the wide-ranging functions each department performs (see Figure 11-6).

11-4b Independent Agencies

Beyond the fifteen cabinet departments lies an array of agencies and commissions. **Independent agencies** exist outside the cabinet departments—hence the name "independent." They report directly to the president, and are run by administrators who are appointed by the president and confirmed by the Senate. Independent agency heads also serve at the pleasure of the president, which means they can be removed from office at any time.

Some examples of independent agencies are shown in Table 11-1 on page 338.

Figure 11-5
Bureaucratic Locator

▶ **independent agencies**
Bureaucratic organizations that report directly to the president rather than through cabinet secretaries, and whose administrators serve at the pleasure of the president.

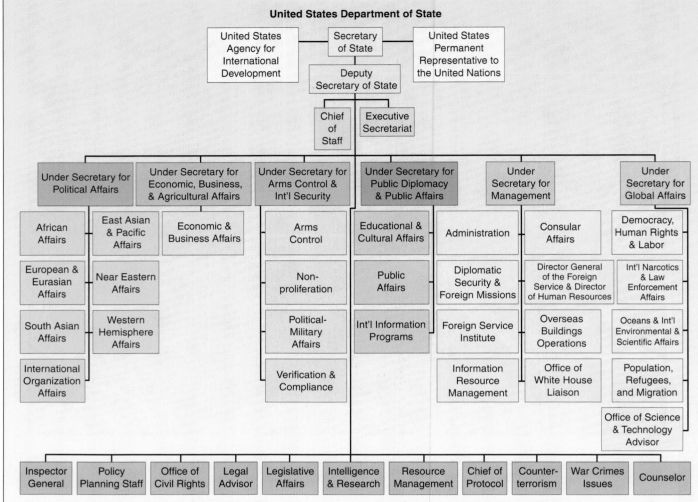

United States Department of State

The Department of State is headed by the secretary of state, who is served by a deputy secretary of state. An executive secretariat coordinates the internal workings of the department's bureaus and offices. The United States ambassador to the United Nations reports directly to the secretary of state, who gives foreign policy direction to the director of the United States Agency for International Development. Six under secretaries report to the secretary of state. The under secretaries are specialists and are served by assistant secretaries who preside over bureaus that do the work of that specialization. For instance, the under secretary for political affairs is a crisis manager who troubleshoots problems involving the United States and different regions of the world.

The under secretary for political affairs is served by seven assistant secretaries, each of whom runs a bureau specializing in a geographic region. The same structure is in place for the remaining five under secretaries, who handle matters ranging from international trade and agricultural policy to arms control policy and strengthening democratic institutions abroad. In addition, eleven offices report directly to the secretary of state. They cover a range of matters—from lobbying Congress to reviewing intelligence information to providing legal advice to the department.

(a)

Figure 11-6
Organizational Charts for Two Federal Departments
(a) The Department of State.
(b) The Department of the Interior.

Sources: Organizational chart of the Department of State at http://www.state.gov/r/pa/ei/rls/dos/7926.htm; and organizational chart of the Department of the Interior at http://www.doi.gov/org.htm.

11-4c Independent Regulatory Commissions and Boards

Like independent agencies, **independent regulatory commissions and boards** report to the president, and are headed by commissioners who are appointed by the president with Senate approval. However, they are more independent of the president than independent agencies because their members serve fixed terms and cannot be removed from office by the president. In fact, they're designed to be as free of political control as possible. By law, they are composed of a fixed number of members, typically between five and ten, and appointees must be divided between the two major political parties.

These commissions perform a regulatory function, which means they oversee a sector of society like banking, commerce, or communications, and are expected to act in the pub-

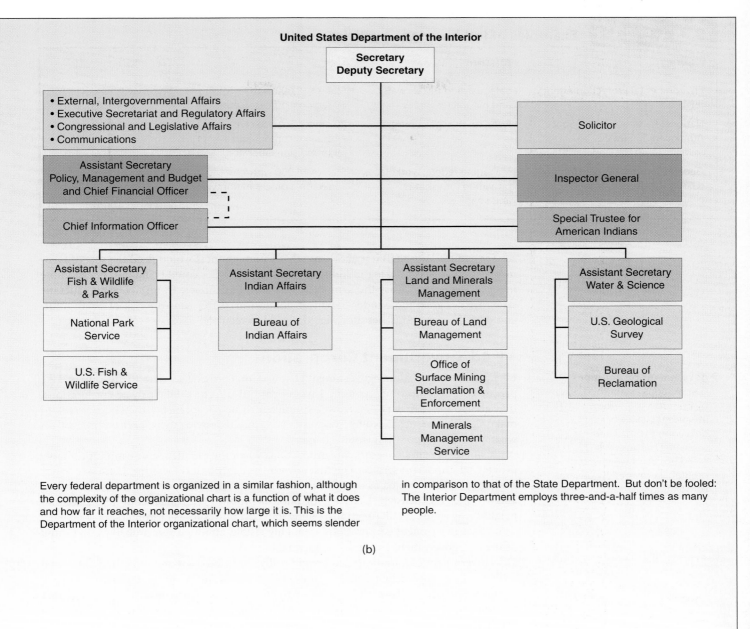

Every federal department is organized in a similar fashion, although the complexity of the organizational chart is a function of what it does and how far it reaches, not necessarily how large it is. This is the Department of the Interior organizational chart, which seems slender in comparison to that of the State Department. But don't be fooled: The Interior Department employs three-and-a-half times as many people.

(b)

lic interest. That's why they're supposed to be sheltered from political pressures. They have the authority to make and enforce rules, which makes them quite powerful. For instance, the Federal Reserve Board (FRB) has the authority to set interest rates, the Federal Communications Commission (FCC) licenses multimillion-dollar television and radio stations, and the Securities and Exchange Commission (SEC) oversees the stock market.

Other prominent independent regulatory commissions and boards are shown in Table 11-2.

Because independent regulatory commissions wield so much power, they are the focus of great attention from the groups they regulate. In some cases, a "revolving door" can develop between commissioners and the industries they regulate, whereby commissioners are selected from the regulated industry and then return to it after their term of

▶ **independent regulatory commissions and boards** (see p. 336) Panels designed to oversee the conduct of various segments of the economy. Members are appointed by the president and confirmed by the Senate. They serve fixed terms and cannot be removed by the president.

TABLE 11-1 Examples of Independent Agencies

Agency	Mission	Size	Website
Environmental Protection Agency (EPA)	Safeguarding the air, water, and natural resources	Staff of 18,000 with 10 regional offices nationwide	http://www.epa.gov/
National Aeronautics and Space Administration (NASA)	Running the space program	20 offices, 5 space centers, 4 research centers, and a jet propulsion laboratory	http://www.nasa.gov/
General Services Administration (GSA)	Managing federal workplaces, providing furnishings and supplies	Staff of 14,000 with 11 regional offices nationwide	http://www.gsa.gov/

service expires. Although it makes sense that commissioners would need the sort of technical expertise that working in industry provides, close ties could bring into question the independence or at least the sympathies of a commissioner. Ironically, a bureaucratic structure designed to be independent of political pressures runs the risk of being influenced by the very industries they were designed to regulate.

11-4d Government Corporations

▶ **government corporations**
Corporations established by Congress to perform important services, like delivering the mail and operating rail lines, which could not be or were not profitably provided by private corporations.

Like private corporations, **government corporations** provide services to customers. Like private corporations, they typically have a board of directors. Like private corporations, they charge for their services. However, unlike private corporations, they do not seek to make a profit, are subsidized by Congress, and typically provide their services for less than what a private corporation would charge.

Congress creates government corporations when the private sector cannot profitably provide an important service. The first government corporation was the Tennessee Valley Authority (TVA), created as part of Franklin D. Roosevelt's New Deal to control flooding and produce inexpensive electricity for poor, depression-era residents of Tennessee and neighboring states. It still functions, selling low-cost power to its customers.[16]

Some government corporations are highly visible, although you probably don't think of them as government corporations (see Table 11-3).

Government corporations can be politically controversial. For a long time, the postal service ran up huge deficits, which required Congress to make up the difference. Amtrak continues to frustrate lawmakers who find themselves faced with subsidizing a service that has not found a way to break even. This is a particular irritant to members of Congress who feel they should not be in the business of running a railroad.

Members of Congress take some political cover from the fact that expenditures on public corporations are "off budget," meaning money spent on them doesn't count against official government budget figures. So, when the postal service was created from what had

TABLE 11-2 Examples of Independent Regulatory Commissions and Boards

Commission or Board	Mission	Board Composition	Website
National Labor Relations Board (NLRB)	Regulating relations between unions and employers	5 members, staggered 5-year terms	http://www.nlrb.gov/
Federal Trade Commission (FTC)	Enforcing consumer protection laws	5 commissioners, staggered 7-year terms	http://www.ftc.gov/
Equal Employment Opportunity Commission (EEOC)	Ending workplace discrimination	5 commissioners, staggered 5-year terms	http://www.eeoc.gov/

TABLE 11-3	Examples of Government Corporations		
Government Corporation	**Mission**	**Interesting Fact**	**Website**
United States Postal Service (USPS)	Providing mail delivery	Largest government corporation	http://www.usps.com/
Amtrak (National Railroad Passenger Corporation)	Providing passenger rail service	Created in 1971 from troubled private rail lines	http://www.amtrak.com/

been a cabinet-level department called the U.S. Post Office, Congress could spend to cover its shortfall without appearing to dip into general revenues.

11-5 What the Bureaucracy Does

The bureaucracy performs three fundamental functions: implementation, regulation, and administration. Collectively, these functions give bureaucrats an enormous amount of influence over the shape of public policy.

11-5a Implementation

When Congress passes and the president signs a bill, they approve words on a piece of paper. It's up to the executive branch to give life to those words. **Implementation** is the process by which departments and agencies enact the law, turning legal language into functioning policies. We briefly visited the concept of implementation when we were talking about the iron triangle in Chapter 8, when we said the power to implement legislation was one of the resources the bureaucracy has that interest groups want.

> **implementation**
> The bureaucratic function of taking the legal language of legislation and turning it into functioning programs.

Because the people who write the laws are different from the people who put them into effect, implementation is not a straightforward process. In theory, bureaucrats would implement legislation exactly as Congress intended. In practice, the intent of Congress is often not intelligible in the wording of legislation. Quite often, there is no single intent; rather, there are multiple perspectives of what the legislation would be from the members who voted to make it law. None of this is reflected in the wording of a bill. It falls to bureaucrats to put their imprint on legislation by deciding how it should be carried out. There's a saying that it's easy to agree on broad principles, but "the devil is in the details." Implementation is about the details.

So, bureaucrats go about the business of formulating the rules that give shape to policy, resting decisions that shape policy in the hands of individuals who never face voters at the polls. In the most clear-cut cases—say, a presidential executive order, a carefully written congressional statute, or a detailed court decision—bureaucrats are given sufficient direction on how to act that the rules they create are little more than instructions on how to follow through on the order, statute, or decision. However, ambiguity often clouds the process. When Congress provides bureaucrats with few details, bureaucratic rule making determines what those policies will look like.[17] Similarly, bureaucrats are the ones who reinterpret policies created in the past as new, unforeseen conditions arise, such as when laws regulating radio and television communication suddenly need to be applied to the Internet. This ambiguity can be a great source of bureaucratic influence (see Box 11-3).

Beyond ambiguity, a host of factors conspire to make implementation a complex process. Political scientist George C. Edwards points out several impediments to effective implementation, including problems with communication, insufficient resources, attitudes of bureaucrats, obstacles posed by standard operating procedures, and the fragmentation of the bureaucracy.[18]

Communication   For starters, you can't assume that bureaucrats responsible for implementing policy understand what they should be doing. Lines of communication between policy makers and bureaucrats are not always clear and open. Many agencies are

> ### Box 11-3   What Does It Mean?
>
> When the president, in his capacity as commander-in-chief, issues an order to move troops, there's no room for interpretation. When he formally recognizes another nation in his capacity as chief of state and instructs the United States to commence diplomatic relations, it gets done.
>
> But what does it mean when Congress passes legislation "to assure so far as possible every working man and woman in the Nation safe and healthy work conditions?"* That language comes directly from the Occupational Safety and Health Act. It fell to the administering agency, the Occupational Safety and Health Administration (OSHA), to create rules that it felt captured the intent of the words "as far as possible," "safe," and "healthy." Obviously, these terms can be interpreted in a multitude of ways, and the manner of interpretation determines how far-reaching the legislation will be. Then, once OSHA gave legal meaning to these legislative abstractions, it was up to the agency to determine how broadly the act would be applied by figuring out exactly when and how health and safety could be—and should be—protected.†
>
> With so much latitude, bureaucrats can shape public policy in ways elected officials never intended. In the extreme, they can gut legislation by the way they implement it. That's the charge that was leveled against the Federal Election Commission (FEC) by supporters of the McCain-Feingold Campaign Finance Reform Act. Senator John McCain has been a vocal critic of the way the FEC has interpreted the legal language in the bill, asserting they intentionally took the teeth out of it, but there's little he can do beyond trying to draw media attention to the issue or challenging the FEC in court. His name may appear on the bill, but once the legislation left Congress, the shape it assumed was out of his hands.
>
> *Cornelius M. Kerwin, *Rulemaking: How Government Agencies Write Law and Make Policy* (Washington, DC: CQ Press, 1994), 6.
> †Ibid.

very large and, as you can probably imagine from having looked at the organizational chart for the Department of State, messages often have to be communicated through multiple bureaucratic layers. The result can be like a game of "telephone," where a message whispered from person to person gets distorted in transit.

Even when messages are communicated clearly, they may not always be welcome. Remember, career civil servants can have strong views about their policy area, and may disregard or alter directions from policy makers if they're at odds with the civil servant's preferences or beliefs.[19]

Insufficient Resources   Everywhere we've turned, we've seen the relationship between resources and effectiveness, and the relationship certainly holds true for bureaucrats. It's difficult for bureaucrats to effectively implement policy when they're lacking these resources:

- *Staff*—When Americans complain about the size of government, as many tend to do, they're looking for a reduction in the size of the bureaucracy. In practical terms, this would mean reducing the size of the staff that's available to implement policy. Ironically, many departments and agencies find themselves calling out for more assistance, not cutbacks. In addition to sheer numbers, workers have to be skilled and effectively trained. If you don't know how to monitor food-processing plants, for instance, you'll be of little use to the Food and Drug Administration, which has to check the conditions of tens of thousands of plants using only four thousand food inspectors.

- *Information*—Bureaucrats need to know how to put a policy into effect, and the information required to do so can be technical and complex. If you're in the Environmental Protection Agency and Congress tells you that you're supposed to come up with standards for clean air, you'd better have some basis for determining how to do it. Because information is so critical to bureaucrats, they're happy to turn to sympathetic interest groups for assistance. As we saw in Chapter 8, this can cement a relationship of mutual dependence and tilt implementation decisions in the group's favor.

- *Facilities*—It may sound basic, but if a department or agency lacks the space to work effectively, or lacks supplies and equipment, it will have trouble getting things accomplished.[20]

Attitudes of Bureaucrats   When bureaucrats and lawmakers see eye-to-eye on a policy, implementation typically goes smoothly. When they do not, things can get interesting. Largely because career civil servants do not have to indulge the wishes of their politically appointed superiors, they can act with some discretion when it comes to making decisions about how something is to be done.[21]

Standard Operating Procedures   Bureaucrats are guided in their work by **standard operating procedures (SOPs),** which are routines that are put in place to direct everyday decision making. If your task is to determine if someone is eligible for welfare benefits, for instance, established practices help you make the decision. Recorded in thick manuals, SOPs (as they're called) can play on the stereotyped image of bureaucrats mindlessly following a protocol that seems—well, bureaucratic. In most cases, though, SOPs make perfect sense to the people following them, and the ability to standardize decision making across a huge government lends an element of fairness to the implementation process. It also keeps bureaucrats from having to start from scratch every time they're faced with a new task. On the downside, SOPs may contribute to agency inflexibility when faced with a new mission that doesn't fit neatly within existing procedures.[22]

▶**standard operating procedures (SOPs)** Guidelines that provide uniformity to bureaucratic decision making.

Fragmentation   Because the bureaucracy developed in a piecemeal fashion in response to a host of unrelated political demands, it is highly fragmented. It's not uncommon for multiple agencies to have overlapping responsibilities. For instance, no less than a dozen agencies share responsibility for implementing legislation that prohibits discriminatory lending practices. This makes it difficult—at times, impossible—for implementation to proceed in a coordinated manner, and it contributes to the widely held sentiment that the bureaucracy is inefficient.

However, fragmentation serves a political purpose. Remember, for every bureaucratic function there is a corresponding congressional committee engaged in policy making, and those committees are centers of congressional power. Widening the scope of responsibility for any piece of legislation is a way of spreading around the resources. This makes bureaucratic reorganization a daunting task because congressional toes (and those of companion interest groups) will get badly bruised in the process.[23] It took a national crisis to get Congress to agree to the biggest bureaucratic reorganization in generations, changing the jurisdiction of all or part of the twenty-two security-related agencies that were combined to form the Department of Homeland Security.

11-5b Regulation

You probably like drinking from a water fountain without thinking twice about whether the water supply is safe, or knowing that food you buy in a supermarket isn't infected with dangerous microorganisms. It's the bureaucracy's job to monitor things like these and impose standards to maintain safe water and food, clean air, and a wide range of other things. This is called **regulation,** and although there may not be a lot of dissent about the value of some things regulations attempt to protect, regulation is one of the bureaucracy's more controversial functions.

That's because regulation is about control, with implications for personal liberty. Everyone values clean air. Not everyone wants to be told they have to pay for an expensive annual automobile emissions test, or for a catalytic converter when they buy a car. Corporate polluters will not appreciate being told they have to pick up the tab for maintaining a particular level of air or water quality. It's a source of tension that often plays out in our politics, as we'll see when we talk about domestic policy making in Chapter 15.

▶**regulation** The bureaucratic function of placing standards or restrictions on the actions of private individuals or companies in order to protect the general welfare of the public.

Regulations are also pervasive, which in its own right can be a source of political conflict. Some people simply object to the long regulatory reach of the federal government (see Box 11-4). Beyond food, water and air quality, the bureaucracy has a hand in regulating workplace safety, consumer products, toxic waste disposal, business practices, highway safety, discriminatory hiring practices, cable television rates, and many less salient matters.

When an agency proposes a new regulation, it is publicly posted in the **Federal Register** in advance of public hearings to solicit feedback. When a regulation goes into effect, it

▶**Federal Register** A publicly available list of all proposed and existing federal regulations.

Box 11-4 Roller Coaster Regulations

Should the regulatory reach of the federal government follow you to Disney World? That was the topic of a recent congressional debate on the National Amusement Ride Safety Act, designed to make roller coaster safety the regulatory responsibility of the federal government. The act was written in response to a loophole in federal law that left roller coaster inspections to individual states, resulting in a wide variety of regulatory policies ranging from extensive to lax to none.

The International Association of Amusement Parks and Attractions opposed the measure, arguing that the odds of injury or death on a roller coaster are infinitesimal, and are more likely to result from careless riders than technical malfunctions. Executives from large theme parks likewise argued

for the right to police themselves, claiming they had too much at stake economically to permit unsafe rides. Congressional advocates of the measure countered with the argument that because amusement park operators are under pressure to make a profit, safety and maintenance procedures could be at risk.*

What do you think? Do you believe roller coaster safety is an appropriate matter for federal regulation, or is it a case of excessive or unwarranted government involvement?

*"Lawmakers Seek Federal Regulation of Roller Coasters," CNN, May 16, 2000, at http://www.cnn.com/2000/ALLPOLITICS/stories/05/16/roller.coaster/.

---

is published in the Federal Register as well. You can get a sense of the range and extent of federal regulations by browsing through the Federal Register online. The next time you log on, go to http://www.archives.gov/federal_register/the_federal_register/indexes.html, and click on the current year under "Daily Table of Contents." A list of dates will appear on the screen. Click on today's date; you'll get a list of every new regulation that was proposed or put into effect today, in alphabetical order, by agency.

Political pressures against government regulation have resulted in the occasional **deregulation** of some industries. Deregulation arose out of the sentiment that government reaches too far into the activities of the private sector, and that the marketplace rather than government is an adequate mechanism for regulating corporate behavior. Although this perspective gained currency during the Reagan administration and is favored by the current Republican congressional majority, one of the first major efforts at deregulation occurred in 1978, during the administration of Democrat Jimmy Carter, with deregulation of the airline industry.

Prior to deregulation, airlines had to adhere to strict bureaucratic guidelines for setting airfares and routes. Following deregulation, airlines had more freedom to set fare and route structures. Lower fares and new low-budget airlines emerged as the industry was deregulated. As a consequence, air travel became more affordable, and many people who used to rely on ground transportation found they could take to the skies. However, a deregulated airline industry also encountered a host of consumer complaints that hadn't existed before, among them long lines at airports, frequent delays, an inequitable fare structure, and insufficient service to remote locations. Box 11-5 discusses the pros and cons of airline deregulation.

The Bush administration is highly sympathetic to deregulation. In areas ranging from telecommunications to energy to environmental concerns, the administration has put its weight squarely behind deregulation efforts. The approach is consistent with President Bush's hands-off policy toward private industry, which reflects his philosophy that the federal government should stand aside whenever possible so that market forces may take effect. This approach has its supporters and its detractors. For instance, some place the blame for the corporate accountability scandals of 2002 on deregulation of the financial markets, and environmentalists worry that too great an emphasis on business interests at the expense of environmental regulations will result in lasting damage to the earth's ecosystem.

deregulation The lifting of federal regulations that had been previously imposed on private industry.

administration The bureaucratic function of tending to the details of executing public policy.

11-5c Administration

One of the least glamorous but more critical functions of the bureaucracy is **administration**—carrying out the routine tasks that any organization must conduct in order to func-

> ### Box 11-5   Airline Deregulation: A Good Idea?
>
> I f you've ever traveled by airplane, or if you have friends or relatives who have, you're probably familiar with what it's like. You can shop for bargain fares, and often you can find them—unless you want to fly during popular travel periods, like over Thanksgiving or Christmas. Chances are, the people sitting on either side of you paid a different price than you did for their tickets—possibly a lot more, conceivably a lot less. Even before additional security restrictions were imposed following the 2001 terror attacks, it wasn't uncommon to wait for a long time at airports to check your bags and to board the plane. On-time arrivals and departures on many routes are rare occurrences, especially if you're traveling during "rush hour," or if you're leaving from or going to a "hub" airport where one airline monopolizes air traffic. Air travel under today's system gets you there, but a number of indignities and inconveniences may be included in the (sometimes low, sometimes not so low) price.
>
> Now, try to imagine a system that's quite different from the one you're used to. When you get to the airport, you find it busy but not frenetic. Lines move swiftly. Your flight leaves on time and arrives on time. You don't have to rearrange your plans to spend a Saturday night at your destination in order to meet the requirements of your fare. In fact, if you change your
>
> mind about your travel plans, you just cancel your ticket and get your money back. On board, you're treated to a hot meal on flights that are scheduled during the time most people eat breakfast, lunch, or dinner. The food probably isn't great, but at least it's more than pretzels or peanuts.
>
> However, you paid a fair amount of money for your ticket—far more than the discounts you're used to paying if you fly home during midsemester break.
>
> Which option do you prefer? Lower fares and more flights are a direct result of deregulation. So, are the inconveniences of contemporary air travel. To get you to fly, airlines will offer some seats at deep discounts. At the same time, they'll try to recoup some of their losses by putting restrictions on your ticket and by offering fewer services. In cities dominated by one airline, competitive pressures are limited, meaning fares are higher and there's little incentive to sell service.
>
> Each system entails trade-offs. It's up to you to decide whether you prefer relative affordability with more hassles and fewer services or higher prices and fewer flights with better services. The way you answer this question may determine whether you believe the federal government should be in the business of regulating the airlines.

tion on a daily basis. The bureaucracy has the responsibility to administer the policies it implements and the regulations it enacts. If Social Security is to function, someone has to print and distribute the checks. If reserves are going to be called to serve during a conflict in Iraq, Afghanistan, or Bosnia, someone has to notify them, someone has to train them, and someone has to equip them. Someone has to put the mail in your mailbox. Someone has to maintain national monuments. We may not like tax audits, but they're a fact of life, and someone has to conduct them, too.

There are countless administrative functions that the government is responsible for performing, with countless bureaucrats participating in the process. It is the end result of executing the law, the realm where things actually happen. Implementation and regulation may be where the bureaucracy has the most say over the shape of public policy, but without people to carry out administrative routines, nothing would get done.

11-6 How the Bureaucracy Has Changed

Since the founding of the republic, the bureaucracy has exploded in size and scope, and has gravitated from being a source of presidential payback for political supporters to an organization structured to keep politics at arm's length. Despite the fact that it hardly resembles the bureaucracy of a hundred (or even sixty) years ago, chronic dissatisfaction with bureaucratic procedures or performance has fueled a merry-go-round of reforms that continue today.

11-6a Bureaucratic Growth

The bureaucracy grew dramatically but not steadily during the nineteenth and twentieth centuries, with the greatest bursts of growth coming in response to expansions in the role of the federal government in American life and the place of America in the world. Before the Civil War, the role of the bureaucracy was small because the federal government performed a limited set of functions and, apart from the Postal Service, experienced little

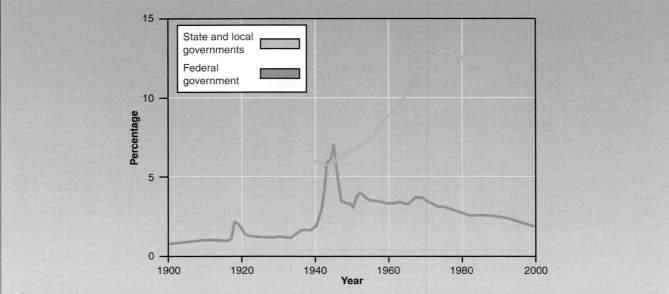

The United States mobilized to fight World War I, but growth in the bureaucracy was temporary. Not so after World War II. Even after the United States dismantled what had been the largest wartime mobilization in its history, the bureaucracy never returned to pre-Depression era levels. The social welfare programs first introduced in the 1930s by Franklin D. Roosevelt's New Deal had created a new, permanent bureaucracy. Simultaneously, the United States had emerged from the war as a global power with a larger military bureaucracy.

The 1960s brought the Johnson administration's Great Society programs, which extended the New Deal philosophy of a government-sponsored social welfare safety net to include programs designed to alleviate social ills. New bureaucratic units followed new social programs in areas like housing, nutrition, and human services.

The bureaucracy has diminished in size to a small degree over the course of the past two decades, largely in response to a decrease in career civil servants working in the Department of Defense following the end of the cold war. Even with this decline, civilian bureaucratic workers in the federal government comprised 2.1 percent of the domestic workforce in 1997, compared with less than 1 percent a century earlier.

Add state and local government bureaucracies to the mix, and you'll get a sense of just how bureaucratic activity took off in the second half of the twentieth century. One reason why state and local bureaucracies appear to have grown so much more than the federal bureaucracy is because the federal bureaucracy utilizes a lot of consultants to do its work, something that states and localities tend not to do. If you were to include all of the planning, training, research, development, and design activities that the federal government outsources to private firms, you'd have a more complete picture of just how large the federal bureaucracy is and how much it has grown since World War II.

Figure 11-7
The March of Bureaucracy

Sources: Data from *Historical Statistics of the United States, Colonial Times to 1970,* Bicentennial Edition (Washington, DC: US Dept. of Commerce, Bureau of the Census, 1975), series Y308; and *Statistical Abstract of the United States:* 1987, Table 741; 1997, Table 537 (see http://www.census.gov/prod/3/97pubs/97statab/fedgov.pdf, p. 349); 1999, Table 539 (see http://www.census.gov/prod/99pubs/99statab/sec09.pdf, p. 342).

expansion. Except for mail delivery and wartime military service, people had little direct contact with Washington.

Social changes following the Civil War and concurrent westward expansion produced the first burst of bureaucratic growth in the period immediately following 1860. Industrialization and economic expansion in the late nineteenth century fueled this trend. The Department of Agriculture, established in 1862, set the stage for the industrial-era Departments of Commerce (1903) and Labor (1913).

The federal bureaucracy grew sharply during World War I as America geared up for the war effort, but that was a temporary condition. When the war was over, the bulk of the bureaucracy that had been put in place during mobilization was dismantled. Not so a generation later, when the changes put into effect by Franklin D. Roosevelt's New Deal policies gave birth to permanent social welfare programs for the first time in American history. Figure 11-7 tells the story of what happened to the bureaucracy as a result.

Notwithstanding the reductions in bureaucratic personnel that followed both world wars, the clear tendency among bureaucracies is to grow. Once a department or agency is established, it takes on something of a life of its own apart from its mission. The natural human tendency toward self-preservation eventually sets in as people affiliated with a department or agency look for ways to maintain the organization that gives them work, and in which they have a long-term investment. Even if a bureaucratic entity successfully achieves its original objectives, its employees will readily alter the organization's goals rather than simply declare victory and go out of business.

This is especially true when careerists like civil servants staff organizations. Important professional benefits like salary, seniority, and rank accrue to people who have been with an organization for a long time. Long-term workers have developed expertise that may not be easily transferable to a position outside the organization. It's difficult and often undesirable to look for work in mid- or late career. People get used to the organizational culture and don't want to change the way they operate. These self-protective mechanisms contribute to what organizational specialist Anthony Downs calls the "Law of Increasing Conservatism," that organizations tend to become more conservative with age when they are staffed by people with many years of service. Unless there's a period of turnover or the organization grows rapidly in size to incorporate people without an investment in the status quo, bureaucratic entities tend toward a self-fulfilling sluggishness that perpetuates their existence while distorting their purpose and reducing their responsiveness.[24]

11-6b From the Spoils System to the Merit System

Individual bureaucratic units may be resistant to change, but the bureaucracy as a whole has undergone revolutionary alterations over the past two centuries. When the nation was young and the bureaucracy was small, federal positions were staffed with the president's political supporters. With little more than several thousand positions to fill—most of them outside Washington in such capacities as postal clerks, surveyors, or land office clerks—early nineteenth-century presidents could strengthen the bonds between national officeholders and local supporters that formed the basis for fledgling mass political parties.

Andrew Jackson used this system of political **patronage** to build the Democratic Party into the first mass-based national political organization. In exchange for a position in the federal bureaucracy, party supporters would kick back a small percentage of their pay to the political party.[25] The ability to offer such enticing rewards to political supporters was considered a perk of winning elections, the spoils of victory. That's why this method of staffing the bureaucracy is called the **spoils system.**

The spoils system had obvious advantages for the party in power, but it had its disadvantages for the operation of the bureaucracy. Changes in political power caused an upheaval to the system as workers loyal to the losing party would be kicked out by the winners. Workers loyal to the president did not have to be people of skill or merit. Also, as the federal government became larger and more specialized following the Civil War, making appointments started to become more of a burden to the president than a reward.

People looking for work hounded each new president. By 1881, President Garfield had 100,000 patronage positions at his disposal, four times the number available just thirty years earlier, reducing him to something of an employment agent for friends and supporters—a clerk who appointed other clerks.[26] As fate would have it, the undignified business of doling out goodies turned out to be the least of his worries. That year, Garfield was assassinated by a disgruntled office seeker who was overlooked for a patronage position.

Something had to give, and it soon did. In 1883, President Chester A. Arthur signed into law the **Pendleton Act,** ending the spoils system and creating the merit-based procedures we use today. It established the **Civil Service Commission** to oversee the process of hiring public employees, taking appointments out of the hands of elected officials and greatly reducing the spoils available to political parties. A **merit system** would replace politics as the basis for hiring government workers. Foremost among the reforms included in the Pendleton Act were the use of objective testing for hiring public employees, the establishment of pay grades, and the restriction against firing civil servants for refusing to support or endorse any political activity. In a further effort to de-politicize the bureaucracy, the **Hatch Act** of 1939 restricted federal workers from engaging in political activity while on the job.[27]

The prevailing philosophy about government embodied in the Pendleton Act is that politics can be taken out of implementation and administration. It's the principle of

patronage Jobs, favors, and other resources that party officials provide in exchange for people's political support.

spoils system The method of staffing the federal bureaucracy, commonplace in the nineteenth century, in which the president offered patronage appointments to political supporters.

Pendleton Act The 1883 law requiring that merit-based criteria be used to hire public employees, ending the tradition of patronage appointments.

Civil Service Commission The commission established by the Pendleton Act to oversee the hiring of career civil servants.

merit system Procedures for hiring civil servants based on objective evaluations of their performance rather than on their political connections.

Hatch Act Legislation enacted in 1939 that prohibits civil servants from engaging in political activities.

▶neutral competence
The philosophy guiding nineteenth-century civil service reform, which states that bureaucrats should be chosen strictly for their ability to perform their job, without political criteria influencing their selection or their actions.

neutral competence, which says that bureaucrats selected for their ability or expertise will provide the best service because an efficient bureaucracy should function apart from the political decisions made elsewhere in government. So, political considerations should not guide the hiring of civil servants, and civil servants should be neutral to political considerations in the performance of their work. To the extent that civil servants are hired on a merit basis, this approach has been successful. However, because we can find politics in any relationship, including the relationships between civil servants and their constituent groups, the expectation that there's a neutral way to conduct bureaucratic business is not always realized.

11-6c Recent Reforms

The Pendleton Act and the Hatch Act weren't the last word on civil service reform. Far from it: For the past half century, every presidential administration has proposed tinkering with the bureaucratic machinery to make it more responsive. Ideas that have been floated during this period include greater disclosure of what the bureaucracy does through "sunshine laws," policing government spending to cut down on waste, introducing incentives to improve the performance of public workers, stimulating competition to produce performance pressures like you'd find in the private sector, using management principles to control and unify the bureaucracy, and making the bureaucracy more efficient by making it client centered.[28]

Clearly, these approaches tackle bureaucratic reform from numerous perspectives. The problem is, every administration has endorsed a different approach, and every approach has a constituency, giving voice to a host of opposing solutions, all of which manage to find their way into new laws and regulations. Instead of a coordinated approach to bureaucratic reform, we've seen piecemeal efforts, which satisfy constituencies with different philosophies about what an overhauled bureaucracy should look like.

11-7 Reinventing Government

The Clinton administration promoted the most recent large-scale effort at bureaucratic reform. It was dubbed "Reinventing Government," borrowing from the title of a 1992 book about applying entrepreneurial principles to the federal bureaucracy to make it more responsive to the shifting demands of a complex and changing economy. Among its core principles, the "Reinventing Government" approach to bureaucratic reform sees the recipients of bureaucratic services—us—as customers, much like a business would, and presents methods that bureaucrats can use to get feedback from the public to create a more "user-friendly" bureaucracy. It argues for an increasingly proactive, innovative bureaucracy, one that frees bureaucrats to pursue the mission of their department or agency rather than stifling creativity with rules and regulations.[29]

So, for instance, reinventing the health care system in an effort to manage spiraling health care costs while extending coverage to the uninsured would entail rethinking a hierarchical medical bureaucracy designed to treat rather than prevent disease. Federal programs like Medicare and Medicaid, with large, centralized bureaucracies, would be retooled to be flexible, decentralized (meaning outside of Washington), proactive units where funding decisions are made based on medical outcomes rather than preexisting payment formulas. In a redesigned health care system, government agencies would set parameters for the medical profession, for instance, by requiring mandatory coverage, then leave it to the marketplace to figure out how best to provide that coverage. The health care institutions that provided the best and most accessible care would be rewarded with government support. Incentives could be offered for preventative care. Government would shape the market, and then let market forces determine what happened from there.[30]

That's a pretty dramatic shift in the way we tend to think about bureaucracy, which means it was bound to generate stiff opposition. As the Clinton administration found out a year after *Reinventing Government* was published, there are a lot of resource-rich groups

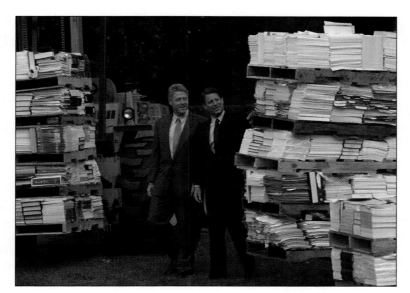

You know an initiative is important when the White House goes to the extent of bringing forklifts filled with documents to the White House lawn to symbolize burdensome government regulations. This media event was designed to focus national attention on the kickoff to the Clinton administration's Reinventing Government effort. It worked beautifully—Reinventing Government was all over the news. The results of the program were more ambiguous.

Source: AP/Wide World Photos.

with a big investment in the way things are run that could successfully block changes to the health care system. As a political matter, it's not easy to get interest groups to think differently about their stake in the system, and, as we said, bureaucracies tend to be conservative.

That didn't keep the administration from trying. The Reinventing Government project was rolled out with great fanfare in 1993 at a big media event on the White House lawn and was promoted as a key administration initiative. Vice President Gore was to take the lead, meeting personally with civil servants across the bureaucracy to solicit their feedback on changes.

So, how did the Clinton administration do in its effort to reinvent government along entrepreneurial lines? Five years after its inception, the Brookings Institution undertook a review of the reinventing-government campaign. Its conclusion: Despite an "A+" for effort, and some notable improvements in "customer service," the overall result was inconsistent.

When Republicans surged to power in Congress after the 1994 election, the reinventing government effort lurched from attempting to revitalize existing bureaucratic structures to questioning the appropriate role of government—what the bureaucracy *should* do—following the political lead of the new conservative congressional majority. When the Republican "revolution" lost steam, Gore refashioned the effort to follow its original purpose,[31] but the dramatic promises and high hopes expressed when the campaign was introduced never materialized. When Al Gore lost the 2000 election, reinventing government faded as a federal priority.

11-8 Bureaucratic Inefficiency

We've said all along that American government was not engineered to be efficient. Quite the opposite: The institutional design of the federal system slows progress and frustrates initiatives to attain the higher goal of resisting public passions and blocking the wishes of large or motivated groups. When it's working as planned, things take a long time to get done.

Now consider the place of the bureaucracy in that system. You might think that any organization engaged in policy implementation, regulation, and administration would be constructed to function efficiently and effectively. At the same time, we've seen how the federal bureaucracy is part of the federal system, even if it wasn't imagined as part of the original federal design. The result is a set of pressures that can work to undermine rational procedures and cost-effective operations.

Box 11-6   The $435 Hammer and the $3,000 Coffeepot

One student of the bureaucracy offers the following explanations for two seemingly outrageous examples of wasteful government spending that have achieved the status of an urban myth: the $435 spent by the navy on a hammer and the $3,000 it spent on a coffeepot.

- The $435 hammer is an example of how billing procedures used by the military can make an item *appear* to be inflated beyond its actual value. The real cost of the hammer was nominal, but it was shipped along with very expensive equipment. The organization that supplied this equipment to the navy was permitted to bill for overhead incurred in the manufacture of each of the items. Rather than calculate a separate overhead figure for each item, federal accounting guidelines directed the supplier to calculate one overhead cost and then divide it equally over each of the items supplied, regardless of how much actual overhead went into making it. The resulting figure made it appear that some of the more complex equipment commanded relatively low overhead costs, but it also produced a billing statement with a $435 hammer.

- The coffeepot really did cost $3,000. But it wouldn't fit on your kitchen counter: It was designed to make coffee for over three hundred soldiers on a navy transport plane. Similar coffeemakers are used by commercial airlines, which often pay a much higher price.[*]

No doubt, journalists would be more attracted to the outrageous dollar figures than to the rational explanations for them, perpetuating the impression that the government brazenly wastes our money. What do you think of these sober and more complex explanations? Do either or both of them satisfy you?

[*]James Q. Wilson, *Bureaucracy: What Government Agencies Do and Why They Do It* (New York: Basic Books, 1989), 319–320.

---

pork barrel   Wasteful or unnecessary spending that can result from logrolling. Whether something is a pork-barrel project or a valuable use of taxpayer dollars may depend on whether you stand to benefit from it.

goldplating   Government purchasing of top-of-the-line items at maximum cost, which can happen when bureaucrats overseeing purchasing decisions have an interest in the items being purchased.

In real terms, this means the bureaucracy will do things that may appear to some of us as wasteful and inefficient. Waste may take the form of money spent to implement programs that result from the **pork-barrel** politics we talked about in Box 9-4 in Chapter 9.

Remember, though, that "wasteful" is in the eye of the beholder: It's easy to target spending on programs or projects that benefit others as wasteful, while accepting spending on programs or projects that benefit *us* as valuable—especially if jobs or tangible benefits come our way as a result.

Sometimes, waste will take the form of outsized government expenditures for ordinary household items, like the fabled $435 hammers and $3,000 coffeepots that get a lot of media attention. These exist for sure, and are harder to rationalize away, although logical explanations have been given. (See Box 11-6 for a reasonable explanation of the cost of the hammer and the coffeepot.) When bureaucrats responsible for overseeing the expenditure of public money have an interest in the result, they have an incentive to engage in "**gold-plating**" their purchases by seeking costly, top-of-the-line items.

So, how wasteful is the bureaucracy in absolute terms? Politicians of both parties are fond of calling for "cutting the fat" out of federal spending, offering it as the way to pay for other programs or to help balance the budget. When you take into account that a lot of what seems like fat has a constituency that presidents dare not offend, how much is left to cut? Figure 11-8 shows how the findings of one commission charged with determining how the federal government might save billions of dollars through greater bureaucratic efficiency could be countered by a close examination of the commission's recommendations. Though the particulars happened a long time ago, the example is just as relevant today as it was when the original claims and counterclaims were made because the same arguments about government waste and inefficiency are still being made.

In fact, a lot of what draws complaints about bureaucratic inefficiency is the product of more subtle forces than civil servants willfully spending hundreds of dollars for small hardware items. These forces include pressure to spend agency money, professional disincentives to operating efficiently, a lack of competition in the bureaucracy, and the political climate under which bureaucrats operate.

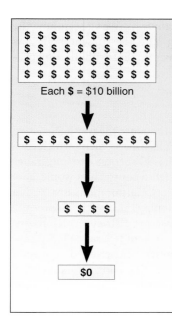

In 1984, the Reagan administration established the President's Private Sector Survey on Cost Control, commonly called the Grace Commission. It recommended ways for the government to save $400 billion through more efficient management of the bureaucracy.

Subsequently, the General Accounting Office (GAO) and the Congressional Budget Office (CBO) issued a joint analysis of the Grace Commission report. In it, they pointed out a number of items where savings were counted twice and suggestions where no savings would be realized at all. Their revised figure was $100 billion in savings.

Of that $100 billion, the report found about $60 billion in savings that would require policy changes rather than managing the bureaucracy more efficiently. These included items like taxing welfare benefits and restricting Medicare benefits.

Most of the remaining $40 billion in savings would come from such things as collecting more in taxes owed the government by hiring more Internal Revenue Service agents—a worthy goal, perhaps, but not something that would come under the heading of improving bureaucratic efficiency or eliminating waste.

Figure 11-8
How Much Can Be Cut?
Source: James Q. Wilson, *Bureaucracy: What Government Agencies Do and Why They Do It* (New York: Basic Books, 1989), 318–319.

11-8a Pressure to Spend

Using a kind of perverse logic, the best way for an agency or department to demonstrate its value is to spend the budget it's been given. This creates a situation where there's greater pressure to spend money than there is to conserve it. The best way to demonstrate the value of a bureaucratic unit to congressional appropriators is to show that every item budgeted was necessary, and because future budget requests will take into account whether present appropriations were necessary, the natural urge to protect agency funding leads bureaucrats to the conclusion that they had best find a way to spend what they've been given.

Often this is not a problem; spending happens naturally. As the fiscal year winds down, though, budgets with unspent funds can pose a problem. Not wanting to give Congress a reason to cut back funding for their agency or office, bureaucrats can find themselves in a situation where they have to "use it or lose it"—spend the funds they have or risk being cut in size the next year. In a counterintuitive exercise that critics claim is quintessential bureaucratic thinking, conserving funds brings on punishment while spending (even for the sake of spending) is rewarded.

11-8b Professional Disincentives to Efficiency

In private enterprise, employees are commonly encouraged to find cost-saving measures, and those who realize effective ways to save money characteristically find themselves in line for advancement. Such incentives are unusual in the federal bureaucracy. People who make decisions about procurement, or purchasing goods and services, are not at the high end of the compensation scale and are not rewarded for doing their job in a way that saves money. Unlike in private businesses, efficiency is not professionally valued.[32]

11-8c Lack of Competition

Businesses respond to competitive pressures by looking for ways to cut costs when they find themselves in a disadvantageous competitive position. There is no analogy for this in the bureaucracy, no competitive situation that would require a bureau or agency to trim down. In fact, a set of contrary forces is at work. We've seen how individual bureaucratic units exist in isolation from each other, and how their congressional and interest group allies are invested in maintaining them and boosting their budgets. We've seen how the best way to garner a budget increase is through making sure the present budget is expended. These factors contribute to a noncompetitive environment without a mechanism for instigating bureaucratic efficiency.

11-8d Political Climate

Lack of competition can also mix with political pressures to influence the way agencies go about making procurement decisions. Take the case of weapons procurement, which constitutes a large portion of federal expenditures. Things like aircraft carriers and long-range missiles don't have a market outside the government, so defense contractors would have nowhere else to turn if they did not have government contracts. Corporations involved in military work have already invested a lot of overhead in developing the capacity to produce weapons, and they employ a lot of people in a lot of congressional districts, which means they and their employees would suffer a great hardship if the flow of federal dollars disappeared. Since members of Congress (and the corporate interests themselves) do not want to see this happen, there's a strong political imperative for keeping contractors supplied with work. Unlike a marketplace where competition would determine how contracts are awarded, strong political pressures underscore the need to maintain or increase military spending.[33] Political pressures are not limited to the Department of Defense. Literally every bureau or agency has congressional patrons who will maintain spending pressures to keep constituents happy. Again, there is no private sector parallel.

11-9 Congressional Influence on the Bureaucracy

You may be getting a sense of how strongly bureaucratic and congressional activities are intertwined. The relationship between Congress and the bureaucracy is in fact quite complex. On one hand, congressional constituents directly profit from services and benefits implemented by the bureaucracy, and as we have seen, much bureaucratic growth is the result of congressional action. On the other hand, because the bureaucracy is so wide-ranging and large, it is hard for Congress to manage and control it. Congress has several tools at its disposal to try to influence the bureaucracy, and while they are not inconsiderable, they are not without their shortcomings.

11-9a Appointments

Some political appointees are subject to Senate approval, which gives senators an opportunity to hold hearings and express their views on the president's nominees. In cases where a nominee is particularly controversial, it's possible for the Senate to withhold action on the nomination in an effort to get the president to withdraw it, but this is a rare occurrence, which points out one of the limitations of Senate consent. Most nominees eventually win approval; some do not require approval at all. Once on the job, appointees are not directly accountable to members of Congress, so regardless of what may have transpired in their confirmation hearings, they can go their own way without fear of congressional reprisals.

11-9b Budgets

The ability of Congress to fund the bureaucracy is more significant than its role in the appointment process. A department or agency's authority to spend money and its actual budget is determined by congressional committees with parallel jurisdiction to the bureaucratic unit. So, for instance, funding for the Department of Agriculture has to pass through the House Agriculture Committee and the Senate Agriculture, Nutrition and Forestry Committee.

At first glance, this would seem to give Congress enormous leverage over the bureaucracy, but when you consider that members of Congress often want to see department and agency budgets increased because of the political benefits they derive from government programs, congressional budgetary authority seems less compelling. A more likely consequence of the congressional role in the budget process is that Congress will direct an agency or department to spend money in a specific way by including legislative language that removes any doubt about what bureaucrats are supposed to do. This is typically done when a powerful member of a congressional committee successfully advances a legislative provision directly benefiting his district. Although the amount of money involved may be significant, this type of pork-barrel legislating offers at best piecemeal congressional control of the bureaucracy.

11-9c Oversight

Congressional **oversight** is one of the most important functions performed by the legislative branch in its dealings with the bureaucracy. Technically speaking, oversight is the method Congress uses to ensure that legislation is implemented the way Congress intended. Setting aside for the moment that it's often impossible to say exactly what Congress intends when it passes a bill, oversight activities give members of Congress perhaps their best opportunity to influence bureaucratic activity.

oversight The process of congressional review of the bureaucracy.

Those same congressional committees whose jurisdictions dovetail with departments and agencies provide the forum for most oversight work. Informally, committee members and their staff communicate regularly with bureaucratic personnel, enabling them to forge and maintain close and influential working relationships. Formally, committees hold hearings on the actions of departments and agencies within their jurisdiction. These provide members of Congress with an opportunity to voice their opinions on how programs are being implemented, a matter of great concern to bureaucrats who are often responsive to members' concerns.[34] As one subcommittee chair said of the agencies in his oversight jurisdiction, "You just have to demonstrate some serious interest . . . serious thoughtful interest, and make suggestions. On the whole, they welcome them. . . . They know that they need you to go to bat for them [in the budgetary process]. So, it can be a very mutually supportive and pretty constructive relationship."[35]

11-10 Judicial Influence on the Bureaucracy

Like the actions of Congress, the president, or state officials, bureaucratic activity is subject to review by the courts. Agencies and bureaus end up in court when someone charges they are acting arbitrarily, failing to carry out the law, or overstepping their authority. More than in the past, the courts have shown a willingness to permit public challenges to bureaucratic actions, and Congress has at times written language permitting court challenges into legislation creating new programs. So, for instance, the Clean Air Act contains a provision permitting anyone to sue the Environmental Protection Agency for failure to properly implement the specific requirements of the act.[36]

The broad range of individuals who can bring suit against departments and agencies has made the courts an influential forum for shaping the way policies are implemented and regulations are enacted. In a manner that the president and Congress cannot match, courts can order written directives mandating bureaucrats to act in a stated fashion. Even so, unless those orders are simple and direct they may not meet with easy compliance.[37] This is because, for all their authority, courts cannot march in and take over an agency. Ultimately, they have to rely on bureaucratic enforcement of court orders.

The lack of direct enforcement powers has broader implications for the place of the courts in the political process. In fact, the dependency of the courts on the bureaucracy to enforce court rulings mirrors a wider problem facing the judiciary, and anticipates a dilemma that has shaped the way courts have acted since the dawn of the republic. We'll visit that issue, among others, in Chapter 12.

Chapter Review

The executive branch or the federal bureaucracy is a large web of departments, agencies, and bureaus charged with carrying out the laws and regulations passed by Congress and signed by the president. It is hierarchical and specialized, but also fragmented and decentralized, with numerous bureaucratic units handling unrelated tasks. Political appointees fill the top administrative spots. They get their jobs through presidential appointment and generally serve at the pleasure of the president. Civil servants fill the vast majority of bureaucratic positions. They get their jobs by scoring well on objective exams. Once tenured, they can serve as long as they wish.

The transient nature of political appointees generally leaves them unfamiliar with the organizational culture of the bureau or agency they are sent to run. This, coupled with the stability of career civil servants, can place political appointees in the position of "going native" and acquiescing to the ways of the department or agency, upending traditional lines of command. It can frustrate the president's desire to exercise control of the bureaucracy. Determined presidents can attempt to circumvent this by placing deeply loyal and ideological appointees at every available leadership level in the bureaucracy. Presidents like Reagan who have followed this strategy and implemented an administrative presidency have achieved some success.

Fifteen cabinet-level departments make up the largest organizational component of the bureaucracy. Independent agencies, like the Environmental Protection Agency (EPA) and the National Aeronautics and Space Administration (NASA), operate outside the cabinet structure, reporting directly to the president. Independent regulatory commissions and boards, like the Federal Trade Commission (FTC), also report directly to the president, but are more independent than the independent agencies. They are composed of a fixed number of members, divided between the two major parties, who serve for a fixed term and cannot be removed by the president. Government corporations, like the U.S. Postal Service, are structured like private corporations and provide a service, though they do not seek to make a profit.

Bureaucracies engage in three primary functions: implementation, regulation, and administration. Implementation entails giving shape to policies, and it can be a complex process, hampered by ambiguous legislative intent, unclear communication between bureaucrats and legislators, insufficient resources, bureaucratic resistance, inflexible standard operating procedures, and bureaucratic fragmentation. Regulation entails monitoring the actions of the private sector to protect the general welfare by maintaining safe water, food, air quality, and the like. Administration involves carrying out routine organizational tasks required to keep the government functioning, like printing Social Security checks and maintaining national monuments.

The bureaucracy has grown as the federal role has expanded. Once largely a patronage system, it became a merit system in the twentieth century with the creation of a professional civil service based on the philosophy of neutral competence. Numerous efforts to reform the bureaucracy have been prevalent over the past half-century. Recently, the Clinton administration's Reinventing Government initiative attempted to bring flexibility to bureaucratic decision making while treating the recipients of bureaucratic services as customers. Some reformers want to reduce bureaucratic inefficiency, which is maintained by a set of forces that include professional disincentives to efficiency, lack of competition in bureaucratic decision making, and political pressures from Congress to spend money.

Congress, for its part, exercises some influence over the bureaucracy through Senate confirmation of some presidential appointees, the ability to fund bureaucratic agencies and departments, and oversight provisions. Since members of Congress benefit politically from bureaucratic activity, their ability to influence the bureaucracy is limited. The courts can also influence bureaucratic behavior by ruling that an agency or department acted arbitrarily, failed to carry out the law, or overstepped its authority. In recent years, the ability to bring suit against the bureaucracy has greatly expanded, in many cases to include ordinary citizens, giving the judiciary additional influence over what the bureaucracy does.

Key Terms

administration (p. 342)
administrative presidency (p. 332)
bureaucracy (p. 327)
civil servants (p. 329)
Civil Service Commission (p. 345)
deregulation (p. 342)
Federal Register (p. 341)
Federal Wage System (FWS) (p. 332)
General Service (GS) (p. 332)
goldplating (p. 348)
"go native" (p. 332)

government corporations (p. 338)
Hatch Act (p. 345)
implementation (p. 339)
independent agencies (p. 335)
independent regulatory commissions and boards (p. 336)
merit system (p. 345)
neutral competence (p. 346)
newsworthy (p. 326)
oversight (p. 351)
patronage (p. 345)

Pendleton Act (p. 345)
Plum Book (p. 330)
political appointees (p. 329)
pork barrel (p. 348)
regulation (p. 341)
Senior Executive Service (SES) (p. 332)
spoils system (p. 345)
standard operating procedures (SOPs) (p. 341)
tenure (p. 331)

Review Questions

Note: You can find the correct answers to these questions by taking the quiz and then submitting your answers in the Online Edition. The program will automatically score your submission. If you miss a question, the program will provide the correct answer, a rationale for the answer, and the section number in the chapter where the topic is discussed.

1. Because the federal bureaucracy handles a large and diverse set of unrelated tasks, we can say that it is
   a. hierarchical.
   b. efficient.
   c. formalized.
   d. decentralized.
2. As a group, career civil servants are characterized by
   a. rapid turnover in their jobs.
   b. people who find work through the Plum Book.
   c. a recent increase in the percentage of college-educated and nonwhite workers.
   d. the tendency to be detached, disconnected, and transient.
3. Each of the following contributes to the temptation for political appointees to "go native" *except*
   a. the bureaucracy is decentralized.
   b. political appointees tend to be loyal to the president.
   c. civil servants have tenure.
   d. departments and agencies tend to have their own organizational culture.
4. A bureaucratic unit that reports directly to the president but whose members cannot be removed by the president best describes
   a. cabinet departments.
   b. independent agencies.
   c. independent regulatory commissions.
   d. government corporations.
5. Insufficient staff and information can complicate the process of
   a. implementation.
   b. regulation.
   c. deregulation.
   d. administration.

6. The Pendleton Act
   a. vastly increased the size of the bureaucracy.
   b. replaced the merit system with the spoils system.
   c. restricted federal workers from engaging in political activity while on the job.
   d. established the Civil Service Commission.
7. The idea that bureaucrats should be selected for their ability or expertise is best expressed in the principle of
   a. reinventing government.
   b. patronage.
   c. standard operating procedures.
   d. neutral competence.
8. Political pressures can generate bureaucratic inefficiency because
   a. Congress often neglects its oversight function.
   b. government spending benefits members of Congress politically.
   c. bureaucrats responsible for procurement tend to be poorly paid.
   d. neutral competence fails to account for bureaucratic ineptitude.
9. Congress exercises its greatest influence over the bureaucracy by
   a. frequently rejecting presidential appointments.
   b. declaring bureaucratic actions to be arbitrary or overreaching.
   c. maintaining regular contact with bureaucratic personnel.
   d. slashing agency budgets.
10. The courts exercise their greatest influence over the bureaucracy by
    a. frequently rejecting presidential appointments.
    b. declaring bureaucratic actions to be arbitrary or overreaching.
    c. maintaining regular contact with bureaucratic personnel.
    d. slashing agency budgets.

In Their Own Words

You might be interested in examining some of what the following authors have said about the topics we've been discussing:

Aberbach, Joel D. *Keeping a Watchful Eye: The Politics of Congressional Oversight.* Washington, DC: Brookings Institution, 1990. A look at how Congress attempts to influence the bureaucracy, and at how congressional oversight has changed over the past decades.

Edwards, George E. *Implementing Public Policy.* Washington, DC: CQ Press, 1980. A comprehensive overview of issues related to implementation.

Golden, Marissa Martino. *What Motivates Bureaucrats? Politics and Administration during the Reagan Years.* New York: Columbia University Press, 2000. President Reagan came to office espousing a philosophy of smaller government, putting him at odds with many bureaucrats. Golden looks at the ways bureaucrats responded to—and resisted—presidential directives they did not agree with.

Goodsell, Charles T. *The Case for Bureaucracy: A Public Administration Polemic.* Chatham, NJ: Chatham House Publishers, 1983. Many of us have negative associations with bureaucracies. Goodsell presents reasons why we might want to reconsider them.

Heclo, Hugh M. *A Government of Strangers: Executive Politics in Washington.* Washington, DC: Brookings Institution, 1977. A look at the sometimes surprising relationship between political appointees and career bureaucrats.

Kerwin, Cornelius M. *Rulemaking: How Government Agencies Write Law and Make Policy.* Washington, DC: CQ Press, 1999. Congress sends laws to bureaucrats, who have to turn laws into policy. Kerwin explains how they do it.

Kettl, Donald F., and others, *Civil Service Reform: Building a Government That Works.* Washington, DC: Brookings Institution Press, 1996. Suggestions for solving dilemmas surrounding the civil service.

Osborne, David, and Ted Gaebler. *Reinventing Government: How the Entrepreneurial Spirit Is Transforming the Public Sector*. New York: Addison-Wesley, 1992. An overview of the client-oriented approach to bureaucracy that informed the Clinton administration's reforms of the same name.

Wilson, James Q. *Bureaucracy: What Government Agencies Do and Why They Do It*. New York: Basic Books, 1989. A wide-ranging look at bureaucratic operations.

Notes

1. Charles T. Goodsell, *The Case for Bureaucracy: A Public Administration Polemic* (Chatham, NJ: Chatham House Publishers, 1983), 3. This is a direct quote from the book.
2. Ibid., 16–37. Data on the postal service may be found on p. 30.
3. Ibid., 82–109.
4. H. H. Gerth and C. Wright Mills, eds., *From Max Weber: Essays in Sociology* (New York: Oxford University Press, 1946).
5. Goodsell, *Case for Bureaucracy*, 83.
6. James Q. Wilson, *Bureaucracy: What Government Agencies Do and Why They Do It* (New York: Basic Books, 1989), 91.
7. Ibid., 93–95.
8. Hugh M. Heclo, *A Government of Strangers: Executive Politics in Washington* (Washington, DC: Brookings Institution, 1977), 84–112.
9. Ibid., 102–105.
10. U.S. Office of Personnel Management, *The Fact Book* (1990–2000 editions), Trend of Employment.
11. Why 3,869 cooks and only one bartender? Sometimes it's hard to figure out the federal government. See Federal Civilian Workforce Statistics, Occupations of Federal White-Collar and Blue-Collar Workers, September 30, 1999, Tables W-A2 and B-A2, at http://www.opm.gov/feddata/ocwcbc99.pdf.
12. Ronald N. Johnson and Gary D. Libecap, *The Federal Civil Service System and the Problem of Bureaucracy* (Chicago: University of Chicago Press, 1994), 4–5.
13. Marissa Martino Golden, *What Motivates Bureaucrats? Politics and Administration during the Reagan Years* (New York: Columbia University Press, 2000), 5–8.
14. Ibid., 151–155.
15. Ibid., 153–160.
16. You can visit TVA online at http://www.tva.gov/.
17. Cornelius M. Kerwin, *Rulemaking: How Government Agencies Write Law and Make Policy* (Washington, DC: CQ Press, 1994), 1–6.
18. George C. Edwards, *Implementing Public Policy* (Washington, DC: CQ Press, 1980), 1–14.
19. Ibid., 17–51.
20. Ibid., 53–87.
21. Ibid., 89–97.
22. Ibid., 125–124.
23. Ibid., 134–141.
24. Paul C. Light, *Thickening Government: Federal Hierarchy and the Diffusion of Accountability* (Washington, DC: Brookings Institution: Governance Institute, 1995), 34–36.
25. Johnson and Libecap, *Federal Civil Service System*, 14–15.
26. Ibid., 17–18.
27. Donald F. Kettl, and others, *Civil Service Reform: Building a Government That Works* (Washington, DC: Brookings Institution Press, 1996), 87–89.
28. Light, *Thickening Government*.
29. David Osborne and Ted Gaebler, *Reinventing Government: How the Entrepreneurial Spirit Is Transforming the Public Sector* (New York: Addison-Wesley, 1992).
30. Ibid., 312–314.
31. Donald F. Kettl, *Reinventing Government: A Fifth-Year Report Card* (Washington, DC: Brookings Institution, 1998).
32. James Q. Wilson, *Bureaucracy: What Government Agencies Do and Why They Do It* (New York: Basic Books, 1989), 320–322.
33. Ibid., 323–325.
34. Joel D. Aberbach, *Keeping a Watchful Eye: The Politics of Congressional Oversight* (Washington, DC: Brookings Institution, 1990), 130–144.
35. Ibid., 196.
36. Wilson, *Bureaucracy*, 279–281.
37. Ibid., 290–294.

The Judiciary

12

12-1 Introduction

Quick: What do you think of when someone says the judiciary? The Supreme Court, perhaps? Justices in long black robes? An imposing marble building? Something totally removed from your everyday experience?

The judiciary has always been the branch of government that seems different from the rest of the political system: more secretive and distant, and removed from the body blows of politics. Its devotion to the law distinguishes the judiciary from the other institutions we've been discussing, not in the sense that it doesn't engage in the process of deciding who gets what, when, and how, but in the way it goes about doing this. The **judiciary** is the place where laws are interpreted and disputes are resolved. It rests at the heart of the **legal system,** which includes members of Congress and the president, who create laws that others may challenge; the bureaucracy, which implements laws in a manner that may cause disputes; individuals or interest groups with grievances; attorneys who argue legal issues on behalf of individuals or interest groups with grievances; and even police officers, who bring conflicts to the attention of the judicial system by enforcing the law on the street.[1]

Its involvement with matters of justice seems to put the judiciary above raw politics, and there are characteristics of the judiciary that you simply won't find anywhere else in the political process. Take the U.S. Supreme Court as an example. Its members are not elected (justices are appointed by the president and confirmed by the Senate). They serve for life, and never have to hire pollsters or media consultants to create a public image or position themselves for the next political campaign. Although they may be strong partisans, they shy away from involvement in partisan gatherings like political party conventions and do not stage media events like elected officials. They deliberate in private and never disclose what is said. This seems nothing like the other two branches of government, where popular participation in regularly scheduled elections is designed to keep officeholders accountable to the electorate.

The trappings of the Court only contribute to this mystique. We'd think it was silly if the president appeared in public in a dark robe, but on a Supreme Court justice, the robe evokes tradition and prestige, suggesting a certain respect for those who walk the imposing marble-laden corridors of the temple-like Supreme Court building. The Court's symbol of "Lady Justice," blindfolded as she balances scales, depicts objectivity and fairness—characteristics rarely on display when Republicans and Democrats face off in a political or policy debate. In form and content, the Supreme Court appears a world apart from the political system we've come to know.[2]

Dark robes and somber expressions contribute to the mystique of the U.S. Supreme Court, which seems more distant and less political than the other two branches of government. *(Back, left to right)* Ruth Bader Ginsburg, David Souter, Clarence Thomas, Stephen Breyer. *(Front, left to right)* Antonin Scalia, John Paul Stevens, Chief Justice William Rehnquist, Sandra Day O'Connor, Anthony M. Kennedy.

Source: The Supreme Court Historical Society.

But is it? If Court actions were only influenced by legal criteria, the answer might be yes, but we will see that this is far from what really happens. As we read on, we'll come to perceive the Court as a highly political institution that may operate differently from other political institutions but that is nonetheless steeped in politics.

There are clues to the Court's political persona, some more obvious than others. For example, the president and senators consider their political agendas when selecting and acting on appointments to the Supreme Court and lower courts in the federal judicial system, and political disputes over appointment confirmations can be ferocious. Nominees themselves may be political figures or individuals with partisan activity in their pasts. Their judgments on the Court are invariably influenced by their political principles, and the decisions they render can put them at the heart of partisan disputes.[3] The Court may be a legal institution, but it exists in a political world.

12-2 A Judiciary without Power

By virtue of its position in this political world, the Court is at something of a disadvantage relative to the legislative and executive branches. The judiciary is, by design, the weakest of the three branches of the federal government. Alexander Hamilton, writing in Federalist #78, called it "the least dangerous to the political rights of the Constitution; because it will be least in a capacity to annoy or injure them." As Hamilton noted, the executive holds the power to enforce the law, and the legislature has the power to tax:

> The judiciary, on the contrary, has no influence over either the sword or the purse; no direction either of the strength or of the wealth of the society; and can take no active resolution whatever. It may truly be said to have neither FORCE nor WILL, but merely judgment; and must ultimately depend upon the aid of the executive arm even for the efficacy of its judgments.[4]

In other words, the Constitution's authors put the judicial function in an institution that would have to rely on a separate institution—the executive—to enforce its rulings. Simultaneously, the Constitution made the judiciary the branch that was to exercise judgment over the decisions of the executive, potentially putting the two branches at odds with each other while making the judiciary dependent on the executive to carry out rulings that could come at the executive's expense. Box 12-1 contrasts this weak judiciary with the earlier lack of a judiciary under the Articles of Confederation.

It took very little time after the ratification of the Constitution for Congress to flesh out the new judiciary, although it would be a while before the judicial and executive

▶ **judiciary** (see p. 356)
The federal and state court systems charged with resolving legal and personal disputes and interpreting the law.

▶ **legal system** (see p. 356)
The web of institutions and individuals involved in bringing legal and personal disputes to the attention of the courts.

Box 12-1 A Weak Judiciary versus No Judiciary

A weak judicial system designed under the doctrine of separation of powers was an upgrade from the mechanism in place for resolving national disputes under the **Articles of Confederation.** That's because there was no mechanism for resolving national disputes under the Articles of Confederation. Recall that the federal government under the Articles centered on a single legislature, which was composed of representatives of the states. The absence of a national judiciary left the young nation without a forum for resolving the numerous disputes that arose among the states, and was widely considered a defect in need of correction by the delegates to the Constitutional Convention.

Like so much to emerge from the Convention, the judicial branch is the product of compromise between those who wished to establish strong federal institutions and those concerned about the rights of smaller states. Federalists who supported the **Virginia Plan** would have established a federal Supreme Court and a multitiered system of lower courts. Supporters of the **New Jersey Plan,** which called only for a federal Supreme Court to act as final arbiter in cases arising in state courts, were worried that a federal court *system* posed a threat to states' rights.* The delegates resolved the issue by punting. In a characteristically vague passage, Article III of the Constitution vests the "judicial power" in the Supreme Court "and in such inferior Courts as the Congress may from time to time ordain and establish." It would be up to the new Congress to determine what, if anything, those "inferior Courts" would look like.

▶ **Articles of Confederation** The first constitution of the United States, which created a loosely functioning national government to which the individual states were supreme. It addressed concerns about a strong national government undermining individual liberty, but it created a national government that was unable to regulate commerce or conduct foreign policy and was abandoned in favor of the United States Constitution just eight years after it was ratified.

▶ **Virginia Plan** A proposal for the new Constitution, supported by large states, that would have based representation on population and provided for a centralized national government that could overrule the states.

▶ **New Jersey Plan** A proposal for the new Constitution, supported by small states, that would have provided for equal representation of large and small states in the national legislature, while limiting the power of the national government over the states.

*Robert A. Carp and Ronald Stidham, *The Federal Courts,* 4th ed. (Washington, DC: CQ Press, 2001), 3–4.

▶ **Judiciary Act of 1789** The act of Congress that established the federal court system. It initially called for a six-person Supreme Court and three circuit courts, each to be administered by two Supreme Court justices and one district court judge.

branches would come into conflict over the enforcement of judicial decisions. That's because it took a while for the nascent court system to find its bearings.

With little in the Constitution to guide them (Article III established the jurisdiction and tenure of justices, but otherwise is silent on the matter of how to organize the court system) and Federalists in command of the debate, Congress established a set of lower courts in the **Judiciary Act of 1789.** It set the number of Supreme Court justices as six (it is now nine), and assigned pairs of Supreme Court justices to each of three new circuit courts (occupying the lower level of the new court system).[5] So, not only would there be lower federal courts, but Supreme Court justices would have a hand in staffing them.

Serving on two courts at once probably sounds like a tall order, but the truth is that for the first decade of its existence, the Supreme Court didn't have much to do. It also didn't have a permanent home or staff, suffered from rapid turnover among justices, and didn't have much of an institutional identity or public prestige.[6] Consider the inaugural session of the Supreme Court, meeting in the Royal Exchange Building in New York City on February 1, 1790. Three justices were absent, and two of those missed the entire court session—which lasted all of ten days.[7] During that time, the justices who were present chose a seal for the Court and appointed a clerk. They didn't rule on any cases because no business was before the Court. In fact, they didn't rule on any cases for three years.[8] Box 12-2 discusses the first appointments to the Court.

Sleepiness was the rule during the Court's first decade. With little prestige and an insignificant role in the federal government, the Court during this time was marked by high turnover and few responsibilities. It ruled on little more than fifty cases during that time and drew little attention to itself.[9] All of that changed with the dawn of the new century and the entrance on the scene of Chief Justice John Marshall, one of the most influential justices in Court history.

> ## Box 12-2 George Washington Sets the Tone
>
> As in so many other areas, George Washington supplied a model for his successors in the way he went about appointing justices to the Supreme Court. Faced with the opportunity to fill every slot on the Court, Washington did a few things that presidents still do today:
>
> - *Appoint ideologically compatible judges.* All six Washington appointees were loyal Federalists. Even though the Federalists were not organized as a formal party, Washington nominated judges who shared his ideological penchant for a strong national government. Presidents throughout history have sought philosophically compatible judicial nominees from their political party.
> - *Offer representation to key interests.* In the late eighteenth century, this meant providing geographic balance: Three of Washington's appointees were southerners, and three were northerners. As political interests changed, the particulars of offering representation to specific groups changed as well. In the twentieth century, religion, race, and gender
>
> replaced regional concerns as factors in court appointments.
> - *Don't expect the best.* Washington's Supreme Court nominees were uneven in their abilities and reputations. Subsequent presidents have found that they can't always get their top choices to serve on the Court, that political criteria like ideological compatibility or satisfying key interests may necessitate settling for a lesser candidate, and that nominees who seem promising may turn out to be disappointing.
> - *Be especially careful when nominating the chief justice.* Washington's choice was John Jay, one of the authors of *The Federalist* and a New York lawyer and judge. Washington believed that the chief justice had to be a widely acclaimed jurist whose ethics were beyond reproach.[*]
>
> [*]Robert A. Carp and Ronald Stidham, *The Federal Courts,* 4th ed. (Washington, DC: CQ Press, 2001), 6–7.

12-3 Judicial Review

John Marshall was appointed chief justice by President Adams in 1801 and served in this capacity for thirty-four years, during which time he fashioned the Court into an equal partner with the executive and the legislature. Many of the procedures in place today were originated under Marshall's tutelage.[10] For instance, before Marshall, it was customary for every justice to write a separate opinion every time the Court ruled on a case, but Marshall recognized the political value of presenting a unified front for the Court by keeping differences among justices behind closed doors. He instituted the practice of hammering out disagreements in private deliberations, then handing down single opinions on cases.[11] Box 12-3 profiles Justice Marshall.

Marshall's most important and enduring contribution to the Court was the practice of **judicial review.** Today we take for granted that the Supreme Court has the authority to review the actions of Congress or the president and declare them unconstitutional. In fact, many people think of constitutional interpretation as the essential purpose of the Supreme Court because the most important thing it does is validate or overturn the acts of others in the political system—but such authority is not expressly granted in the Constitution. It derives from a ruling in the 1803 case *Marbury v. Madison.* It's a complex and important case, involving political power plays, conflicts of interest, and a great twist ending. You can find the facts in Box 12-4 .

The logic behind Marshall's ruling in *Marbury v. Madison*—that Congress overreached by expanding the Court's jurisdiction, and so, the Court must strike down an act of Congress—requires a certain leap of faith. The rationale he gave for saying Congress overstepped its authority when it gave the Court the power to issue writs of *mandamus* was that the Constitution didn't stipulate that Congress had the authority to expand the Court's jurisdiction in this manner. Maybe so, but the Constitution also didn't stipulate that the Court could review an act of Congress and declare it unconstitutional—at least not directly. Marshall was asking us to accept a broad view of constitutional interpretation in the matter of judicial review while he was asking us to take a narrow view of constitutional interpretation in the matter of the Judiciary Act of 1789. Of course, what was

> **judicial review** The authority of the Supreme Court to overrule actions of Congress or the president by declaring them to be unconstitutional.

> **Marbury v. Madison** The Supreme Court case, heard by the Marshall Court in 1803, that established judicial review.

> ## Box 12-3   Chief Justice John Marshall

John Marshall

John Marshall was forty-five years old when President John Adams appointed him to be chief justice of the Supreme Court in 1801. The oldest of fifteen children, Marshall came from modest roots to distinguish himself in several fields of service. A captain in the Revolutionary War, Marshall studied law at the College of William and Mary and practiced law in his native Virginia. He served as a Federalist representative to the Virginia House of Delegates, as an American envoy to France, and briefly as a member of the U.S. Congress. In 1800, Adams tapped Marshall to be his secretary of state. The following year, as Adams' term was about to expire, he appointed Marshall to the Supreme Court, where Marshall served longer than almost anyone in history—until he died in 1835.

Marshall was a bitter political enemy of the man who followed Adams in office, fellow Virginian Thomas Jefferson—who also, by a strange quirk of history, happened to be Marshall's second cousin. Jefferson, who never lacked for the ability to turn a phrase, referred to Marshall as "that gloomy malignity." Adams, in contrast, was more than satisfied with Marshall's long record of service on the Court. Just prior to his death, Adams proclaimed, "My gift of John Marshall to the people of the United States was the proudest act of my life."*

*Abraham, Henry J., *Justices, Presidents and Senators: A History of the U.S. Supreme Court Appointments from Washington to Clinton* (Lanham, MD: Rowman & Littlefield Publishers, 1999), 61–62.

anyone going to do about it? Because the Court could simply refuse the authority to issue writs of *mandamus*, it had the final say in the matter.

During his long tenure as chief justice, Marshall handed down several decisions that shaped the course of our national development by resolving questions about the key political issue of the day, the relationship between the federal government and the states, in favor of the federal government. When we were discussing federalism in Chapter 2, we profiled the case ***McCulloch v. Maryland*** (1819), which was a turning point in the establishment of federal dominance over state governments and an endorsement of a broad constitutional grant of power to the federal government. In ***Gibbons v. Ogden*** (1824), the Marshall Court established the supremacy of the federal government over matters of interstate commerce.

Marshall's durability was so great that he was still presiding over the Supreme Court at the start of Andrew Jackson's administration, during the transition to the second party system that we talked about in Chapter 6, and he was still frustrating chief executives who favored states' rights with his Federalist rulings. Marshall's opinion in the 1832 case *Worcester v. Georgia* upholding federal rather than state jurisdiction over Cherokee land rights so angered President Jackson that the president is alleged to have said, "John Marshall has made his decision, now let him enforce it."[12]

12-4 The Court System

As we mentioned in Section 12-2, "A Judiciary without Power," a system of federal courts began to emerge in the 1790s, when a justice earned his keep by doubling as a judge on a lower "circuit" court since there wasn't much work for the Supreme Court to do. We noted that the Judiciary Act of 1789 created the first lower court system: three circuit courts corresponding to the eastern, middle, and southern sections of the country. The original arrangement called for each circuit to be staffed by two of the six Supreme Court justices, along with a permanent district judge.[13]

The court got its name because the justices would "ride circuit"—they literally covered the territory twice a year on horseback or carriage, hearing cases along the way. And they were miserable. Roads were horrendous, the weather was often bad, and justices had to be away from their families for long stretches of time. One justice, Levi Woodbury, who served in the 1840s, wrote of the "villaneous sea-sickness" he experienced riding circuit in a stagecoach:

McCulloch v. Maryland
The 1819 Supreme Court case that established federal supremacy over the state governments.

Gibbons v. Ogden
The Supreme Court case, heard by the Marshall Court in 1824, that established the federal government's primacy in regulating interstate commerce, saying that the state of New York could not grant an exclusive license to a steamboat company operating between New York and New Jersey.

Box 12-4   *Marbury v. Madison:* The Brief Version

In 1800, John Adams was defeated for re-election by his political rival Thomas Jefferson.

Before leaving office, Adams attempted to fill the federal judiciary with as many sympathetic Federalists as possible. This is also when he appointed John Marshall to be chief justice of the Supreme Court.

John Marshall was also Adams' secretary of state. In that role, it was Marshall's job to deliver Adams' judicial commissions in order for them to become official.

The commissions had to be delivered before Jefferson was sworn in as president. Marshall ran out of time and failed to deliver several commissions, including the appointment of William Marbury, whom Adams had appointed justice of the peace for the District of Columbia. James Madi-

John Adams

son became secretary of state when Jefferson became president. For partisan political reasons, he ignored the appointments of Marbury and his sixteen colleagues, which Marshall had failed to deliver in time. Marbury sued Madison, and the case went to the U.S. Supreme Court.

Marbury asked the Court to issue a **writ of *mandamus,*** a court order commanding an official to act—in this case, an order to Secretary of State Madison to deliver Marbury's judicial appointment. The Supreme Court was granted the authority to issue writs of *mandamus* as part of the Judiciary Act of 1789.

Thomas Jefferson

Setting aside the conflict of interest Marshall faced by having been the individual responsible for Marbury's dilemma, as chief justice, Marshall faced a dilemma of his own. Circumstances made it clear that Marbury was entitled to his appointment, but if Marshall issued the writ, President Jefferson most certainly would have told Secretary Madison to ignore it. If he ruled against Marbury, the Court would have looked weak.

Marshall fashioned a solution in one of the most ingenious Court decisions in American history. He agreed that Marbury was entitled to his appointment, but that Congress had exceeded its constitutional authority when it gave the Court the ability to issue writs of *mandamus*. He therefore struck down the provision of the Judiciary Act of 1789 that gave the court that authority. It was a self-executing order that didn't require Jefferson's enforcement. Marbury didn't get to be justice of the peace, but Marshall had expanded the Court's reach by claiming the power of judicial review.

▶ **writ of *mandamus*** A court order commanding a public official to perform an official act.

I think I never again, at this season of the year, will attempt this mode of journeying. Besides the evils before mentioned I have been elbowed by old women—jammed by young ones—suffocated by cigar smoke—sickened by the vapours of bitters and w[h]iskey—my head knocked through the carriage top by careless drivers and my toes trodden to a jelly by unheeding passengers.[14]

Within ten years of their establishment, more circuits were added along with more district judges but the custom of riding circuit persisted through the nineteenth century, even though justices were required to do it less frequently. In the twentieth century, the circuit court system grew enormously. There are now eleven circuits in the United States, as represented on the map in Figure 12-1.

Today, the federal system is a three-tiered system, with the circuit courts functioning as appeals courts. This parallels the structure in place in each of the fifty states, which have their own state court systems to hear cases arising out of violations of state law. Because each state has its own Constitution, the specifics of the court systems vary from state to state. It's reasonable to picture the federal court system existing in tandem with a system of fifty state courts.

One way to think of the differences among these courts is to consider the differences in their **jurisdiction,** or the types of cases each has the authority to hear. In both the

▶ **jurisdiction** The authority of a court to hear a case.

Figure 12-1
U.S. Court System by Circuit

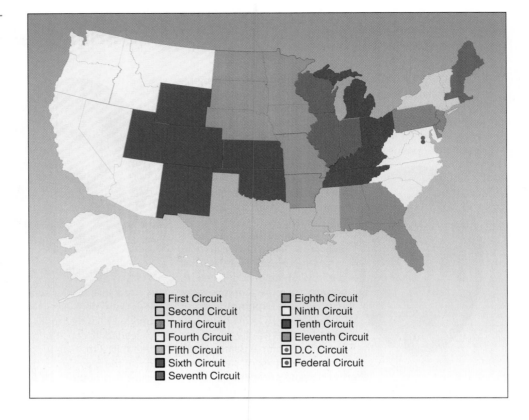

■ First Circuit	■ Eighth Circuit
□ Second Circuit	□ Ninth Circuit
■ Third Circuit	■ Tenth Circuit
□ Fourth Circuit	■ Eleventh Circuit
□ Fifth Circuit	◉ D.C. Circuit
■ Sixth Circuit	◉ Federal Circuit
■ Seventh Circuit	

▶ **original jurisdiction**
The authority of the U.S. Supreme Court to be the first court to hear a case, precluding the need for an appeal from a lower court. The Constitution grants original jurisdiction to cases involving a dispute between the United States and a state; two or more states; citizens of different states; a state and a citizen of another state; and foreign ambassadors.

▶ **appellate jurisdiction**
The authority of a high court to hear cases only after the cases originate in and are appealed from a lower court.

federal and state systems, most cases originate at the bottom level and are appealed upwards. There are exceptions. The Constitution grants the U.S. Supreme Court **original jurisdiction** over certain types of conflicts, meaning they can originate at the top rather than having to work their way through the system. The Supreme Court's original jurisdiction extends to cases where there is a dispute involving:

- The United States and a state
- Two or more states
- Citizens of different states
- A state and a citizen of another state
- Foreign ambassadors

The Supreme Court has **appellate jurisdiction** for all other cases, meaning the cases have to originate in lower courts and work their way through the judicial system on appeal.

Broadly speaking, state courts have jurisdiction over most criminal law and civil law—ranging from serious offenses like murder and robbery to minor offenses like traffic violations to civil issues like divorce and inheritance disputes—because most criminal and civil laws are state laws. For this reason, most trials are held in state courts, and 95 percent of judges are state judges.[15]

Although the federal and state court systems have similar structures, their jurisdictions are so different that it's appropriate to think of them as separate entities. Their paths cross only in rare circumstances. Figure 12-2 demonstrates how the two systems are structured and how they operate.

When the Supreme Court refuses to hear a case on appeal, the word of the lower court is final. Because circuit courts operate under a wide range of judicial philosophies and ideological perspectives, the specific circuit court to hear a case can be critical to the outcome. So, blind justice only tells part of the story. The state or circuit in which a case is heard and the judicial philosophies of the individuals hearing a case all have tremendous bearing on judicial outcomes.

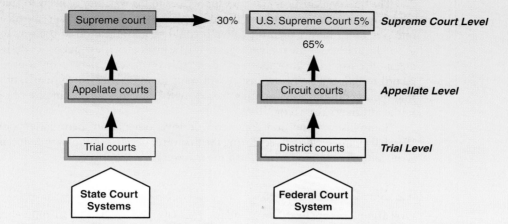

Federalism presents us with fifty state court systems that operate parallel to the federal system we've been discussing. For the most part, each of these systems has three tiers.

The trial level is where most cases originate. State trial courts hear cases involving state law, while federal district courts hear cases involving federal law. There are ninety-four federal district courts.

Appellate courts hear cases appealed by those who lost at the trial level. In the federal court system, there are eleven circuit courts of appeals covering eleven geographic regions of the country, plus a court of appeals for the District of Columbia and one for the federal circuit. Federal circuit courts also hear appeals of decisions by independent regulatory agencies.

Every state has a top-tier court, which is typically the final stop for an appeal. Most—but not all—states call this court the supreme court.

Of course, the U.S. Supreme Court has the final word on cases appealed through the federal court system. About 65 percent of its cases come through this route.

In rare instances, if a case heard in state court raises a contested point of constitutional law, it can be appealed from the state court system to the federal court system, where it is heard directly by the U.S. Supreme Court. Roughly 30 percent of U.S. Supreme Court cases originate this way. Unless a constitutional question is raised in a state trial, there can be no appeal to the federal court system, and the state supreme court has the final word in the matter.

The remaining 5 percent of U.S. Supreme Court cases originate in the Supreme Court itself. These cases fall under the Court's original jurisdiction and involve disputes among or between states, or where the United States or a foreign nation or its representative is a party. Also, some cases involving civil rights or reapportionment claims can be appealed from the trial level directly to the U.S. Supreme Court.

12-5 Deciding Cases

When a court agrees to hear a case, it typically goes through several steps before issuing a judgment. Judges or justices hear arguments from attorneys representing the two sides of the matter, meet privately in conference to discuss the case, and draft their opinions on the case before the final vote is revealed. We'll look at the Supreme Court to get a sense of how this process works.

12-5a Oral Arguments

The first stage of the process is oral argument. Early in its history when the Supreme Court had little work to do, oral arguments could go on for hours or days. Today, unless there's an exception, oral arguments last one hour. They are held in the relatively small courtroom in the Supreme Court building, with the robed justices sitting on an elevated podium, looking down at the attorneys arguing the two sides of the case. You can visit if you like— oral arguments are open to the public. But you may have to wait in a long line for just several minutes of viewing because only about three hundred seats are reserved for the public.[16]

   The atmosphere is solemn and the pace quick. Characteristically, justices will cut off the presenting attorneys in midsentence, challenging a statement they made or raising a related point. Other justices may jump in, taking the questioning in whatever direction they see fit. It's possible for attorneys' time to expire before they get to make the presentation they had prepared. The experience can be overwhelming and breathtaking, much like an intellectual contact sport.

Figure 12-2
**The Court System
and Appeals Process**
Source: Data from David M. O'Brien, *Storm Center: The Supreme Court in American Politics,* 6th ed. (New York: W. W. Norton, 2002), 172 (table).

The questions justices ask can supply clues to the way they're likely to rule. If a justice who is typically in the middle of the ideological spectrum on an issue appears to question one side more sternly than the other, it could be an indication of the way that justice is leaning—at least for the moment. Sympathetic justices may ask questions designed to elicit a response from the attorney arguing the side of the case they favor in order to get the record to reflect a point the justice will want to argue later on. Similarly, hostile justices may hammer the attorney arguing the side of the case they oppose in order to expose flaws in the attorney's reasoning.

Some justices find oral arguments decisive; others find them useless (Justice Oliver Wendell Holmes, who served during the first three decades of the twentieth century, would write letters or doze off while the attorneys were speaking).[17]

12-5b Conferences

Oral arguments are heard on Mondays, Tuesdays, and Wednesdays. Conferences to discuss the week's cases are held on Wednesdays and Fridays. Conferences are private, affording justices a closed setting for the frank exchange of opinions. With the huge workload the Court has to address, there is little time to deliberate at length about any particular case unless it is of exceptional magnitude. Instead, justices gather to see whether there is a consensus opinion. They may reason with each other about the case, or make emotional appeals. They may or may not take a formal vote. If they do, it's understood that their votes may be reversed at any time until the final decision is written and announced.[18]

Even though no one is privileged to the deliberation that occurs among justices, it's not unreasonable to assume that they think and act as strategically as anyone in elected office. This contention is in keeping with the idea of the Court as a political body, as well as with the idea that justices have a view of government and society that they want to advance. Because they don't have to run for office, they're free from the basic strategic decisions that face members of Congress and the president, like what their constituents desire and whether it's too close to an election to take a controversial position.

Instead, a justice's strategy can center on ways to move the law closer to his or her desired position. That entails assessing the likely actions of the other eight people in the room and deciding on a course of action that appears most likely to lead to the justice's desired outcome—an exercise that invariably takes into account the styles and personalities of the other justices as much as the abstract merits of an argument. From this type of reasoning, justices can decide whether their best choice is to advance the position they most desire or, if their position appears to be in the minority, compromise on something less in the hope of building a coalition with other justices.[19]

12-5c Writing Opinions

When justices write opinions, they state their vote on a case and the reasoning behind it. Justices will exchange drafts of opinions before they're made public as a form of negotiation, often making revisions to accommodate other justices they seek to have join them. It's part of a persuasive process in which justices try to get their colleagues to adopt their reasoning. Depending on the mixture of personalities on the Court at any time, this experience can range from collegial to contentious. As in any group of people, justices with a soft touch have often found themselves influential in bringing other justices on board, and have played the role of consensus-builder. In contrast, things can get ugly when dealing with justices who have lesser social skills.[20]

The majority opinion expresses the judgment of the Court, but it may not be the only word on a matter. The legal reasoning behind a decision is as important as the decision itself, and will determine how far reaching a decision will be. Justices who come to the same conclusion may do so for entirely different reasons—and even disagree with each other on the justification for their conclusions. Because of this, a justice may issue a **concurring opinion,** which supports the majority decision but provides a different legal justification for getting there. A justice who disagrees with the majority position explains his or her reasoning in a **dissenting opinion.**

concurring opinion
A statement issued by a justice who agrees with a vote of the Court but differs on the legal or constitutional rationale for the majority decision.

dissenting opinion
A statement issued by a justice who disagrees with a vote of the Court, offering a legal or constitutional rationale for that disagreement.

12-5d Staff

Considering the enormous workload of the Supreme Court—or any court for that matter—trained staff are brought in to assist with the burden. Much of a court's work falls to law clerks, who serve as assistants to justices and judges. There are over 2,000 law clerks in the federal system, working either for individual justices and judges or for an entire court. Law clerks typically engage in legal research, prepare background notes for oral arguments, and assist in drafting opinions.[21] The position of clerk on a high court is a prestigious and competitive one, and can be a valuable stepping stone for someone beginning a legal career. Perhaps because Supreme Court justices hail disproportionately from the Ivy Leagues, there is a strong tendency to select clerks from Ivy League law schools.

12-6 Selecting Cases

When feeling unfairly treated, people sometimes say "I'll take my case all the way to the Supreme Court if I have to!" The assumption, of course, is that that's where we'll finally find justice, and the expectation underlying the claim is that we *could* take any case to the Supreme Court—that everyone who has a grievance is entitled to a hearing.

That's not exactly how it works. In fact, surprisingly few people who petition the Court get a hearing. The Supreme Court has a lot of latitude over its agenda. Sure, others have to bring suit before the Court can hear a case, but the Court can avoid cases in areas of law it doesn't want to address, and select cases in areas of law it wants to decide. It can turn aside cases that it believes raise a political rather than a constitutional question.

It can turn its head away from cases that it feels are not "ripe" because they were brought too early—for instance, if there are other legal avenues available to the person bringing the complaint—or if it feels a case is "moot" because the law has changed in a way that would settle the controversy. Who determines what's "ripe" and what's "moot"? The Supreme Court—and it can make these judgments broadly, using them to circumvent or delay wading into a controversy that it wants to avoid. It doesn't have to give a reason for rejecting a case, and the party bringing the case is out of luck if the Court refuses to listen.[22] Like Marbury, who never got the judgeship he was entitled to, individual outcomes matter less to the Court than legal judgments.

Sometimes, events force the Court to take a case. In 2003, the Supreme Court met in an unusual special session to rule on the constitutionality of the McCain-Feingold campaign finance law, in order to resolve any controversies about the new legislation before the 2004 primaries were held. Once the Court decided it had standing to intervene in the stalemated 2000 presidential election, it had no choice but to act before electoral votes were delivered to Congress. These salient cases are the exception, though. For the most part, the Court can decide its own agenda.

12-6a Reading Tea Leaves

The Court considers only a small number of cases on its **docket,** or list of cases. In 1998, for instance, 8,083 cases were brought to the Supreme Court. The Court heard 90 of them.[23] When the Court agrees to review a ruling of a lower court, it issues a **writ of *certiorari*** ordering the lower court to send all records of the case. If the Court denies *certiorari,* the appeal is not heard, and the ruling of the lower court stands.[24]

The choice of cases at the opening of the Court's annual term (on the first Monday of each October) is typically a strong clue as to the controversies the Court is prepared to consider, and "Court watchers" will speculate about what the justices' choices indicate about the direction the Court will take. This can be a little like trying to predict the future by reading tea leaves, but the Court does send signals that at least will make sense after the fact—by the following spring, when all the term's decisions have been handed down.

The selection of a case that challenges a landmark abortion ruling, for instance, would mean that the Court is prepared to revisit the abortion question. What's less clear is whether it would be looking to reinforce established law or to reconsider it. Overlooking a prominent case on abortion rights that was ripe for appeal would send the message that

> **docket** The list of cases pending before a court.

> **writ of *certiorari*** An order issued by the Supreme Court demanding a lower court turn over all records of a case that the Supreme Court has decided to hear on appeal.

solicitor general The White House official responsible for arguing on behalf of the United States in Supreme Court cases where the United States is a party.

the Court does not wish to engage the issue at this time, although that may mean that the Court is entirely finished hearing cases on this matter, or simply not inclined to do so during the present term.

Members of the Court also send signals to the **solicitor general,** who argues cases on behalf of the administration, that the Court is interested in hearing a case on a particular question. The solicitor general will take these signals to mean that the Court is receptive to deciding a particular question in which the government has an interest and will take action to present an argument to the Court. The solicitor general is responsible for deciding which attorney in his or her office will argue a particular case and will personally argue high-profile cases and cases of particular concern to the administration.

The solicitor general operates out of the Department of Justice, so even though he or she represents "the government," his or her positions will reflect the administration's agenda. This gives the administration influence over the position the government takes before the Court, which in turn can influence the Court's judgment.[25]

12-6b Interest Groups and Case Selection

More than ever before, interest groups of the wide variety we addressed in Chapter 8 engage the judicial system to advance or advertise their causes. This is a sensible strategy for a number of reasons. Interest groups have the resources to engage in protracted court fights as a result of their funding and organization. Legal victories hold the potential to be wide-ranging, broadly advancing the group's goals. Even legal defeats keep the interest group's concerns in the press and therefore on the public agenda. Also, a sympathetic judiciary can prove to be a swifter and more effective route to interest group objectives than working the political side of the federal government, with all its access points designed to slow progress. This was the rationale for the involvement of the National Association for the Advancement of Colored People (NAACP) in the *Brown v. Board of Education* case, discussed in Section 12-9b, "When the Court Overturns Itself," which resulted in advancing the cause of desegregation more swiftly than could have been done through the legislative process.[26]

As with the solicitor general, justices sympathetic to a particular cause may send signals to interest groups advancing that cause that the Court is prepared to hear a case on the issue. If the signal is sent to groups advancing one side of a contentious issue, it can be a strong indication of how the Court would like to rule. Because litigation is commonplace among interest groups, it typically takes little time for the group to get its legal team in place and take advantage of the opportunity the Court is giving them.

amicus curiae Briefs filed by interested parties to a case, whose opinions are offered in an effort to shape the Court's discussion and judgment.

As part of an overall legal strategy, interest groups commonly file *amicus curiae* briefs with the Court, engaging in litigation as a third party to a suit that interests them. Literally "friend of the court," *amicus curiae* briefs can be solicited by a justice who intends to refer to them when writing an opinion in a case. More frequently, interest groups who have a partisan interest in the outcome of a trial voluntarily submit them—and they can be influential. When justices make reference to the arguments in *amicus curiae* briefs in their written decisions on a case, you can tell which groups had an impact on their reasoning.[27]

12-7 Nomination Politics

Because the judicial philosophy of the people in the black robes matters so much to the direction of the Court, political battles can erupt whenever the president has an opportunity to name someone to the Supreme Court or to one of the lower federal courts. This is particularly true during times like the present, when the nation is closely divided politically. It's why conservative Senate Republicans worked hard to delay confirmation hearings on President Clinton's more liberal Court appointees, and why Democrats did the same when they controlled the Senate during the first two years of the Bush administration. More than at any time in memory, confirmation battles over nominees to every level of the federal bench have been marked by divisive, strong-arm tactics.

Truthfully, this jockeying and positioning isn't all that interesting to ordinary people, and with the exception of heated nomination battles that occasionally play out on television, most of us don't pay attention to what goes on when the president sends the Senate a judicial nominee. However, interest groups pay a lot of attention, and if a nominee promises to alter the balance of a court, groups that stand to gain or lose from the shift will organize in a hurry.

In Chapter 9, we saw how the politically charged nominations of Robert Bork and Clarence Thomas to the Supreme Court generated intense resistance from Senate Democrats. They also generated strong lobbying efforts by groups on both sides of the ideological spectrum. In terms of sheer numbers, Bork was actively supported by twenty-one interest groups and actively opposed by seventeen in his unsuccessful bid to join the Supreme Court. Seventeen groups also mobilized to support Thomas, who was opposed by an unprecedented thirty-two interest groups in an unsuccessful effort to keep him off the Court. To put this in historical context, President Eisenhower's 1953 nomination of Earl Warren to be chief justice generated no interest group support and opposition from only two groups, and in the twenty-two years between Warren's nomination and President Ford's lone nomination to the Court (Justice John Paul Stevens) in 1975, a grand total of forty groups mobilized in support and forty-three groups mobilized against seventeen nominees.[28]

Then things heated up in the 1980s, as President Reagan acted on his pledge to appoint conservative justices who would counter the judicial liberals who had controlled the Court's agenda during the preceding three decades. Through the Reagan and first Bush administrations, interest groups battled fiercely over Court nominees. As the second President Bush anticipates filling vacancies in a narrowly divided Supreme Court with conservatives in the Reagan mold, the promise of more hard-fought battles again lies ahead.

Historically, presidents get what they want even when there's a fight—but they don't get everything they want. President Reagan lost the fight over the Bork nomination, and President Nixon had two nominees—Clement Haynsworth, Jr. and G. Harrold Carswell—turned away following widespread questions about their qualifications. Overall, the Supreme Court scorecard favors the president, even if he has to fight hard for his nominee. See Table 12-1.

Presidents can increase the odds of confirmation by considering the prevailing political winds before making a nomination. This may explain the relative ease with which President Clinton's nominees were confirmed. Had Clinton nominated individuals with very liberal views, he no doubt would have antagonized conservatives and sparked confirmation battles. Likewise, President Bush calculated that he would have needed to hold back on his more conservative nominees to the federal bench, had Democrats retained control of the Senate following the 2002 election, or face stiff partisan resistance. When Republicans regained control of the Senate, and with it the confirmation process, those calculations looked quite different, with Bush free to move forward on nominees that Democrats might have blocked.

12-7a Senatorial Courtesy

Regardless of the partisan composition of Congress, presidents as a matter of custom defer to the opinion of senators from the home state of a judicial nominee to one of the lower federal courts before sending the nomination to the full Senate. This custom is called **senatorial courtesy,** and it derives from the Senate's long history of institutional patriotism. Even though the Senate approves most judicial nominees, there's a sense among senators that they do not want to be a rubber stamp for any president. They take their constitutionally mandated role to offer advice and consent seriously, and the most direct way they can protect this is by permitting senators an informal veto over nominees from their home states.

Typically, a senator will object if the president is about to nominate a political adversary from back home. Senators can be particularly influential in derailing a nomination if they share a political party with the president, although senators of the opposing party have been known to influence presidential appointments. Remember, too, that even when a senator successfully blocks an appointment from his home state, there's no guarantee that the president will come back with another nominee from that state. In that regard, presidents always get to make the last move.[29]

senatorial courtesy
The custom that presidents will defer to the wishes of senators from a judicial nominee's home state before making a court appointment.

TABLE 12-1	President	Number of Justices Nominated	Number of Justices Confirmed	Percentage
	Nixon	6	4	66.7%
	Ford	1	1	100%
	Carter	0	n/a	n/a
	Reagan	5	4	80%
	G. H. W. Bush (senior)	2	2	100%
	Clinton	2	2	100%
	G. W. Bush	0	n/a	n/a

Supreme Court Nomination Scorecard: Nixon through G. W. Bush (First Term)

The practice of senatorial courtesy goes back to the first president and the first Congress, when President Washington nominated Benjamin Fishbourn to serve as a naval officer in Savannah, Georgia. Both Georgia senators objected, and the full Senate made it clear that it intended to back its colleagues even though the nominee was qualified to serve. When Washington backpedaled and nominated someone else who was acceptable to the Georgians, he became the first president to engage in the dance of senatorial courtesy that has been repeated many times through history.[30]

12-7b Professional Influences

Senatorial courtesy is the most political of the external influences on the president's choice of a nominee, but it is not the only influence. Members of the court and members of the bar also have their say over nominees at every level of the court system. Presidents have been known to contact sitting judges and justices to solicit opinions about people who would become future colleagues, and it's not unheard of for the communication channels to work in the other direction, with members of the judiciary lobbying the president.

The American Bar Association (ABA), the preeminent legal professional association, routinely offers its opinion on whether a presidential choice is qualified. A favorable nod from the ABA's Federal Judiciary Committee lends a level of professional approval to the political business of judicial nominations. Strategically, it can give a president cover for a controversial nomination by permitting the president to point out that the nominee's peers consider him qualified for service. When President Reagan submitted the nomination of the deeply conservative Antonin Scalia, he knew it would be hard for liberal senators to oppose someone who by reputation was qualified to serve on the Supreme Court (the ABA endorsed him as "well qualified"). Reagan tried a similar strategy with the Bork nomination, but the ABA came back with a mixed verdict, with only 10 of 15 members of the Federal Judiciary Committee giving their approval.[31] This, in turn, gave Bork's opponents an opening to exploit.

12-7c Diversity

As presidents attempt to appeal to diverse constituencies, there is political advantage in selecting high-profile nominees who are not white male Protestants (which the overwhelming majority of Supreme Court justices have been). As a consequence, today's Supreme Court is more diversified than in the past with respect to religion, race, and gender.

Barriers to diversity fell slowly. Although President Jackson appointed the first Roman Catholic to the Court in 1836 (Chief Justice Roger B. Taney), it took until 1894 for President Grover Cleveland to appoint the second (Justice Edward D. White). Three present justices are Roman Catholic—Scalia, Kennedy, and Thomas—but they also represent one-third of all Catholic justices who have ever served on the Court.

Louis Brandeis was the first Jewish justice, appointed by President Wilson in 1916, and for many years thereafter, one seat on the Court was informally considered to be a "Jewish

Roman Catholic Justices	Appointed by	Dates of Service
Roger B. Taney	Andrew Jackson	1836–1864
Edward D. White	Grover Cleveland	1894–1921
Joseph McKenna	William McKinley	1898–1925
Pierce Butler	Warren Harding	1922–1939
Frank Murphy	Franklin D. Roosevelt	1940–1949
William J. Brennan	Dwight D. Eisenhower	1956–1990
Antonin Scalia	Ronald Reagan	1986–
Anthony M. Kennedy	Ronald Reagan	1988–
Clarence Thomas	George H.W. Bush	1991–
Jewish Justices	**Appointed by**	**Dates of Service**
Louis D. Brandeis	Woodrow Wilson	1916–1939
Benjamin N. Cardozo	Herbert Hoover	1932–1938
Felix Frankfurter	Franklin D. Roosevelt	1939–1962
Arthur J. Goldberg	John F. Kennedy	1962–1965
Abe Fortas	Lyndon B. Johnson	1965–1969
Ruth Bader Ginsburg	Bill Clinton	1993–
Stephen G. Breyer	Bill Clinton	1994–

TABLE 12-2

Roman Catholic and Jewish Supreme Court Justices (through 2004)

seat." This tradition was interrupted by President Nixon and restored by President Clinton, who appointed the present Court's two Jewish justices, Ginsburg and Breyer.[32]

Of 108 Supreme Court justices who served through January 2005, a combined 16 have been Roman Catholic or Jewish (see Table 12-2).

The first African American on the Court was former civil rights attorney Thurgood Marshall, appointed by President Johnson in 1967. When he stepped down in 1991, President Bush replaced him with Clarence Thomas, who is the Court's second African American. Although this appeared to establish a "black seat" on the Court, Thomas' conservative orientation couldn't have been more different from Marshall's liberalism, angering some African American activists who felt the Thomas appointment was a cynical ploy to use race to keep liberal senators from blocking the nomination of a conservative.

When President Reagan ran for office, he promised to nominate the first woman to the Court, and he kept his promise with the appointment of Sandra Day O'Connor in 1981. She was joined by Justice Ginsburg twelve years later, making them the only two women to serve on the high court to date.

President Bush has spoken openly about nominating the first Hispanic justice, something he is likely to consider, should a vacancy arise during his second term of office.

Because of this history, the Court at the start of 2005 looked more diverse than at any time in its history, with three Catholics, two Jews, two women, and one African American among its membership. Viewed another way, however, there is a great degree of homogeneity. Seven of the nine justices are Republicans. All attended elite private law schools; five went to Harvard and two went to Stanford. With the exception of Thomas, all are over sixty. Seven are men; eight are white.

Take a second to browse through their profiles in Box 12-5 to get a sense of who was serving on the Court in early 2005.

Diversity on the lower federal courts is a less politically salient matter. These positions get very little public attention, and in some instances, this leads presidents to make different choices than they would for the high-profile Supreme Court. President Reagan, for

Box 12-5 **Who Are the Justices?**

William Hubbs Rehnquist
Source: The Supreme Court Historical Society.

William Hubbs Rehnquist

Title: Chief justice

Year of appointment: 1971; elevated to chief justice in 1986

Appointed by: President Nixon; elevated to chief justice by President Reagan

Home state: Arizona

Political party: Republican

Year of birth: 1924

Religion: Lutheran

Law school attended: Stanford

Approximate net worth (1995): $210,000–$575,000

Ideological position: Conservative

John Paul Stevens
Source: The Supreme Court Historical Society.

John Paul Stevens

Title: Associate justice

Year of appointment: 1975

Appointed by: President Ford

Home state: Illinois

Political party: Republican

Year of birth: 1920

Religion: Protestant

Law school attended: Northwestern

Approximate net worth (1995): $965,000–$2,090,000

Ideological position: Moderate/ liberal

Sandra Day O'Connor
Source: The Supreme Court Historical Society.

Sandra Day O'Connor

Title: Associate justice

Year of appointment: 1981

Appointed by: President Reagan

Home state: Arizona

Political party: Republican

Year of birth: 1930

Religion: Episcopalian

Law school attended: Stanford

Approximate net worth (1995): $1,400,000–$3,900,000

Ideological position: Moderate/conservative

Antonin Scalia
Source: The Supreme Court Historical Society.

Antonin Scalia

Title: Associate justice

Year of appointment: 1986

Appointed by: President Reagan

Home state: Virginia

Political party: Republican

Year of birth: 1936

Religion: Roman Catholic

Law school attended: Harvard

Approximate net worth (1995): $330,000–$760,000

Ideological position: Conservative

Anthony McLeod Kennedy
Source: The Supreme Court Historical Society.

Anthony McLeod Kennedy

Title: Associate justice

Year of appointment: 1988

Appointed by: President Reagan

Home state: California

Political party: Republican

Year of birth: 1936

Religion: Roman Catholic

Law school attended: Harvard

Approximate net worth (1995): $105,000–$635,000

Ideological position: Moderate/conservative

David H. Souter
Source: The Supreme Court Historical Society.

David H. Souter

Title: Associate justice

Year of appointment: 1990

Appointed by: President George H. W. Bush (senior)

Home state: New Hampshire

Political party: Republican

Year of birth: 1939

Religion: Episcopalian

Law school attended: Harvard

Approximate net worth (1995): $530,000–$1,100,000

Ideological position: Moderate

Clarence Thomas
Source: The Supreme Court Historical
Society

Clarence Thomas

Title: Associate justice
Year of appointment: 1991
Appointed by: President George
    H. W. Bush (senior)
Home state: Georgia
Political party: Republican
Year of birth: 1948
Religion: Roman Catholic
Law school attended: Yale
Approximate net worth (1995):
    $80,000–$275,000
Ideological position:
    Conservative

Steven G. Breyer
Source: The Supreme Court Historical
Society

Steven G. Breyer

Title: Associate justice
Year of appointment: 1994
Appointed by: President Clinton
Home state: Massachusetts
Political party: Democrat
Year of birth: 1938
Religion: Jewish
Law school attended: Harvard
Approximate net worth (1995):
    $3,170,000–$6,390,000
Ideological position: Liberal

Ruth Bader Ginsburg
Source: The Supreme Court Historical
Society.

Ruth Bader Ginsburg

Title: Associate justice
Year of appointment: 1993
Appointed by: President Clinton
Home state: New York
Political party: Democrat
Year of birth: 1933
Religion: Jewish
Law school attended: Harvard
Approximate net worth (1995):
    $4,170,000–$7,670,000
Ideological position: Liberal

Source: Lee Epstein, Jeffrey A. Segal, Harold J. Spaeth, and Thomas G. Walker, *The Supreme Court Compendium* (Washington, D.C.: CQ Press, 1996), p. 329.

instance, may have made it a priority to put a woman on the Supreme Court, but less than 8 percent of his 368 lower-court appointments were female.

Among recent past presidents, Bill Clinton did the most to put women and minorities on the federal bench. Despite these efforts, federal judges are overwhelmingly well-to-do middle-aged white male attorneys from elite law schools. The tendency for judges to come from the same elite clique goes a long way toward explaining the other demographics because when the middle-aged appointees of the recent past were in law school, these schools were still largely bastions for well-to-do white men. So, to a large degree the relative lack of diversity on the federal bench can be explained in terms of a long-standing lack of diversity in the elite legal community.[33]

Justice Ruth Bader Ginsburg tells of attending a reception for her class while she was at Harvard Law School in the 1950s. There were over 500 students—and only nine women. She recounts the dean of the law school asking each of the nine "what we were doing at the law school occupying a seat that could have been filled by a man."[34] As elite law school

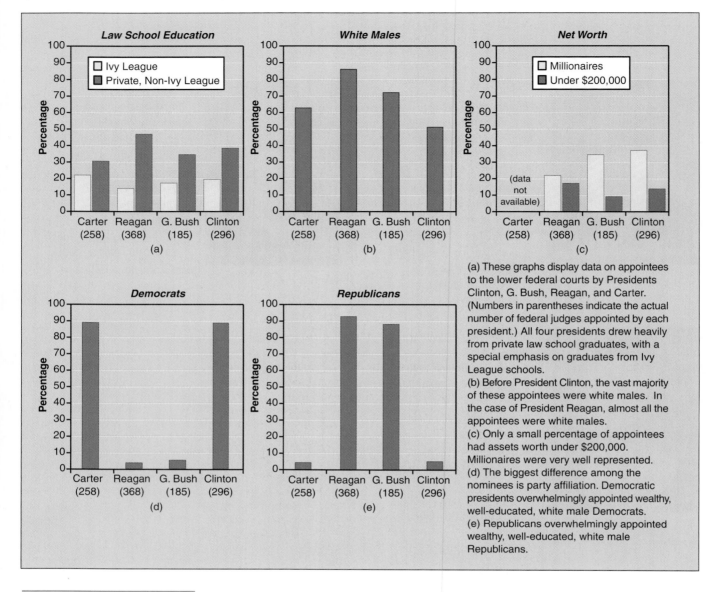

(a) These graphs display data on appointees to the lower federal courts by Presidents Clinton, G. Bush, Reagan, and Carter. (Numbers in parentheses indicate the actual number of federal judges appointed by each president.) All four presidents drew heavily from private law school graduates, with a special emphasis on graduates from Ivy League schools.
(b) Before President Clinton, the vast majority of these appointees were white males. In the case of President Reagan, almost all the appointees were white males.
(c) Only a small percentage of appointees had assets worth under $200,000. Millionaires were very well represented.
(d) The biggest difference among the nominees is party affiliation. Democratic presidents overwhelmingly appointed wealthy, well-educated, white male Democrats.
(e) Republicans overwhelmingly appointed wealthy, well-educated, white male Republicans.

Figure 12-3
Who Are the Federal Judges?
Source: Data from Robert A. Carp and Ronald Stidham, *The Federal Courts,* 4th ed. (Washington, DC: CQ Press, 2001), 71–75.

graduates have become less overwhelmingly white and male, it's possible that the demographics of the lower federal courts will begin to change, but this will also require a commitment to diversity by future presidents, whose appointments will be made out of public view.

Figure 12-3 should give you a good snapshot of the federal judicial elite.

12-7d Judicial Surprises

Republicans appoint Republicans and Democrats appoint Democrats, but that doesn't mean that presidents always get the results they expect from the people they place on the federal bench. There are numerous examples of presidents being surprised (or horrified) at the positions taken by their judicial appointees. Perhaps the most striking example from the twentieth century is President Eisenhower's appointment of Chief Justice Earl Warren, who led the most liberal and activist Court in modern times, particularly in the area of civil rights.

If the moderate Eisenhower had gotten what he was looking for in a chief justice, Earl Warren's activism never would have happened. Eisenhower, a Republican, considered sev-

> ### Box 12-6   One That Got Away
>
> President Bush (senior) was surprised by his first Supreme Court nominee, David Souter. The president was looking for a conservative nominee who was likely to oppose abortion rights, but given the certainty that his nominee's record in adjudicating abortion cases would be a major factor in the pending confirmation battle, he preferred someone who hadn't left a lot of tracks on the issue. Bush's chief of staff John Sununu recommended Souter, a fairly obscure Appeals Court judge from Sununu's home state of New Hampshire. Souter fit the requirements perfectly, leaving little ammunition for congressional supporters of abortion rights to claim that Bush's nominee would tip the delicate Court balance away from the *Roe* decision.
>
> The problem for Bush was that Souter was hard for everyone to judge—including Bush himself. He took it on faith (along with Sununu's judgment) that he had produced a reliably conservative vote for the Court—but that's not how things worked out. Souter turned out to be much more independent than the president had bargained for and frequently votes with the Court's liberal justices. Souter surprised Bush and turned into a disappointment for his conservative supporters, who saw his appointment as one that got away.

eral other moderate Republicans before settling on Warren as his nominee to preside over the Court. Two of these were his Secretary of State John Foster Dulles and New York Governor Thomas E. Dewey.[35] It's highly unlikely that either one would have been an activist chief justice committed to turning the Court into a forum for advancing civil rights the way Warren did.

Then again, few people suspected it of Warren—at least few in the Eisenhower administration suspected it. The president thought he was getting a centrist Republican like himself. Perhaps the broad support Warren had commanded from Republicans *and* Democrats in his three successful campaigns for California governor should have been a clue to his inherent activism, or the fact that his independent streak so distressed the leadership of the California Republican Party that they promoted Warren's appointment to get him out of the state. In any event, Eisenhower was in Warren's debt for the work the governor had done in moving the California delegation behind him in the 1952 Republican Convention, and it is of such political considerations that monumental decisions at times emerge. So, Eisenhower planted Earl Warren at the helm of the Supreme Court believing he had chosen an experienced administrator with moderate tendencies.[36] He later called it the biggest mistake of his presidency.

There are good reasons for judicial surprises like Warren. A president often makes appointments based on the recommendations of aides (particularly to lower court positions) without personally knowing the nominee. While a dossier on a nominee's history can tell a lot, it can't always predict how he or she will behave on the bench. Perhaps nominees at the ideological extremes can be fairly predictable—Antonin Scalia, for instance, had a record of unfaltering conservatism going back to his youth—but between the extremes, where most nominees are found, it can be much harder to predict the future. Box 12-6 talks about a more recent judicial surprise.

Even when the president has a personal history with a nominee, it can be impossible to tell how the nominee will mature on the bench. Judicial philosophies can develop and change over time, and our perspectives on things sometimes alter with age. John Paul Stevens was considered a moderate conservative when President Ford appointed him in 1975, but as the Court became more conservative, he became more liberal.

It's equally impossible to know how a nominee will respond to issues that simply cannot be anticipated at the time of her or his confirmation. Lifetime appointments hold out the possibility, even the probability, that the issues of greatest concern to the president making the appointment will give way to an unexpected set of issues during the nominee's term of service. When Franklin D. Roosevelt named William O. Douglas to the Supreme Court in 1939, it would have been impossible to foresee that he would be at the center of an activist Court that would revolutionize civil rights law before his retirement in 1975. Justices named to the bench fifteen years ago could not have anticipated having to make judgments about privacy on the Internet or human cloning, although these are emerging as important areas of dispute. Knowing a nominee's position on abortion rights doesn't offer a clue as to how he or she might decide cases in other legal areas.

12-8 A Political Court

If personal background and judicial philosophy influence a justice's approach to the law, and if bargaining strategies shape court judgments, it should be clear that the Supreme Court—for that matter, any court—is hardly the neutral arbiter of conflict that its symbols would suggest. Justices may never have to face the judgment of voters, but they are enmeshed in a political process. Perhaps their biggest political challenge is reflected in the dilemma that presented itself to Chief Justice Marshall and which the Court continues to face centuries after *Marbury v. Madison:* In the end, it must rely on the president to enforce its decisions. Marshall may have established the Court as an equal branch of government and begun the long process of developing prestige and admiration for the Court, but at every point in its history the Court has had to be particularly attuned to the politics of the other branches to maintain its precarious place in the federal constellation.

Justice Felix Frankfurter (who served from 1939 to 1962) was attempting to protect the myth of an apolitical Court when he declared, "When a priest enters a monastery, he must leave—or ought to leave—all sorts of worldly desires behind him. And this Court has no excuse for being unless it's a monastery."[37] Frankfurter knew this was hardly the case. Far from being cloistered, the Court survives by reacting to the hardball pursuits of the elected officials populating government's other branches.

The resources it has to bring this about are intangible, but if properly used they can be extremely effective in protecting the Court's political position. One thing the Court has in its favor is the deep well of respect developed over the centuries with generations of Americans. Such legitimacy can make it difficult for presidents to disobey or disregard the Court, as their constituents would not look kindly on a president defying what would be widely perceived as a legitimate act of a respected institution.

Ironically, the symbols we talked about at the opening of the chapter that make the Court seem so removed from politics—the dark robes, the marble building, the secret deliberations—contribute to the mystique that is so much a part of the Court's legitimacy. Put another way, these "nonpolitical" characteristics serve a highly political purpose in protecting the reverence many people feel for the Supreme Court—an opinion that gives the Court leverage with the more powerfully equipped executive and legislative branches. No doubt, Frankfurter was trying to perpetuate this mystique by comparing the Court to a monastery.

To maintain this high level of legitimacy, justices throughout history have been attentive to political currents, often selecting and ruling on cases they feel the public is ready to accept. Recognizing that the large degree of popular good will invested in the Court could be threatened by rulings that took the country where it did not want to go, justices will often keep an eye on the same political trends that elected officials live by. Sometimes events force the Court to hear a controversial case of such magnitude that the results are likely to be met with disapproval from some quarters. By paying attention to popular opinion, the Court can defend its political position by squaring its legal positions with the politicians who will be called upon to enforce the Court's words.

Public opinion and legitimacy interact in a delicate dance, each one reinforcing the other. We can see strains of this in Franklin Roosevelt's infamous "court packing scheme," where the Court's legitimacy was threatened by the actions of an enormously popular president, and in the harrowing case of *United States v. Nixon,* where a Court ruling directed President Nixon to commit political suicide.

12-8a Packing the Court

Although Franklin D. Roosevelt had large numbers of sympathetic Democrats in Congress to pass his New Deal programs during his first term, conservative justices appointed by

Roosevelt's Republican predecessors dominated the Supreme Court. They were philosophically opposed to the New Deal, and during FDR's first four years in office, they struck down much of the president's program, often by a 5–4 vote. It was a classic case of how separation of powers works to impede rapid change, even when a landslide election gives one party control of the other two branches.

Roosevelt, of course, was uninterested in a textbook tutorial on separation of powers and was frustrated by how the Court was thwarting his initiatives. Following his landslide 1936 reelection, he decided to do something about it. Roosevelt asked Congress to give him the authority to expand the size of the Court by adding one new member for every sitting member over the age of 70, a proposal that would have allowed Roosevelt to nominate six new justices and theoretically give his New Deal legislation a 10–5 majority on a new fifteen-member Supreme Court.[38] Supporters called it judicial reform. Opponents called it packing the Court.

Roosevelt's proposal failed even though he had a large partisan advantage in Congress. Democrats who embraced New Deal programs nonetheless had difficulty supporting a plan that would have so blatantly undermined the Court's legitimacy, even though it would have assured the legality of their legislation. Years of building the public's trust by appearing above politics worked to protect the Court from political tampering.

There's a postscript to the story, though. As the Senate Judiciary Committee was preparing to hold hearings on Roosevelt's plan in 1937, Justice Owen Roberts broke away from the anti-New Deal coalition and began ruling in favor of Roosevelt's programs. In *West Coast Hotel Co. v. Parrish* he sided with the New Deal forces in support of a minimum wage law. In *National Labor Relations Board v. Jones and Laughlin Steel Corporation* he voted to uphold the National Labor Relations Act.[39] Recognizing the direction the country was moving and tacitly acknowledging the importance of public opinion to preserving the Court's legitimacy, the conservative Roberts helped stave off a direct assault on the Court by aligning his judgments with public sentiment. It was called the "switch in time that saved nine."[40]

Even though his plan to pack the Court fell through, Roosevelt would exercise enormous influence over the Court's judicial direction. He would nominate eight justices during his tenure as president, leaving a judicial legacy that would outlast his administration. His first appointment came shortly after the Roberts switch. To get back at the Senate for failing to approve his judicial plan, and to make a point with the Court, Roosevelt nominated Senator Hugo Black, who had been at the forefront of the congressional fight in favor of packing the Court. Roosevelt knew that senators would never reject one of their own, and the Supreme Court would have no choice but to welcome one of its more vocal critics.[41]

12-8b The Nixon Tapes

On very rare occasions, the Court is called upon to render a judgment that threatens a confrontation with the president in a way that recalls Marshall's dilemma with *Marbury v. Madison*. It happened again in 1974, in **United States v. Nixon,** when the Supreme Court faced the prospect of issuing a ruling that would jettison President Nixon from office. One key difference between the two cases was the enormous legitimacy the Court could fall back on in making its judgment in the Nixon case. It turns out that it needed all the legitimacy it could muster.

The complex series of events that came to be known as the Watergate scandal originated with a burglary at the Democratic National Committee (DNC) headquarters in Washington's Watergate Hotel. It was 1972, and although President Nixon would win a second term in a landslide later that year, his reelection committee left nothing to chance. Documents had been copied and wiretaps had been placed on telephones at rival Democratic Party offices before a security guard caught five burglars at the DNC headquarters one June evening. They had in their possession telephone numbers for the White House, establishing a connection between the burglars and the administration that would eventually reach to the highest level.

▶ *United States v. Nixon*
The 1974 case in which a unanimous Supreme Court ruled that President Nixon could not use executive privilege to protect the secrecy of incriminating tapes documenting his involvement in the cover-up of the Watergate break-in.

By the next year, congressional and public outcry forced Nixon to appoint a special prosecutor to investigate Watergate. Through that investigation, word surfaced that Nixon had secretly taped all his conversations with aides and visitors to the Oval Office. The audio record could prove vital to the work of the special prosecutor and members of Congress, who by 1973 were holding hearings into whether to impeach the president over his role in Watergate, but they would first have to get Nixon to hand over the tapes.

The scandal was spiraling out of control as it began attaching itself to high-ranking administration officials. Former Attorney General John Mitchell, once head of the Justice Department, was charged with obstruction of justice for his role in trying to block the investigation from reaching the Oval Office. To build his case against Mitchell, Special Prosecutor Leon Jaworski issued a subpoena for Oval Office tape recordings. Nixon refused, claiming his private conversations were protected by executive privilege. This made the matter a constitutional issue that would have to be resolved by the Supreme Court.[42]

Nixon knew the political damage that would result if the tapes were made public because they showed that he was instrumental in planning the cover-up of the Watergate break-in, implicating him in a scheme to obstruct justice. One tape, considered to be a "smoking gun," is a conversation between Nixon and his Chief of Staff H. R. "Bob" Haldeman, recorded just six days after the break-in. It shows that Nixon knew everything that was going on from the start and is chilling in the matter-of-fact way Nixon goes about plotting to break the law (see Figure 12-4).

When you listen to or read a transcript of this tape, you'll probably realize why Nixon fought so hard to keep it from becoming public. Recorded June 23, 1972, just six days after the arrest of the Watergate burglars, the tape reveals that Nixon had intimate knowledge of the break-in and planned from the beginning to obstruct justice in order to make sure the public never found out how much he knew. The plan he considered, as recommended by Attorney General Mitchell, involved getting the FBI's Watergate investigation "under control" to keep it from going in "directions we don't want it to go" by getting FBI Director L. Patrick Gray to "stay the hell out of this."

Nixon's claim of executive privilege raised a constitutional question that would have to be resolved by the Supreme Court. Nixon argued that executive privilege provided the president with confidentiality so that he could speak openly with his confidants about matters of national importance. Jaworski contended that executive privilege did not protect a president from releasing private materials that potentially implicated him in a crime.

As the Supreme Court heard arguments in the case of *United States v. Nixon,* the president's political world was crumbling. Impeachment efforts were moving forward in the House, and the president's support was eroding in the Senate, even among members of his own party. Public opinion stood behind the position that Nixon should release the tapes, as the public widely believed that Nixon had something to hide. The Court would have the public on its side if it ruled against Nixon.

However, it would also have to rely on Nixon to enforce the ruling. There was little doubt that the tapes would incriminate Nixon, since he fought so hard to keep them secret. Would he comply with a court order to release them? What were his options if he did not?

The stakes could not have been higher. Failure to obey the Court would have thrown the nation into an unprecedented constitutional crisis, in which the president put his political survival above the rule of law. What then? Would Nixon use the ensuing crisis to clamp down on the justice system the way the tapes showed he tried to clamp down on the FBI, possibly suspending the Constitution and declaring martial law? That may sound ridiculous to us today, but plenty of people were worried about exactly that scenario. Nixon was under immense political pressure. Those close to him worried that he would see the Court as an enemy and lash out at it.

Under the circumstances, the Court needed to muster all its legitimacy and send the message that the president had no choice but to comply with an order that would lead to his political demise. It did so by ruling unanimously that executive privilege did not apply in this case, and that the president would have to hand over the tapes. Even one dissenting

June 23, 1972

This is the transcript of the recording of a meeting between President Nixon and his chief of staff, H. R. Haldeman, in the Oval Office on June 23, 1972.

Haldeman: Okay—that's fine. Now, on the investigation, you know, the Democratic break-in thing, we're back to the—in the, the problem area because the FBI is not under control because Gray doesn't exactly know how to control them, and they have, their investigation is now leading into some productive areas because they've been able to trace the money, not through the money itself, but through the bank, you know, sources—the banker himself. And, and it goes in some directions we don't want it to go. Ah, also there have been some things, like an informant came in off the street to the FBI in Miami, who was a photographer or has a friend who is a photographer who developed some films through this guy, Barker, and the films had pictures of Democratic National Committee letter head documents and things. So, I guess, so, it's things like that that are gonna, that are filtering in. Mitchell came up with yesterday, and John Dean analyzed very carefully last night and concludes, concurs now with Mitchell's recommendation that the only way to solve this, and we're set up beautifully to do it, ah, in that and that . . . the only network that paid any attention to it last night was NBC . . . they did a massive story on the Cuban . . .

Nixon: That's right.

Haldeman: thing.

Nixon: Right.

Haldeman: That the way to handle this now is for us to have Walters call [FBI director] Pat Gray and just say, "Stay the hell out of this . . . this is ah, business here we don't want you to go any further on it." That's not an unusual development, . . .

Nixon: Um huh.

Haldeman: . . . and, uh, that would take care of it.

Nixon: What about Pat Gray, ah, you mean he doesn't want to?

Haldeman: Pat does want to. He doesn't know how to, and he doesn't have, he doesn't have any basis for doing it. Given this, he will then have the basis. He'll call Mark Felt in, and the two of them . . . and Mark Felt wants to cooperate because . . .

Nixon: Yeah.

Haldeman: he's ambitious . . .

Nixon: Yeah.

Haldeman: Ah, he'll call him in and say, "We've got the signal from across the river to, to put the hold on this." And that will fit rather well because the FBI agents who are working the case, at this point, feel that's what it is. This is CIA.

Figure 12-4
The Smoking Gun Tape
Source: National Archives and Records Administration.

opinion could have given Nixon an opening to make the claim that the Court had ruled in error, but the justices—including four Nixon appointees—did not give him that opportunity.

The nation waited breathlessly for Nixon's response. With popular opinion lined up against him and a Supreme Court that had placed on the line the full measure of public allegiance it had developed over nearly two centuries, the president succumbed to the order. Doing so left him without any more political options. The revelations in the tapes meant certain impeachment by the House and conviction by the Senate. Barely two weeks after the Court's ruling, on August 8, 1974, Nixon announced to the nation that he would become the first president in history to resign the office.

United States v. Nixon demonstrates that judgments can in fact be powerful—that words can have dramatic political repercussions. As with Roosevelt's attempt to pack the Court, it shows how public opinion factors directly into the Court's ability to make controversial rulings (or resist succumbing to the efforts of a popular president), provided that it has been able to build a reservoir of legitimacy with the public. Justices who have been sensitive to keeping the institution in good standing with the public, like Justice Roberts, have been willing to put their judicial philosophy and personal beliefs aside, or at least engage in compromise with other justices, in order to protect the Court's political standing. In rare circumstances where the Court is not able to bridge ideological differences among its members, justices put the Court's legitimacy at risk. We witnessed such an event following the 2000 presidential election.

12-8c Squandering Legitimacy?

In December 2000, the Supreme Court walked into the middle of an entirely different tempest—the biggest presidential election controversy in 124 years—when it agreed to hear the Bush campaign's request to put a halt to manual recounts of Florida ballots that did not clearly register a vote for president. George W. Bush and his Democratic rival Al Gore were separated in the final Florida count by several hundred votes out of millions cast, with the eventual winner to receive all of Florida's electoral votes, and with them the presidency. For weeks America was riveted by the recount battle, as several Florida counties manually reviewed unmarked and poorly marked ballots using different standards for determining the intent of the voter.

Bush v. Gore The controversial 2000 Supreme Court case in which a sharply divided Court ended manual ballot recounts in Florida, following which George W. Bush became president.

The election battle ended abruptly when the U.S. Supreme Court terminated all recounts in the controversial case of *Bush v. Gore* (2000). Seven of the justices felt that the inconsistent recount standards employed in different counties were unconstitutional, but only five of them—all Republican appointees and the Court's most conservative members—argued that the calendar permitted no remedy to correct the inconsistencies because the time had come for electors to report. Four justices with a more liberal voting record strongly disagreed. Unlike the case of *United States v. Nixon,* the Court split into two camps, which were so sharply divided that they were unable to find common ground on which to build consensus. The final vote was 5–4; the recounting would stop, and Bush would become president.

The ruling left the nation as divided as the Court, and it left the Court bitter about what it had done. For a brief time, the Court's veil of secrecy was lifted as justices uncharacteristically displayed their feelings in public, revealing deep disagreements and great resentment. Justice Clarence Thomas, a member of the conservative majority, appeared on C-SPAN within a day of the ruling to deny that partisan considerations had influenced the decision. Chief Justice Rehnquist made the same assertion to reporters.[43]

Meanwhile, the four dissenting justices angrily castigated the majority, writing that the decision "inevitably cast a cloud on the legitimacy of the election."[44] Some openly questioned if the decision would have the same effect on the Court. Justice Ginsburg, who sided with the minority, saw the ruling as a political victory for "the home crowd"—a reference to the conservative majority fashioning what she believed to be a legally questionable ruling in order to put the candidate they preferred in the White House. Justice Breyer, also on the losing side of the case, worried that the partisan overtones of the ruling would undermine the legitimacy of the judicial process, and by extension, the legitimacy of the Court.[45]

Were the dissenters worried for no reason? Although it's true that the Court spoke with two voices on a politically charged, controversial topic while wading into a hotly contested political debate, it isn't clear that it undermined the reverence with which many Americans view the judiciary. In fact, surveys taken shortly after the ruling in *Bush v. Gore* suggest that, overall, the public was no less likely to think well of the Supreme Court than before the ruling.[46] At least in the short term, the Court appears not to have squandered its legitimacy by stepping into the 2000 election firestorm (although certainly many Democrats considered the decision to be suspect and ideologically motivated). Ironically, this could be because while public opinion was divided on who had actually won the election, by the time the Court made its ruling, a consensus was emerging that the recount saga had gone on too long and any resolution would be desirable. Despite the controversy surrounding how they did it, the Court provided the American people with the closure many were seeking.

12-9 Consistency and Legitimacy

To dissenters, one of the more disturbing components of the Court's ruling in *Bush v. Gore* was the requirement that it not be applied to any subsequent case. In other words, the majority made it clear that it was settling a contested election but that it was not establishing a legal precedent. This appeared odd because throughout its history, the Court has operated on the assumption that the collective body of constitutional interpretation contained in the Court's previous rulings provides the basis for making present-day judgments.

This has led the Court to place a premium on consistency. The Court puts a lot of stock in the doctrine of **stare decisis,** or "let the decision stand." *Stare decisis* encourages the Court to use its previous rulings as the basis for making present-day judgments and makes justices generally reluctant to overturn previous decisions, especially judgments that have become part of established law. This can lead justices who disagree with previous Court judgments to uphold them, even as they proclaim their differences with the interpretations of their predecessors.

At the same time, the Court does reverse course, especially in less than monumental matters. By one count, the Court overturned an average of four precedents per year between 1960 and 1999.[47] Some of this is the result of ideological shifting that occurs through turnover, which can account for why the Court might change direction on a precedent it had just recently established. It's generally easier for the Court to reverse itself on a newly decided matter than for it to overturn a long-standing constitutional interpretation. Box 12-7 discusses the continuing battle to reverse the Court's stance on abortion rights.

Reliance on precedent provides the Court with stability that contributes to its legitimacy. Reluctance to make dramatic changes to past rulings despite shifts in the Court's ideological composition distinguishes the Court from the other two federal branches, where swift changes of direction typically characterize partisan shifts. Even when given to ideological motivation, astute justices move slowly to project the appearance of allowing precedent to triumph over self-interest.

Cautious tendencies such as these can paradoxically pose a dilemma when the Court is faced with a previous ruling that was simply a bad judgment. Following *stare decisis* means the Court may take a long time to reverse a burdensome decision, sometimes allowing changes in public opinion to make the outdated ruling untenable. In such cases, the Court eventually protects its legitimacy by changing course or finds its legitimacy tarnished and its judgments discarded by history.

▶ **stare decisis** Literally, "let the decision stand," it is a guiding principle of judicial interpretation that places a premium on letting previous judicial rulings guide current rulings.

12-9a When Events Overturn the Court

Sometimes, events conspire to reverse a bad judgment of the Court. The case of **Dred Scott v. Sanford** (1857) is a profound example. Dred Scott was a slave who had been taken by his owner to Illinois and the Wisconsin territory, where slavery was prohibited under the terms of the Missouri Compromise. When he was returned to the slave state of Missouri, he petitioned the Court to maintain his freedom on the grounds that he had been residing previously in a free state. A judgment in his favor would have undermined the institution of slavery throughout the Union.

Chief Justice Roger Taney had no intention of allowing this to happen. His Court ruled that no person of color, be they free or enslaved, could be considered a citizen of the United States, and therefore Scott had no legal basis to bring suit. Taney's decision referred to Scott (and all black persons) as "an ordinary article of merchandise" that had no rights. Furthermore, in the first direct challenge to Congress since *Marbury v. Madison,* Taney overturned the key provision of the Missouri Compromise that precluded slavery in northern states and territories, effectively making slavery legal nationwide.[48]

Legal scholars widely consider the *Dred Scott* decision to be the Court's lowest moment. Charles Evans Hughes, Chief Justice during the 1930s, called the ruling one of

▶ **Dred Scott v. Sanford** The 1857 Supreme Court case that legalized slavery nationwide, while holding that people of color had no rights or protection under the Constitution. The ruling hastened the Civil War; it was subsequently overturned by constitutional amendment.

Box 12-7   Abortion Rights and Established Law

Prior to 1973, abortion was prohibited in many states. The landmark ruling in the case of **Roe v. Wade** changed that. The Court found that a constitutional right to privacy prohibited states from restricting the availability of abortions during the first three months of pregnancy, and struck down all laws that did so. Abortions were suddenly legal across the country.

Prior to the ruling, the abortion issue was not at the top of the national political agenda, but that quickly changed. As we know, the best way to influence the political process is to organize, and following *Roe v. Wade,* groups seeking to recriminalize abortions organized rapidly. They focused initially on a political and legal strategy, whereby they worked against the election of candidates for high office who were on record as supporting abortion rights, and challenged abortion laws in an effort to get the Supreme Court to reverse or chip away at its decision in *Roe.* The effort eventually bore fruit, and by the early 1980s a sizable congressional contingent and the president, Ronald Reagan, favored reversing the *Roe* decision.*

This did not lead the Court to make an about-face, however. Advocates of reversal argued before the Court that the reasoning used to reach the *Roe* decision was faulty, but this was initially rejected. In *City of Akron v. Akron Center for Reproductive Health* (1983), the Court overturned restrictions imposed on abortion rights by the city of Akron, and in so doing, acknowledged the importance of precedent. In the majority opinion in the *Akron* case, Justice Powell wrote, "Arguments continue to be made . . . that we erred in interpreting the Constitution. Nonetheless, the doctrine of *stare decisis,* while perhaps never entirely persuasive on a constitutional question, is a doctrine that demands respect in a society governed by the rule of law. We respect it today, and reaffirm *Roe v. Wade.*"†

As the 1980s progressed, groups pressing to overturn *Roe* benefited from an effective campaign to keep the abortion issue at the forefront of the political agenda. Meanwhile, President Reagan had the opportunity to appoint to the Supreme Court justices who were philosophically opposed to legal abortion. When the Court again considered the issue in *Webster v. Reproductive Health Services* (1989), advocates of a Missouri law restricting abortions attacked the trimester lan-

guage in *Roe* that decriminalized abortion in the first three months of a pregnancy, contending that it was unworkable, arbitrary, burdensome, and flawed. If their argument held sway in what had become a far more sympathetic Supreme Court, they hoped it would provide the legal rationale for undermining the *Roe* decision. A majority of five justices upheld the Missouri law, but they were divided on the issue of whether their verdict should be used to overturn *Roe,* so the 1973 decision survived what had been its sharpest test to date. With the appointment of two Justices supportive of *Roe* by President Clinton, the status quo continued through the 1990s.‡

We can derive several lessons from this history:

- *Precedent matters:* On major decisions, it takes a lot to move the Court to change what it has established. However, even if the Court is unwilling to reverse itself outright, it may well be open to chipping away at previous decisions.
- *Politics matters:* Who sits on the Supreme Court (a function of who serves as president), whether an interest is well organized, and the climate of public opinion all factor into the receptivity of the Court to a line of argument.
- *Argument matters:* Even when justices come down on the same side of a case, they may do so for different reasons. The way a case is presented to the Court can mean the difference between victory and defeat.

▶ **Roe v. Wade**   The 1973 Supreme Court case that found a constitutional right to privacy applied to reproductive issues, striking down all state laws that prohibited abortions during the first trimester of pregnancy.

---

*Jacob, Herbert, *Law and Politics in the United States,* 2d ed. (New York: HarperCollins College Publishers, 1995), 232–233.

†Lee Epstein and Joseph F. Kobylka, *The Supreme Court and Legal Change: Abortion and the Death Penalty* (Chapel Hill: University of North Carolina Press, 1992), 244–245.

‡Ibid., 203–298.

---

the Court's "self-inflicted wounds."[49] It destroyed the Court's legitimacy in the eyes of abolitionists as it intensified irreparable national divisions over slavery. Within three years, in part because of the effect of the Court's decision, the nation would explode into civil war.

Ultimately, the *Dred Scott* ruling was reversed, not by the action of a future Court, but by constitutional amendments approved in a different political climate. With the passage of the Thirteenth and Fourteenth Amendments following the Civil War, slavery was abolished and blacks were granted full citizenship. Taney's decision was rendered moot and his reasoning discredited, but the *Dred Scott* case remains as a warning about the lasting dangers inherent in any case where the Supreme Court establishes a bad precedent.

12-9b When the Court Overturns Itself

It took almost sixty years, but the Supreme Court eventually jettisoned another racially charged ruling, this time by establishing a new precedent in a subsequent case. The original case in question was ***Plessy v. Ferguson*** (1896), which established the constitutionality of separate public facilities for whites and nonwhites.

Homer Plessy was arrested in 1892 for sitting in the "whites only" car on a Louisiana railroad. Because he had black ancestors, he was considered black under Louisiana law and required to travel in the "coloreds only" car. Plessy went to court to challenge the constitutionality of the segregated railroad, contending it violated the Thirteenth and Fourteenth Amendments. The Court disagreed. Writing for the majority, Justice Henry Billings Brown asserted that the Fourteenth Amendment "could not have been intended to abolish distinctions based on color, or to enforce social, as distinguished from political equality."[50] As long as the facilities available to blacks were on par with those available to whites, segregation was legal.

In a lone dissent that proved to be generations ahead of its time, Justice John Harlan contended, "our Constitution is color-blind, and neither knows nor tolerates classes among citizens. . . . In my opinion, the judgment this day rendered will, in time, prove to be quite as pernicious as the decision made by this tribunal in the *Dred Scott* case."[51] Harlan was right on target. However, it would take until 1954 before a majority of the Supreme Court would agree.

The vehicle for overturning its stand on legal segregation was ***Brown v. Board of Education*** (1954), which revolved around the case of a grade-school girl named Linda Brown, who had to walk to a distant all-black school even though there was an all-white school in her Topeka, Kansas neighborhood. Her father tried to enroll her in the nearby all-white school but was turned down. With legal assistance from the National Association for the Advancement of Colored People (NAACP), the Browns sued the Topeka Board of Education, asking the courts to strike down barriers to integration. Because the ruling in the *Plessy* case clearly made separate educational facilities legal, the lower courts sided with the Board of Education.

It was left to the Supreme Court to stand up to its past, and the politics of the moment made this possible. Earl Warren, just two months into his term as Chief Justice, had an opportunity to correct what the Court had done in 1896 and change the direction of American politics. In a unanimous decision, the Warren Court overturned fifty-eight years of constitutionally sanctioned segregation in a landmark ruling that began breaking down racial barriers in American institutions.

Taking direct aim at *Plessy,* Warren wrote, "Does segregation of children in public schools solely on the basis of race, even though the physical facilities and other 'tangible' factors may be equal, deprive the children of the minority group of equal educational opportunities? We believe that it does. . . . We conclude that in the field of public education the doctrine of 'separate but equal' has no place. Separate educational facilities are inherently unequal."[52]

With those words, the Court made a rare about-face in the wake of changing political conditions, propelling the groundbreaking work of the civil rights movement of the 1950s and 1960s. See Appendix F for the text of key civil rights decisions.

When should the Supreme Court change its mind? Box 12-8 looks at this issue.

12-10 Activism and Restraint

It's probably evident by now that the competing philosophical approaches to the role of the Court that justices hold can make an enormous difference in how much the Court contributes to social change. In this regard, the people wearing the robes matter a lot. John Marshall and Earl Warren were activists who expanded the role of the Court in the political process and in American life. More restrained justices serving during the same periods in history would have done it differently, resulting in less development of federal power in the early nineteenth century and in fewer civil rights advancements in the twentieth century.

12-10a Judicial Activism

As a proponent of **judicial activism,** Warren presided over a revolutionary expansion in minority group rights, criminal defendant rights, voting rights, equal representation, and

▶ ***Plessy v. Ferguson*** The 1896 Supreme Court case that upheld racial segregation. It was reversed in 1954 in the case of *Brown v. Board of Education.*

▶ ***Brown v. Board of Education*** The landmark 1954 Supreme Court case that declared racial segregation unconstitutional, overturning the Court's ruling in *Plessy v. Ferguson.*

▶ **judicial activism** The philosophy that the Court should take an aggressive posture toward politics and the law, striking down presidential and congressional actions whenever it is deemed necessary and instituting far-reaching remedies to social wrongs.

Box 12-8 The Basis for Changing a Bad Decision

What should the Supreme Court do about a ruling that was made by a one-vote margin where the deciding justice subsequently disavowed his position? In the 1986 case *Bowers v. Hardwick*, the Court ruled 5–4 to uphold a Georgia law that made it a crime for two men to engage in consensual sexual relations in private. Justice Lewis Powell later publicly acknowledged that he had made a mistake in supporting the majority view that the constitutional right to privacy did not apply in this situation. In 2002, the Supreme Court agreed to hear another case on the same matter, giving the Court an opportunity to change course. But should it?

In an opinion piece that appeared in the *New York Times*, Yale law professor Kenji Yoshino argued that it should. He reasoned that consistency for consistency's sake is a pointless endeavor and that people recognize that institutions like the Supreme Court can only be as good as the fallible individuals who run them. People will understand that the Court made a mistake, he argued, and correcting it will not undermine the Court's legitimacy. To the contrary, people might appreciate that the justices were able to admit that they were wrong.[*]

In 2003, the Court reversed course and ruled that the state could not make same-sex consensual relations a crime. Do you think this was an appropriate instance for the Court to do an about-face? Does it diminish the Court in your eyes—or does it invite your respect?

[*]Kenji Yoshino, "Can the Supreme Court Change Its Mind?," *New York Times*, December 5, 2002.

---

personal expression. Between 1953 and 1969, the Warren Court acted aggressively, among other things, to

- Desegregate schools
- Draw legislative boundaries so they reflected the "one person, one vote" principle
- Protect individuals accused of crimes from self-incrimination (the famous "Miranda Rights" that police read to suspects prior to arresting them come from the 1966 case *Miranda v. Arizona*)
- Guarantee legal representation to criminal defendants who could not afford it
- Forbid mandatory prayer in public schools
- Expand press freedom by requiring public figures to prove that reporters acted with malice to support a claim of libel.[53]

If you're thinking that all this was controversial, you're right. Critics charge that judicial activists are less interested in interpreting the law than in making it, a role that is constitutionally reserved for Congress. Warren's critics repeatedly charged him with usurping powers that were reserved for others, which—along with the agenda his activism promoted—instigated brisk sales of "impeach Earl Warren" bumper stickers.

If the Court takes a measure of public opinion before acting, though, it should be remembered that the Warren Court served during a period of social upheaval that suited it well. Certainly, the Court's activism contributed to the upheaval, and without a doubt, public opinion was sharply divided over a lot of what it did. Then again, public opinion was sharply divided over everything important happening during the 1960s, when rights for African Americans, women, and young people were at the forefront of the political agenda. It's hard to envision an activist Court taking the positions that the Warren Court did in an era that's more conducive to conservative politics, like what we have today.

Still, it would be a mistake to equate judicial activism with political liberalism. The aforementioned Felix Frankfurter, whose long service included a stint on the Warren Court before his retirement in 1962, was an economic conservative who advanced his preferences by striking down laws that conflicted with his agenda—in other words, through judicial activism.[54] Members of today's conservative Supreme Court who have worked to reverse some of what the Warren Court did could also be seen as conservative activists.

judicial restraint
The philosophy that the Court should defer to the other branches of government and only overturn legislation when it is clearly unconstitutional.

12-10b Judicial Restraint

Today's Court has its share of justices who practice **judicial restraint,** or the philosophy that the judiciary should yield to the actions of the legislature and executive unless they are

> **Box 12-9   Rehnquist and Judicial Restraint**

The 1979 affirmative action case of *United Steelworkers of America v. Weber* provides an example of Justice Rehnquist's judicial restraint (he was simply Justice Rehnquist at the time; President Reagan would elevate him to Chief Justice in 1986). The Steelworkers Union and Kaiser Aluminum had created a plan under which half of thirteen on-the-job training positions available at a Louisiana plant would be reserved for African Americans. Brian Weber was refused employment in one of those positions because he was white. He filed suit, claiming the plan amounted to discrimination and was in violation of the Civil Rights Act of 1964, which states that employers are not to grant preferential treatment to any individual because of his or her race. The Supreme Court ruled 5–2 with two abstentions that while the Louisiana plant violated the letter of the civil rights law, it was true to its spirit, which was to encourage efforts to end traditional patterns of racial discrimination.

Rehnquist was one of the dissenters. In a scathing dissenting opinion, he accused the majority of judicial activism by interpreting the intent of Congress and applying the law in excess of its stated objective to be color-blind in its application. To Rehnquist, whether the Civil Rights Act was good or bad law, it made plain that it sought to avoid preferential treatment—period. In his view, it was not the place of the Court to amend that to permit employers to provide preferential treatment of any kind, regardless of the intent of the action.[*] Rehnquist wrote, "By a tour de force reminiscent ... of escape artists such as Houdini, the Court eludes clear statutory language, 'uncontradicted' legislative history, and uniform precedent in concluding that employers are, after all, permitted to consider race in making employment decisions."[†] It was a clear statement of his restrained judicial philosophy.

[*]Abraham, Henry J., *Justices, Presidents and Senators: A History of the U.S. Supreme Court Appointments from Washington to Clinton* (Lanham, MD: Rowman & Littlefield Publishers, 1999), 271–273.

[†]Ibid., 273.

blatantly unconstitutional. To a justice who practices judicial restraint, a bad policy, an unnecessary policy, even an unfair policy that is permitted under the Constitution should be left alone.[55] Chief Justice Rehnquist is largely perceived to be an advocate of this approach (see Box 12-9). Clearly, someone who takes this approach to the judiciary would never think of using the Court as a vehicle for advancing an activist political agenda. Had someone of Rehnquist's philosophy guided the Court in Warren's place, the social agendas of the 1950s and 1960s might well have played out differently.

Some of the justices who practice judicial restraint are also **constructionists** when it comes to interpreting the Constitution. Constructionists believe that the Constitution should be subject to a literal or narrow interpretation, and understood within the context in which it was written.[56] So, for instance, strict constructionists might oppose the reasoning behind the *Roe* decision that legalized abortion on the basis of a constitutional right to privacy on the grounds that the Constitution does not enumerate privacy as a right, and that the framers of the Constitution did not intend for there to be such a right. A constructionist philosophy is conservative in nature and stands in clear opposition to judicial activism. Not surprisingly, recent conservative presidents like Nixon, Reagan, and both Bushes have favored judicial nominees who hold to this philosophy.

Even so, and despite the prevalence of judicial restraint among justices appointed by recent Republican presidents, the Warren Court was not the high water mark for reversing Supreme Court decisions, acts of Congress, and state laws. Instead, the period since Chief Justice Warren took over the Court in 1953 through the present has been an unparalleled era of judicial activism, in which the Court as a whole has injected itself regularly into the political process. Between 1953 and 2001, the Court reversed 131 of its earlier rulings. In the previous century and a half, it had only done this eighty-eight times. Table 12-3 fills in the details. Despite the conservative direction the Court has taken since Warren's departure, it is now a matter of course that the judiciary is an active, equal—and legitimate—branch of government.

As an equal participant in the political process, the cumulative actions of the courts at every level have tremendous bearing on how we live our lives. The way the courts exercise this influence is itself determined by things beyond the control of the judiciary—like other political actors and the political climate of the times—and by the philosophical leanings of the people in the dark robes. Would the federal government be weaker today if John Marshall had not been Chief Justice for the first three decades of the nineteenth century, when

> ▶ **constructionists** Those who hold to the judicial philosophy that the Constitution should be interpreted strictly and literally, and in the context in which it was written.

TABLE 12-3	Court	Years	Supreme Court Decisions Overturned	Acts of Congress Overturned	State Laws Overturned
Judicial Activism through Time	Marshall	1801–1835	3	1	18
	Taney	1836–1864	4	1	21
	Chase	1865–1873	4	10	33
	Waite	1874–1888	13	9	7
	Fuller	1889–1910	4	14	73
	White	1910–1921	5	12	107
	Taft	1921–1930	6	12	131
	Hughes	1930–1940	21	14	78
	Stone	1941–1946	15	2	25
	Vinson	1947–1952	13	1	38
	Warren	1953–1969	45	25	150
	Burger	1969–1986	52	34	192
	Rehnquist	1986–2001	34	25	86

Source: David M. O'Brien, *Storm Center: The Supreme Court in American Politics,* 6th edition (New York: W. W. Norton, 2003).

clashes over federalism were being resolved? Would the Civil War have occurred when it did had Chief Justice Taney not tried to codify slavery as the law of the land? Would the civil rights agendas of the 1960s have been different without Earl Warren? Would Al Gore have become president had one justice voted differently?

In the courts as everywhere else in the political system, the rules of the game and the way they're interpreted by people in authority determines who gets what—who wins and who loses. Nowhere is this more evident than in the area of public policy, the outcomes produced by the political process in the form of domestic and foreign policy and laws regarding individual rights and liberties. We'll look at those outcomes and what they mean to us personally in the final part of the book, beginning with civil rights policies in Chapter 13.

Chapter Review

The judiciary resolves disputes arising from other branches of government, but it does so without the formal powers of the other branches and has to rely on the executive branch to enforce its rulings. This initially placed the United States Supreme Court in a weak position, which was strengthened enormously with the establishment of the Court's power of judicial review in the 1803 case *Marbury v. Madison.* Other rulings of the Marshall Court helped establish the supremacy of the federal government over the states.

The federal court system is a three-tiered structure with trial courts, circuit courts of appeals, and the Supreme Court. Most cases work their way up this system through an appellate process, although the Supreme Court has original jurisdiction over cases involving the federal government, states, and foreign officials as detailed in the Constitution. State court systems follow this three-tiered structure and have jurisdiction over state criminal and civil law. Cases can only be appealed from a state court to the U.S. Supreme Court if they raise a point of constitutional law.

Courts have a lot of latitude in the cases they select for review, although interest groups try to influence case selection. Deciding cases is a complicated process that starts with oral arguments in court, proceeds with closed conferences, and continues with a period of writing decisions, during which justices attempt to influence each others' opinions and may even change their votes.

Judicial nominations can cause contentious battles between the president and Congress because the direction of the judiciary depends on the philosophy and ideology of the people the president appoints. Historically, presidents get most of the appointments they want, but the Senate takes its consent function seriously and has blocked nominations considered controversial. Presidents will also defer to senatorial courtesy and avoid appointing justices and judges who are not acceptable to their home-state senators.

Although the vast majority of Supreme Court appointees have been white Protestant men, today's Supreme Court reflects more religious, ethnic, and gender diversity. This is less evident on lower federal courts, where President Clinton is alone among his immediate predecessors in the diversity of his appointments.

In order to turn its relatively weak political position to advantage, the Court plays on its mystique to bolster its legitimacy with the public, making it difficult for political officials to defy Court rulings. It also pays attention to public opinion, often taking pains not to get ahead of what the public will accept. So, when Franklin D. Roosevelt attempted to pack the Court with sympathetic justices, the public recoiled at his efforts to play politics with a revered institution, and the scheme failed. However, a justice who had been holding up Roosevelt's New Deal legislation acknowledged its broad public support and began changing his vote, which brought the Court in line with public sentiment.

Justices put a lot of stock in the doctrine of *stare decisis,* making dramatic reversals unusual. But as public opinion changes the Court may become willing to revisit past rulings. The Court may overturn some of its earlier bad judgments, the way *Plessy v. Ferguson* (1896) was reversed by *Brown v. Board of Education* (1954). Events may conspire to reverse the Court, as when the decision affirming slavery in *Dred Scott v. Sanford* (1857) was overturned by constitutional amendment following the Civil War.

Justices differ in judicial philosophy. Judicial activists believe the Court should be a forum for correcting social wrongs. Justices advocating judicial restraint feel the Court should defer to the actions of Congress and the president unless they are blatantly unconstitutional.

Key Terms

amicus curiae *(p. 366)*

appellate jurisdiction *(p. 362)*

Articles of Confederation (p. 358)

Brown v. Board of Education *(p. 381)*

Bush v. Gore *(p. 378)*

concurring opinion (p. 364)

constructionists (p. 383)

dissenting opinion (p. 364)

docket (p. 365)

Dred Scott v. Sanford *(p. 379)*

Gibbons v. Ogden *(p. 360)*

judicial activism (p. 381)

judicial restraint (p. 382)

judicial review (p. 359)

judiciary (p. 356)

Judiciary Act of 1789 (p. 358)

jurisdiction (p. 361)

legal system (p. 356)

Marbury v. Madison *(p. 359)*

McCulloch v. Maryland *(p. 360)*

New Jersey Plan (p. 358)

original jurisdiction (p. 362)

Plessy v. Ferguson *(p. 381)*

Roe v. Wade *(p. 380)*

senatorial courtesy (p. 367)

solicitor general (p. 366)

stare decisis *(p. 379)*

United States v. Nixon *(p. 375)*

Virginia Plan (p. 358)

writ of certiorari *(p. 365)*

writ of mandamus *(p. 361)*

Review Questions

Note: You can find the correct answers to these questions by taking the quiz and then submitting your answers in the Online Edition. The program will automatically score your submission. If you miss a question, the program will provide the correct answer, a rationale for the answer, and the section number in the chapter where the topic is discussed.

1. Alexander Hamilton argued that the judiciary would be the weakest branch of government because it primarily had the power of
   a. force.
   b. will.
   c. judgment.
   d. coercion.

2. In exchange for a claim to the power of judicial review in *Marbury v. Madison,* Chief Justice Marshall gave up
   a. Adams' right to make last-minute judicial appointments.
   b. the power to issue a writ of *mandamus.*
   c. the constitutional right to *stare decisis.*
   d. the Judiciary Act of 1789.

3. The final judgment of the Supreme Court is typically determined
   a. while hearing oral arguments.
   b. in conferences.
   c. when drafting opinions.
   d. when drafting dissenting opinions.

4. A criminal case heard in a state supreme court
   a. can never be appealed to the U.S. Supreme Court.
   b. has original jurisdiction in the U.S. Supreme Court.
   c. has appellate jurisdiction in the U.S. Supreme Court.
   d. has appellate jurisdiction in the U.S. Supreme Court if a point of constitutional law is in question.

5. Despite its increasingly conservative posture, the Supreme Court has been reluctant to overturn *Roe v. Wade* because
   a. not many justices are judicial activists.
   b. justices tend to place a premium on *stare decisis.*
   c. justices are reluctant to issue writs of *certiorari.*
   d. The powerful impact of *amicus curiae* briefs has preserved *Roe.*

6. Although most justices have been white Protestant males from prestigious law schools, the Court has the longest record on which type of diversity?
   a. religious
   b. racial
   c. gender
   d. educational background

7. Justices may surprise and disappoint the presidents who appoint them for all of the following reasons *except*
   a. presidents may not personally know their nominees.
   b. future issues before the Court cannot be anticipated when a nominee is confirmed.
   c. judicial philosophies can change over time.
   d. nominees with strong conservative leanings may move the Court in unpredictable directions.

8. The Supreme Court needed a unanimous ruling in *United States v. Nixon*
  a. to make sure Nixon enforced the decision.
  b. because Nixon's argument for executive privilege was hard to contest.
  c. to be in line with public opinion.
  d. to get Nixon to resign the presidency.
9. *Dred Scott v. Sanford* was overturned by
  a. *Brown v. Board of Education.*
  b. *Plessy v. Ferguson.*
  c. custom and tradition.
  d. constitutional amendment.

10. The rights established in *Miranda v. Arizona* were the result of
  a. judicial activism.
  b. judicial restraint.
  c. strict constructionists.
  d. the influence of Nixon and Reagan court appointees.

In Their Own Words

You might be interested in examining some of what the following authors have said about the topics we've been discussing:

Abraham, Henry J. *Justices, Presidents and Senators: A History of the U.S. Supreme Court Appointments from Washington to Clinton.* Lanham, MD: Rowman & Littlefield, 1999. A colorful account of the nominating process and the Supreme Court through history.

Baum, Lawrence. *The Supreme Court,* 7th ed. Washington, DC: CQ Press, 2001. Baum offers a thorough exploration of the extent to which the Supreme Court operates as a political institution despite appearances to the contrary.

Carp, Robert A., and Ronald Stidham. *The Federal Courts,* 4th ed. Washington, DC: CQ Press, 2001. A detailed overview of the federal court system.

Epstein, Lee, and Jack Knight. *The Choices Justices Make.* Washington, DC: CQ Press, 1998. The authors offer a rational approach to the way Supreme Court justices reach decisions, which should appeal to anyone interested in strategic decision-making.

Epstein, Lee, Jeffrey A. Segal, Harold J. Spaeth, and Thomas G. Walker. *The Supreme Court Compendium: Data, Decisions, and Development,* 2d ed. Washington, DC: CQ Press, 1996. If you have a factual question about the Supreme Court, chances are you can find the answer here. It's everything you've ever wanted to know about the Supreme Court.

Jacob, Herbert. *Law and Politics in the United States,* 2d ed. Boston: HarperCollins, 1995. Jacob examines the interplay between the judicial system and the American political system.

O'Brien, David M. *Storm Center: The Supreme Court in American Politics,* 6th ed. New York: W. W. Norton, 2003. An accessible account of the Supreme Court that emphasizes how the Court functions as a political branch of government.

Notes

1. Herbert Jacob, *Law and Politics in the United States,* 2d ed. (New York: HarperCollins, 1995), 6–18.
2. You can take a virtual tour of the Supreme Court, and even virtually visit a Justice's chambers, by going to oyez.org at http://www.oyez.org/oyez/tour/ginsburgchamber-from-introduction.
3. Lawrence Baum, *The Supreme Court,* 7th ed. (Washington, DC: CQ Press, 2001), 2–4.
4. Alexander Hamilton, *The Federalist,* No. 78. See http://www.constitution.org/fed/federa78.htm.
5. Robert A. Carp and Ronald Stidham, *The Federal Courts,* 4th ed. (Washington, DC: CQ Press, 2001), 4.
6. David M. O'Brien, *Storm Center: The Supreme Court in American Politics,* 6th ed. (New York: W.W. Norton, 2003), 105.
7. Ibid., 106.
8. Carp and Stidham, *The Federal Courts,* 6.
9. Ibid.
10. Baum, *The Supreme Court,* 23–24
11. Carp and Stidham, *The Federal Courts,* 7–8.
12. Ibid., 71. Jackson may not have actually said these words, but there's little doubt that they expressed how he felt about Marshall's Federalist tendencies.
13. Ibid., 16–17.
14. O'Brien, *Storm Center,* 105.
15. Carp and Stidham, *The Federal Courts,* 46–47.
16. Ibid., 248.
17. Ibid., 255.
18. Ibid., 257–267.
19. Lee Epstein and Jack Knight, *The Choices Justices Make* (Washington, DC: CQ Press, 1998), 1–21.
20. O'Brien, *Storm Center,* 267–296.
21. Carp and Stidham, *The Federal Courts,* 32–34.
22. O'Brien, *Storm Center,* 164–182.
23. Carp and Stidham, *The Federal Courts,* 37.
24. If you're curious about the types of cases pending before the Supreme Court right now, you can access the Court's docket at http://www.supremecourtus.gov/docket/docket.html. At the search bar, type in an area that interests you, like "environment," "transportation," or "tax." The website will return all pending and recently decided cases pertaining to that area. If you're a budding lawyer, you can click on the docket number of a case and you'll find the path the case has taken to reach the Supreme Court, and the action taken (or lack thereof), expressed in language only a lawyer could love.
25. You can read more about the solicitor general online at http://www.usdoj.gov/osg/aboutosg/aboutosg.html.
26. O'Brien, *Storm Center,* 222–225.

27. Ibid., 225.
28. Lee Epstein and others, *The Supreme Court Compendium: Data, Decisions, and Development*, 2d ed. (Washington, DC: CQ Press, 1996), 329.
29. Abraham, *Justices, Presidents and Senators*, 18–19
30. Ibid., 19.
31. Ibid., 21–28.
32. Ibid., 46–47.
33. Carp and Stidham, *The Federal Courts*, 69–78.
34. Ibid., 78.
35. Abraham, *Justices, Presidents and Senators*, 191–192.
36. Ibid., 191–194.
37. O'Brien, *Storm Center*, 87
38. Ibid., 56.
39. Ibid.
40. Yes, that's really what it was called.
41. O'Brien, *Storm Center*, 58.
42. Jacob, *Law and Politics*, 79–80.
43. O'Brien, *Storm Center*, 87.
44. Ibid., 251.
45. Ibid., 88 and 96.
46. Ibid., 343.
47. Baum, *The Supreme Court*, 143.
48. O'Brien, *Storm Center*, 29.
49. Ibid., 115.
50. The full text of the ruling may be found at http://usinfo.state.gov/usa/infousa/facts/democrac/33.htm.
51. O'Brien, *Storm Center*, 115.
52. The full text of the ruling may be found at http://usinfo.state.gov/usa/infousa/facts/democrac/36.htm
53. O'Brien, *Storm Center*, 195–197.
54. Lee Epstein and Thomas G. Walker, *Constitutional Law for a Changing America: A Short Course* (Washington, DC: CQ Press, 1996), 39–41.
55. Abraham, *Justices, Presidents and Senators*, 271.
56. O'Brien, *Storm Center*, 14–15.

Establishing Civil Rights

13-1 Introduction

Some people feel passionately about the kind of country they want the United States to be. Others are content to sit on the sidelines as decisions are made about who gets what. For some people, social concerns are of great importance. For others, the stuff of daily experience is enough to keep them occupied, even if that experience is shaped in part by political choices that don't interest them.

Which kind of person are you? Do you think a lot about the kind of society you're living in? Do you think about ways you'd like to maintain it or change it? Do you engage in political action to try to bring it about?

Or do you find questions like these to be uninteresting? Maybe you feel government is too distant from your everyday life to matter much. Do you think that even if you got involved on behalf of what you believe, it wouldn't make much of a difference?

Questions like these are really about values. If you believe we should be a society where we spend heavily on the military, that's a value. If you believe we should be a society where abortions are available to women who want them, that's also a value. If you believe capital punishment is a deterrent to crime, you probably value the death penalty. If you believe traditionally disadvantaged groups should be given extra consideration in college admission decisions, you probably value affirmative action.

It's easy to see how values can conflict with one another because those who want to spend less tax money on the military will clash with those who want to spend more, those who believe abortion is morally wrong will clash with those who feel it is a matter of personal choice, and so on.

People who feel strongly about some of these things and see their positions as moral absolutes might object to having them defined as values. This complicates the battles that ensue when people with different visions of society clash in the political process because it's not unusual for people on *both sides* of an issue to believe that they are simply right. In one regard, the safeguards to the system that we talked about in the first part of the book put a drag on the most aggressive advocates of a political position and deter factions from imposing their will on others. But that doesn't stop the political debate from being intense and ferocious—even if you're personally not involved in it.

Regardless of your personal involvement in politics, all of us live with the results of those who get the political system to successfully respond to their values and their view of society. Politics creates winners and losers. In your parents' generation, advocates of government as a vehicle for bringing about social justice won a lot of battles. Your generation has witnessed the success of those who felt that approach was ineffective or misguided. Even if you didn't participate, if you hold a position on any of the wide range of things government touches, you are a winner or a loser, too.

We're going to explore four arenas where the fury of policy debate determines whose values receive official acknowledgment. It's a fluid process, where winners at one moment could turn into losers at another, and where winners in one area could be losers in another. So, as we look at policies affecting civil rights, civil liberties, domestic affairs and international relations, consider the kind of country you would like to live in, and see how it compares with the kind of country we choose to be. Along the way, think about the things you value, and whether there is any way that you can imagine your voice contributing to the debate over any of the issues we will discuss.

We'll start with issues of civil rights.

13-2 Civil Rights

The Declaration of Independence says, "all men are created equal." **Civil rights** policies are about making sure this is enforced as a matter of law: that the law treats everyone equally, regardless of differences in race, gender, ethnic background, sexual preference, or anything people might be inclined to discriminate against. Because equal treatment does not naturally materialize, ensuring civil rights can be a challenge. Even among people who agree with the principle of equal treatment under the law, there can be strong disagreements over the means to that end. Some would treat everyone the same in order to treat them equally, whereas others would make exceptions for those who have long been the object of discriminatory treatment. This can be the cause of fierce policy disputes.

As we first noted in Chapter 1, there are different ways to define equality, and because they are not entirely compatible with one another, advocates of different conceptions of equality readily clash. Some of the early civil rights struggles were about affording disadvantaged groups the same political rights as others, such as African Americans, who for years were kept out of the political process through legal and violent means, and women, who struggled for decades to win the right to vote. These groups sought **political equality,** which you may recall is a form of **equality of opportunity** because it creates a level playing field for all participants. Although struggles by these groups were ferocious and met with intense resistance by those whites or men who felt threatened by opening the political process to blacks and women, subsequent generations have largely embraced the political gains they made. That's because Americans tend to support equality of opportunity, and widely value the evenhanded application of political rights.

Some of the more recent civil rights battles, however, have been fought over outcomes, which we know to be problematic for many Americans. These battles have sparked enormous controversy because by attempting to advance **equality of outcome,** disadvantaged groups have run headlong into the widely held American preference for not using government to produce **economic equality** or **social equality.** So, people who argue for policies like affirmative action, meant to compensate for past and present discrimination in hiring or college admissions, meet defiance from those who see it as a misguided attempt to mandate economic equality. Women face similar resistance when they argue for comparable worth legislation, mandating equal pay for jobs predominantly performed by women that require similar skill levels and training as other jobs predominantly performed by men.

Compounding matters is the issue of who qualifies as a disadvantaged group. In recent years, Native Americans, Latinos, Asian Americans, gays, people with disabilities, and seniors have prominently organized to demand consideration for past and present discrimination. To some, having so many groups claiming redress for discriminatory practices makes a mockery of civil rights by creating a culture of victimization, whereby anyone with a grievance about how others treat them can turn to the government to rectify it. Their resistance is fueled by the fact that many of these civil rights agendas raise controversial questions about social equality: Should Spanish be used in schools with large Latino populations in order to treat Spanish-speaking children equally, or are Spanish-speaking children treated equally when schools require they learn English? Should monogamous

▶ **civil rights** The promise of equal treatment under the law, regardless of one's race, gender, ethnic group affiliation, sexual preference, or age.

▶ **political equality** Establishing political and legal rights on the basis of the individual, so that everyone has the same right to vote and is equal under the law. An alternative would be to grant political rights to elite individuals based on wealth or social standing.

▶ **equality of opportunity** One of several ways of understanding equality, this way values giving people comparable advantages for succeeding in life, regardless of the unequal outcomes that may result.

▶ **equality of outcome** One of several ways of understanding equality, this way values leveling the social and economic inequities among people, rather than attempting to give people comparable advantages for succeeding in life.

▶ **economic equality** A form of equality of outcome that values using government policy to minimize the economic disparities found in society.

▶ **social equality** A form of equality of outcome that values using government policy to minimize social class distinctions found in society.

homosexual relationships be treated the same as monogamous heterosexual relationships, with gays being allowed to marry? Should seniors be protected from discrimination by employers who may prefer to hire younger people?

In theory, most Americans would agree that everyone should have equal rights before the law and that all people should be treated with equal dignity. In practice, civil rights struggles are always controversial. People do not always accept the legitimacy of a group's grievances, and the aggrieved group's demands for a change in the political, economic, or social order can be perceived to cut against widely held beliefs about equality of outcome. This serves to make civil rights issues among the most heated—and important—controversies that government has to address.

13-3 Equal Protection

The key to civil rights in the United States is laid out in Part 1 of the Fourteenth Amendment, which says "No state shall . . . deny to any person within its jurisdiction the equal protection of the laws." The intent of this **equal protection clause** is that all laws should be applied evenly and without prejudice to all citizens. Note that it is not a mandate for equality of outcomes: The Constitution is silent on the matter of equal results. Rather, the Fourteenth Amendment makes a statement about equal treatment, that everyone is equal in the eyes of the law. This approach is consistent with the long-standing American value of equal opportunity, which is secured in part by equal application of the law.

Groups that have experienced discrimination have used the equal protection clause to rectify inequities. Most prominently, it has been used by African Americans to fight legalized segregation. The Fourteenth Amendment established full citizenship for former slaves while guaranteeing them equal protection of the law. It is one of a trio of post–Civil War amendments designed to give African Americans a legal basis for equal rights. The Thirteenth Amendment abolished slavery in the United States, and the Fifteenth Amendment gave African American males the right to vote.

We saw in Section 12-9a, "When Events Overturn the Court," how slaves prior to the Civil War were treated as property, and how the Supreme Court had affirmed the institution of slavery in the case of ***Dred Scott v. Sanford*** in 1857, just four years before the South seceded from the Union, and just five years before President Lincoln issued the Emancipation Proclamation of 1862, granting freedom to all slaves living in the states of the Confederacy. With the passage of the Thirteenth Amendment in 1865, a revolution in the legal status of African Americans had transpired over the course of eight wrenching years.

Note also how the Fourteenth Amendment says that no *state* shall deny equal protection of the laws to any of its citizens. Not trusting the states of the Confederacy to grant equal protection to freed slaves, the federal government retained the ability to impose the conditions of all three post–Civil War amendments on the states. This language, along with the Union victory in the Civil War, constituted a turning point in a key matter of **federalism** by settling the question of federal supremacy that had been one of the country's hottest political issues since the ratification of the Constitution.

13-4 Civil Rights and African Americans

The authors of the post–Civil War amendments were wise to distrust southern states to implement laws that defied the political culture of the region. Immediately following the Civil War, when Union troops occupied the South, they could impose terms for **Reconstruction** of the Union. Officials of the former Confederacy were initially barred from exercising political power, and could only sit by and watch as the first African Americans (see Figure 13-1) were elected to Congress as Republicans from such states as South Carolina, Mississippi, and Louisiana.

Southern whites did their best to strike back. In 1865, the **Ku Klux Klan** was established in Tennessee as a secret white supremacist organization that regarded freedom for African Americans as a threat to whites. For decades, white-hooded Klansmen would terrorize, torture, and kill blacks, sometimes freely, sometimes despite tepid federal efforts to stop the violence.[1] The Klan disbanded in 1871, only to reemerge in 1915.[2]

equal protection clause
The constitutional restriction against state laws that discriminate, as stated in the Fourteenth Amendment. The equal protection clause served as the legal basis for eliminating laws that permitted racial discrimination.

Dred Scott v. Sanford
The 1857 Supreme Court case that legalized slavery nationwide, while holding that people of color had no rights or protection under the Constitution. The ruling hastened the Civil War; it was subsequently overturned by constitutional amendment.

federalism The division of power between a sovereign federal government and sovereign state governments, which provides that some functions will be performed by the national government, some by the state governments, and some by both the national and state governments. As a feature designed to limit the strength of government, federalism works to decentralize power by creating dual levels of authority.

Reconstruction The period following the Civil War, from 1865 to 1877, during which Union troops occupied the South as states of the Confederacy were readmitted to the Union under conditions established in Washington.

Ku Klux Klan The secret white supremacist society that terrorized and killed African Americans for decades following the Civil War.

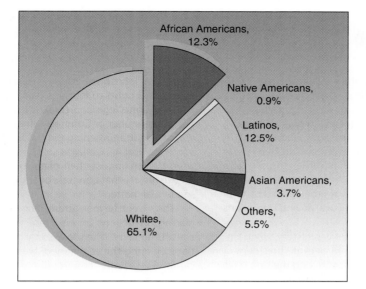

Figure 13-1
**African Americans
in the Population**
In 2000, about 12 of every
100 Americans were of African
American ancestry.

Source: Data from U.S. Census Bureau.

Also in 1865, a number of southern states implemented **"Black Codes"** designed to restrict the civil rights of emancipated slaves. Although the details varied, Black Codes attempted to reinstate the social order that had existed before the Civil War by regulating where African Americans could work, live, and travel, and by preventing them from owning or renting land or from working as anything but laborers.[3] Federal civil rights laws struck down the Black Codes in 1866,[4] but this did not change the fact that millions of newly freed men and women still lived in a white-dominated society that continued to regard them as property, and required their cheap, previously free labor to prop up a devastated economy. Box 13-1 discusses the Reconstruction of the South after the Civil War.

In 1876, the disputed election between Democrat Samuel Tilden and Republican Rutherford B. Hayes appeared to have put a Democrat in the White House for the first time since the start of Reconstruction. Tilden claimed an Electoral College majority, but results from several slates were challenged by Republicans. With the election in doubt, a compromise was hammered out in which Hayes would be given the presidency in exchange for the withdrawal of Union troops from the South. This marked the end of Reconstruction, and the start of a long period in which African Americans saw their civil rights taken away. As Reconstruction ended, the plight of African Americans faded as a political issue in the North. African American representation in Congress began to tail off.[5] Southern blacks were left with few viable avenues for the protection of their civil rights despite the constitutional protections that had been granted a decade earlier.

From this point on, African Americans in the South faced decades of disenfranchisement and institutionalized segregation at the hands of whites who never accepted the terms of Reconstruction. With the Union army and northern Republicans out of the way, repressive measures took hold. Institutionalized segregation in the form of **Jim Crow laws** made discrimination a way of life in the South. Box 13-2 tells who Jim Crow was.

Because you likely never experienced it, you may have trouble imagining just how total and repressive the Jim Crow laws were. Everything from the simplest everyday experiences like going to the park or using a public telephone, everything from birth to schooling to marriage to death was legally segregated. Table 13-1 on page 395 should give you a sense of how this segregation permeated society and denied African Americans their basic civil rights. As you read the table, try to imagine being an African American subjected to Jim Crow laws. Ask yourself what your life would have been like and how you would have felt about yourself if you acquiesced to these laws. There would have been enormous pressures on you to conform, sometimes life-threatening pressures—and a tremendous loss of dignity for doing so. Can you even imagine how you might have behaved?

By the start of the twentieth century, legal segregation so pervaded the South that separate public facilities from rest rooms to drinking fountains to public transportation

▶**Black Codes** An effort by white southerners immediately following the Civil War to restrict the civil rights of emancipated slaves. The codes were overturned by federal civil rights laws, only to become standard practice in the South following Reconstruction.

▶**Jim Crow laws** Laws in place in the South through the middle portion of the twentieth century that legalized segregation in virtually every facet of life.

Box 13-1 The Politics of Reconstruction

When Abraham Lincoln sought a second term as president in 1864, he looked ahead to the conclusion of the Civil War and the need to reconstruct a unified nation. With this in mind, Lincoln—a Republican—selected as his running mate Andrew Johnson, a southern Democrat who believed in states' rights. Johnson represented Tennessee in the Senate even after his state seceded, making him something of a hero to northerners. Even so, Lincoln's move was significant because Democrats at the time were regarded as the party of the South and secession, and Republicans viewed Democrats as the enemy in war.

In one of the great ironies of American history, when Lincoln was assassinated in 1865, Johnson became president of the United States, and the job of reconstructing the Union fell to this southern Democrat. Whatever sympathies he felt toward his home region came through in his approach to reconstruction, or at least were apparent to a Congress dominated by radical Republicans who objected to Johnson's offer of pardons to southerners willing to swear allegiance to the United States, and implementation of a reconstruction program while Congress was out of session.

Congress saw the rise of Black Codes across the South and the return of southern prewar political leaders as clear indica-tions that Johnson's program would undermine efforts to extend civil rights to former slaves. They quickly fought back, with civil rights legislation banning Black Codes, by refusing to seat any member of Congress who had joined the Confederacy, and by strengthening the Union's military presence in the South. Radical Republicans so dominated Congress that they were able to impose their plan over Johnson's veto, the first time in history that Congress overrode the president on a consequential matter.

They went further, attempting to hamstring Johnson by placing restrictions on his office that were of questionable constitutionality. When Johnson violated one of these restrictions by firing the secretary of war—a member of Johnson's cabinet—without congressional authorization, he was impeached by the House—another first—and tried in the Senate, where he was acquitted by one vote in 1868.[*] His anguished tenure in office ended shortly thereafter. Republicans regained the White House with the election of President Ulysses S. Grant, and did not relinquish it until 1885.

[*]See a full account of the Johnson biography at the White House website, http://www.whitehouse.gov/history/presidents/aj17.html.

Box 13-2 Who Was Jim Crow?

Jim Crow was a character from minstrel shows, performed by white entertainers who covered their faces in burnt cork and acted out demeaning stereotypes of African Americans, depicting them as childish and incompetent. By the Civil War, the Jim Crow character was an established part of American popular culture. The exact connection between the racist minstrel show character and the racist laws of the same name is a matter of historical dispute.[*]

[*]Ronald L. F. Davis, "Creating Jim Crow," at http://www.jimcrowhistory.org/history/creating.htm.

Plessy v. Ferguson The 1896 Supreme Court case that upheld racial segregation. It was reversed in 1954 in the case of *Brown v. Board of Education.*

waiting rooms were marked with "Colored Only" signs. As we know from Chapter 12, the Supreme Court had upheld this type of segregation in the 1896 case **Plessy v. Ferguson.** In some southern states, African Americans traveling by train were forced to sit in a separate "Jim Crow car." Interracial marriage was criminalized. Voting rights were taken away through high poll taxes, impossible literacy tests, and laws prohibiting grandchildren of slaves from voting. As a result of these barriers, the number of African Americans casting ballots in South Carolina and Georgia fell by half between 1880 and 1888.[6] Whatever thoughts African Americans may have had about standing up to these racist provisions were dispelled on the one hand through the debilitating effects of widespread illiteracy and poverty, and on the other hand by terrorist acts committed by white lynch mobs.[7]

Although it wasn't as institutionalized, overt, or brutal, color barriers existed nationwide. As industrialization transformed the country in the early twentieth century, manufacturing jobs prompted a mass migration of African Americans from the South to the North and Midwest. There, blacks met with a more subtle form of discrimination. They remained for the most part low-wage earners, confined to live in urban ghettos, often in poor or run-down housing. Job opportunities that held the promise of a better life were

| TABLE 13-1 | Life under Jim Crow Laws |

Subject	Restriction
Nurses	No person or corporation shall require any white female nurse to nurse in wards or rooms in hospitals, either public or private, in which Negro men are placed (Alabama).
Pool and billiard rooms	It shall be unlawful for a Negro and white person to play together or in company with each other at any game of pool or billiards (Alabama).
Barbers	No colored barber shall serve as a barber [to] white women or girls (Georgia).
Burial	The officer in charge shall not bury, or allow to be buried, any colored persons upon ground set apart or used for the burial of white persons (Georgia).
Amateur baseball	It shall be unlawful for any amateur white baseball team to play baseball on any vacant lot or baseball diamond within two blocks of a playground devoted to the Negro race, and it shall be unlawful for any amateur colored baseball team to play baseball in any vacant lot or baseball diamond within two blocks of any playground devoted to the white race (Georgia).
Textbooks	Books shall not be interchangeable between the white and colored schools, but shall continue to be used by the race first using them (North Carolina).
Child custody	It shall be unlawful for any parent, relative, or other white person in this State, having the control or custody of any white child, by right of guardianship, natural or acquired, or otherwise, to dispose of, give or surrender such white child permanently into the custody, control, maintenance, or support, of a Negro (South Carolina).
Buses	All passenger stations in this state operated by any motor transportation company shall have separate waiting rooms or space and separate ticket windows for the white and colored races (Alabama).
Intermarriage	The marriage of a person of Caucasian blood with a Negro, Mongolian, Malay, or Hindu shall be null and void (Arizona).
Parks	It shall be unlawful for colored people to frequent any park owned or maintained by the city for the benefit, use and enjoyment of white persons … and unlawful for any white person to frequent any park owned or maintained by the city for the use and benefit of colored persons (Georgia).
Housing	Any person … who shall rent any part of any such building to a Negro person or a Negro family when such building is already in whole or in part in occupancy by a white person or white family, or vice versa when the building is in occupancy by a Negro person or Negro family, shall be guilty of a misdemeanor and on conviction thereof shall be punished by a fine of not less than twenty-five ($25.00) nor more than one hundred ($100.00) dollars or be imprisoned not less than 10, or more than 60 days, or both such fine and imprisonment in the discretion of the court (Louisiana).
Promotion of equality	Any person … who shall be guilty of printing, publishing or circulating printed, typewritten or written matter urging or presenting for public acceptance or general information, arguments or suggestions in favor of social equality or of intermarriage between whites and Negroes, shall be guilty of a misdemeanor and subject to a fine not exceeding five hundred ($500.00) dollars or imprisonment not exceeding six (6) months or both (Mississippi).
Telephone booths	The Corporation Commission is hereby vested with power and authority to require telephone companies … to maintain separate booths for white and colored patrons when there is a demand for such separate booths. That the Corporation Commission shall determine the necessity for said separate booths only upon complaint of the people in the town and vicinity to be served after due hearing as now provided by law in other complaints filed with the Corporation Commission (Oklahoma).

Sources: Adapted from http://afroamhistory.about.com/cs/jimcrowlaws/.

not forthcoming. Social attitudes in many cities were not much different than they had been in the South.

13-4a The Civil Rights Movement

The Supreme Court ruling in *Brown v. Board of Education* (1954) declaring segregated schools unconstitutional, which we discussed in Chapter 12, foreshadowed one and a half decades of activism on behalf of African American civil rights. It would culminate in the elimination of Jim Crow laws, the triumph of federal over state power, and full implementation of the Fourteenth Amendment one hundred years after its passage. As with any wrenching social change, the human cost was great, both in lives of civil rights activists lost to assassins and lives shattered by riots that decimated African American neighborhoods from Harlem in New York to Watts in Los Angeles.

It started innocuously enough. One year after the *Brown* decision, a forty-two-year-old seamstress named Rosa Parks boarded a bus in Montgomery, Alabama, and sat in the first row of what was called the "Colored" section at the back of the bus. Montgomery's law required that blacks pay their fare at the front of the bus, then leave the bus, reboard in the rear, and sit in the back. If a white patron boarded when the "White" section was full, black passengers seated in the front of the "Colored" section were required to give up their seats and move further back. This happened to Rosa Parks: When a white passenger boarded the crowded bus, the white bus driver insisted that she relinquish her seat as required by law. She refused, and was arrested.

Rosa Parks had been locally active in the National Association for the Advancement of Colored Persons (NAACP), and knew the organization was looking for an opportunity to challenge Montgomery's segregation laws. She presented the organization with an ideal political symbol for the challenge: soft-spoken, demure, gainfully employed, happily married—in short, an utterly sympathetic figure to contrast the brutality of segregation. When Parks agreed to challenge the law, the NAACP immediately organized a boycott by African Americans of Montgomery buses, led by the minister of a local Baptist church, the Reverend Dr. Martin Luther King Jr. The boycott lasted for more than a year, until the Supreme Court ruled bus segregation unconstitutional in December 1956.[8] With that victory, the **civil rights movement** was born. A brief timeline emphasizing key events in the civil rights movement may be found in Table 13-2.

The actions undertaken by Dr. King and other prominent leaders on behalf of civil rights were nonviolent forms of **civil disobedience,** along the lines of Rosa Parks disobeying what she believed to be an illegitimate law. College students were heavily involved. The **Student Nonviolent Coordinating Committee (SNCC)** formed in 1960 and organized **"sit-ins"** at "Whites Only" lunch counters, where black students would simply sit down in seats reserved for whites, to focus national attention on segregated facilities. African Americans and sympathetic whites engaged in **"freedom rides"** throughout the South in 1961, where whites would take the seats at the back of the bus and use "Colored Only" facilities at highway rest stops, while African Americans sat up front and used "Whites Only" facilities.

These activities proved dangerous. Angry mobs attacked the demonstrators, often causing serious harm. Local authorities, sympathetic to the mobs, looked the other way, while local judicial officers sent protesters to prison. The actions of the demonstrators might have gone unnoticed if not for the fact that television, now a decade old and with national reach, was there to record the cruelty of segregation, broadcast it to the country, and help put pressure on the national government to act. Small victories began to pile up, like a 1961 order by the Kennedy Justice Department that outlawed discrimination on interstate buses that was issued in direct response to the treatment of the freedom riders.

As the stakes built, violence escalated. In 1963, civil rights leader Medgar Evers was assassinated. Dr. King organized peaceful demonstrations in Birmingham, Alabama, which were met with violence from angry white mobs. Four black girls attending Sunday School were murdered in the bombing of a Birmingham church. The first of many race riots began in African American sections of major cities, leaving urban centers in ruin for decades to come.

In 1964, SNCC, in conjunction with the NAACP and the largely white-run Congress of Racial Equality (CORE), organized "Freedom Summer," which centered on a voter registration drive in Mississippi to undermine the laws that prevented blacks from voting. White college students from the North were recruited to join southern blacks in a state where less than 7 percent of African Americans were registered to vote, the lowest percentage in the country. It drew an enormous amount of media attention, in part because

▶ civil rights movement
The organized, largely nonviolent, and widely successful efforts of the 1950s and 1960s to bring about social change on behalf of African Americans in the South, whose civil rights were denied by a century-old system of Jim Crow laws.

▶ civil disobedience
A peaceful means of protest whereby individuals draw attention to laws they consider unjust by disobeying them and being arrested for their actions.

▶ Student Nonviolent Coordinating Committee (SNCC) The organization that involved college students in acts of civil disobedience to advance the cause of civil rights for African Americans.

▶ sit-ins A type of civil disobedience popular with civil rights protesters that involved African Americans peacefully sitting at "Whites Only" lunch counters, to focus attention on the injustice of segregation policies.

▶ freedom rides A type of civil disobedience popular with civil rights protesters, where mixed-race groups of bus passengers would ride through the South and disobey laws on racially segregated travel, often at the expense of submitting to mob violence.

TABLE 13-2	**Civil Rights Timeline**

1954	School segregation is ruled unconstitutional in *Brown v. Board of Education* Supreme Court decision.
1955	Dr. Martin Luther King, Jr. leads boycotts against segregated transportation facilities after Rosa Parks defies Montgomery, Alabama, law requiring African Americans to sit at the back of public buses; bus segregation is eventually declared unconstitutional.
1957	President Eisenhower sends federal troops to Little Rock, after Governor Orval Faubus orders the Arkansas National Guard to block nine black students from integrating Central High School in Little Rock.
1960	African American students begin staging "sit-ins" at southern lunch counters that refuse to serve blacks.
1962	President Kennedy sends federal troops to the University of Mississippi to stop riots so that the first black student can attend; all military reserve units are integrated.
1963	Dr. Martin Luther King, Jr. delivers "I have a dream" speech to hundreds of thousands of civil rights protesters who have converged on Washington.
1964	Congress passes the Civil Rights Act following a 75-day long filibuster by southern senators; race riots erupt in New York and Philadelphia.
1965	Civil rights protesters march from Selma to Montgomery, Alabama, to demand voting rights; Congress passes the Voting Rights Act; race riots erupt in Los Angeles.
1968	Dr. Martin Luther King, Jr. is assassinated in Memphis.

Dr. Martin Luther King
Source: AP/Wide World Photos.

President Dwight D. Eisenhower
Source: Library of Congress.

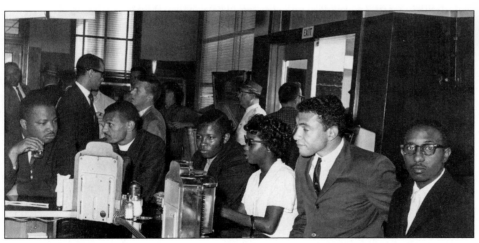

Sit-in at lunch counter
Source: AP/Wide World Photos.

Source: Adapted from CNN.com at http://www.cnn.com/EVENTS/1997/mlk/links.html.

the students were met with a violent response that resulted in over one thousand arrests, at least eighty beatings at the hands of white mobs or police officers, and three murders.[9]

Just as the civil rights movement was generating national sympathy, it was also beginning to fray. The political success of "Freedom Summer" masked racial tensions between black and white activists, as black workers were angered by what they felt was an attitude of superiority among white workers.[10] A radical faction of SNCC, angered at the violence they endured and what they felt was a slow rate of progress, rejected civil disobedience practices in exchange for confronting violence with violence. As the 1960s progressed, violence began to overtake peaceful resistance as a means for change. In 1968, the most visible advocate of peaceful social change, Dr. King, was assassinated in Memphis.

13-4b Legislative Success

Through it all, the civil rights movement realized stunning successes in the legislative arena that effectively ended segregation and stopped voting rights violations. Congress had considered—and failed to pass—civil rights legislation every year from 1945 to 1956. Then in 1957, in reaction to the changing climate of public opinion brought about by the civil rights movement, Congress passed the first civil rights bill in eighty years. The Civil Rights Act of 1957 was narrow in scope, establishing a federal Civil Rights Commission to hear complaints about voting irregularities. It was bolstered three years later by the Civil Rights Act of 1960, which prohibited states from destroying voter registration records.[11] In reality, complaints about voting irregularities took years to process and did not affect practices that disenfranchised African Americans, but these federal acts were valuable for what they presaged.

By 1964, political pressure largely generated by media coverage of the violent response to tactics of peaceful resistance served to bolster public support for legislation that only several years earlier would have been impossible to imagine moving through Congress. The fact that many Americans are naturally sympathetic to the notion of political equality was working to the long-term benefit of the protesters. A coalition of Republicans and non-southern Democrats fought an epic battle in the House and Senate on behalf of this legislation, culminating in a cloture vote that ended a two-month long Senate filibuster. The result was the landmark **Civil Rights Act of 1964,** which:

▶ **Civil Rights Act of 1964**
Landmark legislation arising from the civil rights movement that made racial discrimination a federal crime in the workplace and in public accommodations, while giving the federal government greater power to strengthen voting rights and desegregate public schools.

- Outlawed discrimination in restaurants, hotels, motels, and all public accommodations involved in interstate commerce
- Outlawed discrimination in hiring by businesses employing more than twenty-five people (serving as the basis for the affirmative action policies we'll talk about soon)
- Established the Equal Employment Opportunity Commission (EEOC) to hear complaints about workplace discrimination
- Undermined practices designed to disenfranchise African Americans by mandating the equal application of voter registration requirements
- Authorized withdrawing federal funds from institutions that practiced discriminatory policies
- Authorized the Attorney General to file suit when necessary to desegregate public schools[12]

Although the law was not all encompassing—for instance, it still permitted discrimination in private clubs—it was sweeping in scope and represented a profound political transformation in the area of civil rights. For the first time since Reconstruction, the federal government took an active role against discriminatory policies aimed at African Americans. A sympathetic Supreme Court upheld the legislation. Jim Crow could be heard in the distance, gasping for air.

▶ **Voting Rights Act of 1965**
Landmark legislation arising from the civil rights movement that gave federal officials the power to oversee election practices in southern states where Jim Crow laws disenfranchised African American voters.

The following year, when Congress passed the **Voting Rights Act of 1965,** Jim Crow was effectively dead. By providing for direct federal intervention in state voting and registration procedures, the Voting Rights Act put an end to requirements that disenfranchised African Americans. Specifically, the law empowered the attorney general to send inspectors to supervise voter registration in states that required literacy tests and where less than 50 percent of qualified residents had registered or voted in 1964. By authorizing inspections instead of permitting voters with a complaint to file suit, as had been the case in previous civil rights legislation, the effects were immediate and dramatic.[13]

As with the Civil Rights Act of 1964, the success of the Voting Rights Act could be measured in the rapid changes it brought about. African American voter registration increased markedly. For the first time since Reconstruction, African Americans were returning to Congress and being elected to other offices, in the South and elsewhere. In 1966, Edward Brooke of Massachusetts became the first African American senator in eighty-five years. In 1967, Carl Stokes of Cleveland became the first African American mayor of a major U.S. city; six years later, when Maynard Jackson became the mayor of Atlanta, he became the first African American to lead a southern city.[14] In 1971, there were enough African Americans in the House of Representatives to establish the Congressional Black Caucus, which coordinates the legislative strategy of black members.[15] The first African American governor, Douglas Wilder, was elected in 1989 in Virginia, the state that once housed the capital of the Confederacy.[16]

13-4c Affirmative Action

Although Jim Crow laws have been buried for so long that you may not have been familiar with the term before encountering it in school, today's civil rights advocates charge that the legacy of Jim Crow lingers in unequal access by African Americans to high-quality education, high-paying jobs, and affordable housing. From this perspective, although the turbulence of the 1950s and 1960s is long behind us, Dr. King's dream of a color-blind America remains beyond our grasp. As unequal treatment of African Americans became less blatant than it was during the time of Jim Crow, and as the black civil rights agenda turned from advancing equality of opportunity to equality of outcome, American public opinion began to divide over the remedies to present-day injustices, making contemporary solutions to discriminatory practices highly controversial.

Perhaps no civil rights policy is more controversial than **affirmative action,** which attempts to remedy inequities produced by long-term patterns of discrimination. In Issue Box 13-1, you'll have an opportunity to read about affirmative action policies, and see what supporters and opponents say about them. If you're using the Online Edition, you'll also be able to register your opinion about affirmative action.

As you read through the final four chapters of the book, you'll be presented with eighteen issues like affirmative action—all controversial, all the subject of ongoing debate, all central to the question of what kind of country America should be. At each turn, you'll have an opportunity to read about the issue and decide what your opinion about it is. Some issues deal with civil rights and civil liberties, others with domestic policy and international relations. Together, your opinions about these issues will provide you with a sense of what values you would like to see applied to policy decisions.

In the end, you'll have a chance to decide, once all eighteen controversial issues are considered, whether you feel you'd like to participate in politics in some fashion, or whether you're content to stand aside and let others wage battles for the kind of America they want to see.

> ▶**affirmative action** Federal policies requiring employers to address inequities in hiring and advancement if they appear to unfairly treat disadvantaged groups on the basis of race, religion, gender, national origin, sexual preference, physical disabilities, or Vietnam veteran status.

13-5 Civil Rights and Native Americans

If the civil rights situation of African Americans is distinctive because they were the only immigrant group brought to North America involuntarily, the civil rights situation of Native Americans (see Figure 13-2 on page 402) is unique because of their presence in North America prior to its colonization by European settlers. Before there were states or colonies, there were Native American tribes operating on their own governing principles with a well-established system of rights. When western political structures were superimposed on the territories inhabited by Native Americans, conflict erupted between two sets of values.

Issue Box 13-1 *Affirmative Action*

History and Background

Consider two brief stories:

The first is about a man named Anthony Romero, director of the Ford Foundation's Human Rights and International Cooperation Program, where he is responsible for administering millions of dollars of grant money. His position is light-years removed from his childhood home in a crime-ridden Bronx neighborhood, where an entire family was murdered in the next apartment, his parents would not permit him to play outside out of fear for his safety, and winter nights were spent wearing a hat and gloves because his family's apartment lacked heat and hot water.

By the time he reached high school, Romero's family had scraped together enough money to move to a working-class New Jersey community, trading in a life of crime and poverty for a life of rejection by their white neighbors. Romero responded to feelings of marginalization by throwing himself into his studies, proving his ability to himself and to anyone who cared to notice—including, it turned out, some of the most exclusive universities in the country. He never could have afforded to attend any of them on his family's income, but because he identified himself as "Puerto Rican" on the PSAT application, he was eligible for financial aid and heavily recruited by Ivy League institutions. That's how he was able to attend Princeton and take the first step toward his position at the Ford Foundation.[*]

The second story is about a manager, whom we'll call Alvin, at a utility company. As in many companies, most managers and 85 percent of the employees are white. Alvin has been employed at the company for fifteen years and has an excellent record. In fact, five years ago he received the best performance review in the company. But he's lost out for a promotion he had been expecting to someone who got weaker reviews from his subordinates, despite getting a better review from his superiors—a fact Alvin freely admits. But when he looks at the whole performance picture, Alvin wonders if there isn't something disturbing going on. The person who received the promotion is white. Alvin is African American. He feels the company is racist.[†]

The first story argues for the benefits of affirmative action. The second illustrates what critics say is the psychology of affirmative action gone awry.

Affirmative action is a policy requiring employers to address racial, ethnic, or gender inequalities by ensuring equal opportunities for employment and advancement.[‡] It has been a matter of law since passage of the Civil Rights Act of 1964, which allowed the judiciary to battle discrimination by ordering "such affirmative action as may be appropriate." The following year, President Lyndon Johnson vastly expanded that mandate with an executive order requiring all employers who do more than minimal business with the federal government to apply affirmative action principles.[§]

Originally designed to address past discrimination against racial minority groups, affirmative action has been expanded over the years to include women, people with disabilities, gays, and Vietnam veterans. As affirmative action policies have grown to include more individuals, so have the methods of

Source: AP/Wide World Photos.

implementing them. Under the law, affirmative action requires that there be no artificial barriers to the hiring and advancement of people in the targeted groups, and that if employers underutilize group members they have to take steps to remedy the situation. In practice, affirmative action policies can range from relatively uncontroversial activities like minority recruitment to more explosive approaches like preferential hiring of underrepresented group members and targeted hiring of minority individuals, where a position is advertised for someone in a particular group.[**]

All of these methods aim to address the same objective—correcting past discriminatory practices—but they cover the spectrum from offering equality of opportunity to historically disadvantaged groups (through recruitment procedures, for instance) to compensating for past inequalities with the promise of equal outcomes (preferential hiring). That's where affirmative action is most controversial—when group characteristics are placed ahead of individual talent and ability—because it conflicts with the long-standing American preference for favoring opportunity over outcomes.

The Supreme Court took up the controversy in the 1978 case ***Regents of the University of California v. Bakke.*** The University of California at Davis medical school denied admission to a white applicant while accepting less well qualified minority applicants under a program that set aside a specific number of slots for members of traditionally disadvantaged groups. Bakke, the white student, claimed the policy itself was discriminatory and the Court agreed, backing away from unqualified support of affirmative action policies while upholding the constitutionality of using race as a factor (just not *the* factor) in college admissions.[††]

Since the *Bakke* decision, the debate over affirmative action has simply grown more heated. In 2003, the Supreme Court once again upheld the right of universities to consider an applicant's race in making admissions decisions for the purpose of advancing campus diversity, through a close vote in twin cases involving admissions procedures at the University of Michigan. In *Gratz v. Bollinger*, two white applicants rejected by the University of Michigan despite having been deemed qualified for admission sued the school, claiming its use of racial preferences in making admissions decisions violated the Fourteenth Amendment's equal protection clause. The university countered by pointing to the *Bakke* decision, claiming its admissions procedures included consideration of race in an effort to promote racial diversity on campus.[‡‡] In *Grutter v. Bollinger,* a white applicant rejected by the University of Michigan law school filed a similar claim to the one made in the *Gratz* case, asserting that she had been turned aside because of an application process that treated race as a "predominant" factor in admissions, giving minority applicants an unfair advantage over equally qualified white applicants.[§§]

The Court narrowly reaffirmed that race can be used as a criterion in admissions decisions in the interest of achieving diversity on campus. By a 5–4 vote, it upheld the flexible procedures used by the University of Michigan law school, which considered race as one of a number of "soft" criteria for admission, along with other "soft" criteria like an applicant's letters of recommendation and personal statement. However, it overturned the approach used by the university to admit undergraduates, which consisted of assigning a fixed number of points to applicants who are members of underrepresented minority groups. The Court in essence said that the government has an interest in assuring that universities achieve racial diversity, and because of this race can be considered in the admissions process, but only if consideration is given in a way that's narrowly structured to achieve diversity.

Divisions in the Court reflect divisions in society about affirmative action. Although opponents of affirmative action may still claim a commitment to redressing racist and sexist policies of the past, that's not how it's always viewed by supporters. While supporters may argue that affirmative action is not about favoritism or quotas, that's not how opponents always see it.

Arguments in Support

A lot of arguments have been offered in support of affirmative action policies. Some of the more prevalent ones are:

- It's fair. Americans chafe against inequity, and affirmative action policies correct a long history of discrimination.
- It works. Affirmative action policies have brought people from historically disadvantaged groups into the workforce and have made a difference in countless individual lives.
- It's needed. All the civil rights advances of the late twentieth century have failed to end discrimination.
- It's inclusive. Affirmative action promotes a cultural pluralism that's long been the American antidote to prejudice and discrimination.
- It promotes opportunity. Without affirmative action, many qualified individuals would still face employment barriers, just as women and minorities still face issues of wage equity with white men.
- It's comprehensive. Affirmative action addresses a wide range of discrimination against a host of minority groups.

Arguments Against

There are probably as many arguments against affirmative action policies as there are arguments in support of them. Some of the more prevalent ones are:

- It's unfair. Even though people have long been discriminated against because of group membership, correcting the situation with policies based on group membership is equally discriminatory.

- It stigmatizes. People who get jobs via affirmative action have to live with the fact that ability alone did not get them where they are, and that coworkers might regard them as less qualified.
- It's misguided. You cannot pretend to pursue the goals of a color-blind society with policies that use skin color or gender as a litmus test for opportunity.
- It's divisive. Keying hiring practices to group membership perpetuates differential treatment and resentment.
- It rewards mediocrity. Invariably, the pursuit of diversity will result in some number of less qualified individuals advancing ahead of more qualified individuals.
- It's arbitrary. The issue of who is deserving of affirmative action and even who is a member of a disadvantaged group is open to debate.

My Opinion

When considering your opinion on affirmative action, consider the history of the issue and the arguments supporting and opposing it. In particular, ask yourself if affirmative action:

- Is fair or unfair
- Works effectively or stigmatizes people
- Is needed or misguided
- Is inclusive or divisive
- Promotes opportunity or rewards mediocrity
- Is comprehensive or arbitrary

Then register your opinion to the question that follows. Keep track of your opinions on this and other controversial issues, and they will provide you with a roadmap to the kind of nation you'd like the United States to be.

The most accurate description of my attitude toward affirmative action is:

1—I strongly support it. It's a good idea.
2—I support it, but with some reservations.
3—I oppose it, but with some reservations.
4—I strongly oppose it. It's a bad idea.
5—I haven't thought enough about it to have an opinion.
6—I don't care about it enough to bother.

▶ *Regents of the University of California v. Bakke* The 1978 Supreme Court case that marked a reversal in unlimited support for affirmative action policies by backing the claim of discrimination by a white University of California medical school who was denied admission in favor of less well qualified minority applicants.

[*]Charles R. Lawrence III and Mari J. Matsuda, *We Won't Go Back: Making the Case for Affirmative Action.* New York: Houghton Mifflin Company, 1997.

[†]Richard F. Thomasson, Faye J. Crosby, and Sharon D. Herzberger, *Affirmative Action: The Pros and Cons of Policy and Practice* (Washington, DC: American University Press, 1996), 5–6. The first story in this section is true; the second story is fictional.

[‡]Ibid., 11–12.

[§]Ibid., 12.

[**]Ibid., 12–15 and 135–136.

[††]Ibid., 18–19.

[‡‡]*Gratz v. Bollinger* 539 US 244 (2003).

[§§]*Grutter v. Bollinger* 539 US 306 (2003).

Figure 13-2
Native Americans in the Population
In 2000, fewer than 1 in 100 Americans were of Native American heritage.

Source: Data from U.S. Census Bureau.

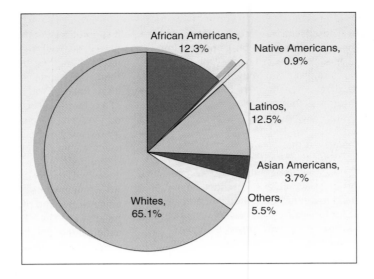

For centuries, the flashpoint for hostility and tension has been the lack of respect and recognition accorded the rights of Native Americans by the federal government. The most basic right that was abridged was tribal sovereignty, or the right of Native American tribes to self-government. Colonial settlers sharply limited tribal sovereignty so that it applied only to internal matters, subjugating tribal autonomy over land rights and affairs with other nations to the will of the colonists and later to the federal government. In many cases, settlers acquired land through treaties that left only hunting and fishing rights to native tribes, in exchange for a promise of protection by settlers that ultimately left once-autonomous Native American nations as wards of the United States. Today, some members of existing tribes practice self-rule on lands set aside by the federal government, and at the same time are subject to the laws and practices of the United States as American citizens.[17] That arrangement was generations in the making.

13-5a Early Policies: Containment and Relocation

The original policy of the American government toward native tribes was to contain them on undeveloped land. It was often implemented violently. In 1830, Congress passed the controversial **Indian Removal Act,** which called for relocating Native American tribes situated east of the Mississippi so that American expansion could continue unabated into that territory. Under the terms of the act, any Native Americans remaining on their land would be forced to leave their tribal nation to become citizens of the state in which they resided. Some moved willingly and some assimilated, although Native Americans who decided to remain sometimes found themselves cheated out of their land by white settlers.

> **Indian Removal Act**
> Legislation passed in 1830 that led to the forced and sometimes violent transfer of Native American nations to areas west of the Mississippi River.

Others resisted and were forced to move or go to war with the United States. Three Seminole wars were fought between 1817 and 1858 over the issue of relocation (fugitive slaves who had been given refuge by the Seminoles fought alongside them in the first two). Ultimately, the Seminoles were killed, driven out, or paid to leave.[18]

In 1836, the Cherokee were given two years to leave their homes in Georgia or face forced relocation. The Supreme Court, in the case of *Worcester v. Georgia* (1832), actually recognized the Cherokee as a sovereign nation, but President Jackson (as we previously learned in Section 12-3, "Judicial Review") had no regard for the decision and negotiated a removal treaty with a small faction of Cherokee, then used it as the legal basis for evicting the entire tribe.

> **"Trail of Tears"** A one-thousand-mile forced march of Cherokee men, women, and children carried out in 1838 to satisfy a federal relocation policy.

The 17,000 Cherokee who wished to remain in their homeland were compelled to leave at gunpoint by American troops as whites looted their belongings. On their forced march west, four thousand Cherokee men, women, and children died of illness and exposure along what became known to Native Americans as the **"Trail of Tears."**[19]

Many whites in the early nineteenth century felt that relocation would resolve territorial issues with Native Americans because they believed the United States would never expand beyond the Mississippi River. Once it did, the idea of separate nations was no longer viable, and national policy embraced reclaiming or dividing up reserved lands in the West and doing battle with Native American tribes.

13-5b Later Policies: "Civilizing" and Assimilating

In the 1890s, the government initiated an effort to "civilize" Native Americans as a means of incorporating them into white Christian society. Children were forced to attend boarding schools where their hair was cut short, they were given Anglo-American clothes, and they were required to speak English. This approach culminated in passage of the **Citizenship Act of 1924,** which made all Native Americans born on American soil citizens of the United States. Passage of the Citizenship Act gave Native Americans rights they lacked before, like the right to vote (a western concept, which not every state honored), but it was really a means of forcing assimilation, viewed by some Native Americans as another step toward undermining the sovereignty of native peoples.[20]

These efforts at assimilation largely failed. Generations of exploitation had left many Native Americans with deplorable living conditions. Poverty, malnourishment, and disease were rampant on reserved lands. In 1934, Congress tried to address this with the passage of the Indian Reorganization Act, which aimed at restoring traditional languages and practices in an effort to reverse the deleterious effects of forced relocation and forced assimilation.

▶**Citizenship Act of 1924**
An effort to assimilate Native Americans into white culture and society through the granting of American citizenship.

13-5c 1960s and 1970s Activism

By the late 1960s, a growing social awareness of civil rights issues gave rise to the "Red Power" movement: waves of activism designed to call attention to discrimination against Native Americans. In 1969, protesters landed on Alcatraz Island in San Francisco Bay and occupied it for nineteen months in a symbolic reclamation of lost native lands. In the decade that followed, activists occupied scores of other federal facilities, including a sit-in at Mount Rushmore, to bring attention to the political and social plight of Native Americans.[21] In 1973, armed members of the American Indian movement staged a seventy-one-day siege at Wounded Knee, South Dakota, the scene of a Sioux massacre eighty-three years earlier.

Native American civil rights activists successfully trained public attention on the long history of discriminatory practices that many white Americans would like to ignore because it is so uncomfortable to acknowledge. In some respects, their work brought about improvements in the status of Native American rights. For instance, while remaining subject to the jurisdiction of the United States government, the Indian Civil Rights Act of 1968 extended to tribal governing bodies the protections granted in the Bill of Rights. Courts upheld the continued legal force of century-old treaties, interpreting ambiguities in a way that favored Native American interests. In 1992, Colorado elected the first Native American to the U.S. Senate: Ben Nighthorse Campbell, who is also a Chief of the northern Cheyenne tribe.[22]

During this period, the courts also began to recognize tribal sovereignty and the right of self-government on reserved lands,[23] including freedom from some state hunting and fishing regulations and special water rights.[24] Exemptions from state gaming regulations have in recent years provided an important (albeit controversial) source of revenue for over two hundred Native American tribes operating casinos and gambling ventures on reserved lands.[25]

Gambling has been an economic windfall for increasing numbers of Native American tribes, although it can hardly be considered a panacea for centuries of civil rights abuses. Poverty, unemployment, and alcoholism are still huge problems in many Native American communities, which bear little resemblance to the stable and thriving civilizations that Europeans encountered when they arrived in North America. Also, notwithstanding protests like Alcatraz and Wounded Knee that attract the national press, the concerns of Native Americans remain relatively low on the national civil rights agenda.

Figure 13-3

Latinos in the Population
As the largest minority group, Latinos constituted 12.5 percent of the American population in 2000.

Source: Data from U.S. Census Bureau.

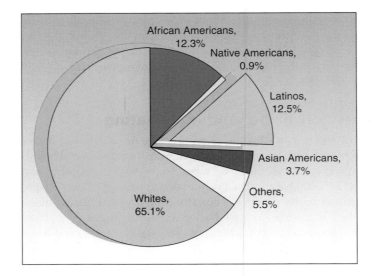

13-6 Civil Rights and Hispanic Americans

Hispanic Americans, or Latinos, are the largest minority group in the United States (see Figure 13-3). Hailing from places as diverse as Mexico, Cuba, Puerto Rico, the Caribbean, and Central America, Hispanic Americans share a Spanish-speaking heritage even though the paths that brought them to the United States are quite varied. Figure 13-4 illustrates the diverse migration patterns of Hispanic groups in the United States. Mexican Americans, for instance, are most likely to have moved to the Southwest, notably California and Texas, and are likely to have come to the United States seeking economic opportunity. Cuban Americans are concentrated in southern Florida, where many arrived seeking political freedom following Fidel Castro's rise to power during the Cuban communist revolution of 1959. Large Puerto Rican communities may be found in the big cities of the Northeast, notably New York. Puerto Ricans hold U.S. citizenship because Puerto Rico is a self-governing commonwealth (it has an elected governor and legislature and its residents participate in federal programs like Social Security and welfare, but it is not represented in Congress or the Electoral College).

Figure 13-4

Where Latinos Have Settled
This map illustrates the diverse migration patterns of Hispanic groups in the United States. The shaded states have the largest Latino communities. The percentages shown indicate the percentage of Latinos in that state's population.

Source: Data from U.S. Census Bureau, 2000 Census.

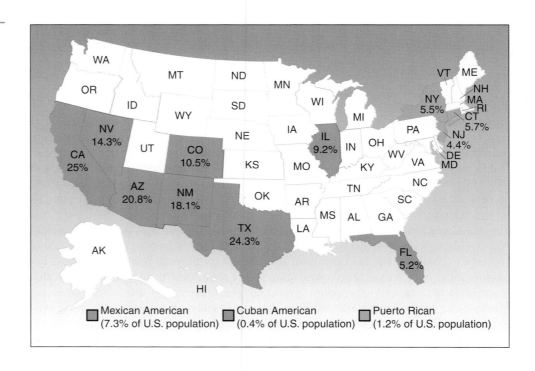

Latinos are also a diverse group economically and politically. Cuban Americans are more likely to be better educated and better off financially, and are more likely than other Hispanic groups to be Republicans. Many Mexican Americans are agricultural workers and, along with Puerto Ricans, experience a higher rate of poverty than the population as a whole.

13-6a Political Struggles and Victories

Although these differences point to a diversity of experiences among Latino groups, discrimination against Hispanic Americans has been a widespread phenomenon. Many Hispanics are Caucasian, but dark skin, Spanish surnames, and a language difference have through the years been a source of discrimination in educational and work opportunities. Widespread illegal immigration by Mexican Americans is an ongoing source of harassment and discrimination toward Latino citizens by resentful Anglos living in areas with large Hispanic American populations. Parents of Latino schoolchildren have been confronted with demands for proof of U.S. citizenship by school officials, a form of discrimination that can dissuade them from enrolling their children in school.[26]

The general public first became aware of these abuses during the civil rights movements of the 1960s, when Hispanic Americans organized for political action. The National Council of La Raza was established in 1968 as an advocacy group to reduce poverty and end discrimination against Latino groups.[27] Union organizer Cesar Chavez fought a lifelong battle against discrimination toward Mexican American laborers that gained national prominence during this time (see Box 13-3).

Workplace discrimination against Latinos continues to be an issue. In 2003, the Mexican American Legal Defense and Education Fund and the Equal Employment Opportunity Commission filed suit against a Texas ductworks factory for segregating Mexican American workers into a department where the wages were less and the working conditions far more dangerous than in other departments. When the workers tried to strike, the company moved against them and attempted to have them fired, only to back off in the face of political pressure.

Latinos have made advances in the political arena in recent years, and this offers the promise of helping to address ongoing discrimination. Republicans and Democrats recognize that by virtue of their rapidly growing numbers, Latinos could one day soon be a decisive political force, and both parties have been reaching out for their allegiance. It's not by chance that President Bush peppered his campaign speeches with liberal amounts of Spanish in parts of Texas, California, and Florida.

Recent years have brought some political milestones. In 2002, both major parties nominated Latino gubernatorial candidates in New Mexico, with the Democrat, former Clinton Energy Secretary Bill Richardson, defeating state representative John Sanchez. In Texas, businessman Tony Sanchez received the active backing of the Democratic Party in his primary campaign for governor because of the expectation that he could mobilize Hispanic voters in a Republican-leaning state. Sanchez lost to popular Republican Governor Rick Perry, but political commentators widely regarded the support he got from establishment Democrats as a harbinger of things to come, as both parties aggressively seek the support of Latino voters.

13-6b Bilingual Education

Because language skills are critical to educational achievement, Hispanic Americans have faced roadblocks to advancement in cases where they speak little or no English. One approach to the language barrier is bilingual education, where classroom learning is conducted in English and Spanish. The rationale for bilingual education is that students who do not comprehend the language of instruction will quickly fall behind in the development of academic skills and are more likely to drop out of school, keeping them trapped in poverty or retarding the economic advancement that education makes possible.

Legally, bilingual education is a permissible alternative when English is a second language because the courts have determined that the circumstances fall under the equal protection umbrella. In the Supreme Court case *Lau v. Nichols* (1974), school districts were

Box 13-3   Cesar Chavez and the United Farm Workers

Agribusiness is vital to California's economy, and for years vegetable and grape growers relied heavily on itinerant Mexican American labor, paying them dirt wages and forcing them to live in deplorable conditions. In 1965, typical Latino farm workers were paid ninety cents an hour and charged by their employers to live in shacks with no plumbing or cooking facilities. Child labor was commonplace. Dangerous conditions led to injury and death. The average life expectancy of a Latino farm laborer was forty-nine years.[*] Despite laws against these conditions, the plight of Hispanic agricultural workers did not register on the national political agenda.

This changed because of the work of Cesar Chavez, a former itinerant worker who painstakingly organized the first union for Hispanic American laborers, the United Farm Workers (UFW). Inspired by the success of the African American civil rights movement, Chavez used nonviolent techniques like hunger strikes and boycotts to focus media attention on the working conditions of Mexican American agricultural workers and to put economic pressure on the businesses that exploited their labor. From the union's inception in 1962 until his death in 1993, Chavez effected social change by successfully raising levels of public awareness about how Latinos were being treated in order to force employers to enter into labor agreements with the union. At the height of the UFW's success between 1973 and 1975, millions of Americans participated in a boycott against Gallo wine for its continued use of nonunion labor.[†]

[*]See the United Farm Workers website at http://www.ufw.org.
[†]Ibid.

---

ordered to accommodate the needs of non-English speaking students in order to assure equal access to educational opportunities. This permitted bilingual teaching, but it did not mandate it.[28]

Bilingual education is a controversial solution, even among Latinos. Some oppose it because they fear it will have the opposite effect to what advocates contend: that students schooled in Spanish and English will simply not learn English the way they would in an all-English environment. Some Anglos oppose it for the same reason, although often in the belief that Hispanic Americans should learn the dominant language of the United States on their own and without what seems like special consideration. This gives the debate over bilingual education a sharp edge because it plays on the emotional issues of assimilation and cultural heritage.

13-7 Civil Rights and Asian Americans

As we saw in Chapter 4, Asian Americans are the fastest growing minority group in the United States (see Figure 13-5). Particularly in the states of the Pacific Rim, the number of Americans of Japanese, Chinese, Vietnamese, and Filipino heritage, among others, has been growing in large numbers. In 2000, 10.9 percent of California's population was of Asian origin, as was 5.5 percent of the population of Washington state (in Hawaii, which as a chain of Pacific islands has always had a large population of Asian Americans, the figure was 41.5 percent).[29] Asian Americans, many well off and politically active, have been able to exercise influence in these regions. When Gary Locke was elected governor of the state of Washington in 1996 he became the first Chinese American governor and the only governor of Asian descent in the United States.

Still, Asian Americans have faced a long history of discrimination in housing, employment, and education at the hands of Caucasians. The most notorious incident was the forced internment of Americans of Japanese descent into "relocation camps" around the country during World War II. The official rationale for rounding up American citizens who showed no loyalty to Japan was to defend against Japanese spying, which was widely feared by American military leaders and ordinary citizens. To Asian Americans, forced relocation was a racist policy. The United States was also at war with Germany and Italy, but American citizens with these European origins were not targeted for removal.

The action appeared to violate the equal protection of Japanese Americans because it was based on a racial classification. In fact, the Supreme Court has been fairly consistent about striking down laws based on group categories as violations of the civil rights of the

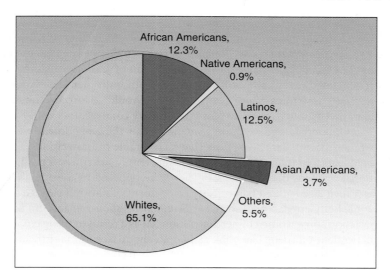

Figure 13-5
Asian Americans in the Population
The fastest growing minority group, Asian Americans constituted 3.7 percent of the American population in 2000.

Source: Data from U.S. Census Bureau.

group singled out for differential treatment. This case was the exception, however. In *Korematsu v. United States* (1944), the Court held that the "military urgency" of the situation justified permitting Congress and the president to use their war powers to justify the relocation.[30] Essentially, because the nation was at war, security arguments bested equal protection arguments. Today, many Americans look back at the government's policy toward Japanese Americans during World War II and regard it as one of the more shameful moments in the nation's history.

13-8 Gender Issues

Imagine that you didn't have the right to vote. You owned some property, but once you got married, control over that property shifted to your husband. If you were fortunate enough to hold a job and earn a salary, chances are it was at a fraction of the pay that a man would earn, and your husband would control that income, too. The larger society believed that you did not have the capability or the right to engage in meaningful work outside the home, and that the proper (or divinely directed) order of things required that you have the protection and guidance of a man, who in turn controlled every significant aspect of your life.

Woman faced these circumstances well into the nineteenth century. Although women were afforded more rights and social standing than slaves, there were enough parallels between the relationship of slave to master and woman to man that it may not be surprising that the original women's rights movement was born of the antislavery movement. When the Civil War ended and the Fifteenth Amendment extended voting rights to freed slaves but not to women, a separate women's rights movement emerged. Through writing, speaking, petitioning, and tireless organizational work, Susan B. Anthony was instrumental in convincing New York State to extend property rights to married women in 1860. In 1869, abolitionists Elizabeth Cady Stanton and Lucretia Mott formed the National Woman Suffrage Association. The right to vote, however, was not extended to women nationwide until the Nineteenth Amendment was adopted in 1920.

13-8a The Equal Rights Amendment

Securing voting rights did not translate into equal rights for women, who faced social and legal obstacles to full equality under the law. Women's rights advocates turned their attention to full constitutional protection for women's civil rights by attempting to win passage of an **Equal Rights Amendment (ERA).** In so doing, women's rights advocates shifted their agenda from political to social and economic equality, introducing a new degree of controversy as their objectives moved from equal opportunity to equal outcomes.

▶**Equal Rights Amendment (ERA)** A proposed constitutional amendment assuring equal rights for women that was first introduced in Congress in 1923, approved by Congress in 1972, and fell three states short of ratification in 1982.

First introduced in Congress in 1923, the ERA was reintroduced every year since, until it was finally approved during the period of civil rights activism in 1972.[31] The Equal Rights Amendment reads: "Equality of rights under the law shall not be denied or abridged by the United States or by any state on account of sex." This is simple enough language, but it generated remarkably stiff opposition from both men and women and therefore took decades to attract mainstream support. Would divorced women lose their right to alimony? Would women be sent into military combat?

Opponents said yes, and contended that the amendment was unnecessary because women's rights were being protected by favorable court decisions. They tapped into widely held fears that the ERA would undermine family structures, a position advocated by traditional religious organizations.[32] They were opposed by a women's rights movement that was revitalized after a half century of dormancy following passage of women's suffrage. In 1963, Betty Friedan published *The Feminine Mystique,* an account of emptiness and dissatisfaction some women of her generation felt as a result of being emotionally and financially dependent on men. The book caused an about-face in mainstream thinking about traditional values and women's roles at a time when civil rights activism was on the rise. In 1966, the **National Organization for Women (NOW)** was formed to advocate for women's equality, and became an influential force for passage of the Equal Rights Amendment.

▶ **National Organization for Women (NOW)** The largest women's rights organization in the United States, which has been an active force for advancing social and economic equality for women.

Congress gave the ERA a seven-year window for ratification, and extended it in 1979 by three years. During that period, the political climate changed dramatically. Ronald Reagan was elected president on a platform that opposed the ERA, and opposition lobbying efforts had taken hold in the few states that had not ratified the amendment, many of which were in the culturally traditional South. When 1982 ended, the ERA was three states short of the three-quarters necessary for ratification. Proponents have tried to keep it alive by introducing it in states that failed to ratify, prepared to challenge the time limit imposed by Congress should three of them sign on. They face an uphill battle in today's conservative political climate.

That said, NOW has a long record of successful activism. It has been behind legal changes protecting women from sexual harassment and discrimination, encouraged unprecedented numbers of female candidates to seek public office, strived to improve conditions for women in the workplace, and promoted equal opportunity for women and men in campus athletics and education (see Box 13-4).

13-8b　Sexual Violence and Harassment

One NOW-affiliated activity with which you may be familiar is the Take Back the Night march. These rallies are held periodically across the country and on many college campuses to draw attention to the issue of violence against women.[33] The issue has also been the subject of legislative action. The 1994 Violence Against Women Act provides for federal penalties for sex crimes and for federal assistance to reduce violent crimes against women and to curb domestic violence.

The political system has also responded to long-standing complaints by women about sexual harassment in the workplace. The U.S. Supreme Court has determined workplace harassment to be a form of discrimination and, as such, it is prohibited by the Civil Rights Act of 1964. It has established that a "hostile and abusive" work environment should be the standard for determining whether sexual harassment exists. Although this standard is to be applied with reason, so that any sensible observer would perceive that a hostile environment exists, determining the presence of sexual harassment in the workplace has been a complex matter subject at times to widely varying perceptions of what qualifies as abusive. This has caused the issue to be hotly debated, and has precipitated an ongoing and evolving public dialogue about how coworkers and subordinates should be treated in the workplace.

13-8c　Workplace Rights

Harassment on the job is one of a cluster of work-related women's rights issues to occupy a central place on the recent political agenda. Although the 1964 Civil Rights Act forbids gender discrimination in hiring, firing, and promoting workers, practical barriers to this objective still exist. Under the law, companies have to demonstrate a compelling business

Box 13-4   Universities and Title IX

The federal government has taken action in matters of sex discrimination on campus. Title IX of the Education Amendments of 1972 (commonly referred to simply as "Title IX") prohibits gender discrimination in education programs receiving federal assistance. Because most colleges and universities receive federal assistance, the language of Title IX effectively makes sexual harassment on campus a federal matter. The same is true of most public school districts. Title IX requires that school officials take action when sexual harassment is severe or ongoing.

Perhaps the most publicized influence of Title IX has been on women's college athletics because it requires colleges and school districts accepting federal funds to provide equal opportunities in sports. The Department of Education has interpreted this provision to mean that the percentage of female athletes at colleges and universities should reflect the percentage of female undergraduates, and that male and female athletics should receive equal funding.*

This interpretation has been controversial and difficult for some universities to implement. Football programs are expensive to run and often provide schools that support them with a large share of the income generated by athletics. With no female counterpart to football, college administrators with football programs face a dilemma of how to control the costs of a profitable venture in order to equalize expenditures with women's athletics. At the same time, Title IX has improved the situation of female student athletes while helping to put some women's sports programs on the map. The growing popularity of women's basketball and gymnastics, for instance, can be attributed in part to decisions universities made to invest in these programs as a result of Title IX regulations.

*U.S. Department of Education, Office for Civil Rights, at http://www.ed.gov/policy/rights/reg/ocr/edlite-34cfr106.html.

reason for providing disparate treatment to men and women. This means pregnancy, childbirth, and marital status are not supposed to be reasons for making employment or promotion decisions.[34]

In practice, obstacles to women's employment and advancement abound. It's not uncommon for women to feel they have to trade-off career opportunities if they want to have a family, or for female employees to comment to each other that their company has an unspoken "mommy track" with fewer opportunities for advancement flowing to women who choose family before career. Companies with a preponderance of men in high-level managerial positions are evidence for those who feel there is an organizational "glass ceiling" above which few women can rise. Typically, conditions such as these exist informally, as part of an amorphous "corporate culture" that favors the advancement of men. In such an atmosphere, unequal treatment may be apparent to those who feel disadvantaged by it, but difficult to rectify through the legal system.

Family and medical leave is one place where legislative advances have worked to protect the employment concerns of women who need to devote attention to seriously ill loved ones or who need time away from work after a pregnancy. Under the **Family and Medical Leave Act of 1993,** eligible employees at companies with more than fifty people have the right to up to twelve weeks of unpaid leave in any calendar year to care for a newborn child, or a spouse, child, or parent with a serious medical condition. Under the terms of the act, a woman who leaves her job for three months after giving birth is assured that her job will still be there when she comes back.[35]

Laws requiring equal pay for equal work have been on the books since the Equal Pay Act of 1963, but intervening factors like differences in seniority between a male and female employee can confound attempts to demonstrate that two circumstances are comparable. Despite the law, women continue to earn on average less than men, although the gap is narrowing. In 1980, women earned roughly 60 percent of what men earned; by 2000, the difference had fallen to about 75 percent.[36] The disparity is commonly attributed to key circumstantial factors: that women as a whole have less education and have been more likely to drop out of the workforce for long stretches to raise a family.

Related to the issue of equal pay is the politically charged matter of comparable worth, which deals with matters of pay equity for comparable labor performed by men and women in different but comparable jobs. See what you think about comparable worth after reading about the history and background of the issue in Issue Box 13-2, and register your opinion on whether you believe it's a policy the government should pursue.

▶**Family and Medical Leave Act of 1993** Legislation designed to permit women working in medium or large companies up to twelve weeks of unpaid leave following childbirth. It also permits employees to take unpaid leave time to care for an ailing relative.

Issue Box 13-2   *Comparable Worth*

History and Background

Although it's been illegal to pay men and women different wages for doing the same work since the passage of the Equal Pay Act of 1963, and illegal to hire or fire someone on the basis of gender since the passage of the Civil Rights Act of 1964, comparable worth, or pay equity, is a more recent issue in our political debate. It addresses wage disparities between men and women who hold comparable jobs. This shouldn't be confused with equal pay for performing the *same* job. Instead, **comparable worth** deals with disparities between jobs held mostly by women that pay less than jobs held mostly by men, despite the fact that the two jobs require comparable skills and training. This makes it a civil rights issue.[*]

For instance, in Washington state, the job of legal secretary is considered to require a comparable level of skill and training to the job of heavy equipment operator. Legal secretaries are overwhelmingly female. Heavy equipment operators are overwhelmingly male. If legal secretaries earn less than heavy equipment operators, there's an issue of comparable worth.[†]

Jobs performed mostly by women include clerical workers, nurses, maids, secondary school teachers, secretaries, social workers, real estate agents, and electronics assembly-line workers. Jobs performed mostly by men include outdoor laborers, doctors, carpenters, electricians, lawyers, upper-level managers, plumbers, and manufacturing assembly-line workers. The "female" jobs require different skill sets from the "male" jobs, but jobs requiring high levels of training and education are neither exclusively "female" nor "male." Electrical engineers (mostly male) average the same number of years of education as librarians (mostly female).[‡] Pay equity supporters contend they should be paid comparably.

As a matter of legislation, comparable-worth measures have an uneven history. Congress considered including a pay-equity provision in the Equal Pay Act of 1963 but found the issue of determining comparable jobs to be too complex. In the 1980s, twenty states considered comparable worth legislation, but only Minnesota and Washington put laws on the books, and these only covered state workers. In the last few years, comparable worth legislation has been proposed in

Congress and in more than half the states, backed by the resources of powerful groups like the AFL-CIO.[§]

The controversy over comparable worth derives partly from differences in how people interpret the evidence of pay disparities, and partly from differences in values. Comparable worth advocates point to persistent gaps in the pay of "female" and "male" occupations.[**] Opponents cite data that suggest negligible or nonexistent differences between pay in "female" and "male" jobs by considering intervening factors, like the fact that men average more hours annually on the job than women.[††] The question of how to determine comparability remains open for debate.

As a matter of values, opponents of comparable worth tend to have more faith in the ability of the free market to set wages than in the ability of government to do so. Proponents of comparable worth laws believe rectifying inequities by

13-8d Women in Public Office

Electoral politics is one place where women have made clear and visible gains. In 1984, when Democratic presidential candidate Walter Mondale selected Representative Geraldine Ferraro as his vice presidential running mate in a losing cause against President Reagan, his choice was considered bold and visionary. Never before had a woman held a place on the national ticket of a major party.

In the intervening generation, women have taken their place alongside men in positions of power. Although the number of women in high office still falls far short of the percentage of women in the population, it is no longer uncommon to see someone like imposing pay standards is an appropriate role for government and something only government can do. Some supporters contend that women still suffer the effects of a cultural predisposition toward women remaining in the home and performing domestic tasks, pointing to data showing women are promoted less quickly than equally qualified men and may hit a "glass ceiling" beyond which they cannot advance in their organizations. Opponents point to salary and employment advances achieved by women in recent years and decry comparable worth initiatives as feeding a culture of victimization that they claim, in the long run, only serves to hold women back.

Arguments in Support

Several arguments are typically offered in support of comparable worth policies. Proponents might say:

- It's important. Although gender discrimination is illegal, it persists in the form of a pay differential where occupations employing mostly women pay less than occupations employing mostly men.
- The market is not a solution. The alternative to pay equity laws is to permit the free market to establish wages, but the market fails women, as evidenced by wage inequities between men and women and "glass ceiling" barriers to workplace advancement.
- It benefits women. No one questions that if gender pay disparities exist in the workforce and can be identified, pay equity laws would eliminate them.
- It's fair. Gender should not be a criterion for determining what someone earns.

Arguments Against

Opponents of comparable worth policies might argue:

- It's not an issue. Proponents of pay equity use incorrect, inappropriate, or misleading statistics to argue that there's a large gender pay gap when in fact inequities between women and men are small.
- It violates market principles. Rectifying pay differences between men and women allows government bureaucracy rather than the free market to establish wages.

- It hurts women. Mandating pay increases for women will simply make employers less likely to hire women.
- It's arbitrary. Trying to classify a multitude of different jobs in order to create comparability standards produces inexact and therefore unfair results.

My Opinion

When registering your opinion on comparable worth, consider the history of the issue and the arguments supporting and opposing it. In particular, ask yourself if comparable worth:

- Is important or not an issue
- Cannot be addressed by the free market or violates free-market principles
- Benefits or hurts women
- Is fair or arbitrary

The most accurate description of my attitude toward comparable worth is:

1—I strongly support it. It's a good idea.
2—I support it, but with some reservations.
3—I oppose it, but with some reservations.
4—I strongly oppose it. It's a bad idea.
5—I haven't thought enough about it to have an opinion.
6—I don't care about it enough to bother.

▶ **comparable worth** A manner of determining pay equity by equalizing pay between jobs held mostly by women that demand comparable training and labor to jobs held mostly by men.

---

[*]Paula England, *Comparable Worth: Theories and Evidence* (New York: Aldine de Gruyter, 1992), 1–2 and 23–24.

[†]Ibid.

[‡]Ibid, 14.

[§]"What Is Comparable Worth?" Employment Policy Foundation paper, at http://www.epf.org/research/newsletters/2000/compworth.asp.

[**]England, *Comparable Worth*, 125.

[††]"What Is Comparable Worth?"

Secretary of State Condoleezza Rice or, before her, Madeleine Albright represent the foreign policy interests of the United States to a world audience.

The year 1992 was a benchmark for women in electoral politics. Dubbed the "Year of the Woman" by women's groups and political reporters, a record twenty-four new women were elected to the House and five to the senate, including both senators from California, the first state to be represented by two women. Ten years later, there were thirteen women in the senate with three states—California, Maine, and Washington—represented by two women. In 1994, ten women won major party gubernatorial nominations, but none of them were elected. By 2002, with voters primed to accept women in executive positions, ten women again won gubernatorial primaries, and were elected in states as diverse as Michigan, Kansas, Arizona, and Hawaii.[37]

One reason why women have achieved growing electoral success is simply that more women are running for office—and one reason for that is women are now taken seriously as political candidates. Before the "Year of the Woman," female candidates were widely regarded as long-shots or jokes, and were often recruited to run against entrenched male officeholders who were assured reelection. Women serving in Congress were likely to have been appointed to their seats upon the death of their husbands. The recent electoral record of female candidates suggests those days are over.

13-9 People with Disabilities

Try for a moment to envision what a staircase looks like to someone in a wheelchair, or what a telephone sounds like to someone who is hearing impaired. For years, most of us were unaware of the obstacles posed by ordinary objects to people with disabilities, and were largely oblivious to the discriminatory treatment that impaired individuals faced in the workplace or in navigating public and private buildings. In fact, the Civil Rights Act of 1964 did not cover people with disabilities.

Over time, lobbying efforts on behalf of disabled individuals helped to bring the circumstances faced by people with disabilities to the forefront of the national agenda, and in 1990 Congress passed the landmark **Americans with Disabilities Act.** The key provisions of the act:

▶ **Americans with Disabilities Act** The landmark 1990 legislation extending equal protection in the workplace and in public accommodations to people with physical and mental disabilities.

- Provide civil rights protection to persons with disabilities on a par with existing protections against discrimination on the basis of race, color, religion, national origin, and gender

- Prohibit job discrimination against persons with disabilities, including discrimination in hiring, firing, compensating, and promoting disabled individuals who can perform essential job functions. Employers are required to make "reasonable accommodations" to the work environment to accommodate the needs of disabled individuals, provided that such changes do not impose "undue hardship" on the employer's business

- Mandate all state and local government agencies provide disabled individuals with equal access to programs and activities, and make public buildings readily accessible to disabled individuals

- Require equal access to public accommodations, such as restaurants, hotels, theaters, stores, doctor's offices, parks, and private schools. Individuals operating such facilities are instructed to modify them for use by disabled individuals, provided that making such modifications does not present the owner with an "undue burden"[38]

The Americans with Disabilities Act is sweeping in scope, covering a wide range of physical and psychological conditions. These conditions include people with impairments that limit major life activities, such as walking, hearing, seeing, and breathing, as well as ailments such as epilepsy, HIV infection, and AIDS. Cancer survivors are protected against discrimination resulting from their medical history, as are people with a history of mental illness. People with learning disabilities are covered by the act, as are recovering alcoholics. Close relatives of people with disabilities are included, so that the spouse of someone with a disability could not be denied employment out of the concern that they might have to spend large quantities of their time caring for their partner instead of working.[39]

If the Americans with Disabilities Act is sweeping, so is it vague, and this has made it controversial. Although the act specifically excludes protection to people with short-term ailments like the flu or a broken leg, there's a large gray area between people who obviously are disabled and people who obviously are not, and this has generated controversy about how broadly to implement the act.

Controversy can be particularly acute when it comes to people with psychological conditions. Should the law cover people with Attention Deficit Disorder (ADD), for instance, who have trouble focusing on their job? The law is broad enough to cover this condition. Supporters say this is appropriate, and that psychological conditions should be afforded the same protection as physical conditions. Opponents contend that conditions like ADD are too frequently diagnosed, and that covering them dilutes the purpose of extending equal protection to people who in their view are obviously disabled.

The Americans with Disabilities Act is equally vague about remedies. At what point does a retail store begin to realize an "undue burden" as it attempts to accommodate people with disabilities? Might an employer have to permit flexible work schedules, modify office equipment, or hire an interpreter to protect disabled employees against workplace discrimination? The Act says yes: Any of these could be an appropriate remedy to discrimination and is considered to be a "reasonable accommodation." Some employers who have to pay the bill experience it differently.

13-10 Gay and Lesbian Rights

The issue of homosexuality is emotionally charged for many Americans. Homophobia is widespread in our culture, leading some people to fear or despise gay men and women. Some believe homosexuality is an abomination against God, while others see it as an abnormality of nature. Sometimes these attitudes provide the basis for discrimination against gays, who face covert and direct obstacles in every walk of life.

At the very least, the hostile climate of public opinion has kept gays and lesbians from realizing the same level of civil rights protections that have been won by other groups that face discrimination. About 40 percent of the states have laws criminalizing sexual activities between persons of the same sex. Some local governments, colleges, and universities have acted to prevent gay and lesbian groups from organizing, holding public events, or educating others about homosexuality.[40]

At the same time, even conservative estimates suggest that homosexuality is fairly prevalent in our society, and is not bounded by socioeconomic status, race, religion, or gender. The exact percentage of gay Americans is impossible to know because many keep their sexual orientation a secret to protect against discrimination and social reprisals. Others, however, have mobilized and organized, in an effort to generate public attention that can translate into political action.

Their work has moved the issue of gay and lesbian rights to the forefront of the policy agenda, and they have realized some success. One of the most noteworthy is the 1993 "Don't Ask, Don't Tell" policy forbidding the Pentagon from asking servicemen to reveal their sexual orientation. In keeping with the emotionally charged nature of the issue, this policy was born of great controversy and protest. The product of a compromise between President Clinton and military leaders, it represented a step back from the president's original intent to end discrimination based on sexual orientation in a military culture where feelings about homosexuality were strong and hostile. Essentially, the policy says that gay servicemen who keep their homosexuality private will not be asked about it or discharged because of it by their commanding officers.

Equally emotional is the issue of gay and lesbian marriage. This, too, is a place where gay rights activists have directed considerable energy and, after years of frustration, have recently experienced some success—and generated a lot of controversy. Take a little while to explore the history and background of same-sex marriages in Issue Box 13-3, and register your opinion about whether you believe gays and lesbians should be given the right to enter into legal partnerships.

13-11 Senior Citizen Rights

Ronald Reagan was elected president in 1980 at the age of sixty-nine. John Glenn, the first American to orbit the earth in 1962, joined the crew of the Space Shuttle Discovery

Issue Box 13-3   *Same-Sex Marriage*

History and Background

When your parents were young, chances are they never heard a discussion about whether people of the same sex should be allowed to marry. That's because homosexuality was in the closet and the only marriages available to gay people were marriages to people of the opposite sex that provided cover for behavior that was considered deplorable and criminal. Then, as part of the sexual revolution of the 1960s, gays became more visible and gradually appeared on the nation's social and political radar. In 1988, *Ms.* magazine published an anonymous article by a woman entitled, "I Left My Husband for the Woman I Love."[*] By 2000, openly gay characters were being featured on prime time television programs and same-sex partnered households numbered close to 600,000.[†] Times had changed dramatically.

As is so often the case with dramatic social shifts, the political system was both the place where gay rights advocates pressed for legal advances and the focus of resistance to the gay rights movement. Initially, political conflicts centered on demands by gay rights groups for civil rights protections and resistance by groups hoping to protect traditional social values. It wasn't until the 1990s that same-sex unions became part of that debate,[‡] when a dramatic judgment by a Hawaii Circuit Court judge opened the door to legalized same-sex marriage in that state and brought the issue to national attention. The 1996 case *Baehr v. Miike* established that Hawaii had no constitutional basis for denying a marriage license to a same-sex couple.[§] With that judgment, Hawaii appeared on the verge of becoming the first state to recognize gay marriages.

The decision sparked a backlash by groups seeking to preserve marriage as a heterosexual institution. By 2001, thirty-five states had passed laws prohibiting the recognition of same-sex unions that might be licensed in other states. These laws were bolstered by federal legislation—the 1996 Defense of Marriage Act—which declared that marriage as a legal matter referred only to heterosexual marriage, and that no state would be obligated to recognize a same-sex marriage from another state. In 1998, Hawaii voters approved a state constitutional amendment giving the legislature the power to overrule the courts and restrict marriage to heterosexual couples. Then the Hawaii Supreme Court threw out the Circuit Court judgment in *Baehr*, ending that state's brief flirtation with same-sex marriage.

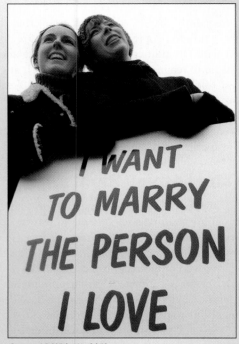

Source: AP/Wide World Photos.

At this point, the battle shifted to Vermont. In late 1999, the Vermont Supreme Court unanimously ruled in the case of *Baker v. State* that the state had unlawfully denied three same-sex couples the rights afforded heterosexual couples, and instructed the state legislature to remedy the situation. Their response was something legally different than same-sex marriage: a new institution called "civil union," which had the effect of extending the benefits of marriage to gay couples without altering existing marriage laws. It applied only to couples living in Vermont, so other states would not have to grapple with whether to recognize the law as they would have had Vermont legalized same-sex marriages. Governor Howard Dean signed it into law in April 2000, and nine months later, legislation was introduced in the Vermont House of Representatives in an unsuccessful effort to repeal it.[**] In 2004, the Massachusetts Supreme Court ruled as the Hawaii Supreme Court had six years earlier, finding nothing in the state Consti-

---

▶**Age Discrimination in Employment Act** The 1967 law that made it illegal for employers to discriminate against people over age forty in hiring, firing, and promotion decisions.

thirty-six years later—at age seventy-seven. Americans are living longer—demographically, people over eighty are the fastest growing group—and as "Baby Boomers" begin to get on in years, the generation weaned on the civil rights movement could be expected to turn its attention and political clout to the rights of seniors.

Age discrimination in its most widespread form occurs in the workplace, where employers are sometimes reluctant to hire older people. This type of discrimination has been illegal since the passage of the **Age Discrimination in Employment Act** of 1967, which makes it a crime to discriminate against people over forty in hiring, firing, and promotion decisions. Additionally, job notices cannot specify age limits or preferences, and tution to prohibit gay marriage and giving the legislature six months to rewrite marriage laws to permit it. The Massachusetts ruling produced another wave of protests from gay marriage opponents like President Bush, culminating in the overwhelming approval in the 2004 election of measures banning gay marriage by voters in eleven states. At the same time, San Francisco responded in solidarity with the Massachusetts ruling by briefly issuing marriage licenses to gay couples.

Deeply held cultural values about marriage, sexuality, justice, and equality lie behind the intense feelings many people have about same-sex marriage. Positions on same-sex marriage are strongly value-driven and can defy one's sexual orientation. Same-sex marriage is opposed by some conservative gays who see it as a threat to bedrock cultural values and by some on the far left who see marriage itself as a patriarchal institution to be rejected.[††] This is the same breakdown of opinion we find among heterosexuals.

Arguments in Support

Supporters and opponents of same-sex marriage make value-based arguments to support their positions. Supporters would argue that:

- It's about discrimination. Denying same-sex couples the rights and privileges stemming from marriage subjects them to differential treatment because of their sexual orientation.
- It's about personal liberty. Sexual orientation is a personal matter, not a public issue. Anyone who wishes to get married should have the freedom to do so regardless of his or her sexual orientation.
- Marriage is defined by relationships. It is about the bonds that hold two people together. Same-sex couples regularly engage in such relationships, but without the legal benefits and protections accorded heterosexual couples that share similar bonds.
- Marriage is good for society. It promotes social stability and provides a suitable environment for raising children, so any couple that marries—regardless of sexual orientation—advances family values.

Arguments Against

Opponents of same-sex marriage invoke a different set of values than supporters to explain their position. They might say:

- Discrimination isn't an issue. Rejecting a behavior one considers morally wrong is not discriminatory, and engaging in it is qualitatively different from being a member of a racial or ethnic group.
- Liberty isn't an issue. Advocates of same-sex marriage want public benefits and public recognition for same-sex couples, placing their efforts in the policy arena—not in the private realm of personal freedoms. Granting those benefits and privileges would amount to publicly sanctioning homosexuality.
- Marriage is defined by the law. Advocates of same-sex marriage seek legal recognition, rendering irrelevant the fact that relationships are involved. On this matter, the law is clear and uniform: Marriage is defined as the union of a husband and a wife.
- Same-sex marriage is bad for society. It undermines core values centered on heterosexual marriage, procreation, and traditional family structures.

My Opinion

When registering your opinion on same-sex marriage, consider the history of the issue and the arguments supporting and opposing it. In particular, ask yourself if same-sex marriage:

- Is or is not about discrimination
- Is or is not about personal liberty
- Is about relationships or laws
- Is good or bad for society

The most accurate description of my attitude toward same-sex marriage is:

1—I strongly support it. It's a good idea.
2—I support it, but with some reservations.
3—I oppose it, but with some reservations.
4—I strongly oppose it. It's a bad idea.
5—I haven't thought enough about it to have an opinion.
6—I don't care about it enough to bother.

[*]Reprinted in Robert M. Baird and Stuart E. Rosenbaum (eds.), *Same-Sex Marriage: The Moral and Legal Debate* (Amherst, NY: Prometheus Books, 1997), 37–41.

[†]William R. Eskridge, Jr., *Equality Practice: Civil Unions and the Future of Gay Rights* (New York: Routledge, 2002), xi.

[‡]Ibid., 1–3.

[§]Baird and Rosenbaum, *Same-Sex Marriage,* 9–10.

[**]Eskridge, *Equality Practice,* 6–82.

[††]Baird and Rosenbaum, *Same-Sex Marriage,* 10–11.

benefits cannot legally be withheld from older employees.[41] Originally, these protections were extended to workers until they reached retirement at age sixty-five. As longevity increased, the mandatory retirement age was raised to seventy in 1978, and eliminated entirely in 1986.

It's not too difficult to expect that as people continue to live and work longer, civil rights for seniors will continue to emerge as an important political issue. In a time that has witnessed an expansion of the personal rights agenda, with groups not previously recognized as disadvantaged speaking out for equal rights, it is easy to imagine a growing, energetic movement supporting the rights of senior citizens.

The Way You Want America to Be — *Civil Rights*

Take a look back at the way you answered the polls in the "Your Opinion" sections of the Issue Boxes. Which answer did you give most often? Read on to see where you stand.

If your primary answer was 1...

...you are a strong supporter of civil rights. Based on your responses to the three issues we discussed, your tendency is to strongly value the rights of individuals who traditionally have been disadvantaged by society. You would probably like America to be a place where social inequities are addressed through public policy, and if you are active in politics—or ever become active—you would support an activist civil rights agenda.

If your primary answer was 2...

...feel free to consider yourself a supporter of civil rights. Based on your responses to the three issues we discussed, your tendency is to value the rights of individuals who traditionally have been disadvantaged by society. You would probably like America to be a place where social inequities are addressed through public policy, and if you are active in politics—or ever become active—you'd probably support an activist civil rights agenda.

If your primary answer was 3...

...perhaps you think of yourself as a traditionalist, or maybe you think that minority groups have made too many demands on society. You may feel that government is not the appropriate arena for working through the agendas of traditionally disadvantaged individuals, or it could be that you don't like the remedies they embrace. You would proba-

bly like America to be a place where government involvement in civil rights issues is limited, and if you are active in politics—or ever become active—you'd probably oppose an extremely activist civil rights agenda.

If your primary answer was 4...

...you are strongly opposed to a number of key issues on the civil rights agenda. Perhaps you think of yourself as a traditionalist, or maybe you think that minority groups have made too many demands on society. You may feel that government is not the appropriate arena for working through the agendas of traditionally disadvantaged individuals, or it could be that you don't like the remedies they embrace. You would probably like America to be a place where government involvement in civil rights issues is limited, and if you are active in politics—or ever become active—you would oppose an extremely activist civil rights agenda.

If your primary answer was 5 or 6...

...you haven't thought much about the civil rights issues we discussed, either because they're not important to you or because you simply never took the time to develop an opinion about things like affirmative action or same-sex marriage. This places you on the sidelines of the intense civil rights debates that sometimes rage in this country. Perhaps that's where you want to be. Or perhaps now that you've read a little about civil rights you would like to know more, so that you can try to influence the direction of this controversial element of our politics. It's totally up to you.

Chapter Review

Civil rights policies are designed to ensure that the law treats everyone equally, regardless of differences in race, gender, ethnic background, or anything people might be inclined to discriminate against. The key to civil rights in the United States is the equal protection clause of the Fourteenth Amendment, which says "No state shall . . . deny to any person within its jurisdiction the equal protection of the laws." The intent of the equal protection clause is that all laws should be applied evenly and without prejudice to all citizens.

When African Americans were granted citizenship following the Civil War, southern states used Black Codes and physical intimidation to deny former slaves their civil rights, even as those states were being reconstructed into the union. Until the 1950s, Jim Crow laws made segregation a way of life in the South. Then the civil rights movement drew national attention to segregation's abuses. A long period of civil disobedience, which was often met with violence, culminated in landmark federal civil rights legislation, notably the Civil Rights Act of 1964 and the Voting Rights Act of 1965.

Since the 1960s, affirmative action programs have been the primary way to address inequalities left from the long history of discriminatory practices against African Americans and other historically disadvantaged minority groups. Under the law, affirmative action requires that there be no artificial barriers to the hiring and advancement of people in groups that have been targets of past discrimination, and that if employers underutilize group members, they have to take steps to remedy the situation. In practice, affirmative action policies can range from minority recruitment to preferential hiring of underrepresented group members and targeted hiring of minority individuals.

Native Americans have suffered discriminatory treatment since the arrival of European settlers in North America. Colonists sharply limited Native American tribal sovereignty so that it applied only to internal matters, subjugating tribal autonomy over land rights and affairs with other nations to the will of the settlers and later to the federal government. For centuries, the federal government tried to subdue Native Americans by alternately containing them on reservations, relocating them to land that settlers hadn't developed, and westernizing them in an effort to get them to assimilate into American culture.

Latino groups have also faced discrimination, notably in education and the workplace. Mexican American farm laborers faced deplorable conditions, leading to the rise of the United Farm Workers Union under Cesar Chavez. Additionally, widespread illegal immigration by Mexican Americans is an ongoing source of harassment and discrimination toward Latino citizens by resentful Anglos living in areas with large Hispanic American populations. Parents of Latino schoolchildren have been confronted with demands for proof of U.S. citizenship by school officials, a form of discrimination that can dissuade them from enrolling their children in school.

At the dawn of the republic, women faced a male-dominated society that felt they were not capable of making decisions for themselves—an attitude manifested in laws restricting married women from owning property or managing finances. These restrictions began to come down in the mid-nineteenth century because of the work of activists like Susan B. Anthony and Elizabeth Cady Stanton.

By 1920, women won the right to vote. A second wave of activism in the 1960s led to the establishment of the National Organization for Women, which works to end sexual violence and harassment, promote gender equality in the workplace and on campus, and advance the cause of women in politics.

A number of other minority groups face or have faced violations of equal protection. Japanese Americans were moved to detention centers during World War II without evidence that they posed a national security risk. Disabled individuals face discrimination in the workplace, although the Americans with Disabilities Act makes such discrimination illegal and attempts to eliminate barriers to navigating public accommodations. Widespread homophobia is the source of discrimination against gays and lesbians, who face housing and workplace discrimination. Senior citizens may face employers who do not want to hire them because of their age, an act that is illegal under the Age Discrimination in Employment Act, which makes it a crime to discriminate against people over forty in hiring, firing, and promotion decisions.

Key Terms

affirmative action (p. 399)

Age Discrimination in Employment Act (p. 414)

Americans with Disabilities Act (p. 412)

Black Codes (p. 393)

Citizenship Act of 1924 (p. 403)

civil disobedience (p. 396)

civil rights (p. 391)

Civil Rights Act of 1964 (p. 398)

civil rights movement (p. 396)

comparable worth (p. 410)

Dred Scott v. Sanford (p. 392)

economic equality (p. 391)

equal protection clause (p. 392)

Equal Rights Amendment (ERA) (p. 407)

equality of opportunity (p. 391)

equality of outcome (p. 391)

Family and Medical Leave Act of 1993 (p. 409)

federalism (p. 392)

freedom rides (p. 396)

Indian Removal Act (p. 402)

Jim Crow laws (p. 393)

Ku Klux Klan (p. 392)

National Organization for Women (NOW) (p. 408)

Plessy v. Ferguson *(p. 394)*

political equality (p. 391)

Reconstruction (p. 392)

Regents of the University of California v. Bakke *(p. 400)*

sit-ins (p. 396)

social equality (p. 391)

Student Nonviolent Coordinating Committee (SNCC) (p. 396)

"Trail of Tears" (p. 402)

Voting Rights Act of 1965 (p. 398)

Review Questions

Note: You can find the correct answers to these questions by taking the quiz and then submitting your answers in the Online Edition. The program will automatically score your submission. If you miss a question, the program will provide the correct answer, a rationale for the answer, and the section number in the chapter where the topic is discussed.

1. The equal protection clause of the Fourteenth Amendment
   a. is a mechanism for protecting liberty.
   b. seeks to advance equality of opportunity.
   c. requires states to advance equal outcomes for groups experiencing discrimination.
   d. granted former slaves the right to vote.

2. Institutionalized segregation was maintained in the South through the first half of the twentieth century by the use of
   a. Black Codes.
   b. Reconstruction policies.
   c. Jim Crow laws.
   d. federal law.

3. The mainstream civil rights movement employed each of the following tactics *except*
   a. sit-ins.
   b. voter registration drives.
   c. organizing angry mobs.
   d. freedom rides.

4. The Civil Rights Act of 1964
   a. encouraged the establishment of affirmative action policies.
   b. permitted federal supervision of state election practices.
   c. markedly increased African American voter registration.
   d. is the primary reason for the sharp increase in the number of African American elected officials.

5. The Native American right of tribal sovereignty
   a. provided a legal basis for the policies of containment and relocation.
   b. was sharply limited by colonial settlers.
   c. protected Native Americans from experiencing civil rights abuses.
   d. permitted Native American tribes to engage in diplomatic relations with other nations.

6. Latinos of Mexican origin
   a. tend to be more conservative than Cuban Americans.
   b. settled mostly in the large cities of the Northeast.
   c. have been more prosperous than Latinos from Puerto Rico.
   d. have faced a long history of workplace discrimination.

7. The Supreme Court upheld the internment of Japanese Americans during World War II on the basis of
   a. Fourteenth Amendment rights.
   b. equal protection.
   c. national security.
   d. Title IX.

8. The Equal Rights Amendment
   a. gave married women the right to own property.
   b. gave women the right to vote.
   c. established laws against sexual harassment in the workplace.
   d. never passed.

9. Comparable worth policies differ from equal pay policies in that
   a. comparable worth policies compare "male jobs" with "female jobs."
   b. equal pay policies are generally more controversial.
   c. comparable worth has been protected by law since 1963.
   d. women already are paid equally to men, but women in "female jobs" are not paid comparably to men in "male jobs."

10. The Americans with Disabilities Act extends civil rights protection to each of the following groups *except*
   a. recovering alcoholics.
   b. spouses of recovering alcoholics.
   c. AIDS patients.
   d. influenza patients.

In Their Own Words

You might be interested in examining some of what the following authors have said about the topics we've been discussing:

On Affirmative Action

Lawrence, Charles R. III, and Mari J. Matsuda. *We Won't Go Back: Making the Case for Affirmative Action.* Boston, MA: Houghton Mifflin, 1997.

Thomasson, Richard F., Faye J. Crosby, and Sharon D. Herzberger. *Affirmative Action: The Pros and Cons of Policy and Practice.* Lanham, MD: American University Press, 1996.

On Comparable Worth

England, Paula. *Comparable Worth: Theories and Evidence.* New York: Aldine de Gruyter, 1992.

On Same-Sex Marriage

Baird, Robert M., and Stuart E. Rosenbaum, eds. *Same-Sex Marriage: The Moral and Legal Debate.* Amherst, NY: Prometheus Books, 1997.

Eskridge, William R., Jr. *Equality Practice: Civil Unions and the Future of Gay Rights.* New York: Routledge, 2002.

Notes

1. For more details, see http://afroamhistory.about.com/library/weekly/aa121900a.htm.

2. See CNN Interactive, "The Civil Rights Movement," at http://www.cnn.com/EVENTS/1997/mlk/links.html.

3. See http://afroamhistory.about.com/library/weekly/aa121900a.htm.

4. For a full timeline of the major events of Reconstruction, see http://www.pinzler.com/ushistory/timeline6.html.

5. See http://www.africana.com/research/encarta/tt_333.asp.

6. Ibid.

7. Ibid.

8. You can read more about Rosa Park's story at Time.com: http://www.time.com/time/time100/heroes/profile/parks01.html.

9. See the Congress of Racial Equality website, at http://www.core-online.org/history/freedom_summer.htm. The murders were later the subject of the film *Mississippi Burning*.

10. Ibid.

11. See CongressLink at http://www.congresslink.org/glossary.html#cR57.

12. See CongressLink at http://www.congresslink.org/civil/essay.html.

13. See CongressLink at http://www.congresslink.org/voting1965.htm.

14. CNN Interactive, "The Civil Rights Movement," at http://www.cnn.com/EVENTS/1997/mlk/links.html.

15. See LawHelpMN.org, Indian Tribal Sovereignty at http://www.lawhelpmn.org/MN/StateChannelResults.cfm/County/%20demoMode/%3D%201/Language/1/State/MN/TextOnly/N/ZipCode/%20/LoggedIn/0/iSubTopicID/1/iProblemCodeID/1920600/sTopicImage/feather.gif/iTopicID/272/bAllState/0/ichannelid/3.

16. CNN Interactive, "The Civil Rights Movement," at http://www.cnn.com/EVENTS/1997/mlk/links.html.

17. See http://dictionary.law.com/.

18. See PBS.org at http://www.pbs.org/wgbh/aia/part4/4p2959.html.

19. North Georgia history, at http://ngeorgia.com/history/nghistt.html.

20. For an overview, see http://www.nebraskastudies.org.

21. See http://ishgooda.nativeweb.org/caged/alcatraz/albckgrd.htm.

22. See http://bioguide.congress.gov/scripts/biodisplay.pl?index=C000077.

23. See, for instance, *United States v. Wheeler* (1978).

24. See LawHelpMN.org, Indian Tribal Sovereignty at http://www.lawhelpmn.org/MN/StateChannelResults.cfm/County/%20demoMode/%3D%201/Language/1/State/MN/TextOnly/N/ZipCode/%20/LoggedIn/0/iSubTopicID/1/iProblemCodeID/1920600/sTopicImage/feather.gif/iTopicID/272/bAllState/0/ichannelid/3

25. Ibid. One prominent example is the Foxwoods Casino in Connecticut, operated by the Mashantucket Pequot nation. The casino website may be found here: http://www.foxwoods.com/. The story of the nation that operates it may be found here: http://www.foxwoods.com/TheMashantucketPequots/Home/.

26. See the NCLR website at http://www.nclr.org.

27. You can get information on La Raza at http://www.nclr.org.

28. See the National Association for Bilingual Education website at http://www.nclr.org.

29. Figures are from the 2000 U.S. Census, at http://factfinder.census.gov.

30. *Korematsu v. United States* 321 US 760 (1944).

31. See the Equal Rights Amendment website, http://www.equalrightsamendment.org/era.htm.

32. Ibid.

33. National Organization for Women website, http://www.now.org/history/history.html.

34. See http://hydra.gsa.gov/eeo/newpage24.htm.

35. The U.S. Department of Labor, at http://www.dol.gov/esa/regs/statutes/whd/fmla.htm.

36. See http://nolo.com/lawcenter/index.cfm/catID/4BEF1F62-722F-435E-98AB18960A6EAB0E.

37. Thomas Hargrove, "Female Candidates Look to Make Electoral Ground." Scripps Howard News Service, October 23, 2002.

38. U.S. Equal Employment Opportunity Commission, "Americans with Disabilities Act Questions and Answers," http://www.ada.gov/q&aeng02.htm.

39. Ibid.

40. American Civil Liberties Union statement on gay and lesbian rights, at http://www.aclu.org/LesbianGayRights/LesbianGayRightsMain.cfm.

41. Equal Employment Opportunity Commission, "Facts about Age Discrimination," at http://www.eeoc.gov/facts/age.html.

Protecting Civil Liberties

14

14-1 Introduction

Some of the most important and controversial questions debated in our political system involve matters of personal liberty. Although few of us question the need to protect individual freedom, actually doing so sometimes requires holding our noses and permitting behaviors we find distasteful or reprehensible. It's not easy to stand by and allow someone to make hostile statements aimed directly at our religious or ethnic group, for instance, much less stand up for their right to do so. You might even say it goes against human nature to defend those who attack us. That's why many people object to the specific liberties people are allowed, even if we agree in the abstract on the importance of maintaining them.

At the most fundamental level, there is little debate about the value of protecting **civil liberties.** The Constitution very clearly restricts government from denying us the liberty to express ourselves, congregate, worship, and protest, affording us the freedom to speak out against the government if we so desire. Remember, the authors of the Constitution were concerned that government be strong enough to protect the weakest among us but not so strong as to overwhelm personal liberty. That's why civil liberties are expressed in the Constitution as actions denied to government.

Most of these liberties were added to the Constitution in the **Bill of Rights.** Toward the end of the Philadelphia convention, George Mason of Virginia moved to include a Bill of Rights in the original document, offering to write one in short order. The delegates were fatigued, however, and in the case of some southerners, concerned that a written declaration of human liberty would conflict with their position on slavery. So, they opted to rely on the protections already included in state constitutions and not include a Bill of Rights in the final document.[1]

As we saw in Chapter 2, the new Constitution was rapidly amended to include a Bill of Rights as a political maneuver to win support for ratification. Table 14-1 quickly reviews the contents of the Bill of Rights as a refresher on the basic civil liberties that are protected from government interference.

14-1a Due Process

The full range of civil liberties provided constitutional protection includes the important right to **due process,** or protection against arbitrary actions of the government. The Fifth Amendment states that no person shall "be deprived of life, liberty, or property, without due process of law." The Fourteenth Amendment echoes this language and

Amendment	Description	
Amendment 1	The First Amendment prevents government from interfering with several key personal freedoms, including the freedom to worship, speak, and assemble peacefully. It also prevents the government from restricting freedom of the press and the freedom to petition government.	**TABLE 14-1** **The Bill of Rights**
Amendment 2	The Second Amendment protects the right to bear arms.	
Amendments 3 and 4	The Third and Fourth Amendments provide a right to privacy from government interference. The Third Amendment prevents government from forcing citizens to house soldiers during peacetime—addressing one of the complaints the colonists had against the British. The Fourth Amendment protects against unreasonable searches and seizures of property or personal effects.	
Amendments 5–8	The Fifth through Eighth Amendments establish a host of protections for individuals accused of a crime. These include the right not to be tried twice for the same crime, the right to be indicted by a grand jury before being tried for a capital crime, the right not to be forced to testify against yourself, the right to due process of law, and the right not to have property confiscated by government without compensation (all in the Fifth Amendment); the right to a speedy and impartial trial, the right to be informed of charges against you, the right to call and confront witnesses, and the right to a lawyer (all in the Sixth Amendment); the right to a jury in civil trials (Seventh Amendment); and the right to be free from excessive bail and from the infliction of cruel and unusual punishments (Eighth Amendment).	
Amendments 9 and 10	The Ninth Amendment is a safety net establishing that any rights not specifically mentioned in the first eight amendments are not necessarily denied. The Tenth Amendment establishes that any powers not granted to the federal government or prohibited to the states are reserved for the states.	

applies it to the states. The presumption behind due process is that conflict between individuals and the government is inevitable and should be resolved through a defined set of legal procedures, where the rules are written to protect the individual from government power.[2]

Some of these requirements are set down in the Constitution itself, while others appear in the Bill of Rights or have been established by the Supreme Court and applied to the states through interpretation of the due process clause of the Fourteenth Amendment. They are outlined in Table 14-2.

You can think of due process as establishing the groundwork for resolving conflicts and protecting civil liberties, based on the presumption that individuals accused of a crime are innocent until proven guilty by the state. The theory is that by following clearly defined and evenly applied procedures, guilt can be assessed while the power of the state is held in check. Of course, this means that in some cases, guilty individuals will be set free because their rights were (purposely or inadvertently) violated at or before trial. This is the consequence of a fundamental choice made by the Constitution's authors: that it is better to let the guilty occasionally go free in the interest of protecting personal liberties than to inadvertently—or purposely—condemn the innocent.

In practice, the constitutionally defined system for a timely, impartial jury trial where defendants have a clear and full set of rights contrasts with the way justice is handled in many courtrooms. Because due process is slow, and courtrooms across the country are

▶**civil liberties** (see p. 420) Constitutional and legal protections against government infringement on a host of personal freedoms.

▶**Bill of Rights** (see p. 420) The first ten amendments to the Constitution, which limit government from denying us a range of personal liberties.

▶**due process** (see p. 420) The protection of individual liberty from the arbitrary or capricious actions of government through a defined set of legal procedures designed to protect the rights of the accused.

TABLE 14-2   Due Process

Item	Constitutional Origin	What This Means
Right to a **writ of habeas corpus**	Article I, Section 9	Before you can be sent to prison, the government has the burden of assuring that your rights were not violated during trial. *Habeas corpus* gives you the right to petition the court if you believe you have been wrongfully imprisoned. The Constitution prohibits suspension of this right except in the extreme case of domestic rebellion or foreign invasion.
Freedom from **bills of attainder**	Article I, Section 9	Congress or other legislatures cannot find you guilty of a crime by passing legislation that convicts you. This reaffirms the basic right of the individual to a jury trial.
Freedom from **ex post facto laws**	Article I, Section 9	Congress or other legislatures cannot pass a law making something illegal after the fact. For instance, if the drinking age was legally 18 before it was raised to 21, anyone who purchased alcohol legally at age 18 cannot subsequently, through legislation, be found guilty of a crime.
Protection against unreasonable searches and seizures	Fourth Amendment	You cannot be arrested or your person or possessions searched without a warrant from the court. The objective is "The right of the people to be secure in their persons, houses, papers and effects," but note the requirement is that searches and seizures be *reasonable*, which has been open to court interpretation. It is reasonable for airport guards to frisk you at a security checkpoint, for the police to search your apartment if you give them consent, or for state troopers to confiscate drugs they find on the front seat of a car they stopped for speeding.
Protection in the form of the **exclusionary rule**	Judicial interpretation	To add weight to the protection against unreasonable searches and seizures, the Supreme Court ruled that any evidence acquired in violation of the Fourth Amendment, such as evidence taken without a warrant, is inadmissible in court.
Grand jury indictments for capital crimes	Fifth Amendment	The protection from being charged with a capital or "infamous" crime without an indictment from a grand jury is a way of dispersing the power to prosecute. It places the ability to charge someone with a serious crime in the hands of a jury of citizens rather than in the hands of a prosecutor.
Protection against **double jeopardy**	Fifth Amendment	No one may be tried twice in the same jurisdiction for the same crime. However, someone who commits a crime that violates federal and state law can be tried in both jurisdictions. Double jeopardy typically doesn't apply to criminal and civil trials either, which is why O. J. Simpson could be acquitted of murder in criminal court yet be convicted in civil court and forced to pay monetary damages.
Protection against self-incrimination	Fifth Amendment	No one may be compelled to take the witness stand in a trial and testify against oneself (this is what people commonly mean when they invoke their "Fifth Amendment rights"). It also forbids the use of involuntary confessions from defendants.
Miranda rights	Judicial interpretation	Noting the inherently intimidating nature of witness interrogation, the Supreme Court ruled in the case of *Miranda v. Arizona* (1966) that for the Fifth Amendment protection against self-incrimination to be fully and fairly applied, individuals in custody need to be informed of—and demonstrate an understanding of—their Fifth Amendment rights (widely called Miranda

overburdened with cases, court officers with nominally adversarial roles will conspire in ways that move defendants through the system without time-consuming trials. Pressure to process a heavy caseload motivates judges to look for shortcuts. Prosecuting attorneys are evaluated for the cases they win and often jump at the chance to avoid the uncertainty of a trial. Defense attorneys, particularly those appointed by the court, tend to be overburdened and wish to avoid the work of a trial. Both can advance their professional interests by striking a plea bargain with the defendant. Box 14-1 discusses plea bargaining, which requires that a defendant waive his or her due process rights.

Item	Constitutional Origin	What This Means
		rights). Before questioning may begin, arresting officers must inform suspects that they have the right to remain silent; that if they speak, anything they say may be used against them in court; and that they have the right to have a lawyer present during interrogation. Separately, the Court decided that suspects who cannot afford a lawyer have a right to have one appointed for them.
Right to a speedy public jury trial	Sixth Amendment	The full provision calls for the right to a speedy and public trial in criminal cases by an impartial jury in the place where the crime was committed. This keeps a prosecutor or judge from having the power to convict someone unilaterally, placing that power in the hands of other citizens who in theory have not made up their minds before trial. If you've ever been called for jury duty, you've experienced an obligation of citizenship placed on you by the Sixth Amendment and applied to the states through the Fourteenth Amendment's requirement of due process.
The right to be informed of a charge against you	Sixth Amendment	This includes the right to confront your accuser and to present witnesses in your defense.
The right to an attorney	Sixth Amendment	Originally, the Constitution simply gave defendants the right to counsel, but it was of little practical use to the vast majority who could not afford to hire a lawyer. Following the 1963 case *Gideon v. Wainwright,* the Supreme Court ruled that an attorney must be provided to anyone who cannot afford one.
Protection against excessive bail	Eighth Amendment	This precludes the punishment of incarceration prior to conviction and allows the accused the freedom to prepare a defense.
Protection against cruel and unusual punishment	Eighth Amendment	Although the Constitution does not specify what makes a punishment cruel and unusual, the Court has interpreted it to mean arbitrary punishment, punishment disproportionate to the crime committed, or torture.

▶ **writ of *habeas corpus*** From the Latin for "you have the body," *habeas corpus* puts the burden on the courts to demonstrate that a defendant's rights have not been violated prior to sentencing. People who believe they have been imprisoned against their constitutional rights have the privilege to petition for their release.

▶ **bills of attainder** Declarations of guilt by legislative decree without benefit of a trial.

▶ **ex post facto laws** From the Latin for "after the fact," legislation that makes something a crime that was legal when it occurred.

▶ **exclusionary rule** To protect against unreasonable searches and seizures, the Supreme Court has established that evidence obtained illegally is not admissible in court.

▶ **double jeopardy** Protection against the state using its power to repeatedly prosecute someone until the person is convicted. Double jeopardy precludes the prosecution of someone for the same crime in the same jurisdiction more than once.

▶ **Miranda rights** The Court requirement, following a judgment in the case *Miranda v. Arizona* (1966), that apprehended individuals know and understand that they have a right against self-incrimination and a right to be represented by an attorney.

▶ ***Gideon v. Wainwright*** The 1963 Supreme Court case that established the right to have an attorney appointed at no charge by the court to defendants unable to afford representation. It was brought by Clarence Earl Gideon, who was sentenced to five years in prison for breaking into a pool hall. From prison, Gideon filed a *habeas corpus* petition, claiming his right to an attorney was violated because he was forced by poverty to represent himself at his trial.

14-1b Due Process and Capital Punishment

The death penalty is one place where the protection against cruel and unusual punishment has been controversial. Although the Court has established the constitutionality of capital punishment, the issue continues to divide Americans as much today as it did early in our history.

Some opponents contend that it is an inhumane violation of fundamental civil liberties for the state to take a life under any circumstances. They bolster their argument by pointing to economic and racial disparities in who is sentenced to death, claiming most

Box 14-1 Plea Bargaining: How the Justice System Often Works

In a **plea bargain,** defendants plead guilty to a lesser crime than the one for which they have been charged and accept a lesser sentence than what they might have expected had they been convicted on the original charge. Instead of a trial, everyone moves right to sentencing. Plea bargains are the result of negotiations where, typically, each attorney tells his or her version of the story, with prosecutors pointing out the most serious facts of the case and defense attorneys minimizing the incident. Sometimes, judges enter the negotiations and explicitly state the sentence they intend to impose. A compromise is hammered out, and if the defendant accepts it, the deed is done. Most felony and misdemeanor cases end in guilty pleas, many of which are the direct result of negotiation.*

Plea bargains serve the interests of the court officers, but we can ask how well they serve the interests of defendants and society as a whole. Because defendants waive their due process rights in accepting a plea bargain, there is no impartial finding of guilt or innocence. In a sense, plea bargaining turns the assumptions behind due process upside-down, presuming guilt on the part of defendants and foregoing the opportunity to permit them to wage a defense. It's possible to imagine innocent people being pressured into accepting a guilty plea by busy defense attorneys who convince them not to take their chances at trial. Maybe it's easier to imagine guilty parties getting a lighter sentence than they would face if they had been convicted in a trial. Does either outcome seem just to you?

▶ **plea bargain** A compromise between a defendant, defense attorney, and prosecutor, whereby the defendant foregoes due process and agrees to plead guilty without a trial to a lesser charge in exchange for a more lenient punishment.

*Herbert Jacob, *Law and Politics in the United States,* 2nd ed. (New York: HarperCollins College Publishers, 1995), 163–175.

death-row inmates are poor individuals lacking in funds to pay expensive lawyers who could have effectively saved their lives through more capable representation. Most of these individuals are African American. The American Civil Liberties Union counts, between 1973 and 2002, 178 African Americans put to death for killing a white person and 12 whites put to death for killing an African American person.[3]

Opponents also argue that the death penalty is carried out in a capricious way that depends largely on the state where you were convicted. The map in Figure 14-1 displays how the number of executions since 1976 varies by state. Be sure to compare Texas with everyone else.

Nonetheless, the death penalty continues to receive strong popular support, either because it is viewed as just or as a deterrent to crime, or both. Take a few minutes to read about the history and background of capital punishment in Issue Box 14-1 on pages 426–427, and consider the arguments made by supporters and opponents.

14-2 Religious Freedom

establishment clause
The language in the First Amendment that serves as the basis for the constitutional separation of church and state.

free exercise clause
The language in the First Amendment that limits government interference in private religious beliefs and practices.

Americans are a religious people. In the 1998 General Social Survey, 91.4 percent claimed a religious identity. About four in ten said their religious affiliation is strong. Half maintained that they attend religious services at least once a month.[4] The United States also boasts a great deal of religious diversity, with Americans claiming to follow over a dozen religions and over twenty-five denominations.[5] Such a wide range of affiliations can cause trouble when religious practices and customs come into conflict with each other and, at times, with nonreligious social values. Constitutional assurances of free religious worship, widely believed to be absolute, have at times been curtailed by the Court to provide for the rights of those opposed to public displays of religious expression or to uphold conflicting social standards.

The First Amendment makes twin statements about religious freedom, which offer two distinct constitutional protections: "Congress shall make no law respecting an establishment of religion, or prohibiting the free exercise thereof." The first of these, the **establishment clause,** is the basis for the widely discussed separation between church and state. The second, typically called the **free exercise clause,** restricts government from interfering with private religious practices. Both of these clauses have been open to interpretation and therefore have been a source of controversy.

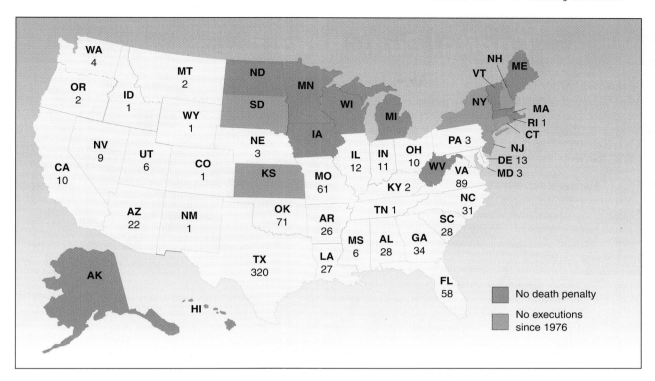

14-2a No Establishment of Religion

In the most fundamental sense, the establishment clause precludes the government from sanctioning a national religion, although it is often taken to mean much more. Thomas Jefferson wrote that the establishment clause built "a wall of separation between church and State." In *Everson v. Board of Education* (1947), Justice Hugo Black elaborated in great detail:

> The "establishment of religion" clause of the First Amendment means at least this: Neither a state nor the Federal Government can set up a church. Neither can pass laws which aid one religion, aid all religions, or prefer one religion over another. Neither can force nor influence a person to go to or to remain away from church against his will or force him to profess a belief or disbelief in any religion. . . . No tax in any amount, large or small, can be levied to support any religious activities or institutions, whatever they may be called, or whatever form they may adopt to teach or practice religion. Neither a state nor the Federal Government can, openly or secretly, participate in the affairs of any religious organizations or groups, and vice versa.[6]

At the same time, the phrase "In God We Trust" appears on the quarter you have in your pocket. A chaplain offers a prayer to start congressional sessions. In fact, the *Everson* decision, in which Justice Black reaffirms Jefferson's "wall of separation," upheld the right of the State of New Jersey to provide public bus service to students of a Catholic school, saying the First Amendment intended government to be neutral—not adversarial—in matters of religion. These are places where religion mixes with government that fall short of establishment. Depending on how thick you feel the wall of separation should be, they may also be points of controversy.

No doubt, the place where the barrier between church and state is put to the greatest test is over the issue of whether prayer should be permitted in public school. It's an emotional concern that moves people on both sides of the question. After reading about the history and background of school prayer in Issue Box 14-2 on pages 428–429, consider the arguments made by supporters and opponents and decide whether you believe religious freedom is the freedom to *permit* prayer in school or the freedom *from* prayer in school.

Figure 14-1
Does Where You Live Influence If You Will Live?
This map shows the number of state executions as of February 2004.

Source: Data from http://people.smu.edu/rhalperi/summary.html.

Issue Box 14-1   *Capital Punishment*

History and Background

In January 2003, as one of his final official acts, Illinois Governor George Ryan commuted the death sentences of all 167 inmates on death row to life in prison, saying the system by which people are sentenced to death was "arbitrary and capricious—and therefore immoral."[*] The sweeping move—unprecedented in its scope—followed an exhaustive study of Illinois death row cases that revealed, among other things, that people had been sentenced to death on the basis of questionable evidence, and that African Americans were far more likely to receive the death penalty than whites. Capital punishment opponents were overjoyed. Victims' rights groups were shocked and appalled.[†]

Governor Ryan's action was one of the more recent turns in America's conflicted history with capital punishment. Through the nineteenth and twentieth centuries, as western countries like England, West Germany, Italy, Switzerland, Norway, Sweden, and Denmark abolished the death penalty, many American states vacillated between abolishing it and reinstating it. The number of executions in the United States plummeted in the 1960s, as the American public, strongly supportive of the death penalty for much of the twentieth century, became less sympathetic. Then, in the 1972 case *Furman v. Georgia,* a fragmented Supreme Court (nine separate opinions were issued) ruled all existing death penalty laws to be unconstitutional, saying they were instituted arbitrarily and capriciously.[‡]

The ruling came at a time when public opinion was beginning to swing back toward support of the death penalty, and it caused a backlash. Many states moved quickly to enact new capital punishment statutes. Within four years of the *Furman* verdict, a more conservative Supreme Court reinstated the death penalty in the case of *Gregg v. Georgia* (1976), ruling that capital punishment does not violate the Eighth Amendment's ban on cruel and unusual punishment and that statutory cor-

rections made by Georgia and other states satisfactorily addressed the inequities that the Court had expressed concern about in its earlier ruling.[§] But *Gregg* didn't put an end to questions about how equitably the death penalty was imposed. In fact, inequities in meting out capital punishment were the reason Governor Ryan commuted all Illinois death sentences twenty-seven years later.

In the wake of the *Gregg* decision, the number of inmates on death row has grown steadily, and although the number of executions carried out has been relatively modest in comparison, they grew from one in 1977 to ninety-eight in 1999.[**] However, subsequent rulings have placed restrictions on how the death penalty may be implemented. *Coker v. Georgia* (1977) banned capital punishment for people convicted of rape.[††] More recently, *Atkins v. Virginia* (2002) did the same for mentally retarded criminals.[‡‡]

Throughout America's uneasy history with the death penalty, the positions taken by opponents and advocates have remained remarkably consistent. Opponents point to what they see as a double standard in the application of the

14-2b Free Exercise of Religion

The idea behind the free exercise clause is that the practice of individual worship should be free from government interference. This is fairly easy to do when religious worship doesn't violate other social values, but since that's not always the case, free exercise has been a matter of dispute over the years, as the Court has held that the free exercise of religion is not absolute.

An early battle of great significance took place between federal authorities and the Mormon Church over the practice of polygamy in the Utah territory. The conflict dated to an 1852 pronouncement by Brigham Young, prophet of the Church of Jesus Christ of Latter-Day Saints, that Mormons would practice polygamy or plural marriage as a part of their religious beliefs. This position enraged official Washington, which found the whole idea of polygamy to be an abomination and criminalized it. The dispute ended up in the Supreme Court in 1878, in the case of *Reynolds v. United States.*[7]

The Mormon Church expected the Court to uphold its right to free exercise of religion as expressed in the Constitution. They were wrong. The Court contended that the Constitution did not define the term "religion," and proceeded to offer its own explanation of the concept, distinguishing between principles and actions. Under this interpretation, the First Amendment protected religious beliefs but not behaviors taken in the death penalty to rich and poor, and to white and nonwhite. Despite the opinion of the Supreme Court in *Gregg v. Georgia,* they hold the opinion that it is cruel and unusual punishment. Supporters regard it as an appropriate penalty for the most violent crimes, a form of justice for crime victims, and a deterrent to violence.

Arguments in Support

Death penalty supporters make the following arguments:

- It deters crime. If people know they face execution, they are less likely to engage in violence.
- It's justice. The death penalty is a punishment of last resort and used only in cases where the most horrendous crimes have been committed. In these cases, it is appropriate for guilty parties to pay with their lives.
- It's equitable. Any past inequities in the implementation of the death penalty have been sorted out, according to the Supreme Court in *Gregg v. Georgia.*
- Victims have rights. People on death row have committed the most gruesome crimes imaginable. The death penalty permits closure for the victims they left behind.

Arguments Against

Opponents of the death penalty contend:

- It's not a deterrent to violent crime. There is no clear-cut evidence to demonstrate that people will think about the repercussions of committing a capital offense.
- It's vengeance. Murdering someone who has committed even the most horrendous crime does not bring the victim back to life or set right the wrong that has been committed.
- It's inequitable. There is a far greater likelihood of being put to death if you're poor, nonwhite, or live in Texas.
- Everyone has rights. The beauty of the American system of justice is that it protects the rights of people who

have done unjustifiable things. For the state to put someone to death, regardless of the circumstances, is the ultimate denial of individual rights.

My Opinion

When registering your opinion on the death penalty, consider the history of the issue and the arguments supporting and opposing it. In particular, ask yourself if you believe the death penalty:

- Does or does not deter crime
- Is justice or vengeance
- Is equitably or inequitably imposed
- Justly accounts for the rights of victims or unjustly denies the rights of the accused

The most accurate description of my attitude toward capital punishment is:

1—I strongly oppose it. It's a bad idea.
2—I oppose it, but with some reservations.
3—I support it, but with some reservations.
4—I strongly support it. It's a good idea.
5—I haven't thought enough about it to have an opinion.
6—I don't care about it enough to bother.

[*]Robert E. Pierre and Kari Lydersen, "Illinois Death Row Emptied," *Washington Post,* January 12, 2003, sec. A.

[†]Ibid.

[‡]Lee Epstein and Joseph F. Kobylka, *The Supreme Court and Legal Change: Abortion and the Death Penalty* (Chapel Hill: University of North Carolina Press, 1992), 34–82.

[§]Ibid., 83–116.

[**]American Civil Liberties website, at http://www.aclu.org/DeathPenalty/DeathPenaltymain.cfm.

[††]Ibid, 120.

[‡‡]See http://supct.law.cornell.edu/supct/html/00-8452.ZS.html.

name of religion that violated the law. Writing for the Court, Chief Justice Waite asked rhetorically,

> Suppose one believed that human sacrifices were a necessary part of religious worship, would it be seriously contended that the civil government under which he lived could not interfere to prevent a sacrifice? Or if a wife religiously believed it was her duty to burn herself upon the funeral pile of her dead husband, would it be beyond the power of the civil government to prevent her carrying her belief into practice?[8]

The logic of the decision makes practical sense if the objective is to maintain the superiority of the law over personal religious practices, or to prohibit behaviors carried out in the name of worship that the broader society finds abhorrent. However, if the goal is to protect one's religious beliefs from government interference, the Court's distinction between beliefs and behaviors may appear a bit academic, for how does one hold a belief if it is not practiced? That dilemma runs through the body of law on the free exercise doctrine.

Other, more recent rulings have limited free exercise of religion when it clashes with deeply held social values. In *Employment Division, Department of Human Resources of Oregon v. Smith* (1990), the Supreme Court ruled that two Native Americans could be fired from their jobs at a drug rehabilitation organization and denied unemployment benefits for using peyote, a controlled substance with important religious significance that could

Issue Box 14-2   *School Prayer*

History and Background

In June 1998, the House of Representatives voted 224–203 to approve a "Religious Freedom Amendment" to the Constitution, permitting prayer in the nation's public schools. The amendment reads in part: "Neither the United States nor any State shall establish any official religion, but the people's right to pray and to recognize their religious beliefs, heritage, or traditions on public property, including schools, shall not be infringed. Neither the United States nor any State shall require any person to join in prayer or other religious activity, prescribe school prayers, discriminate against religion, or deny equal access to a benefit on account of religion."

Because a constitutional amendment requires the approval of two-thirds of each house of Congress before it can go to the states for ratification, the amendment died. Buoyed by having won a simple majority, though, and bolstered by support from some organized religious groups, Oklahoma Republican Representative Ernest Istook reintroduced the measure the following year.[*] It takes a lot to amend the Constitution, and the issue of school prayer is emotionally charged, but its advocates persevere.

Does religious freedom mean having the right to pray in public schools? Or does having religious freedom protect us from public school prayer? The way you answer this question is partly a matter of what you value, and partly a matter of how you interpret the constitutional separation of church and state.

Some view religion as something the government should nurture and support on an evenhanded basis, without establishing a national religion or requiring people to participate in prayer. They see this as a tolerant interpretation of religious freedom consistent with the original intent of the First Amendment.[†] Others view religion as a private matter and understand the establishment clause in the First Amendment to be a statement of every individual's private right to worship or not to worship as he or she pleases. From this perspective, if a teacher leads a class in prayer, social and institutional pressures make it difficult for students who object to express their unwillingness to participate, effectively forcing them to pray against their First Amendment rights.[‡]

In recent years, the Supreme Court has sided with the latter interpretation of the First Amendment. In the 1962 case *Engle v. Vitale,* the Court ruled that the New York State Board of Regents could not give public school teachers the option of leading classes in a voluntary, nondenominational prayer, which read, "Almighty God, we acknowledge our dependence upon Thee, and we beg Thy blessings upon us, our parents, our teachers and our country."[§] In the Court's opinion, any prayer, no matter how neutral, is a religious activity and violates the First Amendment.

The next year, the Court issued a pair of rulings that, together with *Engle v. Vitale,* established the legal framework

Source: PhotoEdit.

for school prayer. The Court struck down a Pennsylvania law in *Abington Township School District v. Schempp* (1963) that required the school day to start with Bible readings and the recital of the Lord's Prayer. In the companion case *Murray v. Curlett* (1963), the Court struck down a similar Maryland law that required unison prayer and Bible reading in public school.[**]

However, none of these cases made mention of voluntary private personal prayer in public schools, which remained constitutional, and in the *Schempp* decision the Court recognized the importance of teaching about religion in the context of history as part of a well-rounded public school education.

More recent Court decisions have interpreted religious freedom the same way. In 1985, the Court struck down an Alabama law in *Wallace v. Jaffree* that required the school day to begin with a moment of silent meditation or voluntary prayer, on the grounds that prayer, even if voluntary, has a religious purpose. In *Lee v. Weisman* (1992), the Court struck down the recital of a prayer at public school graduation ceremonies as a form of coerced religious participation.[††]

Blocked by the Court for decades, school prayer advocates turned to the constitutional amendment process as a way of overturning what has become established law. Its promoters seek to establish protection for what they regard as the majority of Americans who wish to have their faith expressed in schools. They believe the Court's interpretation of the First Amendment violates the wishes of that majority in the name of freedom. Students who object to classroom prayer would still have the right to sit quietly or leave the room, as they may now if they oppose the recital of the nonreligious Pledge of Allegiance, but they wouldn't have the right to silence those who wish to pray.[‡‡]

Opponents say a constitutional amendment is unnecessary because the law already protects an individual's right to private prayer on school property. In that regard, students who wish to pray in school are not being silenced. Instead, opponents express concern for minority rights, which they believe the amendment would violate. They believe the law needs to protect those individuals, especially impressionable schoolchildren, who would be harmed by having to tolerate the publicly sanctioned expression of ideas they do not share.[§§]

Arguments in Support

Several arguments are typically offered in support of a constitutional amendment permitting school prayer. Proponents say:

- It will put a stop to religious tyranny. Without the liberty to worship in schools, we do not have true religious freedom in America. Religious dissenters should not be compelled to join, but they should not be able to silence those who wish to pray.
- It's what the Constitution intended. Religious freedom means having the right to pray in public schools. This is entirely different from the establishment of a state-sanctioned religion, which is what the First Amendment was designed to prevent.
- It's pro-family. Prayer will reinforce traditional values and the lessons that so many parents try to teach at home, including tolerance of those who desire an outlet for religious expression at school by those who would otherwise stop them.
- It's necessary to instill values. Students learn values at school, and the religious and spiritual values expressed by prayer are among the most important for individuals and society to uphold.
- It's voluntary. Students who don't want to participate can remain silent.
- It's harmless. Permitting prayer in school is entirely different than permitting government to decide what individuals can and cannot believe or how they should worship.

Arguments Against

Opponents of a constitutional amendment permitting school prayer argue:

- It's tyrannical. Sanctioned, organized prayer is a threat to the liberty of nonbelievers and those who believe differently than the majority. The law must protect the rights of minorities, no matter how unpopular that may be.
- It violates the intent of the Constitution. The Court has repeatedly affirmed that having religious freedom protects us from prayer in public school.
- It's intolerant. Those who wish to pray in school should do so without subjecting atheists, nonbelievers, and those of minority faiths to a profoundly disturbing experience.

- It infringes on personal rights. School administrators would be free to impose a religious perspective on those who disagreed.
- It's coercive. Dissenters will have no protection from something they do not believe in. Private, personal prayer, which is permitted by the courts, does not pose this problem.
- It's dangerous. Any step that undermines the separation of church and state is a step in the direction of giving the government the power to sanction religion.

My Opinion

When registering your opinion on whether we should approve a constitutional amendment permitting school prayer, consider the history of the issue and the arguments supporting and opposing it. In particular, ask yourself if prayer in school:

- Will stop religious tyranny or is a form of religious tyranny
- Conforms to or violates the intent of constitutionally protected religious freedom
- Is pro-family or intolerant
- Instills values or infringes on personal rights
- Is voluntary or coercive
- Is harmless or dangerous

The most accurate description of my attitude toward passing a constitutional amendment permitting prayer in public schools is:

1—I strongly oppose it. It's a bad idea.
2—I oppose it, but with some reservations.
3—I support it, but with some reservations.
4—I strongly support it. It's a good idea.
5—I haven't thought enough about it to have an opinion.
6—I don't care about it enough to bother.

[*]See http://religiousfreedom.house.gov/.

[†]See Questions and Answers about the "Religious Freedom Amendment," at http://religiousfreedom.house.gov/rqa.htm.

[‡]See United States Department of State facts about America, at http://usinfo.state.gov/usa/infousa/facts/democrac/47.htm.

[§]William K. Muir, Jr., *Prayer in the Public Schools* (Chicago: University of Chicago Press, 1967), 15.

[**]See http://www.nationalcenter.org/scot63.htm. The Murray suit was filed by an atheist whose son had been told he could sit in the hallway while his classmates prayed. You can read more about it online at the American Atheists website, at http://www.atheists.org/courthouse/prayer.html.

[††]Robert S. Alley, *Without a Prayer: Religious Expression in Public Schools* (Amherst, NY: Prometheus Books, 1996), 34–46, 128–138.

[‡‡]Questions and Answers about the "Religious Freedom Amendment," at http://religiousfreedom.house.gov/rqa.htm.

[§§]See, for instance, the American Civil Liberties Union website, at http://www.aclu.org/news/NewsPrint.cfm?ID=9986&c=139.

be used legally on Native American reservations but not off those reservations in the state of Oregon, where the pair worked. Writing for the majority, Justice Antonin Scalia contended that the free exercise of religion can be limited as the incidental result of a law whose primary purpose is to set legal boundaries for everyone.[9] In other words, Oregon did not make peyote illegal in order to limit Native American worship, but if it has that effect, the rights of a religious minority must take a back seat to broader social interests.

Civil rights issues clashed with religious practices in the 1983 case *Bob Jones University v. United States.* Bob Jones University is a conservative Christian university that forbade interracial dating on religious grounds. Because of this policy, the Internal Revenue Service refused the school tax-exempt status on the basis of federal civil rights laws prohibiting tax exemptions for institutions that practiced discriminatory policies. Bob Jones University sued, claiming that its interracial dating policy was a matter of free exercise of religion, not racial discrimination. The Court disagreed, saying the government's overriding interest in ending discrimination outweighed the school's religious position.[10]

However, when the issue has been something narrower than polygamy, drug policies, and civil rights, the Court has sided with religious groups. In *Cantwell v. Connecticut* (1940), the Court held that states couldn't require religious groups to get a special permit to solicit for religious purposes, even if the group's message is unpleasant to those who hear it. In *Wisconsin v. Yoder* (1972), Amish children were granted the right to be taken out of public school after eighth grade in order to comply with religious teachings. The interest of the state in universal education was in this case considered secondary to Amish religious values. As in many cases involving the free exercise clause, the outcome often depends on how sharply religious practices clash with broader social norms.

14-3 Freedom of Expression

No liberty is more central to an open society than freedom of expression. Even though the First Amendment is unequivocal in stating that "Congress shall make no law . . . abridging the freedom of speech," the issue in practice—like freedom of worship—has many variations. Justice Oliver Wendell Holmes may have penned the most famous line about the margins of free expression when he wrote, "Even the most stringent protection of free speech would not protect a man in falsely shouting fire in a crowded theatre and causing a panic."[11]

14-3a Dangerous and Unpopular Speech

Holmes was writing in the 1919 case *Schenck v. United States,* which arose out of the prosecution of Charles Schenck, a Socialist leader who had printed pamphlets urging young men to resist the draft during World War I. Schenck's actions violated provisions of the Espionage Act of 1917, which made it a crime to call for draft resistance or utter disloyal statements about the United States.

Schenck petitioned the Court to have the Espionage Act declared in violation of the First Amendment, but his efforts were unsuccessful. Nonetheless, in upholding the constitutionality of the Espionage Act as a measure the government was permitted to take during wartime, Holmes set out a specific rule for determining when government could limit free expression: the standard of **clear and present danger.**[12] Government could stifle dissent, Holmes argued, when words "are used in such circumstances and are of such a nature as to create a clear and present danger that they will bring about the substantive evils that Congress has a right to prevent. It is a question of proximity and degree."[13] Wartime created such a circumstance, Holmes argued, when unpopular speech became dangerous. Even if Schenck's pleas to avoid the draft were unsuccessful, the fact that he made them was in the Court's view sufficient to present a public danger.

Around the same time, using similar logic, the Court said antiwar rhetoric in a time of conflict is not protected by the Constitution. Box 14-2 explains.

Eight years after the *Schenck* decision, Justice Louis Brandeis elaborated on and in the process altered the clear and present danger standard. Brandeis contended that unpopular speech is critical to maintaining democratic freedom, and that for people to feel secure

▶**clear and present danger**
The standard established by Justice Oliver Wendell Holmes for determining when the government could limit speech.

> ### Box 14-2   Antiwar Rhetoric and Unprotected Speech

Not surprisingly, people with unpopular ideas are typically the ones caught in the middle of court cases testing free expression. The same year as the *Schenck* decision, Eugene Debs, the Socialist Party presidential candidate, criticized American involvement in World War I and spoke out publicly against the draft. At a 1918 speech in Canton, Ohio, Debs urged his audience to oppose the war. Drawing distinctions between leaders who declare war and workers who die in war, he said (to a blue-collar audience), "You have your lives to lose; you certainly ought to have the right to declare war if you consider a war necessary."*

Debs was arrested under the terms of the Espionage Act and charged with inciting disloyalty, insubordination, and mutiny against the armed forces of the United States. He admitted to the statements he had made in the speech, was convicted, and was sentenced to ten years in prison. The Supreme Court upheld the conviction, using the clear and present danger standard established in *Schenck,* noting that the First Amendment protected the general socialist message in the speech but not the call to resist the draft.

Debs continued his 1920 presidential campaign from prison. He received 2.4 million votes.

Debs v. United States, 249 US 211 (1919).

---

about democratic participation, they have to be assured that unpopular speech will not be punished. To this end, he said an idea has to be dangerous and not just disliked to pose a threat to society, and that if there is time to engage in a full discussion of an idea—which is always the case unless the country faces an immediate crisis—it can never pose a clear and present danger. To Brandeis, the way to defuse the danger posed by most threatening ideas is through more discussion, not suppression of speech.[14]

Brandeis' movement toward greater acceptance of free speech set the stage for Court decisions in the 1960s and 1970s that increased First Amendment protection for unpopular speech. The 1969 case *Brandenberg v. Ohio* established the strict standard that speech had to incite "imminent lawless action" in order for government to have the ability to suppress it. Otherwise, First Amendment protections apply, even to speech that advocates violence (but does not actually instigate violence).[15]

14-3b Unpopular Speech in a Difficult Time

During periods of national tension, though, strict protections on speech have been hard to maintain. The close of World War II found the United States settling into a protracted period of uneasy coexistence with the Soviet Union that would last forty-five years. The start of the cold war brought a hysterical reaction to Communism that was exacerbated and exploited by Republican Senator Joseph McCarthy of Wisconsin, who crusaded against Communists in government and the private sector.

McCarthy made baseless accusations without evidence, but with the backing of the FBI and congressional investigators, he wielded immense power. Employers fired people who were tainted by McCarthy's charges, leaving them blacklisted and unable to get work. People were encouraged to turn in their friends and associates to demonstrate their loyalty to America—and to save their own skin. Moderate voices were silenced by the fear that questioning McCarthy's charges would brand them Communist sympathizers, and that McCarthy would next turn his inquisition on them.[16] The publisher of this book would have placed itself at risk for printing this paragraph. For a period of time, our system failed its most basic test, as an intense minority was able to use the mechanisms of government to tyrannize the majority, quashing criticism of the government.

During this period, it was particularly dangerous to be directly affiliated with the American Communist Party. In 1940, Congress passed the Smith Act (technically the Alien Registration Act), which made it a crime to advocate the violent overthrow of the government—the position taken by the American Communist Party leadership during the time of McCarthy's Red Scare. In this climate, party leaders were prosecuted under the Smith Act, and the Court—in a momentary departure from the trend toward protecting unpopular speech—upheld the constitutionality of the Smith Act and the convictions of the

Communist Party leadership. This happened despite the fact that the American Communist Party was small and ineffectual, making it highly unlikely that its advocacy would turn to action.

In dissent, Justice William O. Douglas anticipated the turn the court would take in the next decade, stating, "Free speech has occupied an exalted position because of the high service it has given our society. Its protection is essential to the very existence of a democracy. The airing of ideas releases pressures which otherwise might become destructive."[17] This was a difficult argument to accept in the icy climate of 1951.

As we move deeper into a time when the fear of terrorism is making inroads into our national psyche, and when free expression facilitates the planning and execution of terrorist plots, we might ask ourselves whether we can embrace Douglas' rationale for the benefits of free expression, or whether we will react as our grandparents' generation did to a different but equally penetrating threat. The flashpoint for this discussion has been the USA Patriot Act (which stands for Uniting and Strengthening America by Providing Appropriate Tools Required to Intercept and Obstruct Terrorism), which was passed in haste following the September 11, 2001, terrorist attacks. In the name of fighting terrorism, the USA Patriot Act gives law enforcement officials sweeping powers to conduct surveillance operations, including the power to secretly trace telephone numbers and email addresses. Supporters say the government needs to retain such authority in order to stay in front of covert terrorist groups. Opponents feel the Patriot Act gives too much coercive power to law enforcement officials, which can be used to undermine civil liberties, and worry that it could have a chilling effect on free expression akin to what the United States experienced during the McCarthy era.

14-3c Symbolic Expression

Protesters through the ages have resorted to the use of images to make strong, emotional statements. Designed to be hard to take and often disrespectful, symbolic expression can be a potent and effective way to lash out at policies and policy makers that people find objectionable. Maybe you've seen footage—there's lots of it—of crowds in foreign cities protesting American policy by burning an effigy of the president. During the Vietnam War, hippies grew their hair long in defiance of the buttoned-down values of their parents' generation—the group that most strongly supported the war. A few desecrated national symbols like the flag as a way of expressing their opposition to the actions of political elites.

How much symbolic expression should be permissible under the First Amendment? The most emotional debate revolves around the question of whether flag burning should be condoned. The Court has narrowly upheld flag burning as a constitutionally permissible form of expression, but opponents have mounted a spirited counterattack by trying to win approval of a constitutional amendment that would overrule the Court. Take a few minutes to explore the positions people have staked out on this issue in Issue Box 14-3 on pages 434–435, then make your judgment on whether you believe flag burning should be permitted or prohibited.

14-3d Political Correctness and Speech Codes

What do you do when someone wants to exhibit a strong attachment to a flag that is reviled by other citizens rather than universally beloved? Some southerners have as deep a connection to the Confederate flag as they do to the American flag, but the Confederate flag is widely regarded as an offensive emblem to African Americans, who see it as an endorsement of white supremacy and a symbol of a racist political regime. So, when a fourteen-year-old white Georgia boy recently arrived at school wearing a T-shirt bearing the Confederate flag, he was suspended for a day for violating a school ban on displaying the controversial symbol. The boy objected, using language that echoes the words of those who *support* a constitutional amendment against desecrating the American flag, saying, "My Confederate ancestors, they died for this flag."

White parents flooded the school district with complaints about the suspension, accusing the district of imposing "politically correct" values on their children. They contended that not permitting their kids to display the Confederate flag simply because it might offend some people was a form of censorship. In so doing, they employed an argument identical to what *opponents* of the flag burning amendment have said, asserting the Constitution does not protect people from being offended, and that their right to free expression should be untouchable. The American Civil Liberties Union agreed, siding with those who seek free expression over those who would restrict it.[18]

Unpopular expression is the hardest to defend. Chances are, you or your friends have been involved in or heard about free expression debates on your campus, which invoked the "politically correct" label that surfaced in the Georgia Confederate flag flap. "Political correctness" has been an emotional topic at many universities for the past several years because it touches on sensitive and important personal matters, like what we get to learn and how we're allowed to act.

Those on the left who are associated with "political correctness" once used the term self-mockingly to deflate their own ideas. However, as advocates of a "politically correct" agenda rose to power in academia, their opponents started using it disparagingly. The debate has enveloped numerous elements of campus intellectual life, and it has often been shrill, but the most tangible manifestation of political correctness in academia has been in the implementation of multicultural curricula and personal codes of conduct.

As a curricular matter, proponents of multiculturalism have advocated—successfully in many places—revamping curricula to emphasize cultural diversity among the writers and thinkers represented in core texts. They contend that to do otherwise is to offer an education that is homogeneous and exclusionary in its emphasis on white male European writers. Critics contend that multiculturalists and feminists have hijacked the curriculum and thrown out valuable contributions simply because they were written by white male Europeans, then justified their actions on the grounds that the writings they discard are inherently racist and sexist. In other words, they equate political correctness with censorship.

The same applies to codes of personal conduct. Some universities implemented speech codes that mandated taking disciplinary action against students who used racist or sexist epithets, broadening the umbrella of harassment to include language that critics contended was commonplace and previously regarded as a minor matter.[19] Proponents of speech codes said the fact that so many people considered offensive language to be insignificant was part of the problem, as it spoke to the level of hostility directed against people with diverse backgrounds and viewpoints. Critics spoke widely of a "thought police" attempting to regulate free expression, and speech codes did not fair well when challenged in the courts.[20]

Ironically, some of the sharpest criticism of political correctness came from liberals who felt it undermines free expression. A former president of the Los Angeles chapter of the National Organization for Women (NOW) described political correctness as indulging the "culture of victimhood" and compared it to the reign of terror in George Orwell's novel *1984*, under the guise of trying to promote social equality.[21] A self-described "bleeding heart liberal" undergraduate at a prominent university endorsed an anti-political-correctness student group called Foundation for Academic Standards and Tradition because of her concern that political correctness sacrificed individual freedom.[22]

One way to understand political correctness is to see it in the context of what's been dubbed the "culture wars" that date to the rise of the counterculture of the 1960s. Political correctness took hold on campuses as conservatives were successfully mobilizing voters—especially white male voters—behind an entirely different set of values that advocates of political correctness regarded as directly threatening to multiculturalism. The real dilemma raised by critics of political correctness, and the thing that makes it so controversial, is whether its advocates, in an effort to create an environment supportive of difference, impose a kind of cultural uniformity that stifles free speech and ironically makes it difficult to embrace a different or opposing perspective.

14-4 Freedom of the Press

The press carries a key constitutional responsibility as the source of the information we need to stay informed and make responsible public choices. Even though we questioned

Issue Box 14-3 *Flag Burning*

History and Background

Few symbols move Americans like the flag. To many it is a special icon: an emblem that represents the living nation, which should be accorded the utmost respect. Consequently, few acts of civil disobedience gall Americans like burning the American flag. It's an action that has happened rarely in our history—about two hundred times in over 225 years[*]—but in the 1960s it became the most powerful symbol of anger and protest against the Vietnam War. During that time, many who supported the war felt American values were under attack by a militant counterculture for which flag burning became a potent form of protest. In some important respects, the social wounds opened by that conflict have yet to heal, and the sense of permissiveness and diminished respect for authority, which some people see as stemming from that time, still rubs raw. The intensity surrounding the flag-burning debate may be understood in this context.[†]

In 1989, the Supreme Court issued a 5–4 decision in the case of *Texas v. Johnson* upholding the right of a protester to burn the American flag at the 1984 Republican National Convention in Dallas, overturning a Texas law that had made flag burning a crime punishable by a $2,000 fine and a year in prison. The Court held that flag burning is a constitutionally protected form of political expression, and Texas could not prosecute Johnson for burning the flag without violating his First Amendment rights.[‡]

Congress responded immediately by passing the Flag Protection Act of 1989, which cleared both houses by a lopsided margin and was signed into law by President Bush (senior). The next year, the Court struck down the Flag Protection Act as unconstitutional by the same one-vote margin. That set in motion an organized lobbying campaign determined to overturn the *Johnson* decision with a constitutional amendment. Since 1994, an organization called the Citizens Flag Alliance has been waging a grassroots campaign in conjunction with a coalition of 120 other interests groups to recruit local and national legislative candidates who would support a flag protection amendment permitting federal, state, and local authorities to make it a crime to desecrate the flag.[§]

Members of the Citizens Flag Alliance have been effective, but as of 2003, they have fallen short of their goal. Bolstered by surveys that show large majorities of Americans support their position, they were successful in winning House

Source: Copyright © 2005 Atomic Dog Publishing and its licensors. All rights reserved.

approval for the amendment in 1995 by a vote of 312–120, far surpassing the two-thirds majority required for passage. The amendment failed in the Senate, but only by three votes. Since then, it has fallen short three more times, with the number of House votes in favor dropping from 312 to 310 (in 1997) to 305 (in 1999) to 298 (in 2001). Each time, it failed in the Senate. The American Civil Liberties Union, which opposes the amendment as an infringement on First Amendment freedoms, connects the steady decline in congressional support to vocal opposition to the amendment by prominent Americans like former Secretary of State Colin Powell and former senator and astronaut John Glenn.[**]

Supporters of protecting the flag believe it has a special status as a national icon, something Chief Justice Rehnquist said is regarded by millions with "an almost mystical reverence," and that it can be protected from harm without violating First Amendment freedoms. They argue that burning the flag is a behavior, not an exercise of speech of the sort expressly mentioned in the First Amendment, and that the court erred by regarding the behavior of flag burning as an expression analogous to speech. They also point to opinion polls that repeatedly show overwhelming majorities of Americans stand behind this position.

In turn, opponents argue that the First Amendment was designed to protect noxious behavior in the face of strong popular sentiment against it. To them, the fact that most people support an amendment to protect the flag is all the more

---

how effectively the press performs this function when we discussed the mass media in Chapter 5, the obligation to keep readers and viewers informed is so critical to democracy that news organizations are the only private, for-profit institutions afforded constitutional protection.

14-4a Prior Restraint

prior restraint Censorship of the news by government officials before it is published or broadcast.

Press freedom stems from protection against a practice called **prior restraint,** or censorship of the news by government officials before it is printed or broadcast. The practice dates back to the seventeenth century, when the English King could censor the news before it was published. The rationale behind protecting the press against prior restraint is that reason why we *shouldn't* have one. They contend that conduct is a form of expression long protected by the Court. They feel the greater danger to society is posed by undermining the basic rights for which the flag stands, and that protecting the object at the expense of the rights of the individual tears at a foundational principle of democratic self-rule.[††]

Arguments in Support

Supporters of a constitutional amendment to prohibit flag burning say:

- Nothing could be more American. The flag is a singular icon for America and is entitled to be accorded special protection as a revered symbol of our democracy.
- It's honorable. People die for the American flag and what it represents. It dishonors them to permit the flag to be desecrated.
- It's popular. The will of the people is to protect the flag from destruction.
- It won't violate the First Amendment. Flag burning is an action, not a form of speech. The First Amendment does not specifically protect actions.
- The flag deserves special status. Even if you disagree that flag burning can be outlawed without harming First Amendment rights, the flag still deserves special protection because of its iconic value and the deep attachments Americans have toward it.

Arguments Against

Opponents of a constitutional amendment to prohibit flag burning believe:

- Nothing could be more un-American. Imprisoning people for expressing political opposition is something we'd expect in the former Soviet Union, not here.
- It's intolerant. If we are to be faithful to our core values, we cannot restrict flag burning, no matter how much we may dislike it.
- Democracy is not a popularity contest. The fact that most Americans find flag burning noxious and want to prohibit it is a strong reason for protecting it, because having individual liberty means having the ability to express unpopular sentiments.
- It violates the First Amendment. The Court has consistently upheld political protest as a form of protected expression.

- The First Amendment deserves special status. We dishonor the flag and all it stands for by unraveling the Constitution. Millions have died defending principles that would be destroyed if flag burning were outlawed.

My Opinion

When registering your opinion on whether there should be a constitutional amendment to prohibit flag burning, consider the history of the issue and the arguments supporting and opposing it. In particular, ask yourself if making it illegal to burn the flag:

- Reflects values that are distinctly American —or un-American
- Is honorable or intolerant
- Should happen because it's popular, or should *not* happen because it's popular
- Does or does not violate the spirit of the First Amendment
- Appropriately accords special status to the flag, or inappropriately denies special status to the First Amendment

The most accurate description of my attitude toward a constitutional amendment to prohibit flag burning is:

1—I strongly oppose it. It's a bad idea.
2—I oppose it, but with some reservations.
3—I support it, but with some reservations.
4—I strongly support it. It's a good idea.
5—I haven't thought enough about it to have an opinion.
6—I don't care about it enough to bother.

*"Oppose the Flag Desecration Constitutional Amendment," American Civil Liberties Union website, at http://www.aclu.org/FreeSpeech/FreeSpeech.cfm?ID=9969&c=50.

†Robert Justin Goldstein, *Flag Burning and Free Speech: The Case of Texas v. Johnson* (Lawrence, KS: University Press of Kansas, 2000), xiii–xiv.

‡Ibid, xi.

§Citizens Flag Alliance website, at http://www.cfa-inc.org/about/flag_amend1.htm.

**American Civil Liberties website, at http://www.aclu.org/FreeSpeech/FreeSpeech.cfm?ID=7366&c=50.

††Goldstein, *Flag Burning*, xi–xviii.

the executive, legislature, or courts wield too much power if they are allowed to prevent ideas from entering circulation. Once circulated, however, the press is responsible for the consequences of its actions and can be held accountable for any misstatements of fact.[23] Protection from prior restraint was confirmed in the case of *Near v. Minnesota* (1931), when the Supreme Court struck down a Minnesota law that had been used to stop publication of embarrassing information about local political figures in a tabloid called the *Saturday Press.* In issuing the order, Chief Justice Hughes made it clear that even "miscreant purveyors of scandal" have the constitutional right to publish without government interference.[24] Prior restraint could only be imposed where the public interest was clearly jeopardized by publication, such as in the case of information that would create a major national security breach if released.

The Court has set the national security bar very high. Perhaps the most serious call for prior restraint on national security grounds occurred during the Nixon administration, which tried to block the *New York Times* and the *Washington Post* from publishing a scathing, classified study of the decisions that contributed to American involvement in Vietnam. The Pentagon Papers, as the study was known, showed how a series of presidential administrations had knowingly misled the public about the war. Daniel Ellsberg, a disillusioned senior Defense Department employee who was one of the report's authors, leaked it to the *New York Times* in 1971, and the Nixon administration—which was still prosecuting the Vietnam War—immediately moved to have a series of stories about it suppressed. The Court refused in a 6–3 decision that reaffirmed the need for an urgent national security breach to be threatened before prior restraint could be imposed.[25]

14-4b Libel

Of course, granting the press freedom from prior restraint puts a great responsibility in the hands of publishers, and gives them the power to inflict harm if that power is mishandled. The remedy available to individuals who feel they have been harmed by press coverage lies in **libel** laws, which we discussed in Chapter 5. As we noted, though, libel is difficult to prove—particularly for public figures, who have to show that false statements were published with malice.

> **libel** The legal restriction against the malicious publication of material that knowingly damages an individual's reputation.

In rare situations where sloppy reporting leads to damaging misstatements, the press can get hit hard. For instance, in 1990 the *Philadelphia Inquirer* was ordered to pay $6 million to a Pennsylvania Supreme Court judge for incorrectly accusing him of influence peddling. A year later, a Dallas television station lost a libel suit to a Texas district attorney for falsely reporting he had taken bribes. The station was ordered to pay $58 million.[26] Such judgments, though, are unusual.

14-4c Publishing on the Internet

The advent of the Internet as a device for publishing and communicating has added new wrinkles to traditional notions of press freedom. As neither a print nor an electronic medium, the Internet cuts across previous legal distinctions as it permits us to be our own publishers, sending our ideas across national boundaries where laws on press freedom vary widely.[27] From the standpoint of libel, early indications are that self-publishers can claim to be public figures, requiring those who might sue to restrict cyber content to demonstrate the presence of malice as if they were suing a newspaper or television station.[28]

The Internet is also home to a wide variety of distasteful, troubling, and hateful websites. This can prove to be a difficult test of our tolerance, or of Justice Douglas' remedy to allow expression of offensive ideas, because much of this speech is constitutionally protected.[29]

The Internet is also home to a wide range of material that some would consider obscene. On this point, traditional law is vague and confusing, and Internet postings simply confound the situation. The First Amendment does not protect obscene communication, but there's little agreement over what obscene communication is or the standards that should be used to identify it. Those who have attempted to classify material as obscene can agree on little more than the standard that was penned by Justice Potter Stewart, who wrote in a frustrated effort to define pornography: "I know it when I see it."[30]

Other justices have hardly done better. The Supreme Court has used language like "prurient,"[31] "patently offensive," and "utterly without redeeming social value"[32] as a test of whether something is obscene, leaving it to "the average person, applying contemporary community standards"[33] to determine if something fits this definition. It's problematic how this test applies to the Internet, where in addition to defining obscenity, you have to define the community.

Consider Issue Box 14-4 on pages 438–439, which details a specific example of an Internet posting considered obscene by some, art by others. As you do, see if you can decide where and how you would set the standard for posting potentially obscene material online.

14-5 Freedom of Assembly and Association

In February 2003, tens of thousands of demonstrators rallied against the looming war with Iraq in protests held in cities across the country. They were protected from government retribution by the First Amendment guarantee of "the right of the people to peaceably assemble, and to petition the government for redress of grievances." This may be something we take for granted, but the authors of the Constitution certainly did not. In seventeenth-century England, you could be put in prison for peacefully assembling to advocate ideas that were opposed by the crown.

The Supreme Court has affirmed that the First Amendment protects assembly for the purpose of the lawful exchange of ideas, no matter how unpopular the assembled group may be. This provision has been used to permit meetings of the Communist Party[34] and to enable African Americans to peacefully assemble in southern states during the Civil Rights movement.[35] It has also extended rights to unions, allowing them to form picket lines during labor disputes, provided they do so in an orderly manner.[36]

The right to assemble also covers the right to protest peacefully without repercussions, even if the protest is repugnant to the general public. This is probably the most controversial application of the freedom of assembly, because it can require tolerance of visible displays of vile and hateful expression. When the American Nazi Party chose Skokie, Illinois, as the location for a march in support of fascism in 1977, they knew they were going to evoke a sharp reaction from the residents of the heavily Jewish Chicago suburb, some of whom were Holocaust survivors. Village residents were predictably outraged and went to court to block the march, but the Supreme Court upheld the constitutional rights of the Nazis to stage a public demonstration.[37]

The freedom to associate is closely related to the freedom to assemble. We devoted a lot of attention in Part 3 to group membership in political parties and interest groups, and we talked a little about how Americans like to join organizations. All of this is made possible by the freedom to associate.

While not explicitly stated in the First Amendment, freedom of association has been protected by the Court as an implied right, on the grounds that in order to petition government, people first need the freedom to gather in groups with like-minded citizens. Underlying this logic is the belief that groups of private citizens are necessary to advocate political positions and are valuable mechanisms for checking the power of government.[38]

14-6 Right to Bear Arms

The Second Amendment is one sentence long. It states, "A well-regulated militia, being necessary to the security of a free state, the right of the people to keep and bear arms, shall not be infringed." Those twenty-six simple words have been the basis for some of the most intense political battles in our recent history. The way you interpret them determines where you stand on gun ownership and probably says a lot about how you see the world.

Some people regard the Second Amendment as an unequivocal grant of freedom to possess firearms for everything from hunting to self-defense. They interpret gun ownership as a personal right. Others contend that the amendment's authors had only public defense in mind. They interpret gun ownership as a collective right, one that permits states to form militias—and nothing else.

A recent ABCNews.com poll indicates that three in four Americans take the position that the Second Amendment protects individual gun ownership. At the same time, a majority supports stricter controls on guns.

Websites *You Can Use*

If you'd like more details from this snapshot of public opinion on gun ownership and gun control laws, you can find it at http://abcnews.go.com/sections/us/DailyNews/guns_poll020514.html.

Issue Box 14-4 *Obscenity on the Internet*

History and Background

Barbara Nitke is on the faculty of the School of Visual Arts in New York. She is president of the historic Camera Club of New York, a prestigious 120-year-old institution. Her photography has been critically acclaimed as sensitive in its depiction of sometimes graphic or disturbing subjects. She has been using the camera to reveal the trust and love exhibited by couples engaged in sadomasochistic sex. And she wants to post her images on the Internet.[*]

She knows that doing so will raise legal issues about whether her work is considered obscene because the law permits obscenity to be determined by local community standards—the same criterion applied to other media. But what are local community standards on the Internet? Nitke decided to raise that question in court, with the help of the National Coalition for Sexual Freedom, an organization that bills itself as dedicated to equal rights for "consenting adults who practice forms of alternative sexual expression."[†]

There are a number of ways you could conceivably understand local standards on the Internet. Perhaps the entire Internet is a community. That would be the most general interpretation of the law and would allow virtually anything to be posted. Maybe local community standards are the ones in effect in New York, where she would post her material, or maybe the individuals who self-select to view her work constitute a community. Any of these interpretations would permit Nitke to post her work online for anyone in the world to see. Would these criteria be too permissive, affording constitutional protection to work that some people would definitely find objectionable?

Instead, what if "community" were defined as any place in the world where someone could access her pictures? That would be the most restrictive interpretation of the law because surely there are places were her work would be considered obscene, resulting in her having to remove it from the web. Would imposing that standard constitute censorship?

It's a difficult question because the Internet is so different from any communications medium to come before it. You can enter chat rooms and communicate with people you've never met who could be anywhere in the world. Maybe you have a home page displaying pictures and some of your favorite links that anyone on earth could access. Or perhaps you "instant-message" your friends from your computer— maybe you're doing it right now as a diversion if you're reading this book online. With unlimited access and reach, the

Internet makes location and distance irrelevant to how we communicate, even if the law continues to use pre-information-age constructs for determining obscenity. This raises profound questions about what, if anything, we should be forbidden to communicate, and what should be protected as free expression.

It was inevitable once the Internet became a form of mass communication that lawmakers and the courts would be faced with questions of what constitutes indecent and obscene communication online. The first attempt to regulate Internet communication came in the form of the **Communications Decency Act of 1996,** which prohibited the posting of "patently offensive" or "indecent" material on the web. The language it employs is similar to that applied to broadcast media like radio and television to determine what constitutes offensive material.

Of course, the Internet does not function like a television network, where content is broadcast to receivers for any viewer to watch. Instead, people seek out websites, more in the manner of a pay-per-view television movie. Chat rooms take the form of a public gathering place, an electronic public park where freedom of speech is protected. People who post material on the web could be considered publishers, with their freedom of expression guaranteed.[‡]

These distinctions were not lost on the Supreme Court, which didn't take long to throw out most provisions of the Communications Decency Act on the grounds that it was an unconstitutional attempt to limit free expression. By a vote of 7–2, the Court ruled in the case of *Reno v. ACLU* (1997) that Internet communication was entitled to the same strict consti-

What position do you take? Read both sides of the argument in Issue Box 14-5 on pages 440–441 and decide where you stand.

14-7 Right to Privacy

The Constitution never mentions a right to privacy. Neither does the Bill of Rights. Over time, though, the Court has determined that there is an implied right to privacy that may be found in several constitutional passages, and from this construction, it has secured rights ranging from legal contraceptive use to legalized abortion.

tutional protection as print media because of its decentralized structure with many contributors and no strict gatekeepers.§

However, the Court left in place the section of the law that permitted "local community standards" to determine if something was obscene, without clarifying the issue of what constitutes a community online. Hence Barbara Nitke's dilemma: Should the Internet be viewed as a global or self-selecting community where expression should be tolerated even if some communities with access to the web would find it obscene? Or should any community with access to the web have the right to veto a posting it considers obscene?

Arguments in Support

Those who advocate broad standards for determining what material is permissible to post online make the following arguments:

- The Internet is not an invasive medium. To find something you might consider offensive, you have to look for it.
- The minority should not censor the majority. A parochial interpretation of community standards creates a lowest-common-denominator yardstick for what others can say or post, permitting one small community to veto something it doesn't like or perhaps doesn't understand.
- Society must encourage artistic expression. Sometimes art is designed to offend, and the right to do so must be protected. If people don't like it, they don't have to look at it.
- There is no constitutional morality protection. The First Amendment does not permit one group to impose its ideas about morality on any other group or on the entire nation.

Arguments Against

Those supporting narrow standards for defining online obscenity might say:

- The Internet makes everything available. You can stumble across offensive material by accident or through unclear or deceptive links.
- It's not censorship. Not every place is as permissive as New York City. Individuals should have the right to be protected from material that would be considered offensive in their immediate community.
- It's not art. It's filth. And it shouldn't be online where anyone can come across it.
- There is legislative protection against distributing obscene materials. Even though the law does not

provide uniform standards of obscenity, it does not prohibit Congress from restricting the interstate transmission of items it deems obscene or offensive.

My Opinion

When registering your opinion on whether there should be a broad standard for posting on the web material that some would find obscene, consider the history of the issue and the arguments supporting and opposing it. In particular, ask yourself if:

- You have to seek out potentially obscene material on the Internet, or if just the act of going online puts it in proximity to you
- Narrowly interpreting obscenity constitutes or does not constitute minority censorship of the majority
- Artistic expression should be encouraged even if some consider it obscene, or obscenity should be discouraged even if some consider it art
- The value of restricting any group from imposing its morals on another group is more or less important than the value of prohibiting the distribution of what some would find offensive

The most accurate description of my attitude toward permitting a broad standard for allowing potentially obscene material to be posted online is:

1—I strongly support it. It's a good idea.
2—I support it, but with some reservations.
3—I oppose it, but with some reservations.
4—I strongly oppose it. It's a bad idea.
5—I haven't thought enough about it to have an opinion.
6—I don't care about it enough to bother.

▶ **Communications Decency Act of 1996** A legislative attempt to regulate the transmission of "offensive" or "indecent" material over the Internet. The Supreme Court overturned most of the provisions of the Communications Decency Act.

*Dean Schabner, "Love or Obscenity?: S/M Photographer Challenges Internet Decency Standards," ABCNews.com, June 29, 2002, at http://abcnews.go.com/sections/us/DailyNews/cda_challenge020729.html.

†The National Coalition for Sexual Freedom website, at http://www.ncsfreedom.org/.

‡Yousuf Dhamee, "Obsenity and the Internet: The Communications Decency Act," at http://65.107.211.206/cpace/politics/decency.html.

§CNN Interactive at http://www.cnn.com/US/9703/cda.scotus/. See also Center for Democracy and Technology at http://www.cdt.org/speech/cda/.

The road to this destination was uneven and bumpy. In 1902, a man living in Cambridge, Massachusetts, refused to participate in a smallpox vaccination program that was administered by city officials who feared an outbreak of the disease. He was tried, convicted, fined five dollars, and told that he would have to get a shot. The case reached the Supreme Court, where a judgment was rendered in favor of Massachusetts on the grounds that when any individual refuses to be vaccinated against a contagious disease, he or she passes the risks of vaccination to neighbors but assumes the benefits of immunity by living in an area where an outbreak is unlikely. The Court regarded the situation as a social contract issue, where individuals have to surrender some of their freedom in order for society to function effectively.[39]

Issue Box 14-5 *Gun Control*

History and Background

Gun control is an emotional issue because it is infused with symbolic meaning about deeply held values like security, independence, and state control. Firearms may be the most mythologized and romanticized symbol in our culture. Just look at television and the movies: From the cowboy to the detective to the cop, a gun is an integral part of the image of the individual who knows best, who takes the law into his or her hands, who protects, serves, and works for justice. It is part of the American psyche, part of the mythical image we create for ourselves.*

We saw how powerful myths can be when we looked at the presidency in Chapter 10. So it is in the gun control debate. The individual with the gun acts alone because he or she is a capable person, empowered to follow personal instincts. If we identify with this individual, government proposals to limit our ability to own or use guns feel like repressive restrictions from a distant bureaucracy that wants to deny us a primal self-defense function. Positions taken by opponents of gun control have an antigovernment, libertarian component, a widely held mistrust of centralized authority deeply rooted in Revolutionary War America.† That's why the National Rifle Association (NRA) can attract 4.2 million members by promising to preserve "the right of all law-abiding individuals to purchase, possess, and use firearms for legitimate purposes as guaranteed by the Second Amendment to the U.S. Constitution."‡

Gun control advocates experience the issue so differently that the two sides often appear to talk past each other. Advocates view Second Amendment protections as guarantees to the states, which were given the right to maintain militias as protection against potential abuses of the federal government. From this perspective, the constitutional right to bear arms is a collective one that does not extend to unrestricted personal gun ownership.§ Because guns are supposed to provide communal protection, gun control advocates support federal action to prevent widespread gun use from undermining communities, viewing guns themselves as the things we need to defend against. They emphasize ways they feel the community is endangered by gun ownership, pointing especially to innocent victims killed by people who misuse firearms.

The federal government didn't get into the business of gun control legislation until Franklin D. Roosevelt's election as president. As a former governor of New York, Roosevelt was supportive of that state's law requiring a police permit to possess a handgun (to this day, New York is the only state with a strong and enforced handgun control law), and promoted the National Firearms Act, which was approved by Congress in

1934. The first national gun control law prohibited the interstate shipment of "gangster" firearms like machine guns and limited the shipment of concealed weapons to licensed dealers. It was expanded four years later to include limited controls on a wider range of arms, but a declining crime rate and an administration with many other priorities helped push gun control off the public agenda.**

The issue was revived three decades later, following the assassinations of President John F. Kennedy in 1963 and his brother Senator Robert Kennedy and Dr. Martin Luther King Jr. in 1968. When Congress approved the Gun Control Act of 1968, it was the strongest federal gun control law ever passed. Among its major provisions, it prohibits convicted felons, illegal drug users, inmates in psychological institutions, and minors from owning weapons; sets standards for the licensing of guns; and bans the importation of assault weapons.††

Predictably, Second Amendment advocates began to push back, and in the 1980s found a sympathetic advocate in the White House—despite an assassination attempt against President Ronald Reagan in 1981. The shooting left White House Press Secretary James Brady permanently disabled, and he became an advocate for gun control. His Republican affiliation and heroic story made him an effective symbol for gun control promoters, and Brady lent his name to the decade-long effort to implement a national waiting period for gun purchases. Intense resistance from gun control opponents who saw it as an attack on their Second Amendment rights made for a hard-fought legislative battle, and when President Clinton signed the Brady Gun Control Law in 1993, it marked the first time the federal government would require background checks and a five-day waiting period before handgun purchases could be completed.‡‡

▶**right to privacy** The protection against government interference in private matters, which is not specifically guaranteed by the Constitution but which has been established by the Court and used to legalize contraception and abortion.

However, the Court also recognized that not every situation fits this pattern, and in so doing, established that citizens have the constitutionally guaranteed freedom to be left alone by government, which comes into play when it is not outweighed by prevailing social concerns (like making sure a city is vaccinated against a deadly disease). This was the first step to establishing a **right to privacy,** which was articulated sixty-three years later in *Griswold v. Connecticut.*[40]

One year later, Congress passed a ban on the sale of semi-automatic assault weapons like the AK47. The ban went into effect in 1994, but it carried a "sunset" provision, and it expired in 2004 when Congress failed to renew it.[§§] The National Rifle Association had made ending the ban one of its top legislative priorities.

In May 2000, tens of thousands of women gathered on the Mall in Washington, D.C., under the banner of the "Million Mom March," to demonstrate in favor of tighter gun restrictions. At the same time, a smaller delegation of antigun control advocates staged a counterdemonstration, including a delegation from a group called the "Second Amendment Sisters."

Through it all, the Supreme Court has been reluctant to get involved in the gun control debate. In *United States v. Miller* (1939), the Court upheld the National Firearms Act of 1934 in a ruling widely interpreted to mean the Second Amendment didn't preclude Congress from placing firearms restrictions on individuals. Since then, the Court has been largely unwilling to grant *certiorari* to Second Amendment cases, turning them away without comment. It has been satisfied to sit on the sidelines of a debate whose manifestation is as much cultural as political, as two sides with opposing perspectives on the role and meaning of guns work to advance entirely different views of America.

Arguments in Support

Many arguments have been offered in support of gun control laws. Proponents have said:

- Gun ownership is a collective right. The Second Amendment states that the right to bear arms is limited to forming a militia for the common defense.
- Guns undermine communities. Guns kill people, and the more guns there are in circulation, the more dangerous things are.
- Collective restraints benefit society. We are not all capable of making good judgments about self-defense.
- Guns are a public health risk. They are implicated in countless accidental deaths and injuries, and in suicides.
- Guns are a negative symbol. They represent violence and danger.

Arguments Against

Numerous arguments have been made against gun control. Opponents have said:

- Gun ownership is a personal right. The Second Amendment gives the individual the right to self-defense.
- Guns make us safer. The criminal element will always find a way to get guns. Law-abiding citizens need to be prepared to respond.

- Question authority. Who better than the individual to make decisions about self-defense? Certainly not a government bureaucracy.
- Guns do not injure public health. Many lives are saved because people have access to guns. Gun control advocates who make a public health argument to justify laws requiring trigger locks and other safety devices are only doing so to chip away at Second Amendment rights.
- Guns are a positive symbol. They represent sportsmanship and security.

My Opinion

When registering your opinion on gun control, consider the history of the issue and the arguments supporting and opposing it. In particular, ask yourself if:

- Gun ownership is a collective or personal right
- Guns make communities more dangerous or safer
- Society is better served through collective restraints or by questioning authority
- Guns are or are not a public health risk
- Guns are a negative symbol of violence and danger or a positive symbol of sportsmanship and security

The most accurate description of my attitude toward gun control is:

1—I strongly support it. It's a good idea.
2—I support it, but with some reservations.
3—I oppose it, but with some reservations.
4—I strongly oppose it. It's a bad idea.
5—I haven't thought enough about it to have an opinion.
6—I don't care about it enough to bother.

[*]William J. Vizzard, *Shots in the Dark: The Policy, Politics, and Symbolism of Gun Control* (Lanham, MD: Rowman & Littlefield Publishers, 2000), 3–11.

[†]Ibid, 7.

[‡]National Rifle Association website, at http://www.nraila.org/About/whoWeAre.aspx.

[§]See the American Civil Liberties Union website, at http://www.aclu.org/PolicePractices/PolicePractices.cfm?ID=9621&c=25&Type=s.

[**]Vizzard, *Shots in the Dark*, 87–92.

[††]You can read about the other details of the law at the Brady Campaign to Prevent Gun Violence web page, at http://www.bradycampaign.org/facts/faqs/?page=awb

[‡‡]See U.S. Government Information at http://usgovinfo.about.com/library/bills/blbradyact.htm.

[§§]See The Brady Campaign to Prevent Gun Violence, at http://www.bradycampaign.org/facts/gunlaws/awb.asp.

14-7a Privacy and Birth Control

In the early 1960s, Estelle Griswold, the Executive Director of the Planned Parenthood League of Connecticut, was convicted along with a Yale University medical professor of violating a Connecticut law against advising others in the use of contraceptive devices when they counseled and prescribed birth control for a married couple at the Planned

Parenthood offices. They petitioned the Supreme Court to overturn the conviction on the grounds that the Connecticut law violated their civil liberties.

The Court agreed. Writing for the majority, Justice Douglas acknowledged that the right to marital privacy is not mentioned in the Constitution, but—as we've seen—neither is the right to associate, even though the First Amendment has been interpreted to include that right. Furthermore, Douglas argued that there are places in the Constitution where "Various guarantees create zones of privacy," including:

- The right of association implied by the First Amendment
- The Third Amendment prohibition against being forced by the government to house soldiers during peacetime
- The Forth Amendment guarantee against unreasonable searches and seizures
- The Fifth Amendment protection against self-incrimination
- The Ninth Amendment assurance that personal rights should not be construed to be limited to those enumerated in the Constitution[41]

Douglas concluded that the evidence pointed to a Constitutional right to marital privacy, which, while not expressed in the Constitution, is in keeping with the intent of its authors. "We deal," he wrote, "with a right of privacy older than the Bill of Rights."[42]

The immediate effect of the Griswold decision was to legalize the use of contraceptives among married couples. This right was soon extended to unmarried persons.[43]

14-7b Privacy and Abortion Rights

As we saw in Section 12-9, "Consistency and Legitimacy," the right to privacy was also the basis for legalizing abortion. In the controversial case *Roe v. Wade,* Justice Blackmun established that the right to privacy was "broad enough to encompass a woman's decision whether or not to terminate her pregnancy."[44]

This line of reasoning has become a fault line in the abortion controversy, because it has generated passionate debate about when or whether a fetus should be considered part of a woman's body, permitting abortion to be a private decision. The Court addressed this issue by assigning different conditions to each of pregnancy's trimesters. An unfettered right to privacy was applied to the first trimester, when the abortion decision may be left to a woman in private consultation with her physician. In the second trimester, the state may intervene in the decision for reasons involving the health of the mother. The state can prohibit abortion in the final trimester.[45]

The rationale behind this decision is that at some point the fetus becomes viable, and the choice to have an abortion is no longer without consequences for the developing child. In the absence of a definitive medical determination about when life begins, the Court acted to protect the privacy rights of the mother without making those rights absolute. The problem this generated is that many people have strong beliefs about when life begins despite the absence of medical proof, and those who believe it begins at conception reject as immoral the application of a right to privacy over abortion decisions at any term. Those who subscribe to the Court's logic argue passionately about the immorality of permitting the state to make intimate decisions about a woman's body when a pregnancy is not viable.[46]

14-7c Privacy and Physician-Assisted Suicide

The right to privacy is also a factor in the controversy over whether critically ill individuals should have the right to end their lives. The debate about physician-assisted suicide raises questions arising at the end of life that echo the issues raised in the abortion debate about the start of life: Is it a form of murder or a personal decision without repercussions for anyone but the individual involved? Take a few minutes to read about the history of physician-assisted suicide in Issue Box 14-6 before deciding for yourself whether you believe it should be a personal right.

Issue Box 14-6 *Physician-Assisted Suicide*

History and Background

The last days and weeks of life can be an excruciating ordeal for individuals with terminal illnesses. Even with hospital or hospice care, it's not always possible to manage extreme pain or comfort intense suffering. People confronted with a painful death and no hope of recovery may wish to end their lives by choice; physician-assisted suicide gives them this option. It involves doctors giving terminally ill patients the means for death, usually in the form of a prescription drug. Physician-assisted suicide is not euthanasia, because the doctor does not actively participate in the patient's death. (Perhaps you've heard or read about Dr. Jack Kevorkian, the Michigan physician nicknamed "Dr. Death" for his high-profile participation in euthanasia cases dating back to 1990. This is *not* physician-assisted suicide.) With physician-assisted suicide, the patient must be of sound mind and make a rational decision to approach a doctor for a medical means to suicide, which the patient then applies without assistance.

In a culture that celebrates life and tends not to talk about issues surrounding death, it's not surprising that physician-assisted suicide is controversial. It flies against widely held religious beliefs about the sanctity of life and appears to invert the role of the doctor to do everything possible to save lives, although advocates contend that it is consistent with the physician's obligation to end suffering and that it is a compassionate choice for terminally ill patients in unbearable pain. Opponents worry that it will be abused, with patients who lack access to good medical treatment being forced into it, and patients suffering from depression rather than pain being most interested in it. This gives assisted suicide a complex moral and ethical dimension.[*]

Although assisted suicide became a salient item on the national agenda in the last several years, it isn't new to American politics, and in fact, the issue dates back thousands of years. The ancient Greeks employed physician-assisted suicide (and euthanasia, for that matter) over two thousand years ago for a wide range of ailments for which there was no cure. In the United States, it was debated in the nineteenth century under the terms "patient rights" and "death with dignity"—the same language used by proponents today. However, it never took hold in this country, and disappeared from active discussion with the development of penicillin and other life-sustaining medical advances in the early twentieth century.[†] When it reemerged at the end of the century, it again faced stiff opposition.

Like gun control, the Supreme Court has been reluctant to get involved in the issue of assisted suicide. However, in 1997 the Court heard a pair of cases on the matter. In *Washington v. Glucksberg* and *Vacco v. Quill,* the Court upheld, respectively, a Washington State and a New York State ban on physician-assisted suicide, saying the Constitution does not guarantee terminally ill individuals a right to hasten their deaths.[‡] The ruling left it to the states to determine whether they wanted to legalize physician-assisted suicide.

The first two states to consider the question turned it down. An initiative to legalize physician-assisted suicide was rejected by Washington state voters in 1991 and by California voters in 1992. Then the Hemlock Society, an organization advocating the right to die, secured a spot for a similar initiative on the 1994 Oregon ballot. Oregonians were given the opportunity to pass judgment on whether to legalize suicide for terminally ill individuals who have "voluntarily expressed" a wish to die. Lobbying on both sides of the measure was intense, with groups as diverse as estate lawyers and the Catholic Church in opposition.

In the end, voters divided sharply on the issue, opting to approve it by a slender 51–49 margin. Opponents went to court to block implementation, but their case was dismissed by the U.S. Circuit Court. Opponents then tried to overturn the law with a referendum of their own, but that measure failed by a wide margin, and Oregon became the first state in the union to legalize assisted suicide.[§] The law went into effect in 1997. Ten months later, only eight people had taken advantage of it, suggesting that the Oregon experiment with physician-assisted suicide had not turned the state into a destination for large numbers of people looking for a final alternative to painful terminal illness.[**]

Arguments in Support

Several arguments are typically offered in support of physician-assisted suicide, such as:

- It's compassionate. When suffering is unbearable, the kind and moral thing to do is to give individuals with no hope for survival the opportunity to end their lives.
- It's medically ethical. Doctors have an obligation to do everything to keep patients from suffering.
- It's just. When treatment options have been exhausted and simply refusing care means a slow and painful death, it is right for patients to be able to choose suicide as their only viable option.
- It's a personal matter. The timing and circumstances surrounding one's death should be a matter of private choice, not public policy. It is important to respect the liberty of an individual over matters of personal choice.

Arguments Against

Opponents of physician-assisted suicide policies claim:

- It's immoral. The sanctity of life is absolute, even when someone is in great pain. Regardless of the circumstances, suicide is morally wrong.
- It violates medical ethics. A doctor's foremost obligation is to save lives.

Issue Box 14-6 continued on next page

Issue Box 14-6 continued

- It's unjust. There is no way to guarantee that only patients in great pain will take advantage of assisted suicide, and it would be unjust if individuals who lack good medical care or who are a financial burden on their families were pushed toward suicide as a convenient option.
- It's a social matter. Death may be personal but suicide is a legal issue, and society, not individuals, should have the final say in the matter. The issue is whether to grant legal permission to take a life, something we do not permit individuals to do under any other circumstances.

My Opinion

When registering your opinion on physician-assisted suicide, consider the history of the issue and the arguments supporting and opposing it. In particular, ask yourself if physician-assisted suicide:

- Is compassionate or immoral
- Conforms to or violates medical ethics

- Is just or unjust
- Is a personal or social matter

The most accurate description of my attitude toward physician-assisted suicide is:

1—I strongly support it. It's a good idea.
2—I support it, but with some reservations.
3—I oppose it, but with some reservations.
4—I strongly oppose it. It's a bad idea.
5—I haven't thought enough about it to have an opinion.
6—I don't care about it enough to bother.

*For a more detailed discussion, see http://eduserv.hscer.washington.edu/bioethics/topics/pas.html.

†Ezekiel Emanuel, "Whose Right to Die?," *Atlantic*, March 1997.

‡Melvin I. Urofsky, *Lethal Judgments: Assisted Suicide and American Law* (Lawrence, KS: University Press of Kansas, 2000), 130–153.

§Ibid, 101–104.

**Ibid, 158–159.

The Way You Want America to Be   *Civil Liberties*

Take a look back at the way you answered the polls in the "Your Opinion" sections of the Issue Boxes. Which answer did you give most often? Read on to see where you stand.

If your primary answer was 1...

...you could consider yourself a civil libertarian. With few or no exceptions, on issues ranging from school prayer to flag burning to gun control, you sided with the civil-libertarian perspective, even in instances where that perspective is unpopular. This suggests you would like to see elected officials advance policies that are in line with a liberal reading of the Bill of Rights, even when it means taking positions at odds with public opinion. You would probably find people with similar ideas to yours affiliated with the American Civil Liberties Union.

If your primary answer was 2...

...your tendencies lean toward supporting personal liberties. By and large, you sided with the civil-libertarian perspective that places a premium on individual liberty, even in instances where that perspective is unpopular. Depending on how strongly you feel about a particular issue or a range of issues, you may or may not feel compelled to get involved in the political process to work toward any of the outcomes you've endorsed. However, you would probably be comfortable if elected officials advanced policies that are in line with a liberal reading of the Bill of Rights, even if some of those positions are at odds with public opinion.

If your primary answer was 3...

...your opinions are broadly similar to others who claim that civil liberties should not permit individuals to engage freely in a number of activities you may find offensive (like obscenity on the Internet or flag burning) and/or deny people the liberty to engage in activities you possibly feel are beneficial (like school prayer or gun rights). It's quite possible that you feel advocates for some of these positions simply misunderstand core American values, or at least disagree with you about the kind of country you'd like America to be. If the intensity of your feelings on one or several of these issues motivates you to enter the politi-

cal process, you will find a host of single-issue interest groups that share your perspective.

If your primary answer was 4...

...you strongly object to the claim that civil liberties permit individuals to engage freely in a number of activities you likely find offensive (like obscenity on the Internet or flag burning) and/or deny them the liberty to engage in activities you feel are beneficial (like school prayer or gun rights). It's quite possible that you feel advocates of flag burning and obscenity on the Internet who oppose gun rights and school prayer misunderstand core American values, and would turn the country into something you feel it should not be. If the intensity of your feelings on one or several of these issues motivates you to enter the political process, you will find a host of single-issue interest groups that share your commitment and your perspective.

If your primary answer was 5 or 6...

...you didn't register an opinion on more than half the civil liberties issues, suggesting that you haven't thought much about them or didn't feel qualified to offer an opinion. Maybe you haven't given much consideration to the issues in this group, or maybe they're just not very important to you. So, while you opt out of the debate, others will struggle to set the country's course on civil liberties while you—and all of us—live with the results of their efforts.

If your responses varied widely...

...your responses didn't demonstrate clear support for or opposition to a civil-liberties agenda, suggesting that your positions are determined more on an issue-by-issue basis than by an overarching philosophy. That's fairly typical, as we know from our earlier study of public opinion. It means that you will side with liberals on some civil-liberties matters and with conservatives on others, and that your view of what you'd like America to be cannot easily be reduced to labels. If you feel strongly about any of the positions you took on these issues, you'll need to watch your elected officials closely to make sure they act in concert with your wishes.

Chapter Review

Civil liberties are constitutional and legal protections against government infringement on personal freedoms. Many civil liberties are protected by the Bill of Rights, although some are found in the Constitution and others were established through judicial precedent. Due process, or protection against the arbitrary actions of government, is central to our civil liberties. Due process guarantees fixed and equitable procedures for being charged with and prosecuted for a crime, including the right to a swift jury trial, and protection against double jeopardy, unreasonable searches and seizures, and self-incrimination. Due process also carries constitutional guarantees against cruel and unusual punishment. Opponents of capital punishment have argued that it should be classified as cruel and unusual, although the Court has disagreed.

The First Amendment guarantees a host of personal liberties: religious freedom, freedom of speech, freedom of the press, and freedom of assembly. The First Amendment's establishment clause is the basis for the separation of church and state. This is accepted to mean that the federal government cannot establish a church or force people to attend or not attend a church, but there is disagreement about the height of the barrier between church and state. For instance, advocates of school prayer understand religious freedom to be the freedom to permit prayer in school; opponents of school prayer understand it to mean protection from prayer in school. The First Amendment's free exercise clause restricts government from interfering with religious practices, but this right is not absolute.

Similarly, free expression is constitutionally protected—but not in all instances. The government can limit speech that poses a clear and present danger to others, and in the 1960s, the Court tightened that standard to speech that incited "imminent lawless action." The Court has also affirmed that constitutional safeguards apply to symbolic speech, like flag burning, although the Court was divided over the matter. Efforts to pass a constitutional amendment banning flag burning have come close to passage on several recent occasions. Unpopular expression may be the most difficult to deal with. Speech codes established at some universities in a "politically correct" effort to contend with offensive expression have met opposition in the courts because of the restrictions they placed on free expression.

The press is the only for-profit private business granted constitutional protection, because its obligations to keep people informed and to provide a check on government power are of central importance to democracy. The First Amendment protects the press from prior restraint, or government censorship. Publishing on the Internet adds a new dimension to free expression, especially when it entails hateful material or material some may deem obscene. The Communications Decency Act of 1996 attempted to set guidelines, but the Internet's global reach confounds the traditional legal test of applying contemporary community standards to determine if public communication is protected speech.

The First Amendment also protects freedom of assembly and the right to petition the government, provided that it occurs peacefully. The Court has extended the First Amendment to protect the freedom to form associations, like interest groups and political parties.

The Second Amendment right to bear arms has been understood in different ways over the years, either as an individual grant of freedom to possess firearms or as a collective right to form state militias. The Court has been reluctant to weigh in on the matter, and the controversy over gun control has played out largely in the legislative arena.

One place where the Court has been quite proactive is in establishing a right to privacy, which is not addressed specifically in the Constitution. The right to privacy has been applied to the legalization of contraceptive devices, and was the foundation for the *Roe v. Wade* decision that legalized abortion.

Key Terms

Bill of Rights (p. 420)
bills of attainder (p. 422)
civil liberties (p. 420)
clear and present danger (p. 430)
Communications Decency Act
of 1996 (p. 438)
double jeopardy (p. 422)

due process (p. 420)
establishment clause (p. 424)
ex post facto laws (p. 422)
exclusionary rule (p. 422)
free exercise clause (p. 424)
Gideon v. Wainwright *(p. 423)*
libel (p. 436)

Miranda rights (p. 422)
plea bargain (p. 424)
prior restraint (p. 434)
right to privacy (p. 440)
writ of habeas corpus *(p. 422)*

Review Questions

Note: You can find the correct answers to these questions by taking the quiz and then submitting your answers in the Online Edition. The program will automatically score your submission. If you miss a question, the program will provide the correct answer, a rationale for the answer, and the section number in the chapter where the topic is discussed.

1. Which of the following due process requirements places a specific restriction on the actions of Congress?
   a. the exclusionary rule
   b. freedom from bills of attainder
   c. protection against double jeopardy
   d. protection against unreasonable searches

2. In the 1966 case *Miranda v. Arizona,* the Supreme Court decided that
   a. the government must supply poor suspects with an attorney.
   b. due process guarantees protection against excessive bail.
   c. arresting officers must explain the right against self-incrimination to suspects.
   d. capital punishment is not cruel and unusual.

3. Plea bargains primarily serve the interests of
   a. the defendant.
   b. the public.
   c. the court.
   d. the Constitution.

4. The section of the Bill of Rights typically regarded as the constitutional basis for the separation of church and state is the
   a. establishment clause.
   b. free exercise clause.
   c. due process clause.
   d. prior restraint clause.

5. The "clear and present danger standard" allows government to limit free expression if
   a. it instigates an immediate "substantive evil."
   b. Congress dislikes it.
   c. it has been fully discussed in public.
   d. it will bring about "imminent lawless action."

6. Which of the following best illustrates symbolic speech?
   a. Nazis marching in a predominantly Jewish village
   b. hippies with long hair
   c. Eugene Debs advocating people to resist the draft
   d. speech codes on college campuses

7. The legal remedy for false and damaging press coverage is
   a. to sue for prior restraint.
   b. to sue for libel.
   c. found in the Communications Decency Act of 1996.
   d. not provided by the law or the Constitution.

8. The First Amendment expressly protects the right to
   a. assembly of any kind.
   b. association of any kind.
   c. peaceful assembly.
   d. peaceful association.

9. On the matter of Second Amendment rights, the Supreme Court historically has been
   a. enthusiastically supportive.
   b. emphatically opposed.
   c. intentionally vague and unclear.
   d. reluctant to get involved.

10. Which of the following did the Supreme Court establish under the right to privacy?
   a. the right to free speech on the Internet
   b. the right to opt out of a community vaccination program
   c. legal birth control
   d. unlimited abortion rights

In Their Own Words

You might be interested in examining some of what the following authors have said about the topics we've been discussing:

On Capital Punishment

Epstein, Lee, and Joseph F. Kobylka. *The Supreme Court and Legal Change: Abortion and the Death Penalty.* Chapel Hill, NC: University of North Carolina Press, 1992.

On School Prayer

Alley, Robert S. *Without a Prayer: Religious Expression in Public Schools.* Amherst, NY: Prometheus Books, 1996.

Muir, William K., Jr. *Prayer in the Public Schools.* Chicago: University of Chicago Press, 1967.

On Flag Burning

Goldstein, Robert Justin. *Flag Burning and Free Speech: The Case of Texas v. Johnson.* Lawrence, KS: University Press of Kansas, 2000.

On Hate Speech and Political Correctness

Heumann, Milton, and Thomas W. Church, eds. *Hate Speech on Campus.* Boston: Northeastern University Press, 1997.

On Gun Control

Vizzard, William J. *Shots in the Dark: The Policy, Politics, and Symbolism of Gun Control.* Lanham, MD: Rowman & Littlefield Publishers, 2000.

On Physician-Assisted Suicide

Urofsky, Melvin I. *Lethal Judgments: Assisted Suicide and American Law.* Lawrence, KS: University Press of Kansas, 2000

Notes

1. Howard N. Meyer, *The Amendment That Refused to Die: Equality and Justice Deferred: The History of the Fourteenth Amendment* (Lantham, MD: Madison Books, 2000), 4–5.

2. J. Roland Pennock and John W. Chapman, eds., *Due Process* (New York: New York University Press, 1977), 3–4.

3. American Civil Liberties Union website, at http://www.aclu.org/DeathPenalty/DeathPenaltyMain.cfm.

4. 1998 General Social Survey, at http://www.icpsr.umich.edu: 8080/GSS/homepage.htm.

5. Ibid.

6. *Everson v. Board of Education of the Township of Ewing,* 330 US 1 (1947).

7. Sarah Barringer Gordon, "The Mormon Question: Polygamy and Constitutional Conflict in Nineteenth Century America," *Penn Law Journal,* Spring 2002.

8. *Reynolds v. United States,* 98 US 145 (1878).

9. *Employment Division, Oregon Department of Human Resources v. Smith,* 494 US 872 (1990).

10. *Bob Jones University v. United States,* 461 US 574 (1983).

11. *Schenck v. United States,* 249 US 27 (1919).

12. Nicholas Capaldi, *Clear and Present Danger: The Free Speech Controversy* (New York: Pegasus, 1969), 71–75.

13. *Schenck v. United States,* 249 US 27 (1919).

14. *Whitney v. California,* 274 US 357 (1927).

15. *Brandenberg v. Ohio,* 395 US 444 (1969).

16. Ellen Schrecker, *The Age of McCarthyism* (Boston: Bedford Books, 1994), 92–94.

17. *Dennis v. United States,* 341 US 494 (1951).

18. "Confederate T-Shirts Spark Debate," *Associated Press,* April 6, 2001.

19. Typical of such codes was one adopted in 1988 at the University of Michigan prohibiting "any behavior, verbal or physical, that stigmatizes or victimizes an individual on the basis of race, ethnicity, religion, national origin, sexual orientation, creed, ancestry, age, marital status, handicap, or Vietnam-veteran status." It was struck down as unconstitutional on First Amendment grounds in Federal District Court in 1989. See Milton Heumann and Thomas W. Church, eds., *Hate Speech on Campus* (Boston: Northeastern University Press, 1997), 3, 130–148.

20. Marilyn Friedman and Jan Narveson, *Political Correctness: For and Against* (Lanham, MD: Rowman & Littlefield, 1995).

21. Ibid.

22. Foundation for Academic Standards and Tradition website.

23. Jerome A. Barron and C. Thomas Dienes, *First Amendment Law in a Nutshell* (St. Paul, MN: West Publishing Company, 1993), 47–48.

24. Ibid., 48.

25. Ibid., 52–54.

26. Steven Pressman, "Libel Law in the United States," Department of State International Information Programs at http://usinfo.state.gov/products/pubs/press/press08.htm.

27. Jeremy Harris Lipschultz, *Free Expression in the Age of the Internet: Social and Legal Boundaries* (Boulder, CO: Westview Press, 2000), 10–11. See also 277–304.

28. Mike Godwin, *Cyber Rights: Defending Free Speech in the Digital Age* (New York: Times Books, 1998), 73–100.

29. Ibid., 101–132.

30. Barron and Dienes, *First Amendment Law,* 88.

31. *Roth v. United States,* 354 US 476 (1957).

32. *A Book Named "John Cleland's Memoirs of a Woman of Pleasure" v. Attorney-General,* 383 US 413 (1966). See also *Miller v. California,* 413 US 15 (1973).

33. Ibid.

34. *De Jonge v. Oregon,* 299 US 353 (1937).

35. *Edwards v. South Carolina,* 372 US 229 (1963).

36. *Thornhill v. Alabama,* 310 US 88 (1940).

37. *National Socialist Party of America v. Skokie,* 432 US 43 (1977).

38. Barron and Dienes, *First Amendment Law,* 238–239.

39. *Jacobson v. Commonwealth of Massachusetts,* 197 US 11 (1905).

40. James E. Leahy, *Liberty, Justice and Equality: How These Constitutional Guarantees Have Been Shaped by United States Supreme Court Decisions Since 1789* (Jefferson, NC: McFarland & Co., 1992), 19.

41. *Griswold v. Connecticut,* 381 US 479 (1965).

42. Quoted in Leahy, *Liberty, Justice and Equality,* 20.

43. *Eisenstadt v. Baird,* 405 US 438 (1972).

44. Quoted in Leahy, *Liberty, Justice and Equality,* 22.

45. Ibid., 23.

46. L. J. Macfarlane, *The Theory and Practice of Human Rights* (New York: St. Martin's Press, 1985), 22–23.

Domestic Policy and Policy Making

15-1 Domestic Policies

Should the government spend more money to protect the environment? In one recent survey, 52 percent of Americans said yes. What about more money for health care? That was supported by two-thirds of the population. Education? Seventy-four percent said spend more on that. Fifty-six percent want to spend more on law enforcement. About half want to spend more on Social Security.

How about taxes to pay for all these spending increases? Should taxes be raised? Hardly. Sixty-three percent of survey respondents said taxes are *too high* and should be lowered.[1]

Welcome to the world of domestic policy making, where we ask government officials to make choices on our behalf about how to spend our tax money. Collectively, the guidance we give them is a bit confusing. We want our representatives to support popular programs that benefit a lot of people, like Social Security, and spend money dealing with problems that concern a lot of us, like education and the environment. We also tend to feel we're paying *too much* in taxes and that a lot of that money gets wasted on things that government shouldn't be doing. This feeling is compounded by the fact that we don't have the option of stipulating how we want our tax dollars spent.[2]

Things aren't any less murky when it comes to whether or how government should regulate the way we go about our lives. Many things of value, like clean drinking water, safe workplaces, and cars that don't explode on impact, won't happen without a guiding hand (or a firm shove) from government. Still, many people recoil from the idea of having government place restrictions on their freedom.

You can make the argument that domestic policies should not be the product of a popularity contest. Some programs that assist disadvantaged people, like welfare and Medicaid, are controversial because the taxpayers who support them are not the ones receiving the benefits. That may not be sufficient reason, though, to curtail them. Instead, controversial policies are best developed (or rejected) following protracted political debates about what and how much government should do to assist the needy, or fight crime, or encourage the use of fuel-efficient cars.

We'll focus our attention on those debates because they represent the place where we can have the most influence over the political process. We'll emphasize two controversial types of domestic policy, where the decisions we make define what we're like as a society. The first is regulatory policy, which revolves around issues of how much the government should intervene in the operation of free markets. The second is social welfare policy, which you may be surprised to find is about a lot more than simply helping people in need. We'll also look at the budgetary process and discuss federal taxing and spending policies—two political buzzwords that are never far from domestic political debates.

15-2 Regulatory Policies

If everything the free market produced were beneficial for society, we wouldn't be talking about government managing private affairs, but the quest to maximize self-interest can have undesirable consequences for society as a whole. If you run a manufacturing plant where the cheapest way for you to dispose of industrial waste is to dump it in the river, you're probably going to do it unless someone stops you. If you run an airline and decide you want to fly from New Orleans to Cleveland, imagine the danger and confusion that would result if you just started flying jets without regard to who else might be sharing the skies.

This is where government steps in with **regulatory policies** designed to maximize benefits or minimize hazards that private enterprise alone will not address. You may remember regulatory policies from Chapter 11 (Section 11-5b, "Regulation,"), when we addressed regulations as being among the things the bureaucracy implements.

There are several reasons why government might regulate private activity:

- The market can cause confusion that undermines the public interest.
- The market may not give consumers important, beneficial information that could influence their choices.
- The market may produce undesirable personal outcomes.
- The market may produce undesirable social outcomes.

Let's look at each of these possibilities.

> **regulatory policies** Domestic policies designed to protect the public from harmful conditions that could result from unrestrained free-market competition or to ensure the benefits of a level playing field for private competition.

15-2a Serving the Public Interest

Let's say you wanted to operate a television station in Salt Lake City. You have the necessary financing, so you proceed to put in place the hardware you'll need to set up your station. To give yourself the best possible market position, you'll of course want to broadcast on the most desirable frequency. No doubt, so will your competition. If you and the others were to go ahead and start broadcasting without regard to one another, the result would be chaotic. You know this, of course, and so do your competitors, but why should you be the one to back off and take a less desirable frequency?

Enter government and the requirement that you have to apply for a license before you operate a television station. The Communications Act of 1934 protected the broadcast spectrum as a public resource and established the Federal Communications Commission (FCC) to issue public licenses to private organizations wishing to operate radio and television frequencies.

With the authority to regulate the airwaves by granting broadcasting licenses, the federal government can hold broadcasters to a set of standards that promote the "public interest." If protection against monopoly control of the media is considered to be in the public interest, as it was through the 1980s, the FCC can place limits on the number of licenses it will grant to a single corporation that wants to operate multiple television and radio stations in a given city. If public affairs programming is considered to be in the public interest, the FCC can require that television and radio stations devote a percentage of their broadcast time to news and information programs as a condition of keeping their license. If increased minority ownership of broadcast outlets is considered to be in the public interest, as it has been in recent years, the FCC can give licensing priority to minority-run organizations.[3]

As with any domestic policy, regulation produces winners and losers. When the government regulates in the effort to serve the public interest by determining who can provide a public service like operating a broadcast outlet, winners and losers are narrowly

▶**competitive regulatory policy**   A type of regulatory policy designed to protect the public interest by restricting the provision of a service or good to organizations that win federal licensing approval.

constrained to those elite groups—for instance, broadcast organizations—that apply for government licenses. This type of regulation is called a **competitive regulatory policy** because not every applicant to operate a television or radio station will be granted a license (of course, a corporation denied a license to broadcast in one city can apply to broadcast in another). As part of its regulatory function, a regulatory agency can assess applicants against established "public interest" standards, and decide which applications will be approved.

15-2b Providing Beneficial Information

Do you smoke cigarettes? Even if you don't, you're probably familiar with the warning label that appears on every pack, informing you of the risks of smoking. Warning labels have appeared on cigarettes in some form since the 1960s, when cigarette manufacturers were required to publish the qualified message that "cigarette smoking may be hazardous to your health." The tobacco industry opposed the move to tag their product as a health risk, but Congress authorized the labels under its obligation to notify the public about product hazards once evidence began to mount that cigarette smoking might be linked to health problems. Their intent was to keep cigarettes on the market but to notify smokers that using them could be risky, in order to give consumers the information they would need to make an informed purchasing decision.[4]

▶**protective regulatory policy**   Regulations that supply consumers with information needed to make informed purchasing decisions about such things as cigarettes and home loans or that prevent undesirable personal or social conditions like child labor or unsafe food.

This type of **protective regulatory policy** comes into play when government officials decide the public is best served by being provided with information that would not be supplied voluntarily by manufacturers or service providers. In the case of cigarettes, the requirement to instruct the public about smoking perils falls far short of a policy that would prohibit the sale of cigarettes entirely, resting instead on the principle that consumers can make intelligent purchasing decisions provided they are informed about potential product risks.

Similar logic guides the requirement that food products carry nutrition fact labels, which state how much fat, sodium, cholesterol, and the like is contained in a serving of every packaged item you can find on supermarket shelves. Regulations stipulate that product servings have to be standardized for ease of comparison and dictate the standards a product has to meet before it can be designated "low fat" or "fat free" (see Box 15-1).

Some beneficial information is regulated so that business competition is carried out in an open environment. The Securities and Exchange Commission (SEC) has a long list of requirements for establishing public access to investment information. For instance, if you look for a home loan one day, you'll find that all lending institutions need to make their rates public. That protects you by making sure you've got access to the full range of information you need to find the best terms for your loan.

15-2c Preventing Undesirable Personal Outcomes

Some of our most far-reaching labor laws were protective regulatory provisions that emerged out of the sweatshop conditions found in many industrial facilities during the early part of the last century. Child labor, long a fixture in agrarian, nineteenth-century America, took on a gruesome quality as children as young as six years old would perform factory work for up to thirteen hours a day. Adults and children alike had no choice but to work for measly wages in dirty and often unsafe factories. Today, we would consider these circumstances unthinkable, but at the time, they were the natural outgrowth of an industrial market that required a lot of cheap labor.

It wasn't until 1938 that Congress passed the Fair Labor Standards Act, which imposed meaningful regulations on such things as child labor and compensation. Among other things, it established a minimum wage, overtime pay for long hours, and a minimum age of sixteen for entering the nonagricultural labor force.[5] As a consequence of federal regulation, things we take for granted as being fundamental to the structure of the contemporary workplace—like guaranteed minimum pay, overtime, and safe working conditions—have become commonplace.

> **Box 15-1** **Got Milk?**

In 1998, the Food and Drug Administration (FDA) issued new regulatory guidelines to standardize the use of the terms "fat free," "reduced fat," and "low fat" in food products. The move was designed to make it easier for shoppers to know exactly what they were getting when they bought an item, and to compare the fat content of that item with other products.

The change had the effect of replacing some old, familiar terms with new ones. Take the case of milk labeling. The new FDA regulations provided that:

- "Skim milk" would be known as "fat-free milk." It may also be called "nonfat" milk.

- "Two percent fat-free milk" would be known as "reduced fat milk."
- "One percent fat-free milk" would be known as "low-fat milk." It may also be called "light milk."
- "Whole milk" would be known as ... "whole milk."*

Got that?

*"Milk Gets a Makeover—New Labels Help Make Shopping a Snap," American Dietetic Association, June 1999.

15-2d Preventing Undesirable Social Outcomes

An unregulated market can also produce conditions that are harmful or undesirable to society. The pressure to maximize profits can make cutting corners an attractive option to some companies, provided they don't go too far and undermine public confidence in their products. When producers make decisions about how unsafe to make a product, the temptation remains to push the limits too far, with the consequences being dangerous consumer products, unhealthy food, and unsafe drugs.

The rationale behind imposing government safety standards on everything from kitchens in restaurants to the construction of automobiles is to take safety decisions out of the hands of those who supply goods and services, who must bear the cost of making their products safer, and put them in the hands of government regulators who are positioned to think about the public interest rather than profitability. The next time you hear about a product recall or a restaurant that was shut down for health violations, you'll know it's because of a violation of regulatory guidelines that may not have been picked up if the manufacturer or restaurant had been permitted to self-police.

Regulations also require manufacturers to assume the cost of the unwanted by-products of production that would otherwise be passed along to everyone in the form of pollution. Environmental contamination produced by factory exhaust, toxic waste, and water pollution is a collective problem without a natural market solution. It's rational for producers to forego the often considerable cost and effort of environmental cleanup if they can. Regulatory policies requiring industrial polluters to constrain or repair environmental damage impose a form of social responsibility on industries that otherwise would, out of self-interest, exercise the liberty to avoid or ignore these costs. Essentially, government regulations coerce producers to pay the social costs of doing business rather than permit that cost to be passed on to society.

15-2e How Much Regulation?

We mentioned in Chapter 11 that regulations can be controversial, and you can probably see why. If you're the cigarette manufacturer who has to post warning labels that encourage people not to buy your product or the industrial plant that has to pick up the cost of antipollution devices, you're likely to balk at government regulations. Even if you're not, you may find yourself averse to the idea of regulation. The public has decidedly mixed attitudes toward regulatory policies. We generally want the benefits of clean air and safe food, but many people experience regulatory restrictions as unwelcome government interference—an attitude rooted in our fundamental embrace of liberty.

> **Box 15-2   A "Commonsense" Case against Regulation**
>
> Y ou don't have to regard government as an intrusion into private life to question the value and wisdom of some regulations. It's even possible to oppose regulatory policies while sharing with regulators the objective of maintaining public health and safety, by taking issue with regulations that appear misguided or counterproductive.
>
> Take the example of a thirty-five-page Environmental Protection Agency regulation that required oil refineries to filter smokestacks for the pollutant benzene. An Amoco refinery in Virginia complied with the regulation at a cost of $31 million, only to find that their investment did virtually nothing to cut down on the benzene being emitted by the plant. That was because the pollution was coming from fumes escaping from gasoline being pumped into barges on the loading docks. The regulation missed this simple point.*
>
> There are plenty of other examples available to anyone who wants to make the case that regulations written in Washington run the risk of missing what's going on in the places where they are to be implemented. Critics point to such things as the unanticipated consequences of regulations designed
>
> to scrub toxic waste from land to be reused for industrial purposes. To avoid the expense of complying with this requirement, industries rationally seek to locate on clean sites further away from highly developed urban areas. To reach them, workers have to spend more time in their cars. The result: more pollution.†
>
> Critics of regulatory policies sometimes object to the process by which regulations are developed and implemented. They see individual initiative being hamstrung by rules written by lawyers, and feel the evils that regulations are designed to address could be fought more successfully by the commonsense insights of those who are close to the problem.‡
>
> *Philip K. Howard, *The Death of Common Sense: How Law Is Suffocating America* (New York: Random House, 1994), 7–8.
> †Ibid., 8.
> ‡Ibid.

So environmental interest groups make a popular case when they argue in support of regulatory policies that would promote clean air and water, while President Bush also gets applause when he advocates fewer government regulations. You may even be philosophically inclined toward regulation in general but oppose particular regulations that are personally burdensome. A supporter of clean air who rides a bicycle to work is likely to be more supportive of a $2-per-gallon gasoline tax designed to regulate automobile use than is an environmentalist in an SUV. Your position on regulatory matters may well come down to whether you benefit more than you pay.

Some people don't object to the cost or philosophy of regulation so much as they have a problem with the way regulations are made and the sometimes undesirable effects they have. Their complaints have more to do with regulations that misunderstand and therefore fail to treat the problems they're designed to regulate, and with unintended side effects of regulations. Box 15-2 explains.

Some regulatory costs and benefits are intangible, leaving decisions about whether to regulate open to nonmonetary considerations. The question of whether to open the Arctic National Wildlife Reserve in Alaska to oil drilling is a sensitive issue that pits regulatory tendencies against free-market interests over a course of action that's filled with intangibles. Read on for a discussion of the matter in Issue Box 15-1 on pages 454–455.

15-3 Distributive Policies

> **distributive policies** Domestic policies primarily aimed at directing tax money to a range of public works items. Distributive policies tend not to be controversial because benefits are widely shared.

Regulatory policies are controversial because they create clear winners and losers, and because they invoke the debate over how much government should do to manage private affairs. **Distributive policies** are much less contentious. They entail spending tax dollars on a large host of items that individually benefit specific constituencies but, when taken collectively, offer something for just about everyone. This makes it hard to identify true winners and losers, inasmuch as the costs and benefits of distributive policy are spread around, and easy to make the claim that, in the aggregate, everyone benefits to some degree from distributive policies.[6]

> **pork barrel** Wasteful or unnecessary spending that can result from logrolling. Whether something is a pork-barrel project or a valuable use of taxpayer dollars may depend on whether you stand to benefit from it.

To be sure, some of what we call distributive policy is the end result of **pork-barrel** politics, but that's not to say that distributive policies are simply wasteful. Many distributive policies are **public works** projects: infrastructure development that is undertaken

> **public works** Civic projects built with tax dollars.

Box 15-3   Interstate Highways and the Politics of Distribution

One of the more ambitious public works projects this country ever attempted is the Interstate Highway System, which makes it possible for you to drive from New York to San Francisco, or from Canada to Mexico, without stopping for a traffic light. The idea for an integrated system of highways dates back to the Great Depression (the 1939 New York World's Fair had an exhibit touting the "highway of the future"), but preoccupation with World War II kept plans from moving forward until years later.

The Federal-Aid Highway Act of 1944 authorized the development of a national system of interstate highways, setting the stage for future work. Half the cost of the project was to be funded with federal money, but plans were to be developed and implemented by individual state highway departments, pitting urban against rural interests over the issue of whether federal money would be allocated according to population density or the number of miles that had to be covered. Construction began in 1947, but was bogged down as states diverted federal highway money to other pressing local needs, complained that funding was too low to cover costs, or simply found federal construction guidelines to be too onerous.

The project received a major boost in 1954, as President Eisenhower committed his administration to the completion of a national highway network, couching the initiative in terms of economic need (to promote the transportation of goods and recover billions of dollars in labor lost to traffic jams), safety (to reduce highway deaths), and not insignificantly, national security (as a method of evacuating cities in the event of nuclear war). The latter point may seem ridiculous in today's post–cold war world (or silly to anyone who's been stuck in a highway traffic jam on a holiday weekend). In the political environment of its day, however, Eisenhower's case helped break the political logjam.

It took two years for Congress to work through the contentious issues of how much the federal government would spend, how the funding would be allocated to the states, which taxes would be assessed to pay for the program, and how to calibrate a pay scale for construction workers operating in different parts of the country with widely varying wage rates. Compromises on these matters made possible the Federal-Aid Highway Act of 1956, which produced within a decade the Interstate Highway System that is now a fixture on the American landscape.*

*Richard R. Weingroff, "Creating the Interstate System," U.S. Department of Transportation Federal Highway Administration, at http://www.tfhrc.gov/pubrds/summer96/p96su10.htm.

exclusively or predominantly by government. Many of these are built and maintained by states and localities, and include such facilities as roads, bridges, schools, hospitals, sewer systems, airports, and municipal water plants. However, the federal government supports a long list of public works projects as well, sometimes operating on its own and sometimes providing federal funds to offset the cost of state projects.

The 2004 federal budget contains billions of dollars for public works projects, including:

- $1 billion for highway maintenance
- $14 billion for airport improvements
- $900 million for Amtrak
- $200 million for flood control facilities
- $20 million for watershed improvements[7]

In one way or another, we all benefit from expenditures on national infrastructure. Even if you don't drive a car, you benefit indirectly from expenditures on highways and roads whenever you buy products at a store that were shipped by truck (see Box 15-3). You may never fly on a plane, but you benefit from public expenditures on airports every time you send or receive an overnight package. Because most people recognize these benefits, expenditures on distributive policies of this nature are typically easy to accept.

There are places, though, where the question of how much to spend becomes a matter of public debate. One such place is the military budget. National defense is one of the most important services provided by the government, something we all contribute to through our taxes and something we all benefit from. Because we make it a major national priority, procurement of military items takes up a big portion of the federal budget. In fact, our military budget is the largest on earth, which leads some people to ask how much military spending we need in order to assure our security. We'll take up the issue in Chapter 16, when we talk about defense policy.

Issue Box 15-1   *Environment vs. Oil: Drilling in the Alaskan Wilderness*

History and Background

In the farthest reaches of northeastern Alaska, beyond the majestic mountains of the Brooks Range, lies 19 million acres of wilderness called the Arctic National Wildlife Refuge (ANWR). Most Americans will never see it, but it's home to over 160 species of birds, 36 types of land mammals, and a wide assortment of marine life sharing what the U.S. Fish and Wildlife Service says is "among the most complete, pristine, and undisturbed ecosystems on earth."[*] Wandering caribou share the land with musk oxen, grizzly bears, and wolverines; snow geese and golden eagles dot the horizon. Coastal lagoons, tundra, boreal forests, and snow-capped mountains create an unmatched habitat that supports the rich diversity of wildlife. It is home to the Gwich'in people, who sustain themselves with food and clothing provided by the caribou of the Porcupine River and sustain their culture through intricate links to the coastal plain, which is their sacred ground.[†] All have lived under the protection of the U.S. government, which has maintained the refuge under the direction of the Department of the Interior and has protected it from development.

None of this would be controversial if the Arctic National Wildlife Refuge wasn't sitting on top of a large deposit of oil. Americans, of course, depend heavily on oil to sustain themselves and their culture. Each year Americans consume two and one-half times more energy per capita than Europe and Japan[‡]—one-third of the world's oil consumption goes to meet the needs of 5 percent of the world's population.[§] Although there are productive sources of domestic oil, including Prudhoe Bay in Alaska, America cannot maintain its level of energy consumption without foreign imports, including oil purchased from politically volatile regions like the Middle East. In an era when Americans face the prospect of terrorism from groups that are active in the same parts of the world that supply foreign oil, the prospect of becoming less dependent on overseas oil supplies becomes more pressing and appealing.

In the wake of the attacks of September 11, 2001, President Bush has been making the argument that the United States will become more energy self-sufficient by drilling for oil in the Arctic Refuge. Legislation to do so was approved by the House of Representatives in 2001 before dying in the Senate.[**] A national security crisis, presidential backing, and a sizable share of congressional support translate into the real possibility that the United States will one day permit oil drilling in ANWR. But should it? What are the risks? Would it yield the benefits promised by proponents of drilling? How viable are the alternatives?

Environmental groups like the Alaska Wilderness League warn of catastrophic regional and global damage if oil-drilling

Source: U.S. Fish and Wildlife Service.

equipment is permitted in the Arctic Refuge. They assert that oil drilling would destroy the delicate balance of the regional ecosystem by altering the historic migratory patterns of birds and land animals, threatening species that are dependent on them, and destroying the habitat that sustains the Gwich'in people.[††] The potential for damage from oil spills and drilling-induced temperature increases have environmentalists fearing an epic disaster that could lead to the disappearance of wildlife, lakes, and forests as the permafrost melts through the effects of accelerated climate change.[‡‡]

Oil interests paint a different picture. Chris Kelley, a representative of the American Petroleum Institute, told the British Broadcasting Corporation that oil drilling is now handled in a manner that's safe for the environment, pointing to the smaller size of oil rigs that can drill multiple wells from one location, minimizing the amount of land surface that's affected.[§§] In his view, the environmental risks of drilling are trivial compared to the potential benefit of having the oil.

Still, critics of drilling question whether ANWR would produce enough oil to make a dent in foreign oil dependency. They point to recent government reports that say there is less recoverable oil in the Arctic Refuge than once believed, like a 1995 study from the U.S. Geological Survey that sharply downgrades the amount of oil previously believed to exist in the Arctic Refuge to the point where the best estimates indicate insignificant production—far less than needed to make the United States energy self-sufficient.[***] Journalist and environmentalist Mark Lynas writes that all the oil in ANWR would only keep American homes and industries running for half a year.[†††] A far better alternative for environmentalists would be to encourage energy conservation measures at home. Simply improving car mileage efficiency by 3 mpg would in one year save double the amount of oil that the most optimistic projections say is under ANWR.

▶ **redistributive policies**
Domestic policies, like those promoting social welfare, that take resources from one group in the form of taxes and provide goods or services for another group, typically those in need.

15-4 Social Welfare Policies

Possibly the most contentious domestic policy issues involve promoting social welfare. This is because social welfare policies are **redistributive policies,** where one group (such as working taxpayers) covers the costs while another group (such as the unemployed or poor) receives the benefits.

Oil interests dispute these claims. They say energy conservation can only be one part of a national strategy that includes looking for new sources of oil and natural gas, and that ANWR is perhaps the most promising untapped domestic source. They emphasize the benefits of additional oil drilling, which produces more jobs in the oil industry and throughout the economy from companies that do business with oil interests. They also make the point that residents of Alaska share the economic benefits of oil drilling through payments made by the state from oil royalty funds. These jobs and revenues extend to the Gwich'in, helping to compensate for whatever disruption drilling may cause in their lives.

Arguments in Support

Economic and energy considerations are foremost among those who support drilling for oil in the Arctic National Wildlife Refuge. Proponents say:

- It will promote energy self-sufficiency. ANWR is the last remaining major untapped oil source under American soil, and we need to unearth it if we're going to become less dependent on foreign oil.
- It's safe. Contemporary methods of oil drilling are environmentally sound. Small drilling platforms greatly diminish the amount of land area that's disturbed.
- Conservation alone isn't enough. Although any long-term energy strategy has to include conservation measures, finding additional sources of oil is equally essential.
- It won't harm native people. In fact, the Gwich'in will benefit from the oil dividend realized by the state of Alaska.
- It's about jobs. Additional oil production is good for the economy. It will produce a direct economic benefit to the people of the state of Alaska, expand the workforce, and help the economy overall.

Arguments Against

Environmental and conservation concerns are at the heart of arguments made by those who oppose drilling for oil in the Arctic National Wildlife Refuge. Critics of the plan say:

- It will not promote energy self-sufficiency. Reliable estimates point to at best a six-month supply of oil under ANWR, hardly enough to make a dent in our reliance on foreign oil supplies.
- It's unsafe. Oil drilling is a disaster for the environment locally and globally. It wouldn't take much to permanently disrupt ANWR's delicate ecosystem.
- Conservation is a better alternative. We consume way too much energy and exploiting new oil sources just satisfies our gluttony.

- It will harm native people. The Gwich'in rely on the undisturbed habitat for their survival and spirituality. Drilling for oil threatens to destroy both.
- It's about greed. Oil companies want to drill in ANWR because they see an untapped source of profit.

My Opinion

When thinking about your opinion on drilling for oil in the Arctic National Wildlife Refuge, consider the history of the issue and the arguments supporting and opposing it. In particular, ask yourself if drilling for oil in the Arctic National Wildlife Refuge:

- Will or will not promote energy self-sufficiency
- Is safe or unsafe
- Is or is not a better alternative than conserving energy
- Will or will not harm native people
- Is about jobs or greed

If you're opposed to drilling in the Arctic Refuge, you should also ask yourself if you're ready to alter your lifestyle by using less energy, either voluntarily or through mandated conservation measures. This could mean driving less frequently, or keeping your place a little colder in the winter.

The most accurate description of my attitude toward drilling for oil in the Arctic National Wildlife Refuge is:

1—I strongly oppose it. It's a bad idea.
2—I oppose it, but with some reservations.
3—I support it, but with some reservations.
4—I strongly support it. It's a good idea.
5—I haven't thought enough about it to have an opinion.
6—I don't care about it enough to bother.

---

*U.S. Fish and Wildlife Service website at http://arctic.fws.gov/index.htm.

†Alaska Wilderness League website, at http://www.alaskawild.org/campaigns_arctic.html.

‡Alaska Wilderness League website, "Oil Drilling and the Arctic National Wildlife Refuge," at http://www.alaskawild.org/campaigns_arctic_oil.html.

§BBC Reports: "Head to Head: Arctic Oil Drilling," August 2, 2001, BBC news website at http://news.bbc.co.uk/1/hi/world/americas/1470991.stm.

**Ibid.

††Alaska Wilderness League website, "Oil Drilling."

‡‡BBC Reports: "Head to Head."

§§Ibid.

***Alaska Wilderness League website, "Oil Drilling."

†††BBC Reports: "Head to Head."

Redistributive policies sound like the same thing as *distributive* policies, but they are entirely different. Remember, with distributive policies, there are no clear "winners" or "losers" because the costs and benefits of distributive policies are spread around. In contrast, redistributive policies redistribute resources from one group (which bears the cost) to another (which receives the benefit).

If redistributive policies sound like an attempt to address outcome disparities, you're right, and that adds another layer to the conflict produced by having one group of "winners" and a different group of "losers." Given our historical choice of equal opportunity over equal outcomes, many Americans are uneasy with the government getting heavily involved in programs that redistribute resources, at least up to a point. Welfare, for instance, is at its most controversial when people view it as a "way of life" rather than as short-term assistance, less so when it's viewed as a way to offer greater opportunity to traditionally disadvantaged groups.

There are exceptions to this controversial quality of redistributive policies. Social Security—perhaps the most popular federal program—is redistributive. It's just that most people don't know it (more on this in Section 15-4b, "Social Welfare for Everyone").

transfer payments The direct payment of public money to individuals who qualify for it under the terms of a social welfare program.

Social welfare policies usually involve making **transfer payments** from federal coffers directly to qualifying individuals. Typically, these are direct cash payments to individuals who meet the eligibility requirements for programs like unemployment compensation, veteran's pension and life insurance, Social Security, or welfare benefits. Transfer payments also take the form of food stamps and assistance for medical services offered through Medicare and Medicaid.

Table 15-1 provides a quick overview of the major federal social welfare policies, including who's eligible for them and how they're funded.

15-4a Social Welfare for the Poor

The chief rationale for social welfare policies that aid the disadvantaged is found in the large income disparities that exist in the United States—disparities which grew larger in the last two decades of the twentieth century. As Figure 15-1 on page 458 demonstrates, income during this period increased for Americans across the board, but the richest group got so much richer that the poorest Americans saw their share of total income decline. Disparities in wealth—what people own—are even greater.

In order to design government programs to assist the poor, you need a standardized definition of poverty. This is easier said than done because defining an income boundary that separates the poor from everyone else is an arbitrary exercise, no matter how or where that limit is set. The first to attempt it was a social worker named Robert Hunter, who studied the poor in America at the turn of the twentieth century and determined that an average (for those days) family of five lived in poverty if they earned less than $460 annually in industrial regions of the North, or $300 in the rural South. This was the minimum income that Hunter estimated was necessary to provide subsistence food, clothing, and shelter. To earn less than that, he said, was to live by the "same standard that a man would demand for his horses or slaves."[8]

poverty line A statistical determination of poverty based on income and family size that is used to establish eligibility for some social welfare programs designed to assist those in need.

There have been many attempts since Hunter to calculate a **poverty line.** Under a formula in use for the past two generations, the U.S. Census Bureau placed the poverty line for a family of four at $18,850 in 2004.[9] This figure does not account for people who are living just above the poverty line, who could easily slip below it through an unforeseen reversal of fortune. It also does not indicate how many of these individuals are permanently poor and how many might be able to climb above the poverty line with an improvement in their financial circumstances.

Measured against the poverty line, 34.6 million Americans, or 12.1 percent of the population, lived in poverty in 2002. The rate was double this figure for African Americans and Hispanics, and slightly higher (16.7 percent) among people under the age of 18. Poverty afflicts female-headed households severely, with one in four living below the poverty line. Regardless of whether they are white, African American, or Hispanic, women raising children without partners are more likely than any group to find themselves without the means to make ends meet. In sharp contrast, only 5.3 percent of households headed by married couples live in poverty.[10]

Determining who qualifies as impoverished is only part of the problem surrounding the design and administration of social welfare programs meant to aid the poor. The way you go about dealing with the effects of poverty has a lot to do with what you believe the causes of poverty to be, and on this point there is a great deal of disagreement. Is poverty

TABLE 15-1	Social Welfare Policies		
Policy	**Who Benefits**	**Who Pays**	**How It Works**
Temporary Assistance to Needy Families (TANF)	The poor	Federal taxpayers ($16.6 billion in 2002)	Federal money is provided to states through block grants for the purpose of moving welfare recipients into the workforce. Using federal guidelines, states determine eligibility and benefits.
Medicaid	The poor	Federal and state taxpayers ($160.7 billion in 2003)	Jointly funded by the federal and state governments, it provides medical services to low-income individuals and families, including the elderly and disabled.
Food stamps	The poor	Federal taxpayers ($25.3 billion in 2003)	Recipients receive coupons that can be redeemed like cash for food in grocery stores in order to provide the means for a healthy diet. The program is run by the Federal Department of Agriculture but administered by the states.
Earned Income Tax Credit	The working poor	Federal taxpayers who do not receive the credit ($32 billion in 2003)	Low-income wage earners are eligible for a payment when they file their federal income tax return. The payment either reduces the amount of income tax owed or provides the taxpayer with a refund check that exceeds the amount of tax owed.
Supplemental Security Income (SSI)	The elderly, blind, and disabled	Federal taxpayers ($30.4 billion in 2003)	Money from general tax revenues is provided in the form of monthly cash payments to eligible seniors, the blind, and disabled individuals with limited income. People who get SSI usually also get Medicaid and food stamps.
Social Security	Retired and disabled workers, regardless of income	Workers and employers, through payroll taxes ($453.7 billion in 2002)	Social Security provides retirement benefits in the form of monthly cash payments to workers over age 62 (full benefits kick in at age 65) who have worked a required number of years and to insured families of deceased workers. Social Security also provides disability payments to people under age 65 who cannot work because of physical or mental impairment.
Medicare	The elderly and disabled, regardless of income	Workers and employers, through payroll taxes; federal taxpayers; and Social Security recipients ($273.1 billion in 2003)	There are two parts to Medicare. Medicare Part A provides hospital insurance to persons over 65 and the disabled, with benefits paid to participating hospitals, emergency rooms, and nursing facilities. Workers and employers support it through payroll taxes. Medicare Part B provides voluntary supplementary medical insurance, covering up to 80 percent of outpatient medical expenses in exchange for a monthly premium and a small deductible. The premium is deducted from the recipient's Social Security check, with the balance supported by general tax revenues.
Unemployment insurance	Unemployed people, regardless of income	Employers, through federal and state taxes ($55 billion in 2003)	Workers who lose their jobs involuntarily and are able to work are entitled to payments to offset part of their lost wages for a temporary period of time, up to a maximum of 26 weeks in most states. Recipients pay income tax on the benefits. Each state, under the direction of the Federal Department of Labor, administers its own version of the program.

Source: Budget of the United States.

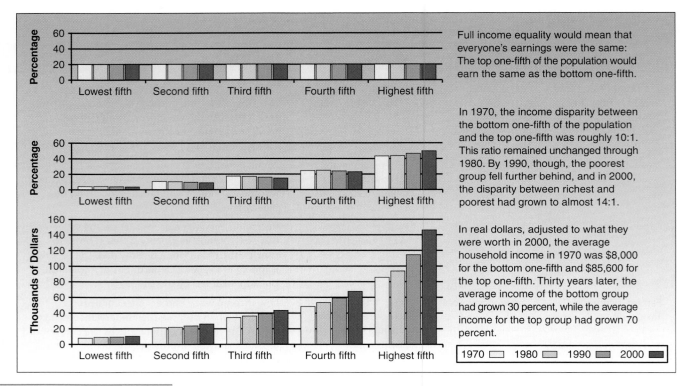

Figure 15-1
Income Inequality
Source: Data from U.S. Census Bureau.

the result of the actions of the impoverished or of the situation in which they find themselves? There are several schools of thought, among them:

Individual Explanations

- The poor lack the skills or motivation necessary to climb out of poverty.
- With well-paying jobs out of reach, the poor lack the motivation to get the training that would make them marketable.

Economic Explanations

- Social programs are generous enough to serve as a disincentive to finding work because they make minimum wage jobs look like an unappealing alternative to welfare.
- The economy does not produce enough well-paying jobs to employ everyone.

Cultural Explanations

- The chronically poor develop a "culture of poverty" apart from mainstream culture, in which initiative and hard work are not valued.[11]

These arguments tend to divide along ideological lines. Conservatives traditionally attributed poverty to the personal characteristics of the poor, whose perceived lack of personal skills or motivation is reinforced by social programs that create a "culture of poverty" that discourages initiative. Liberals traditionally believed poverty was rooted in economics and were more likely to shy away from attributing poverty to cultural attributes, while believing motivational obstacles to overcoming poverty are rooted in a lack of opportunity caused by an economy that cannot produce enough jobs for the poor.

This has caused the two groups to talk past each other. One prominent conservative social theorist called the social welfare programs of the 1960s and 1970s a "trap" that "tried to provide more for the poor and produced more poor instead"[12] by substituting handouts for hard work. Liberals responded by accusing conservative critics of trafficking in mythology about cultural, individual, and economic characteristics when they assert that success comes to those with better values and the free market is the best mechanism for creating economic winners and losers.[13]

These traditional positions have shifted a bit in response to changing economic conditions. Liberals, who in the 1960s tended to blame poverty on bad economic times, were more inclined during the boom years of the 1980s and 1990s to say the changing global economy undermined the desire of the poor to find work because it produced well-paying jobs that they had no hope of attaining. Conservatives, who once derided the poor as lacking initiative, later spoke of how increasingly generous welfare benefits provided a disincentive to working. In essence, the two sides swapped perspectives on how the economy and human nature contributed to poverty, with conservatives speaking more about the economic irrationality of welfare policy and liberals emphasizing the personal effects of poverty.[14]

If this looks to you like an inconclusive and even confusing debate, you probably won't be surprised to learn that public opinion has also fluctuated considerably on the issue of how we view the poor. The moral dimension of poverty leads some to believe that the poor are unworthy of assistance. People holding this view tend to equate welfare recipients with laziness because of their perceived dependence on the state, with socially undesirable behaviors like crime and drug use, or with behaviors that disregard family values, like out-of-wedlock childbirth. Yet, these attitudes vary in prominence in the public debate about poverty, tending to receive more attention during periods when public officials talk about "getting tough" on welfare.[15]

The same uneven pattern of public opinion applies to whether people feel we spend too much money on welfare programs. From 1976 to 1996, majorities twice found welfare spending to be too high: in the late 1970s and again in the early 1990s, with a peak near 60 percent in 1994, just before federal welfare programs were overhauled. These peaks in popular opposition to welfare coincide with peaks in the number of people on welfare. So, while it's possible these fluctuations in public opinion reflect shifting attitudes toward the poor, it's also possible that attitudes toward the poor follow attitudes about the cost of public support for the poor.[16]

It's reasonable to assume that people are aware of increases in spending on social programs for the poor because transfer payments to those in need automatically increase as more people qualify for assistance. Social welfare programs are **entitlements,** meaning everyone who fits a benefit category is eligible for support. The government places a **means test** on programs aiding the poor, like Medicaid, food stamps, and Supplementary Security Income, so that as more individuals fall below the poverty line (or a similar statistical measure of eligibility), they automatically qualify for transfer payments. In contrast, programs designed to address temporary setbacks (like unemployment insurance) or support seniors (like Social Security and Medicare) are entitlements without means tests: If you become unemployed or reach the legal age designated for retirement benefits, you're eligible for those benefits regardless of whether you're rich or poor. As entitlements, social welfare policies are expensive and open-ended.

The high cost of welfare payments in the early 1990s was one factor that contributed to dramatic changes in the way the federal government approaches assistance for the poor. The ascendancy of conservative arguments about the deleterious effects of welfare and the public belief that welfare programs had become too expensive also contributed to a revolution in the relationship between the government and welfare recipients, in which policy goals shifted from long-term support to moving people off welfare and into the job market.

In Issue Box 15-2, you can read about the history of welfare programs in the twentieth century and the welfare reform debate. You'll find that the debate over welfare reform continues to rage, with some people claiming it to be a tremendous success and others finding it merely symbolic, as they seek to return to a policy where the government guaranteed support to the most needy Americans. Then, you'll have an opportunity to record your opinion on whether reforms to the welfare system should be maintained.

15-4b Social Welfare for Everyone

In an age when many people have little faith in the government to operate successful social programs, **Social Security** stands out as the great exception. It is so popular, in fact, that some people don't realize it's a government program! Many others have no idea that it's a

entitlements Social welfare programs targeted to specific groups of individuals, like senior citizens or the unemployed. Benefits are available to all who meet the program requirements, although some entitlements for the poor impose a means test.

means test Eligibility requirements placed on social welfare programs aiding the poor, which restrict participation to individuals whose incomes fall below set levels.

Social Security The popular social welfare program that provides benefits to retirees regardless of need. Social Security also offers insurance payments to families of deceased workers and disability payments to impaired workers.

Issue Box 15-2 *Maintaining Welfare Reform*

History and Background

Welfare is among the most controversial redistributive policies in America, and in the past few years, it has been the subject of tumultuous debate and change. For the last two-thirds of the twentieth century, a key article of faith in the relationship between the government and the people has been the responsibility of the government to provide a safety net for people at the bottom of the economic ladder. By 1996, the philosophy of individual responsibility had replaced the philosophy of government protection. Proponents of that change say it has been a remarkable success. Opponents are not so sure.

Welfare policy dates back to the Great Depression. As part of the Social Security Act of 1935, the federal government established the Aid to Dependent Children program, which originally provided funds to states that wanted to assist children living in poverty. Over time, the program grew into **Aid to Families with Dependent Children (AFDC),** with a fixed set of eligibility rules and benefits extending to families with children living below the poverty line. Because AFDC was means-tested, anyone who met the income standard was eligible. This made AFDC an expensive redistributive program, especially during difficult economic times when more people qualified. It was expanded in the 1960s as part of President Johnson's Great Society efforts to end poverty in America, and began to function in tandem with a handful of other federal benefit programs like **food stamps** (a program to partly defray the cost of food, which was designed to combat malnutrition, not to provide welfare), **Medicaid** (which extended medical care to AFDC families), and the **Earned Income Tax Credit** (a 1975 addition that offers a cash supplement to low-wage earners who leave welfare for work).[*]

In the mid-1990s, a pair of political forces emerged to produce profound changes in how the federal government approached the chronically unemployed and the working poor. In 1992, Bill Clinton campaigned for president as a centrist "new" Democrat, someone who would be willing to rethink the welfare entitlement that had been at the core of Democratic Party philosophy since Franklin D. Roosevelt. His campaign promise to "end welfare as we know it" led to a 1993 task force to explore new approaches to welfare policy, followed by two years of discussions of partisan and bipartisan proposals aimed at moving welfare recipients into the workforce by modifying welfare eligibility rules.

Then in 1994, when free-market Republicans swept to power in the House for the first time in four decades, action on reforming federal welfare policies took a sharp right turn. Their proposal, detailed in the "Contract with America," emphasized using federal money as a form of transitional support to move people quickly off welfare while eliminating welfare as an entitlement. Called the "Personal Responsibility Act," it expressed the philosophy that individuals need to take charge of their own lives and could not look for permanent government support. Opponents charged that they wanted to remove the social safety net that had been a part of the fed-

Source: AP/Wide World Photos.

eral government's promise to our poorest citizens since the 1930s, but congressional Republicans had the momentum. With President Clinton facing reelection without having acted on welfare reform, he knew he had to accept a program that was philosophically in line with what the Republicans were offering. So, in 1996, President Clinton signed the Personal Responsibility and Work Opportunity Reconciliation Act.[†]

The 1996 law ended welfare as an entitlement under AFDC and replaced it with a program called **Temporary Assistance for Needy Families (TANF).** This represented a dramatic shift in the philosophy of welfare assistance. Federal money under TANF is supplied to states in the form of a block grant, which in 2002 amounted to $16.6 billion per year, for administration by the states to welfare families. The assistance is transitional money supplied to welfare recipients for a limited time as they move off the welfare rolls and into the workforce. States have flexibility to determine eligibility for TANF assistance and to decide the conditions recipients have to meet.[‡]

Supporters say welfare reform strengthens families, ends the culture of dependency that developed among long-term welfare recipients, and moves individuals formerly on welfare toward independence and self-reliance. They point to figures showing, since 1996, declining welfare dependency and child poverty, stabilized out-of-wedlock birth rates, and rising employment rates among single mothers—and they attribute this to cultural and economic changes made possible by welfare reform.[§] In fact, statistics show welfare cases plunged from 4.8 percent of the population when the reform measure was signed in 1996 to 2.6 percent by 1999.[**]

Supporters also say that welfare reform reflects the strength of federalism by permitting states the freedom to function as laboratories and experiment with innovative ways to put former welfare recipients to work. The Bush White House even points to figures showing that in the recession of

2001, welfare caseloads did not rise sharply, suggesting that welfare reform can work even in difficult times.[††]

However, others dispute these figures and question how successful welfare reform has been. They say statistics deflect attention from countless individual cases of hardship and adjustment difficulties. Although many people have moved from welfare to work, critics claim that many of the jobs are low-wage positions that don't offer benefits, sometimes leaving workers worse off financially than they would have been on welfare. The difference is still made up by remaining federal assistance programs like food stamps, Medicaid, and the earned income tax credit. At the same time, one-third of welfare-to-work families reported having less money to buy food, and 40 percent had trouble paying rent, mortgage, and utility bills.[‡‡]

They also point to more recent statistics that contradict White House claims about the program holding up during the economic downturn of 2001 and 2002. The nonprofit Center for Law and Social Policy reports that TANF caseloads stabilized between September and December 2001 as the White House contends, but closer inspection indicates that declining welfare cases in a couple of large states masked the fact that in forty states more people were applying for assistance. They trace these increases back to March 2001, when the recession officially began. In a number of states, the increases were significant.[§§]

Because the consequences of major changes in social policy often do not reveal themselves until many years after their inception, the debate over the success and wisdom of welfare reform continues. Welfare policy manifested by AFDC and welfare policy manifested by TANF reflect two sharply different views of America, with different ideas about whether the government should provide a uniform safety net for the poor or encourage those on assistance to find solutions to poverty in the marketplace.

Arguments in Support

Several arguments are typically offered in support of welfare reform. Proponents might say:

- It represents the best of American values. Hard work and individual initiative are backbone American values that were being undermined by traditional welfare policies.
- It strengthens families. Welfare reform has been responsible for declining child poverty, fewer out-of-wedlock births, and rising employment rates among single mothers.
- It encourages self-reliance. Long-term welfare recipients leave behind a culture of dependence on federal assistance for the opportunity to provide for themselves.
- It encourages innovation. Permitting states to function as laboratories for welfare-to-work policies is a creative use of federalism that yields innovative welfare solutions.
- It's recession-proof. Even in difficult economic times, states have successfully moved people off welfare and into jobs.

- It works. The number of people who have moved off welfare and into the marketplace is the best evidence for the success of welfare reform.

Arguments Against

Opponents of welfare reform policies might argue:

- It represents the worst American instincts. Government has a responsibility to provide at least a minimal safety net for the most needy. Welfare reform yanked that safety net out from under millions of people.
- It hurts families. Many welfare-to-work families find poorly paying jobs. They have trouble putting food on the table and paying for necessities like shelter and utilities.
- Government assistance is still needed. Without entitlements like Medicaid and the earned income tax credit, welfare-to-work families would suffer even greater economic hardship.
- It encourages inequity. Permitting states latitude in the implementation of TANF creates a mix of unequal requirements. This would never happen under the uniform federal guidelines in force with AFDC.
- Boom times mask problems. As the fast economy of the late 1990s yielded to the recession of 2001, welfare claims began to rise in most states, putting a drain on strapped budgets.
- It's too soon to know if it works. Many major social changes require years to show unexpected or unintended effects. It remains to be seen whether welfare changes will seem like a good idea several years down the road.

My Opinion

When deciding your opinion on welfare reform, consider the history of the issue and the arguments supporting and opposing it. In particular, ask yourself if welfare reform:

- Represents the best American values or the worst American instincts
- Strengthens or hurts families
- Encourages self-reliance or only appears to
- Encourages policy innovation or inequities
- Is recession-proof or vulnerable to economic downturns
- Works—or whether it's too soon to know

Then record your opinion to the question below:

The most accurate description of my attitude toward welfare reform is:

1—I strongly oppose it. It's a bad idea.
2—I oppose it, but with some reservations.
3—I support it, but with some reservations.
4—I strongly support it. It's a good idea.
5—I haven't thought enough about it to have an opinion.
6—I don't care about it enough to bother.

Issue Box 15-2 continued on next page

Issue Box 15-2 continued

▶ **Aid to Families with Dependent Children (AFDC)**
The original federal welfare program, developed during the
Great Depression as part of the New Deal, which extended
subsistence benefits to families with children living below
the poverty line.

▶ **food stamps**   A federal program designed to fight
malnutrition among people in need by defraying the cost
of food.

▶ **Medicaid**   A social welfare program initiated as part of
President Johnson's Great Society efforts to end poverty in
America, which extended medical care to families receiving
support through Aid to Families with Dependent Children
(AFDC). States are permitted to enact their own Medicaid
eligibility standards, following federal guidelines.

▶ **Earned Income Tax Credit**   A negative income tax for
low-income families, who receive rather than make cash
payments when they file their income tax returns.

▶ **Temporary Assistance for Needy Families (TANF)**
The 1996 welfare reform program that replaced Aid to
Families with Dependent Children (AFDC) and ended
welfare support as a federal entitlement. TANF is designed
as a transitional program that supports welfare recipients
temporarily as they move into the workforce.

*See "A Brief History of the AFDC Program" at http://aspe.hhs.gov/hsp/AFDC/
baseline/1history.pdf.

†American Public Human Services Association website at http://www.aphsa.
org/Policy/HistoryWelfare.asp and CNN/Time online at http://www.cnn.com/
ALLPOLITICS/1997/gen/resources/infocus/welfare/timeline.html.

‡Presidential Welfare Reform fact sheet at http://www.whitehouse.gov/
news/releases/2002/02/20020226.html.

§Ibid.

**Department of Health and Human Services Administration for Children
and Families at http://www.acf.dhhs.gov/news/stats/6097rf.htm.

††Presidential Welfare Reform fact sheet.

‡‡Pamela Loprest, "Long Ride From Welfare to Work." *Washington Post,*
August 30, 1999, sec. A.

§§"Impact of Recession and September 11 Seen on Welfare Caseloads,"
Center for Law and Social Policy, March 20, 2002, at http://www.clasp.org/DMS/
Documents/1011383178.91/doc_Final_2001_Q4_Caseload_discussion.htm.

form of social welfare, a redistributive program that transfers resources from young to old.
But it is.

Social Security provides a retirement safety net for millions of Americans regardless
of need, as well as insurance payments to eligible families of deceased workers and disability payments to people who are kept from working by physical or mental impairment.
Together with the hospital and medical insurance provided to the elderly and disabled
through **Medicare,** seniors and the disabled receive a level of government support that
protects them from having to worry that age or injury will leave them destitute. As entitlements, Social Security and Medicare are available to all, regardless of income or wealth.

Of course, as entitlements Social Security and Medicare are open-ended government
commitments, and that's at the heart of a major political problem. Our aging population
and spiraling medical costs make both programs increasingly expensive. Funding problems are particularly acute with Social Security because of the way the program is structured. You can read about this in Issue Box 15-3, and about a controversial alternative that
has been proposed to keep Social Security solvent into this century. None of the available
options for fixing Social Security is particularly attractive, which makes the politics of
Social Security especially contentious. When you finish reading Issue Box 15-3, you'll be
able to evaluate the alternatives available for maintaining the solvency of the Social Security program, and register your opinion about partial privatization of Social Security—an
option that holds the promise of finding new revenues for retirees at the cost of changing
the ironclad commitment of a retirement safety net.

▶ **Medicare**   The federal social
welfare program that provides
hospital and supplementary
medical insurance to senior
citizens and the disabled.

15-4c "Corporate Welfare"

What would you call a government cash payment to large corporations that protects them
from uneven market conditions? Critics call it "corporate welfare"—and those who
opposed welfare reform measures made a point of contrasting what they saw as the government's generosity to business interests with its stringent treatment of welfare recipients.

Issue Box 15-3   *Privatizing Social Security*

History and Background

Social Security has been called the "third rail of politics"—touch it and you die. Created by the Social Security Act of 1935 during the Great Depression to assure a basic level of subsistence to people in their retirement years, it is arguably the most successful federal program in history. It has achieved its stated purpose and provided generations of seniors with a social safety net that has enabled them to anticipate a basic level of economic stability after retirement. Working people have come to expect that they will not have to endure sudden poverty in old age. Even people who object to big government rarely take aim at Social Security.

The irony is that Social Security is not what it appears to be. Many of us think Social Security works like a pension or retirement account where the money we pay in to the Social Security system during our working years accumulates in value and is there for us to live on after we retire. That would make Social Security a distributive policy. But it isn't.

Social Security provides cash benefits to people who have reached retirement age, survivor benefits to immediate family members of a covered worker who dies before retirement, and disability benefits to injured workers and their families. It's all funded by a payroll tax on workers and employers, which goes into a trust fund that makes Social Security payments. The tax is automatically deducted from every eligible worker's paycheck. When a worker becomes eligible for benefits, the Social Security Trust Fund pays out. But the dollars paid out today are the dollars collected today, making Social Security a redistributive program—essentially a welfare program that doesn't disqualify people based on need that transfers resources from the young to the old.[*]

The fact that Social Security is a redistributive program dressed up to look like a distributive program—the separate trust fund helps recipients feel like they're getting their own money and not a handout from government coffers—makes it palatable to middle-class recipients who might otherwise object to participating in anything resembling welfare (along with Medicare, it's the reason why most social welfare spending goes to the middle class, not the poor). However, the program's structure makes Social Security difficult to sustain. In 1940, the first year the trust fund paid monthly benefits, 222,488 people received a combined $35 million. Since then, an explosion in the population, greater longevity, and cost of living adjustments (COLAs) made annually so payments keep pace with inflation have combined to place a tremendous strain on the system. In 2002, 46.4 million beneficiaries received a combined $453 *billion* in payments.[†]

That's an awful lot of voters receiving an awful lot of money, hence the "third rail" problem. However, long-term demographics are not kind to Social Security, and everyone across the political spectrum recognizes that at some point modifications will have to be made to this popular program. As baby boomers begin to retire in the next decade, demand on the system is only going to increase, and with fewer workers to replace them, the tax base available to provide for this large batch of retirees will shrink. In 1950, when birth rates

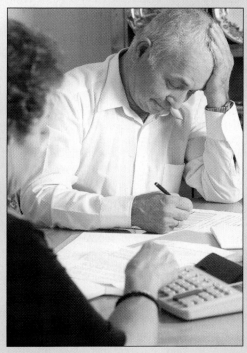

were high and life expectancy much lower than it is today, there were 16.5 workers to pay for every Social Security recipient. In 1990, each retiree was supported by 3.4 workers. By 2050, it's projected that there will be less than 2 workers to pay for every retiree—and more than one-third of those retirees is expected to be over age 80.[‡]

It's no wonder why so many people your age believe you'll never see a penny in Social Security benefits. You'll start paying Social Security taxes as soon as you start working—if you work now you already are—but opinion surveys suggest that if you're like 70 percent of eighteen- to thirty-four-year-olds, you're not confident that Social Security will be solvent when you reach retirement.[§] It's an expression of doubt about the ability of politicians to address the problems that lie ahead.

When the system first faced the prospect of a shortfall as a result of a period of rapid inflation in the 1970s, officials addressed the situation by increasing payroll taxes slightly and cutting benefits at the margins. That was enough to keep the program solvent for a projected fifty years. Now, the fifty-year window is down to twenty years, and the principal choices for restoring the program this century are the same as they were in the 1970s—raise taxes, cut benefits, or push back the retirement age, making people ineligible for benefits until they're older. Not too many politicians will want to propose any of these alternatives. However, if the system is not changed, it will eventually hit a crisis point.

There is one other alternative, but it's controversial. What if Social Security were restructured so that it operated more like a traditional retirement account? In other words, what if

Issue Box 15-3 continued on next page ■

some of that payroll tax money were freed up for investment so that it could potentially grow over the course of time, rather than be transferred to today's recipients? There are a number of ways to do this, with the most widely discussed involving partial privatization of the Social Security system.

Under partial privatization plans circulating around Washington, a percentage of Social Security taxes would be diverted to private accounts that workers would individually control. Depending on the plan, there might be limits on how it could be invested, but workers would have control over what to do with the money. Unlike the transfer payments that characterize the present program, these funds could be invested, leaving them free to rise and fall with the market. The balance of the payroll tax would continue to be used to cover transfer payments to present-day Social Security beneficiaries, but by necessity at a sharply lower level than what is currently provided.

The benefits of doing this are apparent. Over time, markets generally perform very well, and people would stand to earn more for their retirement if they were allowed to become investors. Many Americans have a natural faith in markets, and, in keeping with a deeply felt love of liberty, are willing to take chances provided they also have control over their money. To many, the risks of putting money in the market are preferable to the burden of additional taxation.

Partial privatization plans had a lot of public support in the late 1990s, when the booming stock market was providing middle-class investors with annual double-digit returns. Some people looked at the taxes they were required to pay to the Social Security Trust Fund and complained loudly that if the government would only let them invest that money, they could really make it grow. At the time, they were right. Then, when the high-tech bubble burst at the turn of the century, market forces no longer seemed so friendly, and some who had been enthusiastic about partial privatization had second thoughts.

Still, the issue persists. President Bush campaigned in 2000 on a partial privatization platform, and he remains a supporter. His proposals carry serious political risks, though. Powerful interest groups like the American Association of Retired Persons (AARP) are lined up against partial privatization for fear that it will hurt retired seniors. Even during the fast economic times that were still in place during the 2000 campaign,

the Bush plan had its detractors, and their comments are representative of those who oppose using the market to repair the looming Social Security problem.

Opponents doubt that partial privatization will save money, arguing that the transition from a pay-as-you-go system to a partially private investment system would take hundreds of billions of dollars (some say as much as $1 trillion) out of present-day benefits so funds could be shifted for private investment. They fear today's retirees would bear the brunt of that cost. They also doubt that Americans would quickly abandon the psychology of a social safety net for seniors, and would resist permitting grandma and grandpa to live out in the cold because they invested poorly or suffered a market downturn at the wrong time. This could mean there would be political pressure for an expensive government bailout of hard-luck investors.[**]

One thing both sides agree on is that partially privatizing Social Security would signal a dramatic change from the intent of the original Social Security Act. Instead of having government provide a guaranteed retirement safety net, it would only require that everyone save something for retirement, leaving everyone's bottom-line retirement package up to the way they invest and the direction of the market. These are vastly different social commitments. When we think about which direction to take, it's important to think about the underlying promise we want government to make to us and the nature of the obligation we want to make to one another.

Arguments in Support

Multiple arguments have been made to advance the cause of partially privatizing Social Security. These include:

- It's our money. We know much better than anyone else how to invest it, and we can be responsible for what happens to our investments.
- It's better than tax hikes. Demographics indicate that in the not-too-distant future dramatic increases in costs or cuts in benefits will be needed to keep the system working. Partial privatization eliminates this ugly necessity.
- Partial privatization relieves pressure on the young. Without partial privatization, people entering or about to enter the workforce will bear the brunt of paying for

Supporters call it a safety net for businesses that otherwise could be unfavorably affected by circumstances they cannot control.

This difference of perspective is at the core of the debate over agricultural subsidies, an issue that you may be more familiar with if you live in a rural area. Agricultural subsidies don't grab national headlines, which means Congress can address them in relative anonymity. This gives interested parties greater freedom to operate behind the scenes to lobby for government support. Consequently, agricultural subsidies do not appear to be going away any time soon.

Is this a desirable thing? The matter isn't clear-cut. After you've had a chance to read about it in Issue Box 15-4 on pages 466–467, think about your opinion on the desirability of agricultural price supports and whether you believe they amount to corporate welfare.

- the larger number of retirees that will go ahead of them, either through higher taxes or lower benefits at retirement.
- Market risk is better than political risk. People who don't have faith that politicians will effectively correct what's wrong with Social Security are willing to take a chance on the market as long as they can maintain control over their own money.
- Partial privatization is consistent with liberty. Ours is the largest free-market economy in the world. We should have a retirement program that is consistent with the values of individual initiative and investment choice.
- Look at the stock market. During the 1990s, careful investors would have earned enough to be ahead of the game even during the downturn that followed, and over the long term, the market should outperform the fixed rate of transfer payments currently used by the Social Security system.

Arguments Against

There are as many arguments against partially privatizing Social Security as there are for endorsing it. Opponents might say:

- It's our safety net. Partial privatization would undercut the primary guarantee of retirement security for all, dramatically undermining the program's central promise and purpose.
- Retaining the present system is worth the price. It's not true that there are no alternatives apart from partial privatization that people would be willing to accept. Social Security is so popular that people would embrace a tax increase if that was what it took to keep it solvent.
- Partial privatization hurts the elderly. In order to privatize Social Security, funds presently transferred to retirees would have to be diverted for individual investment. The amount involved could total in the hundreds of billions of dollars, and that money has to come from somewhere. It's most likely to come out of present-day benefits.
- Social Security carries no risk. As structured, the Social Security system is insulated against the capriciousness of the market, it has never missed a payment, and it is popular with the American public.

- Partial privatization is at odds with social responsibility. If we come to see Social Security as an individual retirement program, we sever the collective bonds that come from providing for the whole community.
- Look at the stock market. Perhaps partial privatization looked appealing during the boom years of the 1990s, but not during the down years that followed. Sudden economic downturns can undermine the savings of people about to retire, who can't wait for years for the market to recover.

My Opinion

When registering your opinion on partially privatizing Social Security, consider the history of the issue and the arguments supporting and opposing it. In particular, ask yourself if partially privatizing Social Security:

- Is about our money or our safety net
- Is better or worse than tax hikes
- Relieves pressure on the young or hurts the elderly
- Is or is not worth the risks
- Is consistent with liberty or at odds with social responsibility
- Is a good idea only when the market is doing well

The most accurate description of my attitude toward partially privatizing Social Security is:

1—I strongly oppose it. It's a bad idea.
2—I oppose it, but with some reservations.
3—I support it, but with some reservations.
4—I strongly support it. It's a good idea.
5—I haven't thought enough about it to have an opinion.
6—I don't care about it enough to bother.

---

*History Page, Social Security Online, at http://www.ssa.gov/history/briefhistory3.html.

†Ibid.

‡Susan A. MacManus, *Young v. Old: Generational Combat in the 21st Century* (Boulder, CO: Westview Press, 1996), 3–9.

§"Social Security Poll-tics," *Cato Daily Comment,* May 12, 2000. Data originally cited in May 11 *Roll Call.*

**"Bush and Social Security: The Full Facts," Washington State Democrats online newsroom at http://www.wa-democrats.org/site/news.php.

15-5 Taxing and Spending

Apart from decisions about war and peace, writing a budget and deciding how to pay for it are the most important choices Congress and the president make. That's because budgeting drives substantive determinations about who gets what. Choices about how the tax code is structured and how money is appropriated are often made out of public view. They involve a lot of small, technical, and detailed decisions. Nonetheless, they are worth paying attention to because they determine how the burden of supporting the government is distributed across economic groups and how much money is (or is not) available for government to do the things we say we want it to do. In this regard, taxing and spending decisions may be viewed as social welfare choices that determine how and how much government will redistribute wealth.

Issue Box 15-4   *Subsidizing Agriculture: Farm Aid or Corporate Welfare?*

History and Background

Agriculture is a risky and uncertain business. Drought, floods, temperature extremes, and other natural disasters can play havoc with this critical industry—and with the lives of people dependent on it. Government can step in to try to add an element of stability to agriculture, and has been doing so since the Depression. The Agricultural Adjustment Act of 1933 was the New Deal response to an oversupply of crops that was keeping prices low. Farmers voluntarily agreed to decrease production of such staples as corn, wheat, rice, and cotton in exchange for payments from the government. This was followed a year later by establishment of the Commodity Credit Corporation, a government corporation charged with making favorable loans to farmers in exchange for agreements to control crop production. The Agricultural Adjustment Act of 1938 introduced price supports, or payments to farmers to make up the difference for low market prices.[*]

Farm prices rebounded as a result of these measures, and ever since, farm subsidies have been a part of domestic policy and politics. A subsidy is a government payment for which nothing is expected in return. Such payments have been used to keep farmers from producing a crop that's in abundant supply and to maintain crop price stability. Over time, they've come to be regarded in the agricultural sector as a safety net for farmers akin to welfare for the poor and Social Security for retirees.

They are also highly controversial. In large part, that's because of the changing nature of agriculture and the way farm subsidies are allocated. In recent years, the small, independent farmer has become increasingly rare, as large corporate farms have come to dominate an industry now known as "agribusiness." Because subsidies are distributed on the type and amount of crop a farm produces, big corporate farms that produce more corn, wheat, rice, cotton, and soybeans (the most heavily subsidized crops) can claim a disproportionate share of the subsidy. Small farmers who produce these crops are only eligible for a tiny subsidy, and small farmers who produce other crops are not eligible for anything.[†]

The result: 60 percent of farmers do not get a penny of assistance. Among the others, in 2000, 57,500 farms received subsidies of $100,000, while 150 of the largest farms surpassed $1 million.[‡] Among the top recipients were farms owned by the John Hancock Life Insurance Company, Chevron Oil, banker

David Rockefeller—even basketball millionaire Scottie Pippen.[§] You can probably see why critics call it corporate welfare.

In an effort to address this imbalance, Congress in 1996 passed the Federal Agriculture Improvement and Reform Act, which set limits on how much individual farms could receive from the federal government. However, supporters of farm subsidies argued these limits shredded the agricultural safety net—after all, 40 percent of farmers *did* receive something—and they have had enough political clout to get Congress to bypass its own limits by passing annual emergency supplemental bills every year since 1998. In 2001, supplemental farm subsidies exceeded $5.5 billion. The 2002 farm bill committed $180 billion over ten years.[**]

Still, advocates of farm subsidies point out that the serendipitous nature of the weather is a risk that no other industry faces, making it an economic necessity for the government to regulate agricultural prices. They note that other nations do the same thing, many to a greater extent than the United States,[††] and contend that without government aid, thousands of farmers would go under. If that happened, advocates argue that land prices would plummet, and businesses that rely on farmers would be pulled down with them. From this perspective, there is too much riding on agriculture subsidies for the government to pull them back.

Opponents counter with the argument that other industries that are just as vital to the economy and just as risky do not receive support. The weather doesn't determine the fortunes of the software industry, but try convincing people who

---

We discussed how the federal budget is drafted as part of our discussion of Congress in Chapter 9. Before moving on, you may wish to review the process, which is described in Box 15-4 on page 468.

15-5a Tax Policy

Raising revenue is often controversial. Figure 15-2 on page 468 should give you a sense of where the money comes from to power the federal government.

It's pretty clear that most federal revenue comes from people like you and me. Here's how it breaks down:

lost everything in the "dot-com" bust that their field doesn't carry extreme risk. From this vantage point, there's no obvious reason to bolster farmers, especially as the one-time reality of the small, independent, hard-working farmer recedes into myth. Even if lifting agricultural subsidies hurts businesses that rely on income from farmers, opponents argue that the extra money in our pockets from not having to pay for agricultural relief would more than compensate for the damage to the economy.

The interesting political wrinkle in the farm-subsidy debate is that supporters cut across geographic as well as ideological and partisan lines. Big-government Democrats from rural states regularly team up with limited-government Republicans from rural states to advocate assistance for farmers. In principle, you might expect some of these supporters—those who see government as an instrument for helping the disadvantaged and those who espouse the virtues of the free market—to oppose government aid to agribusiness. Instead, the overarching principle in play is more practical than philosophical.

Arguments in Support

Supporters of farm subsidies point to the importance of agriculture to the economy. They say:

- It's a safety net. Other social programs protect urban and suburban workers; farmers need to know that their livelihood is being protected as well.
- Farming is the backbone of America. Federal dollars help farmers feed America and the world.
- Farming is unusually risky. Unpredictable forces, like extreme weather, regularly buffet agricultural prices. Subsidies are necessary so that farmers can survive hazards that no other industry or business has to face.
- It's good for the economy. Without subsidies, farms would fail, taking farm-related industries along with them.

Arguments Against

Opponents of agricultural subsidies consider them to be a misuse of money. They claim:

- It's corporate welfare. Public money subsidizes huge corporations that successfully lobby for public money they have no right to get.
- Farming has become agribusiness. The largest outlays go to large businesses, not to small, independent farmers.

- Many businesses are risky. Singling out agriculture for assistance is arbitrary and unnecessary.
- It's bad for the economy. The money transferred to agribusiness would benefit the country far more if taxpayers invested it or spent it.

My Opinion

When considering your opinion on farm subsidies, think about the history of the issue and the arguments supporting and opposing it. In particular, ask yourself if farm subsidies:

- Are a safety net for farmers or corporate welfare for big businesses
- Maintain the "backbone of America" or line already-deep pockets
- Help offset unusual risks, or arbitrarily help an industry that's no riskier than others
- Are good or bad for the economy

The most accurate description of my attitude toward subsidizing agriculture is:

1—I strongly oppose it. It's a bad idea.
2—I oppose it, but with some reservations.
3—I support it, but with some reservations.
4—I strongly support it. It's a good idea.
5—I haven't thought enough about it to have an opinion.
6—I don't care about it enough to bother.

To make things a little more interesting, consider this one additional question:

My home region is predominantly

1—Rural
2—Urban or suburban

How do you see this affecting your position?

*Senate Agriculture Committee website at http://agriculture.senate.gov/Legislation/Compilations/AgCom/Cccact.pdf and http://agriculture.senate.gov/Legislation/Compilations/AgCom/Ag38.pdf.

†Brian Riedl, "How Farm Subsidies Became America's Largest Corporate Welfare Program," The Heritage Foundation Policy and Research Analysis, February 25, 2002, at http://www.heritage.org/Research/Budget/BG1520.cfm.

‡Environmental Working Group website at http://www.ewg.org/farm/help/faq.php#workingland.

§Andrew Cassel, "Why U.S. Farm Subsidies Are Bad for the World." *Philadelphia Inquirer,* May 6, 2002.

**Ibid.

††The American Embassy in Paris website at http://www.amb-usa.fr/text/farm_subsidies.htm.

- In 2002, the federal government raised $2.192 trillion, almost half of which came from personal income taxes. That's roughly equal to 9.9 percent of **gross domestic product (GDP),** or the combined value of all the goods and services produced by the United States in 2002.

- Another one-third of revenue ($726 billion) came from Social Insurance payroll taxes, like Social Security and Medicare taxes, unemployment insurance taxes, and federal employee retirement payments.

- One in ten federal dollars ($219 billion) came from corporate income tax payments. At about 2 percent of GDP, the corporate tax burden has fallen considerably over the years; it was 4.5 percent of GDP in 1955.

▶ **gross domestic product (GDP)** A measure of national productivity, the gross domestic product is the total value of goods and services produced by a nation during a fixed period of time.

Box 15-4   Making Budgets

I f you've ever tried to save for something or figure out how you're going to spend limited funds on a bunch of needs, then you know how tricky it can be to write a budget. Add the individual wishes of hundreds of members of Congress and the president into the mix, and it shouldn't be hard to see how writing a budget is one of the most complex, sensitive, and important things Congress has to do. Members who sit on committees with a hand in budget writing find that they are rarely lonely.

Budget writing is an annual affair that typically takes an entire year to complete. A number of committees get into the act, in keeping with the decentralized way the House and Senate function. The process has been more coordinated though, ever since the passage of the **Congressional Budget and Impoundment Control Act of 1974.** A lot of the action happens in the House and Senate Appropriations Committees, which are charged with reporting bills that determine how much money government agencies and programs will have to spend (**appropriations** refer to legislation authorizing the government to spend money).

The procedure is complex, but it follows this outline: First, the House and Senate budget committees set guidelines and budgetary priorities. Then the appropriations committees are supposed to allocate money in line with those priorities. They approve spending bills to cover the variety of items in the federal budget. If the sum of these expenditures exceeds the budgetary guidelines, the expenditures are brought into line

with the budget targets through a process called **reconciliation.** For both houses to end up with the same budget, differences between them are resolved in a conference committee, after which final approval on a budget can be sought in both houses.[*]

If budget guidelines necessitate changes in tax law, the House Ways and Means Committee and the Senate Finance Committee get into the act. As the tax-writing committees of Congress, they draft legislation specifying which taxes will be raised and by how much.

▶ **Congressional Budget and Impoundment Control Act of 1974**   An act designed to centralize the congressional budgeting process, which established current procedures and timetables for writing a budget.

▶ **appropriations**   Legislation permitting the government to spend money that determines how much will be spent and how it will be spent.

▶ **reconciliation**   A procedure in the budget-writing process, whereby appropriations made in a number of congressional committees and subcommittees need to be brought in line with spending targets established early in the process.

[*]Barbara Sinclair, *Unorthodox Lawmaking: New Legislative Processes in the U.S. Congress* (Washington, DC: CQ Press, 1997), 63–69.

Figure 15-2
Where the Money Comes from: Federal Government Revenues, 2002

Source: Data from Office of Management and Budget.

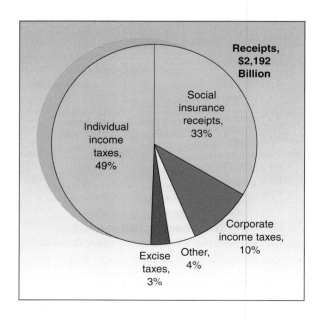

Receipts, $2,192 Billion

Individual income taxes, 49%

Social insurance receipts, 33%

Corporate income taxes, 10%

Excise taxes, 3%

Other, 4%

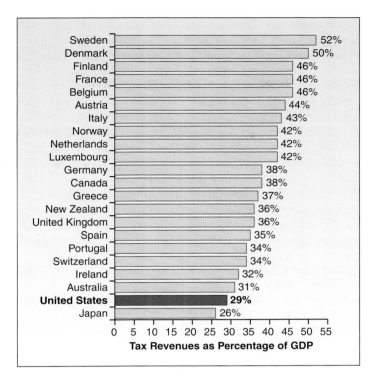

Figure 15-3
**Government Tax Revenues
as a Percentage of GDP**

Source: Data from Organization for
Economic Cooperation and Development,
1999.

- Excise taxes constitute a small portion of the tax pool. These include taxes on specific products and services like alcohol, tobacco, and telephone services. Next time you look at your telephone bill, find the line that lists the federal tax owed—it's a small but regular feature of your bill.

- Other taxes include a miscellaneous group of revenues, like customs duties, estate taxes, and gift taxes.

If you're like most Americans, you probably think that income tax rates are very high. Think again: In comparison to other western nations, the United States Treasury makes relatively few demands on our bank accounts. The United States tax burden ranks second from the bottom in comparison to other industrialized nations, as Figure 15-3 attests.

Not convinced that our taxes are comparatively low? Neither are most Americans. If you were to track attitudes about the appropriate size and scope of government, you'd find that Americans rank at the top of industrialized nations in the belief that private or individual initiative is often preferable to public solutions to social problems. It's a belief with deep roots in the individualistic strains of our political culture that we discussed in Chapter 4, and it helps explain why Americans frequently feel that government takes too much of our hard-earned money, when in fact we pay less in taxes than almost anyone else.[17]

Then there's the issue of how the tax code is structured, which compounds questions about the extent of the tax burden with issues of tax equity and fairness. There is no single or obvious way to tax people. In fact, people were once taxed on the number of windows in their home, on the assumption that more windows meant greater wealth, and windows were harder to hide from the tax collector than assets like money or livestock.[18]

The way government defines what forms of wealth and income are taxable is a political matter that determines how much various social groups will have to pay. Typically, groups with more political power are able to protect their interests most effectively. At the turn of the twentieth century, when the influx of immigrants produced enormous demand for new public works projects, upper-income citizens maneuvered to have their wealth declared tax exempt out of fear that they would have to pay the bill. These efforts hit a roadblock as the Progressive movement gained steam and advanced laws taxing wealth.[19]

tax expenditures Tax breaks in the form of exemptions targeted at groups of taxpayers or, in the case of corporate taxes, at specific industries.

Even when tax laws are on the books, officials can tinker with them by creating exemptions targeted at particular groups of taxpayers. Tax exemptions are officially called **tax expenditures** because, from the government's standpoint, they amount to lost revenue that would have been collected if the exemption had not been in place. Corporate tax breaks go to industries that lobby for favorable treatment, and it's common for states to protect dominant industries with tax exemptions, such as North Carolina providing special treatment to tobacco and Michigan to automobiles.

Private taxpayers are eligible for a host of exemptions as well, some of which are designed to promote a particular type of behavior. For instance, homeowners are permitted to deduct mortgage interest costs from their taxable income. The policy rationale behind this tax expenditure is that it encourages home purchases by making home ownership more affordable. This, in turn, stimulates the economy through increased production of lumber and building supplies, as well as washing machines, refrigerators, and other appliances that homeowners need. Of course, it also benefits the interests of realtors and builders (who lobby to protect it), and is skewed to the upper- and middle-income taxpayers who are most likely to own homes.[20]

Some of the most expensive tax expenditures in terms of their cost to the federal treasury in 2004 were:

- Exclusion of employer pension contributions ($123 billion)
- Exclusion of employer health care contributions ($120 billion)
- Home mortgage interest deduction ($68 billion)
- Capital gains deduction ($54 billion)
- State and local tax deduction ($51 billion)
- Deductions for charitable contributions ($34 billion)
- Exclusion of Individual Retirement Account contributions and earnings ($23.1 billion)
- Child credit ($21.3 billion)
- Exclusion of Social Security benefits ($19 billion)[21]

progressive income tax A tax structure with graduated income rates designed to increase the tax burden on higher-income earners.

regressive tax A tax structure that increases the tax burden on lower-income earners. Sales taxes are regressive because as incomes decline, the tax becomes a larger percentage of total income, and therefore, a greater burden.

Tax rates are also political choices with real consequences for how much people are expected to pay. Ours is a **progressive income tax,** meaning it has a series of graduated rates that increase with one's income. (In contrast, a **regressive tax** imposes a proportionately greater burden on low-income earners. Sales taxes are regressive because a tax everyone pays on food or clothes represents a bigger share of the incomes of low-wage individuals.) In general, the tax structure is redistributive because lower income groups pay proportionately less than upper income groups, and most Americans fall into the lower groups. In 2001, one in four Americans paid no federal taxes at all because their taxable incomes fell below the lowest tax bracket on the progressive income tax scale. Another one in two paid taxes at the lowest marginal rate of 15 percent. In contrast, less than 5 percent combined paid taxes at the top three marginal rates of 31, 36, and 39.6 percent.[22]

Furthermore, although higher levels of income are taxed at higher rates, upper income people also have access to a wider range of deductions and shelters for avoiding tax payments on some of their income. When you take into account adjustments to income, the average taxpayer assessed at the 39.6 percent marginal rate (who averaged $1.1 million in income in 2001) paid 27.4 percent of his or her income in taxes.[23] Adjustments apply to lower wage earners as well. In 1996, a typical person earning between $20,000 and $30,000 paid 7.6 percent of his or her adjusted gross income in taxes. Those earning between $50,000 and $75,000 paid 12.1 percent.[24]

flat tax A proportional tax that would set the tax rate equally for all taxpayers, regardless of their income level.

Not everyone is happy with this structure. In recent years, there has been discussion of replacing the progressive income tax with a **flat tax** that would operate on an entirely different set of assumptions. Issue Box 15-5 discusses this controversial idea with a dedicated following.

Issue Box 15-5 *The Flat Tax*

History and Background

Critics of our complicated tax code joke darkly that if the Internal Revenue System were put in charge of tax simplification, the entire tax form would be reduced to one line that reads, "Enter your income," next to which it would say, "Pay this amount." But advocates of a flat income tax are serious about simplifying the tax code to the point where we would have, as was once advertised on the website flattax.gov, "your tax return on a postcard." It sounds appealing. But is it a good idea—and is it fair?

Advocates say yes—and yes. The idea of replacing our complex income tax structure with a flat tax has gained currency in recent years, most visibly in billionaire publisher Steve Forbes' 1996 presidential campaign. Forbes made a flat tax the centerpiece of his unsuccessful quest for the Republican nomination. Since then, former House majority leader Dick Armey has been an avid and vocal proponent of a flat tax, and it's an idea that has a lot of support among members of the congressional majority. Here's how things would change if flat tax advocates get their way. Our graduated income tax structure would disappear, meaning higher levels of income would no longer be taxed at higher rates. Gone, too, would be the deductions we talked about earlier, including popular deductions for home mortgage interest and charitable contributions, as well as tax credits for the poor and shelters that businesses and wealthy people can take advantage of to protect part of their income from being taxed.

A flat-tax plan like the one promoted by former majority leader Armey would replace the present system with a single, across-the-board rate of 17 percent with almost no deductions. A certain amount of income would be entirely exempt from taxes—the Armey proposal set the floor at $36,800— meaning individuals and families earning less than that amount would pay no taxes. Everyone else would pay a flat 17 percent on everything above $36,800, minus savings, which would not be taxed. Income derived from dividends, interest, and capital gains would no longer be taxed.

Supporters of the flat tax say it offers a number of advantages over the graduated tax system, the most significant of which are simplicity and fairness. It's remarkably simpler than the present system, which appeals to people who struggle with filling out their tax forms every year, or who have to pay considerable sums to someone to do it for them. Simplicity could benefit the overall economy as well. Without deductions, people will not be motivated to skew their spending behavior toward things that will lower their tax burden. If their choices are more natural, the argument goes, the market can operate more efficiently. Because saving money would be the one way to lower your taxable income, there would be extra incentive to put money away, which is also good for the economy.*

The argument about fairness comes from the fact that everyone would pay the same rate. Indeed, this is one way of understanding tax fairness: It's a view based on equality. If everyone is subject to the same tax rate, everyone will shoulder the same share of the tax burden. Some would make the additional argument that a flat tax is the best political meas-

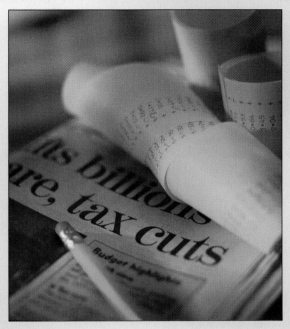

ure for protecting individual liberty against encroachment by public officials, by creating one class of taxpayers who would be united against efforts to raise taxes or tinker with the tax code.†

However, there is another way to regard fairness. Flat-tax opponents contend that the only way for the tax code to be fair is for it to consider that people live under vastly different financial circumstances. They believe people are not entirely responsible for their financial station in life, and taxation is a place where some balance can be regained. This perspective argues for a graduated system like the one we have in place, where people are taxed according to their ability to pay. Progressive income-tax structures place a proportionately greater burden on those who can most afford it, on the assumption that with greater means comes a greater share of the burden to help the poor.‡

This counterargument about fairness dovetails with a counterargument about simplicity. Although no one *likes* to pay taxes, it can be seen as a shared burden or common experience that binds us as a democracy and connects us to the political process. Taxes are the means by which we make collective choices. If we assume that the individual choices we make are somehow better or more valuable than these collective choices—an attitude implicit in the effort to minimize taxation—we can easily find ourselves minimizing government and public life. From this perspective, tax simplification puts a strain on democracy by de-emphasizing collective decision-making.§ In other words, we may not like to eat vegetables, but if we don't, we're going to harm ourselves in the long run.

Issue Box 15-5 continued on next page ▶

Of course, there are those who oppose tax simplification because they believe it's just simplistic—that advocates promise too much when they claim the burden will be equally shared. In this regard, opponents may accept the point made by advocates that equal tax burdens are fair, but reject the premise that the flat tax will deliver. They point to the elimination of taxes on capital gains, interest, and dividends as a windfall to be realized by the wealthiest taxpayers, while everyone else simply loses deductions that had benefited them.

A couple of things make deciphering the flat-tax proposal difficult. Both sides make claims based on projections, using figures that the other side disputes. From these claims, they assert that the flat tax either will or will not burden the middle class, will or will not be good for economic growth, will or will not lead to higher wages, and will or will not spur investment. This is characteristic of many policy struggles, where both sides use figures carefully to make claims that can neither be proved nor disproved unless or until the policy is implemented (and perhaps not even then).

Also, both sides have ideological agendas that go beyond the case they make for simplification and fairness. Conservative supporters of the flat tax would like to see government spend less, and would use tax reform as a vehicle for cutting tax revenues as leverage to cut federal spending. That's why the Armey proposal raises less revenue than what the government takes in under present tax law (he acknowledged this point in his website). Liberal supporters of the present system would like to see the tax code become more progressive, in the belief that the wealthiest Americans should be compelled to contribute disproportionately to the mutual pot. Liberals tend to regard any massive accumulation of wealth as a threat to the opportunities of people with few resources, and would not be unhappy about using tax policy to achieve greater redistribution of wealth.

So there's a lot going on here. Tax law is more than numbers: It's social policy that affects how we behave, how we spend, how we save, and how we regard America as a nation. A lot rides on that little tax-return postcard.

Arguments in Support

Numerous arguments have been made in support of the flat tax. Some of these are:

- It's fair. Everyone would pay the same rate, which is essential to fairness, and it doesn't just benefit the wealthy. People earning below a certain amount would pay no taxes at all.
- It's simple. Tax simplification benefits individuals who struggle with the time and cost of filling out annual returns. It benefits the economy by not forcing people into making spending choices to reap the rewards of a tax deduction, allowing the free market to operate more efficiently.
- Charitable contributions will go up. People will have more to spend as they save a larger share of their income, and historically we give more to charity when we have more to give.
- Homeowners will benefit. Lenders will no longer have to pay a tax on the interest they receive from borrowers and would pass the savings along in the form of lower interest rates. This will permit homeowners to finance their houses at a much lower rate than is presently possible, spurring growth in the housing sector.
- It will impose fiscal discipline. A flat tax rate of 17 percent would generate less revenue than the current system. This will force politicians to spend less money because they will have less on hand.

15-5b Spending Policy

If you've ever had to cover your expenses with money you've earned from working, you know what it's like to budget funds in order to make ends meet. In an ideal world, the amount of money you take in would bear some resemblance to the amount you spend. In the real world, you might have to borrow to pay for a major necessity like tuition or a car, or to afford a luxury you really want, like a spring break vacation. You might take out a loan or run up an unpaid balance on your credit card. In either case, you pay for having additional funds now by making interest payments later. The longer you go without making interest payments, the more you have to pay out over time.

The federal budget works pretty much the same way. Federal budget numbers may be staggeringly large—can you visualize a $2 trillion budget?—but the temptation to spend beyond our means applies just as much to the public sphere as to our private exploits with credit cards. This tendency has been at the center of national political debate for a generation.

One point of confusion in this debate is the difference between the federal deficit and the national debt. Many people confound the two, but as Box 15-5 points out, they're different—and recognizing the difference is fundamental to establishing a reasoned opinion on deficit spending.

Arguments Against

Opponents of the flat tax counter every argument made by its supporters. They say:

- It's unfair. Taxing income at the same rate across the board punishes people at the lower end of the earning scale because a fixed percentage of a small income translates into a greater burden than a fixed percentage of a large income. When wealthier people pay a higher tax on the upper end of their income, it results in redistribution of wealth that benefits those on the bottom end of the earnings scale.
- It's simplistic. Is it realistic to believe that wealthy Americans will give up something for nothing? For instance, only the wealthiest taxpayers face taxation of interest, dividends, and capital gains, and not having to do so offsets the tax shelters they'll give up. Ordinary taxpayers won't have this opportunity.
- Charitable contributions will go down. The flat tax will eliminate the existing deduction for charitable contributions, which is specifically designed to give people an incentive for voluntary giving.
- Homeowners will suffer. The present tax law permits a deduction for mortgage interest payments, permitting people to buy homes that might otherwise be out of their reach by giving them a large tax break as compensation. The flat tax eliminates that break.
- It will raise the deficit. A flat tax rate of 17 percent would generate less revenue than the current system, and since politicians have a poor record of cutting spending, they will end up passing along the difference as deficit spending. Advocates who say that spending would be cut as a product of tax reform have an additional agenda that shouldn't be part of a tax reform plan.

My Opinion

When registering your opinion on the flat tax, consider the history of the issue and the arguments supporting and opposing it. In particular, ask yourself if the flat tax:

- Is fair or unfair
- Is simple or simplistic
- Will help or hurt charitable giving
- Will benefit or harm homeowners
- Will impose fiscal discipline or contribute to deficit spending

The most accurate description of my attitude toward the flat tax is:

1—I strongly oppose it. It's a bad idea.
2—I oppose it, but with some reservations.
3—I support it, but with some reservations.
4—I strongly support it. It's a good idea.
5—I haven't thought enough about it to have an opinion.
6—I don't care about it enough to bother.

*Robert J. Shapiro, "Why Fairness Matters: Progressive versus Flat Taxes," Report of the Progressive Policy Institute, April 1, 1996, at http://www.ppionline.org/ppi_ci.cfm?cp=1&knlgAreaID=125&subsecid=163&contentid=1398.

†"Flat Tax Questions and Answers," at http://www.flattax.gov.

‡Shapiro, "Why Fairness Matters."

§Ibid.

Except for a few years in the late 1990s, the government has run a deficit every year since 1969. There are a number of reasons for deficit spending, some of them arguably more justifiable than others. Sometimes the government runs a deficit accidentally because expenditures or revenue projections were incorrectly estimated when the budget was written. Emergencies like war, a terrorist strike, or a major natural disaster can cause the government to run a deficit because it has no choice but to spend money that wasn't budgeted to address these unexpected circumstances. Congress and the president may even intentionally run a deficit during economic downturns in order to stimulate the economy through increased spending. Each of these circumstances is short-lived and does not add considerably to the national debt.[25]

Sometimes, though, Congress and the president are unwilling to make difficult choices to keep the budget in balance, resulting in long-term deficit spending. This happened in the 1980s, when President Reagan sought to reduce the size of the federal government through cuts in taxes and domestic expenditures while spending more on national defense. Politically popular tax cuts and added defense money proved easy to institute, but curtailing domestic spending meant confronting constituents who benefited from government programs. The result was a policy that spared many domestic programs and looked the other way as deficits climbed to unprecedented levels that regularly

> Box 15-5 Deficits and Debts

When the government takes in less than it spends in a given year, it runs a **deficit.** This is easily confused with the **national debt,** but they are different. The deficit is an imbalance between revenues and expenditures in a given year. After climbing out from under years of deficit spending in the late 1990s, the federal government became heavily indebted again during the second Bush administration; in 2004, the Congressional Budget Office projected a deficit of over $480 billion. When the government runs a deficit, it has to borrow to bridge the gap and to make interest payments on the money it borrows, just like you or I would. The amount the government borrows is its debt, and interest on the debt becomes a budgetary expense. As the government continues to run a deficit, it has to keep borrowing, which increases both the size of the debt and the portion of the budget that goes to paying interest on the debt.

As 2005 began, the national debt was $7.596 trillion, or $7,596,165,867,424.14 to be exact. The debt is owed mostly to domestic banks and financial institutions, and to holders of treasury bonds and savings bonds, although state, local, and foreign governments hold a portion of the debt.*

You can get an exact account of the national debt today from the Treasury Department, at http://www.publicdebt.treas.gov/opd/opdpenny.htm.

▶ **deficit** The gap created in the federal budget when the government takes in less than it spends in a given year.

▶ **national debt** The amount the government borrows to pay for accumulated budget deficits.

*The U.S. Treasury Department has a website for answering frequently asked questions about deficits and the national debt, at http://www.publicdebt.treas.gov/opd/opdfaq.htm#opdfaq33.

surpassed $200 billion per year, which simply deferred the problem for future generations. The roaring economy of the late 1990s brought the government a windfall of unexpectedly high tax revenues and helped end deficit spending temporarily; by 1998, the government was running a small surplus. This was short-lived, however, as large deficits returned with the economic slowdown that set in at the turn of the twenty-first century, coupled with expensive tax cuts favored by the Bush administration and high defense needs following the September 11 terror attacks and the Iraq War.

Strong political and ideological forces make deficit spending hard to stop once it gets started. Although many of us support the idea of a balanced budget in theory, we are more likely to be moved to political action to keep Congress from cutting programs that benefit us rather than to rise up in protest against red ink on a ledger sheet. Interest groups will keep the pressure on legislators to protect their programs, and as we saw in Chapter 8, they have the resources and relationships they need to be persuasive. Consequently, members of Congress are more likely to feel constrained to maintain or increase spending in the face of large deficits while acknowledging the importance of fiscal responsibility in their public remarks. Their words address the widespread constituent desire for responsible budgeting, but they avoid taking actions that would extract a great political cost. As politicians of both parties realized in the 1980s, it's easy to run against an incumbent who voted to cut back a popular program, but it's hard to run against an incumbent who helped run up large, abstract deficit numbers.[26]

Philosophically, arriving at a balanced budget pits different conceptions of the appropriate size and role of government against each other. This, too, can hinder action. Liberals who support social welfare spending are more likely to favor tax increases over spending cuts to achieve balance. Conservatives prefer spending cuts, and some favor tax reductions in part to force the issue of reducing the size of government, hoping to leave Congress with no choice but to reduce domestic spending as a result of lower revenues and higher deficits.[27] This difference reflects a deep philosophical division over what government should be doing, and is a way of using tax policy to legislate social outcomes.

The matter of cutting the budget is complicated by the fact that large portions of it cannot go under the axe. A host of expenditures are mandatory, which means they cannot be touched. These include Social Security and Medicare payments, unemployment insurance, federal retirement benefits, and means-tested entitlements. Interest on the debt is

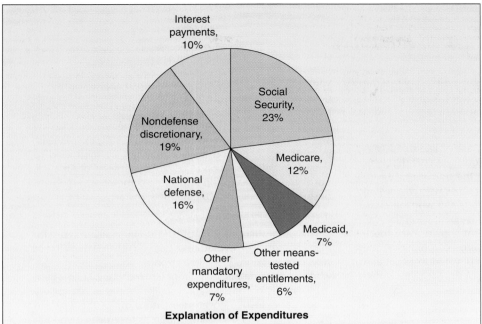

Figure 15-4
Where the Money Goes: Federal Government Expenditures, 2002
Source: Office of Management and Budget, "A Citizen's Guide to the Federal Budget," at http://www.whitehouse.gov/omb/budget/fy2002/guide02.html.

Explanation of Expenditures

- ***Social Security:*** The largest federal program, Social Security provides monthly retirement and disability benefits to 46 million people.

- ***Medicare:*** This provides health-care coverage to 40 million seniors and people with disabilities.

- ***Medicaid:*** This provides health-care coverage to over 34 million poor and disabled Americans. The federal government shares the cost of Medicaid with each state, paying between 50 and 83 percent of the cost.

- ***Other means-tested entitlements:*** The largest programs in this group are food stamps, Supplemental Security Income (SSI), the Earned Income Credit (EIC, a tax credit), veterans' pensions, and the child nutrition program.

- ***Other mandatory expenditures:*** This primarily includes unemployment insurance, payments to farmers, and federal retirement and insurance programs.

- ***National defense:*** This includes the portion of discretionary spending earmarked for the military.

- ***Nondefense discretionary:*** This includes the portion of discretionary spending not earmarked for the military, including all programs for education, training, science, technology, transportation, housing, and foreign aid.

- ***Interest payments:*** This is interest paid on the national debt.

also a fixed cost. With these expenses removed from consideration, you're left with 35 percent of the total budget for discretionary items, and about half of that is earmarked for defense, which is politically unpopular to cut.

Figure 15-4 shows the major spending categories in the 2002 budget. A look at the chart should show you how much of the budget is beyond the control of the budgeters. As more people retire, the percentage of the budget dedicated to Social Security will grow with it. The same is true of Medicare. Programs that help the needy and unemployed become more costly during economic downturns—precisely when tax revenues drop because fewer people are working. The easiest way to pay these costs is to borrow, but as we continue to run deficits, the portion of the budget dedicated to interest payments grows, too, squeezing out the relatively small set of discretionary expenditures. These economic limitations constrain the political options available to the elected officials who write the budget, contributing to the high-stakes nature of budgetary politics.

The Way You Want America to Be | *Domestic Policy*

Take a look back at the way you answered the polls in the "Your Opinion" sections of the Issue Boxes. Which answers did you give most often? Read on to see where you stand.

If your primary answer was 1...

...on domestic policy matters, you are of like mind with many liberals, whether or not you regard yourself that way. Your positions place you strongly on the side of those who see government as a positive force for those who are most in need of assistance: the poor, the elderly, the working class, and possibly even the wildlife and native peoples of the Arctic. You probably feel that government should place these interests ahead of the concerns of large corporations, like agribusiness and big oil. If you felt motivated to engage in political action to advance your view of America, you would find yourself most at home with liberal interest groups or in the Democratic Party.

If your primary answer was 2...

...on domestic policy matters, you tend to agree more than you disagree with liberals, whether or not you regard yourself that way. For the most part, you're open to a view of government as a positive social force. Some of your positions place you on the side of those who need assistance (perhaps the poor, the elderly, the working class, or even the wildlife and native peoples of the Arctic), and you're willing to endorse government action as a way to address their concerns. You may or may not feel motivated to engage in political action to advance your view of America, but if you are, you would find some common ground with liberal interest groups or with the Democratic Party.

If your primary answer was 3...

...on domestic policy matters, you tend to agree more than you disagree with conservatives, whether or not you regard

yourself that way. For the most part, you're open to a view of government as an impediment to initiative—perhaps corporate, individual, or both—and you probably believe that society is well served when government steps out of the way and permits ingenuity and competition to take over, at least in some instances. You may or may not be motivated to engage in political action to advance your view of America, but if you are, you would find some common ground with business groups or with the Republican Party.

If your primary answer was 4...

...on domestic policy matters, you are of like mind with many conservatives, whether or not you regard yourself that way. Your positions place you strongly on the side of those who see government as an impediment to initiative—be it corporate or individual—and you likely believe that society is best served when government steps out of the way and permits ingenuity and competition to take over. If you felt motivated to engage in political action to advance your view of America, you would find yourself most at home with business groups or in the Republican Party.

If your primary answer was 5 or 6...

...you probably place a low priority on things like the way government collects and distributes tax money, or balances the interests of the poor or environmentalists against energy concerns or the desire to put people to work. That leaves it to others to decide whether we should have a flat or a progressive income tax, continue welfare reform initiatives, change the terms of what one day will be your Social Security payments, drill in the Arctic National Wildlife Reserve, and subsidize agricultural concerns with your money—while we all live with the results of the choices they make.

Chapter Review

Regulatory policies depend on government action to minimize hazards or maximize benefits that will not be attended to by the free market. Competitive regulatory policies restrict the provision of a service or good, like operating a television station, to organizations that win federal licensing approval. Protective regulatory policies provide the public with information the government believes is beneficial to disseminate, like health warnings on cigarette packs. Regulation can be controversial because of widely held beliefs about limiting government involvement in the marketplace, even when the results of regulation, like clean air and safe food, are extremely popular.

Distributive policies are typically less controversial because they benefit everyone to some degree. Many distributive policies are public works projects financed by state and local governments, sometimes with federal support like the Interstate Highway System.

In contrast, social welfare policies are redistributive because the beneficiaries are different from the people who pay the bill. Many

social welfare policies, like unemployment compensation, veteran's benefits, Social Security, and Temporary Assistance to Needy Families, involve transfer payments of federal dollars to qualifying individuals. Social welfare policies for the poor are controversial among people who believe they contribute to a "culture of poverty." As entitlements, social welfare programs deliver benefits to everyone who meets the eligibility requirements, like being unemployed or retired. Some programs are means-tested, such that eligibility is dependent on meeting a statistical standard, like having an income below the poverty line in order to receive welfare benefits.

Contrary to popular belief, most social welfare dollars do not go to support the poor. Social Security, which benefits retired workers, is the largest social welfare program and arguably the most popular government program. It is redistributive because today's workers provide the money used to support today's retirees.

Substantive decisions about domestic policy are made through budgetary politics involving raising and spending tax money. The structure of the tax code is a political matter that determines how the tax burden will be shared across income groups. The American tax code is progressive, as higher levels of income are taxed at higher rates, although deductions, or tax expenditures, permit individuals with higher incomes to reduce their payments.

Because tax cuts are politically popular and it's hard to cut funds for programs with a constituency, the federal budget has run a deficit, or spent more than it has taken in, almost every year since 1969. Deficit spending contributes to the national debt, which is the accumulated money owed—with interest—on past deficits. A large percentage of mandatory expenditures, like money earmarked for transfer payments and interest on the debt, compounds the difficulty of making spending cuts and contributes to deficit spending.

Key Terms

Aid to Families with Dependent Children (AFDC) (p. 460)
appropriations (p. 468)
competitive regulatory policy (p. 450)
Congressional Budget and Impoundment Control Act of 1974 (p. 468)
deficit (p. 474)
distributive policies (p. 452)
Earned Income Tax Credit (p. 460)
entitlements (p. 459)
flat tax (p. 470)

food stamps (p. 460)
gross domestic product (GDP) (p. 467)
means test (p. 459)
Medicaid (p. 460)
Medicare (p. 462)
national debt (p. 474)
pork barrel (p. 452)
poverty line (p. 456)
progressive income tax (p. 470)
protective regulatory policy (p. 450)
public works (p. 452)

reconciliation (p. 468)
redistributive policies (p. 454)
regressive tax (p. 470)
regulatory policies (p. 449)
Social Security (p. 459)
tax expenditures (p. 470)
Temporary Assistance for Needy Families (TANF) (p. 460)
transfer payments (p. 456)

Review Questions

Note: You can find the correct answers to these questions by taking the quiz and then submitting your answers in the Online Edition. The program will automatically score your submission. If you miss a question, the program will provide the correct answer, a rationale for the answer, and the section number in the chapter where the topic is discussed.

1. Competitive regulatory policies
   a. alleviate market confusion that can undermine the public interest.
   b. give consumers information on product hazards that might not be provided by the private sector.
   c. give consumers open access to beneficial information that might not be provided by the public sector.
   d. alleviate undesirable personal outcomes like unsafe working conditions.

2. Regulatory policies can be controversial because
   a. they transfer resources from the working class to the poor.
   b. people often object to the results they produce.
   c. they may be regarded as an unwelcome infringement on personal liberty.
   d. warning labels on cigarette packs can be confusing.

3. Public works projects are
   a. distributive policies.
   b. redistributive policies.
   c. protective regulatory policies.
   d. competitive regulatory policies.

4. Transfer payments are
   a. direct payments of cash only to qualified individuals.
   b. direct payments of cash only from the federal government to the states.
   c. indirect payments of cash or benefits from the federal government to the states.
   d. direct payments of cash or benefits to qualified individuals.

5. One argument in favor of social welfare policies for the poor is
   a. social welfare programs create a "culture of poverty."
   b. that without access to well-paying jobs, the poor lack the motivation to find job skills.
   c. welfare pays better than minimum wage jobs.
   d. poor people create their own circumstances through lack of motivation.

6. All of the following programs are means-tested *except*
   a. Medicaid.
   b. food stamps.
   c. Supplementary Security Income.
   d. Medicare.

7. Temporary Assistance for Needy Families (TANF) replaced
   a. Medicaid.
   b. the Earned Income Tax Credit.
   c. Supplementary Security Income.
   d. Aid to Families with Dependent Children (AFDC).

8. Social Security is
   a. a distributive program.
   b. a distributive program dressed up like a redistributive program.
   c. a redistributive program.
   d. not a government program.

9. Most federal revenue comes from
   a. personal income taxes.
   b. payroll taxes.
   c. corporate income taxes.
   d. excise taxes.

10. Each of the following contributes to deficit spending *except*
   a. distaste for cutting mandatory expenditures.
   b. efforts by some conservatives to force spending cuts by running deficits.
   c. the small number of discretionary items in the federal budget.
   d. distaste for cutting programs with constituent support.

In Their Own Words

You might be interested in examining some of what the following authors have said about the topics we've been discussing:

Handler, Joel F. *The Poverty of Welfare Reform.* New Haven, CT: Yale University Press, 1995. A critique of recent welfare reform efforts, which Handler regards as misguided in their assumptions about poverty and more symbolic than substantive.

Harris, Richard A., and Sidney M. Milkis. *The Politics of Regulatory Change: A Tale of Two Agencies.* New York: Oxford University Press, 1989. A look at the politics behind regulation and deregulation.

Howard, Philip K. *The Death of Common Sense: How Law Is Suffocating America.* New York: Random House, 1994. The author makes a case against regulatory policy, contending that regulations written in Washington routinely miss their intended mark while stifling local initiatives that could be far more creative and effective.

Kelso, William A. *Poverty and the Underclass: Changing Perceptions of the Poor in America.* New York: New York University Press, 1994. Kelso considers the changing arguments made by liberals and conservatives about the reasons for poverty in America.

MacManus, Susan A. *Young v. Old: Generational Combat in the 21st Century.* Boulder, CO: Westview Press, 1996. A look at the way changing age demographics may affect the politics of Social Security in the years ahead.

Murray, Charles A. *Losing Ground: American Social Policy, 1950–1980.* New York: Basic Books, 1984. A controversial and influential conservative critique of the social welfare programs of the 1960s and 1970s.

Patterson, James T. *America's Struggle against Poverty, 1900–1994.* Cambridge, MA: Harvard University Press, 1994. A comprehensive look at what it meant to be poor in America in the twentieth century, and how social welfare programs affected poverty.

Rubin, Irene S. *The Politics of Public Budgeting: Getting and Spending, Borrowing and Balancing,* 3rd ed. Chatham, NJ: Chatham House Publishers, 1997. An accessible overview of budgetary politics.

Vedlitz, Arnold. *Conservative Mythology and Public Policy in America.* New York: Praeger, 1988. A liberal rejoinder to conservative critiques of social welfare policies.

Notes

1. All figures come from the 2000 General Social Survey, at http://webapp.icpsr.umich.edu/GSS/homepage.htm.

2. The one notable exception is a federal income tax checkoff that routes three dollars of your tax return to a fund for publicly financing presidential candidates without increasing your overall tax payment. Some states also have tax checkoffs for a variety of publicly financed causes like wildlife protection, child-abuse protection, and senior-citizen support.

3. For an overview of the history and procedures of broadcast licensing, see the Museum of Broadcast Communications website at http://www.museum.tv/archives/etv/L/htmlL/license/license.htm.

4. There are questions about the effectiveness of warning labels. Canada goes much further than the United States to draw the connection between smoking and illness, by requiring the placement of pictures of diseased lungs, gums, and hearts over large portions of its cigarette packs.

5. See the Bureau of Labor Statistics, "Child Labor Laws and Enforcement," *Report on the Youth Labor Force* (U.S. Dept. of Labor, November 2000), at http://www.bls.gov/opub/rylf/pdf/chapter2.pdf.

6. Theodore Lowi, "American Business, Public Policy, Case Studies and Political Theory," *World Politics* 16: 4 (July 1964): 677–715.

7. See the American Public Works Association, "2004 Federal Budget Numbers for Public Works Infrastructure and Programs," at http://www.apwa.net/HotTopics/index.asp?HotID= 457&MODE=ARCHIVE&HotLocator=.

8. James T. Patterson, *America's Struggle against Poverty, 1900–1994* (Cambridge, MA: Harvard University Press, 1994), 7.

9. The 2004 Health and Human Services Poverty Guidelines, at http://aspe.hhs.gov/poverty/04poverty.shtml.

10. U.S. Census Bureau, at http://www.census.gov/hhes/poverty/poverty02/table1.pdf and http://www.census.gov/hhes/poverty/poverty02/table2.pdf .

11. William A. Kelso, *Poverty and the Underclass: Changing Perceptions of the Poor in America* (New York: New York University Press, 1994), 31–45.

12. Charles Murray, *Losing Ground: American Social Policy, 1950–1980* (New York: Basic Books, 1984), 9.

13. Arnold Vedlitz, *Conservative Mythology and Public Policy in America* (New York: Praeger, 1988), 1–15.

14. Kelso, *Poverty and the Underclass,* 42–43.

15. Joel F. Handler, *The Poverty of Welfare Reform* (New Haven, CT: Yale University Press, 1995), 1–6.

16. Elaine B. Sharp, *The Sometime Connection: Public Opinion and Social Policy* (Albany, NY: State University of New York Press, 1999), 177–207.

17. John W. Kingdon, *America the Unusual* (New York: Worth Publishers, 1999).

18. Irene S. Rubin, *The Politics of Public Budgeting: Getting and Spending, Borrowing and Balancing,* 3rd ed. (Chatham, NJ: Chatham House Publishers, 1997), 42.

19. Ibid., 42–43.

20. Ibid., 43–53.

21. *Budget of the United States Government, Fiscal Year 2004: Analytical Perspectives,* U.S. Government Printing Office, Washington, DC, 110 (Table 6-3), online at http://www.gpoaccess.gov/usbudget/fy04/pdf/spec.pdf.

22. Citizens for Tax Justice, at http://www.ctj.org/html/margfaq.htm. Citizens for Tax Justice is a nonprofit, nonpartisan interest group that researches and advocates issues of tax fairness.

23. Ibid.

24. Allen Schick, *The Federal Budget: Politics, Policy, Process,* revised ed. (Washington, DC: Brookings Institution Press, 2000), 158–159. When social insurance, corporate and excise taxes are factored in, the effective tax rate for earners in the $20,000–$30,000 range is 17 percent, and for the $50,000–$75,000 range, 23.9 percent. Individuals with incomes of $1,000,000 or more are taxed at an effective rate of 35.3 percent.

25. Rubin, *Politics of Public Budgeting,* 177–179.

26. Ibid., 182–183.

27. Ibid.

Foreign and Defense Policies

16

16-1 Introduction

In the winter of 2003, as America and the world readied for war in Iraq, the foreign policy apparatus of the United States went into full swing. On the diplomatic front, having won the support of Congress for an invasion, the administration intensely engaged in efforts to get allied nations to endorse its decision to go to war with Iraq by declaring Saddam Hussein in violation of United Nations dictates that he disarm. Simultaneously, on the military front, tens of thousands of American troops gathered in the Persian Gulf, preparing to receive invasion orders. In Washington, battle plans were developed to leverage American military superiority in the pursuit of strategic objectives: removing Hussein from power and replacing his regime, finding and destroying Iraqi weapons of mass destruction, minimizing civilian casualties, and doing it all in the shortest possible time. A successful war, the administration argued, would promote a host of American strategic objectives by bringing democracy to the Middle East, keeping dangerous weapons from terrorists, facilitating a settlement of the Israeli-Palestinian crisis, and stabilizing oil markets.

These simultaneous initiatives represent the full reach and scope of American foreign and domestic policy, which is designed to advance American security interests in an increasingly interdependent world. The buildup to war in Iraq engaged the full weight and attention of the domestic political actors who have a hand in developing and executing foreign policy—the president, American diplomats overseas, and Congress—as well as the American foreign policy establishment, including the Departments of State and Defense, the National Security Council, and the Joint Chiefs of Staff. Likewise, it actively engaged prominent world actors, like the United Nations, NATO, and the European Union.

The American effort encompassed economic, diplomatic, and military planning. Provisions were made for protecting Iraqi oilfields from destruction in the event of an invasion, and for rebuilding Iraq's infrastructure in the aftermath of fighting. On the diplomatic front, the State Department engaged in a months-long, ultimately unsuccessful effort to convince traditional allies France and Germany to back American invasion plans in the United Nations, attempted unsuccessfully to negotiate a foreign aid package with Turkey in exchange for permission from that reluctant nation to house American invasion forces, and stared down Iraqi claims of disarmament, which the United States termed hollow posturing. As diplomacy ran its course, military planners were preparing invasion scenarios in the event that weapons replaced words.

Long-term strategy shaped this diplomatic and military planning. Foreign policy is about first articulating goals for American security, then enacting policies designed to attain

Box 16-1   The Cold War

For over two generations, global politics was defined by the standoff between the United States and the Soviet Union. Allies during World War II when faced with a common threat, the two nations settled into an icy peace following the defeat of Germany and Japan. Each saw the other as having designs on global expansion and conquest. Each felt threatened by the other's ideology—American capitalism and Soviet communism—and each saw the other as attempting to export its ideology around the globe. Each had nuclear weapons and therefore was limited in its ability to fight a "hot" war with the other.

Instead, numerous proxy wars were fought between nations aligned with the two sides, with direct or indirect assistance from the superpowers. The Vietnam War can be understood in terms of the United States coming to the assistance of South Vietnam in its struggle to prevent a takeover by the forces of communist North Vietnam. Additionally, there were ongoing propaganda battles between the two sides, each trying to convince the world that its system was superior. During the 1960s, Americans and Soviets were consumed with the "space race," a show of strength through technology measured by which side would be the first to orbit the earth, send satellites into space, and ultimately land a man on the moon.

Generations raised during this time regarded the cold war struggle between the United States and the Soviet Union as an accepted fact of life. It dominated literature, film, and art; fear of nuclear annihilation was a chronic reality. In fact, the nuclear standoff between the two nations made it seem inconceivable that the cold war would ever end, which made the collapse of the Soviet Union in 1991 a surreal experience for the millions who had been weaned on superpower tensions and a divided world.

them. Strategic interests are typically easy to identify, and tend to be shared by Republican and Democratic lawmakers and by most Americans. During the cold war, there was bipartisan support for containment of the Soviet Union and preventing a Soviet nuclear first strike (see Box 16-1). In the 1990s, liberals and conservatives saw the need to make the American economy competitive in a period of economic globalization. After September 2001, no one questioned the need to protect America from further terrorist attacks.

Articulating goals is typically the easy part of foreign policy development. The challenge comes from reaching agreement on how to achieve them, which is why the real juice in foreign policy making comes from confronting differences over strategies. When the Reagan administration advocated a military buildup to contain the Soviet Union, detractors argued that their policies would lead to a dangerously militarized world and increase the risk of nuclear war. When the Clinton administration pressed for free trade to enhance global markets for American goods, critics said these policies would cost American workers their jobs. When the Bush administration pursued an unprovoked attack on Iraq as a way of making the world safer from terrorism, it sparked global protests with millions of dissenters. See Box 16-2.

As former secretary of state Colin Powell *(left)* pursued diplomatic measures to get allied nations to support a U.S.-led invasion of Iraq, troops stationed in nearby Kuwait awaited the order to advance.

Source: AP/Wide World Photos.

Box 16-2   The Administration against the World

Feelings can run strong when the world's lone superpower threatens preemptive military action against another country, with lives and global power resting in the balance. Although few people around the world expressed sympathy for Saddam Hussein and his brutal regime, millions gathered to protest an American policy that they regarded as misguided and dangerous. Abroad, protestors reacted in anger against what they viewed as American imperialism.* Domestically, protesters objected to the timing and purpose of the war, doubting the administration's contention that it would help prevent the spread of global terror and opposing what they saw as an ominous break from taking military action only in response to provocation. With the advent of war, thousands from San Francisco to New York took to the streets in acts of civil disobedience, chaining themselves to each other, blocking federal buildings, and snarling rush hour traffic.†

The worldwide backlash to the American invasion of Iraq was unusual in its scope and intensity, and signified the great reach and high stakes involved in the American action. Protests against American foreign policy are not uncommon, though, from groups that stand to lose from policy decisions. For instance, environmentalists have demonstrated against policies they feel will facilitate global warming, and workers worried about losing their jobs have protested international trade policies. Issues of this magnitude matter deeply to those directly influenced by American policy, but unless they hit home with a broad section of the electorate, they are unlikely to influence a lot of votes and turn presidential or congres-

Global protests gave voice to those who opposed the American invasion of Iraq, although they weren't strong enough to stop it.

Source: AP/Wide World Photos.

sional elections. This makes protests an appealing instrument to those who wish to affect public opinion about how officials are conducting foreign affairs.

*You can get a sense of the demonstrations that took place around the world from the Stop the War Coalition website, at http://www.stopwar.org.uk/.

†You can get a sense of the demonstrations that took place around the United States at the United for Peace and Justice website, at http://www.unitedforpeace.org/.

In the pages ahead, we'll look more closely at the people and institutions engaged in foreign policy formulation, at the economic, diplomatic, and military initiatives they undertake, and at the sometimes controversial strategies they employ to advance their objectives abroad and at home.

16-2 The Players at Home

Ultimate responsibility for foreign policy formulation—and for its success and failure—rests with elected officials in the executive and legislative branches. They are joined by an extensive foreign policy establishment that bridges the diplomatic and military functions of foreign affairs.

16-2a Domestic Policy Makers

As we saw in Chapter 10, the president maintains chief responsibility for American foreign policy, with vast diplomatic and military authority. The president appoints all American ambassadors, but he also functions as chief diplomat through his constitutional ability to negotiate treaties with other nations and through the power to enter into **executive agreements** on behalf of the United States. In his role as commander-in-chief, the president is civilian head of the armed forces, and has final authority to commit troops to combat (see Box 16-3).

We mentioned in Chapter 10 that the president has over time acquired more range than Congress over the conduct of international affairs. The Constitution gave Congress the power to declare war in a time when formal declarations preceded military action, but as we said in Chapter 10, since World War II, the pattern has been to wage war without

▶ **executive agreements**
Legally binding presidential agreements with other nations that do not require congressional approval.

▶ Box 16-3   One Man's View of the World

Placing primary responsibility for national security in the hands of one person leaves vital decisions about our national welfare at the mercy of how that person views the world. The assumptions the president makes about the intentions, motivations, and actions of our friends and adversaries—beliefs rooted in his approach to human nature—can structure his thinking and, with it, the policies he develops in our name. A lot of things can contribute to the development of a president's "worldview," particularly the experiences he has growing up and in previous offices that permit him to draw conclusions about what makes people tick.* In the end, these remain assumptions and cannot be demonstrated to be definitively right or wrong, even though that is exactly how history will view the actions taken in the name of a worldview.

President Bush (senior) was heavily influenced by his experience fighting in World War II, in the years after European appeasement permitted Adolph Hitler to begin his pursuit of global conquest, and the surprise Japanese attack on Pearl Harbor caught America off guard. Experience taught Bush to be strong and be prepared, and during one of his biggest foreign policy crises, when Iraq invaded Kuwait, these principles guided his reaction. Comparing Saddam Hussein to Hitler, Bush assembled an international coalition and, with America in the lead, launched a war to push back Hussein's aggressive move.

His successor had an entirely different formative experience. Bill Clinton witnessed the debacle of Vietnam, where strength and preparedness led America into a costly guerilla war for reasons many people did not understand. Clinton personally wrestled with serving in that war—many believe he evaded the draft—and like many of his generation he regarded military solutions as a last resort to solving complex problems, perhaps even as a failure of policy. When Clinton

spoke of disseminating humanitarian aid as a way of avoiding conflict, he was expressing a worldview that placed diplomacy and economic assistance ahead of military action.

The second President Bush is more like his father than his predecessor, although he is more inclined to see the world in absolute terms. Following the September 11 attack, he issued his call to other nations that in the fight against terror, you were either "with us or against us."† This view of the world explains his belief that a good regime (the United States) could replace an evil regime (Saddam Hussein's Iraq) with another good regime, and that the Iraqi people would see the difference and embrace the change. It also explains his determination to head toward war even though it meant alienating allies who were bitterly opposed to the American policy (reasoning in absolute terms, he believed they would come around when they saw the United States was successful).

Before action is taken, it's impossible to know if a worldview accurately describes the world and predicts how other national actors will behave. It's entirely possible that worldviews are suited to some situations but are not "one size fits all," leaving little room for knowing how likely it is that policies will be effective. Even after the fact, if things go badly, the side whose view is not supported by events will be tempted to rationalize away what happened. That's because worldviews are so fundamental that it's sometimes easier to challenge what happened than to challenge what we believe.

*For a discussion of the development of presidential "worldview" in the context of the development of a president's character and style, see James David Barber, *The Presidential Character: Predicting Performance in the White House* (Englewood Cliffs, NJ: Prentice Hall, 1992).

†"You Are Either With Us Or Against Us," CNN.com, November 6, 2001, at http://www.cnn.com/2001/US/11/06/gen.attack.on.terror/

declaring it. This is the reason why Congress passed the **War Powers Act of 1973,** in an effort to regain lost authority in military affairs.

Although Congress is not irrelevant to military policy—after all, President Bush asked Congress for formal approval of his Iraq policy to bolster its legitimacy—the blueprint for where and when to use force comes from the executive branch. It was President Bush's decision to disarm Iraq; he approved the plans and gave the go-ahead. Congress had the more constrained function of offering its consent, operating in an important but subsidiary role that is typical of its place in foreign policy making.[1]

> ▶ **War Powers Act of 1973**
> A congressional attempt to reassert the role of the legislature with respect to the president in military affairs by restricting the president's ability to wage war.

16-2b The Foreign Policy Establishment

Presidents make the call on what our foreign policy should be, but they have a lot of assistance in deciding what to do. Some presidents might say they have *too much* assistance because members of the vast foreign policy establishment have been known to fight among themselves and jockey for influence in the Oval Office.

We already know a bit about the major institutions of foreign policy making from our work in Chapter 10, where we discussed the Departments of State and Defense, the National Security Council, the CIA, and the Joint Chiefs of Staff. Let's take a closer look at how officials in foreign policy organizations operate and how they work together (or go after each other's throats).

Department of State The president's foreign policy is formulated and implemented at the State Department. Headed by the **secretary of state,** who is the president's chief foreign policy advisor, the State Department coordinates the activities of federal agencies that have dealings with other nations and is responsible for allocating money to other agencies engaged in foreign affairs. The Department of State is also the lead diplomatic institution, where it represents the president's policies to other nations through the efforts of the secretary of state and through a diplomatic corps operating at over 260 embassies, consulates, and international organization offices in over 180 nations.[2]

Department of Defense What the State Department is to diplomacy, the Department of Defense is to military and national security concerns. The army, navy, air force, and marine corps all report to the Defense Department for matters involving equipping, training, and recruiting personnel. This includes procuring weapons systems for national defense. Overall, the Department of Defense houses 1.37 million active duty forces, 1.28 million reserves, and over 650,000 civilian employees.[3]

Joint Chiefs of Staff The heads of the Army, Air Force, Navy, and Marine Corps also serve as the president's key military advisors in their capacity as members of the **Joint Chiefs of Staff.** Working with an extensive staff, they perform an important research and advisory function, informing the civilian commander-in-chief about the military contingencies of any potential defense policy. As President Bush was developing his policy toward Iraq, former Secretary of State Colin Powell and Defense Secretary Donald Rumsfeld weighed in on the *desirability* of a diplomatic versus military approach to Saddam Hussein; the joint chiefs contributed an analysis of *how* a military approach should be implemented, including estimates of the size and composition of the force, the timing and duration of the conflict, and how it would best be carried out.

At the same time, the civilian leaders were not without a voice on military questions. Widely circulated press reports told of disagreements between Rumsfeld and the joint chiefs over the size of the Iraqi invasion force, with the defense secretary rejecting the joint chiefs' recommendation for a larger troop buildup than what the United States eventually put in place. In the first week of the campaign, as administration hopes for a smooth march to Baghdad faded against initially tenacious Iraqi resistance, Rumsfeld was bombarded with questions by reporters who suggested the American advance might have been more swift and less costly had he not overruled the military advisors. This critique faded from discussion days later when American troops waged a rapid assault on the Iraqi capital; it reemerged during the occupation of Iraq, when a thinly stretched American presence necessitated extending the tour of duty of many soldiers.

National Security Council Established by President Truman in 1947 to coordinate foreign policy in the White House, the **National Security Council (NSC)** is an advisory body to the president that pulls together high-level representatives of the diplomatic and defense establishment. Its purpose is to review national security issues and offer advice on how the president might address them.[4] By bringing together the president, the secretaries of state and defense, the chairman of the Joint Chiefs of Staff, and the director of the CIA, among others, all major diplomatic and military perspectives are represented.

This arrangement can be fruitful when disagreements among the participants are minimal or can be effectively managed. As with the case of Secretary Rumsfeld and the joint chiefs, however, infighting is not uncommon. Historically, friction has not been uncommon between the president's **national security advisor** (who serves as a personal advisor to the president on national security matters) and the secretary of state, who in some administrations have found themselves in competition with each other for the president's attention. Tension derives from the overlapping responsibilities of the two positions, which can place their occupants on a collision course when they have major differences over the direction of foreign policy.

16-2c Players on a Global Stage

International alliances have long been a staple of foreign relations, but international organizations today play a critical role in shaping national policy perhaps more than at any time in history. President Bush spent months trying to win the support of allied nations opposed to an invasion of Iraq, in part because of the desirability of sharing the costs of war and reconstruction, in part because global public opinion matters. The president wanted the legitimacy that comes from having the backing of influential world leaders, and he delayed American invasion plans in February 2003 in an effort to get it.

There are limits, of course, to the restrictions other countries can place on a determined head of state; failing to win the support he sought, Bush forged ahead with his plans anyway. However, in an interdependent world there are also ramifications for unilateral action; as critics in France, Germany, and Russia viewed the American invasion of Iraq as blatantly disregarding their wishes, they made it plain that a lot of repair work would have to be done in order for them to put relations with the United States back on track. This came to pass when Secretary of State Powell struggled to get these nations to contribute to the costs of rebuilding Iraq after the major fighting ended.

Global influences on American foreign policy come from major organizations like the United Nations, NATO, and the European Union. They can also come from interest groups with a multinational base.

The United Nations Although it cannot make laws or guarantee enforcement of its resolutions, the United Nations (UN) is the voice of international opinion and a forum for working through international conflict. With a membership list that includes almost every country on earth, the UN has been the center of international discussion on some of the most problematic conflicts of our time. Established in 1945 in a world that had seen two global wars in the course of thirty years, the UN charter aimed at four objectives: maintaining peace; fostering cooperation among nations; resolving international disputes; and promoting human rights.[5]

Although the United Nations encompasses a host of organizations to advance its objectives, and all member nations are represented in the large General Assembly, the main diplomatic work takes place in the Security Council. There, the United States is one of five permanent members with the power to veto any resolution (China, France, Russia, and Great Britain are the others). Along with ten other nations who serve two-year terms, the Security Council tries to resolve international hostilities by establishing guidelines for conflict resolution, working to arrange ceasefires between warring parties, and in some cases, sending peacekeeping troops to separate hostile armies. Box 16-4 discusses President Bush's appeals to the Security Council as the United States prepared for the American invasion of Iraq.

Since 1948, the Security Council has sent peacekeeping forces to intervene in fifty-four conflicts.[6] In recent years, the Security Council has supported the successful struggle to end apartheid in South Africa, advanced the cause of human rights in Cambodia, negotiated an end to the fighting and supported relief efforts in the former Yugoslavia, overseen free elections in Nicaragua, worked to rebuild Afghanistan following the fall of the Taliban government, and brokered the transition from American occupation to an interim government in Iraq.[7]

Like much of the work of the Security Council, these were all long-term efforts that defied immediate success. Intractable problems can remain before the world community for generations. Security Council Resolutions 242 and 338 are still widely considered to be central components of a potential resolution to the Israeli-Palestinian conflict even though they were passed, respectively, in 1967 and 1973, and a solution to that crisis is nowhere in view.

NATO The **North Atlantic Treaty Organization** (**NATO**) is a throwback to the cold war, when it served as a common security pact for North America and Western Europe against

▶**North Atlantic Treaty Organization (NATO)**
An alliance of the United States, Canada, and Western European nations originally designed as a military pact to counter Soviet expansion. Following the cold war, it has grown to include European nations once aligned with the Soviet Union.

Box 16-4   The United States, Iraq, and the Security Council

In 2002, the Bush administration—arguing that Saddam Hussein had produced weapons of mass destruction he could funnel to terrorists—made a strategic decision to ask the United Nations Security Council to endorse its efforts to get Iraq to dismantle those weapons or face military consequences. The result was Security Council Resolution 1441, which authorized UN weapons inspectors to return to the country that had kicked them out after their first tour following the 1991 Persian Gulf War, threatening "serious consequences" for not complying with the inspectors but stopping short of imposing a deadline for compliance. With American troops mobilizing on his borders, Saddam Hussein permitted the inspectors to return, only to provide them with what the American administration regarded as half-measures designed to conceal more than they revealed.

As 2002 became 2003, the United States beat the drums for war, regularly accusing Hussein of brazenly thwarting serious efforts to disarm and saying the time for action had arrived. However, the inspectors did not see it the same way, periodically reporting to the Security Council that Iraq was allowing them enough access to do their work, and that they had turned up no hard evidence of illegal weapons. Nations opposed to an American first strike on Iraq used these reports to advocate giving the inspectors more time, and strenuously rejected American and British calls for a second resolution advocating the immediate use of force to resolve the conflict. Leaders of some of these countries, like France and Germany, faced stiff public opposition to a war. Even Great Britain, America's strongest ally on the Council, supported the U.S. position at the risk of alienating a majority of its citizens, which is why it was the driving force behind a second resolution authorizing war. Great Britain hoped that a clear endorsement by the United Nations would assuage a divided public that was skittish about being America's only major partner in war.

This put the United States in a tough diplomatic position. Virtually alone against the world, American diplomats took aim at Council members, cajoling them, threatening to end foreign aid, and using whatever carrots and sticks they had in their considerable bag of resources to muster the nine yes votes necessary to win support for a second resolution. They faced stiff opposition because the resolution was wildly unpopular. When it became apparent that France and possibly Russia and China were ready to veto the resolution, the Bush administration said it was willing to settle for majority support to demonstrate it had built a coalition, even though the resolution would fail. When it looked like an extra two weeks would be necessary to win that majority, the administration put its battle plans on hold. Soon it became apparent that majority approval was out of reach. President Bush said he was willing to go ahead with the vote anyway, then reconsidered on the advice of aides who believed if the United States and Great Britain were going to go it alone, it would be better for them to stage an invasion without first facing an embarrassing loss at the UN.

From the start, it was clear to member nations that the United States had decided to invade Iraq even before it asked for the initial Security Council resolution. Why, then, go through so many diplomatic gymnastics? Why go to the United Nations at all? The answer to that question reveals the importance of an organization that cannot dictate the actions of any on its members, but which represents world opinion in an age when world opinion has political value. UN approval would have offered international legitimacy for what otherwise would be a unilateral American invasion of a nation that had not initiated hostilities. It would have permitted the United States to diffuse anger in the Islamic world that was sure to be triggered by a western attack. It would have calmed a nervous public at home, where support for a war without global backing was shaky.

The failure to achieve Security Council support did not stop the Bush administration from implementing a policy it had developed out of its view of national self-interest. That was not going to happen. However, by galvanizing the belief among nations opposed to war that America was never serious about renewed weapons inspections, the Security Council ironically validated the administration's assumption about its relevance.

the Warsaw Pact alliance of the Soviet Union and Eastern Europe. The NATO alliance initially maintained that a Soviet attack on any member nation would be regarded as an attack on the entire alliance in an effort to prevent Soviet expansion in Europe. After the cold war, NATO maintains its relevance by virtue of its size (which has grown to include some former Warsaw Pact members) and strategic position. As the United States and Iraq inched closer to war in February 2003, NATO member Turkey, which borders on Iraq, requested and received surveillance aircraft and missile defenses from the alliance in the event of an Iraqi attack.[8]

European Union (EU)
The framework for integrating previously disparate European economies into a single market.

The European Union   An economic counterpart to NATO, the **European Union** (**EU**) has integrated the previously disparate economies of European nations into a single market with clout in the international economy. Originally a small federation of nine countries when it was established in 1950, the EU grew in size and importance toward the end of the cold war. In May 2004, ten countries—mostly former communist nations of Eastern Europe—joined the EU, bringing its membership to twenty-five countries with a combined 455 million people.[9] The EU formally established a single European market in 1993. In 2002, it introduced a single European currency—the euro—which is recognized as the official currency of many member nations.[10]

Nongovernmental Organizations (NGOs) A host of nonprofit, voluntary **nongovernmental organizations** (**NGOs**) bring local involvement to international concerns. NGOs may perform a number of functions. They lobby governments individually or through the United Nations, encourage participation in matters of international importance, monitor government actions in international affairs, or perform humanitarian work around the world. Many NGOs are issue-oriented and organized around a specific policy area with international applications, like the human rights group Amnesty International or the environmental group Greenpeace.[11] These organizations are probably familiar as some of the interest groups that we talked about in Chapter 8, and some NGOs can be classified in this way. You might think of NGOs as nonprofit interest groups advancing solutions to problems that lie beyond international boundaries. NGOs are based in countries around the world.

The tactics used by NGOs range from organizing international protests to working quietly in diplomatic circles. Operating as they do beyond national borders, NGOs are likely to use the Internet to mobilize international support behind their agendas. In fact, their influence is such that they may be regarded as nonstate actors on the international scene. In recent years, NGOs have engaged in successful efforts to strengthen women's and children's rights around the globe, influence arms control and disarmament agreements, improve the well-being of poor and indigenous people, win international approval to ban land mines, and address numerous other global social and economic concerns.[12]

Corporate Interests Multinational corporations are, like NGOs, transnational actors with great influence over the structure of international affairs. Many of these groups will be familiar from Chapter 8 as well, as corporate interests heavily involved in lobbying Congress and the president. As more and more corporations have become global entities, their lobbying efforts have extended to the international arena, and their influence can be strong because of the resources they command. Multinational energy corporations, for instance, have an interest in maintaining or establishing friendly governments in the oil-rich Middle East and will want a say over policies influencing that region. Corporations doing business around the globe have a direct interest in international business regulations and will lobby to protect their interests in the way these regulations are formulated and implemented.

16-3 Economic Policies

With national borders becoming increasingly smaller obstacles to international trade and finance, economic policies are becoming a more important component of international relations. Global computer networks make it possible for assets to be moved instantaneously around the world, connecting financial markets in a web of interdependency. Trade in services—like telecommunications, banking, and insurance—and trade in ideas—like inventions and other "intellectual property"—have vastly expanded the traffic in international markets, which following World War II, was limited primarily to goods.[13] These changes have moved nations to renegotiate the terms under which they do business.

16-3a Protectionism and Free Trade

Through the first half of the twentieth century, nations commonly followed a policy of **protectionism,** designed to boost the sales of domestic goods in order to protect the jobs of the workers who produced them. The main instrument of protectionism is the **tariff,** or a tax on imports designed to make them more costly and therefore less competitive than domestic products. Protectionism appealed to many policy makers in a world with distinct borders, where nations traded far fewer commodities far less frequently than they do today and where corporations resided within national boundaries. Today,

> **nongovernmental organizations (NGOs)** Nonprofit organizations that promote interests with global ramifications on the world stage.

> **protectionism** The policy of raising the price of imported goods through tariffs in order to make them less attractive than domestic products.

> **tariff** A tax on imports designed to raise their cost and make them less competitive than domestic products, in an effort to protect the jobs of domestic workers.

Box 16-5   Were the NAFTA Critics Correct?

As Congress approached a final vote on NAFTA in 1993, the rhetoric level rose as interest groups on both sides of the issue lobbied hard for the support of legislators in what was shaping up to be a razor-thin vote. Critics of NAFTA in the United States argued that the agreement would cost American jobs as businesses relocated to Mexico, where labor is much less expensive. Supporters promised that NAFTA would create jobs while increasing wages for Mexican workers. A decade later, which group was right?

It depends on who's doing the talking.

The interest group Public Citizen is highly critical of NAFTA, claiming the agreement has fallen well short of the promises made by its advocates. Far from creating the 200,000 new American jobs its supporters had promised, Public Citizen counts double that number of job *losses*, and contends that many workers who lost their jobs to NAFTA remain unemployed or were forced to take jobs that paid less. Rather than raise wages for Mexican workers, critics claim both Mexican wages and the Mexican standard of living have fallen since the implementation of free trade, undermining the bargaining power of employed workers in the United States, who have to compete against Mexicans who work for less.[*]

NAFTA supporters, like the United States-Mexico Chamber of Commerce, paint an entirely different picture. They attribute very few of the 18 million jobs created in the United States during the first five years of NAFTA to the effects of the free trade agreement, but they make the same case for the roughly 7 million American jobs lost during that period. Specifically, they estimate that 350,000 jobs were created in the United States as a direct result of increased exports to Mexico, and a somewhat smaller number of jobs were lost, making the trade agreement essentially a wash when it comes to employment.[†] This may not be the 200,000 new jobs NAFTA proponents promised, but supporters argue it isn't the net negative claimed by opponents.

[*]See the Public Citizen website at http://www.citizen.org/trade/nafta/jobs/.

[†]See the United States-Mexico Chamber of Commerce website at http://www.usmcoc.org/n6.html.

---

multinational corporations defy those boundaries; a Toyota automobile that appears to be an import could easily have been manufactured in Kentucky by American workers using Japanese parts. Arrangements like these have promoted free trade policies aimed at reducing barriers between nations.

The vehicle for negotiating trade agreements is an international body called the **World Trade Organization (WTO),** which establishes the rules for trade among nations, hosts trade negotiations, and settles trade disputes. The WTO was created in 1995 as part of a major overhaul of the **General Agreement on Tariffs and Trade (GATT),** an international treaty that had been in effect since 1948. Between 1948 and 1995, GATT was the source of rules about world trade, implemented on a provisional basis by an international organization also called GATT. Over the years, several rounds of negotiations updated GATT, primarily by reducing tariffs. Then, between 1986 and 1994, the Uruguay Round of negotiations—quite possibly the largest trade negotiation ever—culminated in almost all of the 125 participants agreeing to reduce trade barriers and apply free trade principles to services and intellectual property in addition to goods.[14]

GATT requires all trading partners to be treated equally, so, for instance, if a country wants to do another country a favor and lower the customs duty assessed against one of its products, it would have to extend that treatment to every other WTO nation.[15] One exception to this rule is the case of regional trade zones, like North America, where nations can agree to separate free trade agreements applying only to nations in the region.

A highly controversial effort to create a regional free trade zone in North America, called the **North American Free Trade Agreement (NAFTA),** was negotiated with Canada and Mexico by President Bush (senior) and, following an intense lobbying effort by the Clinton administration (see Box 16-5), was approved by Congress in 1993. NAFTA phased out tariffs on most items traded among the three countries; opened previously protected agricultural, automobile, and textile products to free trade; and provided for free trade in finance and telecommunications services.

World Trade Organization (WTO) The international organization responsible for promoting free trade among nations and settling trade disputes.

General Agreement on Tariffs and Trade (GATT) The 1948 treaty establishing the rules for free trade, which has been revised and dramatically expanded, most recently during the Uruguay round of trade negotiations (1986–1994). GATT was also the name of the international organization that oversaw the treaty; the World Trade Organization (WTO) replaced it in 1995.

North American Free Trade Agreement (NAFTA) A landmark free trade agreement setting up a regional free trade zone in North America.

16-3b The Trade Deficit

The debate over free trade takes place against the backdrop of a stark imbalance between the value of the goods and services the United States imports and the value of the goods

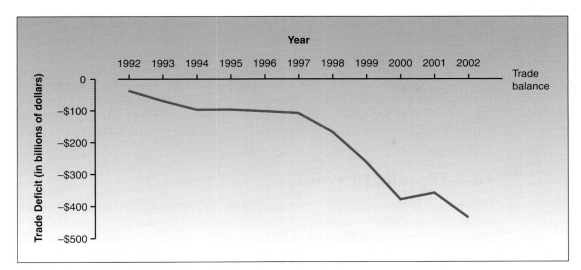

Figure 16-1
The Growing American Trade Deficit, 1992–2002
Source: Data from U.S. Census Bureau.

and services it exports. Since the early 1980s, the United States has run an annual **trade deficit,** meaning that American consumers and businesses have purchased more goods and services from foreign nations than foreign nations have purchased from the United States. This makes the United States a debtor nation because it owes more than it brings in, and contrasts with the situation in place prior to 1980, in which there was a **balance of trade** or a rough equivalence between the value of American exports and the value of imports. The trade deficit began to snowball dramatically in the late 1990s, increasing from $29.5 billion in 1991 to $436 billion in 2002 (see Figure 16-1). In absolute dollar terms and as a percentage of gross domestic product, this is the largest trade deficit in American history.[16]

Whether or not the trade deficit is a huge problem depends a lot on your outlook. Some see the trade deficit as a sign of American prosperity, an indication that low interest rates and low inflation have made the United States an appealing destination for foreign investment. At the same time, American trading partners are relatively weak, explaining why exports are increasing at a much lower rate than imports. Others see in the trade imbalance the deleterious effects of global trade posing a long-term threat to America's standard of living. They blame the trade deficit on unequal rules that give countries like China and Japan access to American markets while maintaining barriers to U.S. imports, multinational corporations moving manufacturing plants to other countries where labor is cheaper, and unfair competition from developing nations that maintain low prices for goods by exploiting workers and disregarding costly environmental standards.[17]

Of course, different perspectives on the meaning of the trade deficit lead to different conclusions about what, if anything, American policy makers should do about it. Conservatives who see the trade imbalance as a sign of American global economic strength do not believe that it will produce long-term, adverse consequences. They do not believe that corrective measures are necessary. Rather, they credit the current trade situation with contributing to economic growth, job creation, low inflation, and high levels of productivity built on foreign investments. Some liberals who regard the trade deficit as problematic advocate policies to regain balance in order to reverse what they see as the detrimental effects of the trade deficit, including rising income inequality, the loss of manufacturing jobs, and declining U.S. competitiveness in world markets because of America's position as the world's largest debtor nation.[18]

▶**trade deficit** A negative balance between the value of goods and services purchased from foreign nations and the value of goods and services sold to foreign nations.

▶**balance of trade** Equilibrium between the value of imports and exports.

16-3c Foreign Aid

Apart from trade policy, money figures into foreign relations in the form of aid to other nations. Foreign aid tends to be one of the least appreciated components of foreign policy.

You're not alone if you don't know a lot about foreign aid. Most Americans believe we give far more than we do in foreign aid, and when asked their opinion on what the proper level of aid should be, often demand cuts in spending—to amounts far *greater* than what we really give. Foreign aid works against an isolationist streak in American public opinion—a streak that advocates that other nations solve their own problems—which is why it can be controversial for representatives to propose increases in aid to other nations. Private contributions from U.S. corporations and foundations are more palatable to some. The argument in favor of foreign aid is that it is a relatively inexpensive way to maintain international stability and advance national interests, particularly by addressing poverty in developing nations, promoting international economic growth, and advancing the cause of human rights abroad.[19]

16-4 Diplomatic Policies

Diplomatic relations are managed through an extensive network of ambassadors to other nations and representatives to organizations like the United Nations, NATO, and the WTO. Although you may (correctly) think of diplomacy as being the first line of defense in a crisis, with former secretary of state Colin Powell, say, jetting to India and Pakistan to quiet a nuclear-charged conflict between those nations over the disputed Kashmir province, the primary purpose of diplomacy is proactive. Effective diplomacy promotes stability in parts of the world where the United States maintains vital security interests, in conjunction with allied nations who have common concerns. In this regard, diplomacy is an ongoing endeavor whose success is often measured by what does *not* happen, as when regional tensions are prevented from bubbling into regional conflict and war.

Promoting stability also involves using diplomatic means to combat global challenges that pose a threat to American interests. Diplomacy is an integral part of the war on terror, as well as the war on drugs. American diplomats work to prevent the development and transport of nuclear, biological, and chemical weapons. When humanitarian concerns are an administration priority, diplomats carry them out, and in recent years, diplomats have worked to battle the African AIDS epidemic and fight international trafficking in women and girls.[20] Diplomats, along with foreign service workers (see Box 16-6), labor to assure the safety of Americans traveling abroad.

Diplomatic activities are also a means for carrying out economic policies. Trade agreements like NAFTA, GATT, and over 250 others finalized in the past two decades were negotiated through diplomatic means, as a way of implementing the policy of expanding free trade. The 1994 Summit of the Americas was a diplomatic function engaging Western Hemisphere nations in negotiations for hemispheric free trade. The Asia-Pacific Economic Cooperation partnership is a long-term diplomatic effort to open trade among Pacific Rim nations.[21]

16-5 Military Policies

As we said in Chapter 15, national defense is one of the most important functions the government performs. We acknowledge this claim by devoting one-sixth of the federal budget to military spending. The manner in which we spend it determines what our military capabilities will be, which in turn is the result of a debate about the type of challenges our military is likely to be asked to confront.

During the cold war, there was consensus over what those challenges were. The United States pursued a policy of containment toward the Soviet Union designed to check the spread of communism around the globe. This required a large, conventional military equipped to fight regional conflicts on behalf of countries like South Vietnam and South Korea as they opposed Soviet-backed communist regimes in North Vietnam and North Korea. It also required a large nuclear force to check the large Soviet nuclear force, following an approach called Mutual Assured Destruction (MAD)—the theory being that the best way to avoid nuclear war between rival superpowers with large nuclear arsenals was to assure that a first strike by either side would be met with a fatal response by the other.[22]

During the forty-five years of the cold war, the United States spent heavily on national defense to secure these goals. In fact, during the Kennedy administration, defense spending accounted for half the federal budget.[23] The end of the cold war brought about widespread discussion of a "peace dividend" in the form of lower defense spending, and in fact,

> ## Box 16-6 Foreign Service Work
>
> Foreign service workers are civilians stationed at American embassies and consulates overseas to assist American citizens who are traveling or living abroad. This may involve anything from arranging emergency funds for U.S. citizens to providing aid to American travelers who become ill while in another country to assisting Americans during an overseas crisis. Foreign service work can be highly rewarding and highly demanding. Workers have to be ready to serve for unspecified periods of time in any country where the United States has diplomatic relations and may have to be prepared to endure hardships.

> ## Websites *You Can Use*
>
> If working abroad for the government sounds interesting to you and you'd like to get more information, contact the State Department online at http://www.state.gov/employment.

the percentage of federal money spent on defense declined slightly during the 1990s, as policy makers tried to determine what our defense needs would be in a world where we were the only remaining superpower.

However, the notion of a "peace dividend" was controversial. As an ideological matter, some conservative members of Congress argued that even without the Soviet threat, the United States risked being unprepared for unforeseen acts of aggression if it permitted the military to atrophy. Liberals, eager to redirect funds to domestic priorities, took the opposite position, arguing that defense budgets had become bloated during the cold war and that national security could be maintained for less money. At the same time, practical considerations cut across ideological lines. Defense contractors are powerful interest groups with an investment in maintaining lucrative government business, and they don't have to remind members of Congress that military equipment is built in congressional districts across the country, providing jobs for constituents. Liberals and conservatives alike recognize the value of keeping these jobs secure.[24]

The September 11 terror attacks brought clarity to national defense policy and provided the basis for a steady increase in defense spending. The fiscal year 2003 military budget of $355 billion represented an increase of 10.6 percent from the previous year. What kinds of things did it provide for? Highlights include:

Intelligence and Surveillance
- The largest one-year increase in spending for the National Foreign Intelligence Program in two decades

Ballistic Missile Defense
- Patriot missile defense system
- Airborne laser development
- Total funding: $7.4 billion

Strategic Mobility
- Fifteen C-17 transport aircraft, totaling $3.3 billion

Personnel
- $93.6 billion to support 1.4 million active duty and 865,000 guard and reservists

Operation and Maintenance
- $114.8 billion for training, spare parts, real property, and maintenance

Major Acquisitions
- Aircraft, including nineteen Blackhawk helicopters, forty-six F/A-18 fighters, and twenty-three F-22 fighters
- Munitions, including Tomahawk cruise missiles and JDAM precision-guided bombs
- Ships, including two AEGIS destroyers and one attack submarine[25]

By any measure, this is an extensive menu of items. Whether it is enough is, of course, a matter of debate. Take a few minutes to see what people on both sides of that debate have to say. You'll find a discussion of increased defense spending in Issue Box 16-1 on pages 494–495.

16-6 Strategic Policies

As we said in the previous section, policy makers try to design the military budget to meet what they consider to be the most likely threats to our security. Doing so requires long-term strategic planning, which by necessity is a matter of making assumptions about the challenges that are likely to come along. If we believe the United States will be called upon to fight two regional wars simultaneously, we need to have the capacity to do so, and therefore would adjust our military planning for that eventuality. If we believe that intelligence information will provide security against terrorist groups, then we need to make the appropriate investments. If we believe that strong alliances—like NATO during the cold war—advance our national security, then we will target the necessary money and diplomatic effort to keep those alliances strong.

16-6a Strategies and Resources

Military and intelligence capabilities and international alliances are among the tools of strategy, some of the things that policy makers can employ in order to chart a course for advancing national interests. Our foreign policy objectives have to be built on a realistic assessment of the resources we have to work with, and, in turn, we make judgments about the size, scope, and allocation of resources with our foreign policy objectives in mind.

When strategic objectives can only be met with resources we don't have, policy debate will center on questions of resource acquisition. President Reagan wanted to counter the Soviet nuclear arsenal with an antiballistic missile capability that would seek and destroy inbound nuclear warheads before they could reach their target. However, the capability to implement this strategy did not exist. Thus began a protracted debate about the strategic desirability and technical feasibility of what became popularly known as "Star Wars" technology. The debate over whether to embark on an expensive research and development campaign to create a missile shield centered on both the rightness of President Reagan's strategy (would it make the United States safer or destabilize the existing nuclear balance of power?) and resource issues (did the huge price tag and uncertain outcome of a missile defense program make "Star Wars" a bad investment?).

Similarly, for several years after the 2001 attack on the World Trade Center and Pentagon, policy makers wrestled with how best to organize American intelligence capabilities to maximize effectiveness against an elusive terror threat. In 2004, an independent commission looking into the September 11 attack suggested restructuring the intelligence community around a new director of national intelligence, setting off a heated political battle with the Pentagon and CIA over their place in the new intelligence bureaucracy. Ultimately, political pressures to address the nation's most pressing foreign policy problem were enough to overcome bureaucratic resistance to change, and Congress approved the restructuring plan in late 2004.[26]

In contrast, when strategic objectives can be met with existing resources, debate will center exclusively on questions of strategy. During the buildup to the Iraq War, questions about resource availability were not at issue. America's military capability was clear. Policy planners in the Bush administration knew they had the personnel and hardware necessary to give the United States an overwhelming advantage in any conflict with Saddam Hussein. As a consequence, the debate within the administration and in the press centered on whether it was strategically advisable for the United States to use its military power against Iraq.

16-6b Strategies and Assumptions

The debate over Iraq was passionately engaged, as advocates of two different approaches faced off against each other in the administration, in homes across America, in the United Nations, and around the world (see Box 16-7). At home, the dividing line was whether a

Box 16-7 Dueling Strategies

As a military matter, timing was everything to the Iraqi campaign. Eager to avoid fighting a war in the scorching desert summer, the Bush administration calibrated the military buildup in the Persian Gulf to coincide with Iraq's cooler winter months, with the aim of having a fighting force in place by February 2003. In order to meet this strategic aim, the administration needed to move an invasion force to the region while it was engaged in diplomatic efforts to resolve matters peacefully, creating a sense among nations opposed to war, like France and Germany, that American military strategy was at odds with American diplomatic efforts.

It was an open secret in Washington and at the United Nations that the American military was following a timetable, even though the Bush administration publicly denied it. Diplomats understood America's strategic military needs, but the sense that American military strategy was driving American diplomatic efforts fueled resistance by nations reluctant to support a war, who felt the United States was not taking their interests seriously. France, Germany, and Russia led the charge for giving UN weapons inspectors—who had returned to Iraq months before under the terms of Security Council Resolution 1441—more time to do their work, claiming that they were slowly but effectively disarming Iraq. The United States brushed this off, aware that negotiating more time for weapons inspections would upend its military strategy.

As a diplomatic matter, the model for building a multinational coalition was the 1991 Persian Gulf War. Following Iraq's march into Kuwait, President Bush senior took time to build a global coalition against Saddam Hussein, using diplomacy backed by the threat of force to pressure Iraq to relinquish Kuwait. The buildup of troops, called "Operation Desert Shield," was designed to put pressure on Iraq, create global legitimacy for military action, and share the manpower and monetary costs of a possible war.

On the surface, the second Bush administration appeared to be doing the same thing, but the circumstances were quite different. Because there had not been a hostile action by Iraq to precipitate war in 2003 as there had been in 1991, President Bush had a far more difficult time selling allied nations on the idea of an invasion than did his father. This would be a preemptive action, designed to forestall what American officials said was an ongoing Iraqi program to develop weapons of mass destruction. With some nations questioning the moral authority of carrying out an attack under these circumstances, advocates of continued weapons inspections found a receptive audience.

Internal administration divisions about the desirability of diplomacy further complicated matters. Secretary of State Colin Powell, as the head of the department responsible for American diplomacy, was an early advocate of building a coalition. Secretary of Defense Donald Rumsfeld, as the head of the department responsible for orchestrating the military campaign, advocated action on a schedule that favored American troops.

Underlying these different departmental perspectives was something deeper: fundamental differences in the strategic *desirability* of building a coalition or going it alone. This is where the assumptions that strategists made about the world most influenced their strategic choices.

Advocates of alliances emphasized the importance of *legitimacy* in international affairs. They believed that a broad group of like-minded nations acting in concert diminished political resistance from opponents and mitigated the unintended consequences of military action. In the case of Iraq, they believed that a worldwide invasion force would look less to the Islamic world like an imperialist action by the United States and would be less likely to stir anti-American anger that could lead to a new wave of terrorism against American interests. For this reason, they believed that American security was advanced by multilateral diplomatic efforts rather than through a unilateral show of strength.

Advocates of unilateral military action emphasized the importance of *strength* in international affairs. They believed that actions determine how nations respond, and that it is more important to be feared than liked. In the case of Iraq, they believed that foes and wayward allies would appreciate a crushing display of American power. The Islamic world might not like the presence of American troops on Iraqi soil but they would respect the results. Nations opposed to American military action before the war would have no choice but to grudgingly accept the results of the invasion, which would leave the United States in a strong position to dictate the terms of Iraqi reconstruction. For this reason, they believed that American security was advanced by a unilateral show of strength rather than through multilateral diplomatic efforts.

As America's traditional allies began to perceive that unilateralists were in charge of American policy, they came to regard the press for war as more than a matter of military strategy, and they dug in their heels. In the end, advocates of strength carried the day. The effectiveness of their strategy depended, like any strategy, on how clearly and accurately their underlying assumptions captured global dynamics. As America faced mounting casualties in Iraq and international resistance to postwar aid, administration proponents of a policy based on strength came under fire from advocates of coalition-building, who argued that American power had not been sufficient to shape conditions in postwar Iraq.

military or a diplomatic strategy would best advance American interests in the Middle East. The military strategy called for quick use of American forces in Iraq, which for logistical reasons would have to occur before international support could be won. The diplomatic strategy called for avoiding rifts in time-tested alliances by not going to war without international support. It was not a simple choice. As is typical of strategic decisions, assumptions by domestic policy makers about how best to advance national interests shaped the debate and its outcome.

Issue Box 16-1 *Increased Defense Spending*

History and Background

At what level have we committed sufficient resources to ensure our national security? When have we spent too much? Are we willing to trade off spending on domestic programs so that we can spend on national defense? Is defense money best spent on the military or on global aid projects?

Questions like these arise every year as Congress and the president negotiate the federal budget, and in an age when homeland security is a top priority, they take on an urgency not seen since the cold war.

Regardless of whether the American military budget is increased or held steady, the United States far outspends everyone else in the world. The military budget for fiscal year 2004 of $399 billion was more than six times as large as Russia's military budget, and Russia ranks number two in the world. China spends $47 billion; Japan, $43 billion; Great Britain, $38 billion. You could add up the twenty nations on the list beneath the United States and their combined military expenditures would not equal ours. The three nations that President Bush identified as forming an "axis of evil"—Iran, Iraq, and North Korea—spend a combined $6.9 billion. There is no question that as a matter of dollars, the United States is in a league by itself.*

Furthermore, global military spending is declining. In 1985, global military expenditures totaled $1.3 trillion. By 2000, that figure had dropped to $812 billion. As a consequence, America's share of global military spending has grown to the point where in fiscal year 2000, 36 percent of the world's military expenses came from Washington.†

Still, many people feel we do not spend enough on national defense. They contend that national security is our number one priority, for which we should spare no expense to protect ourselves. They point out that we live in a complex age when our military has to be prepared for a wide range of demands, including instability in Iraq, military threats in the Middle East and North Korea, peacekeeping missions in the Balkans and Afghanistan, and disrupting terrorist activities around the world. In this global environment, they say, we need to be prepared for the possibility that we will have to fight and win two major regional wars simultaneously.‡

Advocates of increased military spending also raise questions about the condition of our military. They point to the relatively low pay available to military personnel, saying pay and benefit levels make it difficult to attract new recruits to our all-volunteer armed forces. As a candidate for president in 2000, George W. Bush charged that the military had been allowed to decline since the end of the cold war and promised more spending to improve it.

Opponents of increased military spending fall into two groups: those who think a larger military budget is unnecessary and those who think it is misguided. Those in the first

Source: Department of Defense.

group take issue with President Bush's claim that we have experienced a decline in our military preparedness. They point to the fact that defense spending still averages 95 percent of what it did during the cold war§ and contend that it's ridiculous to expect to have to fight two large regional wars at once without allied help.** They do grant the point that personnel should be paid fair wages, but argue that the military could easily redirect some money from procuring weapons systems to make that happen. Doing so would also invite inspection of waste and fraud, conditions that critics claim are inevitable in a budget this large.

Those who believe increased military spending is misguided generally take one of two positions. Some look at the unconventional nature of the terrorist problem and advocate a smaller, flexible, and well-trained military tailored to meet targeted threats. They say massive force is a relic of the cold war and does not make us safer today. They would supplement downsized forces with better intelligence capabilities and diplomacy, none of which requires the kind of spending we devote to maintaining our armed forces.††

Others take the position that a military as large as ours is a threat to world peace. They invite Americans to try to imagine how provocative our military position looks to the rest of the world, and contend that it will only aggravate global tension. Instead of increasing the military budget, they urge consideration of less expensive policies aimed at dealing with global inequity and injustice, which some see as the root of international conflict. They point to the relatively small amount of money the United States devotes to foreign aid and argue that if we spent even a fraction of what we devote to the military toward humanitarian assistance to combat disease, illiteracy, poverty, and hunger, we would reap the benefits of a safer world.‡‡

16-6c Strategies and Crisis Response

Some strategies are long-term and enduring, like the cold war strategy of containment. Others are developed in response to a crisis. During the cold war, the United States faced periodic international crises and had to fashion its response with long-term strategic inter-

No matter which way you come down, you should see military spending as a choice we make as a nation. Whether or not you support an increase in defense spending, remember that every dollar spent on defense is a dollar that is not spent on something else, a dollar that contributes to budget deficits, or a dollar that is not returned to us in tax relief. Because of the stakes involved in protecting national security and the size of the defense budget, military spending is one of the most important collective choices we make.

Arguments in Support

Some people want to increase the defense budget. They claim:

- Nothing is more important. Without the strongest possible defense, our way of life and everything we value is at risk. Given the present global climate, how can we not spend more on our military?
- We have to be prepared. The military already answers the call around the globe, and in an uncertain world it should be ready if need be to fight two major global wars simultaneously.
- We need better pay for military personnel. The only way to guarantee a strong military is to provide the pay and benefits that will attract and hold good people.
- Large forces make us safer. When potential enemies see our size and strength, they are more likely not to confront us.
- We need to be prepared to use massive force. As we saw in the invasion of Afghanistan, strength is necessary if we're going to carry out our strategic goals and protect our interests.
- Peace comes through strength. All the humanitarian aid in the world could not have prevented the September 11 terror attack, and we will weaken ourselves if we divert money from the military to foreign aid.

Arguments Against

Some people do not want to spend more on national defense. They contend:

- We're already well protected. Defense spending didn't decline much after the cold war, and our military expenditures already far exceed every other nation on earth.
- We're prepared. American troops were outnumbered during the first Persian Gulf War and routed Iraq without suffering many casualties. The idea that America may have to fight two major wars simultaneously without allied support is unrealistic.
- We need better pay for military personnel. However, the way to provide it is by cutting waste in the military budget and redirecting some money designated for weapons procurement.

- Large forces put us at risk. We appear threatening to the rest of the world, and that aggravates global tensions.
- We need to be flexible. Today's security risks call for a smaller, more flexible, and less expensive military that can supplement improved intelligence and diplomatic operations.
- Peace comes through understanding. Even a small diversion of funds from the military to humanitarian aid will begin to address the inequities that are the root causes of international conflict and war.

My Opinion

When registering your opinion on defense spending, it's not necessary to agree with all the arguments made by one side or the other. In fact, people on the same side of this issue may differ with each other about the underlying reasons for their beliefs. So, as you evaluate the positions people take, consider the range of arguments for and against increased defense spending. Ask yourself which of them ring true. Do you believe:

- We have to be more prepared, or we're already well prepared?
- We need more money for military personnel, or we can find it in the existing budget?
- A large force makes us safer or puts us at risk?
- We need to rely on massive force or a smaller, flexible response?
- Peace comes through strength or understanding?

The most accurate description of my attitude toward *increased* defense spending is:

1—I strongly oppose it. It's a bad idea.
2—I oppose it, but with some reservations.
3—I support it, but with some reservations.
4—I strongly support it. It's a good idea.
5—I haven't thought enough about it to have an opinion.
6—I don't care about it enough to bother.

*Center for Defense Information, "World Military Expenditures," at http://www.cdi.org/issues/wme/spendersfy04.html. Figures are from 2002.

†Ibid.

‡See Network Justice Watch at http://www.thirdworldtraveler.com/Pentagon_military/Increase_MilitarySpend.html.

§Council for a Livable World, "Making Sense of Defense," at http://www.clw.org/milspend/sophistries.html.

**Network Justice Watch.

††Council for a Livable World, "Why the Military Budget Should Be Cut," at http://www.clw.org/milspend/whycut.html.

‡‡Friends Committee on National Legislation, "A Wasteful, Bloated Military Budget: No Way to Advance Peace or Human Security," March 2002. Article available at http://www.thirdworldtraveler.com/Military_Budget/Wasteful_Military_Bud_2003.html.

ests in mind—foremost among them containing Soviet expansion without triggering nuclear war. For this reason, whenever hostility broke out in a region of the world involving client states of the two superpowers, the United States was constrained in its actions.

For instance, Israel and neighboring Arab countries fought four wars during the cold war era, in which the Soviet Union supported the Arab combatants and the United States supported Israel (in cold war language, Israel was always described as the only democracy in the Middle East). The United States was able to offer Israel economic support and weaponry, but had to temper its involvement to avoid creating a direct conflict with the Soviet Union. Likewise, the "hot" wars America fought in Korea and Vietnam did not threaten to undermine broader national interests as long as they remained surrogate conflicts for the American struggle with the USSR.

Not surprisingly, the most frightening crises of the cold war period came when American and Soviet interests directly clashed. Try to imagine what things felt like in October 1962 when President Kennedy announced to the American public that the Soviet Union was in the process of placing nuclear weapons in Cuba, and that the American response would be a naval quarantine of the island to prevent Soviet ships from reaching Cuban ports. An American invasion of Cuba was threatened if the Soviets disobeyed the quarantine, an act certain to start World War III. Pressure to invade was immense; the chairman of the Joint Chiefs of Staff argued that it was America's only option. Secretary of Defense Robert McNamara reportedly looked closely at the sun shining in the White House Rose Garden, believing he would never see it again.[27]

Never before had the world been as close to nuclear war as during the Cuban missile crisis. What most of Kennedy's advisors didn't know, however, was that the president was engaged in back-channel communications with Soviet Premier Nikita Khrushchev, and was ready to remove antiquated American missiles in Turkey as a fallback compromise had the Soviets rejected outright American demands that they remove their missiles from Cuba. It was an action that would have cost Kennedy prestige and left him vulnerable to political attack from hardliners, but the president saw the need to keep his options open and not embark on an irreversible course to global destruction.

The crisis ended peacefully and victoriously for the United States when the Soviets abandoned their position in Cuba. There was a lot of self-congratulating among the president's advisors, who believed their hard line was the reason why "the other fellow blinked," in Secretary of State Dean Rusk's phrase, or gave in first. In fact, it was strength coupled with flexibility and the willingness to avoid going to the brink of nuclear war that enabled Kennedy to escape the cold war's most dangerous moment.[28]

The American reaction to the September 11 terror attacks constituted a different type of crisis response. When the reality of what had happened settled in, many Americans instinctively agreed with President Bush that we were suddenly at war with a previously unknown adversary. When we learned that the adversary was named al-Qaeda and that they were granted safe haven by a radical Islamic regime in Afghanistan, there was little debate about the Bush administration's decision to invade Afghanistan with the objective of removing the Taliban government and dismantling the terrorists' leadership structure.

However, this crisis reaction created new policy questions for the United States, requiring new strategies to meet the circumstances of living in a world that seemed to have changed in one day. This is not unusual in crisis situations, as every action creates fallout—both intended and unexpected. One of the key questions raised by the American invasion of Afghanistan was what to do once the crisis response had been carried out. Indications were that the United States would have to find a way to put the political structures of Afghanistan back together again, but Americans who objected to maintaining a long-term presence in other nations recoiled at this possibility.

Take a minute and explore the options for American policy in the wake of our response to the September 11 attacks. The situation in Afghanistan is complex and does not lend itself to an easy strategic solution. Read Issue Box 16-2 on pages 498–499 for a discussion of the choices involved.

16-7 Foreign Policy and Domestic Politics

Because every major foreign policy decision has political ramifications, it shouldn't be surprising that politically sensitive administrations pay careful attention to the domestic fallout of the actions they take. Public response to foreign policy choices can cut many ways. As we saw in Section 10-3c, "Malleable Public Opinion," the public regularly rallies behind

Box 16-8   The Information War in the Persian Gulf

During the 1991 Persian Gulf War, the military exercised tight control over battlefield information, leaving reporters to cover—and frame—the war primarily through official briefings and sanctioned images of bombing campaigns. To be sure, one reason for regulating battlefield information is to protect troops in battle. At the same time, however, the Pentagon and the White House are fully aware that contemporary warfare plays out on television and that pictures have the capacity to establish how people will experience the fighting, with the potential to build or undermine public support. For this reason, it is in their interest to present a sanitized version of events devoid of graphic accounts of suffering and death. Critics contend that coverage of the first Persian Gulf War in the American media made it appear to be an easy-to-cheer action movie or video game that existed in surreal contrast to the brutality experienced by combatants and civilians.*

Given the effectiveness of the information campaign during the 1991 conflict, the Pentagon decision to modify it in 2003 and permit reporters to travel with the American invasion force in Iraq is at face value surprising. Select reporters, including television reporters with camera equipment, were "embedded"—to use the official term—with American forces and allowed to beam pictures back to the domestic audience. Of course, anything appearing on CNN in the United States also appeared on CNN in Iraq, which partially explains the shift in strategy. Having planned an initial assault designed to convince Iraqi troops of their inevitable defeat so they would lay down their arms, the Pentagon understood that it could amplify the power of the attack with around-the-clock images of American might. Simultaneously, anticipating the sort of action-adventure coverage that was the hallmark of the 1991 war, the military also assumed that the initial bombing campaign would play well with domestic public opinion. In effect, reporters traveling with American troops served a dual military and domestic public relations purpose.†

Initial events appeared to validate this strategy, as the early bombardment of Iraq was covered as spectacular, overpowering, and remarkable. Coverage of the war's opening days was laced with upbeat images of troops rushing into battle, and of smiling Iraqis greeting Americans as liberators. It was imagery the Pentagon wanted Iraq to see—imagery it was certain would not be featured in Arab-language media—and it framed the battle the way the White House wanted to portray events to nations that had opposed the war and to the domestic audience.

The strategy carried some risk for the Pentagon, though, because permitting journalists into battle meant they would be there if things went wrong for the United States. Military planners assumed that reporters would bond and identify with American troops, leading to a kind of self-censorship that would serve the information management interests of the Pentagon and the White House. There is certainly evidence of this phenomenon. However, just as television reporters could not resist pictures of the aerial bombardment of Baghdad, neither could they resist images of American casualties. Furthermore, because television amplifies experiences while concentrating on only one thing at a time, news of battlefield difficulties for the United States drowned out images of American military superiority as soon as it became clear that there would be Iraqi resistance.

Albeit briefly, on television and in print the storyline shifted overnight from success to setbacks.‡ President Bush tried to get ahead of these changing events by urging Americans to prepare for a longer war with more casualties than might have been anticipated from the opening hours of the conflict. Having cameras in battle, though, made possible the personalization of the war in a manner that was largely absent from the coverage in 1991, and assured that news reporting would be more like a roller coaster of changing events than the steady stream of distantly reported information that characterized the first Persian Gulf conflict.

*See, for instance, Calvin Exoo, *The Politics of the Mass Media* (St. Paul, MN: West Publishing Company, 1994).

†For a discussion of this strategy, see Lucian K. Truscott, "Using the News as a Weapon," *New York Times,* March 25, 2003.

‡See David Carr, "Reporting Reflects Anxiety," *New York Times,* March 25, 2003, at http://www.nytimes.com/2003/03/25/international/worldspecial/25MEDI.html?pagewanted=1&th.

the president immediately following a national crisis or when the president first commits troops to military action. We also saw, however, that rally events are typically short-lived.

Where a president's popularity lands depends on how the public experiences the effectiveness of the administration's response.

Foreign policy decisions are unpredictable because they are only as good as the assumptions behind them and because their outcomes depend on the actions of leaders of other nations. So, presidents will do their best to spin events to their liking. Nowhere is the urge to manage the media message more evident than in wartime, when events are at their most unpredictable and the stakes are at their highest (see Box 16-8). The more an administration is able to exercise control over war coverage, the more likely it is to convince the public to experience conflict on its terms. Working in its favor is the tendency for domestic reporters to identify with the American cause when troops are in battle, but should

Issue Box 16-2   *Maintaining a Presence in Afghanistan*

History and Background

The eyes of the world were trained on Afghanistan in the weeks following the September 11 attacks. In short order, American forces and internal Afghani factions toppled the Taliban government that had provided safe haven to al-Qaeda terrorist leaders. Those not captured or killed were forced to disburse into remote mountain areas. President Bush declared victory for American forces. CNN and other media picked up their cameras and went home.

Then the real trouble began.

Largely out of view, Americans remained in Afghanistan for the process of stabilizing a nation left torn apart by despotic leaders and war. They're still there. Afghanistan has a long history of factional rivalry, making a stable government difficult—some say impossible—to establish. Without political and economic stability, however, the potential is great that a new regime supportive of al-Qaeda will emerge. What should the United States do? Stay and try to rebuild Afghanistan's infrastructure? Attempt to install a democratic government? Offer humanitarian assistance? Return home?

These are among the possibilities facing American policy makers, and it presents a thankless choice. Setting aside for a minute the difficult issue of what the United States should try to achieve in Afghanistan, the simple fact that Americans remain in another country may be viewed in contrasting ways by American policy makers, mission participants, and the world.

One perspective on what the United States is doing is called "nation building." It entails helping devastated countries rebuild their political institutions in a manner that meets the interest of the nation helping them to do so. It's related to "peacekeeping," where the rebuilding efforts focus on humanitarian missions and developing a reliable national defense structure so the country can eventually police itself, but the terms carry entirely different emotional content. "Peacekeeping" can call to mind the image of a good neighbor, while "nation building" may evoke imperialism, where an outside force attempts to mold another country in its image. To some people, nation building and peacekeeping both smack of unwise foreign entanglements, which, once engaged, are difficult to end.

President Bush warned against precisely these entanglements when he was a presidential candidate, but in the wake of September 11, he and others in his administration decided that some sort of American presence in postwar Afghanistan was unavoidable. The result is what many have called "nation building lite," a limited effort to establish legitimate political and economic institutions in Afghanistan.*

Source: AP/Wide World Photos.

The policy faces long odds. It's up against two decades of famine and political strife that have left Afghanistan a humanitarian and political disaster area. When the bombs stopped falling, Americans found themselves in a place where warlords ruled small bits of territory, fighting among themselves for control. Central authority was shaky and did not extend to the entire country. The infrastructure, including hospitals, schools, power plants, and sewer systems, was in ruins. Malnutrition was widespread. There were millions of refugees.[†] The question America faced was: What, if anything, should the United States do in a situation like this?

Some opponents of American involvement contend that we should do nothing. They say that despite our national interest in creating a stable, functioning Afghanistan, the situation is hopeless. They see Afghanistan as three rival ethnic camps—Pashtuns in the south, Uzbeks and Tajiks in the north—who can't stand each other and cannot be expected to work together to rebuild the country. Their answer is to get out of Afghanistan's internal affairs with the warning to whatever government comes to power that if they harbor terrorists, the United States will return with military force.[‡]

Others argue against an American presence in Afghanistan because they do not see a compelling national interest in being there. During congressional debate on America's role in Afghanistan in May 2002, Representative Ron Paul of Texas argued against sending taxpayer money to a country that, in his words, "harbors some of our most virulent enemies."[§] Equating nation building with both colonialism and a form of social engineering that he feels will not work, Representative Paul argued that the best use of our resources would be to keep them at home.

---

things go sour for the United States, as they did in Vietnam, pictures of dead and injured American soldiers can have a negative impact on domestic public opinion.

Presidents can also try to use the political circumstances created by international events to advance their domestic agenda. In the run-up to war with Iraq, President Bush saw his job approval ratings sag under the weight of the uncertainty many Americans felt about the impending conflict, but his political advisors correctly anticipated that he would get a short-term boost in popularity once the war started. Mindful of the overwhelming

The open-ended nature of the Afghanistan mission worries some detractors. They express concern over "mission creep"—that the United States will gradually be drawn into a situation from which there is no clear exit strategy, producing what will become an unending commitment. Because it's impossible to predict how such a mission will play out, this is a real risk. On the other hand, reacting to fears that the mission in postwar Afghanistan will become open-ended by pulling out before establishing stability could plunge the country back into civil strife, once again permitting al-Qaeda to operate freely.**

Some who see Americans as peacekeepers argue that we have a moral imperative to remain in Afghanistan after the war to make sure the nation can rebuild. Doing otherwise would show the world that we're a self-interested bully, quick to start a war but uninterested in putting the pieces back together afterwards. Some who reject the moral argument nonetheless see the propaganda value of keeping the peace and helping Afghanistan to rebuild.†† Even this cuts two ways, though. Those who see Americans as nation builders draw the exact opposite conclusion, worrying that the American presence in Afghanistan looks imperialistic and will inflame the very anger that others fear we would spark by not helping to rebuild.

Arguments in Support

Should we maintain an American presence in Afghanistan? Proponents might say:

- We have no choice. We may have won the war but we'll certainly lose the peace if chaos reigns and al-Qaeda returns to Afghanistan.
- It's in our national interest. A destabilized Afghanistan will become a haven for our worst enemies.
- We have a clear objective. We don't need to build democratic institutions in Afghanistan, but we need to be sure that some type of regular government is functioning reliably before we can leave.
- It's morally right. After waging war, we have an obligation to be peacekeepers in Afghanistan.
- It has propaganda value. We'll look like bullies if we invade Afghanistan and do not attempt to help rebuild.

Arguments Against

Opponents of an American presence in Afghanistan argue:

- It's hopeless. We're facing an impossible situation if we expect to rebuild a country torn by factional strife. The best way to avoid certain catastrophe is to stay out.
- It's not in our national interest. Afghanistan has harbored our worst enemies and so does not deserve American aid.

- "Mission creep" is a real danger. Without realistic or carefully articulated goals, we could end up being unable to extract ourselves from Afghanistan.
- It's morally wrong. We have no business acting like a colonial power by trying to rebuild Afghanistan in our image.
- It has propaganda value. It's wise to resist the urge to appear imperialistic by meddling in Afghanistan's internal affairs.

My Opinion

When deciding whether the United States should continue its postwar presence in Afghanistan, consider the history of the issue and the arguments supporting and opposing it. In particular, ask yourself if rebuilding Afghanistan:

- Is something we have to do or if it's a hopeless mission
- Is or is not in our national interest
- Presents a clear objective or poses the risk of an endless commitment
- Is morally right or morally wrong
- Has more propaganda value than not rebuilding Afghanistan

The most accurate description of my attitude toward maintaining an American presence in postwar Afghanistan is:

1—I strongly support it. It's a good idea.
2—I support it, but with some reservations.
3—I oppose it, but with some reservations.
4—I strongly oppose it. It's a bad idea.
5—I haven't thought enough about it to have an opinion.
6—I don't care about it enough to bother.

---

*See "Nation Building Lite in Afghanistan: A Conversation with Michael Ignatieff," at http://www.fpa.org/topics_info2414/topics_info_show.htm?doc_id=126829.

†"A Natural Fear Increased with Tales: America's Aversion to Nation Building and Peacekeeping," Center for Defense Information, March 8, 2002, at http://www.cdi.org/terrorism/nation-building-pr.cfm.

‡Ted Galen Carpenter, "Flirting with Nation-Building in Afghanistan," The Cato Institute, November 2, 2001, at http://www.cato.org/current/terrorism/pubs/carpenter-011102.html.

§See http://www.house.gov/paul/tst/tst2002/tst052702.htm.

***"A Natural Fear Increased with Tales."

††Ibid.

---

job approval Bush's father received following the first Persian Gulf War, White House strategists anticipated that a successful conclusion to the impending conflict would enhance the president's long-term approval, and that he could use his refreshed public standing to enhance his clout with Congress on domestic matters.[29]

In fact, President Bush didn't wait until the end of the war to advance an important component of his domestic agenda. During the first few days of fighting, while national attention was focused overseas and public debate on domestic matters appeared unseemly,

Issue Box 16-3   *Domestic Surveillance*

History and Background

It's not easy to conduct a widespread domestic search for potential terrorists while maintaining the freedoms and rights we're entitled to under the Constitution. One controversial proposal for domestic surveillance was floated by the Bush administration following the September 11 terrorist attacks. It entailed establishing a network of domestic informants to root out terrorists at home. The Bush Justice Department lobbied hard for it, but had to scale back plans in the face of criticism from civil liberties groups. Ultimately, the administration failed to get its program included in the 2002 Homeland Security Act, which established the new cabinet-level Department of Homeland Security. In fact, language in the Act expressly prohibits the Justice Department from initiating the program.* Nonetheless, President Bush advocated a commitment to expanding domestic surveillance, and it's not at all unthinkable that the administration will revisit the issue in the future.

The domestic surveillance program dubbed "Operation TIPS" (for Terrorism Information and Prevention System) was first introduced by the Justice Department in January 2002. The objective was to recruit and deputize up to one million Americans to gather information for the government, reporting suspect actions of their neighbors and coworkers. The plan would have recruited postal workers, utility workers, cable installers, transit workers, shippers, and truckers to report "suspicious" activity. Under protest, the government dropped the provision to actively recruit postal and utility workers, while still permitting them to volunteer for the program.

Attorney General John Ashcroft offered repeated assurances that the program would not infringe on personal liberty and that it was a necessary step to secure the security of Americans against small terrorist cells that could be operating within our borders. He said law-abiding Americans would not be targeted and that the program would only be a way of alerting the government to suspicious activities. He contended that terrorist cells can be very small—sometimes no more than a few people—but they are capable of doing great damage if they're not stopped. One of the most effective ways to stop them is to bring surveillance to the grassroots level in the form of investigators who would blend in with a neighborhood and get to know residents well. At the same time, the

attorney general vigorously objected to characterizing the program as "spying."†

The prospect of the cable guy being a government snitch didn't sit well with some in Congress. Opponents say Operation TIPS is unnecessary because people can already report suspicious activity on their own. They fear the additional cover of being in a federal program would give untrained ordinary citizens the sense that they can do police work, but inadequate preparation would result in a mountain of blind leads and false charges that would require valuable resources to sort out. They argue that racial profiling would be inevitable, with false accusations creating huge problems for people who would then have to clear their names in an environment where many of us are inclined to assume guilt rather than innocence.‡

If that happened, opponents say, the liberty of people falsely accused of being terrorists would be severely threatened, the accused would face possible incarceration and

Republican congressional leaders worked with the White House to slowly advance the president's proposed $726 billion tax cut through a sharply divided legislature. In peacetime, this would have been a big story, and opponents of the controversial tax cut would have felt emboldened to speak out against it. Instead, the president was able to find cover for his tax plan while the media agenda was saturated with war issues. Subsequently, the president was able to win support for a smaller version of his tax package while his postwar job approval ratings were still high.

Foreign policy decisions can also have ramifications for domestic policy rather than politics. In the period following the attack on the World Trade Center and the Pentagon, the administration wrestled with how to identify suspected terrorists operating in the deportation, and it would all be done, in the words of the executive director of the National Coalition Against Censorship, with "no limits, no controls, no guidelines, no rules, no nothing."§

Does a program like Operation TIPS flirt too closely with creating a police state in a free society as civil libertarians argue? Or is it a reasonable program designed to offer a greater degree of security in an uncertain time, as Attorney General Ashcroft claimed?

Arguments in Support

The Bush Justice Department defended the domestic surveillance proposal known as Operation TIPS by saying:

- It's critical. Without good grassroots surveillance, it may be impossible to root out small terrorist cells operating in American neighborhoods.
- It's not spying. The program would simply alert law enforcement officers to individuals who draw attention to themselves by their actions. If further surveillance turned up nothing, the government would take no action and no harm would have been done.
- It's constitutional. There would not be forced or unwelcome entry to people's homes, and individual rights would not be violated.
- Honest citizens would not be targeted. Americans who mean and do no harm would not be affected.
- Civil rights remain in force. Someone targeted for surveillance would still be innocent until proven otherwise.

Arguments Against

Opponents of domestic surveillance have the following to say about Operation TIPS:

- It's creepy. Do you really want your letter carrier or bus driver working secretly for the government?
- It's spying. What else do you call it when people are reporting information about their neighbors behind their backs?
- It's unethical. Although it may be constitutional, Operation TIPS threatens to undermine personal freedom.
- It would result in racial profiling. Human nature suggests people would be naturally suspicious of those who fit

Middle Eastern profiles, even those who are honest citizens who mean and do no harm.
- Civil rights are at risk. In a climate of fear, those targeted for surveillance will be regarded as terrorists until they can clear their name, and may face incarceration or deportation.

My Opinion

It's difficult to maintain security in an open society. Americans want to feel safe and protect hallmark liberties, but efforts to provide security can quickly bump up against personal rights protections. You should consider whether Operation TIPS crosses the line between liberty and security. When registering your opinion on domestic surveillance, consider the history of the issue and the arguments supporting and opposing it. In particular, ask yourself if Operation TIPS:

- Is critical or creepy
- Is or is not spying
- Is constitutional or unethical
- Would protect honest citizens or result in racial profiling
- Would protect or undermine civil rights

The most accurate description of my attitude toward domestic surveillance of the sort proposed by Operation TIPS is:

1—I strongly oppose it. It's a bad idea.
2—I oppose it, but with some reservations.
3—I support it, but with some reservations.
4—I strongly support it. It's a good idea.
5—I haven't thought enough about it to have an opinion.
6—I don't care about it enough to bother.

*Julia Scheeres, "Fed's Spying Plan Fades to Black." *Wired,* December 4, 2002, at http://www.wired.com/news/politics/0,1283,56701,00.html.

†George Sanchez, "The Furor over TIPS," MotherJones.com, July 17, 2002, at http://www.motherjones.com/web_exclusives/features/news/tips.html.

‡"Stop the Government from Turning Neighbor against Neighbor," American Civil Liberties Union, October 7, 2002, at http://www.aclu.org/SafeandFree/SafeandFree.cfm?ID=10783&c=206.

§Sanchez, "The Furor over TIPS."

United States and what to do once suspects had been detained. Both issues pit safety imperatives against civil rights concerns. The more leeway law enforcement officials are given to spy on and imprison suspects, the more efficiently they can do their jobs. However, we have seen how efficiency can be the enemy of liberty, and in this case, the liberty of potentially innocent suspects was in the crosshairs. How far should we go to protect their liberty when we believe terrorists are plotting to strike again in the United States?

Take a few minutes to read Issue Box 16-3 about domestic surveillance and Issue Box 16-4 about detaining suspected terrorists. What's your opinion on what the government should do in each case to balance the rights of the individual against the needs of the community?

Issue Box 16-4　*Detaining Terror Suspects*

History and Background

When the president swears an oath to uphold the Constitution, he pledges to defend the rights that document entitles us to. He also promises to "faithfully execute his office," which includes doing his best to keep us safe. You could make the case that there are no two greater responsibilities for a president—which makes it all the more complicated when the two conflict.

It was inevitable following September 11 that there would be a dragnet for individuals who were suspected of having knowledge of or involvement with known terror organizations. It was equally inevitable that many of these individuals would be innocent of the charges made against them. In order to defend the country, it would be necessary to detain them until officials could sort through the evidence against them and determine if they were security risks. This is a laborious and time-consuming job, though, and detainees have a right to a speedy trial or to be released pending trial if the government cannot give the courts a compelling reason to hold them in custody. This poses a serious dilemma in which the rights of the accused are in direct conflict with national security interests.

Initially, the Justice Department asked Congress for unilateral powers to indefinitely detain illegal aliens it believed were involved in terrorist activity. Congress refused. The attorney general would have to demonstrate that there were "reasonable grounds" to believe that a suspect was involved in terrorism, unless he could present the court with evidence of the suspect's involvement in a crime. Otherwise, the suspect could only be legally detained for a few days.

This proved complicated. If the Justice Department had evidence against a suspect that came from secret intelligence sources, it would be unable to present it in court without compromising the source. The same problem would arise from evidence that the Justice Department wanted to keep secret so as not to compromise the search for other suspects.*

In the confusion of the ensuing weeks, it was hard to keep track of the more than 1,000 people who were detained by the United States. Many, it turned out, had no terrorist connections, but some were disappearing from public view, and suspicion grew among civil rights groups that suspects were being held against their legal rights. In December 2001, nineteen civil rights groups filed suit against Attorney General Ashcroft under the Freedom of Information Act, asking for immediate release of the records of everyone detained in connection with the September 11 attacks. A lawyer for the American Civil Liberties Union (ACLU) said, "It is absolutely critical that the American public has the information it needs to

Source: AFP/Getty Images.

decide whether the Justice Department's actions are consistent with the freedoms we are now fighting to defend."†

Months passed, but the tension between protecting America and protecting suspects' rights did not dissipate. Hundreds of suspects were detained indefinitely at the U.S. military base at Guantanamo Bay, Cuba, under a controversial policy in which the Justice Department labeled them "unlawful combatants," denying them the rights of prisoners of war. However, the United States was having difficulty putting together a legal case against many of them. The dilemma posed by these detainees, said the State Department ambassador-at-large for war crimes, was that "as long as they live and breathe, they are devoted to killing Americans, yet there is insufficient information to prosecute some of them. We would hate to . . . release such a person, and he's out there on the next plane heading into another tower in the United States."‡

In 2004, the issue went before the Supreme Court in the twin cases of *Rasul v. Bush* and *al Odah v. U.S.* In these cases, relatives of Kuwaiti, British, and Australian prisoners being held at Guantanamo Bay argued that their family members were innocent victims being held indefinitely for no reason. The Court agreed, holding that the detainees had a right to challenge the legality of their detention at Guantanamo Bay and that federal courts have jurisdiction to hear their complaints even though they were being held at a facility outside the United States.§

The detainment policy was not the only controversial effort of its kind by the Bush administration. Later in 2002, the Immigration and Naturalization Service (INS) issued its own contentious policy, requiring all male visitors over the age of sixteen from Iran, Iraq, Libya, Sudan, Syria, and thirteen other countries to report to the INS to be fingerprinted, photographed, and answer questions under oath. The ACLU called it a pretext for the roundup and illegal detention of men of Middle Eastern and Muslim origin, and in early 2003, joined religious and immigrants' rights groups in petitioning Congress to stop it. They claimed that any information the government would need from them would have already been reported on their application for a green card and that the exercise represented "an extended vacation from common sense." Said an ACLU spokesperson: "Not only does it undercut core American conceptions of law and basic decency—it reduces security by alienating the very communities whose cooperation is essential in the fight against terrorism."**

Is the government right in taking aggressive and possibly illegal actions in detaining and corralling terror suspects? Are personal rights universal, and do they apply in all circumstances as prescribed in the Constitution? How should the Justice Department account for the rights of individuals who are believed to be dangerous terrorists? What about the rights of individuals in cases where the Justice Department is not so sure?

Arguments in Support

Those who support any and all means to detain terror suspects are willing to trade off individual rights for collective safety. They argue:

- Openness makes us vulnerable. In a war, certain rights become a luxury. If some people's civil liberties are violated in an effort to keep everyone else safe, that's the price we pay for security.
- The ends justify the means. In a war, sometimes you have to do things that are distasteful in order to win.
- The rights of the many are more important than the rights of the few. Our most important objective is to protect ourselves against future attacks. Doing so is going to create innocent victims, just like there were innocent victims on September 11.

Arguments Against

Those who advocate being circumspect in the treatment of terror suspects are concerned about national security, but tend to view security in terms of human rights protection rather than exclusively in terms of stopping those who would attack us. They say:

- Openness makes us strong. President Bush said terrorists hate us because of what we represent. If we undercut the rights we're trying to protect in our fight to protect them, we weaken society and the terrorists win.

- Means matter. The way a society acts when it is under stress is the greatest measure of its character. If we want to claim to live by a high standard we need to uphold that standard even when it's distasteful or difficult to do so.
- The rights of the many are the sum total of the rights of the few. Each illegal detention diminishes us all. Once we make exceptions to this, we put everyone at risk. One day you could be the one the government is trying to detain.

My Opinion

How to handle terror suspects is an emotionally charged issue. When registering your opinion on how far the government should go in detaining individuals suspected in terrorist activities, try to consider the emotional and rational dimensions of the matter as you explore the arguments supporting and opposing it. In particular, ask yourself if:

- Openness makes us vulnerable or openness makes us strong
- The ends justify the means or means matter
- The rights of the many are more important than—or the sum total of—the rights of the few

The government has gone to great lengths to detain terror suspects. Some contend it has done so at the expense of the civil rights of the accused. The most accurate description of my attitude toward the way the government has acted is:

1—I strongly oppose it. It's a bad idea.
2—I oppose it, but with some reservations.
3—I support it, but with some reservations.
4—I strongly support it. It's a good idea.
5—I haven't thought enough about it to have an opinion
6—I don't care about it enough to bother.

---

*Joseph A. D'Agostino, "Detaining Foreign Terror Suspects Difficult," *WorldNetDaily,* October 15, 2001, at http://www.worldnetdaily.com/news/printer-friendly.asp?ARTICLE_ID=24906.

†"U.S. Government Sued for Detaining Hundreds of Terror Suspects," *Agence France-Presse,* December 6, 2001.

‡Frank Davies, "Detaining Suspects Brings Many Legal Questions," *Miami Herald,* May 9, 2002.

§*Shafiq Rasul, et al., Petitioners v. George W. Bush, President of the United States, et al.* 542 U.S. 334 (2004); and *Fawzi Khalid Abdullah Fahad al Odah, et al., Petitioners v. United States et al.* 542 U.S. 343 (2004).

**"ACLU Urges Congress to Fully Investigate Ill-Conceived Immigration Registration and Detention Program," January 10, 2003, at http://www.aclu.org/SafeandFree/SafeandFree.cfm?ID=11554&c=206.

16-8 Completing the Circle

The first question we raised in this book was, "Should we care about politics?" It was raised with the promise that it would not be answered for you, that you would in the end decide for yourself whether any form of political involvement—the big and small ways available for you to interact with democracy—is a valuable use of your time.

We've now reached the end of the discussion. The past three chapters have concluded with a chance for you to look at a summary of your responses to difficult policy choices about civil rights, civil liberties, and domestic affairs. Shortly, you will have an opportunity to assess your choices about foreign policy.

As you consider the meaning of your opinions, think back over the range of attitudes you expressed in this part of the book, and consider how closely your view of America aligns with the reality of what our policy makers do. If there are places where the United States is moving in a direction you don't like, ask yourself if you feel that any action on your part might make a difference. If you're largely content with the direction of the country, remember that political situations are fluid, and ask yourself if you feel that any political activity would be warranted to counter those who seek to change course.

Even if you don't believe you're in a position to make a difference, think about whether you believe any action on your part would be meaningful. When you do, remember that not all participation is noisy, and not all participation is all-encompassing. True, tens of thousands of Americans took to the streets in vocal demonstrations against the Iraq War or in support of American forces. This may be the most visible form of participation, but it is far from the most common. Sending an email to a senator, voting, and even advocating political action to a friend are all ways to advance your views and make your mark. There are many ways for your voice to be heard.

Remember also that not acting is a choice, for there will always be others ready to take the space that you could fill, others who may differ with your objectives and desires. You've got to decide how much that matters. Some of us hold beliefs about what America should look like, but we don't hold to them very strongly. Some of us care deeply about one or two things. Some are motivated to speak out in moments of crisis. Some are universally committed and actively involved.

And some of us are turned off when we don't get what we want, when the rewards of participation are not forthcoming. This can be discouraging, as we know from considering the plight of individuals without many resources who do not feel the efficacy necessary for participation. Is political participation worth it anyway, even when we lose—even when we fail to achieve our objectives? Is there value in the process, or satisfaction in knowing that our voice was expressed, even if it was not ultimately heard?

The answers to these questions are personal. Ultimately, they shape the choices we make about how or whether to voice our views, the sum total of which determine the kind of future we will have.

The Way You Want America to Be

Foreign Policy

Take a look back at the way you answered the polls in the "Your Opinion" sections of the Issue Boxes. Which answers did you give most often? Read on to see where you stand.

If your primary answer was 1...

... your foreign policy views place you squarely with those who have reservations about military and political might in foreign affairs. Perhaps it's skepticism about turning neighbors into informants, or putting additional resources into military solutions to foreign problems. In either event, you're at home with those who are circumspect about big government power in security and international matters. Should your feelings spur you to political action, you might find yourself in a protest against American military or antiterror policies. In a more conventional setting, you would probably find a home for some of your views among those who take a left-of-center position in the Democratic Party.

If your primary answer was 2...

... your foreign policy views place you generally in line with those who have doubts about military and political might in foreign affairs. Perhaps you have problems with turning neighbors into informants or putting too much money into military solutions to foreign problems. Whatever your specific concerns, your attitudes align you at least in part with those who are circumspect about big government power in security and international matters. Maybe your feelings aren't strong enough to spur you to protest against American military or antiterror policies, but your view of what you would like American foreign policy to look like overlaps with the views of those who would, as well as with some who take left-of-center positions in the Democratic Party.

If your primary answer was 3...

... your foreign policy views place you generally in line with those who support military action and government authority to advance foreign policy objectives. Perhaps you're sympathetic to spending more money on the military, or you're comforted by government efforts to proactively secure our borders from terrorists. In either event, your opinions generally place you with those who believe the way to find security is through strength. Maybe your feelings aren't strong enough to spur you to political action, but your view of what you'd like American foreign policy to look like overlaps with the views of those who take a right-of-center position in the Republican Party.

If your primary answer was 4...

... your foreign policy views place you firmly in line with those who support military action and government author-

ity to advance foreign policy objectives. Perhaps it's your desire to see more resources spent on the military or your wish to see government use the powers available to it in order to secure our borders from terrorists. In either event, you're at home with those that believe the way to find security is through strength. Should your feelings spur you to political action, you would probably find a home for some of your views among those who take a right-of-center position in the Republican Party.

If your primary answer was 5 or 6...

... you're not particularly interested in America's role in the world or you haven't figured out what you think it should be. That's not at all unusual: Many people turn away from foreign affairs, and there's a long history in this country of being more interested in matters that occur close to home. Foreign policy is typically at its most salient when we feel like whatever happens abroad will have a direct impact on us, a sentiment that was widely shared immediately following the September 11 terror attacks. Of course, while you're not thinking much about it or not certain what your positions are, foreign policy is being made by others. They will decide whether American troops should continue to be deployed abroad, how much of your money will be spent on the military, and how we're going to treat our own citizens and terrorist suspects.

If your responses were mixed...

... you didn't demonstrate clear support or opposition for military and government strength as a means to security. That's understandable. Someone could support increased military spending and not want to see the money go to an American presence in Afghanistan, while someone else might want to stay in Afghanistan with a smaller military budget. Likewise, you could see the issue of detaining terrorist suspects and engaging in domestic surveillance as either security or civil rights issues, and neither position would necessarily predict your feelings about military spending. This simply means that you have to pay extra attention if you want the full range of your foreign policy attitudes to be represented. If you feel strongly about any of the positions you took on these issues, watch the president and Congress closely, and feel free to write or send them email if they act against your view of what American foreign policy should be.

Chapter Review

American foreign and defense policy is influenced by domestic and global actors. The president is the leading domestic figure in developing and executing foreign policy, and the way he views the world will shape the policy choices he makes. The president is supported in his decisions by an extensive foreign policy establishment. He receives diplomatic support from the Department of State, military advice from the Department of Defense and the Joint Chiefs of Staff, and policy coordination from the National Security Council. Because of their different missions, perspectives, and ambitions, these actors do not always work together harmoniously.

Globally, American policy is influenced by international organizations. Foremost among these is the United Nations, a diplomatic union that provides a forum for discussing international disputes and engages in peacekeeping work, but which cannot back its decisions with the force of law. Regionally, NATO remains an important strategic organization even though it no longer serves its original cold war purpose as a security pact for Western Europe and North America. Additionally, nongovernmental organizations and multinational corporations function like interest groups on a global scale, operating cross-nationally to advance agendas that go beyond national borders.

Foreign policy encompasses a wide range of economic, diplomatic, and military concerns. Significant steps away from protectionism and toward free trade were made in the 1990s with the creation of the World Trade Organization and the negotiation of the North American Free Trade Agreement. Supporters claim free trade is good for economic growth while detractors assert that it causes corporations to move American jobs to countries where labor is cheap. The debate over free trade takes place against the backdrop of a sharply rising trade deficit, the result of American imports far outpacing exports. Foreign aid is also a controversial item, although as a percentage of gross domestic product, the United States gives less foreign aid than any of the world's wealthiest nations, and far less than most Americans believe.

Diplomatic relations are managed through an extensive network of ambassadors to other nations and representatives to international organizations. Effective diplomacy promotes stability in parts of the world where the United States maintains vital security interests. Military policy is supported by a large defense budget that is protected by advocates of a strong defense and by lawmakers responding to the lobbying efforts of defense contractors. The defense budget is also influenced by assumptions about the country's future strategic needs, just as strategic concerns shape the way the United States relates to other nations and responds to crises. Domestic political strategy may enter into foreign policy considerations, with presidents aware that their effectiveness in handling important international incidents may constrain or enhance the public support they need to advance their domestic agenda.

Key Terms

balance of trade (p. 489)
European Union (EU) (p. 486)
executive agreements (p. 482)
General Agreement on Tariffs and Trade (GATT) (p. 488)
Joint Chiefs of Staff (p. 484)
national security advisor (p. 484)

National Security Council (p. 484)
nongovernmental organizations (NGOs) (p. 487)
North American Free Trade Agreement (NAFTA) (p. 488)
North Atlantic Treaty Organization (NATO) (p. 485)

protectionism (p. 487)
secretary of state (p. 484)
tariff (p. 487)
trade deficit (p. 489)
War Powers Act of 1973 (p. 483)
World Trade Organization (WTO) (p. 488)

Review Questions

Note: You can find the correct answers to these questions by taking the quiz and then submitting your answers in the Online Edition. The program will automatically score your submission. If you miss a question, the program will provide the correct answer, a rationale for the answer, and the section number in the chapter where the topic is discussed.

1. Which of the following policies led critics to contend that it would result in a dangerously militarized world?
   a. President Kennedy's response to the Cuban Missile Crisis
   b. President Reagan's policy toward containment of the Soviet Union
   c. President Clinton's policy toward global markets
   d. President George W. Bush's policy toward Iraq

2. The lead diplomatic arm of the American foreign policy establishment is the
   a. Department of Defense.
   b. Joint Chiefs of Staff.
   c. Department of State.
   d. National Security Council.

3. The United Nations charter aims to achieve each of the following objectives *except*
   a. maintain global peace.
   b. promote international cooperation.
   c. implement Security Council resolutions that have the force of law.
   d. promote human rights.

4. The organization originally established as a defensive alliance for Western Europe is
   a. NATO.
   b. the European Union.
   c. the Warsaw Pact.
   d. the Security Council.

5. Multinational corporations and nongovernmental organizations both
   a. stage protests.
   b. play a leading role in resolving international humanitarian problems.
   c. are primarily concerned with economic interests.
   d. engage in international lobbying efforts.

6. Advocates of protectionism would be most likely to support
   a. NAFTA.
   b. tariffs.
   c. GATT.
   d. the World Trade Organization.
7. The U.S trade deficit
   a. is growing, which makes some conservatives worry about declining U.S. competitiveness in world markets.
   b. is shrinking, which makes some conservatives worry about rising income inequality.
   c. is growing, which makes some liberals worry about the loss of manufacturing jobs.
   d. is shrinking, which some liberals see as a sign of America's global economic strength.
8. The notion of a "peace dividend" was
   a. controversial for defense contractors.
   b. a direct objective of the "MAD" strategy.
   c. derided by liberals, who feared military funds would be used for domestic purposes.
   d. a way for the United States to prepare for unforeseen acts of aggression by spending less money on the military.

9. The relationship between strategies and resources in the conduct of foreign policy is
   a. strategic decisions are independent of resource acquisition decisions.
   b. strategic decisions always take into account resource availability.
   c. resource acquisition decisions always determine strategic decisions.
   d. resources are always available for strategic planners.
10. During the Cuban Missile Crisis, President Kennedy attempted to
   a. develop a crisis response that did not undermine the long-term strategy of containment.
   b. resolve the crisis by ignoring the constraints placed on him by the long-term strategy of containment.
   c. resolve the crisis by avoiding solutions that would undermine his domestic political credibility.
   d. dramatically redefine the strategy of mutually assured destruction.

In Their Own Words

You might be interested in examining some of what the following authors have said about the topics we've been discussing:

Frankel, Benjamin, ed. *The Cold War, 1945–1991.* Detroit: Gale Research, 1992. This multivolume reference profiles the major figures and events of the cold war era.

Halberstam, David. *The Best and the Brightest.* New York: Random House, 1972. The title is an ironic reference to the highly capable and experienced elite that led the United States into the Vietnam War. Halberstam's journalistic account provides insight into a time that continues to cast a shadow over American foreign policy.

Lindsay, James M. *Congress and the Politics of U.S. Foreign Policy.* Baltimore: Johns Hopkins University Press, 1994. Lindsay presents a comprehensive account of the secondary but important role Congress plays in the conduct of American foreign policy.

Nathan, James A. *Anatomy of the Cuban Missile Crisis.* Westport, CT: Greenwood Press, 2001. With the assistance of declassified information, Nathan provides context and meaning for one of history's most dangerous crises.

Nye, Joseph S., Jr., and Roger K. Smith. *After the Storm: Lessons from the Gulf War.* Lanham, MD: Madison Books, 1992. This collection of scholarly articles about the Gulf War draws interesting conclusions about strategy and diplomacy that can be read in the context of events surrounding the Iraq War, including why the first President Bush decided not to remove Saddam Hussein from power.

Wilson, George C. *This War Really Matters: Inside the Fight for Defense Dollars.* Washington, DC: CQ Press, 2000. An inside account of the political maneuvering that shapes the nation's defense budget.

Notes

1. See James M. Lindsay, *Congress and the Politics of U.S. Foreign Policy* (Baltimore: Johns Hopkins University Press, 1994). Lindsay contends that Congress plays the secondary but essential role of legitimizing and criticizing presidential policy decisions.
2. See the U.S. Department of State website at http://www.state.gov/r/pa/ei/rls/dos/4078.htm.
3. Active duty and civilian figures are from 2001; reserve figures are from 2000. See the publication "Department of Defense at a Glance," at http://www.defenselink.mil/pubs/almanac/.
4. For background on the National Security Council, see: http://www.whitehouse.gov/nsc/.
5. See the United Nations website at http://www.un.org/Overview/brief1.html.
6. See the United Nations website at http://www.un.org/Overview/brief2.html.
7. Ibid.
8. See the NATO website at http://www.nato.int.

9. The new additions are Cyprus, the Czech Republic, Estonia, Hungary, Latvia, Lithuania, Malta, Poland, the Slovak Republic, and Slovenia. These nations joined Austria, Belgium, Denmark, Finland, France, Germany, Greece, Ireland, Italy, Luxembourg, the Netherlands, Portugal, Spain, Sweden, and the United Kingdom.
10. See the European Union website at http://europa.eu.int/abc/index_en.htm. Click on "The EU at a Glance" in the upper left of your screen.
11. See information from the UN on NGOs at http://www.un.org/dpi/ngosection/brochure.htm.
12. James A. Paul, "NGOs and Global Policy-Making," *Global Policy Forum,* June 2000, at http://www.globalpolicy.org/ngos/analysis/anal00.htm.
13. See "The World Trade Organization," at http://www.wto.org/english/res_e/doload_e/inbr_e.pdf.
14. Ibid.
15. Ibid.

16. "The U.S. Trade Deficit: Causes, Consequences and Recommendations for Action," U.S. Trade Deficit Review Commission report, November 14, 2000, 1–3. See http://www.ustdrc.gov/reports/tdrc_toc.pdf.

17. Ibid., 17–18. See http://www.ustdrc.gov/reports/tdrc_ch2.pdf.

18. Ibid., 84–85. See http://www.ustdrc.gov/reports/tdrc_ch3.pdf.

19. "Foreign Aid in the National Interest," United States Agency for International Development, at http://www.usaid.gov/fani/.

20. U.S. Department of State website at http://www.state.gov/r/pa/ei/rls/dos/4078.htm.

21. Ibid.

22. For a complete account of the personalities and events that shaped the cold war, see Benjamin Frankel, ed., *The Cold War, 1945–1991* (Washington, DC: Gale Research, 1992).

23. Defense spending declined following the Vietnam War but remained high by present levels. With increases during the Reagan years, defense spending totaled slightly more than one-quarter of federal spending during the 1980s. See Office of Management and Budget, *Budget of the United States Government: Historical Tables,* Table 3-1, at http://w3.access.gpo.gov/usbudget/fy2001/pdf/hist.pdf.

24. See George C. Wilson, *This War Really Matters: Inside the Fight for Defense Dollars* (Washington, DC: CQ Press, 2000).

25. Almanac of Policy Issues: Defense Spending, at http://www.policyalmanac.org/world/defense_spending.shtml.

26. Philip Shenon, "New Phase Begins in Push to Reorganize Intelligence," *New York Times,* December 20, 2004.

27. James A. Nathan, *Anatomy of the Cuban Missile Crisis* (Westport, CT: Greenwood Press, 2001), 93–101.

28. Ibid.

29. In fact, the second Bush administration was looking over its shoulder at the first Bush administration to apply political and policy lessons learned during the first Persian Gulf War. For a look at some of the lessons learned by students of the conflict, see Joseph S. Nye, Jr. and Roger K. Smith, eds., *After the Storm: Lessons from the Gulf War* (Lanham, MD: Madison Books, 1992).

Declaration of Independence

In Congress, 4 July 1776

The Unanimous Declaration of the Thirteen United States of America

When, in the course of human events, it becomes necessary for one people to dissolve the political bands which have connected them with another, and to assume, among the powers of the earth, the separate and equal station to which the laws of nature and of nature's God entitle them, a decent respect to the opinions of mankind requires that they should declare the causes which impel them to the separation.

We hold these truths to be self-evident: That all men are created equal; that they are endowed by their Creator with certain unalienable rights; that among these are life, liberty, and the pursuit of happiness; that, to secure these rights, governments are instituted among men, deriving their just powers from the consent of the governed; that whenever any form of government becomes destructive of these ends, it is the right of the people to alter or to abolish it, and to institute new government, laying its foundation on such principles, and organizing its powers in such form, as to them shall seem most likely to effect their safety and happiness. Prudence, indeed, will dictate that governments long established should not be changed for light and transient causes; and accordingly all experience hath shown that mankind are more disposed to suffer, while evils are sufferable, than to right themselves by abolishing the forms to which they are accustomed. But when a long train of abuses and usurpations, pursuing invariably the same object, evinces a design to reduce them under absolute despotism, it is their right, it is their duty, to throw off such government, and to provide new guards for their future security. Such has been the patient sufferance of these colonies; and such is now the necessity which constrains them to alter their former systems of government. The history of the present King of Great Britain is a history of repeated injuries and usurpations, all having in direct object the establishment of an absolute tyranny over these states. To prove this, let facts be submitted to a candid world.

He has refused to assent to laws, the most wholesome and necessary for the public good.

He has forbidden his governors to pass laws of immediate and pressing importance, unless suspended in their operation till his assent should be obtained; and, when so suspended, he has utterly neglected to attend to them.

He has refused to pass other laws for the accommodation of large districts of people, unless those people would relinquish the right of representation in the legislature, a right inestimable to them, and formidable to tyrants only.

He has called together legislative bodies at places unusual, uncomfortable, and distant from the depository of their public records, for the sole purpose of fatiguing them into compliance with his measures.

He has dissolved representative houses repeatedly, for opposing, with manly firmness, his invasions on the rights of the people.

He has refused for a long time, after such dissolutions, to cause others to be elected; whereby the legislative powers, incapable of annihilation, have returned to the people at large for their exercise; the state remaining, in the mean time, exposed to all dangers of invasions from without and convulsions within.

He has endeavored to prevent the population of these states; for that purpose obstructing the laws for naturalization of foreigners; refusing to pass others to encourage their migration hither, and raising the conditions of new appropriations of lands.

He has obstructed the administration of justice, by refusing his assent to laws for establishing judiciary powers.

He has made judges dependent on his will alone, for the tenure of their offices, and the amount and payment of their salaries.

He has erected a multitude of new offices, and sent hither swarms of officers to harass our people and eat out their substance.

He has kept among us, in times of peace, standing armies, without the consent of our legislatures.

He has affected to render the military independent of, and superior to, the civil power.

He has combined with others to subject us to a jurisdiction foreign to our constitution, and unacknowledged by our laws, giving his assent to their acts of pretended legislation:

For quartering large bodies of armed troops among us;

For protecting them, by a mock trial, from punishment for any murders which they should commit on the inhabitants of these states;

For cutting off our trade with all parts of the world;

For imposing taxes on us without our consent;

For depriving us, in many cases, of the benefits of trial by jury;

For transporting us beyond seas, to be tried for pretended offenses;

For abolishing the free system of English laws in a neighboring province, establishing therein an arbitrary government, and enlarging its boundaries, so as to render it at once an example and fit instrument for introducing the same absolute rule into these colonies;

For taking away our charters, abolishing our most valuable laws, and altering fundamentally the forms of our governments;

For suspending our own legislatures, and declaring themselves invested with power to legislate for us in all cases whatsoever.

He has abdicated government here, by declaring us out of his protection and waging war against us.

He has plundered our seas, ravaged our coasts, burned our towns, and destroyed the lives of our people.

He is at this time transporting large armies of foreign mercenaries to complete the works of death, desolation, and tyranny already begun with circumstances of cruelty and perfidy scarcely paralleled in the most barbarous ages, and totally unworthy the head of a civilized nation.

He has constrained our fellow-citizens, taken captive on the high seas, to bear arms against their country, to become the executioners of their friends and brethren, or to fall themselves by their hands.

He has excited domestic insurrections among us, and has endeavored to bring on the inhabitants of our frontiers the merciless Indian savages, whose known rule of warfare is an undistinguished destruction of all ages, sexes, and conditions.

In every stage of these oppressions we have petitioned for redress in the most humble terms; our repeated petitions have been answered only by repeated injury. A prince, whose character is thus marked by every act which may define a tyrant, is unfit to be the ruler of a free people.

Nor have we been wanting in our attentions to our British brethren. We have warned them, from time to time, of attempts by their legislature to extend an unwarrantable jurisdiction over us. We have reminded them of the circumstances of our emigration and settlement here. We have appealed to their native justice and magnanimity; and we have conjured them, by the ties of our common kindred, to disavow these usurpations, which would inevitably interrupt our connections and correspondence. They, too, have been deaf to the voice of justice and of consanguinity. We must, therefore, acquiesce in the necessity which denounces our separation, and hold them, as we hold the rest of mankind, enemies in war, in peace friends.

We, therefore, the representatives of the United States of America, in General Congress assembled, appealing to the Supreme Judge of the world for the rectitude of our intentions, do, in the name and by the authority of the good people of these colonies, solemnly publish and declare, that these United Colonies are, and of right ought to be, FREE AND INDEPENDENT STATES, that they are absolved from all allegiance to the British crown, and that all political connection between them, and the state of Great Britain is, and ought to be, totally dissolved; and that, as free and independent states, they have full power to levy war, conclude peace, contract alliances, establish commerce, and do all other acts and things which independent states may of right do. And for the support of this declaration, with a firm reliance on the protection of Divine Providence, we mutually pledge to each other our lives, our fortunes, and our sacred honor.

John Hancock *[President]*

New Hampshire
Josiah Bartlett
William Whipple
Matthew Thornton

Massachusetts Bay
Samuel Adams
John Adams
Robert Treat Paine
Elbridge Gerry

Rhode Island
Stephen Hopkins
William Ellery

Connecticut
Roger Sherman
Samuel Huntington
William Williams
Oliver Wolcott

New York
William Floyd
Philip Livingston
Francis Lewis
Lewis Morris

New Jersey
Richard Stockton
John Witherspoon
Francis Hopkinson
John Hart
Abraham Clark

Pennsylvania
Robert Morris
Benjamin Rush
Benjamin Franklin
John Morton
George Clymer

James Smith
George Taylor
James Wilson
George Ross

Delaware
Caesar Rodney
George Read
Thomas M'Kean

Maryland
Samuel Chase
William Paca
Thomas Stone
Charles Carroll, of Carrollton

Virginia
George Wythe
Richard Henry Lee
Thomas Jefferson

Benjamin Harrison
Thomas Nelson, Jr.
Francis Lightfoot Lee
Carter Braxton

North Carolina
William Hooper
Joseph Hewes
John Penn

South Carolina
Edward Rutledge
Thomas Heyward, Jr.
Thomas Lynch, Jr.
Arthur Middleton

Georgia
Button Gwinnett
Lyman Hall
George Walton

Resolved. That copies of the Declaration be sent to the several assemblies, conventions, and committees, or councils of safety, and to the several commanding officers of the continental troops; that it be proclaimed in each of the United States, at the head of the army.

Constitution of
the United States

We the People of the United States, in Order to form a more perfect Union, establish Justice, insure domestic Tranquility, provide for the common defense, promote the general Welfare, and secure the Blessings of Liberty to ourselves and our Posterity, do ordain and establish this Constitution for the United States of America.

Article I

Section 1

All legislative Powers herein granted shall be vested in a Congress of the United States, which shall consist of a Senate and House of Representatives.

Section 2

The House of Representatives shall be composed of Members chosen every second Year by the People of the several States, and the Electors in each State shall have the Qualifications requisite for Electors of the most numerous Branch of the State Legislature.

No Person shall be a Representative who shall not have attained to the age of twenty-five Years, and been seven Years a Citizen of the United States, and who shall not, when elected, be an Inhabitant of that State in which he shall be chosen.

Representatives and direct Taxes shall be apportioned among the several States which may be included within this Union, according to their respective Numbers, which shall be determined by adding to the whole Number of free Persons, including those bound to Service for a Term of Years, and excluding Indians not taxed, three fifths of all other Persons.[1] The actual Enumeration shall be made within three Years after the first Meeting of the Congress of the United States, and within every subsequent Term of ten Years, in such Manner as they shall by Law direct. The Number of Representatives shall not exceed one for every thirty Thousand, but each State shall have at Least one Representative; and until such enumeration shall be made, the State of New Hampshire shall be entitled to chose three, Massachusetts eight, Rhode-Island and Providence Plantations one, Connecticut five, New-York six, New Jersey four, Pennsylvania eight, Delaware one, Maryland six, Virginia ten, North Carolina five, South Carolina five, and Georgia three.

When vacancies happen in the Representation from any State, the Executive Authority thereof shall issue Writs of Election to fill such Vacancies.

The House of Representatives shall chose their Speaker and other Officers; and shall have the sole Power of Impeachment.

Section 3

The Senate of the United States shall be composed of two Senators from each State, *chosen by the Legislature thereof,*[2] for six Years; and each Senator shall have one Vote.

Immediately after they shall be assembled in Consequence of the first Election, they shall be divided as equally as may be into three Classes. The Seats of the Senators of the first class shall be vacated at the Expiration of the second Year, of the second Class at the Expiration of the fourth Year, and of the third Class at the Expiration of the sixth Year, so that one third may be chosen every second Year; *and if Vacancies happen by Resignation, or otherwise, during the Recess of the Legislature of any State, the Executive thereof may make temporary Appointments until the next Meeting of the Legislature, which shall then fill such Vacancies.*[3]

No Person shall be a Senator who shall not have attained to the Age of thirty Years, and been nine Years a Citizen of the United States, and who shall not, when elected, be an Inhabitant of that State for which he shall be chosen.

The Vice President of the United States shall be President of the Senate, but shall have no Vote, unless they be equally divided.

The Senate shall chuse their other Officers, and also a President pro tempore, in the Absence of the Vice President, or when he shall exercise the Office of President of the United States.

The Senate shall have the sole Power to try all Impeachments. When sitting for that Purpose, they shall be on Oath or Affirmation. When the President of the United States is tried the Chief Justice shall preside: and no Person shall be convicted without the Concurrence of two thirds of the Members present.

Judgment in Cases of Impeachment shall not extend further than to removal from Office, and disqualification to hold and enjoy any Office of honor, Trust or Profit under the United States: but the Party convicted shall nevertheless be liable and subject to Indictment, Trial, Judgment and Punishment, according to Law.

Section 4

The Times, Places and Manner of holding elections for Senators and Representatives, shall be prescribed in each State by the Legis-

Note: Those portions of the Constitution set in italic type have been superseded or changed by later amendements.

lature thereof; but the Congress may at any time by Law make or alter such Regulations, except as to the Places of choosing Senators.

The Congress shall assemble at least once in every Year, and such Meeting shall be on the *first Monday in December, unless they shall by Law appoint a different Day.*[4]

Section 5

Each House shall be the Judge of the Elections, Returns and Qualifications of its own Members, and a Majority of each shall constitute a Quorum to do Business; but a smaller Number may adjourn from day to day, and may be authorized to compel the Attendance of absent Members, in such Manner, and under such Penalties as each House may provide.

Each House may determine the Rules of its Proceedings, punish its Members for disorderly Behavior, and, with the Concurrence of two thirds, expel a Member.

Each House shall keep a Journal of its Proceedings, and from time to time publish the same, excepting such Parts as may in their Judgment require Secrecy; and the Yeas and Nays of the Members of either House on any question shall, at the Desire of one fifth of those Present, be entered on the Journal.

Neither House, during the Session of Congress, shall, without the Consent of the other, adjourn for more than three days, nor to any other Place than that in which the two Houses shall be sitting.

Section 6

The Senators and Representatives shall receive a Compensation for their Services, to be ascertained by Law, and paid out of the Treasury of the United States. They shall in all Cases, except Treason, Felony and Breach of the Peace, be privileged from Arrest during their Attendance at the Session of their respective Houses, and in going to and returning from the same; and for any Speech or Debate in either House, they shall not be questioned in any other Place.

No Senator or Representative shall, during the Time for which he was elected, be appointed to any civil Office under the Authority of the United States, which shall have been created, or the Emoluments whereof shall have been increased during such time; and no Person holding any Office under the United States, shall be a Member of either House during his Continuance in Office.

Section 7

All Bills for raising Revenue shall originate in the House of Representatives; but the Senate may propose or concur with Amendments as on other Bills.

Every Bill which shall have passed the House of Representatives and the Senate, shall, before it become a Law, be presented to the President of the United States; If he approve he shall sign it, but if not he shall return it, with his Objections to that House in which it shall have originated, who shall enter the Objections at large on their Journal, and proceed to reconsider it. If after such Reconsideration two thirds of that House shall agree to pass the Bill, it shall be sent, together with the Objections, to the other House, by which it shall likewise be reconsidered, and if approved by two thirds of that House, it shall become a Law. But in all such Cases the Votes of both Houses shall be determined by yeas and Nays, and the Names of the Persons voting for and against the Bill shall be entered on the Journal of each House respectively. If any Bill shall not be returned by the President within ten Days (Sundays excepted) after it shall have been presented to him, the Same shall be a Law, in like Manner as if he had signed it, unless the Congress by their Adjournment prevent its Return, in which Case it shall not be a Law.

Every Order, Resolution, or Vote to which the concurrence of the Senate and House of Representatives may be necessary (except on a question of Adjournment) shall be presented to the President of the United States; and before the Same shall take Effect, shall be approved by him, or being disapproved by him, shall be repassed by two thirds of the Senate and House of Representatives, according to the Rules and Limitations prescribed in the Case of a Bill.

Section 8

The Congress shall have Power To lay and collect Taxes, Duties, Imposts and Excises, to pay the Debts and provide for the common Defence and general Welfare of the United States; but all Duties, Imposts and Excises shall be uniform throughout the United States;

To borrow Money on the credit of the United States;

To regulate Commerce with foreign Nations, and among the several States, and with the Indian Tribes;

To establish an uniform Rule of Naturalization, and uniform Laws on the subject of Bankruptcies throughout the United States;

To coin Money, regulate the Value thereof, and of foreign Coin, and fix the Standard of Weights and Measures;

To provide for the Punishment of counterfeiting the Securities and current Coin of the United States;

To establish Post Offices and post Roads;

To promote the Progress of Science and useful Arts, by securing for limited Times to Authors and Inventors the exclusive Right to their respective Writings and Discoveries;

To constitute Tribunals inferior to the Supreme Court;

To define and punish Piracies and Felonies committed on the high Seas, and Offenses against the Law of Nations;

To declare War, grant Letters of Marque and Reprisal, and make Rules concerning Captures on Land and Water;

To raise and support Armies, but no Appropriation of Money to that Use shall be for a longer Term than two Years;

To provide and maintain a Navy;

To make Rules for the Government and Regulation of the land and naval Forces;

To provide for calling forth the Militia to execute the Laws of the Union, suppress Insurrections and repel Invasions;

To provide for organizing, arming, and disciplining, the Militia, and for governing such Part of them as may be employed in the Service of the United States, reserving to the States respectively, the Appointment of the Officers, and the Authority of training the Militia according to the discipline prescribed by Congress;

To exercise exclusive Legislation in all Cases whatsoever, over such District (not exceeding ten Miles square) as may, by Cession of particular States, and the Acceptance of Congress, become the Seat of the Government of the United States, and to exercise like Authority over all Places purchased by the Consent of the Legislature of the State in which the Same shall be, for the Erection of Forts, Magazines, Arsenals, dock-Yards and other needful Buildings;—And

To make all Laws which shall be necessary and proper for carrying into Execution the foregoing Powers, and all other Powers vested by this Constitution in the Government of the United States, or in any Department or Officer thereof.

Section 9

The Migration or Importation of such Persons as any of the States now existing shall think proper to admit, shall not be prohibited by the Congress prior to the Year one thousand eight hundred and eight, but a Tax or duty may be imposed on such Importation, not exceeding ten dollars for each Person.

The Privilege of the Writ of Habeas Corpus shall not be suspended, unless when in Cases of Rebellion or Invasion the public Safety may require it.

No bill of Attainder or ex post facto Law shall be passed.

No Capitation, or other direct, Tax shall be laid, *unless in Proportion to the Census or Enumeration herein before directed to be taken.*[5]

No Tax or Duty shall be laid on Articles exported from any State.

No Preference shall be given by any Regulation of Commerce or Revenue to the Ports of one State over those of another; nor shall Vessels bound to, or from, one State, be obliged to enter, clear or pay Duties in another.

No Money shall be drawn from the Treasury, but in Consequence of Appropriations made by Law; and a regular Statement and Account of the Receipts and Expenditures of all public Money shall be published from time to time.

No Title of Nobility shall be granted by the United States: And no person holding any Office of Profit or Trust under them, shall, without the Consent of the Congress, accept of any present, Emolument, Office, or Title, of any kind whatever, from any King, Prince, or foreign State.

Section 10

No State shall enter into any Treaty, Alliance, or Confederation; grant Letters of Marque and Reprisal; coin Money; emit Bills of Credit; make any Thing but gold and silver Coin a Tender in Payment of Debts; pass any Bill of Attainder, ex post facto Law, or Law impairing the Obligation of Contracts, or grant any Title of Nobility.

No State shall, without the Consent of the Congress, lay any Imposts or Duties on Imports or Exports, except what may be absolutely necessary for executing its inspection Laws: and the net Produce of all Duties and Imposts, laid by any State on Imports or Exports, shall be for the Use of the Treasury of the United States; and all such Laws shall be subject to the Revision and Controul of the Congress.

No State shall, without the Consent of Congress, lay any Duty of Tonnage, keep Troops, or Ships of War in time of Peace, enter into any Agreement or Compact with another State, or with a foreign Power, or engage in War, unless actually invaded, or in such imminent Danger as will not admit of delay.

Article II

Section 1

The executive Power shall be vested in a President of the United States of America. He shall hold his Office during the Term of four Years, and, together with the Vice President, chosen for the same Term, be elected, as follows

Each State shall appoint, in such Manner as the Legislature thereof may direct, a Number of Electors, equal to the whole Number of Senators and Representatives to which the State may be entitled in the Congress: but no Senator or Representative, or Person holding an Office of Trust or Profit under the United States, shall be appointed an Elector.

The Electors shall meet in their respective States, and vote by Ballot for two Persons, of whom one at least shall not be an Inhabitant of the same State with themselves. And they shall make a List of all the Persons voted for, and of the Number of Votes for each; which List they shall sign and certify, and transmit sealed to the Seat of the Government of the United States, directed to the President of the Senate. The President of the Senate shall, in the Presence of the Senate and House of Representatives, open all the Certificates, and the Votes shall then be counted. The Person having the greatest Number of Votes shall be the President, if such Number be a Majority of the whole Number of Electors appointed; and if there be more than one who have such Majority, and have an equal Number of Votes, then the House of Representatives shall immediately chuse by Ballot one of them for President; and if no Person have a Majority, then from the five highest on the List the said House shall in like Manner chuse the President. But in chusing the President, the Votes shall be taken by States, the Representation from each State having one Vote; a quorum for this Purpose shall consist of a Member or Members from two thirds of the States, and a Majority of all the States shall be necessary to a Choice. In every Case, after the Choice of the President, the Person having the greatest Number of Votes of the Electors shall be the Vice President. But if there should remain two or more who have equal Votes, the Senate shall chuse from them by Ballot the Vice President.[6]

The Congress may determine the Time of chusing the Electors, and the Day on which they shall give their Votes; which Day shall be the same throughout the United States.

No Person except a natural born Citizen, or a Citizen of the United States, at the time of the Adoption of this Constitution, shall be eligible to the Office of President; neither shall any person be eligible to that Office who shall not have attained to the Age of thirty five Years, and been fourteen Years a Resident within the United States.

In Case of the Removal of the President from Office, or of his Death, Resignation, or Inability to discharge the Powers and Duties of the said Office, the Same shall devolve on the Vice President, and the Congress may by Law provide for the Case of Removal, Death, Resignation or Inability, both of the President and Vice President, declaring what Officer shall then act as President, and such Officer shall act accordingly, until the Disability be removed, or a President shall be elected.[7]

The President shall, at stated Times, receive for his Services, a Compensation, which shall neither be encreased nor diminished during the Period for which he shall have been elected, and he shall not receive within that Period any other Emolument from the United States, or any of them.

Before he enter on the Execution of his Office, he shall take the following Oath or Affirmation:—"I do solemnly swear (or affirm) that I will faithfully execute the Office of President of the United States, and will to the best of my Ability, preserve, protect and defend the Constitution of the United States."

Section 2

The President shall be Commander in Chief of the Army and Navy of the United States, and of the Militia of the several States, when called into the actual Service of the United States; he may require the Opinion, in writing, of the principal Officer in each of the executive Departments, upon any Subject relating to the Duties of their respective Offices, and he shall have Power to grant Reprieves and Pardons for Offences against the United States, except in Cases of Impeachment.

He shall have Power, by and with the Advice and Consent of the Senate, to make Treaties, provided two thirds of the Senators present concur; and he shall nominate, and by and with the Advice and Consent of the Senate, shall appoint Ambassadors, other public Ministers and Consuls, Judges of the supreme Court, and all other Officers of the United States, whose Appointments are not herein otherwise provided for, and which shall be established by Law: but the Congress may by Law vest the Appointment of such inferior Officers, as they think proper, in the President alone, in the Courts of Law, or in the Heads of Departments.

The President shall have Power to fill up all Vacancies that may happen during the Recess of the Senate, by granting Commissions which shall expire at the End of their next Session.

Section 3

He shall from time to time give to the Congress Information of the State of the Union, and recommend to their Consideration such Measures as he shall judge necessary and expedient; he may, on extraordinary Occasions, convene both Houses, or either of them, and in Case of Disagreement between them, with Respect to the Time of Adjournment, he may adjourn them to such Time as he shall think proper; he shall receive Ambassadors and other public Ministers; he shall take Care that the Laws be faithfully executed, and shall Commission all the Officers of the United States.

Section 4

The President, Vice President and all civil Officers of the United States, shall be removed from Office on Impeachment for, and Conviction of, Treason, Bribery, or other high Crimes and Misdemeanors.

Article III

Section 1

The judicial Power of the United States, shall be vested in one supreme Court, and in such inferior Courts as the Congress may from time to time ordain and establish. The Judges, both of the supreme and inferior Courts, shall hold their Offices during good Behaviour, and shall, at stated Times, receive for their Services, a Compensation, which shall not be diminished during their Continuance in Office.

Section 2

The judicial Power shall extend to all Cases, in Law and Equity, arising under this Constitution, the Laws of the United States, and Treaties made, or which shall be made, under their Authority;—to all Cases affecting Ambassadors, other public Ministers and Consuls;—to all Cases of admiralty and maritime Jurisdiction;—to Controversies to which the United States shall be a Party;—to Controversies between two or more States;—*between a State and Citizens of another State;*[8]—between Citizens of different States;—between Citizens of the same State claiming Lands under Grants of different States, and between a State, or the Citizens thereof, and foreign States, Citizens or Subjects.

In all Cases affecting Ambassadors, other public Ministers and Consuls, and those in which a State shall be Party, the supreme Court shall have original Jurisdiction. In all the other Cases before mentioned, the supreme Court shall have appellate Jurisdiction, both as to Law and Fact, with such Exceptions, and under such Regulations as the Congress shall make.

The Trial of all Crimes, except in Cases of Impeachment, shall be by Jury; and such Trial shall be held in the State where the said Crimes shall have been committed; but when not committed within any State, the Trial shall be at such Place or Places as the Congress may by Law have directed.

Section 3

Treason against the United States, shall consist only in levying War against them, or in adhering to their Enemies, giving them Aid and Comfort. No Person shall be convicted of Treason unless on the Testimony of two Witnesses to the same overt Act, or on Confession in open Court.

The Congress shall have Power to declare the Punishment of Treason, but no Attainder of Treason shall work Corruption of Blood, or Forfeiture except during the Life of the Person attainted.

Article IV

Section 1

Full Faith and Credit shall be given in each State to the public Acts, Records, and judicial Proceedings of every other State. And the Congress may by general Laws prescribe the Manner in which such Acts, Records and Proceedings shall be proved, and the Effect thereof.

Section 2

The Citizens of each State shall be entitled to all Privileges and Immunities of Citizens in the several States.

A person charged in any State with Treason, Felony, or other Crime, who shall flee from Justice, and be found in another State, shall on Demand of the executive Authority of the State from which he fled, be delivered up, to be removed to the State having Jurisdiction of the Crime.

No Person held to Service or Labour in one State, under the Laws thereof, escaping into another, shall, in Consequence of any Law or Regulation therein, be discharged from such Service or Labour, but shall be delivered up on Claim of the Party to whom such Service or Labour may be due.[9]

Section 3

New States may be admitted by the Congress into this Union; but no new State shall be formed or erected within the Jurisdiction of any other State; nor any State be formed by the Junction of two or more States, or Parts of States, without the consent of the Legislatures of the States concerned as well as of the Congress.

The Congress shall have Power to dispose of and make all needful Rules and Regulations respecting the Territory or other Property belonging to the United States; and nothing in this Constitution shall be so construed as to Prejudice any Claims of the United States, or of any particular State.

Section 4

The United States shall guarantee to every State in this Union a Republican Form of Government, and shall protect each of them against Invasion; and on Application of the Legislature, or of the Executive (when the Legislature cannot be convened) against domestic Violence.

Article V

The Congress, whenever two thirds of both Houses shall deem it necessary, shall propose Amendments to this Constitution, or, on the Application of the Legislatures of two thirds of the several States, shall call a Convention for proposing Amendments, which, in either Case, shall be valid to all Intents and Purposes, as Part of this Constitution, when ratified by the Legislatures of three fourths of the several States, or by Conventions in three fourths thereof, as the one or the other Mode of Ratification may be proposed by the Congress; Provided that no Amendment which may be made prior to the Year One Thousand eight hundred and eight shall in any Manner affect the first and fourth Clauses in the Ninth Section of the first Article; and that no State, without its Consent, shall be deprived of its equal Suffrage in the Senate.

Article VI

All Debts contracted and Engagements entered into, before the Adoption of this Constitution, shall be as valid against the United States under this Constitution, as under the Confederation.

This Constitution, and the Laws of the United States which shall be made in Pursuance thereof; and all Treaties made, or which shall be made, under the Authority of the United States, shall be the supreme Law of the Land; and the Judges in every State shall be bound thereby, any Thing in the Constitution or Laws of any State to the Contrary notwithstanding.

The Senators and Representatives before mentioned, and the Members of the several State Legislatures, and all executive and judicial Officers, both of the United States and of the several States, shall be bound by Oath or Affirmation, to support this Constitution; but no religious Test shall ever be required as a Qualification to any Office or public Trust under the United States.

Article VII

The Ratification of the Conventions of nine States, shall be sufficient for the Establishment of this Constitution between the States so ratifying the Same.

Done in Convention by the Unanimous Consent of the States present the Seventeenth Day of September in the Year of our Lord one thousand seven hundred and Eighty seven and of the Independence of the United States of America the Twelfth In witness whereof We have hereunto subscribed our Names,

G^o WASHINGTON—*Presid^t and deputy from Virginia*

New Hampshire	JOHN LANGDON NICHOLAS GILMAN
Massachusetts	NATHANIEL GORHAM RUFUS KING
Connecticut	W^M SAM^L JOHNSON ROGER SHERMAN
New York	ALEXANDER HAMILTON
New Jersey	WIL: LIVINGSTON DAVID BREARLEY W^M PATERSON JONA: DAYTON
Pennsylvania	B FRANKLIN THOMAS MIFFLIN ROB^T MORRIS GEO. CLYMER THO^S FITZSIMONS JARED INGERSOLL JAMES WILSON GOUV MORRIS

Delaware	GEO: READ GUNNING BEDFORD jun JOHN DICKINSON RICHARD BASSETT JACO: BROOM
Maryland	JAMES M^{C}HENRY DAN OF S^T THO^S JENIFER DAN^L CARROLL
Virginia	JOHN BLAIR— JAMES MADISON Jr.
North Carolina	W^M BLOUNT RICH^D DOBBS SPAIGHT HU WILLIAMSON
South Carolina	J. RUTLEDGE CHARLES COTESWORTH PINCKNEY CHARLES PINCKNEY PIERCE BUTLER
Georgia	WILLIAM FEW ABR BALDWIN

Amendment I *[The first ten amendments, known as the "Bill of Rights," were ratified in 1791.]*

Congress shall make no law respecting an establishment of religion, or prohibiting the free exercise thereof; or abridging the freedom of speech, or of the press; or the right of the people peaceably to assemble, and to petition the Government for a redress of grievances.

Amendment II

A well regulated Militia, being necessary to the security of a free State, the right of the people to keep and bear Arms, shall not be infringed.

Amendment III

No Soldier shall, in time of peace, be quartered in any house, without the consent of the Owner, nor in time of war, but in a manner prescribed by law.

Amendment IV

The right of the people to be secure in their persons, houses, papers, and effects, against unreasonable searches and seizures, shall not be violated, and no Warrants shall issue, but upon probable cause, supported by Oath or affirmation, and particularly describing the place to be searched, and the persons or things to be seized.

Amendment V

No person shall be held to answer for a capital, or otherwise infamous crime, unless on a presentment or indictment of a Grand Jury, except in cases arising in the land or naval forces, or in the Militia, when in actual service in time of War or public danger; nor shall any person be subject for the same offence to be twice put in jeopardy of life or limb; nor shall be compelled in any criminal case to be a witness against himself, nor be deprived of life, liberty, or property, without due process of law, nor shall private property be taken for public use, without just compensation.

Amendment VI

In all criminal prosecutions, the accused shall enjoy the right to a speedy and public trial, by an impartial jury of the State and district wherein the crime shall have been committed, which district shall have been previously ascertained by law, and to be informed of the nature and cause of the accusation; to be confronted with the witnesses against him; to have compulsory process for obtaining witnesses in his favor, and to have Assistance of Counsel for his defence.

Amendment VII

In Suits at common law, where the value in controversy shall exceed twenty dollars, the right of trial by jury shall be preserved, and no fact tried by a jury, shall be otherwise reexamined in any Court of the United States, than according to the rules of the common law.

Amendment VIII

Excessive bail shall not be required, nor excessive fines imposed, nor cruel and unusual punishments inflicted.

Amendment IX

The enumeration in the Constitution, of certain rights, shall not be construed to deny or disparage others retained by the people.

Amendment X

The powers not delegated to the United States by the Constitution, nor prohibited by it to the States, are reserved to the States respectively, or to the people.

Amendment XI *[Ratified in 1795]*

The Judicial power of the United States shall not be construed to extend to any suit in law or equity, commenced or prosecuted against one of the United States by Citizens of another State, or by Citizens or Subjects of any Foreign State.

Amendment XII *[Ratified in 1804]*

The Electors shall meet in their respective states and vote by ballot for President and Vice President, one of whom, at least, shall not be an inhabitant of the same state with themselves; they shall name in their ballots the person voted for as President, and in distinct ballots the person voted for as Vice President, and they shall make distinct lists of all persons voted for as President, and of all persons voted for as Vice President, and of the number of votes for each, which lists they shall sign and certify, and transmit sealed to the seat of the government of the United States, directed to the President of the Senate;—The President of the Senate shall, in the presence of the Senate and House of Representatives, open all the certificates and the votes shall then be counted;—The person having the greatest number of votes for President, shall be the President, if such number be a majority of the whole number of Electors appointed; and if no person have such majority, then from the persons having the highest numbers not exceeding three on the list of those voted for as President, the House of Representatives shall choose immediately, by ballot, the President. But in choosing the President, the votes shall be taken by states, the representation from each state having one vote; a quorum for this purpose shall consist of a member or members from two-thirds of the states, and a majority of all the states shall be necessary to a choice. *And if the House of Representatives shall not choose a President whenever the right of choice shall devolve upon them, before the fourth day of March next following, then the Vice President shall act as President, as in the case of the death or other constitutional disability of the President.*—[10] The person having the greatest number of votes as Vice President, shall be the Vice President, if such number be a majority of the whole number of Electors appointed, and if no person have a majority, then from the two highest numbers on the list, the Senate shall choose the Vice President; a quorum for the purpose shall consist of two-thirds of the whole number of Senators, and a majority of the whole number shall be necessary to a choice. But no person constitutionally ineligible to the office of President shall be eligible to that of Vice President of the United States.

Amendment XIII *[Ratified in 1865]*

Section 1

Neither slavery nor involuntary servitude, except as a punishment for crime whereof the party shall have been duly convicted, shall exist within the United States, or any place subject to their jurisdiction.

Section 2

Congress shall have power to enforce this article by appropriate legislation.

Amendment XIV *[Ratified in 1868]*

Section 1

All persons born or naturalized in the United States and subject to the jurisdiction thereof, are citizens of the United States and of the State wherein they reside. No State shall make or enforce any law which shall abridge the privileges or immunities of citizens of the United States; nor shall any State deprive any person of life, liberty, or property, without due process of law; nor deny to any person within its jurisdiction the equal protection of the laws.

Section 2

Representatives shall be apportioned among the several States according to their respective numbers, counting the whole number of persons in each State, excluding Indians not taxed. But when the right to vote at any election for the choice of electors for President and Vice President of the United States, Representatives in Congress, the Executive and Judicial officers of a State, or the members of the Legislature thereof, is denied to any of the male inhabitants of such State, being *twenty-one*[11] years of age, and citizens of the United States, or in any way abridged, except for participation in rebellion, or other crime, the basis of representation therein shall be reduced in the proportion which the number of such male citizens shall bear to the whole number of male citizens twenty-one years of age in such State.

Section 3

No person shall be a Senator or Representative in Congress, or elector of President and Vice President, or hold any office, civil or military, under the United States, or under any State, who, having previously taken an oath, as a member of Congress, or as an officer of the United States, or as a member of any State legislature, or as an executive or judicial officer of any State, to support the Constitution of the United States, shall have engaged in insurrection or rebellion against the same, or given aid or comfort to the enemies thereof. But Congress may by a vote of two-thirds of each House, remove such disability.

Section 4

The validity of the public debt of the United States, authorized by law, including debts incurred for payment of pensions and bounties for services in suppressing insurrection or rebellion, shall not be questioned. But neither the United States nor any State shall assume or pay any debt or obligation incurred in aid of insurrection or rebellion against the United States, or any claim for the loss or emancipation of any slave; but all such debts, obligations and claims shall be held illegal and void.

Section 5

The Congress shall have power to enforce, by appropriate legislation, the provisions of this article.

Amendment XV *[Ratified in 1870]*

Section 1

The right of citizens of the United States to vote shall not be denied or abridged by the United States or by any State on account of race, color, or previous condition of servitude.

Section 2

The Congress shall have power to enforce this article by appropriate legislation.

Amendment XVI *[Ratified in 1913]*

The Congress shall have power to lay and collect taxes on incomes, from whatever source derived, without apportionment among the several States, and without regard to any census or enumeration.

Amendment XVII *[Ratified in 1913]*

The Senate of the United States shall be composed of two Senators from each State, elected by the people thereof, for six years; and each Senator shall have one vote. The electors in each State shall have the qualifications requisite for electors of the most numerous branch of the State legislatures.

When vacancies happen in the representation of any State in the Senate, the executive authority of such State shall issue writs of election to fill such vacancies: *Provided,* That the legislature of any State may empower the executive thereof to make temporary appointments until the people fill the vacancies by election as the legislature may direct.

This amendment shall not be so construed as to affect the election or term of any Senator chosen before it becomes valid as part of the Constitution.

Amendment XVIII *[Ratified in 1919]*

Section 1

After one year from the ratification of this article the manufacture, sale, or transportation of intoxicating liquors within, the importation thereof into, or the exportation thereof from the United States and all territory subject to the jurisdiction thereof for beverage purposes is hereby prohibited.

Section 2

The Congress and the several States shall have concurrent power to enforce this article by appropriate legislation.

Section 3

This article shall be inoperative unless it shall have been ratified as an amendment to the Constitution by the legislatures of the several States, as provided in the Constitution, within seven years from the date of the submission hereof to the States by the Congress.[12]

Amendment XIX *[Ratified in 1920]*

The right of citizens of the United States to vote shall not be denied or abridged by the United States or by any State on account of sex.

Congress shall have power to enforce this article by appropriate legislation.

Amendment XX *[Ratified in 1933]*

Section 1

The terms of the President and Vice President shall end at noon on the 20th day of January, and the terms of Senators and Representatives at noon on the 3d day of January, of the years in which such terms would have ended if this article had not been ratified; and the terms of their successors shall then begin.

Section 2

The Congress shall assemble at least once in every year, and such meeting shall begin at noon on the 3d day of January, unless they shall by law appoint a different day.

Section 3

If, at the time fixed for the beginning of the term of the President, the President elect shall have died, the Vice President elect shall become President. If a President shall not have been chosen before the time fixed for the beginning of his term, or if the President elect shall have failed to qualify, then the Vice President elect shall act as President until a President shall have qualified; and the Congress may by law provide for the case wherein neither a President elect nor a Vice President elect shall have qualified, declaring who shall then act as President, or the manner in which one who is to act shall be selected, and such person shall act accordingly until a President or Vice President shall have qualified.

Section 4

The Congress may by law provide for the case of the death of any of the persons from whom the House of Representatives may choose a President whenever the right of choice shall have devolved upon them, and for the case of the death of any of the persons from whom the Senate may choose a Vice President whenever the right of choice shall have devolved upon them.

Section 5

Sections 1 and 2 shall take effect on the 15th day of October following the ratification of this article.

Section 6

This article shall be inoperative unless it shall have been ratified as an amendment to the Constitution by the legislatures of three-fourths of the several States within seven years from the date of its submission.

Amendment XXI *[Ratified in 1933]*

Section 1

The eighteenth article of amendment to the Constitution of the United States is hereby repealed.

Section 2

The transportation or importation into any State, Territory, or possession of the United States for delivery or use therein of intoxicating liquors, in violation of the laws thereof, is hereby prohibited.

Section 3

This article shall be inoperative unless it shall have been ratified as an amendment to the Constitution by conventions in the several States, as provided in the Constitution, within seven years from the date of the submission hereof to the States by the Congress.

Amendment XXII *[Ratified in 1951]*

Section 1

No person shall be elected to the office of the President more than twice, and no person who has held the office of President, or acted as President, for more than two years of a term to which some other person was elected President shall be elected to the office of the President more than once. But this Article shall not apply to any person holding the office of President when this Article was proposed by the Congress, and shall not prevent any person who may be holding the office of President, or acting as President, during the term within which this Article becomes operative from holding the office of President or acting as President during the remainder of such term.

Section 2

This article shall be inoperative unless it shall have been ratified as an amendment to the Constitution by the legislatures of three-fourths of the several States within seven years from the date of its submission to the States by the Congress.

Amendment XXIII *[Ratified in 1961]*

Section 1

The District constituting the seat of Government of the United States shall appoint in such manner as the Congress may direct:

A number of electors of President and Vice President equal to the whole number of Senators and Representatives in Congress to which the District would be entitled if it were a State, but in no event more than the least populous State; they shall be in addition to those appointed by the States, but they shall be considered, for the purposes of the election of President and Vice President, to be electors appointed by a State; and they shall meet in the District and perform such duties as provided by the twelfth article of amendment.

Section 2

The Congress shall have power to enforce this article by appropriate legislation.

Amendment XXIV *[Ratified in 1964]*

Section 1

The right of citizens of the United States to vote in any primary or other election for President or Vice President, for electors for President or Vice President, or for Senator or Representative in Congress, shall not be denied or abridged by the United States or any State by reason of failure to pay any poll tax or other tax.

Section 2

The Congress shall have power to enforce this article by appropriate legislation.

Amendment XXV *[Ratified in 1967]*

Section 1

In case of the removal of the President from office or of his death or resignation, the Vice President shall become President.

Section 2

Whenever there is a vacancy in the office of the Vice President, the President shall nominate a Vice President who shall take office upon confirmation by a majority vote of both Houses of Congress.

Section 3

Whenever the President transmits to the president pro tempore of the Senate and the Speaker of the House of Representatives his written declaration that he is unable to discharge the powers and duties of his office, and until he transmits to them a written declaration to the contrary, such powers and duties shall be discharged by the Vice President as Acting President.

Section 4

Whenever the Vice President and a majority of either the principal officers of the executive departments or of such other body as Congress may by law provide, transmit to the President pro tempore of the Senate and the Speaker of the House of Representatives their written declaration that the President is unable to discharge the powers and duties of his office, the Vice President shall immediately assume the powers and duties of the office as Acting President.

Thereafter, when the President transmits to the President pro tempore of the Senate and the Speaker of the House of Representatives his written declaration that no inability exists, he shall resume the powers and duties of his office unless the Vice President and a majority of either the principal officers of the executive department[s] or of such other body as Congress may by law provide, transmit within four days to the President pro tempore of the Senate and the Speaker of the House of Representatives their written declaration that the President is unable to discharge the powers and duties of his office. Thereupon Congress shall decide the issue, assembling within forty-eight hours for that purpose if not in session. If the Congress, within twenty-one days after receipt of the latter written declaration, or, if Congress is not in session, within twenty-one days after Congress is required to assemble, determines by two-thirds vote of both Houses that the President is unable to discharge the powers and duties of his office, the Vice President shall continue to discharge the same as Acting President; otherwise, the President shall resume the powers and duties of his office.

Amendment XXVI [Ratified in 1971]

Section 1

The right of citizens of the United States, who are 18 years of age or older, to vote shall not be denied or abridged by the United States or by any State on account of age.

Section 2

The Congress shall have power to enforce this article by appropriate legislation.

Amendment XXVII [Ratified in 1992]

Section 1

No law, varying the compensation for the services of the senators and representatives, shall take effect until an election of representatives shall have intervened.

Notes

1. Changed by the Fourteenth Amendment, Section 2.
2. Changed by the Seventeenth Amendment.
3. Changed by the Seventeenth Amendment.
4. Changed by the Twentieth Amendment, Section 2.
5. Changed by the Sixteenth Amendment.
6. Superseded by the Twelfth Amendment.
7. Modified by the Twenty-fifth Amendment.
8. Modified by the Eleventh Amendment.
9. Changed by the Thirteenth Amendment.
10. Changed by the Twentieth Amendment, Section 3.
11. Changed by the Twenty-sixth Amendment.
12. Repealed by the Twenty-first Amendment.

Federalist No. 10

James Madison
22 November 1787

To the People of the State of New York

Among the numerous advantages promised by a well constructed Union, none deserves to be more accurately developed than its tendency to break and control the violence of faction. The friend of popular governments, never finds himself so much alarmed for their character and fate, as when he contemplates their propensity to this dangerous vice. He will not fail therefore to set a due value on any plan which, without violating the principles to which he is attached, provides a proper cure for it. The instability, injustice and confusion introduced into the public councils, have in truth been the mortal diseases under which popular governments have every where perished; as they continue to be the favorite and fruitful topics from which the adversaries to liberty derive their most specious declamations. The valuable improvements made by the American Constitutions on the popular models, both ancient and modern, cannot certainly be too much admired; but it would be an unwarrantable partiality, to contend that they have as effectually obviated the danger on this side as was wished and expected. Complaints are every where heard from our most considerate and virtuous citizens, equally the friends of public and private faith, and of public and personal liberty; that our governments are too unstable; that the public good is disregarded in the conflicts of rival parties; and that measures are too often decided, not according to the rules of justice, and the rights of the minor party; but by the superior force of an interested and over-bearing majority. However anxiously we may wish that these complaints had no foundation, the evidence of known facts will not permit us to deny that they are in some degree true. It will be found indeed, on a candid review of our situation, that some of the distresses under which we labor, have been erroneously charged on the operation of our governments; but it will be found, at the same time, that other causes will not alone account for many of our heaviest misfortunes; and particularly, for that prevailing and increasing distrust of public engagements, and alarm for private rights, which are echoed from one end of the continent to the other. These must be chiefly, if not wholly, effects of the unsteadiness and injustice, with which a factious spirit has tainted our public administrations.

By a faction I understand a number of citizens, whether amounting to a majority or minority of the whole, who are united and actuated by some common impulse of passion, or of interest, adverse to the rights of other citizens, or to the permanent and aggregate interests of the community.

There are two methods of curing the mischiefs of faction: the one, by removing its causes; the other, by controlling its effects.

There are again two methods of removing the causes of faction: the one by destroying the liberty which is essential to its existence; the other, by giving to every citizen the same opinions, the same passions, and the same interests.

It could never be more truly said than of the first remedy, that it is worse than the disease. Liberty is to faction, what air is to fire, an ailment without which it instantly expires. But it could not be a less folly to abolish liberty, which is essential to political life, because it nourishes faction, than it would be to wish the annihilation of air, which is essential to animal life, because it imparts to fire its destructive agency.

The second expedient is as impracticable, as the first would be unwise. As long as the reason of man continues fallible, and he is at liberty to exercise it, different opinions will be formed. As long as the connection subsists between his reason and his self-love, his opinions and his passions will have a reciprocal influence on each other; and the former will be objects to which the latter will attach themselves. The diversity in the faculties of men from which the rights of property originate, is not less an insuperable obstacle to a uniformity of interests. The protection of these faculties is the first object of Government. From the protection of different and unequal faculties of acquiring property, the possession of different degrees and kinds of property immediately results: and from the influence of these on the sentiments and views of the respective proprietors, ensues a division of the society into different interests and parties.

The latent causes of faction are thus sown in the nature of man; and we see them every where brought into different degrees of activity, according to the different circumstances of civil society. A zeal for different opinions concerning religion, concerning Government and many other points, as well of speculation as of practice; an attachment to different leaders ambitiously contending for pre-eminence and power; or to persons of other descriptions whose fortunes have been interesting to the human passions, have in turn divided mankind into parties, inflamed them with mutual animosity, and rendered them much more disposed to vex and oppress each other, than to cooperate for their common good. So strong is this propensity of mankind to fall into mutual animosities, that where no substantial occasion presents itself, the most frivolous and fanciful distinctions have been sufficient to kindle their unfriendly passions, and excite their most violent conflicts. But the most common and durable sources of factions, has been the various and unequal distribution of property. Those who hold, and those who are without property, have ever formed distinct interests in society. Those who are creditors, and those who are debtors, fall under a like discrimination. A landed interest, a manufacturing interest, a mercantile interest, a monied interest, with many lesser interests, grow up of necessity in civilized nations, and divide them into different classes, actuated by different sentiments and views. The regulation of these various and interfering interests forms the principal task of modern Legislation and involves the spirit of party and faction in the necessary and ordinary operations of Government.

No man is allowed to be a judge in his own cause; because his interest would certainly bias his judgment, and, not improbably, corrupt his integrity. With equal, nay with greater reason, a body of men, are unfit to be both judges and parties, at the same time; yet, what are many of the most important acts of legislation, but so many judicial determinations, not indeed concerning the rights of single persons, but concerning the rights of large bodies of citizens, and what are the different classes of legislators, but advocates and parties to the causes which they determine? Is a law proposed concerning private debts? It is a question to which the creditors are parties on one side, and the debtors on the other. Justice ought to hold the balance between them. Yet the parties are and must be themselves the judges; and the most numerous party, or, in other words, the most powerful faction must be expected to prevail. Shall domestic manufactures be encouraged, and in what degree, by restrictions on foreign manufactures? are questions which would be differently decided by the landed and the manufacturing classes; and probably by neither, with a sole regard to justice and the public good. The apportionment of taxes on the various descriptions of property, is an act which seems to require the most exact impartiality; yet, there is perhaps no legislative act in which greater opportunity and temptation are given to a predominant party, to trample on the rules of justice. Every shilling with which they over-burden the inferior number, is a shilling saved to their own pockets.

It is in vain to say, that enlightened statesmen will be able to adjust these clashing interests, and render them all subservient to the public good. Enlightened statesmen will not always be at the helm: Nor, in many cases, can such an adjustment be made at all, without taking into view indirect and remote considerations, which will rarely prevail over the immediate interest which one party may find in disregarding the rights of another, or the good of the whole.

The inference to which we are brought, is, that the causes of faction cannot be removed; and that relief is only to be sought in the means of controlling its *effects*.

If a faction consists of less than a majority, relief is supplied by the republican principle, which enables the majority to defeat its sinister views by regular vote: It may clog the administration, it may convulse the society; but it will be unable to execute and mask its violence under the forms of the Constitution. When a majority is included in a faction, the form of popular government on the other hand enables it to sacrifice to its ruling passion or interest, both the public good and the rights of other citizens. To secure the public good, and private rights, against the danger of such a faction, and at the same time to preserve the spirit and the form of popular government, is then the great object to which our enquiries are directed: Let me add that it is the great desideratum, by which alone this form of government can be rescued from the opprobrium

under which it has so long labored, and be recommended to the esteem and adoption of mankind.

By what means is this object attainable? Evidently by one of two only. Either the existence of the same passion or interest in a majority at the same time, must be prevented; or the majority, having such co-existent passion or interest, must be rendered, by their number and local situation, unable to concert and carry into effect schemes of oppression. If the impulse and the opportunity be suffered to coincide, we well know that neither moral nor religious motives can be relied on as an adequate control. They are not found to be such on the injustice and violence of individuals, and lose their efficacy in proportion to the number combined together; that is, in proportion as their efficacy becomes needful.

From this view of the subject, it may be concluded, that a pure Democracy, by which I mean, a Society, consisting of a small number of citizens, who assemble and administer the Government in person, can admit of no cure for the mischiefs of faction. A common passion or interest will, in almost every case, be felt by a majority of the whole; a communication and concert results from the form of Government itself; and there is nothing to check the inducements to sacrifice the weaker party, or an obnoxious individual. Hence it is, that such Democracies have ever been spectacles of turbulence and contention; have ever been found incompatible with personal security, or the rights of property; and have in general been as short in their lives, as they have been violent in their deaths. Theoretic politicians, who have patronized this species of Government, have erroneously supposed, that by reducing mankind to a perfect equality in their political rights, they would, at the same time, be perfectly equalized and assimilated in their possessions, their opinions, and their passions.

A republic, by which I mean a government in which the scheme of representation takes place, opens a different prospect, and promises the cure for which we are seeking. Let us examine the points in which it varies from pure democracy, and we shall comprehend both the nature of the cure and the efficacy which it must derive from the union.

The two great points of difference, between a democracy and a republic, are, first, the delegation of the government, in the latter, to a small number of citizens, elected by the rest; secondly, the greater number of citizens, and greater sphere of country, over which the latter may be extended.

The effect of the first difference is, on the one hand, to refine and enlarge the public views, by passing them through the medium of a chosen body of citizens, whose wisdom may best discern the true interest of their country, and whose patriotism and love of justice, will be least likely to sacrifice it to temporary or partial considerations. Under such a regulation, it may well happen, that the public voice, pronounced by the representatives of the people, will be more consonant to the public good, than if pronounced by the people themselves, convened for the purpose. On the other hand the effect may be inverted. Men of factious tempers, of local prejudices, or of sinister designs, may by intrigue, by corruption, or by other means, first obtain the suffrages, and then betray the interest of the people. The question resulting is, whether small or extensive republics are most favorable to the election of proper guardians of the public weal, and it is clearly decided in favor of the latter by two obvious considerations.

In the first place, it is to be remarked that, however small the republic may be, the representatives must be raised to a certain number, in order to guard against the cabals of a few; and that however large it may be, they must be limited to a certain number, in order to guard against the confusion of a multitude. Hence, the number of representatives in the two cases not being in proportion to that of the constituents, and being proportionally greatest in the small republic, it follows, that if the proportion of fit characters be not less in the large than in the small republic, the former will present a greater option, and consequently a greater probability of a fit choice.

In the next place, as each Representative will be chosen by a greater number of citizens in the large than in the small Republic, it will be more difficult for unworthy candidates to practise with success the vicious arts, by which elections are too often carried; and the suffrages of the people being more free, will be more likely to center on men who possess the most attractive merit, and the most diffusive and established characters.

It must be confessed, that in this, as in most other cases, there is a mean, on both sides of which inconveniences will be found to lie. By enlarging too much the number of electors, you render the representative too little acquainted with all their local circumstances and lesser interests; as by reducing it too much, you render him unduly attached to these, and too little fit to comprehend and pursue great and national objects. The Federal Constitution forms a happy combination in this respect; the great and aggregate interests being referred to the national, the local and particular, to the state legislatures.

The other point of difference is, the greater number of citizens and extent of territory which may be brought within the compass of Republican, than of Democratic Government; and it is this circumstance principally which renders factious combinations less to be dreaded in the former, than in the latter. The smaller the society, the fewer probably will be the distinct parties and interests composing it; the fewer the distinct parties and interests, the more frequently will a majority be found of the same party; and the smaller the number of individuals composing a majority, and the smaller the compass within which they are placed, the more easily will they concert and execute their plans of oppression. Extend the sphere, and you take in a greater variety of parties and interests; you make it less probable that a majority of the whole will have a common motive to invade the rights of other citizens; or if such a common

motive exists, it will be more difficult for all who feel it to discover their own strength, and to act in unison with each other. Besides other impediments, it may be remarked, that where there is a consciousness of unjust or dishonorable purposes, communication is always checked by distrust, in proportion to the number whose concurrence is necessary.

Hence it clearly appears, that the same advantage, which a Republic has over a Democracy, in controlling the effects of faction, is enjoyed by a large over a small Republic—is enjoyed by the Union over the States composing it. Does this advantage consist in the substitution of Representatives, whose enlightened views and virtuous sentiments render them superior to local prejudices, and to schemes of injustice? It will not be denied, that the Representation of the Union will be most likely to possess these requisite endowments. Does it consist in the greater security afforded by a greater variety of parties, against the event of any one party being able to outnumber and oppress the rest? In an equal degree does the increased variety of parties, comprised within the Union, increase this security? Does it, in fine, consist in the greater obstacles opposed to the concert and accomplishment of the secret wishes of an unjust and interested majority? Here, again, the extent of the Union gives it the most palpable advantage.

The influence of factious leaders may kindle a flame within their particular States, but will be unable to spread a general conflagration through the other States: a religious sect, may degenerate into a political faction in a part of the Confederacy but the variety of sects dispersed over the entire face of it, must secure the national Councils against any danger from that source: a rage for paper money, for an abolition of debts, for an equal division of property, or for any other improper or wicked project, will be less apt to pervade the whole body of the Union, than a particular member of it; in the same proportion as such a malady is more likely to taint a particular county or district, than an entire State.

In the extent and proper structure of the Union, therefore, we behold a Republican remedy for the diseases most incident to Republican Government. And according to the degree of pleasure and pride, we feel in being Republicans, ought to be our zeal in cherishing the spirit, and supporting the character of Federalists.

Publius

Federalist No. 51

James Madison
6 February 1788

To the People of the State of New York

To what expedient then shall we finally resort for maintaining in practice the necessary partition of power among the several departments, as laid down in the constitution? The only answer that can be given is, that as all these exterior provisions are found to be inadequate, the defect must be supplied, by so contriving the interior structure of the government, as that its several constituent parts may, by their mutual relations, be the means of keeping each other in their proper places. Without presuming to undertake a full development of this important idea, I will hazard a few general observations, which may perhaps place it in a clearer light, and enable us to form a more correct judgment of the principles and structure of the government planned by the convention.

In order to lay a due foundation for that separate and distinct exercise of the different powers of government, which to a certain extent, is admitted on all hands to be essential to the preservation of liberty, it is evident that each department should have a will of its own; and consequently should be so constituted, that the members of each should have as little agency as possible in the appointment of the members of the others. Were this principle rigorously adhered to, it would require that all the appointments for the supreme executive, legislative, and judiciary magistracies, should be drawn from the same fountain of authority, the people, through channels, having no communication whatever with one another. Perhaps such a plan of constructing the several departments would be less difficult in practice than it may in contemplation appear. Some difficulties however, and some additional expense, would attend the execution of it. Some deviations therefore from the principle must be admitted. In the constitution of the judiciary department in particular, it might be inexpedient to insist rigorously on the principle; first, because peculiar qualifications being essential in the members, the primary consideration ought to be to select that mode of choice, which best secures these qualifications; secondly, because the permanent tenure by which the appointments are held in that department, must soon destroy all sense of dependence on the authority conferring them.

It is equally evident that the members of each department should be as little dependent as possible on those of the others, for the emoluments annexed to their offices. Were the executive magistrate, or the judges, not independent of the legislature in this particular, their independence in every other would be merely nominal.

But the great security against a gradual concentration of the several powers in the same department, consists in giving to those who administer each department, the necessary constitutional means, and personal motives, to resist encroachments of the others. The provision for defense must in this, as in all other cases, be made commensurate to the danger of attack. Ambition must be made to counteract ambition. The interest of the man must be connected with the constitutional right of the place. It may be a reflection on human nature, that such devices should be necessary to control the abuses of government. But what is government itself but the greatest of all reflections on human nature? If men were angels, no government would be necessary. If angels were to govern men, neither external nor internal controls on government would be necessary. In framing a government which is to be administered by men over men, the great difficulty lies in this: You must first enable the government to control the governed; and in the next place, oblige it to control itself. A dependence on the people is no doubt the primary control on the government; but experience has taught mankind the necessity of auxiliary precautions.

This policy of supplying by opposite and rival interests, the defect of better motives, might be traced through the whole system of human affairs, private as well as public. We see it particularly displayed in all the subordinate distributions of power; where the constant aim is to divide and arrange the several offices in such a manner as that each may be a check on the other; that the private interest of every individual, may be a sentinel over the public rights. These inventions of prudence cannot be less requisite in the distribution of the supreme powers of the state.

But it is not possible to give to each department an equal power of self defense. In republican government the legislative authority, necessarily, predominates. The remedy for this inconveniency is, to divide the legislature into different branches; and to render them by different modes of election, and different principles of action, as little connected with each other, as the nature of their common functions, and their common dependence on the society, will admit. It may even be necessary to guard against dangerous encroachments by still further precautions. As the weight of the legislative authority requires that it should be thus divided, the weakness of the executive may require, on the other hand, that it should be fortified. An absolute negative, on the legislature, appears at first view to be the natural defense with which the executive magistrate should be armed. But perhaps it would be neither altogether safe, nor alone sufficient. On ordinary occasions, it might not be exerted with the requisite firmness; and on extraordinary occasions, it might be perfidiously abused. May not this defect of an absolute negative be supplied, by some qualified connection between this weaker department, and the weaker branch of the stronger department, by which the latter may be led to support the constitutional rights of the former, without being too much detached from the rights of its own department?

If the principles on which these observations are founded be just, as I persuade myself they are, and they be applied as a criterion, to the several state constitutions, and to the federal constitution, it will be found, that if the latter does not perfectly correspond with them, the former are infinitely less able to bear such a test.

There are moreover two considerations particularly applicable to the federal system of America, which place that system in a very interesting point of view.

First. In a single republic, all the power surrendered by the people, is submitted to the administration of a single government; and usurpations are guarded against by a division of the government into distinct and separate departments. In the compound republic of America, the power surrendered by the people, is first divided between two distinct governments, and then the portion allotted to each, subdivided among distinct and separate departments. Hence a double security arises to the rights of the people. The different governments will control each other; at the same time that each will be controlled by itself.

Second. It is of great importance in a republic, not only to guard the society against the oppression of its rulers; but to guard one part of the society against the injustice of the other part. Different interests necessarily exist in different classes of citizens. If a majority be united by a common interest, the rights of the minority will be insecure. There are but two methods of providing against this evil: The one by creating a will in the community independent of the majority, that is, of the society itself, the other by comprehending in the society so many separate descriptions of citizens, as will render an unjust combination of a majority of the whole, very improbable, if not impracticable. The first method prevails in all governments possessing an hereditary or self appointed authority. This at best is but a precarious security; because a power independent of the society may as well espouse the unjust views of the major, as the rightful interests, of the minor party, and may possibly be turned against both parties. The second method will be exemplified in the federal republic of the United States. While all authority in it will be derived from and dependent on the society, the society itself will be broken into so many parts, interests and classes of citizens, that the rights of individuals or of the minority, will be in little danger from interested combinations of the majority. In a free govern-

ment, the security for civil rights must be the same as for religious rights. It consists in the one case in the multiplicity of interests, and in the other, in the multiplicity of sects. The degree of security in both cases will depend on the number of interests and sects; and this may be presumed to depend on the extent of country and number of people comprehended under the same government. This view of the subject must particularly recommend a proper federal system to all the sincere and considerate friends of republican government: Since it shows that in exact proportion as the territory of the union may be formed into more circumscribed confederacies or states, oppressive combinations of a majority will be facilitated, the best security under the republican form, for the rights of every class of citizens, will be diminished; and consequently, the stability and independence of some member of the government, the only other security, must be proportionally increased. Justice is the end of government. It is the end of civil society. It ever has been, and ever will be pursued, until it be obtained, or until liberty be lost in the pursuit. In a society under the forms of which the stronger faction can readily unite and oppress the weaker, anarchy may as truly be said to reign, as in a state of nature where the weaker individual is not secured against the violence of the stronger. And as in the latter state even the stronger individuals are prompted by the uncertainty of their condition, to submit to a government which may protect the weak as well as themselves: So in the former state, will the more powerful factions or parties be gradually induced by a like motive, to wish for a government which will protect all parties, the weaker as well as the more powerful. It can be little doubted, that if the state of Rhode Island was separated from the confederacy, and left to itself, the insecurity of rights under the popular form of government within such narrow limits, would be displayed by such reiterated oppressions of factious majorities, that some power altogether independent of the people would soon be called for by the voice of the very factions whose misrule had proved the necessity of it. In the extended republic of the United States, and among the great variety of interests, parties and sects which it embraces, a coalition of a majority of the whole society could seldom take place on any other principles than those of justice and the general good; and there being thus less danger to a minor from the will of the major party, there must be less pretext also, to provide for the security of the former, by introducing into the government a will not dependent on the latter; or in other words, a will independent of the society itself. It is no less certain than it is important, notwithstanding the contrary opinions which have been entertained, that the larger the society, provided it lie within a practicable sphere, the more duly capable it will be of self government. And happily for the *republican cause,* the practicable sphere may be carried to a very great extent, by a judicious modification and mixture of the federal principle.

Publius

Anti-Federalists and the Constitution

Anti-Federalists opposed ratification of the Constitution because they feared it would create a strong national government that would trample the rights of individual citizens. In the following selection, George Mason, a leading Anti-Federalist who participated in the Constitutional Convention but who refused to sign the final document, systematically details his objections to the Constitution. Like most Anti-Federalists, Mason concentrates his criticisms on the risks of giving too much power to the national government. James Madison, a leading Federalist, responded to Mason's objections in a letter to George Washington.

George Mason, "Objections to the Constitution"

Circulated early October 1787, published in full in the Virginia Journal **(Alexandria), November 22, 1787**

Objections to the Constitution of Government formed by the Convention

There is no declaration of rights; and the laws of the general government being paramount to the laws and constitutions of the several States, the declarations of rights in the separate States are no security. Nor are the people secured even in the enjoyment of the benefits of the common law, which stands here upon no other foundation than its having been adopted by the respective acts forming the constitutions of the several States.

In the House of Representatives there is not the substance, but the shadow only of representation; which can never produce proper information in the Legislature, or inspire confidence in the people; the laws will therefore be generally made by men little concerned in, and unacquainted with their effects and consequences.

The Senate have the power of altering all money-bills, and of originating appropriations of money, and the salaries of the officers of their own appointment in conjunction with the President of the United States; although they are not the representatives of the people, or amenable to them.

These with their other great powers (viz. their power in the appointment of ambassadors and other public officers, in making treaties, and in trying all impeachments) their influence upon and connection with the supreme executive from these causes, their duration of office, and their being a constant existing body almost continually sitting, joined with their being one complete branch of the Legislature, will destroy any balance in the government, and enable them to accomplish what usurpations they please upon the rights and liberties of the people.

The judiciary of the United States is so constructed and extended as to absorb and destroy the judiciaries of the several States; thereby rendering law as tedious, intricate and expensive, and justice as unattainable by a great part of the community, as in England, and enabling the rich to oppress and ruin the poor.

The President of the United States has no constitutional council (a thing unknown in any safe and regular government) he will therefore be unsupported by proper information and advice; and will be generally directed by minions and favorites—or he will become a tool to the Senate—or a Council of State will grow out of the principal officers of the great departments; the worst and most dangerous of all ingredients for such a council in a free country; for they may be induced to join in any dangerous or oppressive measures, to shelter themselves, and prevent an inquiry into their own misconduct in office; whereas had a constitutional council been formed (as was proposed) of six member, viz. two from the eastern, two from the middle, and two from the southern States, to be appointed by vote of the States in the House of Representatives, with the same duration and rotation in office as the Senate, the Executive would always have had safe and proper information and advice, the President of such a council might have acted as Vice-President of the United States, pro tempore, upon any vacancy or disability of the chief Magistrate; and long continued sessions of the Senate would in a great measure have been prevented.

From this fatal defect of a constitutional council has arisen the improper power of the Senate, in the appointment of public officers, and the alarming dependance and connection between that branch of the Legislature and the supreme Executive.

Hence also sprung that unnecessary and dangerous officer the Vice-President; who for want of other employment is made President of the Senate; thereby dangerously blending the executive and legislative powers; besides always giving to some one of the States an unnecessary and unjust preminence over the others.

The President of the United States has the unrestrained power of granting pardons for treason; which may be sometimes exercised to screen from punishment those whom he had secretly instigated to commit the crime, and thereby prevent a discovery of his own guilt.

By declaring all treaties supreme laws of the land, the Executive and the Senate have, in many cases, an exclusive power of legislation; which might have been avoided by proper distinctions with respect to treaties, and requiring the assent of the House of Representatives, where it could be done with safety.

By requiring only a majority to make all commercial and navigation laws, the five southern States (whose produce and circumstances are totally different from that of the eight northern and eastern States) will be ruined; for such rigid and premature regulations may be made, as will enable the merchants of the northern and eastern States not only to demand an exorbitant freight, but to monopolize the purchase of the commodities at their own price, for many years: To the great injury of the landed interest, and impoverishment of the people: And the danger is the greater, as the gain on one side will be in proportion to the loss on the other. Whereas requiring two-thirds of the members present in both houses would have produced mutual moderation, promoted the general interest and removed an insuperable objection to the adoption of the government.

Under their own construction of the general clause at the end of the enumerated powers, the Congress may grant monopolies in trade and commerce, constitute new crimes, inflict unusual and severe punishments, and extend their power as far as they shall think proper; so that the State Legislatures have no security for the powers now presumed to remain to them; or the people for their rights.

There is no declaration of any kind for preserving the liberty of the press, the trial by jury in civil causes; nor against the danger of standing armies in time of peace.

The State Legislatures are restrained from laying export duties on their own produce.

The general Legislature is restrained from prohibiting the further importation of slaves for twenty odd years; though such importations render the United States weaker, and more vulnerable, and less capable of defence.

Both the general Legislature and the State Legislatures are expressly prohibited making ex post facto laws; though there never was nor can be a Legislature but must and will make such laws, when necessity and the public safety require them, which will hereafter be a breach of all the constitutions in the Union, and afford precedents for other innovations.

This government will commence in a moderate aristocracy; it is at present impossible to foresee whether it will, in its operation, produce a monarchy, or a corrupt oppressive aristocracy; it will most probably vibrate some years between the two, and then terminate between the one and the other.

James Madison to George Washington, "A 'Prolix' Comment on Mason's 'Objections'"

New York, October 18, 1787

I have been this day honoured with your favor of the 10th instant, under the same cover with which is a copy of Col. Mason's objections to the Work of the Convention. As he persists in the temper which produced his dissent it is no small satisfaction to find him reduced to such distress for a proper gloss on it; for no other consideration surely could have led him to dwell on an objection which he acknowledged to have been in some degree removed by the Convention themselves—on the paltry right of the Senate to propose alterations in money bills—on the appointment of the vice President—President of the Senate instead of making the President of the Senate the vice President, which seemed to be the alternative—and on the *possibility,* that the Congress may misconstrue their powers & betray their trust so far as to grant monopolies in trade &c. If I do not forget too some of his other reasons were either not at all or very faintly urged at the time when alone they ought to have been urged; such as the power of the Senate in the case of treaties & of impeachments; and

their duration in office. With respect to the latter point I recollect well that he more than once disclaimed opposition to it. My memory fails me also if he did not acquiesce in if not vote for, the term allowed for the further importation of slaves; and the prohibition of duties on exports by the States. What he means by the dangerous tendency of the Judiciary I am at some loss to comprehend. It never was intended, nor can it be supposed that in ordinary cases the inferior tribunals will not have final jurisdiction in order to prevent the evils of which he complains. The great mass of suits in every State lie between Citizen & Citizen, and relate to matters not of federal cognizance. Notwithstanding the stress laid on the necessity of a Council to the President I strongly suspect, though I was a friend to the thing, that if such an one as Col. Mason proposed, had been established, and the power of the Senate in appointments to offices transferred to it, that as great a clamour would have been heard from some quarters which in general echo his Objections. What can he mean by saying that the Common law is not secured by the new Constitution, though it has been adopted by the State Constitutions. The Common law is nothing more than the unwritten law, and is left by all the Constitutions equally liable to legislative alterations. I am not sure that any notice is particularly taken of it in the Constitutions of the States. If there is, nothing more is provided than a general declaration that it shall continue along with other branches of law to be in force till legally changed. The Constitution of Virga. drawn up by Col. Mason himself, is absolutely silent on the subject. An *ordinance* passed during the same Session, declared the Common law as heretofore & all Statutes of prior date to the 4 of James I. to be still the law of the land, merely to obviate pretexts that the separation from G. Britain threw us into a State of nature, and abolished all civil rights and obligations. Since the Revolution every State has made great inroads & with great propriety in many instances on this *monarchical* code. The "revisal of the laws" by a Coˉmitte of wch. Col. Mason was a member, though not an acting one, abounds with such innovations. The abolition of the *right of primogeniture,* which I am sure Col. Mason does not disapprove, falls under this head. What could the Convention have done? If they had in general terms declared the Common law to be in force, they would have broken in upon the legal Code of every State in the most material points: they would have done more, they would have brought over from G.B. a thousand heterogeneous & antirepublican doctrines, and even the *ecclesiastical Hierarchy itself,* for that is a part of the Common law. If they had undertaken a discrimination, they must have formed a digest of laws, instead of a Constitution. This objection surely was not brought forward in the Convention, or it wd. have been placed in such a light that a repetition of it out of doors would scarcely have been hazarded. Were it allowed the weight which Col. M. may suppose it deserves, it would remain to be decided whether it be candid to arraign the Convention for omissions which were never suggested to them—or prudent to vindicate the dissent by reasons which either were not previously thought of, or must have been willfully concealed—But I am running into a comment as prolix, as it is out of place.

I find by a letter from the Chancellor (Mr. Pendleton) that he views the act of the Convention in its true light, and gives it his unequivocal approbation. His support will have great effect. The accounts we have here of some other respectable characters vary considerably. Much will depend on Mr. Henry, and I am glad to find by your letter that his favorable decision on the subject may yet be hoped for.—The Newspapers here begin to teem with vehement & virulent calumniations of the proposed Govt. As they are chiefly borrowed from the Pennsylvania papers, you see them of course. The reports however from different quarters continue to be rather flattering.

Race and the U.S. Constitution

Race has been a fundamental issue in American politics since the founding of the Republic. As the following excerpts from the Supreme Court's rulings in four landmark cases show, our understanding of the civil rights guaranteed by the Constitution has changed dramatically over the past two centuries.

Dred Scott v. Sanford
19 How. 393; 15 L. Ed. 691 (1857)

[Dred Scott was an African American slave who moved with his owner from Missouri, a slave state, first to Illinois, a free state, and then to the Wisconsin territory, where slavery was illegal under the terms of the Missouri Compromise of 1820. In 1846, Scott asked a state court in Missouri to grant him his freedom on the grounds that he had lived for two years in a free state and a free territory. Scott initially won his case, but the judgment was overturned on appeal and eventually made its way to the Supreme Court. In 1857, the Court's southern majority ruled against Scott, arguing that the Missouri Compromise was unconstitutional because Congress had no power to ban slavery in federal territories. As the following excerpt shows, the Court went even further and argued that African Americans descended from slaves were not American citizens and thus had no right to sue in court.]

MR. CHIEF JUSTICE TANEY delivered the opinion of the Court:

. . . .

The question is simply this: Can a Negro, whose ancestors were imported into this country, and sold as slaves, become a member of the political community formed and brought into existence by the Constitution of the United States, and as such become entitled to all the rights, and privileges, and immunities, guaranteed by that instrument to the citizen? One of which rights is the privilege of suing in a court of the United States in the cases specified in the Constitution. . . .

The words "people of the United States" and "citizens" are synonymous terms, and mean the same thing. They both describe the political body who, according to our republican institutions, form the sovereignty, and who hold the power and conduct the Government through their representatives. They are what we familiarly call the "sovereign people," and every citizen is one of this people, and a constituent member of this sovereignty. The question before us is, whether the class of persons described in the plea in abatement compose a portion of this people, and are constituent members of this sovereignty? We think they are not, and that they are not

included, and were not intended to be included, under the word "citizens" in the Constitution, and can therefore claim none of the rights and privileges which that instrument provides for and secures to citizens of the United States. On the contrary, they were at that time considered as a subordinate and inferior class of beings, who had been subjugated by the dominant race, and, whether emancipated or not, yet remained subject to their authority, and had no rights or privileges but such as those who held the power and the government might choose to grant them. . . .

[A review of] the legislation of the States . . . shows, in a manner not to be mistaken, the inferior and subject condition of that race at the time the Constitution was adopted, and long afterward, throughout the thirteen States by which that instrument was framed. . . . It cannot be supposed that they intended to secure to them rights, and privileges, and rank, in the new political body throughout the Union, which every one of them denied within the limits of its own dominion. More especially, it cannot be believed that the large slaveholding States regarded them as included in the word citizens, or would have consented to a Constitution which might compel them to receive them in that character from another State. For if they were so received, and entitled to the privileges and immunities of citizens, it would exempt them from the operation of the special laws and from the police regulations which they considered to be necessary for their own safety. It would give to persons of the Negro race, who were recognised as citizens in any one State of the Union, the right to enter every other State whenever they pleased, singly or in companies, without pass or passport, and without obstruction to sojourn there as long as they pleased, to go where they pleased at every hour of the day or night without molestation, unless they committed some violation of law for which a white man would be punished; and it would give them the full liberty of speech in public and in private upon all subjects upon which its own citizens might speak; to hold public meetings upon political affairs, and to keep and carry arms wherever they went. And all of this would be done in the face of the subject race of the same color, both free and slaves, and inevitably producing discontent and insubordination among them, and endangering the peace and safety of the State. . . .

Undoubtedly, a person may be a citizen, that is, a member of the community who form the sovereignty, although he exercises no share of the political power, and is incapacitated from holding particular offices. Women and minors, who form a part of the political family, cannot vote; and when a property qualification is required to vote or hold a particular office, those who have not the necessary qualification cannot vote or hold the office, yet they are citizens.

So, too, a person may be entitled to vote by the law of the State, who is not a citizen even of the State itself. And in some of the States of the Union foreigners not naturalized are allowed to vote. And the State may give the right to free negroes and mulattoes, but that does not make them citizens of the State, and still less of the United States. And the provision in the Constitution giving privileges and immunities in other States does not apply to them. . . .

No one, we presume, supposes that any change in public opinion or feeling, in relation to this unfortunate race, in the civilized nations of Europe or in this country, should induce the court to give to the words of the Constitution a more liberal construction in their favor than they were intended to bear when the instrument was framed and adopted. Such an argument would be altogether inadmissible in any tribunal called on to interpret it. If any of its provisions are deemed unjust, there is a mode prescribed in the instrument itself by which it may be amended; but while it remains unaltered, it must be construed now as it was understood at the time of its adoption. It is not only the same in words, but the same in meaning, and delegates the same powers to the Government, and reserves and secures the same rights and privileges to the citizen; and as long as it continues to exist in its present form, it speaks not only in the same words, but with the same meaning and intent with which it spoke when it came from the hands of its framers, and was voted on and adopted by the people of the United States. Any other rule of construction would abrogate the judicial character of this court, and make it the mere reflex of the popular opinion or passion of the day. This court was not created by the Constitution for such purposes. Higher and graver trusts have been confided to it, and it must not falter in the path of duty. . . .

[T]he court is of opinion, that, . . . Dred Scott was not a citizen of Missouri within the meaning of the Constitution of the United States, and not entitled as such to sue in its courts. . . .

Plessy v. Ferguson
163 U.S. 537; 16 Sup. Ct. 1138; 41 L. Ed. 256 (1896)

[*In 1890, the Louisiana state legislature followed the lead of several other southern states and passed a law requiring that "all railway companies carrying passengers in their coaches in this State, shall provide equal but separate accommodations for the white, and colored, races." Homer Adolph Plessy, who was one-eighth African American by descent, was arrested for violating the statute. He was tried in the Criminal District Court of New Orleans, where Judge John H. Ferguson found him guilty. In 1896, the Supreme Court upheld Ferguson's verdict, finding that "separate but equal" laws did not violate the Fourteenth Amendment, as Plessy had argued.*]

MR. JUSTICE BROWN delivered the opinion of the Court:

. . . .

The constitutionality of this act is attacked upon the ground that it conflicts both with the Thirteenth Amendment of the Constitution, abolishing slavery, and the Fourteenth Amendment, which prohibits certain restrictive legislation on the part of the States.

1. That it does not conflict with the Thirteenth Amendment, which abolished slavery and involuntary servitude, except as a punishment for crime, is too clear for argument. . . .

A statute which implies merely a legal distinction between the white and colored races—a distinction which is founded in the color of the two races, and which must always exist so long as white men are distinguished from the other race by color—has no tendency to destroy the legal equality of the two races, or reestablish a state of involuntary servitude. Indeed, we do not understand that the Thirteenth Amendment is strenuously relied upon by the plaintiff in error in this connection.

2. By the Fourteenth Amendment, all persons born or naturalized in the United States, and subject to the jurisdiction thereof, are made citizens of the United States and of the State wherein they reside; and the States are forbidden from making or enforcing any law which shall abridge the privileges or immunities of citizens of the United States, or shall deprive any person of life, liberty, or property without due process of law, or deny to any person within their jurisdiction the equal protection of the laws. . . .

The object of the amendment was undoubtedly to enforce the absolute equality of the two races before the law, but in the nature of things it could not have been intended to abolish distinctions based upon color, or to enforce social, as distinguished from political equality, or a commingling of the two races upon terms unsatisfactory to either. Laws permitting, and even requiring, their separation in places where they are liable to be brought into contact do not necessarily imply the inferiority of either race to the other, and have been generally, if not universally, recognized as within the competency of the state legislatures in the exercise of their police power. The most common instance of this is connected with the establishment of separate schools for white and colored children, which has been held to be a valid exercise of the legislative power even by courts of States where the political rights of the colored race have been longest and most earnestly enforced.

It is . . . suggested by the learned counsel for the plaintiff in error that the same argument that will justify the state legislature in requiring railways to provide separate accommodation for the two races will also authorize them to require separate cars to be provided for people whose hair is of a certain color, or who are aliens, or who belong to certain nationalities, or to enact laws requiring colored people to walk upon one side of the street, and white people upon the other, or requiring white men's houses to be painted white, and colored men's black, or their vehicles or business signs to be of different colors, upon the theory that one side of the street is as good as the other, or that a house or vehicle of one color is as good as one of another color. The reply to all this is that every exercise of the police power must be reasonable, and extend only to such laws as are enacted in good faith for the promotion of the public good, and not for the annoyance or oppression of a particular class. . . .

So far, then, as a conflict with the Fourteenth Amendment is concerned, the case reduces itself to the question whether the statute of Louisiana is a reasonable regulation, and with respect to this there must necessarily be a large discretion on the part of the legislature. In determining the question of reasonableness it is at liberty to act with reference to the established usages, customs, and traditions of the people, and with a view to the promotion of their comfort, and the preservation of the public peace and good order. Gauged by this standard, we cannot say that a law which authorizes or even requires the separation of the two races in public conveyances is unreasonable, or more obnoxious to the Fourteenth

Amendment than the acts of Congress requiring separate schools for colored children in the District of Columbia, the constitutionality of which does not seem to have been questioned, or the corresponding acts of state legislatures.

We consider the underlying fallacy of the plaintiff's argument to consist in the assumption that the enforced separation of the two races stamps the colored race with a badge of inferiority. If this be so, it is not by reason of anything found in the act, but solely because the colored race chooses to put that construction upon it. The argument necessarily assumes that if, as has been more than once the case, and is not unlikely to be so again, the colored race should become the dominant power in the state legislature, and should enact a law in precisely similar terms, it would thereby relegate the white race to an inferior position. We imagine that the white race, at least, would not acquiesce in this assumption. The argument also assumes that social prejudices may be overcome by legislation, and that equal rights cannot be secured to the Negro except by an enforced commingling of the two races. We cannot accept this proposition. If the two races are to meet upon terms of social equality, it must be the result of natural affinities, a mutual appreciation of each other's merits, and a voluntary consent of individuals. . . . Legislation is powerless to eradicate racial instincts or to abolish distinctions based upon physical differences, and the attempt to do so can only result in accentuating the difficulties of the present situation. If the civil and political rights of both races be equal one cannot be inferior to the other civilly or politically. If one race be inferior to the other socially, the Constitution of the United States cannot put them upon the same plane. . . .

[Justice John Marshall Harlan dissented from the majority's ruling in Plessy v. Ferguson. *He argued that the "Constitution is color-blind" and requires that all citizens be treated equally under the law.]*

MR. JUSTICE HARLAN, dissenting:

. . . .

. . . It was said in argument that the statute of Louisiana does not discriminate against either race, but prescribes a rule applicable alike to white and colored citizens. But this argument does not meet the difficulty. Everyone knows that the statute in question had its origin in the purpose, not so much to exclude white persons from railroad cars occupied by blacks, as to exclude colored people from coaches occupied by or assigned to white persons . . . No one would be so wanting in candor as to assert the contrary. The fundamental objection, therefore, to the statute is that it interferes with the personal freedom of citizens . . . If a white man and a black man choose to occupy the same public conveyance on a public highway, it is their right to do so, and no government, proceeding alone on grounds of race, can prevent it without infringing the personal liberty of each.

. . . In view of the Constitution, in the eye of the law, there is in this country no superior, dominant, ruling class of citizens. There is no caste here. Our Constitution is color-blind, and neither knows nor tolerates classes among citizens. In respect of civil rights, all citizens are equal before the law. The humblest is the peer of the most powerful. The law regards man as man, and takes no account of his surroundings or of his color when his civil rights as guaranteed by the supreme law of the land are involved.

. . . The sure guaranty of the peace and security of each race is the clear, distinct, unconditional recognition by our governments,

National and State, of every right that inheres in civil freedom, and of the equality before the law of all citizens of the United States without regard to race. State enactments regulating the enjoyment of civil rights upon the basis of race, and cunningly devised to defeat legitimate results of the war, under the pretence of recognizing equality of rights, can have no other result than to render permanent peace impossible, and to keep alive a conflict of races, the continuance of which must do harm to all concerned.

. . . The arbitrary separation of citizens, on the basis of race, while they are on a public highway, is a badge of servitude wholly inconsistent with the civil freedom and the equality before the law established by the Constitution. It cannot be justified upon any legal grounds.

. . . We boast of the freedom enjoyed by our people above all other peoples. But it is difficult to reconcile that boast with a state of the law which, practically, puts the brand of servitude and degradation upon a large class of our fellow-citizens, our equals before the law. The thin disguise of "equal" accommodations for passengers in railroad coaches will not mislead anyone, nor atone for the wrong this day done. . . .

I am of opinion that the statute of Louisiana is inconsistent with the personal liberty of citizens, white and black, in that State, and hostile to both the spirit and letter of the Constitution of the United States. . . .

Brown et al. v Board of Education
347 U.S. 483; 74 Sup. Ct. 693; 98 L. Ed. 591 (1954)

[In 1950, Oliver Brown, a railroad worker in Topeka, Kansas, attempted to enroll his daughter Linda in the third grade at the Sumner School, a public school for whites located only four blocks from his home. When school officials refused to admit Linda because she was African American, Brown sued the Board of Education for the city of Topeka. Brown's lawsuit eventually reached the Supreme Court, where it was considered along with several other cases challenging the constitutionality of segregated public schools. In 1954, a unanimous Court ruled that segregated school systems denied African American children equal protection under the law, thereby violating the Fourteenth Amendment. The Court's decision in Brown et al. v. Board of Education *effectively overturned the decision it had reached fifty-eight years earlier in* Plessy v. Ferguson.]*

MR. CHIEF JUSTICE WARREN delivered the opinion of the Court:

. . . .

These cases come to us from the States of Kansas, South Carolina, Virginia, and Delaware. They are premised on different facts and different local conditions, but a common legal question justifies their consideration together in this consolidated opinion.

In each of the cases minors of the Negro race, through their legal representatives, seek the aid of the courts in obtaining admission to the public schools of their community on a nonsegregated basis. In each instance, they had been denied admission to schools attended by white children under laws requiring or permitting segregation according to race. This segregation was alleged to deprive the plaintiffs of the equal protection of the laws under the Fourteenth Amendment. In each of the cases other than the Delaware case, a three-judge federal district court denied relief to the plaintiffs on the so-called "separate but equal" doctrine announced by this Court in *Plessy v. Ferguson.* . . .

The plaintiffs contend that segregated public schools are not "equal" and cannot be made "equal," and that hence they are deprived of the equal protection of the laws. Because of the obvious importance of the question presented, the Court took jurisdiction. Argument was heard in the 1952 Term, and reargument was heard this Term on certain questions propounded by the Court.

Reargument was largely devoted to the circumstances surrounding the adoption of the Fourteenth Amendment in 1868. It covered exhaustively consideration of the Amendment in Congress, ratification by the states, then existing practices in racial segregation, and the view of the proponents and opponents of the Amendment. This discussion and our own investigation convince us that, although these sources cast some light, it is not enough to resolve the problem with which we are faced. At best, they are inconclusive. The most avid proponents of the postwar Amendments undoubtedly intended them to remove all legal distinctions among "all persons born or naturalized in the United States." Their opponents, just as certainly, were antagonistic to both the letter and the spirit of the Amendments and wished them to have the most limited effect. What others in Congress and the state legislatures had in mind cannot be determined with any degree of certainty.

An additional reason for the inclusive nature of the Amendment's history, with respect to segregated schools, is the status of public education at that time. In the South, the movement toward free common schools, supported by general taxation, had not yet taken hold. Education of white children was largely in the hands of private groups. Education of Negroes was almost nonexistent, and practically all of the race were illiterate. In fact, any education of Negroes was forbidden by law in some states. Today, in contrast, many Negroes have achieved outstanding success in the arts and science as well as in the business and professional world. It is true that public education had already advanced further in the North, but the effect of the Amendment on northern states was generally ignored in the congressional debates. Even in the North, the conditions of public education did not approximate those existing today. The curriculum was usually rudimentary; ungraded schools were common in rural areas; the school term was but three months a year in many states; and compulsory school attendance was virtually unknown. As a consequence, it is not surprising that there should be so little in the history of the Fourteenth Amendment relating to its intended effect on public education.

In the first cases in this Court construing the Fourteenth Amendment, decided shortly after its adoption, the Court interpreted it as proscribing all state-imposed discriminations against the Negro race. The doctrine of "separate but equal" did not make its appearance in this Court until 1896 in the case of Plessy v. Ferguson . . . involving not education but transportation. American courts have since labored with the doctrine for over half a century . . . in the field of public education. In *Cumming v. County Board of Education* . . . and *Gong Lum v. Rice* . . . the validity of the doctrine itself was not challenged. In more recent cases, all on the graduate-school level, inequality was found in that specific benefits enjoyed by white students were denied to Negro students of the same educational qualifications. . . In none of these cases was it necessary to re-examine the doctrine to grant relief to the Negro plaintiff. And in *Sweatt v. Painter* . . . the Court expressly reserved decision on the question whether *Plessy v. Ferguson* should be held inapplicable to public education.

In the instant cases, that question is directly presented. Here, unlike *Sweatt v. Painter,* there are findings below that the Negro and white schools involved have been equalized, or are being equalized, with respect to buildings, curricula, qualifications and salaries of teachers, and other "tangible" factors. Our decision, therefore, cannot turn on merely a comparison of these tangible factors in the Negro and white schools involved in each of the cases. We must look instead to the effect of segregation itself on public education. . .

We come then to the question presented: Does segregation of children in public schools solely on the basis of race, even though the physical facilities and other "tangible" factors may be equal, deprive the children of the minority group of equal educational opportunities? We believe that it does.

. . . [I]n finding [in *Sweatt v. Painter*] that a segregated law school for Negroes could not provide them equal educational opportunities, this Court relied in large part on "those qualities which are incapable of objective measurement but which make for greatness in a law school." In *McLaurin v. Oklahoma State Regents* . . . the Court, in requiring that a Negro admitted to a white graduate school be treated like all other students, again resorted to intangible considerations: ". . . his ability to study, to engage in discussions and exchange views with other students, and, in general, to learn his profession." Such considerations apply with added force to children in grade and high schools. To separate them from others of similar age and qualifications solely because of their race generates a feeling of inferiority as to their status in the community that may affect their hearts and minds in a way unlikely ever to be undone. The effect of this separation on their educational opportunities was well stated by a finding in the Kansas case by a court which nevertheless felt compelled to rule against the Negro plaintiffs:

"Segregation of white and colored children in public schools has a detrimental effect upon the colored children. The impact is greater when it has the sanction of the law; for the policy of separating the races is usually interpreted as denoting the inferiority of the Negro group. A sense of inferiority affects the motivation of a child to learn. Segregation with the sanction of law, therefore, has a tendency to retard the educational and mental development of Negro children and to deprive them of some of the benefits they would receive in a racially integrated school system."

Whatever may have been the extent of psychological knowledge at the time of *Plessy v. Ferguson,* this finding is amply supported by modern authority. Any language in *Plessy v. Ferguson* contrary to this finding is rejected.

We conclude that in the field of public education the doctrine of "separate but equal" has no place. Separate educational facilities are inherently unequal. Therefore, we hold that the plaintiffs and others similarly situated for whom the actions have been brought are, by reason of the segregation complained of, deprived of the equal protection of the laws guaranteed by the Fourteenth Amendment. . . .

Brown v. Board of Education
[Brown II—The Implementation Decision]
349 U.S. 294; 75 S. Ct. 753; 99 L.Ed. 1083(1955)

[*Although* Brown et al. v. Board of Education *held that segregated public schools violated the Fourteenth Amendment, the case did not address the question of relief, that is, how the nation should desegregate its public schools. Instead, the Supreme Court scheduled further arguments on the question of relief. After hearing new arguments from the original parties to the lawsuit as well as from the attorney general of the United States and the attorneys general of six states, the Court ruled in 1955 that the federal courts should oversee desegregation efforts. While recognizing that practical considerations made it impossible to end segregation immediately, the Court ruled that desegregation should proceed with "all deliberate speed."]*

MR. CHIEF JUSTICE WARREN delivered the opinion of the Court:

. . . .

These cases were decided on May 17, 1954. The opinions of that date, declaring the fundamental principle that racial discrimination in public education is unconstitutional, are incorporated herein by reference. All provisions of federal, state, or local law requiring or permitting such discrimination must yield to this principle. There remains for consideration the manner in which relief is to be accorded. . . .

Full implementation of these constitutional principles may require solution of varied local school problems. School authorities have the primary responsibility for elucidating, assessing, and solving these problems; courts will have to consider whether the action of school authorities constitutes good faith implementation of the governing constitutional principles. Because of their proximity to local conditions and the possible need for further hearings, the courts which originally heard these cases can best perform this judicial appraisal. Accordingly, we believe it appropriate to remand the cases to those courts.

In fashioning and effectuating the decrees, the courts will be guided by equitable principles. Traditionally, equity has been characterized by a practical flexibility in shaping its remedies and by a facility for adjusting and reconciling public and private needs. These cases call for the exercise of these traditional attributes of equity power. At stake is the personal interest of the plaintiffs in admission to public schools as soon as practicable on a nondiscriminatory basis. To effectuate this interest may call for elimination of a variety of obstacles in making the transition to school systems operated in accordance with the constitutional principles set forth in our May 17, 1954, decision. Courts of equity may properly take into account the public interest in the elimination of such obstacles in a systematic and effective manner. But it should go without saying that the vitality of these constitutional principles cannot be allowed to yield simply because of disagreement with them.

While giving weight to these public and private considerations, the courts will require that the defendants make a prompt and reasonable start toward full compliance with our May 17, 1954, ruling. Once such a start has been made, the courts may find that additional time is necessary to carry out the ruling in an effective manner. The burden rests upon the defendants to establish that such time is necessary in the public interest and is consistent with good faith compliance at the earliest practicable date. To that end, the courts may consider problems related to administration, arising from the physical condition of the school plant, the school transportation system, personnel, revision of school districts and attendance areas into compact units to achieve a system of determining admission to the public schools on a nonracial basis, and revision of local laws and regulations which may be necessary in solving the foregoing problems. They will also consider the adequacy of any plans the defendants may propose to meet these problems and to effectuate a transition to a racially nondiscriminatory school system. During this period of transition, the courts will retain jurisdiction of these cases.

The [cases are accordingly remanded to the lower courts] to take such proceedings and enter such orders and decrees consistent with this opinion as are necessary and proper to admit to public schools on a racially nondiscriminatory basis with all deliberate speed the parties to these cases. . . .

The Presidents and Vice Presidents of the United States

APPENDIX G

Year	President and Vice President	Party of President
1789–1797	**George Washington** John Adams	None
1797–1801	**John Adams** Thomas Jefferson	Federalist
1801–1809	**Thomas Jefferson** Aaron Burr (to 1805) George Clinton (to 1809)	Democratic-Republican
1809–1817	**James Madison** George Clinton (to 1813) Elbridge Gerry (to 1817)	Democratic-Republican
1817–1825	**James Monroe** Daniel D. Tompkins	Democratic-Republican
1825–1829	**John Quincy Adams** John C. Calhoun	Democratic-Republican
1829–1837	**Andrew Jackson** John C. Calhoun (to 1833) Martin Van Buren (to 1837)	Democratic
1837–1841	**Martin Van Buren** Richard M. Johnson	Democratic
1841	**William H. Harrison*** John Tyler	Whig
1841–1845	**John Tyler** (VP vacant)	Whig
1845–1849	**James K. Polk** George M. Dallas	Democratic
1849–1850	**Zachary Taylor*** Millard Fillmore	Whig
1850–1853	**Millard Fillmore** (VP vacant)	Whig
1853–1857	**Franklin Pierce** William R. King	Democratic
1857–1861	**James Buchanan** John C. Breckinridge	Democratic
1861–1865	**Abraham Lincoln*** Hannibal Hamlin (to 1865) Andrew Johnson (1865)	Republican
1865–1869	**Andrew Johnson** (VP vacant)	Democratic
1869–1877	**Ulysses S. Grant** Schuyler Colfax (to 1873) Henry Wilson (to 1877)	Republican
1877–1881	**Rutherford B. Hayes** William A. Wheeler	Republican
1881	**James A. Garfield*** Chester A. Arthur	Republican
1881–1885	**Chester A. Arthur** (VP vacant)	Republican
1885–1889	**Grover Cleveland** Thomas A. Hendricks	Democratic
1889–1893	**Benjamin Harrison** Levi P. Morton	Republican
1893–1897	**Grover Cleveland** Adlai E. Stevenson	Democratic
1897–1901	**William McKinley*** Garret A. Hobart (to 1901) Theodore Roosevelt (1901)	Republican
1901–1909	**Theodore Roosevelt** (VP vacant, 1901–1905) Charles W. Fairbanks (1905–1909)	Republican
1909–1913	**William Howard Taft** James S. Sherman	Republican
1913–1921	**Woodrow Wilson** Thomas R. Marshall	Democratic
1921–1923	**Warren G. Harding*** Calvin Coolidge	Republican

532

Year	President and Vice President	Party of President	Year	President and Vice President	Party of President
1923–1929	**Calvin Coolidge** (VP vacant, 1923–1925) Charles G. Dawes (1925–1929)	Republican	1969–1974	**Richard M. Nixon**[†] Spiro T. Agnew[‡] (1969–1973) Gerald R. Ford[§] (1973–1974)	Republican
1929–1933	**Herbert Hoover** Charles Curtis	Republican	1974–1977	**Gerald R. Ford** Nelson A. Rockefeller[§]	Republican
1933–1945	**Franklin D. Roosevelt**[*] John N. Garner (1933–1941) Henry A. Wallace (1941–1945) Harry S. Truman (1945)	Democratic	1977–1981	**Jimmy Carter** Walter Mondale	Democratic
			1981–1989	**Ronald Reagan** George Bush	Republican
1945–1953	**Harry S. Truman** (VP vacant, 1945–1949) Alben W. Barkley (1949–1953)	Democratic	1989–1993	**George Bush** J. Danforth Quayle	Republican
1953–1961	**Dwight D. Eisenhower** Richard M. Nixon	Republican	1993–2001	**William J. Clinton** Albert Gore, Jr.	Democratic
1961–1963	**John F. Kennedy**[*] Lyndon B. Johnson	Democratic	2001–	**George W. Bush** Richard Cheney	Republican
1963–1969	**Lyndon B. Johnson** (VP vacant, 1963–1965) Hubert H. Humphrey (1965–1969)	Democratic			

[*]Died in office.

[†]Resigned from the presidency.

[‡]Resigned from the vice presidency.

[§]Appointed vice president.

APPENDIX

H

Presidential Election Results, 1789–2004

Year	Candidates	Party	Popular Vote	Electoral Vote
1789	**George Washington**			69
	John Adams			34
	Others			35
1792	**George Washington**			132
	John Adams			77
	George Clinton			50
	Others			5
1796	**John Adams**	Federalist		71
	Thomas Jefferson	Democratic-Republican		68
	Thomas Pinckney	Federalist		59
	Aaron Burr	Democratic-Republican		30
	Others			48
1800	**Thomas Jefferson**	Democratic-Republican		73
	Aaron Burr	Democratic-Republican		73
	John Adams	Federalist		65
	Charles C. Pinckney	Federalist		64
1804	**Thomas Jefferson**	Democratic-Republican		162
	Charles C. Pinckney	Federalist		14
1808	**James Madison**	Democratic-Republican		122
	Charles C. Pinckney	Federalist		47
	George Clinton	Independent-Republican		6
1812	**James Madison**	Democratic-Republican		128
	DeWitt Clinton	Federalist		89
1816	**James Monroe**	Democratic-Republican		183
	Rufus King	Federalist		34
1820	**James Monroe**	Democratic-Republican		231
	John Quincy Adams	Independent-Republican		1
1824	**John Quincy Adams***	Democratic-Republican	108,740 (30.5%)	84
	Andrew Jackson	Democratic-Republican	153,544 (43.1%)	99
	Henry Clay	Democratic-Republican	47,136 (13.2%)	37
	William H. Crawford	Democratic-Republican	46,618 (13.1%)	41
1828	**Andrew Jackson**	Democratic	647,231 (56.0%)	178
	John Quincy Adams	National Republican	509,097 (44.0%)	83

Year	Candidates	Party	Popular Vote	Electoral Vote
1832	**Andrew Jackson**	Democratic	687,502 (55.0%)	219
	Henry Clay	National Republican	530,189 (42.4%)	49
	William Wirt	Anti-Masonic		7
	John Floyd	National Republican	33,108 (2.6%)	11
1836	**Martin Van Buren**	Democratic	761,549 (50.9%)	170
	William H. Harrison	Whig	549,567 (36.7%)	73
	Hugh L. White	Whig	145,396 (9.7%)	26
	Daniel Webster	Whig	41,287 (2.7%)	14
1840	**William H. Harrison**	Whig	1,275,017 (53.1%)	234
	Martin Van Buren	Democratic	1,128,702 (46.9%)	60
1844	**James K. Polk**	Democratic	1,337,243 (49.6%)	170
	Henry Clay	Whig	1,299,068 (48.1%)	105
	James G. Birney	Liberty	63,300 (2.3%)	0
1848	**Zachary Taylor**	Whig	1,360,101 (47.4%)	163
	Lewis Cass	Democratic	1,220,544 (42.5%)	127
	Martin Van Buren	Free Soil	291,163 (10.1%)	0
1852	**Franklin Pierce**	Democratic	1,601,474 (50.9%)	254
	Winfield Scott	Whig	1,386,578 (44.1%)	42
1856	**James Buchanan**	Democratic	1,838,169 (45.4%)	174
	John C. Fremont	Republican	1,335,264 (33.0%)	114
	Millard Fillmore	American	874,534 (21.6%)	8
1860	**Abraham Lincoln**	Republican	1,865,593 (39.8%)	180
	Stephen A. Douglas	Democratic	1,381,713 (29.5%)	12
	John C. Breckinridge	Democratic	848,356 (18.1%)	72
	John Bell	Constitutional Union	592,906 (12.6%)	79
1864	**Abraham Lincoln**	Republican	2,206,938 (55.0%)	212
	George B. McClellan	Democratic	1,803,787 (45.0%)	21
1868	**Ulysses S. Grant**	Republican	3,013,421 (52.7%)	214
	Horatio Seymour	Democratic	2,706,829 (47.3%)	80
1872	**Ulysses S. Grant**	Republican	3,596,745 (55.6%)	286
	Horace Greeley	Democratic	2,843,446 (43.9%)	66
1876	**Rutherford B. Hayes**	Republican	4,036,571 (48.0%)	185
	Samuel J. Tilden[†]	Democratic	4,284,020 (51.0%)	184
1880	**James A. Garfield**	Republican	4,449,053 (48.3%)	214
	Winfield S. Hancock	Democratic	4,442,035 (48.2%)	155
	James B. Weaver	Greenback-Labor	308,578 (3.4%)	0
1884	**Grover Cleveland**	Democratic	4,874,986 (48.5%)	219
	James G. Blaine	Republican	4,851,931 (48.2%)	182
	Benjamin F. Butler	Greenback-Labor	175,370 (1.8%)	0
1888	**Benjamin Harrison**	Republican	5,444,337 (47.8%)	233
	Grover Cleveland[†]	Democratic	5,540,050 (48.6%)	168
1892	**Grover Cleveland**	Democratic	5,554,414 (46.0%)	277
	Benjamin Harrison	Republican	5,190,802 (43.0%)	145
	James B. Weaver	People's	1,027,329 (8.5%)	22

Table continues ▶

▶ *Table continued*

Year	Candidates	Party	Popular Vote	Electoral Vote
1896	**William McKinley**	Republican	7,035,638 (50.8%)	271
	William J. Bryan	Democratic; Populist	6,467,946 (46.7%)	176
1900	**William McKinley**	Republican	7,219,530 (51.7%)	292
	William J. Bryan	Democratic; Populist	6,356,734 (45.5%)	155
1904	**Theodore Roosevelt**	Republican	7,628,834 (56.4%)	336
	Alton B. Parker	Democratic	5,084,401 (37.6%)	140
	Eugene V. Debs	Socialist	402,460 (3.0%)	0
1908	**William H. Taft**	Republican	7,679,006 (51.6%)	321
	William J. Bryan	Democratic	6,409,106 (43.1%)	162
	Eugene V. Debs	Socialist	420,820 (2.8%)	0
1912	**Woodrow Wilson**	Democratic	6,286,820 (41.8%)	435
	Theodore Roosevelt	Progressive	4,126,020 (27.4%)	88
	William H. Taft	Republican	3,483,922 (23.2%)	8
	Eugene V. Debs	Socialist	897,011 (6.0%)	0
1916	**Woodrow Wilson**	Democratic	9,129,606 (49.3%)	277
	Charles E. Hughes	Republican	8,538,211 (46.1%)	254
1920	**Warren G. Harding**	Republican	16,152,200 (61.0%)	404
	James M. Cox	Democratic	9,147,353 (34.6%)	127
	Eugene V. Debs	Socialist	919,799 (3.5%)	0
1924	**Calvin Coolidge**	Republican	15,725,016 (54.1%)	382
	John W. Davis	Democratic	8,385,586 (28.8%)	136
	Robert M. La Follette	Progressive	4,822,856 (16.6%)	13
1928	**Herbert C. Hoover**	Republican	21,392,190 (58.2%)	444
	Alfred E. Smith	Democratic	15,016,443 (40.8%)	87
1932	**Franklin D. Roosevelt**	Democratic	22,809,638 (57.3%)	472
	Herbert C. Hoover	Republican	15,758,901 (39.6%)	59
	Norman Thomas	Socialist	881,951 (2.2%)	0
1936	**Franklin D. Roosevelt**	Democratic	27,751,612 (60.7%)	523
	Alfred M. Landon	Republican	16,681,913 (36.4%)	8
	William Lemke	Union	891,858 (1.9%)	0
1940	**Franklin D. Roosevelt**	Democratic	27,243,466 (54.7%)	449
	Wendell L. Wilkie	Republican	22,304,755 (44.8%)	82
1944	**Franklin D. Roosevelt**	Democratic	25,602,505 (52.8%)	432
	Thomas E. Dewey	Republican	22,006,278 (44.5%)	99
1948	**Harry S. Truman**	Democratic	24,105,812 (49.5%)	303
	Thomas E. Dewey	Republican	21,970,065 (45.1%)	189
	J. Strom Thurmond	States' Rights	1,169,063 (2.4%)	39
	Henry A. Wallace	Progressive	1,157,172 (2.4%)	0

Year	Candidates	Party	Popular Vote	Electoral Vote
1952	**Dwight D. Eisenhower**	Republican	33,936,234 (55.2%)	442
	Adlai E. Stevenson	Democratic	27,314,992 (44.5%)	89
1956	**Dwight D. Eisenhower**	Republican	35,590,472 (57.4%)	457
	Adlai E. Stevenson	Democratic	26,022,752 (42.0%)	73
1960	**John F. Kennedy**	Democratic	34,227,096 (49.9%)	303
	Richard M. Nixon	Republican	34,108,546 (49.6%)	219
1964	**Lyndon B. Johnson**	Democratic	43,126,233 (61.1%)	486
	Barry M. Goldwater	Republican	27,174,989 (38.5%)	52
1968	**Richard M. Nixon**	Republican	31,783,783 (43.4%)	301
	Hubert H. Humphrey	Democratic	31,271,839 (42.7%)	191
	George C. Wallace	American Independent	9,899,557 (13.5%)	46
1972	**Richard M. Nixon**	Republican	46,632,189 (61.3%)	520
	George McGovern	Democratic	28,422,015 (37.3%)	17
1976	**Jimmy Carter**	Democratic	40,828,587 (50.1%)	297
	Gerald R. Ford	Republican	39,147,613 (48.0%)	240
1980	**Ronald Reagan**	Republican	42,941,145 (50.7%)	489
	Jimmy Carter	Democratic	34,663,037 (41.0%)	49
	John B. Anderson	Independent	5,551,551 (6.6%)	0
1984	**Ronald Reagan**	Republican	53,428,357 (58.8%)	525
	Walter F. Mondale	Democratic	36,930,923 (40.6%)	13
1988	**George Bush**	Republican	48,881,011 (53.4%)	426
	Michael Dukakis	Democratic	41,828,350 (45.6%)	111
1992	**Bill Clinton**	Democratic	44,908,233 (43.0%)	370
	George Bush	Republican	39,102,282 (37.4%)	168
	Ross Perot	Independent	19,741,048 (18.9%)	0
1996	**Bill Clinton**	Democratic	45,628,667 (49.2%)	379
	Robert Dole	Republican	37,869,435 (40.8%)	159
	Ross Perot	Reform	7,874,283 (8.5%)	0
2000	**George W. Bush**	Republican	50,456,141 (47.87%)	271
	Albert Gore[†]	Democrat	50,996,039 (48.38%)	266
	Ralph Nader	Green	2,882,807 (2.73%)	0
2004	**George W. Bush**	Republican	62,008,619 (50.7%)[‡]	286
	John F. Kerry	Democrat	59,012,107 (48.3%)	252

*Decided by a vote of the House of Representatives.

[†]Popular vote winner.

[‡]Preliminary totals.

Party Control of the Senate and House of Representatives, 1901–2007

Congress	Years	President	Senate			House		
			D	R	Other*	D	R	Other*
57th	1901–1903	McKinley T. Roosevelt	29	56	3	153	198	5
58th	1903–1905	T. Roosevelt	32	58	—	178	207	—
59th	1905–1907	T. Roosevelt	32	58	—	136	250	—
60th	1907–1909	T. Roosevelt	29	61	—	164	222	—
61st	1909–1911	Taft	32	59	—	172	219	—
62nd	1911–1913	Taft	42	49	—	228‡	162	1
63rd	1913–1915	Wilson	51	44	1	290	127	18
64th	1915–1917	Wilson	56	39	1	231	193	8
65th	1917–1919	Wilson	53	42	1	210	216	9
66th	1919–1921	Wilson	47	48‡	1	191	237‡	7
67th	1921–1923	Harding	37	59	—	132	300	1
68th	1923–1925	Coolidge	43	51	2	207	225	3
69th	1925–1927	Coolidge	40	54	1	183	247	5
70th	1927–1929	Coolidge	47	48	1	195	237	3
71st	1929–1931	Hoover	39	56	1	163	267	1
72nd	1931–1933	Hoover	47	48	1	216	218	1
73rd	1933–1935	F. Roosevelt	59	36	1	313	117	5
74th	1935–1937	F. Roosevelt	69	25	2	322	103	10
75th	1937–1939	F. Roosevelt	75	17	4	333	89	13
76th	1939–1941	F. Roosevelt	69	23	4	262	169	4
77th	1941–1943	F. Roosevelt	66	28	2	267	162	6

Congress	Years	President	Senate			House		
			D	R	Other*	D	R	Other*
78th	1943–1945	F. Roosevelt	57	38	1	222	209	4
79th	1945–1947	Truman	57	38	1	243	190	2
80th	1947–1949	Truman	45	51‡	—	188	246‡	1
81st	1949–1951	Truman	54	42	—	263	171	1
82nd	1951–1953	Truman	48	47	1	234	199	2
83rd	1953–1955	Eisenhower	46	48	2	213	221	1
84th	1955–1957	Eisenhower	48‡	47	1	232‡	203	—
85th	1957–1959	Eisenhower	49‡	47	—	234‡	201	—
86th†	1959–1961	Eisenhower	64‡	34	—	283‡	154	—
87th	1961–1963	Kennedy	64	36	—	262	175	—
88th	1963–1965	Kennedy Johnson	67	33	—	258	176	—
89th	1965–1967	Johnson	68	32	—	295	140	—
90th	1967–1969	Johnson	64	36	—	248	187	—
91st	1969–1971	Nixon	58‡	42	—	243‡	192	—
92nd	1971–1973	Nixon	54‡	44	2	255‡	180	—
93rd	1973–1975	Nixon Ford	56‡	42	2	242‡	192	—
94th	1975–1977	Ford	61‡	37	2	291‡	144	—
95th	1977–1979	Carter	61	38	1	292	143	—
96th	1979–1981	Carter	58	41	1	277	158	—
97th	1981–1983	Reagan	46	53	1	243‡	192	—
98th	1983–1985	Reagan	46	54	—	268‡	167	—
99th	1985–1987	Reagan	47	53	—	253‡	182	—
100th	1987–1989	Reagan	55‡	45	—	258‡	177	—
101st	1989–1991	Bush (senior)	55‡	45	—	260‡	175	—
102nd	1991–1993	Bush (senior)	56‡	44	—	267‡	167	1
103rd	1993–1995	Clinton	57	43	—	258	176	1
104th	1995–1997	Clinton	47	53‡		204	230‡	1
105th	1997–1999	Clinton	45	55‡	—	207	227‡	1
106th	1999–2001	Clinton	45	55‡	—	211	223	1
107th	2001–2003	Bush, G.W.	50	49	1	212	221	2
108th	2003–2005	Bush, G.W.	48	51	1	205	229	1
109th	2005–2007	Bush, G.W.	44	55	1	202	232	1

*Excludes vacancies at beginning of each session and reflects distribution of seats immediately following election.

†The 437 members of the House in the 86th and 87th Congresses are attributable to the at-large representative given to both Alaska (January 3, 1959) and Hawaii (August 21, 1959) prior to redistricting in 1962.

‡Chamber controlled by party other than that of the president.

Twentieth-Century Justices of the Supreme Court

Name	Nominated by	Service	Name	Nominated by	Service
John M. Harlan	Hayes	1877–1911	William O. Douglas	F. Roosevelt	1939–1975
Horace Gray	Arthur	1882–1902	Frank Murphy	F. Roosevelt	1940–1949
Melville W. Fuller	Cleveland	1888–1910	**Harlan F. Stone**	F. Roosevelt	1941–1946
David J. Brewer	Harrison	1890–1910	James F. Byrnes	F. Roosevelt	1941–1942
Henry B. Brown	Harrison	1890–1906	Robert H. Jackson	F. Roosevelt	1941–1954
George Shiras, Jr.	Harrison	1892–1903	Wiley B. Rutledge	F. Roosevelt	1943–1949
Edward D. White	Cleveland	1894–1910	Harold H. Burton	Truman	1945–1958
Rufus W. Peckham	Cleveland	1895–1909	**Fred M. Vinson**	Truman	1946–1953
Joseph McKenna	McKinley	1898–1925	Tom C. Clark	Truman	1949–1967
Oliver W. Holmes	T. Roosevelt	1902–1932	Sherman Minton	Truman	1949–1956
William R. Day	T. Roosevelt	1903–1922	**Earl Warren**	Eisenhower	1953–1969
William H. Moody	T. Roosevelt	1906–1910	John M. Harlan	Eisenhower	1955–1971
Horace H. Lurton	Taft	1910–1914	William J. Brennan, Jr.	Eisenhower	1956–1990
Edward D. White	Taft	1910–1921	Charles E. Whittaker	Eisenhower	1957–1962
Charles E. Hughes	Taft	1910–1916	Potter Stewart	Eisenhower	1958–1981
Willis Van Devanter	Taft	1911–1937	Byron R. White	Kennedy	1962–1993
Joseph R. Lamar	Taft	1911–1916	Arthur J. Goldberg	Kennedy	1962–1965
Mahlon Pitney	Taft	1912–1922	Abe Fortas	Johnson	1965–1969
James C. McReynolds	Wilson	1914–1941	Thurgood Marshall	Johnson	1967–1991
Louis D. Brandeis	Wilson	1916–1939	**Warren E. Burger**	Nixon	1969–1986
John H. Clarke	Wilson	1916–1922	Harry A. Blackmun	Nixon	1970–1994
William H. Taft	Harding	1921–1930	Lewis F. Powell, Jr.	Nixon	1971–1987
George Sutherland	Harding	1922–1938	William H. Rehnquist	Nixon	1971–1986
Pierce Butler	Harding	1922–1939	John Paul Stevens	Ford	1975–
Edward T. Sanford	Harding	1923–1930	Sandra Day O'Connor	Reagan	1981–
Harlan F. Stone	Coolidge	1925–1941	**William H. Rehnquist**	Reagan	1986–
Charles E. Hughes	Hoover	1930–1941	Antonin Scalia	Reagan	1986–
Owen J. Roberts	Hoover	1930–1945	Anthony M. Kennedy	Reagan	1988–
Benjamin N. Cardozo	Hoover	1932–1938	David H. Souter	Bush	1990–
Hugo L. Black	F. Roosevelt	1937–1971	Clarence Thomas	Bush	1991–
Stanley F. Reed	F. Roosevelt	1938–1957	Ruth Bader Ginsburg	Clinton	1993–
Felix Frankfurter	F. Roosevelt	1939–1962	Stephen G. Breyer	Clinton	1994–

Note: Boldface type indicates service as chief justice.

Glossary

A

access The ability to maintain personal contact with public officials. Many lobbying strategies depend on maintaining an open door to contacts in the legislative and executive branches.

administration The bureaucratic function of tending to the details of executing public policy.

administrative presidency A strategic approach to the bureaucracy relying on ideological political appointees and tight presidential management to combat the tendency for political appointees to "go native."

affective Existing in the realm of emotion or feeling.

affirmative action Federal policies requiring employers to address inequities in hiring and advancement if they appear to unfairly treat disadvantaged groups on the basis of race, religion, gender, national origin, sexual preference, physical disabilities, or Vietnam veteran status.

Age Discrimination in Employment Act The 1967 law that made it illegal for employers to discriminate against people over age forty in hiring, firing, and promotion decisions.

agenda setting The tendency for topics given great weight by the media to be given equally great weight by those who use the media, such that the people and events considered important by those who determine media coverage will become the people and events that the public considers important.

agents of socialization External influences that shape the way we are socialized to politics, including parents and siblings in the home, friends and coworkers outside the home, and institutions like schools and the media.

Aid to Families with Dependent Children (AFDC) The original federal welfare program, developed during the Great Depression as part of the New Deal, which extended subsistence benefits to families with children living below the poverty line.

Americans with Disabilities Act The landmark 1990 legislation extending equal protection in the workplace and in public accommodations to people with physical and mental disabilities.

amicus curiae Briefs filed by interested parties to a case, whose opinions are offered in an effort to shape the Court's discussion and judgment.

apathy A sense of indifference to or lack of interest in politics.

appellate jurisdiction The authority of a high court to hear cases only after the cases originate in and are appealed from a lower court.

apprenticeship The legislative norm that says freshmen members of Congress should limit their activity and defer to senior members as they learn the ways of the institution. Apprenticeship is no longer enforced in Congress.

appropriations Legislation permitting the government to spend money that determines how much will be spent and how it will be spent.

Articles of Confederation The first constitution of the United States, which created a loosely functioning national government to which the individual states were supreme. It addressed concerns about a strong national government undermining individual liberty, but it created a national government that was unable to regulate commerce or conduct foreign policy and was abandoned in favor of the United States Constitution just eight years after it was ratified.

attack journalism A form of aggressive coverage in which reporters latch onto an allegation of misdoing by a candidate or public official and engage in a "feeding frenzy" in which they cover it intensely and to the exclusion of other news.

attitudes A component of public opinion that measures people's orientations toward politics.

authority The right to act in an official capacity by virtue of holding an office like president or member of Congress.

B

backgrounders Off-the-record exchanges between the president or administration officials and reporters. Whatever a reporter learns at a backgrounder can be used in a story, but the source of the information cannot be revealed.

balance of trade Equilibrium between the value of imports and exports.

beliefs A component of public opinion that measures what people think is true about politics.

bicameral A legislature composed of two houses.

Bill of Rights The first ten amendments to the Constitution, which limit government from denying us a range of personal liberties.

bills of attainder Declarations of guilt by legislative decree without benefit of a trial.

Black Codes An effort by white southerners immediately following the Civil War to restrict the civil rights of emancipated slaves. The codes were overturned by federal civil rights laws, only to become standard practice in the South following Reconstruction.

Boston Massacre A precursor to the war that was still five years away, it was the first mortal conflict between colonists and British troops in Boston and resulted in the deaths of five colonists in 1770.

Boston Tea Party A protest against the Tea Act of 1773 in which fifty colonists dressed as Native Americans boarded British trade ships loaded with tea and threw the contents into the water.

Brown v. Board of Education The landmark 1954 Supreme Court case that declared racial segregation unconstitutional, overturning the Court's ruling in *Plessy v. Ferguson.*

Budget and Accounting Act of 1921 The act providing the legal basis for presidential participation in the budget process, by requiring the president to submit an annual budget to Congress for its consideration.

bureaucracy Another name for the executive branch of government, the institutional component of the presidency, which is charged with carrying out laws passed by Congress.

Bush v. Gore The controversial 2000 Supreme Court case in which a sharply divided Court ended manual ballot recounts in Florida, following which George W. Bush became president.

C

cabinet The name given to the collection of secretaries of the executive departments. Despite commonly held beliefs to the contrary, the cabinet rarely serves as an advisory body to the president.

casework Service performed by members of Congress for constituents with individual problems or complaints that they would like the government to address.

caucus A method of candidate selection in which party identifiers gather in a series of meetings to select delegates to the national convention.

census An accounting or, as Article I Section 2 of the Constitution puts it, an "actual Enumeration" of the residents of the United States, taken every ten years by constitutional decree to assess population growth and population shifts. Census figures are used to determine representation in Congress, as states that lose population between censuses stand to lose House seats to states that gain population.

checks and balances The ability of any one of several equal and independent branches of government to keep the others from acting, designed to prevent power from being consolidated in any one branch. Because any branch can put a check on the others, government can only act when there is cooperation between the branches, a situation that necessitates compromise.

chief diplomat A constitutional role of the president, in which he has the power to recognize ambassadors from other nations.

chief executive The role the president plays as head of the executive branch, in which he carries out the constitutional directive to "take Care that the Laws be faithfully executed."

chief legislator The role the president plays when he offers a legislative agenda and attempts to win congressional approval for it.

chief of staff One of the president's top political advisors and the formal head of the White House staff.

chief of state The role the president plays as ceremonial head of the United States.

Citizenship Act of 1924 An effort to assimilate Native Americans into white culture and society through the granting of American citizenship.

civic responsibility A sense of duty or obligation to society that some people believe comes along with citizenship.

civil disobedience A peaceful means of protest whereby individuals draw attention to laws they consider unjust by disobeying them and being arrested for their actions.

civil liberties Constitutional and legal protections against government infringement on a host of personal freedoms.

civil rights The promise of equal treatment under the law, regardless of one's race, gender, ethnic group affiliation, sexual preference, or age.

Civil Rights Act of 1964 Landmark legislation arising from the civil rights movement that made racial discrimination a federal crime in the workplace and in public accommodations, while giving the federal government greater power to strengthen voting rights and desegregate public schools.

civil rights movement The organized, largely nonviolent, and widely successful efforts of the 1950s and 1960s to bring about social change on behalf of African Americans in the South, whose civil rights were denied by a century-old system of Jim Crow laws.

civil servants Career employees who staff the bureaucracy in a wide range of positions and who get their jobs independent of political considerations.

Civil Service Commission The commission established by the Pendleton Act to oversee the hiring of career civil servants.

classical liberalism A term given to the philosophy of John Locke and other seventeenth- and eighteenth-century advocates of the protection of individual rights and liberties by limiting government power.

clear and present danger The standard established by Justice Oliver Wendell Holmes for determining when the government could limit speech.

cloture The procedure for ending a filibuster. A cloture vote requires a 60 percent majority of the Senate.

coalition A government formed as a partnership among several victorious parties in a multiparty system, following negotiations about the agenda that each party will be allowed to pursue in exchange for its participation in the new government.

coattails The ability of a victorious presidential candidate to sweep congressional candidates of the same party into office on the strength of people voting for one political party.

Coercive Acts Called the Intolerable Acts in the colonies, the Coercive Acts represented the British attempt to clamp down on the colonies following the Boston Tea Party.

cognitive A factual awareness or appreciation of someone or something. Cognition implies knowledge and the ability to exercise judgment. This is why we would say that a young child's understanding of the president is not cognitive because kids' awareness of the president as an important figure lacks appreciation of what the president does and why he is important.

collective goods Benefits stemming from the work of an interest group that are available to everyone, whether or not they join the group.

commander-in-chief The president's constitutional role as civilian leader of the armed forces.

committee chair The member of Congress responsible for running a committee, who can have great influence over the committee agenda and, by extension, the legislative process.

Communications Decency Act of 1996 A legislative attempt to regulate the transmission of "offensive" or "indecent" material over the Internet. The Supreme Court overturned most of the provisions of the Communications Decency Act.

Communications Office The White House office responsible for coordinating the president's media operations, including speechwriting and liaison with national and local reporters.

comparable worth A manner of determining pay equity by equalizing pay between jobs held mostly by women that demand comparable training and labor to jobs held mostly by men.

competitive regulatory policy A type of regulatory policy designed to protect the public interest by restricting the provision of a service or good to organizations that win federal licensing approval.

compromise A form of reciprocity in which members of Congress exhibit flexibility over their legislative objectives in exchange for future flexibility from their colleagues.

concurring opinion A statement issued by a justice who agrees with a vote of the Court but differs on the legal or constitutional rationale for the majority decision.

confederal system An arrangement for establishing a government out of a set of component states, in which the national government is the creation of the states and subservient to them. The Articles of Confederation established a system like this in the United States. In today's world, the United Nations may be the most prominent example of a confederation.

conference committee A committee made up of members of both houses of Congress, assembled when the House and Senate pass different versions of the same legislation. If the conference committee can iron out the differences, a compromise version of the legislation is sent back to both houses for final passage. If it cannot arrive at a compromise, the legislation dies.

Congressional Budget and Impoundment Control Act of 1974 An act designed to centralize the congressional budgeting process, which established current procedures and timetables for writing a budget.

Connecticut Compromise A compromise between the Virginia and New Jersey Plans that broke the deadlock over representation at the Constitutional Convention by providing for a bicameral legislature. Large states would get their demand for representation based on population in the House of Representatives, while every state, regardless of size, would have two senators, which pleased small states.

conservatism An ideology that advocates limits on government power to address economic and social problems, relying instead on economic markets and individual initiative to address problems like health care and education, while promoting government involvement in moral matters to, for instance, minimize or eliminate abortions or permit prayer in public schools.

constituents Individuals living in a district represented by an elected official.

Constitutional Convention A meeting of representatives from twelve of the thirteen states held in Philadelphia in 1787, which produced the federal system of government outlined in the United States Constitution.

constructionists Those who hold to the judicial philosophy that the Constitution should be interpreted strictly and literally, and in the context in which it was written.

cooperative federalism One of several perspectives on federalism, popular during the first two-thirds of the twentieth century, which was defined by joint endeavors between the federal and state governments. Typically, state governments would carry out federal initiatives, using federal money and federal guidelines.

courtesy The legislative norm that members of Congress should treat each other with respect and avoid personal attacks, regardless of how much they may disagree.

critical election An election that heralds a realignment, during which large numbers of voters deviate from their traditional party allegiances in what turns out to be a lasting change.

cue taking Looking to other members of Congress for guidelines on how to cast a vote on a technical or unfamiliar matter.

cynicism A pervasive attitude of mistrust about politics that may lead people to withdraw from political participation.

D

dealignment The weakening of party affiliation, signified by an increase in the number of people who call themselves independents.

Declaration of Independence The document drafted by Thomas Jefferson and approved by the Continental Congress in July 1776, stating the reasons for the Revolutionary War and declaring a formal break with Great Britain.

deficit The gap created in the federal budget when the government takes in less than it spends in a given year.

delegate A philosophy of representation that says officials are elected to carry out constituent interests, even when these interests conflict with what the representative believes is the right thing to do.

democracy A government created by the people over whom it rules.

deregulation The lifting of federal regulations that had been previously imposed on private industry.

diplomatic recognition Formal acceptance of the legitimacy of another nation or its representatives.

direct democracy Democracy without representation, where each eligible individual participates in decision making.

directional An aspect of public opinion that measures whether people feel favorably or unfavorably toward a political figure, institution, or policy.

discharge petition A House procedure that forces a floor vote on legislation stalled in committee. To succeed, a discharge petition must be signed by half the House membership.

disenfranchised Losing or being denied the legal right to vote by intentional or unintentional means.

dissenting opinion A statement issued by a justice who disagrees with a vote of the Court, offering a legal or constitutional rationale for that disagreement.

distributive policies Domestic policies primarily aimed at directing tax money to a range of public works items. Distributive policies tend not to be controversial because benefits are widely shared.

divided government Partisan division of the national government, in which each of the two major parties can claim control of one branch (or one legislative house) of the federal government.

docket The list of cases pending before a court.

double jeopardy Protection against the state using its power to repeatedly prosecute someone until the person is convicted. Double jeopardy precludes the prosecution of someone for the same crime in the same jurisdiction more than once.

Dred Scott v. Sanford The 1857 Supreme Court case that legalized slavery nationwide, while holding that people of color had no rights or protection under the Constitution. The ruling hastened the Civil War; it was subsequently overturned by constitutional amendment.

dual federalism One of several perspectives on federalism, popular during the early years of the republic, which stated that the federal and state governments operated concurrently in separate arenas, and that each had the final say in those areas where it had a clear grant of authority.

due process The protection of individual liberty from the arbitrary or capricious actions of government through a defined set of legal procedures designed to protect the rights of the accused.

E

Earned Income Tax Credit A negative income tax for low-income families, who receive rather than make cash payments when they file their income tax returns.

economic equality A form of equality of outcome that values using government policy to minimize the economic disparities found in society.

efficacy The attitude that you can be effectual and effective in your dealings with government.

electorate The portion of the public eligible to vote in elections.

elitism The theory that government responds to a small, stable, centralized hierarchy of corporate and academic leaders, military chiefs, people who own big media outlets, and members of a permanent government bureaucracy. People who subscribe to this position believe the actions of regular citizens, like voting and joining groups, simply mask the real power exercised by elites.

empirical Any statement based on the assessment of data or the analysis of information, without regard to value judgments.

entitlements Social welfare programs targeted to specific groups of individuals, like senior citizens or the unemployed. Benefits are available to all who meet the program requirements, although some entitlements for the poor impose a means test.

enumerated powers Powers directly granted to Congress by the Constitution.

equal protection clause The constitutional restriction against state laws that discriminate, as stated in the Fourteenth Amendment. The equal protection clause served as the legal basis for eliminating laws that permitted racial discrimination.

Equal Rights Amendment (ERA) A proposed constitutional amendment assuring equal rights for women that was first introduced in Congress in 1923, approved by Congress in 1972, and fell three states short of ratification in 1982.

equal time provision The federal requirement that broadcast outlets selling commercial time to a political candidate must make equal time available to other candidates running for office.

equality of opportunity One of several ways of understanding equality, this way values giving people comparable advantages for succeeding in life, regardless of the unequal outcomes that may result.

equality of outcome One of several ways of understanding equality, this way values leveling the social and economic inequities among people, rather than attempting to give people comparable advantages for succeeding in life.

establishment clause The language in the First Amendment that serves as the basis for the constitutional separation of church and state.

European Union (EU) The framework for integrating previously disparate European economies into a single market.

ex post facto laws From the Latin for "after the fact," legislation that makes something a crime that was legal when it occurred.

exclusionary rule To protect against unreasonable searches and seizures, the Supreme Court has established that evidence obtained illegally is not admissible in court.

executive agreements Legally binding presidential agreements with other nations that do not require congressional approval.

executive branch The institutional component of the branch of government we think of as the presidency, charged with carrying out laws passed by Congress. Sometimes, the executive branch is referred to as the bureaucracy.

Executive Office of the President (EOP) The large staff of advisors to the president that comprises the president's political and policy operation.

executive orders Presidential directives to the bureaucracy that are legally binding and do not require congressional approval.

executive privilege The power of the president, established by custom, to keep Congress, the courts, and the public from having access to presidential documents and communications.

expectations The benchmark for how well a campaign needs to perform in presidential primaries in order to receive positive horserace coverage, based on reporter assessments of the campaign's viability.

F

faction A group of individuals who are united by a desire that, if realized, would threaten the liberty of the larger community—in James Madison's words, individuals who are "united and actuated by some common impulse of passion, or of interest, adverse to the rights of other citizens, or to the permanent and aggregate interests of the community." A faction may be defined by size, such as when a majority of citizens threatens the liberty of the minority, or by intensity, such as when a minority of citizens with intensely held preferences threatens the liberty of a disinterested majority.

Fair Deal The name given to the domestic policies of President Harry S Truman, which built on the popularity of the New Deal.

fairness doctrine The FCC requirement, no longer in force, that electronic media provide a balanced forum for controversial public discourse.

faithless elector A member of the Electoral College who does not cast a vote for the plurality winner of the popular vote in his or her state.

Family and Medical Leave Act of 1993 Legislation designed to permit women working in medium or large companies up to twelve weeks of unpaid leave following childbirth. It also permits employees to take unpaid leave time to care for an ailing relative.

fascism A militant, ultra-nationalistic ideology of the extreme right that rejects liberal ideas about personal rights.

Federal Communications Act of 1934 The act of Congress that established the Federal Communications Commission (FCC) and the equal time provision.

Federal Communications Commission (FCC) The federal agency responsible for regulating broadcast communications, including radio, television, wire, satellite, and cable transmissions. The FCC is directed by five commissioners who are appointed by the president and confirmed by the Senate for five-year terms.

Federal Election Campaign Act The 1974 act aimed at limiting the influence of big-money contributions on political campaigns.

Federal Election Commission (FEC) The federal regulatory agency that administers and enforces campaign finance laws.

Federal Register A publicly available list of all proposed and existing federal regulations.

federal system The arrangement created by the United States Constitution, in which the national government and the states share authority over citizens. States may act autonomously to do such things as create school districts, levy taxes, or assemble a police force; at the same time, powers are reserved for the national government, which is supreme to state laws. In addition to the United States, only Canada, Germany, India, and a small group of other nations have federal systems.

Federal Wage System (FWS) The system used to determine salaries for blue-collar civil servants.

federalism The division of power between a sovereign federal government and sovereign state governments, which provides that some functions will be performed by the national government, some by the state governments, and some by both the national and state governments. As a feature designed to limit the strength of government, federalism works to decentralize power by creating dual levels of authority.

The Federalist A collection of essays written by Alexander Hamilton, James Madison, and John Jay in an effort to persuade a reluctant public to support the Constitution.

filibuster The strategy available to senators to delay or derail legislation by refusing to relinquish their time on the Senate floor. The filibuster is possible only in the Senate, where rules permit unlimited time for debate.

fireside chats The term given to Franklin Roosevelt's radio addresses to the American public, which demonstrated Roosevelt's ability to master the medium and build a sense of rapport with ordinary Americans.

First Continental Congress A gathering of representatives from twelve of the thirteen colonies in Philadelphia in 1774 to protest the Coercive Acts and chart a unified colonial response.

flat tax A proportional tax that would set the tax rate equally for all taxpayers, regardless of their income level.

focus groups A small group of voters chosen by a political campaign for their demographic similarities who are brought together to gauge how the group they represent feels about the candidate.

food stamps A federal program designed to fight malnutrition among people in need by defraying the cost of food.

frame The frame of reference for a news story, or the context around which the facts of a story are organized. If a news story is thematic, like most television news stories, the frame determines what the specific theme of the story will be.

free exercise clause The language in the First Amendment that limits government interference in private religious beliefs and practices.

free media The news coverage that major candidates for high office can expect to receive on a regular basis. Although free, candidates cannot control the content of this coverage or guarantee that it will be favorable.

free rider Someone who is sympathetic to the objectives of an interest group and enjoys the benefits produced by that group without making a contribution. Accordingly, he or she "rides free" on the backs of dues-paying members.

freedom rides A type of civil disobedience popular with civil rights protesters, where mixed-race groups of bus passengers would ride through the South and disobey laws on racially segregated travel, often at the expense of submitting to mob violence.

front-runner The presidential candidate who leads the primary horserace, based on media assessments of the campaign.

G

gatekeepers Television producers, newspaper editors, and prestigious reporters and anchors who make the decisions about what stories will be published or aired. Think of the imagery of a guard who decides who will be allowed to pass through a gate. In this case, news gatekeepers determine which information will be allowed to pass through the medium.

gender gap A difference in the voting pattern of men and women, evident since 1980, whereby men are more likely than women to support Republican presidential candidates.

General Agreement on Tariffs and Trade (GATT) The 1948 treaty establishing the rules for free trade, which has been revised and dramatically expanded, most recently during the Uruguay round of trade negotiations (1986–1994). GATT was also the name of the international organization that oversaw the treaty; the World Trade Organization (WTO) replaced it in 1995.

General Service (GS) The system of eighteen grade levels (GS1 through GS18) that determine the pay level of white-collar civil servants.

generational effects Historical influences felt by an entire generation during their formative years, which shape the way they are socialized to politics.

gerrymandering Drawing district lines in a way that favors the electoral prospects of the party in power.

Gibbons v. Ogden The Supreme Court case, heard by the Marshall Court in 1824, that established the federal government's primacy in regulating interstate commerce, saying that the state of New York could not grant an exclusive license to a steamboat company operating between New York and New Jersey.

Gideon v. Wainwright The 1963 Supreme Court case that established the right to have an attorney appointed at no charge by the court to defendants unable to afford representation. It was brought by Clarence Earl Gideon, who was sentenced to five years in prison for breaking into a pool hall. From prison, Gideon filed a *habeas corpus* petition, claiming his right to an attorney was violated because he was forced by poverty to represent himself at his trial.

"go native" The tendency for political appointees to adhere to the organizational culture of the department they are sent to run, making them advocates of the department rather than advocates of the president.

going public The presidential strategy of using the media to appeal directly to the public to support presidential initiatives.

goldplating Government purchasing of top-of-the-line items at maximum cost, which can happen when bureaucrats overseeing purchasing decisions have an interest in the items being purchased.

government corporations Corporations established by Congress to perform important services, like delivering the mail and operating rail lines, which could not be or were not profitably provided by private corporations.

Great Society The name given to the programs of President Lyndon B. Johnson, which elevated the federal government to the most prominent role it would play in the twentieth century. The philosophy of the Great Society was that government should try to solve large social problems like hunger and poverty.

gridlock The term given to legislative inaction, when members of Congress are unable to reach agreement and legislation stalls.

gross domestic product (GDP) A measure of national productivity, the gross domestic product is the total value of goods and services produced by a nation during a fixed period of time.

H

hard money Funds contributed directly to candidates or national parties by individuals or PACs for the purpose of electing candidates to federal office. Federal law regulates hard-money contributions.

hard news Traditional news items that derive their value from recent, relevant events that have some bearing on the lives of readers or viewers.

Hatch Act Legislation enacted in 1939 that prohibits civil servants from engaging in political activities.

Hobbes, Thomas (1588–1679) The seventeenth-century British social thinker and author of *Leviathan* who believed that people need to trade off liberty for a strong government that can protect their fundamental right to live.

home style The way legislators approach constituents, determined partly by how they size up their support in the district.

honeymoon The initial weeks of a new presidential administration when enthusiasm and good press typically translate into high public-approval ratings.

horserace That element of a political campaign that deals with winning and losing, whether a candidate is leading or trailing an opponent, and what the candidate may be doing to improve or solidify his or her electoral prospects.

I

ideological parties Third parties that form around a broad ideology not represented by the two major American parties. They endure from election to election despite the fact that they rarely achieve electoral success.

ideology A wide-ranging set of beliefs that logically fit together.

impeachment The power granted to Congress to remove from office the president, vice president, judges, and other federal officials.

implementation The bureaucratic function of taking the legal language of legislation and turning it into functioning programs.

implied powers The broad constitutional grant of power to Congress that allows it to make all laws that are "necessary and proper" to carry out its enumerated functions.

incumbent An official presently serving in office.

independent agencies Bureaucratic organizations that report directly to the president rather than through cabinet secretaries, and whose administrators serve at the pleasure of the president.

independent regulatory commissions and boards Panels designed to oversee the conduct of various segments of the economy. Members are appointed by the president and confirmed by the Senate. They serve fixed terms and cannot be removed by the president.

Indian Removal Act Legislation passed in 1830 that led to the forced and sometimes violent transfer of Native American nations to areas west of the Mississippi River.

influence The ability to shape political outcomes to your liking.

infotainment News reports and information-based programs that use information to entertain by playing on sensational topics, such as celebrities, violence, and the like.

inside strategies Lobbying approaches that rely on direct relationships between lobbyists and officials.

institutional patriotism The legislative norm that precludes members of Congress from acting or speaking in ways that would discredit the institution.

integrity A key component of reciprocity in which members of Congress are expected to keep their word with each other and honor their commitments.

intensity An aspect of public opinion that measures how strongly people feel toward a political figure, institution, or policy.

interest aggregation The process by which groups with different and potentially conflicting agendas are brought together under the umbrella of a political party.

interest groups Organized associations that seek to promote common objectives through government action.

inverted pyramid A style of reporting typical of twentieth-century newspaper coverage, in which stories were constructed with the most important factual material in the first paragraph, followed by successively less important facts.

iron triangle The ongoing, mutually beneficial relationship among an interest group, members of Congress sharing the interest group's objectives, and bureaucrats in federal agencies responsible for carrying out legislation pertaining to the interest group's field. Iron triangles can develop in any policy area, and many distinct iron-triangle relationships form because the federal government is responsible for a large number of policies.

issue network A fluid policy community permeable to a wide range of interest groups, permitting a broad array of policy outcomes.

issue voting Choosing a candidate in an election on the basis of his or her proximity to your position on an issue or issues you consider important.

J

Jim Crow laws Laws in place in the South through the middle portion of the twentieth century that legalized segregation in virtually every facet of life.

Joint Chiefs of Staff The group of military advisors comprised of the heads of the army, air force, navy, and marines.

joint committees Committees composed of members of the House and Senate that consider matters of interest to both houses.

judicial activism The philosophy that the Court should take an aggressive posture toward politics and the law, striking down presidential and congressional actions whenever it is deemed necessary and instituting far-reaching remedies to social wrongs.

judicial restraint The philosophy that the Court should defer to the other branches of government and only overturn legislation when it is clearly unconstitutional.

judicial review The authority of the Supreme Court to overrule actions of Congress or the president by declaring them to be unconstitutional.

judiciary The federal and state court systems charged with resolving legal and personal disputes and interpreting the law.

Judiciary Act of 1789 The act of Congress that established the federal court system. It initially called for a six-person Supreme Court and three circuit courts, each to be administered by two Supreme Court justices and one district court judge.

jurisdiction The authority of a court to hear a case.

K

"Know-Nothing" movement An anti-Catholic movement that formed in the 1840s as a reaction to the first large wave of Irish immigration.

Ku Klux Klan The secret white supremacist society that terrorized and killed African Americans for decades following the Civil War.

L

legal system The web of institutions and individuals involved in bringing legal and personal disputes to the attention of the courts.

legislative liaison White House lobbyists who maintain regular contacts with members of Congress and congressional committees, in order to help guide the president's legislative agenda.

legislative work The legislative norm that members of Congress should stay on top of the work required by the committee that deals with their area of specialization.

legitimacy Widespread public acceptance of the official standing of a political figure or institution.

libel The legal restriction against the malicious publication of material that knowingly damages an individual's reputation.

liberalism An ideology that advocates the use of government power to address economic and social problems, like unemployment and environmental protection, while limiting government involvement in moral matters like abortion rights and prayer in public schools.

libertarianism An ideology centered on the reduction of government power to advance personal liberty.

liberty The ability to pursue your ends and objectives, tempered by socially defined boundaries and limited government impediments.

life cycle effects Changes to the way we relate to politics and society that naturally occur during the course of aging, which typically leave us less open to political and social change as we get older.

limited government The idea that power can be denied to government and the people who serve in it, in order to restrict those in positions of authority from infringing upon individual liberty.

lobbying Attempting to influence the content of policy by exerting influence on government officials.

lobbyists Professionals hired by interest groups to influence the political process on behalf of the group.

Locke, John (1632–1704) A seventeenth-century British social contract theorist whose ideas about government getting its authority from the consent of the governed in order to protect fundamental human rights greatly influenced the leaders of the American Revolution.

logrolling A form of reciprocity in which members of Congress exhibit mutual cooperation for each other's pet projects.

long shot A presidential candidate who is not expected to fare well in the primary horserace, based on media assessments of the campaign.

M

majoritarian principle Procedures, such as those in place in the House of Representatives, that limit the ability of the minority party to influence the shape of legislation or the direction of the legislative agenda.

majority Winning more than half the votes in an election, or 50 percent plus one.

majority leader The number-two leadership position in the House of Representatives and the number-one leadership position in the Senate. In the House, the majority leader is the chief assistant to the Speaker; in the Senate, the majority leader is the chief leader on a par with the House Speaker.

majority whip The number-three leadership position in the House of Representatives and the number-two leadership position in the Senate. In both instances, the whip is responsible for mobilizing party members to support the leadership on key issues.

mandate A directive by voters to the president to move ahead with the program he promised when he was a candidate. A large mandate produced by a lopsided vote gives the president a strong bargaining position with respect to Congress to set and advance the agenda in Washington.

Marbury v. Madison The Supreme Court case, heard by the Marshall Court in 1803, that established judicial review.

mass media Vehicles, such as television, radio, newspapers, magazines, and the Internet, capable of rapidly communicating information to large numbers of people over large distances. Note that *media* is the plural form of *medium*: Television *is* a *medium*, whereas television and the Internet *are media*.

McCain-Feingold Act The name commonly used to describe the Bipartisan Campaign Reform Act of 2002, which prohibits the use of soft money in federal elections in an attempt to close a loophole in the 1974 Federal Election Campaign Act.

McCulloch v. Maryland The 1819 Supreme Court case that established federal supremacy over the state governments.

McGovern-Fraser Commission The commission organized by the Democratic Party following its 1968 convention to democratize the process of delegate selection to party conventions.

means test Eligibility requirements placed on social welfare programs aiding the poor, which restrict participation to individuals whose incomes fall below set levels.

media events Activities staged by campaigns or political officials that have enough news value to draw press attention to a message the politician wants to communicate.

Medicaid A social welfare program initiated as part of President Johnson's Great Society efforts to end poverty in America, which extended medical care to families receiving support through Aid to Families with Dependent Children (AFDC). States are permitted to enact their own Medicaid eligibility standards, following federal guidelines.

Medicare The federal social welfare program that provides hospital and supplementary medical insurance to senior citizens and the disabled.

merit system Procedures for hiring civil servants based on objective evaluations of their performance rather than on their political connections.

minority leader The number-one leadership position for the opposition party in the House of Representatives and Senate, whose responsibilities mirror those of the majority leader but without the ability to set or advance the legislative agenda.

minority rights Procedures, such as those in place in the Senate, that permit members of the minority party the opportunity to resist legislative actions they oppose.

minority whip The number-two leadership position for the opposition party in the House of Representatives and Senate, whose responsibilities mirror those of the majority whip.

Miranda rights The Court requirement, following a judgment in the case *Miranda v. Arizona* (1966), that apprehended individuals know and understand that they have a right against self-incrimination and a right to be represented by an attorney.

momentum The ability of a presidential campaign to maintain viability by meeting or exceeding press-generated expectations during the long primary period.

Montesquieu, Baron de (1689–1755) An eighteenth-century French political theorist whose ideas about decentralizing power to ensure personal liberty greatly influenced the government created by the Constitution.

muckraking Investigative reporting prevalent during the turn of the twentieth century, which centered on uncovering corruption in government and industry for the purpose of promoting progressive reforms.

multimember district The structure of electoral districts in proportional representation systems, in which each electoral district sends several representatives to the legislature.

multiparty system Political systems in which more than two parties have a realistic chance to win representation in government.

N

name recognition An informal measure of how much the public is aware of a candidate or elected official, based on how widely people are able to identify who the candidate or official is.

narrowcasting Programming oriented to a small segment of viewers, like that found on cable television stations. It contrasts with broadcasting, like that found on traditional television networks, which seeks to reach a larger audience with programming that has wide appeal.

nation-centered federalism One of several perspectives on federalism, which argues for the supremacy of the Constitution and federal law over state actions.

national debt The amount the government borrows to pay for accumulated budget deficits.

National Organization for Women (NOW) The largest women's rights organization in the United States, which has been an active force for advancing social and economic equality for women.

national security advisor The president's counselor on national security matters. In some administrations, the national security advisor has competed with the secretary of state for the president's attention.

National Security Council (NSC) The group of senior policy advisors responsible for helping the president shape national security policy.

national supremacy The doctrine that the federal government has the final word in disputes with the states. National supremacy was established through court rulings, precedent, and the victory of the North in the Civil War, eventually resolving the conflict between nation-centered federalism and state-centered federalism in favor of the former.

National Voter Registration Act Passed in 1993 to simplify and standardize voter registration requirements, the "Motor Voter Act" allows residents of most states to register to vote at the same time as they apply for or renew their driver's license. It also provides for a standardized, national registration form that can be downloaded from the Internet.

natural rights Inalienable rights inherent to every individual that cannot be taken away by individuals or government, and that government should be designed to protect.

"necessary and proper" clause A constitutional provision (Article I, Section 8) giving Congress a broad grant of authority to make laws that are binding on the states.

neutral competence The philosophy guiding nineteenth-century civil service reform, which states that bureaucrats should be chosen strictly for their ability to perform their job, without political criteria influencing their selection or their actions.

New Deal The name given to the programs of President Franklin D. Roosevelt, which vastly expanded the role of the federal government in an effort to deal with the debilitating effects of the Great Depression on American society.

New Deal coalition The political coalition composed of urbanites, ethnic and racial minorities, unions, liberals, and southerners that made the Democratic Party the majority party during the fifth party system.

New Federalism The name given to the programs of Presidents Richard M. Nixon and Ronald Reagan, which started as an effort to streamline the federal government produced by the Great Society and ended up as a movement to reverse fifty years of federal growth by returning authority to the states.

New Jersey Plan A proposal for the new Constitution, supported by small states, that would have provided for equal representation of large and small states in the national legislature, while limiting the power of the national government over the states.

news cycle The time between when an event happens and when it gets press coverage. With twenty-four-hour news services setting the pace, the demand for new information is enormous and immediate, greatly accelerating the news cycle.

news leaks The tactic used widely by White House officials of releasing information to the press on an anonymous basis when it serves their interests to have the information publicized. Some leaks are unauthorized and unwanted by the White House.

newsworthy The conditions under which a story warrants publication or dissemination, based on a set of values applied by newspaper editors and television producers. Newsworthy stories typically have conflict, proximity and relevance to the audience, timeliness, and familiarity.

nomination The official endorsement of a candidate by a political party, making that candidate the one whose name will appear on the ballot next to the party label in the next general election.

nongovernmental organizations (NGOs) Nonprofit organizations that promote interests with global ramifications on the world stage.

normative Any statement that invokes a judgment or evaluation. Think of the word *norm*, which implies a standard for evaluating something.

norms Unspoken rules of behavior that people adhere to in an institution like Congress that allow people to fit in and help the institution run smoothly.

North American Free Trade Agreement (NAFTA) A landmark free trade agreement setting up a regional free trade zone in North America.

North Atlantic Treaty Organization (NATO) An alliance of the United States, Canada, and Western European nations originally designed as a military pact to counter Soviet expansion. Following the cold war, it has grown to include European nations once aligned with the Soviet Union.

O

Office of Management and Budget (OMB) The executive office responsible for developing the president's annual budget proposals by evaluating requests for funding among departments and setting the president's spending priorities.

original jurisdiction The authority of the U.S. Supreme Court to be the first court to hear a case, precluding the need for an appeal from a lower court. The Constitution grants original jurisdiction to cases involving a dispute between the United States and a state; two or more states; citizens of different states; a state and a citizen of another state; and foreign ambassadors.

outside strategies Lobbying approaches that rely on mobilizing group members to influence the actions of officials.

override The congressional power to overturn a presidential veto by a two-thirds vote of both houses of Congress.

oversight The process of congressional review of the bureaucracy.

P

paid media Radio and television ads paid for and produced by political campaigns.

pardon power The unilateral power of the president to grant unconditional clemency to anyone for any reason.

party caucus The group of all members of a political party in the House or Senate that meets to discuss and formulate legislative priorities.

party identification An individual's association with a political party. The most common parties Americans identify with are the two major parties, Republican and Democrat. Party identification—also called party I.D.—varies in intensity such that it may be strong or weak. Those who do not identify with any party are typically called independents.

party in government That component of political parties composed of elected officials that organizes and runs our governing institutions like Congress, the presidency, state governorships and assemblies, and the like.

party in the electorate Party identifiers who make up the rank-and-file membership of the political parties.

party press Newspapers functioning as an arm of a political party, communicating information about partisan politics from party leaders to their supporters. Newspapers functioned in this capacity from the inception of political parties in America around 1790 through the 1830s.

party system The regular, over-time competition of the same major political parties, composed of the same groups of identifiers.

patronage Jobs, favors, and other resources that party officials provide in exchange for people's political support.

Pendleton Act The 1883 law requiring that merit-based criteria be used to hire public employees, ending the tradition of patronage appointments.

penny press High-circulation newspapers, emerging after 1830, that kept costs down by selling advertising. These newspapers brought in large numbers of readers with lurid and sensational reporting.

persuasion An informal source of presidential power that gives skilled presidents the opportunity to influence the decisions of members of Congress and others in Washington whose support the president needs to accomplish his political objectives.

photo opportunities Staged appearances by politicians in visually appealing settings designed to produce images that will be widely disseminated in the press.

platform The official document produced at the major party conventions that serves as a philosophical and policy blueprint for the party's presidential nominee.

plea bargain A compromise between a defendant, defense attorney, and prosecutor, whereby the defendant foregoes due process and agrees to plead guilty without a trial to a lesser charge in exchange for a more lenient punishment.

Plessy v. Ferguson The 1896 Supreme Court case that upheld racial segregation. It was reversed in 1954 in the case of *Brown v. Board of Education.*

Plum Book The congressional publication listing all top-level political positions in the bureaucracy.

pluralism The theory that government responds to individuals through their memberships in groups, assuring that government is responsive to a wide range of voices. People who subscribe to this position believe that the wide distribution of resources in society drives the decisions government officials make.

plurality Winning the most votes in an election, or at least one more vote than the next closest candidate or party.

pocket veto The presidential prerogative to veto a bill without taking action. Presidents may issue pocket vetoes only if Congress has passed legislation within ten days of adjournment. A pocket veto cannot be overridden.

political action committees (PACs) Organizations formed by interest groups such as labor unions, businesses, and ideological groups for the purpose of contributing money to political candidates.

political appointees Top-level bureaucratic officials whom the president appoints, typically pending Senate confirmation, and who serve at the pleasure of the president.

political culture The common set of attitudes, beliefs, and values that provide the foundation of support for a political system.

political equality Establishing political and legal rights on the basis of the individual, so that everyone has the same right to vote and is equal under the law. An alternative would be to grant political rights to elite individuals based on wealth or social standing.

political machines The name given to urban political parties that used patronage to overrun their competition and maintain power.

political participation The range of activities people can engage in to influence the political process. While voting is the most commonly performed political act, participation encompasses a host of things—from writing letters to public officials to contributing time or money to a campaign or protesting the actions of government.

political party An organized group of individuals with common interests seeking to gain power in government by electing officials to public office.

political socialization The process by which we acquire political knowledge, attitudes, and beliefs.

politics The process of determining who gets what, when, and how.

popular sovereignty Rule by the people based on the consent of the governed.

popular vote The votes individuals cast in a presidential election. Technically, these are votes for a slate of electors representing the candidate. A candidate who wins a plurality of the popular vote in a state gets all the electoral votes allocated to that state.

pork barrel Wasteful or unnecessary spending that can result from logrolling. Whether something is a pork-barrel project or a valuable use of taxpayer dollars may depend on whether you stand to benefit from it.

poverty line A statistical determination of poverty based on income and family size that is used to establish eligibility for some social welfare programs designed to assist those in need.

power The ability to make others act in a way that they otherwise might not have done.

president pro tempore The senator charged with the honorary duty of presiding over the Senate in the absence of the vice president of the United States.

press briefings Formal exchanges of information between the press secretary and the national press covering the president.

press conferences Scheduled meetings between reporters and political figures like the president, which give the press access to the official and an opportunity to ask him or her questions firsthand.

press secretary The liaison between the White House and the national press covering the president.

pressure groups Another term for interest groups that emphasizes the demands interest groups make on the political system.

primary A method of candidate selection in which party identifiers vote for the candidate who will run on the party label in the general election. In presidential primaries, voters select delegates to the national convention.

primary agent of socialization Parents and siblings exert disproportional influence on the political development of children by virtue of the initial influence they have on kids, giving the family a primary role in the process of political socialization.

priming A media effect whereby the context in which a political figure is presented in the news can create a positive or negative cue for how viewers think about and evaluate that figure.

prior restraint Censorship of the news by government officials before it is published or broadcast.

professional reputation The sense among Washington officials of the president's political skills and abilities. It is one of the keys to effective persuasion, as it enhances the president's ability to bargain.

progressive income tax A tax structure with graduated income rates designed to increase the tax burden on higher-income earners.

proportional representation Electoral systems that encourage the participation of many parties by awarding representation on the basis of the share of the vote won by each party in an electoral district.

protectionism The policy of raising the price of imported goods through tariffs in order to make them less attractive than domestic products.

protective regulatory policy Regulations that supply consumers with information needed to make informed purchasing decisions about such things as cigarettes and home loans or that prevent undesirable personal or social conditions like child labor or unsafe food.

public opinion A collection of opinions people hold on matters relating to government, politics, and society.

public prestige The sense among Washington officials about whether the president is well regarded by the public. It is one of the keys to effective persuasion, as it enhances the president's ability to bargain.

public works Civic projects built with tax dollars.

purposive benefit The gratification an interest group member gets by contributing to a cause.

push polls Surveys that appear legitimate but in fact are a dirty campaign trick designed to generate negative opinion about an opponent in a political contest.

Q

Quartering Act An act of the British Parliament requiring colonists to house British troops; first imposed in 1765 and then again in 1774 as part of the Coercive Acts.

R

racial gerrymandering Drawing district lines in a way that combines disparate populations of minority groups in order to guarantee representation by those groups in Congress.

rally effect The tendency for Americans to unite around the president during a crisis, temporarily bolstering his job-approval ratings.

random sample The basis for a scientifically accurate public opinion poll, in which everyone in the community being polled has an equal chance of being selected to give their opinions to pollsters. In a poll of national opinion, everyone in the country would have to have an equal chance of being selected to participate in it.

ranking minority member The minority party counterpart to the committee chair, but without the power to influence the direction of the committee.

realignment A shift from one party system to another, the result of a lasting, long-term adjustment in the groups that identify with the major political parties.

recess appointments The constitutional power granted to the president to make nominations while Congress is out of session that do not require Senate approval. The appointments stand until the end of the congressional term.

reciprocity The legislative norm that encourages members of Congress to support each other's initiatives, even if there is no direct political benefit in doing so.

reconciliation A procedure in the budget-writing process, whereby appropriations made in a number of congressional committees and subcommittees need to be brought in line with spending targets established early in the process.

Reconstruction The period following the Civil War, from 1865 to 1877, during which Union troops occupied the South as states of the Confederacy were readmitted to the Union under conditions established in Washington.

redistributive policies Domestic policies, like those promoting social welfare, that take resources from one group in the form of taxes and provide goods or services for another group, typically those in need.

redistricting   The process by which congressional districts are redrawn every ten years following the release of new census data.

Reform Party   The organization built by businessman Ross Perot in a mostly unsuccessful attempt to create a competitive third party.

Regents of the University of California v. Bakke   The 1978 Supreme Court case that marked a reversal in unlimited support for affirmative action policies by backing the claim of discrimination by a white University of California medical school applicant who was denied admission in favor of less well qualified minority applicants.

regressive tax   A tax structure that increases the tax burden on lower-income earners. Sales taxes are regressive because as incomes decline, the tax becomes a larger percentage of total income, and therefore, a greater burden.

regulation   The bureaucratic function of placing standards or restrictions on the actions of private individuals or companies in order to protect the general welfare of the public.

regulatory policies   Domestic policies designed to protect the public from harmful conditions that could result from unrestrained free-market competition or to ensure the benefits of a level playing field for private competition.

Reinventing Government   The name given to President Bill Clinton's initiative to make the federal government smaller by making it more efficient.

Religious Right   Ideological interest groups promoting a conservative political agenda consistent with an evangelical religious perspective.

representative democracy   A form of democracy in which eligible individuals choose others to make decisions on their behalf.

republic   Any nation with provisions for the selection of representatives who make decisions on behalf of those who select them. James Madison said a republic was "a government in which the scheme of representation takes place," as compared to direct democracy.

resources   Anything of value to others that can be used to sway another individual.

responsible parties   Political parties whose legislative members act in concert, taking clear positions on issues and voting as a unit in accordance with their stated positions.

retrospective voting   Evaluating the past performance of an incumbent to make a judgment about the future—whether the incumbent should be retained or replaced.

revolving door   A consequence of the close relationships between interest groups and government officials that makes it possible for lobbyists to become government officials charged with regulating the organizations they once worked for, or for government officials to become lobbyists who influence friends in their former agency.

right to privacy   The protection against government interference in private matters, which is not specifically guaranteed by the Constitution but which has been established by the Court and used to legalize contraception and abortion.

Roe v. Wade   The 1973 Supreme Court case that found a constitutional right to privacy applied to reproductive issues, striking down all state laws that prohibited abortions during the first trimester of pregnancy.

Rules Committee   The committee of the House that channels legislation to the floor for debate and a vote on passage.

S

Second Continental Congress   A gathering of representatives from the colonies in Philadelphia in 1775, necessitated by the need to coordinate planning during the Revolutionary War, that functioned as the first central government in colonial America.

secondary agent of socialization   Schools and the media have an effect on political socialization, but the effect is less than from primary agents like the family because we do not form close interpersonal bonds with either institution.

secretary of state   The head of the Department of State, who functions as the president's chief foreign policy advisor.

select committee   A House or Senate committee established on a temporary basis to review a specific matter. Typically, select committees make recommendations but do not move legislation.

selective benefits   Incentives offered exclusively to interest group members as a means of getting people to join.

selective exposure   The tendency to pay attention to messages that are consistent with existing attitudes or beliefs, while overlooking messages that conflict with them.

selective perception   An unconscious process by which we filter information that we deem irrelevant, uninteresting, or inconsistent with our attitudes and beliefs, while absorbing information that conforms to our self-perception.

senatorial courtesy   The custom that presidents will defer to the wishes of senators from a judicial nominee's home state before making a court appointment.

Senior Executive Service (SES)   The payment scale used for a small group of upper-level government managers and technical experts. Most positions covered by the Senior Executive Service are in the civil service, although the SES covers select political appointees whose jobs do not require Senate confirmation.

seniority   The custom of awarding committee chairs on the basis of length of service.

separation of powers   The division of political power among several equal and independent branches of government to prevent power from being consolidated in any one branch.

Shays' Rebellion   A rebellion by debtor farmers in western Massachusetts, led by Revolutionary War Captain Daniel Shays, against Boston creditors. It began in 1786 and lasted half a year, threatening the economic interests of the business elite and contributing to the demise of the Articles of Confederation.

single-issue parties   Third parties that form to advance a specific issue agenda, like environmentalism, that members feel is not being adequately addressed by the two major American parties. They endure from election to election despite the fact that they rarely achieve electoral success.

single-member district   The structure of electoral districts in winner-take-all electoral systems, in which each electoral district sends only one representative to the legislature.

sit-ins   A type of civil disobedience popular with civil rights protesters that involved African Americans peacefully sitting at "Whites Only" lunch counters, to focus attention on the injustice of segregation policies.

social contract   The arrangement in which people agree to give up some of their liberty to establish a government that will protect basic rights that are threatened in the state of nature.

social desirability bias   A form of error in public opinion polls, whereby opinions or behaviors that could be considered undesirable are not fully reported in the data.

social equality   A form of equality of outcome that values using government policy to minimize social class distinctions found in society.

social responsibility   Concern for the protection of the rights of individuals in a community or society, at the expense of some degree of personal liberty.

Social Security   The popular social welfare program that provides benefits to retirees regardless of need. Social Security also offers insurance payments to families of deceased workers and disability payments to impaired workers.

socialism   A left-leaning ideology centered on the use of government power to advance equal outcomes.

socioeconomic status (SES) A measure of an individual's social position based primarily on education, income, and occupation. High socioeconomic status individuals are more likely to have advanced education, high incomes, and occupations that award high status and demand great responsibility, like professional or managerial work. The abbreviation for socioeconomic status is SES.

soft money Funds contributed to state and local parties or to national parties for the purpose of running state elections or conducting local "grassroots" political activity.

soft news Feature stories, stories about celebrities, and other news items that do not derive their news value from proximity, timeliness, or relevance to the reader or viewer.

solicitor general The White House official responsible for arguing on behalf of the United States in Supreme Court cases where the United States is a party.

Speaker of the House The leader of the majority party in the House of Representatives who exercises control over the operation of that branch through formal and informal means.

special interest groups Another term for interest groups that emphasizes the narrow scope of their concerns.

specialization The legislative norm that members of Congress should become experts in a legislative field.

spin A technique used by political figures to characterize events in a favorable way in order to get the media to report them in a favorable way—regardless of what the facts of a story may indicate.

splinter parties Third parties that split away from one of the major parties in protest against the direction taken by the Republicans or Democrats. They often form around a charismatic leader and last a short time, after which the major parties address their concerns and they lose their reason to continue.

spoils system The method of staffing the federal bureaucracy, commonplace in the nineteenth century, in which the president offered patronage appointments to political supporters.

stability An aspect of public opinion that measures how much change or variability there is in the way people feel toward a political figure, institution, or policy.

Stamp Act A particularly vexing tax levied by the British on scores of legal documents, which led to a colonial boycott of British goods.

standard operating procedures (SOPs) Guidelines that provide uniformity to bureaucratic decision making.

standing committees Permanent congressional committees that handle matters related to a specific legislative topic.

stare decisis Literally, "let the decision stand," it is a guiding principle of judicial interpretation that places a premium on letting previous judicial rulings guide current rulings.

state of nature The condition of total liberty in which people are free to act on their impulses, but where individual rights are afforded no protection.

state-centered federalism One of several perspectives on federalism, which argues that the Constitution and the federal government are creations of the states and therefore can be overruled by the states.

structural bias The possibility that news stories are skewed toward the limited set of sources and topics selected by gatekeepers for publication and broadcast.

Student Nonviolent Coordinating Committee (SNCC) The organization that involved college students in acts of civil disobedience to advance the cause of civil rights for African Americans.

subcommittees Subunits of standing committees that do the detail work involved in writing legislation.

subgovernments Another term for iron triangles, which captures the specialized (and often hidden) relationship among lobbyists, members of Congress, and bureaucrats, who share mutual professional and policy interests and objectives.

substantive representation The ability of a legislator to represent the agenda or interests of a group to which he or she does not personally belong.

Sugar Act The first in a string of taxes levied by Great Britain on the American colonies. Formally called the American Revenue Act of 1764, it taxed a number of colonial imports, including sugar.

supremacy clause A constitutional provision (Article VI) establishing the relationship between the federal and state governments. The supremacy clause asserts that any conflict between the federal government and the states will be decided in favor of the federal government.

T

tariff A tax on imports designed to raise their cost and make them less competitive than domestic products, in an effort to protect the jobs of domestic workers.

tax expenditures Tax breaks in the form of exemptions targeted at groups of taxpayers or, in the case of corporate taxes, at specific industries.

Telecommunications Act of 1996 Legislation that overhauled the Federal Communications Act of 1934 by deregulating a range of communications technologies in an effort to promote competition in the development and provision of telecommunications services. If your local telephone company now offers long-distance service, or if your cable television provider also offers high-speed Internet access, it's because the opportunity for them to do so was made possible by this law.

Temporary Assistance for Needy Families (TANF) The 1996 welfare reform program that replaced Aid to Families with Dependent Children (AFDC) and ended welfare support as a federal entitlement. TANF is designed as a transitional program that supports welfare recipients temporarily as they move into the workforce.

tenure Job security afforded to civil servants following a probationary period, to protect them against losing their jobs for political reasons.

Three-Fifths Compromise A compromise between northern and southern states that broke the deadlock over how slaves should be counted for purposes of representation. Three-fifths of slaves would be included in population totals, benefiting southern states that had the largest concentration of slaves by inflating their representation in the House of Representatives.

ticket splitting Voting for candidates of different parties for different offices, rather than voting a "party line" for all Republicans or all Democrats. Ticket splitting, which has increased in recent years, is a sign of how Americans have been growing independent from political parties.

trade associations Groups that advance the concerns of specific business interests, such as banks, energy companies, real estate firms, and car manufacturers.

trade deficit A negative balance between the value of goods and services purchased from foreign nations and the value of goods and services sold to foreign nations.

"Trail of Tears" A one-thousand-mile forced march of Cherokee men, women, and children carried out in 1838 to satisfy a federal relocation policy.

transfer payments The direct payment of public money to individuals who qualify for it under the terms of a social welfare program.

trustee A philosophy of representation that says officials are elected for their wisdom and to exercise their judgment of the national interest, even when it is at odds with their constituents' wishes.

two-party system A political system, like ours in the United States, in which only two parties have a realistic chance to win most elections.

tyranny The denial of liberty to individuals through the actions of a faction or through the actions of government itself.

U

unitary system   The inverse of a confederal system, in which a centralized national government creates subnational units like states, provinces, and counties, which derive their authority from the national government. Most nations are unitary systems. In the United States, the relationship between each individual state and its counties, townships, and cities is a unitary relationship, with the states creating and empowering the local governments.

United States v. Nixon   The 1974 case in which a unanimous Supreme Court ruled that President Nixon could not use executive privilege to protect the secrecy of incriminating tapes documenting his involvement in the cover-up of the Watergate break-in.

V

veto power   The constitutional power granted to the president to block an act of Congress. It takes a two-thirds vote of both houses of Congress to override a presidential veto.

Virginia Plan   A proposal for the new Constitution, supported by large states, that would have based representation on population and provided for a centralized national government that could overrule the states.

Voting Rights Act of 1965   Landmark legislation arising from the civil rights movement that gave federal officials the power to oversee election practices in southern states where Jim Crow laws disenfranchised African American voters.

W

War Powers Act of 1973   A congressional attempt to reassert the role of the legislature with respect to the president in military affairs by restricting the president's ability to wage war.

White House Office   That portion of the Executive Office of the President organized to serve the president's immediate needs.

winner-take-all system   The electoral system in use in the United States, whereby the candidate of the party receiving the most votes in an electoral district gets to represent that district.

World Trade Organization (WTO)   The international organization responsible for promoting free trade among nations and settling trade disputes.

writ of *certiorari*   An order issued by the Supreme Court demanding a lower court turn over all records of a case that the Supreme Court has decided to hear on appeal.

writ of *habeas corpus*   From the Latin for "you have the body," *habeas corpus* puts the burden on the courts to demonstrate that a defendant's rights have not been violated prior to sentencing. People who believe they have been imprisoned against their constitutional rights have the privilege to petition for their release.

writ of *mandamus*   A court order commanding a public official to perform an official act.

Y

yellow journalism   The term given to the sensational newspaper coverage prevalent during the turn of the twentieth century, noteworthy for its emphasis on violence, sex, human-interest stories, and exposés of official corruption.

Z

zero-sum policy   A policy debate in which any victory by one side comes at the expense of the opposing side, negating the possibility of compromise.

Name Index

Author names are referenced to the pages where their works are cited. An italic *n* and number following a page number (e.g., 241*n*13) indicate the end-of chapter note where the work is listed.

A

Aberbach, Joel D., 351*nn*34–35, 353
Abraham, Henry J., 360, 367*n*29, 368*nn*30–31, 369*n*32, 373*nn*35–36, 383, 386
Abramson, Paul R., 115*n*33, 183*n*1, 213
Aldrich, John H., 115*n*33, 183*n*1, 213
Alger, Dean, 124*n*4, 134*n*18, 137*n*24, 138, 154
Alley, Robert S., 428, 446
Almond, Gabriel A., 87, 88*n*3, 119

B

Baird, Robert M., 418
Balz, Dan, 244*n*52
Barber, James David, 301, 323, 483
Barron, Jerome A., 435*nn*23–24, 436*nn*25,30, 437*n*38
Baumgartner, Frank R., 229*n*29
Baum, Lawrence, 357*n*3, 359*n*10, 379*n*47, 386
Beck, Paul Allen, 167*n*13, 173, 174*n*232, 175, 177*n*26, 180
Behr, Roy L., 160*n*3, 163*n*6, 165, 180
Berelson, Bernard R., 53, 55*n*6, 83
Berry, Jeffrey M., 222
Bibby, John F., 178
Birnbaum, Jeffrey H., 242*nn*50–51, 246
Blessing, Robert K., 292
Bond, John, 312*n*41
Brace, Paul, 297*n*12, 298*nn*16–17, 299, 323
Burke, John P., 315*nn*46–47, 323

C

Campbell, Angus, 69*n*11, 83, 115*n*32
Capaldi, Nicholas, 430*n*12
Carlson, Darren K., 50*n*1
Carpenter, Ted Galen, 498
Carp, Robert A., 358, 359, 360*nn*12–13, 362*n*15, 363*n*16, 364*nn*17–18, 365*nn*21,23, 371*nn*33–34, 372, 386
Carr, David, 497
Carter, Amy, 99*n*11
Cassel, Andrew, 466
Chapman, John W., 421*n*2
Chatterjee, Pratap, 240
Church, Thomas W., 433*n*19, 446

Cigler, Allan J., 89*n*4, 223*n*20, 227*n*26, 231*n*34, 241, 242*n*49, 246
Clark, Terry Nichols, 87, 119
Converse, Philip E., 69*n*11, 83, 115*n*32
Cramer, Richard Ben, 213
Crosby, Faye J., 400, 418

D

D'Agostino, Joseph A., 502
Dahl, Robert, 10, 19
Davidson, Roger H., 251*nn*4–5, 253*nn*8–10, 255, 256, 259*n*17, 260, 261*nn*19,21, 262, 266*nn*25–26, 269*n*27, 271*n*28, 276, 279*n*33, 280*n*35, 284*n*41, 288
Davies, Frank, 502
Davis, James W., 183*n*2, 213
Davis, Richard, 124*n*5, 125*n*9, 126*n*10, 128, 133, 134*n*17, 185*n*3, 186*n*5, 187*n*6, 190*n*9
Davis, Ronald L. F., 394
Dawson, Richard E., 99*n*14, 100*n*17, 119
DeClerico, Robert E., 213
Deering, Christopher J., 277*n*32
Delli Carpini, Michael S., 53*n*4, 54, 56, 83
Dhamee, Yousuf, 438
DiClerico, Robert E., 183*n*2, 185*n*3, 186*n*5, 187*n*6, 190*n*9
Dienes, C. Thomas, 435*nn*23–24, 436*n*25, 436*n*30, 437*n*38
Dodd, Lawrence C., 250*nn*1–2, 288

E

Edsall, Thomas B., 234*n*41
Edwards, George C., 323, 339*n*18, 340*nn*19–20, 341*nn*21–23
Edwards, George C. III, 290*n*1, 293*n*3, 298*n*13, 303*nn*22–23, 304*nn*24–25
Edwards, George E., 353
Eggen, Dan, 127*n*12
Eliasoph, Nina, 110*n*28, 119
Emanuel, Ezekiel, 443
England, Paula, 410, 418
Epstein, Lee, 364*n*19, 367*n*28, 371, 380, 382*n*54, 386, 426, 446
Epstein, Leon D., 156*n*1, 161*n*5

Eskridge, William R., 418
Exoo, Calvin, 149*n*47, 497

F

Fenno, Richard, 276*n*31, 282*n*39, 288
Fiorina, Morris P., 115*n*34, 119
Fleisher, Richard, 312*n*41
Fowler, Linda L., 252*n*7, 285*n*43
Frankel, Benjamin, 490*n*22, 507
Friedman, Marilyn, 433*nn*20–21

G

Gaebler, Ted, 346*nn*29–30, 354
Gans, Herbert J., 149*n*49
Gerth, H. H., 328*n*4
Gesell-Streeter, Carla, 135*n*23
Godwin, Mike, 436*nn*28–29
Golden, Marissa Martino, 333*nn*13–14, 334*n*15, 353
Goldstein, Robert Justin, 434, 435, 446
Goodsell, Charles T., 326*n*1, 327*nn*2–3, 328*n*5, 353
Gordon, Sarah Barringer, 426*n*7
Graber, Doris A., 123*n*3, 131*n*13, 154
Greenberg, Anna, 171
Greenstein, Fred I., 99*nn*9–10, 101*n*20
Grossman, Michael Baruch, 304*n*26, 305*n*27, 323
Guth, James L., 223*n*20

H

Halberstam, David, 507
Hamilton, Alexander, 357*n*4
Handler, Joel F., 459*n*15, 478
Hargrove, Thomas, 412*n*37
Harris, Richard A., 478
Hart, Roderick P., 63, 151*n*50, 154
Heclo, Hugh M., 329*n*8, 330*n*9, 333, 353
Herrnson, Paul S., 178*nn*27–28, 198, 201*n*18, 202, 204*n*19
Hershey, Marjorie Randon, 175
Hertzgaard, Mark, 146*n*41
Herzberger, Sharon D., 400, 418
Heumann, Milton, 433*n*19, 446

Subject Index

Page numbers in italics identify illustrations. An italic *t* next to a page number (e.g., 241*t*) indicates information that appears in a table. An italic *n* and number following a page number (e.g., 241*n*13) indicate information that appears in an end-of-chapter note and the number of the note where the material can be found.